GOOD HOUSEKEEPING

COOKERY BOOK

GOOD HOUSEKEEPING

COOKERY
BOOK

The Cook's Classic Companion

EBURY PRESS LONDON

First published in 1948
by Ebury Press
an imprint of the Random Century Group
Random Century House
20 Vauxhall Bridge Road
London SW1V 2SA

Completely revised and reset
1962, 1966, 1976, 1985, 1992

Catalogue record for this book is available from
The British Library

ISBN 0 09 175356 2

General Editor: Janet Illsley
Designed by Clive Dorman
Illustrations by Terry Pottle, Julie Carpenter, Gabriel Izen

Typeset by Clive Dorman
Printed and bound in Italy by
New Interlitho S.p.a., Milan

FOREWORD

What better way to celebrate Good Housekeeping's 70th birthday than with a new edition of the Good Housekeeping Cookery Book? With over two million copies sold since the first edition in 1948, it remains unrivalled as an indispensable source of reference and inspiration for all cooks, novice and experienced alike.

We are proud of the excellent reputation Good Housekeeping has built up over the years for exceptional cookery, and it's thanks to the unique Good Housekeeping Institute that we remain one of the leading authorities on food and cookery today.

In this new edition you'll find over 1000 recipes, many of them illustrated in beautiful colour photographs. You have the added reassurance that all the recipes have been originated and double-tested in the Good Housekeeping Institute kitchens.

Choose from popular everyday recipes, British classics and a range of international dishes, many inspired by regional cuisines and the ever increasing range of ingredients now available. Whether traditional, classic or contemporary, all the recipes reflect current cookery methods and our changing attitudes to nutrition and diet.

But, the Good Housekeeping Cookery Book is far more than a comprehensive collection of tried, tested and trusted recipes: it guides the cook from the shop, to the cooker, to the table. You'll find up-to-date information on choosing, buying and storing food in each recipe chapter. There are also practical guides to healthy eating, successful entertaining, including catering for large numbers, and choosing wine. In addition, the many questions which arise today over health and hygiene in the kitchen, freezing, microwave cooking and preserving are also answered.

I'm sure that this comprehensive volume will provide all the necessary practical information and inspiration you need to prepare and serve with confidence, a multitude of memorable meals.

Moyra Fraser

CONTENTS

EATING FOR HEALTH   **9**
Nutritional Information; Guidelines for Healthy Eating; Vegetarianism; Weight Reducing Diets

SOUPS   **17**
Stocks; Vegetable Soups; Bean and Pasta Soups; Hearty Soups; Fish Soups; Chilled Soups

STARTERS   **33**
Fruit, Vegetable and Salad Starters; Seafood Starters; Pâtés, Terrines and Mousses; Dips; Savoury Finger Food; Pastry Starters; After-dinner Savouries

FISH   **53**
Preparation and Cooking Techniques; Sea Fish; Freshwater Fish; Smoked Fish; Shellfish

MEAT   **92**
Meat Cuts, Cooking Methods and Carving Techniques; Beef Dishes; Veal Dishes; Lamb Dishes; Pork Dishes; Bacon and Ham Dishes; Offal Dishes

POULTRY   **146**
Buying, Handling and Storing; Jointing and Boning Poultry; Roasting; Chicken Dishes; Turkey Dishes; Duckling; Goose; Guinea Fowl

GAME   **171**
Seasons for Game Birds, Preparation and Cooking Methods; Game Bird Dishes; Preparing Hare and Rabbit; Hare and Rabbit Dishes

STUFFINGS   **181**
Herb and Fruit Stuffings; Mixed Stuffings

HERBS, SPICES, FLAVOURINGS AND ESSENCES   **187**
Herbs and their Uses; Spices and their Uses; Flavourings and Essences

SAUCES   **197**
White Sauce and Variations; Béchamel and Velouté Sauces; Brown Sauce; Egg-based Sauces; Traditional Sauces; Savoury Butters; Sweet Sauces

VEGETABLES   **211**
A-Z of Vegetables: Varieties, Preparation, Cooking and Serving; Vegetable Dishes; Vegetarian Cooking; Grains and Pulses; Vegetarian Dishes

SALADS   **250**
Salad Leaves; Salad Dressings; Side Salads; Main Course Salads

EGGS   **267**
Buying and Storing Eggs; Cooking Methods; Soufflés; Roulades; Egg Dishes; Omelettes

CHEESE   **279**
Buying, Storing and Serving Cheese; Hard and Soft Cheeses; Cheese Varieties; Cheese Snacks and Light Meals

PIZZAS AND SAVOURY FLANS   **288**
Basic Pizza Doughs; Pizzas and Pizza Snacks; Savoury Flans

PASTA, RICE AND GNOCCHI   **295**
Different Types of Pasta; Making and Shaping Pasta Dough; Pasta Dishes; Types of Rice and Cooking Methods; Rice Dishes; Gnocchi Dishes

FRUIT AND NUTS 314
A-Z of Fruit: Varieties, Preparation and Serving; Dried Fruit; Nuts

DESSERTS 326
Baked Puddings; Steamed Puddings; Batter Puddings; Pies, Flans and Pastries; Fruit Desserts; Cheesecakes; Milk, Custard and Cream Puddings; Hot Sweet Soufflés; Cold Soufflés, Jellies and Mousses; Ices and Iced Desserts; Meringues

PASTRY 376
Shaping Pastry; Short Pastries; Flaked Pastries; Choux, Filo and Other Pastries

CAKES 392
Cake Ingredients and Methods; Cake Tins and Preparation; Small Cakes; Scones and Teabreads; Large Cakes and Gâteaux; Celebration and Seasonal Cakes; Decorating Cakes; Icings

BISCUITS AND PETITS FOURS 435
Rolled, Shaped, Drop, Piped, Bar and Refrigerator Biscuits; Petits Fours

BREAD 448
Breadmaking; Loaf Bread and Rolls; Crumpets; Danish Pastries; Breakfast Breads; Coffee and Teatime Breads; Quick Breads

JAMS, JELLIES AND MARMALADES 464
Equipment and Techniques; Fruit Jams; Fruit Jellies; Marmalades; Fruit Butters, Cheeses and Curds; Mincemeat; Fruits in Alcohol

CHUTNEYS, RELISHES AND PICKLES 484
Chutneys; Relishes; Pickles

SWEETS 493
Equipment and Techniques; Fondants; Marzipan; Toffee; Fudge; Truffles; Dipped Chocolates and Fruit; Chocolate Easter Eggs

PRESENTING FOOD 505
Garnishes and Decorations

CATERING FOR LARGE NUMBERS 509
Planning Ahead; Quantities for Buffet Parties; Buffet Menu for 20; Buffet Menu for 50

WINES AND LIQUEURS 520
A Guide to Wines; Fortified Wines; Liqueurs

COCKTAILS, CUPS AND PUNCHES 528
Cocktail, Cup and Punch Recipes

TEA, COFFEE AND SOFT DRINKS 534
A Guide to Teas: Types of Coffee and Coffee Making; Soft Drinks

EQUIPPING YOUR KITCHEN 541
Cookers; Other Electrical Appliances; Food Preparation Machines; Pots and Pans; Kitchen Utensils

MICROWAVE COOKING 550
Choosing and Using a Microwave Cooker; Cookware; Accessories; Microwave Cooking Techniques; Cook's Microwave Tips; Microwave Time Savers

FOOD STORAGE 556
Kitchen Hygiene; Refrigerator Storage; Freezing; Freezer Storage; Freezing Vegetables and Fruit

GLOSSARY 566

INDEX 574

COOKERY NOTES

1. Follow either metric or imperial measures for the recipes in this book as they are not interchangeable.

2. All spoon measures are level unless otherwise stated. Sets of measuring spoons are available in both metric and imperial size to give accurate measurement of small quantities.

3. Ovens should be preheated to the specified temperature. Grills should also be preheated.

4. Where margarine is stated use either block or soft tub margarine. Otherwise use as specified in the recipe.

5. Size 3 eggs should be used except where otherwise stated.

6. Plain or self raising flour can be used unless otherwise stated. Use white, brown or wholemeal flour but see individual chapters for use in pastry, bread and cake making.

7. Use white or brown granulated sugar unless otherwise stated.

8. Brown or white breadcrumbs can be used unless one type is specified.

9. Use freshly ground black pepper unless otherwise stated.

METRIC CONVERSION CHARTS

LIQUID			SOLID		
Imperial	Exact conversion	Recommended conversion	Imperial	Exact conversion	Recommended conversion
¼ pint	142 ml	150 ml	1 oz	28.35 g	25 g
½ pint	284 ml	300 ml	2 oz	56.7 g	50 g
1 pint	568 ml	600 ml	4 oz	113.4 g	125 g
1½ pints	851 ml	900 ml	8 oz	226.8 g	225 g
1¾ pints	992 ml	1 litre	12 oz	340.2 g	350 g
			14 oz	397.0 g	400 g
			16 oz (1 lb)	453.6 g	450 g

FOR QUANTITIES OF 1¾ PINTS AND OVER, LITRES AND FRACTIONS OF A LITRE HAVE BEEN USED

1 KILOGRAM (KG) EQUALS 2.2 LB

OVEN TEMPERATURE SCALES

°Celsius Scale	Electric Scale °F	Gas Oven Marks
110°C	225°F	¼
130	250	½
140	275	1
150	300	2
170	325	3
180	350	4
190	375	5
200	400	6
220	425	7
230	450	8
240	475	9

EATING FOR HEALTH

'You are what you eat'– it's an old saying but like many proverbs it contains a great deal of truth. There have been far too many reports in the last few years for us to ignore the fact that what we eat can have a significant effect on our health later on in life.

The term malnutrition has different meanings in different parts of the world. In many third world countries it refers to the problem of under-nutrition, not having enough food to satisfy needs. However, in westernized countries it usually refers to the problem of overnutrition, consuming too much of the wrong type of food.

In this country both the type of food we eat and the pattern of eating have changed significantly in recent years. We tend to eat far more processed foods than we used to and more snacks and fast food. 70% of the food we now eat is processed in some way.

Medical experts agree that most people eat too much fat, sugar and salt and not enough dietary fibre. There is an increasing amount of evidence to suggest that this is at least partly responsible for many of the diseases common in this country today. Diseases such as coronary heart disease, certain types of cancer, dental caries, obesity and many more are all related to our poor eating habits. In Britain we are now in the unenviable position of being among the world leaders in deaths caused by these diseases.

But, by making a few simple changes to your diet, combined with other changes like taking more exercise, you can take an important step towards enjoying a long and healthy life. Fortunately healthy eating doesn't mean you're condemned to a life of eating cottage cheese – it's simply a question of eating less of some foods and more of others. There are no 'good' and 'bad' or 'healthy' and 'unhealthy' foods. It's your diet in its entirety that is important – an occasional chocolate bar won't do any damage.

FAT AND CHOLESTEROL

Although a small amount of fat is essential for good health, most people in this country consume far too much. Fat currently provides approximately 40% of our total calorie intake. A high fat intake is known to be a risk factor for a number of diseases, particularly coronary heart disease and certain types of cancer.

The latest Government guidelines on healthy eating recommend that we reduce our fat intake to a level at which it supplies no more than 35% of our total energy intake.

All fats are made up of smaller units called fatty acids. There are three types of fatty acid: saturated, monounsaturated and polyunsaturated. Each type differs slightly in terms of its chemical structure. All fats are made up of a combination of the three types of fatty acid. Butter for example contains 63% saturated fatty acids, 3% polyunsaturated fatty acids and 34% monounsaturated fatty acids. Soya oil contains 57% polyunsaturated, 15% saturated and 24% monounsaturated fatty acids.

SATURATED FATS are made up predominantly of saturated fatty acids. They tend to be solid at room temperature and are found mainly as animal fats such as butter, dairy products, meat.

POLYUNSATURATED FATS are made up predominantly of polyunsaturated fatty acids. They tend to be liquid at room temperature and are found mainly as vegetable oils such as sunflower oil, corn oil etc. The two exceptions are palm oil and coconut oil both of which are saturated fats.

MONOUNSATURATED FATS are found predominantly in olive oil, ground nut (peanut) oil, grapeseed oil and avocado pears.

A diet which is high in saturated fat raises the level of cholesterol in the blood, a risk factor for coronary heart disease.

Polyunsaturated fats can help to lower blood cholesterol levels but the effect is only half as strong as the cholesterol raising ability of saturated fat. The effect of monounsaturated fats is less certain, but there is increasing evidence to suggest that they may play a beneficial role in lowering blood cholesterol levels.

Fat, whatever type, is a very concentrated source of energy (calories). Ounce for ounce it contains almost twice as many calories as protein or carbohydrate, which is why foods that contain large amounts of fat are highly calorific.

CHOLESTEROL

Cholesterol is a fatty substance that occurs naturally in all animal tissues, including the blood stream. Most of the cholesterol in our body is made by the liver from saturated fatty acids, but smaller amounts are obtained from the diet, particularly from eggs, liver, kidney, shellfish and fish roes. Cholesterol is an important constituent of all cell membranes and the fatty sheath that protects nerves; it is involved in the manufacture of hormones, particularly the sex hormones and those which regulate the body's metabolism.

It is transported around the body via the blood linked to proteins called lipoproteins. Low density lipoproteins (LDL's) transport most of the cholesterol and deliver it to cells in the body. When the diet contains large amounts of saturated fats the liver correspondingly produces large amounts of LDL's. Cholesterol associated with LDL's is easily deposited in the arteries. This results in the arteries becoming clogged or furred which will lead to atherosclerosis (narrowing of the arteries which restricts the flow of blood). High density lipoproteins (HDL's) carry a smaller amount of cholesterol, which they transport to the liver where it is excreted. HDL's are therefore considered to be 'good' lipoproteins and LDL's to be 'bad'. Unsaturated fat, particularly polyunsaturates promote the production of the beneficial HDL's. The level of HDL's can also be increased by taking regular exercise, maintaining ideal body weight and giving up smoking.

The amount and type of fat in the diet is more important than the amount of cholesterol in determining blood cholesterol levels.

CARBOHYDRATES

These can be divided into two groups: simple carbohydrates or sugars (eg glucose, sucrose, fructose and dextrose) and complex carbohydrates or starch (cereals, potatoes, rice, etc).

To achieve a healthy diet we should be getting less of our calories from the former and more from the later. Many people still believe that starchy foods are fattening. This is not true. Nutritionists agree that we should all be aiming to eat more starchy foods.

DIETARY FIBRE

In the next few years we should see the term 'fibre' replaced by a new name, Non starch polysaccharides (NSP). This is simply a way of providing a more accurate name for what is not, simply one, but a number of different compounds. NSP are the major components of plant cell walls and as such are found in foods such as cereals, fruits and vegetables. NSP can be further divided into two groups: soluble and insoluble. Soluble NSP which is found in cereals (especially oats), vegetables (particularly beans) and some fruits is believed to help in lowering high blood cholesterol levels. Insoluble NSP which is also found in cereals (particularly wheat bran) and vegetables has the effect of holding or absorbing water thereby making the stools larger, softer and easier to pass. This helps to prevent problems such as constipation, diverticular disease and haemorrhoids. NSP also speeds up the rate at which waste material is passed through the gut; this is believed to play an important role in preventing bowel cancer.

NSP-rich foods are good news for weight watchers too. They are generally less energy dense, and more filling than their low fibre counterparts. In the UK the average intake of NSP is 12 g/day, experts suggests that we should aim to increase this to a level of 18 g/day.

Increasing our intake of NSP doesn't mean adding bran to everything we eat. It's much better to eat foods which are naturally good sources of NSP such as wholegrain cereal (wholemeal bread, pasta, brown rice), fruit, vegetables, beans and pulses.

SUGAR

Sugars can be divided into two groups:
INTRINSIC SUGARS: These are naturally incorporated into the cellular structure of food, for example the sugar present in fruit (fructose).
EXTRINSIC SUGARS such as sucrose, honey and glucose are not present in foods as part of the cellular structure. They are usually added to foods during processing.

Extrinsic sugars are known to be a major factor contributing to tooth decay. However, many experts argue that it is the form in which sugar is taken and the frequency with which it is eaten that is more important than the total amount. Nevertheless sugar is not essential in the diet. It provides what nutritionists refer to as 'empty calories', in other words, it provides the body with calories but no other nutrients. Healthy eating guidelines recommend that we should reduce our consumption of extrinsic sugars to a level at which they provides no more than 10-11% of our total energy intake. For the average person this amounts to a maximum intake of approximately 60 g (2 oz) sugar a day.

PROTEIN

Protein is required for growth and the maintenance and repair of all body tissue. The main dietary sources of protein are meat, fish, eggs, milk, cheese, yogurt, nuts, beans and pulses. The average requirement for protein is between 50-70 g (2-3 oz)/day or about 10% of the total energy intake. Most people in this country get approximately 15% of their energy from protein and so get more than the required amount, but there is no evidence to suggest that it is harmful.

SALT

Although salt (sodium chloride) is an essential part of all body cells, the average intake is 12 times higher than the amount needed. In fact if we didn't add salt to anything we cooked or ate, our needs would still be met. We could easily get the 1 g of salt we need each day from the tiny amounts which occur naturally in most foods.

Nutritionists are still debating the effects of eating too much salt. For people suffering from hypertension (high blood pressure) reducing the level of salt in the diet can help. But it is not yet absolutely certain whether a high salt intake causes hypertension. In Britain, 1 person in five will develop high blood pressure which is a known risk factor for a number of diseases including coronary heart disease and strokes.

Approximately a third of all the salt we eat is added to food during cooking or at the table. One of the easiest ways to reduce the amount of salt in the diet is to stop putting the salt cellar on the table!

VITAMINS AND MINERALS

Walk into any health food shop, pharmacy or chemist and you'll find the shelves positively groaning under the weight of dietary supplements. All manner of pills and potions, promising all sorts of miracle cures. One in four adults in Britain take some form of food supplement, multivitamins being the most common.

VITAMINS

The word vitamin is derived from the Latin *vita* (life) and *amine* (a chemical group once believed to be part of all vitamins). There are some 20 vitamins, most of which cannot be synthesized by the body, and must therefore be obtained from the diet. Each vitamin performs one or several essential functions within the body. Vitamins can be divided into two groups, fat soluble vitamins (A,D,E,K) and water soluble (B complex and C). Water soluble vitamins leach out of food into cooking water and are easily destroyed by heat. The fat soluble vitamins are less vulnerable to losses during cooking and processing. The body is capable of storing some vitamins (A, D, E, K and B12), the rest need to be provided by the diet on a regular basis. In theory a well balanced diet, comprising a wide variety of different foods will provide all the vitamins and minerals you need.

However there may be occasions, for example after an illness when it may be of benefit to take a vitamin supplement. But you should be aware that an excessive intake of some vitamins can be dangerous. The vitamins that are most likely to reach toxic levels are the fat soluble vitamins (A, D, E and K), which the body is unable to excrete. The other vitamins are water soluble and any excess can be eliminated in the urine. If you do decide to take a vitamin supplement it is best to discuss the matter with your doctor or a pharmacist who will be able to advise you as to the most suitable type for your particular needs.

VITAMIN A (RETINOL)

Necessary for growth, good vision in dim light and healthy skin. Vitamin A deficiency is rare in Western countries but it is a major cause of blindness in many third world countries. If consumed in excessive quantities (more than 10 times the recommended levels) it may reach toxic levels. An excessive intake of Vitamin A during early pregnancy may cause birth defects. As a precaution pregnant women or anyone trying to conceive should not take Vitamin A supplements or eat liver, which contains large amounts of the vitamin.

The main dietary sources of retinol are dairy products (cheese, milk, butter and margarine), offal (especially liver), eggs and oily fish, and beta carotene, which is present in many green, orange and yellow vegetables.

BETA-CAROTENE is the pigment found in highly

coloured vegetables. Carrots and dark green vegetables such as spinach contain the most. The body can convert beta carotene into Vitamin A, but besides acting as a source of Vitamin A, Beta carotene may also have an important role to play as an antioxidant in its own right. It helps to prevent cell damage by free radicals, thereby helping to protect against coronary heart disease and certain types of cancer.

VITAMIN B COMPLEX

Vitamin B was originally thought to be one vitamin, but it is now known to be a number of different substances. Many of the B vitamins occur together in the same foods. The three that are best known are Thiamin (Vitamin B1), Riboflavin (Vitamin B2) and Niacin or Nicotinic acid (Vitamin B3). These three are usually referred to by their chemical names, but most of the others are known by their numbers.

VITAMIN B1 (THIAMIN): Helps the release of energy from carbohydrates. Thiamin requirements are increased by alcohol, caffeine, antibiotics and the contraceptive pill. Good sources of thiamin include milk, offal, meat (especially pork), potatoes, wholegrain and fortified cereals, nuts and pulses. This vitamin can also be obtained from yeast, yeast extract and wheatgerm.

VITAMIN B2 (RIBOFLAVIN): Vital for growth, the release of energy from food and the maintenance of healthy skin and eyes. Vitamin B2 is fairly stable to heat but losses can occur as a result of leaching into water; use the cooking water for gravies or sauces. It is also destroyed by ultra violet light, a factor which becomes relevant if milk bottles are left standing on the doorstep. Good sources are milk, meat, offal, eggs, cheese, fortified breakfast cereals and yeast extract.

VITAMIN B3 (NIACIN/NICOTINIC ACID/NICOTINAMIDE): Plays an important role in the release of energy within the cells. Unlike the other B vitamins, niacin can be made by the body from the essential amino acid tryptophan (present in large quantities in milk).

Niacin is not easily destroyed by heat but large losses can occur as a result of leaching into the cooking water. Large doses of niacin (in excess of 3 g/day) are sometimes recommended to help lower blood cholesterol levels, but such treatment should not be embarked upon without medical supervision.

Good sources of niacin are meat, offal, fish, fortified breakfast cereals, and pulses.

VITAMIN B6 (PYRIDOXINE): Helps the body utilize protein and contributes to the formation of haemoglobin for red blood cells. It is found in a wide range of foods including meat, liver, fish, eggs, wholegrain cereals, some vegetables, pulses and yeast extract.

Vitamin B6 supplements are sometimes helpful in relieving the symptoms associated with premenstrual tension.

VITAMIN B12 (COBALAMIN): Vital for growth, the formation of red blood cells, and the maintenance of a healthy nervous system. Vitamin B12 is unique because it is only found in foods of animal origin. Vegetarians who eat dairy products will get enough but vegans may become deficient (however this is rare since many vegan foods are fortified with B12).

Vitamin B12 is fairly stable to heat but like other B vitamins considerable losses can occur as a result of leaching. Deficiency of the vitamin causes a form of anaemia known as pernicious anaemia. Good sources of B12 include liver, kidney, oily fish, meat, cheese, eggs and milk.

FOLIC ACID: Involved in the manufacture of amino acids and the production of red blood cells. Large amounts of folic acid can be lost during cooking and processing since it is unstable at high temperatures and is easily leached into the cooking water.

Deficiency of folic acid can cause a type of anaemia, and there is evidence to suggest that a deficiency prior to conception and in the early stages of pregnancy may cause foetal malformations, particularly spina bifida.

Good sources of folic acid are green leafy vegetables, liver, pulses, eggs, wholemeal cereal products, yeast, wheatgerm and wheat bran.

VITAMIN B5 (PANTOTHENIC ACID): Involved in a number of metabolic reactions, including energy production. This vitamin is present in so many foods that a deficiency is extremely rare; notable exceptions are fat, oil and sugar. Cooking will destroy a certain amount but only if the temperature rises above boiling point.

Good sources include liver, kidney, yeast, egg yolk, fish roe, wheatgerm, nuts, pulses and fresh vegetables. It is also present in relatively large quantities in royal jelly.

BIOTIN: Involved in various metabolic reactions and the release of energy from foods. In adults biotin, unlike most other vitamins, can be synthesized by bacteria that live in the intestines.

Good sources of biotin include liver, oily fish, yeast, kidney, eggs yolks and brown rice.

VITAMIN C (ASCORBIC ACID)

Essential for growth and the formation of collagen (a protein necessary for healthy bones, teeth, gums, blood capillaries and all connective tissue). It plays an important role in the healing of wounds and fractures. It also acts as an antioxidant and as such it may have a role to play in the prevention of certain types of cancer and coronary heart disease.

Many people take Vitamin C supplements, often as an attempt to protect against colds. However the evidence that Vitamin C protects against colds is far from conclusive. Very large doses should be avoided by people who are susceptible to kidney stones, because this vitamin is converted to oxalic acid in the body, which can form stones.

Vitamin C is found mainly in fruit and vegetables. It is the least stable of all the vitamins and large amounts can be lost during preparation and cooking. It is destroyed by heat, alkaline conditions (for example adding bicarbonate of soda to the water when cooking vegetables), and large amounts are lost through leaching into water.

To preserve their Vitamin C content, foods should be steamed or cooked in the minimum amount of water, for as short a time as possible and served immediately. When possible the cooking water should be used for making gravy, stock or soup.

VITAMIN D (CHOLECALCIFEROL)

Essential for growth, the absorption of calcium and the formation of healthy bones. It is also involved in maintaining a healthy nervous system. The amount of Vitamin D occurring naturally in foods is small and it is restricted to very few foods. Good sources are oily fish (fish liver oil supplements), eggs and liver. Some foods like margarine are fortified. Most of our Vitamin D, however, does not come from the diet but is made by the body when the skin is exposed to sunlight.

Vitamin D, like Vitamin A, is stored in the liver. This ensures a constant supply throughout the winter months when there is less sunlight. A deficiency can cause joint problems and brittle bones. Elderly housebound people often have low levels of Vitamin D because of poor food intake and lack of sunshine. Vitamin D can have toxic effects at high doses but this only applies to oral Vitamin D as the body regulates against overproduction of Vitamin D by sunshine.

VITAMIN E (TOCOPHEROLS)

Vitamin E is not one but a number of related compounds usually called tocopherols. They all function as antioxidants, which protect fats from damage by free radicals. There is an increasing amount of evidence to suggest that Vitamin E has an important role to play in the prevention of degenerative diseases, coronary heart disease and certain types of cancer.

Good sources of Vitamin E are vegetable oils, polyunsaturated margarines, wheatgerm, sunflower seeds, nuts, oily fish, eggs, wholegrain cereals, avocado pears and spinach.

VITAMIN K

Essential for the production of several proteins including prothombin, which is involved in the clotting of blood. It has been found to exist in three forms, one of which is obtained from food while the other two are synthesized by the bacteria in the intestine. Vitamin K1, which is the form found in food is present in broccoli, cabbage, spinach, cereals, liver, alfalfa, and kelp.

MINERALS

Minerals are metallic or non-metallic elements that are essential to the body and must be provided by the diet.

Their main functions are as components of bone and teeth, regulators for the composition of body fluids and as necessary substances for the correct functioning of many enzymes.

CALCIUM

Calcium plays a vital role in the formation of bones and teeth. It also helps to control nerve impulses and muscle contractions.

Good sources of calcium are milk, cheese, yogurt, sardines and white flour (fortified with calcium). Dark green leafy vegetables contain calcium but they also contain oxalic acid which interferes with calcium absorption. Calcium in nuts and pulses is also poorly absorbed because of phytic acid. Calcium is no longer deposited in the bones after the age of about 35. It is important to ensure that calcium intakes are adequate prior to this happening, since large deposits of calcium in the bone are believed to protect against the development of osteoporosis (brittle bones) later on in life.

MAGNESIUM

Together with calcium, magnesium forms an integral part of bones and teeth. Also involved in energy supply, nerve and muscle function and in the utilization of calcium and potassium.

Magnesium is present in a wide variety of foods, especially those of vegetable origin. Particularly good sources are nuts, wholegrain cereals, green vegetables and cocoa powder.

PHOSPHORUS
Vital to the formation of bones and teeth, phosphorus is also involved in the release and storage of energy in the body. It is supplied by a wide variety of foods. Good sources include, cheese, liver, lentils, wholegrain cereals, eggs, meat, fish, milk and yeast extract.

POTASSIUM
Along with sodium, potassium is responsible for regulating the levels of acidity and alkalinity within the body and maintaining the correct water balance.

Potassium deficiency due to poor dietary intake is rare, but deficiency can occur as a result of prolonged diarrhoea or repeated vomiting or by regular use of diuretics (particularly in the elderly). Potassium is found in nearly all foods except sugar, fats and oils. Fruits and vegetables are a particularly rich source.

FLUORIDE
Helps children to develop strong bones and teeth and protects against dental caries. Good dietary source are tea, seaweed and fluoridated drinking water. Fluoride is toxic in excess and causes degeneration of tooth enamel.

IODINE
Necessary for the production of thyroid hormones. The best source of iodine is kelp but it is not eaten in sufficient amounts to make a reliable contribution. In the UK most iodine is obtained from milk, dairy products, fish and meat. Iodine deficiency does occur in localized areas where there is a low concentration of iodine in the soil, but it is rare in the UK.

IRON
An important component of haemoglobin (the compound in red blood cells that transports oxygen to all parts of the body). The best sources of iron in the diet are red meat and liver. Reasonable amounts of iron are found in eggs, some vegetables, wholegrain cereals and pulses. But the iron from these foods is not as easily absorbed as that from meat and liver. The absorption of iron is increased in the presence of Vitamin C, so eat foods rich in this vitamin at the same time as iron containing foods.

Absorption is reduced by tannin (a constituent of tea) and so it's best to take tea after a meal rather than at the same time.

An iron deficiency causes anaemia, which is still relatively common in the UK. People most likely to be affected are women of child-bearing age, particularly those who do not eat meat.

ZINC
Vital for growth and sexual maturation. It also plays an important role in wound healing. Zinc is found in greatest amounts in meat, milk, liver, cheese, yogurt, eggs, fish and shellfish. One of the richest sources is oysters.

MAKING THE MOST OF YOUR VITAMINS
There are various ways you can improve the vitamin and mineral content of your diet by buying, storing and preparing food wisely. Follow these tips to get the most from your food.

- The water soluble vitamins B and C are very easily destroyed by storage, heat and light. Try to buy fruit and vegetables little and often rather than in huge quantities. Look for firm produce, avoid limp wilting greens. Buy from a shop that you know has a quick turnover.
- Store vegetables in a cool dark place, ideally for no more than 3 days.
- Never leave vegetables standing in water before cooking.
- Do not add bicarbonate of soda to the water when cooking vegetables.
- Ideally cook vegetables using little or no water. Boiling vegetables in large quantities of water can destroy up to 70% of the Vitamin C. If you do boil vegetables you should keep the water to an absolute minimum, only add the vegetables to the water once it is boiling, and when they are cooked use the water to make gravy, soup or stock.
- Keep peeling to a minimum, since the highest concentrations of vitamins are found directly under the skin. Cut vegetables into large chunks so less surface area is exposed (Vitamin C is lost when cut surfaces are in contact with air).
- Eat food soon after it is prepared; keeping food warm results in vitamin loss.
- Never leave your milk outside all day on the doorstep as up to 70% of the riboflavin can be lost in this way.

GUIDELINES FOR HEALTHY EATING
The following simple changes will help you to improve your diet.

EAT LESS FAT, PARTICULARLY SATURATED FAT
- Use skimmed or semi-skimmed milk instead of full fat.
- Spread butter, margarine or low fat spread thinly.
- Choose lean meat. Trim away any visible fat before cooking. Eat more poultry and white fish both of which are lower in fat. Remove the skin from chicken before eating.
- Avoid fatty meat products such as burgers, sausages and pies.
- Use less fat in cooking. Grill, bake, boil or microwave rather than fry. When you do use oil for cooking use an oil that is high in polyunsaturated fat or olive oil.
- Use low and reduced fat alternatives when available, eg reduced fat pâté, cheese, crisps etc. But be aware that most of these products still contain significant amounts of fat.
- Cut back on foods such as cakes, biscuits, pastry etc, all of which are high in fat.

EAT LESS SUGAR
- About half the sugar we eat is added to food at the table, ie sugar in tea, on breakfast cereal, etc. Aim to reduce the sugar you add to foods, better still don't add any at all.
- Avoid sweet fizzy drinks and squash. Choose the low calorie or sugar-free varieties.
- Eat fewer sugary snacks such as cakes, sweets and biscuits.
- Choose reduced sugar products where available, eg reduced sugar jam, sugar-free muesli, fruit canned in natural juice not syrup.
- Don't be misled into thinking that honey is better for you than sugar or that brown sugar is better than white.

EAT LESS SALT
- Add less salt to your food during cooking and at the table.
- Eat fewer salty foods such as cheese, bacon, crisps, peanuts etc.

EAT MORE FIBRE
- Eat more bread, especially wholemeal bread.
- Eat more wholemeal pasta, brown rice and wholegrain breakfast cereals.
- Eat plenty of fresh fruit and vegetables.
- Eat more beans and pulses.

VEGETARIANISM
The term vegetarian covers a broad spectrum of diets, all of which are based around the avoidance of meat and fish.

LACTO-VEGETARIANS will include milk and milk products in their diet.

LACTO-OVO VEGETARIANS will include milk, dairy products and eggs in their diet.

VEGANS sometimes referred to as 'strict vegetarians' consume no animal products whatsoever, sometimes even excluding products such as honey from their diet.

There are currently in excess of 3 million people in this country who follow a vegetarian diet, that is 7% of the adult population and the number of people becoming vegetarian is ever-increasing.

People choose to become vegetarian for many different reasons. Hindu, Sikh and 7th day Adventist religions all advocate vegetarianism. Many people choose to avoid meat because they believe it's wrong to rear and slaughter animals simply for food. Others choose to become vegetarian because they see it as a way to a healthier diet.

A vegetarian diet is a more economical way of producing food in the context of the limited world food resources. Obtaining food from plants is a much more economical way of using land than using it to rear animals.

People often make the mistake of assuming that vegetarian diets are automatically healthier than diets that include meat. This isn't always the case – there are good and bad vegetarian diets. However, a properly planned vegetarian diet can be a very healthy way of eating; it is low in saturated fat, high in fibre and contains all of the essential vitamins and minerals needed for a healthy life. Vegetables, nuts, pulses, eggs, cheese and cereals are all good sources of protein and, provided vegetarians eat a good variety of these foods, they will get enough protein.

WEIGHT REDUCING DIETS
In this country 40% of men and 32% of women are overweight (ie a total of 21 million people – or one in three). Obesity is not simply a cosmetic problem. Anyone who is more than a stone and a half overweight (11 kg/25 lb) has an increased risk of a number of diseases: heart disease, gall stones, diabetes and high blood pressure to name just a few.

Weight gain occurs when energy (calories) consumed exceeds the energy you expend. In this situation the end result is that excess energy is stored in the body as fat. In order to lose weight you need to create an energy deficit, in this situation the body will draw on fat reserves to provide the energy it needs. The easiest way to do this is by reducing energy consumed (ie restricting calorie intake) and increasing energy expenditure (ie exercise).

The basis of any weight reducing diet is to reduce the number of calories that you consume. But what exactly is a calorie?

A calorie is a scientific term used to describe the quantity of heat required to raise the temperature of 1 g of water by 1°C. The body's energy requirements and the energy value of foods are measured as kilocalories (one kilocalorie is equivalent to 1000 Calories) or kilojoules (a kilojoule is a metric calorie 1 kcal = 4.183 kj). In practice the term calorie is used to describe what is in actual fact a kilocalorie, while the term kilojoule (kj) is rarely used in this country.

To lose weight you should reduce your present calorie intake by between 500 and 1000 calories a day (depending on how much weight you need to lose). It is never a good idea to restrict your intake to a level of less than 1000 calories a day without seeking medical advice. A lower calorie intake than this could lead to loss of lean tissue as well as fat.

Our metabolic rate is determined partly by the amount of lean tissue that we have, so losing lean tissue may make it harder to maintain energy balance in the future.

To maintain weight loss, you need to make permanent changes to your diet. Crash diets and miracle cures may promise rapid and spectacular weight loss but they are rarely successful in the long term.

Dieting is never easy, and when you have to combine watching your weight with feeding your family it can seem impossible! But counting calories doesn't have to mean endless cottage cheese salads. The key to successful dieting is knowing what foods to eat and in what quantities to eat them.

Some foods, particularly fatty foods, such as cheese, cream, butter, oil, etc are highly calorific, but this doesn't necessarily mean that you need to avoid them completely, simply that they should be consumed in much smaller quantities. Other foods, such as fruit, vegetables, lean meat, white fish and chicken, are much lower in fat and calories and therefore can be consumed in more generous quantities.

Starchy foods such as bread, potatoes, pasta, cereals and rice are often wrongly accused of being fattening. In fact a slice of bread has only 80 calories. It's what you put with them that does the damage – spread a generous helping of butter or margarine on your bread and you could easily double the calorie content.

Calorie Saving Tips

- Weight for weight, fat provides more than twice as many calories as carbohydrates, so it's best to concentrate your efforts on cutting right back on the amount of fat you eat.
- Choose lean meat and trim away any visible fat before cooking.
- Use more poultry, game and white fish, all of which are reasonably low in fat and calories. Remove the skin from poultry before cooking.
- Extend or bulk savoury dishes by adding plenty of vegetables, which are low in calories and contain plenty of vitamins.
- Use low fat cooking methods, ie grilling, baking, boiling, steaming or microwave cooking rather than frying. When you do use oil for cooking use either a vegetable oil which is high in polyunsaturated fats or olive oil. To reduce the amount of oil needed when softening vegetables etc, use a heavy based non-stick pan.
- Use fat reduced alternatives where available, eg reduced fat cheddar, skimmed or semi-skimmed milk, low fat yogurts etc.
- Use butter, margarine or low fat spread sparingly. The term 'low fat spread' is slightly misleading: although most contain less than half the fat and calories of butter or margarine they do still contain a significant amount of fat and should be thought of as a high fat food.
- To make gravies and sauces creamy, add low fat natural yogurt or fromage frais rather than cream. Stir in at the end of cooking to prevent curdling.
- Don't be afraid to occasionally use high calorie foods such as cheese and bacon. You only need to use small quantities to add a lot of flavour.
- Choose high fibre accompaniments, eg brown rice, wholemeal pasta, when possible. Experiments have proved that high fibre foods, such as wholemeal bread, are more filling than their refined alternatives and are therefore more satisfying.

Soups

There is nothing as satisfying as a really good homemade soup packed with flavour. Soups range from light consommés and creamed soups to thick hearty potages which are a meal in themselves. They are a great way to use up odds and ends of vegetables and, if you use a homemade stock, you'll find it adds a special flavour.
Soups are relatively quick and easy to make, too. Creamy soups can be worked to a velvety smooth texture within a few minutes in a blender or food processor.

SERVING SUGGESTIONS

When serving soup as a starter, allow about 250-300 ml (8-10 fl oz) per person; for soup that's a meal in itself, allow 300-350 ml (10-12 fl oz), depending on appetite and how substantial the soup is.

Hot soup should be served piping hot. Warm the soup bowls beforehand and, if possible, don't pour it out until people are seated and ready to eat. Chilled soup should not be so cold that its flavour is masked.

GARNISHES AND ACCOMPANIMENTS

Soups, especially those served in wide soup plates, generally look better garnished, while others can be made more substantial or given a contrasting texture by adding an extra ingredient or serving with an accompaniment.
CRUSTY BREAD is the ideal accompaniment for most soups. As a change from a French stick or rolls, try serving a flavoured bread such as olive or cheese bread.
CROÛTONS are fried or toasted cubes of bread. For fried croûtons, cut the bread into small dice and fry in vegetable oil until golden brown.

For garlic-flavoured croûtons, add a crushed garlic clove to the oil. Drain on absorbent kitchen paper and serve in a separate bowl so they remain crisp.

For toasted croûtons, toast the bread and then cut it into dice. Croûtons can be made in advance and stored in an airtight container. Add to the soup just before serving.

CREAM OR YOGHURT swirled on top of a soup just before serving looks attractive.
RICE AND PASTA make a soup more substantial. Either add cooked leftovers and heat through or cook the rice or pasta in the soup itself. Use small pasta shapes in soups or break up large varieties so that it is easy to eat them with a soup spoon.
FRIED VEGETABLES such as onion rings, chopped leeks and sliced mushrooms add colour, texture and flavour to bland soups. Cook, then drain well before using.
BACON STRIPS can be fried or grilled until crisp and then crumbled over a soup to add flavour and texture, but take care that the soup will not be too salty.
FRESH VEGETABLES such as thin slices of cucumber, snipped celery tops and julienne strips of carrot make an attractive garnish and add a crunchy texture. They are particularly good on chilled soups.
LEMON SLICES or curls of lemon rind are good with clear soups. Orange slices and rind go well with tomato soup.
GRATED HARD CHEESE such as Cheddar and Parmesan melts deliciously into hot soups. Serve separately in a bowl and sprinkle on the soup just before serving.
FRESH HERBS will liven up almost any hot or cold soup. Choose your herbs to complement the soup: try freshly chopped basil, coriander, chervil, chives, dill or parsley, or use a mixture of different herbs.

MELBA TOAST

4 slices of ready-sliced white or brown bread

1. Preheat the grill to high and toast the bread lightly on both sides. Cut off the crusts, then holding the toast flat, slide the knife between the toasted edges to split the bread.
2. Cut each piece into 4 triangles, then toast under the grill, untoasted side uppermost, until golden and the edges curl. Serve warm. Alternatively make earlier in the day and warm for a short time in the oven at 170°C (325°F) mark 3 before serving.
SERVES 4

Hold the toast flat, and, using a sharp knife, cut the slices in half.

DUMPLINGS

125 g (4 oz) self raising flour
50 g (2 oz) shredded suet
salt and pepper

1. In a bowl, mix the flour, suet and seasoning with sufficient cold water to make an elastic dough.
2. Divide into about 16 portions and with lightly floured hands, roll into small balls.
3. Add the dumplings to the soup and simmer for about 15-20 minutes.
SERVES 4

VARIATIONS
Flavour the dough with any of the following:
25 g (1 oz) Cheddar cheese, finely grated
½ small onion, skinned and finely chopped
15 ml (1 level tbsp) grated Parmesan cheese
2.5 ml (½ level tsp) mild curry powder
15 ml (1 level tbsp) chopped fresh watercress
7.5 ml (1½ tsp) chopped fresh parsley or chives
5 ml (1 tsp) chopped fresh tarragon
2.5 ml (½ level tsp) mixed dried herbs
2.5 ml (½ level tsp) paprika
5 ml (1 level tsp) caraway seeds

STOCKS

Homemade stocks will undoubtedly produce a better flavoured soup – and stock-making needn't be a chore. Get into the habit of using leftover bones, poultry carcasses and vegetables to make full-flavoured stocks. Use whatever stock is required and freeze the remainder in sensible quantities for future occasions.

If you haven't time to make your own stock, then try one of the milder-flavoured stock cubes, but remember that they are inclined to be strong and salty, so make sure you adjust the seasoning.

The range of stock products available has increased in recent years and you can now buy fish, lamb, veal, ham and vegetable stocks, as well as beef and chicken. Most come in cube form and contain a variety of vegetables and herbs, plus ingredients such as yeast extract and spices. Some products, including a range of stocks sold fresh in cartons, contain no added salt, sugar or artificial additives.

TIPS FOR STOCK-MAKING
1. Use the whole chicken carcass for a jellied chicken stock.
2. Don't cover your stock pot completely. It does need to reduce well and if you keep the steam in it will go cloudy.
3. Make sure you skim your stock frequently: scum and fat in the stock will cause cloudiness.
4. When straining, allow the stock to drip through a sieve, conical if possible. If you try to squeeze the vegetables through you will lose the clarity of the stock.
5. Allow stock to cool and remove the layer of fat from the surface before storing.
6. To freeze, reduce stocks well by boiling, then cool and freeze in ice cube trays.
7. If you store stock, particularly chicken, in the refrigerator, boil it up every day. Meat and chicken stocks will keep refrigerated for up to 4 days, fish stocks 2 days.

BEEF STOCK

450 g (1 lb) shin of beef, cut into pieces
450 g (1 lb) marrow bone or knuckle of veal, chopped
bouquet garni
1 medium onion, skinned and sliced
1 medium carrot, scrubbed and sliced
1 celery stick, washed and sliced
2.5 ml (1 level tsp) salt

1. To give a good flavour and colour, brown the bones and meat in the oven before using them. Put in a sauccpan with 1.7 litres (3 pints) water, the herbs, vegetables and salt. Bring to the boil, skim, partially cover and simmer for 2 hours.
2. Or pressure cook on High (15 lb) pressure for 1 hour, using 1.4 litres (2½ pints) water. If using marrow bones, increase the water to 1.7 litres (3 pints) and cook for 1¼ hours. Strain the stock and when cold remove any trace of fat.
MAKES ABOUT 900 ML (1½ PINTS)

VARIATION
Replace the shin of beef with fresh or cooked meat bones.

CHICKEN STOCK

1 chicken carcass
1 medium onion, skinned and sliced
1 medium carrot, scrubbed and sliced
1 celery stick, washed and sliced
1 bay leaf

1. Break up the carcass and put in a large saucepan with any skin and chicken meat. Add 1.7 litres (3 pints) water, the flavouring vegetables and bay leaf. Bring to the boil, skim, partially cover and simmer for about 2 hours.
2. Or pressure cook on High (15 lb) for about 1 hour using 1.4 litres (2½ pints) water.
3. Strain the stock and, when cold, remove all traces of fat.
MAKES ABOUT 900 ML (1½ PINTS)

FISH STOCK

1 fish head or fish bones and trimmings
salt
bouquet garni
1 medium onion, skinned and sliced

1. Put the head and fish trimmings into a saucepan, cover with 450 ml (¾ pint) water and season with salt. Bring to the boil, then skim.
2. Reduce the heat and add the bouquet garni and onion. Cover and simmer for 20 minutes. Strain.
3. Use on the same day, or store in the refrigerator for not more than 2 days.
MAKES ABOUT 300 ML (½ PINT)

VEGETABLE STOCK

30 ml (2 tbsp) vegetable oil
1 medium onion, skinned and finely chopped
1 medium carrot, scrubbed and diced
50 g (2 oz) turnip, scrubbed and diced
50 g (2 oz) parsnip, scrubbed and diced
4 celery sticks, washed and chopped
vegetable trimmings, eg celery tops, cabbage leaves,
*   mushroom peelings, tomato skins*
bouquet garni
6 black peppercorns

1. Heat the oil in a saucepan, add the onion and fry gently for about 5 minutes until soft and lightly coloured.
2. Add the vegetables with the trimmings and 1.7 litres (3 pints) water. Add the bouquet garni and peppercorns.
3. Bring to the boil, partially cover and simmer for 1½ hours, skimming occasionally.
4. Strain the stock and leave to cool. Store in the refrigerator and use within 1-2 days.
MAKES ABOUT 1.1 LITRES (2 PINTS)

Consommé

A classic consommé is a completely clear, well flavoured broth, made from good brown stock. Both the stock and the utensils must be quite free from any trace of grease, to prevent droplets of fat forming on the surface of the soup.

1.4 litres (2½ pints) Beef Stock (see page 19)
125 g (4 oz) lean beef steak, eg rump
150 ml (¼ pint) cold water
1 medium carrot, peeled and quartered
1 small onion, skinned and quartered
bouquet garni
1 egg white
salt
10 ml (2 tsp) dry sherry (optional)

1. Remove any fat from the stock. Shred the meat finely and soak it in the water for 15 minutes. Put the meat and water, vegetables, stock and bouquet garni into a deep saucepan and add the egg white. Heat gently, whisking continuously until a thick froth starts to form. Stop whisking and bring to the boil. Reduce the heat immediately, cover and simmer for 2 hours. If the liquid boils too rapidly, the froth will break and cloud the consommé.

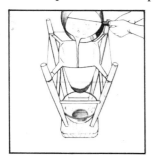

Pour through a jelly bag.

2. Scald a clean cloth or jelly bag, by pouring boiling water through it, wring it out, tie it to the four legs of an upturned stool and place a bowl underneath. Pour the soup through the cloth, keeping the froth back at first with a spoon, then let it slide out on to the cloth. Again pour the soup through the cloth and through the filter of egg white. The consommé should now be clear and sparkling.

3. Reheat the consommé, season with salt if necessary, and if you like, a little sherry to improve the flavour.

Serves 4

NOTE: Consommé may be served hot or cold, plain or with one of the following variations – in which case the consommé takes its name from the garnish. To prevent the consommé becoming cloudy, rinse the garnish in water and add it to the hot liquid just before it is served.

VARIATIONS
Consommé Julienne
Cut small quantities of vegetables such as carrot, turnip and celery into thin strips and boil separately; rinse well before adding to the soup.

Consommé à la Jardinière
Prepare a mixture of vegetables such as finely diced carrots and turnips, tiny florets of cauliflower and green peas. Cook in boiling salted water until just tender, rinse and add to the soup before serving.

Consommé à la Royale
The garnish consists of steamed savoury egg

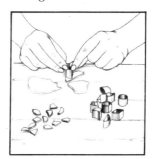

Cut the savoury custard into decorative shapes.

custard cut into tiny fancy shapes. Make the custard by mixing 1 egg yolk, 15 ml (1 tbsp) beef stock, milk or cream and salt and pepper to taste; strain it into a ramekin dish, cover with foil or greaseproof paper and stand the basin in a saucepan containing enough hot water to come half-way up its sides. Steam the custard slowly until it is firm; turn it out and cut into fancy shapes. Add to the soup before serving.

Jellied Consommé
Cold consommé should be lightly jellied. It makes a good soup for summer days. Leave the consommé to cool, then chill until set. Chop roughly and serve in individual dishes.

VARIATIONS FOR JELLIED CONSOMMÉ
1. Add 30-45 ml (2-3 tbsp) chopped fresh herbs (chives, parsley and tarragon) to the consommé. Garnish with whipped cream flavoured with curry powder or sprinkled with toasted flaked almonds.
2. Add 30-45 ml (2-3 tbsp) chopped fresh mint leaves to the consommé. Garnish with whipped cream mixed with chopped mint.

CREAM OF ARTICHOKE SOUP

900 g (2 lb) Jerusalem artichokes, peeled
salt
2 lemon slices
25 g (1 oz) butter or margarine
1 medium onion, skinned and chopped
30 ml (2 level tbsp) cornflour
450 ml (¾ pint) milk
15-30 ml (1-2 tbsp) lemon juice
15-30 ml (1-2 tbsp) chopped fresh parsley
60 ml (4 tbsp) single cream (optional)
pepper
croûtons, to garnish

1. Place the artichokes in a large saucepan with 900 ml (1½ pints) cold salted water and the lemon slices. Bring to the boil, cover and simmer gently for 25 minutes, until tender.

2. Drain, reserving 600 ml (1 pint) of the cooking liquid. Discard the lemon slices and mash the artichokes.
3. Melt the butter in a saucepan, add the onion and cook for about 5 minutes, until soft but not coloured. Remove the pan from the heat, stir in the cornflour and gradually add the artichoke cooking liquid and the milk.
4. Add the artichokes and bring to the boil, stirring. Cook for 2-3 minutes.
5. Cool the soup slightly, then purée in a blender or food processor or rub through a sieve. Return the purée to the rinsed out pan and stir in the lemon juice, parsley and cream if using, and season with salt and pepper.
6. Reheat gently but do not boil. Garnish with croûtons and serve immediately.
SERVES 6

LETTUCE SOUP

50 g (2 oz) butter or margarine
350 g (12 oz) lettuce leaves, roughly chopped
125 g (4 oz) spring onions, trimmed and sliced
15 ml (1 level tbsp) flour
600 ml (1 pint) Chicken Stock (see page 19)
150 ml (¼ pint) milk
salt and pepper

1. Melt the butter in a saucepan, add the lettuce and spring onions and cook until very soft.
2. Stir in the flour, then add the stock. Bring to the boil, cover and simmer for about 20 minutes.
3. Allow the soup to cool slightly, then sieve or purée in a blender or food processor until smooth. Return to the pan and add the milk and seasoning. Reheat gently.
SERVES 4

FRESH TOMATO SOUP WITH BASIL

50 g (2 oz) butter or margarine
2 medium onions, skinned and thinly sliced
900 g (2 lb) tomatoes
45 ml (3 level tbsp) flour
900 ml (1½ pints) Chicken Stock (see page 19)
30 ml (2 level tbsp) tomato purée
7.5 ml (1½ tsp) chopped fresh basil or 2.5 ml
  (½ level tsp) dried
salt and pepper
150 ml (5 fl oz) single cream (optional)

1. Melt the butter in a saucepan, add the onions and fry gently until golden brown.
2. Meanwhile, wipe and halve the tomatoes, scoop out the seeds into a sieve placed over a bowl. Press seeds to remove all tomato pulp and

juice; discard the seeds and reserve the juice.
3. Remove the pan from the heat. Stir in the flour and cook gently for 1 minute, stirring. Remove the pan from the heat and gradually stir in the stock. Bring to the boil slowly and continue to cook, stirring, until thickened.
4. Stir in the tomato purée, herbs and the tomatoes with reserved juice; season. Cover the pan and simmer gently for about 30 minutes.
5. Leave the soup to cool slightly, then sieve or purée in a blender or food processor. Strain through a sieve into a clean pan and reheat gently. Taste and adjust seasoning if necessary.
6. Ladle the soup into individual soup bowls and, if wished swirl a little cream through each bowl just before serving.
SERVES 6

WATERCRESS SOUP

2 bunches of watercress
50 g (2 oz) butter or margarine
1 medium onion, skinned and chopped
25 g (1 oz) flour
568 ml (1 pint) milk
450 ml (¾ pint) Chicken Stock (see page 19)
salt and pepper
90 ml (6 tbsp) single cream (optional)

Watercress Soup

1. Wash the watercress and reserve a few sprigs for garnish. Cut away any coarse stalks. Chop the leaves and remaining stalks.
2. Melt the butter in a large saucepan, add the watercress and onion and cook gently for about 5 minutes, until soft but not browned.
3. Stir in the flour and cook gently for 1 minute, stirring. Remove pan from the heat and gradually stir in milk, stock and seasoning. Bring to the boil slowly and continue to cook, stirring, until thickened. Simmer gently for about 30 minutes, stirring occasionally.
4. Allow to cool slightly, then purée in a blender or food processor.
5. To serve hot, return to the pan, reheat gently, adjust seasoning and stir in the cream, if using.

Garnish with watercress sprigs.
6. To serve the soup chilled, allow to cool, then place in the refrigerator for at least 4 hours or overnight. Serve garnished with swirls of cream, if using, and watercress sprigs.
SERVES 6

CARROT AND ORANGE SOUP

25 g (1 oz) butter or margarine
700 g (1½ lb) carrots, peeled and sliced
2 medium onions, skinned and sliced
1.1 litres (2 pints) Chicken Stock (see page 19)
salt and pepper
1 medium orange

1. Melt the butter in a saucepan, add the carrots and onions and cook gently until the vegetables begin to soften.
2. Add the stock, season with salt and pepper and bring to the boil. Reduce the heat, cover and simmer for about 40 minutes, until the vegetables are tender.
3. Allow the soup to cool slightly, then sieve or purée in a blender or food processor.
4. Finely grate half the rind from the orange and add to the soup. Thinly pare the remainder of the rind, using a potato peeler, and cut into fine shreds. Cook the shreds in simmering water for 2-3 minutes until tender, then drain.
5. Squeeze the juice from the orange and add to the pan. Reheat gently and adjust seasoning, if necessary. Garnish with shreds of orange rind just before serving.
SERVES 6

CAULIFLOWER AND ALMOND CREAM SOUP

few saffron strands
60 ml (4 tbsp) boiling water
125 g (4 oz) flaked almonds
50 g (2 oz) butter or margarine
1 medium onion, skinned and chopped
1 small cauliflower, broken into florets
1.3 litres (2¼ pints) Chicken Stock (see page 19)
freshly grated nutmeg
salt and pepper
150 ml (5 fl oz) single cream

1. Soak the saffron in the boiling water for 2 hours. Toast half the almonds on a sheet of foil under the grill, turning them frequently. Leave to cool.
2. Melt the butter in a large saucepan, add the onion and fry gently until soft. Add the cauliflower and the untoasted almonds and stir, cover and cook gently for 10 minutes.
3. Add the stock and stir well, then strain in the yellow saffron liquid. Add a pinch of nutmeg and season to taste. Bring to the boil, lower the heat, cover and simmer for 30 minutes, or until the cauliflower is very tender.
4. Purée the soup in a blender or food processor until very smooth (you may have to do this twice to break down the almonds). Return to the rinsed out pan, add half the cream and reheat

Cauliflower and Almond Cream Soup

gently. Taste and adjust seasoning, then pour into a warmed tureen.
5. Swirl in the remaining cream and sprinkle with the toasted almonds and a little nutmeg, if liked. Serve immediately.
SERVES 6

FRENCH ONION SOUP

50 g (2 oz) butter or margarine
2 medium onions, skinned and sliced
30 ml (2 level tbsp) flour
900 ml (1½ pints) Beef Stock (see page 19)
salt and pepper
1 bay leaf
4 slices of French bread
75 g (3 oz) Gruyère cheese, grated

1. Melt the butter in a saucepan, add the onions and fry for 5-10 minutes, until browned.
2. Stir in the flour and cook gently for 1 minute, stirring. Remove pan from the heat and gradually stir in the stock, seasoning and bay leaf. Bring to the boil slowly and continue to cook, stirring, until thickened. Cover and simmer for about 30 minutes. Remove the bay leaf. Adjust the seasoning.
3. Put a slice of bread into each individual soup

bowl, pour on the soup and top with cheese. Alternatively, put all the soup into a flameproof casserole, float the slices of bread on it, cover with cheese and put under the grill, or in a hot oven, until the cheese is melted and bubbling.
SERVES 4

NOTE: Gruyère is the cheese traditionally used in this soup. Cheddar is a good alternative.

Cover the surface of the soup with French bread slices, sprinkle over the grated cheese and brown under the grill.

CURRIED PARSNIP SOUP

40 g (1½ oz) butter or margarine
1 medium onion, skinned and sliced
700 g (1½ lb) parsnips, peeled and finely diced
5 ml (1 level tsp) curry powder
2.5 ml (½ level tsp) ground cumin
1.1 litres (2 pints) Chicken Stock (see page 19)
salt and pepper
150 ml (5 fl oz) single cream or milk
paprika, to garnish

1. Melt the butter in a large saucepan, add the onion and parsnips and fry gently for about 3 minutes.
2. Stir in the curry powder and cumin and cook for a further 2 minutes.
3. Add the stock, season and bring to the boil, then reduce the heat, cover and simmer for about 45 minutes, until the vegetables are tender.
4. Allow to cool slightly, then sieve or purée in a blender or food processor until smooth.
5. Return the purée to the pan and adjust the seasoning. Add the cream and reheat but do not boil. Serve sprinkled with paprika.
SERVES 6

CREAM OF SPINACH SOUP

50 g (2 oz) butter or margarine
450 g (1 lb) fresh spinach, washed and roughly chopped, or 175 g (6 oz) packet frozen spinach, thawed
1 medium onion, skinned and finely chopped
25 g (1 oz) flour
450 ml (¾ pint) Chicken Stock (see page 19)
450 ml (¾ pint) milk
salt and pepper
pinch of freshly grated nutmeg
150 ml (¼ pint) single cream

1. Melt the butter in a large saucepan, add the spinach and onion and fry gently for 5-6 minutes. Stir in the flour and cook gently for 1 minute, stirring, then remove from the heat and gradually stir in the stock. Bring to the boil slowly and continue to cook, stirring, until the mixture thickens.
2. Carefully blend in the milk and bring back to the boil, stirring. Cover and simmer for 15-20 minutes, then add the seasoning and nutmeg.
3. Allow to cool slightly, then sieve or purée in a blender or food processor until smooth. Thin with a little milk if necessary. Reheat gently and adjust the seasoning.
4. Pour into a warmed soup tureen or individual soup dishes and stir or swirl in the cream just before serving.
SERVES 6

CELERY AND STILTON SOUP

40 g (1½ oz) butter or margarine
4 celery sticks, trimmed and chopped
45 ml (3 level tbsp) flour
300 ml (½ pint) milk
600 ml (1 pint) Chicken Stock (see page 19)
225 g (8 oz) Stilton cheese, crumbled
salt and pepper

1. Melt the butter in a saucepan, add the celery and cook gently for about 5 minutes, until softened but not coloured.
2. Stir in the flour and cook gently for 1 minute, stirring. Remove from the heat and gradually stir in the milk and stock. Bring to the boil, cover and simmer for about 15 minutes, until the celery is tender.
3. Gradually add the Stilton and stir in until melted. Season to taste and reheat gently.
SERVES 4 AS A MAIN COURSE

SHROPSHIRE PEA SOUP

50 g (2 oz) butter or margarine
1 small onion, skinned and finely chopped
900 g (2 lb) fresh peas, shelled
1.1 litres (2 pints) Chicken Stock (see page 19)
2.5 ml (½ level tsp) sugar
2 large sprigs of fresh mint
salt and pepper
2 egg yolks
150 ml (5 fl oz) single cream or milk
mint sprig, to garnish

1. Melt the butter in a large saucepan, add the onion and cook for 5 minutes, until soft. Add the peas, stock, sugar and sprigs of mint. Bring to the boil, cover and cook for about 30 minutes.
2. Allow to cool slightly, then sieve or purée in a blender or food processor until smooth. Return to the pan and season to taste.
3. In a bowl, beat together the egg yolks and cream and add to the soup. Heat gently, stirring, but do not boil otherwise it will curdle. Adjust the seasoning.
4. Transfer to a soup turecn and garnish with a sprig of fresh mint.
SERVES 6

MUSHROOM SOUP

25 g (1 oz) butter or margarine
25 g (1 oz) flour
600 ml (1 pint) Chicken Stock (see page 19)
300 ml (½ pint) milk
15 ml (1 tbsp) chopped fresh parsley
175 g (6 oz) mushrooms, wiped and finely chopped
salt and pepper
15 ml (1 tbsp) lemon juice
30 ml (2 tbsp) cream (optional)

1. Place all the ingredients except the lemon juice and cream in a large saucepan. Bring to the boil over a moderate heat, whisking continuously. Cover and simmer for about 10 minutes.
2. Remove from the heat and add the lemon juice and cream, if using, stirring well. Adjust seasoning and reheat gently without boiling.
3. Pour the soup into a warmed tureen or individual soup bowls and serve immediately.
SERVES 4

MULLIGATAWNY SOUP

50 g (2 oz) butter or margarine
1 medium onion, skinned and finely chopped
1 medium carrot, peeled and finely chopped
125 g (4 oz) swede, peeled and finely chopped
1 small eating apple, peeled, cored and finely chopped
50 g (2 oz) streaky bacon, rinded and finely chopped
25 g (1 oz) flour
15 ml (1 level tbsp) mild curry paste
15 ml (1 level tbsp) tomato purée
30 ml (2 level tbsp) mango chutney
1.4 litres (2½ pints) Beef Stock (see page 19)
5 ml (1 level tsp) dried mixed herbs
pinch of ground mace
pinch of ground cloves
salt and pepper
50 g (2 oz) long grain white rice

1. Melt the butter in a saucepan, add the onion, carrot, swede, apple and bacon and fry until lightly browned.
2. Stir in the flour, curry paste, tomato purée and chutney and cook gently for 1 minute, stirring. Remove from the heat and gradually stir in the stock, herbs, spices and seasoning. Bring to the boil slowly and continue to cook, stirring, until thickened.
3. Cover and simmer for 30-40 minutes.
4. Cool slightly, then sieve or purée in a blender or food processor until smooth. Return the soup to the pan, bring to the boil, add the rice and boil gently for about 12 minutes or until the rice is cooked, stirring occasionally.
5. Adjust seasoning, then pour the soup into a warmed tureen or individual soup bowls and serve immediately.
SERVES 6

LEFT: *Winter Lentil Soup.* RIGHT: *Bean and Coriander Potage*

WINTER LENTIL SOUP

30 ml (2 tbsp) oil
125 g (4 oz) streaky bacon, rinded and chopped
225 g (8 oz) carrots, peeled and cut into small chunks
225 g (8 oz) parsnips, peeled and cut into small
*   chunks*
450 g (1 lb) leeks, trimmed and sliced
225 g (8 oz) red lentils
1.7 litres (3 pints) Vegetable Stock (see page 19)
15 ml (1 level tbsp) tomato purée
salt and pepper
juice of 1 large orange
grated cheese, to serve (optional)

1. Heat the oil in a large saucepan. Add the bacon and cook until lightly browned, stirring occasionally.
2. Mix in the carrots, parsnips, leeks and lentils. Fry for 1-2 minutes, stirring occasionally.
3. Pour in the stock, adding the tomato purée and seasoning. Bring to the boil, cover and simmer for about 25 minutes or until the lentils and vegetables are tender.
4. Stir in the orange juice and adjust seasoning. If wished, top each portion with a sprinkling of grated cheese to serve.
SERVES 4

TRADITIONAL ITALIAN PASTA SOUP *(Pasta in brodo)*

1.4 litres (2½ pints) Chicken or Beef Stock (see page 19)
*   or three 450 ml (15 fl oz) cans consommé*
400 g (14 oz) medium pasta shapes, eg shells or bows
salt and pepper
freshly grated Parmesan cheese, to serve

1. In a large saucepan, bring the stock or consommé to the boil. Add the pasta and cook until just tender.
2. Taste and adjust seasoning, then pour into six soup bowls and serve immediately with freshly grated Parmesan cheese handed separately.
SERVES 4 AS A MAIN COURSE

Bean and Coriander Potage

small bunch of fresh coriander
30 ml (2 tbsp) oil
225 g (8 oz) onion, skinned and chopped
350 g (12 oz) fennel, trimmed and chopped
10 ml (2 level tsp) ground coriander
1.4 litres (2½ pints) Chicken or Vegetable Stock
   (see page 19)
400 g (14 oz) can chopped tomatoes
30 ml (2 level tbsp) tomato purée
1 garlic clove, skinned and crushed
salt and pepper
400 g (14 oz) can cannellini beans
fresh coriander sprigs, to garnish

1. Tie the coriander stalks into a bundle; chop the leaves, cover and refrigerate.

2. Heat the oil in a saucepan. Add the onion and fennel and fry over a moderate heat until starting to brown.
3. Stir in the ground coriander and cook for 1 minute. Mix in the stock, tomatoes, tomato purée, garlic and seasoning. Add the coriander stalks and bring to the boil. Cover and simmer for 30 minutes.
4. Drain the beans then stir into the soup. Cover and simmer for about 10 minutes or until the vegetables are tender and the beans heated through.
5. Remove the coriander stalks. Stir about 45 ml (3 level tbsp) chopped coriander leaves into the soup. Adjust seasoning and garnish with sprigs of coriander to serve.
Serves 4

Chicken Soup with Dumplings

1.1-1.4 kg (2½ -3lb) oven-ready chicken, skinned
1 medium onion, skinned and chopped
1 litre (1¾ pints) Chicken Stock (see page 19)
350 g (12 oz) carrots, peeled and sliced
salt and pepper
125 g (4 oz) celery sticks with leaves, chopped
FOR THE DUMPLINGS
75 g (3 oz) matzo meal
120 ml (8 tbsp) boiling water
1 egg, beaten
salt

1. Put the chicken, onion, stock, carrots and seasoning into a large saucepan and bring to the boil. Reduce the heat, cover and simmer for about 1 hour, until the chicken is tender. Remove the chicken and leave to stand for a few minutes. Strain the stock into a saucepan and heat to just simmering while you make the dumplings.
2. Mix together the matzo meal, boiling water, egg and salt. Shape the mixture into small marble-sized dumplings with your hands.
3. Add the dumplings and celery to the simmering soup and cook gently for about 20 minutes.
4. Meanwhile, carve the chicken off the bones. Cut the meat into small chunks, stir into the soup and heat through. Taste and adjust seasoning and serve immediately.
Serves 4 as a main course

Chicken Soup with Dumplings

LEEK AND SPLIT PEA SOUP

75 g (3 oz) green split peas, washed
75 g (3 oz) streaky bacon, rinded and chopped
1.1 litres (2 pints) Chicken Stock (see page 19)
salt and pepper
700 g (1½ lb) leeks, trimmed and sliced

1. Cover the split peas with boiling water and leave to soak for 2 hours. Drain thoroughly.
2. Put the bacon in a large saucepan and heat gently until the fat runs out of the bacon.
3. Add the split peas, stock and seasoning. Bring to the boil, cover and simmer gently for about 45 minutes.
4. Add the leeks to the pan and continue cooking for a further 30 minutes, until the leeks are tender. Adjust the seasoning.
SERVES 4 AS A MAIN COURSE

SCOTCH BROTH

700 g (1½ lb) shin of beef, trimmed of excess fat and
    cut into small pieces
salt and pepper
1 medium carrot, peeled and chopped
1 medium turnip, peeled and chopped
1 medium onion, skinned and chopped
2 medium leeks, trimmed and thinly sliced
45 ml (3 level tbsp) pearl barley
15 ml (1 tbsp) chopped fresh parsley, to garnish

1. Put the meat in a saucepan, cover with 2.3 litres (4 pints) water and season. Bring to the boil, cover and simmer for 1½ hours.
2. Add the vegetables and the barley. Cover and simmer for about 1 hour, until the vegetables and barley are soft.
3. Skim off any fat from the surface and adjust seasoning. Serve the soup garnished with parsley.
4. Traditionally, the meat is served with a little of the broth and the remaining broth is served separately.
SERVES 4 AS A MAIN COURSE

MINESTRONE

25 g (1 oz) butter or margarine
2 rashers streaky bacon, rinded and diced
1 small leek, trimmed and sliced
1 small onion, skinned and chopped
1 garlic clove, skinned and crushed
1 small carrot, peeled and cut into thin strips
1 medium turnip, peeled and cut into thin strips
1 celery stick, trimmed and sliced
1.4 litres (2½ pints) Chicken Stock (see page 19)
175 g (6 oz) cabbage, washed and shredded
125 g (4 oz) runner beans, thinly sliced
45 ml (3 tbsp) fresh or frozen peas
25 g (1 oz) short cut macaroni
5 ml (1 level tsp) tomato purée or 4 tomatoes,
    skinned, seeded and chopped
salt and pepper
freshly grated Parmesan cheese, to serve

1. Melt the butter in a large saucepan, add the bacon and fry gently until brown. Remove the bacon from the pan with a slotted spoon and set aside.
2. Add the leek, onion and garlic to the fat in the saucepan and cook gently for about 8 minutes, until beginning to soften.
3. Add the carrot and turnip strips to the pan with the celery and the stock. Bring to the boil, cover and simmer for about 20 minutes.
4. Stir in the cabbage, beans and peas and the macaroni. Cover and simmer for a further 20 minutes until the ingredients are tender.
5. Add the tomato purée or tomatoes and the bacon. Bring back to the boil and season to taste. Serve with grated Parmesan cheese.
SERVES 4 AS A MAIN COURSE

FRENCH BEAN SOUP

30 ml (2 tbsp) oil
125 g (4 oz) onion, skinned and finely chopped
450 g (1 lb) frozen whole French beans
30 ml (2 level tbsp) flour
15 ml (1 level tbsp) chopped fresh or frozen parsley
900 ml (1½ pints) Chicken Stock (see page 19)
150 ml (¼ pint) milk
45 ml (3 level tbsp) soured cream or natural yogurt
  (optional)
salt and pepper
snipped grilled bacon or garlic croûtons, to garnish

1. Heat the oil in a large saucepan and stir in
the onion. Cook for 3-4 minutes until soft but
not coloured. Mix in the beans, flour, parsley
and stock. Bring to the boil, cover and simmer
for 10-12 minutes, stirring occasionally or until
the beans are quite tender.
2. Allow the soup to cool slightly, then purée in
a blender or food processor. Return to the
rinsed-out saucepan, add the milk and reheat
gently.
3. Stir in the soured cream or yogurt and adjust
seasoning before serving. Garnish with snipped
grilled bacon or croûtons.
SERVES 4-6

NOTE: Look out for packets of ready-prepared
garlic croûtons in supermarkets to save
making your own.

French Bean Soup

CHESTNUT AND ORANGE SOUP

450 g (1 lb) fresh whole chestnuts or a 238 g (10 oz)
  can whole chestnuts (drained weight)
40 g (1½ oz) butter or margarine
1 medium carrot, peeled and finely chopped
2 medium onions, skinned and finely chopped
125 g (4 oz) mushrooms, wiped and finely chopped
5 ml (1 level tsp) flour
1.4 litres (2½ pints) Beef Stock (see page 19)
salt and pepper
15 ml (1 level tbsp) finely grated orange rind
chopped fresh parsley, to garnish

1. If using fresh chestnuts, nick the brown outer
skins of the chestnuts with a pair of scissors, or
the tip of a sharp knife. Cook the chestnuts in
boiling water for 3-5 minutes, then lift out using

a slotted spoon, a few at a time. Peel off both the
brown and inner skins and discard.
2. Melt the butter in a large saucepan, add the
vegetables and fry together until lightly browned.
Mix in the flour and cook, stirring for a further
3-4 minutes, or until the flour begins to colour.
3. Off the heat, stir in the stock, prepared
chestnuts and seasoning. Bring slowly to the
boil, stirring. Simmer, covered, for 40-45
minutes, or until the chestnuts are quite tender.
4. Cool a little, then sieve or purée the soup in
batches in a blender or food processor until
smooth. Add half the orange rind and reheat to
serve.
5. Adjust seasoning, add the remaining orange
rind and garnish with the parsley.
SERVES 6

BOUILLABAISSE

900 g (2 lb) mixed fish and shellfish, eg monkfish, red
*   mullet, John Dory, bass, prawns*
few saffron strands
150 ml (¼ pint) olive oil
2-3 medium onions, skinned and sliced
1 celery stick, trimmed and chopped
225 g (8 oz) tomatoes, skinned and sliced
2 garlic cloves, skinned and crushed
1 bay leaf
2.5 ml (½ level tsp) dried thyme or fennel
few fresh parsley sprigs
finely shredded rind of ½ an orange
salt and pepper
about 1.1 litres (2 pints) Fish Stock (see page 19)
French bread, to serve

1. Clean and wash the fish and pat dry with
absorbent kitchen paper. Skin and fillet if
necessary, then cut into fairly large, thick pieces.
If using shellfish, remove them from their shells.
2. Put the saffron in a small bowl. Pour in
150 ml (¼ pint) boiling water and leave to soak
for 30 minutes.
3. Heat the oil in a large saucepan, add the
onions and celery and fry gently for 5 minutes,
until beginning to soften.
4. Stir in the tomatoes with the garlic, herbs,
orange rind and seasoning.
5. Arrange the fish in a layer over the vegetables,
pour over the saffron liquid and just enough
stock to cover the fish. Bring to the boil and
simmer uncovered for about 8 minutes.
6. Add the shellfish and cook for a further
5-8 minutes, until the fish pieces are cooked but
still hold their shape. Serve with French bread.
SERVES 6 AS A MAIN COURSE

MIXED FISH CHOWDER

450 g (1 lb) smoked haddock fillet, skinned
25 g (1 oz) desiccated coconut
50 g (2 oz) butter or margarine
175 g (6 oz) onion, skinned and roughly chopped
6 sticks celery, trimmed and roughly chopped
350 g (12 oz) old potatoes, peeled and cut into small
*   chunks*
1 small green pepper, seeded and chopped
salt and pepper
300 ml (½ pint) milk
125 g (4 oz) peeled prawns
chopped parsley or dill, to garnish

1. Cut the haddock into bite-size pieces. Place
the coconut in a measuring jug and make up to
300 ml (½ pint) with boiling water.
2. Heat the butter in a large pan. Add the
onion and celery, cover and cook for about
5 minutes until starting to soften. Add the
potato and pepper and cook for 1-2 minutes.
3. Strain the coconut liquid and add to the pan
with a further 600 ml (1 pint) water. Bring to
the boil, season, cover and simmer for about
20 minutes or until the vegetables are tender.
4. Add the haddock and milk; simmer, covered,
for 5-10 minutes, or until the fish is flaking apart.
Mix in the prawns, warm gently and adjust
seasoning. Garnish with chopped herbs.
SERVES 4

Mixed Fish Chowder

MUSSEL BISQUE

40 g (1½ oz) butter or margarine
45 ml (3 level tbsp) flour
900 ml (1½ pints) milk
150 ml (¼ pint) white wine
3.4 litres (6 pints) mussels, cooked (see page 82)
2 egg yolks
45 ml (3 tbsp) double cream
salt and pepper
15 ml (1 tbsp) chopped fresh parsley, to garnish

1. Melt the butter in a saucepan, stir in the flour and cook gently for 1 minute, stirring. Remove pan from the heat and gradually stir in the milk. Bring to the boil slowly and continue to cook, stirring, until thickened slightly.
2. Add the wine and mussels and, stirring all the time, cook over low heat for 10 minutes to reheat the fish thoroughly.
3. Mix the egg yolks with the cream in a small bowl. Add a little of the fish soup to the cream, then pour into the soup. Reheat without boiling, stirring all the time.
4. Adjust the seasoning. Sprinkle with the parsley to serve.
SERVES 4 AS A MAIN COURSE

NOTE: If you wish, use four 113 g (4 oz) cans mussels; drain and add with the wine.

BORSHCH

6 small raw beetroot, about 1 kg (2¼ lb), peeled
2 medium onions, skinned and chopped
1.1 litres (2 pints) Beef Stock (see page 19)
salt and pepper
30 ml (2 tbsp) lemon juice
90 ml (6 tbsp) dry sherry
150 ml (5 fl oz) soured cream or natural yogurt and
    snipped fresh chives or dill, to garnish

1. Grate the beetroot coarsely and put in a saucepan with the onions, stock and seasoning. Bring to the boil, cover and simmer for about 45 minutes.
2. Strain, discarding the vegetables, then add the lemon juice and sherry to the liquid and adjust the seasoning. Leave to cool, then chill in the refrigerator. Serve well chilled, garnished with a whirl of soured cream and snipped chives.
SERVES 4

GAZPACHO

30 ml (2 level tbsp) fresh breadcrumbs
15 ml (1 tbsp) olive oil
25 ml (5 tsp) red wine vinegar
450 g (1 lb) tomatoes, skinned
225 g (8 oz) cucumber, skinned and finely chopped
1 medium green pepper, seeded and chopped
1 medium onion, skinned and chopped
450 ml (¾ pint) water
salt and pepper
3 slices fresh white bread
vegetable oil for frying
1 garlic clove, skinned and crushed

1. Place the breadcrumbs, olive oil and vinegar together in a large mixing bowl. Leave to soak for 20 minutes.
2. Halve the tomatoes, remove the seeds and finely chop the flesh.
3. Reserve about 30 ml (2 tbsp) of each chopped vegetable. Cover and refrigerate.
4. Purée the remaining vegetables with half the water until very smooth.
5. Gradually stir into the oil and breadcrumb mixture until thoroughly combined. Stir in the remaining water. Season well.
6. Cover and chill in the refrigerator for at least 2 hours before serving.
7. Evenly dice the bread. Heat the oil with the garlic, add the bread and fry until golden brown. Drain well on absorbent kitchen paper.
8. Serve the soup well chilled with the chopped vegetables and croûtons served in separate dishes. Place one or two ice cubes in each soup bowl before serving, if wished.
SERVES 4

Vichyssoise

25 g (1 oz) butter or margarine
2 medium leeks, trimmed and sliced
1 small onion, skinned and finely chopped
350 g (12 oz) potatoes, peeled and finely sliced
600 ml (1 pint) Vegetable or Chicken Stock (see
    page 19)
salt and pepper
1 blade of mace
150 ml (5 fl oz) single cream
30 ml (2 tbsp) snipped fresh chives or finely chopped
    watercress, to garnish

1. Melt the butter in a saucepan, add the leeks and onion and cook gently without browning for 7-10 minutes. Add the potatoes with the stock, seasoning and mace.
2. Bring to the boil, cover and simmer very gently for 20-30 minutes, until the vegetables are tender.
3. Allow to cool slightly, then sieve or purée in a blender or food processor until smooth. Chill thoroughly.
4. To serve, stir in the cream, adjust the seasoning and sprinkle with snipped chives or chopped watercress.
Serves 4

Chilled Asparagus Soup

700 g (1½ lb) asparagus
salt
125 g (4 oz) butter or margarine
2 medium onions, skinned and thinly sliced
1.4 litres (2½ pints) Vegetable or Chicken Stock (see
    page 19)
pepper
150 ml (5 fl oz) single cream or natural yogurt
small brown uncut loaf
lemon slices, to garnish

1. Wash the asparagus thoroughly under running cold water. Cut off the heads and simmer them very gently in salted water for 3-5 minutes, until just tender. Drain carefully and leave to cool.
2. Scrape the asparagus stalks with a potato peeler or knife to remove any scales and cut off the woody ends. Thinly slice the stalks.

3. Melt 50 g (2 oz) butter in a large saucepan. Add the asparagus stalks and the onions, cover and cook for 5-10 minutes, until beginning to soften.
4. Add the stock and seasoning and bring to the boil. Cover and simmer for about 30-40 minutes, until the asparagus and onion are tender.
5. Allow to cool slightly, then purée in a blender or food processor until smooth. Sieve, to remove any stringy particles, then stir in the cream and adjust the seasoning. Cover and chill in the refrigerator for 2-3 hours.
6. To make asparagus rolls: cut thin slices of brown bread and cut off the crusts; halve lengthways, then butter. Place one asparagus head, on each piece of bread and roll up with the asparagus inside. Cover and chill until required.
7. Serve the soup chilled, garnished with lemon slices and accompanied by the asparagus rolls.

Chilled Avocado Soup

2 ripe avocados
1 small onion, skinned and chopped
grated rind and juice of 1 lemon
150 g (5 oz) natural yogurt
150 ml (5 fl oz) soured cream
600 ml (1 pint) Vegetable or Chicken Stock (see
    page 19)
salt and pepper
snipped fresh chives, to garnish

1. Halve the avocados, remove the stones and scoop out the flesh.
2. Put in a blender or food processor with the onion, lemon rind and juice, yogurt and soured cream and purée until smooth.
3. Turn out into a large bowl and gradually whisk in the stock. Season to taste.
4. Cover tightly and chill well in the refrigerator. Serve the soup garnished with snipped chives.
Serves 6

Starters

Starters are a very important part of a meal because they stimulate the appetite and set the scene for the rest of the meal that is to follow. Starter portions should be small, so they do not take the edge off the appetite, and attractively presented.
Also included in this chapter are canapés – little cocktail savouries – and other savoury finger food that can be eaten with drinks before a meal, hors d'oeuvres, and after-dinner savouries to eat at the end of a formal meal.

Soups, salads, mousses, pâtés, fruit, seafood, cold meats – the choice of starters is endless, but should be made with the other courses in mind. In that way you can achieve a balance of flavour, colour and texture, and if you know you are serving a substantial main course, you can make sure the first course is light. Check also that it does not include the same ingredients as other courses.

Cold starters are probably the easiest as they can usually be prepared well in advance; a hot starter may require a little attention just before the meal. Soups are always popular; a hot soup is obviously a good idea in winter or if the other courses are cold. If serving large numbers choose a starter which can be put on the table before guests sit down.

FINGER FOOD WITH DRINKS

Savoury finger food can be served in small quantities with pre-meal drinks or a selection can be served as the starter before sitting down at the table. Some of the simplest foods to serve with drinks can be bought ready to eat. These include small savoury biscuits and crackers, olives (black, green or stuffed with pimientos or anchovies) and different kinds of nuts. Small cocktail onions and sausages can be served on cocktail sticks, radishes can be served whole and pickled cucumber and gherkins can be chopped into bite-sized pieces.

Dips make excellent accompaniments to pre-meal drinks and if you serve a variety of dips in reasonable quantities they can act as the starter to the meal.

It is very easy to make your own dips, using a blender or food processor. Hot dips are usually based on white sauce, while cold ones are often based on soft cheese, mayonnaise or yogurt. They should be light and full of flavour and soft enough for people to be able to dip food into easily.

Suitable foods for dipping include crudités – sticks of fresh vegetables – such as celery, cucumber, carrot, courgettes, fennel, peppers cauliflower florets and whole radishes. Crackers, tortilla chips, garlic-flavoured croûtons, grissini (crisp Italian bread sticks), small chunks of French bread and thin strips of warm pitta bread are also good for serving as dippers.

For more filling dippers, serve tiny chipolatas, fried scampi, chicken goujons or small meat balls on cocktail sticks.

CANAPÉS

Canapés are probably the most widely served cocktail savoury, consisting of a base made from either fried or toasted bread, small shapes of shortcrust, cheese or puff pastry or ready-prepared bases, such as water biscuits.

The base is spread with a Savoury Butter (see page 207) or a soft cheese and topped with one or more of the following: thin slices of cold meat, rolled or chopped; flaked fish or very small whole fish; grated or sliced cheese; sun-dried tomatoes or fresh tomato slices; cucumber slices; fruit segments; plain or stuffed olives and whole or chopped nuts.

Canapés can be decorated with piped savoury butter or any simple savoury garnish. For a more formal occasion, garnish canapés with a thin coating of aspic jelly – these should be served fairly quickly, so that the base does not become soggy.

HORS D'OEUVRES

These are small dishes, served cold, as a starter. A mixed hors d'oeuvre consists of five or six dishes with contrasting colours and flavours.

HORS D'OEUVRE VARIÉS

It is usual to include at least one meat and one fish dish which can be bought ready-prepared from your local delicatessen – sliced cooked meats (see opposite) and fresh, canned or pickled fish – plus one or two salads or vegetable dishes. Suitable dishes include: potato salad, artichoke hearts, Tomato Salad with Basil (see page 257), palm hearts, Mixed Bean Salad (see page 261), Mushrooms à la Grecque (see page 37), stuffed eggs and Crab Salad (see page 264).

Serve hors d'oeuvre varies in a series of small dishes, or choose a large tray, line it with lettuce or other salad leaves and arrange hors d'oeuvres on top.

MEAT HORS D'OEUVRE

Choose from slices of ham or cured pork, tongue and salami. Smoked chicken, smoked turkey and smoked venison are equally suitable. Arrange on a serving plate, folding and rolling some for an attractive finish. Garnish simply with black olives, lemon wedges and parsley.

FISH AND SHELLFISH HORS D'OEUVRE

ANCHOVIES: Choose from fresh (see page 58), salted in jars or canned (in brine or oil). Because they are salty, serve anchovies in small amounts with bread.

CAVIAR: This is the salted hard roe of the sturgeon fish. Most is caught in the Caspian Sea, by the Russians in the North and the Iranians in the South. In colour it varies from yellow brown to soft grey to grey black, and the quality is judged by the time of year, age of the fish and method of preservation. Also, the less salt the better the caviar. Red caviar is much cheaper than the black. However, even less expensive lump fish roe is often substituted for caviar.

Caviar should be served ice-cold from the jar it comes in, embedded in cracked ice or turned out into a glass dish and surrounded by ice, with freshly made toast or crisp biscuits and chilled butter. It deteriorates when exposed to the air so should not be opened until serving time. Lemon juice may be sprinkled over it if you wish, or serve with wedges of lemon.

Fish Hors d'Oeuvre: Gravad Lax, Smoked Mackerel, Pickled Herring, Prawns and Smoked Eel

Alternatively, spread the caviar directly on croûtes of fried bread or toast and sprinkle with cayenne pepper.

COCKLES, WHELKS AND WINKLES: Choose fresh (see page 85) or purchase cooked. Season and add a little vinegar. Serve with brown bread and butter.

EEL, SMOKED: Serve smoked eel slices on a bed of lettuce with thin brown bread and butter, lemon wedges and pepper.

HERRINGS: Choose pickled or soused herrings (see page 64).

MUSSELS: Choose from fresh (see page 82) or smoked mussels, available in cans and jars. Serve fresh in the half shell with tomato mayonnaise or a light horseradish sauce.

OYSTERS: Serve raw oysters on the half shell (see page 82) and, if possible, on a bed of chopped ice. Thin brown bread and butter, slices of lemon and cayenne or freshly ground black pepper are the usual accompaniments. Smoked oysters, available canned and in jars are a good alternative.

PRAWNS: Serve freshly cooked king prawns in their shells with lemon wedges, brown bread and butter.

SALMON, FRESH: Cold poached salmon can be divided into small portions, dressed with mayonnaise and served on a bed of lettuce. Garnish with cucumber slices.

SALMON, SMOKED: Choose thin slices of smoked salmon or Gravad Lax, available in packets. Serve with lemon wedges, thin brown bread slices and butter.

SARDINES: Buy fresh if available (see page 60) or alternatively use canned ones (in brine, oil or tomato sauce). Drain and serve on a bed of lettuce, garnished with strips of pimiento and chopped parsley.

TROUT AND MACKEREL, SMOKED: Serve fillet of smoked trout or mackerel on lettuce leaves with lemon wedges, Horseradish Cream Sauce (see page 206) and brown bread.

WHITEBAIT: Cook and serve with lemon wedges.

AFTER-DINNER SAVOURIES

Although after-dinner savouries are rarely served these days, they may occasionally be offered at formal dinner parties after the dessert and instead of the cheese course. After-dinner savouries include dishes such as Devils on Horseback and Scotch Woodcock (see page 52).

FRUIT, VEGETABLE AND SALAD STARTERS

GRAPEFRUIT

2 grapefruit
caster sugar, for sprinkling
4 maraschino or glacé cherries (optional)

1. Cut each grapefruit in half and cut around each half, loosening the flesh from the outer skin. Cut between the segments to loosen the flesh from the membranes, sprinkle with sugar and chill before serving.
2. If liked, decorate the centre with a maraschino or glacé cherry.
SERVES 4

SPICED HOT GRAPEFRUIT

2 grapefruit
30 ml (2 level tbsp) brown sugar
2.5-5 ml (½ -1 level tsp) ground cinnamon
a little butter or margarine

1. Prepare the grapefruit as above.
2. Mix the brown sugar and cinnamon together and sprinkle over the grapefruit; dot with butter.
3. Grill lightly under a medium grill until the sugar has melted and the grapefruit is heated through; serve hot.
SERVES 4

FLORIDA COCKTAILS

2 small grapefruit
2 large oranges
curaçao or any orange-flavoured liqueur, to taste
sugar, to taste

1. Working over a plate, prepare the grapefruit: remove all the skin. Holding the fruit in one hand, remove the flesh of each segment by cutting down at the side of the membrane and then scraping the segment off the membrane on the opposite side on to the plate.
2. Repeat the process for the oranges. Mix the segments, together with any of the juice collected on the plate, in a bowl. Add the curaçao and sugar to taste.
3. Divide the fruit between four glasses and pour a little juice into each. Serve chilled.
SERVES 4

MINTED PEAR VINAIGRETTE

125 g (4 oz) streaky bacon, rinded
120 ml (8 tbsp) French Dressing (see page 255)
30 ml (2 tbsp) chopped fresh mint
3 large ripe dessert pears
1 small lettuce, washed

1. Grill the bacon until crisp, cool and snip into tiny pieces.
2. Place the French Dressing in a bowl or screw-topped jar with the chopped mint and whisk or shake well until thoroughly combined.
3. One at a time, peel and halve the pears and scoop out the cores with a teaspoon. Brush both sides of each pear half immediately with a little of the dressing to prevent discoloration.
4. To serve, arrange lettuce leaves on six individual serving plates. Place a pear half, cut-side up, on each plate and spoon over the dressing. Sprinkle with the bacon.
SERVES 6

STUFFED TOMATOES

4 large tomatoes
salt and pepper
15 ml (1 tbsp) vegetable oil
1 small red pepper, halved, seeded and finely chopped
125 g (4 oz) mushrooms, wiped and finely chopped
4 spring onions, trimmed and finely chopped
90 ml (6 tbsp) Mayonnaise (see page 254)
a few lettuce leaves
fresh parsley sprigs, to garnish

1. Cut the tops off the tomatoes, scoop out the seeds using a teaspoon and discard. Roughly chop the tops and put them in a bowl.
2. Sprinkle the insides of the tomatoes with salt, turn upside-down and leave to drain.
3. Heat the oil in a frying pan, add the pepper and mushrooms and fry gently for about 5 minutes, until soft.
4. Remove from the pan, drain on absorbent kitchen paper and add to the bowl with the spring onions and plenty of seasoning. Add the Mayonnaise and mix well.
5. Spoon the mixture into the tomato cases. Place on lettuce leaves on individual serving plates and garnish with parsley sprigs.
SERVES 4

TOMATO AND MOZZARELLA SALAD

2 ripe avocados
150 ml (¼ pint) French Dressing (see page 255)
175 g (6 oz) mozzarella cheese, thinly sliced
6 medium tomatoes, thinly sliced
30 ml (2 tbsp) chopped fresh basil
fresh basil sprigs, to garnish

1. Halve the avocados lengthways and remove the stones. Peel and cut the avocados into slices. Pour the French Dressing over the avocado. Stir to coat thoroughly and prevent discoloration.
2. Arrange slices of mozzarella, tomato and avocado on four individual serving plates.
3. Spoon over the dressing and sprinkle with the chopped basil. Garnish with the basil sprigs.
SERVES 4

Dressed Avocados

2 ripe avocados
lemon juice for sprinkling
a few lettuce leaves (optional)
150 ml (¼ pint) Herb Dressing (see page 255)
fresh herb sprigs, to garnish

1. Halve the avocados lengthways using a stainless steel knife and remove the stones. Brush the cut surfaces of the avocados with lemon juice to prevent discoloration.
2. Place the avocado halves in avocado dishes, or on serving plates lined with lettuce leaves. If serving on flat plates, cut a thin slice from the rounded side of each avocado so that they will sit firmly on the plates.
3. Spoon a little of the dressing into each cavity and garnish with fresh herbs.

VARIATIONS
In place of the Herb Dressing, fill the avocado with shrimps, prawns, lobster or crabmeat, mixed with mayonnaise, or diced tomatoes.

Stuffed Mushrooms with Dill

125 g (4 oz) long grain brown rice
salt and pepper
8 large flat or cup mushrooms, total weight about
_ 450 g (1 lb), wiped_
25 g (1 oz) butter or margarine
1 medium onion, skinned and finely chopped
198 g (7 oz) can sweetcorn niblets, drained
15 ml (1 tbsp) chopped fresh dill or 5 ml (1 level tsp)
_ dried dill weed_
175 g (6 oz) blue cheese, eg Gorgonzola, cut into small
_ pieces_
30 ml (2 tbsp) lemon juice
fresh dill, to garnish

1. Cook the rice in plenty of boiling salted water for about 35 minutes until tender. Drain well.
2. Ease out the mushroom stalks and finely chop them.
3. Melt the butter in a frying pan. Add the chopped mushroom stalks and onion. Fry for 2-3 minutes, stirring occasionally, until the onion is beginning to brown and all excess moisture has been driven off.
4. Remove from the heat and stir in the sweetcorn, cooked rice, dill and cheese. Season with plenty of pepper.
5. Place the mushrooms stalk side up in a large shallow ovenproof dish. Spoon the sweetcorn mixture on top of each one. Sprinkle over the lemon juice.
6. Bake in the oven at 200°C (400°F) mark 6 for about 20 minutes. Serve hot, garnished with dill.
SERVES 8

Mushrooms à la Grecque

30 ml (2 tbsp) olive or vegetable oil
1 medium onion, skinned and chopped
1 garlic clove, skinned and crushed
30 ml (2 level tbsp) tomato purée
300 ml (½ pint) red wine
bouquet garni
15 ml (1 tbsp) coriander seeds, lightly crushed
5 ml (1 level tsp) sugar
salt and pepper
450 ml (1 lb) button mushrooms, wiped
225 g (8 oz) tomatoes, skinned, quartered and seeded
chopped fresh coriander, to garnish

1. Heat the oil in a large frying pan, add the onion and garlic and cook for 5 minutes.
2. Stir in the tomato purée, wine, bouquet garni, coriander seeds, sugar and seasoning.
3. Add the mushrooms and tomatoes and cook gently, uncovered, for about 10 minutes, until just tender.
4. Remove the bouquet garni and spoon the mushrooms and cooking liquid into a serving dish. Chill thoroughly. Serve sprinkled with coriander and accompanied by crusty bread.
SERVES 4

Smoked Chicken and Orange Appetiser

Smoked Chicken and Orange Appetiser

900 g (2 lb) smoked chicken
4 oranges
135 ml (9 tbsp) sunflower or vegetable oil
juice of 1 orange
1.25 ml (¼ level tsp) ground allspice or mixed spice
pinch of sugar
salt and pepper
sprigs of curly endive, to garnish

1. Remove all the meat from the chicken carcass, cutting the slices as thinly and evenly as possible.
2. Remove the skin and pith from the oranges with a sharp, serrated knife, working in a spiral and using a sawing action.
3. Cut the oranges crossways into thin, even rounds.
4. Arrange the chicken and orange slices in a fan shape on four individual serving plates.
5. For the dressing, put the oil, orange juice, spice and sugar in a screw-topped jar with salt and pepper to taste. Shake vigorously to combine, then taste and adjust seasoning.
6. Pour the dressing over the salad, then chill in the refrigerator for at least 30 minutes so that the flavours are absorbed. Garnish each plate with a sprig or two of endive just before serving.
Serves 6

Melon Balls

1 medium melon, such as Cantaloupe, Charentais or
  Ogen
caster sugar, to dredge
30 ml (2 tbsp) Madeira or sherry

1. Cut the top off the melon, remove the seeds from the centre and scoop out the flesh with a melon baller or a teaspoon.
2. Dredge the melon balls with sugar, sprinkle with Madeira or sherry and chill.
3. Serve in small bowls or stemmed glasses, set if possible in crushed ice.
Serves 4

Melon Slices

1 medium melon, such as Cantaloupe, Charentais
  or Ogen
ground ginger and caster sugar, to serve

1. Chill the melon thoroughly and cut into wedge-shaped slices. Remove the seeds and loosen the flesh from the skin. Cut the flesh at right angles to the skin into wedge-shaped

pieces. Leave the melon on the skin.
2. Serve with ground ginger and caster sugar.
Serves 4

Variation
These melon slices are also delicious flavoured with finely crushed almonds or walnut halves or freshly grated nutmeg.

MELON AND PARMA HAM

900 g (2 lb) Cantaloupe melon, chilled
8 thin slices Parma ham
juice of 1 lemon
pepper

1. Cut the melon in half lengthways and scoop out the seeds. Cut each half into four wedges.
2. With a sharp knife and a sawing action, separate the flesh from the skin, keeping it in position on the skin.
3. Cut the flesh across into bite-sized slices, then push each in opposite directions to make an attractive pattern.
4. Roll up each slice of ham into a cigar shape. Place on serving dishes with the melon wedges and sprinkle with lemon juice and pepper.
SERVES 4

Melon and Parma Ham

SALADE TIÈDE

135 ml (9 tbsp) olive oil
30 ml (2 tbsp) wine vinegar
2 garlic cloves, skinned and crushed
5 ml (1 level tsp) French mustard
salt and pepper
8 streaky bacon rashers, rinded
4 thick slices of white bread, crusts removed
30 ml (2 tbsp) single or double cream
1 small head of curly endive, leaves separated

1. Put 90 ml (6 tbsp) of the oil in a salad bowl with the wine vinegar, garlic, mustard and salt and pepper to taste. Whisk with a fork until thick.
2. Cut the bacon and bread into small dice. Heat the remaining oil in a frying pan, add the bacon and bread and fry over brisk heat until crisp and golden brown on all sides. Remove with a slotted spoon and drain on absorbent kitchen paper.
3. Stir the cream into the dressing, then add the endive and warm bacon and croûtons. Toss quickly to combine and serve immediately.
SERVES 4

SEAFOOD STARTERS

SMOKED SALMON PÂTÉ

175 g (6 oz) smoked salmon scraps
75 g (3 oz) unsalted butter or margarine
20 ml (4 tsp) lemon juice
60 ml (4 tbsp) single cream
pepper
cucumber slices, to garnish

1. Cut up the salmon pieces, reserving a few for garnishing, and place in a blender or food processor.
2. Melt the butter and add the lemon juice and cream. Pour into the blender or food processor.
3. Blend mixture until smooth. Season to taste with pepper. Salt is not usually needed.
4. Spoon into a 300 ml (½ pint) dish and refrigerate to set.
5. Leave at room temperature for 30 minutes before serving. Garnish the pâté with twists of smoked salmon and cucumber slices.
SERVES 6

BAKED CRAB RAMEKINS

25 g (1 oz) butter or margarine
1 small onion, skinned and finely chopped
225 g (8 oz) white crab meat or white and brown mixed
50 g (2 oz) fresh brown breadcrumbs
10 ml (2 level tsp) French mustard
150 g (5 oz) natural yogurt
45 ml (3 tbsp) single cream or milk
cayenne pepper
salt
40 g (1½ oz) Cheddar cheese, grated

1. Melt the butter in a saucepan, add the onion and fry until golden brown.
2. Flake the crab meat, taking care to remove any membranes or shell particles. Mix the onion, crab meat and breadcrumbs well together.
3. Stir in the mustard with the yogurt and cream. Sprinkle generously with cayenne pepper, then add salt to taste.
4. Spoon the mixture into six ramekin dishes and sprinkle a little cheese over the surface of each.
5. Stand the dishes on a baking sheet. Bake in the oven at 170°C (325°F) mark 3 for 25-30 minutes, until really hot. Serve with crispbreads.
SERVES 6

SEAFOOD PANCAKES

125 g (4 oz) plus 30 ml (2 level tbsp) plain flour
pinch of salt
1 egg
600 ml (1 pint) milk
vegetable oil for frying
350 g (12 oz) smoked haddock fillets
1 bay leaf
onion slices for flavouring
40 g (1½ oz) butter or margarine
150 ml (5 fl oz) single cream
2 eggs, hard-boiled, shelled and chopped
45 ml (3 tbsp) chopped fresh parsley
snipped fresh chives, to garnish

1. Sift 100 g (4 oz) flour and the salt into a mixing bowl. Make a well in the centre and break in the egg. Gradually add 150 ml (¼ pint) milk, vigorously beating in the flour with a wooden spoon until a thick smooth batter is formed.

Pour in 150 ml (¼ pint) milk, and beat again until quite smooth.
2. Heat a little oil in a small frying pan or omelette pan and when it is very hot pour in a small amount of batter. Tip the pan quickly so the batter runs over the bottom of the pan. Cook over a high heat until the underside is

Cook pancake until golden on bottom, then turn over.

golden brown, then turn the pancake over either by tossing it, or using a fish slice. Cook the other side until golden brown. Cook eight pancakes and keep warm.
3. Place the fish in a saucepan, pour over the remaining milk and add the bay leaf and onion slices. Cover the pan and simmer until the fish begins to flake. Strain off and reserve the milk. Flake the fish and discard the skin and bones.
4. Melt the butter in a pan, stir in the remaining flour and cook gently for 1 minute, stirring. Remove pan from the heat and gradually stir in the reserved milk. Bring to the boil slowly and cook, stirring, until the sauce thickens.
5. Off the heat, stir in the cream, fish, three-quarters of the chopped egg, and the parsley; season with pepper. Cool slightly.
6. Divide the fish mixture between the pancakes, fold over and place in individual dishes or one large ovenproof dish. Cover with buttered foil and cook in the oven at 200°C (400°F) mark 6 for about 20 minutes. Scatter over the remaining egg and chives to serve.
MAKES 8

VARIATIONS
Substitute the smoked haddock fillets with any of the following:
- 350 g (12 oz) peeled prawns, cooked
- 200 g (7 oz) can each of tuna, and sweetcorn niblets, drained and mixed
- 600 ml (1 pint) cockles, cooked and drained
- 350g (12 oz) cooked cod, flaked

SHELLFISH COCKTAILS

60 ml (4 level tbsp) Mayonnaise (see page 254)
60 ml (4 tbsp) single cream
10 ml (2 level tsp) tomato purée
10 ml (2 tsp) lemon juice
dash of Worcestershire sauce
dash of dry sherry
salt and pepper
225 g (8 oz) peeled prawns or shrimps or flaked crab
few lettuce leaves, shredded
lemon slices, to garnish

1. In a small bowl, mix together the Mayonnaise, cream, tomato purée, lemon juice, Worcestershire sauce and sherry. Season to taste. Add the fish and stir well to coat.
2. Place the shredded lettuce in four glasses and top with the fish mixture.
3. Garnish each glass with a lemon slice. Serve with brown bread.
SERVES 4

PÂTÉS, TERRINES AND MOUSSES

VEGETABLE TERRINE

900 g (2 lb) turnips, peeled and cut into chunks
450 g (1 lb) carrots, peeled and sliced
450 g (1 lb) fresh spinach, trimmed, or 300 g (10 oz) packet frozen spinach
50 g (2 oz) butter or margarine
1 medium onion, skinned and thinly sliced
350 g (12 oz) flat mushrooms, sliced
finely grated rind and juice of ½ a lemon
4 eggs
salt and white pepper
1.25 ml (¼ level tsp) ground coriander
1.25 ml (¼ level tsp) freshly grated nutmeg
30 ml (2 tbsp) chopped fresh parsley
2 ripe tomatoes, skinned
200 ml (7 fl oz) French Dressing (see page 255)

1. Put the turnips into a saucepan, cover with cold water and bring to the boil. Lower the heat and simmer for 10-15 minutes, until tender.
2. Meanwhile, cook the carrots in a separate saucepan of cold water for 10 minutes or until tender. Drain both turnips and carrots.
3. Wash the fresh spinach and place in a saucepan with only the water that clings to the leaves. Cook gently for 5 minutes until wilted, 7-10 minutes if using frozen spinach. Drain well.
4. Melt 40 g (1½ oz) of the butter in a frying pan, add the onion and fry gently for about 10 minutes until very soft. Add the mushrooms and fry, stirring constantly, for a further 5 minutes. Stir in the lemon rind and juice.
5. Put the mushroom mixture in a blender or food processor and work until smooth. Transfer to a small heavy-based pan. Cook over moderate heat, stirring constantly, until all the liquid has evaporated and the purée is fairly thick and dry. Watch that the mixture does not catch and burn.
6. Purée and dry the turnips, carrots and spinach in the same way and place each purée in a separate bowl. Add one egg to each purée and mix well. Season each with salt and pepper to taste. Stir the coriander into the carrot purée, the grated nutmeg into the spinach and the chopped parsley into the mushroom.
7. Brush a 1.1 litre (2 pint) terrine or loaf tin with the remaining butter. Put a layer of turnip purée in the bottom, making sure it is quite level. Cover with a layer of carrot, followed by spinach and finally mushroom. Cover the tin tightly with foil.
8. Place the terrine in a roasting tin and pour in enough hot water to come three-quarters of the way up the sides of the terrine. Bake in the oven at 180°C (350°F) mark 4 for 1 hour 20 minutes or until firm. Remove and allow to cool slightly, then turn out carefully on to a serving plate.
9. Just before serving, put the tomatoes and French Dressing in a blender or food processor and work until smooth. Do not let the dressing stand before serving or it will separate.
10. Serve the terrine hot or cold, cut into slices, on top of the tomato vinaigrette.
SERVES 6-8

VARIATIONS
Other vegetables may be used when in season, such as cauliflower, fennel, watercress, parsnips, celeriac and even peas. Try to balance colour and flavour.

DUCK AND ORANGE TERRINE

1.8 kg (4 lb) oven-ready duckling
350 g (12 oz) belly of pork, skin and bones removed
125 g (4 oz) lamb's liver
1 medium onion, skinned and quartered
2 oranges
1 garlic clove, skinned and crushed
salt and pepper
2.5 ml (½ level tsp) ground mace
15 ml (1 tbsp) chopped fresh parsley
30 ml (2 tbsp) sherry
half a 25 g (1 oz) packet aspic jelly
celery leaves, to garnish (optional)

Duck and Orange Terrine

1. Prepare two days ahead. Discard the skin and fat layer from the duckling. Cut away the breast portion and set aside. Remove rest of flesh – about 350 g (12 oz).
2. Finely mince the duckling flesh with the pork, liver and the onion. Grate in the rind of one orange.
3. Segment this orange, removing the membrane, over a bowl to collect any juice. Cut the segments into small pieces.
4. Combine the meat mixture with the orange juice and segments, garlic, seasoning, mace, parsley and sherry.
5. Press half the mixture into a 1.1 litre (2 pint) terrine. Lay the breast portions on top and spread over the remaining mixture.
6. Cover with foil or a lid. Put the dish in a roasting tin half filled with boiling water. Cook in the oven at 170°C (325°F) mark 3 for 3 hours.
7. Place a weight on top of the pâté and refrigerate until cold. Scrape off any solidified fat and drain away the juices.
8. Make up the aspic jelly to 300 ml (½ pint) with water, according to the manufacturer's instructions. Garnish the pâté with the remaining orange, sliced, and celery leaves. Spoon over the aspic when it is nearly set. Leave at room temperature for 30 minutes before serving.
SERVES 8-10

AVOCADO MOUSSE

15 ml (1 tbsp) gelatine
150 ml (¼ pint) chicken stock
150 ml (5 fl oz) double cream
3 small or 2 large ripe avocados
salt and pepper
10 ml (2 tsp) Worcestershire sauce
150 ml (¼ pint) Mayonnaise (see page 254)
thinly sliced cucumber, to garnish

1. Sprinkle the gelatine in 150 ml (¼ pint) water in a small bowl and leave to soak. Place the bowl over a saucepan of simmering water and stir until dissolved.
2. Stir in the chicken stock and set aside to cool for a few minutes.
3. Lightly whip the cream.
4. Halve the avocados and remove the stones, scoop out the flesh with a fork and mash until smooth, or purée in a blender or food processor. Season with salt and pepper and Worcestershire sauce.
5. Slowly pour the gelatine mixture into the avocado mixture and stir until just beginning to thicken. Then gently fold in the Mayonnaise and the cream.
6. Pour into a dampened 1 litre (1¾ pint) mould and chill until firm. Just before serving, remove from the mould and place on a serving platter. Garnish with cucumber slices.
SERVES 6

SALMON MOUSSE

350 g (12 oz) salmon steaks
1 small onion, skinned and sliced
1 medium carrot, peeled and sliced
2 bay leaves
4 black peppercorns
salt and pepper
75 ml (5 tbsp) white wine
15 ml (1 level tbsp) gelatine
300 ml (½ pint) milk
25 g (1 oz) butter or margarine
30 ml (2 level tbsp) flour
75 ml (5 level tbsp) Mayonnaise, made with lemon
  juice (see page 254)
150 ml (5 fl oz) whipping cream
1 egg white

ASPIC JELLY FOR GARNISH
7.5 ml (1½ level tsp) gelatine
60 ml (4 tbsp) white wine
15 ml (1 tbsp) medium sherry
5 ml (1 tsp) rosemary vinegar
5 cm (2 inch) piece cucumber

1. Place the salmon steaks in a small shallow pan. Add half the onion and carrot slices, 1 bay leaf, 2 peppercorns and a good pinch of salt. Spoon over the wine with 75 ml (5 tbsp) water and bring slowly to the boil. Cover the pan and simmer gently for 10-15 minutes, until the fish flakes easily when tested with a knife. Flake the fish, discarding bones and skin. Place the fish in a small bowl and set aside. Boil the cooking liquid until reduced by half, strain and reserve.
2. Sprinkle the gelatine in 45 ml (3 tbsp) water in a small basin and leave to soak.
3. Place the milk in a saucepan with the remaining sliced onion, carrot, bay leaf and peppercorns. Bring to the boil slowly, remove from the heat, cover and leave to infuse for 30 minutes.
4. Melt the butter in a pan, stir in the flour and cook gently for 1 minute, stirring. Remove the pan from the heat and gradually strain in the infused milk, stirring until smooth. Bring to the boil slowly and continue to cook, stirring, until the sauce thickens. Pour into a bowl and while still warm add the soaked gelatine and stir until dissolved.
5. Stir the fish into the cool sauce with the reserved cooking juices. Spoon half at a time into a blender or food processor and switch on

for a few seconds only; the fish should retain a little of its texture. Pour into a large mixing bowl and repeat with the remaining sauce and fish mixture.
6. Stir the mayonnaise gently into the salmon mixture. Whip cream until soft peaks form and fold into the mousse; adjust seasoning. Whisk the egg white until stiff and fold lightly into the mousse until no traces of egg white are visible.
7. Pour the mousse into an oiled 18 cm (7 inch) soufflé dish, smooth the surface, cover and refrigerate for about 2 hours, until set.
8. Meanwhile, make the aspic jelly: soak the gelatine in 30 ml (2 tbsp) water in a small bowl and leave to soak. Place the bowl over a pan of simmering water and stir until dissolved. Stir in the white wine, sherry, vinegar, 90 ml (6 tbsp) water and seasoning. Refrigerate until set.
9. Turn out on to a flat platter and gently dab the surface with absorbent kitchen paper to absorb any oil. Turn the aspic out on to a sheet of damp greaseproof paper and chop roughly with a wet knife. Run a canelle knife or fork down the cucumber to form grooves; slice thinly. Garnish the mousse with cucumber and aspic.
SERVES 6

Salmon Mousse

SMOKED TROUT MOUSSE

300 ml (½ pint) milk
1 piece of carrot
1 piece of onion
1 bay leaf
3 black peppercorns
225 g (8 oz) smoked trout
7.5 ml (1½ level tsp) gelatine
25g (1 oz) butter or margarine
30 ml (2 level tbsp) flour
15 ml (1 tbsp) creamed horseradish
30 ml (2 tbsp) lemon sauce
75 ml (5 tbsp) double cream
salt and pepper
2 egg whites
watercress sprigs or cucumber slices, to garnish

1. Put the milk in a saucepan with the carrot, onion, bay leaf and peppercorns. Bring to the boil slowly, remove from the heat, cover and leave to infuse for 30 minutes.
2. Meanwhile, skin the smoked trout and flake the flesh finely, discarding any bones. Keep the flesh covered until required.
3. Sprinkle the gelatine in 30 ml (2 tbsp) water in a small bowl and leave to soak for at least 10 minutes.
4. Melt the butter in a small pan, stir in the flour and cook gently for 1 minute, stirring. Remove the pan from the heat and gradually strain in the infused milk, stirring until smooth. Bring to the boil slowly and continue to cook, stirring, until the sauce thickens.
5. Remove from the heat and stir in the soaked gelatine until dissolved. Pour into a bowl, cover with a sheet of dampened greaseproof paper and set aside to cool.
6. Mix the flaked fish into the sauce with the horseradish and lemon juice. Whip the cream to soft peaks and fold into the fish mixture. Adjust the seasoning.
7. Whisk the egg whites until stiff, then fold them gently into the fish mixture. Spoon into six 150 ml (¼ pint) individual soufflé dishes, cover and chill until lightly set. Garnish with watercress or slices of cucumber.
SERVES 6

PRAWN AND ASPARAGUS MOUSSE

300 ml (½ pint) milk
1 piece of carrot
1 piece of onion
1 bay leaf
3 black peppercorns
1 mace blade
25 g (1 oz) butter or margarine
30 ml (2 level tbsp) flour
15 ml (1 level tbsp) gelatine
425 g (15 oz) can green asparagus
salt and pepper
75 ml (5 tbsp) double cream
225 g (8 oz) peeled prawns
2 egg whites
tomato slices, to garnish

1. Put the milk into a saucepan with the carrot, onion, bay leaf, peppercorns and mace. Bring to the boil slowly, remove from the heat, cover and leave to infuse for 30 minutes. Strain, reserving the milk.
2. Melt the butter in a saucepan, stir in the flour and cook gently for 1 minute, stirring. Remove the pan from the heat and gradually stir in the milk. Bring to the boil slowly and continue to cook, stirring, until the sauce thickens.
3. Meanwhile, sprinkle the gelatine in 45 ml (3 tbsp) water in a small bowl and leave to soak. Place the bowl over a pan of simmering water and stir until dissolved.
4. Beat the gelatine mixture into the hot sauce. Turn into a bowl, cover closely with a sheet of dampened greaseproof paper and allow to cool but not set.
5. Reserve a few pieces of asparagus for the garnish, then purée the rest in a blender or food processor with the sauce. Season.
6. Softly whip the cream. Whisk the egg whites until stiff. First fold the cream into the puréed mixture, then carefully fold in the egg whites with the prawns. Pour into individual dishes. Chill until set. Garnish with the remaining asparagus and tomato.
SERVES 6

SMOKED MACKEREL PÂTÉ

275 g (10 oz) smoked mackerel
50 g (2 oz) butter or margarine, softened
45 ml (3 level tbsp) creamed horseradish sauce
30 ml (2 tbsp) single cream
pepper
parsley sprig, to garnish

1. Skin the mackerel and discard the bones. Mash the flesh in a bowl.
2. Mix the butter with the fish and add the horseradish sauce and cream. Season with pepper. Salt is not usually needed.
3. Spoon the mixture into a serving dish, cover tightly and refrigerate until required.

4. Leave the pâté at room temperature for 30 minutes before serving. Decorate the surface of the pâté with indentations made using a blunt edged knife. Garnish with parsley.
SERVES 6

VARIATION
HERBY MACKEREL PÂTÉ
1. Cream together 100 g (4 oz) butter or margarine, 30 ml (2 tbsp) chopped fresh parsley and 5 ml (1 tsp) lemon juice and beat well.
2. In a 600 ml (1 pint) dish, layer the fish mixture and parsley butter, beginning and ending with a thick layer of fish.

CHICKEN LIVER PÂTÉ

450 g (1 lb) chicken livers
50 g (2 oz) butter or margarine
1 medium onion, skinned and chopped
1 garlic clove, skinned and crushed
75 ml (5 tbsp) double or single cream
15 ml (1 level tbsp) tomato purée
15 ml (1 tbsp) brandy
salt and pepper
parsley sprigs, to garnish

1. Clean the chicken livers and dry with absorbent kitchen paper.
2. Melt the butter in a saucepan, add the onion

and garlic and cook for about 5 minutes, until the onion is soft. Add the chicken livers and cook for a further 5 minutes.
3. Cool, then add the cream, tomato purée and brandy and season well.
4. Purée the mixture in a blender or food processor, then transfer to a serving dish and chill in the refrigerator. Garnish with parsley sprigs and serve with Melba Toast (see page 18) or crusty French bread.
SERVES 8

NOTE: Melted butter can be poured over the pâté to prevent it drying out.

PORK AND LIVER PÂTÉ WITH BLACK OLIVES

275 g (10 oz) streaky bacon, rinded
450 g (1 lb) belly of pork
275 g (10 oz) diced pie veal
175 g (6 oz) lamb's liver
2 medium onions, skinned and quartered
1 garlic clove, skinned and crushed
*75 g (3 oz) black olives, halved, stoned and roughly
   chopped*
salt and pepper
5 ml (1 tsp) chopped fresh sage
30 ml (2 tbsp) olive oil
15 ml (1 tbsp) lemon juice
30 ml (2 tbsp) brandy

1. Make the pâté one day before needed. Stretch the bacon rashers with the back of a knife. Finely mince the belly of pork, veal, liver and onion. Add remaining ingredients, except the bacon, and mix well.
2. Layer the bacon and minced ingredients in a 1.1 litre (2 pint) terrine, topping with rashers.
3. Cover with foil or a lid and place in a roasting tin, half filled with boiling water. Cook at 170°C (325°F) mark 3 for about 2 hours.
4. Pour off the juices; reserve. Place a weight on top of the pâté and refrigerate overnight.
5. Skim the fat off the jellied juices, warm the juices to liquefy, then spoon over the pâté. Refrigerate to set. Leave at room temperature for 30 minutes before serving.
SERVES 10-12

POTTED PRAWN PÂTÉ

225 g (8 oz) peeled prawns
75 g (3 oz) butter, softened
10 ml (2 tsp) lemon juice
20 ml (4 tsp) chopped fresh parsley
salt and pepper
peeled prawns and lemon slices, to garnish
French bread, to serve

1. Finely chop the prawns. Beat into 50 g (2 oz) butter with the lemon juice, parsley and seasoning.
2. Spoon into a serving dish and level the surface. Melt the remaining butter and pour over the prawn mixture. Chill in the refrigerator for 1 hour. Garnish with prawns and lemon slices. Serve with French bread.
SERVES 4

Potted Prawn Pâté

COARSE GARLIC PÂTÉ

450 g (1 lb) ox liver
60 ml (4 tbsp) milk
450 g (1 lb) belly of pork, skinned and boned
225 g (8 oz) pork fat
225 g (8 oz) stewing steak
1 medium onion, skinned and quartered
125 g (4 oz) mushrooms, wiped and roughly chopped
4 garlic cloves, skinned and crushed
45 ml (3 tbsp) red wine
1.25 ml (¼ level tsp) freshly grated nutmeg
salt and pepper

1. Make the pâté one day before needed. Soak the liver in the milk for about 1 hour, then drain.

2. Mince the liver with the belly pork, pork fat, steak and onion. Stir the mushrooms into the minced mixture.
3. Add the garlic to the pâté ingredients with the wine, nutmeg and seasoning.
4. Pack mixture tightly into a 1.4 litre (2½ pint) terrine. Cover tightly with the lid or foil and stand in a roasting tin with sufficient water to come halfway up the sides. Bake in the oven at 170°C (325°F) mark 3 for about 2 hours.
5. When cooked, remove from the roasting tin and place a heavy weight on the pâté.
6. Refrigerate until required. Leave at room temperature for 30 minutes before serving.
SERVES 10-12

DIPS

TZAZIKI

½ a medium cucumber, diced
150 ml (5 fl oz) natural yogurt (preferably firm set)
10 ml (2 tsp) olive oil
15 ml (1 tbsp) chopped fresh mint
1 garlic clove, skinned and crushed
salt and pepper

1. Place the cucumber in a serving bowl. Pour over the yogurt and olive oil. Add the mint and garlic, season and mix well. Cover and chill before serving.
SERVES 4 AS A SIDE SALAD

TARAMASALATA

225 g (8 oz) smoked cod's roe, skinned and broken up
1 garlic clove, skinned and crushed
50 g (2 oz) fresh breadcrumbs
1 small onion, skinned and finely chopped
grated rind and juice of 1 lemon
150 ml (¼ pint) olive oil
pepper
lemon slices, to garnish
pitta bread or toast, to serve

1. Place the cod's roe in a blender or food processor and blend to form a purée. Add the garlic with the breadcrumbs, onion, lemon rind and juice; blend for a few more seconds.
2. Gradually add the oil, blending well after each addition until smooth. Blend in 90 ml (6 tbsp) hot water with the pepper.
3. Spoon into a serving dish and chill for at least 1 hour. Garnish with lemon slices and serve with pitta bread or toast.
SERVES 6

GUACAMOLE

2 avocados
2 medium tomatoes, skinned
1 small onion, skinned and chopped
15 ml (1 tbsp) chopped fresh parsley
1 green chilli pepper, seeded and chopped
salt and pepper
wholemeal toast or corn chips, to serve

1. Peel, stone and mash the avocado flesh.
2. Halve the tomatoes and discard the seeds. Chop the flesh and add with the onion, parsley and green chilli to the avocado pulp.
3. Adjust the seasoning and serve in small bowls with fingers of wholemeal toast or corn chips.
SERVES 4

MUSTARD DIP

45 ml (3 level tbsp) Mayonnaise (see page 254)
60-90 ml (4-6 tbsp) soured cream
45 ml (3 level tbsp) wholegrain mustard
30 ml (2 level tbsp) finely chopped gherkins

1. Whisk together the Mayonnaise and cream until blended.
2 . Stir in the mustard and gherkins. Leave for several hours for the flavours to develop.
3. Serve with crudités or small meat balls.
SERVES 4

BLUE CHEESE DIP

150 ml (5 fl oz) soured cream
1 garlic clove, skinned and crushed
175 g (6 oz) Blue Stilton cheese, crumbled
juice of 1 lemon
salt and pepper
snipped fresh chives, to garnish

1. Blend all the ingredients, except the chives, to a smooth paste. Sprinkle over the chives and serve with chunks of French bread or crudités.
SERVES 6-8

SPICY CHEESE AND TOMATO DIP

125 g (4 oz) Cheddar or Cheshire cheese, grated
50 g (2 oz) butter or margarine, softened
1 small onion, skinned and finely grated
5 ml (1 level tsp) mustard powder
15 ml (1 tbsp) tomato ketchup
30 ml (2 tbsp) single cream
few drops of Worcestershire sauce
pinch of cayenne pepper

1. In a bowl, beat together the cheese and butter with a wooden spoon.
2. Mix in the onion, then add the mustard powder, tomato ketchup, cream, Worcestershire sauce and cayenne pepper. Mix well.
3. Transfer to a serving dish and chill before serving, with corn chips or crudités.
SERVES 4

HUMMUS

225 g (8 oz) dried chick peas, soaked overnight and
    drained, or two 400 g (14 oz) cans chick peas,
    drained
juice of 2 large lemons
150 ml (¼ pint) tahini paste
60 ml (4 tbsp) olive oil
1-2 garlic cloves, skinned and crushed
salt and pepper
black olives and chopped fresh parsley, to garnish
warm pitta bread, to serve

1. Place the dried chick peas in a saucepan and
cover with cold water. Bring to the boil and

simmer gently for 2 hours or until tender.
Drain, reserving a little of the cooking liquid.
2. Put the drained, cooked chick peas in a
blender or food processor, reserving a few for
garnish, then gradually add the lemon juice,
blending well after each addition in order to
form a smooth purée.
3. Add the tahini paste, all but 10 ml (2 tbsp) of
the oil, the garlic and seasoning. Blend until
smooth.
4. Spoon into a serving dish and sprinkle with
the reserved oil and chick peas. Garnish with
olives and parsley. Serve with warm pitta bread.
SERVES 8

SAVOURY FINGER FOOD

CHEESE AND OLIVE PICK-UPS

125 g (4 oz) blue Stilton cheese
125 g (4 oz) cottage cheese
15 ml (1 tbsp) snipped fresh chives
50 g (2 oz) black olives, stoned and finely chopped
15 ml (1 tbsp) brandy
50 g (2 oz) chopped almonds, browned
buttered cracker biscuits, to serve

1. Blend the cheeses together. Work in the
chives, olives and brandy and shape into a roll
about 2.5 cm (1 inch) across. Roll in the nuts,
coating evenly, then chill on a plate.
2. Just before serving, slice with a sharp knife
and serve with crackers.
MAKES 30-36

SMOKED SALMON PINWHEELS

1 large brown sliced loaf, crusts removed
125 g (4 oz) butter or margarine, softened
350 g (12 oz) smoked salmon, thinly sliced
lemon juice
pepper

1. Butter each slice of bread and cover with
salmon. Sprinkle with lemon juice and season
with pepper.
2. Roll up, then wrap in foil and chill for up to
1 hour before slicing.
MAKES ABOUT 96

ASPARAGUS ROLLS

25 slices of fresh brown bread, crusts removed
50 g (2 oz) butter or margarine, softened
salt and pepper
350 g (12 oz) can asparagus tips, drained

1. Spread each slice with butter, sprinkle with
salt and pepper and roll up with an asparagus tip

inside. Wrap in foil until required and chill. Cut
each roll in half to serve.
MAKES ABOUT 50

NOTE: The bread slices can be lightly rolled with
a rolling pin before buttering; this gives a
thinner roll and prevents the bread cracking.

STILTON BITES

50 g (2 oz) butter or margarine
50 g (2 oz) flour
300 ml (½ pint) milk
175 g (6 oz) Stilton cheese, crumbled
salt and pepper
paprika
4 gherkins, each cut into 16 pieces
1 egg, beaten
50 g (2 oz) dry white breadcrumbs
vegetable oil for frying

1. Melt the butter in a saucepan, stir in the flour and cook gently for 1 minute, stirring. Remove the pan from the heat and gradually stir in the milk. Bring to the boil slowly and continue to cook, stirring, until the sauce thickens, then add the cheese and seasonings and stir well.
2. Turn into a non-stick 18 cm (7 inch) square tin. Chill for several hours.

Cut the cheese bites into dice, then press a piece of gherkin into each one.

3. Remove from the tin and cut into 64 dice. Using floured hands, press a piece of gherkin into each dice, then carefully coat in egg and breadcrumbs.
4. Heat the oil in a deep-fat fryer to 190°C (375°F) and cook the Stilton Bites in batches for several minutes until golden. Drain on absorbent kitchen paper and keep warm in a low oven whilst frying the others.
MAKES 64

NOTE: For a more economical version, use Danish blue cheese instead of the Stilton.

CHEESE STRAWS

75 g (3 oz) flour
salt and pepper
40 g (1½ oz) butter or margarine
40 g (1½ oz) Cheddar cheese, finely grated
1 egg, beaten
5 ml (1 level tsp) French mustard

1. Mix the flour and seasoning together and rub in the butter until the mixture resembles fine breadcrumbs. Add the cheese and stir until mixed evenly.
2. Combine half the egg with the mustard and stir into the flour mixture to form a soft dough. Turn out on to a floured work surface and knead lightly until just smooth.
3. Roll out the dough to a 15 cm (6 inch) square and place on a baking sheet. Brush with the remaining beaten egg. Divide the dough into 7.5 x 1 cm (3 x ½ inch) oblongs and separate them.
4. Bake in the oven at 180°C (350°F) mark 4 for 12-15 minutes, until golden. Cool on a wire rack. Store in an airtight container.
MAKES ABOUT 24

INDIVIDUAL QUICHES

100 g (4 oz) plain flour
pinch of salt
25 g (1 oz) butter or block margarine, diced
25 g (1 oz) lard, diced
75 g (3 oz) matured Cheddar cheese, grated
150 ml (¼ pint) milk
1 egg
5 ml (1 tsp) chopped fresh parsley or 1.25 ml
    (¼ level tsp) mixed dried herbs
salt and pepper

1. Place the flour and salt in a bowl. Add the butter and lard to the flour. Using both hands, rub in until the mixture resembles fine breadcrumbs. Add enough cold water to bind the mixture together. Knead lightly for a few seconds to give a firm, smooth dough.
2. Roll out the pastry on a floured surface and use it to line twelve to fourteen 5 cm (2 inch) patty tins. Divide the cheese between the pastry cases.
3. Lightly whisk together the milk, egg and parsley. Season to taste.
4. Spoon the mixture evenly over the cheese. Bake in the oven at 180°C (350°F) mark 4 for 20-25 minutes. Serve warm.
MAKES 12-14

CHEESE PALMIERS

212 g (7 fl oz) packet frozen puff pastry, thawed
beaten egg, to glaze
75 g (3 oz) Gruyère cheese, finely grated
salt and pepper
paprika

1. Roll out the pastry to an oblong 30 x 25 cm (12 x 10 inches). Brush with beaten egg.
2. Scatter over the grated cheese and sprinkle with salt, pepper and paprika.
3. Roll up tightly lengthways, rolling from each side until the rolls meet in the centre. Cut across into ten pieces.
4. Place on a greased baking sheet and flatten with a round-bladed knife.
5. Bake in the oven at 200°C (400°F) mark 6 for 15-18 minutes, until brown and crisp. Ease off the baking sheet and cool on a wire rack.
MAKES 10

SMOKED SALMON SAMOSAS

225 g (8 oz) smoked salmon (or salmon trimmings)
225 g (8 oz) full fat soft cheese or curd cheese
45 ml (3 tbsp) chopped fresh dill
30 ml (2 tbsp) lemon or lime juice
pepper
8 long slices from a side of smoked salmon, halved
    lengthways
fresh dill sprigs, to garnish
lime or lemon wedges, to serve

1. Chop the 225 g (8 oz) smoked salmon into tiny pieces and mix with the cheese. Stir in the dill and season with lots of black pepper and lemon juice to taste.
2. Cut the long salmon slices in half widthways to give 32 pieces. Place a teaspoonful of the cheese on one end of each slice of smoked salmon. Fold over to form the beginning of a triangle. Keep folding in this manner, forming a triangle each time until the filling is completely enclosed. Cut each samosa in half.

ABOVE: Prawn and Feta Purses. BELOW: Smoked Salmon Samosas

3. Arrange on a flat serving dish, cover and chill until ready to serve. Garnish with sprigs of dill and serve with lime or lemon wedges.
MAKES 64

PRAWN AND FETA PURSES

125 g (4 oz) peeled prawns, thawed and well drained
    if frozen, roughly chopped
225 g (8 oz) feta cheese, crumbled
1 cm (½ inch) piece fresh root ginger, peeled and grated
salt and pepper
30 ml (2 tbsp) chopped fresh chives or dill
pinch of freshly grated nutmeg
1 packet of filo pastry, cut into seventy-five 10 cm
    (4 inch) squares
melted butter for brushing
fresh chives, to garnish

1. Mix the chopped prawns with the feta cheese, ginger, seasoning, chives and nutmeg.
2. Brush each square of pastry with butter and lay three on top of each other to make 25 piles. Place a teaspoonful of filling in the middle of each square. Draw the pastry up around the filling, pinching the middle to form a money bag shape. Pull out and arrange frilly tops.
3. Place on greased baking sheets and brush lightly with melted butter. Bake in the oven at 200°C (400°F) mark 6 for 10-15 minutes until golden brown.
4. Cool slightly and serve while still warm or when completely cold, garnished with chives.
MAKES 25

Savoury Choux Puffs

50 g (2 oz) Choux Pastry (see page 388)
125 g (4 oz) full fat soft cheese or curd cheese
FOR THE FILLING
30 ml (2 tbsp) soured cream
125 g (4 oz) smoked salmon trimmings, finely chopped
15 ml (1 tbsp) lemon juice
pepper
fresh parsley sprigs, to garnish

1. Put the pastry into a piping bag fitted with a 1 cm (½ inch) plain nozzle and pipe about 24 walnut-sized balls on to a dampened baking sheet.
2. Bake in the oven at 200°C (400°F) mark 6 for 15-20 minutes, until golden brown and crisp.

Remove from the oven and make a short slit in the side of each to let out the steam. If necessary, return the cases to the oven to dry out completely.
3. For the filling, cream together the soft cheese, soured cream, smoked salmon trimmings, lemon juice and pepper.
4. Either spoon or pipe the filling into the cases. Arrange on a serving plate and garnish with parsley to serve.
MAKES ABOUT 24

VARIATION
Replace the filling with 175 g (6 oz) liver pâté mixed with 5 ml (1 level tsp) French mustard and 30 ml (2 tbsp) soured cream.

Mushroom Bouchées

368 g (13 oz) packet frozen puff pastry, thawed
beaten egg to glaze
FOR THE FILLING
40 g (1½ oz) butter
75 g (3 oz) button mushrooms, wiped and chopped
45 ml (3 level tbsp) flour
150 ml (¼ pint) milk
salt and pepper
dash of Worcestershire sauce

1. Roll out the pastry to a 5 mm (¼ inch) thickness and cut out twenty-five 5 cm (2 inch) rounds, using a plain cutter. Place the rounds on dampened baking sheets.
2. Using a 4 cm (1¼ inch) plain cutter, cut partway through the centre of each round. Glaze the tops with beaten egg. Bake in the oven at 230°C (450°F) mark 8 for 10 minutes, until well risen and golden brown.
3. To make the filling, melt a knob of butter in a small saucepan and fry the mushrooms until softened. Remove and set aside. Melt the remaining butter in a clean pan, stir in the flour and cook for 2 minutes. Remove from the heat and gradually stir in the milk. Bring to the boil and cook for about 2 minutes, stirring

continuously. Fold in the mushrooms and cream. Season to taste with salt, pepper and a dash of Worcestershire sauce.
4. Remove the cooked Bouchées from the oven and carefully lift off the lids. Scoop out the soft pastry centres and fill the cases with the hot mushroom filling. Serve immediately.
5. Alternatively, cool them on a wire rack and use with a cold filling.
MAKES 25

NOTE: When making Bouchées for a party, it is better to fill cold cases with a cold filling and reheat in the oven at 180°C (350°F) mark 4 for about 15 minutes before serving.

VARIATIONS
CHICKEN BOUCHÉES: For the filling, replace the cooked mushrooms with 1 small sautéed finely chopped onion and 100 g (4 oz) diced chicken meat. Replace the Worcestershire sauce with a dash of Tabasco.

PRAWN BOUCHÉES: For the filling, omit the mushrooms and Worcestershire sauce. Add 100 g (4 oz) peeled prawns, a little lemon juice and 5 ml (1 tsp) chopped fresh parsley.

AFTER-DINNER SAVOURIES

An after-dinner savoury may be served instead of a cheese course after the dessert. They are usually hot and should have a distinctive flavour that contrasts with the main course. The portions should be small. The recipes in this section are some of the most popular after-dinner savouries.

SCOTCH WOODCOCK

two 50 g (1¾ oz) cans anchovies, drained
2 bread slices
butter or margarine
60-90 ml (4-6 tbsp) milk
2 eggs
salt and pepper
pieces of canned pimiento or paprika, to garnish

1. Reserve 2 anchovy fillets for a garnish and sieve the rest.
2. Toast the bread, remove the crusts, and spread with butter, then cut into triangles and spread with the anchovy purée. Keep warm.

3. Melt a knob of butter in a pan. Whisk together the milk, eggs and seasoning, pour into the pan and stir slowly over a gentle heat until the mixture begins to thicken. Remove from the heat and stir until creamy.
4. Spread the mixture on top of the anchovy toast; garnish with thin strips of anchovy fillet and add pieces of pimiento or a sprinkling of paprika to serve.
MAKES 8

NOTE: Gentleman's Relish may be used in place of the sieved anchovies.

DEVILS ON HORSEBACK

8 blanched almonds
a little olive oil
salt and cayenne pepper
8 large prunes, stoned
4 thin rashers of streaky bacon, rinded
8 rounds of bread, about 5 cm (2 inches) in diameter
50 g (2 oz) butter or margarine
watercress, to garnish

1. Fry the almonds for 2-3 minutes in a little oil, until they are golden brown, then toss in a little salt and cayenne pepper. Place an almond in each stoned prune.
2. Stretch the bacon rashers with the back of a knife, cut in half and roll around the prunes.

Secure with a wooden cocktail stick or small skewer and cook under a medium grill, turning, until all the bacon is golden brown.
3. Meanwhile, fry the bread for 2-3 minutes in the butter, until golden. Put a prune on each piece, garnish with watercress and serve at once.
MAKES 8

VARIATION
ANGELS ON HORSEBACK
Omit the almonds and prunes and replace with 8 oysters sprinkled with cayenne pepper and lemon juice. Place one oyster and bacon roll on top of each croûte of bread and bake in the oven at 200°C (400°F) mark 6 for about 15 minutes, or until the bacon is lightly cooked.

CHICKEN LIVERS ON TOAST

125 g (4 oz) chicken livers
15-30 ml (1-2 level tbsp) seasoned flour
4 rounds of bread, about 5 cm (2 inches) in diameter
50 g (2 oz) butter or margarine
30 ml (2 tbsp) sherry or Madeira
50 g (2 oz) mushrooms, wiped and sliced (optional)

1. Wash and dry the livers, cut them in small pieces and coat with the seasoned flour.
2. Toast the bread and lightly butter.
3. Melt the remaining butter in a frying pan, add the livers and cook until browned, stirring. Add the sherry and the mushrooms if using, mix well and cook slowly for 10-15 minutes.
4. Place the livers on the toast and serve at once.
MAKES 4

FISH

Fish is both nutritious and versatile. It provides a valuable source of protein, plus minerals and vitamins, and comes in a variety of forms – whole, and as cutlets, steaks and fillets. These can be used in a variety of recipes to suit all the family.

Fish are classified into three groups: white fish, oily fish and shellfish. There are two types of white fish: round species, such as cod, haddock and whiting; and flat fish, such as halibut, plaice and sole. White fish have a more delicate flavour than oily fish. They have less than 2 per cent fat and contain only 50-80 calories per 125 g (4 oz).

Oily fish, such as trout, herring and mackerel, generally have darker, richer flesh. They have 8-20 per cent fat and contain 80-160 calories per 125 g (4 oz). These fish are particularly good sources of vitamins A and D. The fat contained in oily fish is mainly polyunsaturated; indeed the fatty acids in fish oils are believed to help prevent heart disease.

This chapter includes some of the exotic species, previously unavailable in this country; try experimenting by using them in recipes instead of the more familiar ones. Some fish are available all year around, others have a close season (period when they cannot be fished) which is usually the spawning time. General availability for each fish is given in the individual entries, but it can vary depending on region and weather conditions.

BUYING FRESH FISH

Look for fish that is as fresh as possible and preferably cook on the day it is bought. Whole fish should have clear, bright eyes, bright red or pink gills, shiny bodies and close-fitting scales. Fillets, steaks and cutlets should have a white transluscent colour and show no signs of dryness or discoloration, nor should they be wet and shiny. All fresh fish should have a mild, clean smell; do not buy any strong smelling fish. If necessary fresh fish can be stored overnight; simply rinse, pat dry with absorbent kitchen paper, cover and store in the refrigerator.

Shellfish should be eaten very fresh as they are more perishable than other fish. They should have a clean sea smell and clear fresh colour; avoid any that are dull looking. Prawns and shrimps should have tails curled well under them. Look for tightly closed undamaged shells where applicable (see individual entries).

BUYING FROZEN FISH

Frozen fish are sold in a variety of ways—whole, filleted, as cutlets or as fingers or cakes. Shellfish are also available frozen. Make sure you buy frozen fish which is frozen hard, with no sign of partial thawing or damaged packaging. Fish and shellfish are best thawed in the refrigerator overnight. Frozen fish may also be defrosted in the microwave. Use fish soon after defrosting.

CLEANING FISH

The fishmonger will nearly always prepare fish for you, but you can do it yourself if you follow these instructions:
1. Using the back of a knife, remove any scales, scraping from tail to head (the opposite way to the direction the scales lie). Rinse frequently under cold running water.
2. To remove the entrails from round fish, such

Scrape off the scales.

Slit along abdomen to gut.

as herrings or trout, make a slit along the abdomen from the gills to the tail vent. Draw out the insides and clean away any blood. Rub with a little salt to remove the black skin and blood. Rinse under cold running water and pat dry with absorbent kitchen paper.

3. To remove the entrails from flat fish, such as sole and plaice, open the cavity which lies in the upper part of the body under the gills and clean out the entrails in the same way. Rinse under cold running water.

4. Cut off the fins and gills, if wished, if the fish is to be served whole. The head and tail may also be cut off, if wished. Rinse the fish under cold running water and pat dry with absorbent kitchen paper.

5. Fish fillets and cutlets should be rinsed under cold running water, then patted dry with absorbent kitchen paper.

SKINNING FISH

WHOLE FLAT FISH

1. Rinse the fish and cut off the fins, if not already removed. Make an incision across the tail, slip the thumb between the skin and the

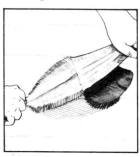

To skin flat fish, make an incision across the tail. Use salted fingers and pull the skin away.

flesh and loosen the dark skin around the sides of the fish. Salt your fingers, then hold the fish down firmly with one hand and hold the skin with the other hand. Then pull the skin upwards towards the head. The white skin can be removed in the same way, but unless the fish is particularly large, this layer of skin is usually left on.

FILLETS OF FLAT FISH

1. Lay the fillet on a board, skin side down. Salt your fingers and hold the tail end of the skin firmly. Insert a sharp knife between the flesh and the skin and work from head to tail, sawing with the knife from side to side and pressing the flat side of the blade

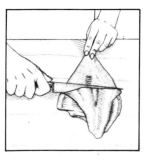

Firmly hold tail while skinning the fish.

against the skin. Keep the edge of the blade close to the skin while cutting, but do not press it down at too sharp an angle or you will slice through the skin.

With salted fingers, carefully pull the skin towards the tail.

ROUND FISH

These are usually cooked with the skin on, but may be skinned if wished.

1. Using a sharp knife, cut along the spine and across the skin just below the head. Loosen the skin under the head with the point of the knife. Salt the fingers, then gently pull the skin down towards the tail, working carefully to avoid breaking the flesh. Skin the other side in the same way.

FILLETING FISH

FLAT FISH

1. Four fillets are taken from flat fish, two from each side. Using a small sharp pointed knife, make an incision straight down the back of the fish, following the line of the bone and keeping the fish flat on the board.

2. Insert the knife between the flesh and the bone and carefully remove the flesh with long,

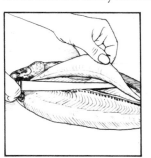

Place a knife between the flesh and bones and slice away the fillet.

clean strokes, cutting the first fillet from the left-hand side of the fish, carefully working from the head to the tail.

3. Turn the fish and cut off the second fillet from tail to head. Fillet the other side using the same method. There should not be any flesh left on the fish's bone.

KEY
1. Sardine
2. St. Peter's Fish
3. Sea Bass
4. Mackerel
5. Parrotfish
6. Red Snapper
7. Snapper (Job Gris)
8. Emperor Bream

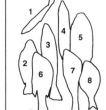

ROUND FISH
1. Two fillets are taken from round fish. Keeping the fish flat on the board, cut along the centre of the back to the bone, using a sharp knife. Then cut along the abdomen of the fish.
2. Remove the flesh cleanly from the bones, working from the head down, pressing the knife against the bones and working with short, sharp strokes. Remove the fillet from the other side in the same way. If the fish is large, cut the fillets into serving size pieces.

HERRING AND MACKEREL: These small round fish are often cooked whole. To remove the bones:
1. Cut off head, tail and fins. Split fish along the underside and remove entrails. Salt fingers and rub off the black inner skin and blood.
2. Put the fish on a board, cut side down, and press lightly with the fingers down the middle of the back to loosen the bone.
3. Turn the fish over and ease the backbone up with the fingers, removing with it as many of the small bones as possible.

POACHED FISH

Fish should be poached very gently, so that it does not break up and the texture is not spoilt by overcooking. It can be poached on the top of the stove in a fish kettle or saucepan, or in the oven. The poaching liquid may be wine, milk or fish stock, flavoured with parsley sprigs, a small piece of onion and/or carrot, a few mushroom stalks, a squeeze of lemon juice, a bay leaf and some peppercorns. Alternatively, poach in Court Bouillon (see below).

Fillets, steaks or whole fish, eg halibut, turbot, haddock, flounder, salmon, sea trout,

smoked haddock and kippers can be poached.
1. Heat the liquid in a fish kettle or saucepan until simmering, then add the fish. Cover and simmer very gently until tender, allowing 10-15 minutes per 450 g (1 lb) for whole fish or large cuts, according to thickness. For steaks and fillets cooking times vary enormously according to size and thickness; refer to individual recipes.
2. Drain the fish, carefully transfer to a warmed serving dish and serve with a sauce made from the cooking liquid. Alternatively, serve the fish cold, in aspic or with Mayonnaise (see page 254).

COURT BOUILLON

1 litre (1¾ pints) water or dry white wine and water
1 small carrot, scrubbed and sliced
1 small onion, skinned and sliced
1 small celery stick, washed and chopped (optional)
15 ml (1 tbsp) wine vinegar or lemon juice
few fresh parsley sprigs
1 bay leaf
3-4 black peppercorns
10 ml (2 level tsp) salt

1. Place all the ingredients in a saucepan and simmer for about 30 minutes. Allow to cool and strain the liquid before using, if wished.
MAKES ABOUT 900 ML (1½ PINTS)

GRILLED FISH

Small fish, thin fillets and thicker cuts, eg sole, plaice, halibut, turbot, hake, brill, cod, haddock, flounder, salmon, sea trout, trout, herring, mackerel, kippers, red mullet and monkfish, can be grilled.
1. Put the prepared fish in the grill pan, season and make two or three diagonal cuts in the body on each side, to allow the heat to penetrate through the flesh.
2. Brush with melted butter, oil or margarine and cook under a moderate heat, allowing 4-5 minutes for thin fillets, 10-12 minutes for

thicker fillets, steaks and small whole fish, adjusting times according to size and thickness. Turn whole fish and thick fillets during cooking.

BARBECUED FISH
Many types of fish can be barbecued – trout, bass, red mullet, sardines and shellfish such as lobster, oysters, prawns and scallops are all suitable. Use a special grilling basket or wrap in foil to prevent the fish breaking up. Alternatively, thread fish on to long skewers. Leave the shells on shellfish to protect the delicate flesh during cooking.

STEAMED FISH

Fillets, eg sole, trout and monkfish, and small whole fish can be steamed.
1. Season the prepared fish with salt and pepper. Heat the water in the base of a steamer to simmering point (line top of steamer with buttered foil to keep in the flavour, if wished).
2. Put the fish into the steamer and cover with a tight fitting lid. Steam for 5-10 minutes for thin fillets or 15-20 minutes for thicker pieces or small whole fish; the fish should be firm to touch and just flaking from the bones. Transfer to a warmed serving dish and serve immediately.

NOTE: If you do not have a steamer, the fish can be placed between two greased plates over a saucepan of simmering water.

SHALLOW-FRIED FISH

Fillets, steaks and whole fish, eg sole, plaice, dab, bass, monkfish, bream, cod, haddock, mackerel, herring, trout, perch and pike, can be shallow-fried.
1. Coat the prepared fish with either a coating of seasoned flour, or egg and breadcrumbs.
2. Heat either clarified butter (see page 568), vegetable oil, or oil and butter until fairly hot.
3. Add the fish and fry for 3-4 minutes for small fillets, steaks or whole fish and 8-10 minutes for larger cuts, turning once.
4. Drain well on crumpled absorbent kitchen paper and serve with lemon and parsley or Maître d'Hôtel Butter (see page 207).

DEEP-FRIED FISH

Fillets from large fish coated with batter or egg and breadcrumbs, and small whole fish, eg cod, haddock, hake, whiting, coley, monkfish and skate, can be deep-fried.
1. Heat vegetable oil in a deep-fat fryer to 190°C (375°F). Coat the fish with flour, egg and breadcrumbs or fritter batter (see page 334).
2. Lower the fish gently into the oil, using a basket for egg-and-crumbed pieces, and deep-fry for 4-5 minutes or until golden brown and crisp. (Take care when cooking small fish like whitebait, as they will cook in little more than a minute.)
3. Drain well on absorbent kitchen paper before serving.

BAKED FISH

Fillets, steaks, whole fish and cuts from large fish, eg cod, haddock, hake, whiting, sole, plaice, trout, halibut, herring and monkfish, can be baked. For salmon, see page 76.
1. Place the prepared fish in a single layer in an ovenproof dish, season, add a knob of butter or margarine and pour over a little water, milk, lemon juice, stock or wine. Cover with foil.
2. Alternatively, wrap the prepared fish in greased foil and add a squeeze of lemon juice and a sprinkling of salt and pepper. Place the fish on a baking sheet.
3. Bake in the oven at 180°C (350°F) mark 4 allowing about 40-50 minutes for whole fish; 15-30 minutes for fillets and steaks. Delicate thin fillets and whole flat fish will take much less time to cook than dense fish. Refer to individual recipes for timings.

NOTE: The cooking liquid must never be allowed to boil otherwise the fish will have a rather unpleasant dry, flaky texture.

MICROWAVE COOKING FISH

Fish cooks particularly well in a microwave oven. Small whole fish, eg sole, plaice and trout; cutlets, steaks and fillets are suitable. Always cover with a lid and use less liquid than for conventional cooking. Season after cooking. Cooking times vary according to quantity and thickness: 450 g (1 lb) fillets would take 4-5 minutes, plus 2 minutes standing time.

SEA FISH

ANCHOVY

The anchovy is a small round fish, which is usually filleted and cured, by salting or brining, and then canned or bottled. Because they are very salty, cured anchovies are only used in small amounts in appetisers and cocktail nibbles, as pizza topping and in Salade Nicoise (see page 262). They can also be used to make Anchovy Butter (see page 207) for use in savouries.

Anchovies are rarely available fresh, but they are easily recognised by their extraordinarily large mouth, which stretches back almost as far as their gills. They have a strong flavour, but are not salty like the cured ones.

BASS

Bass is a round fish, similar to salmon in shape, which can weigh up to 4.5 kg (10 lb). It has steel grey or blue scales covering the back and sides and a white or yellowish belly. It has white flesh and is sold whole or as steaks or fillets. Large bass, which have a good flavour, are usually poached or baked; small fish can be grilled or fried. Available August to March.

BREAM (EMPEROR)

This family of exotic fish, also known simply as emperors, includes *capitaine rouge* and *lascar*.

BREAM (SEA)

Bream is a round, red-backed fish with a silvery belly and red fins. It has firm white flesh which has a mild flavour. It is usually sold whole and can be stuffed and baked, poached, fried or grilled. Available June to February.

BRILL

This is a flat fish with a good flavour and texture resembling turbot. The flesh is firm and slightly yellowish; avoid any with a bluish tinge. It is sold whole or as fillets and may be poached, served cold with Mayonnaise (see page 254), or cooked like turbot (see page 61). Available June to February.

CATFISH

Catfish gets its name from its head, which has cat-like whiskers. The flesh is firm and white with a pinkish tinge and has a strong flavour. It is ideal for casseroles or stews. It can also be grilled or cooked as for Cod (see below). It is sold as fillets, portions or cutlets. Available February to July.

COD

Cod is a large round fish with close, white flesh. Small cod are known as codling. Cod may be sold whole when young and small, or as fillets or steaks when large. It can be grilled, baked, fried in batter or used in various cooked dishes. Available all year, best from June to February.

COD'S ROE is available fresh, canned or smoked.

SALT COD FILLETS are sold in some ethnic shops. Look for fillets that are thick and have white flesh; when not fresh, salt cod takes on a yellow appearance. To use: soak for 24 hours in cold water, changing the water several times. Drain and remove any skin and bones before cooking with well flavoured ingredients.

COLEY (SAITHE)

Coley is a member of the cod family with bluish-black skin. It is usually sold as fillets or cutlets, but may be sold whole. The well-flavoured meaty flesh is pinkish-grey and turns white when cooked. Use in the same way as Cod (see above), but as it is inclined to be dry, add moisture during cooking. Best August to February.

CONGER EEL

The conger eel is a sea fish which is a greyish-brown colour on top and silver underneath. The full-flavoured flesh is white and firm; larger eels have a coarser texture than small ones. The conger eel is larger than the common (freshwater) eel, but it can be prepared and cooked in the same way. Eels can be jellied, fried, grilled, poached or baked. Available March to October.

CUTTLEFISH

The cuttlefish is a member of a group of aquatic creatures known as cephalopods – a name which comes from the Greek words for head and feet – so called because they have tentacles protruding from their heads. Octopus and squid are also cephalopods. Cuttlefish and squid have ten tentacles, octopus eight. In prehistoric times, they had external shells and, although they no longer have them, they are still regarded as part of the mollusc family (see Shellfish, page 81). Cuttlefish are mostly sold frozen. If buying fresh, prepare as for Squid (see page 61).

DAB

Dab is a small member of the plaice family with white flesh and is good fried or baked. It is sold whole or as fillets. Season: September to May.

FLOUNDER
Flounder is a flat fish which resembles plaice, but does not have such a good texture and flavour. It is sold whole or as fillets and cooked like Plaice (see page 60). Season: March to November.

GURNET, GURNARD
This is a small round fish with a large, distinctive, boney head and three rays of the pectoral fins extending downwards. There are three types of gurnet, the grey, yellow and red. It has firm white flesh and can be baked, grilled or poached and is especially good for fish soups. Season: July to February.

HADDOCK
This round fish is a cousin of the cod and is distinguished from it by a dark streak, which runs down the back, and the two black 'thumb marks' above the gills. Haddock has firm, white flesh and may be cooked by any method suitable for white fish; it is particularly useful for cooked dishes such as fish pie. It is sold as fillets or cutlets. Available all year, best May to February. Haddock does not take salt as well as cod does, and it is traditionally cured by smoking.

HAKE
Hake belongs to the same family as cod and is similar in shape, but has a closer white flesh and a better flavour. It can be cooked like Cod (see page 58). Small hake are sold whole; large ones are sold as fillets, steaks or cutlets. Available June to March.

HALIBUT
Halibut is a very large flat fish and like turbot is regarded as one of the best flavoured fish. It is sold as fillets or steaks. It is usually baked or grilled, but may also be cooked by any recipe suitable for Turbot (see page 61) or Cod (see page 58). Season: June to March.

HERRING
Herring is a fairly small, round, oily fish with creamy-coloured flesh which has a distinctive flavour. It is usually grilled, fried, sautéed or stuffed and baked. Though generally sold whole, the fishmonger will fillet them for you on request. Season: May to September. Herrings are also sold prepared in various ways:
SALT HERRINGS are gutted and preserved in wooden casks between layers of salt. Salt herrings are usually sold at delicatessen counters.
MATJES HERRINGS are herrings cured in salt, sugar and a little saltpetre. They are sold whole or as fillets and are considered to have a better flavour than salt herrings.

ROLLMOPS AND BISMARCKS are boned herrings marinated in spiced vinegar. Rollmops are rolled with chopped onions, gherkins and peppercorns. Bismarcks are flat fillets covered with sliced onion.
CANNED HERRINGS are most popular in tomato sauce. Canned kippers and bloaters are available too, as are herring roes.

HUSS
Huss is a long, pointed fish with light brown skin and a cream-coloured belly. It is also known as dogfish and rock salmon. The firm flesh is white with a tinge of pink and is excellent fried. It is usually sold as fillets or cutlets. Available all year, best September to January.

JOHN DORY
This ugly, flat fish has very large jaws and a body that is nearly oval in shape and olive-brown skin with a black 'thumb mark' on each side just behind the head. It has firm, white flesh with a delicate flavour. The head and fins can be removed and the fish poached or baked whole, but it is more usually filleted and cooked like Sole (see page 60). Available all year.

MACKEREL
Mackerel is a fairly small, round, oily fish with blue-black markings on the back, cream-coloured flesh and a very distinctive flavour. It is sold whole. It can be cooked whole or filleted and cooked by any method suitable for Herring (see left). Mackerel must be eaten very fresh. Available all year.
HORSE MACKEREL (SCAD) are sometimes available. They are a darker colour than ordinary mackerel and their flavour is not as good.

MONKFISH (ANGLER FISH)
A round fish with a very large, ugly head. Only the tail is eaten and it is sold as fillets. The firm white flesh is not unlike lobster. Available all year, best October to January.

MULLET (GREY)
Grey mullet is a round fish which looks and tastes similar to sea bass. It is sold whole or as fillets. The firm white flesh has a mild, nutty flavour and is suitable for baking, grilling, steaming or poaching. Season: September to February.

MULLET (RED)
No relation to the grey mullet, red mullet is smaller, crimson in colour with a unique and delicate flavour. The liver is a delicacy and should not be discarded. Red mullet is sold whole and may be grilled, fried or baked. Available May to November.

OCTOPUS

The octopus is a member of the cephalopod group (see Cuttlefish, page 58) and has eight tentacles. Octopus vary in size and can grow up to 3 metres (12 feet). Small octopus may be sold whole; larger ones, ready-prepared in pieces. Octopus can be poached in water or red wine, then skinned and served cold or reheated in a sauce. It can also be used in soups and casseroles.

TO PREPARE OCTOPUS

1. Rinse the octopus, then hold the body in one hand and with the other firmly pull off the head and tentacles. The soft contents of the body will come out and can be discarded. Cut the tentacles just in front of the eyes.

2. Rinse the body and the tentacles, then beat well with a wooden mallet. Cut the flesh into rings or pieces or keep whole for stuffing. The ink sac has a musky flavour and is not usually used.

PARROTFISH

This round tropical fish has a brilliant blue skin and a beak-like snout. It is usually sold whole and is best steamed or poached. Available all year.

PILCHARD

This is a small, round, oily fish, called sardine when young and pilchard when mature. Most pilchards are caught off the coasts of Devon and Cornwall and are sold canned. Fresh pilchards can be grilled or fried whole. Available November to April.

PLAICE

Plaice is a flat fish with warm brown skin with orange or red spots on the top side. The underside is white. The flesh is soft and white with a very delicate flavour. It is sold whole or as fillets and can be cooked by most methods, including steaming, frying, grilling and baking. Available all year, best May to February.

RED FISH (OCEAN PERCH/NORWAY HADDOCK)

This is a fish with a flattened body and bright orange-red skin with dark blotches. It is sold whole or as fillets. The white flesh is lean and firm and has a good flavour. It is excellent for soup, but can also be cooked like Bream (see page 58). Available all year.

SARDINE

Sardines are strictly speaking young pilchards, but the name is also applied to the young of other fish (sprats and herrings). The majority are canned in olive oil or tomato sauce but fresh sardines are becoming more readily available. Sardines can be grilled or baked or fried like Smelts, Sprats and Whitebait (see below). They are available November to April.

SHARK

This giant fish is becoming more readily available from fishmongers. It has a pale creamy pink flesh, with a distinctive flavour and dense texture. It is usually sold in steaks or fillets and is best grilled, braised or casseroled. Available all year.

SKATE

Skate is a flat-bodied, kite-shaped fish. Its upper side is bluish-grey and its belly is greyish-white. Only the wings (side parts) and nuggets of flesh known as 'nobs' are eaten and they are usually sold already cut from the body. They can be fried, grilled or poached. The wings of small skate are often sold whole, but those of larger fish are usually sold cut into slices. Pieces of small skate can be cooked without any preparation, but large skate tend to be rather tough and flavourless and are better if first simmered in salted water or Court Bouillon (see page 56) until just tender. They can then be skinned, cut into 5-7.5 cm (2-3 inch) pieces and cooked in any way you wish. Skate nobs are nuggets of flesh cut from under the boney part of the fish and sold separately. Season: May to February.

SMELT

This is a small round, silvery fish, which can be very oily. Its flavour is similar to trout. Smelts are usually served as a starter. They are prepared by making a small cut with scissors just below the gills and gently pressing out the entrails. They can be threaded on to skewers through the eye sockets and deep fried or larger ones may be baked. Available November to February.

SNAPPER

The tropical snapper family includes the *red snapper, bourgeois, job gris* and *therese*. These round fish have a distinctive red or pinkish skin and delicious white flesh. Snappers are usually sold whole, but steaks and fillets are also available. Whole fish may be baked with scales left on, or stuffed and baked. Alternatively, grill, braise or steam with scales removed. Available all year.

SOLE

The name sole is given to several species of flat fish which resemble the sole of a sandal. Dover sole is the only true sole. Sold whole or as fillets, sole is delicious grilled, fried, baked or steamed.

DOVER SOLE is considered one of the finest flat fish. It has dark brown-grey skin and pale, firm flesh with a delicious flavour. Season: May to February.

LEMON SOLE is lighter in colour, slightly longer and its head is more pointed than Dover sole. The flesh is more stringy and has less flavour. Season: May to February.

WITCH OR TORBAY SOLE is shaped like Dover sole and has slightly greyish-pinkish skin. Its flesh is similar to that of lemon sole. Season: May to February.

SPRAT

A fairly small, round fish of the same family as the Herring (see page 59). To prepare sprats, wash and draw them through the gills, as for Smelt (see left). Coat in seasoned flour and fry as for Whitebait (see right), but allow 4-5 minutes frying. They may also be grilled. Available October to March.

SQUID

Squid is the most commonly available member of the cephalopod group (see Cuttlefish, page 58) in Britain. There are several species, varying in size. Only the tentacles and body pouch are eaten, the other parts are discarded. The tentacles are usually chopped and the body is either sliced into rings, cut into sections or kept whole and the body cavity stuffed.

A popular practice in Mediterranean cookery is to cook the squid in their ink, the ink sac must, therefore, be removed intact. Small squid can be sautéed, poached, grilled or deep-fried; larger ones are often stewed.

TO CLEAN SQUID

1. Rinse the squid, then hold the body in one hand and with the other, firmly pull on the head and tentacles. As you do this, the soft contents

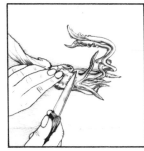

Firmly holding the squid, pull on the head and tentacles to remove the body cavity's contents, then discard.

Using a small sharp knife, cut the tentacles away from the head just in front of the eyes, then discard.

of the body will come out and can be discarded. Cut the tentacles just in front of the eyes. Remove the ink sac from the head, if wished.

2. Remove the plastic-like quill and rinse the body under cold running water to remove any white substance.

3. Rub the fine dark skin off the outer body and rinse again under cold running water. Cut the flesh into rings, pieces or keep whole for filling with stuffing.

STURGEON

Sturgeon is not usually available in Britain. It is a large fish – it can grow up to 4 metres (13 feet) – and has a head covered with hard boney plates and a snout with four barbels (thin feelers) hanging from it. Its flesh is white to pink with a flavour similar to veal. Caviar (see page 34) is the roe of the female sturgeon.

TUNA (TUNNY)

Fresh tuna is not widely available in Britain – it is usually sold canned. Tuna is a very large round fish with a dark blue back and silvery grey sides and belly. The deep reddish-pink flesh is oily and much heavier than the flesh of other fish, it is almost like meat. It may be sold in slices or pieces, the belly is the best part. Fresh tuna can be braised, poached in foil, grilled or fried. Canned tuna fish can be used in both hot and cold dishes.

TURBOT

Turbot is a flat diamond-shaped fish with very small scales. The upper sides can be various shades of dappled brown. It has creamy white flesh with a delicious flavour and is considered to be the finest of the flat fish. It is usually cut into steaks and grilled, baked or poached – often with wine. In season all year, but it is most tasteful March to August.

WHITEBAIT

This is the tiny, silvery fry (young) of the sprat or herring. Whitebait are eaten whole and require no gutting. Simply rinse thoroughly and drain well. Whitebait are usually coated in flour, either seasoned with salt and pepper and/or cayenne pepper, and deep-fried until crisp. Best February to June.

WHITING

Whiting is a smallish fish with a pale brown to olive-green back and a cream-coloured belly. The flesh is soft, white and flaky with a delicate flavour. Whiting is sold whole or as fillets. It can be poached, steamed or shallow-fried. Season: June to February.

ROLLED PLAICE WITH PESTO

8 small plaice fillets, about 550 g (1¼ lb) total weight
3 spring onions, trimmed
125 g (4 oz) fine asparagus or fine French beans,
  trimmed
125 g (4 oz) carrots, peeled
15 ml (1 level tbsp) pesto sauce
30 ml (2 tbsp) lemon juice
100 ml (4 fl oz) fish stock
salt and pepper
75 g (3 oz) oyster or button mushrooms, trimmed
125 g (4 oz) whole baby sweetcorn, halved lengthwise
125 g (4 oz) mangetouts, topped and tailed
30 ml (2 tbsp) vegetable oil (optional)

1. Skin the plaice fillets and divide each one along the natural centre line into two fillets. Roll up loosely (keeping the skin side inside).
2. Cut the spring onions, asparagus and carrots into 6 cm (2½ inch) lengths.
3. Place the fish, pesto sauce, lemon juice, stock and seasoning in a medium pan. Bring to the boil, cover tightly with damp greaseproof paper and the lid. Simmer gently for about 10 minutes or until the fish is cooked.
4. Meanwhile, steam the prepared vegetables until just tender or heat the oil in a sauté pan and stir fry the vegetables for 3-4 minutes.
5. To serve, spoon the vegetables onto individual serving plates and top with the fish fillets and pan juices.
SERVES 4

LEFT: Spinach and Seafood Pasties.   RIGHT: Rolled Plaice with Pesto

COD IN WHITE WINE

50 g (2 oz) butter or margarine
450 g (1 lb) courgettes, thinly sliced
2 large onions, skinned and sliced
30 ml (2 level tbsp) flour
15 ml (1 level tbsp) paprika
300 ml (½ pint) dry white wine
397 g (14 oz) can tomatoes
15 ml (1 tbsp) chopped fresh basil or 5 ml (1 level tsp)
*   dried*
1 garlic clove, skinned and crushed
salt and pepper
1.1 kg (2½ lb) cod fillets, skinned and cut into
*   5 cm (2 inch) pieces*
190 g (6¾ oz) can pimiento, drained and sliced
fried French bread croûtes, to serve

1. Melt the butter in a large frying pan, add the courgettes, onions, flour and paprika and fry gently for 3-4 minutes, stirring.
2. Stir in the wine, tomatoes, basil, garlic and seasoning. Bring to the boil.
3. In a large ovenproof dish, layer up the fish, pimiento and sauce mixture, seasoning well.
4. Cover the dish and cook in the oven at 170°C (325°F) mark 3 for 50-60 minutes. Garnish with the croûtes.
SERVES 8

VARIATION
Use haddock or other firm white fish.

SPINACH AND SEAFOOD PASTIES

4 cod steaks, about 125 g (4 oz) each
3 eggs
40 g (1½ oz) butter or margarine
350 g (12 oz) frozen leaf spinach, thawed
30 ml (2 tbsp) lemon juice
freshly grated nutmeg
15 g (½ oz) plain white flour
150 ml (¼ pint) milk
salt and pepper
125 g (4 oz) cooked peeled prawns
30 ml (2 level tbsp) chopped fresh parsley
370 g (13 oz) packet puff pastry
sautéed cherry tomatoes, to accompany
watercress, to garnish

1. Skin the cod steaks and carefully remove the central bone. Cook two eggs in boiling water for 8-10 minutes. Cool, shell and rougly chop.
2. Melt 25 g (1 oz) butter in a medium-sized saucepan. Add the spinach and cook over a high heat, stirring frequently, until all excess moisture has evaporated. Remove from the heat. Stir in the lemon juice and a generous grating of nutmeg.

3. Melt remaining butter in a saucepan, stir in the flour and cook for 1 minute. Off the heat, add the milk, then bring to the boil, season and simmer for 1-2 minutes. Mix in the chopped eggs, prawns and parsley. Cool slightly.
4. Divide the pastry into four equal pieces. Roll each piece out to a large square, about 23 cm (9 inches). Place a piece of cod on one half of each pastry square. Top with the spinach and the prawn sauce.
5. Brush pastry edges with beaten egg and fold the pastry over the fish to enclose totally, tucking edges under the parcel to neaten. With a sharp knife, carefully score the pastry in one direction only. Place on a baking sheet and glaze with remaining egg.
6. Bake in the oven at 220°C (425°F) mark 7 for 25 minutes or until the pastry is crisp and browned. Serve immediately, accompanied by sautéed cherry tomatoes. Garnish with watercress sprigs.
SERVES 4

VARIATION
Use thickly cut cod fillet in place of the steaks.

HAKE GOUJONS

450 g (1 lb) hake fillets, skinned, boned and cut into
    20 even-sized pieces
1 egg, beaten
50 g (2 oz) fresh breadcrumbs
vegetable oil for deep-frying
Tartare Sauce (see page 254), to serve

1. Coat the fish pieces in egg, then in the
breadcrumbs.

2. Heat the oil in a deep-fat fryer to 180°C
(350°F), add the fish and fry until golden. Drain
on absorbent kitchen paper.
3. Serve the goujons on cocktail sticks with the
sauce handed separately.
SERVES 4

VARIATION
Other firm fish such as haddock, cod, monkfish
and huss can be cooked in the same way.

FISH CAKES

350 g (12 oz) fish, eg cod, haddock or coley, cooked
    and flaked
350 g (12 oz) potatoes, cooked and mashed
25 g (1 oz) butter or margarine
15 ml (1 tbsp) chopped fresh parsley
salt and pepper
few drops of anchovy essence (optional)
milk or beaten egg, to bind
125 g (4 oz) fresh breadcrumbs
vegetable oil for frying

1. Mix the fish with the potatoes, butter, parsley,
seasoning and anchovy essence, if using, binding
if necessary with a little milk or egg.
2. On a lightly floured board, form the mixture
into a roll, cut into eight slices and shape into
flat cakes. Coat with egg and breadcrumbs.
3. Heat the oil in a frying pan, add the fish cakes
and fry, turning once, until crisp and golden.
Drain well on absorbent kitchen paper.
SERVES 4

VARIATIONS
Replace the cod, haddock or coley with smoked
haddock, herrings, canned tuna or salmon.

HERRINGS IN OATMEAL

4 herrings, weighing 175-225 g (6-8 oz) each, cleaned,
    boned and heads and tails removed
salt and pepper
125 g (4 oz) fine oatmeal
½ a lemon, cut into wedges
chopped fresh parsley, to garnish

1. Sprinkle the herrings with salt and pepper
and coat with oatmeal, pressing it well into the
fish.
2. Arrange the herrings in a grill pan. Cook
under a fairly hot grill for 6-8 minutes, turning
once, until tender and slightly flaky.
3. Serve garnished with lemon wedges and
chopped parsley.
SERVES 4

SOUSED HERRINGS

salt and pepper
4 large or 6-8 small herrings, cleaned, boned and heads
    and tails removed
1 small onion, skinned and sliced into rings
6 black peppercorns
1-2 bay leaves
fresh parsley sprigs
150 ml (¼ pint) malt vinegar

1. Season fish, roll up and secure. Arrange in a
shallow ovenproof dish with onion, peppercorns
and herbs.
2. Pour in the vinegar and enough water to
almost cover the fish. Cover with foil and bake
in the oven at 180°C (350°F) mark 4 for about
45 minutes or until tender.
3. Leave the herrings to cool in the liquid
before serving as an appetiser or with salad.
SERVES 4

MONKFISH WITH LIME AND PRAWNS

550 g (1¼ lb) monkfish fillets, skinned, boned and cut
    into 5 cm (2 inch) pieces
30 ml (2 level tbsp) seasoned flour
30 ml (2 tbsp) vegetable oil
1 small onion, skinned and chopped
1 garlic clove, skinned and chopped
225 g (8 oz) tomatoes, skinned and chopped
150 ml (¼ pint) dry white wine
grated rind and juice of 1 lime
pinch of sugar
salt and pepper
125 g (4 oz) cooked peeled prawns
lime slices, to garnish

Monkfish with Lime and Prawns

1. Coat the fish in seasoned flour. Heat the oil
in a flameproof casserole, add the onion and
garlic and fry gently for 5 minutes, until
softened. Add the fish and fry for 5 minutes,
until golden.
2. Stir in the tomatoes, wine, lime rind and
juice, sugar and seasoning. Bring to the boil.
3. Cover and cook in the oven at 180°C (350°F)
mark 4 for 15 minutes. Add the prawns and
continue to cook for a further 15 minutes, until
the monkfish is tender. Garnish with lime slices.
SERVES 4

MONKFISH AND MUSSEL BROCHETTES

36 mussels, cooked (see page 82)
18 streaky bacon rashers, rinded and halved
900 g (2 lb) monkfish fillets, skinned, boned and cut
    into 2.5 cm (1 inch) cubes
50 g (2 oz) butter or margarine, melted
60 ml (4 tbsp) chopped fresh parsley
grated rind and juice of 1 lime or lemon
4 garlic cloves, skinned and crushed
salt and pepper
shredded lettuce, bay leaves and lime or lemon wedges,
    to garnish

Monkfish and Mussel Brochettes

1. Shell the mussels, discarding shells.
2. Roll the bacon rashers up neatly. Thread the
cubed fish, mussels and bacon alternately on to
six oiled kebab skewers.
3. Mix together the melted butter, parsley, lime
rind and juice, garlic and salt and pepper to
taste. (Take care when adding salt as both the
mussels and the bacon are naturally salty.)
4. Place the brochettes on an oiled grill or
barbecue rack. Brush with the butter mixture,
then grill under a moderate grill for 15 minutes,
turning frequently and brushing with the butter.
5. Arrange the hot brochettes on a serving
platter lined with shredded lettuce. Garnish with
bay leaves and lime wedges and serve at once
with saffron rice, if wished.
SERVES 6

RED MULLET IN TOMATO SAUCE

25 g (1 oz) butter or margarine
1 small onion, skinned and finely chopped
1 garlic clove, skinned and crushed (optional)
450 g (1 lb) tomatoes, skinned and quartered
salt and pepper
10 ml (2 level tsp) sugar
1 bay leaf
4 red mullet, about 550 g (1¼ lb) each, cleaned
30 ml (2 level tbsp) seasoned flour
45 ml (3 tbsp) vegetable oil
30 ml (2 level tbsp) fresh breadcrumbs
15 ml (1 tbsp) chopped fresh parsley

1. Melt the butter in a saucepan, add the onion and the garlic, if using, and fry for about 5 minutes, until soft but not coloured. Add the tomatoes, seasoning, sugar and bay leaf. Cover and simmer gently for about 30 minutes, until soft and pulped. Remove the bay leaf.
2. Meanwhile, coat the fish in seasoned flour. Heat the oil in a large frying pan, add the fish and fry for 6-8 minutes, turning them once.
3. Place half the tomato sauce in a shallow ovenproof dish, lay the fish on top, then cover with the rest of the sauce. Sprinkle the breadcrumbs over the top and brown under a hot grill. Sprinkle with parsley and serve at once.
SERVES 4

FRESH SARDINES WITH HERBS

900 g (2 lb) fresh sardines (at least 12), cleaned if
  wished
60 ml (4 tbsp) chopped fresh mixed herbs, eg mint,
  parsley, sage
grated rind of 2 lemons
120 ml (8 tbsp) lemon juice
300 ml (½ pint) olive or sunflower oil
2 medium onions, skinned and finely sliced
salt and pepper
lemon wedges, to garnish

1. Wash the sardines well. Mix together 45 ml (3 tbsp) herbs with the lemon rind and juice, oil, onions and seasoning.
2. Grill the sardines for 5-7 minutes each side, basting with the herb dressing. Serve immediately or leave in the dressing to cool completely.
3. Sprinkle with the reserved herbs before serving. Garnish with lemon wedges.
SERVES 4

SKATE WITH BLACK BUTTER

700-900 g (1½-2 lb) skate wings
salt
50 g (2 oz) butter
15 ml (1 tbsp) white wine vinegar
10 ml (2 level tsp) capers
10 ml (2 tsp) chopped fresh parsley

1. Put the fish in a saucepan and cover with salted water. Bring to the boil, then simmer for 10-15 minutes, until tender. Drain and place on a warm serving dish. Cover and keep warm.
2. Melt the butter in a saucepan, cook until it turns golden brown, add the vinegar and capers

and cook for a further 2-3 minutes. Pour over the fish, sprinkle with parsley and serve immediately.
SERVES 4

VARIATION
SKATE IN PEPPER BUTTER
1. Cook the skate as described (see left).
2. Melt 75 g (3 oz) butter in a saucepan, add 30 ml (2 level tbsp) black peppercorns, crushed; 1 small garlic clove, crushed; and 5 ml (1 level tsp) dried sage. Stir over a medium heat for about 1 minute, until the butter is golden brown. Pour over skate and serve immediately.

PARCHMENT BAKED FISH

50 ml (2 fl oz) dry white wine
125 g (4 oz) cucumber, thinly sliced
4 fish steaks, eg cod, halibut, turbot or salmon, about
*   150 g (5 oz) each*
5 ml (1 level tsp) fennel seeds or 2.5 ml (½ level tsp)
*   dried dill seeds*
25 g (1 oz) butter or margarine
salt and pepper
fresh dill, to garnish

1. Take 4 pieces of non-stick parchment or greaseproof paper, each about 28 cm (11 inches) square, and crumble them together into a small bowl. Pour over the wine and leave to soak for 1 hour. Push down into the wine occasionally.

2. Separate and open out the parchment sheets. Arrange a circle of cucumber rounds in the centre of each sheet. Place a fish steak on top. Sprinkle with fennel or dill seeds and dot with a small piece of butter. Season. Drizzle over any remaining wine.

3. Lift up opposite sides of the parchment and fold together. Twist and tuck under the two shorter ends.

4. Place the parcels on a baking sheet. Bake in the oven at 200°C (400°F) mark 6 for about 15 minutes. Serve at once, garnished with dill.

SERVES 4

OLD FASHIONED FISH PIE

450 g (1 lb) haddock, cod or coley fillets
300 ml (½ pint) milk
1 bay leaf
6 black peppercorns
onion slices for flavouring
salt and pepper
65 g (2½ oz) butter or margarine
45 ml (3 level tbsp) flour
150 ml (5 fl oz) single cream
2 eggs, hard-boiled, shelled and chopped
30 ml (2 tbsp) chopped fresh parsley
90 ml (6 tbsp) milk
900 g (2 lb) potatoes, cooked and mashed
1 egg, beaten, to glaze

1. Put the fish in a frying pan, pour over the milk and add the bay leaf, peppercorns, onion slices and a good pinch of salt. Bring slowly to the boil, cover and simmer for 8-10 minutes, until the fish flakes when tested with a fork.

2. Lift the fish out of the pan using a fish slice and place on a plate. Flake the fish, discarding the skin and bone. Strain and reserve the milk.

3. Melt 40 g (1½ oz) butter in a saucepan, stir in the flour and cook gently for 1 minute, stirring. Remove the pan from the heat and gradually stir in the reserved milk. Bring to the boil slowly and continue to cook, stirring until the sauce thickens. Season.

4. Stir in the cream and fish, with any juices. Add the chopped egg and parsley and adjust the seasoning. Spoon the mixture into a 1.1 litre (2 pint) pie dish or similar ovenproof dish.

5. Heat the milk and remaining butter in a saucepan, then beat into the potato. Season and leave to cool slightly.

6. Spoon the cooled potato into a large piping bag fitted with a large star nozzle. Pipe shell-shaped lines of potato across the fish mixture. Alternatively, spoon the potato on top and roughen the surface with a fork.

7. Place the dish on a baking sheet and cook in the oven at 200°C (400°F) mark 6 for 10-15 minutes or until the potato is set.

8. Beat the egg with a good pinch of salt then brush over the pie. Return to the oven for about 15 minutes, until golden brown.

SERVES 4

VARIATIONS
- Stir 125 g (4 oz) grated Cheddar cheese into the sauce.
- Beat 125 g (4 oz) grated Cheddar or Red Leicester cheese into the mashed potatoes.
- Stir 175 g (6 oz) canned sweetcorn, drained, and 1.25 ml (¼ tsp) cayenne pepper into the fish mixture.
- Fry 125 g (4 oz) sliced button mushrooms in 25 g (1 oz) butter for 3 minutes. Stir into the fish mixture.
- Sprinkle the potato topping with 50 g (2 oz) mixed grated Parmesan cheese and fresh breadcrumbs after the first 10-15 minutes.
- Cover the pie with puff pastry instead of the mashed potatoes.

INDONESIAN FISH CURRY

1 small onion, skinned and roughly chopped
1 garlic clove, skinned and chopped
2.5 cm (1 inch) piece root ginger, skinned and chopped
5 ml (1 level tsp) ground turmeric
2.5 ml (½ level tsp) laos powder (see page 192)
1 dried red chilli or 1.25 ml (¼ level tsp) chilli powder
30 ml (2 tbsp) vegetable oil
salt
450 g (1 lb) haddock fillets, skinned and cut into bite-sized pieces
450 ml (¾ pint) coconut milk
juice of 1 lime
shredded coconut, to garnish

1. Put the first seven ingredients in a blender or food processor with 2.5 ml (½ level tsp) salt. Work to a thick paste.
2. Transfer the paste to a flameproof casserole and fry gently, stirring, for 5 minutes. Add the haddock pieces and fry for a few minutes more, shaking the pan constantly.
3. Pour in the coconut milk, shake the pan and turn the fish gently in the liquid. (Take care not to break up the pieces of fish.) Bring to the boil slowly, then lower the heat, cover and simmer for 10-15 minutes, until the fish is tender.
4. Add the lime juice, taste and adjust seasoning, then transfer to a warmed serving dish and sprinkle with coconut. Serve immediately.
SERVES 4

STUFFED SOLE PAUPIETTES

75 g (3 oz) butter or margarine
1 small onion, skinned and chopped
225 g (8 oz) button mushrooms, wiped and trimmed
75 g (3 oz) fresh breadcrumbs
finely grated rind of 1 lemon
15 ml (1 tbsp) chopped fresh tarragon leaves
salt and pepper
18 lemon sole quarter-cut fillets (two from each side of fish), skinned
300 ml (½ pint) dry white wine
30 ml (2 level tbsp) flour
about 90 ml (6 tbsp) double cream, at room temperature
fresh tarragon sprigs, to garnish

1. Make the stuffing. Melt 25 g (1 oz) of the butter in a saucepan, add the onion and fry gently until lightly coloured.
2. Meanwhile, slice half the mushrooms and chop the remainder very finely. Put the chopped mushrooms in a bowl with the breadcrumbs, lemon rind and tarragon.
3. Stir in the onion and seasoning.
4. Place a sole fillet, skinned side uppermost, on a board. Put a teaspoonful of stuffing on one end of the fillet. Roll the fish up around it. Secure with a wooden cocktail stick.
5. Stand in an upright position in a well buttered baking dish. Repeat with remaining sole fillets, placing them side by side in the dish.
6. Mix the wine with 150 ml (¼ pint) water and pour over fish. Cover loosely with foil and bake in oven at 190°C (375°F) mark 5 for 15 minutes.
7. Remove the fish from the cooking liquid with a slotted spoon and discard the cocktail sticks. Place the fish in a single layer in a warmed serving dish, cover and keep warm. Strain the liquid and reserve.
8. Melt 25 g (1 oz) butter in a saucepan, sprinkle in the flour and cook for 1-2 minutes, stirring. Remove from the heat, then gradually stir in the reserved cooking liquid. Bring to the boil, reduce the heat and simmer gently for 5 minutes, stirring until thick.
9. Meanwhile, melt remaining butter in a pan, add the finely sliced mushrooms and fry gently.
10. Whisk the cream into the sauce. Pour a little sauce over each paupiette, then garnish with sliced mushrooms and tarragon, to serve.
SERVES 6

Stuffed Sole Paupiettes

MARINATED COD STEAKS

30 ml (2 tbsp) grapeseed oil
30 ml (2 tbsp) white wine vinegar
10 ml (2 level tsp) sesame seeds
pinch of dry mustard powder
salt and pepper
4 cod steaks, about 175 g (6 oz) each
175 g (6 oz) onion, skinned and finely sliced into rings
mangetout to garnish

1. In a jug, whisk together the oil, vinegar, sesame seeds, mustard powder and seasoning for the marinade.
2. Place the cod steaks in a shallow dish into which they just fit, add the onion rings and pour over the marinade. Cover and leave to marinate overnight in the refrigerator, turning once.
3. Line the grill pan with foil and carefully place the cod steaks and onion on it. Cook under a hot grill for about 4 minutes each side, brushing well with the marinade. Garnish with mangetout and serve immediately.
SERVES 4

Marinated Cod Steaks

CEVICHE

450 g (1 lb) haddock fillets, skinned and cut
  diagonally into very thin strips
5 ml (1 level tsp) coriander seeds
5 ml (1 level tsp) black peppercorns
juice of 6 limes
1-2 green chilli peppers, chopped
5 ml (1 level tsp) salt
30 ml (2 tbsp) olive oil
bunch of spring onions, washed, trimmed and sliced
4 tomatoes, skinned and chopped
dash of Tabasco sauce, or to taste
30 ml (2 tbsp) chopped fresh coriander
1 avocado, lime slices and fresh coriander, to garnish

1. Place the fish strips in a bowl. Using a pestle and mortar, crush the coriander seeds and peppercorns to a fine powder, mix with the lime juice, chilli and salt, then pour over the fish. Cover and chill in the refrigerator for 24 hours, turning the fish occasionally.

2. The next day, heat the oil in a frying pan, add the spring onions and fry gently for 5 minutes. Add the tomatoes and Tabasco sauce to taste and toss together over brisk heat for 1-2 minutes. Remove from the heat and cool for 20-30 minutes.
3. To serve, drain the fish from the marinade, discarding the marinade, and mix with the spring onion and tomatoes and the chopped coriander.
4. Halve the avocado, peel and remove the stone. Slice the flesh crossways. Arrange the slices around the inside of a serving bowl and pile the fish mixture in the centre. Garnish with lime slices and coriander. Serve chilled.
SERVES 4

NOTE: The lime juice in the marinade effectively 'cooks' the fish so it requires no further cooking after marinating. It is essential to use really fresh fish in prime condition for this Latin American dish.

LEMON AND MUSTARD MACKEREL

40 g (1½ oz) butter or margarine
1 small onion, skinned and finely chopped
75 g (3 oz) fresh breadcrumbs
30 ml (2 level tbsp) mustard seeds
grated rind and juice of 1 lemon
15 ml (1 level tbsp) French mustard
1 egg yolk
salt and pepper
2 mackerel, each weighing 350 g (12 oz), cleaned,
    boned and heads removed
15 ml (1 level tbsp) flour
lemon rind shreds, to garnish

1. Heat 15 g (½ oz) butter in a frying pan, add the onion and fry until softened. Remove from the heat and stir in the breadcrumbs, mustard seeds, lemon rind, the mustard and egg yolk. Season with salt and pepper.
2. Press the breadcrumb mixture well into the cavity of the fish. Place in a greased shallow ovenproof dish just large enough to hold the mackerel and make deep slashes along each fish.
3. Dust the mackerel lightly with the flour. Pour over the lemon juice and dot with the remaining butter. Cook, uncovered, in the oven at 190°C (375°F) mark 5 for about 30 minutes. Baste frequently during cooking. Serve garnished with lemon rind shreds.
SERVES 2

SOLE VÉRONIQUE

700 g (1½ lb) Dover or lemon sole fillets, skinned
2 shallots, skinned and chopped
fresh parsley sprigs
1 bay leaf
salt and pepper
150 ml (¼ pint) dry white wine
25 g (1 oz) butter or margarine
30 ml (2 level tbsp) flour
about 150 ml (¼ pint) milk
125 g (4 oz) seedless white grapes, peeled
squeeze of lemon juice
30 ml (2 tbsp) single cream (optional)

1. Arrange the fish in a shallow ovenproof dish with the shallots, herbs, salt and pepper, wine and 150 ml (¼ pint) water. Cover with foil and bake in the oven at 200°C (400°F) mark 6 for about 15 minutes, until tender.
2. Strain the liquid from the fish and reduce it slightly by boiling rapidly. Transfer the fish to a serving dish and keep warm.

3. Melt the butter in a saucepan, stir in the flour and cook for 1 minute, stirring. Remove the pan from the heat and gradually stir in the reduced fish liquid, made up to 300 ml (½ pint) with the milk. Bring to the boil slowly and continue to cook, stirring, until the sauce thickens.
4. Remove from the heat and stir in most of the grapes, the lemon juice and the cream.
5. Pour over the fish and serve decorated with the remaining grapes.
SERVES 4

NOTE: Fillets of plaice and John Dory or large dabs may also be cooked in the same way.

VARIATION
SOLE BONNE FEMME
Omit grapes and lemon juice. Add the finely chopped stalks of 125 g (4 oz) button mushrooms to the shallots, herbs, salt and pepper, wine and water. Fry the mushroom caps lightly in 20 g (¾ oz) butter and serve as a garnish.

SOLE MEUNIÈRE

4 small Dover or lemon soles, skinned and fins removed
30 ml (2 level tbsp) seasoned flour
75g (3 oz) Clarified Butter (see page 571)
15 ml (1 tbsp) chopped fresh parsley
juice of 1 lemon
lemon slices or wedges, to garnish

1. Coat the fish with seasoned flour. Fry in 50 g (2 oz) clarified butter for 5 minutes each side. Drain and keep warm.
2. Wipe the pan clean. Melt the remaining butter in the pan and heat until lightly browned. Add the parsley and lemon juice and pour over fish. Garnish with lemon to serve.
SERVES 4

HOT FISH TERRINE WITH GRUYÈRE SAUCE

65 g (2½ oz) butter or margarine
1 garlic clove, skinned and crushed
60 ml (4 level tbsp) flour
700 ml (1¼ pints) milk
550 g (1¼ lb) hake fillets, skinned and cut into pieces
150 ml (5 fl oz) double cream
10 ml (2 tsp) anchovy essence
3 eggs
1 egg yolk
salt and pepper
30 ml (2 tbsp) chopped fresh parsley
125 g (4 oz) cooked peeled prawns, finely chopped
125 g (4 oz) Gruyère cheese, grated

1. Grease and base-line a 1.6 litre (2¾ pint) loaf tin or terrine.
2. Melt 40 g (1½ oz) butter in a saucepan, add the garlic and 45 ml (¾ level tbsp) flour and cook for 1 minute, stirring. Remove from the heat and gradually stir in 450 ml (¾ pint) milk. Bring to the boil, stirring, until the sauce thickens.
3. Put the sauce, raw fish, cream, anchovy essence, eggs and egg yolk in a blender or food processor. Work to a purée, then season lightly.
4. Spoon half the mixture into the tin. Sprinkle with parsley and half the prawns. Spoon in the rest of the fish mixture.
5. Cover tightly with greased greaseproof paper. Place in a roasting tin with water to come halfway up the sides of the terrine and cook in the oven at 150°C (300°F) mark 2 for about 1¾ hours.
6. Just before the end of the cooking time, make the cheese sauce. Melt the remaining butter in a saucepan. Stir in 15 ml (1 level tbsp) flour and cook gently for 1 minute, stirring. Remove the pan from the heat and gradually stir in the remaining milk.
7. Bring to the boil stirring and continue to cook, stirring, until the sauce thickens. Simmer for 3 minutes. Remove from the heat and stir in the grated cheese and the remaining prawns. Check the seasoning. Invert the terrine on to a warmed serving dish and tilt slightly to drain off the juice.
8. To serve, spoon a little sauce over the terrine and hand the rest of the sauce separately.
SERVES 6

CHUNKY FISH CASSEROLE

125 g (4 oz) small dried pasta shells
50 g (2 oz) butter or margarine
1 medium green pepper, seeded and cut into squares
1 medium yellow pepper, seeded and cut into squares
2 medium onions, skinned and sliced
225 g (8 oz) button mushrooms, wiped and sliced
450 g (1 lb) sole fillets, skinned and cut into
    finger-sized strips
6 scallops, prepared (see page 83) and halved
60 ml (4 level tbsp) seasoned flour
1 garlic clove, skinned and crushed
300 ml (½ pint) dry vermouth
150 ml (¼ pint) fish or chicken stock
15 ml (1 tbsp) chopped fresh sage, or 5 ml (1 level tsp)
    dried
salt and pepper
200 g (7 oz) can whole artichoke hearts, drained and
    quartered
225 g (8 oz) cooked peeled prawns
chopped fresh parsley, to garnish

1. Cook the pasta shells in boiling salted water for three quarters of the time recommended on the packet. Drain in a colander and run cold water over the pasta.
2. Melt 25 g (1 oz) butter in a large frying pan, add the peppers, onions and mushrooms and fry over a high heat for a few minutes. Remove from the pan with a slotted spoon and place in a deep 2.8 litre (5 pint) ovenproof dish.
3. Toss the prepared fish in the seasoned flour. Melt the remaining butter in the pan, add the sole and scallops with the garlic and fry gently for a few minutes, turning gently to avoid breaking up the fish.
4. Stir in the vermouth, stock, sage and seasoning and bring to the boil. Pour over the vegetables. Add the artichoke hearts, prawns and pasta shells and stir gently to mix the ingredients.
5. Cover the dish and bake in the oven at 180°C (350°F) mark 4 for about 40 minutes. Serve garnished with chopped parsley.
SERVES 6

MIXED FISH STIR-FRY

225 g (8 oz) monkfish fillet
225 g (8 oz) scallops, prepared (see page 83)
5 ml (1 level tsp) flour
10 ml (2 level tsp) ground coriander
10 ml (2 level tsp) ground cumin
30 ml (2 tbsp) vegetable oil
1 small green pepper, seeded and finely sliced
1 small yellow pepper, seeded and finely sliced
1 medium onion, skinned and finely sliced
225 g (8 oz) tomatoes, skinned and cut into eighths
125 g (4 oz) bean sprouts
75 ml (5 tbsp) dry white wine
chopped fresh coriander or parsley, to taste
salt and pepper
rice or noodles, to accompany

1. Slice the monkfish into thin strips and the
scallops into thin rounds, removing their orange
roe to cook separately. On a plate, mix the flour
and spices together. Lightly coat all the fish in
this mixture.
2. Heat 15 ml (1 tbsp) oil in each of two
medium frying pans. Place the peppers and
onion in one pan and stir-fry over a high heat
until beginning to brown. Add the fish to the
other pan and stir-fry for 2-3 minutes or until
tender.
3. Add the tomatoes and bean sprouts to the
vegetables and cook for 2-3 minutes or until the
tomatoes begin to flop.
4. Stir the contents of both pans together. Mix
in the wine with coriander and seasoning and
allow to bubble up. Serve with rice or noodles.
SERVES 4

Mixed Fish Stir-fry

SPICED FISH STEAKS

30 ml (2 level tbsp) chopped fresh mint
1 medium onion, or 2 large spring onions, skinned
  and roughly chopped
2 garlic cloves, skinned and crushed
5 ml (1 level tsp) paprika
30 ml (2 level tbsp) coriander seeds
10 ml (2 level tsp) ground cumin
10 ml (2 level tsp) dried dill
150 ml (5 fl oz) natural yogurt
salt and pepper
4 thick cod or haddock steaks or fillets, each
  about 175 g (6 oz)

1. First make the marinade mixture. Put the
mint, onion, garlic, paprika, cumin, dill and
yogurt in a blender or food processor and
process until a thick paste is formed. Season the
mixture to taste with salt and pepper.
2. Place the fish in a single layer in a shallow
dish. Spread the paste all over the top of the
fish and leave in a cool place to marinate for
2-3 hours.
3. Cook under a hot grill, basting occasionally,
until the fish is cooked and the yogurt mixture
has formed a crust. Serve straight away with rice
and chutney, accompanied by a green salad.
SERVES 4

FRITTO MISTO DI MARE

450 g (1 lb) squid, cleaned
225 g (8 oz) whitebait
4 small red mullet, cleaned and heads and tails
*   removed, sliced*
225 g (8 oz) firm white fish fillets, eg cod, haddock or
*   sole, skinned, and cut into long thin strips*
8-12 large raw prawns, peeled
60 ml (4 tbsp) seasoned flour
vegetable oil for deep-frying
fresh parsley sprigs and lemon wedges, to garnish

1. Slice the body of the squid into rings 5 mm (¼ inch) thick and the tentacles into 1 cm (½ inch) pieces. Toss all the fish in seasoned flour to coat.
2. Heat the oil in a deep-fat fryer to 190°C (375°F). Add the fish pieces a few at a time and fry until crisp and golden brown. Drain on absorbent kitchen paper and keep each batch warm while frying the rest.
3. Divide the fish between six warmed plates and garnish with sprigs of parsley and lemon wedges.
SERVES 6

VARIATION
Dip the fish in Fritter Batter (see page 334) before frying.

FISH KOULIBIAC

350 g (12 oz) whiting fillets
150 ml (¼ pint) dry white wine
salt and pepper
75 g (3 oz) butter or margarine
125 g (4 oz) spring onions, trimmed and chopped
75 g (3 oz) long grain white rice
1.25 ml (¼ level tsp) dried dill weed
125 g (4 oz) small button mushrooms, wiped and
*   quartered*
213 g (7½ oz) can red salmon, drained
3 eggs, hard-boiled and chopped
30 ml (2 tbsp) lemon juice
225 g (8 oz) Puff Pastry (see page 385) or
*   368 g (13 oz) packet frozen puff pastry, thawed*
1 egg, lightly beaten
lime wedges and parsley sprigs, to garnish

1. Place the whiting in a shallow saucepan. Pour over the wine with 150 ml (¼ pint) water, season and bring to the boil. Cover and poach gently for 5-8 minutes or until tender, then strain and reserve the juices. Flake the fish and place in a large bowl, discarding skin and any bones.
2. Melt the butter in a saucepan, add the spring onions and fry until lightly browned. Stir in the rice with the reserved fish juices, dill weed and seasoning. Bring to the boil, then cover and simmer for 10 minutes. Stir in the mushrooms

and cook until the rice is tender and the liquid absorbed.
3. Flake the salmon, discarding any skin and bone. Combine the salmon, eggs, whiting and rice mixture. Stir in the lemon juice and adjust the seasoning; allow to cool.
4 . Roll one third of the pastry to an oblong about 36 x 15 cm (14 x 6 inches) and place on a large baking sheet. Spoon the filling down the centre of the pastry, leaving a 2.5 cm (1 inch) strip round the edge. Dome the filling up well – the finished koulibiac should look high and narrow.
5. Brush the rim of pastry with beaten egg. Roll out the remaining dough to a rectangle 43 x 23 cm (17 x 9 inches) and wind loosely round a floured rolling pin. Unroll over filling and press edges well together. Neaten them with a sharp knife, leaving a 2.5 cm (1 inch) pastry rim all round.
6. Roll cut edges inwards, and press firmly. Mark new edge at regular intervals with the back of a knife. Chill for at least 30 minutes.
7. Add a pinch of salt to the beaten egg and use to glaze the pastry. Bake in the oven at 220°C (425°F) mark 7 for 35 minutes or until well browned. Serve hot, garnished with lime wedges and parsley sprigs.
SERVES 6-8

Quenelles

450 g (1 lb) whiting, pike or brill fillets, skinned and
  bones removed
1 egg white
1 quantity of Choux Pastry (see page 388), chilled
salt and pepper
150 ml (5 fl oz) double cream
18 fresh cooked prawns (in the shell)
125 g (4 oz) butter
150 ml (¼ pint) dry white wine
30 ml (2 level tbsp) flour

Spoon the quenelle mixture into simmering water.

1. Mince the fish twice, using the finest blade of the mincer, or purée in a blender or food processor. Cover and chill in the refrigerator for 1 hour.
2. Place the fish mixture in a large bowl placed in a saucepan of iced water. Break up the egg white with a fork. Beat into the fish, a little at a time, using a wooden spoon or electric hand mixer and keep the mixture stiff. Steady the bowl with one hand to prevent any iced water splashing into it.
3. Gradually add the choux paste, beating well between each addition. Add 2.5 ml (½ level tsp) salt and plenty of pepper, then beat into the fish with 60 ml (4 tbsp) cream, a little at a time. The mixture should be the consistency of creamed cake mixture. Cover and refrigerate for at least 1 hour.
4. Meanwhile, twist the heads off the prawns and discard them. Carefully ease the body shell and any roe away from the prawn flesh. Reserve the prawns for garnish. Pound the shells and roes with 50 g (2 oz) butter until well mixed, using a pestle and mortar or the end of a rolling pin in a strong bowl. Sieve the prawn butter to remove shells. Cover and refrigerate with the prawns.

5. Pour 900 ml (1½ pints) water into a large frying pan and add the wine with 1.25 ml (¼ level tsp) salt. Bring to the boil. Using two wet dessertspoons, shape the quenelle mixture into ovals and push them gently out of the spoons into the simmering liquid. Add sufficient quenelle shapes to half fill the pan; they will swell on cooking.
6. Cover the pan and simmer very gently for 10-12 minutes. Do not boil or the quenelles will break up. When the quenelles are well puffed up and firm to the touch, lift them out of the pan using slotted spoons. Drain on absorbent kitchen paper, then transfer to a warm serving dish, cover and keep warm while poaching the remaining quenelles.
7. Boil the cooking liquid until reduced to 250 ml (8 fl oz). Melt the remaining butter in a saucepan, stir in the flour and cook gently for 1 minute, stirring. Remove the pan from the heat and gradually add the reduced stock, stirring constantly.
8. Bring to the boil slowly and continue to cook, stirring, until the sauce thickens. Cook for 1-2 minutes. Remove from the heat, stir in the remaining cream, then whisk in the prawn butter. Reheat gently without boiling. Adjust seasoning. Spoon over the quenelles. Garnish with prawns.
Serves 6 as a starter, 4 as a light meal

Fried Whitebait

450 g (1 lb) whitebait
90 ml (6 level tbsp) seasoned flour
vegetable oil for deep-frying
fresh parsley sprigs, to garnish
lemon wedges and brown bread and butter, to serve

1. Toss the whitebait in the seasoned flour until well coated.
2. Heat the oil in a deep-fat fryer to 180°C (350°F). Add the whitebait, about one quarter at a time, and fry for 2-3 minutes, until crisp. Drain on absorbent kitchen paper. Keep warm, uncovered, in the oven set at 200°C (400°F) mark 6 until all the fish are cooked.
3. Garnish with parsley and lemon and serve with brown bread and butter.
Serves 4

FRESHWATER FISH

Salmon and trout are the main freshwater fish sold – though other varieties are available.

CARP

There are several varieties of carp found in ponds, lakes and rivers in most parts of the world. Carp feeds on vegetation in the mud and its flesh tends to have a slightly muddy flavour: soak in salted water for 3-4 hours and rinse well before cooking. Some carp are very scaley and need careful scaling (see page 53). Carp can be baked, poached or braised over vegetables.

CHAR

Char belongs to the salmon family. It has firm white to pink flesh, similar in flavour to salmon and trout. Cook as for Trout (see right).

EEL

A long, snake-like fish with shiny, dark skin and dense, fatty flesh which is enhanced by strong flavoured sauces. As eels must be fresh, they are sold alive and should be cooked soon after killing. Eels can be jellied, fried, stewed or made into pies. Young eels, called elvers, are best eaten stewed in garlic, sautéed or deep-fried. Eels are also sold jellied, whole or as fillets.

GRAYLING

A silvery fish belonging to the salmon family. It has a thyme-like scent and firm white flesh, like trout. It can be cooked as for Trout (see right).

PERCH

A large round fish with firm, sweet white flesh, perch should be cleaned and scaled as soon as possible after being caught (see page 53). Treat the dorsal fins with respect as they can wound. Fry or poach. If poaching, cook first, then scale.

PIKE

Pike is a sharp-nosed, duck-billed fish with large jaws and sharp teeth. It is found in lakes and streams, where it feeds on other fish – hence its other names of waterwolf and fresh water shark. The flesh is quite dry, but has an excellent flavour. Smaller fish up to 900 g (2 lb) are best. Typically used for quenelles and stuffings, pike can also be poached or stuffed and baked. If the fish has a muddy film on it, it can be soaked in cold water for a few hours before cooking.

SALMON

Salmon is a round fish with bright, silvery scales and flesh which is deep pink when raw and pale pink when cooked. The flesh is firm and rich. It is sold whole, as steaks and cutlets. It is also available smoked. When buying a whole fish, look for a small head and broad shoulders, as the head can be up to one fifth of the weight. Check that the skin is glistening, the eyes are bright and the gills are bright red. Home-caught salmon has such a delicious flavour and excellent texture that the simplest cooking is the best. Whole fish can be baked or poached, and steaks and cutlets can be baked, poached or grilled. Canadian, Norwegian, Alaskan and Japanese salmon tend to be less tender and delicate, but can be made more interesting with sauces. Salmon is in season in England and Scotland from February to August and in Ireland from January to September, but it is imported and sold frozen all year round. Farmed Scottish salmon, reared in large numbers in the remote lochs of the Western Highlands and Islands, is always available.

ST. PETER'S FISH

A charcoal grey fish with a firm, white flesh and a good flavour. It weighs about 450 g (1 lb).

TROUT

There are several different varieties of trout.

SEA TROUT (SALMON TROUT): Sea trout is a trout which has spent a season or more in the sea, living on a diet of crustaceans so that its flesh takes on a pink colour and flavour similar to that of salmon. However, because its flesh is coarser and less succulent than salmon, it is slightly cheaper. Sea trout can be prepared and cooked like Salmon (see page 76).

RAINBOW TROUT: This trout spends all its life in fresh water. It is readily available all year round, as it is reared on trout farms. The delicate flavoured flesh may be white or pink. Farmed fish which are fed on shrimps have pinkish-red flesh and may be called red trout. Rainbow trout is sold, and usually cooked, whole. It can be either grilled, poached or baked in foil.

RIVER OR BROWN TROUT: River trout is a golden brown fish with whitish flesh. It spends all its life in rivers or streams and is considered to have a better flavour than rainbow trout. It is rarely available in the shops. It can be cooked like rainbow trout. Best March to September.

POACHED SALMON

This is the classic way to cook a whole salmon whether serving hot or cold. As a rough guide, a 3 kg (6½ lb) salmon will feed 20 people as part of a buffet or 12-15 as a main dish.

Traditionally whole fish or middle cuts are poached in a fish kettle but a large preserving pan, roasting tin or flameproof casserole can be used. Use the grill rack or crumpled foil to raise fish off bottom of pan, as the poaching liquid should circulate round the fish during cooking.
1. To prepare the salmon, slit along the underside between the head and rear gill opening and clean the belly cavity under cold running water.
2. Snip off the fins and trim the tail into a neat 'V' shape. Leave head on if wished. Pat dry with absorbent kitchen paper and weigh the fish.
3. Place the salmon in the pan and add enough Court Bouillon (see page 56) to cover. If planning to serve the salmon cold, cover with a lid and bring to the boil slowly. For fish weighing up to 2.3 kg (5 lb), allow to boil for 1 minute only; allow 2 minutes for larger fish. Turn off the heat and leave to cool in the liquor.
4. To serve hot, cover and bring to the boil as

above. Simmer for about 7-8 minutes per 450 g (1 lb). When cooked, the salmon skin should peel away easily from the flesh. Allow the salmon to stand in the cooking liquor for 10 minutes before serving, with Hollandaise Sauce (see page 203) or Maître d'Hôtel Butter (see page 207).

SKINNING AND BONING A COOKED SALMON
Whilst still hot, snip the skin below the head and above the tail. Gently peel off the skin. Loosen the flesh along the ridge of the backbone and use scissors to cut the bone through just below the head and above the tail. Gently pull and ease out the bone.

VARIATION
POACHED SALMON STEAKS OR FILLETS
Place salmon steaks, cutlets or fillets in a deep sauté pan. Cover with Court Bouillon (see page 56). Bring to the boil, cover and simmer very gently for about 10 minutes for a 175 g (6 oz) steak. To test when cooked, press the point of a knife into the thickest part of the fish - the flesh should just begin to flake.

BAKED SALMON

Cooking the salmon in its own juices preserves the flavour and nutrients. This is one of the simplest methods, as no special container is required, but take care to avoid overcooking.
1. Clean the fish as above. Wrap loosely in a piece of well buttered foil with some slices of lemon, fresh herbs if available and a sprinkling of dry white wine. Seal the edges of the foil well to keep in the juices.
2. Place on a baking sheet and bake in the oven

at 180°C (350°F) mark 4 for the following times: whole fish and middle cuts between 900 g-2.3 kg (2-5 lb) – about 15 minutes per 450 g (1 lb) plus 15 minutes – cook for a minimum of 45 minutes; whole fish over 2.3 kg (5 lb) – about 10 minutes per 450 g (1 lb); 175 g (6 oz) steaks, cutlets and fillets – about 20-25 minutes in total.
3. If serving the salmon hot, leave in the foil for 15 minutes before serving. If eating cold, remove the skin while still warm.

GRILLED SALMON

This is the quickest conventional method of cooking steaks, cutlets and fillets. Avoid grilling thin cuts as they will become dry and tough.
1. Brush salmon with oil and season with pepper.

2. Place on the grill pan and grill under a medium heat. Allow about 8 minutes for a 175 g (6 oz) portion, turning once and brushing with oil during cooking. Test with a knife (as above).

MICROWAVE COOKING SALMON

Salmon steaks, cutlets and fillets are excellent cooked by microwave.
1. Season with pepper and wrap in buttered greaseproof paper.

2. Refer to your microwave handbook for cooking instructions, allowing about 3 minutes on HIGH for a 125 g (4 oz) fillet and 2-3 minutes per 450 g (1 lb) for larger cuts.

SALMON WITH FENNEL SAUCE

4 salmon steaks, about 175 g (6 oz) each
2 shallots, skinned and chopped
1 small fennel bulb, finely chopped
1 bay leaf
2 stalks fresh parsley, crushed
150 ml (¼ pint) dry white wine
2 egg yolks
125 g (4 oz) butter, softened
salt and pepper
lemon juice, to taste
fresh fennel sprigs, to garnish

1. Place the salmon steaks in a shallow ovenproof dish. Scatter the shallots, fennel, bay leaf and parsley over the top. Pour in the wine, cover tightly and bake in the oven at 180°C (350°F) mark 4 for 15 minutes, until the fish is tender.
2. Strain off 100 ml (4 fl oz) of the cooking liquor. Turn off oven, re-cover the salmon and keep warm.
3. Boil the strained liquor until reduced to 15 ml (1 tbsp). Beat the egg yolks together in a medium heatproof bowl, then stir in the reduced liquor and work in half of the butter.
4. Place the bowl over a saucepan of hot water and whisk with a balloon whisk until the butter has melted. Gradually whisk in the remaining butter, whisking well after each addition, to make a thick, fluffy sauce. Remove the pan from the heat.
5. Add 10 ml (2 tsp) of the cooked fennel to the sauce and season to taste, adding a little lemon juice, if necessary.
6. Transfer the salmon to a warmed plate. Spoon the sauce over and garnish with fennel sprigs to serve.
SERVES 4

Salmon with Fennel Sauce

SALMON IN ASPIC

1 small salmon or sea trout about 1.8 kg (4 lb),
  cleaned with head and tail left on
450 ml (¾ pint) aspic jelly
radishes, cucumber, tomato skins, olives, parsley sprigs
  and prawns, to garnish

1. Poach or bake the salmon (see page 76). Remove the skin, leaving on the head and tail.
2. Place the fish on a wire rack with a large plate or tray underneath, then leave to cool. Make up the aspic according to the packet instructions and when it is just beginning to thicken, coat the fish thinly.
3. Meanwhile, prepare the garnish. Cut the radishes into thin rings, cut strips of cucumber skin or thin cucumber slices, diamonds or strips of tomato skin and rings of olive.
4. Decorate the fish with the prepared garnishes and the parsley sprigs and prawns. Cover with

Chop the remaining aspic and use it as a garnish.

further layers of aspic until the decoration is held in place. When the aspic has set, transfer the fish to a large serving dish.
5. Leave any remaining aspic to set, chop it on damp greaseproof paper and use as a garnish.
SERVES 4

NOTE: For a really professional finish and easy carving, remove the salmon bones before the fish is glazed. Loosen the flesh along the ridge of the backbone and use scissors to cut the bone through just below the head and above the tail. Gently pull and ease out the bone.

BAKED TROUT WITH LEMON

6 rainbow or river trout, cleaned
75 g (3 oz) butter
90 ml (6 tbsp) lemon juice
90 ml (6 tbsp) chopped fresh parsley
salt and pepper
watercress sprigs, to garnish

1. Make three or four diagonal slashes about 5 mm (¼ inch) deep on either side of each fish. Place the fish, side by side, in a shallow, ovenproof dish.

2. Melt the butter in a small saucepan. Leave to cool, then mix in the lemon juice, parsley and seasoning and pour over the fish.
3. Cover the dish and leave in a cool place – not the refrigerator – for 2 hours, turning and basting once.
4. Cover the dish with foil and bake in the oven at 180°C (350°F) mark 4 for about 40 minutes or until the fish is tender.
5. Garnish with watercress sprigs to serve.
SERVES 6

TROUT AND ALMONDS

4 rainbow or river trout, cleaned with heads left on
30 ml (2 tbsp) seasoned flour
65 g (2½ oz) butter
50 g (2 oz) flaked almonds
juice of ½ a lemon

1. Coat the fish with seasoned flour. Melt 50 g (2 oz) butter in a large frying pan, add the fish two at a time, and fry for 12-15 minutes,

turning them once, until they are tender and golden on both sides.
2. Drain on absorbent kitchen paper, transfer to a serving dish and keep warm. Clean out the pan with absorbent kitchen paper.
3. Melt the remaining butter in the pan, add the almonds and fry until lightly browned, add a squeeze of lemon juice and pour over the fish. Serve at once, with the remaining lemon juice.
SERVES 4

SMOKED FISH

There are two methods of smoking – hot and cold. Cold smoking is done at relatively low temperatures and most cold-smoked fish need to be cooked before eating. The exception is salmon, which is smoked for a long period and can be eaten raw. Hot smoking is done at higher temperatures and the fish is ready to eat. Smoking is done more for flavour than as a means of preserving these days and smoked fish should only be kept in the refrigerator for up to 3 days.

SMOKED COD
SMOKED FILLETS: These are taken from large fish, skinned and cold smoked. They are sometimes dyed, often to a bright orange yellow. To cook, poach the fillets in milk, water or Court Bouillon (see page 56) for 10-15 minutes.
SMOKED COD'S ROE: This is firm roe taken from a large cod and smoked for a long period with slight heat. It does not need cooking. It is used to make Taramasalata (see page 46).

SMOKED EEL
Smoked eel is not widely available, but may be found either whole or as chunks of fillet in some delicatessens and fishmongers. It is ready to eat. Serve as a starter with cayenne pepper, lemon wedges and brown bread and butter.

SMOKED HADDOCK
SMOKED FILLETS: These are taken from large fish and cold smoked with the skin on. They are sometimes dyed, often to a bright orange yellow. Cook as for Smoked Cod (see above).
FINNAN HADDOCK: These are named after the village of Findon near Aberdeen in Scotland. Before smoking, the fish are split and lightly brined, but not usually dyed. They are a light straw colour and darken during cooking. Cook as for Smoked Cod (see above).
GOLDEN CUTLETS: These are small haddock with the heads removed, which are split and boned before smoking. Cook as for Smoked Cod (see above).
SMOKIES: These are also whole haddock, or whiting, with the heads removed. They are hot smoked and only need reheating in the oven or under the grill. Originally, smokies came from Arbroath in Scotland and were very dark in colour. They are now smoked mechanically and are much lighter.

SMOKED HALIBUT
This is not widely available, but may be found as slices of fillet. It does not need cooking.

SMOKED HERRING
BLOATER: This is a lightly smoked, dry salted herring with bones, head and tail removed. Bloaters should be eaten within 24 hours of buying. Lightly grill or fry.
BUCKLING: This is a whole smoked herring which is ready to eat.
KIPPER: The fish are split, lightly brined, then cold smoked. To cook, grill or poach for about 5 minutes, or place in a jug of boiling water and leave in a warm place for 5-10 minutes, or wrap in foil and bake in the oven at 190°C (375°F) mark 5 for 10-15 minutes.
RED HERRING: These are heavily smoked and highly salted. They are rarely available. Lightly grill or fry.

SMOKED MACKEREL
Mackerel may be whole or filleted and some are coated with peppercorns. They are hot or cold smoked. Cold smoked mackerel may also be known as kippered mackerel. They can be poached or grilled.

SMOKED SALMON
Smoked salmon is cold smoked for a long period and is ready to eat. Scottish smoked salmon, which is quite pale in colour, is the best quality. Canadian and Pacific smoked salmon are a deeper colour.

SMOKED SPRATS
These are smoked whole and are grilled or fried.

SMOKED STURGEON
This is not widely available, but is sometimes sold sliced very thinly. It does not need cooking.

SMOKED TROUT
Smoked trout is usually rainbow trout, cleaned with the head left on. It is hot smoked and does not need cooking.

SMOKED TUNA
This is not widely available, but may be found as slices of fillet. It does not need cooking.

SMOKED HADDOCK KEDGEREE

175 g (6 oz) long-grain rice
salt
450 g (1 lb) smoked haddock fillets
2 hard-boiled eggs, shelled
75 g (3 oz) butter or margarine
cayenne pepper
chopped fresh parsley, to garnish

1. Cook the rice in a saucepan of fast-boiling salted water until tender. Drain well and rinse under cold water.
2. Meanwhile, put the haddock in a large frying pan with just enough water to cover. Bring to simmering point, then simmer for 10-15 minutes, until tender. Drain, skin and flake the fish, discarding the bones.
3. Chop one egg and slice the other into rings. Melt the butter in a saucepan, add the cooked rice, fish, chopped egg, salt and cayenne pepper and stir over a moderate heat for about 5 minutes, until hot. Pile on to a warmed serving dish and garnish with parsley and the sliced egg.
SERVES 4

SMOKED HADDOCK GOUGÈRE

FOR THE CHOUX PASTRY
100 g (4 oz) plain or strong white flour
75 g (3 oz) butter or margarine
200 ml (7 fl oz) water
3 eggs, lightly beaten
FOR THE FILLING
450 g (1 lb) smoked haddock fillets
25 g (1 oz) butter or margarine
1 medium onion, skinned and chopped
25 g (1 oz) flour
300 ml (½ pint) milk
10 ml (2 level tsp) capers
2 eggs, hard-boiled, shelled and chopped
2 tomatoes, skinned, seeded and cut into thin strips
salt and pepper
about 30 ml (2 tbsp) lemon juice
15 ml (1 level tbsp) fresh breadcrumbs
15 ml (1 level tbsp) grated hard cheese
chopped fresh parsley, to garnish

1. Make the choux pastry. Sift the flour on to a plate or piece of paper. Put the fat and water together in a saucepan, heat gently until the fat has melted, then bring to the boil. Remove from the heat. Tip all the flour at once into the hot liquid. Beat thoroughly with a wooden spoon, then return the pan to the heat.
2. Continue beating the mixture until it is smooth and forms a ball in the centre of the pan (take care not to over-beat or the mixture will become fatty). Remove from the heat and leave the mixture to cool for a minute or two.
3. Beat in the egg, a little at a time, adding just enough to give a piping consistency.
4. Using a 1 cm (½ inch) plain nozzle, pipe the mixture in two circles (one on top of the other) round the bottom of each of four 12 cm (5 inch) diameter ovenproof dishes. Bake in the oven at 220°C (425°F) mark 7 for about 25 minutes.
5. Meanwhile, put the haddock in a large frying pan with just enough water to cover. Bring to simmering point, then simmer for 10-15 minutes, until tender. Drain, skin and flake the fish, discarding the bones.
6. Melt the butter in a saucepan, add the onion and fry gently until golden brown. Stir in the flour and cook for 1 minute, stirring. Remove the pan from the heat and gradually stir in the milk. Bring to the boil slowly and continue to cook, stirring, until the sauce thickens.
7. Stir in the capers, chopped hard-boiled eggs, fish and tomatoes. Season well; add the lemon juice to taste.
8. Spoon the mixture into the centre of each choux ring, dividing it equally between them. Combine the breadcrumbs and cheese, sprinkle over the gougères and cook in the oven for a further 10 minutes. Garnish with chopped parsley and serve immediately.
SERVES 4

SHELLFISH

Shellfish can be divided into two different types – molluscs and crustaceans. Molluscs, such as cockles and winkles, have soft bodies and live inside a solid, hard shell. Some molluscs, such as clams and mussels, have a pair of shells and are known as bivalves. The exceptions are the cephalopods, such as Cuttlefish, Octopus and Squid (see pages 58, 60 and 61), which belong to the mollusc family, but have no shells. Crustaceans have hard external skeletons, which are segmented to allow for movement. All shellfish, except crayfish, are sea fish.

CLAM

There are many different species of this bivalve, varying considerably in size. The *carpet shell (little-neck/palourde)* is creamy or light brown in colour, sometimes with darker brown markings. It grows up to about 6 cm (2½ inches), but is generally sold smaller. The *manilla clam* is very similar to the *carpet shell* in size and appearance. It is extensively farmed in this country and other parts of Europe.

The *American hard-shell clam (quahog)* is dirty white, greyish or brown. It grows up to about 12 cm (5 inches), but is generally sold before it reaches this size. The *venus shell (praire clam)* is creamy red or pink and looks as if it has been varnished. It grows up to about 7.5 cm (3 inches), but is invariably sold smaller.

Clams are sold live in their shells and smaller ones can be eaten raw. Large ones can be cooked as for Mussels (see page 82). Available all year, clams are best in the autumn. They are also available frozen, canned and smoked throughout the year from supermarkets.

Use a cloth to protect your hands and prise open the clam shell.

TO PREPARE RAW CLAMS
1. Scrub the clams with a stiff scrubbing brush. Hold each clam in a cloth or glove in the palm of one hand and prise open the shells at the hinge (it is helpful if you use a special clam knife for this).
2. Loosen the clams, leaving them in one half shell.

CRAB

There are many different species of this crustacean. All are encased in a hard shell which is shed periodically to allow the crab to grow.

The *blue crab (Atlantic blue crab)* gets its name from its blue claws. It has the finest flavour of all the crabs. It is extremely popular in America, where it is eaten in the soft-shell state when it has shed its shell and before it grows a new one. It is also found in the Mediterranean. It grows to a maximum width of about 20 cm (8 inches).

The *common crab* has a brownish-red shell. It grows to a width of about 20 cm (8 inches). The *rock crab* has a yellowish shell marked with purple or brown spots. It grows to a width of about 10 cm (4 inches). The *shore (green crab)* has a green shell, sometimes with yellow spots. It grows up to a width of about 7.5 cm (3 inches). In Venice, the *shore crab* is very popular in its soft-shell state.

The *southern stone crab* has a greyish shell and enormous claws in proportion to its size; one claw is bigger than the other. It grows to a width of about 12 cm (5 inches). The *spider crab (spiny crab)* has a shell which varies in colour from brown to reddish orange and is covered with prickly spines. It has a round body and long legs – hence its name. This variety of crab grows up to a width of about 20 cm (8 inches).

Crabs are sometimes sold alive, but more often they are ready-cooked. When buying a crab, choose one which feels heavy for its size and make sure the shell is not cracked. There are two types of meat in a crab: white meat in the claws and legs, and brown meat in the shell. Season: April to December. Crab meat is also available canned and frozen.

CRAWFISH

Often called the *spiny lobster,* the crawfish resembles a lobster without the big claws. Prepare and cook like Lobster (see page 82). It is also delicious cooked in casseroles and stews. Often used in creole-style cooking. Available May to October. Crawfish is also available canned and frozen.

CRAYFISH

The crayfish is a freshwater crustacean which looks like a miniature lobster. It varies in colour from dark purple to red. Small crayfish can be used for soups and garnishes, larger ones can be served hot in a cream sauce or cold with salad and brown bread and butter.

TO PREPARE CRAYFISH

1. Rinse well, then remove the intestinal tube under the tail, using a pointed knife. Put the fish in a saucepan of cold salted water, bring to the boil and cook for about 10 minutes.

LOBSTER

There are several types of this crustacean; the most common are the *European lobster*, which has the finest flavour, the *spiny lobster (crawfish)* and the *flat lobster*. Lobster is dark blue when alive and bright pink when cooked. It is often sold ready-boiled. Female lobsters may contain eggs in the form of an orange coral. Available all year, lobster is best in the summer months; it may be difficult to obtain from December to April. Lobster meat is often available frozen.

TO PREPARE LOBSTER

If a lobster has been bought alive, ask the fishmonger to weigh it, then kill and cook by one of the following methods.

1. Boil a large saucepan of water vigorously, then let it become completely cold. Immerse the lobster in the water and leave for 30 minutes. The lack of oxygen renders the lobster unconscious before it is put over the heat. Bring to the boil slowly, then simmer gently for 8 minutes per 450 g (1 lb). Lift the lobster out of the pan, set it aside and leave to cool completely.

2. Or bring a large saucepan of water to the boil, grasp the lobster by the back and drop it into the water, covering the pan with a lid and weight it down for the first 2 minutes. Then simmer gently for 12 minutes for the first 450 g (1 lb), 10 minutes for the next 450 g (1 lb) and 5 minutes more for each additional 450 g (1 lb). Lift out of the pan, set aside and leave to cool completely.

3. Or you can kill a lobster before cooking it or before grilling it, so it is not overcooked. Keeping your hands clear of the claws, put the lobster, shell side up on a work surface. Place a cleaver in the centre of the cross-shaped mark behind the head and hammer it down with one sharp blow. The lobster may still twitch a little, but that is only reflex action. Cook the lobster in the same way as for method 2 above or prepare and grill it (see page 87).

MUSSELS

Mussels are bivalves with blue-black to golden tortoiseshell coloured shells. They are usually sold by the quart (1.1 litres) which is approximately the same as 900 g (2 lb). Never buy mussels with cracked or open shells. Season: September to March.

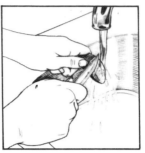

Scrape the mussels clean under cold running water.

TO PREPARE MUSSELS

1. Put the mussels in a large bowl and, under running cold water, scrape off any mud, barnacles, seaweed and 'beards' with a small sharp knife. Discard any that are open and do not close when sharply tapped with the back of a knife. Rinse again until there is no trace of sand in the bowl.

2. Put the mussels in a frying pan and cover. Cook on a high heat for about 5 minutes, until the shells open. Discard any whose shells do not open.

3. Alternatively, put the mussels in a saucepan of water or wine, flavoured with onion and herbs. Cover and cook for 3-5 minutes, until the mussels open, shaking the pan frequently. Discard any whose shells do not open and do not attempt to prise open.

OYSTERS

Oysters are bivalves which are farmed intensively in oyster beds and sea lochs. There are many species: in Britain, the smaller ones from the Essex and Kent beds are the best for eating raw, while *Portuguese oysters* or the *American blue points* (now cultivated in Britain) are best cooked.

The shells should be firmly closed. To keep fresh oysters, pack in a bowl, deep shell downwards and cover with a damp cloth. Place in the refrigerator and eat on the day of purchase. Under no circumstances should the oysters be covered with water while they are in the refrigerator.

Oysters can be served raw 'on the half-shell'; open as for Clams (see page 81). Alternatively, they can be cooked in various ways – as patties, as oysters au gratin, or added to steak and kidney puddings. Season: September to April. Shelled (shucked) oysters are available frozen or canned, or dried from oriental shops. Oysters stuffed with various fillings are also available frozen, as are canned smoked oysters.

PRAWNS

Prawns are crustaceans which are available in a variety of sizes, called by many different names. The *common prawns* from the cold waters of the North Atlantic have a better flavour than those from the warm waters of the Indian and Pacific Oceans, such as *Malaysian prawns* and *Pacific (jumbo) prawns*. The Mediterranean has several different species, known as *Mediterranean prawns*.

Fresh prawns are usually sold ready-boiled in the shell and may be sold by volume or weight. Frozen prawns come from different areas around the world and are usually peeled. Available all year. Also available canned, or dried from oriental stores.

TO PEEL PRAWNS

1. Hold the head of the prawn between the thumb and forefinger of the right hand. Using the fingers of the left hand, hold the tail and gently pinch and pull off the tail shell. Holding the body, gently pull off the head, the body shell and the claws.

2. To de-vein large prawns, use a skewer or the point of a knife to carefully remove the black intestinal vein running down the prawn's back.

SCAMPI (DUBLIN BAY PRAWN)

This crustacean, which is related to the lobster, has a variety of names. It is known as *Norway lobster, languostine* in France, *cigale* in Spain and *scampi* in Italy. In Britain it is usually called *Dublin Bay prawn* when whole and the peeled, uncooked tail meat is known as *scampi*.

It can be cooked whole as for Lobster (see page 82) and served cold with Mayonnaise (see page 254), or the tail meat can be fried or used in hot dishes. Available all year.

SCALLOPS

Scallops are bivalves with ribbed shells that are almost circular. There are several types which vary in size; the *great scallop* and the *queen scallop* are the varieties most commonly available in Britain. The colour of their shells varies from whitish, brown, yellow or orange to pinkish or purple.

Look for shells that are tightly closed. If slightly open, tap the shell sharply and, if fresh, they will close up instantly. Do not buy any that do not close. Scallops are in season October to March. Frozen scallops are available all year from supermarkets.

TO PREPARE SCALLOPS

1. Scrub the scallop shells under cold running water to remove as much sand as possible. Discard any that are open and do not close when

sharply tapped. Place on a baking sheet with their rounded side uppermost. Cook in the oven at 150°C (300°F) mark 2 for about 10 minutes, or until the shells open, then set aside and leave until they are cold.

Slide knife into shells.

2. Using your fingers, gently push the shells slightly apart until there is a gap into which a knife blade can be slipped. Slide the blade through the opening against the rounded upper shell, then gradually ease the scallop flesh away from the top shell.

3. Detach the scallop from the top shell and prise apart the top and bottom shells by pushing the shell backwards until the small black hinge at its back snaps. Rinse the scallops, still attached to the lower shells, under cold running water to remove as much sand as possible.

4. Using a small knife, cut and ease away all the grey-coloured beard-like fringe surrounding the scallop. Make sure that you don't detach the orange roe and try not to tear the flesh.

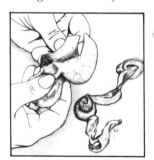

Gently pull off the scallop's intestinal bag.

5. Slide the point of a small knife under the black thread on the side of the scallop. Ease this up and gently pull it off, with the attached black intestinal bag. Ease the scallop away from the bottom shell, wash in a bowl of cold water until all traces of sand have gone. Scrub the rounded shells thoroughly to remove all traces of sand and grit; drain carefully under cold running water and gently pat dry with absorbent kitchen paper.

SHRIMPS

In Britain, only very small crustaceans are called shrimps. They are greyish-brown and translucent when alive and pink when cooked. In America, larger crustaceans – which are known as prawns in Britain – are called shrimps. Shrimps are available fresh nearly all the year. They are also available frozen, canned and potted in butter from supermarkets.

WHELKS

These are molluscs with greyish or brownish shells. They are usually sold ready-cooked and shelled and can be eaten plain with vinegar. Available all year, best September to February.

TO PREPARE RAW WHELKS

Wash the whelks in several changes of water, then leave to soak for 2-3 hours. Cook in boiling salted water for 15-20 minutes, until tender.

WINKLES

Small molluscs usually sold ready-cooked, with or without shells. A long pin is needed to remove the flesh from the shells. Prepare and cook raw winkles as Whelks (see left). Eaten with vinegar and bread. Available September to April.

COCKLES

These molluscs are usually sold cooked and shelled. They are normally eaten plain or with vinegar and bread, like whelks and winkles. Cockles are available all year, best September to December.

TO PREPARE COCKLES

1. Rinse the cockles thoroughly under cold running water, then leave to soak for 2-3 hours before cooking.
2. Place the cockles in a saucepan with a little water and heat gently, shaking the pan, for about 5 minutes, until the shells open. Discard any which remain closed.
3. Take cockles out of their shells and cook for a further 4 minutes.

Dressed Crab

DRESSING A CRAB

1 medium uncooked crab, weighing about 900 g (2 lb)
salt
1 bay leaf
15 ml (1 tbsp) lemon juice

1. Place the crab in a large saucepan in enough cold, salted water to cover. Add the bay leaf and lemon juice. Bring slowly to boiling point, cover and boil fairly rapidly for 10-20 minutes. Allow the crab to cool in the water.

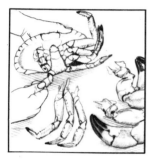

Hold the crab securely and twist off claws.

2. Place the crab on its back on a large chopping board. Take a claw firmly in one hand, holding it as close to the body of the crab as possible. Twist it off, steadying the body with the other hand.

3. Remove the other claw and the legs in the same way. Snap the claws in half by bending them backwards at the joint.

4. Hold the claws at the top end and, with a hammer or heavy weight, tap the shell smartly on the rounded edge to crack the claws open. Try to avoid shattering the shell. Repeat with the second claw.

Use a blunt knife to ease meat out of claws.

5. Using a blunt knife, ease the white meat out of the claws. Keep the blade as close to the edges of the shell as possible.

6. Using a teaspoon handle or skewer, reach well into the crevices to make sure all the white meat is removed. Discard any membrane.

7. Crack the larger legs open and scrape out the white meat. Keep the small legs for decoration. Reserve all the scooped-out white meat in one bowl.

Press the shell down firmly to ease out the body.

Remove grey feather-like gills from the crab's body.

8. Place the crab on its back with the tail flap towards you, head away from you. Hold the shell firmly and press the body section upwards from beneath the tail flap and ease out with your thumbs until the body is detached.

9. Pull off the inedible, grey feather-like gills (known as dead men's fingers) from the body section and discard them.

10. Use a spoon to remove the stomach bag and mouth which are attached to the back shell. If the bag breaks, make sure you remove all the greenish or grey-white matter.

11. Ease the brown meat out of the shell, running a knife around the edge to bring it out smoothly. Put in a separate bowl.

12. Discard any membrane and carefully scrape out the corners of the shell, using the handle of a teaspoon.

13. Protect your hand with a cloth. Hold the shell firmly and tap with a hammer just inside the natural line of the shell until the inner shell breaks smoothly away.

14. Scrub the shell well under cold running water. Then dry the empty shell with absorbent kitchen paper and rub the outside of the shell lightly with oil.

15. Place the body on its back on the board. Cut through the body to divide it in two.

16. Spoon any creamy brown meat out of the body and add it to the rest of the brown meat. Discard the body pieces. Complete dressing the crab as described on page 86.

DRESSED CRAB

shell and meat from 1 medium cooked crab, weighing
about 900 g (2 lb) (to remove the crab meat and
prepare the shell, see Dressing a Crab, page 85)
salt and pepper
15 ml (1 tbsp) lemon juice
30 ml (2 level tbsp) fresh breadcrumbs
1 egg, hard-boiled and shelled
chopped fresh parsley, to garnish
lettuce or curly endive, to serve

1. Using two forks, flake all the white crab meat,
removing any shell or membrane. Season and
add about 5 ml (1 tsp) lemon juice.
2. Pound the brown meat and work in the
breadcrumbs with the remaining lemon juice
and seasoning to taste.
3. Using a small spoon, place the white meat in
both ends of the crab's empty shell, making sure
that it is well piled up into the shell. Keep the
inside edges neat.
4. Spoon the brown meat in a neat line down
the centre, between the sections of white meat.

5. Hold a blunt knife between the white and
brown crab meat and carefully spoon lines of
parsley, sieved egg yolk and chopped egg white
across the crab, moving the knife as you go to
keep a neat edge.
6. To serve, place the shell on a bed of lettuce or
endive, surrounded by the small crab legs.
SERVES 2-3

Arrange white meat in
sides of the empty shells.

Neatly spoon brown meat
down the shell's centre.

LOBSTER SALAD

1 medium lobster, weighing 450 g (1 lb), cooked
1 lettuce, washed
fresh parsley sprigs, to garnish
French Dressing (see page 255) or Mayonnaise
(see page 254), to serve

1. Place the cooked lobster on a firm surface
and twist off the claws and pincers.
2. Crack open the large claws and remove the
flesh, discarding the membrane from the claw
centre. Reserve the smaller claws, which are
used only for garnishing.
3. Using a sharp pointed knife split the lobster
in two from head to tail.
4. Remove and discard the intestine (which
looks like a small vein running through the
centre of the tail), the stomach (which lies near
the head), and the spongy-looking gills, which
are not edible.
5. Take out the tail flesh, reserving the coral if
there is any. Scrape the meat from the rear legs
with a skewer.
6. Wash and dry the two halves of the shell. Pile

the meat back into the shell halves.
7. Line a serving dish with the lettuce leaves,
arrange the lobster on top, garnish with the
claws, parsley and chopped coral if there is any.
Serve with French Dressing or Mayonnaise.
SERVES 2

Remove the lobster meat
from the cracked claws.

VARIATION
LOBSTER MAYONNAISE
1. Remove the meat
from the lobster (see
left) retaining the
claws and coral for
garnish.
2. Flake the flesh and
mix with 150 ml
(¼ pint) Mayonnaise
(see page 254).
3. Arrange the
shredded lettuce

leaves in a salad bowl and pile the lobster in the
centre. Garnish with the claws and the coral,
sieved if liked.

GRILLED LOBSTER

1 medium lobster, killed by method 3 on page 82 but
not precooked
melted butter for brushing
salt and cayenne pepper

1. Split the lobster lengthways and remove the intestine, stomach and gills.

2. Brush the shell and flesh with melted butter and grill the flesh side for 8-10 minutes, then turn and grill the shell side for 5 minutes.
3. Dot the flesh with small pieces of butter, sprinkle with a little salt and cayenne pepper and serve with melted butter.
SERVES 2

LOBSTER NEWBURG

2 small lobsters, weighing 225 g (8 oz) each, cooked
25 g (1 oz) butter or margarine
salt and cayenne pepper
60 ml (4 tbsp) Madeira or sherry
2 egg yolks
150 ml (5 fl oz) single cream
chopped fresh parsley, to garnish

1. Cut the lobsters in half lengthways and remove the lobster meat from the shells (see left).
2. Melt the butter, add the lobster, season and heat gently for 5 minutes.

3. Pour over the Madeira or sherry, increase the heat and cook until liquid is reduced by half.
4. Beat the egg yolks with a little seasoning and add the cream. Remove the lobster from the heat, pour over the cream mixture and mix gently over a low heat until the sauce is the consistency of cream.
5. Adjust the seasoning, sprinkle with parsley and serve with hot buttered toast or boiled rice.
SERVES 2

VARIATION
As an alternative, make Prawns Newburg, using 225 g (8 oz) peeled prawns or shrimps.

LOBSTER THERMIDOR

2 small lobsters, weighing 225 g (8 oz) each, cooked
50 g (2 oz) butter or margarine
15 ml (1 tbsp) chopped shallot
10 ml (2 tsp) chopped fresh parsley
5-10 ml (1-2 tsp) chopped fresh tarragon
60 ml (4 tbsp) dry white wine
300 ml (½ pint) Béchamel Sauce (see page 200)
45 ml (3 level tbsp) grated Parmesan cheese
mustard powder, salt and paprika

1. Cut the lobsters in half lengthways and remove the lobster meat from the shells. Chop

the claw and head meat roughly and cut the tail meat into thick slices.
2. Melt half the butter, add the shallot, parsley and tarragon and fry gently for a few minutes. Add the wine and simmer for 5 minutes.
3. Add the Béchamel Sauce and simmer until it is reduced to a creamy consistency. Add the lobster meat to the sauce, with 30 ml (2 tbsp) of the cheese, the remaining butter, in small pieces, and mustard, salt and paprika to taste.
4. Arrange the mixture in the shells, sprinkle with the remaining cheese and put under the grill to brown the top quickly. Serve at once.
SERVES 2

OYSTERS AU NATUREL

12 oysters
salt and pepper
brown bread and butter, lemon wedges and Tabasco
sauce, to serve

1. Scrub the oysters with a stiff scrubbing brush, then prise open.
2. Remove the beard from each and loosen the oysters, leaving them in the deeper half-shell. Season lightly and serve with brown bread, lemon wedges and Tabasco sauce.
SERVES 4

STIR-FRIED PRAWNS

pinch of ground chilli powder
60 ml (4 level tbsp) desiccated coconut
1 garlic clove, skinned and crushed
2.5 cm (1 inch) piece fresh root ginger, peeled and
  grated
60 ml (4 tbsp) vegetable oil
450 g (1 lb) raw jumbo prawns in or out of shell
60 ml (4 tbsp) sherry
30 ml (2 level tbsp) tomato ketchup
shredded spring onion tops, to garnish

1. Beat together the chilli powder, coconut, garlic, ginger and 15ml (1 tbsp) oil.
2. Toss the prawns in the coconut mixture. Cover and leave to marinate in the refrigerator for 2-3 hours.
3. Heat the remaining oil in a wok or large frying pan. Add the prawns. Toss over a high heat for 3-4 minutes or until the prawns are no longer opaque and the shells are bright pink.
4. Stir in the sherry and tomato ketchup. Toss and stir over the heat for a further minute before serving. Serve garnished with spring onion tops. Have finger bowls on the table for each guest.
SERVES 4 AS A STARTER

PRAWNS FRIED IN GARLIC

50 g (2 oz) butter
30 ml (2 tbsp) olive oil
12 raw Dublin Bay prawns in shell
3 garlic cloves, skinned and crushed
60 ml (4 tbsp) brandy
salt and pepper
lemon wedges and shredded lettuce, to serve

1. Melt the butter with the oil in a large heavy-based pan. Add the prawns (cook half at a time if your pan is not large enough) and the garlic and fry over high heat for 5 minutes, tossing the prawns constantly.
2. Sprinkle the brandy over the prawns with salt and pepper to taste. Serve immediately, garnished with lemon wedges and lettuce. Provide finger bowls for each guest.
SERVES 2

MALAYSIAN-STYLE PRAWNS

30 ml (2 tbsp) vegetable oil
1 medium onion, skinned and very finely chopped
2 garlic cloves, skinned and crushed
2.5 cm (1 inch) piece root ginger, skinned and crushed
2 dried red chillis, finely chopped
15 ml (1 level tbsp) ground coriander
10 ml (2 level tsp) ground turmeric
salt
700 g (1½ lb) cooked peeled prawns
half a 200 g (7 oz) block creamed coconut, crumbled
about 300 ml (½ pint) boiling water
juice of 1 lime or lemon
15-25 g (½ -1 oz) coconut shreds or shredded coconut
  (optional)
lime or lemon slices, whole prawns (optional) and fresh
  coriander sprigs, to garnish

1. Heat the oil in a wok or large frying pan, add the onion, garlic and ginger and fry gently for 5 minutes. Sprinkle in the chillis, spices and salt and stir-fry for 2-3 minutes more.
2. Add the prawns to the pan and stir-fry for 2-3 minutes until heated through and evenly coated in the spice mixture.
3. Crumble in the creamed coconut, then gradually add the water and bring to the boil, stirring all the time (add just enough water to make a thick gravy that coats the prawns). Simmer for 5 minutes, stirring frequently. Taste and add more salt, if necessary.
4. Transfer to a warmed serving dish and sprinkle the juice from the lime evenly over the top. Scatter over the coconut shreds, if using, then garnish with lime or lemon slices, whole prawns, if using, and coriander sprigs. Serve immediately.
SERVES 6

MOULES MARINIÈRES

1.8 kg (4 lb) fresh mussels
40 g (1½ oz) butter or margarine
1 medium onion, skinned and finely chopped
1 small garlic clove, skinned and crushed
300 ml (½ pint) medium dry white wine
1 bay leaf
salt and pepper
10 ml (2 level tsp) plain flour
15-30 ml (1-2 tbsp) chopped fresh parsley

1. Clean the mussels (see page 82) thoroughly under running cold water. Melt 25 g (1 oz) butter in a large heavy-based saucepan, add the onion and fry gently until lightly browned. Add the mussels, garlic, wine, bay leaf, salt and plenty of pepper.
2. Cover, bring to the boil, and cook for 3-5 minutes, until the mussels open, shaking the pan frequently.
3. Pour off the cooking juices into a small saucepan, discarding the bay leaf, and boil until reduced by about one third.

4. Lift the mussels out of the pan and discard any that have not opened. Pull away and discard each empty shell, leaving the mussel attached to the half-shell. Do this over the pan to catch any juices. Transfer the mussels to a warmed soup tureen or individual soup bowls, cover and keep warm.
5. Work the remaining butter and the flour together, using a blunt-edged knife on a flat plate, until a smooth paste is formed. Off the heat, whisk the kneaded butter into the reduced cooking juices.
6. Return to the heat and bring to the boil, stirring constantly. Adjust the seasoning and add the parsley. Pour over the mussels and serve immediately.
SERVES 4 AS A STARTER OR 2 AS A MAIN COURSE

NOTE: Marinièr is a French term meaning 'in the style of the fisherman'. Moules Marinières is a classic French dish suitable to be served as a starter or main course. Hot garlic bread is the perfect accompaniment.

MUSSELS AND CLAMS WITH TOMATOES

900 g (2 lb) fresh mussels
450 g (1 lb) small clams, such as venus clams
25 g (1 oz) butter
1-2 large garlic cloves, skinned and crushed
1 small onion, skinned and finely chopped
150 ml (¼ pint) dry white wine
225 g (8 oz) ripe tomatoes, chopped
finely grated rind of 1 lemon
30 ml (2 tbsp) chopped fresh parsley
salt and pepper

1. To prepare the mussels, wash them thoroughly under running cold water, then scrape off any barnacles with a small sharp knife. Cut off the fibrous beards that protrude from between the shells. Wash in several changes of water. Discard any cracked mussels, or any that do not close when tapped sharply with a knife.
2. Scrub the clams thoroughly and discard any that are cracked or open.
3. Melt the butter in a large pan, add the garlic and onion and cook gently for a few minutes, until the onion is softened. Add the wine, tomatoes, lemon rind and half of the parsley. Bring to the boil.
4. Add the mussels and the clams to the pan, cover and cook over a high heat for 3-4 minutes or until the mussels and clams are open, shaking the pan occasionally. Discard any mussels or clams that have not opened.
5. Season to taste. Transfer to large bowls or soup plates and sprinkle with the remaining parsley. Serve with lots of crusty bread.
SERVES 2-3

NOTE: If clams are unavailable, simply use all mussels instead.

DEEP-FRIED SCAMPI

225 g (8 oz) scampi, fresh or frozen, thawed if frozen
15-30 ml (1-2 tbsp) seasoned flour
125 g (4 oz) plain flour
pinch of salt
15 ml (1 tbsp) vegetable oil
1 egg, separated
30-45 ml (2-3 tbsp) water or milk and water
vegetable oil for deep-frying
Tartare Sauce (see page 254), to serve
lemon wedges, to garnish

1. If fresh scampi are used, discard their heads, remove the flesh from the shells and remove the dark veins.
2. Dip the scampi in the seasoned flour. Mix

the plain flour, salt, oil and egg yolk with enough liquid to give a stiff batter which will coat the back of a spoon. Beat until smooth.
3. Just before cooking, whisk the egg white until stiff and fold into the batter.
4. Heat the oil in a deep-fat fryer to 180°C (350°F). Dip the scampi in the batter, then fry, a few at a time, until golden brown. Drain on absorbent kitchen paper and keep warm while frying the rest. Serve with Tartare sauce and lemon wedges.
SERVES 2

VARIATION
Coat the scampi with beaten egg and 25-50 g (1-2 oz) fresh breadcrumbs and fry until golden.

SCAMPI PROVENÇAL

45 ml (3 tbsp) olive oil
1 medium onion, skinned and finely chopped
1 garlic clove, skinned and finely chopped
450 g (1 lb) tomatoes, skinned and chopped, or
    397 g (14 oz) can tomatoes, drained
90 ml (6 tbsp) dry white wine
salt and pepper
15 ml (1 tbsp) chopped fresh parsley
450 g (1 lb) frozen scampi, thawed and drained

1. Heat the oil in a saucepan, add the onion and garlic and fry gently for about 5 minutes, until soft but not coloured.
2. Stir in the tomatoes, wine, seasoning and parsley and simmer gently for about 10 minutes.
3. Add the scampi and continue simmering for about 5 minutes, or until they are just heated through. Serve with crusty French bread or boiled rice.
SERVES 4

COQUILLES ST. JACQUES

8 medium scallops, prepared (see page 83)
60 ml (4 tbsp) medium white wine
1 bay leaf
salt and pepper
40 g (1½ oz) butter or margarine
45 ml (3 level tbsp) flour
60 ml (4 tbsp) single cream
50 g (2 oz) Gruyère cheese, grated
450 g (1 lb) potatoes, boiled and mashed

1. Reserve four of the round scallop shells. Place the scallops in a small saucepan; add 150 ml (¼ pint) water, the wine, bay leaf and a good pinch of salt.
2. Bring slowly to the boil, cover, and simmer gently for about 5 minutes or until the scallops are just tender when tested with a sharp knife. Lift out the scallops with a slotted spoon. Strain

and reserve the juices.
3. Melt the butter in a saucepan. Stir in the flour and cook gently for 1 minute, stirring. Remove the pan from the heat and gradually stir in the reserved juices.
4. Bring to the boil slowly and continue to cook, stirring, until the sauce thickens. Season and simmer gently for 4-5 minutes. Lower the heat and stir in the cream and half the grated cheese. Cut each scallop into two or three pieces and stir into the sauce.
5. Pipe a border of mashed potato around the edges of the rounded scallop shells. Spoon the sauce mixture into the centre and sprinkle the remaining grated cheese over the top.
6. Bake in the oven at 220°C (425°F) mark 7 for about 15 minutes or until the sauce and piped potato are golden.
SERVES 4

GLAZED SEAFOOD PLATTER

225 g (8 oz) haddock fillet, skinned
450 g (1 lb) halibut fillet, skinned
75 g (3 oz) Florence fennel
300 ml (½ pint) dry white wine
150 ml (¼ pint) fish stock
1 bay leaf
225 g (8 oz) queen scallops, cleaned
125 g (4 oz) shelled fresh mussels
125 g (4 oz) cooked peeled prawns
40 g (1½ oz) butter
40 g (1½ oz) plain flour
1 egg yolk
150 ml (¼ pint) double cream
salt and pepper
50 g (2 oz) Emmenthal cheese, coarsely grated

Glazed Seafood Platter

1. Cut the fish fillets into bite-sized pieces. Remove the feathery tops from the fennel, finely chop and reserve. Cut the fennel into wafer-thin slices.
2. Place the fish and fennel in a large shallow pan and pour on the wine, stock and bay leaf. Bring to the boil, cover and simmer for 7-8 minutes or until the fish is just cooked.
3. With a slotted spoon, remove the fish and fennel from the cooking liquor and arrange in a single layer on a large heatproof platter. Add the scallops and mussels to the liquid, return to the boil and immediately remove with a slotted spoon. Scatter over the fish with the prawns.

4. Cover the platter with foil and keep warm in the oven at 170°C (325°F) mark 3. Melt the butter in a saucepan. Stir in the flour and cook, stirring, for 1-2 minutes. Strain in the poaching liquor, bring to the boil, stirring all the time, then simmer for 2-3 minutes until thickened.
5. Heat the grill. Beat the egg yolk and cream into the sauce. Season with salt and pepper, then spoon evenly over the seafood and sprinkle with cheese. Place the platter under the grill until golden brown. Serve immediately, garnished with the reserved fennel tops.
SERVES 4

MIXED SEAFOOD BROCHETTES

100 ml (4 fl oz) olive oil
pared zest of ½ a lemon
1 thyme sprig
1 bay leaf
6 parsley stalks
salt and pepper
125 g (4 oz) turbot steak
125 g (4 oz) salmon steak
450 g (1 lb) shelled scallops
125 g (4 oz) shelled scampi
1 lemon, quartered, and parsley sprigs, to garnish
Hollandaise Sauce (see page 203), to serve (optional)

1. For the marinade, mix the olive oil with the lemon zest, herbs and seasoning.
2. Cut the turbot and salmon into pieces equal in size to the scallops and scampi.
3. Skewer the pieces of fish alternately on four metal skewers and place in a shallow dish. Pour the marinade over and leave in a cool place for at least 2 hours, turning frequently.
4. Remove the brochettes from the marinade and drain off excess liquid. Place them under a preheated grill and cook for about 15 minutes, turning the brochettes frequently.
5. Serve the brochettes on a bed of white, brown or saffron rice, garnished with lemon quarters and parsley sprigs. Hand the Hollandaise Sauce separately, if serving.
SERVES 4

Meat

In this country beef, lamb and pork are the most popular meats, while veal is eaten to a lesser extent. The flavour and texture of meat is determined by the breed of the animal, its environment and feed. Meat from cattle reared on lush pastures will taste quite different from that derived from corn fed animals. With the exception of veal, meat is hung before it is sold to improve texture and develop flavour.

Modern methods of transport and developments in cold storage have done away with seasons for meat and you can buy good-quality beef, lamb and pork at any time of the year. Most butchers and large supermarkets sell both fresh and frozen meat and it is worth searching out a good local supplier who is prepared to offer a wide choice of cuts. Bear in mind that he should be an expert on meat and take advantage of this. A friendly butcher can take away a lot of preparation problems by being prepared to bone, chop or mince to your requirements.

Meat is not just the basis of a good satisfying meal, it is a major supplier of nutrients including protein, some of the B vitamins and iron. It need not be the most expensive ingredient in a dish since price varies according to the type of cut. You pay most for those parts of the animal which are least exercised and thus tender enough to roast, fry or grill. Tougher cuts, which have more muscle, are cheaper and need long, gentle, moist cooking to soften them. Nutritionally there is nothing to choose between tender and tougher cuts, and the flavour of both is good if correctly cooked.

CHOOSING MEAT

Obviously it is essential to select a cut of meat which is suitable for the particular recipe. Details of cuts and suitability for different cooking methods are given in individual sections (see Beef, Lamb, Pork etc).

Meat should always look and smell fresh, with a clear but not necessarily bright colour. Bright red does not necessarily indicate good eating quality. The colour of cut lean beef displayed in butchers' shops will, for example,

vary from bright red to dark brown. Exposure to atmosphere makes meat develop a brownish-red shade so some butchers use red-tinted lighting to disguise it.

It is important to cut down the amount of fat we eat, but when cooking meat a little fat is essential to prevent the meat drying out. It also enhances the flavour. Fat on meat should be firm and free from dark marks or discoloration. Meat for roasting, frying and grilling should be finely grained, firm and slightly elastic, with a fine marbling of fat throughout. Meat that is to be stewed or braised will have coarser grained, lean areas and more fat. Trim off all but a little of the fat before cooking.

STORING MEAT

Meat which has not been pre-packed should always be removed from the wrappings in which it was bought. Re-wrap in greaseproof paper and place on a plate. Pre-packed meat on a film-covered tray can be left in its container; loosen the wrapping initially to dry the surface moisture, then re-wrap. Always store meat in the coldest part of the refrigerator, which is usually just below the frozen food storage compartment. To avoid the risk of bacterial cross contamination, never allow raw meat to come into contact with cooked food. If your refrigerator has wire shelves, rather than solid ones, store cooked food at the top of the refrigerator and raw meat below, to prevent blood dripping from raw on to cooked meat.

The refrigerator should not be regarded as a place for the long term storage of meat. The lower temperature merely slows down the process of deterioration; it does not completely prevent it. Minced raw meat and offal are especially perishable and should be used within a day of being purchased.

Leftover casseroles should first be allowed to cool and then put into the refrigerator in a covered dish. They should be used within 2 days and reheated thoroughly before they are eaten. Bring the dish to boiling point and simmer gently for at least 10 minutes.

BOILING MEAT

The term boiling is a misnomer since meat cooked by this method should not be boiled but gently simmered. Boiling produces tough and tasteless meat. For this type of cooking the meat should be covered with liquid in a pan with a well-fitting lid so that evaporation is kept to a minimum. Vegetables and herbs added to the cooking liquid will make ideal stock for soup.

Meat for boiling is usually salted and should first be soaked in cold water for several hours or overnight to remove excess salt. Change the water before bringing it slowly to the boil, then reduce to a gentle simmer. Large salted joints should be cooked for 25 minutes per 450 g (1 lb) plus an extra 30 minutes. Small joints should be cooked for a minimum of 1½ hours. Calculate the cooking time from the moment the water reaches the boil. With vacuum packs, follow the instructions given.

Pressure cooking will cut the time needed to 'boil' meat by about two thirds, and less liquid is needed; follow the manufacturer's instructions for exact times and quantities.

GRILLING AND BARBECUING MEAT

Grilling is a quick method of cooking by radiant heat which is only suitable for top quality tender cuts of meat, such as cutlets, chops, steaks, liver, kidneys, gammon, back and streaky bacon. Grilling toughens inferior cuts of meat as the fibres cannot be broken down.

An electric grill and, of course, a barbecue, should be preheated but this is not necessary with a gas grill. As the heat is fierce the meat must be basted with oil or melted butter before cooking. Meat for grilling or barbecuing is often greatly improved by first being marinated for at least 2 hours.

FRYING MEAT

It is the heat of the fat that cooks the meat during frying, and as it cooks, the meat absorbs some of the fat. Frying is therefore not a suitable cooking method for anyone who is trying to cut down on fat.

Frying may be done in shallow fat that comes about halfway up the sides of the meat or deep fat in which it is completely immersed.

BRAISING MEAT

Braising is a combination of stewing, steaming and roasting. The meat is cooked in a saucepan or casserole, over a bed of vegetables, with just sufficient liquid for the steam to keep it moist. This gives a good flavour and texture to meat that otherwise would be tough and flavourless.

STEWING AND CASSEROLING MEAT

Strictly speaking, both stewing and casseroling describe a long, slow method of cooking in a simmering liquid. The only difference between the two is that casseroling refers to the actual dish in which the food is cooked. This method of cooking is particularly suitable for tougher cuts of meat and since all the liquid is served, none of the flavour or food value is lost. A strong heavy-based saucepan or casserole is needed to avoid burning; it should have a tightly fitting lid to prevent evaporation. Keep the temperature below boiling – as boiling can often cause meat to become tough to chew.

ROASTING MEAT

The process known as oven-roasting is in fact baking. It is essential to choose a good quality tender cut which is suitable for roasting. High temperature roasting at 450°F (230°C) mark 8 is only suitable for the most expensive prime cuts, such as tenderloin of beef. Roasting at 180°C (350°F) mark 4 will produce succulent meat with minimum shrinkage.

When purchasing a joint for roasting, allow about 225 g (8 oz) per person for a boned and rolled joint; 300-350 g (10-12 oz) per person for meat on the bone.

Bring the meat to room temperature before cooking. Preheat the oven to 180°C (350°F) mark 4. Weigh the joint in order to calculate the cooking time (see chart overleaf).

If the meat doesn't have a natural layer of fat it should be barded (see page 566). Season the joint and apply flavourings. Beef is often rubbed with a coating of dry mustard. Lamb can be studded with slivers of garlic and rosemary sprigs. Pork should be rubbed with oil and salt.

Place the meat, fat side up, on a wire rack in a roasting tin. Baste frequently during cooking.

ROASTING MEAT AT 180°C (350°F) MARK 4		
	COOKING TIME	INTERNAL TEMPERATURE
BEEF		
Rare	20 minutes per 450 g (1 lb) plus 20 minutes	60°C (140°F)
Medium	25 minutes per 450 g (1 lb) plus 25 minutes	70°C (160°F)
Well Done	30 minutes per 450 g (1 lb) plus 30 minutes	80°C (175°F)
VEAL		
Well Done	25 minutes per 450 g (1 lb) plus 25 minutes	70°C (160°F)
LAMB		
Medium	25 minutes per 450 g (1 lb) plus 25 minutes	70-75°C (160-170°F)
Well Done	30 minutes per 450 g (1 lb) plus 30 minutes	75-80°C (170-175°F)
PORK		
Medium	30 minutes per 450 g (1 lb) plus 30 minutes	75-80°C (170-175°F)
Well Done	35 minutes per 450 g (1 lb) plus 30 minutes	80-85°C (175-180°F)

To check whether or not the meat is cooked to the correct degree of doneness, insert a meat thermometer into the thickest part of the joint, making sure the tip of the thermometer is not touching the bone. The internal temperature readings relating to the required degree of doneness are given on the chart above.

NOTE: Meat cooked to an internal temperature of 60°C (140°F) at an oven temperature of 180°C (350°F) mark 4 will have a surface temperature in excess of 70°C, thus minimising any food hygiene risk. However expectant mothers, the very young, elderly or sick may wish to avoid rare meat because they may be more susceptible to infection.

SPIT-ROASTING MEAT

For spit-roasting or rotisserie cooking, the meat is placed on a revolving spit or skewers and cooked under (or over) a direct source of heat, either in the oven, on a grill attachment or over a barbecue. Cooking times vary, depending on the strength of the heat source.

CARVING MEAT

Carving is not the mystery some people like to pretend it is provided you understand a few basic facts. The only things needed are a large, sharp carving knife, a knife sharpener and a two-pronged carving fork with a finger guard.

Boned and rolled joints are simply sliced through. The backbone of rib or loin cuts of lamb and pork helps to keep the joint in shape during cooking. Get the butcher to 'chinc' it (partially chop through the bone lengthways)

when you buy it so you can then remove the bone just before serving, for easier carving.

Place the cooked joint on a meat dish, wooden board or spiked metal carving dish with recesses to catch the meat juices and leave to stand for 15 minutes before carving. Always carve on a non-slip surface. Before starting to carve, loosen the cooked meat from any exposed bones. Take off all or at least some of the crackling before carving pork.

Aim to cut across the grain of the lean in order to shorten the muscle fibres. This makes the meat easier to chew and thus more tender. This procedure will usually mean cutting at right angles to the bone.

CARVING BEEF

FORE RIB: Ask the butcher to chine the backbone. After cooking, remove the backbone and run a sharp knife between meat and bone. Carve the meat downwards, on to and between the rib bones.

SIRLOIN: Sirloin of beef comprises the fillet and sirloin muscles with a T-shaped bone between and a portion of flank. Sometimes the fillet is removed and sold separately. When carving, gradually loosen the meat from the bones with a sharp knife as you carve along the joint. Carve slices of meat down to the bone, first on one side, then the other. If the entire joint is to be carved at one time, it may be easier to remove the three pieces of meat first.

CARVING LAMB

LEG: With the meatier side of the leg uppermost, carve a narrow, wedge-shaped piece of meat

To carve a leg of lamb, begin by cutting a narrow, wedge-shaped piece of meat from the middle of the leg through the meat down to the bone. Continue carving from either side, cutting at an angle.

from the middle of the leg right down to the bone. Then carve slices from either side of the cut, slanting the knife to obtain larger slices. The underside of the joint can be carved, after removing any excess fat, by slicing along the length of the leg.

SHOULDER: Secure the joint at the shank end, with the crisp skin uppermost. Cut a wedge-shaped slice through the middle of the joint in the angle between the shoulder blade and the leg bone. Carve slices from each side of the first

cut until the shoulder blade and shank bones are reached. Turn the joint over and carve horizontal slices from the underside.

BEST END OF NECK: Get the butcher to chine the joint. After cooking, remove the chined bone and cut the meat into cutlets between the rib bones.

CARVING PORK

LOIN: Ask the butcher to chine the bone. After cooking, remove it and cut through the fat just beneath the crackling and remove a section or all of it before carving thinly, downwards to the bones.

LEG (SHANK END): Remove some of the crackling. Cut thin slices down to and around the bone as far as possible. When the shank bone is reached, carve slanting slices over the top of the bone. Turn the whole joint over and cut slanting slices down towards the thin end of the bone.

LEG (FILLET END): Carve slices through to the bone, on either side of it.

BEEF

The quality of beef is very dependent on all sorts of factors, such as the age, breed and sex of the animal and the hanging, storing and the cutting up of the joints. It is worth seeking out a butcher who supplies the sort of beef you like.
Beef should look fresh and moist but not watery, with small flecks of fat through the lean – this fat (called marbling) helps to keep the meat moist and tender when cooking. Choose meat with little gristle between the fat and the lean.

CUTS AND METHODS OF COOKING

SHIN (FORELEG) AND LEG (HINDLEG) are lean meat with a high proportion of connective tissue. Suitable for stews, casseroles, stock and soups.

NECK AND CLOD are usually cut into pieces and sold as stewing 'steak' or mince.

SILVERSIDE is a boneless joint traditionally salted and sold for boiling. Today it is more often sold for roasting but, because it is lean it needs constant basting. Note that uncooked salted beef is grey, but turns pink during cooking.

FORE RIB is the traditional large roasting joint sold on the bone or boned and rolled. It may also be sold as 'rib eye' steaks.

WING RIB is a popular roasting joint, but often boned, sliced and sold as frying or grilling steaks.

SIRLOIN is a tender and delicious cut of beef, sold on the bone or boned and rolled with or without the fillet, for roasting or more often as steaks.

FILLET is the smaller 'eye' on the inside of the rib bone, which is usually removed and sold in slices as fillet steak or whole for Beef Wellington. It is regarded as the prime beef cut.

CHUCK AND BLADE STEAK is a large, fairly lean cut of high-quality meat, removed from the bone and sold sliced, or cubed as 'chuck steak'. Suitable for braising, stewing and pie fillings.

THICK FLANK (TOP RUMP) is a lean boneless cut suitable for roasting, pot roasting and braising or, when sliced, for braising and frying.

THIN FLANK is ideal for braising and stewing. It is frequently sold minced.

BRISKET is sold either on the bone or more commonly boned and rolled, and it is suitable for braising or pot-roasting. It is also sold salted. Good served cold.

THIN RIBS AND THICK RIBS are usually sold boned and rolled; ideal for braising and pot roasting

RUMP is an excellent large lean and tender cut from the hind quarter. It is usually sold in slices for grilling and frying.

TOPSIDE is a lean cut of beef, with little or no fat. It is often sold with a layer of fat tied around it. Rump can be roasted or pot roasted.

FLASH-FRY STEAKS are cut from the thick flank, topside or silverside. The steaks are beaten out and passed between spiked rollers. This process tenderises the meat so it can be quick-fried.

BRAISING STEAK is normally sold sliced or cubed and is taken from chuck, blade and thick rib cuts.

STEWING STEAKS requires long slow cooking and is usually sold cubed or sliced. It is taken from shin, leg, neck and clods.

MINCED BEEF may be coarse or finely cut. It is produced from thin flank, thin rib, clod and neck. Extra lean mince is widely available.

ROASTING

For general instructions, refer to page 94.

STEAKS

Steaks are lean slices taken from the tenderest cuts of beef. They take very little time to cook and care must be taken to ensure they do not overcook.

Steaks need very little preparation; trim them to a good shape if necessary and wipe well. Trim off excess fat but do not remove it all, then slash the remaining fat at regular intervals before cooking to prevent the meat curling while it is cooking.

TRADITIONAL STEAK CUTS

RUMP is one of the commonest cuts used for grilling or frying. The 'point' is considered the best part for tenderness and flavour.

FILLET is the undercut of the sirloin. It is probably one of the best-known and the most expensive of the cuts used for grilling or frying. Fillet is very tender, although it usually has less flavour than rump steak.

The 'centre' or 'eye' of the fillet is considered the best part. The fillet is often cut and shaped into small rounds, known as tournedos, weighing 125 g (4 oz) each. A *filet mignon tournedos* is a small round steak, weighing 75 g (3 oz), cut from the end of the fillet.

CHATEAUBRIAND is a thick slice taken from the middle of the fillet. It is generally regarded as the most superb cut of all. It can weigh up to 350 g (12 oz).

SIRLOIN (OR CONTRE FILET) is cut into two parts.

Porterhouse steak is cut from the thick end of the sirloin and can weigh as much as 800 g (1¾ lb); when it is cooked on the bone it is called T-bone steak. *Minute steak* is a very thin steak from the upper part of the sirloin, weighing 125-150 g (4-5 oz), without any trimmings of fat.

ENTRECÔTE by definition, is the part of the meat between the ribs of beef, but a slice cut from the sirloin or rump is often served under this name.

GRILLING AND BARBECUING STEAKS

Brush with melted butter or oil and cook under a preheated medium grill, or barbecue, turning the steaks regularly with a blunt tool so as not to pierce the meat and allow the sealed in juices to escape.

FRYING STEAKS

Use a heavy-based frying pan, heating it well before adding the fat. If the steak is large, brown it quickly on both sides in hot shallow oil and/or butter, then reduce the heat and cook gently for the remaining time. With small steaks, fry over medium heat for half the cooking time on one side, then turn them and cook for remaining time.

To make quick sauces for fried steaks remove them from the pan and keep warm. Add whisky or brandy to the pan juices and ignite. Pour the sauce over the steaks. Alternatively add mustard and cream to the pan juices and heat without boiling, then pour over the steaks.

GRILLING AND FRYING TIMES FOR STEAKS	
Sirloin/Rump [2 cm (¾ inch) thickness]	
Rare	2½ minutes each side
Medium	4 minutes each side
Well Done	6-7 minutes each side
Fillet [2-3 cm (¾ -1¼ inch) thickness]	
Rare	3-4 minutes each side
Medium	4-5 minutes each side
Well Done	6-7 minutes each side
Flash-fry [1 cm (½ inch) thickness]	
Medium	2-4 minutes each side

ACCOMPANIMENTS

A piece of Maître d'Hôtel Butter (see page 207) placed on each steak before it is served, is one traditional accompaniment. Other accompaniments are matchstick or chipped potatoes, grilled tomatoes and fried mushrooms, or a green or mixed salad, or green vegetables.

ROAST BEEF WITH YORKSHIRE PUDDING

Traditionally, beef was roasted at a high temperature to allow the Yorkshire pudding to be cooked with the joint. If you are roasting at the lower temperature of 180°C (350°F) mark 4, you will need to keep the joint warm and covered, while cooking the Yorkshire pudding. If cooking roast potatoes, leave them in the oven while cooking the Yorkshire pudding to give them a crisp finish.

Yorkshire pudding is made from a batter mixture and should be cooked in a baking or small roasting tin (not an ovenproof dish as this tends to make it soggy); avoid opening the oven door during cooking. Roast the meat according to the chart on page 94. Make the gravy as directed on page 202.

piece of sirloin, rib, rump or topside (see note)
50 g (2 oz) beef dripping (optional)
.pepper
5 ml (1 tsp) mustard powder (optional)
FOR THE YORKSHIRE PUDDING
125 g (4 oz) plain flour
pinch of salt
1 egg
200 ml (7 fl oz) milk
25 g (1 oz) lard or dripping or 30 ml (2 tbsp)
  vegetable oil

1. Weigh the meat and calculate the cooking time (see page 94). Put the meat into a shallow roasting tin, preferably on a grid, with the thickest layer of fat uppermost and the cut sides exposed to the heat. Add dripping if the meat is lean. Season with pepper and mustard, if wished.

2. Roast the joint at 180°C (350°F) mark 4 and cook for the calculated time, basting occasionally with the juices from the tin.

3. To make the Yorkshire pudding, mix the flour and salt in a bowl, make a well in the centre and break in the egg.

4. Add half the milk and using a wooden spoon gradually work in the flour. Beat the mixture until it is smooth then add the remaining milk and 100 ml (3 fl oz) water. Beat until well mixed and the surface is covered with tiny bubbles.

5. Put the fat in a small roasting or other baking tin and place in the oven at 220°C (425°F) mark 7 for about 10 minutes until the fat shows a haze.

6. Pour in the batter and return to the oven to cook for 40-45 minutes, until risen and golden brown.

NOTE: Refer to page 94 for serving quantity guide and general advice on roasting.

VARIATION
For individual Yorkshire Puddings or Popovers, use 50 g (2 oz) plain flour, a pinch of salt, 1 egg, 150 ml (¼ pint) milk and water mixed. Use to fill 12 patty tins. Cook for 15-20 minutes.

BRAISED BRISKET WITH RED WINE

1.1 kg (2½ lb) piece of lean boned and rolled brisket
15 ml (1 level tbsp) seasoned flour
15 ml (1 tbsp) vegetable oil
2 medium carrots, peeled and cut into chunks
2 medium parsnips, peeled and cut into chunks
2 medium onions, skinned and diced
150 ml (¼ pint) beef stock
15 ml (1 level tbsp) tomato purée
60 ml (4 tbsp) red wine
2.5 ml (½ level tsp) dried thyme
1 bay leaf
salt and pepper
10 ml (2 level tsp) cornflour

1. Roll the brisket joint in the seasoned flour until well coated.

2. Heat the oil in a 2.3 litre (4 pint) flameproof casserole and brown the joint well. Remove.

3. Stir the vegetables into the fat remaining in the pan and fry gently for 2 minutes, then add the stock, tomato purée, wine, thyme, bay leaf and seasoning. Bring to the boil. Replace the meat, placing it in the centre of the vegetables.

4. Cover tightly and cook in the oven at 170°C (325°F) mark 3 for about 2¼ hours, until the meat is tender when pierced with a fine skewer.

5. Remove the meat and carve into slices. Arrange on a warmed serving dish with the vegetables, cover and keep warm.

6. Mix the cornflour to a smooth paste with 30 ml (2 tbsp) water. Stir into the meat juices, then bring slowly to the boil. Boil for 1 minute, adjust seasoning and serve separately.
SERVES 6

Fillet of Beef Wellington

FILLET OF BEEF WELLINGTON (*Boeuf en Croûte*)

1.4 kg (3 lb) fillet of beef
pepper
30 ml (2 tbsp) vegetable oil
225 g (8 oz) button mushrooms, wiped and sliced
50 g (2 oz) butter or margarine
175 g (6 oz) smooth liver pâté
368 g (13 oz) packet frozen puff pastry, thawed
beaten egg, to glaze

1. Trim and tie up the fillet at intervals to retain its shape. Season with pepper. Heat the oil in a large frying pan, add the meat and fry briskly on all sides to brown. Press down with a wooden spoon while frying to seal the surface well.
2. Roast in the oven at 220°C (425°F) mark 7 for 20 minutes, then cool the beef and remove the string. Fry the mushrooms in the butter until soft; leave until cold, then blend with the pâté.
3. On a lightly floured surface roll out the pastry to a large rectangle about 33 x 28 cm (13 x 11 inches) and 5 mm (¼ inch) thick.
4. Spread the pâté mixture down the centre of the pastry. Place the meat in the centre. Brush the edges of the pastry with egg.
5. Fold the pastry edges over lengthways and turn the parcel over so that the join is underneath. Fold the ends under the meat and place on a baking sheet.
6. Decorate with leaves cut from the pastry trimmings. Glaze with beaten egg and bake in the oven at 220°C (425°F) mark 7 for 50 minutes, covering with foil after 25 minutes.
SERVES 8

CLASSIC BEEF STEW

50 g (2 oz) lard or 45 ml (3 tbsp) vegetable oil
700-900 g (1½-2 lb) stewing steak, trimmed and cut
*   into 4 cm (1½ inch) cubes*
4 medium onions, skinned and halved lengthways
350 g (12 oz) carrots, peeled and cut into chunks
30 ml (2 level tbsp) flour
600 ml (1 pint) beef stock
15 ml (1 level tbsp) tomato purée
salt and pepper
2 bay leaves

Classic Beef Stew

1. Melt the lard in a medium flameproof
casserole. Increase the heat and when the fat is
just beginning to smoke, add the meat about one
quarter at a time. Fry each batch until well
browned. Remove with a slotted spoon.
2. Reduce the heat, add the onions and carrots
and fry until the vegetables are lightly browned.
Remove from the casserole.
3. Sprinkle the flour into the fat remaining in
the pan and stir well until evenly blended.
Return the pan to the heat and cook slowly,
stirring constantly, until the roux begins to turn
a light brown colour.
4. Add the stock, tomato purée and seasoning
and stir until the mixture is quite smooth. Bring
slowly to the boil, stirring, then add the meat
and vegetables with their juices and the bay
leaves.
5. Cover the casserole tightly and cook in the
oven at 170°C (325°F) mark 3 for about
2½ hours. Uncover and stir once during
cooking; recover and return to the oven.
Alternatively, cover and simmer gently on top of

the stove for about 2 hours, stirring occasionally
to prevent the stew from sticking. Remove the
bay leaves before serving.
SERVES 4

VARIATION
CARBONADE OF BEEF
Omit the carrots and slice the onions after
halving them. Add 300 ml (½ pint) brown ale
and 5 ml (1 tsp) cider or wine vinegar to the
stock; cover and cook for 2 hours only. Cut
8 medium-sized slices of French bread and
spread one side with French mustard. Uncover
the casserole and push the bread down into the
meat juices, with the mustard side up. Return to
the oven and cook, uncovered, for about 30 minutes, or until the bread forms a good crust.

SPICED SILVERSIDE

1.8 kg (4 lb) piece of boned salted silverside
1 medium onion, skinned and sliced
4 medium carrots, peeled and sliced
1 small turnip, peeled and sliced
1-2 celery sticks, trimmed and chopped
8 cloves
125 g (4 oz) soft brown sugar
2.5 ml (½ level tsp) mustard powder
5 ml (1 level tsp) ground cinnamon
juice of 1 orange

1. Soak the meat in cold water for several hours
or overnight, then rinse and put in a large
saucepan with the vegetables. Cover with water

and bring slowly to the boil. Remove any scum,
cover with a lid and simmer for 3-4 hours until
tender. Allow to cool in the liquid.
2. Drain well, then put the meat into a roasting
tin and stick cloves into the fat. Mix together the
remaining ingredients and spread over the meat.
3. Bake in the oven at 180°C (350°F) mark 4 for
¾ -1 hour, basting occasionally. Serve hot or cold.
SERVES 6

NOTE: If you wish, you can press the meat after
cooking. Fit it snugly into a casserole or foil-
lined tin, spoon a little of the liquid over and
cover with a board or plate. Put a heavy weight
on top. Leave in a cold place for several hours.

BEEF STEWED IN RED WINE

1.4 kg (3 lb) piece top rump or chuck steak, trimmed
150 ml (¼ pint) red wine
1 medium onion, skinned and finely sliced
3 garlic cloves, skinned and sliced
3 parsley stalks, lightly crushed
8 black peppercorns
sprig of fresh thyme or 2.5 ml (½ level tsp) dried thyme
30 ml (2 tbsp) olive oil
about 150 ml (¼ pint) beef stock
125 g (4 oz) lean gammon, cut into cubes
salt and pepper

1. Place the piece of beef in a polythene bag or bowl, pour in the wine and add the onion, garlic, parsley stalks, peppercorns and thyme. Mix well.
2. Seal the bag or cover the dish, and leave in a cool place to marinate for 4-5 hours.
3. Remove the beef from the marinade. Set aside. Strain the marinade and set aside.

Reserve the onion slices.
4. Heat the oil in a heavy flameproof casserole, add the reserved onion slices and fry gently for 5 minutes until soft but not coloured. Add the beef and fry for about 10 minutes, until brown on all sides.
5. Pour over the marinade and the stock, then add the gammon. Season. Bring to the boil and boil rapidly for 2-3 minutes.
6. Cover tightly and cook in the oven at 180°C (350°F) mark 4 for 2¼-3 hours, until the beef is tender. Check every 30 minutes, turning the beef and making sure there is enough liquid. If necessary, top up with a little stock.
7. To serve, remove the cooked beef from the casserole and slice neatly. Arrange the slices overlapping on a warmed serving plate. Taste and adjust the seasoning of the sauce, then serve immediately with the sliced beef.
SERVES 6

BOEUF BOURGUIGNONNE

50 g (2 oz) butter or margarine
30 ml (2 tbsp) vegetable oil
125 g (4 oz) streaky bacon rashers, rinded and diced
900 g (2 lb) topside, rump or lean braising steak, cut into 2.5 cm (1 inch) cubes
1 garlic clove, skinned and crushed
45 ml (3 level tbsp) flour
salt and pepper
bouquet garni
150 ml (¼ pint) beef stock
300 ml (½ pint) burgundy or other red wine
12 small onions, skinned
175 g (6 oz) button mushrooms, wiped
chopped fresh parsley, to garnish

1. Melt half the butter and oil in a large

flameproof casserole. Quickly brown the bacon, then drain on absorbent kitchen paper.
2. Reheat the fat and brown the meat in batches. Return the bacon to the casserole with the garlic. Sprinkle in the flour and stir well.
3. Add salt and pepper, the bouquet garni, stock and wine. Bring to the boil, stirring, then cover and cook in the oven at 170°C (325°F) mark 3 for about 2½ hours.
4. Meanwhile, fry the onoins in the remaining butter and oil until glazed and golden brown. Remove from the pan and fry the mushrooms.
5. Add the mushrooms and onions to the casserole and cook for a further 30 minutes. Remove the bouquet garni, adjust the seasoning. Serve garnished with chopped parsley.
SERVES 6

FONDUE BOURGUIGNONNE

700 g (1½ lb) fillet or rump steak, trimmed of excess fat and cut into 2.5 cm (1 inch) cubes
vegetable oil for deep frying
Spicy Cheese and Tomato, Mustard and Blue Cheese dips (see page 47)
1 onion or shallot, finely chopped
finely chopped fresh parsley

1. Arrange the steak on individual plates.

2. Fill a fondue dish one-third full of oil and heat on a fondue burner on the table to 190°C (375°F).
3. Put the dips and onion in individual bowls.
4. Each guest has a two-pronged fondue fork with which they spear the meat cubes, and immerse in the hot oil for a few minutes. The cooked meat is then served with the dips and onions.
SERVES 4

STEAK DIANE

4 pieces of fillet steak, 5 mm (¼ inch) thick, trimmed of
    excess fat
25 g (1 oz) butter or margarine
30 ml (2 tbsp) vegetable oil
30 ml (2 tbsp) Worcestershire sauce
15 ml (1 tbsp) lemon juice
1 small onion, skinned and grated
10 ml (2 tsp) chopped fresh parsley

1. Fry the steaks in the butter and oil for
1-2 minutes on each side. Remove with a slotted
spoon and keep warm. Stir the Worcestershire
sauce and lemon juice into the pan juices.
2. Warm through, then add the onion and
parsley and cook gently for 1 minute. Serve the
sauce spooned over the steaks.
SERVES 4

STEAK AU POIVRE

30 ml (2 level tbsp) black or green peppercorns
4 sirloin, rump or fillet steaks, trimmed of excess fat
salt
25 g (1 oz) butter or margarine
15 ml (1 tbsp) vegetable oil
30 ml (2 tbsp) brandy
150 ml (¼ pint) double cream

1. Crush the peppercorns coarsely using a pestle
and mortar, or in a polythene bag, or on a board
with a rolling pin.
2. Place the steaks on the peppercorn mixture
and press hard to encrust the surface of the
meat; repeat with the other side.
3. Heat the butter and oil in a frying pan and fry
the steaks for 2 minutes on either side. Reduce

the heat and continue cooking until cooked to
taste (see page 96 for cooking chart). Season
with salt.
4. Remove the steaks from the pan and keep
warm. Add the brandy to the pan, remove from
the heat and set it alight. Take off the heat until
the flames have died
down, then stir in the
cream. Season and
reheat gently. Pour
over the steaks.
SERVES 4

*Encrusting steaks with
coarsely crushed
peppercorns.*

BEEF OLIVES

75 g (3 oz) streaky bacon, rinded and chopped
10 ml (2 tsp) chopped fresh parsley
125 g (4 oz) fresh breadcrumbs
50 g (2 oz) shredded suet
1.25 ml (¼ level tsp) dried mixed herbs
rind and juice of 1 lemon
salt and pepper
1 egg, beaten
8 thin slices beef topside, 700 g (1½ lb) total weight
45 ml (3 level tbsp) seasoned flour
60 ml (4 tbsp) vegetable oil
450 ml (¾ pint) beef stock
2 medium onions, skinned and sliced into rings

1. Combine the first six ingredients for the
stuffing, season and bind with the egg. Spread
each slice of meat with stuffing, roll up, secure
with string and toss in seasoned flour.
2. Heat the oil in a frying pan and fry the beef
olives gently, turning, until lightly browned.

Remove and place in a casserole.
3. Add remaining seasoned flour to the frying
pan, brown well, then gradually add the stock
and bring to the boil, stirring. Season and pour
over the beef olives.
4. Add the onion slices, cover and cook in the
oven at 180°C (350°F) mark 4 for 1½ hours until
tender. Remove the strings before serving the
beef olives.
SERVES 4

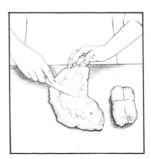

*Spread each slice of meat
with stuffing, leaving a
small space around the
edge. Roll up and secure
neatly with fine kitchen
string.*

STEAK AND STILTON PARCELS

2 quick-fry steaks, about 450 g (1 lb) total weight
30 ml (2 tbsp) oil
75 g (3 oz) blue Stilton cheese
15 ml (1 level tbsp) chopped fresh tarragon or 2.5 ml
    (½ level tsp) dried
60 ml (4 tbsp) single cream
pepper
5 large sheets filo pastry, about 45.5 x 25.5 cm
    (18 x 10 inch) each
50 g (2 oz) butter, melted
lemon juice, to serve

1. Halve each steak. Heat the oil in a frying pan, then seal the meat quickly in the hot oil; allow to cool.
2. Grate the cheese or soften with a fork. Mix with the tarragon, cream and black pepper (the Stilton should add sufficient salt). Spread the mixture over the cold steaks.
3. Brush one sheet of filo pastry with butter and wrap around one steak to enclose it completely like a parcel. Place on a baking sheet and brush with butter. Repeat with the rest of the steaks.
4. Brush the last sheet of filo with butter and fold it over and over to form a strip about 2.5 cm (1 inch) wide. Cut into diamond shapes and use to decorate the parcels. Brush with melted butter. Chill for about 20 minutes.
5. Bake in the oven at 220°C (425°F) mark 7 for 15-20 minutes or until well browned. Squeeze lemon juice over the parcels and serve accompanied by a mixed leaf salad.
SERVES 4

STEAK AND KIDNEY KEBABS

225 g (8 oz) button onions, peeled
salt and pepper
125 g (4 oz) button mushrooms
450 g (1 lb) rump steak
225 g (8 oz) lamb's kidneys, skinned, halved and cored
bay leaves
300 ml (½ pint) red wine
30 ml (2 tbsp) brandy
2 large garlic cloves, skinned and sliced
olive oil for brushing
150 ml (¼ pint) beef stock
15 ml (1 level tbsp) cornflour
watercress, to garnish

Steak and Kidney Kebabs

1. Put the button onions in a saucepan, cover with cold, salted water, bring to the boil and cook until almost tender, about 10-15 minutes. Drain and refresh under cold running water.
2. Cut the rump steak and kidneys into bite-sized pieces.
3. Thread the steak, kidney, onions, mushrooms and bay leaves on to wooden skewers – don't pack the ingredients too tightly together. Place the skewers in a large non-metallic dish.
4. Pour over the wine and brandy and add the garlic and plenty of pepper. Cover tightly and marinate in the refrigerator for about 24 hours, turning occasionally.
5. Lift the skewers out of the marinade and place on a grill pan. Protect the ends of the skewers with foil to prevent them burning.

Brush the kebabs with oil and grill, turning occasionally, until cooked through.
6. Pour the stock and marinade into a saucepan and simmer for about 10 minutes. Mix the cornflour to a smooth paste with a little water. Off the heat, stir into the pan juices, then bring to the boil, stirring all the time. Cook for 1 minute, then adjust seasoning before serving with the kebabs.
7. Garnish with watercress and serve with rice and broad beans.
SERVES 4

ABOVE: *Steak and Stilton Parcels.* BELOW: *Peppered Beef Sauté*

PEPPERED BEEF SAUTÉ

350 g (12 oz) sirloin steaks
10 ml (2 level tsp) green peppercorns in brine, drained
15 ml (1 tbsp) olive oil
25 g (1 oz) butter
175 g (6 oz) red onion, skinned and thinly sliced
90 ml (6 tbsp) single cream
15 ml (1 tbsp) lemon juice
salt
lemon slices, to garnish
fine noodles tossed with chives, to accompany

1. Cut the steaks into fine, thin strips. Finely chop the peppercorns.
2. Heat the oil and butter together in a medium-sized sauté pan. Add the onion and fry until just beginning to soften.
3. Stir in the beef and peppercorns and cook over a high heat for about 2-3 minutes or until the meat is tender, stirring frequently.
4. Lower the heat and stir in the cream and lemon juice with salt to taste. To serve, garnish with lemon slices and accompany with noodles.
SERVES 2–3

BOEUF STROGANOFF

*700 g (1½ lb) rump or fillet steak, trimmed of excess fat
    and thinly sliced into 5 mm x 5 cm (¼ x 2 inch)
    strips*
45 ml (3 level tbsp) seasoned flour
50 g (2 oz) butter or 60 ml (4 tbsp) vegetable oil
1 medium onion, skinned and thinly sliced
225 g (8 oz) mushrooms, wiped and sliced
salt and pepper
300 ml (10 fl oz) soured cream

1. Coat the steak strips with the seasoned flour,
then fry in half the butter or oil for about
5-7 minutes, until golden brown.
2. Cook the onion and mushrooms in another
pan in the remaining butter or oil for 3-4 minutes; season to taste and add to the beef.
3. Stir the soured cream into the meat mixture
and warm through gently. Serve with boiled or
buttered noodles.
SERVES 4

STEAK AND KIDNEY PUDDING

*550 g (1¼ lb) piece stewing steak, trimmed and cut into
    1 cm (½ inch) cubes*
225 g (8 oz) ox kidney, cut into small even-sized cubes
1 medium onion, skinned and finely chopped
30 ml (2 tbsp) chopped fresh parsley
45 ml (3 level tbsp) flour
grated rind of 1 lemon
salt and pepper
275 g (10 oz) self raising flour
150 g (5 oz) shredded suet
butter or margarine for greasing
parsley sprig, to garnish

1. Place the beef and kidney in a bowl with the
onion and the chopped parsley. Sprinkle in the
plain flour and lemon rind and season liberally.
Stir well.
2. Mix together the self raising flour, suet and a
good pinch of salt. Stir in about 200 ml (7 fl oz)
water, until a soft dough is formed. Knead
lightly, then on a lightly floured surface, roll out
to a 35 cm (14 inch) round. Cut out one-quarter
of the dough in a fan shape to within 2.5 cm
(1 inch) of the centre; set aside for the lid.
3. Lightly grease a 1.7 litre (3 pint) pudding
basin. Dust the top surface of the pastry with
flour and fold the dough in half, then in half
again. Lift the dough into the basin, unfold,
press into the base and up the sides, taking care
to seal the join well. The pastry should overlap
the basin top by about 2.5 cm (1 inch).
4. Spoon the meat mixture into the lined
pudding basin. Spread the meat out evenly.
Add about 120 ml (8 tbsp) water. This should
come about two thirds of the way up the meat
mixture.
5. Roll out the remaining piece of dough to a
round 2.5 cm (1 inch) larger than the top of the

basin. Dampen the exposed edge of the dough
lining the basin. Lift the round of dough on top
of the filling and push the pastry edges together
to seal. Trim around the top of the basin to
neaten. Roll the sealed edges inwards around
the top of the basin.
6. Cut a piece of greaseproof paper and a piece
of foil large enough to cover the basin. Place
them together and pleat across the middle.
Lightly butter the greaseproof side and put them
over the pudding, greaseproof side down. Tie
securely on to the basin, running the string just
under the lip. Make a string handle across the
basin top.
7. Bring a large pan of water to the boil. Fit a
steamer over the pan and put the pudding
inside. Cover with lid. Steam for about 5 hours.
Top up with boiling water as necessary and do
not allow the water to go off the boil.
8. To serve, uncover and place on a serving
plate. Garnish with parsley.
SERVES 6

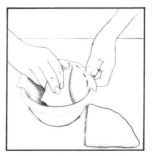

*Cut out one quarter of
the dough. Fold remain-
ing dough in half, then
in half again. Lift into
basin, unfold and seal.*

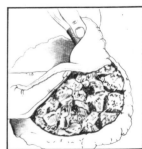

*Spoon the filling into
pastry lined basin. Roll
out reserved quarter of
dough and place on top
of the filling.*

STEAK AND MUSHROOM PIE

700 g (1½ lb) stewing steak, cut into small even pieces
30 ml (2 level tbsp) seasoned flour
1 medium onion, skinned and sliced
450 ml (¾ pint) beef stock
salt and pepper
125 g (4 oz) button mushrooms, wiped
212 g (7½ oz) packet frozen puff pastry, thawed
1 beaten egg, to glaze

1. Coat the meat with seasoned flour, then put in a large saucepan with sliced onion and stock.
2. Bring to the boil, reduce the heat and simmer for 1½-2 hours, until the meat is tender. Season with salt and pepper to taste. Alternatively, cook for 2 hours in a covered casserole in the oven at 170°C (325°F) mark 3.

3. Chill the meat and the mushrooms, then put into a 1.1 litre (2 pint) pie dish with enough of the gravy to half fill it.
4. Roll out the pastry 2.5 cm (1 inch) larger than the top of the dish. Cut off a 1 cm (½ inch) strip from round the edge of the pastry and put this strip round the dampened rim of the dish. Dampen the edges of the pastry with water and put on the top of the pie, without stretching the pastry; trim if necessary and knock up the edges (see page 379). Use the trimmings to make decorations if wished. Brush the top of the pie with beaten egg.
5. Bake in the oven at 220°C (425°F) mark 7 for 20 minutes. Reduce the heat to 180°C (350°F) mark 4 and cook for about a further 20 minutes.
SERVES 4

CORNISH PASTIES

450 g (1 lb) stewing steak, trimmed and cut into small
   pieces
175 g (6 oz) potatoes, peeled and diced
175 g (6 oz) swede, peeled and diced
1 medium onion, skinned and chopped
2.5 ml (½ level tsp) dried mixed herbs
salt and pepper
400 g (14 oz) Shortcrust Pastry made with 400 g
   (14 oz) plain flour (see page 381)
25 g (1 oz) butter or margarine
1 egg, beaten, to glaze

1. Place the meat, potato, swede and onion in a bowl and mix in the herbs and seasoning.
2. Divide the pastry into six equal portions and roll out each piece to a 20 cm (8 inch) circle. Spoon the filling on to one half of each circle

and top with a little butter.
3. Brush the edges of the pastry with water, then fold over and press edges firmly together to seal.
4. Place the pasties on a baking sheet. Brush with the beaten egg and bake at 220°C (425°F) mark 7 for 15 minutes. Reduce the heat to 170°C (325°F) mark 3 and cook the pasties for a further 1 hour. Serve warm or cold.
SERVES 6

Divide pastry into six and roll out each piece to a 20 cm (8 inch) circle. Spoon filling on to half of each circle, top with butter and moisten pastry edges. Fold over and seal.

RISSOLES

225-350 g (8-12 oz) cooked beef, minced
1 small onion, skinned
450 g (1 lb) potatoes, boiled and mashed
dash of Worcestershire sauce
salt and pepper
1 egg, beaten
25 g (1 oz) fresh breadcrumbs
45 ml (3 tbsp) vegetable oil

1. Mince together the meat and onion. Add the potatoes, the Worcestershire sauce and season well. Stir until well blended.
2. Using floured hands, form into eight round patties, coat with the beaten egg and then with breadcrumbs.
3. Heat the oil in a frying pan, add the rissoles and fry on both sides until golden brown. Drain well on absorbent kitchen paper before serving.
SERVES 4

COTTAGE PIE (Shepherd's pie)

900 g (2 lb) potatoes, peeled
45 ml (3 tbsp) milk
knob of butter or margarine
salt and pepper
15 ml (1 tbsp) vegetable oil
1 large onion, skinned and chopped
450 g (1 lb) cold cooked beef or lamb, minced
150 ml (¼ pint) beef stock
30 ml (2 tbsp) chopped fresh parsley or 10 ml
*   (2 level tsp) dried mixed herbs*

1. Cook the potatoes in boiling salted water for 15-20 minutes, then drain and mash with the milk, butter and seasoning.
2. Heat the oil in a frying pan, add the onion and fry for about 5 minutes, then stir in the minced meat with the stock, seasoning and parsley.
3. Spoon the meat mixture into an ovenproof dish and cover the top with the mashed potato. Mark the top with a fork and bake in the oven at 190°C (375°F) mark 5 for 25-30 minutes, until the surface is crisp and browned.
SERVES 4

VARIATION
Use 450 g (1 lb) fresh minced beef in place of the cooked meat, add it to the softened onion and cook until well browned. Add 30 ml (2 level tbsp) flour and cook for 2 minutes, then add 300 ml (½ pint) beef stock. Bring to the boil and simmer for 30 minutes. Put the meat in an ovenproof dish and proceed as above.

BEEFBURGERS

450 g (1 lb) lean beef, eg chuck, shoulder or rump
*   steak, minced*
½ a small onion, skinned and grated (optional)
salt and pepper
melted butter or oil for coating or a little fat for shallow
*   frying*

1. Mix the minced beef well with the onion, if using, and a generous amount of salt and pepper. Shape lightly into 4-8 round flat patties.
2. To cook, brush sparingly with melted butter or oil and grill for 4-6 minutes for small burgers and 8-10 minutes for larger ones, turning once, or fry in a little fat in a frying pan, turning them once and allowing the same amount of time.
SERVES 4

NOTE: Burgers can be served rare or well done, according to personal preference.

VARIATIONS
Traditionally, beefburgers contain no other ingredients, but they can be varied by adding any of the following to the basic mixture:
- 50-125 g (2-4 oz) grated cheese
- 15 ml (1 tbsp) sweet pickle
- 5-10 ml (1-2 level tsp) prepared mustard
- 5 ml (1 level tsp) dried mixed herbs

CHILLI CON CARNE

225 g (8 oz) dried red kidney beans, soaked in cold
*   water overnight*
15 ml (1 tbsp) vegetable oil
2 medium onions, skinned and chopped
700 g (1½ lb) minced beef
1 garlic clove, skinned and crushed
salt and pepper
2.5 ml (½ level tsp) hot chilli powder or 30-45 ml
*   (2-3 level tbsp) chilli seasoning*
15 ml (1 level tbsp) flour
30 ml (2 level tbsp) tomato purée
793 g (28 oz) can tomatoes

1. Drain the beans, rinse, then put into a large saucepan with enough water to cover. Bring to the boil, boil rapidly for 10 minutes, then reduce the heat and simmer gently for about 35 minutes, until tender. Drain.
2. Heat the oil in a large saucepan, add the onions and fry until softened, then add the mince and cook until browned.
3. Add the garlic, salt, pepper and chilli powder.
4. Sprinkle in the flour and stir well, then add the tomato purée and tomatoes with their juice. Bring to the boil and add the drained beans.
5. Simmer for 30 minutes, stirring occasionally.
SERVES 6

CHILLI BEEF WITH NOODLES

450 g (1 lb) rump steak
225 g (8 oz) red pepper, halved and seeded
225 g (8 oz) broccoli
30 ml (2 tbsp) oil
1 medium onion, skinned and roughly chopped
2.5 ml (½ level tsp) chilli powder or few drops of
    Tabasco sauce
10 ml (2 level tsp) dried oregano or dried mixed herbs
50 g (2 oz) dried tagliarini (thin pasta noodles)
30 ml (2 tbsp) sherry or medium white wine
300 ml (½ pint) beef stock
5 ml (1 tbsp) soy sauce
pepper

1. Trim the steak of any excess fat. Cut into
bite-sized pieces. Cut the pepper into similar-
sized pieces. Thinly slice the broccoli stalks, and
divide the remainder into small florets.
2. Heat the oil in a large sauté pan and brown
the beef well on all sides for about 2-3 minutes.
Remove with a slotted spoon. Add the
vegetables, chilli powder and oregano. Sauté,
stirring, for 1-2 minutes.
3. Mix in the tagliarini, sherry, stock and soy
sauce. Cover and simmer for 5 minutes or until
the noodles and broccoli are tender.
4. Return the beef to the pan. Bring to the boil
and simmer for 1 minute to heat through. Adjust
seasoning, adding pepper as necessary.
SERVES 4

Chilli Beef with Noodles

MEAT BALLS IN TOMATO SAUCE

150 g (5 oz) crustless stale white bread
150 ml (¼ pint) milk
15 g (½ oz) butter or margarine
20 ml (4 level tsp) flour
200 ml (7 fl oz) beef stock
397 g (14 oz) can tomatoes, sieved
5 ml (1 level tsp) sugar (optional)
2.5 ml (½ level tsp) dried thyme
salt and pepper
1 large onion, skinned and finely chopped
450 g (1 lb) minced beef
5 ml (1 level tsp) paprika
45 ml (3 tbsp) vegetable oil

1. Crumble the white bread into a bowl, pour
over the milk and leave to soak for 30 minutes.
2. Melt the butter in a large saucepan, stir in the
flour and cook gently for 1 minute, stirring.
Remove from the heat and gradually stir in the
stock. Return to the heat, bring to the boil and
continue to cook, stirring, until the sauce
thickens. Add the tomatoes, sugar, if using, and
thyme. Season well and simmer, covered, for
30 minutes.
3. Meanwhile, put the onion and the mince in a
bowl and add the soaked bread with any remaining milk, the paprika and seasoning. Using
floured hands shape the mixture into 18 balls.
4. Heat the oil in a frying pan and fry the meat
balls a few at a time until browned all over.
5. Place the meat balls in a single layer in a
shallow ovenproof dish and pour over the sauce.
Cover and bake at 180°C (350°F) mark 4 for
about 30 minutes.
SERVES 6

VEAL

Veal comes from a young animal so it is naturally a very lean, tender meat. The young calf produces a fine-textured, pale pink, soft meat. The palest veal comes from calves which have been reared on milk rather than grass. The fat – of which there is very little – should be firm and pinkish or creamy white. Veal bones make excellent jellied stock or gravy when simmered – they impart a special flavour to veal stews and fricassées.

CUTS AND COOKING METHODS

LEG is a prime cut, used mainly for escalopes (also known as *schnitzels*) for frying. Occasionally sold as small joints for roasting.

FILLET is usually the most expensive cut and is generally sold in a piece for roasting. It can also be cut in thin slices, which are beaten and fried. It is also sold as medallions.

KNUCKLE is usually sold as osso buco, already sawn into 5 cm (2 inch) pieces, for stewing.

LOIN is usually sold as cutlets (with rib in) and chops. It can be boned and sold as entrecôte steak. Otherwise rolled for roasting.

SHOULDER is usually boned and rolled into oyster and shoulder roasting joints. The oyster cut is slightly leaner than the shoulder.

BEST END OF NECK is a good value cut. It can be chined and roasted on the bone, or boned, stuffed and rolled for roasting, or used for braising and stewing. Cutlets can be cut if the 'eye' muscle is sufficiently large.

BREAST is usually the least expensive cut. It is divided into breast and flank joints, boned and rolled and sometimes ready stuffed for roasting.

PIE OR DICED VEAL consists of trimmings and small pieces of shoulder, breast, neck or knuckle, sold ready cut up. It needs long slow cooking.

MINCED VEAL is becoming increasingly available. It is ideal for pasta sauces and stuffings.

ROASTING

For general instructions, refer to page 94.

VEAL CHOPS WITH SPINACH PURÉE

6 veal chops, weighing about 175 g (6 oz) each, trimmed
finely grated rind of 2 lemons
90 ml (6 tbsp) lemon juice
150 ml (¼ pint) dry vermouth
1 large garlic clove, skinned and crushed
salt and pepper
225 g (8 oz) fresh spinach, trimmed
50 g (2 oz) butter or margarine
2.5 ml (½ level tsp) grated nutmeg
45 ml (3 tbsp) vegetable oil
1 egg, hard-boiled and finely chopped
bunch of spring onions, trimmed and shredded

1. Place the chops in a large shallow dish. Whisk together the lemon rind and juice, vermouth, garlic and seasoning and pour over the chops. Cover and marinate in a cool place overnight.
2. Wash the spinach well in several changes of cold water. Put in a saucepan with just the water that clings to the leaves, cover and cook for 3-4 minutes. Drain well in a colander, pressing the spinach with the back of a wooden spoon to

extract as much liquid as possible. Finely chop.
3. Heat 25 g (1 oz) butter in a pan and sauté the spinach with the nutmeg for 1-2 minutes to dry off any excess moisture. Transfer to a bowl. Cool and cover.
4. Remove chops from marinade, drain and pat dry with absorbent kitchen paper. Heat oil with the remaining butter in a large pan until foaming. Brown the chops well on both sides, one or two at a time. Place in a single layer in one or two shallow ovenproof dishes.
5. Pour the marinade into the pan. Bring to the boil, stirring any sediment from the base. Strain over the chops. Cover tightly and cook in the oven at 180°C (350°F) mark 4 for about 50 minutes, or until chops are tender.
6. Transfer the chops to a warmed serving dish and keep warm. Purée the spinach mixture with the reserved pan juices in a blender or food processor until smooth. Pour into a small saucepan and simmer gently for 5-10 minutes, until hot.
7. Garnish the chops with the chopped egg and spring onion. Serve the purée separately.
SERVES 6

ESCALOPES FINES HERBES

4 veal escalopes, weighing about 450 g (1 lb)
60 ml (4 level tbsp) seasoned flour
50 g (2 oz) butter or margarine
10 ml (2 level tsp) tomato purée
60 ml (4 tbsp) sherry
100 ml (4 fl oz) red wine
50 g (2 oz) mushrooms, sliced
2.5 ml (½ level tsp) dried mixed herbs
60 ml (4 tbsp) single cream
salt and pepper
225 g (8 oz) tomatoes, skinned and chopped
50 g (2 oz) mature Cheddar cheese, grated

1. Flatten each escalope between two sheets of damp greaseproof paper, then coat in seasoned flour.
2. Melt 25 g (1 oz) of the butter in a frying pan and fry the escalopes gently for 3-5 minutes on each side, then remove and keep warm.
3. Add the remaining flour to the frying pan, stir in the tomato purée, sherry and wine and bring the mixture slowly to the boil. Add the mushrooms, herbs and the cream. Season and cook very gently for about 5 minutes, without boiling.
4. Heat the remaining butter in a pan, add the tomatoes and heat through. Pour the tomato mixture into a shallow ovenproof dish, arrange the meat on top, pour over the sauce, sprinkle with the cheese and brown under the grill.
SERVES 4

WIENER SCHNITZEL (Fried Veal Escalopes)

4 veal escalopes, weighing about 450 g (1 lb)
salt and pepper
1 egg, beaten
150 g (5 oz) fresh breadcrumbs
75 g (3 oz) butter or margarine
30 ml (2 tbsp) vegetable oil
8 anchovy fillets, drained and halved (optional)
1 egg, hard-boiled and the yolk and white chopped separately (optional)
lemon slices and capers, to garnish

1. Flatten each escalope thinly between two sheets of damp greaseproof paper.
2. Season the meat, then coat in beaten egg and breadcrumbs, pressing the crumbs on well.
3. Heat the butter and oil in a large frying pan and fry the escalopes, two at a time, for 3-5 minutes each side, until golden. Drain on absorbent kitchen paper and keep warm whilst cooking the remaining escalopes.
4. Serve garnished with the anchovy fillets, egg, if using, the lemon slices and capers.
SERVES 4

VEAL ESCALOPES WITH HAM AND MARSALA (Saltimbocca alla Romana)

8 veal escalopes, weighing about 900 g (2 lb)
15-30 ml (1-2 tbsp) lemon juice
pepper
8 fresh sage or basil leaves or sprigs of marjoram
8 thin slices of prosciutto (Parma ham)
50 g (2 oz) butter or margarine
15 ml (1 tbsp) vegetable oil
30 ml (2 tbsp) Marsala
fried croûtons, to garnish

1. Flatten escalopes between two sheets of greaseproof paper.
2. Season each escalope with lemon juice and pepper. Place a sage, basil or marjoram sprig in the centre and cover with a slice of prosciutto Roll up and secure with a cocktail stick.

3. Heat the butter and oil in a frying pan, add the veal rolls and fry gently until golden brown. Stir in the Marsala, bring to simmering point, then cover the pan and simmer gently for about 10 minutes. Serve with the juices poured over and surround with croûtons.
SERVES 8

Roll the escalopes.

VEAL AND HAM PIE

450 g (1 lb) minced veal
125 g (4 oz) boiled ham, minced
30 ml (2 tbsp) chopped fresh parsley
2.5 ml (½ level tsp) ground mace
1.25 ml (¼ level tsp) ground bay leaves
finely grated rind of 1 lemon
2 medium onions, skinned and finely chopped
salt and pepper
125 g (4 oz) lard, plus extra for greasing tin
350 g (12 oz) plain wholemeal flour
1 egg yolk
3 eggs, hard-boiled and shelled
10 ml (2 level tsp) aspic jelly powder

Veal and Ham Pie

1. Grease a 1.4 litre (2½ pint) loaf tin and line the base with greased greaseproof paper.
2. Put the first 7 ingredients in a bowl with 5 ml (1 level tsp) salt and 1.25 ml (¼ level tsp) pepper. Mix well to combine.
3. Put the lard and 200 ml (7 fl oz) water in a saucepan and gently heat until the lard has melted. Bring to the boil, remove from the heat and tip in the flour with 2.5 ml (½ level tsp) salt. Beat well to form a soft dough.
4. Beat the egg yolk into the dough. Cover with a damp tea towel and rest in a warm place for 20 minutes, until the dough is elastic and easy to work. Do not allow the dough to cool.
5. Pat two-thirds of the pastry into the base and sides of the prepared tin, making sure it is evenly distributed. Press in half of the meat mixture and arrange the eggs down the centre. Fill with the remaining meat mixture.
6. Roll out the remaining pastry for the lid.

Cover the pie with the pastry and seal the edges. Use the pastry trimmings to decorate the top, then make a large hole in the centre of the pie.
7. Bake at 180°C (350°F) mark 4 for 1½ hours. If necessary, cover the pastry with foil towards the end of cooking to prevent overbrowning. Leave to cool for 3-4 hours.
8. Make up the aspic jelly as directed on the packet to 300 ml (½ pint) with water. Cool for about 10 minutes.
9. Pour the liquid aspic through the hole in the top of the pie. Chill the pie for about 1 hour. Leave to stand at room temperature for about 1 hour before removing from the tin.
SERVES 8-10

VEAL GOULASH

50 g (2 oz) butter or margarine
1.4 kg (3 lb) stewing veal or braising steak, cut into
    4 cm (1½ inch) pieces
700 g (1½ lb) onions, skinned and thinly sliced
450 g (1 lb) carrots, peeled and thinly sliced
45-60 ml (3-4 level tbsp) paprika
30 ml (2 level tbsp) flour
900 ml (1½ pints) veal or chicken stock
60 ml (4 tbsp) dry white wine
salt and pepper
150 ml (5 fl oz) soured cream

1. Melt the butter in a frying pan and fry the veal, a little at a time, until browned. Remove from the pan with a slotted spoon and place in an ovenproof dish.
2. Fry the onions and carrots in the fat remaining in the pan for about 5 minutes until lightly browned. Add the paprika and flour and fry for 2 minutes. Gradually stir in the stock, wine and seasoning. Bring to the boil; pour over the veal.
3. Cover tightly and cook in the oven at 150°C (300°F) mark 2 for 2¾ hours. Pour the soured cream over the goulash to serve.
SERVES 8

Veal Escalopes in Mushroom Sauce

VEAL ESCALOPES IN MUSHROOM SAUCE

4 veal escalopes, about 175 g (6 oz) each
2 slices cooked ham, halved
50 g (2 oz) butter
1 celery stick, trimmed and chopped
1 eating apple, peeled and chopped
25 g (1 oz) Cheddar cheese, grated
1 small onion, skinned and chopped
125 g (4 oz) button mushrooms, sliced
25 g (1 oz) plain flour
300 ml (½ pint) fresh milk
salt and pepper
30 ml (2 tbsp) fromage frais
celery leaves, to garnish

1. Put each escalope between two sheets of greaseproof paper and beat until thin with a meat mallet or rolling pin.
2. Place a ham slice on each escalope.
3. Melt 15 g (½ oz) of the butter in a large frying pan and lightly fry the celery and apple for 3-4 minutes. Stir in the cheese.
4. Place some of the stuffing on each escalope and roll up, securing with wooden cocktail sticks, fine string or strong cotton.
5. Melt the remaining butter in the pan. Add the veal rolls, brown on all sides and cook for 10 minutes. Remove from the pan, place on a warmed serving plate and keep hot.
6. Add the onion and mushrooms to the pan and cook for about 5 minutes, until softened. Stir in the flour and cook for 2 minutes, then gradually add the milk, stirring continuously, until the sauce thickens, boils and is smooth. Simmer for 1-2 minutes. Season to taste.
7. Stir in the fromage frais. Pour the sauce over the escalopes and garnish with celery leaves. Serve at once.
SERVES 4

BLANQUETTE DE VEAU

700 g (1½ lb) pie veal, trimmed and cubed
2 medium onions, skinned and chopped
2 medium carrots, peeled and chopped
squeeze of lemon juice
bouquet garni
salt and pepper
25 g (1 oz) butter or margarine
45 ml (3 level tbsp) flour
1 egg yolk
30-45 ml (2-3 tbsp) single cream
4-6 bacon rolls, cooked
chopped fresh parsley, to garnish

1. Put the meat, onions, carrots, lemon juice, bouquet garni and seasoning into a large saucepan with enough water to cover. Cover and simmer gently for about 1 hour, until the meat is tender.
2. Strain off the cooking liquid, reserving 600 ml (1 pint) and keep the meat and vegetables warm.
3. Melt the butter in a pan, stir in the flour and cook gently for 1 minute, stirring. Remove from the heat and gradually stir in the reserved liquid. Return to the heat, bring to the boil slowly and cook, stirring, until the sauce thickens.
4. Adjust the seasoning, remove from the heat and when slightly cooled stir in the egg yolk and cream. Add the meat, vegetables and bacon rolls and reheat without boiling for 5 minutes. Serve garnished with parsley.
SERVES 4-6

OSSO BUCO

50 g (2 oz) butter or margarine
15 ml (1 tbsp) olive oil
1 medium onion, skinned and finely chopped
4 large or 8 small ossi buchi (veal shin, hind cut), weighing about 1.75 kg (3½ lb) sawn into 5 cm (2 inch) lengths
45 ml (3 tbsp) seasoned flour
300 ml (½ pint) dry white wine
300 ml (½ pint) veal or chicken stock
finely grated rind of 1 lemon
1 garlic clove, skinned and finely chopped
45 ml (3 tbsp) chopped fresh parsley
Risotto alla Milanese, to serve (see page 311)

1. Melt the butter with the oil in a flameproof casserole, add the onion and fry gently for 5 minutes, until soft but not coloured.
2. Coat the veal in the flour, add to the casserole and fry for about 10 minutes, until browned.
3. Pour over the wine and boil rapidly for 5 minutes, then add the stock.
4. Cover pan tightly and simmer for 1½-2 hours, basting and turning the meat occasionally.
5. Transfer the meat to a warmed serving dish, cover and keep warm. If necessary, reduce the sauce by boiling, then pour over the meat.
6. Mix the lemon rind, garlic and parsley and sprinkle over the dish. Serve with the risotto.
SERVES 4

VITELLO TONNATO (Veal in Tuna Fish Sauce)

700 g (1½ lb) leg of veal, boned, with bone reserved
1 small carrot, peeled and sliced
1 medium onion, skinned and quartered
1 celery stick, trimmed and chopped
4 black peppercorns
salt and pepper
99 g (3½ oz) can tuna in oil, drained
4 anchovy fillets, drained
2 egg yolks
15 ml (1 tbsp) lemon juice
150 ml (¼ pint) olive oil
capers, black olives and lemon slices, to garnish

1. Tie the meat into a neat roll and put into a saucepan with the bone, carrot, onion, celery, peppercorns, 5 ml (1 level tsp) salt and 300 ml (½ pint) water. Bring to the boil.
2. Cover and simmer for about 1 hour, or until tender. Remove the meat and cool.
3. Meanwhile, mash together the tuna and anchovies with a fork or in a blender or food processor. Stir in the egg yolks, pepper and lemon juice. Add the oil, a little at a time, until the sauce resembles thin cream. Season.
4. Cut the meat into thin slices, arrange in a shallow dish and coat completely with the sauce. Cover and leave overnight.
5. Garnish with capers, olives and lemon.
SERVES 4-6

L AMB

Lamb is a particularly tender meat and all the joints can be roasted. This is because lambs
are slaughtered before their connective tissues become tough, so the tissues dissolve
easily in the meat's natural moisture during cooking. Cuts such as chops and cutlets from the
neck, are also suitable for grilling or frying. Other neck cuts are ideal for casseroles, stews
and pies. The fat in lamb should be crisp and white with the lean meat fine-grained, firm
and pinky brown. There is usually very little gristle. Freshly cut surfaces should look
slightly moist and the bones should be pinkish-white.

CUTS AND METHODS OF COOKING

SCRAG AND MIDDLE NECK are usually sold as neck cuts on the bone and used for stewing or braising. These are the traditional cuts for Irish stew and Lancashire hot pot. The main 'eye' of lean meat from the middle neck is sold as neck fillet. This tender cut is ideal for grilling and frying.

SHOULDER is sold whole or halved into blade and knuckle, with bone in or boned and rolled, for roasting or braising. Chops and steaks can also be cut from the shoulder or forequarter, these are ideal for grilling or braising.

BEST END OF NECK is sold as individual cutlets and as a whole roasting joint with a row of 6 or 7 rib bones, called rack of lamb. The butcher will chine the backbone, to make carving easier. Two best end necks joined together are used for speciality joints: Crown roast and Guard of honour. Both of these can be stuffed before roasting.

Cutlets are sold with one rib bone to each, for grilling or frying. When boned and rolled, they are called *noisettes*.

LOIN: The whole loin consists of both chump and loin chops. It can be roasted in the piece, or boned, stuffed and rolled. Loin is more often divided into loin end and chump end, and cut into chops. Chump chops are recognisable by the small round bone in the centre. Loin chops are recognisable by the small T bone. These chops are suitable for grilling, frying and barbecuing.

SADDLE OF LAMB is a large roasting joint for special occasions, comprising the whole loin from both sides of the animal, in one piece.

Double loin chops, also known as Barnsley chops, are cut from a saddle of lamb.

LEG is an excellent roasting joint either on the bone, or boned and rolled. The leg is often divided into fillet end and shank end. Lean leg steaks are suitable for grilling, frying and barbecuing.

BREAST is usually sold boned and rolled. It is also available ready stuffed. It is the most ecomonical cut for roasting or braising. Riblets are short ribs cut from the breast. These are a suitable alternative to pork spare ribs for barbecuing, pan roasting etc.

CUBED LAMB is a convenient way to purchase lamb for casseroles and kebabs. It is usually cut from the shoulder, leg or chump.

MINCED LAMB is becoming more widely available. It is ideal for moussaka, meatballs, burgers and kebabs.

ROASTING LAMB

Leg, shoulder, best end of neck and breast are suitable joints. Refer to general instructions for roasting meat (see page 94).

Traditional accompaniments are mint sauce or jelly, redcurrant jelly and Onion Sauce (see page 199).

GRILLING AND BARBECUING LAMB

When grilling or barbecuing, trim away excess fat and preheat grill or barbecue. Brush with oil and grill under a medium heat for 6-8 minutes each side, depending on thickness.

FRYING LAMB

Trim excess fat from chops or steaks. Heat 15 ml (1 tbsp) oil in a frying pan and fry lamb for 6-8 minutes each side depending on thickness.

CROWN ROAST OF LAMB

2 best end necks of lamb, chined, each with 6 cutlets
25 g (1 oz) butter or margarine
1 medium onion, skinned and chopped
3 celery sticks, trimmed and chopped
1 eating apple, peeled, cored and chopped
40 g (1½ oz) dried apricots, soaked overnight
125 g (4 oz) fresh breadcrumbs
30 ml (2 tbsp) chopped fresh parsley
finely grated rind of ½ a lemon
15 ml (1 tbsp) lemon juice
1 egg
salt and pepper
50 g (2 oz) lard or 30 ml (2 tbsp) vegetable oil
30 ml (2 level tbsp) flour
450 ml (¾ pint) lamb stock

1. Trim each cutlet bone to a depth of 2.5 cm (1 inch) and trim off excess fat. Bend the joints around, fat side inwards, and sew together using strong cotton or fine string to form a crown. Cover the exposed bones with foil.
2. Melt the butter in a saucepan and cook the onion, celery and apple until brown. Drain, dry and chop the apricots and stir into the pan with the breadcrumbs, parsley, lemon rind and juice, egg and seasoning. Allow to cool, then fill the centre of the joint with the stuffing and weigh.
3. Place the joint in a small roasting tin with the lard or oil. Roast at 180°C (350°F) mark 4 for 25 minutes per 450 g (1 lb) plus 25 minutes. Baste occasionally and cover with foil if necessary.
4. Transfer the crown roast to a warmed serving dish and keep warm. Drain off all but 30 ml (2 tbsp) of the fat in the roasting tin, add the flour and blend well. Cook for 2-3 minutes, stirring continuously. Add the stock and boil for 2-3 minutes. Season and serve hot with the joint.
SERVES 6

VARIATION
GUARD OF HONOUR
This is also prepared from two best ends of neck. Trim as above but interlace the bones, fat side outwards, to form an arch. Fill the cavity with the stuffing (as above) and fasten together with strong thread or fine string.

Crown Roast of Lamb

1. Bend joints around, fat side inwards.

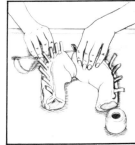

2. Sew joints together using strong cotton or fine kitchen string to form a crown.

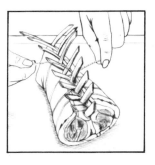

3. For Guard of Honour, interlace the bones, fat side outwards, to form an arch.

ROLLED STUFFED BREASTS OF LAMB

25 g (1 oz) butter or margarine
1 medium onion, skinned and chopped
411 g (14½ oz) can apricot halves in natural juice
175 g (6 oz) fresh breadcrumbs
45 ml (3 tbsp) chopped fresh parsley
25 g (1 oz) chopped mixed nuts
finely grated rind of ½ a lemon
30 ml (2 tbsp) lemon juice
salt and pepper
1 egg, beaten
2 large breasts of lamb, boned and trimmed
45 ml (3 tbsp) vegetable oil

1. Melt the butter in a saucepan and lightly brown the onion. Drain and roughly chop three-quarters of the apricots, reserving the rest for garnishing.
2. Mix together the onion, chopped apricots, breadcrumbs, parsley and nuts and stir in the lemon rind and juice, seasoning and egg.
3. Lay the breasts of lamb fat side down on a work surface, overlapping slightly, and spread the stuffing evenly over them. Roll up the lamb breasts loosely and tie in several places with string to hold their shape. Weigh the joints.
4. Heat the oil in a small roasting tin and roast the joint at 180°C (350°F) mark 4 for 25 minutes per 450 g (1 lb) plus 25 minutes, basting occasionally. Serve garnished with the reserved apricots.

Roll up the breasts loosely. SERVES 4

LAMB CUTLETS EN CROÛTE

25 g (1 oz) butter or margarine
1 medium onion, skinned and chopped
25 g (1 oz) fresh breadcrumbs
1 egg, beaten
30 ml (2 tbsp) chopped fresh mint
salt and pepper
squeeze of lemon juice
12 lamb cutlets, trimmed
two 368 g (13 oz) packets frozen puff pastry, thawed
beaten egg, to glaze
fresh mint sprig, to garnish

1. To make the stuffing, melt the butter in a pan and fry the onion for about 5 minutes, until soft but not brown. Remove from the heat. Stir in the breadcrumbs and bind with the egg. Mix in the mint, seasoning and lemon juice.
2. Grill or fry the cutlets for 3 minutes on each side until browned, but still pink inside. Leave to cool.
3. Thinly roll out each piece of pastry on a lightly floured surface and cut six squares.
4. Place each of the lamb cutlets on a square of pastry so that the bone extends over the edge of the pastry.
5. Press even amounts of stuffing on the eye of each cutlet. Dampen the pastry edges, wrap the pastry over the cutlets and seal.
6. Place on a dampened baking sheet, folded sides underneath. Use any pastry trimmings to decorate the cutlets. Brush with a little beaten egg.
7. Bake in the oven at 220°C (425°F) mark 7 for 15-20 minutes, then reduce the temperature to 190°C (375°F) mark 5 and bake for a further 15 minutes, until the pastry is golden. Serve hot, garnished with a sprig of fresh mint.

SERVES 6

LAMB KORMA

75 g (3 oz) ghee or butter
1 large onion, skinned and thinly sliced
1-2 garlic cloves, skinned and crushed
2.5 cm (1 inch) piece fresh root ginger, peeled and very
*   finely chopped*
15 ml (1 level tbsp) coriander seeds
10 ml (2 level tsp) whole cloves
10 ml (2 level tsp) black peppercorns
6 green cardamoms
900 g-1.1 kg (2-2½ lb) boneless lamb fillet, trimmed
*   and cut into cubes*
10 ml (2 level tsp) ground turmeric
finely grated rind and juice of 1 lime or lemon
50 g (2 oz) ground almonds
salt
200 ml (7 fl oz) double cream
25-50 g (1-2 oz) flaked blanched almonds
grated lemon or lime rind, to garnish

1. Heat the ghee in a heavy-based saucepan or flameproof casserole, add the onion, garlic and ginger and fry very gently, stirring frequently, for about 10 minutes until soft and lightly coloured.
2. Meanwhile, finely grind the coriander seeds, cloves, peppercorns and cardamoms in a small electric mill or with a pestle and mortar. Add to the pan and stir well to mix. Fry for 1-2 minutes, stirring all the time.
3. Increase the heat and add the lamb to the casserole a few pieces at a time. Fry until well browned on all sides before adding the next batch. Stir in the turmeric, lime or lemon juice and ground almonds, then add salt to taste. Cover the pan and simmer gently for 45 minutes to 1 hour until the lamb is tender.
4. Slowly stir the cream into the casserole, then heat through. Taste and adjust seasoning, then turn into a warmed serving dish. Sprinkle with the flaked almonds and the grated lime or lemon rind and serve immediately.
SERVES 4-6

KASHMIRI-STYLE LAMB

1.4 kg (3 lb) leg of lamb
15 ml (1 level tbsp) poppy seeds
45 ml (3 level tbsp) grated fresh or desiccated coconut
2 medium onions, skinned and coarsely chopped
5 cm (2 inch) piece fresh root ginger, peeled and
*   coarsely chopped*
25 g (1 oz) blanched almonds, chopped
1 cinnamon stick, 5 cm (2 inch) long
6 green cardamoms
3 black cardamoms, ground
4 cloves
small piece of mace
2.5 ml (½ level tsp) grated nutmeg
7.5 ml (1½ level tsp) mild chilli powder
5 ml (1 level tsp) salt
150 ml (5 fl oz) natural yogurt
75g (3 oz) ghee or butter, melted
4 bay leaves, crushed
30 ml (2 level tbsp) ground aniseed

1. Remove all traces of fat and the white membrane from the meat. Prick the meat thoroughly with a sharp knife so that the fibres are completely broken up. It should virtually be falling off the bone. Place in a deep baking dish or a roasting tin.
2. Soak the poppy seeds and the coconut in a little warm water for 10 minutes. Drain and put in a blender or food processor with the next 11 ingredients and blend to a smooth paste.
3. Pour the paste over the meat and spread all over coating well. Again, prick the meat with a knife all over to help the mixture to penetrate.
4. Mix together the yogurt and remaining ingredients and spread it over the lamb. Cook in the oven at 170°C (325°F) mark 3 for 2¼-2½ hours, basting frequently. Turn the leg over once, halfway during cooking time. Remove from the oven and transfer to a warmed serving dish. Carve and serve hot.
SERVES 6

SPINACH STUFFED SHOULDER OF LAMB

2 medium onions, skinned and finely chopped
15 ml (1 tbsp) vegetable oil
227 g (8 oz) packet frozen chopped spinach, thawed
   and drained
2-3 garlic cloves, skinned and thinly sliced
2.5 ml (½ level tsp) grated nutmeg
salt and pepper
1.4 kg (3 lb) shoulder of lamb, boned
10 ml (2 level tsp) flour
300 ml (½ pint) lamb stock
15 ml (1 level tbsp) redcurrant jelly
dash of gravy browning

1. Soften the onion in the oil in a saucepan, then add the spinach, 1 garlic clove, nutmeg and seasoning, adding plenty of pepper. Cool.
2. Fill the bone cavity of the lamb with the spinach mixture and sew up using cotton or fine string. Make small cuts in the fat and insert the remaining garlic slices into them.
3. Place the lamb on a rack in a roasting tin. Roast in the oven at 180°C (350°F) mark 4 for about 2¼ hours, basting several times during cooking.
4. Transfer the joint to a shallow serving plate and keep warm. Drain off all but 15 ml (1 tbsp) fat from the roasting tin, stir in the flour and cook for 1-2 minutes, stirring. Add the stock, jelly, seasoning and a dash of gravy browning and boil for 2-3 minutes, stirring. Serve the gravy separately.
SERVES 6

NAVARIN OF LAMB

30 ml (2 tbsp) vegetable oil
1 kg (2¼ lb) best end of neck or shoulder of lamb,
   trimmed and cut into 2.5 cm (1 inch) cubes
5 ml (1 level tsp) sugar
15 ml (1 level tbsp) flour
900 ml (1½ pints) lamb stock
30 ml (2 level tbsp) tomato purée
salt and pepper
bouquet garni
225 g (8 oz) button onions, skinned
4 medium carrots, peeled and sliced
1-2 small turnips, peeled and quartered
8 small, even-sized potatoes, peeled
125 g (4 oz) frozen peas (optional)
chopped fresh parsley, to garnish

1. Heat the oil in a large flameproof casserole. Add the lamb and lightly fry on all sides. Stir in the sugar and heat until it browns slightly, then add the flour, stirring until it browns.
2. Remove from the heat and gradually stir in the stock. Bring to the boil, add the tomato purée, seasoning and bouquet garni, then cover and simmer for about 1 hour.
3. Remove the bouquet garni, add the onions, carrots and turnips and continue cooking for a further 30 minutes. Add the potatoes and continue cooking for about 20 minutes, until tender. Add the peas for the last 10 minutes, if using.
4. Transfer the meat to a warmed serving dish and garnish with the parsley.
SERVES 4

LAMB PAPRIKA

40 g (1½ oz) butter or margarine
8 best end of neck chops, trimmed
2 medium onions, skinned and chopped
450 g (1 lb) tomatoes, skinned, quartered and seeded
15 ml (1 tbsp) chopped fresh parsley
5-10 ml (1-2 level tsp) paprika
salt
150 ml (5 fl oz) soured cream or natural yogurt

1. Melt the butter in a large frying pan and brown the chops on both sides, then remove from the pan. Fry the onions in the fat for about 5 minutes, or until golden brown.
2. Add the tomatoes, parsley, paprika and salt to taste, replace the chops, cover and simmer gently for about 30 minutes, until tender.
3. Stir in the cream, adjust the seasoning and reheat without boiling.
SERVES 4

LAMB ESCALOPES WITH OATMEAL

2 lamb leg steaks, about 550 g (1¼ lb) total weight
    (bone in) and about 2-2.5 cm (¾-1 inch) thick
Dijon mustard
about 150 g (5 oz) medium oatmeal
15 ml (1 level tbsp) dried rubbed sage
salt and pepper
1 egg, beaten
150 ml (5 fl oz) soured cream
15-30 ml (1-2 level tbsp) paprika
oil
25 g (1 oz) butter

1. Trim excess fat off lamb and cut out the
bone. Place the meat between sheets of
greaseproof paper and, using a rolling pin, bat
out until 5 mm (¼ inch) thick. Divide each steak
into 5 pieces.
2. Spread a little mustard over one side of each

piece of lamb. Mix the oatmeal, sage and
seasoning together.
3. Brush the meat with beaten egg and coat with
the oatmeal mixture; cover and chill for about
30 minutes.
4. Mix the soured cream and 15 ml (1 level tbsp)
mustard together in a small bowl. Sprinkle with
a little paprika; cover and chill.
5. Heat a little oil in a frying pan. Mix in the
butter and, when foaming, add about half the
meat. Fry over a moderate heat until browned
and tender, about 3 minutes each side. Drain on
kitchen paper. Keep warm, covered, while frying
the remaining lamb, adding more oil if
necessary.
6. Serve the lamb with the soured cream sauce
and accompanied by a green leaf, orange and
onion salad.
SERVES 4

ROAST LAMB FILLETS WITH GARLIC

450 g (1 lb) lamb neck fillet
2 large garlic cloves, skinned and thinly sliced
20 ml (4 level tsp) fresh chopped rosemary or 5 ml
    (1 level tsp) dried
salt and pepper
8 rashers streaky bacon, rinded
15-30 ml (1-2 tbsp) oil
10 ml (2 level tsp) flour
300 ml (½ pint) lamb stock
10 ml (2 level tsp) Dijon mustard
dash of gravy browning (optional)
lime wedges and herbs, to garnish

1. Trim the lamb fillet and divide into four
pieces. Split horizontally, without cutting right
through, and open out like a book.
2. Sprinkle with the garlic, rosemary and
pepper. Close the fillets.
3. Stretch the bacon rashers with the back of a
blunt-edged knife. Wrap around the fillets,
securing with wooden cocktail sticks.
4. Heat the oil in a small roasting tin. Add the
lamb and then bake at 200°C (400°F) mark 6 for
30-35 minutes or until the lamb is tender.
5. Slice the lamb into 5 mm (¼ inch) thick
pieces, discarding the cocktail sticks. Cover and
keep warm.
6. Pour all but 30 ml (2 tbsp) juice out of the
tin. Stir in the flour and cook until lightly

Roast Lamb Fillets with Garlic

browned. Add the stock, mustard, gravy
browning, if using, and seasoning and let bubble
for a few minutes. Serve garnished with lime
wedges and herbs. Accompany with potatoes
and salad.
SERVES 4

ABOVE: Lamb Escalopes with Oatmeal. BELOW: Lamb Chops with Leeks and Lentils

LAMB CHOPS WITH LEEKS AND LENTILS

4 loin lamb chops, about 450 g (1 lb) total weight and
*   about 2.5 cm (1 inch) thick*
1 small onion, skinned and finely chopped
100 ml (4 fl oz) fresh orange juice
salt and pepper
15 ml (1 tbsp) oil
450 g (1 lb) leeks, trimmed and cut into 1 cm
*   (½ inch) slices*
125 g (4 oz) split red lentils
5 ml (1 level tsp) paprika
300 ml (½ pint) lamb stock
fresh coriander, to garnish

1. Trim the chops of fat; place in a non-metallic dish. Sprinkle the onion over the lamb. Pour over the orange juice and season with pepper. Cover and refrigerate for at least 12 hours, turning once.
2. Lift the chops out of the marinade; pat dry on absorbent kitchen paper. Heat the hot oil in a medium-sized sauté pan and brown the chops on both sides. Drain on kitchen paper.
3. Add the leeks, lentils and paprika to the pan and stir over a moderate heat for 1 minute. Place the chops on the lentils. Pour in the marinade and stock and bring to the boil.
4. Cover and simmer for 20 minutes. Adjust the seasoning. Serve garnished with coriander and accompanied by steamed or boiled potatoes.
SERVES 4

SPICED LAMB WITH WHOLEWHEAT

350 g (12 oz) wholewheat grain, washed and soaked
  in cold water overnight
75 ml (5 tbsp) vegetable oil or ghee
2 medium onions, skinned and finely chopped
2 garlic cloves, skinned and finely chopped
5 cm (2 inch) piece fresh root ginger, peeled and finely
  chopped
5 ml (1 level tsp) black cumin seeds
4 green cardamoms
4 cloves
5-7.5 ml (1-1½ level tsp) mild chilli powder
2.5 ml (½ level tsp) ground turmeric
30 ml (2 tbsp) chopped fresh coriander leaves
15 ml (1 tbsp) chopped fresh mint leaves
700 g (1½ lb) fillet of lamb, cut into 2.5 cm (1 inch)
  pieces
7.5 ml (1½ level tsp) salt
300 ml (10 fl oz) natural yogurt
75 ml (5 tbsp) lemon juice
fresh coriander, to garnish

1. Drain the wheat and place in a saucepan.
Add 1.4 litres (2½ pints) water and boil for about
40 minutes, until tender. Drain.
2. Heat the oil in a large heavy-based saucepan.
Add the onions and fry for about 10 minutes,
stirring, until a deep golden colour. Remove
with a slotted spoon and place in a blender or

food processor. Add the garlic and the ginger
and blend to a smooth paste.
3. Reheat the oil in the pan, add the ground
onion mixture and continue frying for another
few minutes. Then add the cumin seeds,
cardamoms, cloves, chilli powder, turmeric and
the chopped coriander and mint. Fry for a
further 8-10 minutes, stirring frequently, until a
rich golden colour.
4. Add the meat and salt and fry for about
40 minutes, stirring frequently, until the meat is
well browned and nearly tender. Stir in the
yogurt and fry for another 10 minutes, stirring,
until the meat is tender and the yogurt well
blended. Add 300 ml (½ pint) water, stir well
and simmer for another 10 minutes.
5. Add the reserved wheat and the lemon juice
and stir well. Reheat but do not allow to boil.
Garnish with fresh coriander and serve with
chapatis and poppadums.
SERVES 4

CHAPATIS are large unleavened griddle cakes
which can be bought from shops specialising in
Eastern foods, or made at home (see page 462).
POPPADUMS are wafer-thin savoury biscuits that
can be bought dried. To cook, fry one at a time
in a little hot fat until crisp, holding each down
with a spoon during cooking; alternatively heat
for 1-2 minutes under a hot grill.

LANCASHIRE HOT POT

8 middle neck chops, about 900 g (2 lb) total weight,
  trimmed
175 g (6 oz) lamb's kidneys
40 g (1½ oz) lard or dripping or 45 ml (3 tbsp)
  vegetable oil
450 g (1 lb) leeks, trimmed, cut into 1 cm (½ inch)
  slices and washed
2 medium carrots, peeled and thickly sliced
900 g (2 lb) potatoes, peeled and thinly sliced
5 ml (1 level tsp) dried thyme
salt and pepper
600 ml (1 pint) lamb stock

1. Skin, halve and core the kidneys and divide
each half into three or four pieces.
2. Heat the lard in a frying pan and brown the
lamb, a few chops at a time. Lightly brown the
kidneys.
3. In a 3.4 litre (6 pint) ovenproof casserole,
layer the meats, leeks, carrots and three quarters
of the potatoes, sprinkling the thyme and
seasoning between the layers. Pour in the stock
and top with a neat layer of overlapping potato
slices. Brush with the lard remaining in the
frying pan.
4. Cover the casserole and cook in the oven at
170°C (325°F) mark 3 for 2 hours. Uncover,
increase the temperature to 220°C (425°F)
mark 7 and continue cooking for about
30 minutes, until the potatoes are golden
brown and crisp.
SERVES 4

IRISH STEW

8 middle neck chops, about 900 g (2 lb) total weight,
   trimmed
900 g (2 lb) potatoes, peeled and sliced
2 large onions, skinned and sliced
15 ml (1 level tbsp) pearl barley
salt and pepper
chopped fresh parsley, to garnish

1. Place alternate layers of meat and vegetables in a flameproof casserole, sprinkling each layer with a little pearl barley; season and finish with a layer of potatoes.
2. Add sufficient water to half cover. Cover and simmer very slowly for 3 hours. Alternatively, cook the stew in the oven at 180°C (350°F) mark 4 for about 2½ hours. Serve sprinkled with chopped parsley.
SERVES 4

MOUSSAKA

450 g (1 lb) aubergines, sliced
salt and pepper
2 large onions, skinned and sliced
1 garlic clove, skinned and finely chopped
90 ml (6 tbsp) vegetable oil
700 g (1½ lb) minced lamb
15 ml (1 level tbsp) flour
397 g (14 oz) can tomatoes
300 ml (10 fl oz) natural yogurt
2 eggs, beaten
1.25 ml (¼ level tsp) grated nutmeg
25 g (1 oz) grated Parmesan cheese

1. Place the aubergine slices in a colander, sprinkling each layer with salt. Cover and leave for 30 minutes to extract the bitter juices.
2. Meanwhile, fry the onions and garlic in 30 ml (2 tbsp) oil for 5 minutes, until golden. Add the meat and fry for a further 10 minutes, until browned, then add the flour and cook for 1 minute. Add the tomatoes with their juice, season and simmer for 20 minutes.
3. Drain the aubergine slices, rinse and pat dry. Heat the remaining oil in a frying pan and fry the aubergine slices in batches for 4-5 minutes, turning once. Add more oil, if necessary.
4. Arrange a layer of aubergine in the bottom of a large ovenproof dish and spoon over a layer of meat. Continue the layers until all the meat and aubergines are used.
5. Beat the yogurt, eggs, seasoning and nutmeg together and stir in half the Parmesan. Pour over the dish and sprinkle with the remaining cheese. Bake in the oven at 180°C (350°F) mark 4 for about 45 minutes, until golden.
SERVES 4-6

STUFFED VINE LEAVES (Dolmas)

227 g (8 oz) packet vine leaves in brine
15 ml (1 tbsp) olive oil
1 medium onion, skinned and finely chopped
450 g (1 lb) minced lamb
50 g (2 oz) long grain white rice, cooked
30 ml (2 tbsp) chopped fresh mint or 5 ml (1 level tsp)
   dried mint
salt and pepper
450 ml (¾ pint) lamb or chicken stock
natural yogurt, to serve

1. Drain the brine from the vine leaves, put them in a large bowl and pour over boiling water. Rinse well to remove excess salt.
2. Heat the oil in a frying pan, add the onion and cook for 5 minutes, until browned. Remove from the heat and add the lamb, rice, mint and seasoning. Mix well.
3. Spread out three quarters of the vine leaves on a flat surface and spoon a little of the lamb mixture on to each. Fold the leaves over to make small, neat parcels. Arrange some of the remaining vine leaves in a large saucepan.
4. Arrange half the dolmas close together in a single layer in the pan, then cover with more vine leaves. Add another layer of dolmas. Pour over the stock and cover with a small plate. Bring to the boil and simmer for 45 minutes.
5. Lift the dolmas from the cooking liquid and arrange on a warmed serving dish. Serve with natural yogurt.
SERVES 4-6

LAMB KEBABS

45 ml (3 tbsp) olive oil
15 ml (1 tbsp) lemon juice
15 ml (1 tbsp) chopped fresh rosemary
salt and pepper
1 garlic clove, skinned and crushed
700 g (1½ lb) boned leg of lamb, trimmed and cut into
 2.5 cm (1 inch) cubes
8 small tomatoes, halved
16 button mushrooms
bay leaves
4 small onions, quartered
1 sweetcorn cob, boiled and sliced

1. Mix together the olive oil, lemon juice,
rosemary, seasoning and garlic. Add the lamb
and marinate for 2 hours, (or preferably
overnight).
2. Remove with a slotted spoon, reserving the
marinade.
3. Thread eight skewers alternately with meat
cubes, tomatoes, mushrooms, bay leaves, onions
and slices of sweetcorn.
4. Brush with the marinade and cook under a
low grill for 10-15 minutes, turning the kebabs
about three times, until the meat is tender.
Serve with boiled rice.
SERVES 4

Lamb Kebabs

MIDDLE EASTERN MEATBALLS

2 medium aubergines, sliced
salt and pepper
150 ml (¼ pint) vegetable oil
450 g (1 lb) boneless lamb
2 thick slices of white bread, crusts removed
1 small onion, skinned
10 ml (2 level tsp) ground cumin
plain flour, for coating
450 g (1 lb) tomatoes, skinned and chopped
15 ml (1 tbsp) tomato purée
150 ml (¼ pint) lamb or chicken stock
2.5 ml (½ level tsp) ground allspice
vegetable oil for deep-frying

1. Layer the aubergine slices in a colander,
sprinkling each layer with salt. Cover with a
plate, weight down and leave for 30 minutes.
2. Drain the aubergine slices, rinse and dry well.
Heat some of the oil in a large frying pan, and
fry the aubergine slices in batches for 4-5 minutes. Drain on absorbent kitchen paper.

3. Finely mince the lamb with the fried
aubergines, bread and onion, using a food
processor or mincer.
4. In a bowl, mix the minced meat with the
cumin and seasoning to taste. Chill for
30 minutes until firm.
5. Meanwhile put the tomatoes, tomato purée,
allspice and stock in a large flanged casserole.
Season. Bring to the boil and simmer for
30 minutes until thick.
6. With well-floured hands, form the meat
mixture into 30 balls. Chill in the refrigerator
for 30 minutes.
7. Heat the oil for deep-frying and fry the meatballs in batches until golden, about 3 minutes.
Drain and add to the casserole.
8. Bring slowly to boiling point, then cover and
simmer gently for 30 minutes. Shake the
casserole frequently during this time so that the
meatballs become saturated in the sauce. Adjust
the seasoning before serving.
SERVES 6

OXFORD JOHN STEAKS WITH CAPER SAUCE

4 lamb leg steaks, about 175 g (6 oz) each
salt and pepper
25 g (1 oz) butter
5 ml (1 tsp) plain flour
300 ml (½ pint) lamb stock
30 ml (2 tbsp) drained capers
15 ml (1 tbsp) vinegar from the capers

1. Season the lamb steaks to taste. Heat the butter in a frying pan and fry the steaks gently for 10-15 minutes, turning occasionally, until browned on both sides. Remove from the pan with a slotted spoon and transfer to a warmed dish.

2. Stir to loosen any sediment at the bottom of the pan, then stir in the flour and cook for 1-2 minutes. Gradually add the stock, stirring all the time, then cook until the sauce thickens, boils and is smooth. Add the capers and vinegar and simmer for 1-2 minutes.

3. Return the lamb steaks to the pan and simmer for 5 minutes or until the lamb is cooked to your liking. Serve hot.
SERVES 4

VARIATION
LAMB IN REDCURRANT SAUCE
Replace the capers and vinegar with 30ml (2 tbsp) red wine and 15 ml (1 level tbsp) redcurrant jelly.

Oxford John Steaks with Caper Sauce

LAMB AND KIDNEY BEAN CASSEROLE

125 g (4 oz) dried red kidney beans, soaked overnight
15 ml (1 tbsp) vegetable oil
1 large breast of lamb, trimmed and cut into 5 cm
    (2 inch) pieces
450 g (1 lb) leeks, washed, trimmed and cut into 1 cm
    (½ inch) pieces
1 bay leaf
450 ml (¾ pint) lamb or chicken stock
1 garlic clove, skinned and crushed
salt and pepper
125 g (4 oz) garlic sausage, cut into bite-size pieces

1. Drain the kidney beans and place in a large saucepan. Cover with fresh water, bring to the boil and boil for 10 minutes, then reduce the heat and simmer for 30 minutes. Drain.

2. Meanwhile, heat the oil in a flameproof casserole and fry the lamb until browned. Remove from the casserole with a slotted spoon, then brown the leeks in the remaining fat.

3. Return the meat to the casserole and add the drained beans, bay leaf, stock, garlic and seasoning and bring to the boil.

4. Add the garlic sausage to the casserole. Cover tightly and simmer gently for about 1¼ hours.
SERVES 4

PORK

Pork can be bought all the year round. All joints can be roasted and the individual cuts
from them can be grilled or fried. In addition, the forequarter cuts can be used for
casseroles, stews and pies. The lean part of pork should be pale pink, moist
and slightly marbled with fat. There should be a good outer layer of firm,
white fat with a thin, elastic skin.

CUTS AND METHODS OF COOKING

NECK END (SPARE RIB AND BLADE BONE) is a large,
economical roasting joint which is sold bone-in
and boneless. It is particularly good when
boned, stuffed and rolled. This joint is often
divided into blade and spare rib. These two
smaller cuts can also be roasted, braised or
stewed. Spare rib pork makes the best filling for
pies. Spare rib chops are suitable for braising,
grilling, frying and barbecuing.

SHOULDER (HAND AND SPRING) is a large roasting
joint, often divided into the smaller cuts, hand
and shank. As well as being suitable for roasting,
hand and shank can be cubed for casseroles and
stews. Shoulder steaks for grilling and frying are
also available.

BELLY can be sold as a boned and rolled joint,
with excess fat removed or cut into slices, for
grilling, barbecuing and casseroling. Slices are a
popular alternative to traditional belly pork.

SPARE RIBS are from the lower part of the belly
and/or loin. They are sold as single rib bones or
a rack. Chinese spare ribs tend to have less meat
on them than American cut ribs. Spare ribs are
suitable for barbecuing, grilling and roasting.

LEG is usually sold divided into fillet end and the
knuckle shank end. Both cuts are often sold
boned and rolled for roasting. The fillet end
(the top of the leg) is the prime roasting joint. It
is sometimes sliced into steaks for grilling and
frying. Escalopes are very lean slices, cut across
the grain so they are tender. The feet (trotters)
are usually salted and boiled or used to make
brawn.

LOIN is a popular roast on the bone or boned,
stuffed and rolled. It is also cut into loin chops,
large meaty chump chops and boneless steaks,
all of which are excellent for grilling, frying or
roasting. Loin produces good crackling.

TENDERLOIN is a tender, lean cut, found just
underneath the backbone of the loin, in the
same position as beef fillet. It is sometimes
called pork fillet, not to be confused with the
fillet end of the leg. It can be stuffed and rolled
for roasting. Tenderloin is also often sold sliced
as medallions. These are suitable for grilling
and frying.

CUBED PORK is usually cut from the trimmed
shoulder or leg. It is convenient for casseroles
and kebabs.

MINCED OR GROUND PORK is becoming more
widely available and can be used in all mince
dishes.

ROASTING PORK

Loin, fillet, shoulder, leg and neck end are
suitable. Refer to general instructions for
roasting meat (see page 94).

For good crackling, score the rind deeply
and evenly. Brush the cut surface with oil and
rub salt into the scoring. Place the joint, with
the rind uppermost, in a roasting tin. Do not
baste the pork during cooking. Alternatively, the
rind can be removed before cooking, treated in
the same way, and roasted separately until crisp
and golden.

ACCOMPANIMENTS:
Sage and Onion Stuffing (see page 182), and
Apple, Gooseberry or Cranberry Sauce (see
pages 204-6) are traditional accompaniments.
Try baked apples or onions as an alternative.

GRILLING AND BARBECUING PORK

Trim any excess fat from the chops. Large loin
chops often have a thick strip of fat around the
edge. To prevent it curling during cooking, snip
with scissors at 2.5 cm (1 inch) intervals. Brush
the chops with oil and preheat grill or barbecue.
Cook for about 8-10 minutes each side.

FRYING PORK

Trim chops as above. Heat the oil in a large
frying pan and add the chops. Cook for about
20 minutes, turning them frequently.

ROAST PORK TENDERLOIN

3 pork tenderloins, about 900 g (2 lb) total weight
125 g (4 oz) streaky bacon, rinded
150 ml (¼ pint) dry white wine
300 ml (½ pint) chicken stock
10 ml (2 level tsp) arrowroot
FOR THE STUFFING
175 g (6 oz) mushrooms, wiped and roughly chopped
1 medium onion, skinned and finely chopped
50 g (2 oz) butter or margarine
125 g (4 oz) fresh breadcrumbs
15 ml (1 tbsp) chopped fresh sage or 5 ml (1 level tsp)
dried rubbed sage
salt and pepper
1 egg, beaten

1. To make the stuffing, fry the mushrooms and onion in 25 g (1 oz) butter until golden, then remove from the heat. Mix in the breadcrumbs and sage with seasoning and bind with egg; cool.
2. Carefully trim any skin and excess fat from the pork tenderloins and slit lengthways, three quarters of the way through each tenderloin. Open the meat out so that it is as flat as possible.
3. Spread one piece of meat with half of the mushroom mixture. Top with another of the tenderloins. Spread over the remaining stuffing and top with remaining tenderloin.
4. Stretch out each bacon rasher thinly, using a knife. Wrap up the meat in the bacon rashers and tie with string to form a joint.
5. Put the pork parcel in a small roasting tin, spread the remaining butter over the top and season well. Pour the wine around and roast in the oven at 180°C (350°F) mark 4 for about 1¾ hours, basting frequently. Lift on to a warmed serving platter, and remove string. Keep warm.
6. Add the stock to the pan and bring to the boil. Blend the arrowroot with 20 ml (4 tsp) water to a smooth paste and add to the pan, stirring. Boil for 1 minute, then adjust the seasoning.
7. Carve the pork into thin slices and serve with the sauce.
SERVES 6

CROWN ROAST OF PORK

two 2-2.3 kg (4½-5 lb) fore loins of pork, chined, each
with 7-8 cutlets
salt
½ quantity Sage and Onion Stuffing (see page 182)
watercress, to garnish

1. With fat side of pork skin uppermost, slice skin across the width into 5 mm (¼ inch) strips. Then slice into 6 cm (2½ inch) lengths. Retain a third, placing the rest on a mesh wire trivet in a roasting tin. Sprinkle with salt. Roast below the joint until the crackling is crisp, 1½-2 hours.
2. Cut along length of joint through to the bones and trim each bone to a depth of 1 cm (½ inch) – not further as flesh shrinks during cooking. Finely chop the lean meat and add to the stuffing.
3. Lay the joint on the board with the fat side down, eye towards you. Make a narrow incision between cutlet bones. Slice down through the eye of the meat to a

Cut around the bones.

depth of 2.5 cm (1 inch). Cut through the fat at base of the joint.
4. Prepare the second loin in the same way as the first. Sew the joints together to form one long piece using a trussing needle and fine string. Make sure that the string goes around the end bone on each joint to prevent it tearing the flesh away.
5. Stand the joints up with the eye of the meat as the base, bend around with the fat inside and sew together to form a crown shape.
6. Place the crown in a large roasting tin and tie two rows of string around the base. Spoon the stuffing into the centre, pushing down well to plump out the crown shape. Shape the stuffing into a dome at the level of the bone tips. Cover the exposed bones with foil and place the reserved strips of pork on top of the stuffing. Sprinkle with salt and weigh the joint.
7. Roast in the oven at 180°C (350°F) mark 4 for 30 minutes per 450 g (1 lb) plus 30 minutes, basting frequently. (When done the juices should run clear, not pink.) To serve, lift on to a serving plate. Remove foil and string and garnish with watercress.
SERVES 7-8

GOLDEN GRILLED PORK STEAKS

8 pork loin steaks, about 75g (3 oz) each
finely grated rind and juice of 1 large orange
45 ml (3 tbsp) dry sherry
2 bay leaves
salt and pepper
1 bunch spring onions, trimmed and cut into 1 cm
   (½ inch) lengths
4 dried apricots, shredded
2 garlic cloves, skinned and sliced
oil
300 ml (½ pint) stock
5 ml (1 level tsp) cornflour
dash of soy sauce (optional)
orange slices and fresh herbs, to garnish

1. Trim steaks and shape into rough rounds, securing with a cocktail stick. Place in a non-metallic dish.
2. Add the orange rind with the strained juice, sherry, bay leaves and seasoning.
3. Add the spring onions, apricots and garlic to the dish with the pork steaks and stir well. Cover tightly and refrigerate for at least 2 hours, preferably overnight.
4. Lift the pork onto a grill rack, reserving marinade. Brush lightly with oil and grill for about 7 minutes each side or until tender and well browned. Remove cocktail sticks.
5. Meanwhile, simmer the marinade ingredients in a saucepan with the stock for 10 minutes. Mix the cornflour to a smooth paste with a little water, then off the heat, stir into the pan. Return to heat and boil for 1-2 minutes, stirring all the time. Adjust seasoning, and add a dash of soy sauce, if using.
6. To serve, spoon the sauce over the pork steaks, garnish with orange slices and fresh herbs and serve with mashed potato and cabbage.
SERVES 4

QUICK PORK CASSOULET

450 g (1 lb) pork streaky rashers, about 2 cm (3 inches)
   thick
15-30 ml (1-2 tbsp) oil
350 g (12 oz) onion, skinned and sliced
1 green pepper, seeded and roughly chopped
6 celery sticks, trimmed and chopped
2.5 ml (½ level tsp) chilli powder
5 ml (1 level tsp) dried mixed herbs
400 g (14 oz) can chopped tomatoes
450 ml (¾ pint) stock
salt and pepper
432 g (15¼ oz) can red kidney beans, drained
fried white breadcrumbs, to top (optional)
chopped fresh parsley, to garnish

1. Cut the rind and any excess fat off the pork rashers and then divide the flesh into bite-sized pieces. Heat a little oil in a flameproof casserole and lightly brown the pork.
2. Remove the pork from the casserole. Add the vegetables, with a little more oil if necessary, and stir-fry the mixture for about 2-3 minutes.
3. Add the chilli powder and cook for 1 minute before mixing in the herbs, tomatoes and juice, stock and seasoning. Return the meat to the casserole and bring to the boil. Cover tightly and simmer for about 45 minutes or until the meat is tender.

Quick Pork Cassoulet

4. Uncover, stir in the kidney beans and simmer to reduce and thicken slightly. Adjust seasoning before serving, topped with fried breadcrumbs if desired. Garnish with chopped parsley.
SERVES 4

LEFT: Golden Grilled Pork Steaks. RIGHT: Pork and Pasta Stir-fry

PORK AND PASTA STIR-FRY

450 g (1 lb) pork tenderloin (fillet)
75 g (3 oz) streaky bacon, rinded and chopped
*225 g (8 oz) onions, preferably red, skinned and finely
    sliced*
15 ml (1 level tbsp) wholegrain mustard
100 ml (4 fl oz) dry cider
1 garlic clove, skinned and crushed
45-60 ml (3-4 tbsp) oil
salt and pepper
175 g (6 oz) green beans, topped, tailed and halved
1 green pepper, seeded and cut into strips
75 g (3 oz) dried pasta shells or bows
15 ml (1 tbsp) soy sauce
60 ml (4 tbsp) stock

1. Cut the pork into strips, about 5 cm x 5 mm
(2 x ¼ inch), discarding skin and excess fat.
Place in a bowl with the bacon and onions. Add
the mustard, cider, garlic, 15 ml (1 tbsp) oil and
seasoning. Stir well. Cover and leave to
marinate in the refrigerator for at least 1 hour,
preferably overnight.
2. Blanch the green beans and pepper together
in boiling salted water for 2 minutes, drain; run
under cold water, cool.
3. Cook the pasta in boiling salted water until
just cooked, about 7-10 minutes. Drain and toss
in a little oil to prevent the pasta sticking.
4. Drain the meat and the onions from the
marinade, reserving juices. Heat 30 ml (2 tbsp)
oil in a large sauté or frying pan. Add the meat
and onions and stir-fry over a high heat for
3-4 minutes or until the meat is lightly browned
and the onions are beginning to soften.
5. Put the beans, pepper and pasta into the pan
with the marinade, soy sauce, stock and seasoning. Bring to the boil, stirring, then simmer for
about 5 minutes or until piping hot.
SERVES 4

SOMERSET PORK STEW

450 g (1 lb) lean belly pork, rinded, boned and cut into
  chunky cubes
225 g (8 oz) dried black-eye or haricot beans, soaked
  overnight
15 ml (1 tbsp) clear honey
600 ml (1 pint) chicken stock
300 ml (½ pint) apple juice
1 medium onion, skinned and stuck with a few cloves
bouquet garni
3 medium carrots, peeled and sliced
2 leeks, trimmed and sliced
2 celery sticks, sliced
30 ml (2 tbsp) Worcestershire sauce
15 ml (1 tbsp) tomato purée
salt and pepper

1. Cook the pork in a flameproof casserole over
a brisk heat until the fat runs.
2. Drain the beans and add to the pork with the
honey, stock, apple juice, onion and bouquet
garni. Slowly bring to the boil, then cover and
simmer for 1 hour or until the beans are just
becoming tender.
3. Add the carrots, leeks and celery to the
casserole with the Worcestershire sauce and
tomato purée. Season with salt and pepper to
taste. Continue simmering for a further
15-30 minutes or until the beans are really
tender. Discard the bouquet garni before
serving. Accompany with crusty bread.
SERVES 4-6

BAKED STUFFED PORK CHOPS

50 g (2 oz) long grain brown rice
salt and pepper
30 ml (2 tbsp) vegetable oil
4 spare rib pork chops, trimmed and boned
1 small onion, skinned and finely chopped
50 g (2 oz) raisins
225 g (8 oz) can pineapple pieces in natural juice,
  drained with juice reserved
45 ml (3 tbsp) chopped fresh parsley

1. Cook the rice in plenty of boiling salted water
for about 35 minutes, until tender. Drain well.
2. Heat the oil in a large frying pan and brown

the chops. Allow to cool slightly, then slit three
quarters of the way through each chop to form a
large pocket.
3. Meanwhile, brown the onion in the oil
remaining in the pan. Stir in the raisins with the
pineapple, cooked rice, parsley and seasoning.
4. Place the chops in a shallow ovenproof dish
and spoon the rice mixture into the prepared
pockets. Spoon over 60 ml (4 tbsp) pineapple
juice. Season.
5. Cover the dish tightly and cook in the oven at
180°C (350°F) mark 4 for 4 for 1-1¼ hours. Baste
once with the juice during cooking.
SERVES 4

NORMANDY PORK

300 ml (½ pint) dry white wine
225 g (8 oz) button mushrooms, wiped and sliced
900 g (2 lb) pork fillet, cut into thick strips
30 ml (2 level tbsp) seasoned flour
25 g (1 oz) butter or margarine
15 ml (1 tbsp) vegetable oil
30 ml (2 tbsp) Calvados
2 large cooking apples, peeled, cored and thinly sliced
30 ml (2 tbsp) chopped fresh parsley
150 ml (5 fl oz) double cream
salt and pepper

1. Bring the wine to the boil in a small
saucepan, add the mushrooms and simmer,
covered, for 10-15 minutes.
2. Toss the pork strips in the seasoned flour.
3. Heat the butter and oil in a frying pan and
brown the pork. Warm the Calvados in a small
pan, set it alight and when the flames die down,
pour it over the meat.
4. Add the wine, mushrooms and apples to the
pork and simmer, covered, for 30 minutes, until
tender.
5. Add the parsley and cream to the juices in the
pan and simmer without boiling until the sauce
thickens slightly. Adjust the seasoning.
SERVES 6

PORK ESCALOPES WITH SAGE

450g (1 lb) pork fillet, trimmed and cut into 5 mm
   (¼ inch) slices
1 egg, beaten
125 g (4 oz) fresh breadcrumbs
10 ml (2 level tsp) dried sage
grated rind of 1 lemon
50 g (2 oz) butter or margarine
15 ml (1 tbsp) vegetable oil
lemon wedges, to garnish

1. Flatten the pork between two sheets of damp greaseproof paper into thin escalopes.
2. Dip the escalopes in the egg.
3. Mix together the breadcrumbs, sage and lemon rind and coat the pork escalopes.
4. Heat the butter and oil in a large frying pan, add half the escalopes and cook for 2-3 minutes each side, until golden brown. Keep warm whilst cooking the remaining escalopes. Garnish with lemon wedges to serve.
SERVES 4

BARBECUED SPARE RIBS

30 ml (2 tbsp) vegetable oil
2 medium onions, skinned and chopped
1 garlic clove, skinned and crushed
30 ml (2 level tbsp) tomato purée
60 ml (4 tbsp) malt vinegar
1.25 ml (¼ level tsp) dried thyme
1.25 ml (¼ level tsp) chilli seasoning
45 ml (3 level tbsp) honey
150 ml (¼ pint) beef stock
1 kg (2¼ lb) American-cut spare ribs

1. Heat the oil in a saucepan, add the onions and cook for 5 minutes, until softened. Add all the remaining ingredients, except the spare ribs, and simmer gently for 10 minutes.
2. Place the spare ribs in a roasting tin in a single layer and brush with a little of the sauce.
3. Roast in the oven at 190°C (375°F) mark 5 for 30 minutes, then pour off the fat and spoon the remaining sauce over the meat. Cook for a further 1-1¼ hours, basting occasionally.
SERVES 4

SWEET-SOUR PORK BALLS

450 g (1 lb) pork, minced
1 garlic clove, skinned and crushed
45 ml (3 level tbsp) flour
50 g (2 oz) fresh breadcrumbs
salt and pepper
1 egg yolk, beaten
30 ml (2 tbsp) vegetable oil
FOR THE SAUCE
75 g (3 oz) soft brown sugar
60 ml (4 tbsp) cider vinegar
45 ml (3 tbsp) soy sauce
45 ml (3 level tbsp) tomato ketchup
227 g (8 oz) can pineapple pieces in natural juice,
   drained with juice reserved
30 ml (2 level tbsp) cornflour
1 green pepper, blanched and cut into thin strips

1. Mix together the minced pork, garlic, 15 ml (1 level tbsp) flour, the breadcrumbs and seasoning. Stir in the egg yolk and mix well.
2. Form into twenty four balls and toss in the remaining flour.
3. Heat the oil in a frying pan, add the pork balls and fry gently for 20 minutes, turning frequently, until golden. Drain on absorbent kitchen paper.
4. Meanwhile, put the sugar, vinegar, soy sauce and tomato ketchup in a saucepan. Make up the pineapple juice to 300 ml (½ pint) with water, blend in the cornflour and add to the pan. Bring to the boil, stirring, then simmer gently for 5 minutes. Add the pineapple and green pepper and simmer for a further 5-10 minutes.
5. Transfer the pork balls to a warmed dish and pour over the sauce.
SERVES 4

Pork Steaks with Peppers

PORK STEAKS WITH PEPPERS

15 ml (1 tbsp) vegetable oil

15 g (½ oz) butter

1 medium onion, skinned and chopped

2.5 cm (1 inch) piece fresh root ginger, peeled and finely grated

1 garlic clove, skinned and crushed

4 boneless pork loin steaks, 150 g (5 oz) each

1 red pepper, seeded and thinly sliced

1 green pepper, seeded and thinly sliced

45 ml (3 tbsp) dry sherry

30 ml (2 tbsp) soy sauce

150 ml (¼ pint) unsweetened pineapple juice

salt and pepper

1. Heat the oil and butter in a large frying pan, add the onion, ginger and garlic and gently fry for 5 minutes, until soft. Push to one side of the pan.

2. Add the pork steaks and brown on both sides, then add the remaining ingredients and mix thoroughly together.

3. Cover tightly and simmer gently for 8-10 minutes, until the steaks are tender and the peppers are soft. Transfer the steaks and peppers to warmed serving plates. Bring the remaining liquid in the pan to the boil and boil for 2-3 minutes until reduced slightly. Spoon over the steaks and serve with boiled rice.

SERVES 4

FRIKADELLER

450 g (1 lb) lean pork, cubed
1 small onion, skinned and quartered
salt and pepper
30 ml (2 level tbsp) flour
1 egg, beaten
a little milk
vegetable oil for deep-frying
Basic Tomato Sauce (see page 207), to serve

1. Finely mince the meat and onion together using a food processor or mincer. Season and stir in the flour, egg and enough milk to give a soft mixture that holds its shape. Divide into small pieces and roll into balls.
2. Heat the oil in a deep-fryer to 190°C (375°F) and cook the meat balls in batches for about 6 minutes, until brown. Drain on absorbent kitchen paper and serve with Tomato Sauce.
SERVES 4

PORK KEBABS

450 g (1 lb) minced pork or lamb
1 large onion, skinned and grated
2 garlic cloves, skinned and crushed
1 green chilli pepper, seeded and finely chopped
5 ml (1 level tsp) ground cumin
salt and pepper
grated rind and juice of 1 lemon
vegetable oil
lemon wedges and pitta bread, to serve

1. Place all the ingredients except the oil in a bowl and mix thoroughly. Cover and chill for at least an hour.
2. Divide the meat mixture into 16 pieces and shape each into a thin strip about 10 cm (4 inches) long and then roll up; or form into tight balls.
3. Place four meat rolls on each lightly greased skewer and brush lightly with the oil.
4. Place the skewers under a hot grill and grill for about 10 minutes, turning frequently for even browning. Serve with lemon wedges and pitta bread.
SERVES 4

PORK AND OAT BURGERS

45 ml (3 level tbsp) mango chutney
450 g (1 lb) minced pork
50 g (2 oz) rolled oats
5 ml (1 level tsp) dried sage
salt and pepper
1 egg, beaten
flour for dusting
oil for brushing
burger buns, salad leaves and tomato slices, to serve
tomato ketchup or Apple Sauce (see page 205), to
*   accompany (optional)*

1. Chop up any coarse particles of mango chutney and mix all the chutney with the pork, oats, sage, seasoning and sufficient egg to bind. Beat well to combine thoroughly.
2. With lightly floured hands, shape into about eight flat burgers. Place on a foil-lined baking sheet and cover. Leave in the refrigerator for about 30 minutes.
3. Brush the burgers lightly with oil and grill under a moderate heat for 7-8 minutes each side until well browned and cooked through, turning once.
4. Serve in burger buns with salad leaves and tomato slices. Accompany with tomato ketchup or apple sauce.
SERVES 4

Bacon

Bacon is made by curing fresh pork. There are several methods of curing which result in different flavours of bacon. The most common is the 'Wiltshire' cure which involves injecting whole sides, under pressure, with a special 'brine' or 'pickle'. This ensures even distribution of the curing salts throughout the muscles of the carcass. The brine contains permitted preservatives, which colour and flavour the meat.

A side of bacon (half a carcass, without the head and feet) may be cured whole, as in the Wiltshire cure, or cuts such as the middle may be cured separately, with or without their bones. Bacon may be smoked after curing – hung over smouldering wood sawdust. Oak chippings or sawdust give the most distinctive flavouring. Unsmoked bacon is known as 'green', 'pale' or 'plain' bacon.

QUICK CURES: Smaller cuts of meat may be cured by modern 'quick' cures. Parts of the side, such as middle and shoulder are cured separately. The curing solution is injected by machine into the lean and, unlike the Wiltshire method, the bacon is not then immersed in brine. The pieces are simply hung for 2-3 days. Bacon sold in vacuum packs as 'sweet', 'mild' or 'tender cure' has had sugar added to the curing brine.

TRADITIONAL CURES: As well as modern quick methods of curing, there are other traditional methods. In Scotland, the 'Ayrshire' method is as old as the Wiltshire cure. Instead of curing the whole side, the carcass is skinned, jointed, boned and formed into rolls, usually called Ayrshire gigot (hind leg), Ayrshire middle or Ayrshire shoulder. The rolls are injected with brine and then immersed in a brine cure.

CUTS AND METHODS OF COOKING

Bacon is sold sliced and unpacked ('loose') or in airtight vacuum packs. Vacuum-packed bacon will remain moist until opened. After being opened it will gradually dry and deteriorate in a similar way to 'loose' bacon. Fresh 'loose' bacon has moist, lean, firm white fat and smooth rind. Green bacon has a pale rind and smoked bacon a deep brown rind. Local methods of cutting bacon sides make it difficult to describe all the available cuts. Gammon is the name given to whole hind legs cut from a side of bacon after curing. Joints of gammon and bacon vary in saltiness.

PRIME BACK is lean and usually sold as rashers or boneless chops (thick rashers), which are grilled or fried. Alternatively, a thick piece can be used for boiling, braising or roasting.

PRIME STREAKY RASHERS combine lean and fat and are best grilled or fried. Streaky bacon is used to line pâté dishes and can be chopped for casseroles, soups and rice dishes; stretched and rolled to make bacon rolls; or crispy fried snippets can be used as a garnish. A joint of streaky bacon is excellent boiled and pressed, to eat cold.

MIDDLE OR THROUGHCUT RASHERS are the back and streaky cut together, giving a long rasher with a balanced mix of lean and fat – an economical buy. Use them for grilling or have a piece of middle cut rolled and use for boiling or baking – delicious used as a stuffed joint. With the rind removed, this is sometimes called Ayrshire Roll, as it is traditionally prepared in Scotland.

LONG BACK LEAN RASHERS are best cut fairly thin for frying or grilling. Thick slices cut up well for casseroles, flans or pies.

MIDDLE GAMMON is a prime, lean, meaty cut for boiling, braising or baking. Gammon rashers or steaks, about 1 cm (½ inch) thick, are usually cut from this joint. They are excellent grilled or fried.

CORNER GAMMON is an economical buy. It is a triangular cut off the gammon which can be boiled and served hot, with a parsley sauce, or sliced when cold for sandwiches.

GAMMON HOCK gives succulent meat as a small boiling joint or cut up meat for casseroles, soups, pies and mincing.

PRIME COLLAR makes a good joint boiled or braised. The collar joint can also be sliced into rashers. As a joint it may need to be soaked.

PRIME FOREHOCK is another bacon joint that is sometimes better soaked. A good meaty cut for casseroles or boiling as a joint, it is also a suitable cut for mincing.

Bacon pieces: These offcuts, if available, are worth buying for the occasions when you need small amounts of bacon to lard lean joints of meat or poultry, or to add to casseroles, etc. Don't buy if they look dry.

Vacuum-packed Bacon

Bacon is widely sold in vacuum packets, which are hygienic and convenient both for the customer and the shopkeeper. Mostly rashers come packed in this way, but also small joints and gammon steaks. Vacuum packing extends the keeping qualities of bacon and packets are marked with a 'sell by' or 'best before' date. Once opened, use and treat as loose bacon. As a guide, vacuum-packed rashers, chops, steaks and joints keep for up to 15 days in the refrigerator.

Storage of Bacon

Store loose bacon in the refrigerator in an airtight plastic container or wrapped closely in kitchen foil. Do not use greaseproof paper, which is porous and allows bacon to dry out. Refrigerate for up to a week.

Preparing rashers

If the bacon is bought with rind, the easiest way to remove it is with kitchen scissors or a sharp knife. Remove any bone. Thick rashers, steaks or chops should be snipped at intervals along the fat edge to help them remain flat during cooking. If you suspect that chops, collar or gammon steaks are salty, soak them for a short time or poach in water for a few minutes, then throw away the water. Pat dry, using absorbent kitchen paper, and cook as desired.

For bacon rolls, use thin cut streaky rashers and remove the rind. Stretch each rasher by running the back of a knife along its length. Do this on the work surface or a board. Either roll up the whole rasher or cut it in half crossways before rolling.

Cooking Rashers

For frying, overlap back bacon rashers in a cold pan with the lean parts over the fat. For grilling, heat the pan gently first, then arrange the bacon rashers on the rack with the fat parts overlapping the lean. Turn rashers halfway through cooking time, 3-5 minutes. Grill under a high heat, reducing the heat and turning the bacon over halfway through cooking. Allow 3-5 minutes for rashers, 12-15 minutes for chops and 10-15 minutes for bacon steaks, depending on thickness.

Ham

Ham, strictly speaking, is the hind leg of a pig cut from the whole carcass, then cured and matured separately. Nowadays, cooked gammon is often described as ham. When selecting a whole ham, choose a short, thick leg without too much fat and a thin rind. Hams are usually cooked prior to purchase; if not cook as for bacon. Some of the best-known cures are described below.

York ham is cured with dry salt and lightly smoked before being boiled. York ham is cut from the side near the oyster bone, which makes it a long shape. It is then rounded off. The meat is pale with a mild, delicate flavour. Average weight is 7-11 kg (16-24 lb).

Bradenham ham is less widely available than it used to be and it is expensive. It is cured in a similar way to York ham and then pickled in molasses for a month. The cure turns the skin black and the meat rather red with a slightly sweet flavour. To cook, soak for 48-72 hours, drain and put in fresh cold water. Boil as for bacon (see page 134).

Suffolk ham is sweet cured and has a rich red-brown meat with a 'blue' bloom. This ham, cured in beer and sugar or black molasses, has a deep golden, toasted look to the skin. It is less widely available today.

Cumberland ham is dry salted, with the addition of brown sugar.

Belfast ham is now almost entirely found in the West of Scotland. These hams are dry salted and traditionally smoked over peat.

Honey-baked ham is baked with a coating of honey, or honey and brown sugar.

Virginia ham is an American ham. A true Virginia ham comes from pigs fed on peanuts and peaches.

Kentucky ham is an American ham from pigs fattened on acorns, beans and cloves.

Raw hams: All English hams need to be cooked but there are several hams from other countries produced specially for eating raw. The most famous is the proscuitto (raw ham) from Parma in Italy, which is regarded as the best. Bayonne in France and Westphalia in Germany also produce notable raw hams.

BOILED BACON JOINT

piece of gammon, collar or forehock bacon
2 medium onions, skinned
2 medium carrots, peeled and thickly sliced
1 bay leaf
4 black peppercorns
Parsley or Onion Sauce (see page 199), to serve

1. Weigh the joint. To remove the salt, place the joint in a large saucepan with enough cold water to cover, bring to the boil, then drain and discard the water.
2. Calculate the cooking time allowing 20 minutes per 450 g (1 lb) plus 20 minutes. If the joint is over 4.5 kg (10 lb), allow 15-20 minutes per 450 g (1 lb) plus 15 minutes.
3. Place the joint in a large saucepan or preserving pan, add the flavouring vegetables, bay leaf and peppercorns, cover with cold water and bring slowly to the boil. Remove any scum with a slotted spoon. Cover and calculate the cooking time from this point.
4. When the bacon is cooked, ease off the rind and any excess fat and serve hot, sliced, with Parsley or Onion Sauce.

VARIATIONS
1. Add 300 ml (½ pint) cider after the flavouring vegetables and peppercorns and cover the joint with cold water.
2. To serve the joint cold, remove the rind and excess fat and roll it in toasted breadcrumbs. Leave to cool.

BRAISED BACON

1.4 kg (3 lb) piece of gammon, collar or forehock bacon
1 medium onion, skinned and sliced
4 medium carrots, peeled and sliced
1 small turnip, peeled and sliced
2 celery sticks, trimmed and sliced
45 ml (3 tbsp) vegetable oil
chicken stock
bouquet garni
salt and pepper
Parsley or Onion Sauce (see page 199), to serve

1. Soak the gammon or bacon in plenty of cold water for 2-3 hours or place the joint in a large saucepan with enough cold water to cover, bring to the boil, then discard the water. Weigh the joint and calculate the cooking time, allowing 20 minutes per 450 g (1 lb) plus 20 minutes.
2. Place the joint in a large saucepan, cover with cold water and bring slowly to the boil. Remove any scum from the surface, cover and calculate the cooking time from this point.
3. Lightly fry the vegetables in the oil for 3-4 minutes. Put them in a casserole, put the bacon on top and add enough stock to cover the vegetables. Add the bouquet garni and the seasoning, cover and cook in the oven at 180°C (350°F) mark 4 for the remainder of the cooking time.
4. About 30 minutes before the end of the cooking time, remove the rind and continue cooking, uncovered, for the final 30 minutes. Remove the bouquet garni and serve with Parsley or Onion Sauce.
SERVES 6-8

NOTE: Some gammon or bacon joints are more salty than others and the soaking time will therefore vary accordingly. If possible, ask your butcher which cure was used and he will be able to advise more specifically on the length of the soaking time.

BAKED AND GLAZED BACON

Gammon and bacon joints may be boiled for half their cooking time as calculated in Boiled Bacon Joint (see page 134) and then baked for the remainder of the cooking time.

1. Weigh the joint to calculate the cooking time and boil as above. Drain and wrap in foil. Place in a roasting tin and bake in the oven at 180°C (350°F) mark 4 until 30 minutes before the cooking time is complete. Increase the oven temperature to 220°C (425°F) mark 7.

Score the bacon fat and stud with cloves.

2. Remove foil and rind from the bacon. Score the fat in diamonds and stud with cloves. Sprinkle the surface with demerara sugar and pat in. Return the joint to the oven for 30 minutes, until crisp and golden. Or glaze (see below), and serve with Cumberland Sauce (see page 207).

SPICED MARMALADE AND HONEY GLAZE: In a small bowl, blend together 60 ml (4 level tbsp) fine shred marmalade, 75 ml (5 tbsp) clear honey and 4-5 drops Tabasco sauce. Brush about one third of the glaze over the bacon fat 30 minutes before the end of cooking time. Return to the oven for 10 minutes, then repeat. Don't use the glaze that has run into the pan as this will dull the shine. Repeat with the final third.

Baked Ham

SHARP HONEY GLAZE: In a small saucepan, warm 15 ml (1 tbsp) clear honey and 30 ml (2 tbsp) vinegar. Pour the glaze over the bacon fat. Mix together equal quantities of brown sugar and golden breadcrumbs and sprinkle over the top. Return to the oven, basting frequently.

HAM AND LEEKS AU GRATIN

8 medium leeks, washed and trimmed
salt and pepper
50 g (2 oz) butter or margarine
75 ml (5 level tbsp) flour
600 ml (1 pint) milk
125 g (4 oz) Cheddar cheese, grated
8 thin slices of cooked ham
25 g (1 oz) fresh breadcrumbs

1. Cook the leeks in boiling salted water for 10-15 minutes, until soft. Drain and keep warm.
2. Meanwhile, melt 40 g (1½ oz) butter, stir in the flour and cook gently for 1 minute. Remove the pan from the heat and gradually stir in the milk. Bring to the boil slowly and continue to cook, stirring until the sauce thickens. Stir in 75 g (3 oz) of the cheese and season.
3. Wrap each leek in a slice of ham, place in a flameproof dish and coat with sauce.
4. Mix together the breadcrumbs and remaining cheese and sprinkle over the top. Dot with the remaining butter and brown under the grill until golden and bubbling.
SERVES 4

VARIATION
Use 4 heads of chicory instead of the leeks, cooking for 15 minutes, until tender. Use only 4 slices of ham for wrapping the chicory heads.

OFFAL

Offal is one of the most economical meats to buy; the strong flavour and lack of bones in most offal means that only small amounts are needed. Liver and kidney are the varieties most commonly eaten, but other offal can be used to make interesting and nutritious meals. Offal must be very fresh and should be cooked as soon as possible as it goes off more quickly than other meat. It must not be overcooked or it will be tough.

The availability and popularity of certain types of offal has declined in recent years. This is partly due to the occurence of BSE (Bovine Spongiform Encephalopathy) or mad cow disease. This is a slowly progressive, ultimately fatal disorder of adult cattle. Those parts of the cow which harbour the BSE agent are now banned for human consumption in this country. These include the brain, thymus (sweetbreads), spleen, spinal cord and intestines.

TYPES OF OFFAL

LIVER: The best liver is calf's, followed by lamb's, pig's and ox, which is coarse and strong flavoured. Calf's, lamb's and pig's liver can be grilled, fried or used in braised dishes. Pig's and ox livers are mainly used in stews and casseroles or minced for pâtés and stuffings. The strong flavour of ox and pig's livers can be mellowed by soaking in milk for an hour.

KIDNEY: Calf's kidney is light in colour, delicately flavoured and considered the best. Lamb's kidney is darker than calf's, and smaller; it also has an excellent flavour. These kidneys should be cooked quickly to be tender and are most frequently grilled or fried. Pig and ox kidneys have a much stronger flavour; ox kidney needs slow moist cooking. They are traditionally used in casseroles and pies. To prepare kidneys, remove the outer membrane, split in half lengthways and, using scissors, remove the white core and as many of the tubes as possible.

HEART: Whole lamb's and pig's hearts are the most commonly available and one per portion is usually sufficient. Best results are achieved by pot roasting, braising or casseroling. An ox heart will weigh up to 1.8 kg (4 lb) and is best cut into cubes for stews and casseroles. Whole hearts are frequently stuffed. Wash thoroughly in cold water, trim away fat and tubes and snip the cavity walls. Leave to soak for an hour in clean, salted water. Rinse and drain. Cut across an ox heart and thus across the grain to increase tenderness.

TRIPE: Tripe is the stomach linings from the ox. The smooth first stomach is known as 'blanket', the second 'honeycomb' and the third 'thick seam'. All should be thick, firm and white and there is no difference in taste. Tripe is sold bleached (dressed) and partly boiled.

TONGUE: Ox and lamb's tongues are the most common, calf's and pig's usually being sold with the head. Lamb's and ox tongues can be bought fresh or salted. Lamb's tongues weigh about 225 g (8 oz) but an ox tongue can weigh from 1.8-3 kg (4-6½ lb). Lamb's tongue: soak for 1-2 hours if fresh or 3-4 hours if salted. Ox tongue: soak 2-3 hours if fresh or overnight if salted. Drain, place in cold water (salt only if fresh) and bring slowly to the boil. Skim, then add peppercorns, bay leaves and root vegetables. Simmer gently for 2-3 hours, until tender. Remove skin carefully and use as required.

TAIL: Oxtail is usually the main type sold, ready skinned and jointed (pigs' tails are sometimes available). There should be a good proportion of lean with a layer of firm, white fat. One oxtail weighs about 1.4 kg (3 lb).

SWEETBREADS: These consist of two portions of the thymus gland. Lamb's sweetbreads are sold in pairs and are considered a delicacy. Buy 450 g (1 lb) sweetbreads to serve 3-4 people. Soak in cold water or milk for 2 hours. Rinse. Cover with cold water, flavoured with the juice of half a lemon and 5 ml (1 level tsp) salt and bring to a simmer. Simmer for 15 minutes and plunge into cold water to firm the meat. Remove tubes and outer membrane. Use as required.

BRAINS: Lamb's brains have a delicate flavour. They are usually sold in sets: one set of lamb's brains is sufficient for 1 portion. When fresh, they should look shiny, pinkish-grey, plump and moist. Soak for 1-2 hours in cold water to remove all traces of blood. Remove arteries and membranes with a sharp, pointed knife. Cover with water and parboil for 5-15 minutes, depending on size. Vinegar or lemon juice can be added to the cooking water to help retain the colour. Add other ingredients for flavour, such as an onion or bay leaf. After parboiling, plunge into cold water or cool in the cooking liquid to firm the meat. Discard the water and any loose particles of meat which will have solidified.

HEAD: Rarely available now, although pig's and sheep's heads were once common. The best brawn is made from boiled pig's head. Pig's cheek is sold as Bath Chaps. In the past, a pig's head was sometimes roasted whole, glazed and decorated as a Boar's head for festive occasions.

FEET: When cooked, trotters (feet) produce a protein-rich gelatin. Pig's trotters are the most frequently available, either fresh or salted. Calf's foot and cow heel, once widely used for jellied stock and meat moulds, are now rarely seen. Pig's trotters may be boned, stuffed and roasted, or the meat from them used in brawn.

Singe off any hairs over an open flame. Scrub well and pat dry. Parboil in salted water for 5 minutes before using in a recipe.

LUNGS: Also known as 'lights', lungs are not commonly eaten in this country but can be used as an ingredient in forcemeats or stuffing.

LIVER AND ONIONS

25 g (1 oz) butter or margarine
450 g (1 lb) onions, skinned and chopped
salt and pepper
2.5 ml (½ level tsp) dried sage or mixed herbs (optional)
450 g (1 lb) calf's or lamb's liver, cut into thin strips

1. Melt the butter in a frying pan, add the onions and fry gently until they begin to colour, then add the seasoning and the herbs, if using. Cover the frying pan and simmer very gently for about 10 minutes, until the onions are soft.

2. Add the liver strips to the onions, increase the heat slightly and continue cooking, stirring for about 5-10 minutes, until the liver is just cooked. Transfer to a warmed serving dish.
SERVES 4

LIVER MARSALA

450 g (1 lb) lamb's liver, cut into wafer-thin strips
30 ml (2 tbsp) Marsala or sweet sherry
salt and pepper
225 g (8 oz) tomatoes, skinned
30 ml (2 tbsp) vegetable oil
1 large onion, skinned and finely sliced
150 ml (¼ pint) beef stock

1. Place the liver in a shallow bowl with the Marsala and season well with pepper. Cover and leave to marinate for 2-3 hours in a cool place.

2. Quarter the tomatoes, discard seeds and slice into fine strips, reserving juice.

3. Heat the oil in a frying pan and add the liver strips, a few at a time. Shake the pan briskly for about 1 minute so that the strips cook quickly. Remove from the pan and keep warm.

4. Add the onion to the oil remaining in the pan and cook, covered, for about 5 minutes. Add the stock and seasoning, return the liver to the pan and add the tomatoes and their juice. Bring to the boil, adjust seasoning and serve immediately.
SERVES 4

CHINESE-STYLE FRIED LIVER

4 fresh mushrooms, wiped and chopped, or 25 g (1 oz) dried mushrooms
450 g (1 lb) lamb's liver, cut into thin strips
10 ml (2 level tsp) cornflour
30 ml (2 tbsp) sherry
2.5 cm (1 inch) piece fresh root ginger, peeled and sliced
1 small onion, skinned and finely chopped
30 ml (2 tbsp) vegetable oil
175 g (6 oz) can bamboo shoots, drained
10 ml (2 tsp) soy sauce

1. If using dried mushrooms, soak in hot water for 10 minutes, until soft, then cut into small pieces.

2. Mix the liver with the cornflour, sherry, ginger and onion.

3. Heat the oil in a frying pan and fry the liver briskly for about 1 minute, then add the vegetables. Stir until every piece is golden, about 3-4 minutes, then pour in the soy sauce and toss well. Serve immediately.
SERVES 4

Lamb's Liver and Mushrooms

LAMB'S LIVER AND MUSHROOMS

15 g (½ oz) butter
1 medium onion, skinned and sliced
450 g (1 lb) lamb's liver, cut into strips
15 ml (1 tbsp) plain flour
125 g (4 oz) button mushrooms
150 ml (¼ pint) lamb or beef stock
4 tomatoes, skinned and roughly chopped
30 ml (2 tbsp) Worcestershire sauce
salt and pepper
150 ml (5 fl oz) soured cream

1. Melt the butter in a large frying pan and gently fry the onion for 5 minutes, until softened.
2. Coat the liver strips with the flour and add to the pan with the mushrooms. Fry for 5 minutes, stirring, then add the stock and bring to the boil.
3. Stir in the tomatoes and Worcestershire sauce. Season to taste, then simmer for 3-4 minutes. Stir in the soured cream, and reheat without boiling. Serve hot with noodles.
SERVES 3-4

GRILLED KIDNEYS

550-700 g (1¼-1½ lb) lamb's kidneys, washed, skinned
  and cored
45 ml (3 tbsp) vegetable oil
salt and pepper
grilled bacon, to serve

1. Thread the kidneys on to 4 skewers, cut side uppermost. Brush with oil and sprinkle with salt and pepper.
2. Cook under a hot grill for 3 minutes, uncut side uppermost, then turn over to allow the juices to gather in the cut side and grill a further 3 minutes. Serve immediately with grilled bacon.
SERVES 4

SAUTÉED LIVER WITH SAGE AND APPLE

450 g (1 lb) thinly sliced calves' liver
25 g (1 oz) plain white flour
45 ml (3 tbsp) oil
125 g (4 oz) leeks, trimmed and sliced
*5 ml (1 level tsp) dried rubbed sage or dried mixed
   herbs*
15 ml (1 level tbsp) mustard, preferably wholegrain
150 ml (5 fl oz) single cream
300 ml (½ pint) apple juice
salt and pepper

1. Cut the liver into slightly smaller slices.
Sprinkle the flour onto a flat plate and coat the
liver slices well on all sides.
2. Heat 30 ml (2 tbsp) oil in a large sauté pan
(preferably non-stick) and brown the liver well
for about 30 seconds on each side. Remove with
a slotted spoon.
3. Heat the remaining oil in the pan. Add the
leeks and sage and sauté, stirring well, for
2-3 minutes. Mix in the mustard, cream and
apple juice, then bring to the boil and allow to
bubble for about 5 minutes or until the sauce is
reduced by about half.
4. Return the liver to the pan, season and
simmer very gently for 1-2 minutes or until hot
through. Serve immediately, with creamed
potatoes and steamed broccoli.
SERVES 4

Sautéed Liver with Sage and Apple

BRAISED KIDNEYS IN PORT

8 lamb's kidneys
25 g (1 oz) butter
1 medium onion, skinned and sliced
125 g (4 oz) mushrooms, sliced
45 ml (3 tbsp) plain flour
150 ml (¼ pint) port
150 ml (¼ pint) lamb or chicken stock
15 ml (1 tbsp) chopped fresh parsley
bouquet garni
salt and pepper

1. Skin the kidneys, then cut each one in half
lengthways. Snip out the cores with scissors.
2. Heat the butter in a large frying pan or
flameproof casserole and fry the onion for
3-4 minutes, until softened. Add the mushrooms
and fry for a further 3-4 minutes.
3. Stir in the kidneys and cook for 5 minutes,
stirring occasionally.
4. Stir in the flour, then gradually stir in the
port and stock. Slowly bring to the boil. Stir in
the parsley and bouquet garni. Season to taste.
5. Cover and simmer for 15 minutes, stirring
occasionally. Discard the bouquet garni. Serve
hot, with boiled rice or mashed potatoes and a
mixed salad.
SERVES 3-4

CREAMED KIDNEYS IN WINE

25 g (1 oz) butter
12 lamb's kidneys, cored and halved
225 g (8 oz) mushrooms, sliced
3 celery sticks, diced
1 medium onion, skinned and finely chopped
25 g (1 oz) plain flour
300 ml (½ pint) dry red wine
5 ml (1 tsp) mustard powder
salt and pepper
150 ml (5 fl oz) double cream

1. Melt the butter in a medium saucepan. Add the kidneys, mushrooms, celery and onion and fry gently for 10 minutes, until tender.
2. Stir in the flour and cook for 1-2 minutes. Gradually stir in the wine, mustard and salt and pepper. Cook for a further 5 minutes. Stir in the cream and gently reheat.
3. Serve the creamed kidneys on a bed of boiled rice with a green vegetable.
SERVES 4

LAMB'S HEART CASSEROLE

50 g (2 oz) butter or margarine
1 medium onion, skinned and chopped
125 g (4 oz) mushrooms, wiped and chopped
125 g (4 oz) streaky bacon, rinded and chopped
2.5 ml (½ level tsp) dried sage or thyme
225 g (8 oz) fresh breadcrumbs
finely grated rind of 1 lemon
salt and pepper
1 egg, beaten
8 lamb's hearts, washed and trimmed
60 ml (4 level tbsp) flour
30 ml (2 tbsp) vegetable oil
300 ml (½ pint) lamb or chicken stock
45 ml (3 tbsp) sherry

1. Melt half the butter in a saucepan and cook the onion, mushroom and bacon until browned. Remove from the heat and stir in the sage or thyme, breadcrumbs, lemon rind and seasoning. Bind with the egg.
2. Fill the hearts with the stuffing and sew up neatly with strong cotton.
3. Toss the hearts in the flour and brown well in the remaining butter and oil in a flameproof casserole. Pour over the stock and sherry, season well and bring to the boil.
4. Cover the casserole and cook in the oven at 150°C (300°F) mark 2 for about 2 hours or until tender. To serve, slice the hearts and pour over the juices.
SERVES 8

LANCASHIRE TRIPE AND ONIONS

450 g (1 lb) dressed tripe, washed
225 g (8 oz) shallots, skinned
600 ml (1 pint) milk
salt and pepper
pinch of grated nutmeg
1 bay leaf (optional)
25 g (1 oz) butter or margarine
45 ml (3 level tbsp) flour
chopped fresh parsley, to garnish

1. Put the tripe in a saucepan and cover with cold water. Bring to the boil, then drain and rinse under running cold water. Cut into 2.5 cm (1 inch) pieces.
2. Put the tripe, shallots, milk, seasonings and bay leaf (if using) into the rinsed out pan. Bring to the boil, cover and simmer for about 2 hours, until tender. Strain off the liquid and reserve 600 ml (1 pint).
3. Melt the butter in a pan, stir in the flour and cook gently for 1 minute, stirring. Remove pan from the heat and gradually stir in the cooking liquid. Bring to the boil and continue to cook, stirring, until the sauce thickens.
4. Add the tripe and shallots and reheat. Adjust the seasoning and sprinkle with parsley.
SERVES 4

BRAISED OXTAIL

2 oxtails, total weight about 1.6 kg (3½ lb), trimmed
*   and cut into pieces*
30 ml (2 level tbsp) seasoned flour
60 ml (4 tbsp) vegetable oil
2 large onions, skinned and sliced
900 ml (1½ pints) beef stock
150 ml (¼ pint) red wine
15 ml (1 level tbsp) tomato purée
finely grated rind of ½ a lemon
2 bay leaves
salt and pepper
2 medium carrots, peeled and chopped
450 g (1 lb) parsnips, peeled and chopped
chopped fresh parsley, to garnish

1. Coat the oxtail pieces in the seasoned flour. Brown a few pieces at a time in the oil in a large flameproof casserole. Remove from the casserole with a slotted spoon.
2. Add the onions to the casserole and lightly brown. Stir in any remaining flour, the stock, red wine, tomato purée, lemon rind and bay leaves and season well. Bring to the boil and replace the meat. Cover and simmer for 2 hours, then skim well.
3. Stir the carrots and parsnips into the casserole.
4. Re-cover the casserole and simmer for a further 2 hours, until the meat is quite tender.
5. Skim all fat off the surface of the casserole, adjust seasoning and garnish with parsley.
SERVES 6

FRICASSÉE OF LAMB'S TONGUES

900 g (2 lb) lamb 's tongues
salt and pepper
1 medium onion, skinned and sliced
1 medium carrot, peeled and sliced
1 bay leaf
6 black peppercorns
50 g (2 oz) butter or margarine
60 ml (4 level tbsp) flour
60 ml (4 tbsp) double cream
45 ml (3 tbsp) chopped fresh parsley
20 ml (4 tsp) lemon juice
bacon snippets and bread croûtons, to garnish

1. Rinse the tongues under cold water. Turn into a large bowl and cover with cold water, add 2.5 ml (½ level tsp) salt and leave to soak for 1-2 hours.
2. Rinse and drain well. Place in a large saucepan with the onion and carrot, bay leaf and peppercorns and water to cover. Add a large pinch of salt, bring slowly to the boil and skim off any scum rising to the surface. Cover and simmer gently for about 2 hours, or until tender.
3. Remove the tongues with a slotted spoon and place in a large bowl of cold water. Leave to go quite cold. Boil the cooking liquid to reduce and strengthen the flavour, strain off and reserve 450 ml (¾ pint).

4. When the tongues are cold, ease a finger or thumb between the skin and flesh and gradually peel the skin off. Using a small pointed knife, gradually ease out the small bones and pieces of gristle lying at the base of the tongue.
5. Place the tongues on a chopping board and, using a very sharp knife, slice diagonally into 1 cm (½ inch) slices, starting from the tip end.
6. Melt the butter in a pan, stir in the flour and cook gently for 1 minute, stirring. Remove the pan from the heat and gradually stir in the reserved stock. Bring to the boil slowly and cook, stirring until the sauce thickens. Blend in the cream and season. Lower the heat and stir in the parsley.
7. Stir the tongue into the sauce, cover the pan and leave over a low heat for 10-15 minutes to warm through, stirring occasionally to prevent sticking. Just before serving, stir in the lemon juice and adjust seasoning. Garnish the dish with bacon snippets and small croûtons.
SERVES 6

NOTE: To make bacon snippets, remove the rinds from six prime streaky bacon rashers and chop into small pieces using kitchen scissors. Fry in a heavy-based frying pan with no extra fat until crisp and golden. Drain on absorbent kitchen paper and keep hot until required.

PRESSED OX TONGUE

1.6-1.8 kg (3½-4 lb) pickled ox tongue
1 medium onion, skinned and thickly sliced
1 medium carrot, peeled and thickly sliced
4 celery sticks, trimmed and thickly sliced
30 ml (2 tbsp) wine vinegar
2 bay leaves
12 black peppercorns
5 ml (1 level tsp) gelatine

1. The day before, scrub and rinse the tongue under cold water. Place in a large bowl, cover with cold water and leave to soak overnight. Drain the tongue, then roll into a neat shape and secure with a skewer. Wrap in a single thickness of muslin, tying the ends together.
2. Next day, place the tongue in a large pan. Cover with cold water, bring to the boil and boil for 1 minute. Drain, rinse with cold water, then cover with fresh water. Add vegetables to pan with vinegar, bay leaves and peppercorns. Bring to the boil, cover and simmer for about 4 hours.
3. Lift the tongue on to a large plate, reserving the cooking liquid. Unwrap, ease out the skewer and use to pierce the thickest piece of flesh; if it slips in easily, the tongue is cooked.

4. Place the tongue in a colander and rinse with cold water until cool enough to handle. This will help to loosen the skin. Using a sharp knife, make a shallow slit along the underside. Peel the skin off in strips, starting from the tip end. Ease out the bones and gristle lying at the base.
5. Tightly curl the warm tongue and put into a 15 cm (6 inch) deep-sided soufflé dish or non-stick cake tin into which it fits tightly.
6. Strain the stock, reserving 600 ml (1 pint). Pour into a saucepan and boil rapidly to reduce to 150 ml (¼ pint). Meanwhile, pour 30 ml (2 tbsp) water into a small bowl and sprinkle on the gelatine. Soak for 10 minutes, then spoon the gelatine into the stock; stir gently and cool.
7. Gently pour the stock over the tongue. Put a small plate that will just fit inside the soufflé dish on top of the tongue. Put weights on the plate and chill overnight.
8. Lift the weights off the tongue and then ease off the plate. To release the tongue, run a blunt-edged knife around the inside of the dish, then immerse the base and sides in hot water for a few seconds only. Invert on to a serving plate, shaking to release tongue. Slice tongue to serve.
SERVES 10-12

OXTAIL PAPRIKA

2 oxtails, total weight about 1.6 kg (3½ lb), trimmed
*   and cut into pieces*
75 ml (5 tbsp) vegetable oil
2 medium onions, skinned and sliced
30 ml (2 level tbsp) paprika
60 ml (4 level tbsp) flour
700 g (1½ lb) fresh tomatoes, skinned and chopped or
*   397 g (14 oz) can tomatoes*
2 caps canned pimiento, sliced
600 ml (1 pint) beef stock
salt and pepper
150 ml (5 fl oz) soured cream
chopped fresh parsley, to garnish

1. The day before heat the oil in a large flame-proof casserole and brown the oxtail pieces, a few at a time. Remove with a slotted spoon.
2. Brown the onions in the oil remaining in pan. Stir in paprika and flour and cook gently for 1 minute. Stir in tomatoes, pimientos, stock and seasoning. Bring to the boil. Replace the meat.
3. Cover tightly and cook in the oven at 170°C

Oxtail Paprika

(325°F) mark 3 for about 3 hours, until the meat is really tender. Cool and refrigerate.
4. Next day, shortly before serving, skim all fat from the surface. Bring slowly to the boil, cover and simmer gently for 10 minutes. Stir in the cream and heat gently. Garnish with parsley.
SERVES 6

Creamed Sweetbreads

CREAMED SWEETBREADS

450 g (1 lb) sweetbreads, rinsed and soaked in cold
  water for 2 hours
1 small onion, skinned and chopped
1 medium carrot, peeled and chopped
few parsley stalks
1 bay leaf
salt and pepper
40 g (1½ oz) butter or margarine
60 ml (4 level tbsp) flour
300 ml (½ pint) milk
squeeze of lemon juice
chopped fresh parsley, to garnish

1. Put the sweetbreads, vegetables, herbs and seasoning in a saucepan with water to cover and simmer gently for about 15 minutes, until the sweetbreads are tender. Drain, reserving 300 ml (½ pint) of the cooking liquid, and keep hot.
2. Melt the butter in a saucepan, stir in the flour and cook gently for 1 minute, stirring. Remove from heat and gradually stir in milk and cooking liquid. Bring to the boil and cook, stirring, until thickened. Season and add lemon juice.
3. Add the sweetbreads to the sauce and simmer gently for 5-10 minutes. Garnish with parsley.
SERVES 4

BRAINS IN BLACK BUTTER SAUCE

4 sets of lamb's brains
30 ml (2 tbsp) wine vinegar
salt and pepper
125 g (4 oz) butter or margarine
chopped fresh parsley, to garnish

1. Soak the brains for 1-2 hours in cold water. Remove as much of the skin and membrane as possible and put the brains into a saucepan with half the vinegar, 2.5 ml (½ level tsp) salt and enough water to cover well. Bring to simmering

point and cook gently for 15 minutes.
2. Drain and place in cold water, then dry on absorbent kitchen paper.
3. Melt half of the butter in a frying pan, add the brains, brown on all sides and put on to a very hot dish. Add the rest of the butter to the pan and heat until dark brown, without allowing it to burn. Add the remaining vinegar, then pour it over the brains and sprinkle with salt, pepper and parsley.
SERVES 4

BRAWN

2 large pig's trotters
900 g (2 lb) belly of pork
30 ml (2 tbsp) white wine vinegar
10 ml (2 level tsp) salt
12 black peppercorns
8 whole allspice berries
2 cloves
5 ml (1 level tsp) dried mixed herbs
1 medium onion, skinned and roughly chopped
2 eggs, hard-boiled

1. Ask your butcher to split the trotters. Put them and the belly of pork into a large saucepan. Pour over 1.7 litres (3 pints) water and add the vinegar, salt, peppercorns, allspice, cloves, mixed herbs and onion.

2. Bring slowly to the boil, cover and simmer for 2½ hours. Skim off any scum every 20-30 minutes.
3. Remove the meat and strain the liquid into a clean saucepan. Boil to reduce to about 300 ml (½ pint). Leave until cool but not set, then skim.
4. When the meat is cool enough to handle, skin and dice the belly of pork, discarding bones, and remove all the meat from the trotters.
5. Slice the hard-boiled eggs and arrange on the bottom and sides of a 900 ml (1½ pint) bowl or soufflé dish. Arrange the meat in layers on top.
6. Gently pour in enough of the reduced liquid to cover the meat. Place a small saucer and light weight on top. Chill until set into a firm but not solid jelly. Remove any fat from the surface before turning out for serving.
SERVES 6

SAUSAGES

FRIED SAUSAGES
Melt a little fat in the frying pan, add the sausages and fry for 15-20 minutes, keeping the heat low to prevent them burning and turning them several times to brown evenly.

GRILLED SAUSAGES
Heat the grill to hot, put the sausages on the grill rack in the pan and cook until one side is lightly browned, then turn them; continue cooking and

turning frequently for about 15-20 minutes, until the sausages are well browned.

BAKED SAUSAGES
Heat the oven to 200°C (400°F) mark 6. Put the sausages in a greased baking tin and cook in the oven for about 30 minutes. Alternatively, make kilted sausages by wrapping rinded streaky bacon rashers around pairs of chipolatas and baking in the same way at 190°C (375°F) mark 5.

SAUSAGE ROLLS

175 g (6 oz) Shortcrust Pastry, made with 175 g (6 oz)
*   plain flour (see page 381)*
225 g (8 oz) pork sausagemeat
flour, for dusting
a little milk
beaten egg, to glaze

1. On a lightly floured surface, roll out the pastry thinly to an oblong, then cut it lengthways into 2 strips. Divide the sausagemeat into 2 pieces, dust with flour, and form into 2 rolls the length of the pastry.
2. Lay a roll of sausagemeat down the

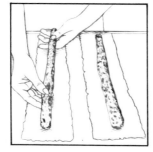

Lay a sausagemeat roll down the centre of each strip of pastry.

centre of each strip, brush the edges of the pastry with a little milk, fold one side of the pastry over the sausagemeat and press the two long edges firmly together to seal.
3. Brush the length of the two rolls with egg, then cut each into slices 4-5 cm (1½-2 inches). Place on a baking sheet and bake in the oven at 200°C (400°F) mark 6 for 15 minutes. Reduce the temperature to 180°C (350°F) mark 4 and cook for a further 15 minutes. Serve hot, or cool on a wire rack and serve cold.
MAKES 16

VARIATION
Sausage rolls can also be made with bought frozen puff pastry. Use a 212 g (7½ oz) packet and allow it to reach room temperature before rolling out and shaping. Cook these at 220°C (425°F) mark 7 for 10-15 minutes.

SAUSAGE AND BEAN STEW

15 ml (1 tbsp) vegetable oil
15 g (½ oz) butter
450 g (1 lb) pork sausages
1 large onion, skinned and sliced
two 397 g (14 oz) cans red kidney beans, drained
227 g (8 oz) can tomatoes
30 ml (2 tbsp) tomato purée
350 ml (12 fl oz) dry cider
salt and pepper

1. Heat the oil and butter in a large flameproof casserole and fry the sausages for about 5 minutes, until browned. Cut each sausage in half crossways.

2. Add the onion to the casserole and fry for 5 minutes, until golden brown. Drain off any excess fat. Return the sausages to the casserole together with the beans, tomatoes and their juice, tomato purée, cider and salt and pepper to taste.

3. Cover and cook gently for about 15 minutes or until the sausages are tender. Accompany with crusty bread, boiled rice or potatoes.
SERVES 4

TOAD IN THE HOLE

30 ml (2 tbsp) vegetable oil
450 g (1 lb) sausages
125 g (4 oz) plain flour
pinch of salt
1 egg
300 ml (½ pint) milk and water mixed

1. Put the vegetable oil in a small roasting tin and add the sausages. Place the tin in the oven at 220°C (425°F) mark 7 for about 10 minutes, until browned and the fat is hot.

2. Meanwhile, sift the flour and salt into a bowl and make a well in the centre. Add the egg and half the liquid.

3. Gradually mix the flour into the centre of the bowl and add the remaining liquid. Beat until smooth.

4. Pour into the roasting tin and bake in the oven for 40-45 minutes, until the batter is well risen and golden.
SERVES 4

LAYERED SAUSAGE PIE

225 g (8 oz) self raising flour
salt
125 g (4 oz) lard
1 small onion, skinned and grated
225 g (8 oz) pork sausagemeat
15 ml (1 tbsp) snipped fresh chives
225 g (8 oz) potatoes, peeled and sliced
50 g (2 oz) streaky bacon, rinded and chopped
225 g (8 oz) cooking apples, peeled, cored and sliced
beaten egg, to glaze

1. Place the flour and 1.25 ml (¼ level tsp) salt in a bowl. Cut the lard into small pieces and add to the flour. Using both hands, rub the fat into the flour until the mixture looks like fine breadcrumbs. Add the onion and enough water to bind the mixture together. Knead lightly for a few seconds to give a firm, smooth dough.

2. On a lightly floured surface roll out three quarters of the pastry and use to line a 20 cm (8 inch) sandwich tin.

3. Mix together the sausagemeat and chives. Layer up the potatoes, sausage mixture, bacon and apples in the pastry shell, seasoning lightly between the layers.

4. Roll out the remaining pastry to make a lid and place on top of the filling, sealing the edges well.

5. Place on a baking sheet. Glaze with the egg. Bake in the oven at 200°C (400°F) mark 6 for about 1 hour, covering lightly if overbrowning. Turn out of the tin and serve hot or cold.
SERVES 4

POULTRY

Chicken, turkey, duckling and goose are all classified as poultry. Guinea fowl, which used to be reared as game, is included because it is farmed nowadays. Poultry was once a rare luxury food, served only on special occasions. Developments in breeding and intensive methods of rearing have radically changed this, and most poultry is now plentiful and no longer expensive. Chicken is now the most popular meat in this country. This is partly because a growing awareness of healthy eating has encouraged people to eat more low fat white meat and less red meat.

Nutritionally poultry is an excellent food. It is a good source of protein and the B vitamins. Chicken and turkey are relatively low in fat, especially if the skin is not eaten.

CHICKEN

Fresh and frozen chickens are sold in a range of sizes. In addition a wide variety of fresh and frozen portions including breasts, drumsticks, thighs and mixed packs, are available. Convenience products, such as ready-prepared breadcrumbed portions, Chicken Kiev and marinated chicken pieces are highly popular.

OVEN-READY CHICKENS are sold completely eviscerated, chilled or frozen, with or without giblets. They range in weight from 1.4-3.2 kg (3-7 lb). Allow at least 375 g (12 oz) per person. In addition to standard oven-ready birds, pre-basted chickens are also sold.

Apart from roasting, oven-ready chickens can be steamed, poached or braised.

POUSSINS are very small chickens, 4-6 weeks old, weighing 450-575 g (1-1½ lb). One poussin serves 1-2 people.

SPRING CHICKENS are small birds, 12 weeks old, weighing 1.1 kg (2½ lb). One serves 2-3 people.

BOILING FOWL are not widely available these days. They are older, tougher birds, weighing 2.3-3.2 kg (5-7 lb). They are not suitable for roasting, but can be used in casseroles.

CORN-FED CHICKENS are a distinctive yellow colour because they are reared on a diet of sweetcorn (maize). Available fresh, and to a lesser extent frozen, they are slightly more expensive than chickens fed on standard feed.

CHICKEN HALVES AND QUARTERS are available whole or skinned and can be used for grilling, frying or casseroling.

CHICKEN BREASTS are often bought with the skin and some bones attached. Also sold as fillets and escalopes, with or without skin. Can be grilled, fried, barbecued or baked. Suprêmes are a French cut, with the wing bone attached.

CHICKEN THIGHS, DRUMSTICKS AND WINGS are dark meat portions which are available whole; or skinless; or with skin and bone removed. They can be baked, fried, grilled or casseroled.

FREE-RANGE CHICKENS

Consumer demand for free-range chickens has grown steadily. EEC regulations define four methods of free-range poultry production and labelling. These are summarised below.

EXTENSIVE OUTDOOR (BARN REARED): A maximum of 12 birds are kept per sq metre. They cannot be slaughtered before they are 8 weeks old.

FREE RANGE: A maximum of 13 birds are kept per sq metre and they must have access to open air runs. Feed must contain at least 70% cereals. Minimum slaughter age: 8 weeks.

TRADITONAL FREE RANGE: A maximum of 12 birds sq per metre, continuous daytime access to open air runs from 6 weeks and feed with at least 70% cereals. Minimum slaughter age: 11½ weeks.

FREE RANGE TOTAL FREEDOM: Must conform to all above criteria, but runs must be unlimited.

TURKEY

Turkey is now on sale all year round in a range of sizes and as a boneless roast. Turkey portions, sausages and burgers are also widely available.

OVEN-READY TURKEYS are available fresh and frozen in sizes ranging from 2.3 kg (5 lb) to as much as 13.5 kg (30 lb). For a guide to calculating serving quantities, see page 168. The cheapest way to buy turkey is frozen, but it is essential to allow plenty of time for thawing (see page 148). Allow for a weight loss of 5% during thawing owing to the extra water content. 'Chilled' turkeys do not contain extra water.

SELF-BASTING TURKEYS: These have a basting ingredient, such as butter, placed under the skin to keep the bird moist during cooking.

TURKEY ROAST: Boned and rolled joint of a convenient size. Usually serves 4–6.

TURKEY JOINTS: Drumsticks, wings and thighs are sold in packets. Suitable for pies and casseroles.

TURKEY ESCALOPES: These are thin slices from the breast of the bird. Suitable for grilling or frying.

HANDLING AND STORING POULTRY

To avoid the potential risk of food poisoning, particular care must be taken when handling poultry. Bacteria which can cause food poisoning, especially salmonella and campylobacter, may be present in low levels in raw birds. Provided that poultry is correctly stored, these bacteria will remain at low levels and, as long as it is then cooked properly, the bacteria will be killed by heat and rendered harmless.

* Always buy poultry from a reliable retailer and check the 'use by' date.
* Transfer poultry to the refrigerator or freezer as soon as possible. In warm weather carry poultry home in an insulated cool bag.
* Fresh chicken should be stored, covered, in the refrigerator on a plate. Open the seal and remove the giblets if there are any. Cook within 2 days.
* Frozen poultry should be transfered to the freezer while still frozen solid in its original wrapping. Store for up to 3 months. Defrost thoroughly before cooking. Cook quickly after thawing. Never re-freeze raw chicken.
* To avoid cross-contamination, always wash hands before and after preparing poultry. Never use the same utensils or chopping board for preparing raw poultry as for cooked foods without washing them in between.
* Always cook poultry thoroughly. Cool leftover meat quickly; refrigerate. Use within 2 days.

JOINTING AND BONING POULTRY

JOINTING POULTRY

1. With the bird breast side up and using poultry shears or a sharp knife, cut through the skin between leg and breast. Bend leg back until the joint cracks. Remove leg from body by cutting through thigh joint. Repeat with the other leg.

2. Separate the thighs from the drumsticks by bending each leg to crack the joint. Cut through the joint with the poultry shears or sharp knife to separate. Remove wings by bending them back and cutting the joint at the breast.

3. Place the carcass on its side. Cut from leg joint to backbone and along backbone to neck. Turn and cut along the other side to detach the breast. (The backbone will remain intact.)

4. Hold the breast skin-side down and bend it back to crack the breastbone. Cut along each side of the breastbone and remove.

HALVING A BIRD

1. With the bird breast side up, using poultry shears or a sharp knife, cut straight along one side of the breastbone from body cavity to neck cavity. Spread open, then cut along the side of the backbone to halve.

BONING POULTRY

Use a small very sharp knife, strong scissors, a darning or trussing needle with a large eye.

1. If using a frozen bird, first remove the giblets. Snip off the wing pinions at the second joint and remove the parson's nose. Wipe and pat dry.

2. Place the bird on its breast, and cut straight down the back to the bone. Ease flesh and skin away from backbone and rib-cage. Work down towards the joints, turning the bird as you go.

3. Clasping one leg in each hand, press firmly outwards to release the ball and socket joints. Ease the knife point into the joints and separate the legs from the body. Repeat for the wings.

4. Return to the main body and fillet flesh from breastbone. There is little flesh below the skin. Work down both sides and continue along the tip until the whole carcass is free.

5. Taking hold of the thigh end of the leg joint in one hand, scrape the flesh down from the bone towards the hinge joint. Continue filleting flesh off the lower leg joint until the knobbly end is reached. Clasp exposed bones in one hand, the skin and flesh in the other. Pull leg inside out to remove the bone, snipping any sinews.

6. Remove the wing bones in the same way and take out the wishbone.

ROASTING TURKEY (FRESH OR FROZEN)

Oven-ready weight	Approximate thawing time (at cool room temperature) if applicable	Cooking time (without foil)	Cooking time (foil wrapped)	Approximate No.of servings
550 g–1.4 kg (1¼-3 lb)	4–10 hours	1½–1¾ hours	1¾–2 hours	2–4
1.4–2.3 kg (3-5 lb)	10–15 hours	1¾–2 hours	2–2½ hours	4–6
2.3–3.6 kg (5-8 lb)	15–18 hours	2–2½ hours	2–2½ hours	6–10
3.6–5 kg (8-11 lb)	18–20 hours	2½–3¼ hours	3½–4 hours	10–15
5–6.8 kg (11-15 lb)	20–24 hours	3¼–3¾ hours	4–5 hours	15–20
6.8–9 kg (15-20 lb	24–30 hours	3¾–4¼ hours	5–5½ hours	20–30
9–11.3 kg (20-25 lb)	30–36 hours	4¼–4¾ hours	not recommended	30–40
11.3–13.5 kg (25-30 lb)	36–48 hours	4¾–5½ hours	not recommended	40–50

PREPARING POULTRY FOR ROASTING

THAWING

Frozen chickens and turkeys must be thoroughly thawed before cooking. They should be left in their bags and thawed at cool room temperature, not in the refrigerator. Remove giblets as soon as they are loose – these can be used to make stock for the gravy. To check that the bird is thawed, make sure there are no ice crystals in the cavity and that the legs are quite flexible. Once it is thoroughly thawed, cover and store in the refrigerator. Cook as soon as possible.

STUFFING

Loosely stuff the neck end only of the bird to ensure heat penetrates the centre more quickly. Allow 225 g (8 oz) stuffing for each 2.3 kg (5 lb) dressed weight and stuff bird just before cooking. Sew up neck skin or use skewers: truss bird.

TRUSSING

Trussing is done to keep the bird in a compact shape. You need a trussing needle or fine skewer and thin thread.
1. Fold the neck skin under the body and fold the wing tips back towards the backbone so they hold the neck skin in position. Put the bird on its back and press the legs well into the side. Slit skin above vent, push the parson's nose through.
2. Thread the needle with a length of string and insert it close to the second joint of the right wing; push it right through the body, to catch the corresponding joint on the left side.
3. Insert the needle again in the first joint of the left wing, pass it through the flesh at the back of the body, catching the tips of the wings and the neck skin, and pass it out through the first joint of the wing on the right side. Tie ends in a bow.
4. To truss the legs, re-thread the needle and insert it through the gristle at the right side of the parson's nose. Pass the string over the right leg, over the left leg, through the gristle at the left side of the parson's nose, carry it behind the parson's nose and tie ends of the string firmly.
5. If using a skewer, insert it right through the body of the bird just below the thigh bone and turn the bird over on to its breast. First, catching in the wing tips, pass the string under the ends of skewer and cross it over the back. Turn the bird over and tie the ends of the string together around the tail, at the same time securing each of the drumsticks.

ROASTING TURKEY

Weigh the bird and calculate the cooking time, to be ready 30 minutes before carving. Spread the turkey with butter or margarine and grind over pepper. Wrap the turkey loosely in foil or put it straight into a roasting tin. Preheat oven to 180°C (350°F) mark 4 and put the turkey in. Fold back foil about 45 minutes before end of cooking time to brown. Baste regularly.

TESTING

To test when the bird is cooked, push a fine skewer into the thickest part of the thigh. If the juices run clear, the bird is cooked but if they are still pink, it needs longer cooking.

CARVING

1. Remove the trussing thread and place the bird so that one wing is towards your left hand, with the breast diagonally towards you. Prise the leg outwards with the fork. Sever the leg.
2. Divide thigh from drumstick by cutting through the joint; in a big bird it is further divided. Hold wing with fork and cut through outer layer of breast and wing joint. Ease wing away from body. Repeat with other wing.
3. Slice the breast, cutting parallel with the bone. Slice stuffed birds from front of breast.

ROAST CHICKEN

1.4-1.8 kg (3-4 lb) oven-ready chicken
stuffing (see pages 182-186)
1 onion, skinned
1 lemon wedge
melted butter or vegetable oil for brushing
salt and pepper
streaky bacon rashers (optional)
ACCOMPANIMENTS
Forcemeat Balls (see page 183)
Bread Sauce (see page 206)
Gravy (see page 202)

1. Wash bird, dry thoroughly and put stuffing in the neck end before folding the neck skin over. Put the onion and lemon in the body cavity.
2. Truss the bird (see page 148) and weigh. Put in a deep roasting tin, brush with melted butter or oil and season. Lay a few strips of bacon over the breast to prevent it from becoming dry, if desired. Roast in the oven at 200°C (400°F) mark 6, basting occasionally, allowing 20 minutes per 450 g (1 lb) plus 20 minutes. Cover the breast with foil if it shows signs of over browning.
3. Serve with the accompaniments.
SERVES 4-6

FRENCH-STYLE ROAST CHICKEN

1.4 kg (3 lb) oven-ready chicken
50 g (2 oz) butter or margarine
salt and pepper
5-6 fresh tarragon or parsley sprigs
melted butter for brushing
2 rashers bacon, rinded
300 ml (½ pint) chicken stock or 150 ml (¼ pint)
  chicken stock and 150 ml (¼ pint) white wine

1. Prepare the bird as for ordinary roasting.

2. Cream the butter with seasoning and put inside the bird with the herbs.
3. Brush the breast with melted butter and cover with the rashers of bacon.
4. Place the bird in a roasting tin and add the stock. Roast in the oven at 190°C (375°F) mark 5 for about 1 hour 20 minutes, basting with the stock every 15 minutes. Remove the bacon during the last 15 minutes to brown the breast. Use the stock to make gravy.
SERVES 4

ITALIAN STUFFED CHICKEN

75 g (3 oz) butter or margarine
1 medium onion, skinned and finely chopped
45 ml (3 tbsp) Marsala
450 g (1 lb) minced pork
125 g (4 oz) fresh breadcrumbs
50 g (2 oz) green olives, stoned and roughly chopped
50 g (2 oz) pine nuts, roughly chopped
15 ml (1 tbsp) chopped fresh marjoram or 5 ml
  (1 level tsp) dried
pinch of freshly grated nutmeg
salt and pepper
1 egg, beaten
3 kg (6½ lb) chicken, boned (see page 147)
450 g (1 lb) piece Italian salami, skinned

1. Melt 25 g (1 oz) of butter in a frying pan and cook the onion for 5 minutes, until soft but not brown. Add the Marsala and boil rapidly for 2 minutes. Cool for 5 minutes.
2. Mix together the onion, pork, breadcrumbs, olives, pine nuts, marjoram, nutmeg and salt and

pepper to taste. Bind with the egg.
3. Place the chicken, skin side down, on a work surface. Push the legs and wings inside and flatten with a rolling pin to evenly distribute the flesh. Spread half the stuffing mixture over the centre of the chicken, then place the salami on top. Cover with the remaining stuffing mixture.
4. Tuck the neck end in towards the filling, draw the long sides of the bird over the stuffing and sew it neatly together with fine string or cotton, reshaping the bird. Use overlapping stitches and do not roll too tightly or the bird will burst during cooking. Secure the string loosely for easy removal. Weigh the bird.
5. Place the chicken in a roasting tin. Sprinkle with salt and pepper, then dot with the remaining butter. Roast in the oven at 190°C (375°F) mark 5, basting occasionally, allowing 25 minutes per 450 g (1 lb).
6. Cool, then refrigerate overnight. Remove the string before slicing.
SERVES 12-16

CHICKEN GALANTINE

50 g (2 oz) butter or margarine
125 g (4 oz) button mushrooms, wiped and coarsely
    chopped
1 medium onion, skinned and coarsely chopped
3 celery sticks, trimmed and coarsely chopped
225 g (8 oz) fresh breadcrumbs
5 ml (1 level tsp) dried marjoram
1 egg, beaten
salt and pepper
1.4 kg (3 lb) oven-ready chicken, boned (see page 147)
125 g (4 oz) piece of garlic sausage

1. Melt half the butter in a large frying pan, add the vegetables and fry for about 4 minutes, then leave to cool.
2. Place the breadcrumbs in a mixing bowl, add the marjoram and cooked vegetables. Mix well with a wooden spoon, adding enough egg to bind. Season well.

3. Spread the bird out, skin side down and spoon some of the stuffing into the leg and wing cavities. Spread the remaining stuffing over the bird. Place the garlic sausage lengthways down the centre.
4. Tuck the neck end in towards the filling, draw the long sides of the bird over the stuffing and sew it neatly together with fine string or strong thread. Use overlapping stitches and do not roll too tightly or the bird will burst during cooking. Secure the string loosely for easy removal.
5. Weigh the chicken and calculate the cooking time, allowing 25 minutes per 450 g (1 lb). Place the chicken in a roasting tin and dot with the remaining butter. Season well. Roast in the oven at 180°C (350°F) mark 4, basting frequently. When cooked, remove from the tin and leave to cool. Remove skewers, then chill in the refrigerator. To serve, remove the thread and thinly slice the chicken.
SERVES 6-8

DEVILLED POUSSINS

15 ml (1 level tbsp) mustard powder
15 ml (1 level tbsp) paprika
20 ml (4 level tsp) ground turmeric
20 ml (4 level tsp) ground cumin
60 ml (4 level tbsp) tomato ketchup
15 ml (1 tbsp) lemon juice
75 g (3 oz) butter or margarine, melted
3 poussins, about 700 g (1½ lb) each
15 ml (1 level tbsp) poppy seeds

1. Put the mustard powder, paprika, turmeric and ground cumin into a small bowl. Add the tomato ketchup and lemon juice and beat well to form a thick, smooth paste. Slowly pour in the melted butter, stirring all the time.
2. Place the poussins on a chopping board, breast side down. With a small sharp knife cut right along the backbone of each bird through the skin and flesh. With scissors cut through the backbone to open them up. Turn the birds over, breast side up. Continue cutting along the breastbone which will split the birds into two equal halves. Lie them skin side uppermost in a roasting tin.

3. Spread the paste evenly over the surface of the birds. Sprinkle with the poppy seeds. Cover loosely and leave in a cool place for at least 1-2 hours. Cook the poussins, uncovered, in the oven at 220°C (425°F) mark 7 for 15 minutes.
4. Remove from the oven and place under a hot grill until the skin is well browned and crisp. Return to the oven, reduce temperature to 180°C (350°F) mark 4 for a further 20 minutes.
SERVES 6

VARIATIONS
HERBY ORANGE POUSSINS
Replace the spicy marinade with a mixture of 150 ml (¼ pint) dry white wine, 45 ml (3 tbsp) olive oil, juice of 2 oranges, 5 ml (1 tsp) each chopped fresh rosemary, thyme and marjoram and 1 skinned and crushed garlic clove.

ORIENTAL-STYLE POUSSINS
Replace the spicy marinade with 100 ml (4 fl oz) soy sauce, 30 ml (2 tbsp) dry sherry, 2 thinly sliced spring onions, 30 ml (2 tbsp) soft light brown sugar, 2.5 ml (½ tsp) salt and 2.5 ml (½ tsp) ground ginger.

BAKED CHICKEN QUARTERS

4 chicken quarters or pieces
salt and pepper
45 ml (3 level tbsp) flour
50-75 g (2-3 oz) butter or margarine

1. Wipe the chicken quarters and pat dry with absorbent kitchen paper. Season.
2. Toss in the flour until completely coated and place in a roasting tin. Melt the butter and pour it over the chicken. Bake in the oven at 200°C (400°F) mark 6 for 45 minutes, turning once, until tender.
SERVES 4

VARIATION
For a crisp coating, dip the chicken pieces in 1 lightly beaten egg and then in 50 g (2 oz) dry breadcrumbs. Bake as above.

FRIED CHICKEN

4 chicken quarters or pieces
salt and pepper
45 ml (3 level tbsp) flour
50 g (2 oz) butter or margarine or 45 ml (3 tbsp)
*   vegetable oil*

1. Wipe the chicken quarters or pieces and pat dry with absorbent kitchen paper. Season to taste with salt and pepper.
2. Toss the chicken in the flour until completely coated.

3. Heat the butter in a frying pan or flameproof casserole and add the chicken pieces. Cook until golden brown on both sides, then lower the heat and cook for about 30-40 minutes, until tender. Drain on absorbent kitchen paper.
SERVES 4

NOTE: To ensure that the chicken pieces remain moist the surface should be browned at a high temperature to seal in the juices and give a good colour, then the heat reduced for the remainder of the cooking time.

GRILLED CHICKEN OR POUSSIN

4 chicken quarters or whole poussins
salt and pepper
50-75 g (2-3 oz) butter or margarine, melted, or
*   45-60 ml (3-4 tbsp) vegetable oil*

1. If using chicken quarters, season and brush with melted butter, margarine or oil and grill under a medium heat for 20 minutes.

2. To prepare poussins for grilling, place them breast side down on a board. Cut through the backbone, open the bird out and flatten.
3. Brush all over with the melted butter or oil and season lightly. Place in the grill pan.
4. Grill under a medium heat, turning once or twice for about 30 minutes, until tender.
SERVES 4

POACHED CHICKEN

1.4 kg (3 lb) oven-ready chicken
juice of ½ a lemon
salt
1 medium onion, skinned and stuck with 3-4 cloves
1 medium carrot, peeled
6 black peppercorns
bouquet garni

1 Rub the bird with lemon juice. Put in a large pan and just cover with water. Add the salt, onion, carrot, peppercorns and bouquet garni.
2. Bring to the boil, cover and simmer for about 50 minutes, until tender. Remove from the stock and allow to cool.
3. Dice and use for fricassées, curries or salads. Use the cooking liquid to make sauce or soup.
SERVES 4

VARIATION
POACHED CHICKEN BREASTS
Poach chicken breasts in a deep frying pan (as above). Cook for 20-25 minutes until tender.

CHICKEN WITH CUMIN AND CIDER

15 ml (1 tbsp) vegetable oil
50 g (2 oz) butter or margarine
4 chicken quarters
2 small cooking apples, peeled and sliced
1 small onion, skinned and sliced
5 ml (1 level tsp) ground cumin
15 ml (1 level tbsp) flour
300 ml (½ pint) chicken stock
150 ml (¼ pint) dry cider
salt and pepper
1 large red-skinned eating apple

1. Heat the oil and 25 g (1 oz) butter in a flame-proof casserole, add the chicken quarters and fry until golden. Remove from the pan with a slotted spoon.
2. Add the cooking apples and onion to the pan, cook for 3 minutes, then stir in the cumin and flour and cook for 1 minute, stirring. Remove from the heat and gradually stir in the stock and cider.
3. Bring to the boil slowly and continue to cook, stirring, until thickened. Return the chicken to the pan and adjust the seasoning.
4. Cover the pan and simmer gently for 15 minutes. Turn the chicken pieces over. Re-cover the pan and cook for a further 15 minutes, until the chicken is quite tender.
5. Meanwhile, quarter and core the eating apple, halve each quarter lengthways. Melt the remaining butter and fry the apple slices until golden but still crisp.
6. Garnish the dish with the fried apple slices and serve immediately.
SERVES 4

CHICKEN WITH TARRAGON SAUCE

6 chicken breast fillets, skinned
75 g (3 oz) butter or margarine
25 g (1 oz) flour
450 ml (¾ pint) chicken stock
30 ml (2 tbsp) tarragon vinegar
10 ml (2 level tsp) French mustard
15 ml (1 tbsp) chopped fresh tarragon, or
  5 ml (1 level tsp) dried
50 g (2 oz) Cheddar cheese, grated
150 ml (5 fl oz) single cream
salt and pepper

1. Wipe the chicken breasts and pat dry with absorbent kitchen paper.
2. Melt 50 g (2 oz) butter in a frying pan or flameproof casserole and add the chicken breasts. Cook until golden on both sides, then lower the heat and cook for about 20 minutes until tender, turning once.
3. Meanwhile, melt the remaining butter in a saucepan, stir in the flour and cook gently for 1 minute, stirring. Remove the pan from the heat and gradually stir in the stock and tarragon vinegar. Bring to the boil slowly and continue to cook, stirring constantly, until the sauce thickens.
4. Stir in the mustard, tarragon, cheese and cream. Season with salt and pepper and heat gently without boiling.
5. Drain the chicken breasts on absorbent

Chicken with Tarragon Sauce

kitchen paper, then transfer to a warmed serving dish. Spoon over the tarragon sauce and serve immediately.
SERVES 6

SPICED CHICKEN WITH CASHEW NUTS

8 chicken breast fillets, skinned
2.5 cm (1 inch) piece fresh root ginger, peeled and
roughly chopped
5 ml (1 level tsp) coriander seeds
4 cloves
10 ml (2 level tsp) black peppercorns
300 ml (10 fl oz) natural yogurt
1 medium onion, skinned and roughly chopped
50 g (2 oz) cashew nuts
2.5 ml (½ level tsp) hot chilli powder
10 ml (2 level tsp) ground turmeric
40 g (1½ oz) ghee or clarified butter (see page 568)
salt
chopped toasted cashew nuts and chopped fresh
coriander, to garnish

1. Make shallow slashes across each chicken breast. Put the ginger, coriander seeds, cloves, peppercorns and yogurt in a blender or food processor and purée until almost smooth. Pour the yogurt mixture over the chicken, cover and leave to marinate in the refrigerator for about 24 hours, turning once.
2. Put the onion, cashew nuts, chilli powder, turmeric and 150 ml (¼ pint) water in a blender or food processor and purée until almost smooth.
3. Lift the chicken out of the marinade. Melt the ghee in a large frying pan, add the chicken and fry until browned.
4. Stir in the marinade with the nut mixture and bring slowly to the boil. Season with salt.
5. Cover the pan and simmer for about 20 minutes, until the chicken is tender, stirring occasionally. Adjust seasoning. Serve garnished with cashew nuts and coriander.
SERVES 8

CHICKEN KIEV

175 g (6 oz) butter, softened
grated rind of ½ a lemon
15 ml (1 tbsp) lemon juice
salt and pepper
15 ml (1 tbsp) chopped fresh parsley
1 garlic clove, skinned and crushed
6 large chicken breast fillets, skinned
25 g (1 oz) seasoned flour
1 egg, beaten
125 g (4 oz) fresh breadcrumbs
vegetable oil for deep-frying
lemon wedges and parsley sprigs, to garnish (optional)

1. Combine the butter with lemon rind, juice, salt and pepper, parsley and garlic. Beat well together, form into a roll and chill well.
2. Place the chicken breasts on a flat surface and pound them to an even thickness with a meat mallet or rolling pin.
3. Cut the butter into six pieces and place one piece on the centre of each chicken breast.
4. Roll up, folding the ends in to enclose the butter completely.
5. Secure the rolls with wooden cocktail sticks, then coat each one with seasoned flour.
6. Dip the rolls in the beaten egg, then coat them with breadcrumbs, patting the crumbs firmly on to the chicken.
7. Place the rolls on a baking sheet, cover lightly with non-stick or greaseproof paper and refrigerate for 2 hours or until required, to allow the coating to dry.
8. In a deep-fryer, heat the oil to 160°C (325°F). Put two chicken rolls in a frying basket and lower into the oil. Fry for 15 minutes. The chicken is cooked when it is browned and firm when pressed with a fork. Do not pierce.
9. Remove from the fryer, drain on absorbent kitchen paper and keep warm while cooking the remaining chicken. Remove the cocktail sticks before serving.
SERVES 6

VARIATION
SPICY CHICKEN KIEV
To make the spicy butter filling, sauté 1 finely chopped shallot with 20 ml (2 level tsp) cayenne pepper in 15 ml (1 tbsp) butter or oil until soft but not brown. Stir in 15 ml (1 tbsp) chopped fresh parsley. Mix with 175 g (6 oz) softened butter and season. Proceed from step 2 above.

CHICKEN MARYLAND

1.4 kg (3 lb) oven-ready chicken, jointed (see page 147)
salt and pepper
45 ml (3 level tbsp) flour
1 egg, beaten
125 g (4 oz) fresh breadcrumbs
25 g (1 oz) butter or margarine
45-60 ml (3-4 tbsp) vegetable oil
4 Fried Bananas, Corn Fritters and 4 Bacon Rolls
   (see right), to serve

1. Divide the chicken into fairly small pieces, coat with seasoned flour, dip in beaten egg and coat with breadcrumbs.
2. Heat the butter and oil in a large frying pan, add the chicken joints and fry until lightly browned. Continue frying gently, turning the pieces once, for about 20 minutes, until tender. Alternatively, fry them in hot oil in a deep-fat fryer for 5-10 minutes at a frying temperature of 190°C (375°F).
3. Serve the chicken with Fried Bananas, Corn Fritters and Bacon Rolls.

SERVES 4

FRIED BANANAS

Peel and slice the bananas lengthways and fry gently for about 3 minutes in a little hot butter or margarine until lightly browned.

CORN FRITTERS

Make up a batter from 100 g (4 oz) flour, a pinch of salt, 1 egg and 150 ml (1 pint) milk. Fold in a 312 g (11 oz) tin sweetcorn kernels, drained. Fry spoonfuls in a little hot fat until crisp and golden, turning them once. Drain well on absorbent kitchen paper.

BACON ROLLS

Roll up rashers of rinded streaky bacon, thread on a skewer and grill for 3-5 minutes, until crisp.

SESAME LEMON CHICKEN

8 small chicken drumsticks, about 75 g (3 oz) each
30 ml (2 level tbsp) cornflour
1 egg, beaten
1 lemon
15 ml (1 tbsp) soy sauce
15 ml (1 tbsp) cider vinegar
15 ml (1 level tbsp) demerara sugar
60 ml (4 tbsp) dry sherry
15 ml (1 tbsp) sesame oil
30 ml (2 tbsp) peanut oil
2 medium leeks, washed, trimmed and cut into 1 cm
   (½ inch) slices
45 ml (3 level tbsp) sesame seeds
salt and pepper

1. Put the drumsticks in a large saucepan and cover with cold water. Bring to the boil, cover and simmer for about 30 minutes. Drain and dry with absorbent kitchen paper.
2. Mix together the cornflour and egg; use to thoroughly coat the chicken drumsticks.
3. Grate the lemon rind and whisk together with the soy sauce, cider vinegar, sugar and sherry. Peel and thinly slice the lemon and reserve for the garnish.
4. Heat the sesame and peanut oils in a wok or large frying pan until just beginning to smoke. Brown the drumsticks a few at a time. Remove with a slotted spoon and keep warm.
5. Fry the leeks and sesame seeds in the oil remaining in the pan for 1-2 minutes, adding more oil if necessary. Return the drumsticks with the sauce mixture to the pan. Bring to the boil, then simmer for 3-4 minutes, stirring occasionally. Season.
6. Transfer to a warmed serving dish. Lightly fry the lemon slices in the wok or frying pan. Garnish the drumsticks with the lemon.

SERVES 4

TANDOORI CHICKEN

4 chicken quarters, skinned
30 ml (2 tbsp) lemon juice
1 garlic clove, skinned
2.5 cm (1 inch) fresh root ginger, peeled and chopped
1 green chilli pepper, seeded
60 ml (4 tbsp) natural yogurt
5 ml (1 level tsp) ground cumin
5 ml (1 level tsp) Garam Masala (see page 196)
15 ml (1 level tbsp) paprika
5 ml (1 level tsp) salt
30 ml (2 tbsp) melted ghee or vegetable oil
lemon wedges and onion rings, to garnish

1. Using a sharp knife or skewer, pierce the chicken pieces all over. Put the chicken in an ovenproof dish, add the lemon juice and rub it into the flesh. Cover and leave for 30 minutes.
2. Meanwhile, put the garlic, ginger and chilli in a blender or food processor with 15 ml (1 tbsp) water and grind to a smooth paste.
3. Add the paste to the yogurt with the cumin, garam masala, paprika, salt and melted ghee. Mix well, then use to coat the chicken.
4. Cover and leave to marinate at room temperature for 5 hours, turning once or twice.
5. Roast in the oven at 170°C (325°F) mark 3 for 1¾-2 hours, basting frequently. Garnish with lemon wedges and onion rings.
SERVES 4

CHICKEN AU GRATIN

4 chicken quarters, skinned
6 black peppercorns
1 bay leaf
1 medium carrot, peeled and sliced
1 medium onion, skinned and sliced
2 cloves
thinly pared rind of 1 lemon
salt and pepper
25 g (1 oz) butter or margarine
25 g (1 oz) flour
pinch of grated nutmeg
125 g (4 oz) Cheddar cheese, grated
30 ml (2 tbsp) lemon juice
30 ml (2 level tbsp) fresh breadcrumbs

1. Put the chicken quarters in a large saucepan with the peppercorns, bay leaf, carrot, onion, cloves, lemon rind and a pinch of salt. Cover with cold water and bring to the boil. Cover and simmer gently for 45 minutes, until tender. Remove joints and keep warm. Boil stock until reduced to 300 ml (½ pint), strain and reserve.
2. Melt the butter in a pan, stir in the flour and nutmeg and cook for 1 minute, stirring. Remove from heat and gradually stir in the reserved stock. Bring to the boil slowly and cook, stirring, until thick. Remove from heat and add lemon juice and three quarters of the cheese. Season well.
3. Arrange chicken in a shallow ovenproof serving dish. Coat with the sauce. Combine remaining cheese and breadcrumbs. Scatter over the sauce. Grill until golden and bubbling.
SERVES 4

FRICASSÉE OF CHICKEN

1.6 kg (3½ lb) oven-ready chicken
1 medium onion, skinned and chopped
2 celery sticks, sliced
salt and pepper
bouquet garni
30 ml (2 tbsp) lemon juice
65 g (2½ oz) butter or margarine
175 g (6 oz) button mushrooms, wiped and sliced
50 g (2 oz) flour
45 ml (3 tbsp) double cream

1. Put the chicken in a large pan with the onion, celery, seasoning, bouquet garni and half the lemon juice. Add just enough water to cover. Bring to the boil, cover and simmer for 1 hour.
2. Drain, reserving the vegetables and 600 ml (1 pint) of the stock. Dice the chicken flesh.
3. Melt 15 g (½ oz) butter in a saucepan, add the mushrooms and fry for 2-3 minutes.
4. In a separate pan melt the remaining butter, stir in the flour and cook, stirring, for 1 minute. Remove from heat and gradually stir in reserved stock. Bring to the boil and cook, stirring, until thickened. Add 15 ml (1 tbsp) lemon juice, the chicken, vegetables and mushrooms. Stir in the cream and adjust the seasoning.
SERVES 4

Stir-fried Chicken with Courgettes

STIR-FRIED CHICKEN WITH COURGETTES

30 ml (2 tbsp) vegetable oil
1 garlic clove, skinned and crushed
450 g (1 lb) chicken breast fillets, skinned and cut into
*   thin strips*
450 g (1 lb) courgettes, cut into thin strips
1 red pepper, seeded and cut into thin strips
45 ml (3 tbsp) dry sherry
15 ml (1 tbsp) soy sauce
60 ml (4 tbsp) natural yogurt
pepper

1. Heat the oil in a large frying pan or a wok and fry the garlic for 1 minute. Add the chicken and cook for 3-4 minutes, stirring continuously.
2. Add the courgettes and pepper and continue to cook for 1-2 minutes, until the chicken is cooked and the vegetables are tender but still crisp.
3. Stir in the sherry and soy sauce and cook for 1 minute, until hot. Stir in the yogurt and season to taste with pepper. Serve immediately with boiled rice or noodles.
SERVES 4

SHREDDED CHICKEN WITH MUSHROOMS AND WALNUTS

*4 chicken breast fillets, skinned and cut into
    thin strips*
*5 cm (2 inch) piece fresh root ginger, peeled and thinly
    sliced*
45 ml (3 tbsp) soy sauce
60 ml (4 tbsp) dry sherry
5 ml (1 tsp) five spice powder
45 ml (3 tbsp) vegetable oil
125 g (4 oz) mushrooms, halved
¼ cucumber, cut into chunks
75 g (3 oz) walnut pieces, roughly chopped
pepper

1. Put the chicken in a bowl with the ginger, soy sauce, sherry and five spice powder. Stir well, cover and leave to marinate for at least 1 hour.

2. Remove the chicken from the marinade with a slotted spoon, reserving the marinade.
3. Heat the oil in a large frying pan or wok. Add the chicken and cook for 3-4 minutes, stirring continuously.
4. Add the mushrooms, cucumber and walnuts and continue to cook for 1-2 minutes, until the chicken is cooked and the vegetables are tender but still crisp.
5. Stir in the reserved marinade and cook for 1 minute, until hot. Season to taste with pepper. Serve immediately with rice or noodles.
SERVES 4

VARIATION
Replace the walnut pieces with cashew nuts and sprinkle with a little sesame oil before serving.

Shredded Chicken with Mushrooms and Walnuts

POULET EN COCOTTE

1.4 kg (3 lb) oven-ready chicken
50 g (2 oz) butter or margarine
225 g (8 oz) lean back bacon in one slice
450 g (1 lb) potatoes, peeled and cut into 2.5 cm
*   (1 inch) cubes*
3 celery sticks, trimmed and sliced
450 g (1 lb) small new carrots, peeled
50 g (2 oz) button mushrooms, wiped
25 g (1 oz) shelled walnuts
chopped fresh parsley, to garnish
FOR THE STUFFING
125 g (4 oz) sausagemeat
30 ml (2 level tbsp) fresh breadcrumbs
1 chicken liver, chopped
30 ml (2 tbsp) chopped fresh parsley
salt and pepper

1. To make the stuffing, mix all the ingredients together in a bowl until well blended. Season well.
2. Stuff the chicken at the neck end, then truss the bird as for roasting. Season well.
3. Melt the butter in a large frying pan, add the chicken and fry, turning it until well browned all over.
4. Place the chicken and butter in a large ovenproof casserole.
5. Remove the rind from the bacon, then cut into 2 cm (¾ inch) cubes. Add to the casserole, cover, and cook in the oven at 180°C (350°F) mark 4 for 15 minutes.
6. Remove the casserole from the oven and baste the chicken. Surround it with the vegetables and walnuts, turning them in the fat.
7. Return the casserole to the oven and cook for a further 1½ hours. Transfer the chicken to a warmed serving plate and garnish with chopped parsley. Serve with the vegetables and juices from the casserole.
SERVES 4

CHICKEN WITH VERMOUTH AND OLIVES

8 chicken thighs, skinned, total weight about 900 g
*   (2 lb)*
40 g (1½ oz) seasoned flour
50 g (2 oz) butter or margarine
300 ml (½ pint) chicken stock
150 ml (¼ pint) dry French vermouth or dry white wine
1 small garlic clove, skinned and crushed
150 ml (5 fl oz) soured cream
50 g (2 oz) black olives, stoned and sliced
salt and pepper
Pastry Crescents (see right) and parsley sprigs, to
*   garnish*

1. Toss the chicken thighs in seasoned flour and reserve any remaining flour. Melt the butter in a flameproof casserole and brown the chicken well all over. Carefully remove the chicken with a large slotted spoon and set aside; keep warm.
2. Stir in the reserved seasoned flour and cook gently for 1 minute, stirring. Remove pan from the heat and gradually stir in the stock, vermouth and crushed garlic. Bring to the boil slowly and continue to cook, stirring constantly, until the sauce is thickened.

3. Return the chicken to the pan, cover and simmer gently for about 1 hour.
4. Transfer the chicken to a serving dish and keep warm. Stir the cream into the pan juices. Heat gently for 3-4 minutes, without boiling.
5. Just before serving, add the olives, adjust the seasoning and spoon the sauce over the chicken. Garnish with pastry crescents and parsley.
SERVES 4

Using a biscuit cutter, cut crescent shapes from thinly rolled pastry.

PASTRY CRESCENTS (FLEURONS)
Use 50 g (2 oz) Short-crust Pastry made with 50 g (2 oz) flour (see page 381). Cut into crescents, place on a dampened baking sheet and bake in the oven at 220°C (425°F) mark 7 for about 12 minutes, until golden brown and well risen.

CHICKEN MARENGO

4 chicken quarters
½ a lemon, cut into wedges
50 g (2 oz) flour
60 ml (4 tbsp) vegetable oil
50 g (2 oz) butter or margarine
30 ml (2 tbsp) brandy
salt and pepper
397 g (14 oz) can tomatoes, with their juice
1 garlic clove, skinned and crushed
150 ml (¼ pint) chicken stock
125 g (4 oz) button mushrooms, wiped
30 ml (2 tbsp) chopped fresh parsley

Chicken Cacciatora

1. Rub the chicken quarters all over with the lemon and coat in the flour.
2. Heat the oil in a large frying pan, add the chicken joints and fry on both sides, until golden brown, about 5-10 minutes.
3. Remove from the frying pan and place, skin-side up, in a large saucepan or flameproof casserole together with 25 g (1 oz) of the butter. Sprinkle with the brandy and seasoning, then turn the joints over. Roughly chop the tomatoes and add them to the chicken with the garlic and stock.
4. Cover and simmer gently for about 1 hour, until the meat is tender.
5. Ten minutes before serving, melt the remaining butter in a pan and cook the mushrooms for about 5 minutes, until soft. Drain and add to the chicken.
6. When the chicken is cooked, add the parsley and stir. Adjust the seasoning.
7. Transfer the chicken joints to a warmed serving dish. If the sauce is too thin, boil briskly to reduce. Spoon the sauce over the chicken and serve garnished with the fried bread.
SERVES 4

VARIATION
CHICKEN CACCIATORA
To make Chicken Cacciatora, increase the mushrooms to 225 g (8 oz) and fry with 1 skinned and finely chopped onion. Replace the stock with dry white wine.

STOVED CHICKEN

25 g (1 oz) butter
15 ml (1 tbsp) vegetable oil
4 chicken quarters, halved
125 g (4 oz) lean back bacon, rinded and chopped
1.1 kg (2½ lb) floury potatoes, such as King Edwards, peeled and cut into 5 mm (¼ inch) slices
2 large onions, skinned and sliced
salt and pepper
10 ml (2 tsp) chopped fresh thyme or 2.5 ml (½ tsp) dried thyme
600 ml (1 pint) chicken stock
fresh chives, to garnish

1. Heat half of the butter and the oil in a large frying pan and fry the chicken and bacon for 5 minutes, until lightly browned.
2. Place a thick layer of potato slices, then onion slices, in the base of a large ovenproof casserole. Season well, add the thyme and dot with half the remaining butter.
3. Add the chicken and bacon, season to taste and dot with the remaining butter. Cover with the remaining onions and finally a layer of potatoes. Season and dot with butter. Pour over the stock.
4. Cover and bake at 150°C (300°F) mark 2 for about 2 hours, until the chicken is tender and the potatoes are cooked, adding a little more hot stock if necessary.
5. Sprinkle with snipped chives to serve.
SERVES 4

ITALIAN-STYLE POUSSIN

15 ml (1 tbsp) vegetable oil
25 g (1 oz) butter or margarine
4 small poussins
450 g (1 lb) potatoes, peeled and cut into small fingers
175 g (6 oz) button onions, skinned
125 g (4 oz) button mushrooms, wiped
450 ml (¾ pint) chicken stock
30 ml (2 level tbsp) tomato purée
45 ml (3 tbsp) dry sherry
5 ml (1 level tsp) dried oregano
salt and pepper
50 g (2 oz) cooked ham, shredded
30 ml (2 level tbsp) cornflour

1. Heat the oil and butter in a large flameproof casserole, add the poussins and fry until browned. Remove with a slotted spoon and drain on absorbent kitchen paper.
2. Add the potatoes to the casserole with the onions and mushrooms and cook until golden brown. Return the poussins to the casserole, arranging them side by side.
3. Mix together the stock, tomato purée, sherry and oregano and season well. Pour over the poussins, cover and cook in the oven at 180°C (350°F) mark 4 for about 1 hour, until tender.
4. Transfer the birds and vegetables to a warmed serving plate, leaving the juices in the pan. Add the ham to the juices, adjust the seasoning and stir in the cornflour blended with a little water. Bring to the boil, stirring, until thickened. Spoon over the poussins and serve.
SERVES 4

COQ AU VIN

1 large chicken, jointed, or 6-8 chicken joints
30 ml (2 level tbsp) flour
salt and pepper
90 g (3½ oz) butter or margarine
125 g (4 oz) lean bacon, diced
1 medium onion, skinned and quartered
1 medium carrot, peeled and quartered
60 ml (4 tbsp) brandy
600 ml (1 pint) red wine
1 garlic clove, skinned and crushed
bouquet garni
1 sugar lump
30 ml (2 tbsp) vegetable oil
450 g (1 lb) button onions, skinned
pinch of sugar
5 ml (1 tsp) wine vinegar
225 g (8 oz) button mushrooms, wiped
6 slices of white bread, crusts removed

1. Coat the chicken pieces with 15 ml (1 tbsp) of the flour, liberally seasoned with salt and pepper.
2. Melt 25 g (1 oz) of the butter in a flameproof casserole, add the chicken pieces and fry gently until they are golden brown on all sides. Add the bacon, onion and carrot and fry until softened.
3. Heat the brandy in a small saucepan, pour over the chicken and ignite, shaking the pan so that all the chicken pieces are covered in flames. Pour on the wine and stir to remove any sediment from the bottom of the casserole. Add the garlic, bouquet garni and sugar lump. Bring to the boil, cover and simmer for 1-1½ hours, until tender.
4. Meanwhile, melt another 25 g (1 oz) of the butter with 10 ml (2 tsp) of the oil in a frying pan. Add the onions and fry until they begin to brown. Add the sugar and the vinegar, together with 15 ml (1 tbsp) water. Cover and simmer for 10-15 minutes, until just tender. Keep warm.
5. Melt 25 g (1 oz) of the butter with 10 ml (2 tsp) oil in a pan and add the mushrooms. Cook for a few minutes. Keep warm. Remove chicken from the casserole and place in a serving dish. Surround with the onions and mushrooms. Keep hot.
6. Discard the bouquet garni. Skim the excess fat off the cooking liquid and boil the liquid in the casserole briskly for 3-5 minutes to reduce it.
7. Add the remaining oil to the fat in the frying pan and fry the pieces of bread until golden brown on both sides. Cut each slice into triangles.
8. Work the remaining 15 ml (1 level tbsp) flour and 15 g (½ oz) butter to make a beurre manié (see page 570). Take the casserole off the heat and add the beurre manié in small pieces to the cooking liquid. Stir until smooth, then bring just to the boil. The sauce should now be thick and shiny. Adjust the seasoning and pour over the chicken. Garnish with fried bread.
SERVES 6-8

CHICKEN PUFF PIE

900 g (2 lb) oven-ready chicken
1 bay leaf
2 fresh rosemary or marjoram sprigs, or 10 ml
    (2 level tsp) dried
salt and pepper
4 medium leeks, trimmed, cut into 2 cm (¾ inch)
    lengths and washed
2 large carrots, peeled and thickly sliced
125 g (4 oz) boiled ham, cut into bite-sized pieces
25 g (1 oz) butter or margarine
1 medium onion, skinned and chopped
45 ml (3 level tbsp) flour
150 ml (¼ pint) milk
60 ml (4 tbsp) single cream
225 g (8 oz) frozen puff pastry, thawed
1 egg, beaten, to glaze

1. Put the chicken in a large saucepan with the herbs and salt and pepper to taste. Cover with water and bring to the boil, then reduce the heat, cover and simmer for 45-60 minutes, until the chicken is tender.
2. Remove the chicken from the liquid and leave to cool slightly. Meanwhile, add the leeks and carrots to the liquid, bring to the boil and simmer for about 7 minutes, until tender but still crunchy. Remove from the pan with a slotted spoon. Strain the cooking liquid and reserve 600 ml (1 pint).
3. Remove the chicken meat from the bones, discarding the skin. Cut into bite-sized chunks.
4. Mix the chicken with the ham, leeks and carrots in a 1.1 litre (2 pint) pie dish.
5. Melt the butter in a clean saucepan, add the onion and fry gently until soft. Stir in the flour and cook gently for 1 minute, stirring, then gradually add the reserved cooking liquid.
6. Bring to the boil and simmer, stirring, until thick, then stir in the milk and cream, with salt and pepper to taste. Pour the sauce into the pie dish and leave for about 50 minutes, until cold.
7. Roll out the pastry on a floured surface until about 2.5 cm (1 inch) larger all round than the pie dish. Cut off a strip from all round the edge of the pastry. Place the strip on the rim of the pie dish, moisten, then place pastry lid on top.
8. Press the edge firmly to seal, then knock up and flute. Make a hole in the centre of the pie and use the pastry trimmings to make decorations, sticking them in place with water.
9. Brush the pastry with the egg, then bake in the oven at 190°C (375°F) mark 5 for 30 minutes, until puffed up and golden brown. Serve hot.
SERVES 4-6

CHICKEN CHAUDFROID

15 g (½ oz) aspic jelly powder
6 chicken breast fillets, skinned and poached
300 ml (½ pint) Béchamel Sauce (see page 200)
cucumber, pickled walnuts, radishes and strips of
    lemon rind, to garnish

1. Make up the aspic to 300 ml (½ pint) as directed on the packet and leave it until it has almost reached setting point.
2. Place the cold chicken portions on a wire rack over a tray or large plate.
3. Add half the aspic to the Béchamel Sauce, stir in lightly and allow it to thicken but not set. (Keep the remaining aspic in a basin standing in a bowl of warm water.) Coat the chicken portions by pouring the sauce steadily over them to give a smooth, even surface, allowing the excess to run off and collect in the tray.
4. Decorate the chicken portions with strips of cucumber skin, or pieces of pickled walnut, slices of radish and strips of lemon rind, then carefully spoon over the remaining aspic (which should be at setting point), so that the coated chicken portions are completely covered with aspic, but the decorations are not disturbed.
SERVES 6

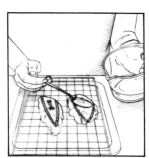

Place the chicken portions on a wire rack and pour over the sauce to give a smooth, even coating. Collect the excess sauce in a tray under the rack.

Use finely cut strips of cucumber skin, radishes, lemon rind and pickled walnuts to decorate the chicken pieces. Then spoon over aspic.

PANCAKE ROLLS

225 g (8 oz) cooked chicken, boned and skinned
15 ml (1 tbsp) sesame or vegetable oil
1 small bunch spring onions, trimmed and chopped
3 garlic cloves, skinned and crushed
2.5 cm (1 inch) piece root ginger, peeled and crushed
125 g (4 oz) beansprouts
1 medium carrot, peeled and grated
15 ml (1 tbsp) soy sauce
2.5 ml (½ level tsp) soft brown sugar
salt and pepper
8 squares of frozen spring roll pastry (available from oriental food stores), thawed
vegetable oil for deep-frying

Pancake Rolls

1. Cut the chicken into thin strips. Set aside.
2. Heat the 15 ml (1 tbsp) oil in a wok or frying pan, add the spring onions, garlic and ginger and fry gently for 5 minutes until soft. Add the beansprouts and carrot; stir-fry for 2 minutes.
3. Turn the vegetables into a bowl and mix with the chicken, soy sauce, sugar and seasoning.
4. Divide the filling mixture equally into eight, then form each portion into a roll shape.
5. Place one roll on one sheet of pastry, towards the nearest corner. Fold the corner over the roll.
6. Fold in the corner at right angles to the first corner, then fold in the opposite corner.
7. Roll up the filling in the pastry until the last corner is reached, completely enclosing the filling. Seal the end with a little water.
8. Heat the oil in a deep-fryer to 180°C (350°F) and fry the rolls in batches for about 10 minutes until golden. Drain before serving.
MAKES 8

ROASTING TURKEY

When roasting a turkey, remember you are cooking two different types of meat, the delicate light breast meat, which must not be allowed to dry out, and the darker leg meat which takes longer to cook. The turkey must be roasted long enough for the legs to cook, so frequent basting is necessary.

ROAST TURKEY

1 oven-ready turkey (see note)
a little melted butter or vegetable oil
salt and pepper
streaky bacon rashers, rinded (optional)
ACCOMPANIMENTS
Bacon Rolls (see page 154)
Forcemeat Balls (see page 183)
Bread Sauce (see page 206)
Cranberry Sauce (see page 206)

1. Wash the inside of the bird and stuff at the neck end before folding the neck skin over.
2. Make the turkey plump and as even in shape as possible, then truss it with the wings folded under the body and the legs tied together.
3. Weigh the turkey and calculate the cooking time (see page 148).
4. Place the turkey in a roasting tin, brush with melted butter and sprinkle with salt and pepper.
5. Place streaky bacon rashers over the breast to prevent it from becoming dry, if wished. Roast in the oven at 180°C (350°F) mark 4, basting from time to time. Put a piece of foil over the bird if it shows signs of becoming too brown.
6. Serve with gravy and accompaniments.

NOTE: Refer to page 148 for serving quantity guide and general advice on preparing turkey.

Ballontine of Turkey

BALLONTINE OF TURKEY

5.5 kg (12 lb) oven-ready turkey
125 g (4 oz) butter or margarine
225 g (8 oz) onion, skinned and roughly chopped
225 g (8 oz) button mushrooms, roughly chopped
2 large garlic cloves, skinned and crushed
700 g (1½ lb) pork sausagemeat
125 g (4 oz) fresh breadcrumbs
90 ml (6 tbsp) chopped fresh parsley
60 ml (4 tbsp) Dijon mustard
grated rind and juice of 2 lemons
1 egg, beaten
salt and pepper
450 g (1 lb) smoked loin of pork, in one piece
bacon rolls and chipolata sausages, to serve

1. First bone the turkey. Place the bird breast side down on a large chopping board. Using a small sharp knife, cut straight along the backbone. Fillet the flesh away from the carcass, keeping the knife as close to the bones as possible. Take great care not to puncture the skin.
2. Loosen the leg and wing ball-and-socket joints with the point of the knife. Push these joints away from the carcass until they loosen and partially come away. Carefully split the leg flesh and ease out the bones and sinews. Ease out the large wing joint. Run your fingers all over the flesh to ensure no bones or sinews remain.
3. You should have a large oblong of skin covered with turkey meat. Remove the parson's nose. Trim most of the leg and thigh meat from one side of the bird and any excessively fat

portions of breast flesh (you should have about 900 g (2 lb) trimmed meat to use in casseroles). (It is not essential to trim this flesh, but without it the ballontine will have a better shape, with even distribution of both turkey meat and stuffing.) Cover and refrigerate the boned turkey while preparing the stuffing.
4. Heat 50 g (2 oz) butter in a sauté pan. Add the onion and fry until beginning to brown. Increase heat, add the mushrooms and garlic and fry until the liquid has evaporated, stirring frequently. Turn into a large bowl and cool.
5. Stir the sausagemeat, breadcrumbs, parsley, mustard, lemon rind, 30 ml (2 tbsp) lemon juice and plenty of seasoning into the mushroom mixture. Mix thoroughly.
6. Lay the boned turkey flat on a board, flesh side up, and spread the stuffing mixture over the flesh. Place the smoked loin on top and then fold the turkey skin around to enclose the stuffing completely. Secure with fine skewers or cocktail sticks, or sew the skin together.
7. Spread the turkey generously with butter and season liberally with pepper. Wrap in foil and place in a roasting tin.
8. Bake at 180°C (350°F) mark 4 for 2½ hours. Fold back the foil and return to the oven for about 1 hour or until well browned. Test with a fine skewer; if cooked, the juices will run clear.
9. Lift the ballontine onto a serving plate. Let stand for about 20 minutes before slicing thickly. Serve with the bacon rolls and chipolatas.
SERVES 8

STUFFED TURKEY DRUMSTICKS

2 turkey drumsticks, at least 900 g (2 lb) total weight
225 g (8 oz) pork sausagemeat
15 ml (1 tbsp) chopped fresh tarragon or 5 ml (1 level tsp) dried
10 ml (2 tsp) chopped fresh parsley
salt and pepper
50 g (2 oz) mushrooms, wiped and thinly sliced
flour for dusting
1 egg white, beaten
175 g (6 oz) fresh breadcrumbs
125 g (4 oz) butter or margarine, softened
15 ml (1 level tbsp) French mustard
Onion Sauce (see page 199), to serve

1. Skin the turkey drumsticks, slit the flesh and ease out the bone and large sinews.
2. Mix the sausagemeat, herbs and seasoning and spread one quarter in each boned leg. Cover with a layer of sliced mushrooms and top with more sausagemeat stuffing. Reshape the legs and sew up neatly.
3. Dip joints in flour, brush with the egg white and place seam-side down in a greased roasting tin.
4. Beat together the breadcrumbs, butter and mustard, then spread it over the top and sides of the drumsticks.
5. Bake in the oven at 190°C (375°F) mark 5 for about 1 hour 40 minutes, until the meat is tender and has a crisp, golden crust. Remove the string and serve sliced with Onion Sauce.
SERVES 6

DEVILLED TURKEY DRUMSTICKS

2 cooked turkey drumsticks
50 g (2 oz) butter or margarine, melted
5 ml (1 level tsp) French mustard
5 ml (1 level tsp) prepared English mustard
10 ml (2 level tsp) chutney, finely chopped
pinch of ground ginger
pinch of cayenne pepper
salt and pepper
watercress sprigs, to garnish

1. Score the drumsticks with a sharp knife, then brush with melted butter.
2. Mix together the French and English mustards, chutney, ground ginger, cayenne and salt and pepper.
3. Spread the mixture over and into the cuts and leave the turkey legs to marinate for at least 1 hour.
4. Grill the drumsticks on a greased grid under a medium heat until crisp and brown, turning regularly to ensure even cooking. Serve halved, garnished with watercress.
SERVES 4

TURKEY STROGANOFF

15 ml (1 tbsp) vegetable oil
50 g (2 oz) butter or margarine
450 g (1 lb) turkey fillets, cut into pencil-thin strips
30 ml (2 tbsp) brandy
1 garlic clove, skinned and crushed
salt and pepper
225 g (8 oz) button mushrooms, wiped and sliced
1 medium green pepper, seeded and thinly sliced
60 ml (4 tbsp) soured cream

1. Heat the oil and butter in a large frying pan and brown the turkey strips. Pour over the brandy and set alight, then add the garlic and seasoning.
2. Cover the pan and simmer for 4-5 minutes, or until the turkey is just tender.
3. Increase the heat, add the mushrooms and pepper and cook for 3-4 minutes, turning occasionally.
4. Reduce the heat, stir in the soured cream (if on the thick side, stir before adding to the pan) and adjust seasoning.
SERVES 4

Turkey Kebabs with Chilli Peanut Sauce

450 g (1 lb) turkey fillets, cut into 2.5 cm (1 inch)
cubes
225 g (8 oz) button mushrooms, wiped
150 ml (¼ pint) vegetable oil
30 ml (2 tbsp) lemon juice
5 ml (1 level tsp) ground cumin
5 ml (1 level tsp) sugar
5 ml (1 level tsp) salt
300 ml (½ pint) milk
45 ml (3 level tbsp) desiccated coconut
60 ml (4 level tbsp) crunchy peanut butter
pinch of mild chilli powder or 20 ml (4 level tsp) chilli
seasoning
pepper
beansprouts and spring onions, to garnish

Thread the turkey cubes and mushrooms on to eight long skewers.

1. Thread eight skewers alternately with turkey meat and whole mushrooms.
2. Mix together the oil, lemon juice, cumin, sugar and salt. Pour over the kebabs, and turn them to coat. Cover and leave to marinate for at least 2 hours, turning occasionally.
3. Bring the milk to the boil and add the coconut. Remove from the heat, cover and leave to infuse for 10 minutes, then strain.
4. In a heavy-based saucepan, heat the peanut butter with the chilli powder. Cook gently for 1 minute. Gradually stir in the coconut milk, bring to the boil, then simmer for 2-3 minutes. Add pepper to taste.
5. Cook the kebabs under a low grill for 10-15 minutes, turning two or three times and basting with the marinade.
6. Spoon a little sauce over the kebabs and serve the rest separately. Garnish the kebabs with beansprouts and spring onions.
Serves 4

Turkey in Spiced Yogurt

7.5 ml (1½ level tsp) ground cumin
7.5 ml (1½ level tsp) ground coriander
2.5 ml (½ level tsp) ground turmeric
2.5 ml (½ level tsp) ground ginger
salt and pepper
300 ml (10 fl oz) natural yogurt
30 ml (2 tbsp) lemon juice
900 g (2 lb) turkey meat, cut into 2.5 cm (1 inch)
cubes
45 ml (3 tbsp) vegetable oil
2 medium onions, skinned and sliced
45 ml (3 level tbsp) desiccated coconut
30 ml (2 level tbsp) flour
150 ml (¼ pint) chicken stock
chopped fresh parsley, to garnish

1. In a large bowl, mix the spices with the seasoning, yogurt and lemon juice. Stir well until evenly blended.
2. Fold in the turkey meat to coat with the yogurt mixture. Cover and leave to marinate in the refrigerator for several hours.
3. Heat the oil in a medium flameproof casserole, add the onions and fry until lightly browned. Add the coconut and flour and fry gently, stirring, for about 1 minute.
4. Remove from the heat and stir in the turkey with its marinade and the stock. Return to the heat and bring slowly to the boil, stirring all the time. Cover tightly and cook in the oven at 170°C (325°F) mark 3 for 1-1¼ hours until the turkey is tender.
5. Adjust the seasoning and serve garnished with chopped fresh parsley.
Serves 6-8

TURKEY WITH CASHEW NUTS AND MUSHROOMS

450 g (1 lb) turkey or chicken breast fillets
30 ml (2 tbsp) oil
50 g (2 oz) shallots or onion, skinned and chopped
50 ml (4 tbsp) dry sherry
350 g (12 oz) button mushrooms, thinly sliced
1 garlic clove, skinned and crushed
25 g (1 oz) toasted salted cashew nuts
150 ml (5 fl oz) soured cream
salt and pepper
30 ml (2 level tbsp) chopped fresh parsley or spring
    onion tops
lemon slices, to garnish

1. Cut the turkey or chicken into small, thin escalopes. Bat out lightly between sheets of greaseproof paper.
2. Heat the oil in a large sauté pan (preferably non-stick). Fry the turkey escalopes a few at a time, with the shallots or onion, until lightly browned on both sides.
3. Return all the turkey and shallot mixture to the pan with the sherry, mushrooms, garlic, cashew nuts and soured cream. Bring to the boil, stirring continuously, then simmer gently for a further 3-4 minutes or until the turkey is tender. Season.
4. Garnish with lemon slices and serve with plain boiled rice or mixed white and wild rice flavoured with spring onion and parsley.
SERVES 4

Turkey with Cashew Nuts and Mushrooms

TURKEY SAUTÉ WITH LEMON AND WALNUTS

450 g (1 lb) turkey fillets or escalopes, cut into thin
    5 cm (2 inch) long strips
30 ml (2 level tbsp) cornflour
30 ml (2 tbsp) vegetable oil
40 g (1½ oz) walnut halves or pieces
1 medium green pepper, seeded and cut into strips
25 g (1 oz) butter or margarine
60 ml (4 tbsp) chicken stock
30 ml (2 tbsp) lemon juice
45 ml (3 level tbsp) lemon marmalade
5 ml (1 tsp) malt vinegar
1.25 ml (¼ tsp) soy sauce
salt and pepper

1. Toss the turkey in the cornflour until coated.
2. Heat the oil in a large sauté or deep frying pan, add the walnuts and green pepper and fry for 2-3 minutes. Remove from the pan with a slotted spoon.
3. Melt the butter in the residual fat, add the turkey strips a few at a time and fry until golden.
4. Return all the turkey to the pan and stir in the stock and lemon juice, stirring well to remove any sediment at the bottom of the pan. Add the lemon marmalade, vinegar, soy sauce and seasoning. Stir in the walnuts and pepper.
5. Cook gently for a further 5 minutes. Adjust seasoning if necessary, and serve at once.
SERVES 4

Turkey Escalopes with Asparagus

TURKEY ESCALOPES WITH ASPARAGUS

225 g (8 oz) thin asparagus spears
2 turkey escalopes, about 225 g (8 oz) each, skinned and halved
30 ml (2 tbsp) plain flour
salt and pepper
15 g (½ oz) butter
15 ml (1 tbsp) vegetable oil
300 ml (½ pint) chicken stock
5 ml (1 tsp) chopped fresh sage or 2.5 ml (½ tsp) dried
60 ml (4 tbsp) dry white wine
150 ml (5 fl oz) soured cream

1. Snap off the ends of the asparagus if they are tough and woody. Trim them all to the same length. Cut off the tips and set aside. Cut the stalks into 3 pieces.
2. Bat out each turkey escalope slightly with a rolling pin or meat mallet. Coat in the flour seasoned with salt and pepper, shaking off any excess. Heat the butter and oil in a large frying pan and fry the turkey until lightly browned on both sides. Add the chicken stock, asparagus stalks, sage and wine. Cover and cook gently for 15-20 minutes, until tender.
3. Five minutes before the end of the cooking time, add the reserved asparagus tips and the cream. Season to taste. Serve with new potatoes.
SERVES 4

TURKEY À LA KING

50 g (2 oz) butter or margarine
125 g (4 oz) mushrooms, wiped and sliced
1 medium green pepper, chopped, or 1 small canned pimiento, chopped
50 g (2 oz) flour
600 ml (1 pint) milk or milk and chicken stock, mixed
450 g (1 lb) skinned, cooked turkey meat, diced
salt and pepper
paprika and grated nutmeg
15-30 ml (1-2 tbsp) sherry (optional)

1. Melt the butter in a saucepan, add the mushrooms and green pepper and fry until soft.
2. Stir in the flour and cook gently for 1 minute, stirring. Remove the pan from the heat and gradually stir in the milk. Bring to the boil slowly and continue to cook, stirring constantly, until the sauce thickens.
3. Add the turkey, season to taste with salt, pepper, paprika and nutmeg. Add the sherry, if using. Heat through, stirring occasionally. Serve with boiled rice or buttered noodles.
SERVES 4

DUCKLING

Duckling is sold both fresh and frozen ready for the oven and is available all year round.
Commercial ducklings are killed before the second feather stage, at about 7-8 weeks. After this stage
a duckling becomes a duck. A smaller number of ducks are sold New York dressed or 'rough
plucked' (with heads and feet on and not drawn). When choosing a rough plucked bird check
that the beak and feet are pliable and the breast plump.
Oven-ready weights range from 1.4-2.7 kg (3-6 lb) and you should allow a minimum
of 450 g (1 lb) dressed weight per person. Fresh and frozen duckling portions are available.
These include leg portions, duckling breasts, duck breast fillets and quarter ducklings. If buying
frozen duckling allow plenty of time for thawing. Defrost as for Turkey (see page 148).

ROAST DUCKLING

1.8-2.6 kg (4-6 lb) oven-ready duckling
Sage and Onion Stuffing (see page 182)
salt and pepper
Apple Sauce (see page 205), to serve
Thin Gravy (see page 202), to serve

1. Wash the duckling inside and out, pat dry and
stuff with the Sage and Onion Stuffing.
2. Rub the skin with salt and prick it all over
with a sharp skewer or fork to allow the fat to run
during cooking. Weigh the bird.
3. Place the duckling on a wire rack over a
roasting tin and roast in the oven at 180°C
(350°F) mark 4, allowing 30-35 minutes per
450 g (1 lb). Serve with Apple Sauce and thin
brown gravy.
SERVES 4

PORTIONING A DUCKLING
1. Cut off any excess neck skin and discard. Pull
out the clusters of fat from inside the body cavity
and discard.
2. With the bird breast side up, starting at the
vent end, cut along one side of the breastbone to
the neck cavity.
3. Cut along both sides of the backbone to halve
the duckling and remove the bone.
4. Cut each half of the duckling into two to give
equal portions of meat, using poultry shears or a
sharp knife.

DUCKLING WITH ORANGE SAUCE

1.8-2.6 kg (4-6 lb) oven-ready duckling
salt and pepper
150 ml (¼ pint) white wine
4 oranges (use bitter oranges when available)
1 lemon
15 ml (1 level tbsp) sugar
15 ml (1 tbsp) white wine vinegar
30 ml (2 tbsp) brandy or orange-flavoured liqueur
15 ml (1 level tbsp) cornflour
1 bunch watercress, to garnish

1. Rub the duckling skin with salt and prick the
skin all over.
2. Put the duckling in the roasting tin with the
wine and roast in the oven at 180°C (350°F)
mark 4 for 30-35 minutes per 450 g (1 lb),
basting occasionally.

3. Meanwhile, grate the rind from 1 orange and
squeeze the juice from 3 of the oranges and the
lemon. Separate the remaining orange into
segments and reserve for the garnish.
4. Melt the sugar in a pan with the vinegar and
heat until it is a dark brown caramel.
5. Add the brandy and the orange and lemon
juice and simmer gently for 5 minutes.
6. When the duckling is cooked, remove it from
the roasting tin, joint it (see above) and place
the pieces on a serving dish and keep warm.
7. Drain excess fat from the tin and add the
orange sauce and grated rind to the sediment.
8. Blend the cornflour with 30 ml (2 tbsp) water,
stir into the pan juices, bring to the boil and cook
for 2-3 minutes, stirring. Season and pour the
sauce over the joints. Garnish with watercress.
SERVES 4

Crispy Duck Breast with Mangetout

CRISPY DUCK BREAST WITH MANGETOUT

4 duck breast fillets
salt
25 ml (1½ level tbsp) clear honey
45 ml (3 tbsp) vegetable oil
1 bunch spring onions, trimmed and cut into 2.5 cm
   (1 inch) lengths
1 large green pepper, seeded and cut into thin strips
225 g (8 oz) mangetout, topped and tailed
2 garlic cloves, skinned and crushed
2-3 good pinches five spice powder
45 ml (3 level tbsp) caster sugar
45 ml (3 tbsp) dark soy sauce
45 ml (3 tbsp) malt vinegar
16 water chestnuts, sliced
40 g (1½ oz) toasted cashew nuts, chopped

1. Prick the duck breast skin all over with a skewer or fork and rub well with salt to help crisp the skin. Place, skin side uppermost on a rack or trivet in a roasting tin.
2. Bake in the oven at 180°C (350°F) mark 4 for 15 minutes. Brush the skin with the honey and cook for a further 15 minutes or until cooked through. Remove from the oven and leave to cool. When cold, cut into thin strips.
3. In a wok or large frying pan, heat the oil. Add the spring onion, green pepper, mangetout, garlic and five spice powder and stir-fry for 2 minutes. Add the sugar, soy sauce, vinegar and duck strips and toss in the sauce to heat through and glaze. Add the water chestnuts and toss through lightly.
4. Serve at once, sprinkled with toasted cashew nuts and accompanied by Special Fried Rice (see page 309).
SERVES 6

GOOSE

The main season for fresh goose is September to December, but frozen oven-ready goose is increasingly available throughout the year, especially at Easter. A young goose is ready to be eaten when it is six months old and weighs between 3.6-6.3 kg (8-14 lb). By the end of the season a goose will be considerably bigger, weighing up to 9 kg (15 lb). Fresh goose may be sold dressed or 'rough plucked' (with head and feet on and not drawn). Look for a young goose with a plump breast, downy feathers around the legs and soft flexible legs and webs. Avoid any with deep yellow fat as this indicates an old goose. You may find it necessary to order a fresh goose in advance. If buying frozen oven-ready goose, check that the packaging is undamaged and allow plenty of time for thawing before cooking. Defrost as for Turkey (see page 148).

Geese range in weight considerably. Allow about 700 g (1½ lb) per person. As a rough guide, a 4.5 kg (10 lb) goose will serve 6-8 people. Goose is generally roasted whole to drain off the fat from under the skin.

It is important to remember that the breast meat will cook faster than the leg and underside and care must be taken that it does not dry out, so cover it with foil. The legs are cooked if the juices run clear when a skewer is inserted.

ROAST GOOSE

4-5 kg (9-11 lb) oven-ready goose
salt
Sage and Onion Stuffing (see page 182)
Apple Sauce (see page 205), to serve
Thin Gravy (see page 202)

1. Prick the skin of the goose with a fork in several places. Pull the inside fat out of the bird. Rub salt over the skin.
2. Spoon the stuffing into the neck end of the

goose, skewer the neck skin to the back of the bird, then truss (see page 148) or tie up the goose with string. Weigh the bird.
3. Put on a rack placed over a roasting tin. Cover the breast with foil. Roast in the oven at 200°C (400°F) mark 6 for 15 minutes per 450 g (1 lb) plus 15 minutes, basting frequently. Remove foil for the last 20 minutes to brown.
4. Serve the goose with Apple Sauce and gravy.
SERVES 8

GUINEA FOWL

These are available all the year round, but are at their best from February to June. A guinea fowl has grey plumage with white spots and is about the same size as a pheasant, though it can be as large as a small chicken. It has a more gamey flavour than chicken. When choosing one, look out for the same points as in a fresh chicken, especially a plump breast and smooth-skinned feet. An average-sized bird will serve 4 people. All methods for cooking chicken or pheasant are applicable, especially braising or casseroling, but be sure to use plenty of fat when roasting.

ROAST GUINEA FOWL

1 medium guinea fowl
salt
few rashers of streaky bacon, rinded
softened butter, for basting
watercress, to garnish
Bread Sauce (see page 206)
Thin Gravy (see page 202)

1. Singe, draw and wipe the bird, then truss it for roasting (see page 148). Lay the bacon rashers over the breast.
2. Roast in the oven at 200°C (400°F) mark 6, allowing 15 minutes per 450 g (1 lb) plus 15 minutes, basting frequently with butter.
3. Garnish with watercress and serve with Bread Sauce and gravy.

Game

Game is the name given to wild birds and animals which are hunted for food rather than farmed, but which at certain times of the year are protected by law. Also included in this chapter are pigeon, though strictly only wood or wild pigeon counts as game; quail, which is farmed; rabbit, which is also farmed but cooked in the same way as hare; and venison which is now extensively farmed. Game has a distinctive flavour.

Game Birds

Game birds are best eaten young. The plumage is a guide as all young birds have soft even feathers. With pheasants and partridge, the long wing feathers are V-shaped in a young bird, as distinct from the rounded ones of an older bird. Smooth, pliable legs, short spurs and a firm, plump breast are other points to look for. Most game birds need to be hung so ask the butcher or poulterer if the bird has been hung and for how long. If it is not hung, the flesh will be tough and tasteless.

It is normally advisable to order game from your butcher or poulterer and he will hang the bird for the specified time and supply it ready plucked and drawn on the required day. If you are given game, you can hang it yourself in a cold, dry, airy place for the time specified in the chart overleaf. The birds should be hung by the neck without being plucked or drawn. If you are given a bird that has been damaged by shot or is wet, it will not keep as long as a bird in good condition. Check it frequently and cook it as soon as the tail feathers will pluck out easily.

STORING GAME BIRDS

A bird that has been hung and is ready for cooking can be stored for 1-2 days in the refrigerator, or it can be frozen, plucked and drawn.

COOKING AND SERVING

The more simply game is cooked, the better. For a young bird, there is no better way than roasting, but for older birds, which are likely to be tough if plainly roasted, braising or stewing is preferable. If in doubt about the age of the bird, opt for braising or casseroling.

Game birds lack fat, so it is usual to bard the breast before roasting; ie, to cover it with pieces of fat bacon, and to baste frequently with butter or margarine during the cooking. When the bird is nearly cooked, the bacon can be removed in order to brown the meat.

TRADITIONAL ACCOMPANIMENTS

THIN GRAVY: This can be served with any roast game bird. Add 150 ml (¼ pint) water or meat stock to the roasting tin and, with a spoon, stir up any cooking juices left in the tin. Bring to the boil and boil for 2-3 minutes. Remove all grease from the surface with a metal spoon, season to taste and strain before serving.

FRIED CRUMBS: These are sprinkled over fried game. Fry 50-125 g (2-4 oz) fresh breadcrumbs in 25 g (1 oz) butter or margarine until golden brown, stirring occasionally to brown evenly.

GAME CHIPS: To prepare, peel and cut potatoes into very thin slices, then deep-fry until golden.

BREAD SAUCE: See page 206.

TOAST: Small birds such as grouse are roasted directly on a slice of toast or on a rack over a slice of bread brushed with melted butter. The bird is served on the toast, which acquires a delicious flavour from the dripping.

CARVING GAME

Large game birds are carved in the same way as chicken (see page 148). Small birds such as partridges and pigeons are usually cut in half. If very small, the whole bird may be served as one portion; woodcock, snipe and quail are among the birds which are served whole, on the toast or fried bread on which they were cooked.

Special poultry shears are available for cutting birds in half. Alternatively use a game carver or a short, pointed knife instead. Insert

OPEN SEASONS FOR GAME BIRDS

Bird	Shooting Season	Hanging (Days)	Cooking	Number of Servings
Blackgame (black grouse)	20 Aug-10 Dec	3-10	Roast at 190°C (375°F) mark 5 for about 45 minutes	2 servings
Capercaillie	1 Oct-31 Jan	7-14	Roast at 200°C (400°F) mark 6 for about 40 minutes	2-3 servings
Grouse	12 Aug-10 Dec	2-4	Roast at 200°C (400°F) mark 6 for about 40 minutes	1 per person
Partridge (Grey and Red-legged)	1 Sept-1 Feb	3-5	Roast at 200°C (400°F) mark 6 for 40 minutes	1 per person
Pheasant	1 Oct-1 Feb (10 Dec in Scotland)	3-10	Roast at 230°C (450°F) mark 8 for 10 minutes, then reduce to 200°C (400°F) mark 6 for 30-50 minutes	Female birds give 2 servings, male birds give 3 servings
Ptarmigan	12 Aug-10 Dec	2-4	Braise or casserole at 190°C (375°F) mark 5 for 40 minutes	1 per person
Quail	not applicable	not applicable	Roast at 190°C (375°F) mark 5 for 15-20 minutes	2 per person
Snipe	12 Aug-31 Jan	3-4	Roast at 190°C (375°F) mark 5 for 15-20 minutes	1-2 per person
Wild Duck (Mallard, Teal and Wigeon)	1 Sept-31 Jan	2-3 (may be drawn before hanging)	Roast at 220°C (425°F) mark 7 for about 30 minutes	2 servings
Wild Geese (Pink Footed and Greylag)	1 Sept- 31 Jan	2-9	Roast at 220°C (425°F) mark 7 for 20 minutes. Reduce heat to 180°C (350°F) mark 4 allowing 13-15 minutes per 450 g (1 lb).	A 4.5 kg (10 lb) bird will serve 6-8 people
Woodcock	1 Oct-31 Jan (1 Sept-31 Jan in Scotland)	3-5	Roast at 190°C (375°F) mark 5 for 15-20 minutes	1 per person
Woodpigeon	No close season (best May-Oct)	Requires no hanging	Roast at 230°C (450°F) mark 8 for about 15-20 minutes	1 per person

CASSEROLED PIGEONS WITH CIDER AND APPLE

4 oven-ready pigeons
1 large onion, skinned and sliced into rings
2-3 celery sticks, washed and chopped
450 g (1 lb) apples, peeled, cored and thinly sliced
pinch of cayenne pepper
pinch of freshly grated nutmeg
1 bay leaf
salt
600 ml (1 pint) medium or dry cider
Worcestershire sauce (optional)
watercress sprigs and apple slices, to garnish

1. Put the pigeons into a large casserole, either whole or cut in half.
2. Arrange the vegetables and apples round them, add the cayenne, nutmeg and bay leaf and season well with salt. Pour over the cider.
3. Cover the casserole and cook in the oven at 150°C (300°F) mark 2 for 2 hours, until the birds are quite tender and the vegetables soft.
4. Remove the birds and the bay leaf with a slotted spoon and keep warm. Purée the cooking liquid and the vegetables in a blender or food processor until smooth.
5. Taste the sauce and if it is too sweet (which will depend on the apples and cider used) add a dash of Worcestershire sauce.
6. Pour the sauce over the birds and garnish with watercress and apple slices.
SERVES 4

ROAST QUAIL

8 quail
8 rounds of bread, toasted or fried
thin rashers of fat bacon
Thin Gravy (see page 202)
Game Chips (see page 171), to serve
watercress, to garnish

1. Pluck and singe the birds but do not draw. Cut off the head and neck and take out the crop.
2. Place each bird on a round of toast or fried bread and cover the breast with thin rashers of fat bacon. Roast in the oven at 220°C (425°F) mark 7 for about 25 minutes, basting with butter.
3. Serve on the toast or fried bread with the bacon, gravy and Game Chips. Garnish with watercress sprigs.
SERVES 4

CREAMED QUAIL CASSEROLE

4 quail
30 ml (2 tbsp) seasoned flour
50 g (2 oz) butter or margarine
125 g (4 oz) button mushrooms, wiped
60 ml (4 tbsp) dry sherry
salt and pepper
150 ml (5 fl oz) soured cream
chopped fresh parsley, to garnish

1. Coat the quail in the seasoned flour.
2. Melt the butter in a flameproof casserole, add the quail and fry until evenly browned.
3. Add the mushrooms and fry until softened, then add the sherry and seasoning.
4. Cover and cook in the oven at 190°C (375°F) mark 5 for 40 minutes.
5. Stir in the soured cream, adjust the seasoning and serve sprinkled with chopped parsley.
SERVES 2

Roast Pheasant

ROAST PHEASANT

brace of young pheasants, oven-ready
½ onion, skinned
butter for basting
salt and pepper
few rashers of streaky bacon
watercress, to garnish
Thin Gravy (see page 171)
Bread Sauce (see page 206)
Game Chips (see page 171)

1. Wash the pheasants inside and out and pat dry. Put the onion and a knob of butter inside each body cavity, season inside well, then truss.
2. Cover the breast with the bacon and roast in the oven at 230°C (450°F) mark 8 for 10 minutes, then reduce the heat to 200°C (400°F) mark 6 and cook for a further 30-50 minutes, until tender, basting frequently with butter.
3. Serve garnished with watercress and accompany with the gravy, Bread Sauce, Game Chips and a green vegetable.
SERVES 4

PHEASANT WITH PORT

30 ml (2 tbsp) vegetable oil
3 young pheasants, well wiped
300 ml (½ pint) chicken stock
120 ml (8 tbsp) port
finely grated rind and juice of 2 oranges
50 g (2 oz) sultanas
salt and pepper
20 ml (4 level tsp) cornflour
25 g (1 oz) flaked almonds, toasted, to garnish

1. Heat the oil in a large flameproof casserole. When hot, add the pheasants and brown all over.

2. Pour over the stock and port, add the orange rind and juice with the sultanas and season well. Bring to the boil. Cover tightly and cook in the oven at 170°C (325°F) mark 3 for 1-1½ hours.
3. Remove pheasants from casserole, then joint each into two or three pieces, depending on size, and arrange on a serving dish; keep warm.
4. Mix the cornflour to a smooth paste with 60 ml (4 tbsp) water. Stir into the juices in the casserole and bring to the boil. Adjust the seasoning and spoon over the pheasant. Garnish with toasted flaked almonds.
SERVES 6

PHEASANT WITH CHESTNUTS

30 ml (2 tbsp) vegetable oil
50 g (2 oz) butter or margarine
brace of pheasants, oven-ready
225 g (8 oz) fresh chestnuts, peeled
2 medium onions, skinned and sliced
45 ml (3 level tbsp) flour
450 ml (¾ pint) beef stock
100 ml (4 fl oz) red wine
salt and pepper
grated rind and juice of ½ an orange
10 ml (2 level tsp) redcurrant jelly
bouquet garni
chopped fresh parsley, to garnish

1. Heat the oil and butter in a large frying pan, add the pheasants and fry for about 5-6 minutes until golden brown. Remove from the pan with a slotted spoon and put into a casserole.
2. Fry the chestnuts and onions in the oil and butter for about 5 minutes, until golden brown, and add to the pheasant.
3. Stir the flour into the remaining fat and cook gently for 1 minute, stirring. Remove the pan from the heat and gradually stir in the stock and wine. Bring to the boil slowly and continue to cook stirring until it thickens. Season and pour over the pheasant.
4. Add the orange rind and juice, redcurrant jelly and bouquet garni, cover and cook in the oven at 180°C (350°F) mark 4 for 1 hour, until the pheasant is tender.
5. Remove the bouquet garni before serving and adjust the seasoning to taste, if necessary. Sprinkle with chopped parsley.
SERVES 4

SALMIS OF PHEASANT

brace of older pheasants, oven-ready
about 75 g (3 oz) butter or margarine
salt and pepper
300 ml (½ pint) chicken stock
slices of carrot and onion for flavouring
1 bay leaf
225 g (8 oz) carrots, peeled
1 medium onion, skinned
3 celery sticks, washed and trimmed
45 ml (3 level tbsp) flour
60 ml (4 tbsp) port
fried croûtons (see page 17), to garnish

1. Place the birds in a small roasting tin. Rub a small knob of butter over the breast of each bird. Season well and pour the chicken stock into the tin. Roast at 200°C (400°F) mark 6 for 40 minutes, basting occasionally.
2. Lift the birds out on to a large chopping board. Pour off the pan juices and reserve. Slice through the flesh, cutting through the breast of the bird to the bone. Using strong scissors or game shears, snip right through the breast bone to open out the bird.
3. Cut through the skin around the legs then push the joints away from the carcass until completely detached. Snip firmly down either side of the backbone to remove it; reserve the bone. Divide each breast portion into two, snipping through the bone. Place the joints on a plate, cover loosely and store in a cool place.
4. Place the backbones in a small saucepan. Pour over the reserved roasting juices. Add the flavouring vegetables with the bay leaf and seasoning and sufficient water to just cover the bones. Bring slowly to the boil, then simmer uncovered for about 30 minutes, until about 450 ml (¾ pint) stock remains. Strain off and reserve.
5. Cut the carrots, onion and celery into 5 mm (¼ inch) slices.
6. Melt 50 g (2 oz) butter in a flameproof casserole. Add the prepared vegetables, cover and cook over a moderate heat until the vegetables soften, about 10 minutes. Stir in the flour and cook gently for 1 minute, stirring. Remove the casserole from the heat and gradually stir in the 450 ml (¾ pint) stock and the port. Season, then bring to the boil and continue to cook, stirring, until thickened.
7. Remove from the heat and add the pheasant joints. Bring slowly to the boil, cover and cook in the oven at 170°C (325°F) mark 3 for about 1¼ hours. Garnish with the croûtons.
SERVES 4-6

HARE AND RABBIT

Hares and rabbits belong to the same family, but hares are larger and have longer legs. Hare is available from late summer to early spring. Rabbit is available all the year around and may be tame (farmed) or wild. Hare has a darker more gamey flavoured flesh than rabbit.

HARE

Hare is best eaten young. An undressed young hare weighs about 3 kg (6½ lb) and will serve four. Hares are hung by the hind feet without being paunched (entrails removed) for 5-7 days to improve the flavour. During this time, the blood collects in the chest cavity. When paunching (see below) collect the blood if using for Jugged Hare (see page 177) and add 5 ml (1 tsp) malt vinegar to it to stop it coagulating. It can be stored, covered, in the refrigerator for 2-3 days. If you want the butcher to collect the blood, you will probably have to order the hare and ask for the blood to be put aside. Add vinegar to it as above. The butcher will skin and paunch the hare after hanging.

Very young hares (leverets) may be roasted whole but for larger hares, the body alone is used. This is known as saddle or baron of hare.

RABBIT

Rabbits are available both fresh and frozen. Unlike hares, they are paunched within a few hours of killing and are not hung. Tame rabbits, which have a delicate flavour, are always tender. Wild rabbits have darker stronger flavoured flesh and they should be eaten young. Fresh rabbit can be cooked in the same way as hare. Frozen rabbit is best used for pies and casseroles. It must be defrosted thoroughly before cooking.

PREPARING A HARE OR RABBIT

SKINNING
1. Cut off the feet at the first joint. Loosen the skin round the back legs. Hold the end of one leg and bend at the joint, then pull the skin over the hind leg. Do the same with the other legs.
2. If keeping the head on for roasting, cut the skin around the eyes and mouth and remove the eyes (if not, cut the head off), then pull the skin towards the head, stripping it off inside out.

PAUNCHING
1. Using kitchen scissors, snip the skin at the fork and cut it up the breastbone, then open the paunch by cutting the inside skin in the same direction. Draw out entrails. Cut away the gall-bladder and flesh it rests on and discard. Reserve kidneys and liver. Cut the diaphragm and draw out the heart and lungs. Discard lungs but keep the heart. For Jugged Hare, reserve the blood.

TRUSSING
1. Cut the sinews in the hind legs at the thigh, bring the legs forward and press closely against the body. Bend forelegs back in the same way. Secure with two skewers or truss with thread.

JOINTING
1. Cut off the hind legs at the thighs and the forelegs round the shoulder bone. Cut off the head. Cut the back into pieces, giving the knife a sharp tap with a hammer to cut through the bone, then cut the ribs in two lengthways.

ROAST HARE

1.6 kg (3½ lb) hare or saddle of larger hare
Veal Stuffing (see page 184)
streaky bacon rashers
dripping or margarine
gravy and redcurrant or guava jelly, to serve

1. Stuff the hare, fold the skin over and sew in position (see Trussing, above). Lay slices of bacon over the back and cover with greased greaseproof paper.
2. Put in a roasting tin, dot with dripping and roast in the oven at 180°C (350°F) mark 4 for

1½-2 hours, basting frequently.
3. Remove paper and bacon 15 minutes before end of cooking time to allow the joint to brown.
4. Remove the skewers and trussing thread and serve the hare with gravy and redcurrant or guava jelly.
SERVES 4

NOTE: The heart, liver and kidneys may be added to the stuffing, if wished. Wash well, put into a saucepan, cover with cold water, bring to the boil, then strain and chop finely.

Jugged Hare

1.6 kg (3½ lb) hare, paunched and jointed, with its
  blood (see page 176)
75 ml (5 level tbsp) seasoned flour
125 g (4 oz) streaky bacon, rinded and diced
50 g (2 oz) butter or margarine
900 ml (1½ pints) beef stock
150 ml (¼ pint) port
5 ml (1 level tsp) dried marjoram
45 ml (3 level tbsp) redcurrant jelly
2 medium onions, skinned and stuck with 12 cloves
salt and pepper
chopped fresh parsley, to garnish

1. Wipe the hare and toss in the seasoned flour.

2. Brown the bacon in its own fat in a large flameproof casserole, then remove and drain.
3. Add the butter to the casserole and lightly brown the hare portions. Add the stock, port, marjoram and redcurrant jelly with the onions. Replace the bacon and season.
4. Bring to the boil, cover and cook in the oven at 170°C (325°F) mark 3 for 3 hours.
5. Transfer the hare to a deep serving dish, cover and keep warm. Discard onions.
6. Mix the blood with the cooking juices until smooth. Pour into the casserole and heat gently, without boiling. Adjust seasoning and pour over the hare. Garnish with parsley.
Serves 6

Poacher's Pie

4 rabbit portions, total weight about 550 g (1¼ lb),
  boned and cut into cubes
125 g (4 oz) bacon rashers, rinded and chopped
2 medium potatoes, peeled and sliced
1 medium leek, trimmed, sliced and washed
salt and pepper
15 ml (1 tbsp) chopped fresh parsley
1.25 ml (¼ level tsp) mixed dried herbs
about 300 ml (½ pint) chicken stock
225 g (8 oz) Shortcrust Pastry made with 225 g (8 oz)
  plain flour (see page 381)
beaten egg, to glaze

1. Fill a 1.7 litre (3 pint) pie dish with alternate layers of rabbit, bacon and vegetables, sprinkling with seasoning and herbs. Half-fill with stock.
2. Roll out the pastry to 5 cm (2 inches) wider than the top of the dish. Cut a 2.5 cm (1 inch) strip from outer edge and line the dampened rim of the dish. Dampen pastry rim and cover with the pastry lid. Trim and seal edges. Make a hole in the centre to let the steam escape.
3. Decorate with pastry leaves and brush with egg. Bake in the oven at 190°C (375°F) mark 5 for 30 minutes. Cover loosely with foil, reduce to 180°C (350°F) mark 4 for a further 1 hour.
Serves 4

Sweet-sour Rabbit with Prunes

1 kg (2¼ lb) rabbit, jointed
2 medium onions, skinned and sliced
300 ml (½ pint) dry white wine
300 ml (½ pint) chicken stock
1 bay leaf
30 ml (2 tbsp) redcurrant jelly
a few black peppercorns
8 whole prunes, stoned
15 ml (1 tbsp) malt vinegar
10 ml (2 level tsp) cornflour
salt and pepper
chopped fresh parsley and toasted almonds, to garnish

1. Put the rabbit in a dish with the onions, pour over the wine and marinate overnight.

2. Discard the onions, then place the rabbit and wine in a flameproof casserole and add the stock, bay leaf, redcurrant jelly and a few peppercorns. Bring to the boil.
3. Add the prunes and submerge them in the liquid. Cover the casserole tightly and cook in the oven at 170°C (325°F) mark 3 for about 1½ hours, until the rabbit is really tender and the prunes plump.
4. Remove the meat from the joints and discard the bones. Blend the vinegar with the cornflour and add to the liquid in the pan. Adjust the seasoning, then boil for 1-2 minutes.
5. Arrange the rabbit and prunes in a hot casserole and pour over the thickened juices. Garnish with parsley and toasted almonds.
Serves 4

FRICASSÉE OF RABBIT

1 kg (2¼ lb) rabbit, jointed
3 medium onions, skinned
bouquet garni
450 ml (¾ pint) chicken stock
25 g (1 oz) butter or margarine
125 g (4 oz) bacon rashers, rinded and chopped
45 ml (3 level tbsp) flour
150 ml (¼ pint) white wine
2 egg yolks
salt and pepper
pinch of freshly grated nutmeg
sliced lemon, to garnish

1. Place the rabbit joints in a saucepan with one onion, the cloves and bouquet garni. Add the stock and simmer for about 45 minutes.

2. Slice remaining onions. Melt the butter in a large saucepan, add bacon and sliced onions and cook for 5 minutes, until browned. Stir in the flour and cook for 1 minute. Remove from heat.
3. Strain the stock from the rabbit and stir gradually into the flour. Bring to the boil and continue to cook, stirring, until it thickens.
4. Add the rabbit and simmer for 30 minutes.
5. Remove the rabbit joints to a serving plate, cover and keep warm. Blend the wine and egg yolks together to a smooth cream, add a little of the sauce and return the blended mixture to the pan. Add salt, pepper and nutmeg and allow to heat through, but do not boil.
6. Pour the sauce over the rabbit joints. Garnish with lemon slices and serve with boiled rice.
SERVES 4

RAISED GAME PIE

1 pheasant
4 rabbit joints, total weight about 450 g (1 lb)
500 g (1 lb) shoulder venison
1 medium onion, skinned
450 g (1 lb) pork sausagemeat
1 garlic clove, skinned and crushed
5 ml (1 level tsp) dried marjoram
pinch of ground mace
6 juniper berries, crushed
salt and pepper
slices of onion, carrot, 6 black peppercorns and 1 bay
   leaf for flavouring
450 g (1 lb) hot water crust pastry, made with
   450 g (1 lb) flour (see page 386)
5 ml (1 level tsp) gelatine

1. Remove the flesh from the pheasant and rabbit joints and cut into small pieces, discarding skin. Reserve the pheasant carcass and rabbit bones. Cut the venison into similar sized pieces. Put the meats in a bowl, add the onion, sausagemeat, garlic, spices, juniper and seasoning. Cover and leave in a cool place for 2-3 hours.
2. Place the pheasant carcass and rabbit bones in a large saucepan, add the flavouring ingredients and 1.4 litres (2½ pints) water. Bring to the boil, skim, then cover and simmer for about 2½ hours. Strain, then if necessary, boil to reduce the stock to 300 ml (½ pint). Cool.
3. Let the pastry rest for 30 minutes, then use the pastry whilst still warm.

4. Keep one quarter of the pastry covered. On a lightly floured surface, roll out the remaining pastry to a 35 cm (14 inch) circle. Fold loosely over the rolling pin, then lift over a 20 cm (8 inch) spring release tin. Ease the pastry into the corners and press evenly up the sides of the tin. Fold excess pastry outwards.
5. Spoon the meat mixture into the lined tin, pressing down with the back of the spoon. Roll out the remaining pastry to a 23 cm (9 inch) round and use to top the pie. Seal well, then trim the edges and reserve the trimmings.
6. Flute the edges and make a small hole in the centre of the pie, and two near the edge – to pour the stock through later. Use trimmings to make 'leaves', arrange on top of the pie.
7. Place the pie on a baking sheet and brush with the beaten egg. Bake in the oven at 220°C (425°F) mark 7 for 20 minutes, then reduce the temperature to 180°C (350°F) mark 4 and cook for a further 2¾ hours, covering with foil if necessary. To test, insert a skewer through the centre hole – the meat should feel tender. Cool.
8. Soak the gelatine in 20 ml (4 tsp) water. Place the bowl over a pan of simmering water until dissolved. Heat reserved stock in a pan and add the gelatine. Remove from the heat and leave to cool until beginning to set.
9. Place the pie on a plate, then ease off the tin. Pour in the stock, cover loosely, then refrigerate overnight. Serve cold.
SERVES 10-12

VENISON

Venison is the meat of the red, fallow or roe deer. It is a dark, firm, fine-textured meat with very little fat, which should be clear and white. The meat from mature deer aged 1½-2 years is considered to have the best flavour. As it is inclined to be tough it is hung for 1-2 weeks before cooking. A wide variety of venison cuts is available. Loin, saddle and leg or haunch are prime cuts suitable for roasting and braising. Tenderloin chops and medallions are cut from the boned loin; these can be sautéed or grilled. Shoulder, neck and breast are best diced for stewing, or minced. As there is only a little fat on venison, the meat tends to be dry, so additional fat or liquid is added for cooking. This is done either by marinating the meat overnight or adding melted fat or oil and basting frequently during cooking.

ROAST VENISON

saddle, leg or loin of venison
melted butter or vegetable oil
Thick Gravy (see page 202) and redcurrant jelly

1. Pat the joint dry with absorbent kitchen paper and place on a large piece of foil. Brush generously with butter. Fold the foil to make a parcel. Weigh.
2. Place the parcel in a roasting tin and roast in the oven at 170°C (325°F) mark 3 allowing 25 minutes per 450 g (1 lb), basting frequently. Fold back the foil 20 minutes before the end of the cooking time to allow to brown. Serve with gravy and redcurrant jelly.

VARIATION
MARINATED VENISON
Place 2 chopped carrots and small onions, 1 chopped celery stick, 6 black peppercorns, parsley stalks, 1 bay leaf and 3 blades mace in a large dish. Add venison and sufficient wine to half-cover. Marinate for 12 hours, turning the meat 2-3 times. Remove meat and cook as above. Boil marinade to reduce by half; use for gravy.

RICH VENISON CASSEROLE

1 kg (2 lb) stewing venison, trimmed and cut into
*   cubes*
150 ml (¼ pint) red wine
100 ml (4 fl oz) vegetable oil
12 juniper berries, lightly crushed
4 cloves
8 black peppercorns
1 garlic clove, skinned and crushed
125 g (4 oz) streaky bacon rashers, rinded
2 medium onions, skinned and sliced
30 ml (2 level tbsp) flour
150 ml (¼ pint) beef stock
30 ml (2 tbsp) redcurrant jelly
salt and pepper
chopped fresh parsley, to garnish

1. Place the venison in a bowl and add the wine, half the oil, the juniper berries, cloves, peppercorns and garlic. Stir well and leave to marinate for 24 hours, stirring occasionally.
2. Stretch each bacon rasher using a knife, cut in half and roll up. Heat the remaining oil in a flameproof casserole, add the bacon rolls and fry for about 3 minutes, until coloured. Remove from the casserole with a slotted spoon.
3. Remove the venison from the marinade and quickly fry the meat pieces in the casserole, in several batches, until coloured. Add the onions and cook for 3 minutes. Then add the flour and cook for 2 minutes, stirring.
4. Remove casserole from heat and gradually stir in the stock, redcurrant jelly and the marinade.

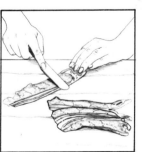

Using the back of a knife, stretch each bacon rasher.

Bring to the boil slowly and cook, stirring, until thickened. Return venison to casserole. Season and place bacon rolls on top.
5. Cover and cook in oven at 170°C (325°F) mark 3 for 3 hours, until the venison is tender. Garnish with chopped parsley.
SERVES 4

Venison Escalopes with Red Wine

VENISON ESCALOPES WITH RED WINE

6 escalopes of venison cut from the haunch (leg), about
   175 g (6 oz) each
1 small onion, skinned and finely chopped
1 bay leaf
2 fresh parsley sprigs
8 juniper berries
300 ml (½ pint) dry red wine
15 g (½ oz) butter
15 ml (1 tbsp) vegetable oil
30 ml (2 tbsp) redcurrant jelly
salt and pepper
Game Chips (see page 171), to serve

1. Put the venison escalopes in a large shallow dish and sprinkle with the onion, bay leaf, parsley and juniper berries. Pour on the wine, cover and leave to marinate in the refrigerator for 3-4 hours or overnight, turning the escalopes occasionally.
2. Remove the escalopes from the marinade, reserving the marinade. Heat the butter and oil in a large frying pan and fry the escalopes for 3-4 minutes on each side. Transfer to a warmed serving dish and keep warm while making the sauce.
3. Strain the reserved marinade into the frying pan and stir to loosen any sediment. Increase the heat and boil rapidly for 3-4 minutes, until reduced. Stir in the redcurrant jelly and season the mixture to taste. Cook, stirring, for 1-2 minutes. Pour over the escalopes.
4. Serve immediately with Game Chips, Brussels sprouts and carrots.
SERVES 6

STUFFINGS

Stuffings, also known as forcemeats, fillings and sometimes farces, may be used in various ways. They can help keep a dry food moist during cooking or absorb some of the fat and juices from meat, or they can be used to extend small amounts of ingredients into meal-sized portions. They can also be used to provide contrasting colour, flavour or texture to a dish. Stuffings are most commonly used with meat and poultry, but they are equally good with fish or vegetables such as peppers and tomatoes.

STUFFING INGREDIENTS

Most stuffings are based on one of the following basic ingredients:

BREADCRUMBS: It is preferable to make your own breadcrumbs rather than use bought ones, which tend to be dry and powdery. Use brown or white bread that is 2-3 days old and make the breadcrumbs in a blender or food processor, or use a grater. To prepare dry breadcumbs, dry them in a low oven.

RICE: This should be cooked first (see page 302), then mixed with a little fat, egg or liquid to bind it with the other ingredients.

SUET: This adds flavour and moisture to a stuffing. Suet is sold in packets, shredded, ready for use. Vegetarian suet is also available.

SAUSAGEMEAT: This can be bought fresh from the butcher or frozen. If unobtainable, simply use pork sausages, removing the skins and pressing the sausagemeat together.

Small amounts of other foods such as meat, sausagemeat, fish, nuts, vegetables and cheese can be added to the basic ingredient. Depending on the mixture, it may need moistening with a little water, stock or fruit juice or binding with egg.

MAKING STUFFINGS

When making a stuffing, assemble all the ingredients but do not mix with any egg or liquid until ready to use. Do not put the stuffing into poultry, meat or fish until ready to cook it; bacteria could penetrate the stuffing which might not reach a sufficiently high temperature during cooking to kill them.

When cooking poultry and other stuffed foods, it is necessary to calculate the cooking time on the total weight of the food including the stuffing, to make absolutely sure that it will be cooked thoroughly.

WATCHPOINTS

- Do not make the stuffing too wet or too dry; if too wet it will be stodgy and if it is too dry it will be crumbly and difficult to handle.
- It is advisable to season stuffings well as the flavours may well need to penetrate a fairly solid mass.
- When stuffing poultry, loosely stuff the neck end of the bird only, otherwise it might prevent heat penetrating through to the centre of the body cavity.
- Do not pack the stuffing too tightly into meat and poultry as the meat juices will make the stuffing swell during cooking and it may burst the skin and spill out.
- If you have too much stuffing, cook the surplus in a separate casserole or form into small balls and cook in the oven with the meat for about 1 hour.

NOTE: It is not advisable to stuff meat or poultry prior to freezing.

CALCULATING QUANTITIES

As an approximate guide, allow about 225 g (8 oz) stuffing for each 2.3 kg (5 lb) dressed weight of turkey or other large poultry. For small birds, allow approximately 125 g (4 oz) stuffing per 450 g (1 lb).

Turkey with Festive Turkey Stuffing and Forcemeat Balls

FESTIVE TURKEY STUFFING

45 ml (3 tbsp) oil
50 g (2 oz) butter or margarine
350 g (12 oz) onion, skinned and roughly chopped
6 celery sticks, trimmed and roughly chopped
2 eating apples
175 g (6 oz) fresh breadcrumbs
125 g (4 oz) coarse oatmeal
50 g (2 oz) suet
45 ml (3 level tbsp) fresh chopped sage or 5 ml
  (1 level tsp) dried rubbed sage
finely grated rind and juice of 2 oranges
salt and pepper
1 egg, beaten

1. Heat the oil and butter in a frying pan and fry the vegetables until beginning to brown. Meanwhile, quarter, core and roughly chop the apples. Stir into the pan and fry for 1-2 minutes. Turn out into a large bowl to cool.
2. Stir in the breadcrumbs, oatmeal, suet and sage. Add the orange rind with 45 ml (3 tbsp) orange juice. Season well, add the egg and mix thoroughly.
SUFFICIENT FOR A 4.5-5.4 KG (10-12 LB) OVEN-READY TURKEY

SAGE AND ONION STUFFING

50 g (2 oz) butter or margarine
450 g (1 lb) onions, skinned and chopped
30 ml (2 tbsp) chopped fresh sage or 10 ml (2 level tsp)
  dried rubbed sage
225 g (8 oz) fresh breadcrumbs
125 g (4 oz) medium oatmeal
salt and pepper

1. Melt the butter in a saucepan, add the onions and sage and fry for 4-5 minutes. Stir in the breadcrumbs.
2. Toast the oatmeal under the grill for a few minutes, then stir into the breadcrumb mixture and season well. Cool before use.
SUFFICIENT FOR A 4-5 KG (9-11 LB) OVEN-READY GOOSE

MINT AND ROSEMARY STUFFING

75 g (3 oz) butter or margarine
2 medium onions, skinned and finely chopped
2 celery sticks, trimmed and finely chopped
225 g (8 oz) fresh breadcrumbs
30 ml (2 level tbsp) mint sauce
15 ml (1 tbsp) chopped fresh rosemary or 10 ml
    (2 level tsp) dried rosemary
grated rind of 1 lemon
salt and pepper
1 egg, beaten

1. Melt the butter in a saucepan, add the onions and celery and fry gently for about 10 minutes.
2. Put the breadcrumbs, mint sauce, rosemary and lemon rind in a bowl. Stir in the celery and onion and season. Mix well together, then bind with the beaten egg.
SUFFICIENT FOR A 4.5-5.4 KG (10-12 LB) OVEN-READY TURKEY

Mint and Rosemary Stuffing

FORCEMEAT BALLS

50 g (2 oz) butter or margarine
175 g (6 oz) onion, skinned and roughly chopped
50 g (2 oz) walnut pieces, roughly chopped
2.5 ml (½ level tsp) chilli powder
900 g (2 lb) pork sausagemeat
chopped fresh parsley
salt and pepper
flour for dusting
about 30 ml (2 tbsp) oil

1. Heat the butter in a frying pan. Add onion and fry until beginning to brown. Add the nuts and chilli powder and stir-fry for 1 minute. Cool.
2. Place the sausagemeat in a bowl. Stir in the cold onions with 60 ml (4 level tbsp) parsley. Season well. With floured hands shape the sausagemeat into about 32 balls. Place on a flat baking sheet, cover and chill.
3. Heat a thin film of oil in a large roasting tin. Add the sausagemeat balls. Bake at 180°C (350°F) mark 4 for about 45 minutes, turning occasionally. Drain on kitchen paper before tossing quickly in parsley and serving as an accompaniment to roast turkey.
SERVES 14-16

RICE STUFFING

50 g (2 oz) long grain rice, cooked
1 medium onion, skinned and chopped
50 g (2 oz) raisins
50 g (2 oz) almonds, blanched and chopped
30 ml (2 tbsp) chopped fresh parsley
25 g (1 oz) butter or margarine, melted
salt and pepper
1 egg, beaten

1. Combine all the ingredients in a bowl, except the egg, then season. Add sufficient egg to bind.
2. Use for meat, fish, vegetables or chicken.
SUFFICIENT FOR A 1.4 KG (3 LB) OVEN-READY CHICKEN

VARIATIONS
1. Replace onion with 1 celery stick, finely chopped.
2. Replace parsley with chopped fresh coriander.

OATMEAL AND PRUNE STUFFING

125 g (4 oz) prunes
60 ml (4 tbsp) port
175 g (6 oz) fresh brown breadcrumbs
125 g (4 oz) shelled Brazil nuts, chopped
125 g (4 oz) coarse oatmeal
1 large cooking apple, peeled and cored
50 g (2 oz) butter or margarine, melted
50 g (2 oz) shredded suet
salt and pepper
2 eggs, beaten

1. Soak the prunes in the port and 300 ml (½ pint) water overnight. Drain, reserving the liquid. Chop the prunes into small pieces.
2. In a bowl, mix together the prunes, breadcrumbs and nuts. Toast the oatmeal for a few minutes under the grill, then stir into the breadcrumb mixture. Coarsely grate the cooking apple into the mixture.
3. Stir in the butter, suet and seasoning and bind together with the eggs.
SUFFICIENT FOR A *4.5-5.4 KG (10-12 LB) OVEN-READY TURKEY*

NOTE: Use the reserved liquid for the gravy.

VEAL STUFFING

125 g (4 oz) lean veal
75 g (3 oz) lean bacon, rinded
25 g (1 oz) butter or margarine
1 small onion, skinned and finely chopped
75 g (3 oz) fresh breadcrumbs
25 g (1 oz) mushrooms, wiped and finely chopped
30 ml (2 tbsp) chopped fresh parsley
salt and pepper
pinch of cayenne pepper
pinch of ground mace
1 egg, beaten

1. Finely mince the veal and bacon using a food processor or mincer, then transfer to a bowl and beat well.
2. Melt the butter in a saucepan, add the onion and fry for 2-3 minutes, until soft but not coloured, then add to the meat.
3. Add the breadcrumbs, mushrooms, parsley and seasonings. Mix together well, then bind with the egg.
SUFFICIENT FOR A LARGE VEAL OR LAMB JOINT

NOTE: Double the quantities for a 6 kg (13 lb) oven-ready turkey.

NUT STUFFING

50 g (2 oz) butter or margarine
2 small onions, skinned and finely chopped
125 g (4 oz) mushrooms, wiped and finely chopped
50 g (2 oz) shelled walnuts, finely chopped
45 ml (3 tbsp) shelled cashew nuts, finely chopped
6 shelled Brazil nuts, finely chopped
pinch of dried mixed herbs
15 ml (1 tbsp) chopped fresh parsley
175 g (6 oz) fresh breadcrumbs
1 egg, size 2, beaten
salt and pepper

1. Melt the butter in a saucepan, add the onions and fry for 5 minutes. Add the mushrooms and fry for a further 5 minutes. In a bowl, mix together the nuts, mixed herbs, parsley and breadcrumbs.
2. Stir in the mushroom mixture with the egg. Season to taste.
SUFFICIENT FOR A *4-4.5 KG (9-10 LB) OVEN-READY TURKEY*

VARIATIONS
Replace cashew nuts with peanuts. If preferred, use one type of nut only. Almonds could be used in this stuffing.

APPLE AND CELERY STUFFING

50 g (2 oz) butter or margarine
125 g (4 oz) bacon, rinded and chopped
4 medium onions, skinned and chopped
4 celery sticks, trimmed and chopped
700 g (1½ lb) cooking apples, peeled, cored and sliced
175 g (6 oz) fresh breadcrumbs
60 ml (4 tbsp) chopped fresh parsley
5 ml (1 level tsp) sugar, or to taste
salt and pepper

1. Melt the butter in a frying pan, add the bacon and fry for 2-3 minutes, until golden brown. Remove from the pan with a slotted spoon and put in a bowl.
2. Fry the onions and celery for 5 minutes, then remove from the pan with the slotted spoon and add to the bacon.
3. Fry the apples for 2-3 minutes, until soft, then add to the bowl.
4. Stir in all the remaining ingredients and mix well together. Season well.
SUFFICIENT FOR A 4-5 KG (9-11 LB) OVEN-READY GOOSE

BACON OR HAM STUFFING

15 ml (1 tbsp) vegetable oil
1 small onion, skinned and chopped
25 g (1 oz) mushrooms, wiped and chopped
50-75 g (2-3 oz) cooked bacon or ham, chopped
25 g (1 oz) fresh breadcrumbs
salt and pepper
pinch of mustard powder
few drops of Worcestershire sauce
1 egg, beaten

1. Heat the oil in a frying pan, add the onion and fry gently for 1-2 minutes. Add the mushrooms and bacon and fry until the onion is soft but not coloured.
2. Remove from the heat and add the breadcrumbs, seasoning, mustard powder and Worcestershire sauce. Mix together well, then bind with the egg.
SUFFICIENT FOR A 1.4 KG (3 LB) OVEN-READY CHICKEN

NOTE: This can also be used for vegetables, such as tomatoes, small marrows, peppers, etc.

CHESTNUT STUFFING

450 g (1 lb) fresh chestnuts or 225 g (8 oz) can whole chestnuts (unsweetened), drained and roughly chopped
25 g (1 oz) butter or margarine
2 medium onions, skinned and chopped
350 g (12 oz) fresh breadcrumbs
75 g (3 oz) shredded suet
45 ml (3 level tbsp) creamed horseradish
5 ml (1 tsp) lemon juice
salt and pepper

1. If using fresh chestnuts, make a small cut along the flat side of each. Bake in the oven at 200°C (400°F) mark 6 for 10 minutes, until the skins crack. Peel when cooled. Simmer the chestnuts in salted water for 20 minutes or until tender. Drain and chop roughly.
2. Melt the butter in a frying pan, add the onions and fry until soft but not coloured.

3. Remove from the heat and stir in the chestnuts, breadcrumbs, suet, horseradish, lemon juice and seasoning.
4. Continue to fry slowly on top of the cooker, stirring occasionally, for 15-20 minutes, or spoon into an ovenproof dish, cover and bake in the oven at 200°C (400°F) mark 6 for 30-35 minutes. Uncover and bake for a further 15 minutes. Cool before use.
SUFFICIENT FOR A 4.5-5.4 KG (10-12 LB) OVEN-READY TURKEY

VARIATION
SAUSAGEMEAT AND CHESTNUT STUFFING
Put 225 g (8 oz) fresh breadcrumbs, 450 g (1 lb) pork sausagemeat, finely grated rind of 1 orange, 5 ml (1 level tsp) dried sage, salt and pepper in a large bowl. Stir well. Drain and roughly chop a 440 g (15½ oz) can whole chestnuts. Add to the bowl with juice of 1 orange and gently bind.

PEACH AND NUT STUFFING

50 g (2 oz) long grain brown rice
10 ml (2 level tsp) ground turmeric
25 g (1 oz) butter or margarine
125 g (4 oz) spring onions, trimmed and finely
   chopped
25 g (1 oz) Brazil nuts, finely chopped
2.5 ml (½ level tsp) ground ginger
1 fresh peach, skinned and chopped
salt and pepper

1. Cook the brown rice with the turmeric in boiling salted water for about 45 minutes. Drain well.
2. Melt the butter in a saucepan, add the spring onions, nuts and ginger and fry gently for 5 minutes.
3. Remove from the heat and stir in the rice and peach. Season and cool.
SUFFICIENT FOR A 1.4 KG (3 LB) OVEN-READY CHICKEN

MUSHROOM STUFFING

25 g (1 oz) butter or margarine
125 g (4 oz) mushrooms, wiped and chopped
1 small onion, skinned and chopped
30 ml (2 tbsp) chopped fresh parsley or coriander
salt and pepper
125 g (4 oz) fresh breadcrumbs
1 egg, beaten

1. Melt the butter in a saucepan, add the mushrooms and onion and fry gently for 2-3 minutes, until soft but not coloured.
2. Add the parsley, seasoning and breadcrumbs and mix together well, then bind with a little beaten egg.
SUFFICIENT FOR A 1.4-1.8 KG (3-4 LB) OVEN-READY CHICKEN

NOTE: Double these amounts for a 4.5 kg (10 lb) goose or turkey. The mixture may also be used to stuff tomatoes or green peppers, but reduce the amount of breadcrumbs to 50 g (2 oz).

APRICOT STUFFING

175 g (6 oz) fresh breadcrumbs
125 g (4 oz) dried apricots, finely chopped
50 g (2 oz) salted peanuts, finely chopped
15 ml (1 tbsp) chopped fresh parsley
50 g (2 oz) butter or margarine
1 large onion, skinned and finely chopped
grated rind and juice of 1 small orange
5 ml (1 level tsp) curry powder
salt and pepper
1 egg, beaten

1. Place the breadcrumbs in a bowl and add the apricots, peanuts and parsley.
2. Melt the butter in a small saucepan, add the onion and orange rind, cover and cook gently until soft. Remove from the pan and add to the breadcrumb mixture.
3. Sprinkle in the curry powder and cook gently

for 1 minute, then pour over the orange juice and boil gently for 30 seconds.
4. Stir the curry-flavoured orange juice into the breadcrumbs. Season liberally, then bind with the beaten egg.
SUFFICIENT STUFFING FOR A 1.8 KG (4 LB) OVEN-READY DUCKLING

VARIATION
APRICOT, APPLE AND PRUNE STUFFING
Cut 125 g (4 oz) soaked and stoned prunes into quarters. Mix the prunes, 50 g (2 oz) chopped dried apricots, 175 g (6 oz) peeled, cored and roughly chopped cooking apples, 125 g (4 oz) cooked rice, 50 g (2 oz) shredded suet and 50 g (2 oz) blanched and chopped almonds in a bowl. Season to taste. Add the grated rind and juice of ½ lemon, and bind with 1 beaten egg.
SUFFICIENT FOR A 1.4 KG (3 LB) ROLLED PORK JOINT

Herbs, Spices, Flavourings and Essences

Herbs and spices have been used with food since time immemorial. Originally, one of their main purposes was to disguise the flavour and colour of perishable foods which were past their best. Today, they are appreciated for the distinctive tastes they impart to meat, fish, vegetables, rice, pulses and fruit. The spread of ethnic foods has increased the selection of fresh and dried herbs available.

Herbs

Herbs are sold fresh or dried; fresh have a better appearance than dried and are essential for adding to salads, but many dried herbs have a good flavour when used in cooked dishes such as casseroles. Dried herbs have a stronger flavour than fresh and should be used more sparingly; as a rule, you need about one third the amount specified for fresh herbs if substituting dried.

The majority of herbs, even if they do not originate in this country, can be grown successfully in the garden or in window boxes. Some are annuals and need to be sown each year, others are perennial.

Ideally, fresh herbs should be picked just before using, or used soon after buying. If necessary they can be stored in the refrigerator for 1-2 days: seal in a polythene bag enclosing plenty of air. Large bunches of herbs, such as parsley and coriander, which still have their roots on should be stored in a jug of water with a plastic bag inverted over the leaves. Herbs can also be dried or frozen and used in soups or casseroles. To freeze, chop finely and freeze in ice cube trays.

DRYING AND STORING HERBS

Dry home-grown herbs in a very slow oven, in the sun or by hanging them in a cool airy place, covered with muslin to keep the dust off. Alternatively, dry in the microwave between sheets of absorbent kitchen paper: put a glass of water in the oven at the same time.

When dry, strip the leaves carefully from the stems and leave them whole. This will preserve more flavour than crumbling them.

Dried herbs keep best in airtight jars away from the light. Choose wood, earthenware or dark-coloured glass.

In a cool place, dried herbs will keep their flavour for 6-8 months. After that, any left can be scattered around the herb garden or sprinkled round pot plants to keep away insects.

HERBS AND THEIR USES

ANGELICA: Tall plant with all parts used for flavouring, though only the candied stem is available commercially. Use the leaves as a vegetable, add to salads or cook with fish. The stems can be eaten raw like celery or candied and crystallised and used in ice creams, cakes and as a cake decoration. The root is good for stewing with acid fruits such as rhubarb.

BALM (LEMON BALM): This has green, heart-shaped leaves and a tendency, like mint, to take over a garden unless controlled by planting it in a bottomless container sunk in the earth to contain the roots. It has a lemony smell and taste and is good with fish, poultry and ham dishes and in marinades. It also adds flavour to punches and fruit drinks and makes an excellent herbal tea.

BASIL (SWEET BASIL): Has a distinctive, pungent taste and aromatic scent and is generally used with tomatoes and in Italian cookery. It is also good in salads, with lamb, grilled meat, green vegetables, in tomato soup and in Pesto Sauce (see page 256). Basil grows for a short period in summer and needs plenty of sun.

Bay: Has a strong, spicy flavour and can be used fresh or dried – when the flavour is even more pronounced. One or two leaves are all that is needed to flavour a dish. Bay is one of the ingredients used in a bouquet garni. Although mainly used in meat and fish casseroles and marinades for fish and poultry, it is also used in soups and stocks and to flavour infusions of milk for use in sauces such as Béchamel or milk puddings. Bay trees are very ornamental and can be pruned like hedges to a desired shape.

Borage: Both the slightly hairy leaves and the bright blue flowers have a flavour of salt and cucumber. It is mainly used in claret cup, Pimms and other cool drinks, but can be used in salads. The flowers can be candied and used as decorations for cakes and sweets. Borage is easy to grow and is not sold dried.

Burnet (salad burnet): Has a nutty flavour with a hint of cucumber and is good in salads, especially in winter when it continues to flourish. It can also be used in soups and stews.

Chervil: Has a delicate, sweet flavour and is used in a similar way to parsley, especially in French dishes. It is good in salads, as a garnish, with a variety of vegetables, especially new potatoes, and as a flavouring for sauces such as Hollandaise. It also blends well with egg, cheese and chicken dishes.

Chives: Members of the onion family with narrow, green leaves which are the part you eat. They are best used raw to flavour salads and dressings and as a garnish for soups and savoury dishes. They should be snipped into short lengths before use.

Coriander: Also grown for its seeds (see page 191) but the leaves have an unusual flavour and are good in Middle Eastern and Indian dishes, salads and chilled soups.

Curry plant: The spiky leaves of this shrubby perennial have a strong curry flavour. It is not used in Indian curries, but the fresh or dried leaves are added sparingly to soups and stews.

Dill: The feathery leaves (known as dill weed) are used as a herb and the dried dill seeds as a spice. Dill weed has a mild, sweet, caraway flavour and needs to be used in fairly large quantities. The dried dill seeds are more pungent. Dill is used in salads, as a garnish, in scrambled eggs, white meat dishes and, classically, with salmon.

Fennel: Both the feathery leaves and seeds are used. It has a slightly aniseed flavour and the seed is a good aid to digestion. It is a classical flavouring for fish – especially oily fish where it counteracts the richness – and in marinades, soups and sauces.

Fines herbes: A mixture of finely chopped leaves of chives, chervil, parsley and tarragon which are used in omelettes, with fish, poultry and salads.

Garlic: This is not a herb but is often used in conjunction with fresh herbs. Garlic is the most pungent of the onion family and is available in three varieties: white, red and pink. Choose cloves that are hard and firm. It is used widely in savoury dishes, usually only a clove at a time. See page 207 for Garlic Butter.

Lemon Grass: Grown mostly in tropical and sub-tropical countries but is imported to the West, in fresh and dried forms and as a powder (sereh). It has thick, grass like leaves which smell and taste strongly of lemon. It is most often used in the cooking of Sri Lanka and South Asia to flavour curries and meat dishes. It can also be used with fish and to flavour sweet puddings.

Lovage: Has a sharp peppery flavour, which is good in all strong tasting savoury dishes and soups. Lovage leaves add an unusual tang to salads cold roast beef sandwiches.

Marjoram: Belongs to the same family as Oregano (see page 190) and has similar uses. It has a distinctive powerful flavour and is good in stuffings, rubbed over roasts such as pork, in meat soups, on pizza and in homemade sausages. It is also used on vegetables and in cream soups.

Mint: There are many culinary varieties of mint with different flavours and scents, eg peppermint, spearmint, applemint. It is sold fresh and dried but is very easy to grow. Use fresh for Mint Sauce (see page 205) or mint jelly with lamb, as a flavouring for potatoes, peas and other vegetables and to garnish wine and fruit cups.

KEY:
1. Sage
2. Parsley
3. Chives
4. Garlic
5. Bay Leaves
6. Rosemary
7. Tarragon
8. Basil
9. Dill
10. Marjoram
11. Mint
12. Chives
13. Fennel
14. Curly-leafed parsley
15. Flat-leafed Parsley
16. Coriander
17. Thyme

MIXED HERBS: A mixture of dried herbs, usually parsley, sage, thyme, marjoram and tarragon, used for seasoning savoury dishes such as soups and casseroles.

OREGANO: A member of the marjoram family, also known as Wild Marjoram. The two herbs are interchangeable, although oregano is much more aromatic and strongly flavoured. Use with meat, sausages, soups, pizza and other Italian dishes, tomatoes, in salads, with cooked vegetables and in egg and cheese dishes.

PARSLEY: There are two varieties of parsley now widely available: the familiar curly-leafed parsley and continental or flat-leafed parsley. The curly parsley has a milder flavour. The strong flavoured stalks are a classic ingredient in bouquet garni and fines herbes. Use parsley in sauces for chicken, ham, fish and shellfish, with vegetables, in stuffings and butters, soups, salads and as a garnish.

ROSEMARY: Strong pungent herb with spikey leaves. The flavour overpowers other herbs so use it on its own and sparingly in meat, fish, poultry and some sweet dishes. It marries well with all lamb dishes and is excellent used with barbecued meats.

SAGE: A large-leaved herb with a strong, slightly bitter taste. Use sparingly on its own, in stuffings, casseroles, salads, meat dishes, especially pork, and sausages, egg and cheese dishes.

SAVORY: Comes in summer and winter varieties and is best when fresh. It has a distinctive peppery flavour which has a particular affinity with beans and brings out their taste. Use also with egg dishes, tomatoes and other vegetables, soups and cheese.

TARRAGON: Has a distinctive, unusual flavour. There are two main species, the French variety being better than the Russian. It is one of the herbs used in the fines herbes mixture and is also used in Hollandaise, Bearnaise and Tartare Sauces. Use also to flavour wine vinegar, in marinades, with fish and chicken, in aspic glaze, tarragon butter and sauce for ham.

THYME: Comes in many varieties of which garden and lemon are the most common. It has a strong aromatic flavour and is used in bouquet garni. Rub over beef, lamb and veal before roasting and use in soups, stuffings, Bread Sauce, with carrots, onions and mushrooms. Lemon thyme is especially good in stuffings for veal, and in egg and fish dishes.

SPICES

Spices are the dried parts of aromatic plants and may be the fruit, bark, seed, root or flower bud. Most come from hot countries. Once rare and expensive commodities, spices are now some of the most useful ingredients available to every cook.

Most spices are sold dried, either whole or ground. Whole spices which you grind yourself will give a more pungent flavour than those which are ready ground. For the strongest flavour, grind the spice immediately before use. Use either a pestle and mortar or an electric coffee bean grinder. If the latter, first clean it by grinding a slice of stale bread which will absorb any coffee flavour. If you grind spices regularly keep a separate grinder for this purpose. Buy spices in small quantities as their flavour deteriorates quite quickly. Keep them in small, airtight glass jars – preferably coloured – away from the light as this affects flavour. Discard any that are not used within a year of purchase.

SPICES AND THEIR USES

ALLSPICE: Also called Jamaica Pepper, it is sold as small dried berries or ready ground. The whole spice is an ingredient of pickling spice. Its flavour is a mixture of cloves, cinnamon and nutmeg and it can be used whole in marinades, meat dishes, pickles, chutneys and with poached fish or ground in pickles, relishes, soups, sauces, vegetable dishes, beef stews, baked ham, lamb dishes, cakes, milk puddings and fruit pies.

ANISEED (ANISE): These small seeds have a strong, distinctive flavour. Used mainly to flavour cakes and biscuits, but also in salad dressings, with red cabbage, in cheese, fish and shellfish dishes. Aniseed is the main flavouring ingredient in drinks such as Pernod, Anisette, Ouzo and Raki.

ANISE PEPPER: Also called Szechuan pepper, it is a hot aromatic spice made from the dried red berries of a Chinese tree. It is one of the ingredients of Five-spice Powder (see page 195).

ASAFOETIDA: This is not a true spice but is derived from the resin of a plant native to Afghanistan and Iran. It can be bought in solid form but as it is very hard it is best bought ground, in powder form. The flavour is pungent, so it is used in very small quantities, mainly in Indian cooking for pickles, fish and vegetables. It is often used as a substitute for salt in India.

CARAWAY: Small brown seeds with tapering ends with a pleasant, sharp, liquorice-like taste. Widely used in central European and Jewish cookery. Used mainly for flavouring cakes, biscuits and bread but also in soups, salads, sauerkraut, with vegetables, in cheese dishes, omelettes and pork dishes. It is also an ingredient of the liqueur Kummel. Like aniseed, caraway aids digestion.

CARDAMOM: A member of the ginger family sold both whole either green or black, and ground. It has a strong, bitter sweet, slightly lemony flavour and should be used sparingly. Widely used in Indian, Eastern and continental European cooking. Cardamom is an expensive spice as the seed pods must be snipped individually from the plant by hand. It is an ingredient of most curry powders and can also be used in pickles, soups, beef and pork dishes, with sweet potato, pumpkin and apples and in bread, buns, biscuits and cakes, with iced melon and in custard and rice pudding. It is also added to Turkish coffee.

CAYENNE: This comes from the red pepper (capsicum) family and is prepared from the smallest, hottest chillies. It is always sold ground and is sweet, pungent and very hot. Use it sparingly to flavour meats and sauces, especially barbecue and devilled recipes, eggs, fish, vegetables, cheese sauces and pastry, chicken croquettes, cheese and vegetable soups. Unlike paprika, it cannot be used for colouring as it is far too strong.

CELERY SEEDS: These are seeds from a different plant than salad celery and have a strong taste which resembles the vegetable. They are sold whole or ground and can be used sparingly in pickles and chutney, meat and fish dishes, salads, bread, marinades, dressings and dips.

CHILLI POWDER: A very hot spice which should be used extremely sparingly in Mexican dishes, pickles, chutneys, ketchups, soup, tomato dishes, casseroles, spaghetti and meat sauces. Some pre-mixed commercial chilli powders, often called mild chilli powder or seasoned chilli powder, contain a mixture of chilli and other spices such as cumin, oregano, salt and garlic and are less hot. Test before using.

CINNAMON: Available ground or in sticks of bark. It has a sweet, pungent flavour and is widely used in all sweet, spicy baking, as a flavouring for chocolate dishes, on cheesecakes, in pork dishes, pickles and chutneys and to flavour hot drinks, mulled wine and punches.

CLOVES: These are available whole, and are also sold ground. They have a distinctive, pungent flavour and are used mainly to flavour apple dishes, Christmas pudding, mincemeat, Bread Sauce and to stud ham and pork. They are good with pumpkin and in mulled wine. Whole cloves are best removed before a dish is eaten.

CORIANDER: Coriander seeds have a mild, sweet, orangey flavour and are sold whole or ground. Coriander is an ingredient of most curry powders and pickling spice and is also used in chutney, meat dishes, especially pork, in casseroles, Greek-style dishes, apple pies, pea soup and baked goods.

CUMIN: Seeds with a strong, spicy, slightly bitter taste which are sold whole or ground. An ingredient of curry powders and some chilli powder mixtures, they are also used in pickles, chutney, cheese dishes, soups, with cabbage and rice dishes, in Mexican and Eastern dishes, meat loaves, marinades and fruit pies.

FENUGREEK: Seeds with a slightly harsh, hot flavour which are an ingredient of commercial curry powders. Also used in chutneys, pickles and sauces, but rarely as the sole spice.

GINGER: A root with a hot sweetish taste sold in various forms. Root ginger is available fresh or dried, or it may be dried and ground. Stem (green) ginger is available preserved in syrup or crystallised. Root ginger needs to be cooked to release the true flavour; peel and slice and use in marinades, curries, sauces, chutneys and Chinese cooking. Ground ginger is used in curries, sauces, preserves, cakes and sprinkled on to melon. Preserved ginger is used in sweet dishes.

HORSERADISH: A root of the mustard family, which has a hot, biting, pungent taste and should be used sparingly. It is used raw, grated into dressings of cream and is classically served with roast beef. Horseradish is also good with some fish and as a sandwich flavouring.

JUNIPER: Small purple-black berries with an aromatic scent and pine tang. They should be crushed before being added to a dish to release maximum flavour. Use with game, venison, pork and mutton, in marinades and casseroles with these ingredients, also in pâtés and sauerkraut. Juniper is a flavouring agent in gin.

LAOS POWDER: Is related to ginger and is similar in that the root is the part used. It has a peppery ginger taste and is used in the hot dishes of South-east Asia. In Europe it is used to flavour liqueurs and bitters. It is also known as *galangal* or *galingale.*

MACE: The outer covering of the nutmeg which is bright red when harvested and dries to a deep orange. Is sold as blades (useful for infusing) or ground. It has a stronger flavour than nutmeg. Use it in mulled wine and punches, potted meat, fish dishes, Béchamel sauce, meat loaf, stews, pies and some puddings and cooked fruit dishes.

MUSTARD: Made from the black, brown and white seeds of the mustard plant. The dark seeds give aroma and white ones pungency and most made-up mustards are a combination of the two in varying proportions. The seeds are either left whole for whole-grain mustard or are ground to make mustard flour and then liquid such as wine, vinegar and cider are added to moisten it and add the characteristic flavours. Some English mustard is sold as a dry yellow powder made from black mustard seeds which you mix up with water; other mustards are sold ready mixed. Mustard is used as a condiment like salt and pepper with a wide variety of savoury dishes and also to flavour dressings and sauces, with cheese dishes, especially Welsh rarebit and in beef, ham and bacon dishes.

NUTMEG: The seed of the nutmeg fruit. Nutmeg is sold whole or ground. As the flavour evaporates quickly, it is best bought whole and a little grated when required. Use it in chicken and cream soups, sprinkled on buttered corn, spinach, carrots, beans, and Brussels sprouts, in cheese dishes, with chicken and veal, in custards, milk puddings, Christmas pudding and cakes.

PAPRIKA: A sweet mild spice which is always sold ground to a red powder. It is good for adding colour to pale egg and cheese dishes. Some varieties (particularly Hungarian) are hotter than others. It keeps poorly so buy little and often. Use it in salads, fish, meat and chicken dishes, with vegetables, on canapés and, classi-cally, in Goulash where it adds the characteristic rich red colour.

PEPPER: The berry of the pepper tree is sold in several forms; green, black or white. Green or unripe berries are picked and either dried, canned or bottled. They have a milder flavour than black or white pepper and are used whole as a separate spice in pâtés, with rich meat like duck and in sauces and casseroles. They are

sometimes lightly crushed.

Black pepper consists of berries which are picked while green and dried in the sun which shrivels and darkens them. It has a strong, pungent, hot flavour and is best used freshly ground to season virtually all savoury dishes.

White pepper is made from the fully-ripened berries and is more aromatic and less hot in flavour than black pepper. It can be interchanged with it, but its main use is in light-coloured dishes and sauces whose appearance could be marred by dark flecks.

POPPY SEEDS: Small black seeds from the opium poppy, which have no narcotic effect, but are nutty flavoured, very hard and usually sold whole. They are used to add flavour and give an attractive appearance to baked goods, also in curry powder, dips, spreads, onion soup, salads and dressings and pasta dishes. They are widely used in Jewish and central European cookery. Cream coloured poppy seeds are also available.

SAFFRON: The most expensive of the spices, saffron is the dried stigmas of the saffron crocus flower. It has an aromatic, slightly bitter taste and only a pinch is needed to flavour and colour dishes such as bouillabaisse, chicken soup, rice and paella, fish sauces, buns and cakes – traditionally Cornish saffron cake. Where just a touch of colour is needed, a pinch of turmeric can be used, but the flavour will not be the same.

SESAME SEEDS: Small seeds with a rich, sweet, slightly burnt flavour which is enhanced by toasting or frying in butter. Use in salads and dressings, with mashed potato, sprinkled on to fish and chicken dishes, in fruit salads, pastry for meat pies and baked goods.

STAR ANISE: The star-shaped fruit of an evergreen tree native to China. When dried it is a red-brown colour and the flavour is one of pungent aniseed. It can be used to flavour stewed and simmered duck, beef, chicken and lamb. It can

KEY:
1. White Peppercorns 2. Fennel seeds
3. Ground white pepper 4. Black peppercorns 5. Ground black pepper
6. Vanilla Pods 7. Juniper berries
8. Cinnamon sticks 9. Coriander seeds
10. Ground coriander 11. Whole nutmeg 12. Blade mace 13. Cardamom pods 14. Whole dried chillies 15. Ch Powder 16. Cumin seeds 17. Ground Cumin 18. Ground Mace 19. Dill seed
20. Black and white mustard seeds
21. Dried root ginger 22. Ground ging 23. Ground Turmeric 24. Fenugreek seeds 25. Poppy seeds 26. Caraway see 27. Saffron 28. Cloves

also be placed under whole fish for steaming. It is used whole and one star is quite sufficient to flavour a large dish. Star anise is one of the ingredients of Five-spice Powder (see page 195).

Tamarind: This is the large pod of the Indian tamarind tree. It is seeded, peeled and pressed into a dark-brown pulp which is sold dried. Tamarind juice (see page 196) is used to add a sour flavour to chutneys, sauces and curries.

Turmeric: The dried root of a plant of the ginger family. Whole pieces of turmeric are available – they look like fresh ginger but are bright orange inside the peel – but it is most commonly sold ground. It has an aromatic, slightly bitter flavour and should be used sparingly in curry powder, pickles and relishes and to colour cakes and rice dishes.

Vanilla: The dried pods of a climbing orchid which are sold whole or as a synthetic bottled flavouring. Infuse a pod in the milk or cream when making custard or sweet sauces. A pod left in a jar of caster sugar will impart its flavour to it, creating 'vanilla sugar'. Use in ice cream, chocolate and coffee dishes and custards.

Flavourings and Essences

There are some concentrated flavourings that do not fall into the category of herbs or spices. These include flavouring agents such as salt and monosodium glutamate as well as the most common bottled flavourings and essences. True essences are made by naturally extracting the flavour from the food itself, flavourings are synthetic and tend to be cheaper. Both flavourings and essences have very strong flavours and usually only a few drops are needed in a recipe.

Almond: The essence is made from bitter almonds. It is not widely available but is sold at herbalists. Almond flavouring is sold in most supermarkets. Either can be used in baking.

Anchovy essence: A strong salty essence made from cured anchovies. Should be used sparingly.

Angostura bitters: A liquid made from a secret formula which includes cloves, cinnamon, citrus peel, nutmeg, prunes, quinine and rum. Originally medicinal; now used in drinks mixtures and sometimes as a flavouring in casseroles.

Coffee essence: Bottled coffee concentrate used to impart flavour to both sweet and savoury dishes, and also for making quick iced coffee.

Monosodium glutamate (msg): A powder with little taste of its own but it enhances the flavour of meat and vegetables. It is widely used in processed foods for home use. It is also called taste powder and gourmet powder, particularly when used in Chinese cooking.

Orange flower water: Orange-flavoured water used in small quantities in baking and desserts.

Rose water: Highly fragrant rose-flavoured water, used in Turkish Delight, baking and sweet dishes and in other Middle Eastern dishes.

Salt: A mineral used for seasoning. Sea salt and bay salt are fairly coarse and are evaporated naturally or over heat. Rock salt is mined or pumped up with water, then evaporated. Table salt is mixed with magnesium carbonate and ground finely so that it flows freely.

Salt substitutes are available for people who want to reduce their salt intake. These may be low sodium or sodium reduced and are bulked out with potassium chloride.

Soy sauce: Light or dark brown sauce with a salty sweetish taste made from soya beans which have been boiled and then fermented. Light soy sauce has a more delicate flavour and is not as salty as the dark soy sauce. It is widely used in oriental cookery and a variety of savoury dishes.

Tabasco: This is a hot strong sauce made from chillies, spirit vinegar and salt, to a secret recipe. It is used in spicy dishes and drink mixes.

Tahini: A creamy-textured paste made from finely ground sesame seeds, widely used in Middle Eastern dishes.

Vanilla: True vanilla essence is extracted from vanilla pods. It is not widely available but is sold at some high-class food shops and herbalists. It may be sold as an essence or natural vanilla. Vanilla flavouring is made from an ingredient in clove oil; it is widely available. Both can be used to flavour sweet dishes, particularly to bring out the flavour of coffee and chocolate.

Worcestershire sauce: Pungent sauce made from a secret recipe. Can be used to flavour sauces, meat casseroles and cheese dishes.

HERB AND SPICE MIXTURES

BOUQUET GARNI

This is a small bunch of herbs, tied together with string so it can be suspended in soups, casseroles and sauté dishes and removed before serving. The classic ingredients are bay leaves, parsley stems and thyme, but other herbs can be added to suit a particular dish.

When dried herbs are used for a bouquet garni they are tied in a small muslin bag. Tie together 5 ml (1 level tsp) dried parsley, 2.5 ml (½ level tsp) dried thyme and a bay leaf, broken in half.

- If liked, 1 sprig of fresh marjoram can be added with the thyme; or 2.5 ml (½ level tsp) dried.
- To go with lamb, add 1 rosemary sprig to the basic bunch of fresh herbs; 1.25 ml (¼ level tsp) dried crumbled rosemary leaves to the muslin bag.
- To go with pork, add 1 sprig each of sage and savory; or 1.25 ml (¼ level tsp) each of dried.
- To go with beef, add 1 thinly pared strip of orange rind and 1 sprig of celery leaves.
- To go with chicken, use lemon thyme instead of thyme and tie in 1 strip lemon rind; or add 2.5 ml (½ level tsp) dried lemon thyme.
- To go with fish, replace the thyme with lemon thyme and add a sprig of fresh fennel; or add 2.5 ml (½ level tsp) dried lemon thyme and 1.25 ml (¼ level tsp) dried fennel.

You can buy bouquet garni made from dried herbs; these should be stored in dark airtight jars and used up quickly.

FINES HERBES

90 ml (6 level tbsp) finely chopped fresh parsley
45 ml (3 level tbsp) finely chopped fresh chervil
45 ml (3 level tbsp) finely chopped fresh chives
30 ml (2 level tbsp) finely chopped fresh tarragon

1. Mix the chopped herbs together and use to flavour omelettes and other egg dishes, fish, poultry and salads.

NOTE: The fines herbes mixture can be frozen in ice cube trays.

CURRY POWDER

The flavourings for authentic Indian curries are made up of different mixtures of ground spices which include cumin, coriander, chilli powder and other aromatics.

Besides using it in ethnic dishes, curry powder can add spice to many other types of dishes. Add it to salad dressings, sprinkle it into sauces and casseroles, and rub it into chicken skin before cooking.

Bought curry powders are available but for the best flavour make your own.

30 ml (2 level tbsp) cumin seeds
30 ml (2 level tbsp) whole fenugreek
7.5 ml (1½ level tsp) mustard seeds
15 ml (1 level tbsp) black peppercorns
120 ml (8 level tbsp) coriander seeds
15 ml (1 level tbsp) poppy seeds
15 ml (1 level tbsp) ground ginger
5 ml (1 level tsp) hot chilli powder
60 ml (4 level tbsp) ground turmeric

1. Combine all the ingredients in a blender or coffee grinder and blend to a fine powder. Store in an airtight container for up to 3 months.

FIVE-SPICE POWDER

A ground mixture of star anise, anise pepper, fennel seeds, cloves and cinnamon or cassia. Five-spice powder is used in authentic Chinese cookery. It is cocoa coloured and very pungent and should be used sparingly. Five-spice powder is used to season Chinese red-cooked meats (meats simmered in soy sauce) and roast meats and poultry. It can also be added to marinades and sprinkled over whole steamed fish and vegetable dishes.

25 ml (5 tsp) anise pepper
25 ml (5 tsp) star anise
12 cm (5 inch) cassia bark or cinnamon stick
30 ml (6 tsp) whole cloves
35 ml (7 tsp) fennel seeds

1. Grind together all the spices. Store in an airtight jar for up to 1 month.

Garam Masala

This is a mixture of spices used in Indian cookery. Grind together 4 black cardamoms or 10 green cardamoms, 15 ml (1 level tbsp) black peppercorns and 10 ml (2 level tsp) cumin seeds. The amounts can be increased or decreased according to taste and spices such as dried red chillies or whole coriander seeds may be added.

Harissa

Harissa is a hot mixture of chilli and other spices that is used in Middle Eastern cooking. It can be bought in powder and paste form and may contain up to twenty spices. It is often served with Couscous and other North African dishes. The harissa is put into a separate bowl, stock from the main dish is poured on to dilute it, then it is spooned back over the dish to taste.

25 g (1 oz) dried red chillies
1 garlic clove, skinned and chopped
5 ml (1 level tsp) caraway seeds
5 ml (1 level tsp) cumin seeds
5 ml (1 level tsp) coriander seeds
pinch of salt
olive oil

1. Soak chillies in hot water for 1 hour. Drain well, then grind into a paste using a pestle and mortar or coffee bean grinder together with the garlic clove and spices. Add a pinch of salt.
2. Put into a jar, cover with olive oil and seal. It will keep in the refrigerator for up to 2 months. The oil can be used in salad dressings.

Tamarind Juice

15 ml (1 level tbsp) dried tamarind pulp
60 ml (4 tbsp) warm water

1. Soak the dried pulp in warm water for 15 minutes. Strain the liquid through a sieve, pressing down hard with a wooden spoon to extract as much of the pulp as possible.
2. Discard the pulp left in the sieve and use the juice according to the recipe.

NOTE: Substitute lime or lemon juice in recipes calling for tamarind juice if tamarind pulp is unavailable.

Mixed Spice

This is a mixture of sweet-flavoured ground spices. Mixed Spice is most often used in sweet dishes, cakes, biscuits and confectionery, but it can be added sparingly to curries and spiced Middle Eastern dishes.

30 ml (6 level tsp) whole cloves
25 ml (5 level tsp) whole allspice berries
12 cm (5 inch) cinnamon stick
60 ml (4 level tbsp) freshly grated nutmeg
30 ml (6 level tsp) ground ginger

1. Grind the whole spices together and mix with the nutmeg and ginger. Store in an airtight, screw-topped jar. Keeps well for up to 1 month. Use for baking and in puddings.

Pickling Spice

Pickling spice is a pungent mixture of varying spices added to the vinegar when making pickles. Varying proportions of black peppercorns, mace, red chillies, allspice, cloves, ginger, mustard seeds or coriander may be included.

30 ml (2 level tbsp) mace blades
15 ml (1 level tbsp) allspice berries
15 ml (1 level tbsp) whole cloves
18 cm (7 inch) cinnamon stick
6 black peppercorns
1 bay leaf, crumbled

1. Mix all the ingredients together well. Store in an airtight, screw-topped jar. Keeps well for up to 1 month. Tie in a muslin bag to use.

Dry-Frying Spices

Heating in a frying pan will mellow the flavour of spices. Use a small heavy-based pan to prevent them from burning. They can be dry-fried individually or in mixtures before using. Put the hardest ones, such as fenugreek, in first and add softer ones, like coriander and cumin, after a few minutes. Stir constantly until evenly browned. Cool and grind, or crush in a pestle and mortar. Use as required.

Sauces

Sauces provide the finishing touch to many recipes and it is important that their flavour complements the dish they are served with. For this reason it is well worth making your own; commercial packet sauces are often highly seasoned and coloured, lending an inferior flavour.
Once you have mastered the basic techniques of sauce making, the variations are endless and you can easily create original and distinctive sauces.

A great deal of mystique is attached to successful sauce making, but in fact all that is required is a little time and your undivided attention. Roux-based sauces are probably the most common type, but there are also egg-based types and the classic British favourites like bread, mint and apple sauce. Savoury butters and sweet sauces are also included.

ROUX-BASED SAUCES

These are made by melting butter (or another fat), adding flour and cooking, then adding liquid. For a white sauce the butter and flour, ie the *roux,* are cooked but not coloured; for a blond sauce they are allowed to cook to a light biscuit colour; for a brown sauce the roux is cooked until brown.

LIQUID FOR SAUCES

For white and blond sauces, such as Velouté, the liquid used is usually milk or milk and white stock. Brown sauces need meat stock and/or vegetable water. Fish should be served with a sauce made from a liquid produced by boiling up the fish bones in water and adding milk if necessary.

There is no doubt that real stock (see page 19) does add an excellent flavour to sauces. If you are short of time, or do not have any homemade stock, you can use a flavoured stock cube but bear in mind that many contain monosodium glutamate and other sodium compounds and give a salty flavour.

CORNFLOUR SAUCES

Cornflour is used in a different way to wheat flour. Blend the required amount with a little cold liquid, bring the rest of the liquid to the boil and gradually stir in the cornflour mixture and cook for a few minutes.

Cornflour tends to give a more glutinous texture to a sauce than the roux-based sauce.

ARROWROOT SAUCES

Arrowroot can be used in the same way as cornflour to thicken a clear liquid. It gives the sauce a gloss, unlike cornflour which produces a slightly cloudy sauce. Once added to the sauce, bring to the boil, then remove from the heat.

VEGETABLE PURÉE SAUCES

Leaf vegetables can be briefly cooked and puréed to make sauces. Root vegetables and pulses need to be cooked until they are really soft. Purées such as onion, need to be thickened with equal quantities of white sauce to give the desired consistency, while others, like pulses, need thinning with stock or their cooking liquid.

COULIS

A coulis is strictly a purée of fresh or cooked fruit or vegetables, which is thin enough to pour easily. It may be a smooth or rough-textured sauce. Fruit coulis, such as strawberry, mango redcurrant and gooseberry, are popular dessert sauces. Sorbets and ice creams are sometimes served on a pool of fruit coulis.

TIPS FOR SAUCE-MAKING

- You can make a sauce before it is needed and leave it to stand with a piece of dampened greaseproof paper pressed down on the surface to prevent a skin forming. Reheat when required.
- A lumpy sauce can sometimes be rescued by vigorous beating with a wire whisk, although you should not do this in a non-stick pan as it will damage the lining. Otherwise, strain it through a sieve or put it in a blender or food processor and process to remove the lumps.

- Make a sauce slowly, stirring all the time, and avoid turning your back on it until you have finished cooking.
- Give a sauce a glossy finish by adding a spoonful or two of cream, a knob of butter or margarine or an egg yolk at the last minute. Do not allow the sauce to boil after this stage or it may curdle.
- If a cream-based sauce starts to separate, add a splash of boiling water, whisk vigorously and the sauce should return to its original consistency.

WHITE SAUCE (Roux method)

15 g (½ oz) butter or margarine
15 g (½ oz) flour
300 ml (½ pint) milk
salt and pepper

1. POURING SAUCE
1. Melt the butter in a saucepan, stir in the flour and cook gently for 1 minute, stirring.
2. Remove the pan from the heat and gradually stir in the milk. Bring to the boil slowly and continue cooking, stirring all the time, until the sauce comes to the boil and thickens.
3. Simmer very gently for a further 2-3 minutes. Season with salt and pepper.
MAKES 300 ML (½ PINT)

2. COATING SAUCE
Follow recipe for Pouring Sauce (see above), increasing butter and flour to 25 g (1 oz) each.

3. BINDING SAUCE
Follow recipe for Pouring Sauce (see left), increasing butter and flour to 50 g (2 oz) each.

4. ONE-STAGE METHOD
1. Use ingredients in the same quantities as for Pouring or Coating Sauce (see left).
2. Place the butter, flour, milk and seasonings in a saucepan. Heat, whisking continuously, until the sauce thickens and is cooked.

5. BLENDER OR FOOD PROCESSOR METHOD
1. Use ingredients in the same quantities as for Pouring or Coating Sauce (see left).
2. Place the butter, flour, milk and seasonings in the machine and blend until smooth.
3. Pour into a saucepan and bring to the boil, stirring continuously, until the sauce thickens and is cooked.

WHITE SAUCE (Blending method)

25 ml (5 level tsp) cornflour
300 ml (½ pint) milk
knob of butter or margarine
salt and pepper

POURING SAUCE
1. Put the cornflour in a bowl and blend with 75 ml (5 tbsp) milk to a smooth paste. Heat the remaining milk with the butter until boiling, then pour on to the blended mixture, stirring all the time to prevent lumps forming.
2. Return the mixture to the saucepan. Bring to the boil slowly and continue to cook, stirring all

the time, until the sauce comes to the boil and thickens.
3. Simmer gently for a further 2-3 minutes, to make a white, glossy sauce. Add salt and pepper to taste.
MAKES 300 ML (½ PINT)

NOTE: For a savoury sauce, half stock and half milk can be used.

COATING SAUCE
Increase the quantity of cornflour to 30 ml (2 level tbsp) and blend with 90 ml (6 tbsp) milk.

WHITE SAUCE VARIATIONS

PARSLEY SAUCE
A traditional sauce for bacon, ham and fish.
1. Follow the recipe for the Pouring Sauce or Coating Sauce (see opposite).
2. After seasoning with salt and pepper, stir in 15-30 ml (1-2 tbsp) finely chopped fresh parsley.

ONION SAUCE
For grilled and roast lamb, tripe and freshly hard-boiled eggs.
1. Follow the recipe for the Pouring Sauce or Coating Sauce (see opposite).
2. Soften 1 large onion, skinned and finely chopped, in the butter before adding the flour.

ANCHOVY SAUCE
Serve with fish.
1. Follow the recipe for the Pouring Sauce or Coating Sauce (see opposite), using half milk and half fish stock.
2. Before seasoning with salt and pepper, stir in 5-10 ml (1-2 tsp) anchovy essence to taste, a squeeze of lemon juice and a few drops of red colouring to tint a pale pink, if liked.

MUSHROOM SAUCE
Serve with fish, meat or eggs.
1. Follow the recipe for the Pouring Sauce or Coating Sauce (see opposite).
2. Fry 50-75 g (2-3 oz) sliced button mushrooms in the butter before adding the flour.

CAPER SAUCE
Serve with lamb dishes.
1. Follow the recipe for the Pouring Sauce or Coating Sauce (see opposite), using all milk, or to give a better flavour, use half milk and half stock.
2. Before seasoning with salt and pepper, stir in 15 ml (1 level tbsp) capers and 5-10 ml (1-2 tsp) vinegar from the capers, or lemon juice. Reheat gently before serving.

EGG SAUCE
Serve with poached or steamed fish or kedgeree.
1. Follow the recipe for the Pouring Sauce or Coating Sauce (see opposite), using all milk or preferably half milk and half fish stock.
2. Before seasoning with salt and pepper, add 1 hard-boiled egg, shelled and chopped, and 5-10 ml (1-2 tsp) snipped chives. Reheat gently before serving.

CHEESE SAUCE
Delicious with fish, poultry, ham, bacon, egg and vegetable dishes.
1. Follow the recipe for the Pouring Sauce or Coating Sauce (see opposite).
2. Before seasoning with salt and pepper, stir in 50 g (2 oz) finely grated Cheddar cheese or 50 g (2 oz) crumbled Lancashire cheese, 2.5-5 ml (½-1 level tsp) prepared mustard and a pinch of cayenne pepper.

MILD CURRY SAUCE

Use for vegetables such as marrow and cabbage wedges, hard-boiled eggs or combine with pieces of cooked fish, chicken or meat.

50 g (2 oz) butter or margarine
1 medium onion, skinned and finely chopped
15-20 ml (3-4 level tsp) mild curry powder
45 ml (3 level tbsp) flour
450 ml (¾ pint) milk or half stock and half milk
*30 ml (2 level tbsp) mango or apple chutney, roughly
    chopped*
salt and pepper

1. Melt the butter in a saucepan, add the onion and fry until golden.
2. Stir in the curry powder and cook for 3-4 minutes. Add the flour and cook gently for 2-3 minutes.
3. Remove the pan from the heat and gradually stir in the milk. Bring to the boil slowly and continue to cook, stirring, until the sauce thickens.
4. Add the chutney and seasoning. Reheat gently before serving.
MAKES 450 ML (¾ PINT)

NOTE: Curry sauce is useful when you want to make a curry in a hurry, and makes good use of leftovers of meat, poultry and fish. Because some people like a hottish curry flavour and others prefer a very mild taste, it is best to start with the smaller amount of curry powder.

MUSTARD CREAM SAUCE

Use for carrots, celery hearts, herring, mackerel, cheese, ham and bacon dishes.

40 g (1½ oz) butter or margarine
45 ml (3 level tbsp) flour
450 ml (¾ pint) milk
30 ml (2 level tbsp) mustard powder
20 ml (4 tsp) malt vinegar
salt and pepper
30 ml (2 tbsp) single cream

1. Melt the butter in a saucepan, stir in the flour and cook for 1 minute, stirring.
2. Remove the pan from the heat and gradually stir in the milk. Bring to the boil slowly and continue to cook, stirring, until the sauce thickens. Simmer for about 5 minutes.
3. Blend the mustard powder with the vinegar and whisk into the sauce, then season. Stir in the cream. Reheat but do not boil.
MAKES 450 ML (¾ PINT)

NOTE: To vary the flavour, use different mustards, such as wholegrain, Dijon or herb-flavoured mustards, such as tarragon or chive.

BÉCHAMEL SAUCE

This classic sauce is the basis of many other sauces (see below). Use for fish, poultry, egg and vegetable dishes.

300 ml (½ pint) milk
1 shallot, skinned and sliced, or a small piece of onion, skinned
1 small carrot, peeled and sliced
½ celery stick, washed and chopped
1 bay leaf
3 black peppercorns
25 g (1 oz) butter or margarine
25 g (1 oz) flour
salt and white pepper
30 ml (2 tbsp) single cream (optional)

1. Put the milk, vegetables and flavourings in a saucepan and slowly bring to the boil. Remove from the heat, cover and set aside to infuse for 30 minutes, then strain, reserving the milk.

2. Melt the butter in a saucepan. Stir in the flour and cook gently for 1 minute, stirring. Remove the pan from the heat and gradually stir in the flavoured milk.
3. Bring to the boil and continue to cook, stirring, until the sauce thickens. Simmer very gently for 3 minutes. Remove from the heat and season with salt and pepper to taste. Stir in the cream, if using.
MAKES 300 ML (½ PINT)

VARIATIONS
MORNAY SAUCE
Serve with eggs, chicken or fish.
1. Before seasoning, stir in 50 g (2 oz) finely grated, mature Cheddar cheese or 25 g (1 oz) grated Parmesan or 50 g (2 oz) grated Gruyère. Do not reheat this sauce or the cheese will become overcooked and stringy.

CHAUDFROID SAUCE

25 g (1 oz) aspic jelly powder
300 ml (½ pint) warm Béchamel Sauce (see above)
150 ml (¼ pint) single cream
salt and pepper

1. Sprinkle the aspic powder in 150 ml (¼ pint) water. Place the bowl over a pan of simmering water and stir until dissolved, taking care not to overheat the mixture.
2. Add the dissolved aspic to the Béchamel Sauce, beating well, then stir in the cream and

extra seasoning, if necessary.
3. Strain the sauce and leave to cool, stirring frequently, so it remains smooth and glossy. When it reaches the consistency of thick cream, use as a coating sauce.
MAKES ABOUT 450 ML (¾ PINT)

NOTE: This is a classic sauce which is used for coating chicken, fish or eggs. A final decoration of anchovy, pimiento, hard-boiled egg slices or cucumber slices is often added.

SOUBISE SAUCE

Use for fish, egg and meat dishes.

25 g (1 oz) butter or margarine
2 medium onions, skinned and chopped
300 ml (½ pint) Béchamel Sauce (see opposite)
15-30 ml (1-2 tbsp) chicken stock or water
salt and pepper

1. Melt the butter in a saucepan, add the onions and cook gently for 10-15 minutes, until soft.
2. Sieve or purée with the Béchamel Sauce and the stock in a blender or food processor until smooth.
3. Season and reheat gently for 1-2 minutes before serving.
MAKES ABOUT 300 ML (½ PINT)

VELOUTÉ SAUCE

Serve with poultry, fish or veal.

knob of butter
30 ml (2 level tbsp) flour
450 ml (¾ pint) Chicken or other white stock
  (see page 19)
30-45 ml (2-3 tbsp) single cream
few drops of lemon juice
salt and pepper

1. Melt the butter in a saucepan, stir in the flour and cook gently for 1 minute, stirring well, until the mixture is a light golden colour.
2. Remove the pan from the heat and gradually stir in the stock. Bring to the boil and continue to cook, stirring, until the sauce thickens. Simmer until slightly reduced and velvety.
3. Remove from the heat and add the cream, a few drops of lemon juice and seasoning.
MAKES 450 ML (¾ PINT)

VARIATIONS
SUPRÊME SAUCE
Serve with poultry or fish. This sauce is also sometimes used in meat and vegetable dishes.

300 ml (½ pint) warm Velouté Sauce (see above)
1 egg yolk
30-45 ml (2-3 tbsp) single or double cream
knob of butter

1. Remove the Velouté Sauce from the heat and stir in the egg yolk and the cream, then add the butter a little at a time. Reheat if necessary, but do not allow to boil, or the sauce will curdle.
MAKES 300 ML (½ PINT)

AURORE SAUCE
Serve with eggs, chicken or fish.

15-30 ml (1-2 level tbsp) tomato purée
25 g (1 oz) butter or margarine
300 ml (½ pint) warm Velouté Sauce (see left)
salt and pepper

1. Blend the tomato purée with the butter and stir into the Velouté Sauce, a little at a time. Season with salt and pepper.
MAKES 300 ML (½ PINT)

NORMANDY SAUCE
Serve with poached, grilled or steamed white fish dishes, or hot crab and lobster dishes.

300 ml (½ pint) warm Velouté Sauce (see left), made
  with Fish Stock (see page 19)
1 egg yolk
25 g (1 oz) unsalted butter

1. Remove the Velouté Sauce from the heat and beat in the egg yolk.
2. Gradually add the butter, a small piece at a time, rotating the pan in a circular fashion gently until the butter melts. Do not stir or reheat after adding the butter.
MAKES 300 ML (½ PINT)

BROWN SAUCES

Brown sauces are made by cooking a roux until it is brown, thus giving the sauce its colour. Brown sauces range from simple gravies made with meat juices to the classic Espanole Sauce and sauces based on it. For the best flavour, use homemade Beef Stock (see page 19) when making brown sauces.

GRAVY

A rich gravy is traditionally served with all roast joints; it may be thick or thin. If the gravy is made in the baking tin, there should be no need to use colouring. Remove the joint from the tin and keep it hot while making the gravy.

THIN GRAVY

1. Pour the fat very slowly from the tin, draining it off carefully from one corner and leaving the sediment behind. Season well with salt and pepper and add 300 ml (½ pint) hot vegetable stock, water or wine (or a mixture).
2. Stir thoroughly, until all the sediment is scraped from the tin and the gravy is a rich brown; return the tin to the heat and boil for 2-3 minutes to reduce. Serve very hot.
MAKES ABOUT 300 ML (½ PINT)

THICK GRAVY

1. Pour off most of the fat from the roasting tin, leaving about 30 ml (2 tbsp) of the sediment behind.
2. Stir in about 15 ml (1 level tbsp) flour, blend well and cook, stirring, over the heat until it turns brown. Slowly stir in 300 ml (½ pint) beef stock, vegetable water or a mixture of stock and wine, then boil for 2-3 minutes.
3. Season well, strain and serve very hot.
MAKES ABOUT 300 ML (½ PINT)

NOTE: If required a little gravy browning may be added to enrich the colour.

As an alternative to the traditional method, gravy can be thickened by adding gravy granules, which are available unflavoured and flavoured, ie beef, chicken, onion etc.

ESPAGNOLE SAUCE

Serve with red meats and game.

25 g (1 oz) butter or margarine
1 rasher streaky bacon, rinded and chopped
1 shallot, skinned and chopped, or a small piece of
    onion, skinned and chopped
60 ml (4 tbsp) mushroom stalks, wiped and chopped
1 small carrot, peeled and chopped
30-45 ml (2-3 level tbsp) flour
450 ml (¾ pint) Beef Stock (see page 19)
bouquet garni
30 ml (2 level tbsp) tomato purée
salt and pepper
15 ml (1 tbsp) sherry (optional)

1. Melt the butter in a saucepan, add the bacon and fry for 2-3 minutes. Add the vegetables and fry for a further 3-5 minutes, until lightly browned. Stir in the flour, mix well and continue cooking until it turns brown.
2. Remove from the heat and gradually add the stock, stirring after each addition.
3. Bring to the boil slowly and continue to cook, stirring, until the sauce thickens. Add the

bouquet garni, tomato purée, salt and pepper.
4. Reduce the heat and allow to simmer very gently for 1 hour, stirring from time to time to prevent it sticking; alternatively, cook in the oven at 170°C (325°F) mark 3 for 1½-2 hours.
5. Strain the sauce, reheat and skim off any fat, using a metal spoon. Adjust seasoning and add the sherry, if using, just before serving.
MAKES ABOUT 300 ML (½ PINT)

VARIATIONS
DEMI-GLACE SAUCE
This is a simplified version of the classic demi-glace, but gives quite a satisfactory result. Serve with red meats and game.

150 ml (¼ pint) jellied stock from under beef dripping
300 ml (½ pint) Espagnole Sauce (see above)

1. Add the stock to the sauce and boil, uncovered, until the sauce has a glossy appearance and will coat the back of a spoon with a shiny glaze.
MAKES 450 ML (¾ PINT)

ROBERT SAUCE

A traditional accompaniment to pork.

25g (1 oz) butter or margarine
1 small onion, skinned and finely chopped
150 ml (¼ pint) dry white wine
15 ml (1 tbsp) wine vinegar
300 ml (½ pint) Espagnole Sauce (see opposite)
5-10 ml (1-2 level tsp) mild prepared mustard
pinch of sugar
salt and pepper

1. Melt the butter in a saucepan, add the onion and fry gently for about 10 minutes, without browning.
2. Add the wine and vinegar and boil rapidly until reduced by half. Stir in the sauce and simmer for 10 minutes.
3. Add the mustard, sugar and extra seasoning, if necessary.
MAKES ABOUT 450 ML (¾ PINT)

REFORM SAUCE

45-60 ml (3-4 tbsp) vinegar
few parsley stalks
1 bay leaf
sprig of fresh thyme
6 black peppercorns
300 ml (½ pint) Espagnole Sauce (see opposite)
1 gherkin, finely sliced
15 g (½ oz) tongue, finely sliced
1 hard-boiled egg white, finely chopped

1. Put the vinegar, parsley stalks, bay leaf, thyme and peppercorns into a saucepan and boil, uncovered, until reduced by half.
2. Stir in the Espagnole Sauce and simmer for 10-15 minutes, then strain.
3. Add the gherkin, tongue and egg white and serve, without further cooking, with lamb or beef.
MAKES ABOUT 300 ML (½ PINT)

EGG-BASED SAUCES

Egg yolks rather than flour are the thickening agent with these sauces. They must be cooked very slowly and gently. The water in the double saucepan should be barely simmering, a fierce heat will produce a granular texture and, if overcooked, the eggs will scramble. If not serving immediately, remove the sauce from the heat and keep warm over warm (not hot) water.

HOLLANDAISE SAUCE

A classic sauce for fish, egg, chicken and vegetable dishes.

30 ml (2 tbsp) wine or tarragon vinegar
15 ml (1 tbsp) water
2 egg yolks
225 g (8 oz) unsalted butter, softened
salt and white pepper

1. Put the vinegar and water into a saucepan. Boil gently until the liquid has reduced by half. Set aside until cool.
2. Put the egg yolks and reduced vinegar liquid into a double saucepan or bowl standing over a pan of very gently simmering water and whisk until the mixture is thick and fluffy.

3. Gradually add the butter, a tiny piece at a time. Whisk briskly until each piece has been absorbed by the sauce and the sauce itself is the consistency of mayonnaise. Season with salt and pepper. If the sauce is too sharp add a little more butter – it should be slightly piquant, and warm rather than hot when served.
MAKES ABOUT 300 ML (½ PINT)

VARIATION
MOUSSELINE SAUCE
This is a richer sauce suitable for asparagus and broccoli and poached fish, egg and chicken dishes.
Stir 45 ml (3 tbsp) whipped double cream into the sauce just before serving.

BÉARNAISE SAUCE

A classic sauce for meat grills and roasts.

60 ml (4 tbsp) wine or tarragon vinegar
1 shallot or ¼ onion, skinned and finely chopped
few fresh tarragon sprigs, chopped
2 egg yolks
75 g (3 oz) butter, softened
salt and white pepper

1. Put the vinegar, onion and tarragon into a saucepan and boil gently until the liquid has reduced by about one-third. Leave to cool.
2. Put the egg yolks and reduced vinegar liquid into a double saucepan or bowl standing over a pan of very gently simmering water and whisk until thick and fluffy.
3. Gradually add the butter, a tiny piece at a time. Whisk briskly until each piece has been absorbed by the sauce and the sauce itself has thickened. Season with salt and white pepper.
MAKES ABOUT 200 ML (⅓ PINT)

NOTE: 15 ml (1 tbsp) vinegar can be replaced by 15 ml (1 tbsp) water – this gives a slightly less piquant sauce, which some people prefer.

RESCUE REMEDIES
• Have ready a bowl containing a little iced water. If the sauce shows signs of curdling, put the pan or bowl of sauce in the cold water and stir briskly. Alternatively, add a small ice cube to the sauce itself, then stir quickly.
• If the sauce curdles, beat 5 ml (1 tsp) lemon juice and 15 ml (1 tbsp) curdled sauce in a warm mixing bowl until it thickens. Then beat in the remaining curdled sauce 15 ml (1 tbsp) at a time.
• If the above remedies do not work, beat two egg yolks with some seasoning in a bowl and beat in 30 ml (2 tbsp) of the curdled sauce. Cook as originally, stirring constantly, adding the rest of the mixture slowly. It will have a stronger egg flavour than usual.

TRADITIONAL SAUCES

Traditional sauces – like bread, apple, horseradish and mint, as well as various hot and cold savoury sauces for serving with fish, cutlets, beefburgers, pasta and croquettes and for barbecues – are included in this section.

GOOSEBERRY SAUCE

A lovely eighteenth century sauce for mackerel and other oily fish.

350 g (12 oz) gooseberries
25 g (1 oz) butter or margarine
25 g (1 oz) sugar
1.25 ml (¼ level tsp) freshly grated nutmeg
salt and pepper

1. Put the gooseberries in a saucepan with 150 ml (¼ pint) water and cook for 4-5 minutes, until tender and pulped. Drain and rub through a sieve or purée in a blender or food processor.
2. Add the butter, sugar, nutmeg and salt and pepper. Reheat and serve.
SERVES 4

Bacon Chops with Gooseberry Sauce

CUCUMBER SAUCE

Serve with trout, mackerel, salmon or sea trout.

½ small cucumber
300 ml (10 fl oz) soured cream
5 ml (1 tsp) tarragon vinegar
5 ml (1 tsp) chopped fresh tarragon
salt and pepper

1. Coarsely grate the cucumber into a bowl.
Add the cream, vinegar and tarragon. Stir until
evenly blended.
2. Season with salt and pepper to taste.
SERVES 4

VARIATION
Replace the tarragon vinegar with wine vinegar
and use chopped dill instead of tarragon.

Trout with Cucumber Sauce

HORSERADISH CREAM

Serve with beef, trout or mackerel.

30 ml (2 level tbsp) grated fresh horseradish
10 ml (2 tsp) lemon juice
10 ml (2 level tsp) sugar
pinch of mustard powder (optional)
150 ml (¼ pint) double cream

1. Mix together the horseradish, lemon juice,
sugar and mustard, if using.
2. Whip the cream to soft peaks, then fold in the
horseradish mixture.
SERVES 4

APPLE SAUCE

This slightly acidic sauce is served with roast pork
and goose to counteract their fattiness.

450 g (1 lb) cooking apples, peeled, cored and sliced
25 g (1 oz) butter or margarine
little sugar

1. Put the apples in a saucepan with 30-45 ml
(2-3 tbsp) water and cook gently, uncovered,
until soft and thick, about 10 minutes.
2. Beat to a pulp with a wooden spoon or potato
masher, then, if you wish, sieve or purée in an
electric blender or food processor.
3. Stir in the butter and add a little sugar if the
apples are very tart.
SERVES 4

MINT SAUCE

Serve with lamb.

small bunch of fresh mint, washed and stalks removed
10 ml (2 level tsp) caster sugar
15 ml (1 tbsp) boiling water
15-30 ml (1-2 tbsp) wine vinegar

1. Chop the mint leaves finely and place in a
sauceboat with the sugar.
2. Stir in the boiling water and leave for about
5 minutes to dissolve the sugar.
3. Add the vinegar and leave for about 1 hour
before serving.
SERVES 4

CUMBERLAND SAUCE

Usually served cold with ham, venison or lamb.

1 orange
1 lemon
60 ml (4 level tbsp) redcurrant jelly
5 ml (1 tsp) Dijon mustard
60 ml (4 tbsp) port
salt and pepper
pinch of ground ginger (optional)

1. Pare the rind thinly from the orange and lemon, free of all the white pith. Cut it into fine strips, cover with water and simmer for 5 minutes. Drain.
2. Squeeze the juice from both fruits. Put the redcurrant jelly, orange juice, lemon juice and mustard in a saucepan and heat gently, stirring, until the jelly dissolves. Simmer for 5 minutes, then add the port. Season with salt and pepper and ginger, if wished.
SERVES 4

CRANBERRY SAUCE

A tasty accompaniment to turkey.

225 g (8 oz) cranberries, washed
225 g (8 oz) sugar
15 ml (1 tbsp) port (optional)

1. Put the cranberries in a saucepan, cover with 300 ml (½ pint) cold water and bring slowly to the boil over a moderate heat.
2. Simmer, uncovered, for a further 10 minutes or until the berries have burst.
3. Add the sugar and port, if using, and cook very gently until the sugar has dissolved. Cool before serving.
SERVES 4-6

BREAD SAUCE

Serve with roast chicken, turkey or pheasant.

2 cloves
1 medium onion, skinned
1 small bay leaf
450 ml (¾ pint) milk
75 g (3 oz) fresh breadcrumbs
salt and white pepper
15 g (½ oz) butter or margarine
30 ml (2 tbsp) single cream

1. Stick the cloves into the onion and place in a heavy saucepan with the bay leaf and milk.

Stick the cloves into the onion.

2. Bring slowly to the boil, remove from the heat, cover and leave to infuse for 10 minutes, then remove the onion and bay leaf.
3. Add breadcrumbs and seasoning, cover and simmer gently for 10-15 minutes, stirring occasionally. Stir in butter and cream.
SERVES 4

BARBECUE SAUCE

Serve with chicken, sausages, burgers or chops.

50 g (2 oz) butter or margarine
1 large onion, skinned and chopped
5 ml (1 level tsp) tomato purée
30 ml (2 tbsp) vinegar
30 ml (2 level tbsp) demerara sugar
10 ml (2 level tsp) mustard powder
30 ml (2 tbsp) Worcestershire sauce

1. Melt the butter in a saucepan, add the onion and fry for 5 minutes, until soft. Stir in the tomato purée and continue cooking for a further 3 minutes.
2. Blend together the remaining ingredients with 150 ml (¼ pint) water until smooth, then stir into the onion mixture. Bring to the boil and boil, uncovered, for a further 10 minutes.
SERVES 4

BASIC TOMATO SAUCE

Serve with pasta, beefburgers, chops and other meats, or use as a pizza topping.

15 ml (1 tbsp) olive oil
1 medium onion, skinned and finely chopped
50 g (2 oz) carrot, peeled and finely chopped
125 g (4 oz) celery, trimmed and finely chopped
1 large garlic clove, skinned and crushed
15 ml (1 level tbsp) chopped fresh mixed herbs, eg
  parsley, thyme, basil and marjoram, or 5 ml
  (1 level tsp) dried mixed herbs
450 g (1 lb) ripe tomatoes, peeled, halved, seeded and
  finely chopped
1 bay leaf
15 ml (1 level tbsp) tomato purée
150 ml (¼ pint) dry white wine or vegetable stock
salt and pepper

1. Heat the oil in a medium saucepan and sauté the onion, carrot and celery with the garlic and mixed herbs for 4-5 minutes until softened and golden.
2. Stir in the tomatoes, bay leaf, tomato purée, wine or stock, and seasoning. Bring to the boil, cover and simmer for 15-20 minutes, or until the vegetables are tender.
3. Uncover the sauce and continue to simmer for a further 4-5 minutes, or until the mixture has the consistency of tomato ketchup. Adjust the seasoning and discard the bay leaf.
4. The sauce is now ready to use, or can be puréed in a blender or food processor for a smoother texture.
SERVES 4

QUICK TOMATO SAUCE

400 g (14 oz) can chopped tomatoes
15 ml (1 level tbsp) chopped fresh mixed herbs, eg
  parsley, thyme, basil and marjoram, or 5 ml
  (1 level tsp) dried mixed herbs
pinch of sugar
15 ml (1 level tbsp) tomato purée
150 ml (¼ pint) dry white wine or vegetable stock
salt and pepper
1 large garlic clove, skinned and crushed

1. Place all the ingredients in a medium saucepan. Bring to the boil, then simmer, uncovered, for 15-20 minutes or until the mixture has the consistency of tomato ketchup. Adjust seasoning. Serve as above.
SERVES 4

SAVOURY BUTTERS

Savoury Butters may be added to sauces, or used as a garnish for meat, fish and vegetable dishes and as toppings for canapés. On average allow 25 g (1 oz) of butter per person. Make them at least a few hours beforehand and leave in a cool place to become firm before you use them.

Add one of the following flavouring ingredients to 125 g (4 oz) softened butter:
ANCHOVY BUTTER: 6 anchovies, mashed with a fork.
BLUE CHEESE BUTTER: 50 g (2 oz) soft blue cheese.
CURRY BUTTER: 10 ml (2 level tsp) curry powder.
GARLIC BUTTER: 2 cloves garlic, skinned and crushed and 5-10 ml (1-2 tsp) chopped fresh parsley.
GOLDEN BUTTER: Sieved yolks of 2 hard-boiled eggs.
GREEN BUTTER: 50 g (2 oz) chopped watercress.

HAM BUTTER: 125 g (4 oz) minced cooked ham.
HORSERADISH BUTTER: 30 ml (2 level tbsp) creamed horseradish.
LOBSTER BUTTER: 50 g (2 oz) lobster coral.
MAÎTRE D'HÔTEL (PARSLEY) BUTTER: 30 ml (2 tbsp) finely chopped fresh parsley and a squeeze of lemon juice, with salt and cayenne pepper to taste.
ONION BUTTER: 30 ml (2 level tbsp) finely grated onion.
TARRAGON BUTTER: 30 ml (2 tbsp) chopped fresh tarragon.

SWEET SAUCES

Sweet sauces in this section can be served either hot or cold and you do not necessarily have to serve a hot sauce with a hot dessert; a piping hot pudding tastes delicious with a chilled spicy cream sauce.

SWEET WHITE SAUCE (Roux method)

20 g (¾ oz) butter or margarine
about 30 ml (2 level tbsp) flour
300 ml (½ pint) milk
about 25 ml (5 level tsp) sugar

1. Melt the butter in a saucepan, stir in the flour and cook gently for 1 minute, stirring.
2. Remove the pan from the heat and gradually stir in the milk.
3. Bring to the boil and cook, stirring, until the sauce thickens. Add the sugar to taste.
MAKES 300 ML (½ PINT)

SWEET WHITE SAUCE (Blended method)

25 ml (5 level tsp) cornflour
300 ml (½ pint) milk
about 25 ml (5 level tsp) sugar

1. Place the cornflour in a bowl and blend with 15-30 ml (1-2 tbsp) milk to a smooth paste.
2. Heat the remaining milk until boiling, then pour on to the blended mixture, stirring.
3. Return the mixture to the pan and bring to the boil, stirring continuously. Cook for 1-2 minutes after the mixture has thickened to make a white, glossy sauce. Add sugar to taste.
MAKES 300 ML (½ PINT)

NOTE: For a thicker sauce, increase the quantity of cornflour to 30 ml (2 level tbsp). This will be necessary if you add cream, rum or any other form of liquid when the sauce has been made.

VARIATIONS
Replace 15 ml (1 level tbsp) cornflour with cocoa powder. Or flavour the sauce with any of the following when it has thickened:
• 5 ml (1 level tsp) mixed spice or grated nutmeg
• 30 ml (2 level tbsp) jam
• grated rind of ½ an orange or lemon
• 15-30 ml (1-2 tbsp) rum

EGG CUSTARD SAUCE

2 eggs
15 ml (1 level tbsp) sugar
300 ml (½ pint) milk
few strips of thinly pared lemon rind or ½ a vanilla pod, split

1. In a bowl, beat the eggs, sugar and 45 ml (3 tbsp) milk. Put the rest of the milk in a pan

with the lemon rind and bring slowly to the boil. Remove from heat and infuse for 10 minutes.
2. Pour the milk on to the eggs and strain the mixture into the top of a double boiler or into a heavy-based saucepan.
3. Cook, stirring, until the custard will thinly coat the back of a spoon. Do not boil.
MAKES 300 ML (½ PINT)

BUTTERSCOTCH SAUCE

Serve poured over ice cream.

50 g (2 oz) butter or margarine
60 ml (4 level tbsp) soft brown sugar
30 ml (2 tbsp) golden syrup
90 ml (6 level tbsp) chopped nuts
squeeze of lemon juice (optional)

1. Put the butter, sugar and syrup in a saucepan and heat gently, stirring until well blended.
2. Bring to the boil and boil for 1 minute, then stir in the nuts and lemon juice, if using. Serve at once.
SERVES 4

RICH CHOCOLATE SAUCE

175 g (6 oz) plain chocolate
50 g (2 oz) light soft brown sugar

1. Break up the chocolate and place in a heavy-based saucepan with the sugar and 150 ml (¼ pint) water.
2. Heat gently until the chocolate and sugar have dissolved. Add a further 150 ml (¼ pint) water, bring to the boil and simmer uncovered for 20-30 minutes, or until of a thick pouring consistency, stirring occasionally.
SERVES 6

Rich Chocolate Sauce

LEMON OR ORANGE SAUCE

Serve hot with baked or steamed puddings or cold with ice cream.

grated rind and juice of 1 large lemon or orange
15 ml (1 level tbsp) cornflour
30 ml (2 level tbsp) sugar
knob of butter or margarine
1 egg yolk (optional)

1. Make up the fruit rind and juice with water to 300 ml (½ pint). Blend the cornflour and sugar with a little of the liquid to a smooth cream.
2. Heat the remaining liquid until boiling, then pour on to the blended mixture, stirring all the time. Return it to the pan and bring to the boil, stirring until the sauce thickens and clears. Add the butter.
3. Cool, beat in the egg yolk, if using, and reheat, stirring, without boiling.
SERVES 4

GINGER SAUCE

Serve over steamed or baked puddings or fruit desserts.

30 ml (2 level tbsp) sugar
squeeze of lemon juice
4-6 pieces of stem ginger, sliced
30 ml (2 tbsp) ginger syrup from the jar

1. Put the sugar in a saucepan with 60 ml (4 tbsp) water and heat gently until the sugar has dissolved. Bring to the boil and boil until thickened.
2. Add the lemon juice, ginger and syrup and serve at once.
SERVES 4

MELBA SAUCE

Serve poured over ice cream.

60 ml (4 level tbsp) redcurrant jelly
50 g (2 oz) sugar
150 ml (¼ pint) raspberry purée, from 225 g (8 oz)
*   raspberries, sieved*
10 ml (2 level tsp) arrowroot or cornflour
15 ml (1 tbsp) cold water

1. Put the jelly, sugar and raspberry purée in a saucepan and slowly bring it to the boil.
2. Blend the arrowroot with the cold water to a smooth cream, stir in a little of the raspberry mixture, then stir into the mixture in the pan off the heat. Bring to the boil, stirring with a wooden spoon, until the sauce thickens and clears. Cool before serving.
SERVES 4

SWEET MOUSSELINE SAUCE

Serve over light steamed or baked puddings, fruit desserts or Christmas pudding.

1 egg
1 egg yolk
45 ml (3 level tbsp) sugar
15 ml (1 tbsp) sherry
60 ml (4 tbsp) single cream

1. Place all the ingredients in a bowl over a pan of boiling water and whisk until pale and frothy and of a thick creamy consistency. Serve at once.
SERVES 4

SABAYON SAUCE (COLD)

Serve with cold fruit desserts.

50 g (2 oz) caster sugar
2 egg yolks, beaten
grated rind of ½ a lemon
juice of 1 lemon
30 ml (2 tbsp) rum or sherry
30 ml (2 tbsp) single cream

1. Put the sugar in a saucepan with 60 ml (4 tbsp) water and heat gently until the sugar has dissolved. Bring to the boil and boil for 2-3 minutes, until syrupy. Pour slowly on to the egg yolks, whisking constantly until pale and thick.
2. Add the lemon rind, lemon juice and rum and whisk for a further few minutes. Fold in the cream and chill well.
SERVES 4

BRANDY BUTTER (HARD SAUCE)

Traditionally served with Christmas pudding and mince pies.

75 g (3 oz) butter
75 g (3 oz) caster sugar
30-45 ml (2-3 tbsp) brandy

1. Cream the butter until pale and soft.
2. Beat in the sugar gradually, then add the brandy few drops at a time, taking care not to allow the mixture to curdle. The finished sauce should be pale and frothy.

3. Pile into a small dish and chill before serving.
SERVES 6-8

NOTE: If you prefer a smoother texture, use sifted icing sugar or half icing and half caster sugar.

VARIATION
RUM BUTTER
Make this as for Brandy Butter, but use soft brown sugar, replace the brandy with 60 ml (4 tbsp) rum and add the grated rind of ½ a lemon and a squeeze of lemon juice.

CRÈME PÂTISSIÈRE

The traditional pastry cream, used as a filling for flans and pastries.

2 eggs
50 g (2 oz) caster sugar
30 ml (2 level tbsp) plain white flour
30 ml (2 level tbsp) cornflour
300 ml (½ pint) milk
few drops of vanilla flavouring

1. Whisk the eggs and sugar together in a large bowl, using an electric whisk, until pale and thick enough to leave a trail when the whisk is lifted. Sift the flour and cornflour into the bowl and

beat in with a little cold milk until smooth.
2. Heat the rest of the milk in a pan until almost boiling. Pour on to the egg mixture, stirring well.
3. Return the custard to the saucepan and stir over a low heat until the mixture boils. Add vanilla flavouring to taste and cook for a further 2-3 minutes. Cover the surface with greaseproof paper and allow to cool before using.
MAKES 300 ML (½ PINT)

VARIATIONS
Flavour the cold custard with a little kirsch or brandy.

VEGETABLES

The variety of vegetables available has never been greater than it is today. New varieties and hybrids are constantly being introduced to provide a diverse range of colours, shapes and sizes, including baby vegetables. Organic vegetables – grown without chemical aids – are becoming more widely available.

Vegetables are highly nutritious; they are a particularly valuable source of vitamins and minerals. These are usually concentrated just under the skin, so peel thinly and cook in the minimum of liquid to minimise the loss of water-soluble nutrients. For information on storing and freezing vegetables refer to the chapters on Food Storage and Home Freezing.

ARTICHOKE (GLOBE)

A type of thistle native to North Africa but now grown in Europe and America as a vegetable.
TO BUY: Look for heads with a clear green colour and leaves which have no dry edges. Choose artichokes which are

tightly curled rather than wide open.
TO PREPARE: Cut off the stalks and remove a few of the rough outer leaves with scissors so that any brown or dried edges are removed.
TO COOK: Cook in boiling salted water or steam for 35 minutes or until you can pull out a leaf easily.
TO EAT: Serve hot with melted butter or Hollandaise Sauce (see page 203) or cold with Mayonnaise (see page 254) or French Dressing (see page 255). Pull off the leaves one by one, dip in the dressing, then suck off the fleshy part. Once all the leaves are off, slice off or spoon out the hairy choke (easily visible) and use a knife and fork to eat the base (fond).

Allow 1 artichoke per person as a starter or light lunch dish. If only the hearts are being served, allow 2-3 per person.

ARTICHOKE (JERUSALEM)

This is a tuber with a nut-like taste, which ranges in colour from beige to brownish-red.
TO BUY: Choose the smoothest ones

available as they are easier to peel.
TO PREPARE: Scrub well and peel thinly. If they are very knobbly and difficult to peel, cook them first and then peel. Like other tubers, Jerusalem artichokes can be cubed, diced, sliced or cut into julienne slices.
TO COOK: Cook in boiling salted water with 15 ml (1 tbsp) lemon juice or vinegar added to prevent discoloration for 15-20 minutes.
TO EAT: Serve as a vegetable accompaniment, purée or make into soup.
Allow 175-225 g (6-8 oz) per person.

ASPARAGUS

There are two basic types, blanched (white) asparagus which is cut below the soil when the tips are 5 cm (2 inches) above it, and green asparagus which is cut at soil level.
TO BUY: Choose stems which look fresh and tender. Avoid wilted stems, ones with brown patches or coarse looking woody ones.
TO PREPARE: Bend each stem until it snaps, which will be the point where it begins to toughen. Peel the ends of thicker stems.
TO COOK: Use a special asparagus pan or wedge the bundles upright in a deep saucepan. Cover the tips with a cap made of foil and simmer gently for about 8-12 minutes, until tender. This way the stalks are poached while the delicate tips are gently steamed. Untie the bundles.

TO EAT: Serve hot with melted butter or Hollandaise Sauce (see page 203), or cold with Mayonnaise (see page 254) or French Dressing (see page 255). Asparagus is eaten with the fingers. Dip one stem at a time into the sauce.

Allow 6-10 stems each depending on size.

AUBERGINE (EGG PLANT)

Aubergines range in colour from white and whitish green through dark green to yellowish purple to red purple or black.

TO BUY: Choose firm, shiny aubergines free from blemishes. They may be round or oval.

TO PREPARE: Cut off the stem, trim the ends and halve or slice. Sprinkle the flesh with salt and leave for half an hour to extract the bitter juices. Rinse and dry with absorbent kitchen paper.

TO COOK: Grill or fry the slices and serve as accompaniments, or stuff and bake and serve as a starter or main dish. Aubergine is included in many dishes, such as ratatouille and moussaka.

Allow 175-225 g (6-8 oz) per person.

BAMBOO SHOOTS

These are the conical-shaped shoots of a bamboo plant native to Asia. The shoots are cut when they are 15 cm (6 inches) long. Fresh bamboo shoots are available in Chinese stores.

TO PREPARE AND COOK: They should be peeled and cooked in boiling water for about 40 minutes or until tender. Canned bamboo shoots are more readily available and these are already cooked. Either sort are excellent in stir-fried dishes or salads.

Allow 50-75 g (2-3 oz) per person.

BEANS, BROAD

TO BUY: Choose young, small, tender pods.

TO PREPARE AND COOK: Where the pods are less than 5-7.5 cm (2-3 inches) long, both pods and beans can be cooked and eaten. Larger than that, the beans should be removed from the pods. Cook beans in boiling salted water or steam for 8-10 minutes, then serve with melted butter or in a Béchemel Sauce (see page 200). Old large beans should be cooked, then made into soup or puréed.

Allow about 225-275 g (8-10 oz) weight of whole beans per person.

BEANS, FRENCH (GREEN BEANS)

These are slim, tender beans. Other varieties include *bobby beans,* which are shorter and fatter, and *haricot verts* which are slim and delicate. Cook both as for French beans, for about 8 minutes.

TO BUY: Choose slim French beans which break with a crisp snap.

TO PREPARE AND COOK: Cut off the ends and steam or cook in boiling salted water for about 10 minutes.

TO EAT: Serve hot or cold in a French Dressing (see page 255).

Allow 100-175 g (4-6 oz) per person.

BEANS, RUNNER

TO BUY: Choose beans that break with a crisp snap.

TO PREPARE: Cut off the ends and remove the strings from the sides. Cut into chunks or lengths (a bean slicer makes this task quicker).

TO COOK: Steam or cook in boiling salted water for about 10 minutes. Serve hot.

Allow 125-175 g (4-6 oz) per person.

BEAN SPROUTS

TO BUY: Choose crisp, small, fresh shoots or grow them yourself at home. Bean sprouts take only 5-6 days to sprout from mung beans (see page 242).

TO PREPARE AND COOK: Cook as soon as possible after buying or harvesting. Rinse in cold water, then either blanch for 30 seconds in boiling salted water or stir-fry for 1-2 minutes. Serve hot as an accompaniment, cold in salads or stir-fried with other ingredients.

Allow about 125 g (4 oz) per person.

BEETROOT

TO BUY: Choose firm, smallish beetroots with crisp tops. There are two types of beetroot

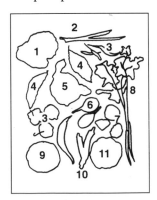

KEY
1. Savoy Cabbage
2. Asparagus
3. Chilli Peppers
4. Karella
5. Baby Cauliflower
6. Baby Aubergines
7. Baby Squash
8. New Carrots
9. Pumpkin
10. Okra
11. Custard Marrow

available: long and globe shape. Small, globe-shaped beetroots, available in early summer, are usually sold in bunches. Maincrop beetroot, which grow larger, are sold by weight and it is common practice for them to be sold cooked.

To PREPARE: Cut off the stalk about 2.5 cm (1 inch) above the root and wash the beetroot. Take care not to pierce the skin or juices will bleed into the cooking water.

To COOK: Cook in boiling salted water until soft, this may take up to 1½ hours for large beetroot. Alternatively, bake in the oven at 180°C (350°F) mark 4 for 2-3 hours. Peel, slice or dice and serve hot or cold with a sauce or dressing.

Allow 125-175 g (4-6 oz) per person.

BROCCOLI

There are several types of broccoli, the sprouting ones which produce many purple, white or green shoots and the heading type with one large close head like a cauliflower. Originally from Italy  *Calabrese* is another variety with green heads.

To BUY: Choose firm, tightly packed heads with strong stalks. The purple and green varieties have a more delicate flavour than the white.

To PREPARE: Trim the stalks and leaves. Halve the shoots if large.

To COOK: Simmer upright in boiling salted water for 7-10 minutes, or steam for 10-15 minutes. Broccoli florets can be stir-fried or added to casseroles. Serve hot.

Allow 125-175 g (4-6 oz) per person.

BRUSSELS SPROUTS

To BUY: Choose small round sprouts with tightly packed heads and no wilted leaves.

To PREPARE: Remove any damaged or wilted leaves and cut off the stem. Cut a cross on the stump to allow the thick part to cook as quickly as the leaves. Wash and drain.

To COOK: Cook in boiling salted water for 8-10 minutes, or steam for about 15 minutes. Serve hot. Very young Brussels sprouts can be served raw in salads.

Allow 125-175 g (4-6 oz) per person.

CABBAGE, SEASONAL

To BUY: Available all year round. In spring the thinnings from the main crop are sold as spring

greens before the heart has formed. Spring cabbages are on sale a little later and these have a small heart. The summer cabbages are firm and green. The winter cabbages are coarser, not as sweet as the summer ones, and are more strongly flavoured. Choose fresh looking cabbage with no wilted leaves.

To PREPARE AND COOK: See Dutch cabbage (below).

Allow 175-225 g (6-8 oz) per person.

CABBAGE, RED AND WHITE

To BUY: Choose those with either a deep, bright red or pale yellowish-white colour, which are round, heavy for their size and firmly packed.

To PREPARE: Cabbage can be shredded for using raw in salads or, for cooking briefly, cut into thick wedges, or the centre can be removed and the cabbage stuffed.

To COOK: Cook in boiling salted water or steam for 3-5 minutes if shredded; 10 minutes for wedges. Serve hot, immediately.

Allow 175-225 g (6-8 oz) per person.

CABBAGE, DUTCH (SAVOY)

To BUY: Choose one that is heavy for its size.

To PREPARE: Remove the coarse outer leaves and cut the rest in half. Take out the centre stalk, wash, shred finely or cut into wedges.

To COOK: Cook in boiling salted water or steam for 3-5 minutes if shredded; 10 minutes for wedges. Serve hot, immediately.

Allow 175-225 g (6-8 oz) per person.

CARDOON

An edible thistle related to the artichoke, which grows in the Mediterranean. Its stalks are like celery and it can be eaten in the same way.

To PREPARE: To eat raw, separate the stalks and remove the strings and inner white skin. Cut the stalks into lengths and thinly slice the heart. Leave in cold water acidulated with lemon juice to prevent browning until ready to serve.

To COOK: Separate the heart and stalks and slice. Cook in boiling salted water with added lemon juice for 25-30 minutes, until tender, then peel away the strings and skin. Serve hot.

Allow 225-275 g (8-10 oz) per person.

Carrots

To buy: Choose firm carrots which are brightly coloured, well shaped and with smooth skins.

To prepare: Leave tiny new carrots whole with a stub of the green stalks attached and scrub well. Pare the skins from older carrots and cut lengthways or slice.

To cook: Steam for 12-18 minutes or cook in boiling salted water for 10-15 minutes.

Serve hot as an accompaniment or make into purée or soup. Carrots can also be eaten raw, either grated or cut into sticks.

Allow 125-175 g (4-6 oz) per person.

Cassava (Manioc, Yucla)

A long, brown-skinned tuber with white starchy flesh. In the Caribbean there are two varieties: a sweet one and a bitter one, which is poisonous unless it is specially prepared. Only the sweet variety is available in Britain.

To prepare: Peel and cut into slices.

To cook: Cook in boiling salted water for 20 minutes or until tender.

Allow 125-175 g (4-6 oz) per person.

Cauliflower

To buy: Choose cauliflowers with firm white heads surrounded by fresh green leaves. Cauliflowers can be eaten raw in salads or cooked. Cook as soon as possible after buying.

To prepare: To cook whole, cut away the outer leaves and chop off the stem. Cut a cross on the stump to help the thick part cook more quickly, or divide into florets. Wash and drain.

To cook: Cook in boiling salted water or steam for 10-15 minutes for whole cauliflower; 5-7 minutes for florets. Keep the stem immersed, but the florets out of the water. Cover the pan so that the florets cook in the steam.

A medium cauliflower serves 4 people.

Celeriac

Sometimes known as turnip rooted celery, celeriac is a swollen root with a pronounced celery flavour.

To buy: Choose bulbs which are firm, heavy and free from blemishes.

To prepare: Scrub well, cut off the roots and peel thickly. Leave whole, grate or slice into julienne strips. Leave in cold water with a little lemon juice until you are ready to cook.

To cook: Cook in boiling salted water for about 20 minutes (slices and strips), 35-45 minutes (whole). Drain well. Serve hot with melted butter or a sauce. Alternatively blanch strips and use in salads.

Allow 125-225 g (4-8 oz) per person.

Celery

To buy: Pale green celery is available all year round, while white winter celery is usually available from October through the new year. Winter celery is usually sold with black soil still attached. Choose celery with thick unblemished sticks and fresh leafy tops. The green tops will tell you if the plant is fresh.

To prepare: Separate the stalks and scrub well to remove any dirt. Leave whole or cut into slices. Serve raw in salads or with cheese.

To cook: To serve hot, boil or steam for about 15 minutes. The leaves can be used as a garnish.

Allow 3-4 celery sticks per person.

Chayote (Chow-chow/vegetable pear)

Pear-shaped gourd with a smooth or ridged skin and white to green flesh with a high water content. They have a delicate flavour which becomes more insipid as they become larger. Also known as christophene or vegetable pear, chayote is available from West Indian shops and some supermarkets.

To buy: Avoid ones with blemishes or soft spots.

To prepare and cook: Small ones can be cooked like courgettes. Peel larger ones and cook in boiling salted water for 15-20 minutes until tender; stuff and bake; or make into chutney.

Allow 2-3 small ones per person, 175-225 g (6-8 oz) for larger ones.

Chicory

To buy: Choose heads with crisp white leaves. Too much green on them indicates a bitter flavour.

To prepare: Remove any damaged outer leaves and cut off the root end. Chop into pieces or leave whole.

To COOK: Plunge the heads into boiling salted water and cook for 5 minutes, drain and braise in about 60 ml (4 tbsp) water and a little lemon juice for about 25 minutes; serve hot. Alternatively serve raw in salads.

Allow half a head per person in salads and 1 head per person when cooked.

CHINESE LEAVES

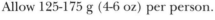

To BUY: Choose heads that are heavy and look fresh. Chinese leaves can be served raw in salads or cooked and served hot.
To PREPARE: Cut off the stem and cut the leaves widthways into about 8 thin slices.
To COOK: Cook as for cabbage or stir-fry.

Allow 125-175 g (4-6 oz) per person.

COURGETTES

There are green and yellow varieties of this miniature marrow, which is a member of the squash family. Baby courgettes are particularly tender and delicately flavoured. Courgette flowers can be eaten too. They may be stuffed and baked, or deep-fried; they are especially popular in Italy.
To BUY: Choose small, tender courgettes with smooth skins that are free from blemishes. Large ones tend to be tough and are best stuffed and baked.
To PREPARE: Slice off both ends, wash or wipe the skin and slice or dice.
To COOK: Cook in boiling salted water for about 5 minutes; steam for 5 minutes; coat in batter and deep-fry for 2-3 minutes; or slice and sauté in butter for about 5 minutes. Serve hot.

Allow 125-175 g (4-6 oz), 1-3 courgettes, depending on size, per person.

CUCUMBER

To BUY: Choose smallish cucumbers with skins that are free from blemishes.
To PREPARE: They may be sliced or diced.
To COOK: Cucumber is usually served raw but may also be boiled, steamed or sautéed and eaten hot.

Allow 125-175 g (4-6 oz) per person if serving as a hot vegetable, 50-125 g (2-4 oz) per person in salads. Cucumber goes well with chervil, dill, chives, fennel or parsley.

DUDI

The dudi is a member of the marrow family. It grows up to 60 cm (2 feet) long and is thinner at the stalk end, becoming wide at the other end. It has a yellowy-green skin and a creamy taste.
To BUY: Choose smooth-skinned ones with no bruising.
To PREPARE: Top and tail and cut into thick slices (there is no need to peel), leaving the seeds in.
To COOK: Cook in boiling salted water for 10-20 minutes, until tender, or shallow-fry. If boiled, eat with melted butter.

1 dudi will serve 4 people.

EDDOE AND DASHEEN

These two root vegetables are related and can be treated in the same way. Eddoe has a small central bulb surrounded by tuberous growths. Dasheen normally consists of a large, irregularly shaped main tuber. Both have a white flesh and a potato-like flavour.
To PREPARE AND COOK: Peel, cut into pieces, cook and use like potatoes. Both vegetables can be boiled, baked, or chopped and fried.

Allow 175-225 g (6-8 oz) per person.

FENNEL

Known as Florence fennel to distinguish it from the herb. The bulb resembles celery but is more bulbous at the base with long green feathery leaves. Fennel has a distinctive aniseed flavour.
To BUY: Choose heads with white or pale green bulbs. A dark green bulb indicates a sharp bitterness.
To PREPARE: Trim both root and stalk ends. Chop or grate if it is to be eaten raw.
To COOK: Quarter, cook in boiling salted water for about 15-20 minutes, then drain and slice. If liked, the slices can then be sautéed in butter. Serve hot or raw in salads. Use the feathery leaves as a garnish, or add to salads.

Allow 125-175 g (4-6 oz) per person.

KALE

There are many varieties, both flat and curly, of this leafy winter vegetable. It has a tough texture but is a good source of vitamins in the winter.

To BUY: Choose kale that is firm and green with no wilted yellow leaves.

To PREPARE AND COOK: Trim off the tough stalks and cook the leaves in boiling salted water for 8-10 minutes, until tender but still crisp. Drain and shred. Serve hot.

Allow 175-225 g (6-8 oz) per person.

KARELLA

Long pod-like vegetable which comes from Kenya. It looks like a large okra with knobbly skin and edible red seeds.

To BUY: Choose firm green pods, avoid brown or withered ones.

To PREPARE AND COOK: Top and tail and scrape off the knobs. Slice the pods, place in a colander, sprinkle with salt and leave for 1 hour. Wash, drain and pat dry, then fry gently until tender. Sprinkle with a little sugar and serve as a side dish with curry.

Allow 125 g (4 oz) per person.

KOHLRABI

An unusual looking white or purple skinned vegetable, similar in size to a turnip. It is a swollen stalk, not a root, with leaves growing out from the surface.

To BUY: Choose small ones, no more than 5 cm (2 inches) in diameter as larger ones can be very tough. Do not buy any with decaying leaves.

To PREPARE: Trim the base, cut off the leaves and stalks and peel the globe thinly. Cut into 1 cm (½ inch) slices or strips.

To COOK: Cook in boiling salted water for 8-12 minutes; steam or fry and serve hot. Kohlrabi can also be sliced very thinly and eaten raw.

Allow 125-175 g (4-6 oz) per person.

LEEKS

To BUY: Choose small young firm leeks which have white stalks and fresh green leaves.

To PREPARE: Trim the root and top and slit down the length or slice crossways. Wash well under cold running water to remove all dirt. It may require several rinses to remove all the grit between the layers.

To COOK: Cook in boiling salted water for 8-10 minutes, steam for 12-15 minutes or braise whole, in enough stock to cover, for about 30 minutes. Serve hot, with herbs or a sauce. Alternatively, allow to cool and serve with French Dressing (see page 255) or serve raw in salads.

Allow 1-2 leeks per person.

LETTUCE

To BUY: Choose lettuce with crisp green leaves and no brown or slimy patches. Large compact varieties and cos lettuces stay crisp. Soft round and loose-leaved lettuces are more delicate and have a tendency to bruise. For further information on varieties of lettuce and other salad leaves, refer to Salads (see pages 250-252).

To PREPARE: Trim the base of the stalk and remove any damaged outer leaves. Separate the remaining leaves and wash in a bowl of cold water, not under running cold water which could wilt them. Dry thoroughly and tear the leaves into pieces. Try not to cut with a knife as this damages them, causing loss of vitamins and may cause discoloration.

To COOK: Lettuce is usually served raw in salads but can be braised for 25-30 minutes or stir-fried. Lettuce also makes a good soup.

Allow 1 small lettuce per person when cooked, rather less when serving raw.

MARROW

To BUY: Look for firm marrows with no blemished or soft parts. Choose ones which are about 30 cm (12 inches) long and weigh about 900 g (2 lb). Over this size they tend to be full of seeds and rather fibrous.

To PREPARE: Wash the skin and if thick, peel it off. Cut into small pieces or into halves, lengthways if the marrow is to be stuffed. Discard the seeds and centre fibres. Place in a colander and sprinkle with salt. Leave for 30 minutes to extract the bitter juices. Rinse and pat dry with absorbent kitchen paper.

To COOK: Cook in boiling salted water for 10-15 minutes, steam for 20-25 minutes or sauté for 5-10 minutes. Stuffed marrow should be baked in the oven covered with foil at 190°C (375°F) mark 5 for about 45 minutes, until tender.

Allow 175-225 g (6-8 oz) per person.

Mushrooms

There are many edible species of mushrooms. Those described below are the most common varieties in Britain.

Cultivated mushrooms are the most commonly available. They may be gathered young as *button mushrooms,* as *cup mushrooms* when the cap has partially opened or as *flat mushrooms* when the cap has opened out and become flat. *Chestnut mushrooms,* which have a stronger flavour, are becoming more widely available.

Several oriental mushrooms are now cultivated in this country, including the pale fan-shaped *oyster mushroom,* and the tan coloured velvety *shiitake* mushroom.

Cèpes and Chanterelles grow in woodlands throughout Europe but cannot be cultivated and are usually only sold dried or canned in Britain. When these wild mushrooms are in season, you may be able to buy them fresh from specialist shops and markets. They have a delicious delicately perfumed flavour.

Morels also have a very delicate flavour and are used in many European dishes. They are usually only available dried.

Truffles, which are renowned for their flavour and scent, are actually tubers which grow near the roots of oak and beech trees, particularly in France and Italy. The two main, highly prized, varieties are the black *Perigord* which is used as a garnish (for *pâté de foie gras* in particular) and the white *Piedmontese* which is usually used grated raw on pasta or egg dishes.

To buy: Choose mushrooms which are firm, textured, with fresh looking stalks that are not brown or withered. Use fresh mushrooms as soon as possible since they deteriorate quickly.

To prepare: Wipe with a damp cloth. If very dirty, wash them quickly but do not leave fresh mushrooms to soak.

Soak dried mushrooms for 15-20 minutes in warm water before using in cooked dishes.

To cook: Sauté in butter or oil, steam or cook in a little salted water for 3-5 minutes and serve hot. Young mushrooms can be eaten raw in salads.

Allow 125 g (4 oz) fresh mushrooms per person. 75 g (3 oz) dried mushrooms when reconstituted will be equal to about 450 g (1 lb).

Okra

These are dark green podded vegetables which rather look like ribbed chillies. They are about 7.5 cm (3 inches) in length and both pods and seeds are eaten.

To buy: Choose those without brown marks which indicate staleness.

To prepare: Top and tail and if the ridges are tough or damaged, scrape them. Slice or leave whole.

To cook: Cook in boiling salted water for 5 minutes or sauté for about 10 minutes, until tender. Serve hot.

Allow 125 g (4 oz) per person.

Onions

There are different varieties of onions, some more strongly flavoured than others.

Globe onions are the most commonly used variety for cooking.

Spanish onions are larger and more delicately flavoured. They are more suitable for frying or serving raw.

Italian red onions are oblong-shaped and smaller than globe onions. They have a mild, sometimes sweet flavour, and are attractive cut into thin rings raw.

Pickling (button) onions are about 2.5 cm (1 inch) in diameter.

Shallots are also small and have a stronger flavour than globe onions.

Silverskin onions have white flesh and a silver skin. They are very small and are popular for pickling.

Spring onions are nearly always used raw. They are slim and mild in flavour when young, with a more pronounced taste as they increase in size.

To buy: Choose clean, firm onions with dry, papery skins.

To prepare: Cut a slice from the top and peel off the skin. Cut the onion in half lengthways and cut each half separately. Laying it flat on the chopping board, slice it through in one direction; turn and slice it in the other direction for chopped onion.

To prepare spring onions, cut off the roots and trim the green part to about 2.5 cm (1 inch) above the white. Use whole or sliced in salads or chop and add to stir-fried dishes.

To cook: Boil whole onions for 20-30 minutes, bake for 1-1½ hours, steam for 40 minutes, braise for 30-40 minutes or slice and gently fry in butter until soft.

Allow 1 onion or 125 g (4 oz) shallots per person if serving as a vegetable. Allow 2-3 spring onions per person in salads.

PALM HEARTS

These are the edible
inner part of palm tree
shoots. The firm,
creamy coloured flesh
has a delicate flavour
rather like artichoke or
asparagus. They are
rarely found fresh in
Britain but canned ones are available. They can
be added to salads or eaten hot as a vegetable.

PARSNIP

A root vegetable with a nutty, sweet flavour
which improves if harvested after several frosts.
To BUY: Choose those which are small and
young with firm clean skins and no side shoots
or brown marks.
To PREPARE: Scrub well, trim the top and root
ends and peel thinly. Either leave young
parsnips whole or slice large old ones into
quarters and remove the central core.
To COOK: Boil or steam for 15-20 minutes, or
blanch and sauté in butter or oil, or roast around
a joint of meat after first boiling in water for
2 minutes. Serve hot.
Allow 175-225 g (6-8 oz) per person.

PEAS

To BUY: Choose crisp, well filled pods with some
air space between the peas. Very full pods may
have tough peas inside. The fresh pea season is
short but they are available all year round frozen.
Tiny *petit pois* are prepared in the same way.
To PREPARE: Shell the peas and discard any that
are discoloured or blemished. Wash and cook
immediately.
To COOK: Cook in a little boiling salted water for
5-10 minutes, depending on size. Serve hot with
butter, sprinkled with chopped fresh mint.
Allow 125-175 g (4-6 oz) prepared weight
per person. You will need to buy about 225-350 g
(8-12 oz) per person in the pods.

PEAS, MANGETOUT

In French, mange tout means eat all. The whole
pods are eaten very young when the peas are
under-developed.
To BUY: Choose pods in which the peas are very
small and underdeveloped.
To PREPARE: Trim the ends and wash.
To COOK: Cook in boiling salted water for 2-4
minutes, or include in stir-fried dishes.
Allow about 125 g (4 oz) per person.

PEAS, SUGAR SNAP

This is an American variety of edible-podded
pea. It has a crisp stringless pod with well-
developed seeds, and a sweet flavour. Prepare,
cook and serve as for mangetout peas (see left).

PEPPERS

Peppers belong to the capsicum family. There is
a great variety of colours ranging from white,
yellow, red and green to purple. Red peppers
are sweeter than green ones, while the other
varieties tend to have a milder flavour.
To BUY: Choose those with firm shiny skins and
no sign of shrivelling. They can be eaten cooked
or raw.
To PREPARE: Rinse the skins, then slice off the
stem and remove the seeds and membrane.
Leave whole, slice into rings or dice. When
peppers are to be eaten raw they are more
digestible with the skins removed: grill or turn
the whole pepper over a gas flame until the skin
is charred, then plunge into cold water; the skin
will rub off between your fingers.
To COOK: Blanch or stuff and bake in the oven
at 190°C (375°F) mark 5 for about 45 minutes.
Allow 1 stuffed pepper per person.

PEPPERS, CHILLI

Red, green and yellow chilli peppers are available all year round. There are numerous kinds,
varying in shape, size and strength of flavour.
To BUY: Choose those which are free from
wrinkles and brown patches.
To PREPARE AND COOK: The volatile oils in the
flesh and seeds of the chilli can irritate your skin,
so treat with care. Either wear rubber gloves or
prepare chillies in a bowl of cold water. Avoid
touching your eyes and wash hands immediately
afterwards.
Chillies are sometimes eaten on their own
in Indian and Far Eastern cookery but otherwise
they are added in small quantities to soups and
casseroles for flavour. Remove stems, then
discard seeds if you don't want a very hot flavour.

PLANTAIN

This belongs to the same family as the banana,
which it resembles, but is cooked and eaten as a
vegetable – especially in the West Indies.
To BUY: Choose firm, undamaged plantains
which are still green or partly green.
To PREPARE AND COOK: Peel, slice and fry gently in
butter and oil.
Allow 175 g (6 oz) per person.

POTATOES

New or early British potatoes are available from May to August. Maincrop British potatoes are lifted during September and October and stored for sale over the next eight months.

TO BUY: Choose potatoes with smooth, firm skins. New potatoes should have skins that can be rubbed off. Buy new potatoes in small quantities and use up quickly. See varieties for the best methods of cooking.

NEW POTATOES

ARRAN PILOT has creamy white flesh which does not break up when cooked. Good for boiling, sautéeing, potato salad and chips.

HOME GUARD has creamy white flesh which does not break up or discolour when cooked. Good for boiling, frying and potato salad.

JERSEY ROYAL has creamy coloured, tender flesh. It can be boiled, steamed and used in salads.

MARIS PEER has pale yellow firm flesh. Good for boiling, steaming, sautéeing, potato salad, chips or roasting.

PENTLAND JAVELIN has very white firm flesh. Good for boiling and potato salad.

ULSTER SCEPTRE is a very early variety with white flesh which does not discolour. Good all rounder.

WILJA has pale yellow flesh and a soft texture. Good for boiling or steaming and potato salad.

MAINCROP POTATOES

DESIRÉE has pinkish-red skin and pale yellow flesh which is consistently good quality and not as dry as many maincrop varieties. Good all-rounder.

KING EDWARD has a patchy red skin and pale yellow floury flesh. Good all rounder.

MARIS PIPER has a pale skin and creamy white floury flesh which does not discolour after cooking. Good for chips, cooking in its jacket, boiling, sautéeing, mashing and roasting.

MAJESTIC has a white skin and creamy white floury flesh, which tends to discolour after cooking. Good for chips, sautéeing and roasting.

PENTLAND DELL has a pale skin and tends to disintegrate. It is best for jacket potatoes.

PENTLAND HAWK has pale skin and creamy flesh but only moderate cooking quality. It is best for boiling, mashing and cooking in its jacket.

PINK FIR APPLE has a pinkish flesh and a firm, waxy texture. Excellent flavour – use in salads, boil or steam.

ROMANO is a popular red-skinned maincrop variety with cream flesh. Fairly good all-rounder.

TO PREPARE: Prepare potatoes just before you cook them; leaving them in water after peeling causes loss of their vitamin C. Scrub or scrape new potatoes.

Cook as below, allowing 175-225 g (6-8 oz) per person.

BOILED POTATOES: Peel and, if necessary, cut into smallish, even-sized pieces. Place in cold salted water and bring to the boil. Cook for about 10-15 minutes for new potatoes; 15-20 minutes for maincrop; or until tender.

CHIPPED POTATOES: Peel and cut into slices, then into sticks. Put into a bowl of cold water for 30 minutes to remove excess starch. Drain and dry in a clean tea towel or on absorbent kitchen paper. In a deep frying pan or electric deep fat fryer, heat the oil to 190°C (375°F). If you do not have a thermostat on the pan, nor a cooking thermometer, check the temperature by dropping in one chip which should rise to the surface immediately, surrounded by bubbles.

Put enough chips into the frying basket to quarter-fill it, lower into the oil and cook for 6-7 minutes, until starting to colour. Raise the basket and drain the chips on absorbent kitchen paper. When all the chips have had their first frying, repeat the process and fry this time for 3 minutes, until they are golden and crisp. Drain and serve at once.

GAME CHIPS: Cut very thin slices, then deep-fry until golden.

JACKET POTATOES: Wash, dry and prick with a fork or impale on a potato baking spike. For crisp skins, brush with oil or melted butter. Bake near the top of the oven at 200°C (400°F) mark 6 for 1-1½ hours, until tender right through. Cut a cross in the top or cut in half and serve with a knob of butter.

MASHED AND CREAMED POTATOES: Boil, then mash until smooth with a fork or potato masher. Season, then put on a low heat and dry for 2-3 minutes, stirring continuously. For creamed potatoes, add a little butter or margarine with a little warm milk and beat until fluffy.

STEAMED POTATOES: Scrub the potatoes and remove a 1 cm (½ inch) strip of peel from around the centre of each. Steam for about 45 minutes, until tender.

SAUTÉED POTATOES: Boil the potatoes for 15 minutes, until just cooked. Drain, peel and cut into large chunks. Sauté gently in hot butter and oil until golden and crisp on both sides. Drain thoroughly on absorbent kitchen paper and sprinkle with salt.

ROAST POTATOES: Place peeled potatoes in cold salted water and bring to the boil. Cook for 2-3 minutes, then drain thoroughly. Either add to the fat around a joint at 180°C (350°F) mark 4 for about 1¼-1½ hours or heat vegetable oil or dripping in a roasting tin in the oven at 220°C (425°F) mark 7 and put the potatoes into it. Cook for about 45 minutes to 1 hour, basting regularly and turning once or twice, until golden brown all over.

PUMPKIN

One of the largest of the squashes (the same family as the marrow), pumpkin can be used as a vegetable or a fruit.

TO BUY: Choose firm pumpkins weighing about 4.5-6.8 kg (10-15 lb).

TO PREPARE: Cut in half and scoop out the seeds. Cut into sections and peel and chop the flesh into even-sized pieces. Alternatively, you can buy slices of pumpkin, sold by weight.

TO COOK: Cook pumpkin in boiling salted water for about 15 minutes, until tender; or steam; or roast like potatoes around a joint or in hot fat. Pumpkin can also be stuffed and baked or used in soups or stews.

Allow 225 g (8 oz) per person.

RADISHES

There are several varieties of this root vegetable.

RED RADISH: The cultivated varieties of this small radish are sold all year round. They have a peppery flavour which is milder in the spring. They are usually eaten raw in salads, as an hors d'oeuvre, or they can be made into attractive garnishes (see page 506). The leaves add a pungent flavour to salads.

DAIKON RADISH is the traditional white Japanese variety, often sold in oriental food shops. It is milder than other types and is grated and used as a garnish, or pickled.

MOOLI is a long, white parsnip-shaped vegetable which can be grated and eaten raw or cooked.

SPANISH BLACK RADISH is a round radish the size of a small turnip. It can be eaten raw or cooked.

TO BUY: Choose those with fresh green tops or, if these have been cut off, look for ones with firm bright flesh.

Allow 3-4 red radishes per person; 175-225 g (6-8 oz) raw weight, 125-175 g (4-6 oz) cooked weight white or black radish per person.

SALSIFY AND SCORZONERA

These two root vegetables are closely related. They both have long, tapering roots. Salsify has a white skin and a flavour similar to oysters – it is also known as oyster plant or vegetable oyster. Scorzonera has a brownish black skin and is also known as black salsify. It has a stronger flavour than salsify and is at its best in the late autumn.

TO BUY: Choose roots that are as smooth as possible and firm. Avoid flabby ones.

TO PREPARE: Top and tail the roots and scrub well under cold running water.

TO COOK: Cook in boiling salted water with a little added lemon juice for 25-30 minutes, until tender but still crisp. Drain well. Serve hot with lemon juice, melted butter and chopped herbs, or purée for soups; use in casseroles or salads.

Allow 125-175 g (4-6 oz) per person.

SEAKALE

This looks like a cross between blanched forced rhubarb and celery. It has crisp white stalks topped with tiny green leaves. The forced variety is most commonly available. Outdoor grown seakale is available in specialist shops in the spring.

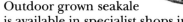

TO BUY: Choose stalks which are not discoloured or wilting. Trim the stalks and wash well.

TO COOK: Tie in bunches of five or six stalks as for asparagus. Steam for 20-25 minutes, or alternatively, boil in lightly salted water with a little lemon juice for 15-20 minutes. Drain well.

TO EAT: Serve hot, topped with melted butter, Hollandaise or cheese sauce.

Allow 125-175 g (4-6 oz) per person.

SORREL

There are several varieties but the main ones are wild sorrel and French sorrel.

TO BUY: Choose leaves which are small, fresh looking and bright green. Sorrel is not widely available, but is easily grown in a garden. It should be picked when young before it flowers.

TO PREPARE: Wash well and tear up any large leaves into smaller pieces. Use raw in salads or soften the leaves in butter or margarine and use in soups, sauces or as a filling for omelettes. Sorrel has a distinctive acidic flavour and cannot be used alone in a salad.

Allow 50 g (2 oz) per person.

SPINACH

Summer spinach is light green and fine textured, while winter spinach is darker and coarser.

As spinach can be quite a difficult vegetable to grow, hardier varieties have been developed. The 'spinach substitutes' available are listed here; they are plants that produce leaves similar in colour, texture and flavour:

SPINACH BEET: Also called perpetual spinach, this looks very much like winter spinach but the leaves have a coarser centre rib and stalk and a stronger flavour.

SEAKALE BEET: Although unrelated, the leaves are used as spinach and the centre ribs cooked as for seakale.

GOOD KING HENRY: This vegetable is native to Britain. The plant produces leaves on a centre stalk rather than many leaves grown from the root.

TO BUY: Choose bright green leaves and avoid spinach that is yellow or wilted.

TO PREPARE: Wash spinach well as it collects dirt. Use several changes of water and handle the leaves gently as they bruise easily.

TO COOK: Summer spinach is best steamed for 5-10 minutes in just the water that clings to it after rinsing. Winter spinach needs to have the stalks and central ribs removed before boiling in salted water for 5-10 minutes, until tender. Drain well and press the water out of the leaves with the back of a wooden spoon.

Allow at least 225 g (8 oz) per person.

SQUASH

There are many different varieties of squash, including the familiar pumpkin, marrow and courgette (see individual entries). These are summer squashes, which are generally thin-skinned, immature and tender. Other summer varieties are the *patty pan* and *custard marrow*. Winter squashes are larger, more mature and have hard skins. Varieties include the *spaghetti marrow* and *butternut squash*.

TO BUY: Select firm, uncut squash which are blemish free.

TO PREPARE AND COOK: Summer squash can be prepared in the same way as courgettes. Winter squash are often halved and baked with a tasty filling. Otherwise they are peeled, cut into chunks and steamed or boiled, or added to soups and stews. Spaghetti squash is boiled whole, then halved before serving to allow the fibres to be scooped out.

Allow 175-225 g (6-8 oz) per person.

SWEDE

A heavy, coarse-skinned root vegetable with orange flesh.

TO BUY: Choose small swedes as large ones can be tough. Avoid those with damaged skins.

TO PREPARE: Peel thickly to remove all the skin and roots, then cut into chunks.

TO COOK: Place in cold salted water and boil for 20 minutes or steam for the same amount of time, then mash or purée with a knob of butter and seasoning. Alternatively, roast chunks of swede in hot fat or around a joint of meat at 200°C (400°F) mark 6 for 1-1½ hours.

Allow 175-225 g (6-8 oz) per person.

SWEETCORN

Sweetcorn originated in America but it is now grown all over the world. The cob's sweet nutty flavour is at its best just after picking. Once the cob is cut from the plant the natural sugar in the kernels changes to starch and the cob loses the sweetness and flavour quite quickly.

BABY SWEETCORN which looks like miniature corn on the cob, is now wideley available. It has a delicious sweet flavour. When cooked, the whole cob is eaten.

TO BUY: Choose cobs with a pale green, tightly fitting husk with creamy coloured kernels inside that are not dry. Once they turn gold some of the sweetness goes and the corn becomes tougher.

TO PREPARE: Remove the stem, leaves and silky fibres. Trim the pointed end if the corn is not fully formed there.

TO COOK: Cook in boiling unsalted water (salt makes corn tough) for 5-15 minutes, until a piece of corn comes away from the cob easily. Boil baby corn for a few minutes only, or stir-fry.

TO EAT: Serve with melted butter. The easiest way to eat corn on the cob is from special cob-shaped dishes, holding it between two forks or special tiny skewers.

If the corn is to be served off the cob, remove it by holding the cob upright on a work surface and cutting off the corn with a sharp knife, working downwards. Cook the loose corn kernels in a little unsalted boiling water for 5-10 minutes, then drain.

Serve hot with melted butter, or cool and add to salads. Serve baby corn whole or halved, with butter as an accompaniment, in soups, casseroles, stir-fries or salads.

Allow 1 whole cob per person and 75-125 g (3-4 oz) loose corn or baby corn.

SWEET POTATOES

Despite their name, these are not related to potatoes. They are a tuber vegetable, usually an elongated shape though there are some round varieties. The flesh is usually white and is sweet and slightly perfumed. The outer skin may be white or purplish red.

TO BUY: Choose those which are small and firm; large ones tend to be fibrous.

TO PREPARE: Scrub them well and if boiling, peel after they are cooked as the flesh is soft and floury.

TO COOK: Boil, bake, fry or roast as for ordinary potatoes.

Allow 225 g (8 oz) per person.

SWISS CHARD

This is related to Seakale beet and is grown mainly for its leaves which look very similar to spinach. The leaves have coarse, crisp central ribs.

TO BUY: Choose fresh looking bulbs with unblemished ribs and crisp leaves.

TO PREPARE AND COOK: The leaves are prepared and cooked in the same way as winter spinach. The central ribs, once removed, are prepared and cooked in the same way as seakale.

Allow 225 g (8 oz) leaves per person and 125-175 g (4-6 oz) ribs per person.

TOMATOES

Although strictly speaking a fruit, the tomato is nearly always used as a vegetable and has come to be classed under that heading. There are many varieties, ranging in colour from red to orange, yellow to green.

HOME-GROWN TOMATOES are available from mid-spring throughout the summer.

SPANISH TOMATOES vary from deep pink to green. They are good raw or stuffed.

ITALIAN PLUM TOMATOES are bright red with a strong flavour. They are excellent for soups, sauces and casseroles.

CHERRY TOMATOES are tiny tomatoes about the size of large marbles, which are very sweet and delicious eaten raw.

BEEF TOMATOES are very large, weighing up to 450 g (1 lb). They can be stuffed or used raw.

MARMANDE TOMATOES from Provence are also large. These have an excellent flavour.

TO BUY: Look for firm unblemished tomatoes.

TO PREPARE: Prepare tomatoes according to their final use. For cooked dishes and some salads, they are skinned: cover with boiling water for about 30 seconds, then plunge into cold water and the skins will slide off. Alternatively, hold on a fork over a gas flame for 15-30 seconds, turning until the skin blisters, then peel.

Slice or quarter tomatoes if using raw. If they are to be stuffed, remove the top and scoop out the seeds and flesh; cut a small sliver from the base. Over-ripe tomatoes can be used to make juice or sauces for pasta, meat, fish and vegetables.

TO EAT: Serve in salads or with herbs and a dressing as a starter. When stuffed, they may be served hot or cold.

Allow 1-2 tomatoes per person when served raw, 1 large one when stuffed.

TURNIPS

Sweet, tender early turnips are slightly mustard flavoured. They have green and white skins and are sold from April to July. Maincrop turnips, which are available for the rest of the year, have thicker skins and coarser flesh.

TO BUY: Choose turnips that are smooth and unblemished.

TO PREPARE: Peel young turnips thinly. Peel older ones thickly, then slice or cut into chunks.

TO COOK: Place in cold salted water and boil for 20-30 minutes until tender. Young turnips can be cooked whole, but older ones should be cut up and served either in chunks or mashed. Their strong flavour benefits from being mashed with an equal part of mashed potato or carrots.

TO EAT: Use older turnips sparingly, diced or thinly sliced, in soups and casseroles. Young turnips can be served raw, sliced thinly or grated into salads; or cooked as an accompaniment.

Allow 175-225 g (6-8 oz) per person.

VINE LEAVES

These are the young leaves of the grape vine which originated in the Mediterranean region and are now found all over the world.

TO BUY: Vine leaves are sold fresh, canned or packed in brine. Choose fresh leaves that are undamaged.

TO PREPARE: If using fresh vine leaves, plunge a few at a time into boiling water for a few minutes

until softened. When using vine leaves packed in brine, drain them, then pour over boiling water and leave to soak for about 20 minutes. Drain, then soak in fresh cold water for a further 20 minutes, drain again, then soak once more to remove any remaining excess salt.
TO EAT: Serve in salads or stuffed with a savoury filling. They can also be wrapped around game or used as an attractive base for fresh fruit dishes, cheese and salads.

   Allow 4-5 stuffed vine leaves per person.

WATERCRESS
TO BUY: Choose watercress that looks fresh with dark green leaves and no sign of yellowing.
TO PREPARE: Wash well and trim off the tough stalks before use.
TO EAT: Watercress is eaten raw in salads, used as a garnish, or used in soups and sauces.

   Allow 1 bunch for four people in a salad.

YAMS
A member of the tuber family, yams originated in Africa but have become widely available in British markets and supermarkets. Yams have a brownish-pink skin and white flesh. Choose undamaged yams when buying.

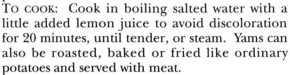

TO PREPARE: Wash and peel, then dice.
TO COOK: Cook in boiling salted water with a little added lemon juice to avoid discoloration for 20 minutes, until tender, or steam. Yams can also be roasted, baked or fried like ordinary potatoes and served with meat.

   Allow 175-225 g (6-8 oz) per person.

VEGETABLE DISHES

ASPARAGUS MALTAISE

450 g (1 lb) asparagus, washed and trimmed
salt and pepper
3 egg yolks
grated rind and juice of 1 orange
125 g (4 oz) unsalted butter, softened
15 ml (1 tbsp) lemon juice
30-45 ml (2-3 level tbsp) double cream
orange twists, to garnish

1. Tie the asparagus in bundles of six to eight stalks. Cover the tips with foil and stand them upright in a pan of boiling salted water and cook for 8-12 minutes, until tender.
2. Meanwhile, make the sauce. Beat together the egg yolks, orange rind and seasoning in a bowl with a knob of the softened butter.
3. Place the bowl over a pan of hot water and whisk in the orange and lemon juice. Cook over a gentle heat and gradually beat in remaining butter, a little at a time.
4. Once the sauce begins to thicken, remove the bowl from the heat and continue beating for 1 minute. Adjust seasoning to taste. Stir the

Asparagus Maltaise

cream into the orange butter sauce.
5. Remove the asparagus from the pan and drain well. To serve, remove the string, arrange on a serving plate and garnish with the orange twists. Serve immediately with the orange butter sauce handed separately.
SERVES 6

STUFFED GLOBE ARTICHOKES

6 medium globe artichokes
45 ml (3 tbsp) lemon juice
salt and pepper
75 g (3 oz) butter or margarine
2 medium onions, skinned and finely chopped
350 g (12 oz) streaky bacon, rinded and finely sliced
700 g (1½ lb) ripe tomatoes, skinned, quartered, seeded and chopped
175 g (6 oz) fresh breadcrumbs
finely grated rind and juice of 2 medium oranges
90 ml (6 tbsp) chopped fresh parsley
2 eggs, beaten
melted butter, to serve

1. Strip away discoloured leaves. Slice off stem of artichoke as close as possible to the base of leaves. Level up so artichokes stand upright.
2. Using scissors, snip off the leaf tips. Soak the artichokes in cold water acidulated with 15 ml (1 tbsp) lemon juice for about 30 minutes while preparing the rest.
3. Drain the artichokes and place them in a large saucepan of boiling salted water with the remaining lemon juice.
4. Cover and boil gently for 30-45 minutes, depending on size. The artichokes will float, so turn them during cooking and keep covered, to steam the leaves above the water.
5. Meanwhile, make the stuffing. Heat butter in a saucepan, add the onions and bacon and fry gently until onions are soft and bacon is golden.
6. Add the tomatoes to the pan, cook for a few minutes, then stir in the breadcrumbs, grated orange rind, parsley, eggs and seasoning, beating well to mix.
7. Test whether the artichokes are cooked. To do this, gently pull an outer leaf; if cooked, it will come out easily.
8. Drain the cooked artichokes upside down in a colander and hold briefly under cold running water to help bring out and set the green colour and cool the leaves for handling.
9. Gradually peel back leaves, working from the outside inwards (be careful not to snap any off). Continue peeling back the leaves until the hairy choke of the artichoke is exposed.
10. With a teaspoon, scrape away and discard hairs. Hollow out heart slightly.
11. Spoon stuffing generously over hearts; divide it evenly between the six artichokes.
12. Gently fold the leaves back around the stuffing. Tie string around each one to hold it together.
13. Pack artichokes into a well-buttered deep ovenproof dish or shallow casserole. Pour over the strained orange juice and cover tightly with buttered greaseproof paper or foil and the lid. Bake in the oven at 190°C (375°F) mark 5 for 25 minutes. To serve, remove string and hand the melted butter separately.
SERVES 6

JERUSALEM ARTICHOKES IN NUTMEG CREAM

700 g (1½ lb) Jerusalem artichokes, washed and peeled
1 lemon
salt and pepper
50 g (2 oz) butter or margarine
150 ml (5 fl oz) single cream
little freshly grated nutmeg

1. Place the artichokes in a saucepan with a slice of lemon. Cover with cold salted water, bring to the boil and simmer gently for 10 minutes. Drain.
2. Melt the butter in a clean pan, add the artichokes with the juice of ½ a lemon. Cover and cook for 10 minutes, shaking occasionally.
3. Remove from the heat, add the cream, seasoning and nutmeg. Heat gently for 5 minutes.
SERVES 4

AUBERGINES WITH HAM

2 even-sized aubergines, 450 g (1 lb) total weight
salt and pepper
vegetable oil, for brushing
1 medium onion, skinned and finely chopped
50 g (2 oz) butter or margarine
1 garlic clove, skinned and crushed
30 ml (2 level tbsp) flour
10 ml (2 level tsp) chopped fresh basil or 2.5 ml
    (½ level tsp) dried
50 g (2 oz) fresh breadcrumbs
125 g (4 oz) cooked lean ham, finely chopped
5 ml (1 level tsp) French mustard
5 ml (1 tsp) lemon juice
60 ml (4 tbsp) single cream or top of the milk

1. Cut the aubergines in half lengthways,
sprinkle with salt and leave for 30 minutes to
extract the bitter juices. Rinse and pat dry.
2. Score the cut side, brush with oil and place in
an ovenproof dish with 60 ml (4 tbsp) water.
Cover with foil or a lid and bake in the oven at
190°C (375°F) mark 5 for about 50 minutes. Do
not overcook.
3. Scoop out as much flesh as possible, leaving
the shell intact. Chop the flesh.
4. Brown the onion in half the butter, add the
crushed garlic and aubergine flesh and fry for a
few minutes.
5. Sprinkle over the flour and basil and cook for
a few minutes, stirring. Reserve 30 ml (2 tbsp) of
the breadcrumbs and add the rest to the pan
with the ham, mustard, lemon juice, cream and
seasoning.
6. Fill the aubergine shells with stuffing.
Sprinkle over the reserved breadcrumbs and dot
with the remaining butter.
7. Bake, uncovered, in the oven at 190°C
(375°F) mark 5 for about 30 minutes.
SERVES 2

BROAD BEANS IN LEMON PARSLEY SAUCE

900 g-1.1 kg (2-2½ lb) broad beans, shelled
salt
FOR THE SAUCE
25 g (1 oz) butter or margarine
45 ml (3 level tbsp) flour
150 ml (¼ pint) chicken stock
60 ml (4 tbsp) milk
salt and pepper
1 egg yolk
30 ml (2 tbsp) single cream
grated rind and juice of ½ a lemon
15 ml (1 tbsp) chopped fresh parsley

1. Cook the broad beans in boiling salted water
for 8-10 minutes, until just tender. Drain well.
2. Meanwhile, make the sauce, melt the butter
in a saucepan, stir in the flour and cook gently
for 1 minute, stirring. Remove the pan from the
heat and gradually stir in the stock. Bring to the
boil slowly and continue to cook for 1-2 minutes,
until the sauce thickens.
3. Stir in the milk and the seasoning.
4. Beat the egg yolk and cream together in a
bowl. Add 45 ml (3 tbsp) of the sauce to the
cream, then stir the mixture into the pan. Cook
over a very low heat, stirring, until the sauce
thickens. Stir in the lemon rind and juice,
parsley and the drained beans.
SERVES 4

FRENCH BEANS WITH THYME

25 g (1 oz) butter or margarine
1 medium onion, skinned and finely sliced
4 rashers streaky bacon, rinded and chopped
700 g (1½ lb) French beans, topped and tailed
5 ml (1 tsp) chopped fresh thyme
salt and pepper

1. Melt the butter in a large saucepan, add the
onion and bacon and cook for 10 minutes, until
the onion begins to colour.
2. Add the beans to the pan with the thyme,
seasoning and 90 ml (6 tbsp) cold water. Cover
and simmer gently for about 10 minutes, until
the beans are tender but still crisp.
SERVES 4

FRENCH BEANS WITH TOMATOES

700 g (1½ lb) French beans, topped and tailed
salt
30 ml (2 tbsp) vegetable oil
4 tomatoes, skinned and chopped
1 garlic clove, skinned
chopped fresh parsley, to garnish

1. Blanch the beans whole in boiling salted water for about 3 minutes. Drain well.
2. Heat the oil in a saucepan, add the tomatoes, garlic and beans. Cover and cook for 10-15 minutes, until the tomatoes and beans are tender.
3. Remove the garlic and turn the beans into a warmed serving dish. Sprinkle with parsley before serving.
SERVES 4

SPICED RUNNER BEANS

700 g (1½ lb) runner beans, topped and tailed
25 g (1 oz) butter or margarine
15 ml (1 tbsp) vegetable oil
1.25 ml (¼ level tsp) mustard powder
1.25 ml (¼ level tsp) ground cumin
5 ml (1 level tsp) ground turmeric
1.25 ml (¼ level tsp) cayenne pepper
salt and pepper

1. Cut the beans into 5 cm (2 inch) lengths and then into thin strips. Heat the butter and oil in a saucepan, add the spices and cook for 1 minute, stirring.
2. Add the beans and seasonings, cover and cook over a very gentle heat for about 10 minutes, until the beans are tender. Shake the pan from time to time to prevent sticking.
SERVES 4

BEAN SPROUTS WITH CHINESE EGG STRIPS

45 ml (3 tbsp) vegetable oil
3 eggs, beaten
1 medium onion, skinned and finely chopped
1 garlic clove, skinned and crushed
1 medium red or green pepper, seeded and sliced
4 celery sticks, washed and chopped
175 g (6 oz) button mushrooms, wiped and sliced
225 g (8 oz) bean sprouts, washed
15 ml (1 tbsp) soy sauce
salt and pepper

1. Heat 15 ml (1 tbsp) oil in a frying pan, add the beaten eggs and cook over a gentle heat for about 5 minutes, until set like a thin omelette. Remove from the pan, cut into thin strips, then cut each strip into three or four pieces.
2. Heat the remaining oil in the pan, add the onion, garlic, pepper and celery and cook for about 10 minutes, until soft. Increase the heat, add the mushrooms and cook until golden brown.
3. Stir in the bean sprouts, soy sauce, seasoning and the egg strips and cook for 3-4 minutes, stirring, until heated through. Serve immediately.
SERVES 4

BEETROOT WITH ORANGE

4 large beetroots
vegetable oil for brushing
25-50 g (1-2 oz) butter or margarine
grated rind of 1 orange
salt and pepper

1. Scrub the beetroots well and place on a baking sheet. Brush the skins with a little oil and cook in the oven at 180°C (350°F) mark 4 for 2-3 hours, according to size. The flesh is cooked when it can be pierced with a knife.
2. While still warm, peel, then slice or chop coarsely. Melt the butter in a saucepan, add the orange rind and the beetroots and heat through.
3. Season to taste and turn into a warmed serving dish.
SERVES 4

BAKED BEETROOT

4 large beetroots, about 225 g (8 oz) each
butter or soured cream, to serve
salt and pepper

1. Wash the beetroots, but do not trim. Wrap them in greased foil or place in a greased ovenproof dish.
2. Cover tightly and bake at 180°C (350°F) mark 4 for 2-3 hours. When the beetroots are cooked the skin will slide off easily. Serve with a slice cut off the top, but not skinned. Top with the butter or soured cream and season to taste.
SERVES 4

BROCCOLI AMANDINE

700 g (1½ lb) broccoli, trimmed and divided into florets
50 g (2 oz) butter or margarine
50 g (2 oz) flaked almonds
30 ml (2 tbsp) lemon juice
pepper

1. Cook the broccoli in boiling salted water for 7-10 minutes. Drain well and turn into a warmed serving dish.
2. Melt the butter in a frying pan, add the almonds and cook over a gentle heat for about 5 minutes, until golden brown.
3. Stir in the lemon juice and seasoning and spoon over the broccoli.
SERVES 4

BRUSSELS SPROUTS AND CHESTNUTS

350 g (12 oz) fresh chestnuts
300 ml (½ pint) chicken stock
1 celery stick, trimmed
5 ml (1 level tsp) sugar
700 g (1½ lb) Brussels sprouts, trimmed
salt
25 g (1 oz) butter or margarine

1. Place the chestnuts in a saucepan of cold water and bring to the boil. Drain and remove skins.
2. Return the chestnuts to the pan, with the stock, celery and sugar. Bring to the boil and allow to simmer gently for about 35-40 minutes, until the nuts are soft. Remove and discard the celery, then drain the nuts.
3. Meanwhile, cook the Brussels sprouts separately in boiling salted water for 8-10 minutes. Drain.
4. Melt the butter and toss the cooked nuts and sprouts together.
SERVES 4

BRAISED RED CABBAGE WITH APPLE

1.1 kg (2½ lb) red cabbage
2 medium onions, skinned and sliced
2 medium cooking apples, peeled, cored and chopped
10 ml (2 level tsp) sugar
bouquet garni
30 ml (2 tbsp) red wine vinegar
25 g (1 oz) butter or margarine

1. Shred the cabbage finely, discarding any discoloured outside leaves and coarse stems.
2. Layer the cabbage in a 3.4 litre (6 pint) casserole with the onions, apples, sugar and seasoning. Put the bouquet garni in the centre and pour over 30 ml (2 tbsp) water and the vinegar.
3. Cover tightly and cook in the oven at 200°C (400°F) mark 6 for 1 hour. Remove the lid and continue cooking for about 30 minutes, until the liquid has evaporated.
4. Add the butter and toss the cabbage just before cooking.
SERVES 6

CABBAGE WITH JUNIPER BERRIES

25 g (1 oz) butter
1 medium onion, skinned and chopped
1 garlic clove, skinned and crushed
6 juniper berries, crushed
450 g (1 lb) cabbage, shredded
salt and pepper

1. Melt the butter in a large saucepan. Add the onion, garlic and juniper berries and lightly cook for 5 minutes, until the onion is soft.
2. Add the cabbage and stir until well coated in butter. Season to taste. Cover and cook the cabbage in its own juice for 10 minutes, stirring occasionally. The cabbage should still be slightly crunchy and not soft. Serve hot.
SERVES 4

SAVOURY WHITE CABBAGE

50 g (2 oz) butter or margarine
700 g (1½ lb) white cabbage, finely shredded
1 medium onion, skinned and grated
2 rashers streaky bacon, rinded and chopped
pinch of freshly grated nutmeg

1. Melt the butter in a large saucepan. Add all the remaining ingredients, cover and cook very gently for 20-30 minutes, until the cabbage is just tender, shaking the pan frequently.
SERVES 4

LEFT: Cabbage with Juniper Berries. RIGHT: Baked Beetroot

CARROTS WITH MINT AND LEMON

700 g (1½ lb) small new carrots, trimmed
*   and scrubbed*
salt and pepper
finely grated rind and juice of ½ lemon
5 ml (1 tsp) light soft brown sugar
15 g (½ oz) butter
30 ml (2 tbsp) chopped fresh mint
lemon slices, to garnish

1. Cook the carrots in boiling salted water for about 10 minutes, until just tender. Drain thoroughly.
2. Return the carrots to the pan with the remaining ingredients and toss together over a high heat until the butter melts. Serve at once, garnished with lemon slices.
SERVES 4

Carrots with Mint and Lemon

CAULIFLOWER CHEESE

1 medium cauliflower, trimmed
40 g (1½ oz) butter or margarine
45 ml (3 level tbsp) flour
300 ml (½ pint) milk
125 g (4 oz) Cheddar cheese, grated
salt and pepper

1. Cook the cauliflower in fast-boiling salted water until just tender, then drain and place in an ovenproof serving dish.
2. Meanwhile, melt the butter in a saucepan, stir in the flour and cook gently for 1 minute. Remove pan from the heat and gradually stir in the milk. Bring to the boil and continue to cook, stirring, until the sauce thickens, then add 75 g (3 oz) cheese and seasoning to taste.
3. Pour the sauce over the hot cauliflower, sprinkle with the remaining cheese and brown under a hot grill.
SERVES 4

CAULIFLOWER POLONAISE

1 medium cauliflower, trimmed and divided
*   into florets*
salt
1 egg, hard-boiled
50 g (2 oz) butter or margarine
50 g (2 oz) fresh breadcrumbs
chopped fresh parsley, to garnish

1. Cook the cauliflower in boiling salted water for 5-7 minutes, until tender but still crisp.

Drain well, then place in a shallow serving dish and keep hot.
2. Sieve the egg yolk, chop the egg white and reserve.
3. Melt the butter in a frying pan, stir in the breadcrumbs and cook until the breadcrumbs are golden brown.
4. Spoon the golden crumbs over the cauliflower, then sprinkle the egg yolk, egg white and parsley in neat rows over the cauliflower.
SERVES 4

CELERIAC AND ONION BAKE

*900 g (2 lb) celeriac, peeled and cut into 5 mm
  (¼ inch) slices*
1 large onion, skinned and thinly sliced
salt and pepper
50 g (2 oz) butter or margarine
150 ml (¼ pint) milk

1. Layer the celeriac and onion slices in a greased ovenproof dish. Sprinkle each layer with seasoning and dot with butter.
2. Pour over the milk and cook, uncovered, in the oven at 190°C (375°F) mark 5 for about 1¼ hours, until the celeriac is soft and golden brown on top.
SERVES 4

BRAISED CELERY WITH WALNUTS

1 large head of celery, trimmed and washed
50 g (2 oz) butter or margarine
1 medium onion, skinned and chopped
150 ml (¼ pint) chicken stock
50 g (2 oz) walnuts, roughly chopped
chopped fresh parsley, to garnish

1. Cut the celery sticks into 2.5 cm (1 inch) lengths.
2. Melt the butter in a saucepan, add the onion and celery and cook for 5-10 minutes, until soft but not coloured. Add the stock, cover and simmer gently for 20 minutes, until the celery is tender and the stock absorbed.
3. Stir in the walnuts and heat through. Turn into a warmed serving dish and sprinkle with parsley to serve.
SERVES 4

BRAISED CHICORY

4 chicory heads, trimmed and washed
25 g (1 oz) butter or margarine
1.25 ml (¼ level tsp) freshly grated nutmeg
juice of ½ a lemon
150 ml (¼ pint) chicken stock
10 ml (2 level tsp) cornflour
salt and pepper
30 ml (2 tbsp) single cream
chopped fresh parsley, to garnish

1. Blanch the chicory in boiling water for 1 minute. Drain, refresh in cold water and drain again. Place the chicory heads in a single layer

in a greased ovenproof dish and dot with the butter.
2. Stir the nutmeg and lemon juice into the stock and pour over the chicory. Cover and cook in the oven at 170°C (325°F) mark 3 for 1-1¼ hours, until the chicory is tender.
3. Blend the cornflour with 30 ml (2 tbsp) water to a smooth paste. Drain the juice from the dish into a small pan, add the cornflour mixture and the seasoning. Bring to the boil, stirring, and cook for 1 minute. Add the cream.
4. Arrange the chicory in a warmed serving dish, pour over the sauce and sprinkle with parsley.
SERVES 4

STIR-FRIED CHINESE LEAVES

1 head Chinese leaves, coarsely shredded
450 g (1 lb) firm tomatoes, skinned
30 ml (2 tbsp) sunflower oil
salt and pepper

1. Wash the Chinese leaves in cold water and drain well, patting dry with absorbent kitchen paper.
2. Quarter the tomatoes, or if large, cut into eighths. Using a teaspoon, scoop out the seeds

and discard.
3. Heat the oil in a wok or large deep frying pan, stir in the Chinese leaves and continue stir-frying for 3-4 minutes, until the leaves are transparent but still crisp.
4. Stir in the tomatoes and season well with salt and pepper. Stir again.
5. Using a large spoon, arrange in a warmed serving dish.
SERVES 6

CREAMY COURGETTES AND ALMONDS

450-700 g (1-1½ lb) courgettes, trimmed and cut into
    1 cm (½ inch) slices
45 ml (3 level tbsp) seasoned flour
25 g (1 oz) butter or margarine
30 ml (2 tbsp) vegetable oil
50 g (2 oz) blanched almonds
150 ml (5 fl oz) soured cream
salt and pepper
paprika, to garnish

1. Coat the courgettes in the seasoned flour.
2. Heat the butter and oil in a frying pan, add
the courgette slices, a few at a time, and fry until
golden brown on both sides. Drain on
absorbent kitchen paper and keep warm.
3. Add the almonds to the pan and fry gently
until golden brown. Stir in the cream and
seasoning and heat gently, stirring.
4. Spoon the courgettes into a warmed serving
dish, pour over the cream and almonds and
sprinkle with paprika.
SERVES 4

Creamy Courgettes and Almonds

SAUTÉED CUCUMBER WITH HERBS

1 cucumber
salt
50 g (2 oz) butter or margarine
2 shallots or 1 small onion, skinned and finely chopped
15 ml (1 tbsp) fresh chopped rosemary or 5 ml
    (1 level tsp) dried
2.5 ml (½ tsp) sugar
pepper
60 ml (4 tbsp) soured cream
fresh rosemary sprigs, to garnish

1. Using a sharp fork, run the prongs down the
length of the cucumber to score the skin.
2. Using a sharp knife, cut the cucumber into
5 cm (2 inch) lengths, then cut each piece
lengthways into quarters.
3. Remove seeds from cucumber, then put in a
colander and sprinkle with the salt. Cover with a
plate and leave to drain for 30 minutes, pressing
the plate down occasionally to press out the
liquid from the cucumber. Rinse and pat dry
with absorbent kitchen paper.
4. Melt the butter in a large, heavy-based frying

Sautéed Cucumber with Herbs

pan. Add the shallots and fry gently for 5 minutes, until they are soft and lightly coloured.
5. Add the cucumber pieces to the pan, together
with the rosemary, sugar and pepper to taste.
Cook for 5 minutes only, stirring frequently.
6. Remove the pan from the heat and stir in the
soured cream. Garnish with rosemary to serve.
SERVES 6

BRAISED FENNEL

25 g (1 oz) butter or margarine
1 medium onion, skinned and chopped
2 large carrots, peeled and chopped
2 celery sticks, trimmed and chopped
4 small fennel heads, trimmed
450 ml (¾ pint) vegetable or chicken stock
salt and pepper
bouquet garni

1. Melt the butter in a saucepan, add the onion, carrots and celery and sauté gently for 5 minutes. Remove the vegetables with a slotted spoon and place in a shallow ovenproof dish. Cut each fennel in half and place, cut side down, on the vegetables.
2. Pour over the stock and add seasoning and the bouquet garni. Cover and cook in the oven at 180°C (350°F) mark 4 for about 1 hour, until the fennel is tender.
3. Transfer the fennel to a warmed serving dish. Remove the bouquet garni and sieve the remaining vegetables or purée in a blender or food processor until smooth. Pour the sauce over the fennel before serving.
SERVES 4

SCALLOPED KOHLRABI

700 g (1½ lb) kohlrabi, washed, peeled and cut
    into 5 mm (¼ inch) slices
1 large onion, skinned and chopped
salt and pepper
50 g (2 oz) butter or margarine
150 ml (¼ pint) milk

1. Arrange the kohlrabi in layers with the onion in a greased ovenproof dish. Sprinkle each layer with seasoning and dot with butter.
2. Pour over the milk, cover, and cook in the oven at 190°C (375°F) mark 5 for 1 hour. Remove the lid and continue cooking for 15 minutes, until the top is golden brown.
SERVES 4

LEEKS AU GRATIN

4 medium leeks, trimmed and halved lengthwise
salt and pepper
25 g (1 oz) butter or margarine
45 ml (3 level tbsp) flour
300 ml (½ pint) milk
2.5 ml (½ level tsp) mustard powder
125 g (4 oz) Cheddar cheese, grated
50 g (2 oz) fresh breadcrumbs

1. Wash the leeks thoroughly under running cold water. Steam or cook in boiling salted water for 10-15 minutes and drain thoroughly.
2. Melt the butter in a saucepan, stir in the flour and cook gently for 1 minute, stirring. Remove the pan from the heat and gradually stir in the milk. Bring to the boil slowly and continue to cook, stirring, until the sauce thickens. Stir in the seasoning, mustard and half the cheese.
3. Arrange the leeks in a greased shallow flameproof serving dish and pour over the cheese sauce.
4. Mix together the remaining cheese and breadcrumbs and spoon over the sauce. Brown under a hot grill or in the oven.

Leeks au Gratin
SERVES 2 FOR SUPPER OR 4 AS AN ACCOMPANIMENT

STIR-FRIED MANGETOUT

30 ml (2 tbsp) vegetable oil
1 small onion, skinned and chopped
50 g (2 oz) button mushrooms, wiped and chopped
450 g (1 lb) mangetout, trimmed
125 g (4 oz) bean sprouts, washed
15 ml (1 tbsp) soy sauce
salt and pepper

1. Heat the oil in a wok, add the onion and cook over a high heat, stirring for 2-3 minutes.
2. Add the mushrooms and cook until lightly browned, then add the mangetout and cook for 2-3 minutes.
3. Stir in the bean sprouts and cook for 1 minute, then add 30 ml (2 tbsp) water, the soy sauce and seasoning. Continue cooking for 2 minutes. Serve.
SERVES 4

SPICED MARROW

1 marrow, about 900 g (2 lb)
15 ml (1 tbsp) vegetable oil
25 g (1 oz) butter or margarine
1 large onion, skinned and chopped
1 garlic clove, skinned and crushed
15 ml (1 level tbsp) paprika
15 ml (1 level tbsp) flour
150 ml (¼ pint) vegetable stock
15 ml (1 level tbsp) tomato purée
salt and pepper
4 large tomatoes, skinned and chopped

1. Peel the marrow thinly. Cut into 7.5 cm (3 inch) pieces and scoop out the seeds, then cube.
2. Heat the oil and butter in a large saucepan, add the onion and garlic and cook for 5 minutes. Stir in paprika and flour and cook for 1 minute, stirring. Remove pan from heat and gradually stir in the stock. Bring to the boil slowly and continue to cook, stirring, until thickened.
3. Stir in the tomato purée, seasoning and tomatoes and simmer, uncovered, for 15 minutes, until thick. Stir in the marrow and cook for a further 10-15 minutes.
SERVES 4

CREAMED MUSHROOMS

25 g (1 oz) butter or margarine
450 g (1 lb) button mushrooms, wiped and sliced
20 ml (4 level tsp) cornflour
150 ml (¼ pint) milk
60 ml (4 tbsp) single cream
salt and pepper
4 large slices of bread
butter or margarine for spreading

1. Melt the butter in a saucepan, add the mushrooms and sauté gently for 5 minutes.
2. Blend the cornflour to a smooth paste with a little of the milk. Stir into the remaining milk, then add to the pan. Bring to the boil, stirring, and cook for 1-2 minutes, until the sauce thickens.
3. Mix in the cream and seasoning, and reheat without boiling. Toast the bread and spread with butter. Pile the creamed mixture on top.
SERVES 4

CURRIED OKRA

15 ml (1 tbsp) vegetable oil
25 g (1 oz) butter or margarine
salt and pepper
5 ml (1 level tsp) ground cumin
5 ml (1 level tsp) ground turmeric
5 ml (1 level tsp) ground coriander
450 g (1 lb) okra, trimmed and sliced
150 ml (5 fl oz) natural yogurt
5 ml (1 level tsp) tomato purée

1. Heat the oil and butter in a large saucepan, stir in the salt and all the spices and cook for 1-2 minutes, stirring. Add the okra, cover and cook for about 10 minutes, until just tender.
2. Stir in the yogurt, tomato purée and pepper and reheat for 2-3 minutes, stirring occasionally.
SERVES 4

JACKET BAKED ONIONS

4 large even-sized onions
25 g (1 oz) butter or margarine
50 g (2 oz) Cheddar cheese, grated
15 ml (1 tbsp) chopped fresh parsley
salt and pepper

1. Wash the onions well and trim off the bases. Place in a baking tin and cook in the oven at 180°C (350°F) mark 4 for 1-1½ hours, until tender.
2. Remove from the oven, cut a cross in the top of each onion, scoop out the centre and chop finely. Mix the chopped onions with the butter, cheese, parsley and seasoning, then spoon the mixture back into the onions. Return to the oven for 10-15 minutes to reheat.
SERVES 4

GLAZED ONIONS

700 g (1½ lb) shallots, skinned
75 g (3 oz) butter or margarine
15 ml (1 level tbsp) sugar
salt and pepper
chopped fresh parsley, to garnish

1. Put the shallots in a saucepan and cover with cold water. Bring to the boil and cook for 10 minutes. Drain the shallots well.
2. Melt the butter in a frying pan, add the sugar, seasoning and shallots. Cover and cook for about 15 minutes, until the shallots are tender and well glazed, stirring occasionally to prevent the sugar from burning.
3. Turn into a warmed serving dish and sprinkle with parsley.
SERVES 4

PARSNIP BAKE

700 g (1½ lb) parsnips, washed and thickly sliced
salt and pepper
75 g (3 oz) butter or margarine
2 medium onions, skinned and sliced
3 eggs
45 ml (3 tbsp) single cream
8 large thin-cut slices brown bread
butter or margarine for spreading
vegetable extract for spreading

1. Cook the parsnips in boiling salted water for 15-20 minutes, until tender. Drain and peel.
2. Melt 50 g (2 oz) butter in a saucepan, add the onion slices and fry until lightly browned. Reserve a few slices for garnishing.
3. Purée the parsnips, onions, eggs, cream and remaining butter in a blender or food processor. Season well.
4. Cut crusts off bread, then roll thinly, using a rolling pin. Butter and spread sparsely with vegetable extract. Cut each into two triangles.
5. Butter four 300 ml (½ pint) ovenproof dishes. Line each dish with four bread triangles. Spoon in the parsnip mixture and top with reserved onion slices. Bake in the oven at 200°C (400°F) mark 6 for 30-35 minutes, until set and golden.
SERVES 4

PETITS POIS À LA FRANÇAISE

1 firm-hearted lettuce
50 g (2 oz) butter or margarine
900 g (2 lb) young peas, shelled
12 spring onions, trimmed and sliced
5 ml (1 level tsp) sugar
salt and pepper
150 ml (¼ pint) chicken or vegetable stock

1. Remove the outer leaves of the lettuce and cut the heart into quarters.
2. Melt the butter in a large saucepan, add the peas, spring onions, lettuce, sugar, seasoning and stock. Bring to the boil, cover and simmer gently for 15-20 minutes.
SERVES 4

RATATOUILLE

450 g (1 lb) aubergines, cut into thin slices
salt and pepper
120 ml (8 tbsp) olive oil
1 garlic clove, skinned and crushed
450 g (1 lb) onions, skinned and chopped
450 g (1 lb) tomatoes, skinned, seeded and chopped, or
*   one 397 g (14 oz) can tomatoes, drained*
30 ml (2 level tbsp) tomato purée
450 g (1 lb) courgettes, cut into thin slices
3 medium red or green peppers, seeded and
*   cut into rings*
bouquet garni

1. Sprinkle the aubergines with salt and leave
for 30 minutes to extract the bitter juices. Rinse
under cold running water and pat dry with
absorbent kitchen paper.
2. Heat the oil and garlic in a large saucepan.
Add the onions and cook gently for about
10 minutes, until soft and golden.
3. Add the tomatoes and tomato purée and
cook for a few more minutes, then add the
aubergines, courgettes, peppers, bouquet garni
and salt and pepper. Cover and simmer gently
for 30 minutes. The vegetables should be soft

Ratatouille

and well mixed, but retain their shape and most
of the cooking liquid should have evaporated.
To reduce the liquid further if necessary, remove
the lid and cook gently for 5-10 minutes. Check
the seasoning and serve hot or cold.
SERVES 6

SCALLOPED POTATOES

700 g (1½ lb) potatoes, peeled and finely sliced
salt and pepper
45 ml (3 level tbsp) flour
25 g (1 oz) butter or margarine
150 ml (¼ pint) milk

1. Arrange the potatoes in layers in a greased
ovenproof dish. Season each layer, dredge with
flour and dot with butter.
2. Repeat the layers until all the slices are used,
then pour over the milk. Cook in the oven at
190°C (375°F) mark 5 for 1¼ hours, or until the
potatoes are cooked and the top golden brown.
SERVES 4

GRATIN DAUPHINOIS

900 g (2 lb) waxy potatoes, eg Ulster Sceptre, La Ratte,
*   Belle de Fontenay or Pentland Javelin, peeled and*
*   cut into very thin slices*
1.1 litres (2 pints) milk
600 ml (1 pint) double cream
salt and pepper
1 garlic clove, skinned and crushed
pinch of freshly grated nutmeg
125 g (4 oz) Gruyère cheese, grated

1. Put the potatoes and milk in a large saucepan,
bring to the boil and simmer for 15-20 minutes;
drain, reserving milk. Arrange in a single layer
in a greased 1.1 litre (2 pint) ovenproof dish.
2. Bring the cream just to the boil, add the
seasoning, garlic and nutmeg, then pour over
the potatoes. If the potatoes are not completely
covered, add some of the milk.
3. Sprinkle with cheese, cover and cook in the
oven at 180°C (350°F) mark 4 for about
1-1¼ hours or until the potatoes are tender.
SERVES 4-6

GREEK-STYLE NEW POTATOES

900 g (2 lb) small new potatoes, scrubbed
225 ml (8 fl oz) vegetable oil
100 ml (4 fl oz) white or red wine
60 ml (4 tbsp) chopped fresh coriander, mint or parsley
salt and pepper

1. With a meat mallet, hit each potato once or twice so that the flesh breaks slightly. Heat the oil in a sauté pan or saucepan, until a stale bread cube turns golden in 2-3 seconds.
2. Add the potatoes to the hot oil and fry over moderate heat, turning frequently, until golden brown on all sides.
3. Pour off the oil, then pour the wine over the potatoes. Add half of the chopped coriander and season liberally. Shake the pan, then cover and simmer for about 15 minutes, until the potatoes are tender.
4. Turn the potatoes into a warmed serving dish and sprinkle with the remaining coriander. Serve immediately, as an accompaniment to roast or grilled lamb; or barbecued meat, especially lamb.
SERVES 4

Greek-style New Potatoes

NEW POTATOES WITH TARRAGON CREAM

15 g (½ oz) butter or margarine
4 spring onions, washed, trimmed and chopped
150 ml (5 fl oz) soured cream
salt and pepper
3 sprigs of fresh tarragon
700 g (1½ lb) cooked new potatoes, drained and
   kept hot

1. Melt the butter in a saucepan, add the onions and cook for 5 minutes, until soft. Stir in the cream, seasoning, and two tarragon sprigs and heat without boiling.
2. Add the cooked potatoes to the creamy onion and tarragon mixture in the pan. Reheat gently, do not boil.
3. Turn the potatoes and the sauce into a warm serving dish and serve garnished with the remaining tarragon sprig.
SERVES 4

New Potatoes with Tarragon Cream

CHÂTEAU POTATOES

50 g (2 oz) butter or margarine
700 g (1½ lb) new potatoes, scraped
salt and pepper
chopped fresh parsley, to garnish

1. Melt the butter in a frying pan and add the potatoes. Cover and cook gently, shaking the pan occasionally, for 15-20 minutes, until golden brown.
2. If the new potatoes are fairly large, pour the butter and potatoes into an ovenproof dish, cover and cook in the oven at 190°C (375°F) mark 5 for about 15 minutes, until cooked.
3. Season well and garnish with parsley.
SERVES 4

HASSELBACK POTATOES

8 potatoes, weighing about 75 g (3 oz) each
vegetable oil for brushing
salt and pepper

1. Cut the potatoes across their width at 5 mm (¼ inch) intervals three-quarters of the way through.
2. Place in a layer in an oiled baking tin. Brush with oil and season. Roast, uncovered, in the oven at 220°C (425°F) mark 7 for 45 minutes.
SERVES 4

SWISS ROSTI

350 g (12 oz) potatoes
salt and pepper
75 g (3 oz) butter or margarine
1 small onion, skinned and grated

1. Scrub the potatoes and cook in boiling salted water for 7 minutes. Drain well, remove the skins and grate the potatoes into a bowl.
2. Melt 25 g (1 oz) butter in a pan, add the onion and cook for 5 minutes, until soft. Stir into the grated potato and add the seasoning.
3. Melt the remaining butter in a 20 cm (8 inch) frying pan, add the potato mixture and form into a cake the size of the pan. Fry for 5-7 minutes, until golden brown.
4. Using a wide spatula, turn and brown the second side. Serve cut into wedges.
SERVES 2

DUCHESSE POTATOES

700 g (1½ lb) potatoes, peeled and cut into pieces
salt and pepper
50 g (2 oz) butter or margarine
1 egg, beaten
freshly grated nutmeg

1. Cook the potatoes in boiling salted water for 15-20 minutes, until tender, then drain well.
2. Sieve or mash the potatoes, then beat in the butter, egg, seasoning and nutmeg. Cool.
3. Spoon into a piping bag fitted with a large rosette nozzle and pipe into pyramids on a greased baking sheet. Cook in the oven at 200°C (400°F) mark 6 for about 25 minutes, until set and golden brown.
SERVES 4

CREAMED SPINACH

900 g (2 lb) spinach, washed, trimmed and chopped
3-4 spring onions, trimmed and finely chopped
25 g (1 oz) butter or margarine
150 ml (5 fl oz) double cream
salt and pepper
freshly grated nutmeg

1. Place the spinach in a pan with the spring onions and butter and cook for about 10 minutes, stirring occasionally, until tender. Drain well.
2. Sieve or chop the spinach and return to the pan with the cream, seasoning and nutmeg. Reheat gently without boiling.
SERVES 4

SWEDE AND BACON BAKE

25 g (1 oz) butter or margarine
1 large onion, skinned and chopped
1 garlic clove, skinned and crushed
6 smoked streaky bacon rashers, rinded and chopped
125 g (4 oz) mushrooms, wiped and sliced
45 ml (3 level tbsp) flour
300 ml (½ pint) vegetable or beef stock
salt and pepper
450 g (1 lb) swede, peeled and cut into 5 mm
    (¼ inch) slices

1. Melt the butter in a saucepan, add the onion, garlic and bacon and fry gently for 5 minutes. Add the mushrooms and continue cooking for 3-4 minutes.
2. Stir in the flour and cook for 1 minute. Remove the pan from the heat and gradually stir in the stock and seasoning. Bring to the boil slowly and continue to cook, stirring, until thickened.
3. Arrange the swede slices in layers with the bacon and mushroom sauce in a 1.1 litre (2 pint) ovenproof dish.
4. Cover and cook in the oven at 190°C (375°F) mark 5 for about 1 hour, until the swede slices are tender.
SERVES 4

SWEET POTATOES WITH ORANGE

900 g (2 lb) medium sweet potatoes, scrubbed
2 large oranges
15 ml (1 tbsp) black peppercorns
30 ml (2 tbsp) vegetable oil
25 g (1 oz) butter or margarine
2.5 ml (½ level tsp) ground cinnamon
30 ml (2 level tbsp) chopped fresh parsley

1. Cook the potatoes in boiling salted water for about 20 minutes, until almost tender.
2. Meanwhile, peel and segment one orange and squeeze the juice from the other. Crush the peppercorns using a pestle and mortar or the end of a rolling pin in a strong bowl.
3. Drain the potatoes and peel off their skins while still hot. Cut the potatoes into large chunks.
4. Heat the oil and butter in a large frying pan and when it is frothing, tip in all the potatoes. Fry, turning occasionally, until the potatoes are golden brown and beginning to flake.
5. Remove the pan from the heat and stir in the cinnamon, peppercorns, parsley, orange juice and segments and salt. Mix well, then transfer to a warmed serving dish and serve immediately.
SERVES 4

TURNIPS IN MUSTARD SAUCE

1 kg (2¼ lb) turnips, peeled and cut into pieces
450 ml (¾ pint) chicken stock
FOR THE MUSTARD SAUCE
25 g (1 oz) butter or margarine
45 ml (3 level tbsp) flour
300 ml (½ pint) milk
15 ml (1 level tbsp) mustard powder
10 ml (2 level tsp) sugar
15 ml (1 tbsp) vinegar
salt and pepper

1. Put the turnip pieces in a saucepan and add the stock. Cover, bring to the boil and cook for about 30 minutes, until tender.
2. Meanwhile, make the sauce: melt the butter in a pan, stir in the flour and cook gently for 1 minute, stirring. Remove pan from the heat and gradually stir in the milk. Bring to the boil slowly and continue to cook, stirring, until the sauce thickens.
3. Blend mustard and sugar with the vinegar, add to the sauce and reheat. Drain the turnips, add to the sauce, season and reheat gently.
SERVES 4-6

VEGETARIAN COOKING

Provided a wide range of foods is eaten, a vegetarian diet should be as nutritionally sound as any other diet. There are plenty of good vegetable sources of protein, including grains, beans and nuts; as well as eggs, cheese, milk and yogurt for non-vegans. In addition, there are a number of high protein products – such as quorn, TVP and tofu – which can be useful for vegetarians.

QUORN

Quorn is a relatively new chilled product; a myco-protein derived from a distant relative of the mushroom. It is very low in fat and calories yet high in fibre and protein. Although unsuitable for vegans, it provides a good source of complete protein for vegetarians. It has a bland flavour and is improved by marinating before cooking. It's also very quick to cook.

TOFU

Also known as soya bean curd, tofu is made from a paste of soya beans which has been pressed into blocks. It is an excellent source of vegetable protein and contains no fat. Although tofu is very bland, it readily absorbs other flavours and benefits from being marinated before cooking.

Silken tofu is soft and creamy and is useful for dressings, cheesecakes, sauces and dips. Firm tofu can be cut into chunks for frying, grilling, and inclusion in stir-fries, stews and curries, or it can be grated or chopped and used in burgers and roasts. Smoked tofu is also available.

T.V.P. (TEXTURED VEGETABLE PROTEIN)

Textured vegetable protein forms the bulk of most vegetarian burger and mince mixtures. It's made from soya flour which is extruded under pressure then cut into chunks or small pieces to resemble mince. Unlike tofu it has a slightly chewy, meat-like texture which makes it unappetising to some vegetarians.

GRAINS

Grains are the edible seeds of different grasses. They are high in vitamins and minerals and, though widely used in the form of flour, they can also be used whole, cracked or flaked to add interest and nutrients to a wide range of dishes. Also included in this section are buckwheat and couscous, which are not grains but are used in the same way. Store grains in airtight containers and use as fresh as possible.

BARLEY

One of the earliest grains to be cultivated, it is now used mainly in Scotch whiskies, malt drinks and malt extract. Pearl barley, which is the husked, polished grain, is used to thicken soups and stews and to make barley water.

BUCKWHEAT

Although cooked and eaten as a cereal grain, buckwheat is actually the fruit of a plant related to rhubarb. It is a triangular-shape, rather like a beech nut. It is widely used in Russia to make porridge known as *kasha*, and in Japan to make noodles called *soba*.

Buckwheat is often sold lightly roasted, which enhances the mild flavour. It can then be used without further preparation. It is also made into flour (see page 450).

BULGHUR, BURGUL OR BULGAR WHEAT

Bulghur is cooked wheat which is spread out to dry, then broken into pieces. It can be used in salads or stuffings.

CORN (MAIZE)

Corn grain has a tough outer layer which makes it difficult to cook whole. It is often ground to a meal or flour. Cornmeal may be yellow or white; Italian yellow cornmeal is called *polenta,* and *masa harina* is a specially processed fine cornmeal which is used for making Tortillas (see page 463). *Hominy* is whole dried corn without the yellow husk. *Grits* are coarsely ground dried corn and may be yellow or white depending on whether the outer husk has been removed. Cornflour is used as a thickening agent. It is lighter than wheat flour.

COUSCOUS

Couscous is made from durum wheat which is processed into tiny granules. It is soaked, then steamed and used to make the North African dish of the same name (see Spiced Vegetable Couscous, page 243). Pre-cooked couscous is also sold in packets; follow pack instructions.

CRACKED WHEAT

Cracked wheat is split from the whole grain with just the husk removed. Coarse and fine ground varieties are available.

MILLET

Millet is the third most important grain in the world after rice and wheat. There are many different varieties. The grains are small round and pale golden to yellow. Millet flakes are also available and can be used in porridge or muesli.

OATS

Oats are available as whole grains, rough cut (sometimes called groats), medium or fine oatmeal or as rolled or flaked oats. Grains are used for porridge; rolled oats for quick porridge; rough cut for thickening stews and making oatcakes; medium oatmeal for cakes (see Oatmeal Parkin, page 405) and for mixing with flours for scones; fine oatmeal for pancakes and coating grilled herrings.

RYE

The grains are seldom cooked on their own, but can be used with other grains in casseroles. Rye flour is used in bread making (see page 450). Rye flakes can be used in porridge or muesli.

WHEAT

This is the world's main grain crop. Its most important use is as flour (see page 450). It is also processed into various types of cereal (see above and below).

WHOLEWHEAT

Wholewheat grains are grains with just the outer husk removed. They look like brown grains of rice with a split down the middle. They can be added to casseroles or breakfast cereals.

WHEATGERM

Wheatgerm is the heart of the grain which is removed when milling white flour. It is high in vitamins and is sold plain or toasted. It can be added to cooked dishes or sprinkled over the top of breakfast cereals.

PULSES

Pulse is the generic name given to dried beans, peas and lentils and there are many varieties in different shapes, sizes and colours. Pulses are very versatile ingredients and can be used in savoury dishes of all kinds. Nutritionally they are an excellent food; they contain plenty of dietary fibre, protein, B group vitamins, iron and potassium, but virtually no fat. When eaten with a cereal such as bread, rice or pasta, they form a complete protein.

Pulses are sold in packets or loose and should be bought in fairly small quantities from a shop with a good turnover. Use them up within 6-9 months, or they will start to shrivel and become tough. Before cooking, wash them thoroughly and pick out any pieces of dirt or damaged beans. All pulses, except lentils, need to be soaked, preferably overnight, before cooking. If you haven't enough time for this, cover the pulses with water, bring to the boil, simmer for 2 minutes, then leave to soak for 2-3 hours.

Cooking times for pulses vary enormously, depending largely on the length of time the beans have been stored. The chart overleaf provides a rough guide only. When cooking, allow double the volume of water to beans, bring to the boil and boil vigorously for 10 minutes. This initial boiling is essential to render any toxins which may be present harmless. Lower the heat and simmer gently until tender. Do not add salt until the end of the cooking time or it will make the pulses tough. After cooking, pulses are approximately double their original dried weight. If preferred, pulses can be cooked in a pressure cooker to save time. Cook at HIGH (15 lb) pressure allowing approximately one third of the cooking time suggested overleaf.

CANNED BEANS

Although canned beans often have sugar and salt added, they're a good quick alternative to cooking your own. Rinse them in a sieve under cold running water before use. As they tend to be quite soft, they should be added to 'chilli', casseroles, stews and curries towards the end of the cooking time or they will disintegrate.

A 425 g (14 oz) can of beans, drained, is equivalent to 225 g (8 oz) cooked beans, or 125 g (4 oz) dried (uncooked) beans.

TYPES OF PULSES

There are numerous varieties of pulses to choose from. The following are the most common.

ADUKI (ADZUKI) BEANS

Small, reddish-brown round shiny beans with a delicious sweet flavour when cooked. They also form the basis of Chinese red bean paste.

BLACK BEANS

Oval beans with a shiny black casing and white flesh. They are used mainly in soups, curries and the Chinese black bean sauce, but can be interchanged with red kidney beans.

BLACK-EYED BEANS

Small, cream-coloured beans with a black spot. They have an earthy taste that goes well with pork and hearty casseroles.

BORLOTTI BEANS

Oval, pinkish beige speckled beans with a bitter-sweet flavour. Ideal for soups, stews and salads.

BUTTER (LIMA) BEANS

Large, oval, flat, creamy coloured beans, which should be cooked gently so they don't break up.

CANNELINI BEANS

These creamy-white beans are very popular in Italian cooking. They are excellent in soups, salads and stews.

CHICK PEAS (GARBANZOS)

These round, beige coloured pulses have a nutty flavour. They are virtually impossible to over-cook. Chick peas are an essential ingredient in Hummus (see page 46).

DRIED PEAS

These may be whole or split, green or yellow. Dried peas cook quickly and are good in soups; they can also be puréed.

FLAGEOLET BEANS

These kidney-shaped beans are small and oval. They may be white or pale green. Equally good served hot or cold.

HARICOT BEANS

Small, white oval beans which come in a number of varieties, the best known being the navy bean.

LENTILS

Small pulses which may be red, yellow, brown or green. The red and yellow lentils cook quickly to a purée and are good in soups and sauces. Brown lentils also cook quickly and keep their shape for use in casseroles or salads; the larger brownish-green continental lentils can be served in the same way. The tiny green *Puy* lentils from France are renowned for their excellent flavour and texture but they are not widely available.

Lentils cooked in India are known collectively as *dals*. There are many different types available; a large selection can be found in Indian shops, and health food stores stock a good range.

Lentils do not need soaking.

MUNG BEANS

These are small, round green beans which are used in Indian cookery or as seeds for sprouting bean sprouts. When cooked, they are sweet and creamy in texture. Mung beans are good in stuffings and salads.

PINTO BEANS

Beige speckled beans extensively used in Mexican cooking.

RED KIDNEY BEANS

Dark red beans with creamy-white flesh and a full, strong flavour. They are typically used in hot spicy stews and bean salads.

SOYA BEANS

Round brown beans which are the most useful of all pulses nutritionally. They contain first class protein and so do not need to be eaten with a cereal to release it. Soya beans are widely used in vegetarian cookery. They are used to make bean curd (tofu) and also for meat substitutes (soya protein or textured vegetable protein). Soya beans with a yellow tinge have a mild flavour; the blacker ones taste sweet. Black soya beans are fermented to make Chinese salted black beans.

COOKING TIMES FOR PULSES

Type	Cooking Time (approximate)
Aduki beans	30 minutes-1 hour
Black beans	1½ hours
Black-eye beans	1½ hours
Butter beans	1½ hours
Cannellini beans	1 hour
Chick peas	1½-2 hours
Flageolet beans	1 hour
Haricot beans	1-1½ hours
Lentils, whole	1 hour
Lentils, split	20-30 minutes
Mung beans	40 minutes
Red kidney beans	1-1½ hours
Soya beans	3-4 hours
Split peas	45 minutes-1 hour

VEGETABLE COUSCOUS

125 g (4 oz) spring onions
15 ml (1 tbsp) oil
225 g (8 oz) parsnips or carrots, peeled and chopped
350 g (12 oz) potato, preferably sweet potato, peeled
    and chopped
225 g (8 oz) frozen broad beans or French beans
50 g (2 oz) creamed coconut
15 ml (1 level tbsp) tomato purée
400 g (14 oz) can spiced lentil dahl
15 ml (1 tbsp) white wine vinegar
salt and pepper
225 g (8 oz) couscous (pre-cooked)

1. Roughly chop the spring onions, reserving the tops for garnish.
2. Heat the oil in a medium saucepan and sauté the spring onions, parsnips or carrots, and potato for 1 minute. Add all the remaining ingredients, except the couscous.
3. Stir in 150 ml (¼ pint) water. Bring to the boil, cover and simmer for about 20 minutes or until the vegetables are tender.
4. Meanwhile, cook the couscous in plenty of boiling salted water for 3-5 minutes or until tender. Drain well.
5. Serve the couscous topped with the spiced vegetables. Garnish with the spring onion tops.
SERVES 4

ABOVE: Vegetable Couscous. BELOW: Walnut Croquettes

WALNUT CROQUETTES

40 g (1½ oz) butter or margarine
1 small onion, skinned and finely chopped
5 ml (1 level tsp) mild curry powder
225 g (8 oz) walnut pieces, finely chopped
75 g (3 oz) Cheddar cheese, coarsely grated
175 g (6 oz) fresh brown breadcrumbs
5 ml (1 level tsp) chopped fresh herbs, eg thyme, sage or
    chives, or pinch of dried mixed herbs
1 egg
about 15 ml (1 tbsp) milk
salt and pepper
oil for shallow-frying
watercress sprigs, to garnish
Tomato Sauce (see page 207) or Ratatouille
    (see page 236) to serve

1. Melt the butter in a medium saucepan and sauté the onion for 2-3 minutes until softened. Add the curry powder and cook, stirring, for a further minute. Remove from the heat.
2. Stir in the nuts, cheese, breadcrumbs, herbs and egg, with enough milk to bind to a firm mixture. Season. Shape into croquettes, about 5 cm (2 inches) long, 2.5 cm (1 inch) in diameter.
3. Heat the oil in a sauté pan and shallow-fry the croquettes in batches for 3-4 minutes until golden and hot through. Drain on absorbent kitchen paper.
4. Serve immediately, garnished with watercress and accompanied by tomato sauce or ratatouille.
SERVES 4

VEGETARIAN ROAST

175 g (6 oz) long-grain brown rice
15 g (½ oz) butter
1 medium onion, skinned and chopped
1 garlic clove, skinned and crushed
2 carrots, peeled and grated
125 g (4 oz) button mushrooms, wiped and finely
    chopped
125 g (4 oz) fresh wholemeal breadcrumbs
125 g (4 oz) nuts, finely chopped
125 g (4 oz) Cheddar cheese, grated
2 eggs
salt and pepper
Tomato Sauce (see page 207) or chutney, to serve

1. Cook the rice in boiling salted water for
30-35 minutes or until tender. Drain well.
2. Meanwhile, heat the butter in a medium
frying pan and fry the onion, garlic, carrots and
mushrooms, stirring frequently, until softened.
Stir in the breadcrumbs, nuts, cooked rice,
cheese and eggs. Season to taste with salt and
pepper and mix thoroughly together.
3. Pack the mixture into a greased 1.7 litre
(3 pint) loaf tin and bake in the oven at 180°C
(350°F) mark 4 for 1-1¼ hours or until firm to
the touch and brown on top. Serve sliced, hot or
cold, with tomato sauce or chutney.
SERVES 4–6

CARROT AND BEAN SOUFFLÉS

450 g (1 lb) carrots, peeled and thinly sliced
salt and pepper
30 ml (2 tbsp) oil
15 ml (1 level tbsp) wholemeal flour
425 g (15 oz) can butter beans, drained
75 g (3 oz) Gruyère cheese
3 eggs, separated
30 ml (2 level tbsp) chopped fresh coriander
10 ml (2 level tsp) medium oatmeal or fresh brown
    breadcrumbs

1. Cook the carrots in boiling salted water for
10-12 minutes or until very soft. Drain well,
reserving 150 ml (¼ pint) cooking liquor.
2. Heat the oil in a saucepan. Add the flour and
cook, stirring, for 1 minute. Add the reserved
liquor and bring to the boil, stirring. Simmer for
2 minutes.
3. Place the carrots, sauce, butter beans, grated
cheese and egg yolks in a food processor. Blend
until smooth, then season. Turn into a bowl.
4. Whisk the egg whites until stiff, then fold into
the carrot mixture with the coriander.
5. Spoon into four well greased individual
soufflé dishes. Sprinkle with the oatmeal or
breadcrumbs.
6. Bake at 190°C (375°F) mark 5 for
20-25 minutes or until golden and just firm
to the touch. Serve with a watercress and
cucumber salad.
SERVES 4

ROASTED PEPPERS WITH LENTILS

125 g (4 oz) split red lentils
salt and pepper
2 green peppers, about 175 g (6 oz) each, halved and
    seeded
25 g (1 oz) butter or margarine
1 medium onion, skinned and finely chopped
75 g (3 oz) celery, trimmed and finely chopped
75 g (3 oz) soft fresh goat's cheese or low-fat soft cheese
1 egg
about 8 pitted black olives, stoned and roughly chopped
fresh basil, to garnish

1. Cook the lentils in boiling salted water for
12-15 minutes until just tender. Drain.
2. Meanwhile, grill the peppers for 10-12 minutes, turning occasionally, until the skin is
browned and the flesh softened.
3. Melt the butter in a saucepan and sauté the
onion and celery for 2-3 minutes. Stir in the
lentils. Off the heat, beat in the cheese, egg,
olives and seasoning. Spoon the filling evenly
into the pepper halves.
4. Grill the peppers for 2-3 minutes until
golden. Garnish with fresh basil and serve with a
tomato and onion salad.
SERVES 2

HOT SPICED CHICK PEAS

15 ml (1 tbsp) oil
1 medium onion, skinned and roughly chopped
10 ml (2 level tsp) ground turmeric
15 ml (1 level tbsp) cumin seeds
two 400 g (14 oz) cans cooked chick peas, drained
450 g (1 lb) tomatoes, skinned and roughly chopped
15 ml (1 tbsp) lemon juice
60 ml (4 level tbsp) chopped fresh coriander
salt and pepper
fresh coriander leaves, to garnish

1. Heat the oil in a medium saucepan and sauté the onion until golden brown.
2. Add the turmeric and cumin seeds. Cook, stirring, for 1-2 minutes, before adding all the remaining ingredients.
3. Sauté for 1-2 minutes, stirring frequently, then adjust the seasoning. Serve garnished with fresh coriander and accompanied by crusty wholemeal bread.
SERVES 4

LEFT: *Hot Spiced Chick Peas.*   RIGHT: *Roasted Peppers with Lentils.*   ABOVE: *Carrot and Bean Soufflés*

RED KIDNEY BEAN HOT-POT

125 g (4 oz) dried red kidney beans, soaked overnight
25 g (1 oz) butter
1 medium onion, skinned and roughly chopped
125 g (4 oz) celery, trimmed and sliced
125 g (4 oz) carrots, peeled and sliced
15 ml (1 level tbsp) plain flour
300 ml (½ pint) vegetable stock
salt and pepper
125 g (4 oz) runner beans, topped and tailed
125 g (4 oz) courgettes, sliced
25 g (1 oz) fresh wholemeal breadcrumbs
75 g (3 oz) Cheddar cheese, grated

1. Drain the kidney beans and rinse well under running cold water. Put in a large saucepan, cover with plenty of fresh cold water and slowly bring to the boil.
2. Skim the surface with a slotted spoon, then boil rapidly for 10 minutes. Half cover the pan and simmer for about 1½ hours, until tender.

3. Melt the butter in a large saucepan, add the onion and gently fry for about 5 minutes, until softened. Add the celery and carrots, cover and gently cook for 5 minutes.
4. Add the flour and gently cook, stirring, for 1-2 minutes. Remove from the heat and gradually blend in the stock. Bring to the boil, stirring constantly, then simmer for 5 minutes. Season to taste.
5. Add the runner beans and simmer for a further 5 minutes, then add the courgettes. Cook for a further 5-10 minutes, until the vegetables are tender but still with a bite.
6. Drain the kidney beans, add to the vegetables and heat through for about 5 minutes. Adjust seasoning, then turn into a deep flameproof dish.
7. Mix the breadcrumbs and cheese together. Sprinkle on top of the bean mixture, then brown under a hot grill until crisp and crusty. Serve hot, with wholemeal bread and a green salad.
SERVES 4

VEGETARIAN MEDLEY

25 g (1 oz) butter
2 carrots, peeled and sliced
1 large onion, skinned and chopped
1 green pepper, seeded and sliced
2 tomatoes, skinned and chopped
1 large cooking apple, peeled and chopped
1 garlic clove, skinned and crushed
15 ml (1 tbsp) chopped fresh sage or 5 ml (1 tsp) dried
125 g (4 oz) lentils, cooked
15 ml (1 level tbsp) raisins
30 ml (2 level tbsp) unsalted peanuts
salt and pepper
300 ml (10 fl oz) natural yogurt
25 g (1 oz) cream cheese

1. Melt the butter in a large frying pan and lightly fry the carrots, onion, green pepper, tomatoes, apple, garlic and sage for 15 minutes, until softened.
2. Add the lentils, raisins and peanuts. Season to taste.
3. Stir the yogurt into the cream cheese and mix well to blend. Stir into the vegetable mixture. Reheat gently for 5 minutes. Serve at once.
SERVES 4

STIR-FRIED MIXED VEGETABLES

4 large, fat carrots, peeled and trimmed
1 bunch of spring onions, trimmed
half a head of Chinese leaves, trimmed
30 ml (2 tbsp) vegetable oil
225 g (8 oz) French beans, trimmed
225 g (8 oz) mangetout, trimmed
50 g (2 oz) cashew nuts
salt and pepper

1. Using a potato peeler, pare each carrot into long thin, ribbons. Cut spring onions into long strips and the Chinese leaves into large chunks.
2. Heat the oil in a large wok, add the beans and fry for 3-4 minutes, stirring all the time. Add the Chinese leaves and carrots and stir-fry for a further 2 minutes, then add the mangetout and nuts; cook for 1 minute. Season to taste. Pile on to a hot serving dish and serve immediately.
SERVES 6

BROAD BEAN BAKE

700 g (1½ lb) fresh broad beans or 225 g (8 oz) frozen
2 medium carrots, peeled and cut into chunks
2 medium parsnips, peeled and cut into chunks
25 g (1 oz) butter
25 g (1 oz) plain wholemeal flour
300 ml (½ pint) milk
30 ml (2 tbsp) chopped fresh mixed herbs, eg savory, chives, parsley, thyme
5 ml (1 level tsp) mild mustard
salt and pepper
30 ml (2 level tbsp) porridge oats
50 g (2 oz) Double Gloucester cheese, grated
25 g (1 oz) chopped mixed nuts

1. Shell the fresh broad beans, if using, then cook in boiling salted water for 5 minutes.
2. Add the carrots and parsnips to the beans and continue to cook for 10-15 minutes or until the vegetables are tender. If using frozen beans, add for the last 5 minutes of cooking. Drain well.
3. Melt the butter in a small saucepan. Stir in the flour and cook for 2 minutes. Remove from the heat, gradually add the milk, then cook, stirring, until the sauce thickens, boils and is smooth. Simmer the sauce for 1-2 minutes.
4. Stir in the herbs, mustard and the vegetables. Add seasoning to taste. Simmer for 2-3 minutes, until heated through, then divide between 2-3 individual flameproof dishes.
5. Mix the oats, cheese and nuts together and sprinkle on top of the vegetable mixture. Brown for 2-3 minutes under a hot grill.
SERVES 2-3

WHOLEMEAL VEGETABLE AND HERB PIE

90 g (3½ oz) butter
3 carrots, peeled and sliced
40 g (1½ oz) plain white flour
300 ml (½ pint) milk
salt and pepper
1 small cauliflower, broken into florets
125 g (4 oz) broccoli
50 g (2 oz) pearl barley, cooked
30 ml (2 tbsp) chopped fresh parsley
125 g (4 oz) plain wholemeal flour
milk, to glaze

1. Melt 40 g (1½ oz) of the butter in a medium saucepan and lightly fry the carrots for 7 minutes. Stir in the white flour and cook for 1 minute. Gradually add the milk, then cook, stirring, continuously, until the sauce thickens, boils and is smooth. Simmer for 1-2 minutes. Season with salt and pepper to taste.
2. Blanch the cauliflower and broccoli in boiling salted water for 5 minutes. Drain.
3. Mix the sauce with the cauliflower, broccoli, pearl barley and parsley. Spoon into a 1.1 litre (2 pint) pie dish.
4. Put the wholemeal flour and salt in a bowl. Rub in the remaining 50 g (2 oz) butter until the mixture resembles fine breadcrumbs. Add 45 ml (3 tbsp) cold water to mix and form a dough.
5. Roll out the pastry on a lightly floured work surface to 5 cm (2 inch) wider than the top of the pie dish. Cut a 2. 5 cm (1 inch) wide strip from the outer edge and place on the dampened rim of the dish. Brush the strip with water. Cover with the pastry lid, press the edges lightly to seal. Trim off excess pastry. Knock the edges back to seal and crimp. Garnish with pastry leaves and brush with milk.
6. Bake in the oven at 200°C (400°F) mark 6 for 30 minutes, until golden.
SERVES 4

QUORN SATAY

450 g (1 lb) quorn, in large even-sized chunks
vegetable oil, for brushing
FOR THE MARINADE
2 garlic cloves, skinned and crushed
2.5 cm (1 inch) piece fresh root ginger, peeled and
*   grated*
45 ml (3 tbsp) soy sauce
10 ml (2 level tsp) brown sugar
FOR THE SAUCE
50 g (2 oz) creamed coconut, roughly chopped
75 ml (5 level tbsp) crunchy peanut butter
30 ml (2 tbsp) soy sauce
5 ml (1 level tsp) brown sugar
1 garlic clove, skinned and crushed
5 ml (1 level tsp) chilli powder, or to taste
5 ml (1 level tsp) chopped fresh lemon grass or
*   finely grated lemon rind*

1. Mix all the ingredients for the marinade in a large shallow dish with 45 ml (3 tbsp) water. Add the quorn and stir until evenly coated. Cover and leave to marinate in the refrigerator for 2-3 hours or overnight.
2. To make the sauce, put the coconut in a bowl, add 150 ml (¼ pint) boiling water and stir until dissolved. Add all the remaining ingredients and mix thoroughly. Cover and set aside.
3. Thread the quorn onto 16 bamboo skewers. Brush with a litttle vegetable oil then cook under a very hot grill, turning occasionally, for about 3-4 minutes or until lightly browned. Serve hot with the cold peanut sauce.
SERVES 4

BOSTON BEANS

275 g (10 oz) dried haricot or cannellini beans
15 ml (1 tbsp) vegetable oil
2 medium onions, skinned and chopped
5 ml (1 level tsp) mustard powder
15 ml (1 level tbsp) black treacle
150 ml (¼ pint) tomato juice
30 ml (2 level tbsp) tomato purée
10 ml (2 level tsp) dark soft brown sugar
300 ml (½ pint) vegetable or beef btock

1. Soak the beans overnight, then cook in boiling water for 25 minutes. Drain.
2. Heat the oil in a flameproof casserole, add the onions and fry until soft.
3. Remove from the heat and stir in the remaining ingredients.
4. Bring contents to the boil, cover and cook in the oven at 140°C (275°F) mark 1 for about 2½-3 hours, until the beans are tender and the sauce is syrup-like. Stir occasionally.
SERVES 4

SAVOURY NUT BURGERS

25 g (1 oz) butter
1 large onion, skinned and chopped
15 ml (1 tbsp) chopped fresh parsley
30 ml (2 level tbsp) plain wholemeal flour
150 ml (¼ pint) milk
225 g (8 oz) chopped mixed nuts
15 ml (1 tbsp) soy sauce
15 ml (1 level tbsp) tomato purée
175 g (6 oz) fresh wholemeal breadcrumbs
1 egg, beaten
pepper
Cheese Sauce (see page 199), to serve

1. Melt the butter in a medium saucepan and lightly fry the onion and parsley until soft. Stir in the flour and cook for 2 minutes.
2. Remove from the heat, gradually add the milk, then bring back to boil, stirring until the sauce thickens, boils and is smooth. Simmer for 1-2 minutes.
3. Add the nuts, soy sauce, tomato purée, breadcrumbs, egg and pepper to taste. Mix well.
4. Divide into 8 portions and shape into rounds. Cook under a preheated grill for 4 minutes each side, until golden and cooked through. Serve with cheese sauce and a tomato salad.
SERVES 4

Vegetable Curry

VEGETABLE CURRY

30 ml (2 tbsp) vegetable oil
10 ml (2 level tsp) ground coriander
5 ml (1 level tsp) ground cumin
2.5-5 ml (½-1 level tsp) chilli powder
2.5 ml (½ level tsp) ground turmeric
2 garlic cloves, skinned and crushed
1 medium onion, skinned and chopped
1 small cauliflower, cut into small florets
2 potatoes, peeled and roughly chopped
2 carrots, peeled and sliced
1 green pepper, seeded and chopped
225 g (8 oz) tomatoes, roughly chopped
150 ml (5 fl oz) natural yogurt
salt and pepper
toasted flaked almonds, to garnish

1. Heat the oil in a large saucepan, then add the coriander, cumin, chilli powder, turmeric, garlic and onion and fry for 2-3 minutes, stirring continuously.
2. Add the cauliflower, potatoes, carrots and green pepper and stir to coat in the spices. Stir in the tomatoes and 150 ml (¼ pint) water. Bring to the boil, cover and gently simmer for 25-30 minutes or until the vegetables are tender.
3. Remove from the heat, stir in the yogurt and season to taste. Serve garnished with toasted almonds and accompanied by rice and chutney.
SERVES 4

SALADS

An ever-increasing range of salad vegetables is available throughout the year, so it is always possible to enjoy interesting and refreshing salads. The main ingredients are described below. Always choose the freshest produce available, and use soon after purchase. A good dressing - made with quality ingredients - will make all the difference to a salad.

AVOCADOS
Although strictly a fruit, avocados are used like a vegetable. Prepare just before serving. Cut in half, remove the stone, peel and slice. Brush with lemon juice to prevent discolouration.

BABY CORN
Cook briefly in unsalted water until tender. Drain and toss in an oil and vinegar dressing while still warm, to absorb the flavours.

BEETROOT
Thinly peel cooked beetroot; dice or grate large ones and thinly slice small ones. Beetroot tends to 'bleed' into salads, so either add at the last minute or serve in a separate dish.

CARROTS
Carrots add colour and a crunchy texture to salads; tender new ones are especially good. Trim and either scrub or scrape. Cut into thin sticks or serve tiny new ones whole.

CABBAGE
Choose young green, white or red cabbage. Wash in salted water, dry well, then shred.

CELERIAC
Peel, wash and slice, dice or cut into julienne strips. Immediately toss in French Dressing, or Mayonnaise flavoured with mustard.

CELERY
Separate the sticks and wash in cold water. Use a small brush to scrub along the grooves to remove any dirt. Slice into the lengths required or make celery curls (see page 505).

CHICORY
Trim off the root end and remove any damaged leaves. Either separate the leaves or slice cross-wise. If the central core is very hard, remove it.

CHINESE LEAVES
Trim off the root end and remove any damaged leaves. Wash thoroughly, then shred finely.

COURGETTES
Trim off ends, then slice thinly, cut into julienne strips, dice or grate. Tender, young baby courgettes are excellent in salads.

CUCUMBER
Wipe the skin and peel if wished, then slice thinly or dice just before serving. Alternatively, pare off strips of peel lengthwise, using a cannelle knife or vegetable peeler before slicing, to create decorative slices.

DANDELION
Dandelion leaves are a good addition to salads. They have a slightly bitter flavour. Buy or pick in early spring while young and tender, well away from roadsides. Wash thoroughly before use.

KEY
1. Chinese Leaves
2. Radicchio
3. Escarole
4. Rocket
5. Lamb's Lettuce
6. Little Gem Lettuce
7. Lollo Rosso
8. Cos Lettuce
9. Chicory
10. Batavia Lettuce

ENDIVE (FRISÉE)

This excellent salad vegetable has narrow curly leaves which are dark green on the outside but pale inside. It has a bitter flavour. To prepare, trim off the root end and remove coarse outer leaves. Separate the remaining leaves, wash and dry well, then tear into bite-sized pieces.

ESCAROLE

A loose-leaved salad vegetable which resembles lettuce, but has a flavour like endive; though less bitter. Prepare as for Endive (above).

FENNEL

Trim off leafy tops and use as a garnish. Slice off the root base. Wash and slice thinly or grate.

LETTUCE

There is an ever increasing variety of lettuces to choose from but there are basically three main types: the compact round lettuce (also known as butterhead or cabbage lettuce; long-leaved cos-type, and loose-leaved lettuce (eg Lollo Rosso).
ROUND LETTUCES: Varieties include the crisp, delicious Webb's Wonderful; the crunchy but less flavoursome Iceberg; red-leaved, tasty Four Seasons (*Quattro Stagioni*); and the large Batavia which has pale red or green tinged leaves.
LONG-LEAVED LETTUCES: Varieties include the crisp-leaved large Cos (including a red-leaved variety) and Little Gem which has a sweet flavour and keeps better than most lettuces.
LOOSE-LEAVED LETTUCES: These include the curly Salad Bowl; the delicately flavoured red Oak Leaf (or *Feuille de Chêne*); the red *Lollo Rosso* and green *Lollo* which both have frilly leaves.

To prepare lettuce, trim base and remove coarse outer leaves. Wash and dry thoroughly. Tear into pieces shortly before using.

LAMB'S LETTUCE (CORN SALAD/MÂCHÉ)

This delicately flavoured salad green is becoming more widely available. To prepare, separate the leaves, wash in cold water and dry thoroughly.

MUSHROOMS

Button mushrooms are excellent eaten raw in salads. Trim base off stalks, wipe and thoroughly dry, if necessary. Halve or thinly slice.

MUSTARD AND CRESS

Snip the tops and stems as low down as possible. Place in a sieve and wash in cold water. Dry and remove any seeds which have stuck to the tops.

NASTURTIUM LEAVES

The round, peppery flavoured leaves of the nasturtium are sometimes added to salads. Choose young, tender leaves and use either whole or shredded. The flowers may be sprinkled over salad as a garnish.

PEPPERS

Red, green, yellow and black peppers add colour to salads. To prepare, cut off the top and stalk and remove the seeds and membrane. Wash, dry and slice thinly or cut into dice. If preferred, the peppers may also be skinned (see page 219).

RADICCHIO

This firm-textured 'red-leaved chicory' has an excellent slightly bitter flavour. It is becoming increasingly popular. To prepare, cut off the root end and separate the leaves, discarding any that are damaged. Wash and dry, then tear into manageable pieces.

RADISHES

Trim off the root end and leaves and wash in cold water. Serve whole or sliced thinly.

ROCKET

This slightly hot, peppery salad leaf is a good addition to salads and is becoming more widely available. Wash thoroughly and tear into pieces. Use sparingly.

SPRING ONIONS

Trim off the root end, slide the onion out of its papery skin and remove the green leaves. Wash and serve whole, chopped into smaller pieces or made into tassels (see page 505).

TOMATOES

Choose flavoursome tomatoes for salads. Remove the stem, wash then slice or cut into wedges. To skin tomatoes, lower into boiling water for 30 seconds, then drain and plunge into cold water; the skin will then slide off easily. Alternatively hold on a fork over a gas flame for about 30 seconds, turning constantly.

Sun-dried tomatoes also make a delicious addition to salads; they are sold in jars (in oil). Drain and cut into thin strips before adding.

WATERCRESS

Snip off the coarse ends of the stalks and remove any yellow leaves. Wash in cold water and drain well before using.

SALAD DRESSINGS

A salad is rarely complete without a light coating of dressing, whether it's a tart, fresh-tasting vinaigrette, a smooth, creamy mayonnaise or simply a squeeze of lemon juice.

SALAD OILS

The foundation of most good dressings is the oil. Olive oil, with its distinctive flavour, has long been regarded as the all-purpose salad oil. Virgin olive oil, which has a dark green colour and a strong rich aroma has the best flavour.

The rich and mellow nut oils – walnut, hazelnut and almond – are becoming more popular. They are delicious, albeit costly, and can be blended successfully with the lighter oils, such as sunflower oil. Walnut oil is considered by many to be the best of all for salad dressings. Hazelnut oil also has a rich, nutty flavour. Almond oil is a pale delicately-flavoured oil. Nut oils tend to go rancid quickly; once opened store them in the refrigerator.

Sunflower, grapeseed and groundnut oils are lighter with blander flavours. They are ideal for combining with strongly flavoured salad ingredients or blending with the richer oils.

VINEGARS

Most dressings combine oil with some acidic element. Lemon, mustard and yogurt can all provide the essential tartness, but the ingredient most often chosen is vinegar, which comes in lots of flavours. The proportion of oil to vinegar varies according to taste. Note that the strength of vinegar varies from one brand to another.

Wine and cider vinegars are suitable for salad dressings. Wine vinegars range from light delicately flavoured ones to rich mellow red wine vinegars. Sherry vinegar is a dark full-flavoured variety. Balsamic vinegar is a dark, mellow vinegar with an excellent flavour. Although expensive, only a small amount is needed to lend a superb flavour to a dressing.

Vinegars flavoured with garlic, herbs such as tarragon, or fruit such as raspberries add unusual flavours to dressings. You can buy them or make your own more cheaply.

For herb vinegars, place the herbs or mixture of herbs in clean bottles. Fill up with good quality red or white wine or cider vinegar, cork or cap the bottles and leave for 6 weeks in a dark place. Strain through muslin and re-bottle, adding a fresh herb sprig if desired.

Fruit vinegars are usually made with soft fruits like raspberries, strawberries, blackberries or blackcurrants. Wash the fruit and mash it gently with a wooden spoon. Place in wide-mouthed jars and add 600 ml (1 pint) white wine vinegar for each 450 g (1 lb) fruit. Cover and leave for 3-4 days, shaking the jars occasionally. Strain through muslin into a saucepan and boil for 10 minutes. Pour into sterilized jars and seal (see page 484).

HERBS AND FLOWERS

Fresh herbs are excellent in salads. They look attractive as well as imparting a delicious flavour. Basil is invariably used in tomato salads, dill is traditionally added to a cucumber salad and savory is particularly good with bean salads. Other suitable herbs for adding to salads are borage, chervil, chives, fennel, parsley, salad burnet and tarragon.

The flowers from herb plants such as borage, fennel, marjoram, rosemary and thyme can also be added to salads. Fresh fragrant petals from edible flowers like marigolds, nasturtiums, clove pinks, primroses and violets can also be sprinkled over salads to impart colour and flavour.

DRESSING A SALAD

When applying a dressing, the most important rule to remember is never to drown the salad. There should be just enough dressing to cling very lightly to each ingredient, so there's no pool of excess in the bottom of the bowl.

For leafy salads, it's a good idea to pour the dressing into a salad bowl – allow about 75 ml (3 fl oz) per six servings. Place the ingredients lightly on top. Cover and refrigerate for up to 40 minutes. Toss just before serving. Cooked vegetables, rice, pasta or pulses for salads are best dressed while still warm. Apply the dressing, stir to mix, cover and leave to cool in the dressing to absorb the flavours.

All dressings should be stored in airtight jars or bottles. Shake well to re-emulsify before using. Those containing rich oils such as walnut or hazelnut, and cream, yogurt or soft cheese should be made in small quantities and kept in the refrigerator for no longer than 2-3 days. Bring to room temperature before using. The Basic French Dressing can be stored at cool room temperature for up to 4 weeks and will retain its full flavour.

MAYONNAISE

1 egg yolk (see note)
2.5 ml (½ level tsp) mustard powder or
*   5 ml (1 level tsp) Dijon mustard*
2.5 ml (½ level tsp) salt
1.25 ml (¼ level tsp) pepper
2.5 ml (½ level tsp) sugar
15 ml (1 tbsp) white wine vinegar or lemon juice
about 150 ml (¼ pint) oil (see opposite)

1. Put the egg yolk into a bowl with the mustard, seasoning, sugar and 5 ml (1 tsp) of the vinegar or lemon juice. Mix thoroughly, then add the oil drop by drop, whisking constantly, until the sauce is thick and smooth. If it becomes too thick, add a little more of the vinegar or lemon juice. When all the oil has been added, add the remaining vinegar or lemon juice gradually and mix thoroughly.
2. Store for up to 3 days in a screw-topped jar in the refrigerator.
MAKES ABOUT 150 ML (¼ PINT)

NOTE: The ingredients for Mayonnaise must be at room temperature. Never use eggs straight from the refrigerator or cold larder as this may result in curdling.

If a recipe requires thin mayonnaise, thin it down with a little warm water, single cream, vinegar or lemon juice. Add the extra liquid slowly – too much will spoil the consistency.

MAYONNAISE IN A BLENDER OR FOOD PROCESSOR

Most blenders and food processors need at least a two-egg quantity in order to ensure that the blades are covered. Put the yolks, seasoning and half the vinegar or lemon juice into the blender or food processor and blend well. If your machine has a variable speed control, run it at a slow speed. Add the oil gradually while the machine is running. Add the remaining vinegar and season.

RESCUE REMEDIES

If the Mayonnaise separates save it by beating the curdled mixture into a fresh base. This base can be any of the following: 5 ml (1 tsp) hot water; 5 ml (1 tsp) vinegar or lemon juice; 5 ml (1 level tsp) Dijon mustard or 2.5 ml (½ level tsp) mustard powder; or an egg yolk. Add the curdled mixture to the base, beating hard. When the mixture is smooth, continue adding the oil as

before. (If you use an extra egg yolk you may find that you need to add a little extra oil.)

VARIATIONS
CAPER MAYONNAISE

Add 10 ml (2 tsp) chopped capers, 5 ml (1 tsp) chopped pimiento and 2.5 ml (½ tsp) tarragon vinegar (see page 253). Caper Mayonnaise makes an ideal accompaniment for fish.

CUCUMBER MAYONNAISE

Add 30 ml (2 tbsp) finely chopped cucumber and 2.5 ml (½ level tsp) salt. This mayonnaise goes well with fish salads, especially crab, lobster or salmon.

BLUE CHEESE DRESSING

Add 150 ml (5 fl oz) soured cream, 75 g (3 oz) crumbled blue cheese, 5 ml (1 tsp) vinegar, 1 crushed garlic clove, and pepper to taste.

RÉMOULADE SAUCE

Add 5 ml (1 tsp) chopped gherkins, 5 ml (1 tsp) chopped capers, 5 ml (1 tsp) chopped fresh parsley and 1 anchovy, finely chopped.

TARTARE SAUCE

Add 5 ml (1 tsp) chopped fresh tarragon or snipped chives, 10 ml (2 tsp) chopped capers, 10 ml (2 tsp) chopped gherkins, 10 ml (2 tsp) chopped fresh parsley and 15 ml (1 tbsp) lemon juice or tarragon vinegar. Allow to stand for at least 1 hour before serving, to allow the flavours to blend.

THOUSAND ISLAND MAYONNAISE

Add 15 ml (1 tbsp) chopped stuffed olives, 5 ml (1 tsp) finely chopped onion, 1 egg, hard-boiled, shelled and chopped, 15 ml (1 tbsp) diced green pepper, 5 ml (1 tsp) chopped fresh parsley and 5 ml (1 level tsp) tomato purée.

CURRY CREAM SAUCE

Sauté 10 ml (2 level tsp) chopped onion and 1 crushed garlic clove in 15 ml (1 tbsp) oil for 2-3 minutes. Stir in 10 ml (2 level tsp) curry powder and 5 ml (1 level tsp) tomato purée. Add 75 ml (3 fl oz) water, 1 lemon slice and 10 ml (2 level tsp) apricot jam. Simmer for 5-7 minutes. Strain and allow to cool. When cold, whisk into the mayonnaise. Adjust seasoning to taste.

FRENCH DRESSING

Make up a large batch of dressing. The flavour can be varied with any of the suggestions given below. Serve with salad leaves or cooked or raw vegetables, if preferred.

175 ml (6 fl oz) olive oil
45 ml (3 tbsp) white wine vinegar
2.5 ml (½ level tsp) caster sugar
10 ml (2 level tsp) Dijon mustard
salt and pepper

1. Place all the ingredients in a bowl or screw-topped jar and whisk together or shake until thoroughly combined.
2. Adjust seasoning to taste.
MAKES ABOUT 200 ML (7 FL OZ)

NOTE: Store in a cool place for up to 4 weeks, but shake vigorously before serving.

VARIATIONS
HERB DRESSING: Whisk 30 ml (2 level tbsp) finely chopped, fresh mixed herbs, eg parsley, thyme, marjoram, chives, sage, etc, into the dressing.

MUSTARD AND PARSLEY DRESSING: Stir in 15 ml (1 level tbsp) wholegrain mustard and 30 ml (2 level tbsp) finely chopped fresh parsley.

SWEET AND SPICED DRESSING: Add 5 ml (1 level tsp) mango chutney, 5 ml (1 level tsp) mild curry paste and 2.5 ml (½ level tsp) ground turmeric.

ROQUEFORT DRESSING: Place the dressing in a blender or food processor. Add 25 g (1 oz) Roquefort cheese and 30 ml (2 tbsp) single cream. Blend until the mixture is smooth.

GARLIC DRESSING: Crush 2 garlic cloves into the dressing. Stir in 15 ml (1 level tbsp) snipped chives if desired.

RICH GARLIC DRESSING

Balsamic vinegar produces a dark sweet-sour dressing, ideal with strong-flavoured foods.

50 ml (2 fl oz) balsamic vinegar
150 ml (5 fl oz) olive oil
2.5 ml (½ level tsp) caster sugar
2 cloves garlic, skinned and crushed
salt and pepper

1. Whisk together the vinegar, oil, sugar and garlic until thoroughly combined.
2. Adjust seasoning to taste.
MAKES ABOUT 200 ML (7 FL OZ)

SPICED HONEY AND CORIANDER DRESSING

This is a very good combination for salads accompanying spicy foods. Or serve with sliced, grilled duckling breasts, orange and onion salad, or mixed beans.

150 ml (5 fl oz) light oil, eg grapeseed, sunflower, etc
10 ml (2 tsp) clear honey
15 ml (1 tbsp) cider vinegar
2 spring onions, trimmed and finely chopped
10 ml (2 level tsp) finely chopped fresh coriander
15 ml (1 level tbsp) chopped salted peanuts
1 red chilli pepper, seeded and finely chopped
salt and pepper

1. Whisk together the oil, honey and vinegar.
2. Stir in the spring onions, coriander and peanuts.
3. Stir the chilli into the dressing mixture and season to taste.
MAKES ABOUT 150 ML (5 FL OZ)

AÏOLI

4 garlic cloves, skinned
1.25 ml (¼ level tsp) salt
2 egg yolks
300 ml (½ pint) olive oil
30 ml (2 tbsp) lemon juice

1. In a bowl, crush the garlic cloves with a little of the salt until a smooth paste is formed. Add the egg yolks and remaining salt and beat well.
2. Gradually beat in the oil, a little at a time, as for Mayonnaise, until the mixture is thick and smooth.
3. When all the oil has been added, beat in the remaining lemon juice. Store for up to 3 days in a screw-topped jar in the refrigerator.
MAKES 300 ML (½ PINT)

Aïoli with a selection of fresh vegetables

PESTO

50 g (2 oz) fresh basil leaves
2 garlic cloves, skinned
30 ml (2 tbsp) pine nuts
salt and pepper
50 g (2 oz) freshly grated Parmesan cheese
100 ml (4 fl oz) olive oil

1. Put the basil, garlic, pine nuts and seasoning in a mortar and grind with a pestle until a paste forms. Add the cheese and blend well.

2. Transfer to a bowl. Beat in the oil, a little at a time, stirring vigorously with a wooden spoon.
MAKES 300 ML (¼ PINT)

NOTE: This sauce can also be made in a blender or food processor. Place the basil, garlic, pine nuts, seasoning and olive oil in a blender or food processor and blend at high speed until very creamy. Transfer the mixture to a bowl, fold in the cheese and mix thoroughly. Store for up to 1 week in a screw-topped jar in the refrigerator.

YOGURT DRESSING

150 g (5 fl oz) natural yogurt
15 ml (1 tbsp) sunflower oil
5-10 ml (1-2 tsp) vinegar
5 ml (1 tsp) wholegrain mustard

1. Place all the ingredients in a bowl and whisk together until well blended, then chill before serving. Store for up to 3 days in a screw-topped jar in the refrigerator.
MAKES 150 ML (¼ PINT)

NOTE: Yogurt can be used as a substitute for soured cream in many recipes. It will give a slightly sharper dressing. Yogurts vary a little in acidity – season to taste.

VARIATION
TOMATO AND YOGURT DRESSING
Place 60 ml (4 tbsp) olive or sunflower oil, 5 ml (1 level tsp) salt, 5 ml (1 level tsp) caster sugar, 30 ml (2 tbsp) vinegar and 300 ml (½ pint) tomato juice in a bowl and whisk well together.

Gradually whisk in 150 ml (5 fl oz) natural yogurt, 10 ml (2 level tsp) grated onion and. 30 ml (2 tbsp) Horseradish Cream (see page 205). Season liberally with pepper. Store the dressing for up to 3 days in a screw-topped jar in the refrigerator.
MAKES 600 ML (1 PINT)

CLASSIC GREEN SALAD

1 lettuce, washed
½ frisée (curly endive), washed
1 bunch watercress, washed and trimmed
2 chicory heads, trimmed, washed and chopped
½ cucumber, thinly sliced
60 ml (4 tbsp) French Dressing (see page 255)
5-10 ml (1-2 tsp) chopped fresh parsley, chives, chervil,
*   tarragon or other herbs, as available*

1. Tear the lettuce and frisée (curly endive) into bite-sized pieces and place in a salad bowl with the other green ingredients.
2. Pour over the French Dressing and toss well to lightly coat the salad. Sprinkle with herbs and serve immediately.
SERVES 4-6 AS A SIDE SALAD

VARIATION
Vary the salad leaves according to taste and availability. Try lamb's lettuce (corn salad), escarole or rocket leaves. Edible flowers (see page 253) make a colourful addition.

TOMATO SALAD WITH BASIL

750 g (1½ lb) ripe tomatoes, skinned
135 ml (9 tbsp) olive oil
45 ml (3 tbsp) wine vinegar
1 small garlic clove, skinned and crushed
30 ml (2 tbsp) chopped fresh basil
salt and pepper

1. Slice the tomatoes thinly and arrange on six individual serving plates.
2. Place the oil, vinegar, garlic, basil and seasoning in a bowl or screw-topped jar and whisk or shake well together. Spoon over the tomatoes. Cover and chill in the refrigerator for about 2 hours before serving.
SERVES 6 AS A SIDE SALAD

VARIATION
TOMATO AND ONION SALAD
Arrange the tomato slices and 3 finely sliced onions alternately on serving plates. Spoon over 90 ml (6 tbsp) French Dressing (see page 255) mixed with 10 ml (2 tsp) snipped fresh chives.

POTATO SALAD

1 kg (2 lb) potatoes
4 spring onions, trimmed and finely chopped
salt and pepper
150 ml (¼ pint) Mayonnaise (see page 254)
15-30 ml (1-2 tbsp) boiling water or milk (optional)
snipped fresh chives, to garnish

1. Place the potatoes in cold salted water, bring to the boil and cook for 15-20 minutes, until just tender. Drain, remove the skins and leave until quite cold.
2. Cut the potatoes into small dice and place in a bowl. Add the spring onions and season to taste with salt and pepper.
3. Thin the Mayonnaise, if wished, with a little boiling water or milk, stir it into the potatoes and toss gently.
4. Leave the salad to stand for at least 1 hour. Sprinkle with snipped chives before serving.
SERVES 6 AS A SIDE SALAD

VARIATION
Replace the Mayonnaise with 150 ml (¼ pint) French Dressing (see page 255).

CRISPY CAULIFLOWER SALAD

1 medium cauliflower, trimmed
1 red eating apple, cored and chopped
2 eggs, hard-boiled, shelled and chopped
50 g (2 oz) walnut pieces, chopped
150 ml (¼ pint) Mayonnaise (see page 254)
15 ml (1 tbsp) lemon juice
salt and pepper

1. Break the cauliflower into small florets, wash and drain well.
2. Put all the ingredients in a salad bowl, season with salt and pepper and toss well together.
SERVE 4 AS A SIDE SALAD

WALDORF SALAD

450 g (1 lb) eating apples
juice of ½ a lemon
2.5 ml (½ level tsp) sugar
150 ml (¼ pint) Mayonnaise (see page 254)
1 lettuce
½ a head of celery, trimmed and sliced
50 g (2 oz) walnut pieces, chopped
a few walnut halves, to garnish (optional)

1. Peel and core the apples, slice one and dice the rest. Dip the slices in lemon juice to prevent discoloration. Toss the diced apples in the lemon juice, the sugar and 15 ml (1 tbsp) Mayonnaise and leave to stand for about 30 minutes.
2. Just before serving, wash and dry the lettuce leaves and use to line a salad bowl. Add the celery, walnuts and remaining Mayonnaise to the diced apples and toss together. Spoon into the salad bowl and garnish with the apple slices and a few whole walnuts, if wished.
SERVES 4 AS A SIDE SALAD

RICE SALAD RING

225 g (8 oz) long grain white rice
1 green pepper, seeded and diced
3 caps canned pimiento, diced
200 g (7 oz) can corn niblets, drained
75 ml (5 tbsp) chopped fresh parsley
50 g (2 oz) salted peanuts
45 ml (3 tbsp) lemon juice
celery salt
pepper
watercress, to garnish

1. Cook the rice in plenty of boiling salted water for 10-15 minutes, until tender, then drain. Rinse through with cold water and drain thoroughly. Leave to cool completely.
2. Blanch the pepper in boiling water for 1 minute, drain, rinse in cold water and drain again.
3. In a large bowl, mix the cold rice, pepper and pimiento, corn niblets, parsley, peanuts and lemon juice, and season well with celery salt and pepper. Press the salad into a lightly oiled 1.4 litre (2½ pint) ring mould and chill well.
4. To serve, turn out on to a flat serving plate and fill the centre of the salad ring with watercress.
SERVES 8 AS A SIDE SALAD

VARIATION
This ring can be made using brown rice; cook for 30-35 minutes.

COLESLAW

½ a white cabbage, about 900 g (2 lb) weight, trimmed and finely shredded
1 large carrot, peeled and grated
1 large onion, skinned and finely chopped
45 ml (3 tbsp) chopped fresh parsley
4 celery sticks, trimmed and sliced
salt and pepper
200 ml (7 fl oz) Mayonnaise (see page 254)
watercress, to garnish (optional)

1. In a large bowl, combine the cabbage, carrot, onion, parsley and celery, tossing well together.
2. Season the Mayonnaise well, pour over the vegetables and toss until well coated.
3. Cover and chill for several hours before serving. Garnish with watercress, if wished.
SERVES 8 AS A SIDE SALAD

NOTE: If preferred, the ingredients can be prepared beforehand and left covered. Add the dressing 2-3 hours before serving.

MANGETOUT AND MUSHROOM SALAD

225 g (8 oz) mangetout, trimmed
salt and pepper
175 g (6 oz) button mushrooms, wiped and sliced
150 ml (¼ pint) Mayonnaise (see page 254)
30 ml (2 level tbsp) natural yogurt
60 ml (4 level tbsp) chopped fresh parsley
30 ml (2 level tbsp) chopped fresh chives

1. Cut the mangetout into diamond slices. Blanch in boiling salted water for 1 minute, drain and rinse under cold running water. Mix with the mushrooms.
2. Beat together the mayonnaise, yogurt, parsley and half the chives in a bowl. Season with salt and pepper to taste. If you have time, leave to stand for a while to allow the flavours to infuse.
3. Arrange the mangetout and mushrooms on individual plates. Top with the dressing and sprinkle with the remaining chives.
SERVES 4

Mangetout and Mushroom Salad

GREEK SALAD

2 marmande or beefsteak tomatoes, cut into eighths
1 medium green pepper, seeded and thinly sliced
½ a medium cucumber, thickly sliced
50 g (2 oz) black or stuffed olives, stoned
125-175 g (4-6 oz) Feta cheese, diced
120 ml (8 tbsp) olive oil
30-45 ml (2-3 tbsp) lemon juice
salt and pepper
pitta bread, to serve

1. Arrange the tomatoes, pepper, cucumber and olives in a salad bowl. Add the cheese to the bowl, reserving a few dice for garnish.
2. Pour over the olive oil, followed by the lemon juice, then season well. Toss the salad together. Crumble over the remaining cheese cubes and serve with pitta bread.
SERVES 4 AS A SIDE SALAD OR 2 AS A MAIN COURSE

RED CABBAGE AND APPLE SALAD

½ a red cabbage, about 900 g (2 lb) weight, trimmed
*   and very finely shredded*
3 eating apples
1 small garlic clove, skinned and crushed
300 ml (½ pint) French Dressing (see page 255)

1. Blanch the cabbage for 1 minute in boiling salted water, taking care not to over-blanch it, otherwise it will lose its crisp texture. Drain and leave to cool.
2. Peel, core and slice the apples and place in a bowl with the cabbage. Add the garlic to the dressing, pour over the salad and toss well.
3. Cover the salad and refrigerate overnight. Toss again to mix well just before serving.
SERVES 8 AS A SIDE SALAD

MARINATED MUSHROOMS

450 g (1 lb) small button mushrooms, wiped
150 ml (¼ pint) French Dressing (see page 255)
chopped fresh parsley or coriander, to garnish

1. Place the mushrooms in a bowl and pour over the dressing. Coat the mushrooms well, then cover and leave to marinate in the refrigerator for 6-8 hours, stirring occasionally.
2. Serve in individual shallow dishes and sprinkle the mushrooms with chopped parsley.
SERVES 4-6 AS A SIDE SALAD

BEAN SPROUT AND BROWN RICE SALAD

225 g (8 oz) long grain brown rice
salt
225 g (8 oz) bean sprouts
1 large green pepper
90 ml (6 tbsp) French Dressing (see page 255)

1. Cook the rice in a large pan of boiling salted water for about 35 minutes, until just tender. Drain and rinse through with hot water.
2. Wash the bean sprouts and drain well. Halve the pepper, discard the seeds, dice and mix in a bowl with the bean sprouts and rice.
3. Spoon the dressing over the salad and stir well. Cover and chill for 2 hours before serving.
SERVES 6 AS A SIDE SALAD

RADICCHIO AND ALFALFA SALAD

2 heads radicchio (see variation)
50-75 g (2-3 oz) alfalfa sprouts
90 ml (6 tbsp) Garlic Dressing (see page 255)

1. Tear the radicchio into bite-sized pieces. Wash, drain and pat dry on absorbent kitchen paper. Wash and dry the alfalfa sprouts.
2. Mix the alfalfa and radicchio together in a large bowl. Pour over the dressing and toss well.
SERVES 6 AS A SIDE SALAD

VARIATION:
As an alternative to radicchio, use 350 g (12 oz) thinly shredded red cabbage.

CAESAR SALAD

1 large garlic clove, skinned and crushed
150 ml (¼ pint) olive oil
75 g (3 oz) stale white bread
1 Cos lettuce
salt and pepper
1 egg
30 ml (2 tbsp) lemon juice
25 g (1 oz) Parmesan cheese, freshly grated
8 anchovies, finely chopped

1. Add the garlic to the oil and leave to stand for 30 minutes. Cut the bread into 5 mm (¼ inch) dice. Heat a little of the garlic oil in a frying pan and fry the bread until golden brown on all sides. Remove and drain on absorbent kitchen paper.
2. Wash and dry the lettuce leaves and tear into bite-sized pieces. Place in a salad bowl. Pour over the remaining garlic oil and toss until the leaves are completely coated. Season well.
3. Boil the egg for 1 minute only, break it into the salad and toss well. Add the lemon juice, cheese, anchovies and croûtons. Toss again and serve immediately.
SERVES 4 AS A SIDE SALAD

FENNEL AND TOMATO SALAD

90 ml (6 tbsp) sunflower oil or half sunflower, half
walnut oil (see page 253)
45 ml (3 tbsp) lemon juice
salt and pepper
12 black olives, halved and stoned
450 g (1 lb) Florence fennel
450 g (1 lb) ripe tomatoes

1. In a medium mixing bowl, whisk the oils, lemon juice and seasoning together. Add the olives to the dressing.
2. Snip off the feathery ends of the fennel and refrigerate them in a polythene bag until required.
3. Halve each bulb of fennel lengthways, then slice thinly crossways, discarding the roots. Blanch in boiling salted water for 1 minute, then drain. While it is still warm, stir into the dressing.
4. Leave to cool, cover and refrigerate until required. Meanwhile, skin and slice the tomatoes, cover and refrigerate.
5. Just before serving, arrange the tomatoes and

Fennel and Tomato Salad

fennel mixture on individual serving plates and snip the fennel tops over them.
SERVES 6 AS A SIDE SALAD

NOTE: This salad can also be made with chicory and garnished with parsley.

BEETROOT IN CARAWAY DRESSING

450 g (1 lb) small beetroots
5 ml (1 level tsp) caraway seeds
30 ml (2 tbsp) boiling water
30 ml (2 tbsp) wine vinegar
5 ml (1 level tsp) salt
10 ml (2 level tsp) caster sugar
pepper

1. Cook the beetroots in boiling salted water for 1-1½ hours according to size. While still warm, remove skins and cut into 5 mm (¼ inch) slices.
2. For the dressing, place the caraway seeds in a bowl, pour over the boiling water and leave for 30 minutes. Stir in the remaining dressing ingredients.
3. Pour over the beetroot slices and leave to marinate for 1-2 hours or overnight.
SERVES 4 AS A SIDE SALAD

MIXED BEAN SALAD

175 g (6 oz) mixed dried beans, eg aduki, red kidney,
black or haricot, soaked separately overnight
2.5 ml (½ level tsp) ground coriander
100 ml (4 fl oz) French Dressing (see page 255)
1 small onion, skinned and very finely sliced
salt and pepper

1. Drain the beans, place in a saucepan and cover with fresh water. Bring to the boil and boil for 10 minutes, then cover and simmer for about 1 hour, until tender. (If aduki beans are included, add them halfway through the cooking time.) Drain and place in a large bowl.
2. Add the coriander to the dressing and pour over the beans while they are still warm. Toss thoroughly and leave to cool.
3. Add the onion to the beans, stir well and season. Chill, then transfer to a salad bowl or individual serving plates.
SERVES 6 AS A SIDE SALAD

FLORIDA CHICORY SALAD

1 small grapefruit
2 medium oranges
225 g (8 oz) tomatoes, skinned
2 chicory heads, trimmed and washed
30 ml (2 tbsp) sunflower or grapeseed oil
15 ml (1 tbsp) lemon juice
10 ml (2 level tsp) light soft brown sugar
salt and pepper
45 ml (3 tbsp) chopped fresh parsley

1. Prepare the grapefruit and oranges over a bowl to catch any juice: using a serrated knife, cut away all the peel and pith and divide the flesh into segments, discarding the pips and as much of the membrane as possible. Add the segments to the juice in the bowl.
2. Quarter the tomatoes, scooping the seeds and juice into a nylon sieve placed over the bowl. Discard the seeds. If large, slice the tomato quarters into eighths and add to the bowl.
3. Slice the chicory diagonally into 1 cm (½ inch) pieces. Open out the slices and add to the tomato, grapefruit and orange mixture.
4. Place the oil, lemon juice, sugar, seasoning and parsley in a bowl or screw-topped jar and whisk or shake well together. Pour over the fruit and vegetable mixture and stir well. Adjust the seasoning and, if the fruit is very acidic, add a little more sugar.
5. Cover and chill well before serving.
SERVES 6 AS A SIDE SALAD

LEMON-DRESSED AVOCADO SALAD

2 ripe avocados
½ a small cucumber, diced
90 ml (6 tbsp) oil (see page 253)
45 ml (3 tbsp) lemon juice
5 ml (1 tsp) thin honey
salt and pepper
4 celery sticks, trimmed and thinly sliced
50 g (2 oz) salted peanuts
paprika, to garnish

1. Peel, halve and stone the avocados. Sprinkle with a little of the lemon juice to prevent discolouration.
2. Place the oil, remaining lemon juice, honey and seasoning in a bowl or screw-topped jar and whisk or shake well together.
3. Place the celery and peanuts in a bowl with the cucumber and avocado, pour over the dressing and toss well. Pile into a serving dish, sprinkle with paprika and serve immediately.
SERVES 6 AS A SIDE SALAD

FRESH SPINACH SALAD WITH HOT BACON DRESSING

225 g (8 oz) fresh young spinach, washed and trimmed
2 large slices of white bread, crusts removed
45 ml (3 tbsp) vegetable oil
1 garlic clove, skinned and crushed
8 rashers streaky bacon, rinded and chopped
15 ml (1 tbsp) white wine vinegar
salt and pepper

1. Shred any large spinach leaves into small strips and place in a salad bowl. Set aside.
2. To make the croûtons, cut the bread into 1 cm (½ inch) cubes. Heat the oil in a frying pan and fry the bread cubes until golden brown.
3. Stir the crushed garlic into the croûtons, then drain them on absorbent kitchen paper.
4. Add the bacon to the pan and fry for about 5 minutes until crisp and golden brown. Pour the bacon and any fat over the spinach leaves.
5. Add the vinegar to the pan, stir well, then pour over the salad. Add seasoning, toss quickly, scatter the croûtons on top and serve at once.
SERVES 4 AS A SIDE SALAD

Smoked Haddock and Bean Salad

SMOKED HADDOCK AND BEAN SALAD

450 g (1 lb) smoked haddock fillet
a little milk and water
439 g (15 oz) can borlotti beans
150 ml (5 fl oz) soured cream
5-10 ml (1-2 level tsp) curry paste
45-60 ml (3-4 tbsp) lemon juice
45 ml (3 level tbsp) chopped fresh parsley
black pepper
3 eggs, hard-boiled and quartered
mixed salad leaves, to serve
fresh herbs, to garnish

1. Put the fish in a pan and add just enough milk and water to cover. Bring to the boil, then lower the heat, cover and gently poach for about 5 minutes, or until tender. Drain, discarding the skin, and divide the fish into large chunks. Add the drained beans.
2. Combine the soured cream, curry paste, lemon juice and parsley in a bowl. Season with pepper. Lightly fold into the haddock mixture.
3. Arrange on a bed of salad leaves, with the hard-boiled egg quarters. Garnish with herbs.
SERVES 4-6

SALADE NIÇOISE

200 g (7 oz) can tuna fish, drained
225 g (8 oz) tomatoes, skinned and quartered
50 g (2 oz) black olives, stoned
½ a small cucumber, thinly sliced
225 g (8 oz) French beans, cooked
2 eggs, hard-boiled, shelled and quartered
15 ml (1 tbsp) chopped fresh parsley
15 ml (1 tbsp) chopped fresh basil
150 ml (¼ pint) Garlic Dressing (see page 255)
8 anchovies, halved lengthways

1. Flake the tuna into fairly large chunks. Arrange in a salad bowl with the tomatoes, olives, cucumber, beans and egg quarters.
2. Add the parsley and basil to the dressing, mix well and pour over the salad.
3. Arrange the anchovy fillets in a lattice pattern over the top of the salad and allow to stand for about 30 minutes before serving.
SERVES 4 AS A SIDE SALAD OR 2 AS A MAIN COURSE

PASTA, PRAWN AND APPLE SALAD

175 g (6 oz) pasta shells
150 ml (¼ pint) unsweetened apple juice
5 ml (1 tsp) chopped fresh mint
5 ml (1 tsp) white wine vinegar
salt and pepper
225 g (8 oz) peeled prawns
2 crisp dessert apples, peeled, cored and roughly
    chopped
lettuce leaves
paprika, to garnish

1. Cook the pasta in plenty of boiling salted water until just tender. Drain well, rinse in cold running water and drain again.
2. To make the dressing, whisk together the apple juice, mint, vinegar and seasoning.
3. Stir the prawns, apples and cooked pasta into the dressing until well mixed. Cover and refrigerate for 2-3 hours.
4. Wash the lettuce leaves, dry and shred finely. Arrange the lettuce in a bowl and spoon the prawn salad on top. Sprinkle with paprika.
SERVES 2 AS A MAIN COURSE

Pasta, Prawn and Apple Salad

CRAB SALAD

15 ml (1 tbsp) lemon juice
15 ml (1 tbsp) mayonnaise
15 ml (1 tbsp) natural yogurt
225 g (8 oz) crab meat
½ cucumber, diced
2 tomatoes, skinned and cubed
50 g (2 oz) pasta shells, cooked
pepper
shredded lettuce, to serve
cucumber and lemon slices, to garnish

1. Mix together the lemon juice, mayonnaise and yogurt for the dressing.
2. Combine the crab meat, cucumber, tomatoes and pasta shells with the dressing. Season with pepper to taste.
3. Serve the crab salad on a bed of shredded lettuce. Garnish with cucumber and lemon slices, and serve accompanied by brown bread and butter if desired.
SERVES 2

SMOKED MACKEREL SALAD

450 g (1 lb) small new potatoes
350 g (12 oz) smoked mackerel fillets, skinned
150 ml (5 fl oz) soured cream
60 ml (4 level tbsp) Mayonnaise (see page 254)
45 ml (3 level tbsp) Horseradish Cream (see page 205)
salt and pepper
½ a head of celery, trimmed and sliced
paprika, to garnish
lemon wedges, to serve

1. Cook the potatoes in their skins in boiling salted water for 10 minutes, or until tender. Drain, halve and leave to cool. Divide mackerel fillets the into bite-sized pieces.
2. In a large bowl, mix the soured cream with the Mayonnaise, Horseradish Cream and seasoning. Stir in the fish, celery and potatoes, cover and chill well in the refrigerator.
3. Serve the salad sprinkled with paprika and accompanied by lemon wedges.
SERVES 4 AS A MAIN COURSE

Warm Seafood Salad

WARM SEAFOOD SALAD

selection of salad leaves, eg radicchio, frisée (curly endive), lamb's lettuce
few fresh chives, snipped
60 ml (4 tbsp) French Dressing (see page 255)
12 medium scallops
25 g (1 oz) butter or margarine
50 g (2 oz) streaky bacon, rinded and cut into strips
50 g (2 oz) peeled prawns
200 g (7 oz) can artichoke bottoms, drained and thickly sliced
salt and pepper
fresh chives, to garnish

1. Arrange the salad leaves on a large platter or individual plates. Sprinkle over the chives and drizzle over the French dressing.
2. Remove and discard the white muscle from each scallop. Separate the corals and reserve. Cut the white flesh into thick slices.
3. Melt the butter in a sauté pan and fry the bacon for 2-3 minutes. Add the scallops and fry for a further 2-3 minutes, or until just cooked through.
4. Add the reserved corals, prawns and artichokes. Stir over the heat for 1 minute or until heated through. Adjust seasoning. Divide the seafood mixture between the serving plates. Garnish with chives and serve immediately, with warm crusty bread.
SERVES 2

WHOLEWHEAT AND APRICOT SALAD

225 g (8 oz) wholewheat grain
125 g (4 oz) dried apricots, washed
3 celery sticks, trimmed and sliced
90 ml (6 tbsp) French Dressing (see page 255)

1. Soak the wholewheat overnight in plenty of cold water. Drain and place in a large saucepan of boiling water. Simmer gently for 25 minutes, or until the grains are tender but retain a little bite. Drain well, rinse under cold running water and place in a bowl.

2. Snip the apricots into small pieces and add to the wholewheat with the celery. Pour the dressing over the salad and toss well.

3. Cover and chill for several hours. Stir again just before serving.

SERVES 4 AS A SIDE SALAD OR 2 AS A MAIN COURSE

SPICED DUCKLING AND ORANGE SALAD

1.8 kg (4 lb) oven-ready duckling
2 medium oranges
salt and pepper
45 ml (3 tbsp) vegetable oil
15 ml (1 tbsp) white wine vinegar
30 ml (2 level tbsp) Mayonnaise (see page 254)
10 ml (2 level tsp) curry powder
30 ml (2 level tbsp) orange marmalade
snipped fresh chives or chopped fresh parsley, to garnish

1. Wipe the duckling and prick well all over with a fork. Using a potato peeler or sharp knife, pare the rind from one orange and place it inside the duckling. Place the duckling on a rack or trivet in a roasting tin. Sprinkle with salt and pepper inside and out, then roast in the oven at 180°C (350°F) mark 4 for about 2 hours, or until the juices run clear and the flesh is tender. While still warm, strip the breast skin off the duck and reserve. Carve off all the meat and shred finely.

2. In a large bowl, mix the oil, vinegar, Mayonnaise, curry powder and marmalade and season with salt and pepper. Stir in the duckling.

3. Using a serrated knife, remove all the peel and pith from the oranges and divide into segments, discarding the pips and as much of the membrane as possible. Add to the duck, then cover and refrigerate.

4. Cut the reserved duck skin into strips and grill until crisp. Just before serving, sprinkle over the salad. Top with the chives or parsley.

SERVES 4 AS A MAIN COURSE

CORONATION CHICKEN

2.3 kg (5 lb) chicken, poached (see page 151)
15 ml (1 tbsp) vegetable oil
1 small onion, skinned and finely chopped
15 ml (1 level tbsp) curry paste
15 ml (1 level tbsp) tomato purée
100 ml (4 fl oz) red wine
1 bay leaf
juice of ½ a lemon
4 canned apricot halves, drained and finely chopped
300 ml (½ pint) Mayonnaise (see page 254)
100 ml (4 fl oz) whipping cream
salt and pepper
watercress, to garnish

1. Remove the flesh from the chicken and cut into small pieces.

2. In a small saucepan, heat the oil, add the onion and cook for about 3 minutes, until softened. Add the curry paste, tomato purée, wine, bay leaf and lemon juice.

3. Simmer, uncovered, for about 10 minutes until well reduced. Strain and leave to cool.

4. Purée the chopped apricot halves in a blender or food processor or through a sieve. Beat the cooled sauce into the Mayonnaise with the apricot purée.

5. Whip the cream to stiff peaks and fold into the mixture. Season, adding a little extra lemon juice if necessary. Fold in the chicken pieces.

6. Garnish with watercress to serve.

SERVES 8 AS A MAIN COURSE

EGGS

Eggs are a highly nutritious, versatile food and they have a wide range of uses in cooking. They are an essential ingredient in most cakes, as well as many hot puddings, cold desserts and sauces. Two eggs contain as much protein as 125 g (4 oz) meat. They also contain vitamins A and B, plus useful amounts of iron and calcium.

EGG SAFETY

Care must be taken when buying, storing, and using eggs because they are particularly susceptible to contamination by salmonella. This is because their shells are porous and can absorb the bacteria if they come into contact with it. Both free-range and standard eggs are vulnerable. Provided that eggs are thoroughly cooked, any salmonella present will be destroyed by heat. However many classic recipes – such as cold soufflés and meringues, lemon curd and mayonnaise, soft-boiled, poached and lightly scrambled eggs – can only be made with raw or lightly cooked eggs. Although the risk is small, 'at risk' people, including the very young, pregnant women, elderly or sick, should avoid these dishes. If for any reason you are particularly anxious about safety, buy pasteurised eggs which have been heat treated; they are available in frozen or dried form. However these are not suitable for making mayonnaise or lemon curd.

BUYING EGGS

Always buy eggs from a reputable supplier with a quick turnover and check the 'use by' date on the pack. Never buy or use cracked or damaged eggs. If an egg is dirty, wipe clean with dry absorbent kitchen paper. Unless using immediately, do not wash otherwise the protective film on the shell will be destroyed, making it more permeable to bacteria.

There is no difference in flavour or nutritional value between brown or white eggs; the simple explanation is that varying breeds of hen produce different coloured eggs. Most of the eggs on sale in this country are produced by 'battery hens' which are raised by intensive farming methods. However free-range eggs, laid by hens which have greater freedom, are now widely available.

EGG SIZES

Eggs are graded for size as follows:

Size 1	over 70 g
Size 2	65-70 g
Size 3	60-65 g
Size 4	55-60 g
Size 5	50-55 g
Size 6	45-50 g
Size 7	below 45 g

Unless a particular egg size is specified in a recipe, use Size 2 or 3 eggs.

STORING EGGS

Store eggs in their container in a cool room if possible. Otherwise store them in a refrigerator keeping them well away from the ice compartment and away from strong-smelling foods like cheese or fish because eggs readily absorb smells. Store pointed end down and use within 2 weeks of purchase. Bring to room temperature before cooking; eggs that are too cold will crack when boiled and are also difficult to whisk.

To test for freshness immediately before use, place the egg in a bowl of water. If it floats to the surface it is likely to be bad. A fresh egg will sink to the bottom.

COOKING WITH EGGS

Eggs can be cooked in numerous different ways. They also have three main functions in cooking. **EMULSIFYING:** Egg yolk is an emulsifying agent and is used together with butter or oil to make Mayonnaise (see page 254), Hollandaise (see page 203), etc.

THICKENING AND BINDING: Beaten eggs are used to thicken sauces, such as custard. They are also used to bind ingredients, as in rissoles, fish cakes, etc. A coating of beaten egg is also applied to foods which are likely to disintegrate during cooking, such as fish for frying and fritters.

RAISING: When eggs – or more notably egg whites – are whisked, they incorporate air, which remains trapped. It is this property which gives soufflés, meringues and whisked cakes their light airy texture.

TO SEPARATE AN EGG

Tap the egg sharply on the side of a cup to break the shell in half. Don't let the yolk break and mingle with the white, because egg whites will not whisk well if any yolk is present. Collect the egg in one half of the shell, then pass the yolk back and forth between the two halves, allowing the white to drop into a bowl below. Put the separated yolk into another container.

When separating more than one egg, transfer the separated white to another container, so that if you do break a yolk you will only spoil one white.

OTHER TYPES OF EGGS

DUCK AND GOOSE EGGS are larger and richer than hens' eggs. They are not widely available. Both kinds must be thoroughly cooked to ensure that all bacteria are killed; allow at least 10 minutes for boiling. They should not be used raw or in any hot dishes which are cooked for a short time or at a low temperature. Both duck and goose eggs should be eaten within 2 days of purchase.

TURKEY EGGS taste similar to hens' eggs but are much larger. They can be cooked by any of the methods given for hens' eggs, but take longer due to their size. Turkey eggs are rarely sold.

QUAIL EGGS which are much smaller than hens' eggs are becoming more widely available. They are usually soft-boiled for 1 minute, partially peeled and served in their attractive speckled shells, as an hors d'oeuvre.

METHODS OF COOKING EGGS

SOFT BOILED EGGS
Although called boiled eggs, these are in fact simmered rather than boiled. Using a spoon, lower them into a pan of simmering water and simmer for 3½ minutes for a light set and up to 5 minutes for a firmer set. The water should be sufficient to cover the eggs. If the egg cracks in

the pan, quickly add a little salt or vinegar to the water to prevent a stream of egg escaping.

Soft-boiled eggs are often eaten from the shell in an egg cup.

HARD-BOILED EGGS
Put the eggs into boiling water, bring back to the boil and simmer gently for 10-12 minutes. Once cooked, drain and cool under cold running water, then tap the shells and leave them until cold (this prevents a discoloured rim forming round the outside of the yolk and enables the shell to be removed easily). Crack the shell all over, then peel it off.

EGGS MOLLET
These soft-boiled eggs have soft yolks and fairly firm whites. They can be served hot in a savoury sauce, or cold in aspic. They can also be used as an alternative to poached eggs.

Put the eggs into a pan of simmering water and simmer gently, allowing about 6 minutes from the time the water comes back to a simmer. Immediately plunge the eggs into cold water, leave for about 8 minutes, then carefully peel away the shell.

CODDLED EGGS
Place the eggs in boiling water, cover, remove from the heat and leave in a warm place for 8-10 minutes until lightly set.

POACHED EGGS
The eggs may be cooked in a poaching pan or in a sauté pan, or deep frying pan.

To use an egg poacher, half-fill the lower container with water, place a small knob of butter in each cup and heat. When the water boils, break the eggs into the cups, season and cover the pan. Simmer gently for about 3 minutes until the eggs are set, then loosen with a knife before turning out.

To use a frying pan, fill to a depth of 7.5 cm (3 inches) with water and add 30-45 ml (2-3 tbsp) vinegar to help the eggs keep their shape. Bring to the boil, swirl the water with a spoon and slip the eggs into the water. Cook gently until lightly set, about 4 minutes. Lift out with a slotted spoon or fish slice.

FRIED EGGS
Melt a little butter or oil in a frying pan. Break each egg separately into a cup and carefully slide into the hot fat. Cook over medium heat, basting with the fat, so the eggs cook evenly on top and underneath. When just set, remove the egg from the pan with a fish slice or broad palette knife. If preferred, the egg can be flipped to brown the underside.

BAKED EGGS

Eggs are baked in ramekin dishes. Place the required number of ovenproof dishes on a baking sheet, with a knob of butter in each dish. Put them in the oven until the butter has melted. Break an egg into each dish, season, and cook at 180°C (350°F) mark 4 for about 8-10 minutes, until the eggs are just set. Serve at once.

SCRAMBLED EGGS

Melt a knob of butter in a small saucepan. Lightly beat the eggs with a little milk or water [15 ml (1 tbsp) to each egg] and season. Pour into the saucepan and stir slowly over a gentle heat until the mixture begins to thicken. Remove from the heat and stir until creamy. Pile on to hot buttered toast and serve immediately.

HOT SAVOURY SOUFFLÉS

A hot soufflé is the true soufflé. The tiny bubbles of air, trapped within the egg whites, expand as they are heated, puffing up the base mixture, to which they were added, by as much as two thirds of its original size. When making hot soufflés, it is important to follow the recipe precisely; do not try to cut corners. This section also includes a roulade – a soufflé mixture baked in a paper case, which is then turned out and rolled up with a filling or sauce inside.

HINTS FOR SUCCESSFUL SOUFFLÉS

- All the equipment must be spotlessly clean and dry. This is especially important when whisking the egg whites, as the volume will be poor if there's a trace of grease in the bowl or on the whisk.
- Either a hand whisk or an electric one can be used but be careful not to overbeat the whites with an electric whisk.
- The mixture should stand in soft peaks. Overbeaten egg whites look dry and powdery and will be difficult to fold in evenly.
- The basic sauce mixture must still be warm when the whisked whites are folded in. If necessary, the sauce can be prepared in advance and gently reheated before adding the egg whites. Much of the volume of the whites will be lost if they are folded into a cold, stiff mixture.
- Quickly fold in one large spoonful of the egg whites first to loosen the basic sauce. Always add the egg whites with a large metal spoon, using a light cutting and folding action.
- Make sure that the dish is well greased – this helps it rise. Before baking, a hot soufflé dish should be two-thirds to three-quarters full.
- Don't open the oven door during cooking. A hot soufflé is cooked when it is risen and golden, and just firm to the touch. The creamy middle should be a little gooey – if it is dry it tastes like overcooked scrambled egg.
- A hot soufflé must be served immediately.

HOT SPINACH SOUFFLÉ

30 ml (2 level tbsp) grated Parmesan cheese
450 g (1 lb) fresh spinach, cooked or 250 g (8 oz)
packet chopped spinach, thawed
50 g (2 oz) butter or margarine
45 ml (3 level tbsp) flour
200 ml (7 fl oz) milk
salt and pepper
3 eggs, separated, and 1 extra egg white
125 g (4 oz) Gruyère or Emmenthal cheese, grated

1. Grease a 1.3 litre (2¼ pint) soufflé dish and dust with the Parmesan cheese.
2. Place the spinach in a sieve and press to remove all moisture.

3. Melt butter in a saucepan, add spinach and cook for a few minutes to evaporate any liquid.
4. Stir in the flour and cook gently for 1 minute, stirring. Remove the pan from the heat and gradually stir in the milk and seasoning. Bring to the boil slowly, and continue to cook, stirring until thickened. Cool slightly. Beat in the yolks one at a time and 75 g (3 oz) grated Gruyère.
5. Stiffly whisk the egg whites and fold into the mixture. Spoon into the soufflé dish. Sprinkle with the remaining cheese.
6. Stand dish on a baking sheet and bake in the oven at 190°C (375°F) mark 5 for 30 minutes or until well risen and just set. Serve immediately.
SERVES 3-4

CHEESE SOUFFLÉ

15 ml (1 level tbsp) grated Parmesan cheese
200 ml (7 fl oz) milk
few slices of onion and carrot
1 bay leaf
6 black peppercorns
25 g (1 oz) butter or margarine
30 ml (2 level tbsp) flour
10 ml (2 level tsp) Dijon mustard
salt and pepper
cayenne pepper
4 whole eggs, separated and 1 extra egg white
75 g (3 oz) mature Cheddar or Gruyére cheese,
    finely grated

Cheese Soufflé

1. Grease a 1.3 litre (2¼ pint) soufflé dish.
Sprinkle the grated Parmesan into the dish. Tilt
the dish, knocking the sides gently until they are
evenly coated with cheese.
2. Place the milk in a medium saucepan
together with the onion and carrot slices, bay
leaf and black peppercorns. Bring slowly to the
boil, remove from the heat, cover, and leave to
infuse for 30 minutes. Strain off and reserve the
milk.
3. Melt the butter in a medium saucepan, stir in
the flour, mustard and seasoning and cook
gently for 1 minute, stirring. Remove from the
heat and gradually stir in the milk. Bring to the
boil slowly and continue to cook, stirring until
the sauce thickens. Cool a little.
4. Beat the egg yolks into the cooled sauce one
at a time. Sprinkle the Cheddar cheese over the
sauce, reserving 15 ml (1 level tbsp). (At this
stage the mixture can be left to stand for several
hours if necessary.) Stir in the cheese until
evenly blended.
5. Using a hand or electric mixer, whisk the egg
whites until the egg whites stand in stiff peaks.
6. Mix one large spoonful of egg white into the
sauce to lighten its texture. Gently pour the
sauce over the remaining egg whites and cut and
fold the ingredients together. Do not overmix;
fold lightly, using a large metal spoon or plastic
spatula, just until the egg whites are evenly
incorporated.
7. Pour the soufflé mixture gently into the
prepared dish. The mixture should come about
three quarters of the way up the side of the dish.
Smooth the surface of the soufflé with a palette
knife and sprinkle over the reserved cheese.

8. Place the soufflé dish on a baking sheet. Bake
in the oven at 180°C (350°F) mark 4 for about
30 minutes until golden brown on the top, well
risen and just firm to the touch with a hint of
softness in the centre. Serve at once.
SERVES 4

VARIATIONS
Don't use too great a weight of filling or the
soufflé will be heavy. Omit the cheese and add
one of the following:

STILTON SOUFFLÉ: Replace the Cheddar with
blue Stilton.

HAM SOUFFLÉ: Add 75 g (3 oz) cooked ham,
diced.

FISH SOUFFLÉ: Add 75 g (3 oz) cooked smoked
haddock, finely flaked.

MUSHROOM SOUFFLÉ: Add 75-100 g (3-4 oz)
mushrooms, chopped and cooked in butter until
tender.

SPICY SPINACH ROULADE

900 g (2 lb) fresh spinach
salt
5 ml (1 level tsp) mustard seeds
5 ml (1 level tsp) coriander seeds
2.5 ml (½ level tsp) cumin seeds
225 g (8 oz) low-fat soft cheese
4 eggs, separated
pepper
15 g (½ oz) butter
175 g (6 oz) button mushrooms, wiped and finely
*   chopped*
1 teaspoon ground turmeric
225 g (8 oz) cooked peeled prawns, thoroughly
*   defrosted if frozen, finely chopped*
whole cooked prawns and fresh parsley sprigs, to
*   garnish*

1. Line a greased 33 x 23 cm (13 x 9 inch) Swiss roll tin with non-stick baking parchment. Set aside.
2. Wash the spinach thoroughly and discard the stalks. Put the leaves in a large saucepan with only the water that clings to them. Add salt to taste and cook over gentle heat for 5 minutes, shaking the pan constantly, until the spinach wilts and shrinks. Drain well.
3. Turn the spinach into a blender or food processor and work to a purée. Crush the spices with a mortar and pestle, then add to the spinach with half of the cheese. Work until evenly mixed. Add the egg yolks and salt and pepper to taste and work again until smooth. Transfer to a large bowl.
4. Whisk the egg whites in a clean bowl until standing in stiff peaks. Fold into the spinach mixture, then immediately spread in the prepared tin with a palette knife. Bake in the oven at 200°C (400°F) mark 6 for 15 minutes or until firm to the touch.
5. Meanwhile, melt the butter in a saucepan, add the mushrooms and turmeric and toss over high heat until the juices have evaporated. Add the prawns and heat through. Turn the mixture into a bowl, add the remaining cheese and salt and pepper to taste. Beat to a soft, spreading consistency. Cover and keep warm.
6. Turn the cooked roulade out on to a large sheet of non-stick baking parchment and carefully peel off the lining paper. Immediately spread with the prawn mixture. Roll up carefully with the help of the parchment.

Spicy Spinach Roulade

7. To serve, lift the roulade carefully on to a warm serving plate and place seam side down. Garnish with prawns and parsley.
SERVES 4-6

Spread the sauce on to the roulade.

Using the paper, carefully roll it up.

EGG DISHES

EGGS FLORENTINE

900 g (2 lb) spinach
salt and pepper
40 g (1½ oz) butter or margarine
45 ml (3 level tbsp) flour
300 ml (½ pint) milk
75 g (3 oz) Gruyère or Cheddar cheese, grated
4 eggs

1. Wash the spinach well in several changes of water. Put into a saucepan with a little salt and just the water that clings to the leaves, cover and cook for 10-15 minutes, until tender. Drain well, chop roughly and reheat with 15 g (½ oz) butter.
2. Melt the remaining 25 g (1 oz) butter, stir in the flour and cook gently for 1 minute, stirring.

3. Remove pan from heat and gradually stir in the milk; bring to the boil and cook, stirring until thickened. Add 50 g (2 oz) cheese and season. Do not allow to boil.
4. Poach the eggs (see page 268). Place the spinach in an oven-proof dish, arrange the eggs on top and pour the cheese sauce over.
5. Sprinkle with the remaining cheese and brown under the grill.

Arrange the eggs decoratively over the spinach then cover with sauce.

BAKED EGGS WITH MUSHROOMS

25 g (1 oz) butter or margarine
125 g (4 oz) button mushrooms, wiped and finely chopped
30 ml (2 tbsp) chopped fresh tarragon or parsley
salt and pepper
2 eggs

1. Melt two thirds of the butter in a frying pan, add the mushrooms and fry until all excess moisture has evaporated. Add the tarragon or parsley and season.

2. Divide the mixture between two ramekin or cocotte dishes; make a well in the centre of each.
3. Carefully break an egg into each dish, dot with reserved butter and stand the ramekins in a roasting tin. Pour boiling water into the tin to come halfway up the sides of the ramekins.
4. Cover the roasting tin tightly with foil and place in the oven. Bake at 180°C (350°F) mark 4 for 10-12 minutes, until the eggs are just set. Serve at once.
SERVES 2

PIPÉRADE

30 ml (2 tbsp) olive oil
2 large onions, skinned and thinly sliced
1 garlic clove, skinned and finely chopped (optional)
1 medium red or yellow pepper, seeded and sliced
1 medium green pepper, seeded and sliced
450 g (1 lb) tomatoes, skinned and roughly chopped
6 eggs
5 ml (1 tsp) finely chopped fresh parsley or basil
salt and pepper
fried bread triangles, to garnish

1. Heat the oil in a deep frying pan or shallow flameproof casserole, add the onions and garlic and fry gently until golden.
2. Add the peppers and cook for 10-15 minutes, until they are soft.
3. Stir in the tomatoes, raise the heat a little and cook until most of the moisture has evaporated and the tomatoes have reduced to a thick pulp.
4. Beat the eggs together with the herbs, adding salt and pepper to taste, and pour it into the pan. Stir gently until they begin to set.
5. Remove the pan from the heat while the mixture is still creamy.
6. Serve garnished with the fried bread triangles.
SERVES 4-6

EGG MAYONNAISE

4 eggs, hard-boiled
few lettuce leaves
150 ml (¼ pint) Mayonnaise (see page 254)
chopped fresh parsley or paprika, to garnish

1. Halve the eggs lengthways. Wash and drain the lettuce and arrange in a shallow dish.
2. Place the eggs on the lettuce, cut side down and coat with the Mayonnaise. Garnish with parsley or paprika to serve.
SERVES 2-4

SCOTCH EGGS

4 eggs, hard-boiled
10 ml (2 level tsp) seasoned flour
a few drops of Worcestershire sauce
225 g (8 oz) sausagemeat
1 egg, beaten
fresh breadcrumbs
vegetable oil for deep-frying

1. Dust the eggs with the seasoned flour.
2. Mix the Worcestershire sauce into the sausagemeat and divide it into 4 equal portions. Form each quarter into a flat cake and shape it round an egg, making it as even as possible, to keep the egg a good shape; make sure there are no cracks in the sausagemeat.
3. Brush with egg and roll in the breadcrumbs.
4. Heat the oil in a deep fat fryer to a temperature of 160°C (325°F), gently lower the Scotch Eggs into the oil and fry for 7-8 minutes. (As the sausagemeat is raw, the fat must not be too hot or the meat will not have time to cook.)
5. When they are golden brown on the outside, remove and drain on absorbent kitchen paper.
6. Cut the eggs in half lengthways and serve either hot with Tomato Sauce (see page 207) or cold with a green salad.
SERVES 4

STUFFED EGGS WITH PÂTÉ

6 eggs, hard-boiled
125 g (4 oz) soft liver pâté
salt and pepper
stuffed green olives, sliced, to garnish

1. Cut the hard-boiled eggs in half lengthways, carefully remove the yolks and rub through a nylon sieve into a bowl.
2. Add the pâté and beat well. Season with salt and pepper.
3. Put the pâté mixture into a piping bag fitted with a 1 cm (½ inch) plain nozzle and pipe into the egg whites.
4. Garnish with slices of olive.
SERVES 2-4

STUFFED EGG MAYONNAISE

4 eggs, hard-boiled
75 g (3 oz) soft blue cheese, eg Cambazola
75 g (3 oz) full fat soft cheese
45-60 ml (3-4 tbsp) single cream
salt and pepper
225 g (8 oz) tomatoes, skinned
150 ml (¼ pint) Mayonnaise (see page 254)
parsley sprigs, to garnish

1. Halve the eggs lengthways, carefully remove the yolks and rub through a nylon sieve.
2. Cut the rind off the Blue Brie and beat the cheese until smooth. Work in the full fat soft cheese with the sieved egg yolks, cream and seasoning, beating until it is a smooth and pipeable consistency.
3. Put the cheese mixture into a piping bag fitted with a 1 cm (½ inch) star nozzle and pipe into the egg whites.
4. Slice half the tomatoes and arrange in four individual serving dishes; place the stuffed eggs on top. Refrigerate for 30 minutes.
5. Halve, seed and roughly chop the remaining tomatoes and stir into the Mayonnaise.
6. Spoon a little Mayonnaise over each egg and garnish with parsley sprigs.
SERVES 4

BAKED EGG AND VEGETABLE POTS

225 g (8 oz) aubergine, chopped
salt and pepper
30 ml (2 tbsp) oil
175 g (6 oz) onion, skinned and thinly sliced
225 g (8 oz) courgettes, thinly sliced
4 medium-sized tomatoes, skinned and roughly chopped
45 ml (3 tbsp) white wine
30 ml (2 level tbsp) tomato purée
1 clove garlic, skinned and crushed
6 eggs
150 ml (¼ pint) Greek-style natural yogurt

1. Place the aubergine in a colander, sprinkle with salt and leave to stand for about 20 minutes. Rinse the aubergine under cold running water, drain and dry on absorbent kitchen paper.
2. Heat the oil in a medium saucepan. Add the onion, aubergine and courgettes and fry until beginning to brown, stirring frequently.
3. Add the tomatoes, wine, tomato purée, garlic and seasoning. Cover and simmer for 10-15 minutes or until the vegetables are tender, but not mushy. Divide the mixture between four 300 ml (½ pint) ovenproof dishes. Cool slightly.
4. Make a well in the centre of the vegetables and break an egg into each. Whisk together the remaining two eggs, the yogurt and seasoning. Carefully spoon over the vegetables.
5. Bake in the oven at 180°C (350°F) mark 4 for 20-25 minutes or until the eggs are lightly set.
SERVES 4

ASPARAGUS SCRAMBLE

350 g (12 oz) asparagus, steamed, or a 284 g (10 oz)
    can asparagus spears, well drained
1 small French loaf, cut into 1 cm (½ inch) slices
about 50 g (2 oz) butter
paprika to taste
6 eggs
60 ml (4 tbsp) milk
salt and pepper

1. Cut off the asparagus tips and reserve; roughly chop the stalks.
2. Toast the bread on both sides; spread with a little butter and sprinkle with paprika. Keep warm in a low oven.
3. Whisk together the eggs, milk and seasoning with a generous pinch of paprika.
4. Melt 25 g (1 oz) butter in a heavy-based saucepan. Add the eggs and stir over a moderate heat until beginning to set.
5. Mix in the chopped asparagus, stirring until the eggs are lightly set.
6. Spoon the eggs into a serving dish. Surround with the bread croûtes and top with asparagus spears. Sprinkle with paprika to serve.
SERVES 3 AS A STARTER, 2 AS A LIGHT LUNCH

EGGS BÉNÉDICT

4 slices bread
4 eggs
150 ml (¼ pint) Hollandaise Sauce (see page 203)
4 thin slices lean ham
parsley sprigs, to garnish

1. Toast the bread on both sides.
2. Poach the eggs (see page 268) and gently warm the Hollandaise Sauce.
3. Top each slice of toast with a folded slice of ham, then the hot poached egg and finally coat with Hollandaise Sauce.
4. Garnish each with a sprig of parsley.
SERVES 4

Eggs Bénédict

BACON AND EGG CROQUETTES

200 ml (7 fl oz) milk

slice of carrot, onion, 1 bay leaf, 6 black peppercorns,
    for flavouring

25 g (1 oz) butter or margarine

125 g (4 oz) streaky bacon rashers, rinded and roughly
    chopped

105 ml (7 level tbsp) flour

30 ml (2 tbsp) single cream

1 egg yolk

4 eggs, hard-boiled and chopped

salt and pepper

1 egg, beaten

50 g (2 oz) fresh white breadcrumbs

oil for deep-frying

parsley sprigs, to garnish

1. Bring the milk to the boil in a saucepan with the flavourings, cover and leave to infuse for at least 15 minutes, then strain.

2. Meanwhile, melt the butter in a heavy-based frying pan, add the bacon and fry until golden brown.

3. Stir in 75 ml (5 level tbsp) flour and cook gently for 1 minute, stirring. Remove pan from heat and gradually stir in the milk. Bring to the boil, stirring, then blend in the cream, egg yolk, hard-boiled eggs and seasoning to taste. Transfer the mixture to a bowl, cool and then chill in the refrigerator until firm.

4. Roll the egg mixture into sausage shapes on a floured board, brush with beaten egg and coat in breadcrumbs – leave for 15 minutes for a crisper coat. At this stage croquettes can be refrigerated for an hour.

5. Heat the oil in a deep fat fryer to a temperature of 180°C (350°F) and fry the croquettes, a few at a time, until golden. Drain on absorbent kitchen paper; serve at once garnished with parsley.

MAKES 12

LEFT: Bacon and Egg Croquettes. RIGHT: Scotch Eggs (see page 273). BELOW: Classic Green Salad (see page 257).

OMELETTES

With care, anyone can master the art of omelette making. Delicate handling and a little practice is needed – don't be discouraged if your first two or three omelettes are not successful. Two good points about omelettes are the short preparation time and the way they can be combined with cooked meat, fish or vegetables – either in the omelette itself, as a filling, or as an accompaniment. Have everything ready before beginning to make an omelette, including a hot plate on which to serve it – an omelette must never wait, but rather be waited for.

THE PAN

Special omelette pans are obtainable and should be kept for omelettes only. If you do not own such a pan, however, a heavy-based frying pan can also be used. Non-stick pans are ideal for omelettes and do not require seasoning before use. Whether of cast iron, copper, enamelled iron or aluminium, the pan should be thick, so that it will hold sufficient heat to cook the egg mixture as soon as it is put in. This means the omelette can be cooked in about 2 minutes; both slow cooking and overcooking make an omelette tough. A 15-18 cm (6-7 inch) pan takes a 2-3 egg omelette.

To season an omelette pan (to treat it before using for the first time), sprinkle 15 ml (1 level tbsp) salt into the pan, heat it slowly, then rub in well with a piece of absorbent kitchen paper. Tip out the salt and wipe the pan. To clean an omelette pan after use, don't wash it, but rub it over with absorbent kitchen paper, then rub the surface again with a clean cloth. Gently heat the pan before use to ensure that it is heated evenly right to the edges – a fierce heat would cause the pan to heat unevenly. When the pan is ready for the mixture it will feel comfortably hot if you hold the back of your hand about 2.5 cm (1 inch) away from the surface.

NOTE: Manufacturers of non-stick pans advise that heating the empty pan will damage the surface, so carefully read the instructions and add the fat before heating the pan.

GREASING OMELETTE PANS

Undoubtedly butter gives the best flavour, but margarine or oil can be used as a substitute. Bacon fat can also be used.

TYPES OF OMELETTE

Basically there are only two different kinds of omelette, the plain, and the soufflé omelette in which the egg whites are whisked separately, then folded into the yolk mixture to give it a fluffy texture. Plain omelettes are usually savoury and soufflé omelettes are most commonly served with a sweet filling but there is no fixed rule and the fillings can be interchanged. There are also many different omelette variations, where the different ingredients are added to the eggs or used in the filling.

PLAIN OMELETTE

2 eggs per person
salt and pepper
butter or margarine for greasing

Whisk the eggs just enough to break them down; don't make them frothy as overbeating spoils the texture of the finished omelette. Season with salt and pepper and add 15 ml (1 tbsp) water or milk. Place the pan over a gentle heat and when it is hot, add a knob of butter or margarine to grease it lightly. Add the beaten eggs. Stir gently with a fork or wooden spatula, drawing the mixture from the sides to the centre as it sets and letting the liquid egg from the centre run to the sides. When the eggs have set, stop stirring and cook for another minute until the omelette is golden underneath and still creamy on top. Tilt the pan away from you slightly and use a palette knife to fold over a third of the omelette to the centre, then fold over the opposite third. Carefully turn the omelette out on to the warmed serving plate, with the folded sides underneath, and serve at once. Don't overcook or the omelette will be tough and leathery.

OMELETTE FILLINGS

FINES HERBES: Add 15 ml (1 tbsp) finely chopped fresh herbs or 5 ml (1 level tsp) mixed dried herbs to the beaten egg mixture before cooking. Parsley, chives, chervil, dill, marjoram and tarragon are all suitable.

CHEESE: Grate 40 g (1½ oz) Gruyère, Cheddar or other hard cheese and mix 45 ml (3 tbsp) of it with the eggs before cooking; sprinkle the rest over the omelette after it is folded.

TOMATO: Skin and chop 1-2 tomatoes and fry in a little butter or margarine in a saucepan for about 5 minutes, until soft and pulpy. Put in the centre of the omelette before folding.

MUSHROOM: Wipe and thinly slice 50 g (2 oz) mushrooms and cook in a little butter in a saucepan until soft. Put in the centre of the omelette before folding.

BACON: Rind and chop 2 rashers of bacon and fry in butter in a saucepan until crisp. Put in the centre of the omelette before folding.

HAM: Add 50 g (2 oz) chopped ham and 5 ml (1 tbsp) chopped fresh parsley to the beaten egg before cooking.

FISH: Flake some cooked fish and heat gently in a little cheese sauce. Put in the centre of the omelette before folding.

SHRIMP OR PRAWN: Thaw 50 g (2 oz) frozen cooked peeled shrimps or prawns and fry gently in melted butter or margarine in a saucepan, with a squeeze of lemon juice. Put into the centre of the omelette before folding.

SOUFFLÉ OMELETTE

2 eggs, separated
salt and pepper
30 ml (2 tbsp) water
knob of butter or margarine

1. Whisk the egg yolks until creamy. Add the seasoning and the water and beat again.
2. Stiffly whisk the egg whites.
3. Melt the butter in an omelette pan over a low heat without browning.
4. Turn the egg whites into the yolk mixture and fold in carefully, using a metal spoon, but don't over-mix.
5. Grease the sides of the pan with the butter by tilting it in all directions, then pour in the egg mixture. Cook over a moderate heat until the omelette is golden brown on the underside. Place the pan under a preheated grill until the

omelette is golden brown on top.
6. Remove at once, as overcooking tends to make it tough. Run a spatula gently around the edge and underneath the omelette to loosen it. Make a mark across the middle at right angles to the pan handle and add any required filling – see suggestions below – then double the omelette over. Turn it gently on to a warmed serving plate and serve at once.
SERVES 1

VARIATIONS
Any of the fillings given for plain omelettes can be used for soufflé omelettes. For sweet fillings: add 50 g (2 oz) chopped fresh or canned fruit, drained and flavoured with a liqueur, if wished (drain again before adding to the omelette); or 15 ml (1 level tbsp) apricot or raspberry conserve. Serve at once.

SPANISH OMELETTE

45 ml (3 tbsp) olive oil
2 large potatoes, peeled and cut into 1 cm (½ inch) cubes
2 large onions, skinned and coarsely chopped
salt and pepper
6 eggs, lightly beaten

1. In a medium frying pan, gently heat the olive oil. Add the potatoes and onions and season with salt and pepper. Fry, stirring occasionally, for 10-15 minutes, until golden brown.

2. Drain off excess oil and quickly stir in the eggs. Cook for 5 minutes, shaking the pan occasionally to prevent sticking. If you wish, place under a hot grill to brown the top. Serve.
SERVES 4

NOTE: This is a basic Spanish Omelette, but other vegetables may be added, such as chopped red pepper, tomatoes, peas, mushrooms, spinach. Either add them raw at the beginning or stir cooked vegetables into the eggs (peas and spinach should be added already cooked).

Prawn and Tarragon Omelette

PRAWN AND TARRAGON OMELETTE

4 eggs
salt and pepper
knob of butter or margarine
125 g (4 oz) cooked peeled prawns
15-30 ml (1-2 level tbsp) chopped fresh tarragon or
*   2.5 ml (½ level tsp) dried*

1. In a bowl, whisk together the eggs, seasoning and 30 ml (2 tbsp) water.
2. Heat the butter in a medium frying pan or omelette pan, preferably non-stick.
3. When the butter is hot and sizzling, tip in the eggs. Cook over a moderate to high heat, drawing a wooden fork through the mixture to allow the raw egg to run through.
4. When the omelette is lightly set, sprinkle over the prawns and tarragon. Cook for a few seconds longer then fold into three and flip out onto a serving plate. Serve immediately.
SERVES 2

OMELETTE ARNOLD BENNETT

125 g (4 oz) smoked haddock
50 g (2 oz) butter or margarine
150 ml (5 fl oz) double or single cream
3 eggs, separated
salt and pepper
50 g (2 oz) Cheddar cheese, grated

1. Place the fish in a saucepan and cover with water. Bring to the boil and simmer gently for 10 minutes. Drain and flake the fish, discarding the skin and bones.
2. Place the fish in a pan with half the butter and 30 ml (2 tbsp) of the cream. Toss over a high heat until the butter melts. Leave to cool.
3. Beat the egg yolks in a bowl with 15 ml (1 tbsp) cream and seasoning. Stir in the fish mixture. Stiffly whisk the egg whites and fold in.
4. Heat the remaining butter in an omelette pan. Fry the egg mixture, but make sure it remains fairly fluid. Do not fold over. Slide it on to a flameproof serving dish.
5. Blend the cheese and remaining fresh cream together, then pour over the omelette and brown under a preheated grill.
SERVES 2

CHEESE

Cheese is a solid derivative of milk. It is produced by coagulating the protein (casein) so that it forms curds – usually by adding rennet – and draining off the liquid (whey). Cheese then undergoes a ripening process, during which its taste, texture and appearance change, and each variety develops its own particular characteristics.

Most cheese is made from cow's milk with a small amount made from ewe's or goat's milk. The type of milk and the different techniques used to separate the curds and whey and ripen the cheese result in the many different types of cheese. Climate, vegetation and seasonal changes can also influence the finished cheese; some varieties can only be produced in a certain area and cannot be produced in large quantities or under factory conditions. Cheddar, however, lends itself well to factory techniques.

Although casein makes up 78 per cent of the milk protein, there are other proteins present in smaller quantities, but they are soluble and are drained out with the whey (they are known as whey proteins). The whey may then be processed to curdle the remaining protein and used to make low fat cheese such as Ricotta – a moist, unsalted Italian cheese. Much of the cheese bought in this country is factory produced but increasingly cheese is being made by the traditional methods on farms using unpasteurised milk. Traditional Cheddar, Double Gloucester, Cheshire, Lancashire, Leicester, Wensleydale and Caerphilly are all being produced as 'farmhouse' cheeses.

BUYING AND STORING CHEESE

At specialist cheese shops, each cheese should be kept in exactly the right conditions for its type and you can often taste a sliver of a particular cheese before you buy. If buying pre-packed cheese, make sure that it does not look sweaty or excessively runny and check the 'use by' date. If the date is many weeks ahead it may indicate that the cheese is immature.

Store cheese in a covered, ventilated china dish or on a plate with a bowl on top. Alternatively wrap in greaseproof paper, then foil or place in an airtight plastic container. Keep in the bottom of the refrigerator or dairy compartment, so it does not get too cold. Leave cheese at room temperature, still in its paper or other wrappings to prevent drying out for about 30 minutes before serving.

If you want hard cheese to become dry for grating, leave it exposed to the air in a cool, dry place for 1-2 days, turning it from time to time. Grated cheese can be stored in a polythene bag in the refrigerator for up to 2 weeks.

Cheese can be frozen, but some varieties – notably higher fat ones – freeze better than others. Once thawed, cheeses should be eaten soon as they deteriorate quickly.

SERVING CHEESE

Cheese may be served at the end of a meal, as a snack or light lunch. When planning a cheese board serve with some of the following:
- Savoury or plain biscuits; French, granary, wholemeal or rye bread or rolls.
- Butter or a low-fat spread.
- Salad vegetables, such as lettuce, celery, chicory, tomato wedges, small whole radishes, watercress, carrot sticks and spring onions.
- Fresh fruit, such as grapes, figs and pears.

Cheese and wine have a natural affinity; they can be served together for informal parties, lunches or dinner parties. For a dinner party, the cheese can either be served French-style between the main course and the dessert (in which case it is eaten with the wine served with the main course) or at the end of the meal. As a general rule for serving wine with cheese, serve richer cheeses with full-bodied wines and lighter, creamier cheeses with lighter red or white wine.

COOKING WITH CHEESE

Cheese goes well with eggs, pasta and many other ingredients, and flavours many sauces and toppings. When cooking cheese, remember that a fierce heat can make it stringy. It should melt gently, and when added to a sauce, it should not be allowed to boil. Hard cheese can be grated for cooking, but softer cheeses are best sliced, shredded or crumbled before adding to a dish.

It is important to think carefully about the actual cheese you use in a dish. If a recipe specifies a particular type of cheese it is usually because of its individual flavour and texture, and substituting another variety may alter the taste of the dish. However, some cheeses can be used as substitutes for each other and the recipes in this chapter indicate which these are. Well matured cheese gives the best flavour; if using a mild Cheddar add a little mustard for extra flavour if wished – adding an extra quantity of a mild cheese will not give a greater depth of flavour. Cheddar and Gruyère are good in baking; use either of these, or Lancashire, Cheshire or Leicester for toasting; Mozzarella is perfect for pizzas, while crumbly cheeses such as Feta and Roquefort are ideal in salads and dressings.

TYPES OF CHEESE

SEMI-HARD AND HARD CHEESES

A semi-hard cheese is produced by removing as much of the whey as possible from the curd, often by mechanical pressing, before moulding and ripening. Hard cheeses undergo a further process which involves heating the curd so that it shrinks and hardens, making it possible to extract even more of the whey. These cheeses are left to mature much longer than the softer cheeses. Semi-hard cheeses include Cheddar and Edam, while the most familiar hard cheeses are Parmesan and Pecorino.

LOWER-FAT HARD CHEESES: These are produced from semi-skimmed milk for those who are cutting down on fat in their diet. There are no legal requirements for the fat content of these cheeses but lower-fat Cheddar contains about half as much fat and approximately two thirds of the calories of traditional Cheddar.

These cheeses tend to be mild flavoured. For use in cooking where a stronger flavour is required, add a pinch of mustard.

VEGETARIAN CHEESES

Vegetarian cheeses produced using vegetarian rennet are becoming more widely available. Vegetarian Cheddar is widely available. Other varieties produced include Cheshire, Double Gloucester, Stilton, Mozzarella and goat's cheese.

FRESH AND SOFT CHEESES

A true soft cheese is made by coagulating milk with rennet. The addition of a 'starter' just before rennet is added ensures a clean acid flavour. The majority of soft cheeses, such as Camembert, are foreign in origin. The British varieties of unripened soft cheese are usually made from cow's milk, but goat's milk can equally well be used.

The British cheeses are usually marketed in a fresh or unripened state, whilst the better known of those made abroad are consumed when fully mature. This requires the growth of specific bacteria and moulds to produce the desired ripening action.

It is these soft mould ripened cheeses – Brie, Camembert, etc and the blue-veined cheeses, such as Danish Blue, which are susceptible to listeria contamination. The risk is mimimal, but 'at risk' groups, especially pregnant women, young children and the elderly should avoid these cheeses.

Today many soft cheeses are made from skimmed milk, which means they are lower in calories and fat content. Varieties of soft cheese are defined and labelled according to the amount of milk fat and water they contain.

SKIMMED MILK SOFT CHEESE must by law contain less than 2 per cent milk fat and not more than 80 per cent water. They are generally low in calories, soft and smooth with a bland or slightly acid taste. Examples include *fromage frais.*

LOW FAT SOFT CHEESE have 2-10 per cent milk fat and up to 80 per cent water. Textures may vary from smooth and yogurt-like to lumpy-textured cottage cheese (see right).

MEDIUM FAT SOFT CHEESE must contain 10-20 per cent milk fat and not more than 10 per cent water. It is white with a smooth but slightly granular texture and lightly acid flavour.

FULL FAT SOFT CHEESES are often called 'creamy' and frequently confused with the higher fat cream cheeses. Full fat means they must contain at least 20 per cent milk fat and not more than 60 per cent water.

The higher fat cream cheeses are often referred to as double cream cheese (see below). One example is Caboc.

CREAM CHEESE can be classified as a soft cheese. Its manufacture is very similar to that described above, but it is made from cream rather than milk. A typical cream cheese is a soft-bodied, unripened cheese with a rich, full and mildly acid flavour. It has a rather granular texture, buttery consistency and a high content of milk fat which gives it a creamy appearance. It is usually moulded into small cylindrical, square, rectangular or round shapes of varying sizes. There are two recognised varieties of cream cheese – single and double cream cheese.

Single cream cheese is made from single cream with an optimum fat content of 20-25 per cent. 1.2 litres (2 pints) of this cream. will yield about six cheeses weighing 125 g (4 oz) each. Carefully prepared, it will keep for a week in a refrigerator, after which it deteriorates quickly both in flavour and appearance.

Double cream cheese is produced from cream containing about 50-55 per cent butter-fat. Usually 1.2 litres (2 pints) of this cream will yield eight double cream cheeses weighing 125 g (4 oz) each. This cheese does not keep quite as long as single cream cheese.

ACID CURD CHEESE

Acid curd cheese is frequently classed as a soft cheese, but is fundamentally different. The curds are formed solely by the action of lactic acid upon the casein. Acid curdling is a completely different action from rennet coagulation and yields a curd of high acidity, quick drainage properties and somewhat granular texture. The cheese has a clean, acid flavour, and a slightly granular, soft, spreadable texture. It has a short shelf life and must be eaten in a fresh state.

COTTAGE CHEESE is an acid curd cheese, but is made from pasteurised, skimmed milk. The curd is cut into small cubes and slowly heated to develop the right body and texture. The whey is drained off, and the curd washed several times and cooled. The washing of the curd produces the familiar lumpy appearance of cottage cheese. Salt and single cream are then added and the cheese is packaged in cartons. The addition of the cream gives a final fat content of 4 per cent. This, combined with the high moisture content gives the cheese its soft velvety texture. Cottage cheese has a short shelf life and must be eaten when it is very fresh.

CHEESE VARIETIES

APPLEWOOD: A type of Cheddar which is smoked over apple branches and coated with paprika. It is very similar to a type called Charnwood.

BEL PAESE: A rich, creamy cheese of mild flavour, made in Italy, weighing about 2.3 kg (5 lb) each.

BLEU DE BRESSE: A soft and creamy blue cheese from France with a rich subtle flavour. It has a grey-coloured rind and should not be allowed to over-ripen as it develops a strong, unpleasant flavour.

BOURSIN: The brand name of a fresh cream cheese made in France – usually flavoured with garlic, or herbs, or rolled in crushed peppercorns.

BRIE: A soft-textured farm cheese, produced in the north of France. It is made from whole milk and is mould-inoculated. Brie is flat and round, usually 35 cm (14 inches) in diameter and about 2.7 kg (6 lb) in weight. It has a white floury crust and should be eaten fresh when soft all through. It doesn't keep well. Brie cheeses flavoured with herbs or peppercorns are available.

CABOC: Originated from the Western Highlands in the fifteenth century. This is a very rich, soft double cream cheese rolled in oatmeal.

CAERPHILLY: Originally a Welsh cheese, this is now made also in Somerset, Wiltshire, Devon and Dorset. It is made from whole milk, pressed only lightly and eaten in its 'green' state, when about ten days old. Caerphilly is soft and white, with a creamy mild flavour.

CAMBAZOLA: A full fat soft German cheese with a white Camembert mould on the rind and a blue Gorgonzola mould internally. Creamy in texture with a light bite coming from the blue.

CAMEMBERT: A French soft cheese, made of cow's milk, the curd being inoculated with a white mould. The cheese was made originally in Normandy, but is made now also in other parts of France. Camembert is at its best when it begins to get soft; if allowed to over-ripen, it develops an aroma which many people find unpleasant.

CHEDDAR: Perhaps the best known and most widely used of the English cheeses. The name 'Cheddar' is given to any cheese which undergoes the 'cheddaring' process, regardless of where it is made. Cheddar is now produced in various other parts of England and also in Scotland, Ireland, Canada, Australia and New Zealand. Flavours vary from mild to quite strong, depending on how long the cheese is left to mature before it is eaten.

English farmhouse Cheddar is made with whole milk from a single herd of cows. The process is the same as ordinary Cheddar but Farmhouse is allowed to mature longer to produce a richer and more mellow flavour.

The mellow, slightly salty Cheddar made in Canada is similar to Farmhouse Cheddar. Its strong, mature flavour makes it excellent for cooking. Australian and New Zealand cheddars are also widely available and are of a mild quality. Cheddar cheese is also available smoked.

CHESHIRE: Said to be the oldest of the English cheeses, Cheshire is another very well known type. Like Cheddar, it is a hard cheese, but rather more crumbly in texture, with a mild yet mellow flavour.

There are two main varieties – the red, which is coloured by the addition of vegetable dye, and the white. There is no significant difference in the flavour. Blue Cheshire is also available. Farmhouse Cheshire, which is made from a single herd of cows, is also available.

CHEVIOT: Cheddar with chives.

CHÈVRE: The French name for various types of cheese made from goat's milk. Cheese given this name should be made from 100 per cent goat's milk, whilst those made from a mixture of goat's and cow's milk are often labelled mi-chèvre, containing a minimum of 25 per cent goat's milk. French goat cheeses are usually small and rounded or cylindrical in shape. The cheese itself is soft, white and somewhat sour in

Selection of Fine French Cheeses in Prime Condition

flavour. Various regional goat's cheeses exist, including *chevret, chevreton, chevrette* and *chevrotin*.

COTSWOLD: A variant of Double Gloucester which is flavoured with chives and chopped onion.

CRÉDIOUX: A processed cheese shaped either as a small cake or round log. It is creamy with a highly refined flavour and is coated with walnuts.

DANISH BLUE: A white softish cheese made in Denmark; it has a blue mould veining and a sharp salty taste.

DEMI-SEL: A fresh cream cheese, usually sold in small squares wrapped in foil. It is made in France, mainly in Normandy.

DERBY: A hard, close-textured cheese, mild in flavour when young, it develops a fuller flavour as it matures and is at its best when it is six months old. Its better-known derivative Sage Derby was originally made by layering with sage leaves to give a pleasant, sharp tangy flavour. It must be eaten fresh or the flavour becomes very sharp. Sage oil is now used in place of leaves.

DOLCELATTE: A mild, blue cheese version of Gorgonzola but slightly softer and creamier.

EDAM: A Dutch ball-shaped deep yellow cheese, with a bright red or yellow wax coating, about 2.3 kg (5 lb) in weight. It is firm and smooth in texture and has a mild flavour.

EMMENTHAL: A Swiss cheese similar to Gruyère but larger and slightly softer in texture, with larger holes.

ESROM: Made in Denmark, this is a semi-hard yellow cheese and has a pleasant, mild flavour.

FETA: Made from ewe's milk originally in Greece but now produced in many other countries. It is stored in brine in barrels which accounts for its salty flavour. It is a fairly hard cheese that crumbles easily for use in salads and other raw dishes. It can also be sprinkled on to stews, used in pastries and in vegetable stuffings.

FONTAINEBLEAU: A French cream type cheese; soft and fresh; it is made in the country round Fontainebleau, mostly in the summer.

FOURME D'AMBERT: A firm but soft French blue cheese made in the Auvergne from cow's milk.

FROMAGE BLANC: A very low fat cheese with a light, fresh, clean taste and a smooth texture.

FROMAGE DE MONSIEUR: A soft French cheese made from cows' milk. It is similar to Camembert, but milder.

FROMAGE FRAIS: Similar to fromage blanc, this is a soft cheese that originated in France but is now made in many other countries and is widely available in Britain. It is sometimes enriched with cream, increasing its fat content, and it is often sold flavoured with fruit. Depending on its fat content, the consistency of fromage frais varies from quite runny to very thick. Some varieties are quite rich and are sold in very small pots. Fruit flavoured fromage frais may be served as a dessert, while plain varieties are often used in cooking.

GLOUCESTER: An orange-yellow, hard cheese with a close, crumbly texture and a good rich flavour, rather similar to that of a mature Cheddar. Originally there were 'double' and 'single' Gloucesters, one being twice the size of the other, but now only the 'double' is made.

GORGONZOLA: A semi-hard, blue-veined sharp flavoured cheese, made in Italy near Milan.

GOUDA: A wheel-shaped Dutch cheese, not unlike Edam in taste and texture, but flatter in shape, with a yellow skin and very much larger, approximately 5 kg (9 lb) in weight. There are also small Goudas, about 450 g (1 lb) in weight. Mature Gouda has a black skin.

GRUYÈRE: A hard, large cheese, weighing anything up to 45 kg (100 lb). Originally it came exclusively from Switzerland but is now made also in France, Italy and other parts of Europe. It is pale yellow in colour and is honeycombed with 'eyes' or holes, caused by the rapid fermentation of the curd; it has a distinctive and fairly sweet taste. Gruyère is normally served uncooked, but it is also used in such classic dishes as fondue.

HUNTSMAN: An attractive looking cheese made from layering Double Gloucester and Stilton.

ILCHESTER: Double Gloucester flavoured with mustard pickle.

JARLSBERG: Originates in Norway. The whole cheese (usually sold in wedges) is wheel-shaped with a yellow wax rind. The cheese itself has a sweet nutty flavour like Emmenthal and has similar holes.

LANCASHIRE: A fairly hard cheese, crumbly in texture when cut. When new it has a mild, tangy flavour, which develops as it matures.

LEICESTER: A hard cheese with a mild, slightly sweet flavour and orange-red colour.

LIMBURGER: A semi-hard, whole milk cheese made in Belgium (and also in Germany and Alsace). It is full flavoured and has a distinctive strong aroma.

LYMESWOLD: The first mild soft blue British cheese. As it matures, Lymeswold develops from a firmer, more curd-textured and fresh-flavoured cheese to a softer, more mellow richness.

MASCARPONE: A rich cream cheese with the texture of thick whipped cream, made in Italy. It is primarily a dessert cheese, but is also used in pasta sauces.

MELBURY: A mild white mould ripened soft cheese. It has a mellow taste and is made in a distinctive loaf shape.

MOZZARELLA: A pale egg-shaped Italian cheese. When fresh, it is very soft, dripping with buttermilk. Traditionally made from buffalo milk, it is now also made from cow's milk.

Mozzarella should be eaten fresh, as the cheese ripens quickly and is past its best in a few days. It can be used in salads and is ideal for pizzas, lasagnes, and other Italian dishes. Bel Paese may be used as a substitute.

MYCELLA: This cheese gets its name from the mould mycelium which produces the blue veins. It is a full fat cheese similar to Danish Blue but has a milder flavour.

NUTWOOD: Cheddar flavoured with cider, nuts and raisins.

PARMESAN: This Italian cheese is the hardest of all cheeses. After being specially processed, the curd is broken up, heated, packed into a large mould the shape of a millstone and matured for at least two and usually three years. When it is ripe the crust is almost black, but the cheese itself should be of a pale straw colour and full of tiny holes.

Parmesan has a strong, distinctive flavour and is used finely grated for cooking or as a traditional accompaniment for soups, such as Minestrone, and for rice and pasta dishes. The flavour of freshly grated Parmesan is far superior to that of ready-grated Parmesan, sold in packets and tubs.

PECORINO: A strong hard Italian cheese, used like Parmesan.

PETIT SUISSE (PETIT GERVAIS): An unsalted cream cheese, cylindrical in shape, made in France. It is very mild in flavour. Often sold in small foil-wrapped packs.

POMMEL: A double cream cheese, unsalted and not unlike Petit Suisse, which is made in France all the year round.

PONT L'EVÊQUE: A soft paste cheese with a thickish orange rind, about 10 cm (4 inches) square and 4 cm (1½ inches) thick. It is made in the Pont l'Eveque district of Normandy. The smell is stronger than the taste.

QUARK: A soft cheese that is often eaten on its own with a spoon. It is sometimes flavoured with fruit or herbs. It may be made from skimmed or whole milk or buttermilk and may also include added cream. The name, which is German, means simply curds and the cheese is also sold as *Buttermilchquark* and *Speisequark*. It has a mild, slightly sour flavour and is used in desserts.

RACLETTE: To most people this means a Swiss method of toasting cheese over an open fire or in a special appliance. But raclette is generally a semi-hard cheese which is golden with a few small holes and a rough, grey-brown rind. It tastes full and fruity and somewhat like Gruyère. There are many local Swiss varieties.

RICOTTA: A fragrant Italian cheese made from the whey left over when producing other cheeses. It has a delicate, smooth flavour and is very suitable for cooking in such dishes as ravioli or cannelloni. It can also be eaten with sugar or used layered in fruit tarts and puddings.

ROQUEFORT: This is the only ewe's milk cheese which has obtained a world-wide reputation. It is made during the lambing season in the village of Roquefort in the Cevennes mountains of France. It can be made only in this district, partly because the sheep-grazing land here is particularly suitable, but also because of the limestone caverns of Roquefort itself, which play a very important part in the maturing process of the cheese. The same mould as that used in the making of Stilton is introduced into the curd as a maturing agent.

This delicious blue cheese has a sharp, pungent flavour and a soft creamy, crumbly texture. It is excellent used in dips and salad dressings.

ROULE: This resembles a Swiss roll in shape and comes in two versions. Both are full fat soft cheese but one is rolled in fines herbes and garlic and the other in spices.

RUTLAND: Cheddar flavoured with beer, garlic and parsley.

SAINT PAULIN: A French semi-hard cheese, round in shape, it was made originally by the monks of Port du Salut and is sometimes sold as Port Salut, but is now made in various other parts of France. It is creamy yellow in colour and has a very mild and delicate flavour; it should be eaten while still slightly soft.

SAMSOE: Named after the Danish island of the same name. It is a firm cheese, made from unskimmed cow's milk with a delicate, nutty flavour. The flavour acquires greater pungency as it matures.

SHERWOOD: Double Gloucester flavoured with chives and onions.

SHROPSHIRE BLUE: A cross between Stilton and Blue Cheshire.

SMOKED CHEESE (AUSTRIAN AND GERMAN): Sold in small rounds or 'sausages' wrapped in brown plastic, the cheese is a pale creamy colour. Mild and smoky in flavour, with a very smooth, soft texture, excellent with wine.

STILTON: One of the best known of English cheeses, it is made in Leicestershire, Nottinghamshire and Derbyshire. Stilton is a semi-hard white cheese with a blue veining, caused by a mould which in most cases is a natural growth throughout the curd, accelerated by the use of stainless steel skewers piercing the cheese to allow the mould to enter. The veins of blue mould should be evenly distributed throughout. The rind, of a dull, drab colour, should be well crinkled, regular and free from cracks. Stilton is at its best when fully ripe, that is 4-5 months after it has been made. If bought in small quantities eat it as soon as possible. A whole or half Stilton keeps well if the cut surface is covered and the cheese is kept in a dry airy larder. It should be cut in slices from the top and not scooped out.

White Stilton bears little resemblance to Blue Stilton in flavour but it is the same cheese before the mould has grown. It has a slightly crumbly texture and a pleasant, mild flavour.

TALEGGIO: An Italian unpressed, uncooked cheese with a pinkish-grey rind and white soft flesh. The flavour becomes stronger and more aromatic as the cheese ripens. Taleggio made with unpasteurised milk is considered a special Italian delicacy.

TOMME: Is the name given to the various small cheeses produced during the summer months in Savoie, mostly from skimmed cow's milk. *Tomme au Raisin* is ripened in a mixture of grape skins, pips and stalks to give the cheese its distinctive flavour. *Tomme de Savoie* is cylindrical in shape and has a pleasant, light flavour.

WINDSOR RED: A mature Cheddar cheese flavoured and coloured with English fruit wine. This produces a cheese with a red veining and a very mature flavour.

WENSLEYDALE: Made in the vale of Wensleydale in Yorkshire. Originally it was a double cream cheese, cylindrical in shape, which matured until it became blue – in this form it was considered one of the best English blue cheeses, next only to Stilton. Much of the Wensleydale production is now sold when white and in this form it is a mild, creamy-coloured cheese with a rather flaky texture. Blue Wensleydale is also obtainable.

WELSH RAREBIT

225 g (8 oz) Cheddar cheese, grated
25 g (1 oz) butter or margarine
5 ml (1 level tsp) mustard powder
salt and pepper
60 ml (4 tbsp) brown ale
4 slices of bread, crusts removed

1. Place all the ingredients except the bread in a heavy-based saucepan and heat very gently until a creamy mixture is obtained.
2. Lightly toast the bread on one side.
3. Pour the sauce over the uncooked sides and put under a hot grill until golden and bubbling.
SERVES 4

VARIATION
BUCK RAREBIT
This is Welsh Rarebit topped with a poached egg.

CROQUE MONSIEUR

16 thin slices bread, crusts removed
5-10 ml (1-2 level tsp) prepared mustard
225 g (8 oz) Gruyère or Cheddar cheese, sliced
225 g (8 oz) cooked ham, thinly sliced
75 g (3 oz) butter or margarine, melted

1. Spread half the slices of bread on one side with the mustard; trim the cheese slices to fit and put them on top.
2. Trim the ham slices to fit and arrange them on top of the cheese. Top with the remaining slices of bread and press lightly.
3. Brush the sandwiches lightly with melted butter and fry for 3-5 minutes, until they are lightly browned.
4. Turn the sandwiches over and fry for a further 3-5 minutes.
5. Cut the sandwiches in half and serve hot.
SERVES 4-8

NOTE: 90 ml (6 tbsp) vegetable oil may be used instead of the butter. Heat in the frying pan and cook the sandwiches as above.

FETA CHEESE PUFFS

225 g (8 oz) Feta cheese, grated
150 ml (5 fl oz) natural yogurt
15 ml (1 tbsp) chopped fresh basil or 5 ml (1 level tsp) dried
pepper
368 g (13 oz) packet puff pastry, thawed
1 egg, beaten
fresh basil leaves, to garnish

1. Mix the cheese with the yogurt, basil and pepper. (Do not add salt as the cheese is salty.)
2. Roll out the pastry thinly on a lightly floured surface and cut out sixteen 7.5 cm (3 inch) rounds. Place half the rounds on two baking sheets. Spoon the cheese mixture into the centre of each one.
3. Brush the pastry edges with beaten egg. Cover with remaining rounds, knocking up the pastry edges to seal. Make a small slit in the top of each puff and glaze the tops with beaten egg.
4. Bake in the oven at 220°C (425°F) mark 7 for about 15 minutes, until well browned and crisp. Serve warm, garnished with basil leaves.
MAKES 8

CHEESE AND POTATO CAKES

450 g (1 lb) potatoes, boiled and mashed
25 g (1 oz) butter or margarine
125 g (4 oz) Cheddar cheese, grated
15 ml (1 tbsp) snipped fresh chives
salt and pepper
15 ml (1 level tbsp) flour
2 eggs, beaten
40 g (1½ oz) fresh breadcrumbs
30-45 ml (2-3 tbsp) oil for frying (optional)

1. Mix the potatoes with the butter, cheese, chives, seasoning, flour and 1 egg and beat until smooth. Leave until cold.
2. Turn on to a lightly floured surface and form into a roll. Cut into 2.5 cm (1 inch) slices and, using lightly floured hands, shape into round cakes.
3. Brush with the remaining egg and coat with breadcrumbs. Place on a greased baking sheet and chill in the refrigerator for 30 minutes. Bake in the oven at 190°C (375°F) mark 5 for about 20 minutes. Alternatively, fry the cakes in the oil until golden brown. Serve hot.
SERVES 4

CHEESE FONDUE

1 garlic clove, skinned
300 ml (½ pint) dry white wine
450 g (1 lb) cheese (half Gruyère and half Emmenthal), coarsely grated
20 ml (4 level tsp) cornflour
pepper
pinch of grated nutmeg
45 ml (3 tbsp) kirsch (optional)
French bread, to serve

1. Rub the inside of a fondue pot or flameproof dish with the garlic. Pour in the wine, place the pot over a fondue burner on the table and warm the liquid.
2. Add the cheese gradually and continue to heat gently, stirring, until the cheese has melted.
3. Blend the cornflour and seasonings to a smooth paste with the kirsch or 45 ml (3 tbsp)

water. Add to the fondue and continue cooking for a further 2-3 minutes. When the fondue reaches a very smooth consistency, it is ready to serve.
4. Fondue is traditionally served in the centre of the table, kept warm over a fondue burner. Crusty cubes of bread are speared on long handled forks and dipped into it.
SERVES 4

NOTE: If liked, small glasses of kirsch can be served with the fondue—guests should dip the cubes of bread first in the kirsch, before dipping in the fondue.

VARIATION
Replace the Gruyère and Emmenthal with mature Cheddar cheese, grated, and use dry cider instead of the white wine.

POTTED CHEESE WITH MINT

75 g (3 oz) butter
225 g (8 oz) Leicester cheese, grated
15 ml (1 tbsp) chopped fresh mint
60 ml (4 level tbsp) soured cream
pepper
fresh mint leaves, to garnish
brown bread or crispbread, to serve

1. Beat the butter until really soft, then gradually beat in the cheese.
2. Stir in the chopped mint and soured cream and add pepper to taste. Salt should not be required as the cheese should add sufficient.
3. Spoon into a serving dish; cover and refrigerate for at least 2 hours.
4. To serve, leave at room temperature for about 20 minutes, to soften a little, then garnish with fresh mint leaves. Spread on slices of brown bread or crispbread.
SERVES 4-6

Pizzas and Savoury Flans

Pizzas at their best are wholesome, nutritious and simply delicious. Use either of the dough recipes below, then add the topping of your choice. For an instant snack, try one of the cheat's pizzas on page 291. Savoury flans also make tasty light meals and fillings can easily be adapted to suit the ingredients to hand.

BASIC PIZZA DOUGH

This mixture will be very sticky initially, but is soon worked into a soft, smooth dough. Don't be tempted to add more flour – it won't be needed.

175 g (6 oz) strong plain white flour
1.25 ml (¼ level tsp) salt
5 ml (1 level tsp) fast-action dried yeast (no need to reconstitute in water)
15 ml (1 tbsp) olive oil

1. In a warm, medium bowl, stir together the flour, salt and yeast. Make a well in the centre of the dry ingredients and add 150 ml (¼ pint) warm water and the olive oil.
2. Stir the mixture by hand until it forms a wet dough. Beat for a further 2-3 minutes.
3. Turn out the dough on to a well floured surface and knead for about 5 minutes, or until the dough becomes very smooth and elastic.
4. Place in a bowl and cover with a clean tea towel. Leave in a warm place until doubled in size, about 45 minutes.
5. Turn out the dough on to a floured surface and knead again for 2-3 minutes.
6. Place a lightly oiled flat baking sheet in a hot oven at 220°C (425°F) mark 7 to heat.
7. Roll out the dough to a circle roughly 25 cm (10 inches) in diameter. Place on the heated baking sheet and press into a rough circle, making the edges slightly thicker than the centre. The pizza dough is now ready to complete and bake with your choice of toppings (see pages 289-290).

QUICK PIZZA DOUGH

Don't overwork this scone-like dough or it will be thin and tough.

200 g (7 oz) plain white flour
1.25 ml (¼ level tsp) salt
5 ml (1 level tsp) baking powder
40 g (1½ oz) butter or margarine
15 ml (1 tbsp) olive oil
1 egg
75 ml (3 fl oz) milk

1. In a medium bowl, stir together the flour, salt and baking powder.
2. Rub in the butter until the mixture resembles breadcrumbs.
3. Whisk together the olive oil, egg and milk in a bowl. Make a well in the centre of the dry ingredients and add the milk mixture.
4. Stir the mixture quickly by hand until it forms a soft dough. (Cover if not using immediately – see recipes, some of which advise you to stop at stage 4 while making up pizza topping.)
5. Turn out the dough on to a well floured surface and knead for about 30 seconds; do not overwork.
6. Place a lightly oiled flat baking sheet in a hot oven at 220°C (425°F) mark 7 to heat.
7. Roll out the dough to a circle roughly 25 cm (10 inches) in diameter. Place on the heated baking sheet and press into a rough circle, making the edges slightly thicker than the centre. The pizza dough is now ready to complete and bake with your choice of toppings (see pages 289-290).

TOMATO AND MOZZARELLA PIZZA

1 quantity Pizza Dough (see page 288)
60 ml (4 level tbsp) chopped mixed fresh herbs, eg
tarragon, parsley, thyme and chives, or 15 ml
(1 level tbsp) dried mixed herbs
1 quantity Tomato Sauce (see page 207)
150 g (5 oz) mozzarella cheese, thinly sliced
few black olives, stoned (optional)
fresh herbs to garnish

1. Prepare either of the pizza doughs to the end
of stage 1. Stir in the mixed herbs. Knead and
shape the dough as directed in stages 2-7 of your
chosen recipe.
2. Using a knife or spoon, spread the tomato
sauce evenly over the surface of the dough, right
to the edges.
3. Arrange the mozzarella evenly over the sauce
and scatter the olives on top if using.
4. Bake in the oven at 220°C (425°F) mark 7 for
25-30 minutes, or until the cheese is melted and
the dough well risen and golden.
5. Garnish with herbs and serve hot.
SERVES 2

PIZZA NIÇOISE

1 quantity Pizza Dough (see page 288)
125 g (4 oz) French beans
salt and pepper
1 quantity Tomato Sauce (see page 207)
200 g (7 oz) can tuna fish in brine, drained
6 green olives, stoned
6 black olives, stoned
15 ml (1 level tbsp) chopped fresh basil
6 anchovy fillets, halved
1 egg
125 g (4 oz) mozzarella cheese, thinly sliced
10 ml (2 level tsp) freshly grated Parmesan cheese
fresh basil to garnish

1. Prepare either of the pizza doughs to the end
of stage 4.
2. Cook the French beans in boiling salted water
until just tender. Drain thoroughly.
3. Knead and shape the dough as directed in
stages 5-7 of your chosen recipe.
4. Using a knife or spoon, spread the tomato
sauce evenly over the surface of the dough, right
to the edges.
5. Sprinkle the beans, tuna fish, olives and basil
over the sauce. Arrange the anchovy fillets on
top.
6. Make a hollow in the centre of the ingredients
on the pizza and carefully crack the egg into it.
Season with pepper.
7. Arrange the mozzarella around the egg.
Sprinkle all over with the Parmesan.
8. Bake in the oven at 220°C (425°F) mark 7 for
about 25-30 minutes or until the dough is well
risen and golden. Garnish with basil and serve.
SERVES 4

HOT SAUSAGE AND SALAMI PIZZA

1 quantity Pizza Dough (see page 288)
1 small green chilli pepper, seeded and finely chopped
200 g (7 oz) can pimiento, drained and finely chopped
1 quantity Tomato Sauce (see page 207)
125 g (4 oz) Kabanos sausage (smoked pork sausage),
skinned and thinly sliced
75 g (3 oz) coarse salami, skinned and roughly
chopped
175 g (6 oz) Emmenthal cheese, thinly sliced

1. Prepare and shape either of the pizza doughs.
2. Stir the chilli and pimiento into the tomato
sauce.
3. Using a knife or spoon, spread the flavoured
tomato sauce mixture evenly over the surface of
the dough, right to the edges.
4. Scatter over the Kabanos sausage and salami.
Top with the cheese slices.
5. Bake in the oven at 220°C (425°F) mark 7 for
about 15-20 minutes or until the cheese is
melted and browned and the dough well risen
and golden. Serve hot.
SERVES 4

NOTE: Remember to wear rubber gloves when
preparing the chilli to avoid skin irritation and
avoid touching your eyes.

SMOKED SALMON AND AVOCADO PIZZA

1 quantity Pizza Dough (see page 288)
2 small ripe avocados
10 ml (2 tsp) olive oil
juice and grated rind of 1 lemon
150 ml (5 fl oz) soured cream
5 ml (1 level tsp) chopped fresh dill or dried dill weed
1 egg yolk
5 ml (1 level tsp) wholegrain mustard
125 g (4 oz) thinly sliced smoked salmon
fresh dill, caviar (optional) and lemon wedges, to
  garnish

1. Prepare either of the pizza doughs to the end of stage 4.
2. Halve, stone and thinly slice the avocados; gently toss them with the olive oil and 5 ml (1 tsp) lemon juice to prevent discolouration.
3. Whisk together the soured cream, dill, egg yolk, mustard and lemon rind.
4. Knead and shape the dough as directed in stages 5-7 of your chosen recipe.
5. Neatly arrange the avocado slices over the surface of the dough, right to the edges. Distribute the smoked salmon evenly over the top.
6. Spoon the soured cream mixture on to the smoked salmon and spread evenly to cover completely.
7. Bake in the oven at 220°C (425°F) mark 7 for 25-30 minutes, until the topping is lightly browned and the dough well risen and golden.
8. Serve warm, garnished with fresh dill, caviar if using, and lemon wedges.
SERVES 4

LEFT: Smoked Salmon and Avocado Pizza. RIGHT: Pizza Niçoise (page 289)

LEFT: Devilled Mushroom 'Pizzas'. RIGHT: Quick Muffin 'Pizzas'.

QUICK MUFFIN 'PIZZAS'

4 muffins
butter or margarine for spreading
45 ml (3 level tbsp) tomato ketchup
200 g (7 oz) can tuna fish, drained
salt and pepper
125 g (4 oz) mozzarella cheese, thinly sliced
8 black olives, stoned and sliced

1. Split the muffins and toast lightly on both sides. Spread the inner sides with a little butter and tomato ketchup.
2. Break the tuna into medium-sized flakes and place on top of the muffins. Season with salt and plenty of pepper.
3. Cover the tuna with the mozzarella slices. Top with the olives. Grill until the cheese is melted and bubbling. Serve immediately.
SERVES 4

DEVILLED MUSHROOM 'PIZZAS'

about 75 g (3 oz) butter
175 g (6 oz) onion, skinned and finely chopped
1 clove garlic, skinned and crushed
350 g (12 oz) button mushrooms, wiped and sliced
30 ml (2 tbsp) vinegar, preferably red wine
5 ml (1 level tsp) mustard powder
dash of Worcestershire or Tabasco sauce
30 ml (2 level tbsp) tomato ketchup
salt and pepper
1 long baguette
30 ml (2 level tbsp) chopped fresh parsley

1. Melt 50 g (2 oz) butter in a small saucepan. Add the onion and garlic and cook until beginning to soften.
2. Mix in the mushrooms and stir over a high heat for a further 3-4 minutes. Add the vinegar, mustard, Worcestershire sauce and ketchup with seasoning to taste. Simmer gently for 1-2 minutes.
3. Meanwhile, cut the baguette in half and then cut each piece in half lengthwise to give 4 long pieces. Toast under the grill, lightly butter and top with the hot mushroom mixture. Sprinkle with parsley to serve.
SERVES 4

VARIATION
Add a little cream or mascarpone to the warm mushroom mixture.

LEEK AND ONION FLAN

175 g (6 oz) Cheese Pastry (see page 383)
40 g (1½ oz) butter
225 g (8 oz) leeks, trimmed and roughly chopped
1 medium onion, skinned and roughly chopped
1 bay leaf
2 fresh rosemary sprigs
25 g (1 oz) plain white flour
300 ml (½ pint) milk or single cream
2 eggs, separated
150 g (5 oz) Gruyère cheese, coarsely grated
salt and pepper

1. Roll out the pastry on a lightly floured surface and use to line a 23 cm (9 inch) loose-based, fluted flan tin (preferably a square one). Chill for 10-15 minutes. Place the flan tin on a flat baking sheet and bake blind (see page 380) for about 20 minutes or until just cooked through.

2. Meanwhile, melt the butter in a saucepan and sauté the leeks and onion with the bay leaf and 1 rosemary sprig until beginning to soften. Remove the herbs. Stir in the flour. Cook, stirring, for 1 minute, then gradually stir in the milk or cream. Bring to the boil. Cook, stirring, for 2-3 minutes until thickened and smooth. Cool slightly.

3. Strip the leaves from the other rosemary sprig and chop finely. Beat the egg yolks, all but 15 ml (1 level tbsp) of the cheese, the chopped rosemary and seasoning into the filling.

4. Whisk the egg whites until stiff but not dry. Fold into the leek mixture with a large metal spoon. Spoon into the prepared flan case. Sprinkle with the reserved cheese.

5. Bake in the oven at 200°C (400°F) mark 6 for 20-25 minutes or until well risen and just set. Serve warm.
SERVES 4-6

PLAICE AND SPINACH FLAN

175 g (6 oz) Rich Shortcrust Pastry (see page 382)
2 medium plaice, skinned and filleted, about 450 g
*   (1 lb) filleted weight*
300 ml (½ pint) milk
few black peppercorns
1 bay leaf
125 g (4 oz) fresh spinach or 50 g (2 oz) frozen
*   chopped spinach*
25 g (1 oz) butter
20 g (¾ oz) plain white flour
salt and pepper
50 g (2 oz) Brie, rinded and roughly chopped
2 small eggs
15 ml (1 level tbsp) freshly grated Parmesan cheese

1. Roll out the pastry on a lightly floured surface and use to line a 34 x 11 cm (13½ x 4½ inch) loose-based, fluted tranche tin. Chill for 10-15 minutes. Place the tin on a flat baking sheet and bake blind (see page 380) for about 20 minutes or until just cooked through.

2. Meanwhile, halve the plaice fillets lengthways to make eight fillets. Roll up skinned side out. Place in a saucepan into which they will just fit and pour over the milk. Add the peppercorns and bay leaf. Cover and bring slowly to the boil, then simmer for about 2 minutes or until the fillets are just cooked. Remove with a slotted spoon and dry on absorbent kitchen paper. Strain and reserve liquid.

3. If using fresh spinach, wash, trim and place in a medium saucepan with just the water clinging to the leaves. Cover and cook over a gentle heat for 3-4 minutes or until wilted. Drain well. Squeeze out any excess liquid and finely chop.

4. Melt the butter in a saucepan. Stir in the flour and cook, stirring, for 1-2 minutes. Gradually stir in 200 ml (7 fl oz) of the reserved poaching liquid, season and bring to the boil. Simmer for 2-3 minutes until thickened and smooth. Off the heat, beat in the Brie, eggs and spinach. Add frozen spinach at this stage, stirring until evenly blended.

5. Arrange the poached fish down the centre of the prepared flan tin. Spoon over the sauce and sprinkle with the Parmesan.

6. Bake in the oven at 180°C (350°F) mark 4 for 25-30 minutes or until just set. Place under a hot grill for 1-2 minutes to brown. Serve warm.
SERVES 4-6

SWEET PEPPER AND BASIL FLAN

1 quantity Rich Shortcrust Pastry (see page 382)
2 large red peppers, about 350 g (12 oz) total weight
few saffron strands (optional)
150 g (5 oz) full-fat soft cheese with garlic and herbs
2 eggs
30 ml (2 level tbsp) chopped fresh basil
15 ml (l level tbsp) chopped fresh parsley
salt and pepper

1. Roll out the pastry on a lightly floured surface and use to line a 20 cm (8 inch) flan tin. Chill for 10-15 minutes. Bake blind (see page 380) for 20 minutes or until just cooked through.

2. Meanwhile, place the peppers under a hot grill and cook for about 10-15 minutes turning frequently until the skin is charred and black. Cool slightly, then rub off the skins under cold running water; pat dry. Halve the peppers and remove seeds. Cut into 5 cm (2 inch) pieces.
3. Grind the saffron with a pestle and mortar. Whisk together the cheese, eggs, herbs and saffron. Stir in the peppers and seasoning.
4. Spoon the mixture into the prepared flan case. Bake in the oven at 180°C (350°F) mark 4 for 25-30 minutes or until just set. Brown under a hot grill for 1-2 minutes if wished. Serve warm.
SERVES 4

LEFT: Sweet Pepper and Basil Flan. RIGHT: Plaice and Spinach Flan.

QUICHE LORRAINE

175 g (6 oz) Shortcrust Pastry (see page 381)
75-125 g (3-4 oz) lean bacon, rinded and chopped
75-125 g (3-4 oz) Gruyère cheese, thinly sliced
2 eggs, beaten
150 ml (5 fl oz) single cream or milk
salt and pepper

1. Roll out the pastry on a lightly floured surface and use to line a 20 cm (8 inch) flan tin. Chill in the refrigerator for 10-15 minutes. Bake blind (see page 380) in the oven at 200°C (400°F) mark 6 for 10-15 minutes, until set.
2. Scatter the bacon over the pastry base and top with the cheese.
3. Beat together the eggs, cream and seasoning and pour into the pastry case. Bake in the oven at 200°C (400°F) mark 6 for about 30 minutes, until well risen and golden. Serve hot or cold.
SERVES 4

CRAB AND RICOTTA QUICHE

175 g (6 oz) Shortcrust Pastry (see page 381)
salt and pepper
2 eggs
150 ml (¼ pint) milk
150 ml (5 fl oz) single cream
225 g (8 oz) crab meat
175 g (6 oz) Ricotta cheese
30 ml (2 level tbsp) grated Parmesan

1. Roll out the pastry and use to line a 20 cm (8 inch) flan tin. Chill for 10-15 minutes.
2. Bake blind (see page 380) in the oven at 200°C (400°F) mark 6 for 10-15 minutes.
3. Whisk the eggs, milk and cream together in a bowl. Flake the crab meat, crumble the Ricotta and add to the egg mixture with the Parmesan and plenty of seasoning. Pour into the flan case and bake in the oven at 190°C (375°F) mark 5 for 35 minutes until golden. Serve hot.
SERVES 6

ROQUEFORT QUICHE

175 g (6 oz) Shortcrust Pastry (see page 381)
75 g (3 oz) Roquefort or other blue cheese, shredded
175 g (6 oz) full fat or low fat soft cheese
2 eggs, beaten
150 ml (5 fl oz) single cream
5-10 ml (1-2 tsp) grated onion or 15 ml (1 tbsp)
   snipped fresh chives
salt and pepper

1. Roll out the pastry and use to line a 20 cm (8 inch) flan tin. Chill for 10-15 minutes.
2. Bake blind (see page 380) in the oven at 200°C (400°F) mark 6 for 10-15 minutes, until set.
3. Cream together the two cheeses and stir in the eggs, cream, onion and salt and pepper.
4. Pour into the pastry case. Bake in the oven at 190°C (375°F) mark 5 for about 30 minutes, until well risen and golden. Serve at once.
SERVES 6

CHEESE AND ASPARAGUS TART

175 g (6 oz) Shortcrust Pastry (see page 381)
25 g (1 oz) butter or margarine
45 ml (3 level tbsp) flour
300 ml (½ pint) milk
125 g (4 oz) Cheddar or Gruyère cheese, grated
salt and pepper
350 g (12 oz) cooked asparagus (fresh or canned)

1. Roll out pastry and use to line a 20 cm (8 inch) flan tin. Chill for 10-15 minutes. Bake blind (see page 380) in the oven at 200°C (400°F) mark 6 for 10-15 minutes, until set. Remove beans. Bake for a further 15 minutes, until firm.
2. Melt the butter in a saucepan, stir in the flour and cook gently for 1 minute, stirring. Remove from heat and gradually stir in the milk. Cook, stirring, until the sauce thickens.
3. Remove from the heat and stir in 75 g (3 oz) of the cheese and salt and pepper to taste.
4. Place the drained asparagus in the pastry case, pour over the sauce and sprinkle with the remaining cheese. Brown under a hot grill.
SERVES 4

Pasta, Rice and Gnocchi

Pasta and rice are cheap, nutritious and extremely versatile; they can be served as accompaniments or used as the main ingredient in a dish. There are numerous types of rice and pasta. Gnocchi – small Italian dumplings – are also included in this section.

Pasta

The word pasta simply means dough in Italian but it is also used to describe spaghetti, macaroni, lasagne and many other pasta shapes made from the basic dough mixture. Also included in this chapter are egg and rice noodles which are widely used in Japanese and Chinese cooking.

There are said to be over 500 different varieties of pasta throughout Italy today, although only about 50 of these are widely known. The best commercially dried pasta is made from 100 per cent hard durum wheat; look for this description, or *'pasta di semola di grano duro'* on the packet. There is a vast selection of dried pasta shapes to choose from. Most dried pastas are made from durum wheat and water, but some are made from *pasta all'uovo* (egg pasta).

Fresh pasta is made from flour and eggs, and is becomming increasingly easy to buy. Most supermarkets stock a good range, and Italian delicatessens invariably make there own. However, nothing can compare with the flavour and freshness of homemade pasta (see page 298).

As for nutritional value, pasta is mainly a carbohydrate food, although good-quality brands can contain as much as 13 per cent protein, and all contain some vitamins and minerals.

DIFFERENT TYPES OF PASTA

There is an increasingly wide choice of flavoured fresh and dried pasta available. Coloured pasta adds interest to meals: green pasta *(pasta verde)* is flavoured with spinach; pink or red pasta *(pasta rosso)* with tomatoes or peppers. Fresh pasta is also available flavoured with basil or garlic. Wholewheat pasta is available too; it contains more fibre than pasta made with ordinary flour and is consequently more chewy.

The variety of pasta shapes is endless and new shapes are constantly being introduced. Here is a guide to the most common ones, although you may see slightly different shapes or the same shape under different names – especially if visiting Italy. This is simply because the different regions of Italy have their own individual pasta shapes and names – and so do the manufacturers.

SPAGHETTI comes in long straight strands of varying thickness. When cooking long dried spaghetti, coil it gently into the pan as it softens on contact with the boiling water.

MACARONI is a thicker hollow tube, sometimes cut into short lengths; *bucatini, tubetti, zite* and *penne* are all short macaroni.

LASAGNE is the widest of the ribbon pastas. It comes in flat strips, rectangles or squares with either a smooth or ridged edge. Some varieties do not need pre-cooking before incorporating into a dish which is to be baked.

NOODLES are narrow flat pasta strips. They are either straight ribbons or folded into a nest-shaped mass, which is easier to drop into boiling water. *Tagliatelle* and *fettucine* are the most common types.

VERMICELLI is the finest ribbon pasta. It comes in a nest-shaped mass and is mostly used in soups.

CANNELLONI are large hollow tubes which can be

stuffed with meat or vegetable mixtures and served with sauce.

RIGATONI are slightly narrower than cannelloni and can be served with a sauce.

SMALL PASTA SHAPES include *lumache* (snails), *conchiglie* (shells), *fusilli* (spirals), *ruotini* (wheels), *farfalle* (bows), and *cappalletti* (hats) and *orecchiette* (ears).

TINY PASTA SHAPES for use in soup include *ditalini* and *orzo* (shaped like rice grains).

STUFFED PASTA SHAPES include *ravioli, tortellini* and *tortelli.*

ORIENTAL NOODLES

Noodles, which feature strongly in Chinese, Japanese and Asian cooking, are very similar to pasta and may be used in the same way as thin ribbon pastas. The following are the varietes most widely available from supermarkets and specialist shops. Fresh noodles are obtainable from Chinese supermarkets.

EGG NOODLES are the best known noodles and are used a great deal in Chinese cooking. They are made from flour, egg and water; usually sold in compressed bundles of varying sizes.

RICE NOODLES come in various thickness. They are made in long strands which are folded over for packaging. Very thin rice noodles are sold in compressed bundles, and these are known as vermicelli.

TRANSPARENT OR CELLOPHANE NOODLES are made from mung bean, pea starch or wheat. Sold in long strands which are folded over for packaging.

Noodles may also be made from soya beans, buckwheat, corn or chick peas.

STORING PASTA

Fresh pasta should be kept in the refrigerator and used within 24 hours of purchase; after this time it begins to dry out. Unopened packets of dried pasta will keep for months in a cool, dry

cupboard, but once opened, the packet should be used up quickly as exposure to the air makes the pasta become brittle and tasteless – this is especially true of pasta made with eggs.

QUANTITIES OF PASTA

When calculating quantities of pasta, you will need to consider appetite and how substantial the other courses are. As a rough guide, when serving as a main course dish, allow 125-150 g (4-5 oz) uncooked fresh pasta per person, or 75-125 g (3-4 oz) dried. If serving as a starter, allow 75-125 g (3-4 oz) fresh pasta per person, 50-75 g (2-3 oz) dried.

MAKING YOUR OWN PASTA

Making pasta at home is very easy – the actual dough is a simple mixture of flour, salt, eggs and olive oil. The best flour to use is semolina flour: a hard, very fine wheat flour. As this is difficult to obtain, a strong flour of the type used for making bread is a satisfactory alternative. General household plain flour can be used, but it produces a dough which cannot be rolled out as thinly by hand.

It is well worth investing in a pasta machine if you regularly make your own pasta. One of these can cut larger quantities more evenly and quickly than you can by hand. It will also cut various shapes, such as spaghetti, macaroni and long strips for lasagne.

COOKING PASTA

Pasta should be cooked in fast-boiling salted water in a large saucepan. Allow about 2-3 litres (3½ -5¼ pints) per 450 g (1 lb) of pasta. Adding 15 ml (1 tbsp) oil to the water will help to prevent the pasta sticking together.

Cooking time depends on the size; long pasta takes about 8-10 minutes, short cut pasta 6-12 minutes and tiny pasta shapes 2-6 minutes. Lasagne takes about 12 minutes. Fresh pasta takes about 2-4 minutes. Brands do vary enormously, so check packet instructions.

Check just before the end of the cooking time by biting a piece of pasta. It should be what the Italians call *al dente,* firm but not too hard or soft. Once it has reached this stage it should be drained thoroughly and served immediately. If the pasta is to be used in a cold dish, rinse under cold running water and drain well. Hot pasta is always best eaten immediately, although it can be kept hot in a colander over a pan of boiling water for a few minutes before serving.

KEY
1. Farfalle. (bows); **2.** Zite (short cut macaroni);
3. Cannelloni; **4.** Spaghetti;
5. Lasagne; **6.** Tagliatelle;
7. Ravioli; **8.** Tortelli and tortellini; **9.** Tagliatelle;
10. Conchiglie (shells);
11. Lasagne;
12. Fusilli (spirals);
13. Ruotini (wheels);
14. Fettucine; **15.** Penne;
16. Tubetti (short cut macaroni)

Homemade Pasta Dough

about 200 g (7 oz) semolina flour or strong
  white flour
2 eggs
pinch of salt
15 ml (1 tbsp) olive oil

1. Sift the flour into a mound on a clean
working surface. With your fist, make a well in
the centre and add the eggs, salt and oil.
2. Using your fingertips, gradually draw in the
flour into the eggs. Continue until the dough
comes together.
3. Then, using both hands, knead the dough on
a lightly floured surface for about 10 minutes
until smooth and not sticky.
4. Form the dough into a ball, place in a
polythene bag and leave to rest for 30 minutes
before shaping as required.
Makes about 350 g (12 oz) dough

Variations
Pasta Verde (Spinach Pasta)
Wash, drain and discard the coarse stalks from
225 g (8 oz) fresh spinach. Cook in a saucepan,
with no additional water until tender, about
5 minutes. Cool, then squeeze out all excess
moisture with your hands. Finely chop. Increase
the flour in the dough to 225 g (8 oz) and add
the spinach with the eggs.

Red Pasta
Skin 1 medium red pepper (see page 219), then
purée in a blender or food processor. Add to
the flour with the eggs and oil, increasing the
flour to 225 g (8 oz).

Herb Pasta
Add 30 ml (2 tbsp) chopped fresh basil or
parsley to the flour with the eggs and oil.

Shaping Dough

If using a pasta machine, put your dough
through on the chosen setting, sprinkling very
lightly with flour if it is becoming sticky.
    Alternatively, roll out the pasta on a floured
work surface to a large rectangle which is nearly
paper thin. If you are making cut pasta, such as
tagliatelle, fettucine or lasagne, the dough must
be allowed to dry. Place the dough on a clean
tea towel, allowing one third to hang over the
edge of a table or work surface and turn every
10 minutes. The pasta is ready to cut when it is
dry to the touch, about 30 minutes.

Tagliatelle
Lightly fold the dough over into a roll about
7.5 cm (3 inches) in depth. With a sharp knife,
cut into 1 cm (½ inch) wide strips; try to cut them
all the same width. Unfold and leave to dry for
about 10 minutes.

Fettucine
Proceed as for tagliatelle but cut the dough into
5 mm (¼ inch) wide strips.

Lasagne
Cut into 10 x 15 cm (4 x 6 inch) rectangles.

Roll out dough on a floured surface until paper thin.

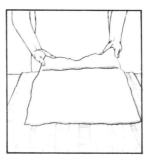

To dry, leave dough on a towel with one third hanging over the edge.

Roll up and cut into noodles. Unfold and dry on a floured tray.

SPAGHETTI WITH BUTTER AND PARMESAN

225-350 g (8-12 oz) spaghetti
50 g (2 oz) butter or margarine
50 g (2 oz) Parmesan cheese, freshly grated

1. Cook the spaghetti in a large saucepan of fast-boiling salted water for about 10 minutes for dried pasta or 3 minutes for fresh pasta or until just tender.
2. Drain well and return to the pan. Add the butter and 15 g (½ oz) of Parmesan cheese. Stir and leave for a few minutes for the butter and cheese to melt. Serve with the remaining cheese in a separate dish.
SERVES 4 AS A STARTER

NOTE: Any form of tubular or ribbon pasta can be cooked and served in this way.

SPAGHETTI BOLOGNESE

25 g (1 oz) butter or margarine
45 ml (3 tbsp) olive oil
2 slices of unsmoked streaky bacon, rinded and finely chopped
225 g (8 oz) minced beef
1 small onion, skinned and finely chopped
1 small carrot, peeled and finely chopped
1 small celery stick, finely chopped
1 small garlic clove, skinned and finely chopped
1 bay leaf
15 ml (1 level tbsp) tomato purée
150 ml (¼ pint) dry white wine
150 ml (¼ pint) beef stock
salt and pepper
450-600 g (1-1¼ lb) spaghetti

1. Heat the butter and oil in a saucepan, add the bacon and cook for 2-3 minutes until soft.
2. Add the minced beef and cook for a further 5 minutes, until lightly browned.
3. Add the onion, carrot, celery, garlic and bay leaf. Stir and cook for 2 minutes. Add the tomato purée, wine, stock and seasoning.
4. Bring to the boil, then simmer uncovered for 1-1½ hours, stirring occasionally.
5. Cook the spaghetti in a large saucepan of fast-boiling salted water for about 10 minutes for dried pasta or 3 minutes for fresh pasta or until just tender. Drain well and mix with the sauce on a warmed dish.
SERVES 4 AS A MAIN COURSE

SPAGHETTI NAPOLETANA

1.1 kg (2½ lb) tomatoes
30 ml (2 tbsp) olive oil
1 small garlic clove, skinned and crushed
7.5 ml (1½ tsp) chopped fresh basil or 2.5 ml (½ level tsp) dried
5 ml (1 level tsp) ground bay leaves
10 ml (2 level tsp) sugar
salt and pepper
450-600 g (1-1¼ lb) spaghetti
small knob of butter or margarine
freshly grated Parmesan cheese, to serve

1. Skin the tomatoes and cut the flesh into quarters. Put the seeds in a nylon sieve placed over a bowl and press lightly to extract any juices.
2. Heat the oil in a heavy based saucepan, add the tomatoes and juices, garlic, herbs, sugar and seasoning and simmer gently, uncovered, until the tomatoes cook down to a thick pulp. Adjust the seasoning.
3. Meanwhile, cook the spaghetti in a large saucepan of fast-boiling salted water for about 10 minutes for dried pasta or 3 minutes for fresh pasta until just tender. Drain, return to the pan and toss in a little butter. Transfer to a warmed serving dish.
4. Pour over the tomato sauce and top with plenty of grated Parmesan cheese to serve.
SERVES 4 AS A MAIN COURSE

SPAGHETTI ALLA CARBONARA

15 ml (1 tbsp) olive or vegetable oil
1 garlic clove, skinned
175 g (6 oz) lean unsmoked bacon, cut into thin strips
450-600 g (1-1¼ lb) spaghetti
4 eggs, lightly beaten
90 ml (6 level tbsp) freshly grated Parmesan cheese
60 ml (4 tbsp) single cream
salt and pepper
50 g (2 oz) butter or margarine

1. Heat the oil and garlic clove in a frying pan, add the bacon and fry for about 10 minutes, until the bacon is golden brown. Discard garlic.
2. Meanwhile, cook the spaghetti in a large saucepan of fast-boiling salted water for about 10 minutes for dried, 3 minutes for fresh, or until just tender. Combine the eggs with the cheese and cream, and season with salt and pepper.
3. Drain the pasta well, return to the saucepan and toss with the butter, then add the bacon. Cook for 1 minute, stirring all the time. Remove

Spaghetti alla Carbonara

from the heat and pour over the egg and cheese mixture. Mix well, then transfer to a warmed serving dish and serve at once.
SERVES 4 AS A MAIN COURSE

PASTA WITH COURGETTES AND BROAD BEANS

175 g (6 oz) dried tagliatelle or spaghetti
salt and pepper
175 g (6 oz) courgettes, thinly sliced
175 g (6 oz) frozen broad beans
150 g (5 oz) carton full-fat soft cheese with garlic and herbs
about 60 ml (4 tbsp) milk or single cream
25 g (1 oz) pine kernels or walnut pieces, toasted

1. Cook the pasta in a large saucepan of fast-boiling salted water for 3 minutes. Add the courgettes and beans and cook for a further 7 minutes, or until the pasta is tender and the beans cooked; drain well.
2. Return the pasta and vegetables to the pan and heat gently while stirring in the cheese and milk; add more milk if necessary. Season.
3. Serve immediately, topped with the nuts.
SERVES 2-3 AS A STARTER

PASTA WITH MUSHROOM AND LEEK SAUCE

450 g (1 lb) dried pasta shapes, eg wheels, shells or bows
25 g (1 oz) butter or margarine
225 g (8 oz) mushrooms, wiped and thinly sliced
125 g (4 oz) leeks, trimmed and thickly sliced
125 g (4 oz) pancetta or streaky bacon, rinded and roughly chopped
1 garlic clove, skinned and crushed
125 g (4 oz) low-fat soft cheese with garlic and herbs
30 ml (2 tbsp) milk or single cream
salt and pepper

1. Cook the pasta in a large saucepan of fast-boiling water for about 10 minutes until just tender.
2. Meanwhile, melt the butter in a saucepan and stir in the mushrooms, leeks, pancetta and garlic. Sauté, stirring, for 3-4 minutes until the leeks are tender but still retain some bite.
3. Lower the heat and stir in the cheese and milk until thoroughly mixed. Season to taste. Drain the pasta thoroughly and mix with the sauce. Serve immediately.
SERVES 4 AS A MAIN COURSE

TAGLIATELLE WITH SUN-DRIED TOMATO SAUCE

*125 g (4 oz) sun-dried tomatoes, drained and finely
 chopped*
*25 ml (1 fl oz) oil (preferably from sun-dried tomato
 jar)*
25 g (1 oz) butter or margarine
75 g (3 oz) onion, skinned and chopped
75 g (3 oz) celery, trimmed and chopped
75 g (3 oz) carrot, peeled and chopped
1 clove garlic, skinned and crushed
400 g (14 oz) can chopped tomatoes
100 ml (4 fl oz) dry white wine
salt and pepper
450-600 g (1-1¼ lb) fresh or dried tagliatelle
slivers of Parmesan and crème fraîche, to serve

1. Heat the oil and butter in a large saucepan.
Add the onion, celery, carrot and garlic and
cook, stirring, for 8-10 minutes or until
beginning to soften.
2. Stir in the canned tomatoes, sun-dried
tomatoes, wine and seasoning. Simmer, covered,
for about 30 minutes, stirring occasionally.
3. Transfer about half the sauce to a food
processor or blender and work until quite
smooth. Stir into the remaining sauce.
4. Cook the tagliatelle in a large saucepan of fast
boiling water for about 3 minutes for fresh pasta,
10 minutes for dried, until just tender. Drain
well.
5. Serve the tagliatelle topped with the sauce,
Parmesan and a spoonful of crème fraîche.
SERVES 4 AS A MAIN COURSE

Tagliatelle with Sun-dried Tomato Sauce

MACARONI CHEESE

225 g (8 oz) short cut macaroni
65 g (2½ oz) butter or margarine
60 ml (4 level tbsp) flour
900 ml (1½ pints) milk
salt and pepper
pinch of freshly grated nutmeg or 2.5 ml (½ level tsp)
   prepared mustard
225 g (8 oz) mature Cheddar cheese, grated
45 ml (3 level tbsp) fresh breadcrumbs

1. Cook the macaroni in a large saucepan of
fast-boiling salted water for about 10 minutes for
dried pasta or 3 minutes for fresh pasta until just
tender and drain well. Keep warm.

2. Meanwhile, melt the butter in a saucepan, stir
in the flour and cook gently for 1 minute.
Remove pan from the heat and gradually stir in
the milk. Bring to the boil and continue to
cook, stirring, until the sauce thickens, then
remove from the heat and add seasoning,
nutmeg or mustard, 175 g (6 oz) cheese and the
macaroni.
3. Pour into an ovenproof dish and sprinkle
with the remaining cheese and breadcrumbs.
4. Place on a baking sheet and bake in the oven
at 200°C (400°F) mark 6 for about 20 minutes,
until golden and bubbling, or brown under a
very hot grill.
SERVES 4 AS A SNACK

TAGLIATELLE WITH PARMA HAM IN CREAM SAUCE

225-350 g (8-12 oz) tagliatelle
50 g (2 oz) butter or margarine
1 large onion, skinned and finely sliced
125 g (4 oz) Parma ham, cut into thin strips
125 g (4 oz) peas, cooked
 60 ml (4 tbsp) single cream
50 g (2 oz) Parmesan cheese, freshly grated
salt and pepper

1. Cook the pasta in a large saucepan of fast-
boiling salted water until just tender. Drain.
2. Meanwhile, melt the butter in a saucepan,
add the onion and cook for about 3 minutes,
until the onion is soft. Add the ham and peas
and cook for a further 5 minutes.
3. Add the drained pasta, stir well, then add the
cream and half the cheese. Toss gently, add
seasoning and serve at once in a warmed serving
dish with the remaining cheese in a separate
dish.
SERVES 4 AS A STARTER

PASTA WITH SPICY SAUSAGE AND TOMATO SAUCE

450 g (1 lb) tomatoes
30 ml (2 tbsp) oil
1 medium onion, skinned and roughly chopped
10 ml (2 level tsp) dried oregano
1 garlic clove, skinned and crushed
450 g (1 lb) Kabanos (spicy pork sausages), skinned
   and thickly sliced
15 ml (1 level tbsp) tomato purée
salt and pepper
dash of Tabasco sauce, or to taste
450 g (1 lb) dried pasta shapes eg orecchiette,
   cappalletti or shells

1. Halve the tomatoes and scoop the seeds into
a sieve over a small bowl. Press the seeds with a
wooden spoon to extract all the juice. Reserve.
2. Place the tomatoes, skin side up, under a hot

grill and cook until well browned and blistered.
Rub to remove the skins and roughly chop the
flesh.
3. Heat the oil in a large saucepan and add the
onion, oregano and garlic. Cook, stirring, for
2-3 minutes until beginning to soften. Add the
sausage slices and cook over a high heat until
well browned.
4. Stir in the chopped tomatoes, reserved
tomato juice, tomato purée, seasoning and
Tabasco sauce. Bring to the boil, lower the heat
and simmer gently, covered, for 10-12 minutes.
Adjust seasoning to taste.
5. Meanwhile, cook the pasta in a large
saucepan of fast-boiling water for about
10 minutes until just tender. Drain well.
6. Serve the pasta topped with the sauce.
SERVES 4 AS A MAIN COURSE

LASAGNE

30 ml (2 tbsp) vegetable oil
1 small onion, skinned and chopped
1 carrot, peeled and chopped
125 g (4 oz) button mushrooms, wiped and sliced
50 g (2 oz) streaky bacon, rinded and chopped
1 garlic clove, skinned and chopped
450 g (1 lb) minced beef
350 g (12 oz) fresh tomatoes, skinned and chopped,
    or 227g (8 oz) can tomatoes
15 ml (1 level tbsp) tomato purée
150 ml (¼ pint) dry white wine
150 ml (¼ pint) beef stock
2 bay leaves
salt and pepper
900 ml (1½ pints) milk
few slices of onion, carrot and celery
6 black peppercorns
225 g (8 oz) lasagne verdi
125 g (4 oz) butter or margarine
75 g (3 oz) flour
75 g (3 oz) freshly grated Parmesan cheese

1. Heat the oil in a large saucepan and add the onion, carrot, mushrooms, bacon and garlic. Fry, stirring, for 1-2 minutes, then add the beef and cook over a high heat for a further 2 minutes. Stir in the tomatoes, tomato purée, wine, stock and a bay leaf. Season with salt and pepper. Bring to the boil, reduce heat to a simmer, cover and cook for about 35 minutes.
2. Meanwhile, pour the milk into a saucepan, add the onion, carrot, celery, peppercorns and remaining bay leaf. Bring slowly to the boil, remove from the heat, cover and leave to infuse for about 15 minutes.
3. Cook the lasagne, several at a time, in a large pan of fast-boiling salted water, for about 12 minutes for dried pasta, 3 minutes for fresh, or until just tender. Stir gently from time to time, to prevent the pasta sticking together.
4. Drain the lasagne and rinse in cold water to prevent further cooking. Drain and lay on a clean cloth.
5. Strain the milk. Melt the butter in a pan, stir in the flour and cook gently for 1 minute, stirring. Remove the pan from the heat and gradually stir in the milk. Bring to the boil slowly and continue to cook, stirring, until the sauce thickens. Season.
6. Grease a 2.8 litre (5 pint) shallow ovenproof dish. Spoon half the meat sauce over the base of the dish. Cover this with half the pasta and spread over half of the sauce. Repeat these layers topping with the sauce to cover the pasta completely. Sprinkle with the Parmesan.
7. Cook in the oven at 180°C (350°F) mark 4 for 45 minutes, or until the top is golden brown.
SERVES 4-6 AS A MAIN COURSE

PASTA BAKED WITH MUSHROOMS AND CHEESE

225 g (8 oz) dried tagliatelle
25 g (1 oz) butter
1 garlic clove, skinned and crushed
225 g (8 oz) mushrooms, wiped and thinly sliced
50 g (2 oz) Stilton cheese
60 ml (4 tbsp) double cream
salt and pepper
1 egg, lightly beaten
125 g (4 oz) mozzarella cheese, thinly sliced

1. Cook the noodles in plenty of fast-boiling salted water for about 7 minutes, until just tender.
2. Meanwhile, melt the butter in a large frying pan and cook the garlic and mushrooms, stirring frequently until just softened. Crumble in the Stilton and cook for 1-2 minutes, stirring continuously. Stir in the cream and seasoning to taste.
3. Drain the pasta and season with lots of pepper. Mix into the mushroom sauce. Stir in the egg and mix together thoroughly.
4. Turn the mixture into a buttered ovenproof dish and top with the mozzarella. Cover with foil and bake in the oven at 180°C (350°F) mark 4 for 10 minutes. Remove the foil and bake at 220°C (425°F) mark 7 for a further 10-15 minutes, until brown and crusty on top. Serve with a green salad.
SERVES 2-3 AS A MAIN COURSE

PASTA, VEAL AND ROSEMARY GRATIN

30 ml (2 tbsp) olive oil
225 g (8 oz) onion, skinned and finely chopped
125 g (4 oz) carrot, peeled and finely chopped
2 sticks celery, trimmed and finely chopped
175 g (6 oz) red pepper, seeded and finely chopped
225 g (8 oz) each minced beef and veal,
   or 450 g (1 lb) beef
45 g (1¾ oz) plain white flour
300 ml (½ pint) beef stock
150 ml (¼ pint) red wine
125 g (4 oz) Parma ham, cut into pieces (optional)
30 ml (2 level tbsp) chopped fresh rosemary or 10 ml
   (2 level tsp) dried
1 bay leaf
salt and pepper
150 g (5 oz) large dried pasta shells, ie about 24
   conchiglie rigate, or about 16 cannelloni
50 g (2 oz) butter or margarine
600 ml (1 pint) milk
50 g (2 oz) Parmesan cheese, freshly grated

1. Heat the oil in a large sauté pan, add the vegetables and cook gently until softened and beginning to colour.

2. Add the beef and veal and cook over a high heat, stirring frequently, until the meat begins to brown. Stir in 5 ml (1 level tsp) flour and cook for a further minute. Pour in the stock and red wine, and add the ham, if using, rosemary, bay leaf and seasoning. Slowly bring to the boil, cover and simmer gently for about 1 hour. (If necessary uncover, increase heat and cook until the mixture has reduced to a thick sauce.)
3. Cook the pasta in plenty of fast-boiling salted water for about 12 minutes until just tender. Drain.
4. Fill the shells with the mince mixture and place in a single layer in a 2.3 litre (4 pint) ovenproof dish.
5. Melt the butter in a small saucepan. Add the remaining 40 g (1½ oz) flour and cook, stirring, for 1-2 minutes. Gradually stir in the milk and bring to the boil, then simmer, stirring occasionally, for 2-3 minutes. Off the heat, beat in half of the grated cheese, adding pepper to taste. Spoon over the pasta and sprinkle with the remaining cheese.
6. Bake in the oven at 180°C (350°F) mark 4 for 40 minutes or until golden and bubbling.
SERVES 6 AS A MAIN COURSE

FISH-STUFFED CANNELLONI WITH CHEESE

50 g (2 oz) butter or margarine
125 g (4 oz) mushrooms, wiped and chopped
115 g (4 oz) can pimientos, drained and diced
1 garlic clove, skinned and crushed
210 g (7½ oz) can salmon or tuna steak, drained and
   flaked
50 g (2 oz) fresh breadcrumbs
12 cannelloni
FOR THE SAUCE
50 g (2 oz) butter or margarine
60 ml (4 level tbsp) flour
600 ml (1 pint) milk
175 g (6 oz) Cheddar cheese, grated
salt and pepper

1. Melt the butter in a saucepan, add the mushrooms and fry gently for 2-3 minutes, until soft. Add the pimientos, garlic, fish and breadcrumbs. Cook over a low heat for 5 minutes, stirring.
2. To make the sauce, melt the butter in a saucepan. Stir in the flour and cook for 1 minute, stirring. Remove the pan from the heat and gradually stir in the milk. Bring to the boil slowly and continue to cook, stirring, until the sauce has thickened. Remove from the heat and stir in 150 g (5 oz) of the cheese until melted. Season well.
3. Spoon the fish filling into the pasta tubes so that it protrudes slightly at each end.
4. Pour enough sauce into an ovenproof dish to just cover the bottom. Arrange the cannelloni side by side in the dish and pour over the remaining sauce. Sprinkle over the rest of the cheese.
5. Bake in the oven at 200°C (400°F) mark 6 for 30 minutes, until golden brown.
SERVES 4 AS A MAIN COURSE

SPRING VEGETABLE PASTA

125 g (4 oz) fresh asparagus or French beans

225 g (8 oz) leeks, trimmed and thinly sliced diagonally

salt and pepper

175 g (6 oz) creamy chèvre or full-fat soft cheese with garlic and herbs

150 g (5 oz) mascarpone cheese or 150 ml (5 fl oz) extra-thick double cream

350-400 g (12-14 oz) dried penne (pasta quills) or rigatoni

50 g (2 oz) butter or margarine

30 ml (2 tbsp) olive oil

1 medium onion, skinned and finely chopped

125 g (4 oz) baby carrots, trimmed and peeled

225 g (8 oz) brown cap mushrooms, wiped and thinly sliced

125 g (4 oz) petit pois

100 ml (4 fl oz) dry white wine

350 g (12 oz) crème fraîche

60 ml (4 level tbsp) chopped fresh herbs, eg parsley, thyme, sage

mascarpone, to serve (optional)

1. Cut the asparagus into 5 cm (2 inch) lengths. Briefly blanch the asparagus or beans, and leeks in boiling salted water for 3-4 minutes. Drain thoroughly.

2. Mix together the chèvre and mascarpone; set aside.

3. Cook the pasta in fast-boiling salted water for about 10 minutes until just tender. Drain well.

4. Meanwhile, in a large sauté pan, heat together the butter and oil. Stir in the onion and cook stirring, for 3-4 minutes. Add the carrots and mushrooms and continue to cook for 2-3 minutes, or until beginning to soften.

5. Stir in the other vegetables, with the wine, crème fraîche and herbs. Simmer very gently until thickened to a good coating consistency. Remove the pan from the heat and gently stir in the cheese mixture until thoroughly mixed. Season to taste.

6. Divide the hot pasta between individual serving plates. Spoon the sauce over the pasta and top each portion with a spoonful of mascarpone, if desired. Serve immediately.

SERVES 4 AS A MAIN COURSE

LEFT: Pasta, Veal and Rosemary Gratin. RIGHT: Spring Vegetable Pasta

TORTELLINI AL FORNO

450 g (1 lb) aubergines, washed and trimmed
salt and pepper
25 g (1 oz) butter or margarine
450 g (1 lb) tomatoes, skinned and chopped
1 garlic clove, skinned and crushed
225 g (8 oz) tortellini
150 ml (¼ pint) milk
225 g (8 oz) full fat soft cheese
15 ml (1 level tbsp) freshly grated Parmesan cheese
30 ml (2 level tbsp) dried breadcrumbs

1. Chop the aubergines, sprinkle with salt and leave for 15-20 minutes. Rinse well and pat dry.
2. Melt the butter in a frying pan, add the aubergines, tomatoes and garlic and cook gently for 5-10 minutes, until very soft. Season well.
3. Cook the tortellini in fast-boiling salted water for about 15 minutes for dried pasta, 8 minutes for fresh pasta or until just tender. Drain well.
4. Spoon the vegetable mixture into a shallow, ovenproof dish. Layer the tortellini on top.
5. In a bowl, gradually beat the milk into the cheese whisking until smooth. Stir in 5 ml (1 level tsp) Parmesan. Spoon evenly over the tortellini. Sprinkle the top with breadcrumbs and the remaining Parmesan.
6. Bake in the oven at 200°C (400°F) mark 6 for 25-30 minutes, until the top is golden brown.
SERVES 4 AS A LIGHT MAIN COURSE

RAVIOLI STUFFED WITH SPINACH

1½ quantities Homemade Pasta Dough
    (see page 298)
75 g (3 oz) butter or margarine
450 g (1 lb) fresh spinach, cooked, or 225 g (8 oz)
    packet frozen spinach, thawed and chopped
50 g (2 oz) Parmesan cheese, freshly grated
pinch of freshly grated nutmeg
salt and pepper
melted butter, freshly grated Parmesan cheese and
    chopped fresh parsley, to serve

1. Make the pasta dough, place in a polythene bag and leave to rest for 30 minutes.
2. Meanwhile, make the filling. Melt the butter and add it to the well-drained spinach with the cheese and nutmeg. Season well.
3. Halve the dough. Roll out each piece and stretch by drawing the fingertips underneath until each measures 32 x 40 cm (13 x 16 inches).

4. Place small mounds of spinach on one sheet of dough, spacing them evenly, about 4 cm (1½ inches) apart. Brush with water around the mounds.
5. Cover with the remaining dough and seal around each spinach mound. Cut with a serrated pastry wheel between the mounds.
6. Cook the ravioli in boiling salted water, about 12 at a time, for about 10 minutes until tender. Remove with a slotted spoon and keep warm while cooking the remainder. Drain well and toss in melted butter, cheese and parsley.
SERVES 4 AS A MAIN COURSE

VARIATION
The cooked ravioli can be layered with Tomato Sauce (see page 207) in a greased ovenproof dish, sprinkled with grated Parmesan cheese and baked in the oven at 200°C (400°F) mark 6 for about 15 minutes, until golden brown.

1. Roll out dough as thinly as possible, then stretch by 'drawing out' with your fingertips.
2. Spoon small mounds of spinach on to the dough.
3. Press firmly around the mounds to seal.

RICE

Rice is the staple food for about half of the world's population. Once harvested, it is processed to remove the inedible outer husk, yielding brown rice, which still retains its outer bran layers. To produce white rice, it is further milled to remove the bran and germ. Rice is classified into long, medium and short-grained types.

Rice is inexpensive, and quick and easy to cook. It contains protein, carbohydrate, B vitamins and minerals. Because it doesn't contain fat, rice is not a high calorie food; 25 g (1 oz) cooked rice provides only 35 calories. Brown rice also provides dietary fibre, although it does take longer to cook than white rice.

Some rice is sold as easy-cook, pre-cooked or pre-fluffed. It has usually been steam treated before the husk is removed, and this helps retain some of the vitamins and minerals which would normally be removed with the husk. The process helps keep the grains separate during cooking.

There are many varieties of rice, each with different characteristics. Some cook to a light separate firmness, others to a creamy texture, while some cook to a sticky mass. Using the correct rice for a particular dish is essential.

TYPES OF RICE

LONG GRAIN RICE consists of slender grains which are about four times as long as they are wide. When cooked it becomes fluffy and dry, with separated grains. Long grain rice is particularly suitable for savoury dishes. The two main varieties are *patna* and *basmati*. Basmati has the most distinctive aromatic flavour and is the best rice to use in pilaffs and to serve in curries. For best results it should be rinsed before cooking to remove excess starch.

MEDIUM GRAIN RICE has plumper grains than long grain rice and absorbs more liquid when cooked. It is therefore often stickier, but can be used in savoury dishes, like long grain rice.

SHORT GRAIN RICE has small, chalky round or oval grains which absorb a large quantity of liquid and produce a moist sticky mass when cooked. It is used mainly for milk puddings and other sweet dishes.

ARBORIO RICE is an Italian short grain rice which is excellent for risottos. As it cooks, the grains readily absorb liquid without becoming too soft. It is this property which gives the risotto its distinctive creamy texture. It is available from Italian delicatessens and larger supermarkets.

GLUTINOUS RICE is also sold as sticky or sweet rice. It has oval cream-coloured grains which cook into a sticky mass. It is popular in Japanese, Chinese and other South-east Asian cuisines.

WILD RICE is not rice at all but the seed of an aquatic grass. It has long dark brown grains which are cooked in the same way as long grain rice. Although expensive, wild rice has an excellent distinctive flavour, and a little goes a long way. About 125 g (4 oz) wild rice will feed 4 people. It makes an ideal accompaniment to shellfish, poultry and game dishes. It can also be combined with white or brown rice, other grains, nuts and flavourings. Depending on whether a chewy or tender texture is preferred, wild rice takes between 35 and 50 minutes to cook in boiling salted water.

RICE QUANTITIES

During cooking, the starch in rice swells, the grain softens and the rice increases to two or three times its original weight and bulk. Allow about 50 g (2 oz) uncooked rice per person as an accompaniment and about 40-50 g (1-2 oz) when it is to be mixed with other ingredients.

COOKING RICE

Rice is usually cooked in boiling salted water, either in a large volume of water, then drained; or in the quantity of water it will absorb during cooking, ie the absorption method. The latter is more suitable for easy-cook rice. Brown rice should be cooked in plenty of water (see recipes overleaf). Rice can also be steamed.

Always follow manufacturer's instructions for cooking. White rice takes about 12 minutes to cook; brown rice about 35 minutes. To test whether it is cooked, bite a grain of the rice. Like pasta it should be *al dente* – tender but firm to the bite, without a hard core.

Rice is best cooked and served immediately. If necessary it can be cooked and reheated later that day in a tightly covered buttered dish in the oven; or steamed in a colander over boiling water until heated through; or in the microwave.

BOILED RICE

3.4 litres (6 pints) water
salt
225 g (8 oz) long grain white or brown rice

1. Bring a large saucepan of water to a fast boil, then add salt and the rice.
2. Stir once to loosen the grains at the base of the pan, then leave to cook, uncovered, for about 12 minutes for white rice, about 35 minutes for brown rice, until tender.
3. Drain well, rinse with hot water and drain again. Pour into a warmed serving dish and separate the grains with a fork.
SERVES 4

VARIATIONS
Although rice is most usually cooked in water, it can also be cooked in stock for extra flavour.

HERBY RICE
Add 15-30 ml (1-2 tbsp) chopped fresh herbs to the cooking liquid, eg parsley, coriander, marjoram, thyme, mixed herbs.

SAFFRON RICE
Add a pinch of ground saffron to the cooking water to give the rice a delicate yellow colour.

Alternatively, soak a good pinch of saffron strands in a little boiling water for 15 minutes, then add to the rice before cooking.

TURMERIC RICE
Turmeric is also used to give rice a yellow colour, but add only a pinch of it to the cooking water as it has a more pronounced colour than saffron.

BOILED RICE (ABSORPTION METHOD)
An alternative method for cooking white rice is to use an exact amount of water which is completely absorbed by the rice. As the various kinds of rice differ in the amount of water they absorb, it is preferable to follow packet directions for the quantity of water to use. As a rough guide, allow 600 ml (1 pint) water, 5 ml (1 level tsp) salt to 225 g (8 oz) long grain white rice.

　　Place the rice, salt and water in a large pan and bring quickly to the boil, stir well and cover with a tight-fitting lid. Reduce the heat and simmer gently for about 15 minutes or until the rice is tender and the water has been absorbed. Remove from the heat and separate the grains with a fork before serving.
SERVES 4

OVEN-COOKED RICE

225 g (8 oz) long grain white rice
600 ml (1 pint) water
5 ml (1 level tsp) salt

1. Place the rice in an ovenproof dish. Bring the water and salt to a fast boil in a saucepan,

pour over the rice and stir well with a fork.
2. Cover tightly with a lid or foil and bake in the oven at 180°C (350°F) mark 4 for 35-40 minutes, or until the grains are just soft and all the cooking liquid has been absorbed by the rice.
SERVES 4

BASIC PILAU RICE

50 g (2 oz) butter
225 g (8 oz) long grain white rice
750 ml (1¼ pints) boiling Chicken Stock (see page 19)
salt and pepper
knob of butter

1. Melt the butter in a saucepan, add the rice and gently fry for about 5 minutes, stirring all the time, until it looks transparent.
2. Add the stock, pouring it in slowly, as it will tend to bubble at first. Add the seasoning, stir well, cover with a tightly fitting lid and leave over a very low heat for about 15 minutes, until the

water has been absorbed and the rice grains are just soft. (The idea is that the rice should cook in its own steam, so don't stir it while it is cooking.)
3. Remove the lid, cover the rice with a cloth, replace the lid and leave in a warm place for at least 15 minutes to dry out before serving. (This is a traditional part of making a pilau, although often omitted in European versions of the dish.)
4. To serve, stir lightly with a fork to separate the grains, add a knob of butter and serve immediately
SERVES 4

BASMATI PILAFF

225 g (8 oz) easy-cook basmati rice, washed
4 cardamom pods, split
4 black peppercorns
3 whole cloves
2.5 cm (1 inch) stick cinnamon
7.5 ml (1½ tsp) cumin seeds
30 ml (2 tbsp) vegetable oil
1 small onion, skinned and finely chopped
5 ml (1 tsp) ground turmeric
2 curry leaves or bay leaves, torn in pieces
salt and pepper
25-50 g (1-2 oz) shelled pistachio nuts, roughly
    chopped
25 g (1 oz) raisins (optional)

1. Put the rice in a bowl, cover with cold water and leave to soak for 30 minutes. Drain off the water, transfer the rice to a sieve and rinse under cold running water until the water runs clear.
2. Put the cardamom pods, peppercorns, cloves, cinnamon stick and cumin seeds in a large, heavy flameproof casserole and dry fry over moderate heat for 2-3 minutes, stirring all the time until they pop and release their flavour. Add the oil and stir until hot, then add the onion and turmeric and cook gently, stirring frequently, for 10 minutes until the onion is softened.
3. Add the rice and stir until coated in the spiced onion mixture, then slowly pour in 1.1 litres (2 pints) boiling water. (Take care as the water may sizzle and splash.) Add the curry or bay leaves and seasoning, bring to the boil and stir well. Lower the heat, cover and cook very gently for 10 minutes, without lifting the lid. Remove from the heat and leave to stand for 15 minutes for the flavours to develop.
4. Uncover the rice, add half the pistachio nuts and the raisins, if using, and gently fork through, to fluff up the grains. Taste and adjust seasoning. Spoon the pilaff on to a warmed serving platter, mounding it up in the centre, then sprinkle over the remaining pistachios. Serve hot.
SERVES 4

SPECIAL FRIED RICE

225 g (8 oz) long grain white rice
salt and pepper
15-30 ml (1-2 tbsp) vegetable oil
1-2 carrots, peeled and coarsely grated
1 garlic clove, skinned and crushed
50 g (2 oz) frozen peeled prawns, thawed
75 g (3 oz) frozen peas, thawed
75 g (3 oz) fresh bean sprouts, soaked in cold water for
    10 minutes and drained
20 ml (4 tsp) light soy sauce
1 bunch spring onions, trimmed and thinly sliced
    diagonally
5 ml (1 tsp) sesame oil

1. Cook the rice in plenty of boiling salted water (see page 308) until almost tender. Drain then rinse with boiling water. Spread out on a large tray and leave to cool.
2. Just before serving, heat the oil in a wok or large frying pan (you may need to do this in two batches). Add the carrots and garlic and stir-fry for 2 minutes. Add the prawns, peas and bean sprouts and stir-fry for 1 minute.
3. Stir in the rice and stir-fry for 3 minutes. Stir in the soy sauce, seasoning and spring onion.

Special Fried Rice

4. Transfer the rice to a serving dish. Sprinkle with the sesame oil and serve at once.
SERVES 4

SAVOURY RICE

25 g (1 oz) butter or margarine
1 medium onion, skinned and chopped
1 medium pepper, seeded and chopped
1 celery stick, trimmed and chopped
2 rashers bacon, rinded and chopped
225 g (8 oz) long grain white rice
salt and pepper
600 ml (1 pint) Chicken Stock (see page 19) or water

1. Melt the butter in a large saucepan, add the vegetables and bacon and fry gently for about 5 minutes, until soft.
2. Add the rice and seasoning and stir well. Cover with the chicken stock or water. Bring to the boil, cover and cook for about 15 minutes, until the rice is tender and the liquid is totally absorbed.
SERVES 4

VARIATIONS
Add any of the following ingredients to the savoury rice and heat through.
50 g (2 oz) salami, finely diced
200 g (7 oz) can tuna, drained and flaked
200 g (7 oz) canned salmon, drained and flaked
125 g (4 oz) cooked peeled prawns
1 medium canned pimiento, chopped
25 g (1 oz) toasted almonds, chopped
50 g (2 oz) button mushrooms, thinly sliced
2 spring onions, finely chopped
50 g (2 oz) frozen peas
15 ml (1 tbsp) soy sauce
1 garlic clove, skinned and crushed
pinch of ground turmeric

THAI FRIED RICE

225 g (8 oz) basmati rice
salt
45 ml (3 tbsp) corn or sunflower oil
15 ml (1 tbsp) nam pla fish sauce
1 hot chilli pepper, seeded and chopped
2 spring onions, trimmed and chopped
2 large eggs, beaten (optional)
15 ml (1 tbsp) soy sauce
5 ml (1 tsp) brown sugar

1. Cook the rice in plenty of boiling salted water (see page 308) until almost tender. Drain, then rinse with boiling water. Spread out on a tray and leave to cool.
2. Heat the oil in a wok, then add the fish sauce, chilli pepper and spring onions and stir-fry for 1-2 minutes to flavour the oil.
3. Add the eggs, if using, and stir-fry until the egg scrambles, stirring all the time so that the egg sets in small pieces rather than one large lump.
4. Stir the rice with a fork to separate the grains, then tip into the hot oil. Stir-fry with the eggs until really hot (the time will depend on whether the rice was cold or warm before stir frying). Mix the soy sauce with the sugar, then stir into the rice. Serve immediately.
SERVES 4

Thai Fried Rice

NOTE: Nam pla fish sauce is available from oriental food stores. If unobtainable anchovy essence can be used instead, although the flavour will not be quite the same.

SPICED RICE WITH CHICKEN

1.4 kg (3 lb) oven-ready chicken
75 ml (5 tbsp) vegetable oil
2 medium onions, skinned and sliced
175 g (6 oz) long grain white rice
15 ml (3 level tsp) ground cumin
10 ml (2 level tsp) ground coriander
1.25 ml (¼ level tsp) chilli powder
2.5 ml (½ level tsp) ground turmeric
300 ml (10 fl oz) natural yogurt
350 ml (12 fl oz) Chicken Stock (see page 19)
salt and pepper
parsley sprigs, to garnish

1. Remove skin and bones from chicken and cut the flesh into 2.5 cm (1 inch) pieces. Heat the oil in a flameproof casserole, add the chicken, half at a time, and fry until browned. Remove from the pan and set aside.
2. Add the onions to the casserole and lightly brown, then stir in the rice, spices, yogurt and stock. Season well and bring to the boil.
3. Return the chicken to the casserole, cover and bake in the oven at 170°C (325°F) mark 3 for about 35 minutes, or until the rice and chicken are tender and the liquid absorbed.
4. Stir the rice with a fork and garnish with parsley sprigs.
SERVES 4

RISOTTO ALLA MILANESE

1.1 litres (2 pints) Chicken or Beef Stock (see page 19)
75 g (3 oz) butter or margarine
1 small onion, skinned and finely chopped
350 g (12 oz) arborio rice (see page 307)
few saffron strands
salt and pepper
50 g (2 oz) Parmesan cheese, freshly grated

1. Bring the stock to the boil in a large saucepan and keep at barely simmering point.
2. Meanwhile, in a large, heavy-based saucepan, melt 25 g (1 oz) butter, add the onion and fry gently for 5 minutes, until soft but not coloured.
3. Add the rice to the pan and stir with a fork

for 2-3 minutes, until it is well coated with butter.
4. Add a ladleful of stock to the pan and cook gently, stirring frequently, until the stock is absorbed. Add more stock as soon as each ladleful is absorbed, stirring frequently.
5. When the rice becomes creamy, sprinkle in the saffron with salt and pepper to taste. Continue adding stock and stirring until the risotto is thick, creamy and tender but not sticky. This process should take about 20-25 minutes to complete; it must not be hurried.
6. Just before serving, stir in the remaining butter and the Parmesan, then taste and adjust seasoning. Serve hot.
SERVES 4

CHICKEN AND PRAWN RISOTTO

175 g (6 oz) chicken breast fillets, cut into
    2.5 cm (1 inch) pieces
1 small onion, skinned and sliced
1 garlic clove, skinned and crushed
1 litre (1¾ pints) Chicken Stock (see page 19)
225 g (8 oz) brown rice
50 g (2 oz) small button mushrooms, wiped
pinch of ground saffron
salt and pepper
125 g (4 oz) cooked peeled prawns
50 g (2 oz) petits pois
12 whole cooked prawns, to garnish

1. Place all the ingredients, except the prawns and petits pois, in a large saucepan. Bring to the boil and simmer, uncovered, for 35 minutes, until the chicken is tender.
2. Stir in the prawns and petits pois. Cook over a high heat for about 5 minutes, stirring occasionally until most of the liquid has been absorbed.
3. Adjust seasoning. Place in a warmed serving dish and garnish with the whole prawns.
SERVES 4

BROWN RICE RISOTTO

45 ml (3 tbsp) vegetable oil
2 medium onions, skinned and sliced
225 g (8 oz) brown rice
5 ml (1 level tsp) ground turmeric
600 ml (1 pint) Chicken or Vegetable Stock (see
   page 19)
salt and pepper
chopped fresh parsley, to garnish

1. Heat the oil in a medium flameproof casserole, add the onions, rice and turmeric and fry gently for 1-2 minutes. Stir in the stock and seasoning and bring to the boil.
2. Cover the dish tightly and cook in the oven at 170°C (325°F) mark 3 for about 1 hour, until the rice is tender and the stock absorbed. Adjust the seasoning and garnish with plenty of chopped parsley to serve.
SERVES 4

PAELLA

60 ml (4 tbsp) olive oil
6 chicken drumsticks
1 medium onion, skinned and chopped
1 garlic clove, skinned and crushed
225 g (8 oz) tomatoes, skinned and chopped
1 medium red or green pepper, seeded and finely sliced
125 g (4 oz) frozen peas
5 ml (1 level tsp) paprika
450 g (1 lb) Italian arborio rice or long grain
   white rice
few saffron strands
900 ml (1½ pints) Chicken Stock (see page 19)
450 g (1 lb) fresh mussels
125 g (4 oz) cooked peeled prawns
salt and pepper
lemon wedges, to garnish

1. Heat the oil in a paella pan or large saucepan, add the chicken drumsticks and fry for 15-20 minutes.
2. Remove from the pan with a slotted spoon and keep warm. Add the onion and garlic to the fat remaining in the pan and fry for 3-5 minutes.
3. Add the tomatoes, pepper, peas and paprika and cook, stirring, for 5 minutes.
4. Return the chicken to the pan, and stir in the rice, saffron and stock. Bring to the boil, stirring all the time. Reduce the heat and simmer uncovered for 20-25 minutes, or until most of the stock has been absorbed and the rice is tender.
5. Meanwhile, to prepare the mussels, scrub them under cold running water, until thoroughly clean, removing their 'beards' with a small sharp knife. Discard any that are open.
6. Put the prepared mussels in a large pan, containing 1 cm (½ inch) of boiling water, cover and cook for 5 minutes until the shells open; discard any which remain closed. Drain.
7. Stir the mussels and prawns into the rice mixture and reheat for a further 5 minutes.
8. Season with salt and pepper. Arrange the lemon wedges around the rim of the pan and serve immediately.
SERVES 6

VARIATION
A more elaborate paella may be made by adding the flesh of 1 small cooked lobster, about 700-900 g (1½ -2 lb) in weight, and 12 clams, scrubbed. Add to the pan for 5 minutes before cooking is complete; the clams should open in the steam, discard any that do not.

GNOCCHI

Gnocchi are small dumplings which are cooked in boiling water and served like pasta with a sauce. The gnocchi mixture may also be spread in a dish, cooled and cut into rounds or squares; these are arranged in a dish, sprinkled with cheese and browned under the grill, then served with a sauce. Gnocchi are sometimes made with flour, water and egg, or some or all of the flour can be replaced with semolina, cornmeal, cooked potato or grated raw potato.

GNOCCHI ALLA ROMANA

600 ml (1 pint) milk
125 g (4 oz) fine semolina
salt and pepper
pinch of freshly grated nutmeg
1 egg, beaten
25 g (1 oz) butter or margarine
75 g (3 oz) Parmesan cheese, freshly grated
little butter and extra grated cheese, for topping
grated cheese and Tomato Sauce (see page 207)

1. In a large saucepan, bring the milk to the boil, sprinkle in the semolina, salt, pepper and nutmeg, and stir over a gentle heat until the mixture is really thick. Beat until smooth.
2. Remove from the heat and stir in the egg, butter and cheese. Return the pan to a low heat and stir for 1 minute.
3. Spread this mixture, about ½-1 cm (¼-½ inch) thick, in a shallow buttered dish and allow to cool. Cut into 2.5 cm (1 inch) rounds or squares and arrange in a shallow greased ovenproof dish.
4. Put a few knobs of butter over the top, sprinkle with a little extra cheese and brown under the grill or towards the top of the oven at 200°C (400°F) mark 6. Serve with cheese and Tomato Sauce.
SERVES 4

CHEESE GNOCCHI

225 g (8 oz) Ricotta, curd or full fat soft cheese, sieved
50 g (2 oz) butter or margarine
60 ml (4 level tbsp) freshly grated Parmesan cheese
2 eggs, beaten
50-75 g (2-3 oz) flour, plus extra for dusting
salt and pepper
pinch of freshly grated nutmeg
melted butter and freshly grated Parmesan cheese, to serve

1. Mix all the ingredients together and beat until smooth.
2. Dust your hands with flour and shape the dough into small balls. Roll them in flour, then chill in the refrigerator for 30 minutes.
3. To cook the gnocchi, poach about ten at a time in boiling salted water for about 5 minutes, until they rise to the top of the pan. Transfer to a warmed serving dish. Serve tossed in melted butter and sprinkled with grated Parmesan.
SERVES 4

SPINACH GNOCCHI

450 g (1 lb) frozen spinach, thawed, drained and finely chopped
225 g (8 oz) Ricotta or curd cheese
2 eggs, beaten
225 g (8 oz) flour, plus extra for dusting
1.25 ml (¼ level tsp) freshly grated nutmeg
125 g (4 oz) Parmesan cheese, freshly grated
salt and pepper
melted butter, to serve

1. Mix together the spinach, Ricotta, eggs, flour, nutmeg, half the Parmesan and seasoning.
2. Dust your hands with flour and shape the dough into small balls. Roll them in flour, then chill in the refrigerator for at least 30 minutes.
3. To cook the gnocchi, poach about ten at a time in boiling salted water for 5-10 minutes, until they rise to the top of the pan.
4. Serve tossed in melted butter and sprinkled with the remaining Parmesan.
SERVES 4

FRUIT AND NUTS

A wide variety of fresh fruit is now available all year round – including homegrown varieties and a colourful range of exotic and Mediterranean fruits. Nutritionally, fruit is important – both as a source of dietary fibre and of Vitamin C, and most fresh fruits are low in calories. This section shows you how to choose and use exotic and unusual fruits, as well as the more familiar ones.

APPLES

The many varieties of apples can be divided into two groups: dessert and cooking. Dessert apples often have more flavour than cooking apples. *Cox's Orange Pippin, Spartan, Laxton Superb, Worcester Pearmain* and *Granny Smith* are all popular dessert apples with distinctive flavours.

Cooking apples are too tart to eat on their own, but are delicious cooked with sugar. Look for *Bramley's Seedling, Lord Derby and Grenadier.*

Choose firm apples with unblemished skins. Keep apples cool and dry. Apples kept at room temperature should be eaten within 2 weeks.

Wipe and wash dessert apples before using. They make good additions to raw fruit salads or they can be used in pies, tarts and puddings or served with cheese. Apple slices should be brushed with lemon juice to prevent browning.

APRICOTS

These are stone fruits, round and about the size of a plum with velvety, yellowish-orange skin and fairly soft, juicy flesh of much the same colour. Unripe apricots are hard and sour; over-ripe ones tend to be mealy and tastless. Choose firm, unwrinkled fruit with a deep colour or leave unripened fruit to ripen at room temperature. Once ripe they should be eaten within 2-3 days.

Prepare apricots by washing, cutting them in half and removing the stone. To peel apricots, blanch in boiling water for 30 seconds to loosen the skins, then peel. Sliced apricots should be brushed with lemon juice to prevent browning.

Serve apricots raw as a dessert or halve, stone and poach in syrup, or use in puddings and pies. They also make very good jam.

AVOCADOS

These are the fruit of a tree grown in sub-tropical climates. They are the same shape as pears and have a shiny green or knobbly purple brown skin  according to variety. They have a soft, oily, pale green flesh and a large stone. Avocados are prized for their delicate creamy texture and subtle flavour.

A ripe avocado always 'gives' slightly when pressed at the pointed end. A hard, under-ripe avocado will ripen in 1-2 days if kept at room temperature. Ripe fruit will keep in the refrigerator for 2-3 days.

To open an avocado, cut in half lengthways and turn the halves in opposite directions until they come apart. Brush the slices with lemon juice to prevent browning.

Avocados are normally eaten as a savoury, either as a starter or in salads, or they can be made into dips and mousses.

BABACO

A large distinctively shaped fruit, about 25 cm (10 inches) long, with an edible skin which is green, turning yellow when ripe. The flesh is pinkish-orange in colour.

Babaco keeps particularly well. When sliced crosswise, it gives attractive star-shaped slices. In flavour and texture it is a cross between strawberry, melon and pineapple. It is usually eaten sliced, sprinkled with sugar, but may be used in drinks and salads.

BANANAS

Tropical fruit with bright yellow skins and pale, sweet flesh. Bananas are picked in large bunches called 'hands' when they are still hard and green, but they have usually turned yellow by the time they reach the shops.

Choose bananas with evenly coloured skins. They are ready to eat when yellow and slightly flecked brown. Black patches on the surface indicate the fruit is over-ripe. Bananas will ripen quickly if kept in the dark, eg in a paper bag at room temperature.

Once peeled, bananas should be brushed with lemon juice to prevent browning. They can be eaten raw, used in sweet and savoury salads, cakes, ice creams, and in various Indian and Chinese dishes. They can also be baked or fried in butter or made into fritters. For cooking, choose slightly under-ripe fruit as they slice better.

Green-cooking bananas are a variety which is always cooked as a vegetable, either by frying, boiling or baking whole in their skins.

Red bananas are another variety; they have deep red skins and a soft, sweet flesh.

Plantains, which are related to bananas, are unsuitable for eating raw but are used widely in West Indian cooking – as a vegetable (see page 219). They have a higher starch and lower sugar content than ordinary bananas.

BILBERRIES

Bilberries are small dark blue berries which grow on open moorland. They may also be sold as whortleberries or huckleberries. Blueberries (see below) are cultivated in preferance to bilberries because they are easier to pick.

To prepare, remove the stalk and any leaves, rinse and dry thoroughly.

Bilberries can be eaten raw, though they have a distinctive acid taste or they can be stewed with sugar, cooked in pies or made into jam.

BLACKBERRIES

These small soft fruit, dark red to black in colour, are available wild and cultivated. The cultivated varieties tend to be larger and juicier.

Once picked, blackberries lose their flavour rapidly and should be eaten on the day of purchase.

To prepare, wash them and remove stalks. They can be eaten raw, stewed (they are good cooked with apple), included in fruit puddings and pies or made into jams and jellies.

BLUEBERRIES

These are small round blue-black berries with a sweet flavour. They are cultivated in Britain, though most supplies come from the USA. Blueberries can be stored in the refrigerator for 3-4 days.

To prepare, rinse and dry thoroughly. Serve with cream or fromage frais, or use in tarts, pies, summer puddings or crêpes.

CAPE GOOSEBERRIES (CHINESE LANTERN)

These are the fruit of the Chinese lantern and get their name from the lantern-shaped papery calyx which surrounds each fruit. They are round and golden with juicy flesh which has a delicate, scented flavour and many edible seeds.

To prepare, peel back the skin and eat raw or cook in pies or compotes.

CHERRIES

Cherries vary in colour from white, through red to a very dark red. They are mainly eaten raw but some varieties have sour flesh and are used for pies and jams. Popular varieties of sweet cherries are *Napoleon Bigarreau, Frogmore Early, Merton Heart* and *White Heart*. The best variety for cooking is Morello.

Avoid split, diseased or immature fruit. Look for large soft berries for eating raw. Remove the stalks and rinse the fruit in a colander. The stones can be removed with a cherry stoner or the fruit can be slit with the point of a knife and the stones prised out.

CRAB APPLES

The common European crab apple is the original wild apple. The small fruit have a shiny red or yellow skin and firm flesh, which is usually very sour. They are chiefly used to make jelly and other preserves.

CRANBERRIES

These small American fruit are similar to bilberries but with pink to dark red skins. The flesh is sharp-tasting and cranberries are mostly used for sauces and jellies to serve with poultry and game or in tarts and puddings. Cranberry Sauce (see page 206) is served with turkey.

To prepare cranberries, remove stalks and leaves and rinse well under cold running water.

CURRANTS

Currants are small berry fruits which may be black, red or white. Blackcurrants and redcurrants are more common than white ones. They are normally sold on their stems and are more expensive when not. Avoid withered or dusty currants; choose only ones with a distinct gloss.

To remove currants from the stems, use a fork to detach them.

Blackcurrants have a rich flavour but tend to be slightly sour; they are best known for their use in making the liqueur *cassis* and other drinks, but can also be used in puddings and pies. Redcurrants are sweeter and can be eaten raw, but are mainly used in preserves, syrups and tarts and puddings. White currants are less common than other varieties, but are similar in flavour to redcurrants, although slightly less acid, and can be used in the same ways.

CUSTARD APPLES

The annona trees produce several tropical fruit, which are known collectively as custard apples. They include the *cherimoya, sugar apple, sour sop* and *bullock's heart.* They look similar to apples with green, purple-green or yellow-brown skin and flesh that varies from sweet to acid. The best known variety is *cherimoya,* which has a patterned skin and pineapple-flavoured flesh, which is the colour and texture of custard.

To prepare, cut off the top and remove the flesh, discarding the seeds. Use in fruit salads, ice cream and creamy sweets.

DATES

Dates are the fruit of the date palm tree with firm sweet flesh and a long inedible stone. They are mainly cultivated in the deserts of Tunisia and Southern Algeria.

Fresh dates should be plump and shiny, with smooth golden brown skins. Squeeze the stem end to remove the tough skin, then slit open and remove the stone. Dates can be eaten raw, used in salads or sweets, or they may be stuffed with cream cheese.

DURIAN

This very large fruit can weigh up to 9 kg (20 lb). It has a thick dull yellow skin covered with rough spines and a cream coloured flesh which has an unpleasant smell but delicious taste.

To prepare, slit the fruit at segment joints with a sharp knife and prise open, taking care of the sharp spines. The flesh can be eaten raw or added to Indonesian savoury dishes. The large seeds can be lightly roasted and eaten like nuts.

ELDERBERRIES

These are the fruit of the elder tree which grows wild in hedgerows and similar places. The berries are small, round and shiny, almost black in colour, and ripen in late summer. Elderberries are mainly used to make elderberry wine and preserves.

FEIJOAS

Also called pineapple guavas, these oval fruits have a tough reddish-green skin, scented flesh and a soft centre containing edible seeds. They taste like a combination of pineapple, strawberry and guava.

Feijoas are ripe when slightly soft and sweet smelling. Peel off the thin outer skin. The rest of the fruit can be eaten, either raw, sliced into fruit salads or made into jams or jellies.

FIGS

There are green, white, purple and black varieties of figs. They have soft creamy-pink juicy flesh full of tiny edible seeds. Most varieties have thin skins which are edible, though some people prefer to peel figs before eating.

Fresh figs should be soft to the touch and have skins with a distinct bloom. They do not keep well and should be eaten soon after purchase. To prepare, rinse, remove the stalks and eat as a dessert.

KEY
1. Pineapple; 2. Papayas; 3. Custard Apples; 4. Mangoes – yellow and green; 5. Green Bananas and Plantain; 6. Guavas; 7. Pomegranates; 8. Kiwi Fruit, 9. Persimmons, 10. Prickly Pears 11. Tamarillos; 12. Medlars; 13. Figs; 14. Dates; 15. Kumquats; 16. Cape Gooseberries (Chinese Lanterns); 17. Passion Fruit.

GOOSEBERRIES

There are many varieties: round or long; hairy or smooth; cooking or dessert. Cooking goose-berries are usually green with very sour, firm flesh and a fairly large number of edible seeds. Dessert gooseberries can be green, yellow-white or russet in colour, often with hairy skin and usually with soft pulpy flesh and large seeds.

Choose evenly coloured fruit, keep it refrigerated and eat within 3 days. To prepare, wash the berries, top and tail. Dessert varieties can be eaten raw; cooking varieties can be used in pies, puddings and preserves.

GRAPEFRUIT

These large citrus fruit have thick yellow skins and either yellow or pink flesh. The pink-fleshed varieties are sweeter than the yellow.

They will keep for 4 days at room temper-ature or 2 weeks in the refrigerator. Prepare grapefruit by cutting in half and separating the flesh from the skin with a serrated knife, then divide the segments.

Grapefruit can be eaten raw on their own, sweetened with a litte sugar if preferred, or with other fruits, or used to make mixed fruit marmalades.

GRANADILLA

A larger, smooth orange-skinned member of the passion fruit family, The creamy-yellow pulp is full of edible seeds.

GRAPES

Grapes range from pale amber to a deep blue colour. Popular dessert varieties include *Muscat* with white or golden coloured berries, *Almeria*, with golden-yellow or pale green berries and *Alphonse Lavallée* with purple-black berries. Commonly available seedless varieties include white *Thompson Seedless* and red *Flame Seedless*.

Choose plump, unbruised grapes with a distinct bloom to them; where possible buy in bunches and avoid any with shrivelled or squashed berries or any with signs of mould near the stem. Keep grapes refrigerated and use within 3 days. They should be left unwashed until ready to serve.

Grapes can be used in fruit salads and other raw fruit dishes; they are rarely cooked. Pips can be removed by halving the fruit with a knife and flicking out the pips with the point of a knife. To leave the fruit whole, push the tip of a skewer into the grape and push out the pips.

GUAVAS

Tropical fruit of South American and Indian origin, which may be round or pear-shaped. They have green to whitish-yellow or dark red skins and creamy-white to pink flesh which contains edible seeds. Guavas have a strong distinctive aroma and sweet flesh.

Choose firm, unblemished fruit. To prepare, cut in half and peel. Guavas can be eaten raw – they have one of the highest vitamin C contents of all fruit – or they can be baked.

JACKFRUIT

Widely cultivated in the tropical lowlands of Asia, Africa and America, jackfruit can grow up to 32 kg (70 lb) in weight. They have a rough, spiky green skin and yellow fibrous flesh which contains juicy pulp surrounding walnut-sized seeds. The pulp tastes like a cross between banana and pineapple with the texture of lychee.

To prepare, remove the skin and eat the pulp, discarding the seeds.

JAPONICAS

The fruit of the japonica tree is the ornamental version of the quince. They do not always ripen on the tree but can be picked whilst green and stored until they begin to turn slightly yellow. They have a distinctive flavour and are often cooked with apples or they can be made into a jelly.

KIWI FRUIT (CHINESE GOOSEBERRY)

Kiwi fruit are egg-shaped fruit with brown hairy skins and bright green flesh pitted with edible black seeds. They are grown mainly in New Zealand and the Canaries.

Choose firm fruit. Cut in half and eat with a teaspoon or peel and slice to use in fruit or savoury salads, or as an attractive decoration. Kiwi fruit is usually eaten raw but can be used in meat dishes. It has a very high vitamin C content.

KUMQUATS

These tiny fruit with smooth, orange, edible skins and a sweet-sour flavour are a close relative of the citrus family. They may be sliced and eaten raw, poached in sugar syrup, candied or made into preserves.

In recent years a number of hybrids have been produced, including the *limequat* and *citrangequat.*

LEMONS

Lemons have many culinary uses, although they are too acid to eat raw on their own. Look for lemons which are a strong 'lemon yellow' colour, have a moist looking skin and feel heavy for their size. A shrivelled skin indicates that some of the juice has evaporated.

When grating lemon rind, make sure that none of the bitter tasting white pith is grated. To thinly pare lemons, peel the rind with a vegetable peeler, avoiding any white pith.

The rind and juice can be used in puddings, cakes, pies, fruit drinks and in preserves such as lemon curd and marmalade, as well as in many savoury dishes and sauces. Lemon juice is an excellent source of pectin and is used in jams.

LIMES

Limes are like small lemons but with greener skin and a stronger, sharper flavour. Prepare in the same way as lemons. The juice and rind are used in some ice creams and sorbets, drinks, curries and preserves.

LOGANBERRIES AND TAYBERRIES

The loganberry is a hybrid of a blackberry and a raspberry. It is dark red with a flavour similar to a raspberry but stronger. The tayberry is a hybrid of loganberry and blackberry. Both fruits can be used in the same way as raspberries.

LOQUATS (JAPANESE MEDLAR)

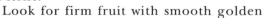

Originally an oriental fruit, loquats are now grown in Mediterranean countries and the USA. They look similar to a small plum with sweet, scented, slightly tart flesh and yellow-orange skins. The seeds are within the large stone.

Look for firm fruit with smooth golden skins. To eat raw, cut crossways and remove the stone. The outer skin can be eaten. To cook, remove the stone, quarter the fruit and poach in a light syrup. Skin if wished, and serve chilled. Loquats can also be made into preserves.

LYCHEES

Originally a Chinese fruit, lychees are now grown in many other countries. They are stone fruit the size of plums, which grow in bunches. They have hard skins, ranging from pink to brown, and sweet, juicy white flesh.

Avoid fruit with shrivelled dry skins. Peel and eat lychees raw, discarding the skin and stone, or poach in syrup and serve chilled on their own with ice cream or a fruit salad.

MANGOES

Mangoes are large stone fruit which grow all over the tropical and sub-tropical regions of the world. Some are round, others long and narrow or pear-shaped. Their juicy fibrous flesh has a distinctive, delicate flavour.

Ripe mangoes are very juicy with a yellow or orange skin and 'give' if gently squeezed. Avoid soft or shrivelled mangoes. Ripe mangoes are best used within 3 days.

To prepare, cut a large slice from one side of the fruit cutting close to the stone. Cut another slice from the opposite side. Cut the flesh in these pieces lengthways and crossways without breaking the skin, then push the skin inside out to expose the cubes of flesh. Peel the remaining centre section and cut the flesh away from the stone in chunks or slices.

Mangoes can be served with ice cream, in fruit salads, or puréed for mousses etc. Green, unripe mangoes, can be made into chutney.

MANGOSTEENS

Tropical fruit with a deep purple, fibrous outer shell and juicy segments of creamy white flesh. It has a sweet delicate flavour. To prepare, cut the thick rind through the centre and remove top part to reveal the fruit which is best eaten raw.

MEDLARS

These are small brown fruit about the size of a crab apple with sharp flavoured flesh. The fruit is eaten when soft and very ripe To prepare, wash  and halve and spoon out the flesh which can be eaten raw or used to make preserves.

MELONS

Depending on the variety, melons can be smooth skinned or have a light or heavy netting. All melons have perfumed, sweet juicy flesh; usually the more fragrant the melon, the sweeter and juicier its flesh.

Melons should feel heavy for their size and slightly soft at the stalk end when ripe. Soft patches on the rind indicate bruising rather than ripeness. Some varieties smell fragrant when ripe. Melons should be stored tightly wrapped in the refrigerator as they can easily pick up the flavours of other foods.

The flesh is usually eaten raw; cut in wedges and discard the seeds. Melon can be served as a starter, sometimes with smoked ham or other cold meat, or as a dessert, or it can be puréed for ice creams and sorbets. The following are the best-known types:

CHARENTAIS: Small round melons with green skin and superb fragrant orange flesh.
CANTALOUPE: Has a green to yellow rough, grooved skin. The flesh is orange-yellow and has a peachy flavour.
GALIA: Round with green flesh and a lightly netted skin which ranges from green to yellow.
HONEYDEW: Oval in shape, usually with bright yellow skin. The flesh is pale green, sweet and refreshing, though less flavoursome than other varieties.
OGEN: Round with yellow to orange skin marked with faint green stripes and very sweet juicy flesh.
WATERMELON: Large round or oblong melon with glossy dark green or striped green and yellow skin. The pink to deep red watery flesh, which contains black seeds, is very refreshing.

MULBERRIES

The most common variety is the black mulberry, which is in fact dark red and has a sharp flavour.

To prepare, wash carefully, then leave to dry in a colander. Mulberries are generally eaten raw or used to make jams and wines.

NECTARINES

Nectarines are a smooth-skinned variety of peach with white-yellow to pinkish-red flesh. White-fleshed nectarines have a particularly fine flavour. Avoid hard, extremely soft or shrivelled fruit. Nectarines will ripen at room temperature but once ripe should be refrigerated and used within a few days.

To prepare, simply wash and brush the exposed flesh with lemon juice to prevent browning. Eat on their own, in fruit salads or make into jams.

ORANGES

These are the best-known of the citrus fruits and are high in vitamin C. There are two main types; bitter and sweet. The two main bitter varieties, which are never eaten raw, are *Seville*, which are used for making marmalade and occasionally in meat and fish dishes; and *Bergamot*, which are used for perfumes and for extracting their oil. Sweet orange varieties include *Shamouti*, *Navel*, *Blood* and *Valencia*. They are very juicy and can be squeezed for their juice or sliced for fruit salads.

Choose firm fruit that feel heavy and have a glossy skin. Avoid ones with hard or dry-looking skins. Oranges will keep for at least 4 days at room temperature.

When serving sliced oranges, remove the white pith and peel. To use orange peel in cooking, peel the rind with a vegetable peeler avoiding any white pith, then blanch the peel for 3 minutes, rinse under cold water and shred before using.

In addition to the bitter and sweet types there are several small varieties of oranges:
MANDARINS AND TANGERINES are generally regarded as being the same thing. They are smaller than oranges and have loose skin which is easy to remove.
SATSUMAS are similar to tangerines with a sweet flesh which is usually seedless.
CLEMENTINES are similar to satsumas and tangerines but are smaller with stiffer skins and they contain pips.
ORTANIQUES are a cross between an orange and a tangerine. They have a thin orange-yellow skin and sweet flesh juicy flesh.
TANGELOS (UGLI FRUIT) are a cross between a tangerine and a grapefruit.
MINEOLAS are a hybrid like tangelos, but they are smaller, with a sweeter and more orangey taste.

Papayas (Paw Paws)

Large tropical fruit with smooth skins which ripen from green to yellow or orange. They have juicy orange-pink flesh the texture of avocado, with lots of black seeds in the centre. These are usually removed because they have a peppery flavour.

Papayas are ripe when the skin is yellow and the fruit feels soft. To prepare, cut in half, remove the seeds and serve in wedges; or cube and add to fruit salads.

Passion Fruit

These tropical vine fruits look like large wrinkled purple plums. The inedible skin is deeply wrinkled when ripe. The yellow flesh is fragrant, sweet and juicy. It is pitted with small edible black seeds.

To eat raw, cut in half and scoop out the flesh with a spoon. The juice can be used to make drinks or to flavour ice cream.

Peaches

There are many varieties of this fruit, including yellow-fleshed, pink-fleshed, and white-fleshed peaches which have a particularly fine flavour. Peaches can be roughly divided into two main types, the 'freestone' type with a stone that separates easily from the flesh, and the 'clingstone' type, in which the stone adheres to the flesh.

Ripe peaches are slightly soft and have a yellow to orange skin. Avoid green, or bruised fruit. Eat within 2 days if kept at room temperature, or if wrapped and kept in the refrigerator within 5 days. Peaches can be eaten raw or cooked. To peel, immerse in boiling water for about 15 seconds, then cool in cold water and skin. As scalding softens and slightly discolours the flesh it is better to simply peel with a sharp knife if eating raw. Brush cut fruit with lemon juice to prevent browning.

Peaches can be eaten on their own as a dessert, added to fruit salads, poached in a light syrup, stuffed and baked Italian-style, or made into jams or chutneys.

Persimmons (Sharon Fruit)

Large tomato-like fruit with leathery skins which turn from yellow to bright orangey red. The most common variety of persimmon is the *sharon fruit.* Unlike other persimmons, it is seedless and both skin and the flesh can be eaten. To prepare, wash the fruit and slice. The flesh can be spooned out and added to fruit salads or puréed and used in ice creams and mousses.

Pears

There are many varieties of pears, each with a different shape, size and colour. Most ripe pears are suitable for eating raw; *Williams Bon Chrétien, Conference, Comice, Packham's* and *Red Bartlett* are good dessert pears.

Choose well formed fairly firm pears. Ripe pears 'give' a little at the stem end. They become over-ripe very quickly so are best eaten within a day or two.

A sweet juicy pear at its peak of ripeness, served simply on its own, is an excellent dessert. Pears can also be eaten with cheese or added to fruit salads. Firm pears can be poached. Prepare pears by washing and peeling. Halve and scoop out the core; brush with lemon juice to prevent browning.

Pineapples

Large distinctive oval fruit with hard knobbly skins that grow in tropical and sub-tropical countries. The skin varies from deep yellow to orange-brown.

When pineapples are fully ripe, they give off a sweet aroma and a leaf can easily be pulled from the crown. Avoid pineapples that are bruised, discoloured or have wilting leaves. Pineapples continue to ripen after picking and are often sold slightly under-ripe. An unripe fruit without an aroma will not ripen properly.

To prepare, cut off the leaf crown and make slanting cuts downwards to remove the skin and brown spots from the flesh. Slice or cut into wedges and remove the central core. The flesh can be eaten raw on its own or in a variety of sweet and savoury dishes.

Pineapple can also be halved lengthways, scooped out, leaving the skin intact, to use as a bowl for fruit salad.

PLUMS

There are many different varieties of this stone fruit, varying in size and colour of skin and flesh. Popular varieties are *Mirabelle, Santa Rosa* and *Victoria* plums. Sweet plums can be eaten raw on their own or added to fruit salads, and all varieties can be cooked. They can be stewed, used in pies and puddings or made into preserves.

Avoid plums that are damaged or very soft. Ripe plums should be eaten soon after purchase. To prepare, wash, halve and stone the plums.
GREENGAGES are small sweet, green-amber coloured plums with a good flavour. They are delicious raw or poached; greengages also make an excellent jam.
DAMSONS are small dark blue to purple coloured plums with yellow flesh. They need to be cooked as they are sour. They are usually stewed, made into pies or preserves, particularly Damson Cheese (see page 480).

POMEGRANATES

These have thin, tough pink or red skins and juicy red flesh packed with seeds.

Buy fruit with hard undamaged skins. To prepare, simply cut in half and scoop out the seeds and juice – the juice is pleasantly sharp. Pomegranates are used in desserts and Middle Eastern soups and stews. The seeds can be used as a garnish.

PRICKLY PEARS

Also known as Indian fig, this pear-shaped fruit with a greenish-orange skin is covered with fine, needle-sharp prickles. The sweet juicy pink flesh has edible seeds.

These have to be prepared carefully because of the prickles.

Wash and scrub off the prickles, cut a slice off each end, then score the skin downwards and peel back. Slice the flesh and serve with a squeeze of lemon juice.

QUINCE

Small, pear-shaped fruit with yellow skin and scented flesh. Avoid scabby, split or very small fruit. Quince make good jams and jellies or they can be stewed with apples and pears. Simply peel and slice.

RAMBUTANS

These are the dark red-brown fruit of an Indonesian tree. The shell, which is covered with soft spines, is peeled off to reveal white translucent flesh, similar in taste to a lychee. It can be eaten on its own, or chopped and added to fruit salads.

RASPBERRIES

Soft juicy fruit with a central hull, raspberries have a delicious sweet, yet slightly acidic, flavour. Most varieties are red; white and black raspberries are now rarely available.

Raspberries are sold hulled which makes them liable to crushing. When buying, avoid stained containers and wet fruit. After picking or purchase, use quickly. They can be eaten fresh with cream, used in desserts with other fruit, or made into preserves.

RHUBARB

Rhubarb is officially a vegetable as it is the stem of a plant, but it is always eaten in sweet dishes. Forced rhubarb is pink and tender looking and sweet tasting; maincrop rhubarb has a stronger colour, a thicker stem and is more acid tasting. Look for young pink rhubarb; once the stems are thick and green they are coarse and tart.

To prepare, cut off the leaves and root, then wash and chop the stems. Rhubarb is always cooked and can be used for pies, puddings and jams. The leaves must not be eaten as they are poisonous.

SLOES

Sloes are the small, round, bluish-black fruit of the blackthorn tree which grows wild. They are used to make sloe gin, wine and preserves.

STAR FRUIT (CARAMBOLA)

Fluted yellow, waxy-looking fruit with a sweet and sour taste, which forms star shapes when sliced. To prepare, peel off the skin and slice. Eat on its own or add to fruit salads.

STRAWBERRIES

Widely grown in the this country, strawberries are one of the most popular summer fruits. The juicy red fruit grows round a central hull and has tiny seeds embedded in the outer surface.

When buying, check the base of the punnet for staining as this indicates squashed fruit. Buy plump glossy berries with the green hulls still attached. Only wash the strawberries just before hulling. Strawberries are best eaten raw, but can be used in flans, pies and preserves.

TAMARILLOS
Originally from South America, these large egg-shaped fruit are now grown in other tropical and sub-tropical countries. They have yellow or red hard skins which must be peeled off. Tamarillos are very acidic and they contain edible seeds. The flesh can be sweetened and eaten raw, but is more often cooked.

DRIED FRUIT

Dried fruits are a useful concentrated source of nutrients; they are also high in dietary fibre. Drying fruit is one of the oldest ways of preserving and, although the methods have changed – most dried fruit is now dried by artificial heat rather than the sun – the principle is the same. The water content is drawn out, preventing the growth of mould and bacteria and leaving the natural sugar in the fruit to act as a preservative.

BUYING AND PREPARING DRIED FRUIT
Dried fruits are sometimes treated with sulphur dioxide to prevent discolouration, and sprayed with mineral oils to enhance their appearance. It is worth searching out untreated fruit.

Most dried fruit needs washing and soaking for at least 3 hours, and preferably overnight, before using. However, some do not require soaking, and certain varieties are pre-soaked, so check packet instructions.

APPLES
Dried apples are usually sold as rings and can be eaten as a snack, added to muesli and other breakfast cereals, or they can be soaked and used to make purées or added to other fruits in crumbles and pies.

APRICOTS
These have an excellent flavour. Some types are specially tenderised so that there is no need to soak them before use. They can be used for fruit salads, purées, pies, sauces and stuffings.

BANANAS
Bananas are peeled and dried whole or sliced lengthways. They may be eaten as a snack, or soaked and used in compotes, or in baking.

DATES
Dried dates are available whole with stones or as pressed blocks of stoned fruit. Whole dates can be stoned and used without soaking for teabreads. The pressed blocks need to be soaked overnight and are best used for puddings, breads and cakes. Chopped dates rolled in sugar are available for use in baking.

FIGS
Dried figs may be sold loose or in pressed blocks. They should not be too sticky. Soak to use in compotes, fruit salads or hot puddings, or use without soaking in biscuits, cakes or scones.

PEACHES AND PEARS
These are usually sold in packets of mixed dried fruits. Soak and use in fruit salads, pies, teabreads, crumble toppings and stuffings for poultry and game.

PRUNES
These are whole dried plums, with or without the stones. Some varieties are tenderised and do not need soaking before using; otherwise, soak in cold tea or red wine rather than water for a better flavour. They can be eaten on their own or used in puddings, cakes and stuffings.

VINE FRUITS
Currants, raisins and sultanas are all types of dried grapes. They do not need soaking and are often sold pre-washed. Currants are dried small black seedless grapes. Seedless raisins are dried seedless grapes; the largest and sweetest raisins come from the Spanish Muscatel grapes. Sultanas are dried small white seedless grapes.

The main use of all the vine fruits is in baking, especially in cakes and puddings.

Nuts

The term nut is used to describe any seed or fruit with an edible kernel inside a hard shell. Nuts are a highly concentrated food, rich in protein, vitamins, minerals, fats and fibre. As well as being popular snacks, they are widely used in baking, sauces and sweet-making. Mixed with vegetables, they make a good substitute for meat, and are therefore popular in vegetarian dishes.

BUYING AND STORING NUTS

Shelled, flaked, chopped and ground nuts are best bought loose, in small quantities or vacuum packed. Store them in airtight containers, preferably in the refrigerator. Nuts bought in their shells should feel heavy; if they feel light they are likely to be stale. Store them in a cool, dark place for up to 3 months.

TOASTING NUTS

Toasting enhances the flavour of nuts, especially almonds and hazelnuts. To toast shelled whole, chopped or ground nuts, place on a baking sheet in an oven at 180°C (350°F) mark 4 for about 10 minutes. Alternatively toast under the grill for 1-2 minutes, turning frequently.

TYPES OF NUTS

ALMONDS

Almonds are the seeds of a tree belonging to the peach family which grows in hot dry climates such as Sicily, Spain and California. There are two varieties of almonds – bitter and sweet. Bitter almonds contain prussic acid and are seldom eaten raw (if they are eaten, they must only be eaten in small quantities). They are used mainly for making essences and oils.

Sweet almonds are available in their shells, and shelled in a variety of forms. Whole and split almonds are used in baking – whole almonds are a traditional decoration for Dundee Cake. Split almonds are traditionally served with trout – in *truite aux amandes*.

Flaked almonds are often toasted and used as a garnish or decoration, while chopped almonds may be sprinkled over desserts and ice cream.

Ground almonds are used to make Almond Paste (see page 426) and macaroons; they are also used in place of flour in cakes to add flavour and moistness.

To blanch almonds, cover with boiling water and leave for 10 seconds, then rinse in cold water and rub off the skin.

BRAZIL NUTS

Brazil nuts are large, oval, creamy-coloured nuts with a high percentage of fat. They grow, grouped together in their individual shells, inside the round fruit of a South American tree. Brazil nuts have a very hard brown shell which is not easy to crack, but shelled Brazil nuts are available from most supermarkets.

They are eaten raw, used in sweet-making or added to vegetarian dishes, such as nut roasts and rissoles.

CASHEW NUTS

These whitish-coloured nuts come from the tropical cashew tree. The tree bears reddish pear-shaped fruit and one kidney-shaped nut grows from the base of each fruit. As there is toxic oil in the shells of cashews, they are always sold shelled.

They are sold whole (often salted), in pieces, or roasted. They have a slightly crumbly texture and delicate sweet flavour. They are often served as an appetiser with drinks or used in stir-fried dishes.

CHESTNUTS

These are the fruit of the sweet chestnut tree, which grows mainly in European countries. Chestnuts are sold in their skins, dried, cooked and canned or as a purée (sweetened or unsweetened) in cans or tubes. Chestnuts in their skins must be peeled and cooked before eating.

To peel chestnuts, make a tiny slit in the skin near the pointed end, then cover with boiling water and leave for 5 minutes. Remove from the water, one at a time, and peel off the thick outer skin and thin inner skin while warm.

To cook chestnuts, simmer the peeled nuts in unsalted water for 30-40 minutes. Alternatively, bake the nuts in their skins in the oven at 200°C (400°F) mark 6 for 20 minutes, then peel.

Chestnuts have a rich flavour and are used to make soups and stuffings, served with vegetables such as Brussels sprouts and cabbage or preserved in sugar to make *marrons glacés*. Chestnut purée is used in gateaux and desserts.

Dried chestnuts are also available. They should be soaked in hot water for 30 minutes, then cooked and used as for raw chestnuts.

COCONUT

The fruit of the coconut palm, a tree native to South-East Asia but which now grows in all tropical areas. In the countries where they grow, coconuts are harvested when young and green, and their watery juice is served as a refreshing drink. It is the mature fruit that is most familiar in Britain. It has a hard, hairy brown shell containing sweet white flesh and a thicker liquid known as coconut milk which also makes a delicious drink.

The flesh of a coconut can be eaten raw, puréed in a blender with the milk to make coconut cream, or it can be shredded and used as an ingredient in baking or oriental cooking. Freshly grated coconut can be toasted in the oven. Fresh coconut milk can be kept, covered, in the refrigerator for up to two days. Coconut flesh is also available flaked or shredded and dried (desiccated).

A version of coconut milk can be made by soaking grated fresh or desiccated coconut in boiling water. Leave until cool, then strain and squeeze through muslin. 'Creamed coconut' is sold in blocks and can be sliced and used in the same way to make coconut milk to use in curries.

When choosing, look for a coconut that is heavy for its size and test it for freshness by shaking it to make sure it contains liquid. There should be no signs of mould around the three indentations (eyes) at the top of the coconut.

To prepare, puncture two of the eyes with a hammer and screwdriver and drain out the milk. Open the coconut by cracking the shell all around at the widest part. Separate halves and prize flesh from the shell with a sharp knife.

HAZELNUTS

Hazelnuts, filberts and cobs are all fruits of different varieties of hazel tree. Cobs are not as common as the other two. Hazelnuts are available in their shells, as shelled whole nuts (plain or roasted), flaked or ground. Remove the skin as for Almonds.

Hazelnuts have a distinct flavour which goes well with chocolate; they are often used in sweets, desserts, cakes and pastries.

PEANUTS (GROUND NUTS, MONKEY NUTS)

Peanuts are a type of underground bean which grows in India, Africa and parts of America and the Far East. They consist of two kernels which grow in a crinkly shell. They are available as whole nuts roasted in their shells or as shelled nuts, which may be plain, dry roasted or roasted and salted. Ground peanuts are used to make peanut butter.

Peanuts are rich in protein and highly nutritious. They are the most popular nuts for eating as snacks. They can be added to salads or used in vegetable dishes. Peanut butter, as well as being a spread, is used in satay sauces.

PECAN NUTS

Pecan nuts belong to the walnut family and grow in North America where they are also known as hickory nuts. They are available in their shells or shelled.

They are used to make Pecan Pie, but can be used instead of walnuts in any recipe.

PINE NUTS (PINE KERNELS, PIGNOLI)

These are the small, pale cream-coloured seeds of the Mediterranean pine tree. They are always sold shelled and may be roasted and salted. They have a delicate flavour and soft oily texture.

They are popular in Middle Eastern rice dishes and stuffings and are also used to make the Italian Pesto Sauce (see page 256). They can also be eaten raw, sprinkled over cooked vegetables or added to fruit salads.

PISTACHIO NUTS

These are the fruit of a small tree native to the Middle East and Central Asia, but now grown in other parts of the world. The bright green kernels have purple skins and beige-coloured shells. The shell splits when the kernels are ripe.

They are available in their shells or shelled (plain or salted). Skin as for Almonds. They can be eaten as a snack or used as a colourful garnish, or in sweets, ices, pâtés, and rice dishes.

WALNUTS

These are one of the most popular nuts and are grown in many parts of the world. They have a round, crinkly shell with a wrinkled kernel.

They are available in their shells, shelled, chopped or ground. Fresh unripe green walnuts are sometimes available pickled in jars.

Walnuts have a moist, oily flavour and are used in cakes, stuffings and salads.

Desserts

From classic baked and steamed puddings to refreshingly light fruit desserts, this chapter provides a collection of the most popular desserts. It includes all the family favourites, from traditional pies, crumbles and charlottes to fresh fruit salads and fools, plus cheesecakes, ices and sorbets, and meringue gâteaux.

Baked Puddings

Baked puddings range from light sponge puddings, flavoured with fruit or jam, to crumbles, charlottes and baked apples filled with brown sugar, mincemeat or dates. Baked puddings take less time to cook than steamed ones as they are cooked in the oven with more direct heat.

BAKED JAM SPONGE

45 ml (3 level tbsp) jam
75 g (3 oz) butter or block margarine
75 g (3 oz) caster sugar
1 egg, beaten
150 g (5 oz) self raising flour
2.5 ml (½ tsp) vanilla flavouring
milk, to mix
Egg Custard Sauce (see page 208), to serve

1. Grease a 600-900 ml (1-1½ pint) pie dish. Spread the jam in an even layer in the bottom of the dish.
2. Cream the fat and sugar together until pale and fluffy. Add the egg, a little at a time, beating well after each addition. Fold in the flour with the flavouring and a little milk to give a smooth dropping consistency.
3. Spoon into the prepared dish and bake in the oven at 180°C (350°F) mark 4 for 30-40 minutes, until well risen and golden. Serve with Egg Custard Sauce.
SERVES 3-4

VARIATIONS
BAKED CASTLE PUDDINGS
Grease eight small individual foil dishes or dariole moulds and put 5-10 ml (1-2 level tsp) jam in the bottom of each. Divide the mixture between the dishes or moulds, and bake for 20 minutes.

ORANGE AND LEMON SPONGE
Add the grated rind of an orange or lemon to the creamed mixture and replace the milk with fruit juice.

CHOCOLATE SPONGE
Add 45 ml (3 level tbsp) cocoa powder, sifted with the flour, or stir 25 g (1 oz) chocolate dots or chips into the mixture. Serve with Rich Chocolate Sauce (see page 209).

GINGER SPONGE
Sift 2.5 ml (½ level tsp) ground ginger with the flour, or add 2 pieces of preserved ginger, finely chopped, and 10 ml (2 tsp) of the ginger syrup.

Eve's Pudding

EVE'S PUDDING

450 g (1 lb) cooking apples, peeled and cored
75 g (3 oz) demerara sugar
grated rind of 1 lemon
75 g (3 oz) butter or block margarine
75 g (3 oz) caster sugar
1 egg, beaten
150 g (5 oz) self raising flour
a little milk, to mix

1. Grease a 900 ml (1½ pint) ovenproof dish. Slice the apples and place in the dish. Sprinkle over the sugar and lemon rind.
2. Cream the fat and caster sugar together until pale and fluffy. Add the egg, a little at a time, beating well after each addition.
3. Fold in the flour with enough milk to give a smooth dropping consistency and spread the mixture over the apples.
4. Bake in the oven at 180°C (350°F) mark 4 for 40-45 minutes, until the apples are tender and the sponge mixture golden brown.
SERVES 4

VARIATION
Add 25 g (1 oz) ground almonds with the flour and sprinkle 25 g (1 oz) flaked almonds over the top of the pudding.

LEMON LAYER PUDDING

grated rind and juice of 2 lemons
50 g (2 oz) butter or block margarine
100 g (4 oz) caster sugar
2 eggs, separated
50 g (2 oz) self raising flour
300 ml (½ pint) milk

1. Grease a 1.1 litre (2 pint) ovenproof dish.
2. Cream together the lemon rind, butter and sugar until pale and fluffy. Add the egg yolks and flour and beat well to combine.
3. Stir in the milk and lemon juice. Whisk the egg whites until stiff and fold into the mixture, then pour into the dish.
4. Stand the dish in a shallow tin of cold water and bake in the oven at 180°C (350°F) mark 4 for about 45 minutes, or until the top is set and spongy to the touch.
SERVES 4

NOTE: This pudding separates out in the cooking into a custard layer with a sponge topping.

FRUIT CRUMBLE

50 g (2 oz) butter or block margarine
100 g (4 oz) plain flour
100 g (4 oz) sugar
450 g (1 lb) prepared fruit (sliced apples, peaches,
*   rhubarb, plums or gooseberries)*
custard, to serve

1. Rub the butter into the flour until the mixture resembles fine breadcrumbs, then stir in 50 g (2 oz) sugar.
2. Arrange half the prepared fruit in a 1.1 litre (2 pint) pie dish and sprinkle evenly with the remaining sugar, then top with the remaining fruit slices.

3. Spoon the crumble mixture over the fruit and lightly press it down.
4. Bake in the oven at 180°C (350°F) mark 4 for about 45 minutes, until the fruit is soft. Serve hot with custard, or cold with cream or yogurt.
SERVES 4

VARIATIONS
1. Add 5 ml (1 level tsp) ground cinnamon, mixed spice or ginger to the flour before rubbing in the fat.
2. Add the grated rind of an orange or lemon to the crumble mixture before sprinkling it over the fruit.

APPLE AND BLACKBERRY CHARLOTTE

450 g (1 lb) cooking apples, peeled and cored
450 g (1 lb) blackberries
finely pared rind and juice of ½ a lemon
1.25 ml (¼ level tsp) ground cinnamon
50-75 g (2-3 oz) sugar, or to taste
30 ml (2 level tbsp) bread or cake crumbs
6 large bread slices
50 g (2 oz) butter or margarine, melted
custard, to serve

1. Grease a 1.4 litre (2½ pint) charlotte mould or a 15 cm (6 inch) round cake tin.
2. Thickly slice the apples and put in a saucepan with the blackberries, lemon rind and juice and cinnamon and cook gently for 10 minutes, until the apples have softened slightly. Add the sugar and crumbs. Discard the lemon rinds.
3. Cut the crusts off the bread. Trim one piece to a round the same size as the base of the tin,

Arrange bread around sides of the mould or tin.

dip it into the melted butter and fit into the bottom of the tin. Dip the remaining slices of bread in the butter and arrange closely around the side of the tin, reserving one piece for the top.
4. Spoon in the stewed fruit and cover with the remaining slice of bread, trimmed to fit the top of the mould.
5. Bake in the oven at 190°C (375°F) mark 5 for about 1 hour. Turn out and serve with custard.
SERVES 4

NOTE: This is the traditional charlotte recipe. It can be made with apples alone.

BAKED APPLES

4 medium cooking apples
demerara sugar
knob of butter or margarine

1. Wipe and core the apples, then make a shallow cut through the skin around the middle of each.
2. Stand the apples in an ovenproof dish. Pour 60 ml (4 tbsp) water around them, fill each apple with sugar and top with a small knob of butter.
3. Bake in the oven at 200°C (400°F) mark 6 for

about 45-60 minutes, until the apples are soft.
SERVES 4

VARIATIONS
1. Stuff the centre of the apples with mincemeat instead of demerara sugar.
2. Stuff the apples with currants, sultanas, stoned raisins, chopped dried apricots, mixed peel or glacé fruits, or with a mixture of chopped dates and walnuts or other nuts.
3. Pack the centres with chopped dates, grated orange rind and soft brown sugar.

WALNUT AND ORANGE PUDDING

125 g (4 oz) soft tub margarine
50 g (2 oz) walnut pieces, chopped
75 g (3 oz) caster sugar
15 ml (1 level tbsp) golden syrup
2 eggs
5 ml (1 tsp) vanilla essence
75 g (3 oz) self-raising flour
5 ml (1 level tsp) baking powder
grated rind of 1 orange
60 ml (4 tbsp) fresh orange juice
custard, to serve

1. Grease six ovenproof ramekins.
2. Place all the ingredients together in a large bowl and beat thoroughly until smooth.
3. Two-thirds fill the ramekins with the mixture. Place on a baking tray and bake in the oven at 180°C (350°F) mark 4 for 20-25 minutes or until firm to the touch.
4. Turn out or leave in the ramekins if preferred, and serve warm with custard.
SERVES 6

Walnut and Orange Pudding

PINEAPPLE UPSIDE-DOWN PUDDING

150 g (6 oz) butter or block margarine
50 g (2 oz) soft dark brown sugar
227 g (8 oz) can pineapple rings, drained
2 glacé cherries, halved
100 g (4 oz) caster sugar
2 eggs, beaten
175 g (6 oz) self raising flour
30-45 ml (2-3 tbsp) pineapple juice or milk

Arrange pineapple rings and cherries in a layer in the bottom of the tin.

1. Grease and base-line an 18 cm (7 inch) round cake tin. Cream together 50 g (2 oz) butter and the brown sugar and spread evenly over the bottom of the tin. Arrange the pineapple rings and cherries on this layer in the bottom of the tin.
2. Cream together the remaining butter and sugar until pale and fluffy. Add the beaten egg, a little at a time, beating well after each addition. Fold in the flour, adding some pineapple juice or milk to give a smooth dropping consistency, then spread the mixture on top of the pineapple rings.
3. Bake in the oven at 180°C (350°F) mark 4 for about 45 minutes. Turn out on to a warmed serving dish and serve.
SERVES 4

VARIATIONS

CHOCOLATE PEAR UPSIDE-DOWN PUDDING
Use canned pear halves instead of pineapple. Substitute 25 g (1 oz) cocoa powder for 25 g (1 oz) flour and sift with the flour into the sponge mixture.

SPICED APRICOT UPSIDE-DOWN PUDDING
Replace the pineapple rings with canned apricot halves, well drained (with a little syrup reserved for giving a smooth dropping consistency). Add 2.5 ml (½ level tsp) ground cinnamon to the pudding mixture.

Steamed Puddings

Steamed puddings are made by a very gentle method of cooking in a bowl in a steamer or saucepan of boiling water or wrapped and boiled in a preserving pan. Follow the rules below and the result will always be soft and moist. These puddings are turned out and often served with a sauce.

GENERAL RULES FOR STEAMING

- Half-fill the steamer with water and heat so that it is boiling by the time the pudding is made. If you haven't got a steamer, fill a large saucepan with water to come halfway up the pudding basin. Cover with a lid and bring to the boil.
- Grease the pudding basin well.
- Cut a double thickness of greaseproof paper or a piece of foil to cover the pudding basin and grease well. Put a pleat in the paper or foil to allow the pudding to rise.

- Fill the basin not more than two-thirds full with mixture. Cover the basin tightly with the paper or foil to prevent steam or water entering. Secure with string and make a string handle to lift the basin in and out of the pan.
- Keep the water in the steamer boiling rapidly all the time and have a kettle of boiling water ready to top it up regularly, or the steamer will boil dry. If you are using a saucepan, put an old saucer or metal pastry cutter in the base to keep the basin off the bottom.

Jam Sponge Pudding

30 ml (2 level tbsp) jam
100 g (4 oz) butter or block margarine
100 g (4 oz) caster sugar
2 eggs, beaten
few drops of vanilla flavouring
175 g (6 oz) self raising flour, sifted
a little milk, to mix
custard, to serve

1. Half-fill a steamer or large saucepan with water and put it on to boil. Grease a 900 ml (1½ pint) pudding basin and spoon the jam into the bottom.
2. Cream together the fat and sugar until pale and fluffy. Add the beaten eggs and the vanilla flavouring, a little at a time, beating well after each addition.
3. Using a metal spoon, fold in half the sifted flour, then fold in the rest, with enough milk to give a dropping consistency.
4. Pour the mixture into the prepared basin, cover with greased greaseproof paper or foil and secure with string. Steam for 1½ hours. Serve with custard.
Serves 4

VARIATIONS
Syrup Sponge Pudding
Put 30 ml (2 tbsp) golden syrup into the bottom of the basin instead of the jam.

Fruit Sponge Pudding
Put a shallow layer of drained canned fruit or a layer of stewed fruit in the basin before adding the sponge mixture.

Mincemeat Surprise Pudding
Line the bottom and sides of the basin with a thin layer of mincemeat and fill with the pudding mixture. When the pudding is cooked, turn it out carefully so that the outside remains completely covered with the mincemeat.

Chocolate Sponge Pudding
Omit jam. Blend 60 ml (4 level tbsp) cocoa powder with 15 ml (1 tbsp) hot water until smooth. Gradually add to the creamed fat and sugar.

Lemon or Orange Sponge
Add the grated rind of 1 orange or lemon when creaming the fat and sugar.

Steamed Castle Pudding
Divide the jam and the sponge mixture between greased dariole moulds, filling them two-thirds full. Cover each mould with greased foil and secure with string. Steam for 30-45 minutes (depending on size) over rapidly boiling water.

Jam Roly-Poly

175 g (6 oz) Suetcrust Pastry (see page 387)
60-90 ml (4-6 level tbsp) jam
a little milk, for brushing
custard, to serve

1. Half-fill a steamer with water and put on to boil. Grease a piece of foil 23 x 33 cm (9 x 13 inches).
2. Roll out the suetcrust pastry on a lightly floured surface to an oblong about 23 x 25 cm (9 x 11 inches). Spread the jam on the pastry, leaving 5 mm (¼ inch) clear along each edge. Brush the edges with milk and roll up the pastry evenly, starting from one short side.
3. Place the roll on the greased foil and wrap the foil around it loosely, to allow room for expansion, but seal the edges well.
4. Steam for 1½-2 hours. Remove from the foil and serve with custard.
Serves 4   *(Illustrated on page 387.)*

Spotted Dick

100 g (4 oz) fresh breadcrumbs
75 g (3 oz) self raising flour
75 g (3 oz) shredded suet
50 g (2 oz) caster sugar
175 g (6 oz) currants
finely grated rind of 1 lemon
75 ml (5 tbsp) milk
custard, to serve

1. Half-fill a preserving pan or large saucepan with water and put on to boil.
2. Place the breadcrumbs, flour, suet, sugar, currants and lemon rind in a bowl and stir well until thoroughly mixed.
3. Pour in the milk and stir until well blended. Using one hand, bring the ingredients together to form a soft, slightly sticky dough.
4. Turn the dough on to a floured surface and knead gently until just smooth. Shape into a neat roll about 15 cm (6 inches) in length.
5. Make a 5 cm (2 inch) pleat across a clean tea towel or pudding cloth. Or pleat together sheets

Encase the Spotted Dick in foil or paper and pleat to close.

of greased greaseproof paper and strong foil. Encase the roll in the cloth or foil, pleating the open edges tightly together.
6. Tie the ends securely with string to form a cracker shape. across the top. Lower the suet roll into the pan of boiling water and boil for about 2 hours.
7. Lift the spotted dick out of the water using the string handle. Place on a wire rack standing over a plate and allow excess moisture to drain off.
8. Snip the string and gently roll the pudding out of the cloth or foil on to a warmed serving plate. Cut the Spotted Dick into slices and serve with custard.
Serves 4

Jam Suet Pudding

30 ml (2 level tbsp) jam
175 g (6 oz) self raising flour
pinch of salt
75 g (3 oz) shredded suet
50 g (2 oz) caster sugar
about 150 ml (¼ pint) milk
custard, to serve

1. Half-fill a steamer with water and put on to boil. Grease a 900 ml (1½ pint) pudding basin and spoon the jam into the bottom.
2. Mix together the flour, salt, suet and sugar. Make a well in the centre and add enough milk to give a soft dropping consistency.
3. Pour into the prepared basin, cover with greased greaseproof paper or foil and secure with string.
4. Steam for 1½-2 hours. Serve with custard.
Serves 4

VARIATION
Add 225 g (8 oz) cooking apples, peeled and finely chopped or grated, to the dry ingredients.

Rich Christmas Pudding

RICH CHRISTMAS PUDDING

100 g (4 oz) prunes
175 g (6 oz) currants
175 g (6 oz) seedless raisins
175 g (6 oz) sultanas
100 g (4 oz) plain flour
1.25 ml (¼ level tsp) grated nutmeg
1.25 ml (¼ level tsp) ground cinnamon
2.5 ml (½ level tsp) salt
75 g (3 oz) fresh breadcrumbs
100 g (4 oz) shredded suet
100 g (4 oz) dark soft brown sugar
25 g (1 oz) blanched almonds, chopped
finely grated rind of ½ lemon
150 ml (¼ pint) brown ale
2 eggs, beaten

1. Snip the prunes into small pieces, discarding the stones.
2. Half-fill a steamer or large saucepan with water and put it on to boil. Grease a 1.3 litre (2½ pint) pudding basin.
3. Place the prunes in a large mixing bowl and stir in the remaining ingredients. Stir well until evenly mixed.
4. Put the mixture into the prepared basin, pushing down well. Cover with greased, pleated greaseproof paper and foil. To cook, steam for about 8 hours.
5. Leave the greaseproof paper in position, allow to cool, then cover with a clean dry cloth or foil and store in a cool place for at least 2 weeks before serving.
6. To reheat, steam for 2½ hours. Turn out on to a warmed serving plate and serve with brandy or Rum Butter (see page 210).
SERVES 8

BATTER PUDDINGS

There are two main types of batter used for puddings: pouring batter, which is used for pancakes and baked batter puddings; and coating batter, which is used for fritters. Coating batter is thicker than pouring batter, so it will cling to fruit dipped into it, which can then be deep-fried. An enriched version is used for waffles.

PANCAKES

125 g (4 oz) plain flour
pinch of salt
1 egg
300 ml (½ pint) milk
vegetable oil for frying
sugar and lemon juice, to serve

1. Sift the flour and salt into a bowl and make a well in the centre. Break in the egg and beat well with a wooden spoon, then gradually beat in the milk, drawing in the flour from the sides to make a smooth batter.
2. Heat a little oil in an 18 cm (7 inch) heavy-based frying pan, running it around the base and sides of the pan, until hot. Pour off any surplus.
3. Pour in just enough batter to thinly coat the base of the pan. Cook for 1-2 minutes, until golden brown, turn or toss and cook the second side until golden.
4. Transfer the pancake to a plate and keep hot. Repeat with the remaining batter to make eight pancakes. Pile the cooked pancakes on top of

each other with greaseproof paper in between.
5. Serve as soon as they are all cooked, sprinkled with sugar and lemon juice.
MAKES 8

NOTE: Pancake batter may also be made in a blender or food processor. Put the egg and liquid in first, then add the flour and process for a few seconds only.

VARIATIONS
1. Add 5-10 ml (1-2 level tsp) icing sugar to the flour before mixing.
2. Add the grated rind of ½ a lemon or orange to the flour before mixing.

APRICOT PANCAKES
Purée 225 g (8 oz) stewed dried apricots in a blender or food processor. Divide between the pancakes then roll up. Place in a greased ovenproof dish, cover and bake at 220°C (425°F) mark 7 for about 20 minutes.

WAFFLES

These crisp, light wafers, made from batter, are cooked in a special waffle iron. The cooking time varies with different kinds of waffle irons; follow manufacturer's instructions carefully.

125 g (4 oz) self raising flour
pinch of salt
15 ml (1 level tbsp) caster sugar
1 egg, separated
30 ml (2 tbsp) butter or margarine, melted
150 ml (¼ pint) milk
2.5 ml (½ tsp) vanilla flavouring (optional)
butter and golden or maple syrup, to serve

1. Heat the waffle iron according to the manufacturer's instructions.

2. Mix the dry ingredients together in a bowl. Add the egg yolk, melted butter, milk and vanilla flavouring and beat to give a smooth coating batter.
3. Whisk the egg white until stiff and fold into the batter. Pour just enough batter into the iron to run over the surface.
4. Close the iron and cook for 2-3 minutes, turning the iron if using a non-electric type. When the waffle is cooked, it should be golden brown and crisp and easily removed from the iron – if it sticks, cook for a minute longer.
5. Serve immediately with butter and golden or maple syrup. Alternatively, layer the waffles with whipped cream or ice cream and fresh fruit.
SERVES 4

CRÊPES SUZETTE

50 g (2 oz) butter or margarine
25 g (1 oz) caster sugar
finely grated rind and juice of 1 large orange
30 ml (2 tbsp) Grand Marnier or other orange-
    flavoured liqueur
45 ml (3 tbsp) brandy or rum
8 freshly cooked pancakes (see page 333)
cream, to serve

1. Melt the butter in a large frying pan. Remove from the heat and add the sugar, orange rind and juice, and the liqueur. Heat gently to dissolve the sugar.
2. Fold each pancake in half and then in half again to form a fan shape. Place the pancakes in the frying pan in overlapping lines.
3. Warm the brandy, pour it over the pancakes and set alight. Shake gently, then serve at once with cream.
MAKES 8

FRITTER BATTER

125 g (4 oz) plain flour
pinch of salt
1 egg
150 ml (¼ pint) milk or milk and water mixed

1. Sift the flour and salt into a bowl and make a well in the centre. Break in the egg and beat well with a wooden spoon, then gradually beat in the liquid, drawing in the flour from the sides to make a smooth batter.
MAKES 200 ML (7 FL OZ)

VARIATION
SWEET FRITTER BATTER
Add 5-10 ml (2-3 tsp) icing sugar to the flour. Replace the milk with beer and add with the egg yolk. Add 15 ml (1 tbsp) oil. Whisk the egg white and fold into the batter. Use immediately.

FRITTERS
Dip pineapple or apple rings, or halved bananas in fritter batter, then deep-fry in hot oil for 2-3 minutes, until golden.

BEIGNETS DE FRUITS

1 quantity Sweet Fritter Batter (see above)
oil for deep-frying
1 large eating apple, peeled, cored and cut into rings
1 firm nectarine, stoned and cut into quarters
1 banana, peeled and cut into chunks
caster sugar, for sprinkling

1. Make up the Sweet Fritter Batter and use immediately.
2. Heat the oil in a deep-fryer to 190°C (375°F). Dip the prepared fruits in the batter and deep-fry in batches. The apple will take about 4 minutes and the nectarine and banana about 3 minutes.
3. Drain on absorbent kitchen paper and keep warm while frying the remainder. Serve hot, sprinkled with caster sugar.
SERVES 4

NOTE: Most fruits make delicious beignets. Remember that soft fruits like apricots or peaches will require a much shorter cooking time than fruits such as apples and pears.

Beignets de Fruits

Pies, Flans and Pastries

Sweet fillings in crispy, light-textured pastry cases make delicious desserts for all occasions. Flans can be made with a pastry or sponge base, or you can use an uncooked case made from biscuits. These desserts have the added advantage that in most cases the cooking can be done beforehand.

Egg Custard Tart

150 g (5 oz) Shortcrust Pastry, made with 150 g (5 oz)
  flour (see page 381)
2 eggs
30 ml (2 level tbsp) sugar
300 ml (½ pint) milk
freshly grated nutmeg

1. Roll out the pastry on a floured surface and use it to line an 18 cm (7 inch) loose-based flan tin or fluted flan dish. Chill for 30 minutes.
2. Meanwhile, whisk the eggs with the sugar; warm the milk and pour on to the egg mixture. Strain the custard into the pastry case and sprinkle the top with nutmeg.
3. Bake in the oven at 220°C (425°F) mark 7 for about 10 minutes, then reduce temperature to 180°C (350°F) mark 4 and cook for 20 minutes, or until the custard is just set. Serve cold.
SERVES 4

Pecan Pie

200 g (7 oz) Shortcrust Pastry, made with 200 g (7 oz)
  flour (see page 381)
3 eggs
15 ml (1 tbsp) milk
175 g (6 oz) demerara sugar
150 ml (¼ pint) maple or corn syrup
50 g (2 oz) butter or margarine, softened
2.5 ml (½ tsp) vanilla flavouring
175 g (6 oz) pecan nuts, halved
cream, to serve

1. Roll out the pastry on a floured surface and use to line a 23 cm (9 inch) loose-based flan tin or fluted flan dish. Chill in the refrigerator for 30 minutes.
2. Meanwhile, make the filling. Beat the eggs and milk together. Boil the sugar and syrup together in a saucepan for 3 minutes. Slowly pour on to the beaten eggs and stir in the butter and vanilla flavouring.
3. Use half the nuts to cover the base of the pastry case, spoon the syrup mixture over and cover with the remaining nuts. Bake in the oven at 220°C (425°F) mark 7 for 10 minutes.
4. Reduce the temperature to 170°C (325°F) mark 3 and cook for a further 45 minutes, until the filling is set. Serve warm or cold with cream.
SERVES 6-8

Bakewell Pudding

212 g (7½ oz) packet frozen puff pastry, thawed
2 eggs
2 egg yolks
100 g (4 oz) butter or margarine, melted
100 g (4 oz) caster sugar
50 g (2 oz) ground almonds
30 ml (2 level tbsp) raspberry jam

1. Roll out the pastry on a floured surface and use to line an 18 cm (7 inch) pie plate or loose-based flan tin.
2. Beat the eggs and extra yolks together, add the butter, sugar and almonds and mix well.
3. Spread the bottom of the pastry case with the jam and pour on the egg mixture.
4. Bake in the oven at 200°C (400°F) mark 6 for 30 minutes, until the filling is firm to the touch.
SERVES 4

ALMOND AND CHERRY FLAN

200 g (8 oz) Flan Pastry (see page 382)
350 g (12 oz) fresh black cherries, stoned
50 g (2 oz) butter or block margarine
50 g (2 oz) caster sugar
125 g (4 oz) ground almonds
5 ml (1 tsp) almond flavouring
15 ml (1 tbsp) almond-flavoured liqueur (optional)
1 egg yolk
50 g (2 oz) self raising flour
2.5 ml (½ level tsp) baking powder
30 ml (2 tbsp) milk
2 egg whites
25 g (1 oz) flaked almonds
cream, to serve

Almond and Cherry Flan

1. Roll out the pastry on a floured surface and use to line a 24 cm (9½ inch) loose-based flan tin or fluted flan dish. Chill in the refrigerator for 30 minutes.
2. Bake blind (see page 380) in the oven at 200°C (400°F) mark 6 for 10-15 minutes, then remove the paper and beans and bake for a further 5 minutes until set. Cool slightly.
3. Scatter the cherries over the pastry. Cream the remaining butter and sugar together and beat in the ground almonds, almond flavouring, liqueur if using, and the egg yolk. Sift together the flour and baking powder and fold into the mixture, then lightly stir in the milk.
4. Whisk the egg whites until they are stiff, and fold them into the creamed mixture.
5. Spread over the cherries in the flan case and scatter the flaked almonds on top. Bake in the oven at 180°C (350°F) mark 4 for about 30 minutes. Serve warm with cream.
SERVES 6

OLD-FASHIONED TREACLE TART

175 g (6 oz) Shortcrust Pastry (see page 381)
225 g (8 oz) golden syrup
finely grated rind and juice of 1 lemon
75 g (3 oz) fresh breadcrumbs
beaten egg, to glaze

1. Roll out the pastry on a floured surface and use to line a 20 cm (8 inch) fluted flan dish. Reserve trimmings. Chill for 30 minutes.
2. Meanwhile, to make the filling, warm the golden syrup in a saucepan with the lemon rind and juice. Sprinkle the breadcrumbs evenly over the pastry base, then slowly pour in the syrup.
3. Make strips from the reserved pastry trimmings and place these over the tart in a lattice pattern, brushing the ends with water to stick them to the pastry case. Glaze with a little egg.
4. Bake in the oven at 190°C (375°F) mark 5 for about 25 minutes until the filling is just set.
SERVES 4-6

Old-fashioned Treacle Tart

FRENCH APPLE FLAN

200 g (8 oz) Flan Pastry (see page 382)
900 g (2 lb) cooking apples
50 g (2 oz) butter or margarine
120 ml (9 level tbsp) apricot jam
50 g (2 oz) sugar
finely grated rind of ½ lemon
30 ml (2 tbsp) Calvados or brandy
225 g (8 oz) eating apples
about 30 ml (2 tbsp) lemon juice
5 ml (1 level tsp) caster sugar

1. Roll out the pastry on a floured surface and use to line a 20 cm (8 inch) loose-based fluted flan tin placed on a baking sheet. Chill in the refrigerator for 30 minutes.
2. Bake blind (see page 380) in the oven at 200°C (400°F) mark 6 for 10-15 minutes, then remove paper and beans and bake for a further 5 minutes until the base is set.
3. Cut the cooking apples into quarters, core and roughly chop the flesh. Melt the butter in a saucepan and add the apples with 30 ml (2 tbsp) water. Cover the pan tightly and cook gently for about 15 minutes until soft and mushy.
4. Rub the apples through a sieve into a large clean pan. Add half the apricot jam with the sugar, lemon rind and brandy. Cook over a high heat for about 15 minutes, stirring, until all excess liquid has evaporated and the mixture is thickened.
5. Spoon the thick apple purée into the flan case and smooth the surface. Peel, quarter, core and slice the dessert apples very thinly. Arrange in an overlapping circle over the apple purée. Brush lightly with lemon juice; sprinkle with the caster sugar.
6. Return the flan to the oven and bake for a further 25-30 minutes, or until the pastry and

French Apple Flan

apples are lightly coloured. Transfer to a serving plate. Cool for 10 minutes.
7. Gently warm the remaining jam with 15 ml (1 tbsp) lemon juice, then sieve. Brush over the top and sides of the flan.
SERVES 6

APPLE PIE

900 g (2 lb) cooking apples, peeled, cored and sliced
50 g (2 oz) sugar
225 g (8 oz) Shortcrust Pastry, made with 225 g (8 oz) flour (see page 381)
caster sugar, for sprinkling

1. Layer the apples and sugar in a 1.1 litre (2 pint) pie dish. Sprinkle over 15 ml (1 tbsp) water.
2. Roll out the pastry on a floured surface to a

circle 2.5 cm (1 inch) larger than the dish. Cut off a strip, dampen the rim of the dish and press on the strip. Dampen the strip and cover with the pastry, pressing the edges well together. Scallop the edges (see page 379) and make a slit in the centre.
3. Bake in the oven at 190°C (375°F) mark 5 for 35-40 minutes, until the pastry is lightly browned. Sprinkle with caster sugar for serving.
SERVES 4-6

APPLE AND HAZELNUT LAYER

75 g (3 oz) hazelnuts, shelled
75 g (3 oz) butter
45 ml (3 level tbsp) caster sugar
115 g (4½ oz) plain flour
pinch of salt
450 g (1 lb) Cox's apples, peeled, cored and sliced
15 ml (1 tbsp) apricot jam or marmalade
grated rind of 1 lemon
15 ml (1 level tbsp) candied peel, chopped
30 ml (2 level tbsp) currants
30 ml (2 level tbsp) sultanas
icing sugar, whipped cream and hazelnuts, to decorate

1. Cut out two 20 cm (8 inch) circles of greaseproof paper. Reserve 8 nuts and finely chop the remainder.
2. Cream the butter and sugar until pale and fluffy. Stir in the flour, salt and chopped nuts, then form into a ball and chill for 30 minutes.
3. Put the apples in a saucepan with the jam and lemon rind and cook over a low heat for 5 minutes, until soft. Add the candied peel and dried fruit and simmer for 5 minutes.
4. Divide the pastry in half, place on the sheets of greaseproof paper and roll out into two circles. Transfer to greased baking sheets.
5. Bake at 190°C (375°F) mark 5 for 7-10 minutes, until light brown. Cut one circle into 8 triangles while warm. Leave to cool.
6. Just before serving, place the complete circle on a serving plate and cover with the apple mixture. Arrange the triangles on top. Dust with icing sugar, pipe cream on top and decorate with hazelnuts.
SERVES 8

FRESH APRICOT FLAN

150 g (5 oz) flour
pinch of salt
50 g (2 oz) ground almonds
75 g (3 oz) butter or block margarine
1 egg yolk mixed with 15 ml (1 tbsp) water
2 eggs
150 ml (5 fl oz) single cream or milk
15 ml (1 level tbsp) caster sugar
few drops of almond flavouring
120 ml (8 level tbsp) apricot jam, sieved
450 g (1 lb) fresh apricots, skinned, halved and stoned
    or 411 g (14 oz) can apricot halves, drained
15 ml (1 tbsp) lemon juice
15 ml (1 tbsp) almond-flavoured liqueur

1. Mix the flour and salt in a bowl with half the ground almonds. Rub in the butter until the mixture resembles fine breadcrumbs. Bind to a firm dough with the egg yolk mixture; knead lightly until smooth.
2. Roll out the dough on a floured surface and use to line a 20 cm (8 inch) loose-based fluted flan tin or flan dish. Chill in the refrigerator for 30 minutes.
3. Bake blind (see page 380) in the oven at 190°C (375°F) mark 5 for 10-15 minutes, then remove paper and beans and bake for a further 5 minutes until set.
4. Meanwhile, mix together the eggs, cream, sugar, remaining ground almonds and almond flavouring.
5. Warm the jam gently in a small saucepan. Spread 45 ml (3 tbsp) jam over the pastry case, then pour the cream mixture into the flan case.
6. Reduce the oven temperature to 170°C (325°F) mark 3 and bake for 20 minutes, or until the filling is just set. Leave for about 1 hour to cool.
7. Arrange the apricot halves neatly over the custard filling in the flan. Add the lemon juice to the remaining jam together with the liqueur and heat the mixture until reduced to a glaze. Brush the glaze over the apricots to cover them completely. Chill in the refrigerator for 2 hours before serving.
SERVES 6

DOUBLE-CRUST BLACKCURRANT PIE

450 g (1 lb) blackcurrants, stringed and washed
75 g (3 oz) sugar
30 ml (2 level tbsp) cornflour
350 g (12 oz) Shortcrust Pastry made with 350 g
   (12 oz) flour (see page 381)
milk, to glaze
caster sugar, for sprinkling

1. Mix together the blackcurrants, sugar and cornflour.
2. Roll out two-thirds of the pastry on a floured surface and use it to line a 20 cm (8 inch) deep pie plate or sandwich tin.
3. Fill the plate with the fruit mixture and roll out the remaining pastry to form a lid, pressing the edges well together. Scallop the edges (see page 379) and make a slit in the centre. Brush the top with milk. Put the plate on a baking sheet and bake in the oven at 190°C (375°F) mark 5 for 40-45 minutes. Cover it loosely with foil after 30 minutes to prevent over-browning. Sprinkle with caster sugar to serve.
SERVES 4-6

MINCE PIES

225 g (8 oz) Shortcrust Pastry (see page 381)
350-450 g (12 oz-1 lb) mincemeat
icing or caster sugar, for dusting

1. Roll out the pastry on a floured surface to about 3 mm (⅛ inch) thickness.
2. Cut out about 20 rounds with a 7.5 cm (3 inch) fluted cutter and 20 smaller rounds with a 5.5 cm (2¼ inch) fluted cutter.
3. Line 6 cm (2½ inch) patty tins with the larger rounds and fill with mincemeat. Dampen the edges of the small rounds with water and place firmly on top. Make a small slit in each top.
4. Bake in the oven at 220°C (425°F) mark 7 for 15-20 minutes, until light golden brown. Leave to cool on a wire rack. Serve dusted with sugar.
MAKES ABOUT 20

VARIATION
PUFF PASTRY MINCE PIES
Mince pies can be made using a 368 g (13 oz) packet puff pastry. Roll out the pastry to 3 mm (⅛ inch) thickness. Cut 16 rounds with a 6 cm (2½ inch) cutter. Re-roll trimmings; cut another 16 rounds to use for the bases.

Place the bases on a dampened baking sheet. Put a heaped 5 ml (1 tsp) mincemeat on each and dampen the pastry edges. Cover with the remaining rounds and press the edges lightly together; glaze with beaten egg.

Bake in the oven at 230°C (450°F) mark 8 for about 20 minutes.
MAKES 16

CHOCOLATE GINGER FLAN

175 g (6 oz) ginger biscuits, crushed
50 g (2 oz) flour
75 g (3 oz) butter or block margarine
200 g (7 oz) natural quark (low fat soft cheese)
3 eggs, separated
30 ml (2 level tbsp) cocoa powder
2 pieces stem ginger, finely chopped
15 ml (1 tbsp) stem ginger syrup or 15 ml (1 level tbsp)
   ginger marmalade
50 g (2 oz) plain chocolate
150 ml (5 fl oz) whipping cream
grated chocolate, to decorate

1. In a bowl, mix together the biscuits and flour. Rub in the butter until the mixture is soft and just begins to bind.
2. Press evenly over the base and up the sides of a 20 cm (8 inch) fluted flan dish or tin. Bake in the oven at 200°C (400°F) mark 6 for 15-20 minutes, or until quite firm to the touch.
3. Whisk together the quark, egg yolks, cocoa, chopped ginger and the syrup. Whisk the egg whites until just holding their shape. Fold into the ginger mixture, then pour into the flan tin.
4. Bake in the oven at 180°C (350°F) mark 4 for about 20 minutes or until just set and firm to the touch. Leave to cool.
5. Melt the chocolate with 30 ml (2 tbsp) water in a small bowl over a pan of simmering water. Spread evenly over cooked flan. Leave to cool.
6. Lightly whip the cream. Spoon over the flan and decorate with grated chocolate.
SERVES 8-10

GLAZED FRUIT SPONGE FLAN

50 g (2 oz) caster sugar plus 10 ml (2 level tsp)
50 g (2 oz) flour plus 5 ml (1 level tsp)
2 eggs, size 2
225 g (8 oz) strawberries, hulled and sliced
45 ml (3 level tbsp) redcurrant jelly

1. Grease a 20 cm (8 inch) raised-based flan tin. Sprinkle over 10 ml (2 tsp) caster sugar and tilt the tin to coat evenly. Add 5 ml (1 level tsp) flour and coat similarly, knocking out any excess
2. Place the eggs and remaining sugar in a deep bowl and whisk until the mixture is very thick. Sift the flour over the surface of the mixture. Fold in gently with a metal spoon, then turn into prepared tin and tilt to level the surface.
3. Place on a baking sheet and bake in the oven at 180°C (350°F) mark 4 for 20-25 minutes, until the sponge springs back when pressed lightly. Turn out on to a wire rack. Leave to cool.
4. Arrange the sliced fruit in the flan case. Put the redcurrant jelly and 15 ml (1 tbsp) water in a small saucepan and heat gently together until liquid. Cool a little, then brush over the fruit.
SERVES 6

VARIATIONS
Use fresh raspberries, apricots, gooseberries or black and green grapes instead of strawberries.

RHUBARB AND ORANGE CHIFFON PIE

175 g (6 oz) digestive biscuits, crushed
50 g (2 oz) demerara sugar
75 g (3 oz) unsalted butter, melted
*450 g (1 lb) fresh rhubarb, trimmed and cut
    into 2.5 cm (1 inch) lengths*
finely grated rind and juice of 1 large orange
2 eggs, separated
50 g (2 oz) caster sugar
30 ml (2 level tbsp) cornflour
2.5 ml (½ level tsp) ground ginger
orange slices, to decorate

1. In a bowl, mix together the biscuits and demerara sugar, then stir in the butter.
2. Press evenly over the base and up the sides of a 20 cm (8 inch) fluted flan dish. Chill in the refrigerator while preparing the filling.
3. Cook the rhubarb with 45 ml (3 tbsp) water in a covered pan until soft and pulpy, stirring occasionally.
4. Purée the rhubarb in a blender or food processor, then pour into a bowl. Put the orange rind and juice into a heavy-based saucepan. Add the egg yolks, caster sugar, cornflour and ginger. Heat gently, stirring, until thick. Stir into the rhubarb purée.

Rhubarb and Orange Chiffon Pie

5. Whisk the egg whites until stiff. Fold into the rhubarb custard, then spoon the mixture into the biscuit crust. Chill in the refrigerator for at least 4 hours, or overnight. Decorate with orange slices just before serving.
SERVES 6

Pineapple Tarte Tatin

PINEAPPLE TARTE TATIN

50 g (2 oz) caster sugar
175 g (6 oz) butter or margarine
2 egg yolks
125 g (4 oz) self raising white flour
125 g (4 oz) granulated sugar
60 ml (4 tbsp) double cream
900 g (2 lb) pineapple, peeled, cored and thinly sliced
15 ml (1 tbsp) Kirsch (optional)
fresh mint sprigs, to decorate
thick yogurt, cream or ginger cream (see note), to serve

1. Beat the caster sugar with 50 g (2 oz) of the butter until pale and light. Beat in the egg yolks, then fold in the flour and knead lightly together to form a smooth dough. Wrap and chill in the refrigerator for 30 minutes.

2. Melt the remaining 125 g (4 oz) butter with the granulated sugar in a small saucepan over a low heat. Bring to the boil, then simmer for 3-4 minutes, beating continuously until the mixture is smooth, dark and fudge-like. (Do not worry if the mixture separates at this stage.)

3. Take off the heat, allow to cool for 1 minute, then stir in the cream, beating until smooth. If necessary, warm gently, stirring, until completely smooth. Spoon into a shallow 22 cm (8½ inch) round non-stick sandwich tin.

4. Arrange the pineapple neatly in overlapping circles on the fudge mixture. Drizzle over the Kirsch if wished.

5. Roll out the prepared pastry to a 25 cm (10 inch) round. Place over the pineapple, tucking and pushing the edges down the side of the tin. Trim off any excess pastry. Stand the tin on a baking sheet.

6. Bake in the oven at 200°C (400°F) mark 6 for about 20 minutes or until the pastry is a deep golden brown. Run the blade of a knife around the edge of the tin to loosen the pastry. Leave to cool for 2-3 minutes, then turn out onto a heatproof serving dish and place under a hot grill for 2-3 minutes to caramelise the top.

7. Decorate with fresh mint sprigs and serve with thick yogurt, cream or ginger cream.
SERVES 6

NOTE: To make ginger cream simply stir together equal quantities of whipped cream and Greek-style natural yogurt. Lightly fold in a little whisked egg white and a few pieces of finely chopped stem ginger.

GÂTEAU ST. HONORÉ

100 g (4 oz) Pâte Sucrée (see page 382)
beaten egg, to glaze
1 quantity Choux Pastry (see page 388)
300 ml (10 fl oz) double cream
45 ml (3 level tbsp) sugar
angelica and glacé cherries, to decorate
FOR THE CRÈME PÂTISSIÈRE
2 eggs
50 g (2 oz) caster sugar
30 ml (2 level tbsp) flour
30 ml (2 level tbsp) cornflour
300 ml (½ pint) milk
few drops of vanilla flavouring

1. Roll out the Pâte Sucrée on a floured surface to an 18 cm (7 inch) round. Place on a baking sheet and prick all over with a fork. Chill in the refrigerator for 30 minutes, then brush a 1 cm (½ inch) band around the edge with beaten egg.
2. Put the choux pastry into a piping bag fitted with a medium plain nozzle and pipe a circle around the edge of the pastry round. Brush with beaten egg. Dampen a baking sheet and pipe about twenty walnut-sized choux balls on to it. Brush with beaten egg.
3. Bake both the flan and the choux balls in the oven at 190°C (375°F) mark 5 for about 15 minutes or until the choux pastry is well risen and golden brown. Make a slit in the side of each bun and the ring to release the steam, then transfer with the flan case on to a wire rack and leave for 15-20 minutes to cool.

4. Meanwhile, to make the Crème Pâtissière, cream the eggs and sugar together until pale and thick. Sift the flour and cornflour into the bowl and beat in with a little cold milk until smooth. Heat the rest of the milk until almost boiling and pour on to the egg mixture, stirring well.
5. Return the custard to the saucepan and stir over a low heat until the mixture boils. Add the vanilla flavouring to taste and cook for a further 2-3 minutes. Cover and allow to cool.
6. Whip the cream until stiff. Reserving a little cream for the top of the gâteau, put the rest into a piping bag fitted with a medium plain nozzle and pipe some into each of the cold choux buns.
7. Put the sugar and 45 ml (3 tbsp) water into a heavy-based saucepan and boil until the edge just begins to turn straw-coloured. Hold the buns with a skewer or tongs and dip the tops into the syrup to coat evenly.
8. Use the remainder of the syrup to stick the

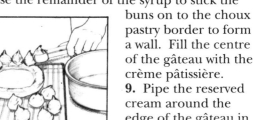

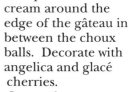

buns on to the choux pastry border to form a wall. Fill the centre of the gâteau with the crème pâtissière.
9. Pipe the reserved cream around the edge of the gâteau in between the choux balls. Decorate with angelica and glacé cherries.

Use the choux buns to form a border around flan.

SERVES 6

BAKLAVA

225 g (8 oz) shelled walnuts, ground
50 g (2 oz) light soft brown sugar
2.5 ml (½ level tsp) ground cinnamon
450 g (1 lb) packet filo pastry
150 g (5 oz) butter, melted
175 g (6 oz) clear honey

1. Grease a 24 x 18 cm (9½ x 7 inch) roasting tin. Mix the walnuts, sugar and cinnamon together in a bowl. Halve each sheet of pastry to make 25 cm (10 inch) squares.
2. Fit one sheet of pastry into the bottom of the prepared tin, allowing it to come up the sides, and brush with melted butter. Repeat with five

more pastry sheets. Sprinkle with one-fifth of the nut mixture.
3. Repeat stage 2 four more times to produce five layers of walnut mixture. Top with the remaining pastry and trim the sheets to fit the tin. Mark the surface of the pastry into 20 squares with the tip of a sharp knife.
4. Bake in the oven at 220°C (425°F) mark 7 for 15 minutes, then at 180°C (350°F) mark 4 for 10-15 minutes, until golden brown.
5. Meanwhile, warm the honey in a saucepan over a low heat, spoon over the cooked baklava, and leave to cool in the tin for 1-2 hours. Cut out the marked squares.
MAKES 20

APPLE STRUDEL

225 g (8 oz) Filo Pastry (see page 389), or ½ x 450 g
(1 lb) packet ready-made filo pastry
700 g (1½ lb) cooking apples, peeled, cored and sliced
50 g (2 oz) currants
50 g (2 oz) sultanas
45 ml (3 level tbsp) caster sugar
5 ml (1 level tsp) ground mixed spice
40 g (1½ oz) butter or margarine, melted
125 g (4 oz) fresh breadcrumbs
25 g (1 oz) flaked almonds
icing sugar, to decorate
cream, to serve

1. Roll out the Filo Pastry as instructed on page 389 and leave to rest on the cloth for 15 minutes.
2. Put the apples, currants, sultanas, sugar and spice in a bowl and mix thoroughly. Brush the dough with half the melted butter and sprinkle with breadcrumbs.
3. Spread the apple mixture over the dough, leaving a 5 cm (2 inch) border uncovered all around the edge. Fold these edges over the apple mixture.
4. With a long side towards you, lift the corners of the cloth and roll up the strudel. Stop after each turn to pat into shape and to keep the roll even.
5. Form the roll carefully into a horseshoe shape and slide on to an oiled baking sheet. Brush with remaining butter and sprinkle with almonds.
6. Bake in the oven at 190°C (375°F) mark 5 for about 40 minutes, until pale golden brown. Dredge with icing sugar to serve. Serve warm or cold with cream.
SERVES 8-10

MILLE FEUILLES

212 g (7 oz) packet frozen puff pastry, thawed,
or ¼ quantity Puff Pastry (see page 385)
125 g (4 oz) raspberry jam
1 quantity Crème Pâtissière (see page 342), or 300 ml
(½ pint) double cream, whipped
175 g (6 oz) Glacé Icing (see page 432), to decorate
few drops of red food colouring

1. Roll out the pastry on a lightly floured surface to a rectangle measuring 25 x 23 cm (10 x 9 inches) and place on a dampened baking sheet. Prick all over with a fork.
2. Bake in the oven at 220°C (425°F) mark 7 for 10 minutes, until well risen and golden brown. Transfer to a wire rack and leave to cool.
3. When cold, trim the pastry edges, cut in half lengthways and cut each half across into six slices. Spread half with raspberry jam, then cover with the crème pâtissière or cream.
4. Spread jam on the bases of the remaining pastry pieces and place jam side down on top of the first layers.
5. Mix 15 ml (1 tbsp) of the glacé icing with the red colouring. Set aside. Spread the remaining glacé icing over the top of the pastries.
6. Pour the pink icing into a greaseproof paper piping bag (see page 424). Cut off the tip and carefully pipe fine pink lines 1 cm (½ inch) apart on top of the white glacé icing, across each pastry. Draw a skewer down the length of the Mille Feuilles at 1 cm (½ inch) intervals to make a 'feathering' design.
7. Leave for 1 hour to set before serving.
MAKES 6

PROFITEROLES

1 quantity Choux Pastry (see page 388)
150 ml (5 fl oz) whipping or double cream
icing sugar, to decorate
Rich Chocolate Sauce (see page 209)

1. Dampen the surface of two or three baking sheets with water. Fill a piping bag fitted with a medium plain nozzle with the choux pastry and pipe small balls, about the size of walnuts, on to the baking sheets.
2. Bake in the oven at 200°C (400°F) mark 6 for 15-20 minutes until crisp. Make a slit in the side of each profiterole to release the steam and leave to cool on a wire rack.
3. Whisk the cream until stiff and spoon into a piping bag fitted with a medium plain nozzle; pipe some into each of the profiteroles. Dredge with icing sugar and pile them into a pyramid.
4. Pour some of the chocolate sauce over and serve immediately with the rest of the sauce handed separately.
SERVES 6

FRUIT DESSERTS

Fruit can be served just as it is, or with cream or yogurt as a quick and simple dessert. It can also be turned into fresh fruit salads or used in a wide range of delectable hot and cold desserts.

POACHED OR STEWED FRUITS IN SUGAR SYRUP

50-125 g (2-4 oz) sugar
450 g (1 lb) fresh firm fruit, eg apples, gooseberries,
   peaches, pears, plums, prepared

1. Slowly dissolve the sugar in 300 ml (½ pint) water in a large heavy-based saucepan over a gentle heat. Bring to the boil and boil for 1 minute.
2. Add the fruit and simmer very gently in the sugar syrup until almost cooked, turning occasionally with a slotted spoon.
3. To prevent the fruit becoming mushy, remove the pan from the heat, cover and leave for several minutes; the fruit will finish cooking in the residual heat.

FLAVOURINGS
APPLES: Add a squeeze of lemon juice, a strip of lemon rind, 1 or 2 cloves, or a small piece of cinnamon stick.
GOOSEBERRY: Add a piece of bruised root ginger or a pinch of ground ginger.
PEACHES: Add 45-60 ml (3-4 tbsp) brandy after the fruit has cooked.
PEARS: Add 1 or 2 cloves or a small piece of cinnamon stick.
PLUMS: Add the plum kernels or a few almonds while the fruit is cooking.
RHUBARB: Add a piece of bruised root ginger, a piece of cinnamon stick or a strip of lemon or orange rind.

STEWED DRIED FRUIT

450 g (1 lb) dried fruit, eg prunes, apricots, peaches,
   figs, apples, pears or a mixture
strip of lemon rind
granulated or demerara sugar, to taste

1. Wash fruit thoroughly, then soak in 600 ml (1 pint) water for 12 hours if necessary.

2. Put the fruit into a saucepan with the soaking water. Add the lemon rind, bring to the boil and simmer gently until tender. Add the sugar.
3. Remove the fruit with a slotted spoon, boil the juice for a few minutes until syrupy, then strain it over the fruit.
SERVES 4

GOOSEBERRY FOOL

450 g (1 lb) gooseberries, washed and topped and
   tailed
125 g (4 oz) sugar
15 ml (1 level tbsp) custard powder
150 ml (¼ pint) milk
few drops of green food colouring
150 ml (5 fl oz) whipping cream
chopped nuts, to decorate

1. Put the gooseberries and sugar in a saucepan with 30 ml (2 tbsp) water, cover and cook for about 20 minutes.
2. Sieve or purée the fruit in a blender or food processor.
3. Blend the custard powder with a little milk and heat the remaining milk. Pour the hot milk

on to the blended custard powder, stirring, then return to the pan and stir over a gentle heat until thickened.
4. Beat the custard into the fruit pulp and allow to cool. Add the food colouring, remembering that the cream will lighten the colour.
5. Whip the cream until stiff, then fold into the purée. Pour into a glass dish or individual glasses and chill in the refrigerator.
6. Decorate with nuts before serving.
SERVES 4

VARIATIONS
Use 450 g (1 lb) raspberries, strawberries, blackberries or damsons instead of gooseberries. Do not cook but purée and add sugar to taste. Sieve if necessary to remove seeds.

FRESH FRUIT SALAD

50-125 g (2-4 oz) sugar
juice of ½ lemon
selection of 4 or 5 fruit, eg 2 red-skinned apples,
   2 oranges, 2 bananas, 125 g (4 oz) black or green
   grapes, 1 small pineapple

1. Dissolve the sugar in 300 ml (½ pint) water over a gentle heat, bring to the boil and boil for 5 minutes. Cool and add the lemon juice.
2. Prepare the fruits: Quarter, core and slice the apples; peel and segment the oranges; slice the bananas; halve and seed the grapes. Cut the pineapple into 1 cm (½ inch) slices, remove the skin and cut flesh into cubes. Put each fruit into the syrup as it is ready.
3. Mix them all together and if possible leave to stand for 2-3 hours before serving, to allow the flavours to blend.
SERVES 4-6

VARIATIONS
1. Add 15-30 ml (1-2 tbsp) Kirsch or other fruit liqueur, brandy or white wine to the syrup.
2. Substitute orange, pineapple or grape juice for the sugar syrup.
3. Any other combinations of fresh fruits can be used, such as dessert pears, strawberries, raspberries, cherries and melon.
4. For a tropical fruit salad, use a mixture of mango, papaya (paw paw), kiwi fruit and pineapple.
5. Fruit salad can be served in a hollowed-out melon or pineapple half; in either case the flesh which has been removed should be cut into chunks and used in the salad.
6. Canned fruit such as apricot halves, peach slices, pineapple chunks, guavas and lychees can also be used in fruit salads. Use some of the juice from the can, with a little lemon juice, to replace the sugar syrup.

ORANGES IN CARAMEL

8 medium juicy oranges
225 g (8 oz) caster sugar
30 ml (2 tbsp) Grand Marnier or other orange-
   flavoured liqueur

1. Thinly pare the rind from half the oranges and cut into very thin julienne strips. Place in a small saucepan and cover with water. Cover the pan and cook for 5 minutes until tender. Drain and rinse under cold water.
2. Cut away the pith from the oranges and both rind and pith from the four remaining oranges.
3. Slice the orange flesh into rounds, reserving any juice and discarding pips; arrange in a serving dish. (If liked, the orange rounds can be

reassembled in the shape of oranges and secured with wooden cocktail sticks.)
4. Place the sugar and 300 ml (½ pint) water in a saucepan and heat gently until the sugar has dissolved. Bring to the boil and boil until the syrup is caramel coloured.
5. Remove the pan from the heat, carefully add 45 ml (3 tbsp) water and return it to a low heat to dissolve the caramel. Add the reserved orange juice and the liqueur.
6. Leave the caramel syrup to cool for 10 minutes, then pour over the oranges. Top with the julienne strips. Chill in the refrigerator for 2-3 hours, turning the oranges occasionally.
SERVES 8

PEARS IN PORT

150 ml (¼ pint) port
75 g (3 oz) sugar
thinly pared rind of 1 lemon
4 large ripe pears
30 ml (2 level tbsp) redcurrant jelly
crisp dessert biscuits, to serve

1. Put the port, sugar and lemon rind in a saucepan with 150 ml (¼ pint) water and heat gently until the sugar dissolves, stirring occasionally. Bring to the boil.

2. Meanwhile, peel the pears and remove the cores. Add to the syrup, bring to the boil, cover and simmer gently until tender, about 15 minutes.
3. Using a slotted spoon, transfer the pears to a serving dish. Add the redcurrant jelly to the syrup and boil rapidly for about 5 minutes until well reduced.
4. Remove the lemon rind and pour the syrup over the pears. Cool. Serve with the biscuits.
SERVES 4

FLAMBÉ BANANAS

25 g (1 oz) butter or margarine
grated rind and juice of 1 large orange
2.5 ml (½ level tsp) ground cinnamon
4 large bananas, peeled
50 g (2 oz) demerara sugar
60 ml (4 tbsp) dark rum
orange rind shreds and slices, to decorate
cream or vanilla ice cream, to serve

1. Melt the butter in a frying pan and add the orange rind and juice. Stir in the cinnamon, then add the bananas and cook for a few minutes, until softened.
2. Add the sugar and stir until dissolved. Add the rum, set alight and stir gently to mix.
3. Decorate with orange shreds and slices and serve immediately with cream or ice cream.
SERVES 4

APRICOT SAVARIN

75 g (3 oz) dried apricots, soaked if necessary
25 g (1 oz) fresh yeast or 15 ml (1 level tbsp) fast-action dried yeast
90 ml (6 tbsp) tepid milk
225 g (8 oz) strong white flour
2.5 ml (½ level tsp) salt
30 ml (2 level tbsp) caster sugar
4 eggs, beaten
100 g (4 oz) butter or block margarine, softened
90 ml (6 tbsp) clear honey
45 ml (3 tbsp) brandy
450 g (1 lb) fresh or canned apricot halves
150 ml (5 fl oz) whipping cream
15 g (½ oz) flaked almonds, toasted

1. Grease a 1.4 litre (2½ pint) ring mould. Drain the soaked apricots and chop roughly.

2. Blend the yeast, milk and 50 g (2 oz) of the flour together in a bowl.
3. Add the remaining flour with the salt, sugar, eggs, butter and dried apricots. Beat thoroughly for 3-4 minutes.
4. Pour into the ring mould and cover with a clean tea towel. Leave to rise in a warm place for 15 minutes.
5. Bake in the oven at 200°C (400°F) mark 6 for about 30 minutes. Turn out on to a plate.
6. Simmer the honey and 90 ml (6 tbsp) water together for 3-5 minutes. Add the brandy and, while still hot, spoon over the savarin. Cool.
7. Transfer carefully to a serving plate and spoon the apricots into the middle of the savarin. Whip the cream until stiff and pipe a border of cream at the top and bottom of the savarin and sprinkle with toasted flaked almonds.
SERVES 4

FRESH PEAR SHORTCAKE

150 g (5 oz) self raising flour
25 g (1 oz) ground rice
grated rind of 1 lemon
50 g (2 oz) dark soft brown sugar
150 g (5 oz) butter or block margarine
3 ripe large, even-sized pears, about 450 g (1 lb) weight
125 g (4 oz) full fat soft cheese
1 egg
few drops of almond flavouring

1. Lightly grease a 20 cm (8 inch) loose-based fluted flan tin and set aside. In a mixing bowl, stir together the flour, ground rice and lemon rind. Sieve the sugar into the bowl.
2. Rub in the butter and continue lightly kneading the mixture until it forms a dough.
3. Press the dough into the prepared tin with floured fingertips. Mark into six portions and prick well with a fork.
4. Bake in the oven at 190°C (375°F) mark 5 for 30-35 minutes until golden brown and cooked through. Leave in the tin to cool slightly.
5. Using a sharp knife, peel and halve the pears. Scoop out the cores using a teaspoon or corer.
6. Cut each pear half crossways into 3 mm (⅛ inch) slices, keeping them together at one edge. Place a sliced pear half on each portion of shortcake, fanning out the slices a little.
7. Beat together the soft cheese, egg and almond flavouring until smooth, then spoon over the pears, completely covering fruit and shortcake.
8. Bake in the oven at 180°C (350°F) mark 4 for 40 minutes until golden. Ease out of the tin and serve warm or cold.
SERVES 6

Autumn Pudding

SUMMER PUDDING

700 g (1½ lb) mixed summer fruit, such as redcurrants,
blackcurrants, raspberries, prepared
about 25 g (1 oz) light soft brown sugar
8-10 thin slices of day-old bread, crusts removed
fresh fruit and mint sprigs, to decorate

1. Stew the fruit gently with 60-90 ml (4-6 tbsp) water and the sugar until soft but still retaining their shape. The exact amounts of water and sugar depend on the ripeness and sweetness of the fruit.

2. Meanwhile, cut a round from one slice of bread to neatly fit the bottom of a 1.1 litre (2 pint) pudding basin and cut 6-8 slices of the bread into fingers about 5 cm (2 inches) wide. Put the round at the bottom of the basin and arrange the fingers around the sides, overlapping them so there are no spaces.

3. When the fruit is cooked, and still hot, pour it gently into the basin, being careful not to disturb the bread framework. Reserve about 45 ml (3 tbsp) of the juice. When the basin is full, cut the remaining bread and use to cover the fruit so a lid is formed.

4. Cover with a plate or saucer which fits just inside the bowl and put a weight on top. Leave the pudding until cold, then put into the refrigerator and chill overnight.

5. To serve, run a knife carefully round the edge to loosen, then invert the pudding on to a serving dish. Pour the reserved juice over the top. Serve cold with cream. Decorate with fruit and mint sprigs.

SERVES 4-6

VARIATION
AUTUMN PUDDING
Replace the summer fruits with a selection of autumn fruits, such as apples or pears, blackberries and plums.

CHEESECAKES

Cheesecakes are a flavoured mixture of cheese, cream and, usually, eggs. There are two basic kinds: the cooked cheesecake, which usually has a pastry or sponge base; and the uncooked cheesecake, which may be set with gelatine and often has a base of crushed biscuits.

TRADITIONAL BAKED CHEESECAKE

50 g (2 oz) self raising flour
2.5 ml (½ level tsp) baking powder
50 g (2 oz) butter or margarine, softened
275 g (10 oz) caster sugar
5 eggs, size 2
450 g (1 lb) full fat soft or curd cheese
40 g (1½ oz) plain flour
grated rind and juice of 1 lemon
150 ml (5 fl oz) soured cream
75 g (3 oz) sultanas

1. Grease and base-line a 20 cm (8 inch) round spring-release cake tin.
2. Sift the self raising flour and baking powder into a bowl. Add the butter, 50 g (2 oz) sugar and 1 egg. Mix well and beat for 2-3 minutes. Spread the mixture evenly over the bottom of the prepared tin.

3. Separate the remaining eggs. Whisk the egg yolks with the remaining sugar until the mixture is thick and creamy.
4. Beat the cheese lightly. Add the whisked egg mixture and mix until smooth. Sift in the plain flour and fold in, then add the lemon rind and juice, soured cream and sultanas; stir until evenly mixed.
5. Whisk the egg whites until stiff, then fold into the mixture. Pour into the tin.
6. Bake in the oven at 170°C (325°F) mark 3 for 1 hour or until firm but still spongy to the touch. Turn off the heat and leave the cheesecake in the oven for 1 hour with the door ajar.
7. Remove from the oven and leave to cool completely for 2-3 hours. Carefully remove the cheesecake from the tin and transfer to a flat plate to serve.
SERVES 8-10

LEMON CHEESECAKE

75 g (3 oz) butter or margarine
175 g (6 oz) digestive biscuits, finely crushed
15 ml (1 level tbsp) gelatine
finely grated rind and juice of 1 lemon
225 g (8 oz) cottage cheese, sieved
150 ml (5 fl oz) soured cream
75 g (3 oz) caster sugar
2 eggs, separated
fresh fruit eg strawberries, sliced, seedless grapes,
*   halved, or kiwi fruit, peeled and sliced, to decorate*

1. Melt the butter in a saucepan and mix in the biscuit crumbs. Press into the base of a 20 cm (8 inch) loose-bottomed or spring-release cake tin. Chill in the refrigerator for 30 minutes.
2. Sprinkle the gelatine in 60 ml (4 tbsp) water in a small bowl. Place over a pan of simmering water and stir until dissolved. Cool slightly.
3. Put the lemon rind, juice and cottage cheese into a bowl, then add the soured cream and sugar and mix well together. Add the egg yolks and gelatine.
4. Whisk the egg whites until stiff, then fold lightly into the mixture. Carefully pour into the tin and chill for several hours, preferably overnight until firm.
5. Remove the cheesecake from the tin and place on a flat serving plate. Decorate with fresh fruit to serve.
SERVES 6

Hot Chocolate Cheesecake

HOT CHOCOLATE CHEESECAKE

FOR THE CHOCOLATE PASTRY
150 g (5 oz) plain flour
75 g (3 oz) butter or margarine
30 ml (2 level tbsp) cocoa powder, sifted
30 ml (2 level tbsp) caster sugar
25 g (1 oz) ground hazelnuts
1 egg yolk
FOR THE FILLING
2 eggs, separated
75 g (3 oz) caster sugar
350 g (12 oz) curd cheese
40 g (1½ oz) ground hazelnuts
150 ml (¼ pint) double cream
25 g (1 oz) cocoa powder, sifted
10 ml (2 tsp) dark rum
icing sugar, for dusting

1. Grease a 20 cm (8 inch) round loose-based cake tin.
2. To make the chocolate pastry, put the flour in a bowl and rub in the butter until the mixture resembles fine breadcrumbs. Stir in the cocoa powder, sugar and hazelnuts. Add the egg yolk and sufficient water to give a soft dough.
3. Roll out the pastry on a lightly floured work surface and use to line the prepared tin. Chill while making the filling.
4. To make the filling, whisk the egg yolks and sugar together in a bowl until thick enough to leave a trail on the surface when the whisk is lifted. Whisk in the cheese, nuts, cream, cocoa powder and rum until blended.
5. Whisk the egg whites until stiff, then fold into the cheese mixture. Pour into the pastry case and fold the edges of the pastry over the filling.
6. Bake in the oven at 170°C (325°F) mark 3 for 1½ hours until risen and just firm to the touch. Carefully remove from the tin and dust the top with icing sugar. Serve while still hot.
SERVES *10-12*

Redcurrant Cheesecake

REDCURRANT CHEESECAKE

65 g (2½ oz) butter, melted
150 g (5 oz) wheatmeal biscuits, finely crushed
175 g (6 oz) redcurrants
15 ml (1 level tbsp) gelatine
125 g (4 oz) cottage cheese
1 egg, separated
40 g (1½ oz) caster sugar
150 ml (5 fl oz) natural yogurt
150 ml (5 fl oz) double cream
15 ml (1 level tbsp) redcurrant jelly
redcurrants, to decorate

1. Mix together the butter and biscuit crumbs. Press the mixture into a 20 cm (8 inch) round loose-bottomed cake tin to line the base and sides.

2. Put the redcurrants in a medium saucepan with 45 ml (3 tbsp) water and simmer gently for 5-6 minutes, until soft. Allow to cool.

3. Sprinkle the gelatine in 45ml (3 tbsp) water in a small bowl and leave to soak. Place the bowl over a saucepan of simmering water and stir until dissolved. Leave until lukewarm.

4. Put the cottage cheese, egg yolk, sugar and yogurt in a food processor or blender and work together until smooth. Whip the cream until it just holds its shape. Fold the cooked redcurrants, redcurrant jelly, gelatine and most of the cream into the cheese mixture. Whisk the egg white until stiff and fold into the mixture.

5. Pour the mixture on to the biscuit base and chill in the refrigerator until set.

6. Carefully remove the cheesecake from the tin and decorate with the remaining cream and redcurrants to serve.

SERVES 4-6

MILK, CUSTARD AND CREAM PUDDINGS

Milk forms the basis of many puddings; on its own as in easy-to digest yogurt for example, or mixed with eggs or cream in a range of ever popular desserts.

MILK

Milk is a nutritious food and a major source of protein and calcium. There are five different varieties of pasteurised milk available: Channel Islands milk which is the richest and creamiest; whole milk with a cream layer; homogenised milk in which the cream is evenly distributed throughout; semi-skimmed milk which contains half the fat of whole milk, and skimmed milk which contains virtually no fat. Sterilised and UHT or long-life milk are also available.

Semi-skimmed milk is becoming more popular. It can be used in milk puddings.

YOGURT

Yogurt is a highly nutritious fermented milk product which is available plain and flavoured in a variety of forms, including low fat yogurt, creamy yogurt, Greek-style yogurt and set yogurt. It can be served as a dessert, or used in place of cream as a topping for puddings. It is also used in savoury dishes. When cooking with yogurt, do not heat it too vigorously or it will curdle.

CREAM

Cream is classified according to its fat content; it is this which determines its uses. To whip, cream must have a minimum fat content of 35 per cent.

Half cream is the thinnest cream and is best used as a pouring cream. Single cream is the most popular pouring cream and has a fat content of 18 per cent. Soured cream has the same fat content as single cream; its flavour is acquired from an added souring culture.

Whipping cream has a fat content of at least 35 per cent and will whip to double its volume. Double cream has a fat content of 48 per cent. It will whip to slightly less volume than whipping cream, but adding 15 ml (1 tbsp) milk to every 150 ml (5 fl oz) will achieve greater volume.

Crème fraîche is fresh cream that has fermented to the point where it is slightly thickened and has a delicious sharp taste.

A range of long-life cream products is available, including UHT cream, extended life cream, sterilized cream and aerosol cream. Lower-fat cream substitute are also available.

YOGURT

Homemade yogurt is easy to make using 'live' yogurt. Use pasteurised, semi-skimmed, sterilised or UHT milk. Yogurt can be made in a vacuum flask or in an electric yogurt maker.

600 ml (1 pint) milk
15 ml (1 tbsp) natural yogurt (not pasteurised)
15 ml (1 level tbsp) skimmed milk powder (optional)

1. Sterilise a vacuum flask and a small saucepan with boiling water. Warm the vacuum flask.
2. Reserve 30 ml (2 tbsp) of the milk and heat the rest to 45°C (113°F).
3. Blend the reserved milk with the yogurt, and skimmed milk powder if using, to a smooth paste. Gradually stir into the warm milk.
4. Pour into the warmed vacuum flask. Replace the lid and leave for about 8 hours, undisturbed. Transfer to a bowl and chill in the refrigerator.
MAKES ABOUT 600 ML (1 PINT)

JUNKET

600 ml (1 pint) pasteurised milk (not UHT or long-life)
15 ml (1 level tbsp) caster sugar
10 ml (2 tsp) rennet essence
freshly grated nutmeg, to serve

1. Gently heat the milk in a saucepan until just warm to the finger. Remove from the heat and stir in the sugar until dissolved. Add the rennet, stirring gently.
2. Pour into a shallow dish and leave in a warm place, undisturbed, for 1-1½ hours until set.
3. Chill in the refrigerator and sprinkle the top with nutmeg to serve.
SERVES 4

BLANCMANGE

60 ml (4 level tbsp) cornflour
600 ml (1 pint) milk
strip of lemon rind
45 ml (3 level tbsp) sugar

1. Blend the cornflour to a smooth paste with 30 ml (2 tbsp) of the milk.
2. Put the remaining milk in a saucepan with the lemon rind, bring to the boil, then strain it on to the blended mixture, stirring well.
3. Return the mixture to the pan and bring to the boil, stirring until the mixture thickens; cook for a further 3 minutes. Add sugar to taste.
4. Pour into a 600 ml (1 pint) dampened jelly mould and leave for several hours until set. Turn out to serve.
SERVES 4

VARIATIONS
Omit the lemon rind and add 50 g (2 oz) melted chocolate or 15-30 ml (1-2 tbsp) coffee essence to the cooked mixture.

RICE PUDDING

50 g (2 oz) short grain white rice
30 ml (2 level tbsp) sugar
600 ml (1 pint) milk
knob of butter or margarine
freshly grated nutmeg

1. Grease a 900 ml (1½ pint) ovenproof dish.
2. Add the rice, sugar and milk and stir; dot with shavings of butter and sprinkle nutmeg on top.
3. Bake in the oven at 150°C (300°F) mark 2 for about 2 hours, stirring after about 30 minutes.
SERVES 4

VARIATION
CREAMED RICE PUDDING
Put the rice, milk and sugar into a double boiler or heavy-based saucepan and cook over a very low heat until creamy, removing the lid halfway through cooking. Cool, then fold in 150 ml (5 fl oz) whipped cream.

SEMOLINA PUDDING

600 ml (1 pint) milk
knob of butter or margarine
60 ml (4 level tbsp) semolina
50 g (2 oz) sugar

1. Heat the milk and butter and sprinkle on the semolina. Bring to the boil, then cook for a further 2-3 minutes, stirring all the time.
2. Remove from the heat and stir in the sugar. Pour the pudding into a greased ovenproof dish.
3. Bake in the oven at 200°C (400°F) mark 6 for about 30 minutes, until lightly browned.
SERVES 4

VARIATION
Add the grated rind of 1 orange or lemon to the milk.

BAKED CUSTARD

600 ml (1 pint) milk
3 eggs
30 ml (2 level tbsp) caster sugar
freshly grated nutmeg

1. Warm the milk in a saucepan but do not boil. Whisk the eggs and sugar lightly in a bowl, then pour on the hot milk, stirring.
2. Strain the mixture into a greased ovenproof dish. Sprinkle the nutmeg on top and bake in the oven at 170°C (325°F) mark 3 for about 45 minutes, until set and firm to the touch. Serve hot or cold.
SERVES 4

CRÈME CARAMEL

125 g (4 oz) sugar plus 15 ml (1 level tbsp)
4 eggs
600 ml (1 pint) milk
1.25 ml (¼ tsp) vanilla flavouring
pouring cream, to serve

1. Place the 125 g (4 oz) sugar in a small
saucepan and carefully pour in 150 ml (¼ pint)
water. Heat gently until all the sugar has
dissolved, stirring occasionally.
2. Bring the syrup to a fast boil and cook rapidly
until the caramel is a golden brown. Remove
from the heat and leave for a few seconds to
darken. Pour into a 15 cm (6 inch) soufflé dish
and cool.
3. Whisk the eggs and remaining sugar in a
bowl. Warm the milk and pour on to the egg
mixture. Whisk in the vanilla flavouring, then
strain the custard on to the cool caramel.
4. Stand the dish in a roasting tin containing
enough hot water to come halfway up the sides
of the dish. Bake in the oven at 170°C (325°F)
mark 3 for about 1 hour. The custard should be
just set and firm to the touch, but not solid.
5. When cold, cover the dish and leave in the
refrigerator for several hours, preferably
overnight. Take out of the refrigerator
30 minutes before serving.
6. Using the fingertips, gently loosen and ease
the edges of custard away from the dish. Take a
rimmed serving dish and invert over the Crème
Caramel dish. Hold the two dishes firmly
together and turn over quickly until the cooking
dish is uppermost.
7. Still holding the dishes together, give a few
sharp sideways shakes until the suction is heard
to release. Leave the cooking dish upturned for
a few minutes until all the caramel has drained

Crème Caramel

out. Stand the dish in a pan of hot water to
soften the remaining caramel, then pour over
the Crème Caramel to serve.
SERVES 4

VARIATION
Divide the mixture between 6 ramekin dishes.
Cook for 40 minutes only.

BREAD AND BUTTER PUDDING

6 thin slices of bread, crusts removed
50 g (2 oz) butter or margarine
50 g (2 oz) currants or sultanas, or mixture of both
40 g (1½ oz) caster sugar
2 eggs
600 ml (1 pint) milk

1. Thickly spread the bread slices with butter.
Cut into fingers or small squares. Put half into a
greased 1.1 litre (2 pint) ovenproof dish.

Sprinkle with all the fruit and half the sugar.
2. Top with the remaining bread, buttered side
uppermost. Sprinkle with the rest of the sugar.
3. Beat the eggs and milk well together. Strain
into the dish over the bread.
4. Leave to stand for 30 minutes, so that the
bread absorbs some of the liquid. Bake in the
oven at 170°C (325°F) mark 3 for 45 minutes-
1 hour, until set and the top is crisp.
SERVES 4

QUEEN OF PUDDINGS

4 eggs
600 ml (1 pint) milk
100 g (4 oz) fresh breadcrumbs
45-60 ml (3-4 level tbsp) raspberry jam
75 g (3 oz) caster sugar

1. Separate three eggs and beat together the three egg yolks and one whole egg. Add to the milk and mix well. Stir in the breadcrumbs.

2. Spread the jam on the bottom of a pie dish. Pour over the milk mixture and leave for 30 minutes.
3. Bake in the oven at 150°C (300°F) mark 2 for 1 hour, until set.
4. Whisk the egg whites until stiff, then fold in the sugar. Pile on top of the custard and return to the oven for a further 15-20 minutes until the meringue is set.
SERVES 4

COFFEE BAVAROIS

125 g (4 oz) well roasted coffee beans
900 ml (1½ pints) milk
6 egg yolks
75 g (3 oz) caster sugar
20 ml (4 level tsp) gelatine
300 ml (10 fl oz) double cream
30 ml (2 tbsp) coffee flavoured liqueur (optional)
grated chocolate, to decorate

1. Put the coffee beans in a saucepan and place over a low heat; warm very gently for 2-3 minutes, shaking the pan frequently. Remove from the heat, pour the milk into the pan, return to the heat and bring to the boil.
2. Remove from the heat, cover and leave to infuse for 30 minutes.
3. Place the egg yolks and caster sugar in a deep mixing bowl and beat until the mixture is thick and light in colour. Strain the coffee infusion on to the egg yolks, stirring well.
4. Return the custard mixture to the rinsed-out saucepan and cook very gently, stirring, until the custard thickens very slightly. Do not boil. Strain into a large bowl and cool.
5. In a small bowl, sprinkle the gelatine over 60 ml (4 tbsp) water. Place over a pan of hot water and stir until dissolved.

6. Stir the gelatine into the cooled custard. Stand the custard in a roasting tin half-filled with water and surround with ice cubes. Stir the custard frequently while it cools to setting point.
7. Meanwhile, lightly whip half the cream and grease a 1.4 litre (2 pint) soufflé dish or mould.
8. When the custard is well chilled and beginning to thicken, fold in the whipped cream. Pour the setting custard into the dish and refrigerate until completely set.
9. With a dampened finger, gently ease the edges of the bavarois away from the dish. Moisten a flat plate and place over the dish. Invert the plate and shake gently. Ease off the dish and slide the bavarois on to the plate.
10. Whisk the remaining cream until it holds its shape, then gradually whisk in the liqueur, if using. Spoon into a piping bag fitted with a 1 cm (½ inch) star nozzle. Pipe the coffee cream around the top edge in a shell pattern. Decorate with grated chocolate.
SERVES 6

VARIATION
CHOCOLATE BAVAROIS
Omit the coffee beans and liqueur. Dissolve 75 g (3 oz) plain chocolate in a little milk, whisk in the remaining milk and complete as above.

SYLLABUB

150 ml (¼ pint) dry white wine
finely grated rind and juice of 1 lemon
75 g (3 oz) caster sugar
300 ml (10 fl oz) double cream

1. Put the wine, lemon rind and juice, and sugar in a bowl. Leave to infuse for at least 3 hours.
2. Add the cream and whisk until the mixture just holds its shape. Do not overwhip or the mixture may curdle.
3. Spoon into six glass dishes and chill in the refrigerator for several hours before serving.
SERVES 6

OLD ENGLISH TRIFLE

600 ml (1 pint) milk
½ vanilla pod
2 eggs, plus 2 egg yolks
30 ml (2 level tbsp) caster sugar plus extra for
    sprinkling
1 Victoria Sandwich Cake (see page 406) or 8 trifle
    sponges
175 g (6 oz) raspberry or strawberry jam
100 g (4 oz) macaroons, lightly crushed
100 ml (4 fl oz) medium sherry
300 ml (10 fl oz) double cream
40 g (1½ oz) flaked almonds, toasted and 50 g (2 oz)
    glacé cherries, to decorate

1. Bring the milk to the boil with the vanilla pod. Remove from the heat, cover and leave to infuse for 20 minutes.
2. Beat together the eggs, egg yolks and sugar and strain on to the milk. Cook gently, without boiling, stirring, until the custard thickens slightly. Pour into a bowl; lightly sprinkle the surface with sugar and cool.
3. Spread the sponge cake with jam, cut up and place in a 2 litre (3½ pint) shallow serving dish with the macaroons. Spoon over the sherry and leave for 2 hours. Pour over the cold custard.
4. Lightly whip the cream. Spread half the cream over the custard. Pipe remaining cream on top and decorate with almonds and cherries.
SERVES 6

CHARLOTTE RUSSE

135 g (4¾ oz) packet lemon jelly
45 ml (3 tbsp) lemon juice
2 glacé cherries, quartered
piece of angelica, cut into triangles
300 ml (½ pint) milk
vanilla pod
15 ml (1 level tbsp) gelatine
3 egg yolks
45 ml (3 level tbsp) caster sugar
18 sponge (boudoir) fingers
300 ml (10 fl oz) whipping cream

1. Dissolve the jelly in a measuring jug making up to 500 ml (1 pint) with the lemon juice and water; cool. Spoon a thin covering of jelly into the base of a 1.1 litre (2 pint) charlotte mould; refrigerate until set.
2. When set, arrange the cherries and angelica on top. Carefully spoon over the liquid jelly to a depth of about 2.5 cm (1 inch). Refrigerate to set, along with the remaining jelly in the jug.
3. Put the milk in a saucepan with the vanilla pod. Bring slowly to the boil, remove from the heat, cover and leave to infuse for 20 minutes.
4. In a small bowl, sprinkle the gelatine in 45 ml (3 tbsp) water and leave to soak for 10 minutes.
5. Beat together the egg yolks and sugar, then stir in the strained milk. Return to the pan and cook gently, stirring, until the custard thickens sufficiently to just coat the back of a spoon. Do not boil. Pour into a large bowl and stir in the gelatine. Cool.

Line inside of mould with sponge fingers trimmed to the correct length.

6. Trim a small amount off each sponge finger so that they just fit the charlotte mould, without rising above the rim; reserve trimmings. Stand the fingers closely together, rounded side down, sugar side out around the edge of the mould.
7. Whip the cream until it just holds its shape and stir into the custard. Place the bowl in a roasting tin containing iced water to come halfway up its sides. Stir occasionally until on the point of setting. Pour into the mould.
8. Trim sponge fingers level with the custard. Lay the trimmings on top of the custard. Cover tightly and refrigerate to set for at least 3 hours.
9. Using fingertips, ease the sponge fingers away from the edge, then tilt it slightly to allow an airlock to form between the two. Dip the base of the mould in hot water for about 5 seconds only, then invert on to a dampened plate to unmould.
10. Take the remaining set jelly out of the refrigerator and loosen by dipping the jug in hot water. Turn out on to a board lined with damp greaseproof paper and chop into small pieces. Spoon around the Charlotte Russe.
SERVES 6

CRÈME BRÛLÉE

600 ml (1 pint) double cream
1 vanilla pod
4 egg yolks
125 g (4 oz) caster sugar

1. Pour the cream into the top of a double boiler or into a mixing bowl placed over a pan of simmering water. Add the vanilla pod and warm gently until almost boiling, then remove from the heat. Remove the vanilla pod.
2. Beat together the egg yolks and 50 g (2 oz) of the caster sugar until light in colour. Gradually pour on the cream, stirring until evenly mixed.
3. Stand 6 individual ramekin dishes in a roasting tin containing enough hot water to come halfway up the sides of the dishes. Pour the custard mixture slowly into the ramekins, dividing it equally between them.
4. Bake in the oven at 150°C (300°F) mark 2 for about 1 hour until set. Do not allow the skin to colour. Remove from the tin and leave to cool, then refrigerate overnight.
5. Sprinkle the remaining sugar evenly over the top of each and put under a preheated hot grill for 2-3 minutes until the sugar turns to a

Crème Brûlée

caramel. Leave to cool, then chill before serving.
SERVES 6

NOTE: Crème Brûlée is delicious served with fruit, such as strawberries, peaches and cherries.

COEURS À LA CRÈME

225 g (8 oz) cottage cheese
25 g (1 oz) caster sugar
300 ml (10 fl oz) double cream
5 ml (1 tsp) lemon juice
2 egg whites
single cream and fresh raspberries or strawberries,
* to serve*

1. Press the cottage cheese through a nylon sieve into a bowl. Add the sugar and mix well.
2. Whip the cream until stiff, then add the lemon juice. Stir into the cheese mixture.
3. Line four or six small heart-shaped moulds with muslin. Whisk the egg whites until stiff and fold into the cheese mixture. Spoon into the moulds and drain overnight in the refrigerator. Turn out and serve with cream and fruit.
SERVES 4-6

BOODLE'S ORANGE FOOL

4-6 trifle sponge cakes, cut into 1 cm (½ inch) thick
* slices*
grated rind and juice of 2 oranges
grated rind and juice of 1 lemon
25-50 g (1-2 oz) sugar
300 ml (10 fl oz) double cream
orange slices or segments, to decorate

1. Use the sponge cake slices to line the bottom and halfway up the sides of a deep dish or bowl.

2. Mix the orange and lemon rinds and juice with the sugar and stir until the sugar has completely dissolved.
3. In another bowl, whip the cream until it just starts to thicken, then slowly add the sweetened fruit juice, continuing to whip until the cream is light and thickened and the juice all absorbed.
4. Pour the mixture over the sponge cakes and refrigerate for at least 2 hours. Decorate with orange slices, or segments.
SERVES 6

CUSTARD CREAM

300 ml (½ pint) Egg Custard Sauce (see page 208)
5-10 ml (1-2 tsp) vanilla flavouring
10 ml (2 level tsp) gelatine
300 ml (10 fl oz) double cream
sugar to taste

1. Make up the custard, add the vanilla flavouring and stir occasionally as it cools. To prevent a skin forming, press a piece of dampened greaseproof paper on to the surface of the custard.
2. In a small bowl, sprinkle the gelatine over 30 ml (2 tbsp) water and leave to soak. Place the

bowl over a pan of simmering water and stir until dissolved. Cool slightly. Pour into the custard in a steady, thin stream, stirring.
3. Whip the cream until stiff, then fold into the custard, check the sweetness and when the mixture is just on the point of setting, pour into a dampened 900 ml (1½ pint) jelly mould and leave to set. Unmould just before serving.
SERVES 4

VARIATION
GINGER CREAM
Add 50 g (2 oz) preserved ginger, chopped.

FLOATING ISLANDS

5 egg yolks, beaten
450 ml (¾ pint) milk
50 g (2 oz) caster sugar plus 75 ml (5 tbsp)
2.5 ml (½ tsp) vanilla flavouring
1 egg white

1. To make the custard, put the egg yolks, milk and 50 g (2 oz) sugar in the top of a double boiler, or in a heavy-based saucepan. Cook gently for about 15 minutes, stirring, until the mixture thickens and coats the back of the spoon. Stir in the vanilla flavouring.
2. Divide the custard between individual dishes. Cover and refrigerate for 1 hour.
3. Meanwhile, whisk the egg white until stiff. Add 30 ml (2 tbsp) sugar and whisk again until

the sugar is dissolved.
4. Pour water into a large frying pan to a depth of 2 cm (¾ inch). Bring to a gentle simmer. Shape the meringue into ovals, using 2 table-spoons as moulds. Carefully slide into the water and poach gently for about 3 minutes until set, turning once.
5. Remove the meringues with a slotted spoon, drain for a minute on absorbent kitchen paper and spoon on to the custard in the dishes.
6. Put the remaining sugar into a heavy-based saucepan and cook, stirring, for about 3 minutes, until it forms a golden syrup.
7. Remove from the heat and leave for 2 minutes to cool slightly, then drizzle a little of the warm syrup over the top of each meringue.
SERVES 4

YOGURT AND BANANA DESSERT

300 ml (10 fl oz) natural yogurt
150 ml (5 fl oz) double cream
3 ripe bananas, mashed
grated rind and juice of 1 lemon
15-30 ml (1-2 level tbsp) caster sugar
1 egg white
grated lemon rind and fresh mint leaves, to decorate

1. In a large bowl, whisk the yogurt and cream together until lightly stiff, then stir in the bananas, lemon rind and juice, and sugar to taste.
2. In a medium bowl, whisk the egg white until stiff, then fold gently into the mixture. Chill until ready to serve.
3. Pour into 4 glass dishes and serve, decorated with lemon rind and fresh mint leaves.
SERVES 4

VARIATION
Replace the bananas with 450 g (1 lb) straw-berries or raspberries, 2 medium mangoes or 4 ripe, skinned nectarines or peaches.

HOT SWEET SOUFFLÉS

Hot soufflés are usually based either on a sweet white sauce called a panada, to which egg yolks and flavourings are added, or on a crème pâtissière, a sauce in which the egg yolks are already incorporated. For hints on making hot soufflés, see page 269.

HOT VANILLA SOUFFLÉ

50 g (2 oz) caster sugar
4 eggs, size 2
60 ml (4 level tbsp) plain flour
300 ml (½ pint) milk
2.5 ml (½ tsp) vanilla flavouring
icing sugar for dusting (optional)

1. Grease a 1.7 litre (3 pint) soufflé dish.
2. In a saucepan, cream the sugar with one whole egg and one yolk until pale cream in colour. Stir in the flour, then pour on the milk and mix until smooth. Bring to the boil, stirring, and simmer for 2 minutes.
3. Cool slightly, then beat in the remaining yolks and vanilla flavouring. Whisk the egg whites until stiff and gently fold into the sauce.
4. Pour into the soufflé dish and bake in the oven at 180°C (350°F) mark 4 for about 45 minutes, until well risen, firm to the touch and pale golden. Dust with icing sugar if desired.
SERVES 4

HOT CHOCOLATE SOUFFLÉ

75 g (3 oz) plain chocolate or chocolate dots
150 ml (¼ pint) milk
50 g (2 oz) caster sugar
60 ml (4 level tbsp) flour
knob of butter or margarine
3 egg yolks
4 egg whites
icing sugar for dusting

1. Grease a 1.1 litre (2 pint) soufflé dish.
2. Put the chocolate in a bowl with 30 ml (2 tbsp) water and melt over a pan of simmering water.
3. Heat the milk, reserving a little, with the sugar, then pour on to the melted chocolate.
4. Blend the flour to a smooth paste with the remaining milk, and stir in the chocolate mixture. Return to the pan, bring to the boil, stirring, then cook for 2 minutes, stirring occasionally. Add the butter, in small pieces, then leave until lukewarm.
5. Stir in the egg yolks. Whisk the egg whites until stiff and fold into the mixture.
6. Pour into the soufflé dish and bake in the oven at 200°C (400°F) mark 6 for about 35 minutes, until well risen and firm to the touch. Dust with icing sugar before serving.
SERVES 4

HOT APRICOT SOUFFLÉ

450 g (1 lb) fresh apricots, halved and stoned
40 g (1½ oz) butter or margarine
60 ml (4 level tbsp) plain flour
150 ml (¼ pint) milk
50 g (2 oz) caster sugar
4 eggs, size 2, separated
15 ml (1 tbsp) apricot brandy
icing sugar for dusting

1. Grease a 2 litre (3½ pint) soufflé dish. Put the apricots in a saucepan with 30 ml (2 tbsp) water and cook until soft. Purée the fruit in a blender or food processor; seive to remove the skins.
2. Melt the butter in a saucepan, stir in the flour and cook for 1 minute, stirring. Remove from heat and gradually stir in the milk and apricot purée. Bring to the boil, and cook, stirring, until the sauce thickens. Remove from heat.
3. Stir in the sugar, egg yolks and brandy. Whisk the egg whites until stiff, then fold into the mixture.
4. Pour into the soufflé dish and bake in the oven at 180°C (350°F) mark 4 for 45 minutes, until well risen. Dust with icing sugar to serve.
SERVES 4

COLD SOUFFLÉS, JELLIES AND MOUSSES

Cold soufflés are not true soufflés but mousses which are set in a dish with a collar as an imitation of a baked soufflé. Mousses are an egg mixture, flavoured with fruit, liqueur or chocolate. They are usually lightened with egg white and may be set with gelatine. They are usually served cold. Homemade jellies containing fresh fruit and fruit juice are very simple to prepare. Their flavour is much better than that of jellies made with commercial jelly tablets and crystals which contain mostly sugar, flavouring and colouring.

USING GELATINE

Gelatine is not difficult to use, providing a few simple rules are followed.

- Before adding it to a mixture it must be softened, by soaking in cold water, this will make it swell; sprinkle the gelatine over the water, never the other way round or you will get lumpy gelatine. Once soaked it can be added to a hot mixture and stirred until dissolved.

- Before soaked gelatine can be added to a cold mixture, it must be dissolved. Do this by standing the bowl over a saucepan of simmering water. Heat gently until it dissolves. Alternatively, dissolve in a microwave oven. Properly dissolved gelatine will be transparent. To test this, dip a teaspoon in, turn it over and any undissolved granules will show on the back of the spoon. Never allow gelatine to boil.

- Always add dissolved gelatine to a mixture which is lukewarm or at room temperature. If added to a cold mixture, it will set on contact, in fine threads. The jelly, mousse or soufflé will not set properly or will set too quickly before you have a chance to fold in the egg whites or cream.

- Allow at least 4 hours for it to set, longer if it contains fruit. For a firm set, allow 12 hours.

POWDERED GELATINE is most commonly used. It is sold loose in cartons or in envelopes each containing exactly 11 g (0.4 oz), which will set 600 ml (1 pint) liquid.

LEAF GELATINE is a more expensive alternative. Four sheets of leaf gelatine is equivalent to 15 ml (1 level tbsp) powdered gelatine and will set 600 ml (1 pint) liquid. Snip into small pieces and soak in about 45 ml (3 tbsp) liquid per four sheets for about 10 minutes before dissolving in the same way as powdered gelatine.

AGAR-AGAR can also be used as a setting agent. It is a tasteless white powder derived from seaweed.

Agar-agar is a vegetarian alternative for gelatine; it is available from health food shops. Follow the manufacturer's instructions if using.

MAKING A JELLY

When making fruit jellies, warm the liquid, sweeten and flavour it, then quickly stir in the dissolved gelatine. The closer these are to being the same temperature, the more easily they can be evenly blended. To hasten the set, heat half of the liquid, add the gelatine, then combine with the remaining cold liquid.

For the best flavour, transfer jellied desserts to room temperature 1 hour before serving.

TO SET FRUIT IN JELLY

Use fresh fruits such as black grapes, bananas, raspberries or orange segments. Do not use fresh pineapple, papaya or kiwi fruit as they contain an enzyme which breaks down gelatine and destroys its setting powers. Boil fresh pineapple juice for 2-3 minutes before using.

Pour about 2.5 cm (1 inch) clear jelly into a mould, and arrange a little of the prepared fruit in this. Refrigerate until the jelly is set. Add more jelly and fruit and allow to set; continue until the mould is filled.

TO LINE OR MASK A MOULD WITH JELLY

First prepare any decorations, eg slice glacé cherries and pistachio nuts, cut angelica. Fill a large basin with chips of ice and rest the dampened mould in it. Pour 30-45 ml (2-3 tbsp) cold but liquid jelly into the mould and rotate this slowly until the inside is evenly coated. Continue pouring in and setting cold liquid jelly until the whole surface is lined with a layer about 3mm (⅛ inch) thick. Using 2 fine skewers, dip the decoration pieces into liquid jelly and position in the mould, allowing each piece to set firmly. Pour a thin coating over the decorations and allow to set before adding the filling.

TO UNMOULD A JELLY OR MOUSSE

Draw the tip of a knife or your finger around the rim of the mould to loosen the edge of the jelly. Immerse the mould in hot water for 2-3 seconds and place a dampened serving plate on top of the mould. Hold in position with both hands, then quickly invert the mould and plate together giving several sharp shakes.

COLD SOUFFLÉS

- The preparation of the dish is all important. Do not tie the paper collar so tightly as to flute the paper and so spoil the final appearance of the soufflé. It should stand upright and be even all round (see right).
- Ideally, beat the egg whites by hand in a copper bowl, using a balloon or rotary whisk. Alternatively use an electric whisk.
- Make sure the bowl and whisk are spotlessly clean, if there is any grease the egg whites will not whisk to maximum volume.
- The mixture should stand in soft peaks, and the tips of the peaks should flop over gently when held upon the whisk. Overbeaten egg whites look dry and powdery and will be difficult to fold in evenly.

- Always add the egg whites with a large metal spoon, using a light cutting and folding action.
- Similarly, cream should be whipped until it just holds its shape. If it is overbeaten it will be impossible to achieve a smooth mixture. Make sure it is well chilled.

TO PREPARE A COLD SOUFFLÉ DISH

- Cut a strip of double greaseproof paper long enough to go right around the soufflé dish with the ends overlapping slightly, and deep enough to reach from the bottom of the dish to about 7 cm (2¾ inches) above the top.
- Tie the paper around the outside of the dish with string, or stick it with adhesive tape, so that it fits closely to the rim of the dish and prevents any mixture escaping.
- Place the prepared soufflé dish on a baking tray. This makes it easier to move the filled dish from the work surface to the refrigerator for chilling.
- To remove the paper from the cold soufflé once the mixture has set, rinse a round-bladed knife in hot water and slip it, upright between the paper and the soufflé, peeling away the paper and the knife.

LEMON SOUFFLÉ

grated rind of 3 lemons
90 ml (6 tbsp) lemon juice
100 g (4 oz) caster sugar
4 eggs, separated
15 ml (1 level tbsp) gelatine
300 ml (10 fl oz) double cream
angelica leaves and mimosa balls, to decorate

1. Prepare a 900 ml (1½ pint) soufflé dish with a paper collar.
2. In a deep bowl, whisk the lemon rind, juice, sugar and egg yolks together over a pan of hot water until thick.
3. Sprinkle the gelatine in 45 ml (3 tbsp) water in a small bowl and leave to soak. Place over a pan of simmering water and stir until dissolved. Stir into the soufflé mixture and chill.
4. Lightly whip the cream. Whisk the egg whites until stiff. Fold half the cream into the soufflé, then the egg whites, until evenly blended.
5. Pour into the soufflé dish and level the

surface. Chill in the refrigerator for at least 4 hours, until set.
6. Remove the paper from the edge of the soufflé. Decorate the soufflé with the remaining cream, angelica leaves and mimosa balls.
SERVES 4

VARIATIONS
STRAWBERRY SOUFFLÉ
Substitute the lemon rind and juice with 450 g (12 oz) strawberries, puréed. Fold into the thickened sugar and egg yolk mixture before folding in the gelatine. Decorate the top of the soufflé with fresh strawberry slices and rosettes of piped cream.

RASPBERRY SOUFFLÉ
Substitute the lemon rind and juice with 450 g (12 oz) raspberries, puréed. Fold into the thickened sugar and egg yolk mixture before folding in the gelatine. Decorate the top of the soufflé with fresh raspberries.

Chocolate Orange Soufflé

CHOCOLATE ORANGE SOUFFLÉ

450 ml (¾ pint) milk
150 g (5 oz) plain chocolate
3 eggs, separated, plus 1 egg white
75 g (3 oz) sugar
15 ml (1 level tbsp) gelatine
grated rind and juice of 1 orange
300 ml (10 fl oz) whipping cream
15 ml (1 tbsp) crème de cacao or other chocolate-
*   flavoured liqueur*
Chocolate Caraque (see page 508) or grated chocolate,
*   to decorate*

1. Prepare a 900 ml (1½ pint) soufflé dish with a paper collar.
2. Put the milk in a saucepan and break the chocolate into it. Heat gently until the chocolate melts, then cook over a high heat until almost boiling.
3. Whisk the egg yolks and sugar together until pale and thick. Gradually pour on the chocolate milk, stirring. Return to the saucepan and cook, stirring continuously, until it coats the back of a wooden spoon; this takes about 20 minutes. Do not boil.
4. Sprinkle the gelatine in 45 ml (3 tbsp) water in a small bowl and leave to soak. Place the bowl over a saucepan of simmering water and stir until dissolved. Stir into the custard with the orange rind and juice. Cool.
5. Whip the cream until it just holds its shape, then fold most of the cream into the cold mixture. Whisk the egg whites until stiff and fold into the mixture.
6. Pour the mixture into the prepared dish and leave to set. Remove the paper collar.
7. Stir the liqueur into the remaining cream and pipe on top of the soufflé. Decorate with caraque or grated chocolate.
SERVES 6-8

BLACKCURRANT MOUSSE

225 g (8 oz) fresh blackcurrants, stringed and washed
caster sugar to taste
4 egg yolks
150 ml (5 fl oz) double cream
2 egg whites

1. Cook the blackcurrants with 30 ml (2 tbsp) water, until soft enough to sieve or purée in a blender or food processor. (This should give 150 ml (¼ pint) purée.)
2. Put the purée, sugar and egg yolks into a large bowl over a saucepan of hot water and whisk until thick and creamy – the mixture should be stiff enough to retain the impression of the whisk for a few seconds.
3. Remove from the heat and whisk until cool. Lightly whip the cream, then fold into mixture.
4. Whisk the egg whites until stiff and gently fold into the blackcurrant mixture.
5. Pour the mixture into a shallow dish or individual soufflé dishes. Chill in the refrigerator for about 2 hours, until set. Serve the same day.
SERVES 4-6

MANGO MOUSSE

2 ripe mangoes, about 350 g (12 oz) each
finely grated rind and juice of 1 orange
3 whole eggs, plus 1 egg yolk
40 g (1½ oz) caster sugar
15 ml (1 level tbsp) gelatine
300 ml (10 fl oz) double cream

1. Stand the mangoes on a board on their long rounded edges. Cut a thick slice down either side of the mango keeping the knife as close to the stone as possible.
2. Scrape the mango flesh out of the skin. Purée in a blender or food processor. Rub through a nylon sieve. Add the orange rind.
3. Place the whole eggs and egg yolk in a large bowl, add the caster sugar and whisk until the mixture is very pale, thick and creamy.
4. Whisk the mango purée, a little at a time, into the mixture, whisking well after each addition.
5. Sprinkle the gelatine over the orange juice in a small bowl and leave to soak. Place the bowl over a pan of simmering water and stir until dissolved.
6. Meanwhile, pour half the cream into a bowl and lightly whip, then, using a metal spoon, lightly fold the cream into the mango mixture. Pour the gelatine in a thin stream into the mango mixture, stirring gently.
7. Pour the mixture into a 2 litre (3½ pint) shallow serving dish. Chill in the refrigerator for about 1 hour until beginning to set, then cover and chill for several hours, or overnight, until set.
8. Lightly whisk the remaining cream until it just holds its shape. Spoon the cream into a piping bag fitted with a star nozzle and pipe small rosettes around the edge of the mousse.
SERVES 6

VARIATION
RHUBARB MOUSSE
In place of mangoes, use 450 g (1 lb) pink rhubarb; wipe, then cut into 2.5 cm (1 inch) pieces. Place the rhubarb in a saucepan with 45 ml (3 tbsp) of water. Cover the pan tightly and cook gently until the rhubarb is soft and pulpy. Purée in a blender or food processor until smooth. (Do not sieve.) Cool, and complete the mousse as from step 2, adding an extra 25 g (1 oz) caster sugar.

ZABAGLIONE

4 egg yolks
65 g (2½ oz) caster sugar
100 ml (4 fl oz) Marsala
sponge fingers, to serve

1. Put the egg yolks and sugar in a large heatproof bowl. Beat together, then add the Marsala and beat until evenly mixed.
2. Place the bowl over a saucepan of simmering water and heat gently, whisking the mixture until it is very thick and creamy and forms soft peaks.
3. Pour the Zabaglione into six glasses and serve immediately, with sponge fingers.
SERVES 6

Tiramisu

TIRAMISU

four 250 g (9 oz) cartons mascarpone cheese
40 g (1½ oz) caster sugar
3 eggs, separated
250 ml (8 fl oz) Kahlua or other coffee-flavoured
*   liqueur*
425 ml (14 fl oz) very strong cold black coffee
about 30 savoiardi (Italian sponge fingers)
cocoa powder, for sprinkling

1. Put the mascarpone cheese, sugar and egg yolks in a bowl and beat with an electric mixer until evenly blended and creamy.
2. Whisk the egg whites until standing in stiff peaks. Fold into the mascarpone mixture until evenly incorporated. Spoon a quarter of the mixture into the base of a glass serving bowl.
3. Mix the liqueur and coffee together in a shallow dish. One at a time, dip one third of the savoiardi in this mixture for 10-15 seconds, turning once so they become soaked through but do not lose their shape. After each one has been dipped, place it on top of the mascarpone in the bowl, making a single layer of savoiardi that covers the mascarpone completely.
4. Cover the savoiardi with one third of the remaining mascarpone, then dip another third of the savoiardi in the liqueur and coffee mixture and layer them in the bowl as before.
5. Repeat with another layer of mascarpone and savoiardi, then spread the remaining mascarpone over the top and swirl with a palette knife. Sift cocoa powder liberally all over the top. Cover the bowl and chill in the refrigerator for 24 hours. Serve chilled.
SERVES 8

CHOCOLATE MOUSSE

350 g (12 oz) plain chocolate
6 eggs, separated
30 ml (2 tbsp) rum or brandy
150 ml (5 fl oz) double cream
Chocolate Caraque (see page 424), to decorate

1. Break the chocolate into a bowl. Place the bowl over a pan of simmering water and heat until melted, stirring occasionally.
2. Remove from heat and beat in the egg yolks and rum. Whisk the egg whites until stiff and fold into the chocolate mixture.
3. Spoon into six ramekin dishes and chill in the refrigerator for 2-3 hours, until set. Whip the cream until stiff. Decorate the mousses with piped cream and Chocolate Caraque.
SERVES 6

STRAWBERRY AND ORANGE MOUSSE

700 g (1½ lb) fresh strawberries, hulled
finely grated rind and juice of 1 large orange
45 ml (3 level tbsp) icing sugar
3 egg yolks and 2 egg whites
125 g (4 oz) caster sugar
15 ml (1 level tbsp) gelatine
300 ml (10 fl oz) double cream
150 ml (5 fl oz) single cream

1. Thinly slice enough strawberries to form a ring around the side of a 2.3 litre (4 pint) shallow glass dish.
2. Purée half the remainder in a blender or food processor with the orange rind, 75 ml (5 tbsp) juice and the icing sugar. Pass through a nylon sieve to give a very smooth texture.

Reserve remaining strawberries for decoration.
3. Whisk the egg yolks and caster sugar until thick and light. Then gradually whisk in the strawberry purée.
4. Sprinkle the gelatine in 45 ml (3 tbsp) water in a small bowl and leave to soak. Place the bowl over a saucepan of simmering water and stir until dissolved. Leave to cool, then stir into the mousse mixture.
5. Lightly whip the creams together. Fold one third into the mousse and keep the rest covered in the refrigerator. Whisk the two egg whites until stiff and fold into the mixture. Pour into the strawberry-lined dish, and chill in the refrigerator for 2-3 hours, until set.
6. Decorate with piped cream and strawberries.
SERVES 6

Stawberry and Orange Mousse

LEMON AND YOGURT MOUSSE

50 ml (2 fl oz) milk
4 eggs, separated
125 g (4 oz) caster sugar
2 drops of vanilla flavouring
25 ml (5 level tsp) powdered gelatine
450 ml (¾ pint) natural yogurt
45 ml (3 tbsp) lemon juice
150 ml (5 fl oz) double cream

1. Put the milk in a small saucepan and bring almost to the boil. Beat the egg yolks and 25 g (1 oz) of the sugar together in a small bowl until pale in colour. Gradually add the milk, mixing well. Return to the pan and stir constantly over a low heat until the mixture begins to thicken and just coats the back of a spoon. Do not boil. Pour into a large bowl and add the vanilla flavouring.
2. Sprinkle the gelatine over 75 ml (5 tbsp) water in a small bowl and leave to soak for 2-3 minutes. Place the bowl over a pan of simmering water and stir until dissolved. Cool slightly, then add to the custard. Stir to mix.
3. Whisk in the yogurt and lemon juice, whisking the mixture until smooth. Leave until cool, beginning to thicken but not set.
4. Whisk the egg whites until stiff but not dry and fold in the remaining sugar. Lightly whip the cream and fold into the yogurt mixture with the egg whites. Pour into a large glass serving dish. Cover and chill for about 3 hours until set.
5. Remove from the refrigerator about 15 minutes before serving.
SERVES 8

CLARET JELLY

300 ml (½ pint) raspberry juice or water
300 ml (½ pint) claret
50 g (2 oz) sugar
finely grated rind and juice of ½ lemon
20 ml (4 level tsp) gelatine
red food colouring (optional)

1. Slowly bring all the ingredients except the food colouring to simmering point. Do not boil. Strain through muslin, add a few drops of colouring if preferred, and pour into a dampened mould.
2. Chill in the refrigerator for several hours until set. Turn out and serve.
SERVES 4

LEMON CHEESE JELLY

135 g (4¾ oz) packet lemon jelly
200 g (7 oz) natural quark (low fat soft cheese)
finely grated rind of 1 lemon
5 ml (1 tsp) lemon juice

1. Make up the jelly according to packet instructions; cool until beginning to set.
2. Purée the jelly with the cheese, grated rind and lemon juice in a blender or food processor. Pour into a shallow dish and chill until set.
SERVES 4

MILK JELLY

50 g (2 oz) caster sugar
3 thin strips of lemon rind
600 ml (1 pint) milk
20 ml (4 level tsp) gelatine
stewed fruit, to serve

1. Add the sugar and lemon rind to the milk and allow to infuse over a gentle heat for 10 minutes. Cool in the refrigerator.
2. Sprinkle the gelatine in 45 ml (3 tbsp) water in a small bowl and leave to soak. Place over a pan of simmering water and stir until dissolved. Leave until lukewarm, then add the cooled milk.
3. Pour into a 600 ml (1 pint) dampened mould and chill in the refrigerator until set. Unmould on to a plate and serve with stewed fruit.
SERVES 4

ICES AND ICED DESSERTS

**There is nothing to beat the rich flavour and creamy texture of home-made ice cream,
or the mouthwatering fruitiness of homemade sorbet.
The secret of successful smooth frozen desserts largely involves making sure that no large ice
crystals form during freezing. This means that it is necessary to periodically whisk the freezing
mixture by hand, if you do not own an ice cream machine, which will do the job for you.**

TO FREEZE ICE CREAM BY HAND

The following freezing times based on 900 ml
(1½ pint) ice cream are given as a guide. If
making a larger quantity of ice cream, the times
should be increased.

- Set the freezer to maximum or fast freeze
  about 1 hour beforehand.
- Make the ice cream as directed in the recipe.
- Pour the mixture into a shallow non-metal
  freezer container. Cover and freeze for about
  3 hours or until just frozen all over. It will
  have a mushy consistency.
- Spoon into a bowl and mash with a fork to
  break down the ice crystals. Work quickly so
  that the ice cream does not melt completely.
- Return the mixture to the container and
  freeze again for about 2 hours or until mushy.
- Mash the ice cream again as before. If any
  other ingredients are to be added, such as
  nuts or chocolate drops, fold in at this stage.
- Return to the freezer and freeze for about
  3 hours or until firm.
- Transfer to room temperature 20-30 minutes
  before serving to soften. Ice cream can be
  stored in the freezer for up to 3 months.

ICE CREAM MACHINES

An ice cream machine will freeze an ice cream
or sorbet mixture and churn it at the same time,
thus eliminating the physical effort. The results
will be smooth and even textured.

There are several types of ice cream
machine available; some use a salt solution and
others a disc which needs to be frozen before
use. Always follow manufacturer's instructions.

Generally speaking, the cooled mixture
should be poured into the machine when the
paddles are moving, otherwise it tends to freeze
on to the base and sides of the bowl, stopping
the paddles working. When making ice cream
this way, if the recipe calls for whipped cream, it
should be ignored. The cream can simply be
added from the carton with the custard. When
making sorbet, any egg white should be lightly
whisked with a fork and added at the start of the
churning process.

Freezing time is usually about 20-30
minutes. The ice cream or sorbet should then
be transferred to the freezer and frozen for 1-2
hours to allow the flavours to develop before
serving. Soften them slightly at room
temperature before serving.

It is vital to clean ice cream machines
thoroughly after use to prevent the development
of bacteria. Wash bowls, lids, paddles and
spatulas in the hottest water temperature
possible. Be sure to wash and dry all parts which
come into contact with salt to prevent corrosion.

FROZEN YOGURT

2 egg whites
25-50 g (1-2 oz) caster sugar
600 ml (1 pint) Greek-style natural yogurt
30 ml (2 tbsp) milk
5 ml (1 tsp) vanilla essence

1. Whisk the egg whites and sugar until stiff.
2. Mix the yogurt, milk and vanilla essence
together in a bowl, then fold in the egg whites.
3. Freeze in an ice cream machine or by hand
(see above).
SERVES 4-6

NOTE: This ice will be more granular if made by
hand rather than in an ice cream machine.

VARIATIONS
FROZEN FRUIT YOGURT
Add 300 ml (½ pint) fruit purée to the yogurt
mixture, then complete as above.

FROZEN MUESLI YOGURT
Blend 125 g (4 oz) muesli, 30 ml (2 tbsp) milk
and 30 ml (2 tbsp) clear honey with the yogurt,
then complete as above.

VANILLA ICE CREAM

1 vanilla pod
300 ml (½ pint) milk
3 egg yolks
50-75 g (2-3 oz) caster sugar
300 ml (10 fl oz) double cream

1. Split the vanilla pod to reveal the seeds. Put the milk and vanilla pod into a heavy-based saucepan and bring almost to the boil. Remove from the heat, cover and leave to infuse for about 20 minutes.
2. Beat the egg yolks and sugar together in a bowl until well blended. Stir in the milk and strain back into the pan. Cook the custard over a gentle heat, stirring all the time, until it thickens very slightly. (Alternatively, cook the custard in a bowl standing over a pan of simmering water.) It is very important not to let the custard boil or it will curdle. Pour out into a bowl and leave to cool.
3. Whisk the cream into the cold custard mixture.
4. Freeze the ice cream mixture by hand or in an ice cream machine (see left). Leave at cool room temperature for 20-30 minutes to soften before serving.
SERVES 4-6

VARIATIONS
COFFEE ICE CREAM
Add 150 ml (¼ pint) strong fresh cooled coffee to the cooled custard or 10 ml (2 tsp) instant coffee granules to the milk. Omit the vanilla.

CHOCOLATE ICE CREAM
Put the milk in a saucepan with 125 g (4 oz) plain chocolate. Heat gently until the chocolate melts, then bring almost to the boil. Continue as left.

CHOCOLATE FLAKE ICE CREAM
Crumble 2 large chocolate flakes. Stir half into the cooled custard with the cream. Complete as left. Stir in the remaining flake just before the ice cream is completely frozen.

CINNAMON ICE CREAM
Add 10 ml (2 tsp) ground cinnamon and a cinnamon stick to the milk. Omit the vanilla.

FRUIT ICE CREAM
Add 300 ml (½ pint) fruit purée, sweetened to taste, to the cooled custard.

COCONUT ICE CREAM
Omit the vanilla. Finely chop 175 g (6 oz) creamed coconut. Add to the milk and warm until dissolved, whisking until smooth, then add 30 ml (2 tbsp) lemon juice.

PRALINE ICE CREAM

50 g (2 oz) whole unblanched almonds
50 g (2 oz) sugar
300 ml (½ pint) milk
1 vanilla pod
1 egg
2 egg yolks
75 g (3 oz) caster sugar
200 ml (7 fl oz) double cream

1. Place the almonds and sugar in a heavy-based saucepan; heat slowly until the sugar caramelises, turning occasionally. Pour on to an oiled baking sheet and leave to cool and harden for about 15 minutes. Then grind to a powder using a blender or food processor, or a rolling pin.
2. Bring the milk and vanilla pod to the boil,

remove from the heat, cover and leave to infuse for 30 minutes.
3. Beat the egg, egg yolks and sugar until pale in colour, then strain in the milk. Cook slowly for about 10 minutes, until the custard coats the back of the spoon. Do not boil. Pour into a chilled freezer container, cool then freeze for 2 hours until mushy.
4. Lightly whip the cream and fold into the custard. Pour into a freezer container and freeze for 2 hours, until mushy.
5. Turn into a large, chilled bowl, beat with a flat whisk or fork, then fold in the praline. Return to the container and freeze until firm.
6. Transfer to the refrigerator to soften 30 minutes before serving.
SERVES 6

ORANGE WATER ICE

125 g (4 oz) caster sugar
15 ml (1 tbsp) lemon juice
finely pared rind of 3 oranges
finely pared rind of 1 lemon
juice of 3 oranges and 1 lemon, mixed, about
    300 ml (½ pint) in total
1 egg white

1. Dissolve the sugar in 300 ml (½ pint) water over a low heat, bring to the boil and boil gently for 10 minutes. Add the lemon juice.

2. Put the fruit rinds in a bowl, pour the syrup over and leave until cold. Add the fruit juices and strain into a freezer container. Freeze for about 2 hours.

3. Whisk the egg white until stiff. Turn the mixture into a bowl and beat gently to break down the ice crystals. Fold in the egg white, then return to the container and freeze until firm.

4. Transfer to the refrigerator about 45 minutes before serving.

SERVES 8

LEMON SORBET

225 g (8 oz) sugar
finely pared rind and juice of 4 lemons
2 egg whites

1. Dissolve the sugar in 600 ml (1 pint) water over a low heat, then bring to the boil and boil for 2 minutes. Remove from heat, add lemon rinds, cover and leave to infuse for 10 minutes.

2. When cool, add the lemon juice, then strain into a shallow freezer container. Freeze for about 2 hours, until mushy.

3. Whisk the egg whites until stiff. Turn the mixture into a bowl and beat gently to break down the ice crystals. Fold in the egg whites, then return to the container and freeze until firm. Transfer to the refrigerator about 45 minutes before serving.

SERVES 8

STRAWBERRY SORBET

700 g (1½ lb) strawberries, hulled
175 g (6 oz) sugar
15 ml (1 tbsp) lemon juice
2 egg whites

1. Purée the strawberries in a blender or food processor, then sieve to remove the seeds.

2. Dissolve the sugar in 300 ml (½ pint) water over a low heat, bring to the boil and boil for 3-4 minutes until syrupy. Stir into the strawberry

purée with the lemon juice. Cool.

3. Pour the mixture into a shallow freezer container and freeze for 3-4 hours, until mushy.

4. Whisk the egg whites until stiff. Turn the mixture into a bowl and beat gently to break down the ice crystals. Fold in the egg whites. Return to the container and freeze until firm.

5. Transfer to the refrigerator about 45 minutes before serving.

SERVES 6

MELON AND GINGER SORBET

75 g (3 oz) sugar
1 medium honeydew melon
45 ml (3 tbsp) lemon juice
1 piece preserved stem ginger, finely chopped
few drops green food colouring (optional)
2 egg whites

1. Dissolve the sugar in 300 ml (½ pint) water over a low heat, bring to the boil for 2 minutes. Allow to cool.

2. Halve the melon, remove the seeds and scoop out the flesh. Purée the flesh in a blender or

food processor until smooth. Stir into the cool syrup with the lemon juice. Add the chopped ginger and food colouring, if wished.

3. Pour the mixture into a freezer container and freeze for 2-3 hours, until mushy.

4. Whisk the egg whites until stiff. Turn the mixture into a bowl and beat gently to break down the ice crystals. Fold in the egg whites. Return to the container and freeze until firm.

5. Transfer to the refrigerator about 45 minutes before serving.

SERVES 6

BROWN BREAD ICE CREAM

125 g (4 oz) fresh fine brown breadcrumbs
50 g (2 oz) soft brown sugar
300 ml (10 fl oz) double cream
150 ml (5 fl oz) single cream
15 ml (1 tbsp) dark rum
50 g (2 oz) icing sugar, sifted

1. Spread breadcrumbs on a baking sheet and sprinkle with the brown sugar. Bake in the oven at 200°C (400°F) mark 6 for 10 minutes, stirring occasionally, until the sugar caramelises and the crumbs are crisp. Cool, then break up.
2. Whisk together the creams until stiff. Gently fold in the rum and icing sugar.
3. Pour into a freezer container and freeze for 2 hours, until mushy.
4. Turn into a chilled bowl and beat with a fork or whisk to break down the ice crystals. Stir in the breadcrumbs. Return to the freezer container and freeze until firm.
5. Transfer to the refrigerator to soften 30 minutes before serving.
SERVES 4

ICED CHRISTMAS PUDDING

225 g (8 oz) mixed dried fruit
50 g (2 oz) glacé cherries, halved
75 ml (5 tbsp) brandy
3 eggs
140 g (4½ oz) caster sugar
450 ml (¾ pint) milk
300 ml (10 fl oz) double cream
150 ml (5 fl oz) single cream

1. Place the mixed dried fruit and glacé cherries in a bowl, spoon over the brandy, cover and leave to soak for 2-3 hours.
2. Beat the eggs and the sugar until well mixed.
Bring the milk nearly to the boil, then stir into the egg mixture.
3. Strain back into the pan and cook gently, without boiling, until the custard coats the back of the spoon. Cool for 30 minutes.
4. Lightly whip the creams together. Fold into the custard with the fruit and brandy mixture.
5. Turn into a large bowl and freeze for 2 hours until mushy. Mix well and pack into a 1.7 litre (3 pint) bombe mould or pudding basin. Freeze for 2-3 hours until firm.
6. Remove from the freezer 20 minutes before serving. Turn out and serve immediately.
SERVES 8

BAKED ALASKA

225 g (8 oz) plus 10 ml (2 level tsp) caster sugar
50 g (2 oz) plus 5 ml (1 level tsp) plain flour
2 eggs, size 2
finely grated rind of 1 orange
225 g (8 oz) fresh or frozen raspberries
30 ml (2 tbsp) orange-flavoured liqueur
4 egg whites, at room temperature
450 ml (15 fl oz) vanilla ice cream

1. Grease a 20 cm (8 inch) non-stick flan tin. Sprinkle over 10 ml (2 level tsp) caster sugar and tilt the tin to give an even coating of sugar. Add 5 ml (1 level tsp) plain flour and coat similarly.
2. Place the eggs and 50 g (2 oz) caster sugar in a bowl and whisk until the mixture is very thick. Fold in the orange rind and sifted flour.
3. Pour the mixture into the tin and level the surface. Bake in the oven at 180°C (350°F) mark 4 for 20-25 minutes, until golden. Turn out on to a wire rack to cool.
4. Place the raspberries in a shallow dish and sprinkle over the liqueur. Cover and leave in a cool place for 2 hours turning occasionally.
5. Place the cold sponge flan on a large oven-proof serving dish and spoon the raspberries with the juice into the centre of the flan.
6. Stiffly whisk the egg whites. Whisk in half the remaining sugar, then carefully fold in the rest.
7. Fit a piping bag with a large star nozzle and fill with the meringue mixture. Place the ice cream on top of the raspberries. Pipe the meringue on top; start from the base and pipe the meringue around and over the ice cream to cover completely.
8. Immediately, bake in the oven at 230°C (450°F) mark 8 for 3-4 minutes, until the meringue is tinged with brown; do not allow to burn. Serve immediately.
SERVES 6-8

INDIVIDUAL COFFEE BOMBES

1½ quantity Coffee Ice Cream (see page 367)
FOR THE FILLING
25 g (1 oz) cake crumbs
25 g (1 oz) ground almonds
50 g (2 oz) plain chocolate
45 ml (3 tbsp) double cream
30 ml (2 tbsp) rum or brandy
Chocolate Leaves, to decorate (see page 508)

1. Set the freezer to fast freeze. Put six 175 ml (6 fl oz) individual freezerproof pie or pudding moulds in the freezer to chill.
2. Leave the ice cream at room temperature for 20-30 minutes or until soft enough to spread.
3. Meanwhile, to make the truffle filling, mix the cake crumbs and almonds together in a bowl. Put the chocolate and cream in a small bowl standing over a pan of simmering water and stir until melted. Add the chocolate mixture to the crumb and almond mixture with the rum. Mix well.
4. Spread the softened ice cream around the base and sides of the pie moulds, leaving a cavity in the centre for the truffle mixture. Freeze for 1 hour or until firm.
5. Fill the centre of each mould with the truffle mixture and level the surface. Cover and freeze for 1 hour or until firm.
6. To serve, dip the moulds briefly in hot water, then unmould on to serving plates. Return to the freezer for 10 minutes to firm up. Decorate with chocolate leaves to serve.
SERVES 6

PERNOD PARFAIT

125 g (4 oz) granulated sugar
4 egg yolks
30 ml (2 tbsp) Pernod
450 ml (15 fl oz) whipping cream
150 ml (5 fl oz) whipping cream, to decorate

1. Place the sugar and 300 ml (½ pint) water in a heavy-based saucepan and heat gently until dissolved. Bring to the boil and boil steadily for 2 minutes.
2. Put the egg yolks in a bowl and beat, using an electric whisk, until pale and fluffy. Pour the hot syrup in a thin stream on to the egg yolks and continue beating until the mixture is cool. Beat in the Pernod.
3. Whip the cream until it just holds its shape, then fold into the egg mixture. Pour into eight freezerproof serving dishes or ramekins. Cover and freeze for 5 hours or overnight until firm.
4. To serve, whip the cream until it just holds its shape, then pipe a swirl on to each parfait. Serve immediately, with crisp dessert biscuits.
SERVES 8

ICED RASPBERRY MERINGUE

700 g (1½ lb) fresh raspberries, hulled
60 ml (4 level tbsp) icing sugar
60 ml (4 tbsp) orange-flavoured liqueur
300 ml (10 fl oz) double cream
150 ml (5 fl oz) single cream
18 meringue nests made from 3 egg whites
  (see page 372)

1. Put half the raspberries into a bowl. Sift over the icing sugar, add the liqueur and mix gently. Cover and leave in a cool place for 3-4 hours or overnight.
2. Purée the raspberry mixture in a blender or food processor, then press through a nylon sieve to remove the pips.
3. Whip the creams together until they just hold their shape. Break up the meringues into 3-4 pieces each and fold into the cream with the raspberry purée until evenly distributed but still marbled in appearance.
4. Oil a 1.7 litre (3 pint) freezerproof mould. Spoon the mixture into the prepared mould, overwrap and freeze for at least 6 hours.
5. Serve straight from the freezer; ease the iced dessert out of the mould and pile the remaining raspberries in the centre.
SERVES 6

ABOVE: Individual Coffee Bombes. BELOW: Pernod Parfait

Meringues

The light, crisp texture of meringues is the perfect foil to creamy fillings and slices of soft fruit. Meringues are made with whisked egg whites to which sugar is incorporated. They are a perfect way to use up leftover egg whites because meringues will keep in an airtight tin for as long as six weeks.

Meringue Suisse is the most common type of meringue. The egg whites must be whisked until they are very stiff and will hold an unwavering peak on the end of the whisk. The sugar can be added in two halves or can be whisked in a little at a time.
Meringue cuite is made by putting the unwhisked whites and sugar in a bowl, then

whisking them over gently simmering water until stiff and thick. As soon as the mixture becomes thick, the bowl should be removed from the heat. This meringue has a smooth texture and wonderful gloss. It also holds its shape well.
Italian meringue is made by whisking a hot sugar syrup into egg whites. It is rarely used in home cooking.

MERINGUES

This recipe uses meringue Suisse; for meringue cuite see below.

3 egg whites, size 2
75 g (3 oz) granulated sugar and 75 g (3 oz) caster sugar or 175 g (6 oz) caster sugar
150 ml (¼ pint) double cream, to serve

1. Line two baking sheets with non-stick baking parchment.
2. Whisk egg whites until stiff. Gradually whisk in half the sugar, whisking after each addition until thoroughly incorporated, then fold in the remaining sugar very lightly with a metal spoon.
3. Spoon the meringue into a piping bag fitted with a large star nozzle and pipe small rounds on to the prepared baking sheet. Alternatively, spoon the mixture into small mounds.
4. Bake in the oven at 110°C (225°F) mark ¼ for about 2½-3 hours, until firm and crisp, but still white. If they begin to brown, prop oven door open a little. Transfer to a wire rack to cool.
5. To serve, whip the cream until thick. Sandwich the meringues together in pairs with cream.
Makes 8-10

MERINGUE BASKET
1. Line three baking sheets with non-stick baking parchment. Draw an 18 cm (7 inch) circle on each and turn the paper over. Spoon one third of the meringue mixture into a piping bag fitted with a large star nozzle.
2. Pipe rings of meringue about 1 cm (½ inch) thick inside two of the circles on the paper. Fill the bag with the remaining meringue and starting from the centre pipe a continuous coil of meringue on to the third circle to make the base.
3. Cook in the oven at 100°C (200°F) mark ¼ for 2½ -3 hours to dry out. Use an extra egg white and 50 g (2 oz) sugar to make more meringue (as above).
4. Remove the cooked meringue rings from the paper and layer on the base, piping fresh meringue between the layers to secure. Return to the oven for a further 1½ -2 hours. Allow to cool, then remove paper.

MERINGUE NESTS
Prepare as above, but draw six 10cm (4 inch) circles on the paper.

MERINGUE CUITE

This can be used in exactly the same way as meringue Suisse.

2 egg whites
125 g (4½ oz) icing sugar

1. Line a baking sheet with non-stick baking parchment.
2. Place the egg whites and icing sugar in a large bowl over a pan of simmering water and whisk until the meringue is very stiff and shiny. Remove from the heat and continue whisking for about 5 minutes.

BROWN SUGAR AND HAZELNUT MERINGUES

25 g (1 oz) hazelnuts
3 egg whites
175 g (6 oz) light brown soft sugar
ice cream or whipped cream, to serve

1. Line two large baking sheets with non-stick baking parchment.
2. Toast the hazelnuts under the grill until golden brown. Tip on to a clean tea towel and rub off the loose skins. Chop roughly.
3. Whisk the egg whites in a bowl until stiff. Whisk in the sugar, 15 ml (1 tbsp) at a time.

Spoon the meringue mixture into a piping bag fitted with a large star nozzle and pipe about 40 small swirls on to the prepared baking sheets. Sprinkle with the hazelnuts.
4. Bake in the oven at 110°C (225°F) mark ¼ for about 2-3 hours or until dry. If the baking sheets are on different shelves, swap them halfway through cooking to ensure even browning. Leave to cool.
5. Sandwich the meringues together in pairs with a little ice cream or whipped cream to serve.
MAKES ABOUT 40

RASPBERRY PAVLOVA

3 egg whites
175 g (6 oz) caster sugar
2.5 ml (½ tsp) vanilla flavouring
2.5 ml (½ tsp) white wine vinegar
5 ml (1 level tsp) cornflour
300 ml (10 fl oz) double cream
350 g (12 oz) fresh raspberries, washed and hulled

1. Draw an 18 cm (7 inch) circle on a sheet of non-stick baking parchment and place the paper mark side down on a baking sheet.
2. Whisk the egg whites until stiff. Whisk in half the sugar, then carefully fold in the remaining sugar, the vanilla flavouring, vinegar and

cornflour, using a large metal spoon.
3. Spread the meringue over the circle and bake in the oven at 150°C (300°F) mark 2 for about 1 hour, until crisp and dry. Transfer to a wire rack to cool, then carefully peel off the non-stick paper.
4. Whisk the cream until stiff. Carefully slide the meringue on to a flat plate, pile the cream on it and arrange the raspberries on top.
SERVES 6

VARIATIONS
Replace the raspberries with strawberries, grapes, passion fruit, pineapple or a mixture of fruit.

LEMON MERINGUE PIE

175 g (6 oz) Shortcrust Pastry made with 175 g (6 oz)
  flour (see page 381)
finely grated rind and juice of 2 lemons
125 g (4 oz) granulated sugar
75 ml (5 level tbsp) cornflour
2 eggs, separated
75 g (3 oz) caster sugar

1. Roll out the pastry on a floured surface and use to line a 20 cm (8 inch) loose-based flan tin or fluted flan dish. Chill in the refrigerator for 30 minutes.
2. Bake blind (see page 380) in the oven at 200°C (400°F) mark 6 for 10-15 minutes, then remove the paper and beans and bake for a further 5 minutes until the base is firm.
3. Put the lemon rind and juice, granulated sugar and 300 ml (½ pint) water in a saucepan.

Heat gently until the sugar dissolves.
4. Mix the cornflour to a smooth paste with 90 ml (6 tbsp) water and stir into the saucepan until well blended. Bring to the boil, stirring and cook for 1 minute, until thickened.
5. Cool slightly, then beat in the egg yolks, one at a time.
6. Pour the warm lemon filling into the pastry case, levelling the surface.
7. Whisk the egg whites until stiff. Whisk in half the caster sugar a little at a time, then carefully fold in the remainder.
8. Spoon the meringue on to the filling and swirl with a palette knife. The filling must be completely covered, but the meringue should not overlap the edge of the flan tin. Bake in the oven at 150°C (300°F) mark 2 for about 35 minutes.
SERVES 4-6

Chocolate and Chestnut Cream Vacherin

6 egg whites

350 g (12 oz) caster sugar

75 g (3 oz) hazelnuts, skinned, toasted and finely chopped

175 g (6 oz) plain chocolate, broken into pieces

500 g (1.1 lb) can sweetened chestnut purée

300 ml (½ pint) double cream

a little icing sugar for dusting

whipped cream and cocoa powder, to decorate

1. Line 3 baking sheets with non-stick baking parchment and draw a 20 cm (8 inch) circle on each.

2. To make the meringue, whisk the egg whites in a bowl until very stiff, but not dry. Gradually whisk in the caster sugar a little at a time, whisking well between each addition until the meringue is smooth and shiny. Very lightly fold in the chopped hazelnuts.

3. Either spread the mixture over the marked circles, or transfer to a piping bag fitted with a plain 1 cm (½ inch) nozzle and pipe the meringue in a spiral over the marked circles, starting from the centre.

4. Bake at 140°C (275°F) mark 1 for 1-1½ hours or until dried out. Change the positions of the baking sheets during cooking so that the meringues dry out evenly. Remove from the oven and leave to cool, then carefully remove the lining papers.

5. Melt the chocolate in a heatproof bowl set over a pan of hot water. Soften the chestnut purée in a bowl and stir in the melted chocolate. Lightly whip the cream until soft peaks form and fold into the chestnut mixture.

6. To assemble the vacherin, sandwich the meringues together with a little of the chestnut cream. Cover the top and sides with the remainder and decorate with whipped cream and cocoa powder.

Serves 8

Chocolate and Chestnut Cream Vacherin

Hazelnut Meringue Gâteau

HAZELNUT MERINGUE GÂTEAU

FOR THE MERINGUE
3 egg whites
175 g (6 oz) caster sugar
50 g (2 oz) hazelnuts, skinned, toasted and finely chopped
FOR THE FILLING
300 ml (½ pint) double cream
350 g (12 oz) raspberries, hulled
icing sugar, for dusting
finely chopped pistachio nuts, to decorate

1. Line two baking sheets with non-stick baking parchment, then draw a 20 cm (8 inch) circle on each one.
2. To make the meringue, whisk the egg whites in a bowl until very stiff, but not dry. Gradually add the caster sugar, a little at a time, whisking well between each addition until stiff and very shiny. Carefully fold in the chopped hazelnuts.

3. Divide the meringue equally between the prepared baking sheets, then spread neatly into rounds. With a palette knife, mark the top of one of the rounds into swirls – this will be the top meringue.
4. Bake in the oven at 140°C (275°F) mark 1 for about 1½ hours until dry. Change the positions of the baking sheets during cooking so that the meringues dry out evenly. Turn the oven off, and allow the meringues to cool in the oven.
5. To make the filling, whip the cream until it will hold soft peaks. Carefully remove the meringues from the paper. Place the smooth meringue round on a large flat serving plate, then spread with the cream. Arrange the raspberries on top of the cream, then place the second meringue on top. Sift icing sugar over the top of the gâteau, then sprinkle with the nuts. Serve the gâteau as soon as possible.
SERVES 6-8

PASTRY

The art of making good pastry lies in paying careful attention to the recipe and using the correct proportion of fat to flour. Pastry doughs, with the exception of choux, hot water crust and filo (strudel), need to be kept cool during making by using cold ingredients and equipment, and by keeping your hands cool for mixing.
It is important to 'rest' pastry before baking as it gets stretched during shaping. If not allowed to 'rest' and firm up, it may shrink away from the sides of the tin during baking. Flaked pastries need 'resting' before and after shaping as they are handled a great deal.
Each kind of pastry produces a different texture and variation in flavour and is suited to a certain range of recipes. Some pastries are more difficult than others but, with practise, you will obtain successful results every time.

PASTRY INGREDIENTS

FLOUR: For most pastries plain flour is the best. Wholemeal flour can be used for shortcrust or suetcrust pastry. Wholemeal flour in shortcrust produces a dough which is more difficult to roll out but has a distinctive flavour and texture when cooked. Shortcrust can also be made with self raising flour but this gives a softer more crumbly texture.

Suetcrust, unlike other pastries, needs a flour and a raising agent to lighten the dough. Puff pastry and filo (strudel) pastry need to be made with strong plain flour, as this contains extra gluten which strengthens the dough for the rolling and folding of puff pastry and allows filo pastry to be stretched out very thinly. Strong plain flour can also be used for choux pastry, making it rise more, but it may also give a slightly tougher result.

RAISING AGENT: Suetcrust pastry needs a raising agent; either plain flour sifted with 12.5 ml (2½ level tsp) baking powder to each 225 g (8 oz), or self raising flour can be used. Do not add baking powder to self raising flour as this produces an unpleasant flavour. Steam acts as the raising agent in flaked pastries in combination with the air enclosed in the layers of dough. In choux pastry the raising agents are eggs and steam.

SALT: The quantity of salt varies according to the type of pastry. Only a pinch of salt is added to shortcrust pastry for flavour, while a measured quantity is added to hot water crust to strengthen the gluten in the flour and allow for the amount of handling during shaping. Salt is also needed to strengthen the gluten in the flour with flaked pastries.

FAT: Butter, margarine and lard are the fats most commonly used, but proprietary vegetable shortenings (both blended and whipped) and pure vegetable oils can give excellent results. When using oil, remember to follow the directions in the recipe on page 383, as a smaller quantity of oil is recommended in proportion to the flour than is usual with other kinds of fat. Generally, the firmer block margarine should be used rather than soft tub margarine. A recipe is given using soft tub margarine, called One Stage Short Pastry (see page 383).

For shortcrust pastry butter, margarine, lard or vegetable fat can be used alone, though margarine tends to give a firmer pastry which is rather yellow in colour. Good results are achieved with an equal mixture of fats – butter or margarine for flavour with lard for shortness. For the richer pastries, it is better to keep to the amount of fat specified in the recipes.

For suetcrust pastry, suet is used. Suet is the fat around the kidneys, heart and liver of beef and mutton. It is available ready shredded in packets from grocers. Vegetarian suet is also available; it is made from white vegetable fat.

LIQUID: Use chilled water to make pastry dough and add just enough to make the dough bind. It is important to add the liquid carefully, as too much will make the cooked pastry tough and too little will produce a crumbly baked pastry. Egg yolks are often used as the binding liquid to enrich the pastry. Lemon juice is added to flaked pastries to soften the gluten in the flour and make the dough more elastic.

SUGAR: Caster sugar may be added to rich shortcrust or flan pastries if the pastry is to be used for a sweet dish.

ROLLING OUT PASTRY

Dust the work surface and the rolling pin – never the pastry – with as little flour as possible. Roll the dough lightly and evenly in one direction only. Always roll away from you, using light but firm strokes, rotating the pastry frequently to keep an even shape. Over-rolled pastry will shrink dramatically when baked.

SHAPING PASTRY

LINING A FLAN CASE

See quantity chart on page 380. Choose a loose-based flan tin, plain or fluted flan ring placed on a baking sheet; a china fluted flan dish or sandwich tin. Loose-based flan tins are ideal, because they make it easier to transfer the flans on to serving plates. Pastry bases will also cook better in a metal tin than a china flan dish.

1. Roll out the pastry thinly to a circle about

Using a rolling pin place the bottom layer of pastry in the flan tin.

Use a rolling pin to trim excess pastry from the top of the flan tin.

5 cm (2 inch) wider than the ring. With a rolling pin, lift the pastry and lower it into the tin or fold the pastry in half and position it in the tin.

2. Lift the edges carefully and ease the pastry into the flan shape, lightly pressing the pastry against the edges – with a fluted edge press your finger edge into each flute to ensure a good finish. No air should be left between the container and pastry.

3. Turn any surplus pastry outwards over the rim and roll across the top with the rolling pin or use a knife to trim the edges.

LINING INDIVIDUAL TARTLET TINS OR MOULDS

1. Arrange the tins close together on a baking sheet. Roll out the pastry to a size large enough to cover the whole area of the tins. Lift the pastry on to the rolling pin and lay loosely over the tins.

2. Using a small knob of dough, press the pastry into each tin. With a rolling pin, roll across the complete set of tins and lift the surplus pastry away.

3. Prick the bases and sides lightly with a fork. With a sheet of patty tins, cut rounds of thinly rolled pastry slightly larger than the top of the tin and ease one round into each shape.

Place a thin strip of pastry on to the dampened rim.

COVERING A PIE DISH

1. Roll out the pastry to the required thickness and 5 cm (2 inch) wider than the pie dish, using the inverted dish as a guide. Cut a 2.5 cm (1 inch) wide strip from the outer edge and place it on the dampened rim of the dish. Seal the join and brush the whole strip with water.

2. Fill the pie dish generously, so that the surface is slightly rounded; use a pie funnel if insufficient filling is available.

3. Lift the remaining pastry on the rolling pin and lay it over the pie dish. Press the lid lightly on to the pastry-lined rim to seal. Trim off any excess pastry with the cutting edge of a knife held at a slight angle away from the dish.

4. Seal the edges firmly so that they do not open up during cooking (see Knock Up, page 379). If you wish, scallop the edges (see page 379). Use trimmings rolled thinly and cut into leaf shapes etc to decorate the pie. Cut a slit in the centre of the pie crust to allow the steam to escape.

Using a rolling pin, place the top crust over the pie filling.

A DOUBLE CRUST PIE

1. Divide the pastry into two parts, one slightly bigger than the other. Shape the larger piece into a ball and roll it out. Rotate the pastry as you roll it, to keep it circular. Pinch together any cracks that appear at the edge. Roll it out to about 2.5 cm (1 inch) wider than the inverted pie plate.

2. To move the pastry, roll the dough loosely around the rolling pin, lift and unroll it over the pie dish. Press into the dish, taking care not to stretch it.

3. Add the cold filling, keeping the surface slightly rounded. Roll out the remaining pastry for the lid, making it about 1 cm (½ inch) wider than the rim.

4. Brush the pastry rim with water, then lift the lid into position as for covering a pie. Seal the edge either by folding the surplus edge of the lid over the rim of the base pastry or by pressing the two layers together and trimming as for covering a pie. Knock up the edges of the pastry (see page 379) and make a short slit in the centre for the steam to escape.

SHAPING FREE STANDING RAISED PIES

This method can be used for small or large pies depending on the size of jar you are using to shape the pastry. Make up 450 g (1 lb) Hot Water Crust Pastry (see page 386) and keep it warm. This is sufficient to make six small pies based on covering six 350 g (12 oz) or 450 g (1 lb) jam jars. You can also use a traditional wooden raised pie mould – available in 450 g (1 lb) or 900 g (2 lb) sizes.

1. Cut off one third of the pastry dough and set aside, covered with a cloth or upturned bowl. Divide the remaining two thirds into six equal portions. Roll each piece into a 15 cm (6 inch) round and trim the edges. Turn a jar upside down and place a round over it. Shape it with your fingertips and smooth down the folds.

Mould the pastry round over an upturned jar.

Gently twist to ease the pastry away from the jar.

Repeat the process with the remaining five jars.

2. Cut out a double thickness of greaseproof paper large enough to fit around the pie. Wrap the paper around the pastry and secure with string. Repeat for all six jars. Cover the jars with a tea towel and leave in a cool place for 2 hours to firm.

3. Turn the jar upright and carefully ease the pastry away from the jar and greaseproof paper, gently twisting to loosen and produce a cup shape. Place the shaped pastry cases on a lightly greased baking sheet.

4. Fill the pastry cases with a meat mixture using a spoon to push firmly down at the base and sides to hold the pie's shape. Brush the edge of the pastry with water.

5. Divide the remaining pastry into six roughly equal portions and roll each portion into a round slightly bigger than the filled case diameter. Place each on top of a pie and press the edges together to seal.

6. Trim away any surplus pastry and paper with a pair of scissors and then cut a cross with a sharp knife in the centre of each pie. Fold back the pastry and glaze and decorate it to taste. Finish with a tassel (see page 379). Bake as directed.

SHAPING A LARGE RAISED PIE IN A MOULD

Use this method for making Raised Game Pie (see page 178).

1. Make up 450 g (1 lb) Hot Water Crust Pastry (see page 386) and keep it warm. Grease a 1.75 litre (3 pint) hinged pie mould or use a loose-based round cake tin or loaf tin with the same capacity. Place the pie mould on a baking sheet.

2. Roll out two thirds of the pastry to a 5 mm (¼ inch) thickness and use to line the tin.

3. Fill and put on the lid as above. Bake as directed in the recipe.

DECORATIVE TOUCHES

Pastry garnishes and decorative borders always look attractive. Remember to glaze the garnish as well as the pie or flan.

Knock up the pastry edge with the blunt edge of a knife.

Use your thumb and a sharp knife to scallop the pastry edge.

Press the pastry against your fingertips to crimp the pastry's rim.

KNOCK UP

After the pastry edges have been trimmed all pies should then be 'knocked up' to seal the edges firmly before decorating. Press your index finger along the rim and holding a knife horizontally, tap the edge of the pastry sharply with the blunt side of the blade to give a 'flaky' appearance.

SCALLOP/FLUTE

Press a thumb on the rim of the pastry and at the same time draw back the floured blade of a round-bladed or table knife about 1 cm (½ inch) towards the centre. Repeat around the edge of the pie. Traditionally sweet dishes should have about 5 mm (¼ inch) scallops and savoury dishes 2.5 cm (1 inch) scallops.

CRIMP

Push the thumb or finger of one hand into the rim of the pastry. Use the thumb and first finger of the other hand to gently pinch the pastry pushed up by this action. Continue around the edge of the pie. Crimp is traditionally used to seal Cornish Pasties as well as to decorate pie edges.

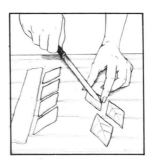

Score diamond shaped pieces of pastry trimmings to make leaves.

Use pastry trimmings to make decorative tassels.

Arrange the top layer of pastry strips diagonally across the first layer.

LEAVES

Cut thinly rolled out pastry trimmings into 2.5 cm (1 inch) wide strips. Cut these diagonally to form diamond shapes and mark the veins of a leaf on each one with the back of a knife blade. Pinch one of the long ends to form a stem.

For festive pies, use a pastry cutter to cut out holly leaves and mould tiny berries with your hands.

TASSEL

Cut a strip from the rolled out pastry trimmings 2.5 cm (1 inch) wide and 10-15 cm (4-6 inches) long. Use a knife to make 2 cm (¾ inch) slits at short intervals to resemble a fringe. Roll up and stand on the uncut end to spread the cut strips.

LATTICE WORK

Lattice is probably the best known decoration for open pie tarts. They may be either simple or interwoven.
1. Use either a knife or pastry wheel to cut the rolled out pastry into 1 cm (½ inch) wide strips of the same length as the tart.
2. Lay half the strips at intervals across the surface an equal distance apart. Place the other half diagonally across the first. Flatten the ends and moisten and press firmly to seal.
3. An interwoven lattice is achieved by folding back alternate strips of the first layer and adding strips at right angles. Replace the folded back strips, lift back the alternate ones and continue.

BAKING BLIND

This is the term used to describe the cooking of pastry cases without any filling. The pastry may be partially pre-baked to be cooked for a further period when filled, or completely cooked if the filling doesn't need further cooking. All short-crust and puff pastries may be baked blind.

The pastry shell is lined with foil or grease-proof paper and then, for larger cases, filled with baking beans before cooking. Baking beans may be any dried pulse or ceramic 'beans'.

1. Make the pastry and line the flan case (see page 377). Chill in the refrigerator for 30 minutes if possible, to 'rest' the pastry.

2. Cut out a piece of foil or greaseproof paper rather larger than the tin. Remove the case from the refrigerator and prick the base thoroughly.

3. Press the paper or foil against the pastry, then form a 1 cm (½ inch) layer of beans.

4. For partially pre-baked cases, bake in the oven at 200°C (400°F) mark 6 for 10-15 minutes until set. Lift out the paper or foil and beans, and bake for a further 5 minutes, until the base is just firm and lightly coloured.

Pastry cases which need complete baking should be returned to the oven for a further 15 minutes or until firm and pale golden brown.

For small pastry cases, it is usually sufficient to prick the pastry well with a fork before baking. Pastry cases which have been baked keep several days in an airtight tin, or they may be frozen.

RECIPE QUANTITIES

When a recipe specifies, for example, 100 g (4 oz) pastry, this means pastry made using 100 g (4 oz) flour, with the other ingredients in proportion, not the combined weight of the ingredients.

NOTE: When you buy ready-made pastry the weight specified on the packet is the combined weight of the ingredients not simply the weight of the flour. See individual pastry recipes for equivalents.

SHORTCRUST PASTRY QUANTITY GUIDE FOR FLANS, TARTLETS AND PIES	
Flan Tin Size (Plain or Fluted)	**Pastry** (Flour weight)
15 cm (6 inch)	100 g (4 oz)
18 cm (7 inch)	150 g (5 oz)
20 cm (8 inch)	175 g (6 oz)
23 cm (9 inch)	200 g (7 oz)
18 x 6 cm (2½ inch) tartlets	225 g (8 oz)
12 x 7.5 cm (3 inch) tartlets	225 g (8 oz)
Pie Dish Size (Plain or Fluted)	**Pastry** (Flour weight)
900 ml (1½ pint)	175 g (6 oz)
1 litre (2 pint)	225 g (8 oz)

Some flan tins are shallower than others and may require less pastry and filling than indicated in the recipe.

Shortcrust Pastry, used here in a pie with cherries

SHORT PASTRIES

Short pastries are some of the easiest to make and the most versatile. They can be plain or flavoured, savoury or sweet, and form the basis of a wide range of flans, pies and tartlets. They are made by rubbing fat into flour until it is broken down into flour-coated crumbs which then bake to a light crisp texture.
Cool ingredients and conditions are essential and the dough should be handled as little as possible. It is not necessary to grease the baking equipment when cooking this type of pastry.

SHORTCRUST PASTRY

This plain short pastry is probably the most widely used of all pastries. For shortcrust pastry, the proportion of flour to fat is 2:1, or twice the quantity. Therefore, for a recipe using quantities of shortcrust pastry other than 225 g (8 oz) simply use half the quantity of fat to the flour weight specified.

This quantity, made with 225 g (8 oz) flour, is approximately equivalent to one 368 g (13 oz) packet ready-made shortcrust pastry.

225 g (8 oz) plain flour
pinch of salt
50 g (2 oz) butter or block margarine, chilled and diced
50 g (2 oz) lard, chilled and diced
chilled water

1. Place the flour and salt in a bowl and add the fat to the flour.
2. Using both hands, rub the fat lightly into the flour until the mixture resembles fine breadcrumbs.
3. Add 45-60 ml (3-4 tbsp) water, sprinkling it evenly over the surface. (Uneven addition may cause blistering when the pastry is cooked.)
4. Stir in with a round-bladed knife until the mixture begins to stick together in large lumps.
5. With one hand, collect the dough mixture together to form a ball.
6. Knead lightly for a few seconds to give a firm, smooth dough. Do not overhandle the dough.
7. To roll out, sprinkle a very little flour on a working surface and the rolling pin (not on the pastry) and roll out the dough evenly in one direction only, turning it occasionally. The usual thickness is 3 mm (⅛ inch). Do not pull or stretch the pastry.
8. The pastry can be baked straight away, but it is better if allowed to 'rest' for about 30 minutes

in the tin or dish, covered with foil or greaseproof paper, in the refrigerator.
9. Bake at 200-220°C (400-425°F) mark 6-7, except where otherwise specified, until lightly browned (see individual recipes).
MAKES 225 G (8 OZ) PASTRY

NOTE: This is the classic shortcrust pastry recipe, but many people now prefer to use all butter or margarine, omitting the lard altogether.

VARIATIONS
WHOLEMEAL PASTRY
Follow the recipe and method for Shortcrust Pastry but use plain wholemeal flour instead of white. You may need a little extra water due to the greater absorbency of wholemeal flour. For a lighter result, use a mixture of half wholemeal and half white flour.

NUT PASTRY
Follow the recipe and method for Shortcrust Pastry but stir in 25 g (1 oz) very finely chopped, shelled walnuts, peanuts, cashew nuts, hazelnuts or almonds before adding the water. When using salted nuts, do not add salt to the flour.

CHEESE PASTRY
Follow the recipe and method for Shortcrust Pastry, but stir in 125 g (4 oz) finely grated Cheddar or other hard cheese and a pinch of mustard powder before adding the water.

HERB PASTRY
Follow the recipe and method for Shortcrust Pastry, but stir in 15-30 ml (1-2 level tbsp) finely chopped fresh herbs, eg parsley, sage or thyme, or 5-10 ml (1-2 tsp) dried herbs to the flour before adding the water.

SHORTCRUST PASTRY MADE IN A FOOD PROCESSOR

A food processor makes shortcrust pastry very quickly and gives good results. It is most important not to overmix the dough as a food processor works in seconds not minutes. For even 'rubbing in', turn the machine on in short bursts rather than letting it run continuously.

Make sure you know the capacity of your food processor and never overload the processor bowl. If making a large quantity of shortcrust pastry, it may be necessary to make the pastry in two batches.

Ingredients: as basic shortcrust recipe (see page 381)

1. Mix the flour and salt together in the bowl of the food processor.
2. Cut the fat into pieces and add it to the flour. Mix for a few seconds until the mixture resembles fine breadcrumbs.
3. Add 45-60 ml (3-4 tbsp) chilled water and switch on until the mixture forms a smooth dough. Roll out as for shortcrust pastry.
MAKES 100 G (4 OZ) PASTRY

RICH SHORTCRUST OR FLAN PASTRY

Rich shortcrust or flan pastry is made by the same rubbing in method as shortcrust, but the liquid used is beaten egg instead of water. It is usually sweetened with caster sugar which improves the flavour and is ideal for flan cases, small tarts and other sweet pastries. The sugar is omitted for savoury flans and tarts.

100 g (4 oz) flour
pinch of salt
75 g (3 oz) butter or block margarine and lard, diced
5 ml (1 level tsp) caster sugar (optional)
1 egg, beaten

1. Place the flour and salt in a bowl. Rub the fat into the flour as for shortcrust pastry, until the mixture resembles fine breadcrumbs. Stir in the sugar if using.
2. Add the egg, stirring with a round-bladed knife until the ingredients begin to stick together in large lumps.
3. With one hand, collect the mixture together and knead lightly for a few seconds to give a firm, smooth dough. Wrap the pastry in greaseproof paper or foil and chill in the refrigerator for at least 30 minutes before use. Roll out as for shortcrust pastry.
4. Bake at 200°C (400°F) mark 6, unless otherwise stated, until lightly browned.
MAKES 100 G (4 OZ) PASTRY

PÂTE SUCRÉE (SWEET PASTRY)

This French rich, sweet, short pastry is the best choice for Continental pâtisserie. Pâte Sucrée is thin, crisp yet melting in texture; it keeps its shape, shrinks very little and does not spread during baking. It is fairly quick and easy to make. Although it can be made in a mixing bowl, the classic way to make it is on a flat, cold surface such as marble.

100 g (4 oz) flour
pinch of salt
50 g (2 oz) caster sugar
50 g (2 oz) butter (at room temperature)
2 egg yolks

1. Sift the flour and salt on to a working surface. Make a well in the centre and add the sugar, butter and egg yolks.
2. Using the fingertips of one hand, pinch and work the sugar, butter and egg yolks together until well blended.
3. Gradually work in all the flour to bind the mixture together.
4. Knead lightly until smooth. Wrap the pastry in foil or greaseproof paper and leave to 'rest' in the refrigerator or a cool place for about 1 hour, or overnight if possible.
5. Bake at 190°C (375°F) mark 5, unless otherwise stated, until lightly browned.
MAKES 100 G (4 OZ) PASTRY

CHEESE PASTRY

There are two types and methods of making cheese pastry. The plainer version is made by the shortcrust pastry technique with grated cheese added (see page 381) and is easy to handle and less liable to crack when shaped. That type is better to use for pies, tarts and flans.

This cheese pastry is a little more difficult to make and handle; the fat and cheese are creamed together, then the flour is worked in. This type is best used for small savouries, such as pastry and cocktail appetisers and savouries. Use a hard, dry, well flavoured cheese with a 'bite', such as Cheddar, Cheshire or Leicester, and grate it finely. A pinch of dry mustard added to the flour with the salt helps to bring out the cheese taste. Another flavour which blends well with cheese pastry is a pinch of cayenne pepper.

40 g (1½ oz) butter or block margarine
40 g (1½ oz) lard or white vegetable fat
75 g (3 oz) Cheddar or other hard cheese, finely grated
100 g (4 oz) flour
pinch of salt

1. Cream the butter, lard and cheese together until soft. Gradually work in the flour and salt with a wooden spoon or a palette knife until the mixture sticks together.
2. With one hand, collect the mixture together and knead very lightly for a few seconds to give a smooth dough. Wrap in greaseproof paper or foil and leave in a cool place until required.
3. Bake at 200°C (400°F) mark 6, unless stated otherwise, until lightly browned.
MAKES 100 G (4 OZ) PASTRY

ONE STAGE SHORT PASTRY

This quick method for making pastry is completely different from the rubbed-in method for shortcrust. Soft tub margarine, water and a little of the flour are creamed together, then the remaining flour is mixed in until a dough is formed. One Stage Short Pastry can be used in any recipe using shortcrust pastry.

100 g (4 oz) soft tub margarine
175 g (6 oz) flour, sifted
15 ml (1 tbsp) chilled water
pinch of salt

1. Place the margarine, 30 ml (2 level tbsp) flour and the water in a bowl.
2. Cream with a fork for about 30 seconds until well mixed. Mix in the remaining flour with the salt to form a fairly soft dough and knead lightly until smooth. Roll out as for shortcrust pastry.
3. Bake at 190°C (375°F) mark 5 until lightly browned, or for the length of time stated in the individual shortcrust pastry recipes.
MAKES 175 G (6 OZ) PASTRY

OIL OR FORK-MIX PASTRY

Oil Pastry is very quick to make and can be used instead of shortcrust pastry. As it is naturally slightly more greasy, it is best used for savoury rather than sweet dishes. Short and flaky in texture, oil pastry should be mixed quickly and used straight away, as it dries out and is too difficult to roll if left for even a short while or chilled.

40 ml (8 tsp) vegetable oil
15 ml (1 tbsp) chilled water
100 g (4 oz) flour
pinch of salt

1. Put the oil and water into a bowl. Beat well with a fork to form an emulsion.
2. Mix the flour and salt together and gradually add to the mixture to make a dough.
3. Roll out on a floured surface or between pieces of greaseproof paper.
4. Bake at 200°C (400°F) mark 6 for the same length of time as shortcrust pastry.
MAKES 100 G (4 OZ) PASTRY

FLAKED PASTRIES

The light layered texture of flaked pastries is achieved by rolling and folding the dough to trap pockets of air between the layers of dough.
The proportion of fat to flour is much higher in all flaked pastries than shortcrust, and the methods of mixing it into the dough vary with the different types of flaked pastries. Remember to rest all flaked pastries in the refrigerator for about 30 minutes after making and again after shaping and before baking. During baking, the air expands and the fat melts and is absorbed by the flour which leaves more air spacing. This gives the pastry its characteristic flaky texture.

FLAKY PASTRY

This pastry can be used instead of puff pastry in many savoury and sweet dishes where a great rise is not needed. The fat should be of about the same consistency as the dough with which it is to be combined, which is why it is 'worked' on a plate beforehand.

225 g (8 oz) plain flour
pinch of salt
175 g (6 oz) butter or a mixture of butter and lard
120 ml (8 tbsp) chilled water and a squeeze of lemon juice
beaten egg, to glaze

Eccles Cakes

1. Mix the flour and salt together in a bowl. Soften the fat by 'working' it with a knife on a plate, then divide it into four equal portions.
2. Add one quarter of the fat to the flour and lightly rub it into the flour between finger and thumb tips until the mixture resembles fine breadcrumbs.
3. Add enough water and lemon juice, stirring with a round-bladed knife, to make a soft, elastic dough. Turn the dough on to a lightly floured surface, knead until smooth, then roll out into an oblong three times as long as it is wide.

Dot the butter and lard over the top two thirds of the rolled pastry.

4. Using a round-bladed knife, dot a second quarter of the fat over the top two thirds of the pastry in flakes, so that it looks like buttons on a card.
5. Fold the bottom third of the pastry up and the top third down, then turn it so that the folded edges are at the sides.
6. Seal the edges of the pastry by pressing with a rolling pin. Wrap the pastry in greaseproof paper and leave in the refrigerator to rest for 15 minutes. Re-roll as before and repeat twice more until the remaining fat has been used up.
7. Wrap the pastry loosely in greaseproof paper and leave it to 'rest' in the refrigerator for at least 30 minutes before using.
8. Roll out the pastry on a lightly floured work surface to 3 mm (⅛ inch) thickness and use as required. Leave to rest in the refrigerator for 30 minutes before baking. Brush the pastry with beaten egg before baking to give the characteristic glaze.
9. Bake at 200°C (400°F) mark 6, unless otherwise stated.

Rough Puff Pastry

Similar in texture to flaky pastry, rough puff can be used instead of flaky, except when even rising and appearance are particularly important. Rough puff is quicker and easier to make than puff or flaky pastry.

225 g (8 oz) plain flour
pinch of salt
75 g (3 oz) butter or block margarine, well chilled
75 g (3 oz) lard
about 150 ml (¼ pint) chilled water and a squeeze of
*   lemon juice*
beaten egg, to glaze

1. Mix the flour and salt together in a bowl. Cut the butter into 2 cm (¾ inch) cubes. Stir into the flour without breaking up the pieces.
2. Add enough water and lemon juice to mix to a fairly stiff dough using a round-bladed knife. On a lightly floured surface, roll out into an oblong three times as long as it is wide.
3. Fold the bottom third up and the top third down, then turn the pastry so that the folded edges are at the sides. Seal the ends of the pastry with a rolling pin. Wrap the pastry in greaseproof paper and chill for 15 minutes.
4. Repeat this rolling and folding process three more times, turning the dough so that the folded edge is on the left hand side each time. Wrap the pastry in greaseproof paper and chill for 30 minutes.
5. Roll out the pastry to a 3 mm (⅛ inch) thickness and use as required. Leave to 'rest' in the refrigerator for 30 minutes before baking. Brush with beaten egg before baking to give the characteristic glaze.
6. Bake at 220°C (425°F) mark 7.

 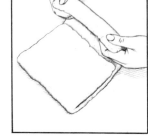

Add butter to the flour.   *Fold up bottom third.*

Puff Pastry

The richest of all the pastries, puff requires patience, practice and very light handling. Whenever possible it should be made the day before use. It is not practical to make in a quantity with less than 450 g (1 lb) flour weight.
    This quantity is equivalent to two 368 g (13 oz) packets of frozen ready-made puff pastry.

450 g (1 lb) strong white flour
pinch of salt
450 g (1 lb) butter or block margarine
300 ml (½ pint) chilled water
15 ml (1 tbsp) lemon juice
beaten egg, to glaze

1. Mix the flour and salt together in a bowl. Cut off 50 g (2 oz) of butter and flatten the remaining butter with a rolling pin to a slab 2 cm (¾ inch) thick.
2. Cut the 50 g (2 oz) butter into small pieces, add to the flour and rub in. Using a round-bladed knife, stir in enough water and lemon juice to make a soft, elastic dough.
3. Quickly knead the dough until smooth and shape into a round. Cut through half the depth in the shape of a cross. Open out to form a star.
4. Roll out, keeping the centre four times as thick as the flaps. Place the slab of butter in the centre of the dough and fold the flaps over the slab envelope-style.
5. Press gently with a rolling pin and roll out into a rectangle measuring about 40 x 20 cm (16 x 8 inches).
6. Fold the bottom third up and the top third down, keeping the edges straight. Seal edges.
7. Wrap the pastry in greaseproof paper and leave in the refrigerator to 'rest' for 30 minutes. Put the pastry on a lightly floured work surface with the folded edges to the sides and repeat the rolling, folding and resting sequence five times.
8. Shape the pastry as required, then leave to 'rest' in the refrigerator for 30 minutes before baking. Brush with beaten egg.
9. Bake at 220°C (425°F) mark 7, for about 15 minutes on its own or longer if filled, except where otherwise specified.

MAKING BOUCHÉES

1. Roll out ½ quantity Puff Pastry (see page 385), 5 mm (¼ inch) thick, or use a 368 g (13 oz) packet of puff pastry, rolled thinner. Using a 5 cm (2 inch) plain cutter, cut out 20-25 rounds and put them on a dampened baking sheet.
2. Cut part-way through the centre of each round with a 4 cm (1¼ inch) plain cutter.
3. Glaze the tops with beaten egg and bake in the oven at 230°C (450°F) mark 8 for 10 minutes, until golden brown.
4. Remove the lid and soft pastry from the centre and cool the cases on a rack. Before serving, reheat in the oven at 180°C (350°F) mark 4 for about 15 minutes, then fill with a hot savoury sauce, or fill cold bouchées with cold sauce and reheat as above.
5. Individual vol-au-vents are made in a similar way but are cut with a 7.5 cm (3 inch) plain cutter and a 5 cm (2 inch) plain cutter is used for marking the lid.

MAKING A LARGE VOL-AU-VENT

1. Roll out ½ quantity Puff Pastry, 2.5 cm (1 inch) thick, or use a 368 g (13 oz) packet of puff pastry, rolled thinner. Put on to a dampened baking sheet and cut into an oval or large round to take in nearly all the pastry. Try not to cut nearer than 1 cm (½ inch) to the edge of the slab of pastry.
2. With a small knife mark an oval or round 1-2 cm (½-¾ inch) inside the larger one, to form a lid, cutting about halfway through the pastry.
3. Brush the top with beaten egg. Bake in the oven at 230°C (450°F) mark 8 for 30-35 minutes, covering the pastry with greaseproof paper when it is sufficiently brown. Remove the lid, scoop out any soft pastry inside and dry out the case in the oven for a further 5-10 minutes.
4. Serve hot or cold, filled with a savoury sauce as suggested for Bouchées (see left), or make a cold sweet by filling with soft fruit, peaches or apricots and whipped cream.

Various Pastries

This section includes the pastries like suetcrust, hot water crust, choux and filo that are not made by either the traditional rubbing in or flaked pastry methods.

HOT WATER CRUST PASTRY

This pastry is used to make savoury raised pies such as Veal and Ham Pie and Game Pie. It is mixed with boiling water, which makes it pliable enough to mould into a raised pie that will hold its shape as it cools and during the baking. It is a 'strong' pastry, fit to withstand the extra handling that it must receive during the shaping and also the weight of the savoury filling it must hold.

Care must be taken when moulding hot water crust pastry to ensure that there are no cracks through which the meat juices can escape during baking. Keep the part of the pastry that is not actually being used covered with a cloth or an upturned bowl, to prevent it hardening before use. If you do not wish to 'raise' the pie by hand (see page 378), you can use a cake tin. For a more elaborate raised pie, you can buy a special metal mould, made in two parts, joined by a hinge, which can easily be removed when the pie is cooked.

450 g (1 lb) plain flour
10 ml (2 level tsp) salt
100 g (4 oz) lard or white vegetable fat
250 ml (9 fl oz) water

1. Mix the flour and salt together in a bowl. Make a well in the centre. In a small saucepan, melt the lard in the water, then bring to the boil and pour into the well.
2. Working quickly, beat the mixture with a wooden spoon to form a fairly soft dough.
3. Use one hand to pinch the dough lightly together and knead until smooth and silky.
4. Cover with greaseproof paper or a damp tea towel. Leave in a warm place to rest for 20-30 minutes so the dough becomes elastic and easy to work. Use as required but do not allow it to cool. See page 378 for the method of shaping a raised pie hand and in a cake tin.
5. Bake at 220°C (425°F) mark 7, reducing to 180°C (350°F) mark 4 (see individual recipes).

SUETCRUST PASTRY

This pastry may be used for both sweet and savoury basin puddings, roly-poly puddings and dumplings. It can be steamed, boiled or baked; the first two methods are the most satisfactory, as baked suetcrust pastry is inclined to be hard. Suetcrust pastry is quick and easy to make, and should be light and spongy in texture – the correct mixing, quick light handling and long, slow cooking will achieve this. For a lighter texture or if using wholemeal flour, replace 50 g (2 oz) of the flour with 50 g (2 oz) fresh breadcrumbs.

225 g (8 oz) self raising flour
2.5 ml (½ level tsp) salt
100 g (4 oz) shredded suet
about 150 ml (¼ pint) chilled water

1. Mix the flour, salt and suet together in a bowl.
2. Using a round-bladed knife, stir in enough water to give a light, elastic dough. Knead very lightly until smooth.
3. Roll out to a 5 mm (¼ inch) thickness and use as required.
4. Steaming or boiling basin and roly-poly puddings takes about 2-4 hours, depending on filling and size. Dumplings cooked in simmering liquid take about 25 minutes.

LINING A PUDDING
BASIN WITH SUETCRUST PASTRY

It is important to use the correct size of heat-proof basin given in a recipe. It should allow a space of about 1 cm (½ inch) at the top. Always grease the basin to prevent the pastry from sticking and if you do not have a steamer cook the pudding on a trivet in a saucepan at least 5 cm (2 inch) wider than the diameter of the basin, in boiling water that comes halfway up the side of the basin.

1. For a 1.7 litre (3 pint) pudding basin, roll out the pastry to a round about 35 cm (14 inches) in diameter. Using a sharp knife cut out one quarter of the dough and reserve. Lightly grease the pudding basin.
2. Dust the top surface of the large piece of pastry with flour and fold in half, then in half again. Lift the pastry into the basin, unfold, press into the base and up the sides, taking care to seal the join well. The pastry should overlap the top of the basin by about 2.5 cm (1 inch).

Jam Roly-poly (see page 331) made with Suetcrust Pastry

3. Spoon the filling into the lined pudding basin, taking care not to puncture the pastry lining. Gently spread out the filling so it is evenly distributed.
4. Roll out the remaining one quarter of pastry to a round 2.5 cm (1 inch) wider than the top of the basin. Dampen the exposed edge of pastry lining the basin.
5. Lift the round of pastry on top of the filling. Push the pastry edges together to seal.
6. Cut a piece of greaseproof paper and a piece of foil large enough to cover the basin. Place them together and pleat across the middle to allow for expansion. Lightly grease the greaseproof side and put them over the pudding with the greaseproof side down.
7. Tie the lid securely on to the basin, running the string just under the rim. Make a string handle across the basin top.
8. Bring a large pan of water to the boil. Fit a steamer over the pan, put the pudding inside and cover. Steam the pudding for the time specified in the recipe.

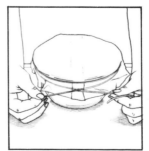

Securely tie pleated greaseproof paper and foil over the pudding basin.

CHOUX PASTRY

This light, crisp-textured pastry is used for making sweet and savoury éclairs, cream puffs, aigrettes and gougère. As long as the recipe instructions are strictly adhered to, choux pastry will always give good results. Always assemble the ingredients together beforehand, as all the flour needs to be added quickly as soon as the mixture has come to the boil.

Raw choux paste is too soft and sticky to be rolled out and is, therefore, piped or spooned on to a dampened baking sheet for baking. During baking, the moisture in the dough turns to steam and puffs up the mixture leaving the centre hollow. Thorough cooking is important; if insufficiently cooked, the choux may collapse when taken from the oven and there will be uncooked pastry in the centre to scoop out.

When the cooked choux has cooled and dried out, it can be filled with whipped cream or a savoury filling. Choux pastry can also be deep fried – pipe or spoon it directly into hot oil.

65 g (2½ oz) plain or strong white flour
50 g (2 oz) butter or block margarine
150 ml (¼ pint) water
2 eggs, lightly beaten (use size 2 when using an
 electric mixer)

1. Sift the flour on to a plate or piece of paper. Put the fat and water together in a saucepan, heat gently until the fat has melted, then bring to the boil. Remove the pan from the heat. Tip the flour at once into the hot liquid. Beat thoroughly with a wooden spoon.
2. Continue beating the mixture until it is smooth and forms a ball in the centre of the pan (take care not to overbeat or the mixture will become fatty). Leave the mixture to cool for a minute or two.
3. Beat in the eggs a little at a time, adding only just enough to give a piping consistency. It is important to beat the mixture vigorously at this stage to trap in as much air as possible. A hand held electric mixer is ideal for this purpose. Continue beating until the mixture develops an obvious sheen and then use as required.
4. Bake in an oven at 200-220°C (400-425°F) mark 6-7. Immediately after the choux pastry is removed from the oven it should be pierced to allow steam to escape.

VARIATIONS
To make a gougère, pipe or spoon the choux pastry into a ring and bake on a baking sheet or in an ovenproof dish. It can also be flavoured with finely grated cheese. Choux pastry can be baked and then filled with a savoury mixture such as fish, kidneys, chicken or ham (see Smoked Haddock Gougère, page 80).

The most elaborate use of choux pastry is the *croquembouche* – the table centrepiece of a French wedding or anniversary celebration. Small choux buns are stuck together with a caramel syrup to form a pyramid and then decorated with either spun sugar or sugared almonds.

PIPING CHOUX PASTRY
1. To fill a piping bag, usually fitted with a plain 1 cm (½ inch) nozzle, place it in a tall jug and turn back the open end over the jug rim. Spoon the pastry mixture into the bag and squeeze it down to eliminate air bubbles.
2. When making éclairs, it may help to mark evenly-spaced lines on the baking sheet with the end of a wooden spoon as a guide for piping.
3. Hold the piping bag in one hand and, with the thumb and one finger of your other hand on the nozzle to guide it, press out the pastry. When the required length is reached, cut off the paste with a dampened knife. Choux puffs and profiteroles can either be piped or spooned into mounds on the baking sheet.

Place the piping bag in a tall jug, turning the open end over the rim.

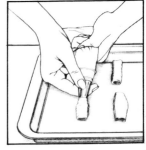

Use one hand to guide the nozzle while piping choux pastry.

FILO (OR STRUDEL) PASTRY

Filo or Phyllo is a pastry of wafer-like thinness from the Middle East which is used for both savoury and sweet pastries, such as Baklava. It is identical to strudel pastry which originated in Europe and is used for the popular Apple Strudel. Filo or strudel pastry is fairly difficult and time consuming to make and for this reason ready-made filo pastry is normally used. It is now widely available and gives excellent results.

Unlike most pastries, filo is made with warm ingredients and, instead of light handling, it has to be kneaded and beaten. The dough is kneaded vigorously to enable the gluten in the flour to develop strength so the pastry can be stretched into a very thin, resilient sheet. For the same reason, strong plain flour is used as it yields more gluten to help produce an elastic dough. The thin sheet is either spread with a filling and rolled or folded, or it is cut into rectangles and stacked with a filling in between.

It is essential to keep filo pastry covered as you work to prevent it from drying out.

225 g (8 oz) strong white flour
2.5 ml (½ level tsp) salt
1 egg, lightly beaten
30 ml (2 tbsp) vegetable oil
1.25 ml (¼ level tsp) lemon juice
25g (1 oz) butter, melted

1. Mix the flour and salt together in a large bowl. Make a well in the centre and pour in the egg, oil and lemon juice. Stirring with a fork, gradually add 75 ml (5 tbsp) lukewarm water or enough to make a soft, sticky dough.
2. Work the dough in the bowl until it leaves the sides. Turn out on to a lightly floured surface and knead for 15 minutes. The dough should feel smooth.
3. Form it into a ball, place on a cloth and cover with a warmed bowl. Leave to 'rest' in a warm place for 30 minutes.
4. Place the ball of dough on a lightly floured clean cotton cloth and roll out into a rectangle about 3 mm (⅛ inch) thick, lifting and turning to prevent it sticking to the cloth.
5. Brush the top of the dough with a little melted butter. Gently stretch the dough by carefully lifting it on the backs of the hands and fingertips, and pulling it from the centre to the outside, trying to keep it in a rectangle.
6. Continue lifting and stretching the dough until it becomes paper thin and the rectangle measures no less than 75 x 50 cm (30 x 20 inches). Trim off uneven thick edges with scissors or a sharp knife.
7. Leave the dough on the cloth to dry and 'rest' for about 15 minutes before lifting off carefully.
8. Bake at 190°C (375°F) mark 5, except where otherwise specified, until lightly browned.

APRICOT AND PISTACHIO ROLLS

400 g (14 oz) 'no-soak' dried apricots
1 bay leaf
grated rind and juice of 1 orange
15 ml (1 tbsp) Grand Marnier
50 g (2 oz) butter, melted
pinch of freshly grated nutmeg
3 sheets filo pastry, about 45 x 28 cm (18 x 11 inches)
25 g (1 oz) pistachio nuts, skinned and roughly chopped
a little icing sugar

1. Place the apricots in a bowl, cover with cold water and leave to soak overnight. Drain, reserving the soaking liquid.
2. Place the apricots in a saucepan with the bay leaf and 150 ml (¼ pint) soaking liquid. Bring to the boil and simmer for 2-3 minutes until most of the liquid has evaporated. Discard the bay leaf. Stir in the orange rind, 30 ml (2 tbsp) orange juice and Grand Marnier. Purée in a blender or food processor and allow to cool.
3. Mix the melted butter with the nutmeg. Halve the filo pastry sheets widthways and separate into 6 single sheets. Brush lightly with half the melted butter. Divide the apricot mixture between the pastry sheets, placing it in a line along one of the shorter edges but leaving about 2.5 cm (1 inch) at each side of the mixture.
4. Fold the sides of the pastry over slightly, then carefully roll up to form thin rolls. Place on a lightly oiled baking sheet and brush with the remaining melted butter. Sprinkle with pistachio nuts and dust lightly with icing sugar. Bake in the oven at 200°C (400°F) mark 6 for 20-25 minutes, or until golden brown and crisp.
5. Serve hot with cream or yogurt.
SERVES 6

ECCLES CAKES

212 g (7½ oz) packet frozen puff pastry, thawed, or
  ¼ quantity Puff Pastry (see page 385)
25 g (1 oz) butter or block margarine, softened
25 g (1 oz) soft dark brown sugar
25 g (1 oz) finely chopped mixed peel
50 g (2 oz) currants
caster sugar, to sprinkle

1. Roll out the pastry on a lightly floured surface and cut into eight to ten 9 cm (3½ inch) rounds.
2. Mix the butter, sugar, mixed peel and currants in a bowl.
3. Place 5 ml (1 tsp) of the fruit and butter mixture in the centre of each pastry round. Draw up the edges of each pastry round to enclose the filling, then re-shape.

Gently fold the edges of the pastry so the filling is completely and securely enclosed.

4. Turn each round over and roll lightly until the currants just show through. Prick the top of each with a fork. Leave to 'rest' for about 10 minutes in a cool place.
5. Transfer the rounds to a dampened baking sheet. Bake in the oven at 230°C (450°F) mark 8 for about 15 minutes until golden. Transfer to a wire rack to cool. Sprinkle with sugar while warm.
MAKES 8-10

PALMIERS

368 g (13 oz) packet frozen puff pastry, thawed, or
  ½ quantity Puff Pastry (see page 385)
caster sugar for dredging
150 ml (5 fl oz) double cream

1. Roll out the pastry on a lightly floured surface to a 30 x 25 cm (12 x 10 inches) rectangle.
2. Dredge with caster sugar. Fold the long sides of the puff pastry halfway towards the centre.
3. Dredge with more caster sugar and fold again, taking the side right to the centre.
4. Dredge with sugar again, and fold in half lengthways to make one long strip of eight

thicknesses of pastry. Press lightly.
5. Cut across the pastry length into 24 equal sized slices. Place the palmiers on a dampened baking sheet, cut-side down. Flatten slightly with a palette knife or the palm of your hand.
6. Bake in the oven at 220°C (425°F) mark 7 for 8 minutes, until golden brown. Turn each one over and bake for a further 4 minutes. Transfer to a wire rack and leave to cool.
7. Whip the cream with a little caster sugar. Sandwich the palmiers together with the cream before serving. Sprinkle with caster sugar.
MAKES 12

CREAM HORNS

212 g (7½ oz) packet frozen puff pastry, thawed, or
  ¼ quantity Puff Pastry (see page 385)
beaten egg, to glaze
raspberry jam
150 ml (5 fl oz) double cream
icing sugar, to dredge

1. Roll out the pastry on a lightly floured surface to a strip measuring 66 x 10 cm (26 x 4 inches). Cut the pastry lengthways with a sharp knife into eight 1 cm (½ inch) ribbons.
2. Grease eight cream horn tins. Moisten one edge of each pastry strip and wind each around a horn tin, starting at the tip, overlapping by 3 mm (⅛ inch) and finishing neatly on the

underside. The pastry should not overlap the metal rim. Brush with beaten egg.
3. Dampen a baking sheet and arrange the cream horns on it, join-side down. Bake in the oven at 220°C (425°F) mark 7 for 10 minutes, until golden.
4. Cool for a few minutes, then carefully twist each tin, holding the pastry lightly in the other hand, to ease it out of the pastry horn. Leave the horns for about 30 minutes to cool completely.
5. When cold, fill the tip of each horn with a little jam. Whip the cream until stiff and fill the horns down to the jam. Sift the icing sugar over the cream horns.
MAKES 8

ÉCLAIRS

1 quantity Choux Pastry (see page 388)
300 ml (10 fl oz) double cream
125 g (4 oz.) plain chocolate

1. Dampen a baking sheet. Put the choux pastry into a piping bag fitted with a medium plain nozzle and pipe 9 cm (3½ inches) long fingers on to the baking sheet. Trim with a wet knife.
2. Bake in the oven at 200°C (400°F) mark 6 for about 35 minutes, until crisp and golden.
3. Make a slit down the side of each bun with a sharp, pointed knife to release the steam, then transfer to a wire rack and leave for 20-30 minutes to cool completely.
4. Just before serving, whip the double cream until stiff and use it to fill the éclairs.
5. Break the chocolate into a bowl and place over simmering water. Stir until melted. Pour into a wide shallow bowl. Dip in the tops of the filled éclairs, drawing each one across the surface of the chocolate to coat evenly.
MAKES 12

Éclairs

FRESH FRUIT TARTLETS

225 g (8 oz) pâte sucrée pastry (see page 382)
300 ml (½ pint) crème pâtissière (see page 210)
125 g (4 oz) dark, well-flavoured cherries, stoned and halved
125 g (4 oz) black grapes, halved and seeded
125 g (4 oz) green grapes, halved and seeded
2 kiwi fruit, peeled and sliced
FOR THE APRICOT GLAZE
225 g (8 oz) apricot conserve
15 ml (1 tbsp) Kirsch
FOR THE REDCURRANT GLAZE
125 g (4 oz) redcurrant jelly

1. Roll out the pastry on a lightly floured surface and cut out twelve 12 cm (5 inch) circles with a plain cutter. Use to line twelve 10 cm (4 inch) tartlet tins. Trim the edges and prick the base of each tartlet with a fork, then place the lined tins on baking sheets and chill for at least 30 minutes.
2. Bake blind (see page 380) in the oven at 200°C (400°F) mark 6 for 20-25 minutes until

very lightly browned. Allow the cases to cool a little in their tins, then carefully transfer to a wire rack to cool.
3. To make the apricot glaze, put the jam and Kirsch in a saucepan and heat gently until softened, then simmer for 1 minute. Sieve, then brush evenly over the inside of each pastry case. Reserve the remaining glaze.
4. Divide the crème pâtissière equally between the pastry cases and spread it evenly. Arrange the cherries in three of the cases, the grapes in six, and the kiwi fruit in the remaining ones.
5. Reheat the remaining apricot glaze until boiling, then carefully brush it over the green grapes and the kiwi fruit to glaze them evenly. Heat the redcurrant jelly until boiling, then carefully brush it over the cherries and the black grapes. Serve as soon as possible.
MAKES 12

VARIATION
Sprinkle the glazed tartlets with finely chopped nuts or a few toasted almonds.

CAKES

Few can resist a freshly baked homemade cake or a batch of warm scones for tea. In this chapter there are cakes and bakes for every occasion from small cakes, teabreads and scones to irresistible gâteaux and rich fruit cakes for weddings and other special occasions. There is also information on decorating and piping techniques, plus recipes for all kinds of icings.

INGREDIENTS FOR CAKE MAKING

FLOUR

A wide range of different types of flour is available (see page 448) and the difference between them is largely due to the varying gluten content. Gluten is an elastic, sticky substance formed when the flour is moistened. It sets when heated, trapping air in the mixture and giving it a light texture.

For cake making, soft flour with a low gluten content is best. It is starchy and absorbs fat well to give a light, soft texture. Soft flour is either plain or self raising. The latter is simply plain flour with added raising agents.

SELF RAISING FLOUR is popular because it eliminates errors; the raising agents are already evenly blended throughout the flour.

PLAIN FLOUR can be used with a raising agent and the raising agent can be varied to suit individual recipes. If you only have plain flour, use 225 g (8 oz) flour and 15 ml (1 level tbsp) baking powder to replace self raising flour in scones; 10 ml (2 level tsp) baking powder for a plain cake mixture, eg rock buns; and 5 ml (1 level tsp) for a rich fruit cake mixture. Sift the flour and baking powder together before use to ensure even blending.

WHOLEMEAL FLOUR can be used in some cake recipes. Both plain and self raising types are available. They give a coarse, dense texture and nutty flavour. Alternatively, a mixture of plain white and wholemeal flour can be used.

It is worth sifting wholemeal flour as any air that can be incorporated will give a better result. Sift the flour, then tip the bran from the sieve back into the bowl. Stir well.

SUGAR AND OTHER SWEETENERS

Sugar is an important ingredient in all cakes and is essential in sponges. Brown sugars and other kinds of sweeteners can be used to add variety and extra flavour.

CASTER SUGAR is the one most commonly used in cakes, especially for creamed mixtures and whisked sponge mixtures. It has a small regular grain size and blends easily to give an even texture.

GRANULATED SUGAR produces a creamed mixture which is slightly reduced in volume, with a reasonably good texture, apart from a slight grittiness and sometimes a speckly appearance. For rubbed-in mixtures, granulated sugar is quite acceptable.

ICING SUGAR is the finest of all sugars. It is not generally used for basic cake mixtures as it produces a poor volume and hard crust. It is used for icing and decorating cakes.

SOFT BROWN SUGAR whether dark or light, gives more flavour than white sugar and has a slightly finer grain. It imparts a caramel taste. When used to replace caster sugar in sandwich cakes, the volume is good. Soft brown sugars cream well.

DEMERARA SUGAR is even coarser grained than granulated sugar, which it can replace in rubbed-in mixtures. It is more suitable for making cakes by the melting method, such as gingerbreads, where heat and moisture help to dissolve it. It is unsatisfactory for creamed mixtures, because its large crystals do not break down during mixing.

BARBADOS SUGAR is a very dark, unrefined sugar of a similar colour to treacle. Molasses, often known as black Barbados or demerara molasses is the least refined and is very dark and sticky.

Too strong in flavour for light cake mixtures, Barbados sugar helps to give a good flavour and colour to rich fruit cakes and gingerbreads. You can modify the flavour by using it half-and-half with white sugar.

GOLDEN SYRUP gives a special flavour which is particularly good with spices.

TREACLE is a dark syrup, which is not as sweet as golden syrup. A little added to rich fruit cakes gives a good dark colour and distinctive flavour; it is also a traditional ingredient for gingerbreads and for the making of malt bread.

HONEY is used in some recipes. It absorbs and retains moisture, keeping cakes and teabreads fresh for longer.

MALT EXTRACT is a thick, sticky brown syrup produced from barley grains.

FAT

BUTTER AND MARGARINE are the commonest fats used in cake making, but lard, blended white vegetable fat, dripping and oil may be used. Butter and block margarine are usually interchangeable, though butter gives a special flavour. The degree of hardness of block margarine varies from brand to brand; some are sold specifically for baking purposes and have been manufactured to cream easily.

As a rule, butter and firm margarine should not be taken direct from the refrigerator; leave them at room temperature for 30 minutes before use. For best results if the fat to be used in a creamed mixture is firm, beat it alone, then add the sugar and cream together.

SOFT TUB MARGARINES are best suited to one-stage recipes (see page 394) but it is possible to experiment with using them in other recipes, though the texture will be different.

OIL is being more often used today, but specially proportioned recipes are needed.

EGGS

These may be used either as a raising agent or to bind the mixture. Use size 2 or 3 eggs, unless otherwise stated.

LIQUID

Moisture is required for the raising agents in the mixture to work.

MILK AND WATER are the most usual liquids used but brewed tea, cider, fruit juice and beer are included in certain specific recipes, or may be used to taste.

BUTTERMILK is used in certain kinds of scones.

RAISING AGENTS

BAKING POWDER is the most commonly used. It usually consists of bicarbonate of soda and an acid-reacting chemical such as cream of tartar, and, when moistened, these react together to give off carbon dioxide. Flour contains gluten, which holds this gas in the form of tiny bubbles when it is wet.

Since all gases expand when heated, these tiny bubbles formed throughout the mixture become larger during the baking, and thus the cake rises. The heat dries and sets the gluten and so the bubbles are held, giving the cake its characteristic light texture.

However, cake mixtures are capable of holding only a certain amount of gas, and if too much raising agent is used the cake rises very well at first, but then collapses, and a heavy, close texture is the final result.

BICARBONATE OF SODA AND CREAM OF TARTAR combined may be used in some recipes to replace baking powder. It is usually in the proportion of one part bicarbonate of soda to two parts cream of tartar.

EGGS By including whisked egg in a cake mixture, air is used as a raising agent, instead of carbon dioxide. When a high proportion of egg is used and the mixture is whisked, as in sponge cakes, very little – if any – other raising agent is needed to obtain the desired result.

In creamed mixtures also, the eggs are beaten in and – as long as the correct proportion of egg is used and the mixture is well beaten – little additional raising agent is needed. In plain cakes, where beaten egg is added together with the liquid, the egg helps to bind the mixture, but it does not act as the main raising agent.

SPICES AND FLAVOURINGS

SPICES which are ready mixed are handy for general flavouring, since they are carefully blended, but for some recipes it's better to have individual spices such as cinnamon, mace and nutmeg. Spices always taste better when freshly ground, or grated in the case of nutmeg.

CAKE FLAVOURINGS are available in a variety of flavours such as coffee, rum, almond and vanilla. They are usually concentrated and should be used sparingly.

NATURAL FLAVOURINGS like lemon or orange, are the most pleasant to use whenever practical. Remember, when using the rind of any citrus fruit, to grate only lightly, so as to remove just the zest – the white pith imparts a bitter flavour.

FRUIT, NUTS AND PEEL

FRUIT: Use good quality dried fruits; if necessary, leave them to plump up in hot water, drain and dry off. You can buy them ready-washed, but it is wise to give them a good looking over. Wash any excess syrup from glacé cherries before use and thoroughly dry.

PEEL: Buy 'caps' of candied orange and lemon peel and cut to the required size or use ready-mixed chopped peel. Ready-cut peel may need chopping into smaller pieces.

NUTS: When nuts are called for in a recipe, check before you start to see whether they are to be blanched or unblanched, whole, split, flaked, chopped or ground. Nibbed, ready chopped nuts are handy, but a blender or food processor will produce chopped or ground nuts.

CAKE DECORATIONS

See page 424 for ingredients for cake decorations.

CAKE MAKING METHODS

RUBBING-IN METHOD

'Rubbing in' is a literal description of the method: the fat is lightly 'worked' into the flour between the fingers and thumbs until the mixture resembles fine breadcrumbs.

Some air is incorporated during this process, which helps to make the cake light, but the main raising agents are chemical. The proportion of fat to flour is half or less.

Add the liquid, using just enough to bring the mixture to the right consistency: too much liquid can cause a heavy, doughy texture and insufficient liquid results in a dry cake. The mixture should drop easily from the spoon when the handle is gently tapped against the side of the bowl. For small cakes and buns that are baked on a flat baking sheet, the mixture should be stiff enough to hold its shape without spreading too much during baking. A stiff consistency describes a mixture which will cling to the spoon.

Because they are low in fat, cakes made by the rubbing-in method do not keep well. They are best eaten the day they are made.

CREAMING METHOD

Rich cakes are made by the creaming method. The fat and sugar are beaten together until as pale and fluffy as whipped cream, the eggs are beaten in and the flour is then folded in. In some recipes the egg whites are whisked separately and folded in with the flour.

You need a mixing bowl large enough to accommodate vigorous beating without any danger of the ingredients overflowing. If beating by hand, use a wooden spoon and warm the bowl first to make the process easier.

Scrape the mixture down from the sides of the mixing bowl from time to time to ensure no sugar crystals are left. An electric mixer or electric hand whisk is a time and labour-saving alternative to creaming by hand, but remember that it should not be used for incorporating the flour.

Use eggs at room temperature and beat thoroughly after each addition to reduce the risk of the mixture curdling. (A mixture that curdles holds less air and produces a heavy dense cake.)

As an extra precaution against the mixture curdling, add a spoonful of the sifted flour with the second and every following addition of egg and beat thoroughly. To keep the mixture light, fold in the remaining flour gradually, using a metal spoon.

ONE-STAGE METHOD

The one-stage method is based on soft tub margarine and this type of cake is wonderfully quick and easy to prepare. There is no need for any creaming or rubbing in: all the ingredients are simply beaten together with a wooden spoon for 2-3 minutes, until well blended and slightly glossy.

This method is also ideal for making cakes in an electric mixer or food processor but take care to avoid overbeating.

Self raising flour is invariably used – often with the addition of a little extra baking powder to boost the rise. You can use either caster or soft brown sugar for these quick cakes because their fine crystals dissolve easily.

These cakes are similar to those made by the creaming method, but their texture is more open and they do not keep as well. Wrap them in foil as soon as they are cold to prevent them going stale.

MELTING METHOD

Gingerbreads and other cakes made by the melting method have a deliciously moist and sticky texture.

The inviting texture and rich dark colour of these cakes are due to the high proportion of sugary ingredients, including liquid sweeteners such as syrup or black treacle. To ensure the liquid sweetener is easily incorporated, it is warmed with the fat and sugar until blended and then added to the dry ingredients together with any eggs and the liquid.

Bicarbonate of soda is often used to raise these cakes – it reacts with natural acids present in liquid sweeteners. Spices are frequently added to enhance the flavour and also counteract the faintly bitter taste of bicarbonate of soda.

Measure the liquid sweetener carefully; too much can cause a heavy, sunken cake. Put the saucepan on the scales, set the dial to zero, then spoon in the required amount of syrup or treacle, or weigh the pan, then add the sweetener until the scales register the weight of the pan plus the required weight of syrup. Warm it very gently, just until the sugar has dissolved and the fat has melted. If allowed to boil, the mixture will become an unusable toffee-like mass.

Allow the mixture to cool slightly before pouring it on to the dry ingredients, or it will begin to cook the flour and a hard tough cake will result. The blended mixture should have the consistency of heavy batter; it can be poured into the prepared tin and will find its own level.

Most cakes made by the melting method should be stored for a day or so before cutting, to allow the crust to soften and give the flavour time to mellow.

WHISKING METHOD

The whisking method produces the lightest of all cakes. The classic sponge is light and feathery and is made by whisking together eggs and caster sugar, then folding in the flour. There is no fat in the mixture, and the cake rises simply because of the air incorporated during whisking. For an even lighter cake, the egg yolks and sugar can be whisked together, with the whites whisked separately and folded in afterwards.

Because they have no fat they always need a filling, and do not keep well. Bake a sponge the day you wish to eat it.

A moister version of the whisked sponge is a Genoese sponge. This is also made by the whisking method, but melted butter is added with the flour. This gives a delicate sponge, lighter than a Victoria sandwich, but with a moister texture than the plain whisked sponge, and a more delicious rich and buttery taste.

When adding melted butter, make sure it is just liquid and pour into the mixture around the sides of the bowl and fold in very lightly. Don't try to substitute margarine for butter in this recipe or the flavour and texture will be lost. A Genoese sponge keeps better than a plain whisked sponge.

To make a really good sponge, the eggs and sugar must be whisked until thick enough to leave a trail when the whisk is lifted from the

Black Forest Gâteau (see page 416)

surface. If you use a rotary whisk or a hand-held electric mixer, place the bowl over a saucepan of hot water to speed the thickening process. When whisking in an electric table top mixer, additional heat is not required.

Do not let the bottom of the bowl touch the water or the mixture will become too hot. When the mixture is really thick and double in volume, take the bowl off the heat and continue to whisk until it is cool.

Add the flour carefully. Sift it first, then add a little at a time to the whisked mixture and fold it in until evenly blended. Do not stir or you will break the air bubbles and the cake will not rise.

Cakes Made Using Oil

Cakes made using oil (corn oil, for example) are very easy to mix and very successful. When using oil for making sandwich cakes, it is essential to add an extra raising agent or to whisk the egg whites until stiff and fold them into the mixture just before baking. This counteracts the heaviness of the cake that sometimes occurs when oil is used.

CAKE TINS

Choose good-quality, strong cake tins in a variety of shapes and sizes. Non-stick surfaces clean most easily and are particularly useful in small awkwardly shaped tins. Some cake tins have a loose bottom or a loosening device to make it easier to remove the cake.

Use the size of tin specified in the recipe. Using too large a tin will tend to give a pale, flat and shrunken-looking cake; cakes baked in too small a tin will bulge over and lose their contours. If you do not have the tin specified, choose a slightly larger one. The mixture will be shallower and will take less time to cook, so test 5-10 minutes early.

FLAN RINGS AND TINS come in many forms. Round tins with plain or fluted sides and removable bases are primarily for pastry flan cases. For sponge flans, use a special flan tin with a raised base.

LOAF TINS are used for cakes as well as bread. The most useful sizes are 900 ml (1½ pint)/450 g (1 lb) and 1. 7 litre (3 pint)/900 g (2 lb).

SANDWICH TINS are shallower round tins with straight sides for making sandwich and layer cakes. They come in a range of sizes: 18-25 cm (7-10 inches). A *moule a manqué* tin is a deep sandwich tin with sloping sides.

SMALL CAKE TINS AND MOULDS are usually called patty tins or bun tins; they come in sheets of six, nine or twelve, or individually. There are shapes for buns, sponge fingers, madeleines, etc.

SPRING-RELEASE TINS or springform tins come complete with seperate loose bottoms.

STANDARD CAKE TINS: For everyday use, 15 cm (6 inch), 18 cm (7 inch) and 20 cm (8 inch) tins are adequate; for celebration cakes you may need larger sizes that come in a variety of shapes.

PREPARING TINS

Follow the manufacturer's special directions regarding non-stick (silicone-finished) tins, which do not usually require greasing or lining.

Greasing

When greasing cake tins, brush lightly with melted margarine or butter (preferably unsalted). They may also be dredged with flour as an additional safeguard against sticking; sprinkle with a little flour in the tin and shake until coated, then shake out any surplus.

For fatless sponges, use a half-and-half mixture of flour and caster sugar. You can also do this to a sponge flan tin for a crisper crust.

Lining

With most cakes it is necessary to line the tins with greaseproof paper, which is usually greased before the mixture is put in, or with non-stick baking parchment, which does not require greasing, and can be used several times.

For a Victoria sandwich cake mixture, it is sufficient to line just the base of the tin. For rich mixtures and fruit cakes, line the whole tin. The paper is usually doubled to prevent the outside of the cake from over-browning and drying out. With the extra rich fruit mixtures used for wedding and other formal cakes, which require a long cooking time, it is also advisable to pin a double strip of thick brown paper or newspaper around the outside of the tin, to help prevent the outside of the cake overcooking.

TO LINE A DEEP TIN: Cut a piece (or 2 pieces, if necessary) of greaseproof paper long enough to reach around the tin and overlap slightly, and high enough to extend about 2.5 cm (1 inch) above the top edge. Fold up the bottom edge of the strip about 2.5 cm (1 inch), creasing it firmly, then open out and snip into this folded portion with scissors; this snipped edge enables the paper band to fit a square, oblong, round or oval tin neatly.

Grease the inside of the paper. Place the strip in position in the greased tin, with the cut edge flat against the base. In a rectangular tin, make sure the paper fits snugly into the corners. Cut a double round of paper to fit inside the base of the tin. (Stand the tin on the paper, draw round it and then cut.) Put the rounds in place – they will keep the snipped edge of the band in position and make a neat lining; brush the base of the lining with melted lard.

TO LINE A SANDWICH TIN: Cut a round of greaseproof paper to fit the bottom of the tin exactly. If the tin's sides are shallow and you want to raise them, fit a band of paper inside the tin, coming about 2.5 cm (1 inch) above the rim.

TO LINE A SWISS ROLL TIN: Cut a piece of paper about 5 cm (2 inch) larger all around than the tin. Place the tin on it and in each corner make a cut from the angle of the paper as far as the corner of the tin. Grease the tin and put in the paper so that it fits closely, overlapping at the corners. Grease the paper and dust with a half and-half mixture of flour and sugar sifted together. Non-stick paper is very satisfactory for lining this type of tin.

TO LINE A LOAF TIN: It is not usually necessary to line a loaf tin fully. Grease the inside, line the base only with an oblong of greaseproof paper and grease the paper.

TO LINE A SPONGE FLAN TIN: Grease the inside well, and place a round of greased greaseproof paper over the raised part only of the tin.

HEATING THE OVEN

Preheat the oven before starting to make cakes so that it will be at the correct temperature by the time the cake is ready to go in. Check that the shelves are in the correct position – place in the centre of the oven where possible.

TO TEST WHETHER A CAKE IS COOKED
Small cakes should be well risen, golden brown in colour and firm to the touch – both on top and underneath – and they should begin to shrink from the sides of the tin on being taken out of the oven.

Larger cakes present more difficulty, although the oven heat and cooking time give a good indication. The following tests are a guide:
* Press the centre top of the cake very lightly with the fingertip. The cake should be spongy and should give only very slightly to the pressure, then rise again immediately, retaining no impression.

* In the case of a fruit cake, lift it gently from the oven and 'listen' to it, putting it closely to the ear. A continued sizzling sound indicates that the cake is not cooked through.
* Insert a warmed long skewer (never use a cold knife) into the centre of the cake and remove it carefully. If any cake mixture is sticking to the skewer, return the cake to the oven as it requires longer cooking.

COOLING

Allow the cake a few minutes to cool before turning it out of the tin; it will shrink away from the sides and is more easily removed. Turn out on to a wire rack. Allow fruit cakes to cool completely in the tin.

CAUSES OF PROBLEMS

TOO CLOSE A TEXTURE
* Too much liquid.
* Too little raising agent.
* Insufficient creaming of the fat and sugar.
* Creamed mixture curdled when the eggs were added (therefore holding less air).
* Heavy-handed folding in of the flour.

PEAKING AND CRACKING
* Too hot an oven.
* The cake was placed too near the top of the oven.
* Too stiff a mixture.
* Too small a cake tin.

FRUIT SUNK TO THE BOTTOM
* Damp fruit.
* Sticky glacé cherries.
* Too soft a mixture so cannot support the weight of the fruit.
* Opening the oven door while the cake is rising.
* Using self raising flour where the recipe requires plain, or using too much baking powder – the cake over-rises and cannot carry the fruit with it.

CAKES SUNK IN THE MIDDLE
* Mixture too soft.
* Too much raising agent.
* Oven too cool, which means that the centre of the cake does not rise.
* Oven too hot, which makes the cake appear to be done on the outside before it is cooked in the centre.
* Insufficient baking.

SMALL CAKES

Small cakes are easy to make. They may be plain or finished with a variety of colourful coatings. As well as traditional small cakes like Fairy Cakes and Maids of Honour, there are recipes for children's favourites, such as Chocolate Crackles.

ALMOND FINGERS

100 g (4 oz) plain flour
pinch of salt
50 g (2 oz) butter or block margarine
5 ml (1 level tsp) caster sugar
1 egg yolk
FOR THE FILLING
45 ml (3 level tbsp) raspberry jam
1 egg white
45 ml (3 level tbsp) ground almonds
50 g (2 oz) caster sugar
few drops of almond flavouring
45 ml (3 level tbsp) flaked almonds

1. Lightly grease a shallow 18 cm (7 inch) square tin. Sift the flour and salt into a bowl and rub in the butter until the mixture resembles fine breadcrumbs. Stir in the sugar and add the egg yolk and enough water to mix to a firm dough.

2. Knead lightly on a floured surface and roll out to an 18 cm (7 inch) square; use to line the base of the tin. Spread the pastry with the jam, almost to the edges.

3. Whisk the egg white until stiff. Fold in the ground almonds, sugar and flavouring. Spread the mixture over the jam.

4. Sprinkle with flaked almonds and bake in the oven at 180°C (350°F) mark 4 for about 35 minutes until crisp and golden. Cool in the tin, then cut into fingers and remove with a palette knife.
MAKES 8-12

LEFT: Maids of Honour. RIGHT: Almond Fingers

MAIDS OF HONOUR

These originated in Henry VIII's palace at Hampton Court where they were popular with the Queen's maids of honour, hence the name.

600 ml (1 pint) milk
15 ml (1 tbsp) rennet
212 g (7½ oz) packet frozen puff pastry, thawed
1 egg, beaten
15 g (½ oz) butter or margarine, melted
50 g (2 oz) caster sugar

1. Gently heat the milk in a saucepan until just warm to the finger. Remove from the heat and stir in the rennet. Leave for 1½-2 hours until set.

2. When set, put the junket into a muslin bag and leave to drain overnight. Next day, chill the curd for several hours or until very firm.
3. Grease twelve 6 cm (2½ inch) patty tins. On a lightly floured surface, roll out the pastry very thinly and using a 7.5 cm (3 inch) plain cutter, cut out 12 rounds. Line the patty tins with the pastry rounds and prick well.
4. Stir the egg, butter and sugar into the drained curd. Divide the mixture between the pastry cases and bake in the oven at 200°C (400°F) mark 6 for 30 minutes, until well risen and just firm to the touch. Serve warm.
MAKES 12

SPONGE FINGERS

1 egg
45 ml (3 level tbsp) caster sugar
60 ml (4 level tbsp) strong white flour

1. Line a baking sheet with non-stick paper. Put the egg and sugar in a deep bowl and whisk until light, creamy and stiff enough to retain the impression of the whisk for a few seconds.
2. Sift half the flour over the mixture and fold in very lightly, using a metal spoon. Add the remaining flour in the same way. Spoon the mixture into a piping bag fitted with a 1 cm

(½ inch) plain nozzle and pipe the mixture on to the baking sheet in 7.5 cm (3 inch) lengths, leaving room for spreading.
3. Bake in the oven at 200°C (400°F) mark 6 for 8-10 minutes, until golden. Remove the sponge fingers carefully and cool on a wire rack.
MAKES 16

NOTE: If you wish, the ends of the fingers may be dipped into melted plain or milk chocolate, or chocolate flavoured cake covering, and allowed to harden before using.

ROCK BUNS

100 g (4 oz) butter or block margarine
225 g (8 oz) plain flour
10 ml (2 level tsp) baking powder
2.5 ml (½ level tsp) ground mixed spice
grated rind of ½ a lemon
100 g (4 oz) demerara sugar
100 g (4 oz) mixed dried fruit
1 egg, beaten
about 5 ml (1 tsp) milk (optional)

1. Grease two baking sheets. Rub the fat into the sifted flour, baking powder and spice until the mixture resembles fine breadcrumbs.
2. Stir in the rind, sugar and fruit. Make a well in the centre, pour in the egg and a little milk if necessary, to give a stiff crumbly consistency. Bind together loosely using a fork.
3. Use two forks to shape the mixture into rough heaps on the baking sheets. Bake in the oven at 200°C (400°F) mark 6 for 15-20 minutes.
MAKES 12

CHOCOLATE CRACKLES

225 g (8 oz) chocolate chips, plain chocolate or chocolate flavoured cake covering
15 ml (1 tbsp) golden syrup
50 g (2 oz) butter or margarine
50 g (2 oz) cornflakes

1. Spread out 12 paper cases on a baking sheet. Melt the chocolate dots with the golden syrup and butter over a very low heat.
2. Fold in the cornflakes. When well mixed, divide between the paper cases and leave to set.
MAKES 12

ENGLISH MADELEINES

100 g (4 oz) butter or block margarine
100 g (4 oz) caster sugar
2 eggs, beaten
100 g (4 oz) self raising flour
30 ml (2 level tbsp) red jam, sieved and melted
50 g (2 oz) desiccated coconut
5 glacé cherries, halved
angelica leaves

1. Grease 10 dariole moulds. Cream the fat and sugar until pale and fluffy. Add the eggs, a little at a time, beating well after each addition before adding more.
2. Fold in the flour, using a metal spoon, then three-quarters fill the moulds.
3. Bake in the oven at 180°C (350°F) mark 4 for

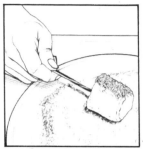

Using a skewer, roll the jam covered Madeleines in the coconut so they are evenly coated.

about 20 minutes, or until firm and browned. Turn them out of the moulds and leave to cool on a wire rack.
4. Trim off the bottoms, so that the cakes stand firmly and are of even height. When they are nearly cold, brush with melted jam, then holding them on a skewer, roll in coconut.
5. Top each madeleine with a glacé cherry half and two angelica leaves.
MAKES 10

FAIRY CAKES

100 g (4 oz) butter or block margarine
100 g (4 oz) caster sugar
2 eggs, beaten
100 g (4 oz) self raising flour
Glacé Icing made with 350 g (12 oz) icing sugar (see page 432)

1. Spread 12 to 16 paper cases out on baking sheets, or if wished put them into patty tins.
2. Cream the fat and sugar until pale and fluffy. Add the eggs, a little at a time, beating well after each addition. Fold in the flour using a metal

spoon. Two-thirds fill the cases with the mixture.
3. Bake in the oven at 190°C (375°F) mark 5 for 15-20 minutes, until golden.
4. When cold, top each cake with a little glacé icing.
MAKES 12-16

VARIATIONS
Add one of the following:
• 50 g (2 oz) sultanas (for Queen cakes)
• 50 g (2 oz) chopped dates
• 50 g (2 oz) chopped glacé cherries
• 50 g (2 oz) chocolate chips

BOSTON BROWNIES

65 g (2½ oz) butter or block margarine
50 g (2 oz) plain chocolate
175 g (6 oz) caster sugar
65 g (2½ oz) self raising flour
1.25 ml (¼ level tsp) salt
2 eggs, beaten
2.5 ml (½ tsp) vanilla flavouring
50 g (2 oz) walnut pieces, roughly chopped

1. Grease and base line a 20 cm (8 inch) square tin.
2. Melt the butter and chocolate in a small bowl over a pan of hot water, then add the sugar.
3. Sift the flour with the salt and add the chocolate mixture, eggs, vanilla flavouring and walnuts.
4. Beat until smooth and pour into the tin. Bake in the oven at 180°C (350°F) mark 4 for 35-40 minutes, until the mixture is risen and beginning to leave the sides of the tin. Leave in the tin to cool, then cut into fingers or squares.
MAKES 12

NOTE: If wished, cover with Chocolate Fudge Frosting (see page 434).

SCONES AND TEABREADS

Scones are quickly and easily made, and always very popular. You can mix and cook them while the rest of the tea is being prepared. The raising agent may be baking powder or bicarbonate of soda and cream of tartar, with fresh milk. Similar mixtures can be used as the basis for quick teabreads.

Self raising flour is satisfactory for scones, but you get a slightly better rise if you include a little extra baking powder, or use plain flour and a raising agent. Scones should be eaten the day they are made as they stale quickly.

In some parts of the country, griddle scones are more popular than oven scones. If you do not possess a traditional griddle or an electrical griddle plate, use a heavy-based frying pan.

CAUSES OF PROBLEMS

HEAVY AND BADLY RISEN
- Insufficient raising agent.
- Heavy handling, especially during kneading.
- Insufficient liquid.
- Oven too cool, or baking position too low.

SCONES SPREAD AND LOSE THEIR SHAPE
- Slack dough, caused by using too much liquid to make the dough.
- Too heavily greased tin. The fat melts on heating in the oven and 'pulls out' the soft dough before it has enough time to set.
- Incorrect kneading (especially of the scraps of dough for the second rolling) or twisting the cutter round as the scones were stamped out (such scones are often oval instead of round when cooked).

VERY ROUGH SURFACE
- Insufficient kneading or badly done.
- Rough handling when transferring to the baking sheet.

Scotch Pancakes or Drop Scones (see page 403)

OVEN SCONES

225 g (8 oz) self raising flour
2.5 ml (½ level tsp) salt
5 ml (1 level tsp) baking powder
25-50 g (1-2 oz) butter or margarine
150 ml (¼ pint) milk
beaten egg or milk, to glaze (optional)

1. Preheat a baking sheet in the oven. Sift the flour, salt and baking powder together into a bowl, then rub in the fat until the mixture resembles fine breadcrumbs.
2. Make a well in the centre and stir in enough milk to give a fairly soft dough. Turn it on to a lightly floured surface, knead very lightly if necessary to remove any cracks, then roll out lightly until about 2 cm (¾ inch) thick, or pat it out with the hand.
3. Cut into 10 to 12 rounds with a 5 cm (2 inch) cutter (dipped in flour) or cut into triangles with a sharp knife. Place on the baking sheet and brush if wished with beaten egg or milk. Bake towards the top of the oven at 230°C (450°F) mark 8 for 8-10 minutes, until golden brown and well risen.
4. Transfer to a wire rack to cool. Serve the scones split and buttered.
MAKES 10-12

VARIATIONS
If plain flour and baking powder are used instead of self raising flour, allow 15 ml (1 level tbsp) baking powder to 225 g (8 oz) flour and sift them together twice before using.
 If you use cream of tartar and bicarbonate of soda in place of baking powder, allow 5 ml (1 level tsp) cream of tartar and 2.5 ml (½ level tsp) bicarbonate of soda to 225 g (8 oz) plain flour with ordinary milk or 2.5 ml (½ level tsp) bicarbonate of soda and 2.5 ml (½ level tsp) cream of tartar with buttermilk.

WHOLEMEAL SCONES
Replace half of the plain flour with wholemeal flour.

EVERYDAY FRUIT SCONES
Add 50 g (2 oz) currants, sultanas, seedless raisins or chopped dates (or a mixture of fruit) to the dry ingredients in the basic recipe.

RICH TEA SCONES
Follow the basic recipe, adding 15-30 ml (1-2 level tbsp) caster sugar to the dry ingredients and using 1 beaten egg with 75 ml (5 tbsp) water or milk in place of 150 ml (¼ pint) milk; 50 g (2 oz) dried fruit may also be included.

CHEESE SCONES

225 g (8 oz) self raising flour
pinch of salt
5 ml (1 level tsp) baking powder
40 g (1½ oz) butter or margarine
75-100 g (3-4 oz) Cheddar cheese, finely grated
5 ml (1 level tsp) mustard powder
about 150 ml (¼ pint) milk

1. Grease a baking sheet. Sift the flour, salt and baking powder together in a bowl and rub in the fat until the mixture resembles fine breadcrumbs. Stir in half the cheese, the mustard and enough milk to give a fairly soft, light dough.
2. On a lightly floured surface, roll out to about 2 cm (¾ inch) thick and cut into rounds with a 5 cm (2 inch) plain cutter. Put on the baking sheet, brush the tops with milk and sprinkle with the remaining cheese.
3. Bake in the oven at 220°C (425°F) mark 7 for about 10 minutes. Cool on a wire rack.
MAKES ABOUT 16

VARIATION
CHEESE AND CHIVE SCONES
Stir in 15 ml (1 level tbsp) snipped fresh chives with the cheese.

GRIDDLE SCONES

225 g (8 oz) self raising flour
pinch of salt
2.5 ml (½ level tsp) freshly grated nutmeg
50 g (2 oz) butter or block margarine
50 g (2 oz) caster sugar
1 egg, beaten
45-60 ml (3-4 tbsp) milk

1. Preheat and grease a griddle, or heavy-based frying pan.
2. Sift the flour, salt and nutmeg together and rub in the fat until the mixture resembles fine breadcrumbs. Stir in the sugar. Mix with the egg and milk to a firm dough.
3. On a lightly floured surface roll out to 1 cm (½ inch) thick and cut into rounds or triangles. Cook on a moderately hot griddle until brown on both sides – about 10 minutes in all.
MAKES 8-10

VARIATION
Add 50 g (2 oz) dried fruit with the sugar.

SCOTCH PANCAKES OR DROP SCONES

100 g (4 oz) self raising flour
30 ml (2 level tbsp) caster sugar
1 egg, beaten
150 ml (¼ pint) milk

1. Preheat and lightly grease a griddle or heavy-based frying pan.
2. Mix the flour and sugar in a bowl. Make a well in the centre and stir in the egg, with enough of the milk to make a batter, the consistency of thick cream; mix as quickly and lightly as possible.
3. Drop the mixture in spoonfuls on to the griddle or pan surface.
4. Keep the griddle at a steady heat and when bubbles rise to the surface of the pancakes and burst – after 2-3 minutes – turn the pancake over, using a palette knife. Continue cooking for a further 2-3 minutes, until golden brown on the other side.
5. Place the cooked pancakes on a clean tea towel, cover with another towel and place on a rack to cool slightly; this keeps in the steam and the pancakes do not become dry.
6. Serve warm with butter, or cold with whipped cream and jam.
MAKES ABOUT 8-10 PANCAKES

VARIATION
For richer drop scones, add about 25 g (1 oz) fat, rubbing it into the flour. If you prefer, use 100 g (4 oz) plain flour, 2.5 ml (1 level tsp) bicarbonate of soda and 5 ml (1 level tsp) cream of tartar instead of the self raising flour.

MUFFINS

15 g (½ oz) fresh yeast or 7 g sachet (1½ level tsp) fast-action dried yeast
300 ml (½ pint) warm milk
450 g (1 lb) strong white flour
5 ml (1 level tsp) salt
5 ml (1 level tsp) plain flour, for dusting
5 ml (1 level tsp) semolina

1. Blend the fresh yeast with the milk.
2. Sift the flour and salt together, then make a well in the centre. Add the yeast liquid or fast-action dried yeast granules and milk to the well, draw in the flour and mix to a smooth dough.
3. Knead the dough on a lightly floured surface for about 10 minutes, until it is smooth and elastic. Place in a clean bowl, cover with a tea towel and leave to rise in a warm place for about 1 hour, until doubled in size.
4. Roll out the dough on a lightly floured surface using a lightly floured rolling pin to about 5 mm-1 cm (¼-½ inch) thick. Leave to rest, covered with a tea towel, for 5 minutes, then cut into rounds with a 7.5 cm (3 inch) plain cutter.
5. Place the muffins on a well-floured baking sheet. Mix together the flour and semolina and use to dust the tops. Cover with a tea towel and leave in a warm place until doubled in size.
6. Grease a griddle, electric griddle plate or heavy frying pan and heat over a moderate heat, until a cube of bread turns brown in 20 seconds.
7. Place the muffins on the griddle or frying pan and cook for about 7 minutes each side, until golden brown.
MAKES ABOUT 12

DATE AND RAISIN TEABREAD

100 g (4 oz) butter or margarine
225 g (8 oz) plain flour
100 g (4 oz) stoned dates, chopped
50 g (2 oz) walnut halves, chopped
100 g (4 oz) seedless raisins
100 g (4 oz) demerara sugar
5 ml (1 level tsp) baking powder
5 ml (1 level tsp) bicarbonate of soda
about 150 ml (¼ pint) milk

1. Grease a 1.7 litre (3 pint) loaf tin and line with greaseproof paper.
2. Rub the fat into the flour until it resembles fine breadcrumbs. Stir in the dates, walnuts, raisins and sugar. Mix the baking powder, bicarbonate of soda and milk together and pour into the centre of the dry ingredients. Mix well together to give a stiff dropping consistency, adding a little extra milk if necessary.
3. Turn the mixture into the prepared tin and bake in the oven at 180°C (350°F) mark 4, for about 1 hour, until well risen and just firm to the touch. Turn out and cool on a wire rack.

MALTED FRUIT LOAF

350 g (12 oz) plain flour
2.5 ml (½ level tsp) bicarbonate of soda
5 ml (1 level tsp) baking powder
250 g (9 oz) sultanas
30 ml (2 level tbsp) demerara sugar
135 ml (9 level tbsp) malt extract
2 eggs, beaten
200 ml (7 fl oz) milk

1. Grease and base-line a 1.7 litre (3 pint) loaf tin, and grease the underside of a baking sheet.
2. Sift the flour, bicarbonate of soda and baking powder together in a bowl. Stir in the sultanas.
3. Slowly heat together the demerara sugar and malt extract. Do not boil. Pour on to the dry ingredients. Add the eggs and milk and beat thoroughly.
4. Turn the mixture into the prepared tin. Cover with the baking sheet, greased side down. Place a weight on top. Bake in the oven at 150°C (300°F) mark 2 for about 1½ hours. Turn out and cool on a wire rack. Wrap and keep for two days before eating.

BANANA AND HONEY TEABREAD

450 g (1 lb) bananas
225 g (8 oz) self raising flour
2.5 ml (½ level tsp) salt
1.25 ml (¼ level tsp) freshly grated nutmeg
125 g (4 oz) butter or block margarine
125 g (4 oz) caster sugar
grated rind of 1 lemon
2 eggs, size 2
120 ml (8 level tbsp) thick honey
8 sugar cubes (optional)

1. Grease and base-line a 1.7 litre (3 pint) loaf tin.
2. Peel the bananas, then mash the flesh using a fork or potato masher. Mix the flour, salt and nutmeg together. Rub in the fat until the mixture resembles fine breadcrumbs.
3. Stir in the sugar, lemon rind, eggs, 90 ml (6 tbsp) honey and mashed banana. Beat well until evenly mixed. Turn the mixture into the prepared tin.
4. Bake in the oven at 180°C (350°F) mark 4 for about 1¼ hours, covering lightly if necessary. Test with a fine skewer which should come out clean when the teabread is cooked.
5. Cool slightly, then turn out on to a wire rack to cool completely. Gently warm the remaining honey, then brush over the teabread. Roughly crush the sugar lumps, if using, and scatter over the top of the teabread.

APRICOT NUT TEABREAD

75 g (3 oz) dried apricots, cut into small pieces
75 g (3 oz) bran breakfast cereal (not flaked)
75 g (3 oz) demerara sugar
300 ml (½ pint) milk
50 g (2 oz) hazelnuts, chopped
1 egg, beaten
175 g (6 oz) self raising flour
5 ml (1 level tsp) baking powder

1. Grease and base-line a 1.7 litre (3 pint) loaf tin.
2. Put the apricots into a large bowl and add the bran, sugar and the milk. Cover and leave in a cool place for 3 hours.
3. Stir the hazelnuts, egg, flour and baking powder into the mixture and stir until well blended.
4. Turn the mixture into the prepared tin and bake in the oven at 190°C (375°F) mark 5 for 1-1¼ hours or until firm to the touch. Cover lightly with foil if necessary.
5. Turn out and cool on a wire rack. Store for a few days before eating.

GINGERBREAD

450 g (1 lb) plain flour
5 ml (1 level tsp) salt
15 ml (1 level tbsp) ground ginger
15 ml (1 level tbsp) baking powder
5 ml (1 level tsp) bicarbonate of soda
225 g (8 oz) demerara sugar
175 g (6 oz) butter or block margarine
175 g (6 oz) black treacle
175 g (6 oz) golden syrup
300 ml (½ pint) milk
1 egg, beaten

1. Grease and line a 23 cm (9 inch) square cake tin. Sift together the flour, salt, ginger, baking powder and bicarbonate of soda into a large mixing bowl.
2. Put the sugar, fat, treacle and syrup in a saucepan and warm gently over a low heat until

melted and well blended. Do not allow the mixture to boil. Remove from the heat and leave to cool slightly, until you can hold your hand comfortably against the side of the pan.
3. Mix in the milk and egg. Make a well in the centre of the dry ingredients, pour in the liquid and mix very thoroughly.
4. Turn into the tin and bake in the oven at 170°C (325°F) mark 3 for about 1½ hours, or until firm to the touch.
5. Turn out on to a wire rack to cool. For optimum flavour, store for a few days wrapped in foil or in an airtight container before eating.

VARIATION
Use half quantities of the above recipe and use a size 6 egg. Bake in an 18 cm (7 inch) deep square tin for 1-1¼ hours.

OATMEAL PARKIN

225 g (8 oz) treacle
225 g (8 oz) golden syrup
100 g (4 oz) butter or block margarine
2.5 ml (½ level tsp) bicarbonate of soda
300 ml (½ pint) milk
1 egg, beaten
450 g (1 lb) plain flour
350 g (12 oz) medium oatmeal
5 ml (1 level tsp) salt
50 g (2 oz) sugar
5 ml (1 level tsp) ground ginger

1. Grease and base-line a 23 cm (9 inch) square cake tin. Melt the treacle, syrup and butter together. Do not boil. Blend the soda with the milk and the egg.
2. Mix all the dry ingredients together, pour in the melted butter mixture, stir well, then add the egg and milk mixture and mix thoroughly.
3. Turn into the prepared tin and bake in the oven at 180°C (350°F) mark 4 for 45 minutes, until firm to the touch.
4. Turn out of the tin when cold. Store in an airtight container for at least one week before slicing and eating.

LARGE CAKES AND GÂTEAUX

Large cakes of the 'everyday type' and gâteaux are included in this section. Choose from deliciously light sponges, moist fruit cakes and a tempting selection of sumptuous gâteaux for special occasions.

VICTORIA SANDWICH CAKE

175 g (6 oz) butter or block margarine, softened
175 g (6 oz) caster sugar
3 eggs, beaten
175 g (6 oz) self raising flour
45-60 ml (3-4 level tbsp) jam
caster sugar, to dredge

1. Grease and base-line two 18 cm (7 inch) sandwich tins.
2. Beat the butter and sugar together until pale and fluffy. Add the eggs, a little at a time, beating well after each addition. Fold in half the flour, using a metal spoon, then fold in the rest.
3. Divide the mixture evenly between the tins and level with a knife. Bake in the oven at 190°C (375°F) mark 5 for about 20 minutes until they are well risen, firm to the touch and beginning to shrink away from the sides of the tins. Turn out and cool on a wire rack.
4. When the cakes are cool, sandwich them together with the jam and sprinkle the top with caster sugar.

VARIATIONS
ONE STAGE SANDWICH CAKE
Sift flour with 5 ml (1 level tsp) baking powder. Replace butter with soft tub margarine and add to the flour with the sugar and eggs. Beat thoroughly, using an electric mixer or food processor, or a wooden spoon, until smooth.

CHOCOLATE
Replace 45 ml (3 level tbsp) flour with cocoa powder. Sandwich the cakes with Vanilla or Chocolate Butter Cream (see page 433).

COFFEE
Add 10 ml (2 level tsp) instant coffee powder dissolved in a little warm water to the creamed mixture with the eggs or use 10 ml (2 tsp) coffee essence. Sandwich the cakes with Vanilla or Coffee Butter Cream (see page 433).

ORANGE OR LEMON
Add the finely grated rind of an orange or lemon to the mixture. Sandwich the cakes together with Orange or Lemon Butter Cream (see page 433).

GENOESE SPONGE

40 g (1½ oz) butter
3 eggs, size 2
75 g (3 oz) caster sugar
65 g (2½ oz) plain flour
15 ml (1 level tbsp) cornflour

1. Grease and line two 18 cm (7 inch) sandwich tins or one 18 cm (7 inch) deep round cake tin.
2. Put the butter into a saucepan and heat gently until melted, then remove from the heat and leave to stand for a few minutes to cool slightly.
3. Put the eggs and sugar in a bowl, place over a pan of hot water and whisk until pale and creamy and thick enough to leave a trail on the surface when the whisk is lifted. Remove from the heat and whisk until cool.
4. Sift the flours together into a bowl. Fold half the flour into the egg mixture with a metal spoon.
5. Pour half the cooled butter around the edge of the mixture. Gradually fold in the remaining butter and flour alternately. Fold in very lightly or the butter will sink and result in a heavy cake.
6. Pour the mixture into the tins. Bake sandwich cakes in the oven at 180°C (350°F) mark 4 for 25-30 minutes, or the deep cake for 35-40 minutes, until well risen, firm to the touch and beginning to shrink away from the sides of the tin. Turn out and cool on a wire rack.

WHISKED SPONGE CAKE

3 eggs, size 2
100 g (4 oz) caster sugar
75 g (3 oz) plain flour
45-60 ml (3-4 tbsp) strawberry or apricot jam, to fill
caster sugar, to dredge

1. Grease and line two 18 cm (7 inch) sandwich tins and dust with a little flour or with a mixture of flour and caster sugar.
2. Put the eggs and sugar in a large bowl and stand it over a pan of hot water. Whisk using an electric hand whisk until doubled in volume and thick enough to leave a thin trail on the surface of the batter when the whisk is lifted.
3. Remove the bowl from the heat and continue whisking for a further 5 minutes, until the mixture is cooler and creamy looking.

4. Sift half the flour over the mixture and fold it in very lightly, using a large metal spoon. Sift and fold in the remaining flour in the same way.
5. Pour the mixture into the tins, tilting the tins to spread the mixture evenly. Do not use a palette knife or spatula to smooth the mixture as this will crush out the air bubbles.
6. Bake in the oven at 190°C (375°F) mark 5 for 20-25 minutes, until they are well risen, firm to the touch and beginning to shrink away from the sides. Turn out and cool on a wire rack.
7. When the cakes are cold, sandwich them together with jam and dredge with caster sugar.

VARIATION
Sandwich the cakes together with whipped cream or Butter Cream (see page 433) and cover the top with Glacé Icing (see page 432).

SWISS ROLL

3 eggs, size 2
100 g (4 oz) caster sugar
100 g (4 oz) plain flour
caster sugar, to dredge
100 g (4 oz) jam, warmed

1. Grease and line a 33 x 23 cm (13 x 9 inch) Swiss roll tin (see page 397); grease the paper. Dust with caster sugar and flour.
2. Put the eggs and sugar in a bowl, place over a pan of hot water and whisk using an electric hand whisk until pale and creamy and thick enough to leave a trail on the surface when the whisk is lifted.
3. Remove the bowl from the heat and whisk until cool. Sift half the flour over the mixture and fold in very lightly with a metal spoon. Sift and fold in the remaining flour, then lightly stir in 15 ml (1 tbsp) hot water.
4. Pour the mixture into the tin and tilt the tin backwards and forwards to spread the mixture in an even layer. Bake in the oven at 200°C (400°F) mark 6 for 10-12 minutes until golden brown, well risen and firm to the touch.
5. Meanwhile, place a sheet of greaseproof paper over a damp tea towel. Dredge the paper thickly with caster sugar.
6. Quickly turn out the cake on to the paper, trim off the crusty edges and spread with warmed jam.
7. Roll up the cake with the aid of the paper.

Make the first turn firmly so that the whole cake will roll evenly and have a good shape when finished, but roll more lightly after this turn.
8. Place seam-side down on a wire rack and dredge with sugar. Leave to cool for 30 minutes before serving.

VARIATIONS
CHOCOLATE SWISS ROLL
Replace 15 ml (1 level tbsp) flour with 15 ml (1 level tbsp) cocoa powder. Turn out the cooked sponge and trim as above, then cover with a sheet of greaseproof paper and roll with the paper inside. When cold, unroll and remove the paper. Spread with whipped cream or Butter Cream (see page 433) and re-roll. Dust with icing sugar.

CHOCOLATE ICE CREAM LOG
Make up the Chocolate Swiss Roll. When cooked, turn out, trim, sprinkle with caster sugar, cover with a tea towel and leave to cool. Halve the sponge horizontally and sandwich with 1 litre (1¾ pint) raspberry ripple ice cream. Serve immediately with hot Rich Chocolate Sauce (see page 209).

GINGER SWISS ROLL
Follow the basic recipe adding 5 ml (1 level tsp) ground ginger with the flour. Spread with 100 g (4 oz) warmed ginger marmalade instead of jam.

CARROT CAKE

225 g (8 oz) butter
225 g (8 oz) light soft brown sugar
4 eggs, separated
finely grated rind of ½ orange
20 ml (4 tsp) lemon juice
175 g (6 oz) self raising flour
5 ml (1 level tsp) baking powder
50 g (2 oz) ground almonds
150 g (5 oz) walnut pieces, chopped
350 g (12 oz) young carrots, peeled and grated
225 g (8 oz) cream cheese
10 ml (2 level tsp) clear honey

1. Grease and line a deep 20 cm (8 inch) round cake tin.
2. Cream the butter and sugar together in a bowl until pale and fluffy. Beat in the egg yolks, then stir in the orange rind and 15 ml (3 tsp) of the lemon juice.
3. Sift in the flour and baking powder, then stir in the ground almonds and 125 g (4 oz) of the walnuts.
4. Whisk the egg whites until stiff, then fold into the cake mixture with the carrots. Pour into the prepared tin and hollow the centre slightly.
5. Bake at 180°C (350°F) mark 4 for about 1½ hours. Cover the top with foil after 1 hour if it starts to brown.
6. Leave to cool slightly, then turn out on to a wire rack and remove the lining paper. Leave to cool.
7. To make the topping, beat together the cream cheese, honey and remaining lemon juice and spread over the top of the cake. Sprinkle the topping with the remaining walnuts.

Carrot Cake

HONEY CAKE

225 ml (8 fl oz) clear honey plus 45 ml (3 tbsp)
75 g (3 oz) butter
350 g (12 oz) plain wholemeal flour
pinch of salt
5 ml (1 level tsp) ground mixed spice
5 ml (1 level tsp) bicarbonate of soda
50 g (2 oz) glacé cherries, halved
50 g (2 oz) chopped mixed peel
3 eggs
45 ml (3 tbsp) milk
grated rind of 1 large lemon
25 g (1 oz) flaked almonds

1. Grease a 20 cm (8 inch) square cake tin and
line the base and sides with greaseproof paper.
2. Put 225 ml (8 fl oz) honey in a saucepan, add
the butter and heat gently, stirring, until smooth.
3. Sift the flour, salt, spice and bicarbonate of
soda into a large bowl, stirring in any bran left in
the sieve. Add the cherries and peel.
4. Beat the eggs and the milk together and stir
into the honey mixture with the lemon rind.
Pour gradually on to the dry ingredients, beating
well after each addition, until well blended.
5. Turn the mixture into the prepared tin and
sprinkle with flaked almonds. Bake at 170°C
(325°F) mark 3 for about 1¼ hours, until the cake
is firm to the touch or a skewer inserted in the
centre of the cake comes out clean.
6. Using a skewer, prick the top of the cake and
spoon over the remaining honey. Turn out and
leave to cool on a wire rack. Do not remove the
lining paper until the cake is cold.

Honey Cake

WALNUT LAYER CAKE

4 eggs, separated
100 g (4 oz) caster sugar
75 g (3 oz) walnuts, finely chopped
25 g (1 oz) fresh brown breadcrumbs
25 g (1 oz) plain flour
½ quantity Butter Cream (see page 433), using coffee
*   essence instead of milk*
10 ml (2 tsp) coffee essence
1 quantity American Frosting (see page 434)
walnut halves, to decorate

1. Grease and base-line two 18 cm (7 inch)
sandwich tins. Dust with caster sugar and flour.
2. Whisk together the egg yolks and caster sugar

until very pale. Fold in the chopped walnuts,
breadcrumbs and flour.
3. Whisk the egg whites until stiff. Stir one large
spoonful into the egg yolk mixture, then fold in
the remainder.
4. Divide the mixture equally between the tins
and level the surface. Bake at 180°C (350°F)
mark 4 for about 30 minutes. Turn out and cool
on a wire rack.
5. When the cakes are cold, sandwich them
together with the Butter Cream.
6. Coat the cake completely with the American
Frosting, working quickly to ensure an even
glossy frosting. Decorate at once with the walnut
halves.

CHOCOLATE BATTENBERG CAKE

175 g (6 oz) butter or block margarine, softened
175 g (6 oz) caster sugar
few drops of vanilla flavouring
3 eggs, beaten
175 g (6 oz) self raising flour
30 ml (2 level tbsp) cocoa powder
a little milk, to mix (optional)
225 g (8 oz) Almond Paste (see page 426)
caster sugar, to dredge
225 g (8 oz) apricot jam, melted

1. Grease and line a 30 x 20 cm (12 x 8 inch) Swiss roll tin and divide it lengthways with a 'wall' of pleated greaseproof paper.
2. Cream the butter and sugar together until pale and fluffy, then beat in vanilla flavouring. Add the eggs, a little at a time, beating well after each addition.
3. Gradually sift the flour over the mixture and fold it in lightly. Turn half the mixture into one side of the Swiss roll tin and level the surface. Sift the cocoa over the other half of the mixture and fold in, adding a little milk if necessary to give a dropping consistency.
4. Turn the chocolate mixture into the other side of the tin and level the surface. Bake in the oven at 190°C (375°F) mark 5 for 40-45 minutes, until well risen, firm to the touch and beginning to shrink away from the sides of the tin. Turn out and leave to cool on a wire rack.

5. When cold, trim cakes to an equal size and cut each in half lengthways. On a working surface sprinkled with caster sugar, roll out the almond paste to a rectangle 30 x 40 cm (12 x 16 inches).
6. Place one strip of cake on the almond paste so that it lies up against the short edge of paste. Place an alternate coloured strip next to it.
7. Brush top and sides of cake with melted jam and layer up with alternate coloured strips.
8. Bring almond paste up and over cake to cover it. Press paste firmly on to cake, then seal and trim join. Place cake seam-side down and trim both ends with a sharp knife. Crimp top edges of almond paste with the thumb and forefinger and mark the top in a criss-cross pattern with a knife. Dredge lightly with caster sugar.

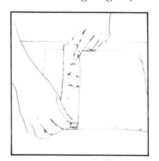 

Place one strip of cake against the short edge of the almond paste.

Arrange cake strips in alternate colours and lift over almond paste.

CHOCOLATE SLAB CAKE

50 g (2 oz) plain chocolate
75 ml (5 level tbsp) cocoa powder
105 ml (7 tbsp) milk
75 g (3 oz) plain white flour
75 g (3 oz) plain wholemeal flour
10 ml (2 level tsp) ground mixed spice
10 ml (2 level tsp) baking powder
250 g (9 oz) caster sugar
3 eggs, beaten
300 g (11 oz) soft tub margarine
225 g (8 oz) icing sugar

1. Grease and base-line a rectangular tin about 30 x 23 cm (12 x 9 inches) top measurement, 25 x 18 cm (10 x 7 inches) base measurement.
2. Break the chocolate into a bowl. Add 45 ml (3 level tbsp) cocoa powder and 60 ml (4 tbsp)

of the milk and place the bowl over a pan of simmering water. Stir until smooth, then leave to cool slightly.
3. Place the flours, spice, baking powder, 175 g (6 oz) caster sugar, the eggs and 225 g (8 oz) margarine in a bowl.
4. Pour in the chocolate mixture and whisk well for about 1 minute. Turn into the prepared tin and bake in the oven at 180°C (350°F) mark 4 for about 50 minutes, until firm to the touch. Turn out and cool on a wire rack.
5. Sieve together the icing sugar and remaining cocoa. Heat the remaining margarine, caster sugar and milk until the sugar dissolves. Bring to the boil, then beat with the icing sugar until the icing begins to thicken.
6. Using a palette knife spread the icing all over the cake. Leave to set before serving.

CHOCOLATE BISCUIT CAKE

125 g (4 oz) plain chocolate or plain chocolate
 flavoured cake covering
15 ml (1 tbsp) golden syrup
125 g (4 oz) butter or block margarine
125 g (4 oz) digestive biscuits, broken up
25 g (1 oz) seedless raisins
25g (1 oz) glacé cherries, halved
50 g (2 oz) flaked almonds, toasted

1. Grease a loose-based 18 cm (7 inch) flan tin.
2. Break the chocolate into a bowl and place over a pan of simmering water. Add the syrup and butter and stir until the chocolate and butter have melted. Remove from the heat and cool slightly.
3. Mix the biscuits, fruit and almonds into the chocolate mixture. Turn the mixture into the tin, lightly level the top, then chill for at least 1 hour before serving.

FARMHOUSE SULTANA CAKE

225 g (8 oz) plain white flour
10 ml (2 level tsp) mixed spice
5 ml (1 level tsp) bicarbonate of soda
225 g (8 oz) plain wholemeal flour
175 g (6 oz) butter or block margarine
225 g (8 oz) soft brown sugar
225 g (8 oz) sultanas
1 egg, beaten
about 300 ml (½ pint) milk
10 sugar cubes (optional)

1. Grease and base-line a 20 cm (8 inch) square cake tin.
2. Sift the plain flour with the spice and soda into a large mixing bowl; stir in the wholemeal flour.
3. Rub in the butter until the mixture resembles fine breadcrumbs, then stir in the sugar and sultanas.
4. Make a well in the centre of the dry ingredients and add the egg and milk. Beat gently until well mixed and of a soft dropping consistency, adding more milk if necessary. Turn into the prepared tin.
5. Roughly crush the sugar cubes with the end of a rolling pin and scatter over the cake, if liked.
6. Bake in the oven at 170°C (325°F) mark 3 for about 1 hour 40 minutes, until cooked. When a fine skewer is inserted into the centre, no traces of moist cake should remain. Turn out and cool on a wire rack.

RICH CHERRY CAKE

225 g (8 oz) glacé cherries, halved
150 g (5 oz) self raising flour
50 g (2 oz) plain flour
45 ml (3 level tbsp) cornflour
45 ml (3 level tbsp) ground almonds
175 g (6 oz) butter or block margarine, softened
175 g (6 oz) caster sugar
3 eggs, beaten
6 sugar cubes (optional)

1. Grease and base-line an 18 cm (7 inch) round cake tin. Wash the cherries and dry thoroughly. Sift the flours and cornflour together. Stir in the ground almonds and cherries.
2. Cream the butter and sugar until pale and fluffy. Add the eggs, a little at a time, beating well after each addition. Fold in the dry ingredients.
3. Turn the mixture into the tin, making sure the cherries are not grouped together, and hollow the centre slightly.
4. Roughly crush the sugar cubes with a rolling pin and scatter these over the cake, if liked.
5. Bake in the oven at 180°C (350°F) mark 4 for hours, until well risen and golden brown. Turn out and cool on a wire rack.

MADEIRA CAKE

100 g (4 oz) plain flour
100 g (4 oz) self raising flour
175 g (6 oz) butter or block margarine, softened
175 g (6 oz) caster sugar
5 ml (1 tsp) vanilla flavouring
3 eggs, beaten
15-30 ml (1 -2 tbsp) milk (optional)
2-3 thin slices citron peel

1. Grease and line an 18 cm (7 inch) round cake tin with greaseproof paper.
2. Sift the plain and self raising flours together. Cream the butter and the sugar together in a bowl until pale and fluffy, then beat in the vanilla flavouring. Add the eggs, a little at a time, beating well after each addition.

3. Fold in the sifted flour with a metal spoon, adding a little milk if necessary to give a dropping consistency.
4. Turn the mixture into the tin and bake in the oven at 180°C (350°F) mark 4 for 20 minutes.
5. Lay the citron peel on top of the cake, return it to the oven and bake for a further 40 minutes until firm. Turn out and cool on a wire rack.

VARIATIONS
ORANGE MADEIRA CAKE
Add the grated rind of 2 oranges to the creamed butter and sugar.

SEED CAKE
Add 10 ml (2 level tsp) caraway seeds with the flour. Omit the citron peel.

DUNDEE CAKE

100 g (4 oz) currants
100 g (4 oz) seedless raisins
50 g (2 oz) blanched almonds, chopped
100 g (4 oz) chopped mixed peel
275 g (10 oz) plain flour
225 g (8 oz) butter or block margarine, softened
225 g (8 oz) light soft brown sugar
finely grated rind of 1 lemon
4 eggs, beaten
25 g (1 oz) split almonds, to decorate

1. Line a 20 cm (8 inch) round cake tin with greased greaseproof paper. Combine the fruit, chopped nuts and mixed peel in a bowl. Sift in a little flour and stir until the fruit is evenly coated.
2. Cream the butter and sugar until pale and fluffy, then beat in the lemon rind. Add the

eggs, a little at a time, beating well after each addition.
3. Sift the remaining flour over the mixture and fold in lightly with a metal spoon, then fold in the fruit and nut mixture.
4. Turn the mixture into the tin and make a slight hollow in the centre with the back of a metal spoon. Arrange the split almonds on top.
5. Bake in the oven at 170°C (325°F) mark 3 for about 2½ hours until a fine warmed skewer inserted in the centre comes out clean. Check near the end of the cooking time and cover with several layers of greaseproof paper if it is over-browning.
6. Cool in the tin for 15 minutes, before turning out on to a wire rack to cool completely for 2 hours. Store in an airtight tin for at least 1 week to mature.

ONE STAGE FRUIT CAKE

225 g (8 oz) self raising flour
10 ml (2 level tsp) ground mixed spice
5 ml (1 level tsp) baking powder
100 g (4 oz) soft tub margarine
100 g (4 oz) soft brown sugar
225 g (8 oz) mixed dried fruit
2 eggs, beaten
30 ml (2 tbsp) milk

1. Grease and base-line an 18 cm (7 inch) round cake tin. Sift the flour, spice and baking powder into a large bowl, add the remaining ingredients and beat until thoroughly combined.
2. Turn the mixture into the tin and bake in the oven at 170°C (325°F) mark 3 for about 1¾ hours, until a warmed fine skewer inserted in the centre comes out clean. Turn out and cool on a wire rack.

LEFT: Madeira Cake. RIGHT: Half-pound Cake

HALF-POUND CAKE

225 g (8 oz) butter or block margarine, softened
225 g (8 oz) caster sugar
4 eggs, beaten
225 g (8 oz) seedless raisins
225 g (8 oz) mixed currants and sultanas
100 g (4 oz) glacé cherries, halved
225 g (8 oz) plain flour
2.5 ml (½ level tsp) salt
2.5 ml (½ level tsp) ground mixed spice
15 ml (1 tbsp) brandy
few walnut halves

1. Line a 20 cm (8 inch) round cake tin with greased greaseproof paper.
2. Cream the fat and sugar until pale and fluffy. Add the eggs, a little at a time, beating well after each addition.
3. Mix together the fruit, flour, salt and spice and fold into the creamed mixture, using a metal spoon. Add the brandy and mix to a soft dropping consistency.
4. Turn the mixture into the tin, level the top and arrange the nuts on top. Bake in the oven at 150°C (300°F) mark 2 for about 2½ hours, until a fine warmed skewer inserted in the centre comes out clean. Turn out and cool on a wire rack.

SOMERSET APPLE CAKE

100 g (4 oz) butter
175 g (6 oz) dark soft brown sugar
2 eggs, beaten
225 g (8 oz) plain wholemeal flour
5 ml (1 level tsp) ground mixed spice
5 ml (1 level tsp) ground cinnamon
10 ml (2 level tsp) baking powder
450 g (1 lb) cooking apples, peeled, cored and chopped
45-60 ml (3-4 tbsp) milk
15 ml (1 level tbsp) clear honey, warmed
15 ml (1 level tbsp) light demerara sugar

1. Grease and line a deep 18 cm (7 inch) round cake tin with greaseproof paper.
2. Cream the butter and sugar together until pale and fluffy. Add the eggs, a little at a time, beating well after each addition. Add the flour, spices and baking powder and mix well. Fold in the apples and enough milk to make a soft dropping consistency.
3. Turn the mixture into the prepared tin and bake at 170°C (325°F) mark 3 for 1½ hours, until well risen and firm to the touch. Turn out on to a wire rack to cool.
4. When the cake is cold, brush the top with the honey and sprinkle with the demerara sugar to decorate.

FROSTED COCONUT CAKE

50 g (2 oz) shelled hazelnuts
225 g (8 oz) butter or block margarine, softened
225 g (8 oz) caster sugar
5 eggs
2.5 ml (½ tsp) vanilla flavouring
125 g (4 oz) plain flour
125 g (4 oz) self raising flour
40 g (1½ oz) desiccated coconut
75 g (3 oz) icing sugar
shredded coconut, to decorate

1. Grease and base line a 20 cm (8 inch) spring-release cake tin with greaseproof paper. Spread the hazelnuts in a grill pan and brown them under a hot grill. Place in a clean tea towel and rub off the skins. Leave to cool, then finely chop.
2. Cream the fat and sugar together until pale and fluffy. Whisk 4 whole eggs and 1 yolk together and gradually beat into the creamed mixture with the vanilla flavouring.
3. Sift the flours together into a large mixing bowl. Fold into the mixture with 25 g (1 oz) of the desiccated coconut, and half the nuts. Spoon into the prepared tin and bake in the oven at 180°C (350°F) mark 4 for 45 minutes.
4. Meanwhile, in a bowl whisk the egg white until stiff. Whisk in half the sifted icing sugar, then fold in the remaining icing sugar, desiccated coconut and hazelnuts.
5. Spoon the meringue topping on to the partially baked cake and scatter with shredded coconut.
6. Return to the oven for 20-30 minutes, or until a fine warmed skewer inserted in the centre comes out clean. Cover lightly with a double layer of greaseproof paper after 15 minutes if necessary. Cool on a wire rack.

Place the browned nuts in a tea towel and rub off the skins.

VARIATION
Use walnuts instead of hazelnuts. There is no need to toast these.

Marbled Chocolate Cake

MARBLED CHOCOLATE CAKE

50 g (2 oz) plain chocolate
5 ml (1 tsp) vanilla flavouring
225 g (8 oz) butter or block margarine
225 g (8 oz) caster sugar
4 eggs, beaten
225 g (8 oz) plain flour
10 ml (2 level tsp) baking powder
50 g (2 oz) ground almonds
30 ml (2 tbsp) milk
Chocolate Frosting (see page 434)

1. Grease a 1.7 litre (3 pint) ring mould. Melt the chocolate with the vanilla flavouring and 15 ml (1 tbsp) water in a bowl placed over a pan of simmering water. Remove from the heat.
2. Cream together the fat and caster sugar until pale and fluffy. Add the eggs, a little at a time,

beating well after each addition.
3. Fold the flour, baking powder and ground almonds into the creamed mixture. Stir in the milk. Spoon half the mixture evenly into the base of the prepared tin.
4. Stir the cooled but still soft chocolate into the remaining mixture. Spoon into the tin. Draw a knife through the cake mixture in a spiral. Level the surface.
5. Bake in the oven at 180°C (350°F) mark 4 for about 55 minutes, until well risen, firm to the touch and beginning to shrink away from sides of the tin. Turn out and cool on a wire rack.
6. Pour frosting over the cooled cake, working quickly to coat top and sides. Leave to set.

NOTE: For a decorative finish, drizzle a little melted chocolate over the top.

BLACK FOREST GÂTEAU

100 g (4 oz) butter
6 eggs
225 g (8 oz) caster sugar
75 g (3 oz) plain flour
50 g (2 oz) cocoa powder
2.5 ml (½ tsp) vanilla flavouring
two 425 g (15 oz) cans stoned black cherries, drained
    and syrup reserved
60 ml (4 tbsp) kirsch
600 ml (20 fl oz) whipping cream
100 g (4 oz) Chocolate Caraque (see page 508), to
    decorate
5 ml (1 level tsp) arrowroot

1. Grease and base-line a 23 cm (9 inch) round cake tin. Put the butter into a bowl, place over a pan of warm water and beat it until really soft but not melted.
2. Put the eggs and sugar into a large bowl, place over a pan of hot water and whisk until pale and creamy and thick enough to leave a trail on the surface when the whisk is lifted.
3. Sift the flour and cocoa together, then lightly fold into the mixture with a metal spoon. Fold in the vanilla flavouring and softened butter.
4. Turn the mixture into the tin and tilt the tin to spread the mixture evenly. Bake in the oven at 180°C (350°F) mark 4 for about 40 minutes, until well risen, firm to the touch and beginning to shrink away from the sides of the tin.
5. Turn out on to a wire rack, covered with greaseproof paper; leave to cool for 30 minutes.
6. Cut the cake into three horizontally. Place a layer on a flat plate. Mix together 75 ml (5 tbsp) cherry syrup and the kirsch. Spoon 45 ml (3 tbsp) over the cake.
7. Whip the cream until it just holds its shape, then spread a little thinly over the soaked sponge. Reserve a quarter of the cherries for decoration and scatter half the remainder over the cream.
8. Repeat the layers of sponge, syrup, cream and cherries. Top with the third cake round and spoon over the remaining kirsch-flavoured syrup.
9. Spread a thin layer of cream around the sides of the cake, reserving a third to decorate. Coat the sides with chocolate caraque, reserving some to decorate the top.
10. Spoon the remaining cream into a piping bag, fitted with a large star nozzle and pipe whirls of cream around the edge of the cake. Top each whirl with a chocolate curl.
11. Fill the centre with the reserved cherries. Blend the arrowroot with 45 ml (3 tbsp) cherry syrup, place in a small saucepan, bring to the boil and boil, stirring, for a few minutes until the mixture is thickened and clear. Brush the glaze over the cherries.

Illustrated on page 395

CHOCOLATE AND VANILLA ROULADE

4 eggs
100 g (4 oz) vanilla-flavoured sugar
60 ml (4 level tbsp) cocoa powder
2.5 ml (½ level tsp) ground cinnamon
caster sugar, to dredge
150 ml (5 fl oz) double cream
icing sugar and strawberries, to decorate

1. Grease a 30 x 20 cm (12 x 8 inch) Swiss roll tin. Line with greaseproof paper and grease the paper. Dust with caster sugar and flour.
2. Whisk the eggs and vanilla sugar in a bowl placed over a pan of hot water until pale and creamy and thick enough to leave a trail on the surface when the whisk is lifted. Sift in the cocoa powder and cinnamon and fold gently through the mixture.
3. Turn the mixture into the tin and bake at 200°C (400°F) mark 6 for 15 minutes, until

Roll up the cake with the paper inside.

golden.
4. Meanwhile, place a sheet of greaseproof paper over a damp tea towel. Dredge the paper thickly with caster sugar.
5. Quickly turn out the cake on to the paper, trim off the crusty edges and roll up with the paper inside. Leave to cool on a wire rack.
6. Whip the cream until it is just holding its shape. When the cake is cold, unroll and remove the paper. Spread with the whipped cream. Roll up and dredge with icing sugar. Decorate with strawberries.

Coffee Gâteau

COFFEE GÂTEAU

75 g (3 oz) caster sugar
3 eggs
100 g (3½ oz) plain flour
1½ quantity Coffee Crème au Beurre (see page 433)
PRALINE
50 g (2 oz) unblanched almonds
50 g (2 oz) caster sugar

1. Grease a 33 x 23 cm (13 x 9 inch) Swiss roll tin and line the base and sides with greaseproof paper.
2. To make the sponge, whisk the sugar and eggs in a bowl over a pan of hot water, using an electric whisk until pale and creamy and thick enough to leave a trail on the surface when the whisk is lifted. Remove the bowl from the heat and whisk until cool.
3. Sift the flour over the mixture and fold in lightly using a metal spoon. Turn the mixture into the prepared tin and gently level the surface.
4. Bake in the oven at 190°C (375°F) mark 5 for

10-12 minutes until well risen and golden brown. Have ready a large sheet of greaseproof paper, sprinkled with a little caster sugar. Turn the sponge out on to the paper, remove the lining paper and leave to cool.
5. To make the praline, gently heat the almonds and sugar in a non-stick frying pan until the sugar melts and turns a rich dark golden brown. Carefully pour on to a well-buttered baking sheet. Quickly coat and separate 8 almonds and leave to one side to set individually; leave the rest of the praline to cool and set.
6. Roughly crush the praline in a blender, or between two sheets of greaseproof paper with a rolling pin.
7. Cut the sponge crossways into 3 equal strips. Sandwich them together with half of the crème au beurre. Spread the remainder over the top and sides of the gâteau. Cover the sides with the crushed praline. Put the remaining crème au beurre into a piping bag fitted with a small star nozzle and pipe on top of the gâteau. Decorate with the caramel coated almonds.

Raspberry Torte

RASPBERRY TORTE

1½ quantity Genoese sponge mixture (see page 406)
1 quantity pâte sucrée (see page 382)
15 ml (1 tbsp) raspberry conserve, sieved
BAVAROIS
20 ml (4 level tsp) powdered gelatine
4 egg yolks
25 g (1 oz) caster sugar
225 ml (8 fl oz) milk
300 ml (½ pint) double cream
30 ml (2 tbsp) icing sugar, sifted
225 g (8 oz) fresh raspberries, sieved
TO DECORATE
450 ml (¾ pint) double cream, whipped
50 g (2 oz) flaked almonds, lightly toasted
few raspberries

1. Grease and line a 25 cm (10 inch) round cake tin. Turn the genoese into the prepared tin and bake in the oven at 180°C (350°F) mark 4 for 30-35 minutes until well risen and firm to the touch. Turn out and cool on a wire rack.
2. Roll out the pâte sucrée on a baking sheet and trim to a neat 25 cm (10 inch) round. Prick all over and chill for 30 minutes. Bake in the oven at 220°C (425°F) mark 7 for 20 minutes.
3. To make the bavarois, soak gelatine in 45 ml (3 tbsp) water in a small bowl. Lightly whisk egg yolks and caster sugar together. Heat milk until almost boiling, then whisk into the egg yolks. Place bowl over a pan of hot water and stir until custard is thick enough to coat back of spoon. Strain into a clean bowl, add gelatine and stir until dissolved. Cool, stirring frequently.
4. Whip the cream with the icing sugar until it forms soft peaks. Mix the custard and raspberry purée together,then fold in the cream.
5. Cut the sponge horizontally into two layers. Place the pastry base on a plate, then spread with the raspberry conserve. Cover with a layer of sponge. Trim the pastry base to the same size as the sponge and place a torten ring or a length of flexible card around them to fit snugly.
6. Pour the bavarois mixture on to the sponge, then chill until beginning to set. Place the other layer of sponge on top and chill until very firm.
7. Remove torten ring or card. Coat the top and sides of the torte with a layer of cream, then cover the sides with flaked almonds. Decorate with remaining cream and raspberries.

SACHERTORTE

150 g (5 oz) plain chocolate, in pieces
100 g (4 oz) unsalted butter or margarine, softened
100 g (4 oz) caster sugar
100 g (4 oz) ground almonds
4 eggs, separated
50 g (2 oz) fresh brown breadcrumbs
30 ml (2 level tbsp) apricot jam, melted
FOR THE ICING
200 g (7 oz) plain chocolate, in pieces
200 ml (7 fl oz) double cream

1. Grease a 23 cm (9 inch) spring-release cake tin, line with greaseproof paper and grease the paper.
2. Melt the chocolate in a heatproof bowl over a pan of simmering water. Remove from the heat.
3. Cream the butter and sugar together in a bowl until pale and fluffy. Stir in the almonds, egg yolks, breadcrumbs and melted chocolate, then beat until well combined.
4. Whisk the egg whites until stiff and fold half into the chocolate mixture, then fold in the other half. Pour the mixture into the prepared tin and level the surface.
5. Bake in the oven at 180°C (350°F) mark 4 for 40-45 minutes until firm to the touch.
6. Cover with a damp tea towel, leave for 5 minutes to cool slightly, then transfer on to a wire rack to cool. When cold, brush the top with the melted apricot jam.
7. To make the icing, place the chocolate in a heatproof bowl with the cream. Stand the bowl over a pan of simmering water and heat until the chocolate melts and blends with the cream. Cool for a few minutes until the icing just coats the back of a spoon.
8. Stand the cake on the wire rack on a baking sheet and pour over the icing. Gently shake the cake to spread the icing evenly and use a palette knife, if necessary to ensure that the sides are completely covered. Leave in a cool place, but not the refrigerator, to set.
SERVES 8-10

Sachertorte

DEVIL'S FOOD CAKE

75 g (3 oz) plain chocolate
250 g (9 oz) light soft brown sugar
200 ml (7 fl oz) milk
75 g (3 oz) butter or block margarine, softened
2 eggs, beaten
175 g (6 oz) plain flour
3.75 ml (¾ level tsp) bicarbonate of soda
FOR THE AMERICAN FROSTING
450 g (1 lb) caster sugar
2 egg whites

1. Grease and base-line two 19 cm (7½ inch) sandwich tins. Grease the paper and dust with caster sugar and flour.
2. Break the chocolate into a small saucepan, add 75 g (3 oz) brown sugar and the milk and heat very gently, stirring. Remove from the heat and leave to cool.
3. Cream the butter and remaining brown sugar. Gradually beat the eggs into the creamed mixture. Slowly pour in the chocolate mixture and beat until well combined.
4. Sift together the flour and bicarbonate of soda and gently fold into the cake mixture, using a large metal spoon.
5. Turn the mixture into the prepared tins and tilt to spread evenly. Bake in the oven at 180°C (350°F) mark 4 for about 35 minutes, until the cakes spring back when lightly pressed with fingertips. Turn out on to a wire rack to cool.
6. Meanwhile, make the frosting. Place the sugar in a large heavy-based saucepan with 135 ml (4½ fl oz) water and heat gently until the sugar has dissolved. Bring to the boil and boil to 115°C (240°F) as registered on a sugar thermometer.
7. Meanwhile, whisk the egg whites in a large deep bowl until stiff. Allow the bubbles to settle, then slowly pour the hot syrup on to the egg whites, whisking constantly. When all the sugar syrup is added, continue whisking until the mixture stands in peaks and just starts to become matt around the edges. The icing sets quickly, so work rapidly.
8. Sandwich the cakes together with some of the frosting. Spread the remainder over the top and sides using a palette knife. Pull the frosting up into peaks all over. Leave to set in a cool place, not in the refrigerator.

RASPBERRY ROULADE

450 g (1 lb) raspberries, hulled
4 eggs, separated
100 g (4 oz) caster sugar
40 g (1½ oz) plain flour
30 ml (2 tbsp) orange-flavoured liqueur
300 ml (10 fl oz) double cream
45 ml (3 level tbsp) icing sugar

1. Grease a 33 x 23 cm (13 x 9 inch) Swiss roll tin. Line with greaseproof paper and grease the paper. Dust with caster sugar and flour.
2. Put half the raspberries into a blender and work until just smooth, then press through a nylon sieve to remove the pips.
3. Whisk the egg yolks in a deep bowl with the caster sugar until pale and creamy and thick enough to leave a trail on the surface when the whisk is lifted. Gradually whisk in the raspberry purée, keeping the mixture stiff.
4. Sift the flour over the surface and fold lightly into the egg and raspberry mixture.
5. Whisk the egg whites until stiff, and fold them gently through the raspberry mixture.
6. Turn into the prepared tin and smooth the surface. Bake in the oven at 200°C (400°F) mark 6 for about 12-15 minutes or until golden brown and firm to the touch.
7. Meanwhile, place a sheet of greaseproof paper over a damp tea towel. Dredge the paper thickly with caster sugar.
8. Quickly turn out the cake on to the paper, trim off the crusty edges and roll up with the paper inside. Carefully place on a wire rack and leave until completely cold.
9. Meanwhile, reserving six raspberries for decoration, sprinkle the rest with the liqueur and sift over the icing sugar. Whip the cream until it is just stiff enough to hold its shape.
10. When the cake is cold, unroll and remove the paper. Spread three quarters of the cream over the top and scatter with raspberries.
11. Roll up the roulade and decorate with piped whirls of cream. Just before serving, dust the top with sieved icing sugar and decorate with the reserved raspberries.

Celebration Cakes

Rich fruit cakes are traditional at weddings and Christenings, anniversaries and Christmas. The centrepiece will most often be a beautiful cake decorated with Royal Icing; beneath the sugar coating will be a dark, glossy cake loaded with fruit, candied peel, nuts and spices and deliciously soaked with brandy.

Like other rich cakes, fruit cakes are made by the creaming method, but the mixture is slightly stiffer to support the weight of the fruit.

If the mixture is too wet, fruit is inclined to sink to the bottom. All dried fruit should be thoroughly cleaned and dried before use; glacé cherries should be rinsed to remove excess syrup, then dried. Toss all fruit in a little of the measured flour to make sure it is quite dry.

All fruit cakes keep well, but the richest actually improve if kept for two or three months before you cut them. Every two or three weeks, get it out, prick the surface with a fine skewer and spoon over a little brandy or other spirit.

Rich Fruit Cake

1. Grease and line the cake tin for the size of cake you wish to make, using a double thickness of greaseproof paper. Tie a double band of brown paper round the outside.
2. Prepare the ingredients for the appropriate size of cake according to the chart overleaf. Wash and dry all the fruit, if necessary, chopping any over-large pieces, and mix well together in a large bowl. Add the flaked almonds. Sift flour and spices into another bowl with a pinch of salt.
3. Put the butter, sugar and lemon rind into a bowl and cream together until pale and fluffy. Add the beaten eggs gradually, beating well.
4. Gradually fold the flour lightly into the mixture with a metal spoon, then fold in the brandy. Finally fold in the fruit and nuts.

5. Turn the mixture into the prepared tin, spreading it evenly and making sure there are no air pockets. Make a hollow in the centre to ensure an even surface when cooked.
6. Stand the tin on newspaper or brown paper in the oven. Bake at 150°C (300°F) mark 2 for time given in chart until a fine warmed skewer inserted in the centre comes out clean. Cover with greaseproof paper after about 1½ hours.
7. When cooked, leave the cake to cool in the tin before turning out on to a wire rack. Prick the top all over with a fine skewer and slowly pour 30-45 ml (2-3 tbsp) brandy over it.
8. Wrap the cake in a double thickness of greaseproof paper and place in an airtight tin or overwrap with foil and store in a cool place.

Planning a Wedding Cake

It is most important for the final overall result to choose the sizes of the tiers carefully, avoiding a combination that would look too heavy. Good proportions for a three-tier cake are 30, 23 and 15 cm (12, 9 and 6 inches); for a two-tier cake 30 and 20 cm (12 and 8 inches), 28 and 18 cm (11 and 7 inches) or 25 and 15 cm (10 and 6 inches).

The bottom tier should be deeper than the upper ones, therefore cakes of 25-30 cm (10-12 inches) diameter are generally made about 7.5 cm (3 inches) deep, while those 18-23 cm (7-9 inches) in diameter are 6.5 cm (2½ inches) deep, and 15 cm (6 inches) diameter cakes are 5 cm (2 inches) deep.

Don't attempt to make the larger sizes of cake unless you have an oven to cope with it, as you should allow at least 2.5 cm (1 inch) space between the oven walls and the tin. For a three-tier cake, bake the two smaller cakes together and the largest one separately. You can expect to cut 8-10 portions of cake from each 450 g (1 lb) cooked weight. (See chart overleaf.)

For a large reception, it is worth making an extra tier for cutting behind-the-scenes.

QUANTITIES AND SIZES FOR RICH FRUIT CAKES

To make a formal cake for a birthday, wedding or anniversary, the following chart will show you the amount of ingredients required to fill the chosen cake tin or tins, whether round or square.

NOTE: When baking large cakes, 25 cm (10 inches) and upwards, it is advisable to reduce the oven heat to 130°C (250°F) mark 1 after two-thirds of the cooking time.

Square tin size	12 cm (5 inches) square	15 cm (6 inches) square	18 cm (7 inches) square	20 cm (8 inches) square
Round tin size	15 cm (6 inches) diameter	18 cm (7 inches) diameter	20 cm (8 inches) diameter	23 cm (9 inches) diameter
Currants	225 g (8 oz)	350 g (12 oz)	450 g (1 lb)	625 g (1 lb 6 oz)
Sultanas	100 g (4 oz)	125 g (4½ oz)	200 g (7 oz)	225 g (8 oz)
Raisins	100 g (4 oz)	125 g (4½ oz)	200 g (7 oz)	225 g (8 oz)
Glacé cherries	50 g (2 oz)	75 g (3 oz)	150 g (5 oz)	175 g (6 oz)
Mixed peel	25 g (1 oz)	50 g (2 oz)	75 g (3 oz)	100 g (4 oz)
Flaked almonds	25 g (1 oz)	50 g (2 oz)	75 g (3 oz)	100 g (4 oz)
Lemon rind	a little	a little	a little	¼ lemon
Plain flour	175 g (6 oz)	215 g (7½ oz)	350 g (12 oz)	400 g (14 oz)
Mixed spice	1.25 ml (¼ level tsp)	2.5 ml (½ level tsp)	2.5 ml (½ level tsp)	5 ml (1 level tsp)
Cinnamon	1.25 ml (¼ level tsp)	2.5 ml (½ level tsp)	2.5 ml (½ level tsp)	5 ml (1 level tsp)
Butter	150 g (5 oz)	175 g (6 oz)	275 g (10 oz)	350 g (12 oz)
Brown soft sugar	150 g (5 oz)	175 g (6 oz)	275 g (10 oz)	350 g (12 oz)
Eggs, beaten	2½	3	5	6
Brandy	15 ml (1 tbsp)	15ml (1 tbsp)	15-30 ml (1-2 tbsp)	30 ml (2 tbsp)
Time (approx.)	2½-3 hours	3 hours	3½ hours	4 hours
Weight when cooked	1.1 kg (2½ lb)	1.6 kg (3¼ lb)	2.2 kg (4¾ lb)	2.7 kg (6 lb)

Square tin size	23 cm (9 inches) square	25 cm (10 inches) square	28 cm (11 inches) square	30 cm (12 inches) square
Round tin size	25 cm (10 inches) diameter	28 cm (11 inches) diameter	30 cm (12 inches) diameter	33 cm (13 inches) diameter
Currants	775 g (1 lb 12 oz)	1.1 kg (2 lb 8 oz)	1.5 kg (3 lb 2 oz)	1.7 kg (3 lb 12 oz)
Sultanas	375 g (13 oz)	400 g (14 oz)	525 g (1 lb 3 oz)	625 g (1 lb 6 oz)
Raisins	375 g (13 oz)	400 g (14 oz)	525 g (1 lb 3 oz)	625 g (1 lb 6 oz)
Glacé cherries	250 g (9 oz)	275 g (10 oz)	350 g (12 oz)	425 g (15 oz)
Mixed peel	150 g (5 oz)	200 g (7 oz)	250 g (9 oz)	275 g (10 oz)
Flaked almonds	150 g (5 oz)	200 g (7 oz)	250 g (9 oz)	275 g (10 oz)
Lemon rind	¼ lemon	½ lemon	½ lemon	1 lemon
Plain flour	600 g (1 lb 5 oz)	700 g (1 lb 8 oz)	825 g (1 lb 13 oz)	1 kg (2 lb 6 oz)
Mixed spice	5 ml (1 level tsp)	10 ml (2 level tsp)	12.5 ml (2½ level tsp)	12.5 ml (2½ level tsp)
Cinnamon	5 ml (1 level tsp)	10 ml (2 level tsp)	12.5 ml (2½ level tsp)	12.5 ml (2½ level tsp)
Butter	500 g (1 lb 2 oz)	600 g (1 lb 5 oz)	800 g (1 lb 12 oz)	950 g (2 lb 2 oz)
Sugar	500 g (1 lb 2 oz)	600 g (1 lb 5 oz)	800 g (1 lb 12 oz)	950 g (2 lb 2 oz)
Eggs, beaten	9	11	14	17
Brandy	30-45 ml (2-3 tbsp)	45 ml (3 tbsp)	60 ml (4 tbsp)	90 ml (6 tbsp)
Time (approx.)	6 hours	7 hours	8 hours	8½ hours
Weight when cooked	4 kg (9 lb)	5.2 kg (11½ lb)	6.7 kg (14¾ lb)	7.7 kg (17 1b)

ICING AND ALMOND PASTE QUANTITIES

The amounts of Almond Paste quoted in this chart will give a thin covering. The quantities of Royal Icing should be enough for two coats. If using ready-to-roll fondant icing, use the quantities suggested for Royal Icing as a rough guide.

Square tin size	12 cm (5 inches) square	15 cm (6 inches) square	18 cm (7 inches) square	20 cm (8 inches) square	23 cm (9 inches) square	25 cm (10 inches) square	28 cm (11 inches) square	30 cm (12 inches) square
Round tin size	15 cm (6 inches) round	18 cm (7 inches) round	20 cm (8 inches) round	23 cm (9 inches) round	25 cm (10 inches) round	28 cm (11 inches) round	30 cm (12 inches) round	33 cm (13 inches) round
Almond Paste	350 g (12 oz)	450 g (1 lb)	550 g (1¼ lb)	800 g (1¾ lb)	900 g (2 lb)	1 kg (2¼ lb)	1.1 kg (2½ lb)	1.4 kg (3 lb)
Royal Icing	450 g (1 lb)	550 g (1¼ lb)	700 g (1½ lb)	900 g (2 lb)	1 kg (2¼ lb)	1.1 kg (2½ lb)	1.4 kg (3 lb)	1.6 kg (3½ lb)

CAKE BOARDS AND PILLARS

The board should be 5 cm (2 inches) larger than the cake. For a very large cake, use a board 10-12 cm (4-5 inches) larger.

Pillars between the base cake and the next tier are usually 9 cm (3½ inches) high and those between the middle tier and top tier 7.5 cm (3 inches) high. White plaster pillars look best.

WEDDING CAKE TIMETABLE

2-3 MONTHS BEFORE: Make the cakes. When cold, prick at intervals with a fine skewer and spoon some brandy evenly over the surface. Wrap the cakes in greaseproof paper and then in double thickness foil. Store in a cool, dry place.

14-20 DAYS BEFORE: The baked cakes should have an even top but if not, they can be levelled with a sharp knife. Cover each cake with Almond Paste (see page 426) and store loosely covered with greaseproof paper in a cool dry place for 4-5 days.
10-15 DAYS BEFORE: Apply the first coat of Royal Icing (see page 426) and leave to dry for 1-2 days. Think about the design of the cake.
8-12 DAYS BEFORE: Apply the second coat of Royal Icing if necessary and leave to dry for 1-2 days. Make all separate or run out decorations for the cake and leave to dry for 1-2 days.
7 DAYS BEFORE: Complete all further decorating a week before the cake is to be served. Do not assemble a tiered cake until the day.

Decorating Cakes

Decorations for informal cakes may be anything from a light dusting of caster sugar or a smooth coat of glacé icing to whirls of butter cream interspersed with nuts or coloured sweets. For formal cakes, you can either use ready-to-roll fondant icing, or master piping techniques and the method of flat icing with Royal Icing.

EQUIPMENT

Simple decorations need no special equipment; all you need are a palette knife, fork and a wire rack; however the right tools do help when you start to attempt more elaborate work.
ICING COMB helps to ice the sides of a deep cake.
ICING NAIL is a small metal or polythene nail with a large head that is designed to hold decorations, such as icing roses, while you make them. It enables you to hold the rose securely, and turn it without damaging it.

ICING RULER is useful for flat icing a large cake. You can use anything with a fine straight edge, long enough to extend both sides of the cake.
ICING TURNTABLE gives you clearance from the working surface and enables you to turn the cake freely. If you do not have a turntable, place the cake board on an upturned plate, to give it a little lift from the working surface.
NOZZLES can be used with paper or fabric piping bags. A fine plain nozzle for writing and piping straight lines and simple designs, plus a star or

shell nozzle, are the basics – you can build up quite a variety using these. More advanced piping work demands a whole range of different shapes and sizes. For use with paper piping bags, choose nozzles without a screw band; the band is useful with a fabric bag.

The following are the most useful: Fine plain (writing) No. 1; medium plain (writing) No. 2; thicker plain (writing) No. 3; six-point star; eight-point star (medium); petal; shell.

PIPING BAGS can be made from greaseproof paper, or bought ready-made in fabric. Special icing pumps are also available.

SILVER CAKE BOARD OR 'DRUM' sets off any iced cake. Some are made from thin card, or stronger ones are about 1 cm (½ inch) thick. Choose a board that is 5 cm (2 inches) larger than the cake, so that a border shows all round.

FINE SANDPAPER can be used to sand down any imperfections on royal icing.

ICING CAKES

Glacé icing and frostings are most commonly used for small cakes and sponges. Royal icing is used with almond paste and an apricot glaze on rich fruit cakes such as Christmas and wedding cakes. Ready-to-roll fondant icing (available in packets) is a convenient alternative to Royal Icing; it can also be applied to sponge cakes. Almond paste can also be used as a decoration in its own right, shaped and coloured if wished.

The cake must be completely cold before you start icing. The surface must be level; if necessary, turn the cake upside down and ice the flat bottom. If making a sandwich or layer cake, fill first. Decorate the sides, then the top.

CAKE DECORATIONS

Add ready-made decorations before the icing hardens completely, or stick them in place with a little dab of fresh icing.

NUTS are a popular decoration, particularly walnuts, hazelnuts, almonds and pistachios.

CRYSTALLISED flowers such as roses and violets are effective. They should be bought in small quantities; keep them in a dark place to avoid discolouring.

ANGELICA can be cut into shapes for decoration. When buying look for a really good colour and a small amount of sugar. To remove sugar, soak briefly in hot water, then drain and dry well.

CHOCOLATE AND COLOURED VERMICELLI are popular. However they stale quickly and become speckled, so buy in small quantities as needed.

SILVER DRAGEES (BALLS) keep well in a dry place; use tweezers for handling. They come in other colours than silver.

HUNDREDS AND THOUSANDS are useful for children's cakes.

SWEETS offer endless possibilities for novelty cakes. Jelly sweets, liquorice, marshmallows, chocolate coins and lollipops can be used to colourful effect.

SUGAR COFFEE BEANS make a sophisticated decoration for gâteaux.

CHOCOLATE DECORATIONS include curls, grated chocolate, cut-out shapes, caraque and leaves (see page 508). Chocolate flavoured cake covering is useful for caraque and curls, but the flavour is not so good. Crumbled chocolate flake makes a useful last minute decoration.

PIPING

Butter cream, crème au beurre, stiff glacé icing and royal icing can all be piped. It is usual to pipe on to a base of the same kind of icing, though butter cream is sometimes piped on to glacé icing.

The icing used for piping must be completely free of lumps, or it will block the nozzle. It must also be exactly the right consistency to force easily through the nozzle, but still retain its shape.

Work with a small quantity at a time, refilling the piping bag frequently if necessary. If you are a beginner, practise on an upturned plate first. The practice icing can be scraped up while still soft and reused. Even on the real cake, if the base icing is hard mistakes can be gently scraped off and corrected by repiping.

MAKING AND USING A PIPING BAG

Fold a 25 cm (10 inch) square of greaseproof paper diagonally in half, then roll into a cone. Fold the points inwards to secure them. To insert a nozzle, snip off the tip of the bag and drop the nozzle securely into position before adding the icing.

For a very fine line, just snip off the end of the bag and use without a nozzle. Never more than half-fill the bag. When using a paper piping bag, fold the top flap down, enclosing the front edge, until the bag is sealed and quite firm; twist a fabric bag firmly closed.

To hold the bag, lay it across the palm of one hand; with a paper bag, place your thumb firmly over the top of the bag, grasp the rest with the other four fingers and apply a steady even pressure until icing starts to come out of the tip of the nozzle. With a fabric bag grasp the bag where it is twisted with thumb and first finger and apply pressure with the remaining fingers.

TO PIPE A STRAIGHT LINE

Place the tip of the nozzle where the line is to start. Apply slight pressure to the bag and as the icing starts to come out of the nozzle, lift the bag about 2.5 cm (1 inch) from the surface. This allows even the shakiest of hands to pipe a straight line. Move your hand in the direction of the line, guiding it with the other hand if you want, allowing the icing to flow evenly. About 1 cm (½ inch) before the end of the line, stop squeezing the bag and gently lower the tip of the nozzle to the surface.

TO PIPE DOTS

Only a slight pressure on the piping bag is required. Place the tip of the nozzle on the surface and hold the bag almost upright. Squeeze the bag gently and at the same time lift the nozzle slightly. Stop squeezing, move the nozzle slightly in a gentle shaking action to avoid a 'tail', and lift the nozzle.

Larger dots can be made by moving the nozzle in a small circle; or use a larger nozzle.

TO PIPE STARS

Fit the bag with a star nozzle. Hold bag upright and just above the surface of the cake. Squeeze the icing out. As soon as the star is formed, stop squeezing and lift the bag away sharply.

TO PIPE ROSETTES

Fit the bag with a star nozzle. Hold the icing bag upright, just above the surface of the cake. Squeeze gently and move the nozzle in a complete circle, filling in the centre. Pull the nozzle away sharply to avoid forming a point on the iced surface which would spoil the appearance of the piped rosette.

TO PIPE A SHELL BORDER

Use either a star nozzle or a special shell nozzle; a shell nozzle will give a flatter, fuller shell with more ridges. In either case the movement is the same. Hold the bag at an angle to the surface and just above it. Squeeze until the icing begins to come from the nozzle and forms a head. Pull the bag gently and at the same time release pressure to form the tail. Pipe the next shell just touching, and remember to release pressure each time to form the tail of the shell.

WRITING

Use a plain writing nozzle and pipe as for a straight line (see left). Practise with simple capital letters at first. Before attempting to write on the cake, draw the letters on greaseproof paper and prick them on to the base icing with a pin; use the pin pricks as a guide.

TO PIPE A ROSE

Place a little icing on the top of an icing nail and stick a small square of non-stick baking parchment on top.

Fit the piping bag with a petal nozzle. Hold the bag with the thin part of the nozzle uppermost. Pipe a cone of icing, twisting the nail between thumb and finger, to form the centre of the rose. Pipe five or six petals around the centre, overlapping each petal and piping the outer ones so that they are more open, and lie flatter.

Lift the square of paper from the nail and leave the rose uncovered for about 24 hours to dry. Attach it to the cake with a dab of icing.

TO PIPE A DAISY

Stick a small square of non-stick baking parchment on top of an icing nail and fit the piping bag with a petal nozzle (as for piping a rose, above). Work with the thick edge of the nozzle to the centre and pipe five even-sized petals. Dry as instructed above.

APRICOT GLAZE

100 g (4 oz) apricot jam

1. Put the jam and 30 ml (2 tbsp) water in a saucepan and heat gently, stirring, until the jam softens. Bring to the boil and simmer for 1 minute.

2. Sieve the glaze and use while still warm.

MAKES 150 ML (¼ PINT)

ALMOND PASTE

Either make your own almond paste following this recipe, or buy ready-made 'white' marzipan rather than the yellow variety. Note that homemade almond paste uses raw eggs.

225 g (8 oz) icing sugar
225 g (8 oz) caster sugar
450 g (1 lb) ground almonds
5 ml (1 tsp) vanilla flavouring
2 eggs, lightly beaten
10 ml (2 tsp) lemon juice

1. Sift the icing sugar into a bowl and mix in the caster sugar and ground almonds.
2. Add the vanilla flavouring, egg and lemon juice and mix to a stiff dough. Knead lightly, then shape into a ball. Cover until ready to use.
MAKES 900 G (2 LB)

NOTE: As an alternative to raw eggs, use water mixed with a little sherry or brandy and the lemon juice to bind the mixture.

COVERING A FRUIT CAKE WITH ALMOND PASTE
1. Measure around the cake with a piece of string. Dust the work surface with icing sugar and roll out two-thirds of the paste to a rectangle, half the length of the string by twice the depth of the cake.

2. Trim the edges, then cut in half lengthways with a sharp knife. Place the cake upside down on a board and brush the sides with apricot glaze. Gently lift the almond paste and place it firmly in position round the cake.
3. Smooth the joins with a palette knife and keep the top and bottom edges square. Roll a jam jar lightly around the cake to help the paste stick more firmly.
4. Brush the top of the cake with apricot glaze and roll out the remaining almond paste to fit. With the help of the rolling pin, lift it on to the cake.
5. Lightly roll with the rolling pin, then smooth the join and leave to dry for up to 4-5 days before starting to ice.

Glaze cake sides then cover with almond paste.   *Use rolling pin to lift almond paste on to cake.*

ROYAL ICING

4 egg whites
900 g (2 lb) icing sugar
15 ml (1 tbsp) lemon juice
10 ml (2 tsp) glycerine

1. Whisk the egg whites in a bowl until slightly frothy. Then sift and stir in about a quarter of the icing sugar with a wooden spoon. Continue adding more sugar gradually, beating well after each addition, until about three-quarters of the sugar has been added.
2. Beat in the lemon juice and continue beating for about 10 minutes, until the icing is smooth.
3. Beat in the remaining sugar until the required consistency is achieved, depending on how the icing will be used.
4. Finally, stir in the glycerine to prevent the icing hardening. Cover and keep for 24 hours to allow air bubbles to rise to the surface.
MAKES ABOUT 900 G (2 LB)

NOTE: As an alternative to raw egg whites, albumen powder can be used. Follow the manufacturer's directions.

FLAT ICING WITH ROYAL ICING
1. Always apply royal icing over a layer of almond paste rather than directly on to the cake. Keep the bowl of icing covered with a damp cloth, to prevent it developing a crusty surface. Spoon almost half the icing on to the top of the cake and spread it evenly with a palette knife, using a padding action to remove any air bubbles.
2. Using an icing ruler or palette knife longer than the width of the cake, draw it steadily, without applying any pressure, across the top of the cake at an angle of 30°. Neaten the edges. Leave to dry for 24 hours before icing the sides.
3. To ice the sides, place the board on an icing turntable or on an upturned plate. Spread the remaining icing on the side of the cake and

smooth it roughly with a small palette knife. Hold the palette knife or an icing comb upright and at an angle of 45° to the cake. Starting at the back, slowly rotate the turntable while moving the knife or comb slowly and evenly towards you to smooth the surface.
4. For a square cake, apply the icing to each side separately.
5. Reserve the surplus icing for decorating.
6. For a really smooth finish, allow to dry for 1-2 days, then apply a second thinner coat of icing. Use a piece of fine sandpaper to sand down any imperfections in the first coat. Allow to dry thoroughly before piping on decorations.

ROUGH ICING WITH ROYAL ICING
1. Use two thirds of the icing to roughly flat ice the top and sides of the cake (see left). Leave to dry for 24 hours.
2. Spoon the remaining icing on top of the flat icing with a palette knife or spatula.
3. Using the palette knife or back of a teaspoon, pull the icing into well formed peaks. Leave to dry for 24 hours.

ROSEBUD WEDDING CAKE

three round cakes of the following sizes, covered in Almond Paste (see page 423): 30 cm (12 inches), 23 cm (9 inches), 15 cm (6 inches); on three round cake boards: 40 cm (16 inches), 28 cm (11 inches), 20 cm (8 inches)
white Royal Icing using 2.7 kg (6 lb) icing sugar (see page 423)
four 9 cm (3½ inch) and four 7.5 cm (3 inch) round pillars
24 roses in pink icing, to decorate

1. Flat ice the cake with two coats of Royal Icing (see left). Place the pillars in position on the base and middle cakes and prick around with a pin for positioning later.
2. Cut a circle of greaseproof paper to the size of the top of each cake; fold the largest two into eight segments, the smallest into six segments. Using a compass or the bottom of a glass of the right diameter, pencil a scallop on the rounded edge between the folds about 5 cm (2 inches) deep for big cakes, and about 2.5 cm (1 inch) deep for the top tier.
3. Cut out the scallops, open paper, place on cake and hold with one hand while pricking scalloped outline on to the icing.
4. Remove paper and, using an icing bag filled with white icing and fitted with a plain No. 2 icing nozzle, pipe a line along the inner edge of the scallops. Pipe a trellis inside each scallop as shown in the photograph.
5. Using an icing bag fitted with a plain nozzle (No. 1) and white icing, pipe a line 5 mm (¼ inch) outside the scalloped edge. Pipe two V's and three dots at the join of each scallop.
6. Place your selected pieces of ribbon and daisy edging in position around the cakes. Secure the ends in position with headed pins.

7. Using an icing bag fitted with a three-point star nozzle and white icing, pipe a shell or star border around the base of the cakes.
8. Carefully position the pillars on top of the bottom cake layer and secure them with icing. Place the second cake layer on top, then pillars, then the top cake layer.
9. Finish the decoration with a rose at the points where the scallops meet, and clusters at the base of the pillars, if wished (optional).

Rosebud Wedding Cake

SIMNEL CAKE

175 g (6 oz) butter or block margarine, softened
175 g (6 oz) caster sugar
3 whole eggs and 1 egg white
225 g (8 oz) plain flour
pinch of salt
2.5 ml (½ level tsp) ground cinnamon
2.5 ml (½ level tsp) grated nutmeg
100 g (4 oz) glacé cherries, washed, dried and cut into
    quarters
50 g (2 oz) cut mixed peel, chopped
250 g (9 oz) currants
100 g (4 oz) sultanas
finely grated rind of 1 lemon
15-30 ml (1-2 tbsp) milk, if necessary
450 g (1 lb) Almond Paste (see page 426)
crystallised flowers, to decorate (optional)

1. Grease an 18 cm (7 inch) round cake tin.
Line with greaseproof paper and grease the
paper.
2. Cream the butter and sugar until pale and
fluffy. Lightly whisk the whole eggs and gradually
beat into the creamed ingredients.
3. Sift the flour, salt and spices over the surface
and fold into the mixture with a metal spoon.
Add all the fruit and the lemon rind, folding
together to give a smooth dropping consistency.
If mixture is a little too firm add a little milk.

4. Divide the Almond Paste in half. Lightly dust
a surface with icing sugar and roll out one half to
a 16 cm (6½ inch) circle.
5. Spoon half the cake mixture into the
prepared tin. Place the round of almond paste
on top and cover with the remaining cake
mixture. Press down gently with the back of a
spoon to level the surface.
6. Tie a double thickness of brown paper round
the outside of the tin. Bake in the oven at 170°C
(325°F) mark 3 for 1 hour, then lower the heat
to 150°C (300°F) mark 2 and bake for a further
2 hours. When cooked the cake should be a rich
brown colour, and firm to the touch.
7. Cool in the tin for about 1 hour, then turn
out. Ease off the greaseproof paper and leave to
cool completely on a wire rack.
8. Divide the remaining Almond Paste in two.
Roll out one half to a 17 cm (7½ inch) circle and
the rest into eleven small balls. Lightly beat the
egg white and brush over the top of the cake.
Place the circle on top, crimp the edges, and
with a little of the egg white fix the balls around
the top edge of the cake.
9. Brush the Almond Paste with the remaining
egg white and place under a hot grill for 1-2
minutes until the paste is well browned. Tie a
ribbon around the cake to serve and decorate
with crystallised flowers if wished.

WHITE CHRISTMAS CAKE

175 g (6 oz) butter or block margarine, softened
175 g (6 oz) caster sugar
3 eggs, size 2, beaten
125 g (4 oz) dried apricots, roughly chopped
125 g (4 oz) Brazil nuts, chopped
50 g (2 oz) candied lemon peel, finely chopped
125 g (4 oz) sultanas
125 g (4 oz) plain flour
125 g (4 oz) self raising flour
Apricot Glaze (see page 425)
225 g (8 oz) Almond Paste (see page 426)
Royal Icing (see page 426), to decorate

1. Grease and line the bottom and sides of a
20 cm (8 inch) round cake tin.
2. Cream the fat and sugar together until pale
and fluffy. Add the beaten eggs, a little at a time,
beating after each addition.
3. Mix all the fruit and nuts together. Sift the
flours together and fold into the creamed
mixture. Fold in the fruit. Spoon into the
prepared tin.
4. Bake in the oven at 180°C (350°F) mark 4 for
about 1¼ hours, covering if necessary, until a fine
warmed skewer inserted in the centre comes out
clean. Cool a little, then turn out on to a wire
rack.
5. To finish, brush top with Apricot Glaze, then
cover with Almond Paste (see page 426).
6. Rough ice the top of the cake (see page 427)
and leave to dry. Decorate if wished with bought
decorations, such as Christmas trees and snow-
men, and tie a festive ribbon around the edge.

CELEBRATION CAKE

This is a simple effortless decorated cake which can be adapted to suit any occasion. It can be completed a day ahead, ready to have the ribbon tied and flowers added just before serving. Illustrated on page 511.

225 g (8 oz) butter or margarine
225 g (8 oz) caster sugar
4 eggs, beaten
225 g (8 oz) self-raising flour
grated rind and juice of 1 lemon
red, blue or yellow edible food colouring
three 225 g (8 oz) packets ready-to-roll fondant icing
300 ml (10 fl oz) double cream
120 ml (8 level tbsp) black cherry conserve or 50 g
(2 oz) sliced strawberries
icing sugar for dusting
fresh flowers and ribbon, to decorate

1. Grease and base-line a 23 cm (9 inch) round cake tin.
2. Cream the butter and sugar together until pale and fluffy. Add the eggs a little at a time, beating well after each addition.
3. Sift the flour and fold into the mixture with the grated lemon rind and juice. Spoon into the prepared tin and level the surface.
4. Bake in the oven at 180°C (350°F) mark 4 for about 1-1¼ hours or until golden and firm to the touch. Cover the top with greaseproof paper, if necessary, towards the end of cooking time. Turn out on to a wire rack and allow to cool.
5. Meanwhile tint the ready-to-roll icing a pale shade by kneading in a little colouring until evenly blended. Wrap tightly in greaseproof paper.
6. Split the cake in half horizontally. Whip the cream until it just holds its shape. Sandwich the cake layers together with jam or fruit and all but 45 ml (3 level tbsp) cream. Place on a serving plate. Spread the reserved cream thinly around the sides and over the top of the cake.
7. Dust the work surface lightly with icing sugar and roll out the icing large enough to cover the cake completely. Fold icing over a rolling pin and carefully lift it onto the cake; gently smooth the sides. Trim excess icing from base of cake.
8. Decorate with a broad ribbon and fresh flowers just before serving.

YULE LOG

3 eggs
100 g (4 oz) caster sugar
100 g (4 oz) plain flour
caster sugar, to dredge
1 quantity Chocolate Crème au Beurre (see page 433)
icing sugar, to decorate

1. Grease a 30 x 20 cm (12 x 8 inch) Swiss roll tin. Line with greaseproof paper and grease the paper. Dust with caster sugar and flour.
2. Put the eggs and sugar in a large bowl, place over a pan of hot water and whisk until pale and creamy and thick enough to leave a trail on the surface of the mixture when the whisk is lifted.
3. Sift half the flour over the mixture and fold in very lightly with a metal spoon. Sift and fold in the remaining flour, then lightly stir in 15 ml (1 tbsp) hot water.

4. Pour the mixture into the prepared tin. Bake in the oven at 220°C (425°F) mark 7 for 8-12 minutes until golden brown, well risen and firm to the touch.
5. Meanwhile, place a sheet of greaseproof paper over a damp tea towel. Dredge the paper with a little caster sugar.
6. Quickly turn out the cake on to the paper, trim off the crusty edges and roll up with the paper inside. Leave to cool on a wire rack.
7. When cold, unroll and remove the paper. Spread one-third of the crème au beurre over the surface and re-roll. Refrigerate for 30 minutes until the roll is firm.
8. Coat with the remaining crème au beurre and mark lines with a fork to resemble tree bark.
9. Chill for 1 hour before serving. Dust lightly with icing sugar and decorate with a sprig of real or artificial holly.

UNUSUAL SHAPED CAKES

If you want to make an unconventionally shaped cake, such as a numeral or a heart shape, use the following guide to calculate how much mixture is required.

FOR THE VICTORIA SANDWICH MIXTURE

50 g (2 oz) butter or block margarine
50 g (2 oz) caster sugar
1 egg
50 g (2 oz) self raising flour

FOR THE FRUIT CAKE MIXTURE

150 g (5 oz) currants
50 g (2 oz) sultanas
50 g (2 oz) seedless raisins
12 glacé cherries, halved
45 ml (3 level tbsp) chopped mixed peel
100 g (4 oz) plain flour
1.25 ml (¼ level tsp) ground mixed spice
75 g (3 oz) butter or block margarine
75 g (3 oz) brown soft sugar
1½ eggs

1. For every 600 ml (1 pint) of water the tin will hold, you will need to make either mixture with the ingredients listed, so multiply as required. Remember to fill the tin only as deep as you want the finished cake to be – not necessarily to the very top.
2. Make either cake in the usual way (see pages 406 and 421). Bake the Victoria Sandwich Mixture in the oven at 180°C (350°F) mark 4 and the fruit cake mixture in the oven at 150°C (300°F) mark 1-2. The time varies according to the shape and depth of the cake. Bake the fruit cake in the centre of the oven and test to see if cooked by piercing with a skewer – the skewer should come out clean. Leave the cake to cool completely in the tin before turning out.

NOTE: It is not really feasible to cook a Victoria Sandwich Cake in a tin larger than 25 cm (10 inches) across, as the edges will overcook long before the middle is done.

NOVELTY CLOWN CAKE

LARGE CAKE
45 ml (3 level tbsp) cocoa powder
350 g (12 oz) self raising flour
10 ml (2 level tsp) baking powder
350 g (12 oz) caster sugar
350 g (12 oz) soft margarine
6 eggs
SMALL CAKE
30 ml (2 level tbsp) cocoa powder
175 g (6 oz) self raising flour
2.5 ml (½ level tsp) baking powder
175 g (6 oz) caster sugar
175 g (6 oz) soft margarine
3 eggs
ICING AND DECORATION
five 227 g (8 oz) packets ready-to-roll icing
red and yellow edible food colouring
coloured paper
liquorice catherine wheels and bootlaces
assorted sweets, such as Smarties
cocktail sticks, satay sticks, coloured pipe cleaners
2 chocolate mini rolls

1. Grease and base-line a 1.6 litre (2¾ pint) and a 2.8 litre (5 pint) pudding basin.
2. Make the cakes one at a time. Put all the ingredients in a food processor and process until smooth; do not over-process. Pour into the prepared basin and bake in the oven at 180°C (350°F) mark 4 for about 1 hour for the small cake and 1½ hours for the large cake, covering the tops of the cakes if they become too brown. Cool on wire racks.
3. To assemble the cake, trim base of large cake, if necessary, so that it stands level. Sit the larger cake, with the flat side down, on a board.
4. Hold the small cake upright in the palm of your hand. Using a sharp knife, trim around the wide top edge so that the cake curves inwards rather than outwards.
5. Colour 1½ packets icing red, and 1½ packets yellow. Roll out the red icing and drape it over the large cake to cover half of it. Trim icing around base of cake. Wrap trimmings in grease-proof paper and set aside. Repeat with yellow icing, covering other half of large cake. Neaten the join in the middle and press lightly together.
6. Cut a ruffle for the clown's neck from the coloured paper. Moisten the top of the large

cake with a little water and arrange the ruffle on top, pressing it in position lightly.

7. Roll out the remaining packets of icing and use to cover the small cake. Trim the icing neatly around the base. Reserve the trimmings as before. Smooth out any creases with your fingers using firm rubbing movements.

8. Roll out the yellow icing trimmings and cut out star shapes with a small cutter. Stick on to the red icing. Unwind a liquorice catherine wheel and use to make stripes or checks on the yellow icing. Stick a Smartie onto the middle of each star. Stick the sweets from the centre of the catherine wheels or other large sweets down the centre of the clown to represent buttons.

9. Roll a piece of the remaining red icing into a ball for the clown's nose. Rub with your fingers until it shines. Stick in position using a cocktail stick to secure if necessary. Cut two short pieces of catherine wheel to make crosses for the eyes. Stick on to cake with water. Make a mouth from a piece of yellow icing and a piece of liquorice.

10. Mould two oval shapes from the icing trimmings to represent hands. Push a satay stick into the sides of the cake where one arm should be. Push a chocolate mini roll on to the satay stick so that it goes all the way through the roll and sticks out just enough at the end to spear the clown's hand. Push the hand into position. Repeat, to make another arm, pushing the stick in at an angle so this arm is raised. Cut two small ruffles from the coloured paper and attach one to each arm between the hand and mini roll.

11. Cut lengths of liquorice boot laces and stick onto his head to make hair (moisten the icing with a little water if necessary to make it stick).

12. Cover an upturned cake tin with coloured paper or kitchen foil and decorate with ribbon. Carefully transfer the clown onto the cake tin. Tie the balloons onto his raised arm.

13. Cut a 23 cm (9 inch) circle from a piece of coloured paper. Make a cut from one edge of the circle to the centre. Curve the paper round to make a hat. Secure with staples. Decorate the top with a pompom of shredded paper.

NOTE: Small helium-filled balloons are best, as they remain airborn. If you can't find these, use the ordinary variety and attach to a coloured pipe cleaner so that the balloon stays up.

Novelty Clown Cake

CAKE ICINGS

Cakes can be covered with a variety of toppings, each of which can be flavoured to suit the cake. Choose from butter cream, glacé icing, crème au beurre or frosting. See page 426 for Royal Icing.

GLACÉ ICING

100 g (4 oz) icing sugar
few drops of vanilla or almond flavouring (optional)
colouring (optional)

1. Sift the icing sugar into a bowl. Add a few drops of vanilla or almond flavouring if wished.
2. Gradually add 15 ml (1 tbsp) warm water. The icing should be thick enough to coat the back of a spoon. If necessary, add more water or sugar to adjust consistency. Add colouring, if liked, and use at once.
MAKES ABOUT 100 G (4 OZ)

VARIATIONS

ORANGE OR LEMON
Replace the water with 15 ml (1 tbsp) strained orange or lemon juice.

MOCHA
Dissolve 5 ml (1 level tsp) cocoa powder and 10 ml (2 level tsp) instant coffee granules in the 15 ml (1 tbsp) hot water.

LIQUEUR
Replace 10-15 ml (2-3 tsp) of the water with the same amount of any liqueur.

CHOCOLATE
Dissolve 10 ml (2 level tsp) cocoa powder in the 15 ml (1 tbsp) hot water.

COFFEE
Flavour with 5 ml (1 tsp) coffee essence or dissolve 10 ml (2 level tsp) instant coffee granules in the 15 ml (1 tbsp) hot water.

ROSEWATER
Use 10 ml (2 tsp) rosewater instead of water.

TO USE GLACÉ ICING
1. If coating both top and sides of cake, stand on a wire rack with a tray underneath to catch the drips. As soon as the icing reaches a coating consistency and looks smooth and glossy, pour it from the bowl on to the centre of the cake.

2. Allow the icing to run down the sides, guiding it with a palette knife. Keep a little icing to fill the gaps. Scrape up any icing which falls under the rack and use this, making sure there are no cake crumbs or it will ruin the appearance.
3. If the sides are decorated and only the top is to have glacé icing, pour the icing on to the centre of the cake and spread it with a palette knife, stopping just inside the edges to prevent it dripping down the sides.
4. If the top is to be iced and the sides left plain, protect them with a band of greaseproof paper tied around the cake and projecting a little above it. Pour on the icing and let it find its own level. Peel off the paper when the icing is hard.
5. Arrange any ready-made decorations, such as nuts, cherries or sweets, in position as soon as the icing has thickened and formed a skin. Except for feather icing, leave the icing until quite dry before applying piped decorations.

TO FEATHER ICE
1. Make a quantity of glacé icing to a coating consistency. Make up a second batch of icing using half the quantity of sugar and enough warm water to mix it to a thick piping consistency.
2. Tint the second batch with food colouring and spoon into a greaseproof paper piping bag.
3. Coat the top of the cake with the larger quantity of icing. Working quickly, before it has time to form a skin, snip the end off the piping bag and pipe parallel lines of coloured icing about 1-2 cm (½-¾ inch) apart, over the surface.
4. Quickly draw the point of a skewer or a sharp knife across the piped lines, first in one direction then in the other, spacing them evenly apart.

SPIDER'S WEB
Alternatively, coat top of cake with the larger quantity of icing as above. Pipe on concentric circles, about 1 cm (½ inch) apart, with coloured icing. Quickly draw the point of a skewer or sharp knife starting from the inner circle out towards the edge, in one direction only.

BUTTER CREAM

75 g (3 oz) butter, softened
175 g (6 oz) icing sugar
few drops of vanilla flavouring
15-30 ml (1-2 tbsp) milk or warm water

1. Put the butter in a bowl and cream until soft. Sift and gradually beat in the icing sugar, then add the vanilla flavouring and milk or water.
MAKES 250 G (9 OZ)

VARIATIONS

ORANGE OR LEMON
Replace the vanilla flavouring with a little finely grated orange or lemon rind. Add a little juice from the fruit instead of the milk, beating well to avoid curdling the mixture.

COFFEE
Replace the vanilla flavouring with 10 ml (2 tsp) instant coffee granules dissolved in some of the hot liquid; cool before adding to the mixture. Or replace 15 ml (1 tbsp) of the liquid with the same amount of coffee essence.

CHOCOLATE
Dissolve 15 ml (1 level tbsp) cocoa powder in a little hot water and cool before adding to the mixture.

MOCHA
Dissolve 5 ml (1 level tsp) cocoa powder and 10 ml (2 level tsp) instant coffee granules in a little hot water taken from the measured amount. Cool before adding to the mixture.

ALMOND
Add 30 ml (2 level tbsp) finely chopped toasted almonds and mix thoroughly.

TO USE BUTTER CREAM
It can be used as a filling or icing. Spread it over the top of the cake only, or over the top and sides. Decorate by making swirls with a palette knife and mark with the prongs of a fork. For more elaborate decoration, butter cream can be piped on top of the cake as well.

CRÈME AU BEURRE

75 g (3 oz) caster sugar
2 egg yolks, beaten
175 g (6 oz) butter, softened

1. Place the sugar in a heavy-based saucepan, add 60 ml (4 tbsp) water and heat very gently to dissolve the sugar, without boiling.
2. When completely dissolved, bring to boiling point and boil steadily for 2-3 minutes, to reach a temperature of 107°C (225°F) as registered on a sugar thermometer.
3. Pour the syrup in a thin stream on to the egg yolks in a deep bowl, whisking all the time. Continue to whisk until the mixture is thick and cold.
4. In another bowl, cream the butter until very soft and gradually beat in the egg yolk mixture.
MAKES ABOUT 275 G (10 OZ)

VARIATIONS
CHOCOLATE
Melt 50 g (2 oz) plain chocolate with 15 ml (1 tbsp) water. Cool slightly and beat into the Crème au Beurre mixture.

FRUIT
Crush 225 g (8 oz) fresh strawberries, raspberries, etc., or thaw, drain and crush frozen fruit. Beat into the Crème au Beurre mixture.

ORANGE OR LEMON
Add freshly grated rind and juice to taste to the Crème au Beurre mixture.

COFFEE
Dissolve 15-30 ml (1-2 tbsp) coffee granules in 15ml (1 tbsp) boiling water. Cool, then beat into the Crème au Beurre mixture. Or add 15-30 ml (1-2 tbsp) coffee essence.

TO USE CRÈME AU BEURRE
Use as butter cream on more elaborate cakes.

COFFEE FUDGE FROSTING

50 g (2 oz) butter or margarine
125 g (4 oz) light soft brown sugar
45 ml (3 tbsp) coffee essence
30 ml (2 tbsp) single cream or milk
200 g (7 oz) icing sugar, sifted

1. Put the butter, sugar, coffee essence and cream in a saucepan and heat gently until the sugar dissolves. Boil briskly for 3 minutes.
2. Remove from the heat and gradually stir in the icing sugar. Beat with a wooden spoon until smooth, then continue to beat for 2 minutes until the icing is thick enough to spread. Use immediately, spreading with a wet palette knife.
MAKES ABOUT 400 G (14 OZ)

VARIATION
CHOCOLATE FUDGE FROSTING
Omit the coffee essence and add 75 g (3 oz) plain chocolate or plain chocolate flavoured cake covering with the butter in the pan.

VANILLA FROSTING

150 g (5 oz) icing sugar, sifted
25 ml (5 tsp) vegetable oil
15 ml (1 tbsp) milk
few drops of vanilla flavouring

1. Put the icing sugar in a bowl and beat in the oil, milk and vanilla flavouring until smooth.
MAKES ABOUT 175 G (6 OZ)

CHOCOLATE FROSTING

25 g (1 oz) plain chocolate or plain chocolate flavoured
    cake covering
150 g (5 oz) icing sugar
1 egg, beaten
2.5 ml (½ tsp) vanilla flavouring
25 g (1 oz) butter or margarine, softened

1. Break the chocolate into pieces and place in a bowl over a pan of simmering water. Heat gently until the chocolate has melted.
2. Stir in the icing sugar, then add the egg, vanilla flavouring and butter and beat until the frosting is smooth.
MAKES ABOUT 200 G (7 OZ)

AMERICAN FROSTING

1 egg white
225 g (8 oz) caster or granulated sugar
pinch of cream of tartar

1. Whisk the egg white until stiff. Gently heat the sugar with 60 ml (4 tbsp) water and the cream of tartar, stirring until dissolved. Then, without stirring, bring to the boil and boil until it reaches a temperature of 120°C (240°F) as registered on a sugar thermometer.
2. Remove the syrup from the heat and immediately when the bubbles subside, pour it on to the egg white in a thin stream, beating the mixture. Leave to cool slightly.
3. When the mixture starts to go dull around the edges and is almost cold, pour quickly over the cake and spread evenly with a palette knife.
MAKES ABOUT 225 G (8 OZ)

SEVEN-MINUTE FROSTING

1 egg white
175 g (6 oz) caster sugar
pinch of salt
pinch of cream of tartar

1. Put all the ingredients into a bowl with 30 ml (2 tbsp) water and whisk lightly.
2. Place the bowl over a pan of hot water and heat, whisking continuously, until the mixture thickens sufficiently to stand in peaks. This will take about 7 minutes.
3. Pour the frosting over the top of the cake and spread with a palette knife.
MAKES ABOUT 175 G (6 OZ)

Biscuits and Petits Fours

Homemade biscuits are quite irresistible. There are six main types of biscuits: rolled, shaped, drop, bar, piped and refrigerator, with dozens of versions of each. The latter part of this chapter includes a selection of petits fours for serving with after-dinner coffee.

Rolled Biscuits

Rolled biscuits are the traditional basic biscuits. If you find it difficult to roll thinly, chill the dough slightly and roll out between sheets of non-stick paper. Adding extra flour to stop the sticking will make the biscuit tough and can spoil the final look. If you do use flour, be sure to brush away the surplus. In a hot kitchen, handle these doughs a little at a time and leave the rest in the refrigerator for about 30 minutes. This prevents the biscuits from shrinking too much during baking.

Shaped Biscuits

These are made from soft doughs that can be moulded with the palms of the hands into small balls or barrels. Dampen your hands if the dough sticks.

Drop Biscuits

These are made from soft doughs which are usually spooned directly onto the baking sheet. They are often irregular in shape as they tend to spread during baking.

Piped Biscuits

These are easy to make and have a delicious melt-in-the mouth texture.

Bar Biscuits

Especially quick and easy to prepare, the mixture is pressed into a tin and cut into bars when cooked. Most types store well.

Refrigerator Biscuits

These are cut from a dough which is chilled until firm.

For Perfect Baking

Have all biscuits even in size and rolled to the same thickness for overall browning.

- Use a flat baking sheet with hardly any sides. High sides prevent proper browning.
- Check the biscuits just before the minimum baking time is up.
- To cool, transfer them with a wide flexible spatula to wire racks. Press down the spatula on the baking sheet and ease it under the biscuits.
- Some biscuits – especially those with syrup or honey as an ingredient – are still soft after baking, so leave them for a few minutes before lifting them off the sheet.
- Do not overlap the biscuits while cooling.

For Ideal Storing

- Line the bottom of an airtight container with greaseproof paper or non-stick baking parchment and place a sheet between each two layers of biscuits or between each single layer of soft ones.
- Store different types of biscuit in separate containers.
- Bar biscuits can be kept in the baking tin and covered tightly with foil to save space.
- Store biscuits un-iced. Before serving dredge with sugar or cover with icing.
- Most homemade varieties will keep for 1-2 weeks. If plain biscuits lose their crispness, return them to a baking sheet and freshen in the oven at 170°C (325°F) mark 3 for 5 minutes without overbrowning.
- Biscuits and cookies keep well in the freezer for several months. Pack fragile ones in rigid boxes; simply wrap others in freezer foil.

SHREWSBURY BISCUITS

125 g (4 oz) butter or block margarine
150 g (5 oz) caster sugar
2 egg yolks
225 g (8 oz) plain flour
grated rind of 1 lemon or orange

1. Grease two large baking sheets.
2. Cream the butter and sugar until pale and fluffy. Add the egg yolks and beat well.
3. Stir in the flour and grated lemon rind and mix to a fairly firm dough with a round-bladed knife.
4. Turn out on to a lightly floured surface and knead lightly.
5. Roll out to about 5 mm (¼ inch) thick. Cut into rounds with a 6.5 cm (2½ inch) fluted cutter and place on the baking sheets.
6. Bake in the oven at 180°C (350°F) mark 4 for about 15 minutes, until firm and a very light brown colour.
MAKES 20-24

VARIATIONS
SPICE BISCUITS
Omit the lemon rind and add 5 ml (1 level tsp) ground mixed spice and 5 ml (1 level tsp) ground cinnamon, sifted with the flour.

FRUIT BISCUITS
Add 50 g (2 oz) chopped dried fruit to the mixture with the flour.

FRUIT SQUARES
Make up the mixture and divide in half. Roll out both portions into oblongs and sprinkle 100 g (4 oz) chopped dried fruit over one piece. Cover with the other piece and roll out the mixture 5 mm (¼ inch) thick. Cut into squares.
MAKES 18-20

CHOCOLATE CREAM SANDWICHES
Omit 45 ml (3 level tbsp) of the flour and sift in 45 ml (3 level tbsp) cocoa powder. When the cooked biscuits are cool, sandwich them together with Butter Cream (see page 433).
MAKES 10-12

RASPBERRY RINGS
Roll out the mixture and cut into rounds, using a 6.5 cm (2½ inch) plain cutter. Place the rounds on a greased baking sheet, remove the centres of half the biscuits, using a 2.5 cm (1 inch) plain cutter, then bake. When the biscuits are cool, spread the solid rounds with jam and dip the rings into white Glacé Icing (see page 432). Place the iced rings on top of the rounds so that the jam shows through.
MAKES 10-12

PINWHEEL BISCUITS

100 g (4 oz) butter or block margarine
50 g (2 oz) caster sugar
50 g (2 oz) cornflour
100 g (4 oz) plain flour
finely grated rind of ½ a lemon
15 ml (1 tbsp) lemon juice
15 ml (1 tbsp) coffee essence
milk for brushing

1. Grease two baking sheets.
2. Cream half of the butter and half of the sugar together in a bowl until pale and fluffy. Gradually work in half the flours with the lemon rind and juice. Knead well, then wrap in foil and chill in the refrigerator for 30 minutes.
3. Meanwhile, cream the remaining butter and sugar together as before. Add the remaining flours and the coffee flavouring. Knead, wrap and chill as above.
4. Roll out both pieces of dough to oblongs 25 x 18 cm (10 x 7 inches). Brush a little milk over one layer and top with second piece of dough. Roll up from the narrow edge, wrap in foil and chill for 30 minutes.
5. Cut the roll into 18 slices and place on baking sheets. Bake in the oven at 180°C (350°F) mark 4 for about 20 minutes. Cool on a wire rack.
MAKES 18

EASTER BISCUITS

100 g (4 oz) butter or block margarine
75 g (3 oz) caster sugar
1 egg, separated
200 g (7 oz) plain flour
pinch of salt
2.5 ml (½ level tsp) ground mixed spice
2.5 ml (½ level tsp) ground cinnamon
50 g (2 oz) currants
15 ml (1 level tbsp) chopped mixed peel
15-30 ml (1-2 tbsp) milk or brandy
a little caster sugar

1. Grease two baking sheets.
2. Cream together the butter and sugar until pale and fluffy and beat in the egg yolk.
3. Sift flour with salt and spices and fold into the creamed mixture, with the fruit and peel. Add enough milk to give a fairly soft dough.
4. Knead lightly on a floured surface and roll out to about 5 mm (¼ inch) thick.
5. Cut into rounds using a 5 cm (2 inch) fluted cutter. Place on the baking sheets and bake in the oven at 200°C (400°F) mark 6 for about 10 minutes.
6. Remove from the oven, brush with beaten egg white and sprinkle lightly with caster sugar.
7. Return to the oven for a further 10 minutes, until golden brown. Cool on a wire rack.
MAKES 16-18

CHOCOLATE NUT SNAPS

1 egg, separated
100 g (4 oz) caster sugar
150 g (5 oz) plain chocolate
125 g (4 oz) hazelnuts, skinned and finely chopped
40 g (1½ oz) plain flour
200 g (7 oz) icing sugar, sifted

1. Grease two baking sheets.
2. Whisk the egg white until stiff but not dry. Fold in the caster sugar.
3. Coarsely grate 75 g (3 oz) chocolate into the mixture and stir in with the hazelnuts, flour and egg yolk. Knead lightly on a well floured surface. Wrap and chill for 30 minutes.
4. Roll out the dough to about 5 mm (¼ inch) thick. Using a 5 cm (2 inch) star cutter, stamp out twenty-four shapes. Knead lightly and re-roll dough as necessary. Place on the baking sheets. Chill again for 30 minutes.
5. Bake in the oven at 190°C (375°F) mark 5 for about 20 minutes. Immediately ease off the baking sheet and cool on a wire rack.
6. Blend the icing sugar to a smooth paste with about 30 ml (2 tbsp) water. Spoon 45 ml (3 level tbsp) into a small greaseproof paper piping bag (see page 425). Melt remaining chocolate with 20 ml (4 tsp) water and stir into remaining icing.
7. Coat the surface of each biscuit with chocolate icing. Pipe on the white icing and pull a skewer back and forth through the icing to create a feathered effect. Leave to set.
MAKES 24

SHORTBREAD ROUNDS

125 g (4 oz) butter or block margarine
50 g (2 oz) caster sugar
125 g (4 oz) plain flour
50 g (2 oz) ground rice
caster sugar, to dredge

1. Grease two baking sheets.
2. Cream the butter until soft. Add the caster sugar and beat until pale and fluffy.
3. Stir in the flour and ground rice, until the mixture binds together. Knead well to form a smooth dough.
4. On a lightly floured surface, roll out the dough thinly. Using a 7.5 cm (3 inch) fluted cutter, stamp out about 20 rounds, re-rolling the dough as necessary.
5. Place the rounds on the baking sheets and prick the surface with a fork. Bake in the oven at 180°C (350°F) mark 4 for about 15 minutes, or until pale golden and just firm to the touch.
6. Transfer to a wire rack to cool. Dredge with caster sugar to serve.
MAKES ABOUT 20

NOTE: Shortbread can also be made in a floured shortbread mould which is turned out on to the baking sheet before baking.

GINGERBREAD MEN

350 g (12 oz) plain flour
5 ml (1 level tsp) bicarbonate of soda
10 ml (2 level tsp) ground ginger
100 g (4 oz) butter or block margarine
175 g (6 oz) light soft brown sugar
60 ml (4 level tbsp) golden syrup
1 egg, beaten
currants, to decorate

1. Grease three baking sheets.
2. Sift the flour, bicarbonate of soda and ginger into a bowl. Rub the butter into the flour until the mixture looks like fine crumbs. Stir in the sugar. Beat the syrup into the egg and stir into the bowl.
3. Mix to form a dough and knead until smooth.
4. Divide into two and roll out on a lightly floured surface to about 5 mm (¼ inch) thick. Using a gingerbread man cutter, cut out figures and place them on the baking sheets. Decorate with currants. Bake in the oven at 190°C (375°F) mark 5 for 12-15 minutes, until golden. Cool slightly, then place on a wire rack.
MAKES 12

Gingerbread Men

GRANTHAM GINGERBREADS

100 g (4 oz) butter or block margarine
350 g (12 oz) caster sugar
1 egg, beaten
250 g (9 oz) self raising flour
5 ml (1 level tsp) ground ginger

1. Grease two or three baking sheets.
2. Cream the butter and sugar in a bowl until pale and fluffy. Gradually beat in the egg.

3. Sift the flour and ginger into the mixture and work in with a fork to a fairly firm dough.
4. Roll the dough into small balls about the size of a walnut and put them on the baking sheets, spaced apart.
5. Bake in the oven at 150°C (300°F) mark 2 for 40-45 minutes, until crisp, well risen, hollow and very lightly browned. Cool on a wire rack.
MAKES 30

PEANUT BUTTER COOKIES

50 g (2 oz) crunchy peanut butter
grated rind of ½ an orange
50 g (2 oz) caster sugar
45 ml (3 level tbsp) light soft brown sugar
50 g (2 oz) butter or block margarine
1 egg
30 ml (2 level tbsp) seedless raisins, chopped
100 g (4 oz) self raising flour

1. Cream together the peanut butter, orange rind, sugars and butter until pale and fluffy.
2. Beat in the egg, add the raisins and stir in the flour to give a fairly firm dough.
3. Roll the dough into small balls about the size of a walnut and place well apart on an ungreased baking sheet. Mark each one with a fork.
4. Bake in the oven at 180°C (350°F) mark 4 for 25 minutes, until risen and golden brown. Cool on a wire rack.
MAKES 25-30

ALMOND CRISPS

125 g (4 oz) butter or block margarine
75 g (3 oz) caster sugar
1 egg yolk
few drops of almond flavouring
150 g (5 oz) self raising flour
75 g (3 oz) chopped almonds

1. Grease two or three baking sheets.
2. Cream the butter and sugar until pale and

fluffy. Beat in the egg yolk and almond flavouring, then the flour to give a smooth dough.
3. Form into a neat log shape and cut into twenty-four even slices. Shape each into a barrel, then roll in chopped almonds.
4. Place well apart on the baking sheets and bake in the oven at 190°C (375°F) mark 5 for 15-20 minutes. Cool on a wire rack.
MAKES 24

MADELEINES

150 g (5 oz) self raising flour
50 g (2 oz) semolina
50 g (2 oz) cornflour
225 g (8 oz) butter or block margarine
75 g (3 oz) icing sugar, plus extra, to dredge

1. Grease eighteen madeleine moulds.
2. Into a bowl, sift the flour, semolina and

cornflour. Cream the butter and icing sugar together until pale and fluffy. Stir in the flour mixture, using a fork to form a soft paste.
3. Press a little of the mixture into each mould and smooth off the top. Bake in the oven at 180°C (350°F) mark 4 for 15-20 minutes. Leave to cool a little in the tins before gently easing out. When cold, dredge with icing sugar.
MAKES 18

CHERRY AND WALNUT BISCUITS

225 g (8 oz) plain flour
pinch of salt
75 g (3 oz) butter or block margarine
100 g (4 oz) caster sugar
grated rind of ½ a lemon
1 egg, separated
45-60 ml (3-4 tbsp) milk
100 g (4 oz) walnut pieces, finely chopped
12 glacé cherries, halved

1. Grease two baking sheets.
2. Sift the flour with the salt, rub in the butter until the mixture resembles fine breadcrumbs, then stir in the sugar, lemon rind, egg yolk and milk to give a fairly firm dough.
3. Form the dough into small balls, dip these in the slightly whisked egg white and roll them in the chopped walnuts.
4. Place the biscuits on the baking sheets and top each with a cherry half.
5. Bake in the oven at 180°C (350°F) mark 4 for 20-25 minutes, until firm and lightly browned. Cool on a wire rack.
MAKES 24

TOP: Cherry and Walnut Biscuits.
LEFT: Madeleines. RIGHT: Almond Crisps

CIGARETTES RUSSES

25 g (1 oz) butter or block margarine
1 egg white
50 g (2 oz) caster sugar
25 g (1 oz) plain flour

1. Grease the handles of several wooden spoons and line two baking sheets with non-stick baking parchment.
2. Melt the butter and leave to cool. Whisk the egg white until stiff and fold in the sugar.
3. Gently stir in the butter with the flour.

4. Spread small spoonfuls of mixture into oblongs about 7.5 x 5 cm (3 x 2½ inches) on the baking sheets, not more than two per baking sheet. Bake one sheet at a time at 190°C (375°F) mark 5 for 6-7 minutes.
5. Allow to stand for 1-2 seconds, then remove with a fish slice and place upside down on a flat surface.
6. Wind tightly round a greased wooden spoon handle. Cool slightly, ease off handles and place on a wire rack to finish cooling.
MAKES 8

COCONUT MACAROONS

2 egg whites
100 g (4 oz) icing sugar, sifted
100 g (4 oz) ground almonds
few drops of almond flavouring
100 g (4 oz) desiccated coconut
30 ml (2 level tbsp) shredded coconut

1. Line two baking sheets with non-stick baking parchment. Whisk the egg whites until stiff but not dry. Lightly fold in the icing sugar.

2. Gently stir in the almonds, almond flavouring and desiccated coconut until the mixture forms a sticky dough.
3. Spoon walnut-sized pieces of mixture on to the baking sheets. Press a few strands of shredded coconut on to the top of each one.
4. Bake in the oven at 150°C (300°F) mark 2 for about 25 minutes. The outer crust should be golden and the inside soft. Cool on a wire rack.
MAKES 18

FLORENTINES

25g (1 oz) hazelnuts, finely chopped
25 g (1 oz) blanched almonds, finely chopped
3 glacé cherries, chopped
30 ml (2 level tbsp) mixed peel, chopped
15 ml (1 level tbsp) sultanas, chopped
50 g (2 oz) butter or block margarine
50 g (2 oz) caster sugar
10 ml (2 tsp) top of the milk
100 g (4 oz) plain chocolate

1. Line three baking sheets with non-stick baking parchment.
2. Mix together the nuts, glacé cherries, peel and sultanas.
3. Melt the butter in a saucepan. Stir in the sugar and bring slowly to the boil, stirring. Remove the pan from the heat immediately, then stir in the fruit and nut mixture with the milk. Allow the mixture to cool slightly, stirring occasionally, until evenly blended and no longer oily in appearance.
4. Spoon the mixture on to the baking sheets, allowing plenty of space to spread. Bake one

sheet at a time in the oven at 180°C (350°F) mark 4 for about 12 minutes, until golden brown.
5. Using a small oiled palette knife immediately push in the edges to give a neat round shape. Allow to cool for 1-2 minutes, then using a fish slice, slide them on to a wire rack to cool.
6. Break up the chocolate and place in a small bowl over a pan of hot water and heat gently until the chocolate melts. Remove the bowl and stir the chocolate until cool, thick and smooth.
7. Spoon a little chocolate on to the smooth side

of each florentine and carefully spread to coat. Leave chocolate until creamy but not set.
8. Draw the prongs of a fork across in a wavy line. Transfer to a baking sheet lined with non-stick baking parchment and leave to set in a cool place.
MAKES 12

Spread chocolate over the smooth side of each.

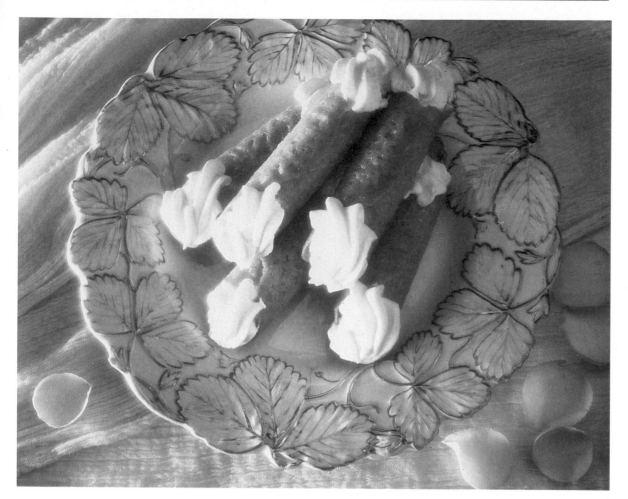

Brandy Snaps

BRANDY SNAPS

50 g (2 oz) butter or block margarine
50 g (2 oz) caster sugar
30 ml (2 level tbsp) golden syrup
50 g (2 oz) plain flour, sifted
2.5 ml (½ level tsp) ground ginger
5 ml (1 tsp) brandy
grated rind of ½ a lemon
150 ml (¼ pint) double cream

1. Grease the handles of several wooden spoons and line two or three baking sheets with non-stick baking parchment.
2. Melt butter with sugar and syrup in a sauce-pan over low heat. Remove from heat. Stir in flour and ginger, brandy and lemon rind.
3. Put small spoonfuls of the mixture about 10 cm (4 inches) apart on the baking sheets, to allow plenty of room for spreading.

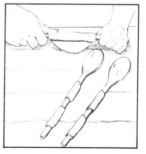

Shape the brandy snaps whilst still warm and malleable.

4. Bake one sheet at a time in the oven at 180°C (350°F) mark 4 for 7-10 minutes, until bubbly and golden. Allow to cool for 1-2 minutes, then loosen with a palette knife and roll them round the spoon handles.
5. Leave until set, then twist gently to remove. (If the biscuits cool too much whilst still on the sheet and become too brittle to roll, return the sheet to the oven for a moment to soften them.) Before serving, whisk the cream until thick and fill the brandy snaps.
MAKES 10

CHOCOLATE VIENNESE FINGERS

125 g (4 oz) butter or margarine
25 g (1 oz) icing sugar
125 g (4 oz) plain flour
1.25 ml (¼ level tsp) baking powder
few drops of vanilla flavouring
50 g (2 oz) plain chocolate or plain chocolate flavour
  cake covering
icing sugar, to decorate (optional)

1. Beat the butter until smooth, then beat in the icing sugar until pale and fluffy.
2. Sift in the flour and baking powder. Beat well, adding the vanilla flavouring.
3. Put into a piping bag fitted with a medium star nozzle. Pipe out finger shapes, about 7.5 cm

When cool, dip the ends of the fingers into the melted chocolate.

(3 inch) long, on to two greased baking sheets, spacing them well apart.
4. Bake in the oven at 190°C (375°F) mark 5 for 15-20 minutes. Cool on a wire rack.
5. Break up the chocolate and place in a bowl over a pan of simmering water. Heat gently until the chocolate melts. Dip

Chocolate Viennese Fingers

the ends of each Viennese Finger in the melted chocolate to coat. Leave to set on the wire rack.
6. Dredge with icing sugar to serve if wished.
MAKES ABOUT 20

GINGER BISCUITS

125 g (4 oz) golden syrup
50 g (2 oz) butter or block margarine
finely grated rind of 1 orange
30 ml (2 tbsp) orange juice
175 g (6 oz) self raising flour
5 ml (1 level tsp) ground ginger

1. Grease two or three baking sheets.
2. Place the syrup, butter and sugar in a medium saucepan.
3. Add the orange rind and juice to the pan. Heat very gently until the ingredients have completely melted and are evenly blended together.
4. Leave the mixture to cool slightly, then add the flour sifted with the ginger. Mix thoroughly until smooth.
5. Place small spoonfuls of the mixture on to the baking sheets, leaving room for spreading.
6. Bake in the oven at 180°C (350°F) mark 4 for about 12 minutes, until golden brown.
7. Leave to stand for 1 minute before easing the biscuits off the baking sheets with a fish slice. Cool completely on a wire rack.
MAKES ABOUT 24

CHOCOLATE CHIP COOKIES

75 g (3 oz) butter or block margarine
75 g (3 oz) caster sugar
75 g (3 oz) light soft brown sugar
few drops of vanilla flavouring
1 egg
175 g (6 oz) self raising flour
pinch of salt
50 g (2 oz) walnut pieces, chopped
50-100 g (2-4 oz) chocolate chips

1. Cream together the butter, sugars and vanilla flavouring until pale and fluffy, then gradually beat in the egg.
2. Sift the flour and salt together and fold in with the nuts and chocolate chips.
3. Drop spoonfuls of mixture on to two greased baking sheets and bake in the oven at 180°C (350°F) mark 4 for 12-15 minutes.
4. Cool on the baking sheets for 1 minute, then transfer to a wire rack to finish cooling.
MAKES 20

LANGUES DE CHATS

50 g (2 oz) butter or block margarine
50 g (2 oz) caster sugar
1 egg
50 g (2 oz) self raising flour
Butter Cream (see page 433)
50 g (2 oz) plain chocolate or plain chocolate flavour cake covering

1. Grease two baking sheets.
2. Cream the butter and sugar until pale and fluffy, then beat in the egg. Work in the flour until the mixture is of piping consistency.
3. Put into a piping bag fitted with a 1 cm (½ inch) plain piping nozzle and pipe on to the baking sheets in fingers about 6-8 cm (2½ -3 inches) long, spaced widely apart.
4. Bake in the oven at 220°C (425°F) mark 7 for about 5 minutes, until the edges of the biscuits are colouring. Cool on a wire rack. When the fingers are cold, melt the chocolate in a bowl over simmering water. Allow to cool slightly. Sandwich the fingers together in pairs with butter cream and dip the ends of each in the melted chocolate. If left plain, these biscuits are good with a rich sweet such as syllabub or soufflé.
MAKES ABOUT 12

CHERRY GARLANDS

225 g (8 oz) soft tub margarine
50 g (2 oz) icing sugar
200 g (7 oz) plain flour
150 g (5 oz) cornflour
few drops of vanilla flavouring
50 g (2 oz) glacé cherries, very finely chopped
glacé cherries, quartered, and angelica pieces, to decorate
icing sugar, to dredge

1. Grease two or three baking sheets.
2. Cream the margarine and icing sugar together in a bowl until the mixture is pale and fluffy.
3. Beat in the flours, vanilla flavouring and cherries. Beat until the mixture is very soft.
4. Spoon half the mixture into a piping bag fitted with a 1 cm (½ inch) star nozzle. Pipe 5 cm (2 inch) rings on to the baking sheets, allowing room for spreading. Decorate with cherry quarters and pieces of angelica. Repeat with remaining mixture.
5. Bake in the oven at 190°C (375°F) mark 5 for about 20 minutes, until pale golden. Allow to firm up slightly on the baking sheets for about 30 seconds before sliding on to a wire rack to cool. Dredge with icing sugar.
MAKES 24

FLAPJACKS

75 g (3 oz) butter or block margarine
50 g (2 oz) light soft brown sugar
30 ml (2 level tbsp) golden syrup
175 g (6 oz) rolled oats

1. Grease a shallow 18 cm (7 inch) square cake tin.
2. Melt the butter with the sugar and syrup in a saucepan over a low heat, then pour it on to the rolled oats. Mix well, turn the mixture into the prepared tin and press down well.
3. Bake in the oven at 180°C (350°F) mark 4 for about 20 minutes, until golden brown. Cool slightly in the tin, mark into fingers with a sharp knife and loosen round the edges.
4. When firm, remove from the tin, and cool on a wire rack, then break into fingers. The flapjacks may be stored in an airtight container for up to a week.
MAKES 8-10

APRICOT OAT CRUNCHIES

75 g (3 oz) self raising wholemeal flour
75 g (3 oz) rolled porridge oats
75 g (3 oz) demerara sugar
100 g (4 oz) butter or margarine
100 g (4 oz) no-soak dried apricots, chopped

1. Lightly grease a shallow tin measuring 28 x 18 x 4 cm (11 x 7 x 1½ inches).
2. Mix together the flour, oats and sugar in a bowl. Rub in the butter until the mixture resembles breadcrumbs.
3. Spread half of the mixture over the base of the prepared tin, pressing it down evenly.
4. Drain and chop the apricots. Spread them over the oat mixture in the tin.
5. Sprinkle over the remaining crumb mixture and press down well. Bake in the oven at 180°C (350°F) mark 4 for 25 minutes until golden brown.
6. Leave in the tin for about 1 hour until cold. Cut into bars to serve. These delicious chewy teatime bars will keep well for several days if well wrapped in foil and kept in an airtight tin.
MAKES 12

DATE CRUNCHIES

175 g (6 oz) self raising flour
175 g (6 oz) semolina
175 g (6 oz) butter or block margarine
75 g (3 oz) caster sugar
225 g (8 oz) stoned dates, chopped
15 ml (1 level tbsp) honey
15 ml (1 tbsp) lemon juice
pinch of ground cinnamon

1. Grease a shallow 18 cm (7 inch) square tin.
2. Mix the flour with the semolina. Melt the butter with the sugar in a saucepan over a low heat, then stir into the flour mixture.
3. Press half of this 'shortbread' mixture into the prepared tin. Meanwhile, heat the dates with the honey, 60 ml (4 tbsp) water, lemon juice and cinnamon, stirring well, until the mixture is soft and smooth. Spread this filling over the mixture in the tin, cover with the remaining 'shortbread' mixture and press down lightly.
4. Bake in the oven at 190°C (375°F) mark 5 for 30-35 minutes. Cut into fingers but do not remove from the tin until cold.
MAKES 12

VARIATION
Use 75 g (3 oz) chopped dried apricots instead of the dates and cook with 200 ml (⅓ pint) water for 10 minutes until softened. Purée if wished in a blender or food processor.

ALMOND CHOCOLATE BISCUITS

200 g (7 oz) self raising flour
150 g (5 oz) caster sugar
1.25 ml (¼ level tsp) freshly grated nutmeg
150 g (5 oz) butter or block margarine
100 g (4 oz) ground almonds
50 g (2 oz) plain chocolate or plain chocolate flavour
   cake covering, coarsely grated
1 egg, beaten

1. Grease two or three baking sheets.
2. Put the flour, sugar and nutmeg into a bowl.
Rub the butter into the flour mixture until it
resembles fine crumbs. Stir in the ground
almonds and 25 g (1 oz) of the chocolate. Bind
the mixture together with egg until smooth.
3. On a lightly floured surface, divide the
mixture into two and roll each part into a 30 cm
(12 inch) long, thin sausage shape, using
greaseproof or non-stick baking parchment.
4. Chill in refrigerator for about 30 minutes,
until firm. Cut slices off about 1 cm (½ inch)
thick and place well apart on the baking sheets.
Flatten lightly with the back of the hand. Bake
one sheet at a time in the oven at 190°C (375°F)
mark 5 for 15-20 minutes.
5. Cool until just warm, then sprinkle the
remaining chocolate over. Transfer to a wire
rack and leave to cool completely.
MAKES ABOUT 48

REFRIGERATOR BISCUITS

150 g (5 oz) caster sugar
150 g (5 oz) soft tub margarine
few drops of vanilla flavouring
grated rind of 1 lemon
1 egg, beaten
225 g (8 oz) plain flour

1. Lightly grease two baking sheets.
2. Cream together the sugar and margarine
until pale and fluffy. Beat in the vanilla
flavouring, lemon rind and egg.
3. Stir in the flour and mix to a firm paste.
Knead lightly, wrap and chill in the refrigerator
for 30 minutes.
4. Roll the dough to a sausage shape about 5 cm
(2 inches) in diameter and 20 cm (8 inches)
long. Wrap in greaseproof paper. Refrigerate
for at least 30 minutes.
5. When required, cut off 5 mm (¼ inch) slices,
place on the baking sheets and bake at 190°C
(375°F) mark 5 for 12-15 minutes. Cool the
biscuits on a wire rack.
MAKES 32

VARIATION
HONEY JUMBLES
Follow the basic recipe above as far as the end of
stage 4. Slice off 5 mm (¼ inch) rounds. Roll
into pencil-thin strips 10 cm (4 inches) long.
Twist into 'S' shapes and place on lightly greased
baking sheets. Chill for 30 minutes. Bake as
above. While still warm, glaze well with thin
honey, sprinkle with demerara sugar and grill for
1-2 minutes until caramelised. Cool.

TOP: Refrigerator Biscuits. ABOVE: Honey Jumbles

PETITS FOURS

Petits fours are the delicious, rich little sweets and biscuits that are served with after-dinner coffee. Traditional petits fours always include little iced cakes made from a Genoese sponge cut into small shapes. They are coated with apricot jam and then covered with fondant, marzipan or glacé icing. They may be decorated with nuts, glacé fruits or crystallised flower petals.
Meringue mixtures are ideal and may be piped into fancy shapes, cooked, then decorated with small pieces of glacé cherry or nuts, or dipped in chocolate. Almost any small rich sweets can be included. A good selection should be colourful and varied in shape, texture and decoration. Serve with truffles, chocolates and fondants.

MERINGUE PETITS FOURS

2 egg whites
125 g (4 oz) icing sugar
10-15 ml (2-3 tsp) coffee flavouring

1. Line a baking sheet with non-stick baking parchment.
2. Place the egg whites and sugar in a mixing bowl over a pan of hot water and whisk until the mixture is very thick and stands in peaks. Remove the bowl from the heat.
3. Place half the mixture in a piping bag fitted with a plain 1 cm (½ inch) nozzle and pipe small

rounds of the mixture, about 2.5 cm (1 inch) in diameter, on the lined baking sheet.
4. Add the coffee flavouring to the remaining mixture and pipe an equal number of rounds. Reserve any uncooked meringue mixture.
5. Bake in the oven at 150°C (325°F) mark 2 for 20-25 minutes, until set but not coloured. Cool.
6. Use a little uncooked meringue mixture to sandwich the white and coffee meringues together in pairs. Place in petits fours paper cases to serve.
MAKES ABOUT 24

LEFT: Meringue Petits Fours. TOP: Almond Stars (see page 447). RIGHT: Iced Petits Fours (see page 447)

ALMOND STARS

2 egg whites
150 g (5 oz) ground almonds
75 g (3 oz) caster sugar
few drops of almond flavouring
24 pieces of angelica and glacé cherries, to decorate

1. Line two baking sheets with non-stick baking parchment. Whisk the egg whites until stiff and use a large metal spoon to fold in the almonds, sugar and almond flavouring.
2. Using a large star nozzle pipe stars, quite close together, on to the lined baking sheets.
3. Decorate each star with a piece of angelica or a glacé cherry. Bake in the oven at 150°C (300°F) mark 2 for 15-20 minutes, until beginning to colour.
MAKES ABOUT 24

FROSTED FRUITS

Soft, juicy fruit such as grapes may be given a crisp, sparkling coating of sugar and served as petits fours.

Wash the fruit and dry carefully. Dip in lightly beaten egg white, toss in caster sugar and leave to dry on a wire rack. Serve the same day.

ICED PETITS FOURS

25 g (1 oz) butter or block margarine
40 g (1½ oz) plain flour
15 g (½ oz) cornflour
2 eggs
50 g (2 oz) caster sugar
apricot jam
50 g (2 oz) Almond Paste (see page 426)
225 g (8 oz) icing sugar, sifted
food colourings
mimosa balls, glacé cherries, angelica, chocolate dots, nuts or crystallised flowers, to decorate

1. For the Genoese sponge, grease and line a 20 cm (8 inch) square tin.
2. Heat the butter gently until it is melted and leave to cool until the sediment has settled. Sift the flour and cornflour together on to a plate.
3. Whisk the eggs and sugar together in a mixing bowl over a pan of hot water until thick and creamy. Remove from the heat and whisk until cool. Re-sift half the flour and cornflour over the surface of the egg mixture and fold in carefully with a large metal spoon.
4. Pour half the melted butter around the edge of the mixture and carefully fold in with the metal spoon. Repeat using the remaining flour and butter.
5. Pour the mixture into the prepared tin and bake in the oven at 180°C (350°F) mark 4 for 20-25 minutes, until risen and golden brown. Turn out and cool on a wire rack.
6. When the cake is cold, cut into shapes about

When cold, cut the cake into a variety of even-sized shapes.

Ice the petits fours in different colours and then decorate. Leave until set.

4 cm (1½ inches) in size, eg rounds, oblongs, squares, diamonds, triangles, crescents. Heat the apricot jam gently, adding a little water if the jam is very thick. Brush each petit four with the apricot glaze.
7. Divide the almond paste and add a ball or roll of almond paste to the top of each petit four.
8. For the decoration, blend the icing sugar with a little water to make glacé icing. Divide the icing and colour pale yellow, pink, green and brown, leaving some white. Spoon the icing over the petits fours, making sure each one is completely covered.
9. Decorate with mimosa balls, glacé cherries, angelica, chocolate dots, nuts or crystallised flowers. Leave to set, then place in petits fours paper cases if desired.
MAKES 25-30

BREAD

The process of bread making has changed very little over the years. Most bread is made with yeast and the dough is kneaded, left to rise, and shaped before baking. A few breads are made with other raising agents and do not have to be left to rise – these are known as quick breads. Bread that has no raising agent is called unleavened bread.

INGREDIENTS FOR BREAD MAKING

YEAST

Yeast is a living plant available fresh or dried. When mixed with flour and liquid it gives off carbon dioxide, which expands, making the dough rise.

FRESH YEAST is rather like putty in colour and texture, and should have a faint 'winey' smell. There should be no discoloration and it should crumble easily when broken. Although it will store for up to a month in a screw-topped jar, the best results are obtained when it is absolutely fresh, so buy in small quantities as required.

Fresh yeast is usually blended with a liquid and then added to the flour all at once. It can also be rubbed directly into the flour or added as a batter. The batter method is known as the 'sponge dough process'; some ingredients are mixed to form a sponge, which is allowed to ferment, then mixed with remaining ingredients to form a dough.

Fresh yeast is easiest measured by weight. The amount of yeast required varies according to the richness of the dough and type of flour used.

DRIED YEAST is more concentrated than fresh yeast. It consists of small granules and is sold in sachets or 100 g (4 oz) tins. It is convenient to use and can be stored in an airtight container in a cool place for up to 6 months.

Ordinary dried yeast requires sugar to activate it; the yeast granules are sprinkled over tepid liquid with the sugar and the mixture is then left to froth for about 15 minutes before using. The sugar used to activate the yeast loses its sweetness in the frothing process. As milk contains sugar in the form of lactose, there is no need to add sugar if milk is the liquid used.

FAST-ACTION DRIED YEAST, also known as 'easy-mix yeast' is readily available and more convenient to use than ordinary dried yeast. It has finer granules which are mixed with bread improvers to make the dough rise more quickly. Fast-action dried yeast is not mixed with liquid but simply mixed into the flour. The dough requires only one rising when made with this yeast.

The recipes in this book give equivalents for fresh and fast-action dried yeast. If using ordinary dried yeast you will need to amend the method accordingly (see left).

Because dried yeast is more concentrated than fresh yeast, as a rough guide you only need to use half as much. Fast-action dried yeast works particularly efficiently as a raising agent. A 7 g sachet of fast-action dried yeast is sufficient to raise 700 g (1½ lb) flour.

OTHER RAISING AGENTS

BICARBONATE OF SODA is the main raising agent for quick breads. When added to liquid and heated, it gives off carbon dioxide which expands and makes the dough rise.

CREAM OF TARTAR is often used with bicarbonate of soda as it reacts with it to help produce carbon dioxide. It also helps to neutralise the slightly soapy taste often given by bicarbonate of soda.

BAKING POWDER is a ready-made mixture of bicarbonate of soda and acid (often cream of tartar) which produces carbon dioxide when it comes in contact with moisture. Also used for quick breads.

RIGHT: A selection of shaped brown and white rolls, including plaits, knots and cottage rolls

FLOUR

Wheat is either hard or soft depending on its gluten content. When hard wheat is milled it produces a strong flour, rich in protein, containing a sticky, rubber-like substance called gluten. In bread making, the gluten stretches like elastic and as it is heated, it expands and traps in the dough the carbon dioxide released by the yeast. The gluten then sets and forms the 'frame' of the bread. It is the gluten content in a strong flour that gives the volume and open texture of bread and best results are obtained by using this flour.

When soft wheats are milled they produce a flour with different gluten properties, more suited to the making of cakes or pastries where a smaller rise and closer, finer texture are required. This ordinary soft flour, which is either plain or self raising, can be used for bread but it will give a smaller rise and closer crumbly texture with a pale, hard crust, and a disappointing result. Self raising flour, ie plain flour with raising agents already added can be used in recipes for quick breads.

Generally, bread made with wholemeal flour has a closer texture and a stronger, more distinctive taste than white bread.

WHOLEMEAL (OR WHOLEWHEAT) FLOUR contains 100 per cent of the wheat (ie the entire grain is milled). Bread made with this flour is coarse textured, has a nutty taste, and is brown in colour. Strong, plain and self raising types of wholemeal flour are available.

BROWN (WHEATMEAL) FLOUR contains 80-90 per cent of the wheat (ie some of the bran is removed) and it is more absorbent than white flour, giving a denser-textured bread than white, but not as coarse as wholemeal. It is available in strong, plain and self raising forms.

WHITE FLOUR contains 72-74 per cent of the wheat. The bran and wheatgerm which give wholemeal and brown flours their brown colour are removed, resulting in the white flour which is used to make fine-textured 'white' bread. Much is bleached chemically; look for the word 'unbleached' for untreated flour. It is available in strong, plain and self raising forms.

STONEGROUND FLOUR takes its name from the specific process of grinding which heats the flour and gives it a slightly roasted, nutty flavour. Both wholemeal and brown flours are available stoneground.

GRANARY FLOUR is strong brown flour with added malted wheat flakes giving a nutty flavour.

RYE FLOUR used on its own produces rather dense, heavy bread as rye lacks sufficient protein for the formation of gluten. Finely milled rye flour gives the densest texture and bread made with coarse rye flour is rougher and more open textured. When baking rye bread, combine the rye flour with a strong flour.

BUCKWHEAT FLOUR is slightly bitter. It lacks gluten, but gives an interesting texture to white flour doughs when mixed with them.

If you wish to eat a bread high in fibre, choose a flour with a high percentage of the wheat grain. Extra fibre can be added to bread recipes in the form of bran, bran flakes or oatmeal. Add in small quantities and use a little extra liquid for mixing.

SALT

Salt improves the flavour of bread. It should be measured accurately, as too little causes the dough to rise too quickly and too much kills the yeast and gives the bread an uneven texture. Salt is used in the proportions of 5-10 ml (1-2 level tsp) to 450 g (1 lb) flour. Low sodium salts may also be used.

FAT

Adding fat to the dough enriches it and gives a moist, close-textured load with a soft crust. It also helps keep the bread fresh and soft for a longer time. It is often rubbed into the flour and salt or, if a large quantity is used, it is melted and added with the liquid ingredients. If using margarine, block margarine is better than soft tub as it is easier to rub in. Oil may be used instead of fat.

LIQUID

Water is suitable for plain bread, producing a loaf with an even texture and a crisp crust. Milk and water, or milk alone, will give a softer golden crust and the loaf will stay soft and fresher.

The amount of liquid used will vary according to the absorbency of the flour. Too much will give the bread a spongy and open texture. Wholemeal and brown flours are usually more absorbent than white.

The liquid is generally added to the yeast at a tepid temperature of 43°C (110°F); it should feel lukewarm. Boiling water will kill the yeast.

GLAZES AND FINISHES

If a crusty finish is desired, bread or rolls can be brushed before baking with a glaze made

Liberally coat the surface with glaze, then with your desired topping.

by dissolving 10 ml (2 level tsp) salt in 30 ml (2 tbsp) water.

For a shiny finish, the surface should be brushed with beaten egg or beaten egg and milk.

For a soft finish, dust the bread or rolls with flour before baking. Some breads and yeast buns are glazed after baking to give them a sticky finish. To do this, brush the bread with warmed honey or a syrup made by dissolving 30 ml (2 level tbsp) sugar in 30 ml (2 tbsp) water and bringing to the boil.

There are many ways of adding interest, variety and extra fibre and vitamins to bread and rolls. After glazing and before baking, lightly sprinkle the surface with one of the following:

- Poppy, caraway, celery or fennel seeds.
- Sesame seeds. Particularly good sprinkled on to the soft baps used with hamburgers.
- Cracked wheat, barley or wheat flakes, wheatgerm, oatmeal or crushed cornflakes. Sprinkle them on wholemeal bread or baps.

MAKING BREAD

MIXING THE DOUGH
Warmed ingredients and bowl will help to speed up the first rising process. Measure all the ingredients carefully into a large bowl. Add the yeast liquid and mix with the dry ingredients, using a wooden spoon or fork, until blended. Work the dough, using your hands, until the mixture is smooth and leaves the sides of the bowl clean.

KNEADING THE DOUGH
Kneading is essential to strengthen the gluten in the flour, thus mak-ing the dough elastic in texture and enabling it to rise more easily.

Turn the dough on to a floured work surface, knead the dough by folding it towards you and quickly and firmly pushing down and away from you with the

Knead until smooth.

heel of the hand. Give the dough a quarter turn and continue kneading for about 10 minutes, until it is firm, elastic and no longer sticky.

USING A DOUGH HOOK: If you have a mixer with a dough hook attachment, it can take the hard work out of kneading. Follow manufacturer's instructions; working with small amounts of dough is more successful than attempting a large batch all at once. Place the yeast dissolved in the liquid in the bowl, add the dry ingredients, begin at the lowest speed and mix to form the dough. Increase the speed for the recommended time.

USING A FOOD PROCESSOR: A food processor also takes the hard work out of yeast mixtures. Follow the manufacturer's instructions on quantities as it is important that the bowl is not overfilled. You may need to halve the recipe and prepare two batches of dough.

RISING
The kneaded dough is now ready for rising. Unless otherwise stated, place in a bowl and cover with a clean tea towel. This will prevent a skin forming during rising. Rising times vary with temperature. Allow 1½-2 hours at room temperature for the dough to rise. It should have doubled in size and the risen dough should spring back when gently pressed with a lightly floured finger. Good results are obtained by allowing the covered dough to rise in the refrigerator overnight or for up to 24 hours. The dough must be allowed to return to room temperature (taking several hours) before it is shaped. The dough can be made to rise in about 45 minutes-1 hour in a warm place such as an airing cupboard or above a warm cooker.

PREPARING TINS
While the dough is rising, grease the tins or baking sheets. Where reference is made to a 450 g (1 lb) loaf tin, capacity 900 ml (1½ pints), the approximate size to use is 16 x 10 cm (6½ x 4 inch) top measurements, and for a 900 g (2 lb) loaf tin, capacity 1.7 litres (3 pints), use one with 20 x 13 cm (8 x 5 inch) top measurements.

KNOCKING BACK
The best texture is obtained by kneading the dough for a second time after rising. Turn the risen dough on to a lightly floured working surface and knead for 2-3 minutes to 'knock' out any large bubbles and ensure an even texture. The dough is then shaped as required (see

below), placed in the prepared tins or on baking sheets, covered with a clean tea towel and left to rise again.

PROVING OR SECOND RISE

This is the last process before baking. The shaped dough should be allowed to 'prove', that is left at room temperature until it has doubled in size and will spring back when lightly pressed with a floured finger. The dough is ready for glazing and baking.

BAKING

Basic breads are baked in the oven at 230°C (450°F) mark 8. When cooked, the bread should be well risen and golden brown and it should sound hollow when tapped underneath with the knuckles. Larger loaves may need to be turned out of the tin and returned to the oven upside down for the last 10-15 minutes of the cooking time to ensure they are cooked through. Allow to cool on wire racks.

TRADITIONAL BREAD AND ROLL SHAPES

LOAF: Only fill the tin two thirds full for a perfect shape. Fold the dough in three, smooth over the top and tuck in the ends, then place into the tin.
TIN: Roll out the dough to an oblong and roll up like a Swiss roll. Tuck the ends under and place in the prepared tin. Before baking, score the top of the loaf with a sharp knife if wished.
BATON: Shape into a long roll with tapering ends, about 20 cm (8 inches) long.
COB: Knead the dough into a ball by drawing the sides down and tucking them underneath to make a smooth top.
CROWN: Divide the dough into 50 g (2 oz) pieces. Knead and place in a greased round sandwich tin. It is usually pulled apart into rolls when served.
COTTAGE: Cut one third off the dough. Knead both pieces well and shape into rounds, place the smaller round on top of the larger one, and place on a baking sheet. Make a hole through the middle of both pieces using the handle of a wooden spoon. Glaze with salt water before baking.
BLOOMER: Flatten the dough and roll up like a Swiss roll. Tuck the ends under and place on a baking sheet. When proved to double its size, make diagonal slits on top with a sharp knife. Glaze with beaten egg or salt water before baking.
PLAIT: Divide the dough into three and shape into three long rolls about 30 cm (12 inches)

ABOVE: Cottage Loaf. BELOW: Granary Stick

long. Pinch the ends together and plait loosely, then pinch the other ends together. Before baking, glaze with beaten egg and sprinkle with poppy seeds.
KNOTS: Shape each piece of dough into a thin roll and tie into a knot.
ROUNDS: Place the pieces on a very lightly floured surface and roll each into a ball. To do this, hold the hand flat almost at table level and move it round in a circular motion, gradually lifting the palm to get a good round shape.
RINGS: Make a thin roll with each piece of dough and bend it round to form a ring; dampen the ends and mould them together.
STICK: Shape into a sausage shape about 40 cm (16 inches) long.
TREFOIL: Divide each piece of dough into three pieces and roll each into a ball. Place the three balls grouped together.
TWIST: Divide each piece of dough into two and shape into thin rolls. Hold one end of the two pieces of dough together and twist. Damp the ends and tuck under.

WHITE BREAD

15 g (½ oz) fresh yeast or 7 g sachet (1½ level tsp) fast-
action dried yeast
450 ml (¾ pint) tepid water
700 g (1½ lb) strong white flour
10 ml (2 level tsp) salt
knob of lard, butter or block margarine

1. Grease a 900 g (2 lb) loaf tin, or two 450 g
(1 lb) loaf tins.
2. Blend the fresh yeast with the water.
3. Mix the flour and salt in a large bowl and rub
in the lard. Make a well in the centre of the dry
ingredients and add the blended fresh yeast, or
fast-action dried yeast granules and liquid. Stir
in with a fork or wooden spoon.
4. Work it to a firm dough using your hand,
adding extra flour if the dough is too slack, until
it leaves the sides of the bowl clean. Do not let
the dough become too stiff as this produces
heavy 'close' bread.
5. Turn the dough on to a floured surface and
knead thoroughly for about 10 minutes, until the
dough feels firm and elastic and no longer sticky.
Shape it into a ball and place in a large mixing
bowl. Cover the bowl with a clean tea towel to
prevent a skin forming and allow to rise (see
page 451) until it has doubled in size and springs
back when pressed gently with a floured finger.
6. Turn the dough on to a lightly floured
surface and knead well for 2-3 minutes,
flattening it firmly with the knuckles to knock
out the air bubbles. Stretch the dough into an
oblong the same width as the length of the tin,

fold it into three and turn it over so that the
'seam' is underneath. Smooth over the top, tuck
in the ends and place in the greased loaf tin.
7. Cover the tin with a clean tea towel and leave
to prove for about 30 minutes, until the dough
comes to the top of the tin and springs back
when pressed gently with a lightly floured finger.
Glaze and finish as desired (see page 450).
8. Place the tin on a baking sheet and bake in
the oven at 230°C (450°F) mark 8 for 30-40
minutes, until well risen and golden brown.
When the loaf is cooked it will shrink slightly
from the sides of the tin. Turn out the loaf; it
will sound hollow if you tap the bottom of it.
Cool on a wire rack.

VARIATIONS
MILK BREAD
Increase the lard, butter or margarine to 50 g
(2 oz) and rub into the dry ingredients. Mix the
dough with 450 ml (¾ pint) milk or a mixture of
milk and water. This will give a close-textured
loaf with a softer crust.

ROLLS
After knocking back the dough, divide it into
about eighteen pieces and roll into any of the
shapes described, left. Place on greased baking
sheets about 2.5 cm (1 inch) apart. Cover the
baking sheets with a clean tea towel and leave to
prove until doubled in size. Remove the cover,
glaze and finish as desired (see page 450). Bake
in the oven at 230°C (450°F) mark 8 for 15-20
minutes, until well risen and golden brown.
Cool on a wire rack.

GRANARY BREAD

900 g (2 lb) granary flour
12.5 ml (2½ level tsp) salt
25 g (1 oz) lard or block margarine
25 g (1 oz) fresh yeast or two 7 g sachets (1 level tbsp)
fast-action dried yeast
15 ml (1 level tbsp) malt extract
600 ml (1 pint) tepid water

1. Grease two 450 g (1 lb) loaf tins.
2. Mix the flour and salt in a bowl and rub in
the lard. Cream the fresh yeast with the malt
extract and water and add to the flour. Simply
add fast-action dried yeast granules to the flour

mixture with the malt extract.
3. Mix to a stiff dough. Turn on to a lightly
floured surface and knead for 10 minutes, until
the dough feels firm and elastic and not sticky.
4. Cover with a clean tea towel and leave to rise
in a warm place until doubled in size. Turn on
to a lightly floured surface and knead for 2-3
minutes.
5. Divide the dough into two pieces and place in
the loaf tins. Cover and leave to prove until the
dough is 1 cm (½ inch) above the top of the tins.
6. Bake in the oven at 230°C (450°F) mark 8 for
30-35 minutes.
7. Turn out and cool on a wire rack.

WHOLEMEAL BREAD

25 g (1 oz) fresh yeast or two 7 g sachets (1 level tbsp)
  fast-action dried yeast
900 ml (1½ pints) tepid water
1.4 kg (3 lb) strong wholemeal flour
30 ml (2 level tbsp) caster sugar
20 ml (4 level tsp) salt
25 g (1 oz) block margarine

1. Grease two 900 g (2 lb) loaf tins.
2. Blend the fresh yeast with 300 ml (½ pint) of the water.
3. Mix together the flour, caster sugar and salt in a large bowl and rub in the fat. Stir the yeast liquid or fast-action dried yeast granules into the dry ingredients, adding enough of the water to make a firm dough that leaves the sides of the bowl clean.
4. Turn it on to a lightly floured surface and knead for about 10 minutes, until the dough feels firm and elastic and no longer sticky. Shape into a ball, place in a bowl, cover and leave until doubled in size.
5. Turn it on to a floured surface and knead until firm, divide into two or four pieces and flatten firmly with the knuckles to knock out any air bubbles. Knead again. Shape to fit the tins.
6. Cover with a clean tea towel and leave to prove until the dough rises almost to the tops of the tins.
7. Brush the tops of the loaves with salt glaze (see page 450) and bake in the oven at 230°C (450°F) mark 8 for 30-40 minutes. Turn out and cool on a wire rack.

QUICK WHOLEMEAL BREAD

15 g (½ oz) fresh yeast or 7 g sachet (1½ level tsp) fast-
  action dried yeast
about 300 ml (½ pint) tepid water
450 g (1 lb) strong wholemeal flour or 225 g (8 oz)
  strong wholemeal flour and 225 g (8 oz) strong
  white flour
5 ml (1 level tsp) sugar
5-10 ml (1-2 level tsp) salt
25 g (1 oz) lard or block margarine

1. Grease two baking sheets.
2. Blend the fresh yeast with the water.
3. Mix together the flour, sugar and salt and rub in the lard. Add the yeast liquid or fast-action dried yeast granules and liquid. Mix to give a fairly soft dough, adding a little more water if necessary.
4. Turn on to a floured surface and knead for about 10 minutes, until the dough feels firm and elastic and no longer sticky. Divide into two, shape into rounds and place on the baking sheets. Cover and leave until doubled in size.
5. Bake in the oven at 230°C (450°F) mark 8 for about 15 minutes, then reduce the oven temperature to 200°C (400°F) mark 6 and bake for a further 20-30 minutes. Turn out and cool on a wire rack.

FLOURY BAPS

15 g (½ oz) fresh yeast or 7 g sachet (1½ level tsp) dried
  yeast
300 ml (½ pint) tepid milk and water mixed
450 g (1 lb) strong white flour
5 ml (1 level tsp) salt
50 g (2 oz) block margarine

1. Lightly flour a baking sheet.
2. Blend the fresh yeast with the liquid.
3. Mix together the flour and salt in a bowl and rub in the fat. Stir in the yeast liquid or fast-action dried yeast granules and liquid. Work to a firm dough, adding extra flour only if necessary, until the dough leaves the sides of the bowl.
4. Knead on a floured surface for about 5 minutes. Place in a bowl, cover with a clean tea towel and leave until doubled in size. Lightly knead, then cut into 8-10 pieces. Shape each into a ball, place on the baking sheet and press to flatten slightly.
5. Cover with a clean tea towel and leave to prove in a warm place until doubled in size.
6. Dredge the tops lightly with flour and bake in the oven at 200°C (400°F) mark 6 for 15-20 minutes. Cool on a wire rack.
MAKES 8-10

SAGE AND ONION BREAD

15 g (½ oz) fresh yeast or 7 g sachet (1½ level tsp) fast-action dried yeast
300 ml (½ pint) warm milk
1 large onion, skinned and finely chopped
25 g (1 oz) butter
225 g (8 oz) strong white flour
225 g (8 oz) strong wholemeal flour
5 ml (1 tsp) salt
pepper
5 ml (1 tsp) dried cracked wheat for sprinkling

1. Blend the fresh yeast with the milk.
2. Meanwhile, gently sauté the onion in the butter for about 5 minutes, until softened.
3. Mix the flours, salt, pepper and sage in a large bowl. Make a well in the centre, then pour in the softened onion and butter, and the yeast liquid or fast-action dried yeast granules and milk. Beat well together until the dough leaves the sides of the bowl clean.
4. Turn on to a lightly floured surface and knead well for about 10 minutes, until smooth and elastic. Place in a clean bowl. Cover with a clean tea towel and leave in a warm place for about 1 hour, until doubled in size.
5. Turn the dough on to a floured surface and knead lightly. Divide into two, shape into rounds and place on a greased baking sheet.
6. Brush with a little milk and sprinkle with cracked wheat. Cover and leave in a warm place for about 30 minutes, until doubled in size.

Sage and Onion Bread

Bake at 230°C (450°F) mark 8 for 15 minutes, then lower temperature to 200°C (400°F) mark 6 and bake for a further 15 minutes. When cooked the loaves will be well risen and golden brown, and sound hollow if tapped on the bottom. Cool slightly and serve warm.
MAKES 2 SMALL LOAVES

DARK RYE BREAD

275 g (10 oz) rye flour
275 g (10 oz) strong white flour
15 g (½ oz) salt
10 ml (2 level tsp) caraway or fennel seeds
150 ml (¼ pint) tepid water
150 ml (¼ pint) tepid milk
15 ml (1 tbsp) black treacle
25 g (1 oz) fresh yeast or 7 g sachet (1½ level tsp) fast-action dried yeast

1. Grease two baking sheets.
2. Mix together the flours and salt in a mixing bowl. Stir in the caraway or fennel seeds.
3. Combine the water, milk and treacle, crumble in the fresh yeast or sprinkle in the fast-action dried yeast granules and stir until blended.

4. Pour into the flour mixture and mix to a firm dough, adding extra flour if required. Turn the dough on to a lightly floured surface and knead for about 10 minutes, until the dough feels firm and elastic and no longer sticky.
5. Place in a bowl, cover with a clean tea towel and leave to rise until doubled in size. Turn the dough on to a lightly floured surface, knead well and divide into two. Shape into traditional cob or baton shapes (see page 452).
6. Place on the greased baking sheets and cover with a clean tea towel. Leave to prove until doubled in size.
7. Bake in the oven at 190°C (375°F) mark 5 for 30 minutes. Brush tops with water, lower temperature to 180°C (350°F) mark 4 and bake for a further 20 minutes. Cool on a wire rack.

CRUMPETS

350 g (12 oz) strong white flour
15 g (½ oz) fresh yeast or 7 g sachet (1½ level tsp) fast-
*   action dried yeast*
300 ml (½ pint) tepid water
2.5 ml (½ level tsp) salt
2.5 ml (½ level tsp) bicarbonate of soda
225 ml (8 fl oz) milk
vegetable oil

1. Sift 175 g (6 oz) flour into a mixing bowl and crumble in the fresh yeast or sprinkle in the fast-action dried yeast granules. Make a well in the centre of the flour mixture and pour in the water. Gradually mix together until smooth, beating well as the flour is worked into the liquid. Cover and leave to stand in a warm place for about 15 minutes, or until frothy.
2. Meanwhile, sift the remaining flour, salt and bicarbonate of soda into a large bowl, make a well in the centre, then pour in the yeast mixture and the milk. Mix to give a thick batter consistency.
3. Using a wooden spoon, vigorously beat the batter for about 5 minutes to incorporate air. Cover and leave in a warm place for about 1 hour, until sponge-like in texture. Beat the batter for a further 2 minutes.
4. Place a large, preferably non-stick frying pan on to a high heat and, using absorbent kitchen paper, rub a little oil over the surface. Grease the insides of three crumpet rings or three 8 cm (3¼ inch) plain metal pastry cutters. Place the rings blunt edge down on to the hot surface and leave for about 2 minutes, or until very hot.

Pour batter into heated rings in frying pan.

5. Pour the batter into a large measuring jug. Pour a little batter into each ring to a depth of 1 cm (½ inch). Cook the crumpets for 5-7 minutes until the surface of each appears dry and is honeycombed with holes.
6. When the batter has set, carefully remove each metal ring. Flip the crumpet over and cook the second side for 1 minute only. Cool on a wire rack.
7. Continue cooking the crumpets until all the batter is used. It is important that the frying pan and metal rings are well oiled each time, and heated before the batter is poured in. When required, toast the crumpets on both sides and serve hot.
MAKES ABOUT 24

CHEESE LOAF

450 g (1 lb) strong white flour
salt and pepper
5 ml (1 level tsp) mustard powder
100-175 g (4-6 oz) Cheddar cheese, grated
15 g (½ oz) fresh yeast or 7 g sachet (1½ level tsp) fast-
*   action dried yeast*
300 ml (½ pint) tepid water

1. Grease two 450 g (1 lb) loaf tins.
2. Mix together the flour, salt, pepper and mustard in a large bowl. Stir in three quarters of the cheese.
3. Blend the fresh yeast and water together. Add the yeast liquid or fast-action dried yeast granules and water to the dry ingredients and mix to a soft dough.
4. Turn on to a floured surface and knead for about 10 minutes, until the dough feels firm and elastic and no longer sticky. Cover with a clean tea towel and leave to rise in a warm place for about 45 minutes, until doubled in size. Turn on to a floured surface and knead for 5 minutes.
5. Divide the dough into two and shape to fit the tins. Cover with a clean tea towel and leave to prove in a warm place, until the dough reaches the top of the tins. Sprinkle the top of the loaves with the remaining cheese.
6. Bake in the oven at 190°C (375°F) mark 5 for 40-45 minutes, until well risen and golden brown on top. Turn out and cool the loaves on a wire rack.

DANISH PASTRIES

25 g (1 oz) fresh yeast or 7 g sachet (1½ level tsp) fast-action dried yeast

150 ml (¼ pint) tepid water

450 g (1 lb) plain white flour

5 ml (1 level tsp) salt

50 g (2 oz) lard

30 ml (2 level tbsp) sugar

2 eggs, beaten

300 g (10 oz) butter or margarine, softened

50 g (2 oz) sultanas

beaten egg, to glaze

Glacé Icing (see page 432) and flaked almonds, to decorate

ALMOND PASTE

15 g (½ oz) butter or margarine

75 g (3 oz) caster sugar

75 g (3 oz) ground almonds

1 egg, beaten

CINNAMON BUTTER

50 g (2 oz) butter

50 g (2 oz) caster sugar

10 ml (2 level tsp) ground cinnamon

1. Blend the fresh yeast with the water.

2. Mix the flour and salt in a large bowl, rub in the lard and stir in the 30 ml (2 level tbsp) sugar. Add the yeast liquid or fast-action dried yeast granules and water, then add the beaten eggs. Mix to an elastic dough, adding a little more water if necessary. Knead well for 5 minutes on a lightly floured surface, until smooth. Return the dough to the rinsed-out bowl, cover with a clean tea towel and leave the dough to 'rest' in the refrigerator for 10 minutes.

3. Shape the butter into an oblong. Roll out the dough on a floured board to an oblong about three times as wide as the butter. Put the butter in the centre of the dough and fold the sides of the dough over the butter. Press the edges to seal.

4. With the folds at the sides, roll the dough into a strip three times as long as it is wide; fold the bottom third up, and the top third down, cover and leave to 'rest' for 10 minutes. Turn, repeat, rolling, folding and resting twice more.

5. To make the almond paste, cream the butter and sugar, stir in the almonds and add enough egg to make a soft and pliable consistency.

6. Make the cinnamon butter by creaming the butter and sugar and beating in the cinnamon.

7. Roll out the dough into the required shapes and fill with almond paste or cinnamon butter.

8. After shaping, cover the pastries with a clean tea towel and leave to prove in a warm place for 20-30 minutes. Brush with beaten egg and bake in the oven at 220°C (425°F) mark 7 for about 15 minutes. While hot, brush with thin Glacé Icing and sprinkle with flaked almonds.

MAKES 16

SHAPING DANISH PASTERIES

CRESCENTS: Cut out a 23 cm (9 inch) round. Divide into four segments and put a little almond paste at the base of each. Roll up from the base and curl round to form a crescent.

IMPERIAL STARS: Cut into 7.5 cm (3 inch) squares and make diagonal cuts from each corner to within 1 cm (½ inch) of the centre. Put a piece of almond paste in the centre of the square and fold one corner of each cut section down to the centre, securing the tips with beaten egg.

FOLDOVERS AND CUSHIONS: Cut into 7.5 cm (3 inch) squares and put a little almond paste in the centre. Fold over two opposite corners to the centre. Make a cushion by folding over all four corners, securing the tips with beaten egg.

PINWHEELS: Cut into a rectangle 25 x 10 cm (10 x 4 inches). Spread with cinnamon butter and sultanas, roll up like Swiss rolls and cut into 2.5 cm (1 inch) slices. Bake cut side upwards.

TWISTS: Cut into rectangles as for pinwheels. Cut each rectangle lengthways to give four pieces. Spread with cinnamon butter and fold the bottom third of each up and the top third down, seal and cut each across into thin slices. Twist these slices and put on a baking sheet.

 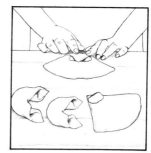

Shaping Imperial stars.   *Rolling up Crescents.*

CROISSANTS

25 g (1 oz) fresh yeast or 7 g sachet (1½ level tsp) fast-
    action dried yeast
225 ml (8 fl oz) tepid water
2 eggs
450 g (1 lb) strong white flour
10 ml (2 level tsp) salt
25 g (1 oz) lard or block margarine
225 g (8 oz) unsalted butter or block margarine at cool
    room temperature
2.5 ml (½ level tsp) caster sugar

1. Blend the fresh yeast with the water.
2. Sift flour and salt into a large bowl and rub in
the lard. Make a well in the centre and pour in
the yeast liquid or fast-action dried yeast granules
and water. Lightly whisk one egg and add to the
well. Mix and then beat in the flour until the
bowl is left clean. Turn on to a lightly floured
surface, knead well for about 10 minutes until
the dough is firm and elastic.
3. Roll out the dough on a clean, dry floured
surface to an oblong about 51 x 20 cm (20 x 8
inches). Keep the edges as square as possible,
gently pulling out the corners to stop them
rounding off. Dust the rolling pin with flour to
prevent it sticking to the dough.

Individual Brioches and Croissants

*Fold over the dough
encasing the butter.*

4. Divide the butter
into three. Dot one
portion over the top
two thirds of the
dough but clear of the
edge. Turn up the
bottom third of the
dough over half the
butter, then fold down
the remainder. Seal
the edges with a rolling
pin. Turn the dough
so that the fold is on
the right.

5. Press the dough lightly at intervals along its
length, then roll out to an oblong again. Repeat
rolling and folding with the other two portions
of butter. Rest dough in refrigerator for 30 minutes, loosely covered with a clean tea towel.
Repeat three more times, cover and chill 1 hour.
6. Roll out the dough to an oblong about 48 x
33 cm (19 x 13 inches), lay a clean tea towel over
the top and leave to rest for 10 minutes. Trim
off 1 cm (½ inch) all around and divide the
dough in half lengthways, then into three

*Roll up each triangle
from the long end.*

squares, then across
into triangles.
7. Beat the remaining
egg, 15 ml (1 tbsp)
water and sugar
together for the glaze
and brush it over the
triangles. Roll each
triangle up from the
long edge finishing
with the tip
underneath. Curve
into crescents and
place well apart on
ungreased baking sheets, allowing room to
spread. Cover loosely with a clean tea towel.
8. Leave at room temperature for about
30 minutes, or until well risen and 'puffy'.
Brush carefully with more glaze. Bake in the
oven at 220°C (425°F) mark 7 for about
15 minutes, until crisp and well browned.
Cool on wire racks.
MAKES 12

MALT BREAD

25 g (1 oz) fresh yeast or 7 g sachet (1½ level tsp) fast-
action dried yeast
150 ml (¼ pint) tepid water
450 g (1 lb) strong white flour
5 ml (1 level tsp) salt
60 ml (4 tbsp) malt extract
15 ml (1 tbsp) black treacle
25 g (1 oz) butter or block margarine
15 ml (1 level tbsp) sugar dissolved in 15 ml (1 tbsp)
water, for glaze

1. Grease two 450 g (1 lb) loaf tins.
2. Blend the fresh yeast with the water.
3. Mix the flour and salt in a large bowl. Warm
the malt, treacle and butter until just melted.
Stir the yeast liquid or fast-action dried yeast
granules and water, malt mixture into the dry
ingredients and mix to a fairly soft, sticky dough,
adding a little more water if necessary.

Roll up firmly and place
in loaf tins. Leave to rise.

4. Turn on to a floured board, knead well
for about 10 minutes,
until the dough is firm
and elastic. Divide
into two pieces. Shape
both into an oblong,
roll up like a Swiss roll
and put into the
prepared loaf tins.
5. Leave to rise in a
warm place until the
dough fills the tins;
this may take about 1½
hours, as malt bread dough usually takes quite a
long time to rise.
6. Bake in the oven at 200°C (400°F) mark 6 for
30-40 minutes until well risen and golden brown.
Brush the loaves with sugar glaze and cool on a
wire rack.

BRIOCHE

15 g (½ oz) fresh yeast or 7 g sachet (1½ level tsp) dried
yeast
25 ml (5 tsp) tepid water
225 g (8 oz) strong white flour
pinch of salt
15 ml (1 level tbsp) caster sugar
2 eggs, beaten
50 g (2 oz) butter or block margarine, melted
beaten egg, to glaze

1. Brush a 1.1 litre (2 pint) fluted brioche
mould with oil.
2. Blend the fresh yeast with the water.
3. Mix together the flour, salt and sugar in a
large bowl. Stir the yeast liquid or fast-action
dried yeast granules and water into the flour,
with the eggs and melted butter. Work to a soft
dough, turn out on to a floured board and
knead for about 5 minutes, until smooth and
elastic.
4. Put the dough in a large bowl, cover with a
clean tea towel and leave in a warm place until it
has doubled in size.
5. Knead the dough well on a lightly floured
surface. Shape three quarters of it into a ball
and place in the bottom of the mould. Press a

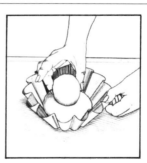

Place three quarters of the
dough in a mould, then
top with remainder.

hole in the centre as
far as the tin base.
Shape the remaining
dough into a 'knob',
put into the hole and
press down lightly.
6. Cover the mould
with a clean tea towel
and leave at room
temperature until the
dough is light and
puffy and nearly
reaches the top edge
of the mould.
7. Brush lightly with
beaten egg and bake in the oven at 230°C
(450°F) mark 8 for 15-20 minutes, until golden.
Turn out and serve at once or cool on a wire
rack. Serve with jam.

VARIATION
INDIVIDUAL BRIOCHES
For small brioches divide the dough into
12 pieces, put into deep 7.5 cm (3 inch) oiled
fluted patty tins, and bake as above for about
10 minutes. Serve hot or cool on wire racks.

Chelsea Buns

CHELSEA BUNS

*15 g (½ oz) fresh yeast or 7 g sachet (1½ tsp) fast-action
dried yeast*
100 ml (4 fl oz) warm milk
225 g (8 oz) strong white flour
2.5 ml (½ tsp) salt
40 g (1½ oz) butter, diced
1 egg, beaten
100 g (4 oz) mixed dried fruit
50 g (2 oz) light soft brown sugar
clear honey, to glaze

1. Grease an 18 cm (7 inch) square tin.
2. Blend the fresh yeast with the milk.
3. Put the flour and salt in a bowl, then rub in
25 g (1 oz) of the butter until the mixture
resembles fine breadcrumbs. Make a well in the
centre, pour in the yeast liquid or fast-action
dried yeast granules and milk, with the egg. Beat
together until the mixture forms a dough that
leaves sides of bowl clean.
4. Turn on to a lightly floured surface and

knead well for 10 minutes, until smooth and
elastic. Cover with a clean tea towel and leave in
a warm place for 1 hour, or until doubled in size.
5. Knead the dough lightly on a floured surface,
then roll it out to a large rectangle, measuring
about 30 x 23 cm (12 x 9 inches). Mix the dried
fruit and sugar together. Melt the remaining
butter, then brush over the dough. Scatter with
the fruit mixture, leaving a 2.5 cm (1 inch)
border around the edges.
6. Roll the dough up tightly like a Swiss roll,
starting at a long edge. Press the edges together
to seal them, then cut the roll into 12 slices.
Place the rolls cut side uppermost in a greased
18 cm (7 inch) square tin.
7. Cover and leave in a warm place for 30 minutes, until doubled in size.
8. Bake in the oven at 190°C (375°F) mark 5 for
30 minutes, until well risen and golden brown.
Brush with honey while still hot. Leave to cool
slightly in the tin before turning out. Serve warm.
MAKES 12

HOT CROSS BUNS

25 g (1 oz) fresh yeast or 7 g sachet (1½ level tsp) fast-action dried yeast

50 g (2 oz) caster sugar

150 ml (¼ pint) tepid milk

75 ml (5 tbsp) tepid water

450 g (1 lb) strong white flour

5 ml (1 level tsp) salt

5 ml (1 level tsp) ground mixed spice

5 ml (1 level tsp) ground cinnamon

2.5 ml (½ level tsp) freshly grated nutmeg

50 g (2 oz) butter, melted and cooled

1 egg, beaten

75 g (3 oz) currants

30 ml (2 level tbsp) chopped mixed peel

50 g (2 oz) Shortcrust Pastry, made with 50 g (2 oz) flour (see page 381)

FOR THE GLAZE

60 ml (4 tbsp) milk and water, mixed

45 ml (3 level tbsp) caster sugar

Hot Cross Buns

1. Grease a baking sheet. Blend the fresh yeast with the milk and water.
2. Sift the flour, salt and spices into a bowl. Stir in the sugar. Make a well in the centre and add the butter, egg, yeast liquid or fast-action dried yeast granules, milk and water. Add the currants and peel and mix to a soft dough.
3. Turn on to a lightly floured surface and knead for about 10 minutes, until smooth and elastic and no longer sticky. Cover with a clean tea towel and leave to rise in a warm place until doubled in size. Turn the dough out on to a floured surface and knead for 2-3 minutes. Divide dough into 12 pieces and shape into buns.
4. Place on the baking sheet, cover and leave in a warm place until doubled in size.
5. Roll out the pastry thinly on a floured surface and cut into thin strips about 9 cm (3½ inches) long. Dampen the pastry strips and lay two on each bun to make a cross.
6. Bake in the oven at 190°C (375°F) mark 5 for 15-20 minutes, until golden brown. For the glaze, heat the milk, water and sugar together. Brush the hot buns twice with glaze, then cool.
MAKES 12

STOLLEN

15 g (½ oz) fresh yeast or 7 g sachet (1½ level tsp) fast-action dried yeast

1.25 ml (¼ level tsp) caster sugar

100 ml (4 fl oz) tepid milk

225 g (8 oz) strong white flour

1.25 ml (¼ level tsp) salt

25 g (1 oz) butter or block margarine

grated rind of 1 small lemon

50 g (2 oz) chopped mixed peel

50 g (2 oz) currants

50 g (2 oz) sultanas

25 g (1 oz) blanched almonds, chopped

½ a beaten egg

icing sugar for dusting

1. Grease a baking sheet. Blend the yeast, sugar and milk with 50 g (2 oz) of flour. Leave in a warm place for about 20 minutes until frothy.
2. Sift remaining flour and salt in a large bowl and rub in the fat. Stir in the fruit and nuts.
3. Add the yeast batter and egg and mix to a soft dough. Knead on a lightly floured surface for about 10 minutes until smooth. Cover with a clean tea towel and leave to rise in a warm place for about 1 hour, until doubled in size.
4. Knead the dough for 2-3 minutes on a lightly floured surface. Roll into an oval, 23 x 18 cm (9 x 7 inches), then mark a line lengthways with the rolling pin and fold dough in half along this line. Place on the baking sheet.
5. Cover with a clean tea towel and leave to prove in a warm place until doubled in size.
6. Bake in the oven at 200°C (400°F) mark 6 for 30 minutes, until golden brown. Cool on a wire rack. Dust thickly with icing sugar.

QUICK BREADS

Quick breads vary from cake-like breads made with bicarbonate of soda to the thin flat breads like chappatis which are unleavened, ie have no raising agent. These breads are quick to make as they do not require the long preparation of yeast doughs. However, they must be eaten quickly as they go stale much sooner than yeast breads.

SODA BREAD

450 g (1 lb) plain white flour
10 ml (2 level tsp) bicarbonate of soda
10 ml (2 level tsp) cream of tartar
5 ml (1 level tsp) salt
25-50 g (1-2 oz) lard or block margarine
about 300 ml (½ pint) soured milk or buttermilk

1. Grease and flour a baking sheet.
2. Sift together the dry ingredients twice. Rub in the lard. Mix to a soft dough with the milk, adding a little at a time.
3. Shape into an 18 cm (7 inch) round and mark into triangles. Place on the baking sheet.
4. Bake in the oven at 220°C (425°F) mark 7, for about 30 minutes. Eat while very fresh.

CARAWAY RYE BREAD

350 g (12 oz) rye flour
10 ml (2 level tsp) caraway seeds
2.5 ml (½ level tsp) salt
5 ml (1 level tsp) baking powder
50 g (2 oz) butter or block margarine
150 ml (5 fl oz) soured cream
150 ml (¼ pint) milk
1 egg
milk and caraway seeds, to garnish

1. Grease and base line two 300 ml (½ pint) Turtle pots or other ovenproof containers.
2. Mix the flour, caraway seeds, salt and baking powder in a large bowl. Rub in the butter.
3. Whisk together the soured cream, milk and egg. Stir into the dry ingredients. Bind to a smooth firm dough, adding a little water if necessary.
4. Halve the dough, and on a lightly floured surface knead each piece lightly, then place in the pots. Brush with milk and sprinkle with caraway seeds.
5. Bake in the oven at 200°C (400°F) mark 6 for 1 hour. Cover loosely with foil towards the end of cooking time if the loaf is browning too quickly. Wrap when cold; best eaten next day but will keep up to three days.

CHAPPATIS

225 g (8 oz) plain wholemeal flour
150-200 ml (5-7 fl oz) tepid water
30 ml (2 level tbsp) ghee or butter

1. Place the flour in a bowl and add enough water to bind. On a lightly floured surface knead the dough until it feels soft and pliable, the consistency should be like that of shortcrust pastry dough. Cover and leave to rest for at least 15 minutes.
2. Heat a heavy-based frying pan or griddle. Divide the dough into 8-10 portions and shape into small balls. Dip the balls into a little flour, sufficient to coat them lightly, then roll into rounds 12 cm (5 inches) in diameter.
3. Place the rolled out chappati in the hot pan and as soon as small bubbles start to appear on the surface, turn it over and repeat the process. Using a clean tea towel, carefully press down the edges of the chappati – so the edges are cooked and the chappati puffs up. It is cooked as soon as both sides have brown spots on the surface.
4. Remove from the frying pan or griddle and smear with a little ghee or butter. Stack the chappatis on top of each other and cover to keep hot. Serve at once.
MAKES 8-10

NOTE: You can make chappatis in advance; store in an airtight container and warm under the grill.

PARATHAS

Plain parathas are similar to chappatis but the addition of ghee or butter and various ways of folding give parathas their distinct character.

225 g (8 oz) plain wholemeal flour
200 ml (7 fl oz) water
45 ml (3 tbsp) ghee, melted

1. Place the flour in a bowl and gradually add the water to form a soft pliable dough. Knead the dough for a few minutes until it leaves the sides of bowl. Cover and leave for 15 minutes.
2. Divide the dough into eight equal portions. Place each portion in the palm of the hand and roll it into a smooth ball. Dip the pieces into a little flour and coat lightly.

3. Roll the dough into 10 cm (4 inch) rounds. Smear a little ghee over the parathas. Fold one third of the round into the centre and then the remaining one third over the first fold, so that you have a rectangle measuring 2.5 cm (1 inch) x 10 cm (4 inches).
4. Smear a little ghee over the rectangle and repeat the folding method as described above, so you now have a small square. Dip the squares into a little flour to coat, then roll out to a larger square no larger than 12 cm (5 inches).
5. Heat a heavy-based frying pan or griddle. Cook the Parathas until bubbles start to appear on the surface. Cook the other side. Turn again, pressing the edges down with a clean tea towel.
Makes 8

TORTILLAS

These are made from *masa harina* (fine corn meal) which can be bought from delicatessens.

250 g (9 oz) masa harina
2.5 ml (½ level tsp) salt
225 ml (8 fl oz) tepid water

1. Mix the masa harina with the salt in a large bowl. Gradually add the tepid water, mixing lightly with a fork to make a dough that is just moist enough to hold together. If necessary, add more water, 15 ml (1 tbsp) at a time. Gather the dough lightly into a ball.
2. Knead the dough quickly and lightly in the bowl with one hand until it is smooth.
3. Divide the dough into 12 equal pieces and shape each one into a small ball. Keep covered to prevent them drying while you roll each out.

4. Flatten each ball until 5 mm (¼ inch) thick, then place between two sheets of greaseproof paper. Roll out to 15 cm (6 inch) rounds and leave between the greaseproof paper.
5. Heat a heavy-based frying pan or griddle. Remove the top sheet from one round and invert it into the frying pan. Peel off the second paper sheet. Cook for 30 seconds, until the edges curl up.
6. Turn the tortilla over and press gently with a fish slice or spatula until bubbles form underneath it. Turn it again and cook for a further minute or until the underside is speckled with brown.
7. Remove from the frying pan. Wrap to keep it hot while you cook the remainder, stacking them in foil as they are cooked.
Makes 12

HERBED CHEESE BREAD

225 g (8 oz) self raising white flour
7.5 ml (1½ level tsp) salt
5 ml (1 level tsp) mustard powder
5 ml (1 level tsp) snipped fresh chives
15 ml (1 tbsp) chopped fresh parsley
75 g (3 oz) double Gloucester or mature Cheddar
   cheese, grated
1 egg, beaten
25 g (1 oz) butter or block margarine, melted

1. Grease a 450 g (1 lb) loaf tin. Mix the flour, salt and mustard in a bowl and stir in the herbs and cheese. Add the egg, 150 ml (¼ pint) water and melted butter and stir until well blended.
2. Spoon into the loaf tin and bake in the oven at 190°C (375°F) mark 5 for about 45 minutes.
3. Turn out and cool on a wire rack. Serve sliced and buttered while still warm.

Jams, Jellies and Marmalades

Preserving fruit in the form of jams, jellies and marmalades was once part of the domestic routine in most homes, so there would be fruit during the winter months when no fresh produce was available. Although this is no longer necessary, people still enjoy making preserves free from artificial colourings and preservatives. This chapter also includes preserving fruits in alcohol, mincemeat and rumpots. Jams and jellies are also a good way of using up gluts of fruit that you do not want to eat or freeze.

EQUIPMENT FOR JAM-MAKING

Some special utensils and tools, though by no means essential, make jam-making easier.

PRESERVING PANS

Also known as maslin pans, these are deep, wide pans that are wider at the top than at the bottom; they usually have a handle on each side, or one curved handle over the top. Choose a preserving pan made from a heavy metal, such as aluminium or stainless steel. There is some concern over the possible link between aluminium and Alzheimer's Disease, but evidence at present is inconclusive. However, it is advisable that people with kidney problems, who are less able to expel aluminium from their systems, should avoid cooking acidic foods in plain, uncoated aluminium pans, and this includes making jams and preserves in unlined aluminium preserving pans.

A good preserving pan should have a fairly thick base to prevent the jam burning, and should be wide enough to allow the jam to boil rapidly without splashing all over the hob. The best size will depend on how much jam you want to make at one time – preferably, the jam should come no more than halfway up the pan.

Old style preserving pans made from unlined copper or brass can be used for jams, providing they are perfectly clean. Any discoloration or tarnish should be removed with a patent cleaner and the pan should be thoroughly washed before use. Tin-lined copper pans cannot be used as the tin lining is likely to be melted by the hot jam.

If a preserving pan is not available, a large thick based saucepan can be used, remembering that, since most saucepans are not as wide as a preserving pan, a longer simmering and boiling period for the fruit may be necessary.

JAM JARS

Jars should be thoroughly clean and free from cracks, chips or other flaws. Those holding 450 g or 1 kg (1 or 2 lb) are the most useful sizes as covers are available for these sizes. Waxed discs, cellophane covers, rubber bands and labels for covering and labelling jars can be bought from most stationery shops and some chemists.

OTHER EQUIPMENT

The following are also useful when making jam:

- A large, long-handled wooden spoon for stirring.
- A slotted spoon for skimming off any scum or fruit stones from the surface of jam.
- A sugar thermometer, though not essential, is very helpful when testing for a set.
- A funnel with a wide tube for filling jars is useful. Failing this, a large heatproof cup or jug can be used.
- A cherry stoner saves time and prevents hands becoming stained with cherry juice.
- Any sieve used in jam-making should be made of nylon, not metal which may discolour the fruit mixture.

JAM

Jam is basically a cooked mixture of fruit and sugar. The high concentration of sugar used in jam making prevents the growth of micro-organisms and allows the jam to be kept for many months.

CHOOSING FRUIT

Fruit for jam should be sound – poor quality fruit will not have as much flavour – and either just ripe or slightly under-ripe. The jam will only set if there are sufficient quantities of pectin, acid and sugar present. Some fruits are naturally rich in pectin (see chart below) and give a good set, while others do not contain as much and may need to have it boosted with added pectin. Lemon juice is most often used for this purpose, since it aids the set and often brings out the flavour of the fruit. Allow 30 ml (2 tbsp) lemon juice to 2 kg (4 lb) of a fruit with poor setting properties. Alternatively, you can buy bottled pectin – follow the manufacturer's instructions for how much to use. Sometimes an acid only is added, such as citric or tartaric acid. These contain no pectin but help to extract the natural pectin from the fruit and improve the flavour of fruits which are lacking in acid. Allow 2.5 ml (½ level tsp) to 2 kg (4 lb) of a fruit with poor setting properties.

HOMEMADE PECTIN EXTRACT can be made from sour cooking apples, crab apples or apple peelings, cores and windfalls, as follows:

Wash 1 kg (2 lb) fruit and chop roughly without peeling or coring. Cover with 600-900 ml (1-1½ pints) water and stew gently for about 45 minutes, until well pulped. Strain through a jelly bag or muslin cloth (see page 472), then carry out a pectin test (see opposite) to ensure that there is sufficient pectin present. Allow 150-300 ml (¼-½ pint) of this extract to 2 kg (4 lb) of fruit which is low in pectin. Pectin extract can also be made using the same method from fresh gooseberries and redcurrants.

SUGAR

Sugar acts as a preservative in jam and also affects its setting quality. The exact amount of sugar needed depends on the pectin strength of the fruit, so it is essential to use the amount specified in a recipe. Too little sugar produces a poor set and the jam may go mouldy when stored. Too much sugar makes a dark sticky jam, overpowers the fruit flavour and may crystallise.

Granulated sugar is the most economical for jam making although less foamy scum is formed on the surface of the jam when lump or preserving sugar is used. However, these are more expensive and the only real benefit is that the end product is slightly clearer than when granulated sugar is used. Caster sugar and brown sugar can also be used but the latter produces a darker jam with a changed flavour. You can also buy preserving sugar crystals with added pectin, specially produced for use with fruits which are low in pectin.

You can make your own reduced sugar jams similar to those on the market. Don't reduce sugar content by more than 20 per cent or the jam will be runny. As it doesn't keep well, make it in small batches and store in the refrigerator (up to 6 weeks) or a cool place (3-4 weeks).

TESTING FOR PECTIN CONTENT

The chart shows the pectin content of fruits and vegetables used in preserving. If you are not sure of your fruit setting qualities, as follows:

When the fruit has been cooked until soft, but before you add sugar, take 5 ml (1 tsp) juice, put it in a glass and, when cool, add 15ml (1 tbsp) methylated spirit. Shake the glass and leave for 1 minute. If the mixture forms a jelly-like clot the fruit has a good pectin content. If it does not form a single firm clot, the pectin content is too low and you will need extra.

PECTIN CONTENT OF FRUITS AND VEGETABLES USED IN PRESERVING		
Good	**Medium**	**Poor**
Cooking apples	Apricots	Bananas
Crab apples	Bilberries	Cherries
Currants (red and black)	Blackberries	Elderberries
Damsons	Cranberries	Figs
Gooseberries	Dessert apples	Grapes
Lemons	Greengages	Marrows
Limes	Loganberries	Melons
Quinces	Mulberries	Nectarines
Seville oranges	Plums	Peaches
	Raspberries	Pineapples
		Rhubarb
		Strawberries

TESTING FOR A SET

Use one of these two methods:

- The temperature test is the most accurate. Stir the jam and insert a sugar thermometer in the middle of the pan. When the reading is 105°C (221°F) a set should be obtained. Some fruits need a degree lower or higher than this, so it is sensible also to carry out the saucer test. Put a tiny amount of jam on a cold saucer or plate (leave in the refrigerator beforehand), allow it to cool, then push a finger gently through it. If the surface of the jam wrinkles, setting point has been reached. Be sure to remove the pan from the heat while doing the test so that the temperature doesn't rise and the jam become over boiled, which weakens its setting property.
- The flake test involves lifting some jam from the pan on a wooden spoon, letting it cool a little, then dropping it back. If it has been boiled for long enough, drops of jam will run together along the edge of the spoon and form flakes which will break off sharply.

POTTING, COVERING AND STORING

As soon as a set has been reached, remove the pan from the heat and with the slotted spoon skim off any scum. Don't pot strawberry and other whole fruit jams immediately or all the fruit will rise to the top. Leave them in the pan for about 15-20 minutes before potting. Spoon the jam into the warm jars, filling them right to the top.

Wipe the outside of the jars with a damp cloth while they are still warm and immediately put wax discs, wax side down, on the surface of the jam, making sure they lie flat.

Either cover the pot immediately with a dampened round of cellophane and secure with a rubber band or string, or leave the jam until it is quite cold before doing this. Label the jars, making sure you include the date, and store in a cool, dry, dark place. Most jams keep well for over a year if properly covered and stored, but their flavour deteriorates after a while.

WATCHPOINTS

Problems with jam making can be eliminated if the following simple tips are followed:

- Mould growth usually occurs because the jam has not been covered with a wax disc while still hot. Alternatively, the pots may have been stored in a place where they picked up bacteria and were not cleaned properly. Other possible causes are insufficient evaporation of water while the fruit is being cooked before sugar is added and/or too short a boiling time after the sugar was added. It is important not to eat jam that has mould growth on it as it produces toxins. Throw away the whole jar if you find any mould on the top surface.
- Bubbles in jam indicate fermentation which is usually because not enough sugar has been used or because the jam was not reduced sufficiently. Fermented jam can be boiled up again and repotted but thereafter should only be used for cooking.
- Crystallisation is usually caused by lack of enough acid or by under or over boiling the jam after the sugar has been added.
- Shrinkage of jam in pots is caused by inadequate covering or failure to store the jam in a cool, dark, dry place.

APRICOT JAM

1.8 kg (4 lb) apricots, washed, halved and stoned
450 ml (¾ pint) water
juice of 1 lemon
1.8 kg (4 lb) sugar
knob of butter

1. Crack a few of the apricot stones with a weight, nutcracker or hammer, take out the kernels and blanch in boiling water for 1 minute.
2. Place the apricots, water, lemon juice and kernels in a preserving pan and simmer for

about 15 minutes until they are soft and the contents of the pan are well reduced. Remove from the heat, add the sugar, stirring until dissolved, then add the knob of butter. Return to the heat, bring to the boil and boil rapidly for about 15 minutes, stirring frequently.
3. Test for a set and, when setting point is reached, take the pan off the heat and remove any scum that has accumulated on the surface with a slotted spoon.
4. Leave to stand for 15 minutes. Pot and cover.
MAKES ABOUT 3 KG (6½ LB)

DRIED APRICOT JAM

450 g (1 lb) dried apricots
1.7 litres (3 pints) water
juice of 1 lemon
1.4 kg (3 lb) sugar
50 g (2 oz) blanched almonds, split
knob of butter

1. Put the apricots in a bowl, cover with the water and leave to soak overnight.
2. Place the apricots in a preserving pan with the soaking water and lemon juice. Simmer for

about 30 minutes until soft, stirring occasionally.
3. Remove the pan from the heat and add the sugar and blanched almonds. Stir until the sugar has dissolved, then add the knob of butter. Bring to the boil and boil rapidly for 20-25 minutes, stirring frequently to prevent sticking.
4. Test for a set and, when setting point is reached, take the pan off the heat and remove any scum with a slotted spoon.
5. Leave to stand for 15 minutes. Pot and cover.
MAKES ABOUT 2.3 KG (5 LB)

BLACKCURRANT JAM

1.8 kg (4 lb) blackcurrants, washed and strung
1.7 litres (3 pints) water
2.7 kg (6 lb) sugar
knob of butter

1. Place the fruit in a preserving pan with the water. Simmer gently for about 45 minutes until the fruit is soft and the contents of the pan are well reduced, stirring from time to time to prevent sticking. (As the skins of currants tend

to be rather tough, it is important to cook the fruit really well before adding the sugar.)
2. Remove the pan from the heat, add the sugar to the fruit pulp, stir until dissolved, then add the knob of butter. Bring to the boil and boil rapidly for about 10 minutes, stirring frequently.
3. Test for a set and, when setting point is reached, take pan off the heat and remove any scum with a slotted spoon. Pot and cover.
MAKES ABOUT 4.5 KG (10 LB)

BLACKBERRY AND APPLE JAM

1.8 kg (4 lb) blackberries, washed
300 ml (½ pint) water
700 g (1½ lb) cooking apples (prepared weight), peeled,
*   cored and sliced*
2.7 kg (6 lb) sugar
knob of butter

1. Place the blackberries in a large saucepan with 150 ml (¼ pint) of the water and simmer gently until soft.
2. Put the apples in a preserving pan with the remaining 150 ml (¼ pint) water and simmer

gently until soft, then pulp with a wooden spoon or a potato masher.
3. Add the blackberries and sugar to the apple pulp, stirring until the sugar has dissolved, then add the knob of butter. Bring to the boil and boil rapidly, stirring frequently, for about 10 minutes.
4. Test for a set and, when setting point is reached, take the pan off the heat and remove any scum with a slotted spoon.
5. Pot and cover.
MAKES ABOUT 4.5 KG (10 LB)

ROSE PETAL JAM

225 g (8 oz) rose heads
450 g (1 lb) sugar
1.1 litres (2 pints) water
juice of 2 lemons

1. Pick the roses when they are in full bloom, remove the petals and snip off the white bases.
2. Place the petals in a bowl and add 225 g (8 oz) sugar. Cover and leave overnight. This

will extract the scent and darken the petals.
3. Pour the water and lemon juice into a saucepan and stir in the remaining sugar. Heat gently until sugar has dissolved, but do not boil.
4. Stir in the rose petals and simmer gently for 20 minutes. Bring to the boil and boil for about 5 minutes, until thick.
5. Pot and cover in the usual way.
MAKES ABOUT 450 G (1 LB)

Strawberry Conserve

1.4 kg (3 lb) strawberries, hulled
1.4 kg (3 lb) sugar

1. Place the strawberries in a large bowl in layers with the sugar. Cover and leave for 24 hours.
2. Put into a large saucepan and bring to the boil, stirring until the sugar dissolves. Boil rapidly for 5 minutes.
3. Return the mixture to the bowl, cover and leave in a cool place for a further 2 days.
4. Return to the pan again and boil rapidly for 10 minutes. Leave to cool for 15 minutes.
5. Pot and cover as for jam.
Makes about 1.4 kg (3 lb)

Left: Gooseberry Jam. Right: Strawberry Conserve

Strawberry Jam

1.6 kg (3½ lb) strawberries, washed and hulled
45 ml (3 tbsp) lemon juice
1.4 kg (3 lb) sugar
knob of butter

1. Place the strawberries in a preserving pan with the lemon juice and simmer gently, stirring occasionally, for 20-30 minutes until really soft.

2. Take the pan off the heat, add the sugar, stirring until dissolved, then add the knob of butter. Bring to the boil and boil rapidly for about 20 minutes, stirring frequently.
3. Test for a set and, when setting point is reached, take the pan off the heat and remove any scum with a slotted spoon.
4. Leave to stand for 15 minutes. Pot and cover.
Makes about 2.3 kg (5 lb)

Gooseberry Jam

2.7 kg (6 lb) gooseberries, topped, tailed and washed
1.1 litres (2 pints) water
2.7 kg (6 lb) sugar
knob of butter

1. Place the gooseberries in a preserving pan with the water. Simmer gently, uncovered, for about 30 minutes, until the fruit is really soft and reduced, mashing it to a pulp with a wooden spoon and stirring from time to time.
2. Remove from the heat, add the sugar to the fruit pulp and stir until dissolved. Add the knob of butter, bring to the boil and boil rapidly for about 10 minutes, stirring frequently.
3. Test for a set and, when setting point is reached, take the pan off the heat and remove any scum with a slotted spoon.
4. Pot and cover.
Makes about 4.5 kg (10 lb)

MARROW AND GINGER JAM

1.8 kg (4 lb) marrow (prepared weight)
1.8 kg (4 lb) sugar
25 g (1 oz) root ginger, peeled
thinly peeled rind and juice of 3 lemons

1. Peel the marrow, remove the seeds and cut into pieces about 1 cm (½ inch) square.
2. Place in a basin, sprinkle with about 450 g (1 lb) of the sugar and allow to stand overnight.
3. Press the ginger with a weight to release the flavour from the fibres, tie it up in a piece of muslin with the lemon rind and place in a preserving pan with the marrow and lemon juice.
4. Simmer for 30 minutes, add the rest of the sugar and boil gently for 15-20 minutes. When setting point is reached and the marrow looks transparent take off the heat and remove scum.
5. Remove the muslin bag. Pot and cover.
MAKES ABOUT 3 KG (6½ LB)

CHERRY JAM

1.8 kg (4 lb) cherries, eg Morello, stoned
juice of 3 lemons
1.4 kg (3 lb) sugar
knob of butter
75 ml (5 tbsp) kirsch (optional)

1. Crack a few of the cherry stones in a nutcracker and remove the kernels.
2. Put the cherries, kernels and lemon juice in a pan and simmer very gently for about 45 minutes until really soft, stirring from time to time to prevent sticking.
3. Remove from the heat, add the sugar, stirring until dissolved, then add the knob of butter. Bring to the boil and boil rapidly for about 30 minutes, stirring frequently.
4. Test for a set and, when setting point is reached, take the pan off the heat and remove any scum with a slotted spoon. Leave to stand for 15 minutes.
5. Stir in the kirsch, if using, then pot and cover.
MAKES ABOUT 2.3 KG (5 LB)

NOTE: Cherry stones are easy to remove with a cherry stoner or the end of a potato peeler, but if you haven't got one, use the cherries with their stones and remove them from the pan with a slotted spoon as they rise to the surface.
As cherries are lacking in pectin, this jam will give only a light set.

PLUM JAM

2.7 kg (6 lb) plums, washed
900 ml (1½ pints) water
2.7 kg (6 lb) sugar
knob of butter

1. Place the plums and water in a preserving pan and simmer gently for about 30 minutes, until the fruit is really soft and the contents of the pan are well reduced.
2. Remove the pan from the heat, add the sugar, stirring until dissolved, then add the knob of butter. Bring to the boil and boil rapidly for 10-15 minutes, stirring frequently.
3. Test for a set and, when setting point is reached, take the pan off the heat.
4. Using a slotted spoon, remove the stones and any scum from the surface of the jam.
5. Leave to stand for 15 minutes. Pot and cover.
MAKES ABOUT 4.5 KG (10 LB)

VARIATIONS
GREENGAGE JAM
Follow the recipe for Plum Jam, using washed greengages, with stalks removed, instead of plums and only 600 ml (1 pint) water.
DAMSON JAM
Follow the recipe for Plum Jam using only 2.3 kg (5 lb) damsons and, after adding the sugar, boil for 10 minutes only.

LIGHT SET RASPBERRY JAM

This jam has only a light set, but has a very good colour and fresh fruit flavour.

1.1 kg (2½ lb) raspberries, washed
1.4 kg (3 lb) sugar

1. Put the raspberries in a preserving pan and simmer very gently for about 10 minutes until the juice flows, then bring to the boil and boil gently for a further 10 minutes.

2. Warm the sugar in a heatproof bowl in the oven and add it to the fruit. Keep stirring until it has dissolved.
3. Bring the jam back to the boil and boil for 2 minutes.
4. Take the pan off the heat and remove any scum with a slotted spoon.
5. Leave to stand for 15 minutes. Pot and cover.
MAKES ABOUT 2.3 KG (5 LB)

RASPBERRY JAM

1.8 kg (4 lb) raspberries, washed
1.8 kg (4 lb) sugar
knob of butter

1. Place the fruit in a preserving pan and simmer very gently in its own juice for about 20 minutes, stirring carefully from time to time, until the fruit is really soft.
2. Remove the pan from the heat and add the sugar, stirring until dissolved, then add the knob

of butter and boil rapidly for about 30 minutes.
3. Test for a set and, when setting point is reached, take the pan off the heat and remove any scum with a slotted spoon.
4. Leave to stand for 15 minutes. Pot and cover.
MAKES ABOUT 3 KG (6½ LB)

VARIATION
LOGANBERRY JAM
Use loganberries instead of raspberries.

RHUBARB AND GINGER JAM

1.1 kg (2½ lb) rhubarb (prepared weight), chopped
1.1 kg (2½ lb) sugar
juice of 2 lemons
25 g (1 oz) root ginger
100 g (4 oz) preserved stem ginger, chopped

1. Place the rhubarb in a large bowl in alternate layers with the sugar and lemon juice, cover and leave overnight.
2. Next day, peel and bruise the root ginger slightly with a weight or rolling pin, and tie it in

a piece of muslin. Put the rhubarb mixture in a preserving pan with the muslin bag, bring to the boil and boil rapidly for 15 minutes, stirring frequently.
3. Remove the muslin bag from the pan, add the stem ginger and boil for a further 5 minutes.
4. Test for a set and, when setting point is reached, take the pan off the heat and remove any scum with a slotted spoon.
5. Pot and cover.
MAKES ABOUT 2 KG (4½ LB)

UNCOOKED FREEZER JAM

1.4 kg (3 lb) raspberries or strawberries, washed and hulled
1.8 kg (4 lb) caster sugar
60 ml (4 tbsp) lemon juice
227 ml (8 fl oz) bottle of commercial pectin

1. Place the fruit in a large bowl and very lightly crush with a fork.
2. Stir in the sugar and lemon juice and leave at room temperature, stirring occasionally, for about 1 hour until the sugar has dissolved.

3. Gently stir in the pectin and continue stirring for a further 2 minutes.
4. Pour the jam into small plastic containers, leaving a little space at the top to allow for expansion.
5. Cover and leave at room temperature for a further 24 hours. Label and freeze for up to 6 months.
6. To serve, thaw at room temperature for about 1 hour.
MAKES ABOUT 3.2 KG (7 LB)

JELLIES

The difference between jams and jellies is that with jellies only the juice is used in the end product. Jellies are slightly more difficult to make and the yield from the fruit is not as high as with jams, but they are well worth the effort. Homemade jellies can be served with meat, used as a glaze on flans and spread on bread and butter.

CHOOSING FRUIT

To make a jelly you need fruit with a high pectin content to give a good set (see chart on page 466). Fruit with low pectin should be combined with high pectin ones.

MAKING JELLIES

Prepare the fruit by washing and chopping; there is no need to peel or core. Don't use damaged fruit.

The amount of water (stated in the recipes) varies according to the water content of the fruit. Hard fruits should always be covered with water. Cooking should be slow and thorough to extract as much juice as possible. After 30 minutes to 1 hour, depending on the softness of the fruit, pour the contents of the pan into a scalded jelly bag suspended on a stand or upturned chair or stool. If you do not have a jelly bag, improvise with a double thickness of fine cloth such as a clean tea towel or muslin. Leave it to drip into a bowl until all the juice is strained off. This may take several hours or overnight if necessary. Do not touch or squeeze the bag while the juices are dripping through or the resulting jelly will be cloudy.

Measure the strained juice and add 450 g (1 lb) sugar for each 600 ml (1 pint) juice extract for pectin rich fruits, and 350 g (12 oz) sugar to 600 ml (1 pint) juice for medium pectin fruits.

Stir the sugar into the juice, return to the pan and heat gently, stirring until the sugar dissolves. Boil for about 10 minutes until setting point is reached, test for this in the same way as for jam (see page 467). Remove any scum from the surface with a slotted spoon, then pot and cover as for jam (see page 467).

MINT AND APPLE JELLY

2.3 kg (5 lb) cooking apples, washed and chopped
1.1 litres (2 pints) water
few fresh mint sprigs
1.1 litres (2 pints) distilled vinegar
sugar
90-120 ml (6-8 tbsp) chopped fresh mint
few drops of green food colouring

1. Place the apples in a large saucepan with the water and mint sprigs. Bring to the boil, then simmer gently for about 45 minutes, until soft and pulpy. Stir from time to time to prevent sticking. Add the vinegar and boil for a further 5 minutes.
2. Spoon the apple pulp into a jelly bag or cloth attached to the legs of an upturned stool, and leave to strain into a large bowl for at least 12 hours.
3. Discard the pulp remaining in the jelly bag. Measure the juice extract and put it in a preserving pan with 450 g (1 lb) sugar for each 600 ml (1 pint) extract. Heat gently, stirring, until the sugar has completely dissolved, then bring to the boil and boil rapidly for about 10 minutes.
4. Test for a set and, when setting point is reached, take the pan off the heat and remove any scum with a slotted spoon.
5. Stir in the mint and add a few drops of green food colouring. Allow to cool slightly, then stir well to distribute the mint.
6. Pot and cover.

VARIATION
HERB JELLIES
Other fresh herbs, such as rosemary, parsley, sage, tarragon and thyme, can be used in place of the mint sprigs.

Strain the juices through a suspended jelly bag.

Rosehip Jelly

ROSEHIP JELLY

900 g (2 lb) cooking apples, washed
450 g (1 lb) ripe rosehips, washed
sugar

1. Remove any bruised portions from apples, then roughly chop without coring or peeling.
2. Put the apples and rosehips in a preserving pan with just enough water to cover. Bring to the boil, then simmer gently for about 45 minutes or until the fruit is soft and pulpy. Stir from time to time to prevent the fruit sticking.
3. Spoon the fruit pulp into a jelly bag or cloth

attached to the legs of an upturned stool, and leave to strain into a large bowl for at least 12 hours.
4. Discard the pulp remaining in the jelly bag. Measure the extract and return to the preserving pan with 450 g (1 lb) sugar for each 600 ml (1 pint) extract.
5. Heat gently, stirring, until the sugar has dissolved, then bring to the boil and boil rapidly for about 15 minutes or until setting point is reached. Remove any scum with a slotted spoon.
6. Pot and cover in the usual way.

BRAMBLE JELLY

1.8 kg (4 lb) slightly under-ripe blackberries, washed
juice of 2 lemons or 7.5 ml (1½ level tsp) citric or
    tartaric acid
450 ml (¾ pint) water
sugar

1. Put the blackberries, lemon juice and water into a preserving pan and simmer gently for about 1 hour, until the fruit is really soft and pulpy, stirring from time to time to prevent sticking.
2. Spoon the blackberry pulp into a jelly bag or

cloth attached to the legs of an upturned stool and leave to strain into a large bowl for at least 12 hours.
3. Discard the pulp remaining in the jelly bag. Measure the juice extract and return it to the pan with 350 g (12 oz) sugar for each 600 ml (1 pint) extract. Heat gently, stirring, until the sugar has dissolved, then bring to the boil and boil rapidly for about 10 minutes.
4. Test for a set and, when setting point is reached, take the pan off the heat and remove any scum with a slotted spoon.
5. Pot and cover.

REDCURRANT JELLY

1.4 kg (3 lb) redcurrants, washed
600 ml (1 pint) water
sugar
45 ml (3 tbsp) port (optional)

1. There is no need to remove the currants from their stalks. Place the currants in a preserving pan with the water and simmer gently for about 30 minutes, until the fruit is really soft and pulpy. Stir from time to time to prevent sticking.
2. Spoon the fruit pulp into a jelly bag or a cloth attached to the legs of an upturned stool, and leave it to strain through into a large bowl for at least 12 hours.
3. Discard the pulp remaining in the jelly bag. Measure the juice extract and return it to the pan with 450 g (1 lb) sugar for each 600 ml (1 pint) extract.
4. Heat gently, stirring, until the sugar has dissolved, then bring to the boil and boil rapidly for about 15 minutes.
5. Test for a set and, when setting point is reached, remove the pan from the heat.
6. Stir in the port, then remove any scum with a slotted spoon.
7. Pot and cover.

ELDERBERRY JELLY

900 g (2 lb) cooking apples, washed
900 g (2 lb) elderberries, washed
sugar

1. Remove any bruised or damaged portions from the apples and roughly chop them without peeling or coring. Place them in a saucepan with just enough water to cover and simmer gently for about 1 hour, until the fruit is very soft and pulpy.
2. Put the elderberries in another saucepan with just enough water to cover and simmer gently for about 1 hour, until the fruit is very soft and tender.
3. Combine the cooked apples and elderberries in a bowl. Stir well, then spoon the fruit pulp into a jelly bag or cloth attached to the legs of an upturned stool, and leave to strain into a large bowl for at least 12 hours.
4. Discard the pulp remaining in the jelly bag. Measure the juice extract and put it in a preserving pan with 350 g (12 oz) sugar for each 600 ml (1 pint) extract. Heat gently, stirring, until the sugar has dissolved, then boil rapidly for about 10 minutes.
5. Test for a set and, when setting point is reached, take the pan off the heat and remove any scum with a slotted spoon.
6. Pot and cover.

VARIATION
BILBERRY JELLY
If preferred, follow the above recipe, using bilberries instead of elderberries.

QUINCE JELLY

1.8 kg (4 lb) quinces, washed and roughly chopped
3.4 litres (6 pints) water
grated rind and juice of 3 lemons
sugar

1. Place the fruit in a preserving pan with 2.3 litres (4 pints) of the water and the lemon rind and juice.
2. Cover with foil or a baking sheet and simmer for 1 hour until the fruit is tender. Stir from time to time to prevent sticking.
3. Spoon the fruit pulp into a jelly bag or cloth attached to the legs of an upturned stool, and leave to strain into a large bowl for at least 12 hours.
4. Return the pulp in the jelly bag to the pan and add the remaining water. Bring to the boil, simmer gently for 30 minutes, then strain again through a jelly bag or cloth for at least 12 hours.
5. Discard the pulp remaining in the jelly bag. Combine the two lots of juice extract and measure. Return to the pan with 450 g (1 lb) sugar for each 600 ml (1 pint) extract. Heat gently, stirring, until the sugar has dissolved, then bring to the boil and boil rapidly for about 10 minutes.
6. Test for a set and, when setting point is reached, take the pan off the heat and remove any scum with a slotted spoon.
7. Pot and cover.

Marmalade

Marmalade is made from citrus fruits. Seville or bitter oranges make the best marmalades. Sweet oranges give marmalade a rather cloudy appearance and are best used in combination with other citrus fruits (see Three Fruit Marmalade, below). Make your marmalade in January or February when Seville oranges are on sale or buy the fruit then and freeze it until required. It is advisable to add one-eighth extra weight of Seville or bitter oranges when freezing for subsequent marmalade making in order to offset pectin loss.

PREPARING THE FRUIT

The peel of citrus fruits is tougher than that of other fruits and needs to be evenly shredded by hand, in the shredder attachment of a food mixer or in a food processor. You can choose the thickness of peel you prefer. To prepare in a food processor, cut the orange peels in half, fit the slicing disc and slice the peel into quarters. Transfer to a bowl. Fit the metal blade and chop batches of the sliced peel, using a pulse action, to the thickness preferred.   For a good appearance, a quarter of the peels can be shredded by hand. Do not put peel through a mincer as this produces a paste-like marmalade. If you are making a large quantity and prepare some fruit a day ahead, leave the peel in water to prevent it drying out.

Marmalade needs to be cooked for much longer than jams; at least 1 hour and often 2-3 hours. Therefore larger quantities of water are needed to allow for evaporation.

The first cooking stage extracts the pectin, reduces the contents of the pan by about half and softens the peel. If this is not done properly the marmalade will not set. Much of the pectin in oranges is contained in the pips and membranes and it is essential to extract all of it for a satisfactory set.

Put all the pips and any loose membrane in a clean piece of muslin, tie it with string and suspend it in the preserving pan so you can easily remove it after the first cooking stage and squeeze all the juice from the muslin bag into the pan.

Add the sugar at the beginning of the second cooking stage and stir until it has dissolved. Boil rapidly for 15-20 minutes until setting point is reached, then test as for jam (see page 467). Remove the pan from the heat, skim off any scum and leave the marmalade to cool for 10-15 minutes. Stir to distribute the peel evenly and pot as for jam (see page 467).

THREE-FRUIT MARMALADE

4 ripe lemons, washed and halved
2 sweet oranges, washed and halved
2 grapefruits, washed
3.4 litres (6 pints) water
2.7 kg (6 lb) sugar

1. Altogether, the fruit should weigh a total of about 1.4 kg (3 lb).
2. Squeeze the juice and pips out of the lemons and oranges. Peel the grapefruit and remove any white pith from the flesh.
3. Tie the pith and pips from all the fruit in a piece of muslin. Thinly cut the peel of all the fruit and chop the grapefruit flesh roughly.
4. Put the peel, flesh, juice, water and muslin bag in a preserving pan. Simmer gently for 1-1½ hours, until the peel is really soft and the contents of the pan are reduced by half.
5. Remove the muslin bag from the pan, squeezing well and allowing the juice to run back into the pan.
6. Add the sugar and heat gently, stirring, until dissolved, then boil rapidly for 15-20 minutes.
7. Test for a set and, when setting point is reached, take the pan off the heat and remove any scum with a slotted spoon. Leave the marmalade to stand for 15 minutes, then stir to distribute the peel.
8. Pot and cover.
MAKES ABOUT 4.5 KG (10 LB)

SEVILLE ORANGE MARMALADE

1.4 kg (3 lb) Seville oranges, washed
juice of 2 lemons
3.4 litres (6 pints) water
2.7 kg (6 lb) sugar

METHOD ONE
1. Halve the oranges and squeeze out the juice and pips. Tie the pips, and any membrane, in muslin.
2. Slice the orange peel and put it in a preserving pan with the fruit juices, water and muslin bag.
3. Simmer gently for about 2 hours until the peel is soft and the liquid reduced by half.
4. Remove the muslin bag.
5. Add the sugar and heat gently, stirring until it has dissolved. Bring to the boil and boil the mixture rapidly for about 15 minutes.
6. Test for a set and, when setting point is reached, take off the heat and remove any scum.
7. Leave to stand for 15 minutes, then stir gently to distribute the peel. Pot and cover.
MAKES ABOUT 4.5 KG (10 LB)

METHOD TWO *(WHOLE FRUIT METHOD)*
1. Place the whole washed fruit in a saucepan with the water.
2. Cover and simmer gently for about 2 hours until tender. Remove the fruit from the pan and leave to cool, then cut it up, thinly or thickly. Tie the pips in a piece of muslin.
3. Put the muslin bag in the liquid in the pan,

add the lemon juice and boil for 5 minutes.
4. Put the fruit in a preserving pan, add the liquid from the saucepan, discarding the muslin bag, and boil off the excess liquid.
5. Add the sugar and heat gently, stirring until it has dissolved, then bring to the boil and boil rapidly for about 15 minutes.
6. Test for a set and, when setting point is reached, take the pan off the heat and remove any scum with a slotted spoon. Leave to stand for about 15 minutes, then stir gently to distribute the peel.
7. Pot and cover.

VARIATIONS
DARK CHUNKY MARMALADE
Follow the recipe for Seville Orange Marmalade. Cut the peel into thick slices. When the sugar is added, stir until it has dissolved, bring to the boil, then simmer gently for a further 1½ hours until the colour of the marmalade has darkened. Test for a set and, when setting point is reached, take the pan off the heat and remove any scum with a slotted spoon. Leave to stand for about 15 minutes. Pot and cover.

WHISKY MARMALADE
Follow the recipe for Seville Orange Marmalade. When setting point is reached, take the pan off the heat, remove any scum with a slotted spoon, then stir in 150 ml (¼ pint) whisky. Leave to stand for about 15 minutes, then stir to evenly distribute the peel. Pot and cover.

DIABETIC MARMALADE

3 large oranges, washed
3 lemons, washed
1.1 litres (2 pints) water
900 g (2 lb) Sorbitol powder
227 ml (8 fl oz) bottle of commercial pectin

1. Pare the rinds from the oranges and lemons as thinly as possible, using a sharp knife or a potato peeler, and shred the rind very finely.
2. Halve the oranges and lemons and squeeze out the juice and pips. Tie the pips and pith in a piece of muslin.
3. Put the fruit juices, shredded rind, muslin bag and water into a preserving pan. Bring to the boil, then simmer gently for 1-1½ hours, until the peel is tender and the contents of the pan have

reduced by about half.
4. Remove the muslin bag, squeezing out as much juice as possible.
5. Add the Sorbitol powder and stir until it has dissolved, then bring to the boil and boil rapidly for 5 minutes.
6. Remove from the heat and stir in the pectin, then remove any scum with a slotted spoon. Leave to cool for 15 minutes, then stir to evenly distribute the peel.
7. Pot the marmalade and cover.
MAKES ABOUT 1.8 KG (4 LB)

NOTE: Small jars are recommended as the marmalade will not keep well once opened. Store in the refrigerator for up to 6 weeks.

Seville Orange Marmalade

ORANGE SHRED MARMALADE

900 g (2 lb) Seville oranges, washed
juice of 2 lemons
2.6 litres (4½ pints) water
1.4 kg (3 lb) sugar

1. Peel off enough rind from the oranges, avoiding the pith, to weigh 100 g (4 oz). Cut the rind into thin strips. Cut up the rest of the fruit and put in a preserving pan with the lemon juice and 1.4 litres (2½ pints) of the water. Cover and simmer for about 2 hours, until the fruit is really soft.
2. Put the shredded rind in another pan with 600 ml (1 pint) of the water, cover and simmer gently until this also is really soft.
3. Drain the shreds, discarding the liquid, and add them to the fruit in the preserving pan.
4. Pour the contents of the pan into a jelly bag or cloth attached to the legs of an upturned stool. Leave to drip into a large bowl for 15 minutes.
5. Return the pulp remaining in the jelly bag to the pan with the remaining 600 ml (1 pint) water, simmer for a further 20 minutes, then pour into the jelly bag again and leave to drip for several hours.
6. Combine the two lots of extract and test for pectin (see page 466). If the liquid does not clot, reduce it slightly by rapid boiling, then test again. Add the sugar and stir until it has dissolved. Add the orange peel shreds from the jelly bag and boil rapidly for about 15 minutes.
7. Test for a set and, when setting point is reached, take the pan off the heat and remove any scum with a slotted spoon. Leave the marmalade to stand for about 15 minutes, then stir to distribute the peel.
8. Pot the marmalade and cover.
MAKES ABOUT 2.3 KG (5 LB)

VARIATION
LEMON SHRED MARMALADE
Substitute the oranges with 900 g (2 lb) lemons.

PRESSURE COOKED MARMALADES, JAMS AND JELLIES

Provided your cooker is one with a three-pressure gauge, it is a good idea to use it for preserving, as it saves quite a bit of time and the fruit retains its flavour and colour.

MARMALADE AND JAMS
There are a few points to remember:
- Always remove the trivet from the pressure pan.
- Never fill the pan more than half-full.
- Cook the fruit at MEDIUM (10 lb) pressure. If you have a cooker which is set to cook only at HIGH (15 lb) pressure, you can obtain alternative weights from the manufacturer which will enable you to alter your cooker to cook at MEDIUM (10 lb) pressure. Cooking preserves at HIGH (15 lb) pressure is not recommended because the pectin will be destroyed.
- Reduce pressure at room temperature.
- Only the preliminary cooking and softening of the fruit must be done under pressure – never cook a preserve under pressure after adding the sugar (and lemon juice, if used), but boil it up in the open pan.
- You can adapt any ordinary marmalade or jam recipe for use with a pressure cooker by using half the stated amount of water and doing the preliminary cooking of the fruit under pressure.
- Soft fruits such as raspberries and straw-berries need very little preliminary softening and are therefore not usually cooked in a pressure cooker.
- When two or more fruits (eg blackberries and apples) are combined, the necessary cooking times may vary somewhat.
- To adapt marmalade recipes, use only a quarter of the recommended amount of the water when the fruit is cooked under pressure. More water is added with the sugar. Marmalades can also be cooked at HIGH (15 lb) pressure because citrus fruits are high in pectin. Refer to your pressure cooker manufacturer's handbook.

JELLIES
The fruit used for making jellies can also be softened in the pressure cooker and this method is particularly useful for fruits which have hard skins, pips and so on.

- Prepare the fruit according to any ordinary jelly recipe.
- Place the fruit in the cooker (without the trivet) and add only half the amount of water stated in the recipe.
- Cook at medium (10 lb) pressure (see chart for the times), then reduce the pressure at room temperature.
- Mash the fruit well and pour it into the prepared jelly bag. Finish in the ordinary way.

PRESSURE COOKING TIMES MEDIUM (10 lb) PRESSURE		
	JAM	JELLY
	Time in minutes	
Apples	5	5
Blackberries and apples combined	7	9
Blackcurrants	3-4	4
Citrus fruits	20	25
Damsons, plums and other stone fruit	5	5
Gooseberries	3	3
Marrow	1-2	–
Pears (cooking)	7	9
Quinces	5	7

Rosemary and Apple Jelly

FRUIT BUTTERS, CHEESES AND CURDS

Fruit butters, cheeses and curds are all traditional country preserves which are usually only made when there is a glut of fruit, as a large quantity of fruit produces only a comparatively small amount of preserve.

BUTTER AND CHEESE

Fruit butters are soft and butter-like and can be used like jam. They do not keep very well so make in small quantities and use up fairly quickly.

Cheeses are very thick preserves that are often served as an accompaniment to meat, poultry and game. The preserve is so thick that it can be potted in small moulds or jars and turned out whole when required. Cheeses store much better than butters and, in fact, improve on keeping.

The fruits most commonly used for fruit butters and cheeses are apples, apricots, black-berries, gooseberries, damsons and medlars.

PREPARATION AND COOKING

Fruit for butter or cheese making only needs picking over and washing, although larger fruits should be roughly chopped. Put the prepared fruit in a preserving pan or large saucepan with just enough water to cover, and simmer until really soft. Press the fruit pulp through a nylon sieve, using a wooden spoon so that the fruit does not discolour. Measure the pulp and allow the following amounts of sugar: For butters, allow 225-350 g (8-12 oz) sugar to each 600 ml (1 pint) pulp. For cheeses, allow 350-450 g (12 oz-1 lb) sugar to each 600 ml (1 pint) pulp.

Return the pulp to the pan, add the sugar and stir until dissolved. Boil gently until the required consistency is reached. Stir constantly to prevent the preserve sticking to the bottom of the pan as it cooks and thickens. Butters should be cooked until they are like thick cream. The cooled butter should be thick so it spreads like jam.

POTTING

For butters, prepare jars or small pots and cover as for jam (see page 467).

For fruit cheeses, brush the inside of small, prepared jars (preferably straight-sided) or moulds with oil. This enables the preserve to be turned out. Pour in the fruit cheese, cover as for jam (see page 467) and store for 3-4 months before using.

CURDS

Made with eggs and butter as well as sugar and fruit, curds are not a true 'preserve' and should only be made in small quantities and eaten fairly quickly. They will keep for up to 2-3 weeks in the refrigerator.

APPLE CHEESE

1.4 kg (3 lb) cooking apples, windfalls or crab apples,
    washed
about 1.1 litres (2 pints) water
2.5 ml (½ level tsp) ground cinnamon
1.25-2.5 ml (¼-½ level tsp) ground cloves
sugar

1. Remove any bruised parts from the apples, then chop them without peeling or coring and put them in a large saucepan. Add just enough water to cover and simmer gently for about 1 hour, until the apples are really soft and pulpy.
2. Using a wooden spoon, press the apple pulp through a nylon sieve and measure the purée. Return the purée to the pan and add the spices and 450 g (1 lb) sugar for each 600 ml (1 pint) purée.
3. Heat gently, stirring, until the sugar has dissolved. Bring to the boil and boil gently, stirring frequently, for 30-45 minutes, until so thick that the wooden spoon leaves a clean line through the mixture when drawn across the bottom of the pan.
4. Pot and cover, or if preferred, prepare and fill a bowl or several small moulds from which the cheese can be turned out and served whole.
MAKES ABOUT 1.4 KG (3 LB)

DAMSON CHEESE

1.4 kg (3 lb) damsons, washed
150-300 ml (¼-½ pint) water
sugar

1. Place the fruit and water in a saucepan, cover and simmer gently for 15-20 minutes, until the fruit is really soft. Scoop out the stones with a slotted spoon as they come to the surface.
2. Using a wooden spoon, press the fruit pulp through a nylon sieve and measure the purée.
3. Return the purée to the pan and add 350 g (12 oz) sugar for each 600 ml (1 pint) purée.
4. Heat gently, stirring, until the sugar has dissolved, then bring to the boil and boil gently, stirring frequently, for 30-40 minutes, until so thick that the wooden spoon leaves a clean line through the mixture when drawn across the bottom of the pan.
5. Pot and cover the cheese or, if preferred, prepare and fill a bowl or several small moulds (see page 479) from which the cheese can be turned out and served whole.
6. Leave to set and cover.
MAKES ABOUT 1.4 KG (3 LB)

VARIATIONS
GOOSEBERRY CHEESE
Make as above, using 1.4 kg (3 lb) gooseberries and 150 ml (¼ pint) water.

DAMSON AND BLACKBERRY CHEESE
Make as above, using 450 g (1 lb) damsons and 900 g (2 lb) blackberries.

LEMON CURD

grated rind and juice of 4 medium lemons
4 eggs
100 g (4 oz) butter
350 g (12 oz) caster sugar

1. Place all the ingredients in the top of a double saucepan or in a bowl standing over a pan of simmering water.
2. Stir until the sugar has dissolved and continue heating gently for about 20 minutes, until the curd thickens; do not boil or it will curdle.
3. Strain into jars and cover.
MAKES ABOUT 700 G (1½ LB)

VARIATIONS
LIME CURD
Replace the lemons with the grated rind and juice of 5 large ripe, juicy limes.

ORANGE CURD

grated rind and juice of 2 large oranges
juice of ½ a lemon
225 g (8 oz) caster sugar
100 g (4 oz) butter
3 egg yolks, beaten

1. Place all the ingredients in the top of a double saucepan or in a bowl standing over a pan of simmering water.
2. Stir until the sugar has dissolved and continue heating gently for about 20 minutes, until the curd thickens; do not boil or it will curdle.
3. Strain into jars and cover.
MAKES ABOUT 450 G (1 LB)

BLUEBERRY CURD

225 g (8 oz) blueberries
50 g (2 oz) butter
225 g (8 oz) caster sugar
3 eggs, beaten

1. Place the fruit and 15 ml (1 tbsp) water in a saucepan, cover and cook gently until tender.
2. Sieve, then return to the pan. Add the butter and sugar and heat gently to dissolve, stirring.
3. Add the eggs and heat gently, stirring, until thick enough to coat back of a wooden spoon; do not boil or it will curdle.
4. Strain into jars and cover.
MAKES ABOUT 450 G (1 LB)

MINCEMEAT

Mincemeat was originally a way of preserving meat without smoking or salting. Today it is a mixture of fruits – mostly dried – preserved in alcohol and sugar. The only reminder of the past is the inclusion of suet. Vegetarians can use vegetable suet.

MINCEMEAT

450 g (1 lb) currants
450 g (1 lb) sultanas
450 g (1 lb) seedless raisins
225 g (8 oz) chopped mixed peel
225 g (8 oz) cooking apples, peeled, cored and grated
100 g (4 oz) blanched almonds, chopped
450 g (1 lb) dark soft brown sugar
175 g (6 oz) shredded suet
5 ml (1 level tsp) grated nutmeg
5 ml (1 level tsp) ground cinnamon
grated rind and juice of 1 lemon
grated rind and juice of 1 orange
300 ml (½ pint) brandy

1. Place the dried fruits, peel, apples and almonds in a large bowl. Add the sugar, suet, spices, lemon and orange rind and juice and brandy, and mix all the ingredients together thoroughly.
2. Cover the mincemeat and leave to stand for 2 days. Stir well and put into jars. Cover. Allow at least 2 weeks to mature before using.
MAKES ABOUT 2.5 KG (5½ LB)

NOTE: For mincemeat that will keep well, use a firm, hard type of apple, such as Wellington; a juicy apple, such as Bramley Seedling, may make the mixture too moist.

Mincemeat

FRUITS IN ALCOHOL

Fruits in alcohol preserve fruit with the minimum of cooking. Although they do not have the keeping qualities of jams and jellies made by the traditional boiling method, the fruits retain a flavour which is very much closer to the original taste of the fruit. Use the same equipment as for jam making, and cover and store in the same way (see page 467). All these preserves make very acceptable gifts.

BRANDIED CHERRIES

450 g (1 lb) cherries, washed
225 g (8 oz) sugar
1 cinnamon stick
about 150 ml (¼ pint) brandy

1. Prick the cherries all over with a fine skewer or darning needle.
2. Make a light syrup by dissolving 100 g (4 oz) of the sugar in 300 ml (½ pint) water. Add the cherries and cinnamon stick and poach gently for 4-5 minutes.

3. Remove the pan from the heat and drain the cherries, reserving the syrup but removing the cinnamon stick. Cool, then arrange the fruit in small jars.
4. Add the remaining sugar to the reserved syrup and dissolve it slowly. Bring to the boil and boil to 110°C (230°F), then allow to cool.
5. Measure the syrup and add an equal quantity of brandy. Pour over the cherries. Cover as for chutneys and relishes (see page 484).
MAKES ABOUT 450 G (1 LB)

Brandied Cherries

BRANDIED PEACHES

450 g (1 lb) fresh peaches or 822 g (1 lb 13 oz) can
*   peach halves*
225 g (8 oz) sugar (if using fresh peaches)
about 150 ml (¼ pint) brandy or orange-flavoured
*   liqueur*

1. If using fresh peaches, skin the peaches by plunging them into boiling water for 30 seconds, then gently peeling off the skins. Halve the peaches and remove the stones.
2. Make a light syrup by dissolving 100 g (4 oz) of the sugar in 300 ml (½ pint) water. Add the peaches and poach gently for 4-5 minutes. Remove from the heat, drain and cool, then arrange the fruit in small jars.

3. Add the remaining sugar to the reserved syrup and dissolve it slowly. Bring to the boil and boil to 110°C (230°F), then allow to cool. Measure the syrup and add an equal quantity of brandy. Pour over the peaches. Cover.
4. If using canned peaches, drain the syrup from the peaches and put it in a saucepan: this size can yields about 450 ml (¾ pint) syrup. Reduce the syrup to half the quantity by boiling gently, remove from the heat and cool.
5. Prick the peaches with a fine skewer or darning needle and place in small jars.
6. Measure the syrup and add an equal quantity of brandy or liqueur and pour over the fruit. Cover and leave for at least 3 months.

RUMPOT

Rumpot or *Rumtopf*, is a delicious concoction of fresh fruit, sugar and rum layered up in a stone or pottery jar. Rumpots do take a while to mature – they're normally started in early summer and the last fruits are added in the autumn, then left to mature for a month or more.

To prepare a rumpot, you'll need a large deep glazed stone or pottery jar with a wide neck and tightly fitting lid; a large glass jar will do. You will also need a small plate or saucer which will fit into the jar and can be easily removed with each addition of fruit. It is important to make sure that as little air as possible is allowed into the jar.

Use only fruit that is in perfect condition: just ripe and with no blemishes. Most fruits are suitable, except rhubarb, which tends to give a bitter taste, or apples, which may ferment. Soft fruits like raspberries, loganberries and currants are delicious but they will disintegrate with time, so don't expect them to remain whole when you come to eat the Rumpot; very watery fruits like melons should be kept to a minimum as they dilute the alcohol, which may result in a layer of mould growth or fermentation.

For every 450 g (1 lb) prepared fruit, you'll need 225 g (8 oz) caster sugar.

Thoroughly clean the jar and plate; if possible, sterilise them with a solution of sodium metabisulphide, which you can get from chemists and suppliers of home wine making equipment.

Carefully wash the fruit and dry on absorbent kitchen paper. Berry fruits should be hulled; currants, gooseberries and grapes should be removed from their stalks. Skin large-stoned fruits if you like, then halve them and remove the stones.

Spread the first fruit on a plate; sprinkle the sugar over and turn gently so that every part of the fruit is covered. After about an hour, transfer the fruit and sugar to the jar and spread evenly. Pour over enough alcohol to cover completely. Place the plate or saucer on top to keep the fruit submerged, then tightly cover the jar. Store in a cool, dry place until you're ready to add the next fruit. Repeat the process, replacing a clean plate or saucer each time and resealing the jar as before.

When the last batch of fruit has been added, top up with more alcohol, cover and store for at least a month. Add more liquid if necessary.

You may find mould growth in your Rumpot if the fruit is over-ripe or damaged, or if the container is stored in unsuitable conditions; unfortunately there's nothing you can do but throw out the contents and start again. If fermentation starts, boil the contents in a saucepan, cool and then eat as soon as possible.

CHUTNEYS, RELISHES AND PICKLES

Making chutneys and pickles is a traditional way of preserving fruit and vegetables with vinegar, spices and flavourings. Chutneys are gently cooked for several hours to produce a sweet and sour mixture like chunky jam. Pickles may be sweet or sharp, or an interesting blend of both. With sharp pickles, the vegetables are usually brined first. Fruits for pickling are usually lightly cooked beforehand.

CHUTNEYS AND RELISHES

Chutneys and relishes differ largely in their finished texture. Chutneys are made from very finely chopped or sliced fruits and/or vegetables which are cooked very slowly to result in a smooth texture and mellow flavour. Relishes have a more chunky texture and are cooked for less time.

Ingredients for chutney are finely chopped, sliced or minced. Bruised and poorly shaped produce can often be used as their appearance will not matter.

Once mixed with vinegar, sugar, spices and salt, the chutney is simmered very slowly, uncovered, so the liquid evaporates and the mixture forms a pulp. The final consistency should be that of a thick sauce.

For relishes, the ingredients should be cut into chunks and cooked for a fairly short time to retain their shape. It is possible to make some relishes without any cooking.

EQUIPMENT

PANS
To make pickles you need a good-sized pan made from enamel, stainless steel or lined aluminium. Recently there has been concern about a possible link between aluminium and Alzheimer's disease. At the time of going to press, research is still inconclusive but, for the time being, it would seem safer to avoid cooking acidic fruits or preserves made with vinegar in unlined aluminium pans. Always make sure that your pan is scrupulously clean, and if it is damaged or pitted, throw it away.

It is not strictly necessary to use a preserving pan unless you are going to cook large quantities, but do remember to allow plenty of time and space for the liquid to evaporate. Do not use brass or copper preserving pans as the vinegar will corrode the metal, giving the pickle a disagreeable taste.

PICKLE JARS
Large, wide-necked bottles are recommended for pickling, though smaller jam jars can be used. Screw-topped jars with plastic-coated linings, such as those used for coffee jars and commercially prepared pickles, are ideal.

The number of jars needed for a specific quantity of pickles varies so much, depending on the size of the vegetables or fruit and how tightly they are packed, that it is not practicable to state exact numbers. Before filling with pickle, jars should be preheated in the oven.

STORING
Chutneys should be stored in a cool, dark, dry place and allowed to mature for 2-3 months before eating.

GREEN TOMATO CHUTNEY

4 small pieces of root ginger, bruised
450 g (1 lb) cooking apples, peeled, cored and minced
2 medium onions, skinned and minced
1.4 kg (3 lb) green tomatoes, thinly sliced
225 g (8 oz) sultanas
225 g (8 oz) demerara sugar
10 ml (2 level tsp) salt
450 ml (¾ pint) malt vinegar
2.5 ml (½ level tsp) cayenne pepper
5 ml (1 level tsp) mustard powder

1. Tie the root ginger in a piece of muslin and place in a preserving pan with all the remaining ingredients.
2. Bring to the boil, then reduce the heat and simmer gently, uncovered, for about 2 hours, stirring occasionally, until the ingredients are tender, reduced to a thick consistency and no excess liquid remains.
3. Remove the muslin bag, spoon the chutney into prepared jars and cover immediately with airtight and vinegar-proof tops.
MAKES ABOUT 1.4 KG (3 LB)

PEACH CHUTNEY

1 small piece root ginger, peeled and bruised
6 ripe peaches, stoned, skinned and sliced
100 g (4 oz) sultanas
2 large onions, skinned and finely chopped
15 ml (1 level tbsp) salt
375 g (12 oz) demerara sugar
300 ml (½ pint) malt vinegar
15 ml (1 level tbsp) mustard seeds
grated rind and juice of 1 lemon

1. Tie the root ginger in a piece of muslin and place in a preserving pan with all the remaining ingredients.
2. Bring to the boil, reduce the heat and simmer, uncovered, for about 1¾ hours, stirring occasionally, until no excess liquid remains and the mixture is thick.
3. Remove the muslin bag. Spoon the chutney into prepared jars and cover immediately with airtight and vinegar-proof tops.
MAKES ABOUT 1.1 KG (2½ LB)

SWEET MANGO CHUTNEY

1.8 kg (4 lb) yellow mangoes, peeled, stoned and sliced
2 small cooking apples, peeled, cored and chopped
2 medium onions, skinned and chopped
100 g (4 oz) seedless raisins
600 ml (1 pint) distilled vinegar
350 g (12 oz) demerara sugar
15 ml (1 level tbsp) ground ginger
3 garlic cloves, skinned and crushed
5 ml (1 level tsp) grated nutmeg
2.5 ml (½ level tsp) salt

1. Place all the ingredients in a preserving pan.
2. Bring to the boil, then reduce the heat and simmer gently, uncovered, stirring occasionally, for about 1½ hours, until no excess liquid remains and the mixture is thick and pulpy.
3. Spoon the mango chutney into prepared jars and cover immediately with airtight and vinegar-proof tops.
MAKES ABOUT 2 KG (4½ LB)

Selection of chutneys, pickles and relishes

APPLE CHUTNEY

1.4 kg (3 lb) cooking apples, peeled, cored and diced
1.4 kg (3 lb) onions, skinned and chopped
450 g (1 lb) sultanas or seedless raisins
grated rind and juice of 2 lemons
700 g (1½ lb) demerara sugar
600 ml (1 pint) malt vinegar

1. Put the apples, onions, sultanas, lemon rind and juice, sugar and vinegar in a preserving pan.
2. Bring to the boil, then reduce the heat and simmer, uncovered, stirring occasionally, for about 3 hours, until the mixture is of a thick consistency, with no excess liquid remaining.
3. Spoon the chutney into prepared jars and cover immediately with airtight and vinegar-proof tops.
MAKES ABOUT 2.7 KG (6 LB)

VARIATIONS
SMOOTH APPLE CHUTNEY
A blender or food processor can be used to produce a smoother texture, if preferred. In this case, bring all the ingredients, except the sultanas or raisins, to the boil and simmer until really soft. Allow to cool slightly, then pour into the blender goblet or processor bowl, a little at a time, and blend until smooth. Return to the saucepan with the sultanas or raisins and cook for a further 15 minutes or until thick. Pot and cover in the usual way.

GOOSEBERRY CHUTNEY
Follow the recipe above, replacing the apples with 1.4 kg (3 lb) gooseberries, topped, tailed and washed.

HOT INDIAN CHUTNEY

700 g (1½ lb) cooking apples, peeled, cored and sliced
450 g (1 lb) onions, skinned and finely chopped
700 g (1½ lb) soft brown sugar
1.3 litres (2½ pints) malt vinegar
450 g (1 lb) seedless raisins, chopped
4 garlic cloves, skinned and crushed
20 ml (4 level tsp) salt
30 ml (2 level tbsp) ground ginger
45 ml (3 level tbsp) mustard powder
30 ml (2 level tbsp) paprika
15 ml (1 level tbsp) ground coriander

1. Place all the ingredients in a preserving pan.
2. Bring to the boil, then reduce the heat and simmer gently for about 3 hours, uncovered, stirring occasionally, until no excess liquid remains and the chutney is thick and pulpy.
3. Spoon into prepared jars and cover immediately with airtight and vinegar-proof tops.
MAKES ABOUT 2 KG (4½ LB)

MARROW AND APPLE CHUTNEY

1.8 kg (4 lb) marrow, peeled and chopped
75 g (3 oz) salt
900 g (2 lb) cooking apples, peeled, cored and finely chopped
450 g (1 lb) shallots or onions, skinned and chopped
450 g (1 lb) soft brown sugar
1.1 litres (2 pints) distilled vinegar
5 ml (1 level tsp) ground ginger
15 g (½ oz) Pickling Spice (see page 196)

1. Put the marrow pieces into a large bowl in layers with the salt and leave for 12 hours or overnight.
2. Next day, rinse the marrow pieces, drain off the water and put them into a preserving pan.
3. Add the apples, shallots, sugar, vinegar, ginger and spice. Bring to the boil, then reduce the heat and simmer gently, uncovered, for about 2 hours, stirring from time to time, until the chutney becomes thick with no excess liquid.
4. Pour into prepared jars while still warm and cover immediately with airtight and vinegar-proof tops.
MAKES ABOUT 2.7 KG (6 LB)

BEET RELISH

900 g (2 lb) cooked beetroot, skinned and diced
450 g (1 lb) white cabbage, finely shredded
75 g (3 oz) fresh horseradish, grated
15 ml (1 level tbsp) mustard powder
600 ml (1 pint) malt vinegar
225 g (8 oz) sugar
pinch of cayenne pepper
salt and pepper

1. Combine all the ingredients in a large saucepan. Bring slowly to the boil, then simmer for 30 minutes, stirring occasionally.
2. Spoon into preheated jars and cover at once with airtight, vinegar-proof tops.
3. Store in a cool, dry, dark place and leave to mature for 2-3 months before eating.
MAKES ABOUT 700 G (1½ LB)

MUSTARD RELISH

175 g (6 oz) cucumber, finely chopped
1 medium onion, skinned and finely chopped
225 g (8 oz) cauliflower, broken into florets
100 g (4 oz) tomatoes, skinned and roughly chopped
1 medium green pepper, seeded and finely chopped
1 medium red pepper, seeded and finely chopped
225 g (8 oz) fresh gherkins, thickly sliced
25 g (1 oz) salt
15 ml (1 level tbsp) mustard seeds
250 g (9 oz) sugar
30 ml (2 level tbsp) flour
2.5 ml (½ level tsp) mustard powder
2.5 ml (½ level tsp) ground turmeric
450 ml (¾ pint) malt vinegar

1. Place all the vegetables in a large bowl. Dissolve the salt in 1.1 litres (2 pints) water and pour over the vegetables. Cover and leave to stand overnight.
2. Next day, drain and rinse the vegetables well. Mix the mustard seeds, sugar, flour, mustard powder and turmeric together in a large saucepan, then gradually stir in the vinegar. Bring to the boil, stirring. Add the drained vegetables and simmer, uncovered, for 30 minutes. Stir gently from time to time to prevent sticking.
3. Spoon the relish into prepared jars and cover immediately with airtight and vinegar-proof tops.
MAKES ABOUT 1.4 KG (3 LB)

TOMATO RELISH

1.4 kg (3 lb) tomatoes, skinned and sliced
450 g (1 lb) cucumber or marrow, peeled, seeded and roughly chopped
50 g (2 oz) salt
2 garlic cloves, skinned and finely chopped
1 large red pepper, seeded and roughly chopped
450 ml (¾ pint) malt vinegar
15 ml (1 level tbsp) mustard powder
2.5 ml (½ level tsp) ground allspice
2.5 ml (½ level tsp) mustard seeds

1. Layer the tomatoes and cucumber in a bowl, sprinkling each layer with salt. Cover and leave overnight.
2. Next day, drain and rinse well and place in a large saucepan. Add the garlic and pepper.
3. Blend the vinegar with the dry ingredients and stir into the pan. Bring slowly to the boil, then reduce the heat and simmer gently, uncovered, for about 1 hour, stirring occasionally, until the mixture is soft.
4. Spoon the relish into prepared jars and cover immediately with airtight and vinegar-proof tops.
MAKES ABOUT 1.4 KG (3 LB)

PICKLES

Pickles are made by preserving raw or lightly cooked vegetables or fruit in clear spiced vinegar. They are usually served as accompaniments to cold meats. Only crisp fresh fruits and vegetables should be pickled.

VINEGAR

You can buy ready spiced vinegar for pickling or make your own (see opposite). It must be of the best quality and have a minimum acetic acid content of 5 per cent. Use distilled malt vinegar for light pickles like onions, and malt vinegar for dark pickles. Wine vinegar can also be used.

BRINING

For a sharp-flavoured pickle, the vegetables are usually brined first to remove surplus water as this dilutes the vinegar and prevents it acting as a preservative. Sweet pickles tend to be made of fruit which does not need brining and is usually cooked lightly before pickling so that the surplus moisture evaporates.

DRY BRINING is used for cucumber, marrow, red cabbage and tomatoes. Prepare vegetables according to recipe and layer in a bowl with salt allowing 15 ml (1 level tbsp) to each 450 g (1 lb) vegetables. Cover and leave overnight.

WET BRINING is used for cauliflower, onions and walnuts. Prepare vegetables according to recipe and place in a large bowl. Cover with a brine solution: 50 g (2 oz) salt dissolved in 600 ml (1 pint) water to each 450 g (1 lb) vegetables. Put a plate over the surface to keep vegetables submerged in liquid, cover and leave overnight.

PACKING AND STORING

After dry or wet brining, rinse the vegetables well in cold water, drain, then pack into jars to within 2.5 cm (1 inch) of the top.

Pour over the spiced vinegar, making sure it covers all the vegetables, and add at least 1 cm (½ inch) to allow for evaporation. Leave a little space at the top of the jar to prevent the vinegar coming into contact with the jar lid.

Cover and store as for chutneys and relishes (see page 484). Allow to mature for 2-3 months before eating: except pickled red cabbage which begins to lose its crispness after 2-3 weeks.

LEFT: Beet Relish.   RIGHT: Spiced Crab Apples

Spiced Vinegar

1.1 litres (2 pints) vinegar
30 ml (2 level tbsp) blade mace
15 ml (1 level tbsp) whole allspice
15 ml (1 level tbsp) cloves
2 cinnamon sticks
6 black peppercorns
1 small bay leaf

1. Place the vinegar, spices and bay leaf in a saucepan, bring to the boil, then allow to cool.
2. Cover to preserve the flavour and leave the

vinegar to marinate for about 2 hours.
3. Strain the vinegar through a piece of muslin into a jug, then pour into bottles and seal with airtight and vinegar-proof tops.

NOTE: A better result is obtained if the spices stand in unheated vinegar for 1-2 months. If the individual spices are not available, use 25-50 g (1-2 oz) pickling spice. Brands of pickling spice vary considerably; for example some contain whole chillies, giving a hotter flavour. See page 196 for homemade Pickling Spice.

Sweet Spiced Vinegar

1.7 litres (3 pints) vinegar
450 g (1 lb) sugar
7.5 ml (1½ level tsp) salt
5 ml (1 level tsp) Mixed Spice (see page 196)
5 ml (1 level tsp) black peppercorns
8-10 cloves

1. Place the vinegar, sugar, salt and spices in a pan, bring to the boil, then pour into a bowl.
2. Cover to preserve the flavour and leave to marinate for 2 hours. Strain the vinegar through a piece of muslin into a jug. Pour into bottles and seal with airtight and vinegar-proof tops.

Spiced Crab-apples

2.7 g (6 lb) crab-apples, trimmed
2-3 strips lemon rind
450 g (1 lb) sugar
450 ml (¾ pint) red wine vinegar
1 cinnamon stick
1-2 whole cloves
3 peppercorns

1. Put the crab-apples in a preserving pan with 900 ml (1½ pints) water and the strips of lemon rind and simmer gently until just tender.
2. Remove the pan from the heat and strain, reserving the liquid. Put the sugar and vinegar

in a pan and add 900 ml (1½ pints) of the liquid from the fruit.
3. Tie the spices in a piece of muslin and add to the liquid. Heat gently, stirring, until the sugar has dissolved, then bring to the boil and boil for 1 minute.
4. Add the crab-apples and simmer gently for 30-40 minutes, until the syrup has reduced to a coating consistency. Remove the muslin bag after 30 minutes.
5. Pack the crab-apples in small jars, pour over the syrup and cover with airtight and vinegar-proof tops.

Spiced Pears

900 g (2 lb) firm eating pears, peeled, cored and
  quartered
450 ml (¾ pint) cider vinegar
450 g (1 lb) sugar
1 cinnamon stick
10 cloves
1 small piece of root ginger

1. Place the pears in a saucepan, cover with boiling water and cook gently for about 5 minutes until almost tender, then drain.

2. Pour the vinegar into a pan and add 300 ml (½ pint) water, sugar, cinnamon, cloves and root ginger. Heat gently, stirring, until the sugar has dissolved, then boil for 5 minutes.
3. Add the pears and continue cooking until the pears are tender.
4. Remove the pears with a slotted spoon and pack into prepared jars. Strain the vinegar syrup to remove spices; pour over the pears to cover.
5. Cover the jars immediately with airtight and vinegar-proof tops.

PICKLED GHERKINS

450 g (1 lb) gherkins
50 g (2 oz) salt
600 ml (1 pint) light malt vinegar
5 ml (1 level tsp) whole allspice
5 ml (1 level tsp) black peppercorns
2 cloves
1 blade of mace

1. Put the gherkins in a large bowl. Dissolve the salt in 600 ml (1 pint) water and pour the brine solution over the gherkins. Leave to soak for 3 days.
2. Rinse, drain and dry the gherkins well, then pack them carefully in large jars. Pour the vinegar into a saucepan, add the spices and boil for 10 minutes. Pour over the gherkins, cover tightly and leave in a warm place for 24 hours.
3. Strain the vinegar out of the jars into a saucepan, boil it up and pour it over the gherkins again. Cover tightly and leave for another 24 hours.
4. Repeat this process until the gherkins are a good green colour.
5. Finally, pack the gherkins in prepared jars, cover with vinegar, adding more if required, and cover with airtight and vinegar-proof tops.

PICKLED ONIONS

1.8 kg (4 lb) pickling onions
450 g (1 lb) salt
1.1 litres (2 pints) Spiced Vinegar (see page 489)

1. Place the onions, without skinning, in a large bowl. Dissolve half the salt in 2.3 litres (4 pints) water, pour the brine over the onions and leave to marinate for 12 hours.
2. Skin the onions, then cover with fresh brine, made with the remaining salt and the same amount of water, and leave for a further 24-36 hours.
3. Drain and rinse the onions well and pack them into jars. Pour the Spiced Vinegar over the onions and cover the jars immediately with airtight and vinegar-proof tops.

PICKLED BEETROOT

beetroot
Spiced Vinegar (see page 489)

1. Weigh the beetroot and wash them carefully, taking care not to damage the skins. Wrap them in foil and bake in the oven at 180°C (350°F) mark 4 for 2-3 hours, depending on size, until tender.
2. Leave the beetroot to cool, then skin and thinly slice them. Pack the slices into jars and cover with cold Spiced Vinegar.
3. Cover the jars immediately with airtight, vinegar-proof tops. For longer keeping, dice the beetroot, pack loosely, cover with boiling vinegar and seal.

VARIATION
Alternatively, make a brine solution, allowing 50 g (2 oz) salt dissolved in 600 ml (1 pint) water to each 450 g (1 lb) beetroot. Put the beetroot in a large saucepan, cover with the brine solution and simmer gently for 1½-2 hours, depending on the size, until tender. Cool, skin and slice. Pack into jars and cover as above.

PICKLED EGGS

600 ml (1 pint) white wine or cider vinegar
6 garlic cloves, skinned
25 g (1 oz) Pickling Spice (see page 196)
small piece of orange rind
1 blade of mace
6 eggs, hard-boiled and shelled

1. Put all the ingredients, except the eggs, in a heavy-based saucepan.
2. Bring to the boil, then reduce the heat, cover and simmer gently for 10 minutes. Leave to cool, then strain some of the spiced vinegar into a large wide-mouthed jar.
3. Put in the eggs and top up the jar with more spiced vinegar.
4. Cover with airtight and vinegar-proof tops and leave for 6 weeks before using.

PICKLED RED CABBAGE

about 1.4 kg (3 lb) firm red cabbage, finely shredded
2 large onions, skinned and sliced
60 ml (4 level tbsp) salt
2.3 litres (4 pints) Spiced Vinegar (see page 489)
15 ml (1 level tbsp) soft brown sugar

1. Layer the cabbage and onions in a large bowl, sprinkling each layer with salt, then cover and leave overnight.
2. Next day, drain the cabbage and onion thoroughly, rinse off the surplus salt and drain again. Pack into prepared jars.
3. Pour the vinegar into a saucepan and heat gently. Add the sugar and stir until dissolved. Leave to cool, then pour over the cabbage and onion and cover immediately with airtight and vinegar-proof tops.

NOTE: Use within 2-3 weeks as the cabbage tends to lose its crispness.

PICKLED PLUMS

450 g (1 lb) granulated sugar
thinly pared rind of ½ a lemon
2 cloves
1 small piece root ginger, peeled and bruised
300 ml (½ pint) malt vinegar
900 g (2 lb) plums

1. Place all the ingredients, except the plums, in a saucepan. Heat gently, stirring, until the sugar has dissolved, then bring to the boil.
2. Remove from the heat, and leave until cold, then strain. Return the plums to the pan and bring back to the boil slowly.
3. Prick the plums, place them in a deep bowl, pour over the spiced vinegar, cover and leave for 5 days.
4. Strain the vinegar into a saucepan, bring to the boil and pour over the fruit again. Cover and leave for another 5 days.
5. Strain the vinegar into a pan and bring to the boil again. Pack the plums into prepared jars, pour the boiling vinegar over and cover the jars immediately with airtight and vinegar-proof tops.

PICKLED MUSHROOMS

900 ml (1½ pints) malt vinegar
2 shallots, skinned and chopped
1 garlic clove, crushed
4 blades of mace
few fresh marjoram sprigs
5 ml (1 level tsp) ground pepper
10 ml (2 level tsp) salt
900 g (2 lb) small button mushrooms, wiped

1. Pour the vinegar into a large saucepan and add the shallots, garlic, mace, marjoram and seasoning.
2. Bring to the boil and add the mushrooms. Simmer gently, uncovered, for about 10 minutes, until tender and slightly shrunk.
3. Remove the mushrooms with a slotted spoon and pack into prepared jars. Pour over the hot vinegar and cover immediately with airtight and vinegar-proof tops.

Pickled Mushrooms

BREAD AND BUTTER PICKLE

3 large ridge or smooth-skinned cucumbers, sliced
4 large onions, skinned and sliced
45 ml (3 level tbsp) salt
450 ml (¾ pint) distilled vinegar
150 g (5 oz) sugar
5 ml (1 level tsp) celery seeds
5 ml (1 level tsp) mustard seeds

1. Layer the cucumber and onion slices in a large bowl, sprinkling each layer with salt. Leave for 1 hour, then drain and rinse well.

2. Put the vinegar, sugar, celery and mustard seeds into a saucepan and heat gently, stirring, until the sugar has dissolved, then bring to the boil and cook for 3 minutes.
3. Pack the vegetable slices into prepared jars and add enough hot vinegar mixture to cover.
4. Cover immediately with airtight, vinegar-proof tops.

NOTE:This pickle must be stored in a dark place or the cucumber will lose its colour.

PICCALILLI

2.7 kg (6 lb) mixed marrow, cucumber, beans, small onions and cauliflower (prepared weight)
350 g (12 oz) salt
250 g (9 oz) sugar
15 ml (1 level tbsp) mustard powder
7.5 ml (1½ level tsp) ground ginger
2 garlic cloves, skinned and crushed
1.4 litres (2½ pints) distilled vinegar
50 g (2 oz) flour
30 ml (2 level tbsp) ground turmeric

1. Seed the marrow and finely dice the marrow and cucumber. Top, tail and slice the French beans, skin and halve the onions and break the cauliflower into individual florets.

2. Layer the vegetables in a large bowl, sprinkling each layer with salt. Add 3.4 litres (6 pints) water, cover and leave for 24 hours.
3. Next day, remove the vegetables, rinse and drain well.
4. Blend the sugar, mustard, ginger and garlic with 1.1 litres (2 pints) of the vinegar in a preserving pan. Add the vegetables, bring to the boil, reduce the heat and simmer, uncovered, for 20 minutes, until the vegetables are cooked but still crisp.
5. Blend the flour and turmeric with the remaining vinegar and stir into the vegetables.
6. Bring to the boil and cook for 2 minutes. Spoon into prepared jars and cover immediately with airtight and vinegar-proof tops.

MIXED PICKLE

1.1 kg (2½ lb) mixed cauliflower, cucumber, small onions, green or red peppers and French beans (prepared weight)
150 g (5 oz) salt
1.4 litres (2½ pints) Spiced Vinegar (see page 489)

1. Break the cauliflower into individual florets, peel and dice the cucumber, skin the onions, seed and slice the green or red peppers and top,

tail and slice the French beans.
2. Layer the vegetables in a large bowl, sprinkling each layer with salt. Add 1.4 litres (2½ pints) water and leave overnight.
3. Next day, rinse the vegetables, drain well and dry on absorbent kitchen paper.
4. Pack the vegetables into jars and cover with spiced vinegar. Cover the jars immediately with airtight and vinegar-proof tops.

PICKLED DATES

1.3 litres (2½ pints) distilled vinegar
40 g (½ oz) pickling spices
350 g (12 oz) soft brown sugar
1.4 kg (3 lb) dates, halved and stoned

1. Place the vinegar, spices and sugar in a saucepan. Heat gently, stirring, until dissolved, then boil for 45 minutes until reduced by half.
2. Place the dates into prepared jars, pour the hot syrup over them and leave to cool. Cover the jars with airtight and vinegar-proof tops.

Sweets

Homemade sweets make attractive presents and they are fun to make. The sweets in this chapter range from simple uncooked peppermint creams which can be made by children with a little supervision, to more complicated fudges and toffees which require undivided attention and patience, as well as a certain amount of special equipment.

ESSENTIAL EQUIPMENT

SUGAR BOILING THERMOMETER is the only really accurate way of measuring the temperature of the liquid when making cooked sweets and can mean the difference between success and failure. Accurate measurement is imperative with some sweets to get the right consistency. Buy one which is easy to read and graduates from 16°C (60°F) to 182°C (360°F) or 232°C (450°F). These thermometers are usually mounted on brass with a brass or wooden handle. Some have a sliding clip so that they can be fixed to the edge of the pan.

A new thermometer should be seasoned by placing in cold water, bringing the pan to the boil and leaving it in the water to cool. Check the reading when the water is boiling to see if it is accurate: it should be 100°C (212°F).

Shake a thermometer well before use, and be sure that the bulb is completely immersed in the mixture. Always read a thermometer at eye level.

It is most important to warm a sugar thermometer before dipping it in the hot liquid; if you put it straight in, the tube could burst. While you are not using the thermometer, stand it in a mug of hot water. Once you have finished measuring, clean the thermometer very thoroughly as any sugar crystals left on it could spoil the next batch of sweets.

SAUCEPAN: Use a strong, heavy-based one to prevent burning and sticking. Make sure it is large enough to allow room for the boiling sugar to rise in the pan. Non-stick pans are not suitable as the high temperatures reached may damage the lining.

WOODEN SPATULA is used for working fondant mixtures and beating fudges.

PALETTE KNIFE should have a flexible stainless steel blade. It is used for lifting and shaping sweets.

CUTTERS: Little shaped cutters make it easy to cut fondants, marzipans and other soft mixtures.

WORKING SURFACE: A marble slab gives the best results for turning toffees and other boiled mixtures, but is expensive to buy new. If you make a lot of sweets (and pastry for which a marble slab is also good) look for stonemasons' offcuts or a piece from an old washstand.

From the left: sugar thermometer, cherry stoner, slotted and long-handled spoons, funnel, nylon sieve, cellophane covers and rubber bands.

Alternatively, use an enamelled surface, or you can use a heavy wooden chopping board as long as it is dampened or well greased before use. Some laminated surfaces can be used but check yours can withstand temperatures of up to 138°C (290°F).

SPECIALIST EQUIPMENT

RUBBER FONDANT MAT is a sheet of rubber about 2.5 cm (1 inch) thick with shaped impressions into which you run liquid fondant, jelly or chocolate. When it is set, you can 'pop' the shapes out like ice cubes by bending the rubber.

CREAM RINGS are useful for moulding round

sweets, such as peppermint creams.

DIPPING FORKS are useful for lifting sweets out of coating fondant or chocolate. The prongs can also be used for making raised designs on the top of sweets.

CARAMEL BARS are used for toffee and caramel making. They are small bar-shaped moulds that can be adjusted to give the exact size and thickness required.

CARAMEL MARKERS are used to mark toffees and fudges into squares before they set. The marked divisions make it easy to break the mixture into individual sweets.

FONDANT FUNNELS are specially designed funnels with a plunger which controls the flow of liquid and make it easy to fill small moulds. An ordinary metal funnel with a small spout may be used instead.

MODELLING TOOLS made of wood or strong plastic with shaped heads are used for shaping and marking marzipan and fondant sweets.

MOULDS come in a wide range of shapes and sizes for making all kinds of sweets from Easter eggs to liqueur chocolates. Available in metal, flexible or rigid plastic or rubber, and give very professional looking results.

TINS: Square or rectangular 2-5 cm (¾-1 inch) deep tins are useful for setting fudges, caramel and toffees. Those with non-stick linings are easiest to work with.

SUGAR BOILING

Sugar boiling is the basis of nearly all sweet making. The sugar is first dissolved in the liquid, then brought to the boil, 100°C (212°F). The temperature continues to rise as the water evaporates and the syrup thickens and becomes darker. The following are the most important stages; they are best checked with a sugar thermometer but simple tests are described for those who do not own one.

THREAD: 102°C-104°C (215°F-220°F). Used for crystallising purposes. The mixture looks syrupy. To test, dip your fingers in water and then very quickly in the syrup. The thumb will slide smoothly over the fingers but sugar will cling to them.

SOFT BALL: 116°C-118°C (240°F-245°F). Used for fondants and fudges. Test by dropping a little of the syrup into very cold water. It should form a soft ball. At 116°C (240°F) the soft ball will flatten when you take it out of the water; the higher the temperature the firmer the ball.

FIRM OR HARD BALL: 120°C-130°C (250°F-265°F).

Used for caramels. When dropped into cold water the syrup forms a ball which is hard enough to hold its shape, although still pliable.

SOFT CRACK: 132°C-143°C (270°F-290°F). Used for toffees. When dropped into cold water the syrup separates into hard but not brittle threads.

HARD CRACK: 149°C-154°C (300°F-310°F). Used for hard toffees. When dropped into cold water the syrup separates into hard and brittle threads.

CARAMEL: 160°C-162°C (320°F-325°F). Used for pralines and caramels. The syrup turns golden brown when it reaches this temperature.

AVOIDING CRYSTALLISATION

Sugar must be dissolved and boiled with great care, as syrup has a tendency to re-crystallise if incorrectly handled. The main causes of crystallisation are agitation of the mixture by stirring or beating whilst the sugar is dissolving and the presence of solid particles during boiling.

WATCHPOINTS

- Make sure the pan is clean.
- Make sure the sugar has dissolved completely before boiling.
- If crystals do form on the sides of the pan, brush around the sides with a pastry brush dipped in cold water.
- Don't stir mixture unless the recipe specifically instructs you to. Recipes which include milk, cream or butter may need an occasional stir to prevent sticking: draw a wooden spoon carefully across the bottom of the pan.
- Once the sugar has dissolved, boil rapidly to the required temperature, then remove the pan from the heat immediately.

STORING SWEETS

Homemade sweets should be stored in a cool place in airtight containers. Uncooked sweets and unboiled marzipan do not keep well – use within a week. Toffees and caramels should be wrapped in greaseproof paper to prevent them going soft. Different types of sweets should be stored separately until served.

Chocolates should be covered with greaseproof paper and stored in an airtight tin. Don't keep them long or they will lose their gloss. Truffles and chocolates with a high percentage of cream should be stored in the refrigerator and eaten within a few days.

Once fudge has been cut, store it between sheets of greaseproof paper in an airtight tin. Cooked fudges will keep for 2-3 weeks.

FONDANTS

Fondants form the basis of many sweets and chocolate centres. The mixture is also used for icing cakes. Fondants may be dipped in melted chocolate (see page 503) or decorated with crystallised flower petals, nuts or glacé fruits. Any fondant that is not required for immediate use may be stored in a covered jar or tin.

BOILED FONDANT

150 ml (¼ pint) water
450 g (1 lb) granulated sugar
45 ml (3 level tbsp) powdered glucose

1. Put the water and sugar in a heavy-based saucepan and heat gently until the sugar has dissolved. Bring the syrup to the boil, add the glucose and boil to a temperature of 116°C (240°F), soft ball stage.
2. Sprinkle a little water on a marble slab, pour on the syrup and leave for a few minutes to cool.
3. When a skin forms round the edges, use a wooden spatula to collect the mixture, then turn and work, using a figure-of-eight movement.
4. Continue to work the syrup, collecting it into as small a mass as possible, until it changes its consistency, becoming opaque and firm. The fondant can be melted down after 'working', poured into a rubber mat and left to set.
5. Scrape it off the slab and knead it in the hands until it is even textured throughout.
MAKES ABOUT 550 G (¼ LB)

NOTE: If a marble slab is not available, leave the fondant in a bowl for 15 minutes to cool, turn and very gently knead it in the bowl until thick, then knead it on greaseproof paper.

UNCOOKED FONDANT

450 g (1 lb) icing sugar, sifted, plus extra for dusting
45 ml (3 tbsp) liquid glucose or good pinch of
*   cream of tartar*
1 egg white, lightly whisked
few drops of flavouring, such as lemon, orange or coffee
few drops of food colouring, such as yellow, orange or
*   brown*

1. Place the icing sugar and glucose in a bowl and stir in sufficient egg white to make a pliable mixture.
2. Transfer to a surface dusted with icing sugar and knead well, then add a few drops of flavouring and colouring and gently knead.
3. Roll out and use as required.
MAKES ABOUT 450 G (1 LB)

PEPPERMINT CREAMS

few drops of peppermint flavouring
25 g (8 oz) fondant (see above)

1. Knead together the peppermint flavouring and the fondant until smooth and evenly coloured.
2. Roll it out to a 5 mm (¼ inch) thickness on a surface lightly dusted with icing sugar and cut into rounds.
3. Put into paper cases and leave for 24 hours until thoroughly dry.
MAKES ABOUT 225 G (8 OZ)

UNCOOKED PEPPERMINT CREAMS

450 g (1 lb) icing sugar, sifted
5 ml (1 tsp) lemon juice
1 egg white, lighty whisked
few drops peppermint flavouring or oil of peppermint
green food colouring (optional)

1. In a bowl, mix the sugar with the lemon juice and enough egg white to make a pliable mixture. Flavour with peppermint and tint a pale green if liked.
2. Knead on a surface dusted with icing sugar and roll out to a 5 mm (¼ inch) thickness. Cut into rounds with a 2.5 cm (1 inch) cutter, or form into balls and flatten slightly with a rolling pin.
3. Leave for 24 hours until thoroughly dry.
MAKES ABOUT 450 G (1 LB)

VARIATION
WALNUT CREAMS
1. Knead a few drops of coffee essence or strong black coffee into some Uncooked Fondant (see page 495).
2. Shape into balls about 2.5 cm (1 inch) in diameter, press a half walnut into each and put the sweets into paper cases.
3. Leave for 24 hours to set and dry. The creams may be half dipped in chocolate.

TOP LEFT: Neapolitan Slices. BELOW: Walnut Creams. RIGHT: Marzipan Fruits and Flowers

MARZIPAN

Marzipan is not difficult to prepare and by using edible colourings, moulding the marzipan into different shapes or combining it with other ingredients such as dried or glacé fruits and nuts, you can make a wide variety of sweets. There are two types of marzipan: boiled, which is best for flowers and sweets that need a good deal of handling (see recipe, below) and uncooked which is quicker to make, but needs careful handling to prevent cracking (for recipe see Simple Marzipan or Almond Paste, below). You can, if wished, use ready-made bought marzipan.

BOILED MARZIPAN

450 g (1 lb) preserving or granulated sugar
150 ml (¼ pint) water
pinch of cream of tartar
350 g (12 oz) ground almonds
2 egg whites
75 g (3 oz) icing sugar, sifted

1. Put the sugar and the water in a heavy-based saucepan and dissolve over a low heat. When the syrup reaches boiling point, add the cream of tartar and boil to 116°C (240°F), soft ball stage.
2. Remove the pan from the heat and stir rapidly until the syrup begins to 'grain'.
3. Stir in the ground almonds and egg whites and cook for a few minutes over a low heat, stirring.
4. Pour on to an oiled marble or enamel slab or wooden chopping board. Add the icing sugar and work well with a palette knife, lifting the edges of the mixture and turning them into the centre.
5. As soon as the mixture is sufficiently cool, knead it until smooth. Additional icing sugar may be kneaded in if the mixture is too wet.
MAKES ABOUT 900 G (2 LB)

SIMPLE MARZIPAN OR ALMOND PASTE (UNCOOKED)

225 g (8 oz) icing sugar, sifted
225 g (8 oz) caster sugar
450 g (1 lb) ground almonds
5 ml (1 tsp) vanilla flavouring
2 eggs, lightly beaten
lemon juice

1. Mix the icing sugar with the caster sugar and ground almonds.
2. Add the vanilla flavouring, with sufficient beaten egg and lemon juice to mix to a stiff dough. Form into a ball and knead lightly.
MAKES 900 G (2 LB)

VARIATIONS
MARZIPAN FRUIT AND FLOWERS
To make these, take small balls of marzipan and mould into the desired shapes with the fingers. Using a small paintbrush and food colourings, tint them all over or add shading. (If making one fruit only, add the colouring to the marzipan before shaping.) Finish as follows:
ORANGES AND OTHER CITRUS FRUIT: To obtain a pitted surface, roll the fruit lightly on the finest part of a grater. Press a clove in one end.

STRAWBERRIES AND RASPBERRIES: Roll them in caster sugar to give them a bumpy surface. Colour a little marzipan green for the hull and assemble or use small pieces of angelica.
APPLES AND PEARS: Press a clove into the top and bottom to resemble stalk and stem.

NEAPOLITAN SLICES
1. Divide some marzipan into three equal pieces and knead a few drops of contrasting food colourings into two of them.
2. Roll out each coloured ball into 2 strips 1 cm (½ inch) thick and 2.5 cm (1 inch) wide.
3. Cut each strip in half lengthways and trim with a sharp knife so that they are exactly the same size.
4. Roll out the uncoloured piece of marzipan very thinly to the same length as the strips and about 11 cm (4½ inch) wide.
5. Lay the coloured bars along it, two underneath and two on top to make a chequered pattern, and wrap the uncoloured marzipan around the bars so that the whole thing resembles a small Battenberg cake. Cut into 5 mm (¼ inch) slices.

TOFFEE

Toffee can be made successfully in your own kitchen, but don't expect it to be exactly like the commercially-made variety. It does, however, need care and accuracy. The temperature to which toffee needs to be boiled varies according to type, and care must be taken to prevent the hot sugar syrup from burning. A large heavy-based saucepan is essential, and to prevent the mixture from boiling over, the inside of the pan should be brushed with water just above the level of the sugar syrup. Do not stir the mixture unless the recipe states that you should, otherwise the toffee will crystallise and spoil the final result.

The toffee should be allowed to boil very slowly indeed. Remove the pan from the heat just before the required temperature is reached to avoid overheating, leaving the thermometer in the syrup just to make certain. The mixture should be poured into the tins immediately and marked into squares or fingers with an oiled knife before the toffee sets. When set, toffees and caramels should be wiped carefully with absorbent kitchen paper to remove any oil, then wrapped individually in waxed papers.

This section also includes Coconut Ice Bars which need careful boiling.

TREACLE TOFFEE

450 g (1 lb) demerara sugar
150 ml (¼ pint) water
1.25 ml (¼ level tsp) cream of tartar
75 g (3 oz) butter
100 g (4 oz) black treacle
100 g (4 oz) golden syrup

1. Lightly oil an 18 cm (7 inch) shallow square tin.
2. Put the sugar and water in a large heavy-based saucepan and heat gently until the sugar has dissolved.
3. Add the remaining ingredients and bring to the boil. Brush the inside of the pan with water just above the level of the sugar syrup. Boil to 132°C (270°F), soft crack stage.
4. Pour into the prepared tin, cool for 5 minutes, then mark into squares with an oiled knife and leave to set.
MAKES ABOUT 800 G (1¾ LB)

PEANUT BRITTLE

350 g (12 oz) unsalted peanuts, chopped
400 g (14 oz) granulated sugar
175 g (6 oz) light soft brown sugar
175 g (6 oz) corn or golden syrup
150 ml (¼ pint) water
50 g (2 oz) butter or margarine
1.25 ml (¼ level tsp) bicarbonate of soda

1. Lightly oil an 18 cm (7 inch) shallow square tin.
2. Spread the peanuts out on a baking tray and warm in the oven at 130°C (265°F) mark 1 for 20 minutes.
3. Put the sugars, syrup and water in a large heavy-based saucepan and heat gently until the sugar has dissolved. Add the butter and bring to the boil. Brush the inside of the pan with water just above the level of the sugar syrup. Boil very gently to 149°C (300°F), hard crack stage.
4. Carefully stir in the bicarbonate of soda and warmed nuts.
5. Pour the toffee slowly into the prepared tin and mark into bars with an oiled knife when almost set.
MAKES ABOUT 1.1 KG (2½ LB)

NOTE: To store, place the pieces of Peanut Brittle in single layers, between sheets of greaseproof paper, in an airtight tin.

VARIATION
Replace the peanuts with toasted almonds.

BUTTERSCOTCH

450 g (1 lb) demerara sugar
150 ml (¼ pint) water
50-75 g (2-3 oz) unsalted butter

1. Lightly oil a 15 cm (6 inch) shallow square tin.
2. Put the sugar and water in a heavy-based saucepan and heat gently until the sugar has dissolved. Bring to the boil and boil to 138°C (280°F), soft crack stage, brushing down the sides of the pan occasionally with a brush dipped in cold water.
3. Add the butter a little at a time, stirring until dissolved before adding more, then pour the mixture into the prepared tin.
4. Cut into pieces when almost set.

MAKES ABOUT 450 G (1 LB)

TOFFEE APPLES

450 g (1 lb) demerara sugar
50 g (2 oz) butter or margarine
10 ml (2 tsp) vinegar
150 ml (¼ pint) water
15 ml (1 tbsp) golden syrup
6-8 medium apples
6-8 wooden sticks

1. Place the sugar, butter, vinegar, water and syrup gently in a heavy-based saucepan and heat until the sugar has dissolved. Bring to the boil, then brush the inside of the pan with water just above the level of the sugar syrup. Boil rapidly for 5 minutes until the temperature reaches 143°C (290°F), soft crack stage.
2. Wipe the apples and push the sticks into the cores, making sure they are secure.
3. Dip the apples into the toffee, twirl around for a few seconds to allow excess toffee to drip off, then leave to cool and set on a buttered baking sheet or waxed paper.

MAKES 6-8

PEPPERMINT HUMBUGS

450 g (1 lb) granulated sugar
150 ml (¼ pint) water
1.25 ml (¼ level tsp) cream of tartar
15 ml (1 tbsp) golden syrup
few drops of peppermint flavouring
few drops of brown food colouring

1. Lightly oil a marble slab or a large wooden chopping board. Oil a pair of kitchen scissors.

Brush pan with cold water.

2. Put the sugar and water in a large heavy-based saucepan and heat gently until the sugar has dissolved. Mix the cream of tartar with 15 ml (1 tbsp) water and add to the pan with the golden syrup. Brush inside of pan with water just above the sugar level. Bring the mixture gently to 154°C (310°F), hard crack stage.
3. Pour the syrup on to the slab and allow to cool a little.
4. Using oiled palette knives, fold the sides of the toffee into the centre and add a few drops of peppermint flavouring. When the mixture is cool enough to handle, cut off one third and, with oiled hands, twist into a rope about 50 cm (20 inches) long. Fold in half and twist and pull out again. Continue to do this until it is pale in colour and elastic and shiny.
5. Add a few drops of food colouring to the remaining toffee and gently form into a thick roll.
6. Divide the pulled toffee into four ropes and press these against the sides of the thick darker rope. Pull out gently to the required thickness and twist. The larger the size of humbug you want, the thicker you will need to make the roll.
7. Using oiled scissors, cut into humbugs or cushions. Leave to set on a buttered baking sheet or waxed paper.

MAKES ABOUT 450 G (1 LB)

COCONUT ICE BARS

450 g (1 lb) granulated sugar
150 ml (¼ pint) milk
150 g (5 oz) desiccated coconut
few drops of red food colouring

1. Lightly oil an 18 cm (7 inch) shallow square tin.
2. Put the sugar and the milk in a heavy-based saucepan and heat gently until the sugar has dissolved. Bring to the boil and boil gently for about 10 minutes, or until 116°C (240°F), soft ball stage is reached.
3. Remove from the heat and stir in the coconut.
4. Pour half the mixture quickly into the tin. Add a few drops of food colouring to the second half and pour quickly over the first layer.
5. Leave until half set, mark into bars and cut or break when cold.
MAKES ABOUT 550 G (1¼ LB)

FUDGE

Fudge is very popular and is also quite simple to make. It can be flavoured with chocolate, coffee, nuts or glacé fruits if desired. Cooked fudge is made from sugar, butter and milk or cream that is gently heated and then boiled to the required temperature. Either caster or granulated sugar may be used. When making fudge, stir the mixture to dissolve the sugar, then bring to the boil without stirring. Continue boiling until the correct temperature is reached, stirring occasionally to prevent sticking. When the required temperature is reached, the mixture is beaten with a wooden spoon to give the characteristic creamy texture. Immediately as the fudge begins to thicken, it should be poured into the prepared tins. Mark it into squares just before it begins to set. A knife dipped in hot water makes cutting easier.

VANILLA FUDGE

450 g (1 lb) granulated sugar
75 g (3 oz) butter or margarine
150 ml (¼ pint) milk
175 g (6 oz) can evaporated milk
2.5 ml (½ tsp) vanilla flavouring

1. Lightly oil an 18 cm (7 inch) shallow square tin.
2. Put the sugar, butter, milk and evaporated milk in a heavy-based pan and heat gently, stirring, until dissolved.
3. Bring to the boil without stirring, then continue boiling until a temperature of 116°C (240°F) is reached, stirring occasionally to prevent sticking.
4. Remove the pan from the heat, add the vanilla flavouring and beat the mixture with a wooden spoon until thick and grainy. Pour the mixture into the prepared tin and leave until almost set, about 5-10 minutes.
5. Using a sharp knife, mark the soft fudge into squares, then leave to cool completely before cutting and removing from the tin. Store for up to 2-3 weeks in an airtight container.
MAKES 800 G (1¾ LB)

VARIATION
CHERRY FUDGE
Follow the above recipe as far as the end of stage 3. Stir in 100 g (4 oz) chopped glacé cherries in place of vanilla flavouring. Complete as above.

LEFT: Cherry Fudge. RIGHT: Walnut and Coffee Fudge

COFFEE FUDGE

300 ml (½ pint) milk
550 g (1¼ lb) sugar
100 g (4 oz) butter
45 ml (3 tbsp) coffee essence

1. Pour the milk, sugar and butter in a heavy-based saucepan, and heat slowly, stirring continuously, until the sugar dissolves and the butter melts. Bring to the boil, cover and boil for 2 minutes.
2. Uncover and continue to boil steadily, stirring occasionally, for 15-20 minutes, until the temperature reaches the soft ball stage 116°C (240°F).
3. Remove from the heat. Stir in the coffee flavouring and leave to cool for 5 minutes.
4. Beat the fudge until it just begins to lose its gloss and is thick.
5. Transfer to a greased 18 cm (7 inch) square tin. Mark into squares when almost set. When firm and set, cut along the marked lines.
MAKES ABOUT 800 G (1¾ LB)

VARIATIONS
WALNUT AND COFFEE FUDGE
Add 50 g (2 oz) chopped walnut pieces with the coffee flavouring.
CHERRY FUDGE
Omit the coffee essence and add 50 g (2 oz) chopped glacé cherries.

CHOCOLATE FUDGE

450 g (1 lb) granulated sugar
150 ml (¼ pint) milk
150 g (5 oz) butter or margarine
150 g (5 oz) plain chocolate
50 g (2 oz) honey

1. Lightly oil an 18 cm (7 inch) shallow square tin.
2. Heat all the ingredients gently in a large heavy-based saucepan, stirring until the sugar has dissolved.
3. Bring to the boil without stirring, then continue boiling until a temperature of 116°C (240°F) is reached, stirring occasionally to prevent sticking.
4. Remove from the heat, stand the pan on a cool surface for 5 minutes, then beat the mixture until thick, creamy and beginning to 'grain'.
5. Pour into the prepared tin, mark into squares when almost set and cut when cold.
MAKES ABOUT 800 G (1¾ LB)

TRUFFLES

Truffles are mouth-watering sweets believed to have originated in France, where larger truffles were served as part of a selection of cakes and biscuits at teatime. Although traditionally associated with Christmas, smaller truffles make ideal after-dinner sweets. They are usually chocolate based with added flavourings such as rum, brandy, coffee, fruit and nuts. When completely set, they are tossed in chocolate or cocoa powder, coconut or chopped nuts, or dipped in chocolate.

RICH CHOCOLATE RUM TRUFFLES

225 g (8 oz) plain chocolate
2 egg yolks
25 g (1 oz) butter
10 ml (2 tsp) rum
15 ml (1 tbsp) single cream
drinking chocolate powder

1. Melt the chocolate in a bowl over a saucepan of hot water making sure the bottom of the bowl does not touch the water, then add the egg yolks, butter, rum and cream.
2. Stir until the mixture is thick enough to handle.
3. Cool slightly, then form into balls and roll in chocolate powder.
4. Leave until firm, then put in paper cases.
MAKES ABOUT 225 G (8 OZ)

VARIATION
RICH CHOCOLATE BRANDY TRUFFLES
Replace the rum with brandy.

MOCHA TRUFFLES

225 g (8 oz) plain chocolate
60 ml (4 tbsp) condensed milk
few drops of coffee flavouring or strong black coffee
cocoa powder

1. Break the chocolate into small pieces and melt it in a bowl over hot water, making sure the bottom of the bowl does not touch the water.
2. Stir in the condensed milk and a few drops of coffee flavouring.
3. Allow the mixture to cool slightly, then form into small balls.
4. Roll in cocoa powder and leave until set.
MAKES ABOUT 225 G (8 OZ)

ALMOND TRUFFLES

100 g (4 oz) fresh or stale cake crumbs
100 g (4 oz) caster sugar
100 g (4 oz) ground almonds
120 ml (8 level tbsp) apricot jam, heated and sieved
10-15 ml (2-3 tsp) rum or sherry
75-100 g (3-4 oz) chocolate vermicelli

1. Crumble the cake crumbs finely and add the sugar, ground almonds and 75 ml (5 tbsp) apricot jam to bind it and give a fairly sticky mixture.
2. Add rum or sherry to taste.
3. Shape into small balls, dip them into the remaining jam and roll them in the chocolate vermicelli. Harden, then put into paper cases.
MAKES ABOUT 350 G (12 OZ)

CHOCOLATE NUT TRUFFLES

100 g (4 oz) plain chocolate, finely grated
25 g (1 oz) chopped mixed nuts
50 g (2 oz) icing sugar
1-2 drops of vanilla flavouring
about 15 ml (1 tbsp) single cream
chocolate vermicelli

1. Put the chocolate, nuts and sugar into a bowl and add vanilla flavouring and enough cream to bind the ingredients together.
2. Form into small balls, roll them in chocolate vermicelli and put into paper cases when firm.
MAKES ABOUT 225 G (8 OZ)

COLLETTES

190 g (6½ oz) plain chocolate
25 g (1 oz) butter
10 ml (2 tsp) brandy
60 ml (4 tbsp) double cream
flaked almonds, glacé cherries and crystallised violets,
*   to decorate*

1. Place 16 small paper cases on a baking sheet.
2. Break 100 g (4 oz) of the chocolate in pieces into a heatproof bowl standing over a saucepan of gently simmering water. Heat gently until the chocolate has melted, stirring only once or twice after the chocolate has started to melt. Remove bowl from pan.
3. Spoon a little chocolate into each case and, using a clean paintbrush, coat inside of the cases. Leave to set in a cool place for about 1 hour.
4. Coat again making sure the chocolate forms an even layer. Leave to set in a cool place for about 1 hour, then carefully peel away the paper from the cases.
5. Melt the remaining chocolate with the butter as in step 2, leave for about 5 minutes until cool but not set, then stir in the brandy until evenly mixed.
6. Whip the cream until stiff and fold into the chocolate mixture. Leave to set for about 5 minutes, until mixture is thick enough for piping.
7. Spoon the chocolate cream into a piping bag fitted with a small star nozzle and pipe into the chocolate cases. Decorate each with a flaked almond, a piece of cherry or a crystallised violet.
8. Arrange in clean paper cases in a box. Store in the refrigerator for up to 1 week.
MAKES 16

ABOVE: Rich Chocolate Rum Truffles and Chocolate Nut Truffles. BELOW: Collettes

CHOCOLATE HAZELNUT CLUSTERS

225 g (8 oz) shelled hazelnuts
225 g (8 oz) plain chocolate
about 7 g (¼ oz) white vegetable fat (optional)

1. Spread the hazelnuts on a baking sheet and toast in the oven at 180°C (350°F) mark 4 for about 10 minutes, turning them or shaking the tray from time to time. Turn into a clean tea towel and rub off the skins. Leave the nuts to cool.
2. Break the chocolate into a bowl and place over a pan of hot water until melted. Add a small knob of vegetable fat if necessary to

achieve a coating consistency. Line a tray with non-stick baking parchment.
3. Remove the pan from the heat. Drop the nuts into the chocolate and stir them around. Using a teaspoon, retrieve four nuts at a time with a good portion of chocolate. Place each cluster in a little heap on the parchment-lined tray. If the chocolate starts to cool and thicken while making the clusters, return the pan to the heat but take care not to overheat the chocolate or it will become too liquid to work with.
4. Leave the hazelnut clusters to dry thoroughly.
MAKES ABOUT 350 G (12 OZ)

DIPPED CHOCOLATES

These are perhaps the most 'professional' looking chocolates you will make at home. Ordinary block or plain or milk chocolate flavoured cake covering will do, but dipping is a time-consuming operation and it is as well to help ensure good results by using couverture chocolate available from specialist suppliers.

When melting the chocolate, it should be broken into small pieces and placed in a bowl over a saucepan of cold water. Make sure that the base of the bowl does not touch the water and that it is wedged into the pan so that no steam escapes round the sides of the bowl. Humidity spoils the texture and gloss of finished chocolates and dipping is best done on a warm, dry day when there is no other steamy cooking taking place in the kitchen.

Heat the water gently but don't allow it to boil. Remove the pan from the heat and stir the chocolate until it is completely melted. If it starts to harden again before you have finished dipping, simply reheat it gently in the same way. If the chocolate is too warm, it will dry cloudy and white; if too cool, it will coat the centres too quickly. The ideal melting temperature for a smooth, shiny result is 38°-40°C (100°-110°F).

Chocolate can also be melted in the microwave, but make sure that the oven has not been used for reheating liquids shortly beforehand, or the residual humidity in the microwave will affect the chocolate. Use a LOW setting and stir frequently to ensure an even result.

Many fondants, fudges and caramels make ideal centres for dipped chocolates. Peppermint creams, walnut creams, marzipan balls and chocolate nut truffles are all suitable. Place the centres on a baking sheet and warm them slightly before you begin.

When the chocolate is ready, lower the centres into it one at a time using a dipping fork. Lift each centre out, shake off any surplus chocolate by knocking the fork gently against the edge of the basin and place the sweet on a baking sheet lined with waxed paper.

While the chocolate is still soft, make a pattern by pressing the dipping fork lightly on the top and lifting it off again gently, or pipe the top of the sweet with a little contrasting chocolate. Alternatively, decorate with walnut pieces, blanched almonds, candied orange peel or chocolate vermicelli. When the chocolates have dried thoroughly, put them into individual paper cases.

CHOCOLATE DIPPED FRUIT

Fresh firm fruit, such as oranges, pineapple, peaches, nectarines or strawberries, can be dipped in chocolate.

To prepare the fruit, remove any skin. Remove all pith and membrane from oranges; cut pineapple into rings and then into wedges; cut peaches and nectarines into quarters or slices. Leave the hulls in strawberries.

Make sure that the surface of the fruit is completely dry before dipping into melted chocolate, or the moisture will spoil the chocolate. Either totally immerse the fruit in the chocolate using a dipping fork, or hold one end of the fruit in your fingers and half dip it. Avoid dipping strawberry leaves. Lift out and hold the coated fruit over the bowl for a moment to drain, then wipe a skewer gently underneath the fork to remove any surplus chocolate. Carefully slide the fruit off the fork on to a baking sheet lined with non-stick baking parchment. Gently push the fruit very slightly with the fork to seal the chocolate underneath.

Leave until completely dry before removing from paper, handling them as little as possible.

CHOCOLATE EASTER EGGS

Tin or plastic moulds are essential for making eggs, they are available in various sizes. Use good quality couverture chocolate or plain or milk chocolate flavoured cake covering and prepare it as for chocolate dipping (see left for detailed instructions).

Polish the inside of the moulds with cotton wool or a soft cloth, then half fill each mould with chocolate and tilt to allow the chocolate to run to the edge of the mould and coat it evenly. Repeat this two or three times, then pour the surplus back into the chocolate pan. Run a finger round the edge of the mould to remove surplus chocolate, then put the mould, domed side up, on a cool flat surface. As the shells cool, they will contract slightly and may be removed by pressing gently at one end. The outer glazed surface caused by contact with the mould must not be handled more than can be helped. The shells can be joined by lightly touching the two halves on to a warm flat tin, so that just sufficient chocolate melts to enable them to set firmly together. Press gently to seal, then set aside to allow the chocolate to harden.

Wrap the eggs in foil, or decorate them with brightly coloured ribbon, sifted icing sugar or fine lines of chocolate piping.

PRESENTING FOOD

One of the secrets of successful entertaining is knowing how to present the food you have so carefully cooked in the most attractive way. And this doesn't mean that you have to be an expert at piping, or adept at carving vegetables.
This chapter includes plenty of ideas for garnishing and decorating, all of which are stunningly effective, yet amazingly simple to do.

GARNISHES

Garnishes add a professional finishing touch to your cooking. They should also look fresh and to be chosen to complement the flavour of the dish. The following kitchen tools are useful for preparing garnishes:

- Canelle knife: for cutting grooves in vegetables.
- Vegetable peeler: for finely peeling citrus rinds.
- Small fluted and fancy cutters: for pastry shapes, fruit and vegetable 'flowers', and chocolate decorations.
- Piping bag and nozzles: for piping cream.

HERBS

The simplest of garnishes are usually the most effective. Fresh sprigs of basil, chervil, chives, coriander, parsley or other herbs, or a scattering of chopped herbs, always looks attractive.

SPRING ONION TASSELS

1. Remove the base and most of the green part from each of the spring onions.

2. Make several parallel slits from the top of each onion to within about 2.5 cm (1 inch) of the base.
3. Allow the spring onions to stand in a bowl of iced water for about 1 hour to curl, then drain thoroughly before using.

LEMON TWISTS

1. Cut thin slices of lemon. Make a cut through to the centre of each slice then twist into an S-shape.
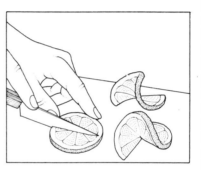
2. A sprig of parsley or another herb may be placed at the centre of the twist for extra colour.
3. This technique can also be used with orange, lime or cucumber slices. If preferred, group two or three cut slices together before twisting.

CELERY CURLS

1. Cut sticks of celery into pieces about 7.5 cm (3 inches) long. Make parallel cuts in each end of the celery about 2.5 cm (1 inch) deep, then flatten out the celery.
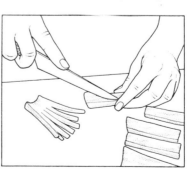
2. At each end, make a careful cut into the 'teeth', so that the teeth are cut in half lengthways.
3. Leave the prepared sticks of celery in a bowl of iced water for about 1 hour so that the frill can curl up.

TOMATO WHIRLS

1. Using a small sharp knife, cut the skin and a very thin layer of flesh from a tomato, starting at the top and working round in the way that you would peel an orange, to give one continuous spiral of skin.

2. Trim the ends of the peel neatly, then curl it up so that it forms a flower shape. Secure with a toothpick until ready to use. Use herbs, such as basil or coriander, to resemble leaves.

RADISH ROSES

1. Trim each radish. Starting at the top of the radish, make rows of small cuts into the radish flesh to make petals. The number of rows will depend on the size of the radish.

2. Submerge the prepared radishes in a bowl of iced water and leave for about 1 hour so that the 'petals' open out to form a rose. Drain thoroughly.

VANDYKING ORANGES

1. Using a small, thin-bladed knife, make a slantwise cut in the equator of an orange to the centre.
2. Without removing the knife, make a series of zig-zag cuts all round the equator of the fruit.
3. Gently twist

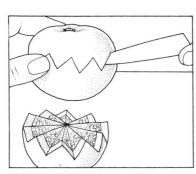

the two orange halves apart.
NOTE: This technique can also be applied to tomatoes, grapefruit, and lemons.

FLUTED OR 'TURNED' MUSHROOMS

1. Choose firm, white button mushrooms. Hold a small sharp knife with the blade parallel to the mushroom stalk.
2. Keeping your thumb and fingers well away from the blade, turn the mushroom

against the knife so that thin, curved strips of the mushroom skin are removed evenly all round.
3. Brush the mushrooms with lemon juice.

GHERKIN FANS

1. Make parallel cuts in each gherkin to within about 1 cm (½ inch) of the base.
2. Open out and flatten into a fan shape.
NOTE: This technique can also be used for avocado halves; brush

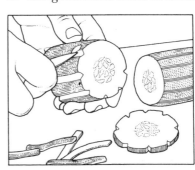

with lemon juice to prevent discoloration.

CARROT CURLS

Using a potato peeler, carefully peel long ribbons of carrot. Roll up each ribbon and secure with a cocktail stick. Leave in a bowl of iced water for about 1 hour. Drain and remove cocktail sticks before using.

CUCUMBER WHEELS

1. Using a canelle knife or a sharp knife, remove thin strips of skin lengthwise at regular intervals all round a cucumber.
2. Slice thinly to create decorative cucumber wheels.

DECORATIONS

Effective decorations for sweet dishes range from the stunningly simple to the sophistication of piped cream or icing. Even if you are not an experienced cook, you can try some of the suggestions shown here.

PIPED CREAM

1. Whip double cream until just stiff enough to

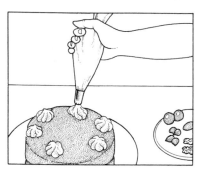

hold its shape. **2.** Using a piping bag, fitted with a star nozzle, pipe rosettes of cream around a dessert or cake. **3.** Top each one with a nut, cherry or some other kind of fruit. Or sprinkle with grated chocolate, toasted chopped nuts, crushed caramel or toasted desiccated coconut.

CITRUS JULIENNE

1. Remove very thin strips of rind from citrus

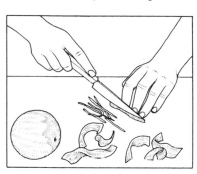

fruit with a canelle knife or vegetable peeler, making sure that the strips contain no traces of pith. **2.** Blanch the strips in boiling water for about 3 minutes, then drain and rinse under cold running water. **3.** Dry thoroughly and cut into julienne strips about 5 mm (¼ inch) thick and about 5 cm (2 inches) long. **4.** Use to sprinkle over desserts; they look especially effective on rosettes of whipped cream or buttercream.

FROSTED FRUITS AND FLOWERS

1. Suitable fruits include clusters of grapes, strawberries and Cape gooseberries. **2.** Whisk together the white of 1 egg with 10 ml (2 tsp) cold water to give a frothy mixture. **3.** Using a small paintbrush, brush the mixture on to small firm fruits or flowers, then dip these

in caster sugar. **4.** Shake off any excess sugar, then spread out on greaseproof paper and leave to dry for at least 24 hours. **5.** Use frosted fruits and flowers to decorate cakes and desserts.

FLOWER DESIGNS

1. Make up some very firm jelly of the colour

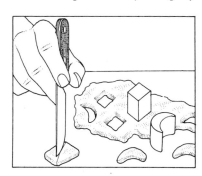

you wish and use aspic cutters or a sharp knife to cut out petal shapes. **2.** Construct flowers using the jelly petals, angelica strips for stems and silver dragees for the centres. Whole blanched almonds can be alternated with the jelly in the flowers. **3.** Arrange the shapes on the top of the dessert or around the edges just before serving. The jelly flowers will keep in the refrigerator for 2-3 days. Store in an airtight container.

MARZIPAN 'ORANGES'

1. Colour batches of marzipan with orange and

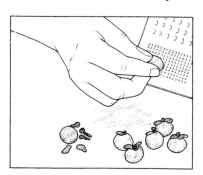

green food colouring. With your fingers, shape small amounts of the orange marzipan into balls. Stick a trimmed whole clove in the end of the fruit. **2.** Roll on the fine side of a conical or box grater to give the texture of orange skin, then roll in caster sugar. **3.** Attach 'leaves' made from the green-coloured marzipan. Use on cakes, or as petits fours, or as presents in sweet cases.

CRUSHED CARAMEL

1. Slowly dissolve 75 g (3 oz) sugar in 75 ml (3 fl

oz) water over gentle heat, then increase the heat and boil until the liquid has turned to a rich caramel colour.
2. Pour the mixture immediately into a shallow baking tin lined with non-stick baking parchment. Leave to set.
3. Crush caramel with a rolling pin. Sprinkle over desserts and cakes.

ICING SUGAR PATTERNS

1. Place a patterned paper doily, or a template

you have cut yourself, on a cake (or get someone to help by holding it just above the surface of a delicate cake or dessert).
2. Sift over icing sugar, then carefully lift off the doily or template. The pattern of holes will be reproduced on the surface of the cake or dessert.

Chocolate powder can be used in a similar way on a lightly coloured cake.

CHOCOLATE SHAPES

1. Melt chocolate in a double boiler or a bowl over a pan of hot water, then pour and spread on to a cold surface (ideally a marble slab) and leave until firm.
2. When the chocolate is set, cut into neat triangles or squares with a sharp knife, or stamp out circles with a small round cutter.

CHOCOLATE LEAVES

1. Melt the chocolate in a double boiler or a

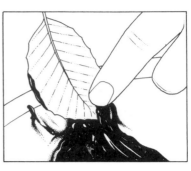

bowl over a pan of hot water.
2. Using rose leaves which have been thoroughly washed and dried, drag the upper surface of each rose leaf through the chocolate, making sure that the underside of the leaf does not become coated with chocolate as well.
3. Turn the leaves chocolate-side up and place on greaseproof paper to set. When the chocolate has set, carefully peel off the leaf.

CHOCOLATE CARAQUE

1. Melt chocolate in a double boiler or a bowl

over a pan of hot water, then pour on to a cold surface (ideally a marble slab) and spread into a rectangular shape, using a palette knife.
Leave to cool until just firm, but not hard or brittle.
2. Hold a sharp long-bladed knife at a slight angle and draw it across the chocolate to make long, thin scrolls.
3. Use chocolate caraque to decorate cakes, mousses and soufflés.

CHOCOLATE CURLS

For a less dramatic, though simpler version of chocolate caraque, shave a bar of chilled chocolate with a vegetable peeler or canelle knife to make chocolate curls.

CATERING FOR LARGE NUMBERS

Parties are made for enjoyment and that goes for the host and hostess as well as your guests. However wonderful the food and ambience may be, few guests will be relaxed and happy if they see their hosts rushing around like scalded cats. So the first rule for party giving is careful pre-planning and organisation. The larger the party is to be, the sooner it should be planned.

What type of party do you want to have? A five-course dinner for eight with all the trimmings? A casual help-yourself supper for a few friends? Early evening drinks for twenty or so? A full-scale celebration with no expense spared? A big, informal, bring-a-bottle party with food and dancing? A Sunday lunchtime buffet in the garden, kids welcome? There are numerous possiblities to choose from depending on how many people you want to invite and how much you want to spend. Whichever type you choose, careful advance organisation will make all the difference.

Having decided on the sort of party, you now have to tackle the tricky bit: how many people and whom to ask. Numbers will depend partly on space, but there are other considerations. For large parties and buffets you will need help. Enlist family or good friends to hand round food or nibbles and keep glasses replenished. You could even consider hiring help. Students from local colleges may be glad of some pocket money.

WHAT WILL YOU NEED?

It's all very well to decide on a huge party and invite 100 people, but you must be able to cater for them. Make a list of everything you'll need, count up what you own and decide in good time if there's anything you need to buy, borrow or hire. You'll use lots of glasses for a big party and it's as well to provide more than one per guest, as people tend to lose them as the evening wears on. A local wine merchant should be able to help out with glass hire, which will often be free if you buy your party wine at the same time.

Depending on the formality of the occasion you can make do with paper plates and plastic cutlery (but make them good quality otherwise they won't stand up to the strain). If you must have the real thing, beg or borrow from friends or hire. Large supplies of paper napkins are essential, especially at barbecues, or if you are serving finger food. And you'll need suitable serving implements for the buffet table. Also on your list should be ashtrays. Large candles left burning at strategic, safe points around the room help to clear unpleasant smoke from the air and you can buy special 'smokers candles' for this purpose.

PLANNING THE MENU

Having decided on the type of party and the number of guests, you can plan the menu. Take into account the time of year as seasonal food will always be the freshest and cheapest available. Then as for all menus, you need to provide a balance of textures, colours and types of foods. Cream of Cucumber Soup followed by Asparagus Mousse and Melon Sorbet might sound delicious until one sees bowls of an indeterminate pale green nature lined up on the table! If you start with a pale creamy soup, serve colourful slices of salmon or beef to follow and then perhaps a fragrant fruit salad to end the meal.

Now think of the ages of your guests, if you're inviting the young or old, simple food would be more acceptable whilst hearty young men will expect something quite substantial. And do think too of vegetarians – very often they find themselves restricted to a tomato slice and a lettuce leaf – hardly a party celebration!

Whilst selecting the menu, think carefully through as to how you're going to cook, store or reheat the food. Do you have big enough saucepans or casseroles to feed a crowd? And more importantly still, do you have space in or on your cooker to reheat these recipes? Friends may offer to lend you large saucepans or preserving pans which sound perfect until you find that only one can fit on the hob at a time. It is better and safer to serve a mainly cold buffet than a selection of lukewarm dishes which could well be breeding dangerous bacteria whilst they sit in a warm room. Your oven too will only have limited capacity. If you cram it full of casseroles and dishes, the heat can't circulate properly and the oven's efficiency will be greatly impaired.

The problem of refrigerator space must also be considered. There will be wine bottles jostling for space besides heaps of salad ingredients, cheeses, cold chickens, cream and much, much more. Here your neighbours can be asked to help by lending you a shelf or two in their refrigerator.

When choosing buffet food, do make sure that all food can be eaten with a fork. There's nothing worse than looking longingly at scrumptious jacket potatoes which stubbornly refuse to be eaten with a fork!

Choose the dishes you want to serve and list them, adding references to cookery books and page numbers where necessary. Highlight the dishes on your list that will freeze successfully and can therefore be cooked in advance. Read through the recipes, plan when to cook each one and start to make shopping lists.

PLANNING AHEAD

Once the menu has been decided make a careful time plan or countdown. This may sound pedantic but it saves all that last minute panic. Include on this all food and general goods to be ordered, the cleaning to be done, staff to be arranged as well as what to do 'on the day'.

- Make detailed shopping lists buying all unperishable items as early as possible.
- Check that you have enough tablecloths, napkins, candles, plenty of rubbish bags, foil, polythene bags, kitchen paper, toilet rolls etc.
- Order wines, beers, soft drinks etc and glasses.
- Arrange extra help.
- Hire tables, chairs, china and cutlery.
- Book space in neighbours' refrigerators and freezers.
- Write a detailed time plan of when to prepare each recipe, reheat it and garnish it.
- Order flowers if wished.

LEFT: *Meringues with Summer Fruits (see page 516)*. RIGHT: *Celebration Cake (see page 429)*

EXTRA HELP

Depending on the formality of your party, you may want to employ professional waiters and waitresses. Either contact them through your Yellow Pages under Caterers or Employment Agencies or most local hotels and clubs will help out in telling you where they hire their temporary staff. For less formal parties, students or older children can be a great help but do give them clear briefs on their duties for the party. For a buffet meal one professional waitress can cope with about 25 guests provided that the drinks, salads etc, are all help yourself. An untrained helper will find 15 people sufficient to cope with. Book all staff early as all the agencies are busy especially in the summer months.

HIRING EQUIPMENT

Here again, look in your Yellow Pages this time under Hire Services for Catering Equipment Hire or Wedding Services. If there's no extra charge, order equipment a day ahead so you've plenty of time to unpack and check it out. Some firms will take equipment back dirty, this adds a bit to the cost but does save a lot of valuable time. Run through your menu ordering plates, glasses, cutlery and serving dishes as necessary. You may need to include jugs for water and fruit juice, ash trays, trestle tables and chairs and tablecloths. Don't forget coffee cups and saucers and even a coffee urn if you are catering for a very large number.

Refrigerators, freezers and hot cupboards

Shredded Red Salad (see page 515)

can be hired too, but do check that you have sufficient power points to plug them in without overloading the system – a black out on the day of the party is not helpful!

THE DRINKS

What drink to serve at parties is very much a personal preference, the important thing is not to run out! Many off licences will sell wine on a sale or return basis which does mean that you can over order just in case your guests are the thirsty type. Ask for advice for wines to suit your menu and don't be tempted by the cheapest available unless you want your guests to suffer from thunderous headaches.

We advise keeping the choice of wines to a minimum, this makes the filling of glasses much easier! Allow at least half a bottle a head, more if all the guests are adults. And order plenty of mineral waters, beers and soft drinks. Many off licences will lend glasses free of charge too – check when you order your wine.

To chill large quantities of wine, line plastic tubs or rubbish bins with plastic sacks and fill with ice and water. Keep in a cool place. Ice can be delivered to the door (see Yellow Pages) or bought in off licences. A 12.6 kg (28 lb) bag of ice should chill a case of wine in about 1 hour – allow longer on hot days. Remember to move chilled bottles up to the top of the container as you put more bottles in. Still white wine can be opened ahead and the corks pressed gently back into the bottles.

COOKING IN QUANTITY

This is not just a question of quadrupling your favourite recipe and then letting it simmer or bake away. Liquids will not reduce at the same speed and cooking times may vary leaving you with a watery casserole or a sunken cake. Unless an experienced caterer we do not advise you to cook recipes for more than 12 people at one time. Few casserole dishes or saucepans will take larger quantities than this and if they do it's often difficult to ensure even heat right through. Just prepare food in smaller batches and chill or freeze for the big day.

HOW MUCH TO COOK

The more people you're feeding the less you'll need to allow per head. For 100 people, 85-90 portions should be enough. Maybe this is because at buffet parties the act of balancing a glass and plate is just too much to cope with. If you're offering a selection of main courses or desserts though, you'll need to over cater a little as people like to 'taste' both. And if it's a 'treat' food like smoked salmon, everyone is bound to indulge so you must be generous.

LAYING OUT THE BUFFET

Have several serving points for the buffet food and the drinks too. This avoids bottlenecks and long delays. Ensure that plates, cutlery and napkins are set out at the start of the buffet table. Don't pile serving platters too high or food will spill over the table. It's better to replenish the dishes as necessary. Keep food tightly covered until it's served and if possible add garnishes at the last minute too. They'll look freshest then. Portion pies and gâteau before the buffet starts or station one of the helpers to serve them out as guests often loathe to be the first to cut into them. And do ensure that there are some seats available for the elderly to sit and eat.

HANDY HINTS

- Make sure you have plenty of rubbish bags and drying up cloths for the aftermath.
- Decide where to stack the dirty plates before the party starts. A kitchen overflowing with washing up looks unsightly.
- To save on time and energy, use good quality bought ingredients such as mayonnaise as a base for sauces and then add a few extra herbs or garlic to liven them up.
- Be ready for the occasional disaster such as a knocked over glass of wine. As it happens mop the stain with cold water then top with several layers of absorbent kitchen paper. Stand on them until no more moisture will blot from the carpet.
- An electric carving knife is useful when slicing bread or creamy cakes.
- Make sure that candles, glasses and bottles are left on sturdy tables, well away from scampering children and pets.
- On the day, allow yourself plenty of time to reheat food or arrange platters of cold food. Always recruit plenty of helpers for this to avoid last minute panic.
- Consider where your guests are going to park and if necessary inform the local police about the volume of traffic.
- It is a good idea to warn neighbours about the party in case guests park in front of their garages or there's a lot of noise.

QUANTITY CHART FOR BUFFET PARTIES

Approximate quantities to serve 12 people.

- For 25 people, multiply the quantities by two.
- For 50 people multiply by four.
- For 75 people multiply by five and a half.
- For 100 people multiply by seven.

COCKTAIL EATS

Allow about 80 small eats to serve before a meal.
Allow about 120 small eats to serve alone.

STARTERS

Soups	2.6 litres (4½ pints)
Pâtés	1.1 kg (2½ lb)
Smoked Salmon	900 g (2 lb)
Prawns	900 g (2 lb)

MAIN DISHES

Chicken/turkey

Boneless chicken or turkey	1.8 kg (4 lb)
Whole chicken	three 1.4 kg (3 lb) (oven-ready birds)
Turkey	one 5.5 kg (12 lb) (oven-ready bird)

Lamb/beef/pork

Boneless	2-2.3 kg (4½ -5 lb)
On the bone	3.2-3.6 kg (7-8 lb)
Mince	2 kg (4½ lb)

Fish

Whole with head	2.3 kg (5 lb)
Steaks	twelve 175 g (6 oz)
Fillets	2 kg (4½ lb)
Prawns	1.4 kg (3 lb)

ACCOMPANIMENTS

Potatoes

Roast & mashed	2 kg (4½ lb)
New	1.8 kg (4 lb)

Rice & pasta	700 g (1½ lb)

Green vegetables

Broccoli, French beans, etc	1.4 kg (3 lb)
Fresh spinach	about 3.6 kg (8 lb)

Salads

Tomato	700 g (1½ lb)
Salad leaves	2-3 medium heads
Celery	2 large heads
Cucumber	1 large

Dressings

French dressing	175 ml (6 fl oz)
Mayonnaise	300 ml (10 fl oz)

Bread

French bread	1 large loaf
Medium sliced bread	1 large loaf (approx 24 slices)

Cheese

For a wine and cheese party	1.4 kg (3 lb)
To serve at the end of a meal	700 g (1½ lb)

Butter

With bread, biscuits and cheese	350 g (12 oz)
With bread or biscuits and cheese	225 g (8 oz)
For sandwiches	175 g (6 oz) softened butter for 12 rounds

Cream

For pudding or dessert	600 ml (20 fl oz) single cream
For coffee	300 ml (10 fl oz) single cream

Milk	450 ml (15 fl oz) (12 cups tea)

Coffee

Ground coffee	about 125 g (4 oz) (12 medium cups)
Instant	about 75 g (3 oz) (12 large cups)

Tea	about 25 g (l oz) (12 medium cups)

BUFFET MENU FOR 20

GARLIC BREAD X 2
EASTERN CASSEROLE OF LAMB X 3
BROWN RICE PILAFF
SHREDDED RED SALAD
THREE BEAN SALAD
MERINGUES WITH SUMMER FRUITS
STRAWBERRIES WITH RASPBERRY SAUCE

COUNT-DOWN TIMETABLE

TWO DAYS BEFORE THE PARTY
THREE BEAN SALAD: Soak the kidney beans in water overnight.
MERINGUES WITH SUMMER FRUITS: Make the meringues (even earlier, if wished). When cold, store in an airtight container or wrap in foil.

ONE DAY BEFORE THE PARTY
GARLIC BREAD: Prepare 2 loaves. Wrap in foil and store in a cool place.
EASTERN CASSEROLE OF LAMB: Make up triple quantities. Cover and refrigerate.
SALADS: Prepare dressing for Shredded Red Salad. Prepare Three Bean Salad, cover and refrigerate.
STRAWBERRIES WITH RASPBERRY SAUCE: Hull the strawberries, keep cool. Pureé and sweeten the raspberries, keep covered in a separate bowl.

ON THE DAY OF THE PARTY
GARLIC BREAD: Place in the oven to warm 15 minutes before serving.
EASTERN CASSEROLE OF LAMB: Remove from the refrigerator 2 hours before the party and allow to come to room temperature. In one large saucepan (or two smaller ones with half the casserole in each), reheat slowly on the top of the stove for 45-60 minutes, stirring occasionally.
BROWN RICE PILAFF: Prepare and bake 1½-2 hours before the party. If the pilaff needs to be kept warm, reduce oven heat to lowest setting 15-30 minutes before the end of the cooking time.
SALADS: Remove bean salad from refrigerator and make Shredded Red Salad 2 hours before serving; keep covered. Stir 1 hour ahead.
MERINGUES WITH SUMMER FRUITS: Whip the cream and assemble the meringues not more than 2 hours beforehand.
STRAWBERRIES WITH RASPBERRY SAUCE: Pour the raspberry sauce over the strawberries and chill in the refrigerator for 1-2 hours before serving.

HOT GARLIC BREAD

1 large French loaf
100-175 g (4-6 oz) butter or margarine
2 garlic cloves, skinned and crushed
salt and pepper

1. Cut the loaf into 2.5 cm (1 inch) thick slices.
2. Cream the butter in a bowl until soft. Add the garlic and salt and pepper and beat together.
3. Spread liberally between the slices. Wrap the loaf loosely in foil and bake at 180°C (350°F) mark 4 for about 15 minutes until soft.
SERVES 8-10

VARIATION
HOT HERB BREAD
Follow the recipe above, omitting the garlic and adding 30 ml (2 tbsp) fresh chopped herbs, eg parsley, chives, thyme.

EASTERN CASSEROLE OF LAMB

450 g (1 lb) tomatoes, skinned and quartered
45 ml (3 tbsp) vegetable oil
1.4 kg (3 lb) lean boned lamb, cut into large chunks
3 medium onions, skinned and sliced
30 ml (2 level tbsp) ground coriander
10 ml (2 level tsp) ground cumin
5 ml (1 level tsp) ground ginger
1.25 ml (¼ level tsp) ground turmeric
1.25 ml (¼ level tsp) cayenne pepper
30 ml (2 level tbsp) flour
15 ml (1 level tbsp) tomato purée
450 ml (¾ pint) chicken stock
75 g (3 oz) sultanas
salt and pepper

1. Rub the tomato seeds through a sieve and reserve the juice.
2. Heat the oil in a large flameproof casserole. Add the meat, a few pieces at a time and fry until well browned, then remove from the casserole. Brown the onions in the fat remaining in the casserole.
3. Add the coriander, cumin, ginger, turmeric and cayenne pepper and cook for 2 minutes, then stir in the flour and cook gently for 2 minutes. Add the remaining ingredients and the reserved tomato juice and season well. Replace the meat, cover the casserole and cook in the oven at 170°C (325°F) mark 3 for about 1¾ hours until tender.
SERVES 6-8

NOTE: The flavour of this casserole is improved if it is made a day ahead, to allow the spices to blend with the lamb, and reheated.

BROWN RICE PILAFF

30 ml (2 tbsp) vegetable oil
4 medium onions, skinned and finely chopped
1 large red pepper, seeded and finely chopped
1 garlic clove, skinned and crushed
5 ml (1 level tsp) ground turmeric
900 g (2 lb) long grain brown rice
1.8 litres (3¼ pints) chicken stock
30 ml (2 tbsp) white wine vinegar
salt and pepper

1. Heat the oil in a large saucepan, add the onion and red pepper and fry gently for 5 minutes.
2. Stir in the garlic, turmeric, rice, stock and vinegar. Bring to the boil and season.
3. Transfer the pilaff to an ovenproof dish and cover tightly with foil. Bake in the oven at 180°C (350°F) mark 4 for about 1¼ hours. Fork through before serving.
SERVES 20

SHREDDED RED SALAD

4 medium red onions, skinned and thinly sliced
5 heads radicchio, shredded
150 g (5 oz) beansprouts
60 ml (4 tbsp) sunflower oil
120 ml (8 tbsp) walnut oil
120 ml (8 tbsp) red wine
60 ml (4 tbsp) red wine vinegar
salt and pepper

1. Mix together the onions, radicchio and beansprouts in a large bowl.
2. Place the sunflower and walnut oils, wine, vinegar and seasoning in a bowl or screw-topped jar and whisk or shake together until thoroughly blended.
3. Add the dressing to the salad and toss well just before serving.
SERVES 20

THREE BEAN SALAD

225 g (8 oz) red kidney beans, soaked overnight
900 g (2 lb) broad beans, shelled
900g (2 lb) French beans, trimmed
300 ml (½ pint) French Dressing (see page 255)
chopped fresh parsley, to garnish

1. Drain the kidney beans and rinse well. Put in a large saucepan, cover with water and bring to the boil. Boil vigorously for 10 minutes, then reduce the heat and simmer for about 1 hour, until tender. Drain well.
2. Meanwhile, cook the broad beans in boiling salted water for 15-20 minutes, until just tender Cook the French beans in boiling salted water for 5-10 minutes. Drain the beans and while still hot combine with the kidney beans and French Dressing. Leave to cool.
3. Sprinkle with parsley just before serving.
SERVES 20

MERINGUES WITH SUMMER FRUITS

6 egg whites
350 g (12 oz) caster sugar
a few drops of rosewater (optional)
600 ml (1 pint) double cream
icing sugar, for dusting
summer fruits, eg peaches strawberries and raspberries
rose leaves (optional) to decorate

1. Cover two flat upturned baking sheets with sheets of non-stick baking parchment.
2. Place the egg whites in a large bowl and whisk until stiff.
3. Gradually whisk in half of the sugar, whisking well after each addition, until the mixture is stiff and shiny. Continue whisking the meringue mixture for a further 5 minutes.

4. Sprinkle the remaining sugar over the meringue mixture and add the rosewater if using. Fold in quickly but gently with a large metal spoon.
5. Shape the mixture into ovals, using two teaspoons. Drop these onto the prepared baking sheet, allowing room for the mixture to spread.
6. Cook in the oven at 110°C (225°F) mark ¼ for about 2 hours until completely dried out. (Transpose the trays if they are on different shelves after 1 hour to ensure even drying.) Transfer the cooked meringues to wire racks and leave to cool.
7. Whip the cream until firm and use to sandwich the meringues together. Pile on to a plate, dust with icing sugar and decorate with fresh strawberries and raspberries, and rose leaves if desired. Refrigerate for up to 2 hours

STRAWBERRIES WITH RASPBERRY SAUCE

1.8 kg (4 lb) small strawberries, hulled
900 g (2 lb) raspberries
100 g (4 oz) icing sugar, sifted

1. Place the strawberries in a large serving bowl.
2. Purée the raspberries in a blender or food processor until just smooth, then rub through a nylon sieve to remove the pips.
3. Whisk in the icing sugar and pour over the strawberries. Chill well before serving.
SERVES 20

Buffet Menu for 50

Pâté en Croûte x 3
Chicken Galatine x 4 (see page 150)
Poached Sea Trout in Aspic with Mayonnaise x 4 (see page 78)
Oriental Salad x 2
Party Coleslaw
Fennel and Radicchio Salad
Green Salad with Croûtons
Breads and Crackers with Butter
Strawberry and Orange Mousse x 4 (see page 364)
Exotic Fruit Salad x 4
Profiteroles x 4 (see page 343)
Whole Ripe Brie

COUNT-DOWN TIMETABLE

Two days before the party
Pâté en Croûte: Prepare and cook triple quantity of filling.
Chicken Galantine: Make four. When cold, wrap each one individually and refrigerate.
Profiteroles: Make four quantities of choux puffs, bake and when cold store, without filling, in an airtight tin.

One day before the party
Pâté en Croûte: Make the pastry, encase the pâté and bake. Leave to cool, then refrigerate.
Poached Sea Trout in Aspic with Mayonnaise: Cook, cool and refrigerate without skinning. Prepare Mayonnaise, cover and refrigerate.
Oriental Salad: Make double quantity. Prepare the vegetables and store in polythene bags in the refrigerator. Make the dressing and refrigerate in a screw-topped jar.
Party Coleslaw: Prepare the vegetables and store in polythene bags in the refrigerator.
Fennel and Radicchio Salad: Prepare vegetables and store in polythene bags in the refrigerator. Make dressing; refrigerate in a screw-topped jar.
Green Salad with Croûtons: Prepare the vegetables and store in polythene bags in the refrigerator. Make the dressing and refrigerate in a screw-topped jar. Make the croûtons and store in an airtight tin.
Strawberry and Orange Mousse: Make four of these, cover and refrigerate, undecorated.

Profiteroles: Make four quantities of chocolate sauce. Cover and keep in a cool place.
Brie: Remove from the refrigerator.

Early on the day of the party
Poached Sea Trout: Finish with aspic and keep in a cool place.

Four hours before the party
Party Coleslaw: Add the dressing and keep covered in a cool place, not necessarily the refrigerator.
Exotic Fruit Salad: Make four quantities, cover and keep in a cool place.

Two hours before the party
Pâté en Croûte: Slice, arrange and cover.
Chicken Galatine: Slice, arrange and cover.
Poached Sea Trout in Aspic: Garnish.
Oriental Salad: Add the peanuts and dressing to the salad, toss well and cover.
Profiteroles: Reheat the chocolate sauce. Fill the profiteroles with cream and chill for 1 hour.

One hour before the party
Fennel and Radicchio Salad: Toss all the ingredients together and cover.
Green Salad with Croûtons: Finish salad and cover. Toss again just before serving and sprinkle with croûtons.
Strawberry and Orange Mousse: Decorate and keep in the refrigerator until ready to serve.

PÂTE EN CROÛTE

450 g (1 lb) chicken livers, trimmed
75 g (3 oz) streaky bacon rashers, rinded
  and chopped
1 medium onion, skinned and chopped
1 garlic clove, skinned and crushed
100 g (4 oz) butter or margarine, softened
salt and pepper
3 eggs
150 ml (5 fl oz) double cream
30 ml (2 tbsp) medium sherry
350 g (12 oz) shortcrust pastry made with 350 g
  (12 oz) flour
beaten egg, to glaze

1. Put the livers, bacon and onion in a blender or food processor with the garlic, butter and seasoning. Blend until smooth. Add the eggs, cream and sherry and blend for 2-3 seconds.
2. Pour into a greased and base-lined 1.1 litre (2 pint) loaf tin, preferably non-stick. Cover, then stand the tin in a roasting tin and add enough water to come half-way up the sides of the loaf tin. Cook in the oven at 150°C (300°F) mark 2 for about 1½ hours.
3. Remove the loaf tin from the roasting tin, place a weight on the top and leave overnight.
4. On a lightly floured surface, roll out the pastry to a rectangle large enough to enclose the pâté completely. Roll out the trimmings and use to make decorations.
5. Turn the pâté out and encase in the pastry, decorate and glaze. Place on a baking sheet and bake in the oven at 200°C (400°F) mark 6 for about 30 minutes.
6. Cool on a wire rack, then chill for 1-2 hours. Serve sliced.
SERVES 12-15

ORIENTAL SALAD

2 heads Chinese leaves, total weight about 2 kg (4½ lb),
  roughly chopped
450 g (1 lb) beansprouts
4 medium red peppers, seeded and finely shredded
300 ml (½ pint) vegetable oil
90 ml (6 tbsp) soy sauce
10 ml (2 tsp) thin honey or soft brown sugar
30 ml (2 tbsp) white wine vinegar
salt and pepper
100 g (4 oz) unsalted peanuts

1. Mix together the Chinese leaves, beansprouts and peppers in a large bowl.
2. Place all the remaining ingredients, except the peanuts, in a bowl or screw-topped jar and whisk or shake together until well blended.
3. To serve, add the peanuts and dressing to the salad and toss well.
SERVES 25

PARTY COLESLAW

1.5 kg (3 lb) white cabbage, finely shredded
6 celery sticks, trimmed and sliced
450 g (1 lb) carrots, peeled and grated
1 medium onion, skinned and chopped
75 g (3 oz) seedless raisins
120 ml (4 fl oz) soured cream
15 ml (1 tbsp) lemon juice
150 ml (¼ pint) Mayonnaise (see page 254)
salt and pepper

1. Mix together the cabbage, celery, carrots, onion and raisins in a large bowl.
2. Blend the soured cream with the lemon juice, Mayonnaise and seasoning. Pour over the salad and mix well.
SERVES 25

FENNEL AND RADICCHIO SALAD

2 large iceberg lettuces, shredded
2 medium heads of radicchio or 450 g (1 lb) red
    cabbage, shredded
2 medium onions, skinned and sliced
1 fennel bulb, trimmed and finely chopped
150 ml (¼ pint) sunflower oil
50 ml (2 fl oz) red wine vinegar
15 ml (1 level tbsp) whole grain mustard
salt and pepper

1. Mix together the lettuces, radicchio, onions and fennel in a large bowl.
2. Place the oil, vinegar, mustard and seasoning in a bowl or screw-topped jar and whisk or shake together until well blended.
3. Stir the dressing into the salad and toss well.
SERVES 25

GREEN SALAD WITH CROÛTONS

8 cos or large Webb's lettuces, torn into bite-sized pieces
4 bunches watercress, washed and trimmed
4 cucumbers, chopped
4 medium peppers, seeded and chopped
3 celery heads, trimmed and chopped
45-60 ml (3-4 tbsp) vegetable oil
4 slices of bread, crusts removed and cut into 1 cm
    (½ inch) cubes
125 g (4 oz) blue cheese, crumbled
900 ml (1½ pints) French Dressing (see page 255)
chopped fresh parsley, to garnish

1. Mix together the lettuces, watercress, cucumbers, peppers and celery in a large bowl.
2. Heat the oil in a frying pan, add the bread and fry until crisp and golden brown. Drain the croûtons on absorbent kitchen paper.
3. Add the blue cheese to the dressing, pour over the salad and toss well.
4. Sprinkle over the croûtons and garnish with parsley just before serving.
SERVES 50

EXOTIC FRUIT SALAD

1 medium pineapple, skin removed and cut into 1 cm
    (½ inch) cubes
1 mango, peeled and sliced
1 papaya, peeled and sliced
3 nectarines, sliced
100 g (4 oz) black or green grapes, halved and seeded
1 Ogen melon, halved and seeded
juice of 3 large oranges
juice of 1 lemon
 45 ml (3 tbsp) orange-flavoured liqueur
fresh mint sprigs, to decorate

1. Mix together the pineapple, mango, papaya, nectarines and grapes in a large bowl.
2. Scoop out the melon flesh with a melon baller and add to the bowl, then scrape out the remaining flesh, chop and add to the fruit.
3. Mix together the orange juice, lemon juice and liqueur. Pour over the fruit, cover and chill in the refrigerator for 2-3 hours. Decorate with mint before serving.
SERVES 10

NOTE: The salad can be kept in a cool place, not necessarily the refrigerator, for 3-4 hours after chilling, before serving.

WINES AND LIQUEURS

The range of wines on offer today is wide in choice and high in quality, thanks to a dramatic improvement in viticulture and winemaking. It has never been easier, or more worthwhile, to experiment with wines from around the world in combination with new or classic dishes.

Wines vary according to the varieties of grape used; where and how they are grown; how the wines are made and aged; and according to the weather pattern of each year. Not only can wines from the same grape varieties grown in different countries be completely different from each other, but the same wine from the same vineyard may vary from vintage to vintage, too.

Wine is fermented grape juice. The fermentation turns grape sugar into alcohol. The amount of alcohol in wine may vary from as little as 5 or 6 per cent by volume (the amount is usually shown on labels) to 16 per cent. In wines such as port and madeira, additional alcohol is added to arrest fermentation and preserve more of the wine's natural sweetness. These are fortified wines, with alcoholic strengths from 15.5 to 22 per cent.

WHAT'S ON THE LABEL

Wine labels provide the consumer with legally approved information about the wine in the bottle. In English-speaking wine-producing countries like America or Australia, back labels, too, can be a useful source of information, and will often contain a tasting indication.

FRANCE: France's best wine-producing regions are given *Appellations d'Origine Contrôlée*. An *Appellation d'Origine Contrôlée* (A.O.C.) is a guarantee of origin, of production method, of grape varieties used and of harvest yields, but not of quality itself. A.O.C. may apply to one small vineyard or to an extensive district. The system varies in importance and complexity from region to region. In Burgundy, for example, the very finest grand cru vineyards benefit from their own A.O.C.s, while in Bordeaux the A.O.C. system is a cruder one based on commune only. The finest

vineyards in Bordeaux are distinguished by the name of the château and its standing in the 1855 'classed growth' classification, rather than by A.O.C. Wine regions without the quality and traditions required for an A.O.C. will be ranked as *Vins Délimités de Qualité Supérieure* (V.D.Q.S.) or as *Vins de Pays*. Anything else can only be described as *Vin de Table*.

GERMANY: German wine law is very different from French. It is based on the ripeness of the grapes at harvest time and a fairly comprehensive system of quality-testing by analysis and tasting. Wine from grapes ripe enough to need no additional sugar in order to produce satisfactory alcohol levels is known as *Qualitätswein mit Prädikat* (Q.m.P.): the *Prädikats* are, in ascending order of richness, *Kabinett, Spätlese, Auslese, Beerenauslese, Eiswein* and *Trockenbeerenauslese*. Wine from specified regions that may have had sugar added to it to increase its alcohol level is known as *Qualitätswein bestimmter Anbaugebiete* (Q.b.A.).

All *Qualitätswein* is officially checked, tested and tasted. The label will show the wine-producing region and either a *Bereich* (district) or a town or parish name (suffixed -er) followed by a vineyard name. Unfortunately, consumers without a reference book or detailed knowledge have no way of telling whether the vineyard name is that of an *Einzellage* (individual vineyard) or of a *Grosslage* (name covering a group of vineyards). *Einzellage* wines are the best. The name of the grape variety may also appear on the label. The pre-eminent grape is Riesling. The lowliest wine is simply described as *Deutscher Tafelwein;* while *Deutscher Landwein,* the German equivalent of France's *Vin de Pays,* falls between *Tafelwein* and Q.b.A. in quality.

ITALY: The would-be equivalent of the French A.O.C. is the *Denominazione di Origine Controllata* (D.O.C.), but D.O.C.s have been awarded to areas whose wines are of only local interest, and some of the best wines do not qualify for D.O.C. A higher category, *Denominazione di Origine Controllata e Garantita* (D.O.C.G.) is restricted to a few better quality zones in Italy. Some of the best Italian wines are, legally, no more than *Vini da Tavola*. This paradoxical situation has arisen because Italy's D.O.C. and D.O.C.G. regulations are based on tradition, and many of the best wines are innovative ones that break with tradition. Labelling and price, however, will leave you in no doubt as to which those innovative wines are. *Classico* means the wine comes from the central, and usually best, part of the region. *Riserva* means the wine has been aged for a statutory period.

SPAIN: The Spanish system *(Denominación de Origen)* like the Italian, delimits many areas that, at present, are of no more than local interest. *Con crianza, Reserva* and *Gran reserva* are terms that indicate wood-ageing of wines, and the last two should also indicate better quality base wine, and bottle ageing before release. *Vinos de la Tierra* indicate Spain's 'country wines'.

PORTUGAL: Portugal's equivalent of France's A.O.C. regions are now known as *Denominações de Origem Controlada*. Many of the best wines appear under the traditional Portuguese term *Garrafeira*, which indicates a wine of good quality given long bottle ageing.

CALIFORNIA: The most important information on the label of California wine is still the producer's name and grape type, but a system of Approved Viticultural Areas (A.V.A.) is in place and A.V.A. names may be increasingly used in future.

AGEING WINE

Most wine is sold when it is ready to drink. But fine wines need bottle age, which may vary from 5 to 20 or more years for great Bordeaux, Hermitage, or vintage port. Your wine merchant's list, or supermarket rack label should advise about the quality and maturity of vintage wines. All but the finest white wines, and all cheap reds, should be drunk as young as possible. Any wine priced at less than £4 per bottle should not be cellared.

HOW TO SERVE WINE

All white wines should be served chilled, dry whites at 9-13°C (48-55°F), sweet and sparkling ones at 5-8°C (41-46°F).

The lighter and younger red wine is, the cooler it should be served. Beaujolais, Loire reds and *Vins de Pays* can be as cool as 13°C (55°F), meaty reds and classic red wines at 16-19°C (61-66°F). Wine temperature should be regulated by placing the wine in a refrigerator or warm room sufficiently in advance of use.

HOW TO STORE WINE

All bottled wine needs is to be kept lying on its side in a cool, dark, draught-free place with the minimum of vibration and no exposure to sudden changes in temperature. A cellar with a steady temperature of 11°C (52°F) is ideal, but a dark situation anywhere with a constant temperature between 8°C (46°F) and 20°C (68°F) will serve.

WINE WITH FOOD

The classically accepted partnerships are:
- with oysters: Chablis or dry Champagne
- with soup: dry sherry or dry madeira
- with fish: dry white wines or dry Champagne
- with roasts or game: red burgundy, full claret, Rioja, Barolo
- with sweets: Sauternes or other dessert wines
- with cheese: port, madeira or claret

However, there are no rules about wines to be served with food; it is a very personal matter. Helpful guidelines are light wines before fuller ones; dry before sweet; red before sweet white; lesser wines before fine ones. When one wine only is served throughout a meal it should be the wine most appropriate to the main course.

DRY WHITE WINES which stimulate the palate are good as an aperitif or with hors d'oeuvres or shellfish (Chablis, Muscadet, Vinho Verde, Champagne or other sparkling wines if dry).

DRY OR MEDIUM DRY WHITE WINES suit plainly cooked veal, chicken and fish dishes and drink well throughout the meal (white burgundy, Sancerre, Alsace, Vouvray, German Trocken and Halbtrocken Q.m.P. wines, Sauvignon Blanc and Chardonnay wines from Australia, New Zealand, California and South Africa).

DRY OR MEDIUM DRY ROSÉ OR BLUSH WINES make pleasant, easy-drinking partners for light summer salads and picnic dishes (Bordeaux Clairet, Tavel, Côtes de Provence, Rioja and Navarra Rosado, Californian Blush wines and South African Blanc de Noir wines).

LIGHTER BODIED RED WINE is pleasant with lamb chops and grilled meats in general, veal escalopes and some of the freshwater fish (light clarets, Beaujolais, Valpolicella, Bardolino).

FULLER RED WINE suits red meats, rich stews, casseroles, game dishes (St Emilion and Pomerol among the clarets; red burgundy, Côtes du Rhône, Australian Shiraz, Rioja).

SWEET WHITE WINES are drunk chilled, on their own or to go with certain sweet puddings and dessert fruits (Sauternes, Muscat de Beaumes de Venise or other French Muscat Vins Doux Naturelles, Moscatel de Valencia, Vouvray or Coteaux du Layon Doux or Moelleux wines, 'botrytised' wines from New Zealand, Australia, California and South Africa).

FRANCE

BORDEAUX: Produces a complete range of quality wines from light, quick-maturing reds to the greatest clarets, and from modest dry whites to some of the world's greatest sweet ones.

The great red wines are the classified growths (*crus classés*) of the Haut-Médoc: St Estèphe, Pauillac, Margaux and St Julien; and of Graves, Pessac-Léognan, St Emilion and Pomerol. Fine reds come from other parts of the Médoc and include the *crus bourgeois, grands bourgeois* and *grands bourgeois exceptionnels* of Haut-Médoc, lesser Graves, outlying districts of St

Emilion, Lalande-de-Pomerol and Fronsac. The reds of Bourg, Blaye and Bordeaux Supérieur, drunk at 3 to 5 years old can be good. Below that, stick to reliable shippers' blends.

The great dessert whites are the classified growths of Sauternes and Barsac. Unclassified wines of those appellations are also good, while those of Sainte Croix-du-Mont, Loupiac, Cérons and Premières Côtes de Bordeaux are sound. The fine dry whites are the classified growths of Graves.

BURGUNDY: The greatest reds come from the Côte de Nuits. *Grands crus* (sold under a vineyard name alone) need 10 years' maturity; *premiers crus* between 5 and 8; village wines (such as Gevrey-Chambertin or Vosne-Romanée) up to 5. The big wines from the Côte de Beaune are the *grands crus* prefixed Corton, and the reds of Pommard, slightly weightier than those of Volnay. Great whites are the *grands crus* of the Montrachet family and the *premiers crus* of Meursault.

CHABLIS: Distinctive white with a greenish glint, often big in character though very dry.

BEAUJOLAIS: Light, short-lived fruity reds. Drink *nouveau* or *primeur* by Easter of the year after the vintage. The *crus,* in increasing order of

Selection of French Wines

seriousness, are: Régnié, Chiroubles, Brouilly, Côte de Brouilly, St Amour, Fleurie, Juliénas, Chénas, Morgon, Moulin-à-Vent (keeps up to about 7 years).

CHAMPAGNE: Comes only from a carefully defined area around Reims, Epernay and in the Aube, and is the world's greatest sparkling wine. Vintages are declared in the best years.

LOIRE: Crisp dry whites from Sancerre and Pouilly Fumé. Similar but less well known are Quincy, Reuilly and Menetou-Salon. Vouvray may be dry, medium or sweet. Most are medium, while the greatest are sweet and capable of long ageing.

Other good sweet whites come from Coteaux du Layon, Bonnezeaux, and Quarts de Chaume. The best dry white of Anjou is Savennières. Good light, dry, quaffing wines are Muscadet and Gros Plant, the former at its best when bottled *sur lie*, ie off the lees produced during fermentation. Top reds are Bourgueil and Chinon, best drunk quite young and cool; the lighter Saumur Champigny; and, in propitious years only, red Sancerre. Rosé d'Anjou is pretty but commonplace, a summer refresher, while red Anjou Rouge can, at its best, match young Chinon and Bourgueil.

RHONE: Good value robust reds, some elegant whites and serious rosés. The great reds come from Côte-Rôtie, St. Joseph, Cornas, Hermitage and some estates of Châteauneuf-du-Pape. Also fine are Gigondas, Vacqueyras and Crozes-Hermitage. Compared with these long-lived wines, Côtes du Rhône-Villages, Lirac and the lesser Côtes du Rhône, or inexpensive Côtes du Ventoux and Côtes du Luberon, are now increasingly made for early drinking.

ALSACE: Fruity and fragrant white wines, named according to grape variety. Pinot Blanc, soft and nutty; Sylvaner, light, crisp and uncomplicated; Muscat, fragrant aperitif wine; Tokay-Pinot Gris, oily, smoky, rich and capable of accompanying meat; Gewürztraminer, powerful spicy flavour; Riesling, classically elegant. Late-harvested sweet wines are made in good years, and labelled *Vendange Tardive* or *Séléction de Grains Nobles*.

SOUTH-WEST FRANCE: Another area of improvement. Seek out Fronton, Buzet, Duras, Marmandais and Bergerac for light, Bordeaux-like wines; Madiran and Cahors for reds of more body; Monbazillac for sweet whites. Skilfully vinified *Vins de Pays* des Côtes de Gascogne deserve promotion for nettle-fresh whites and tasty reds, sometimes given new-oak treatment.

MIDI-PROVENCE, LANGUEDOC, ROUSSILLON: Three-quarters of French wine comes from here, and considerable efforts are being made to improve the better *Vins de Pays*. The best reds are soft, fruity and fresh for early drinking, though increasingly ambitious winemaking is bringing greater depth and texture to Midi reds; whites are, in general, clean and flavoursome. The best options are Coteaux d'Aix-en-Provence, Bandol, Vin de Pays des Sables du Golfe de Lyon, Minervois and Corbières.

GERMANY

RHEINGAU: This region produces the finest Rhine wines, or hocks, largely from Riesling grapes.

RHEINHESSEN AND RHEINPFALZ: Large producing regions, planted principally with Sylvaner and Muller-Thurgau, which produce many Liebfraumilch blends. The best wines of the Rheinhessen are those of the 'Rhein Terrace' near Nierstein and Oppenheim, while the Mittelhaardt area of the Rheinpfalz produces top quality Riesling.

BADEN: Straightforward, rather heavy or soft wines. Many successful German trockens come from here.

MOSEL-SAAR-RUWER: Mittel Mosel, the central area, produces the best of the German wines – more acid and zesty than Rhine wines. Bernkastel has the best wines. Piesport is also justifiably famous. Saar wines, including those of Wiltingen, Ayl and Ockfen, are brilliant and austere. Ruwer wines (Eitelsbach, Mertesdorf and Kasel) are fine and delicate.

ITALY

ALTO ADIGE: Wines with this D.O.C. can be of any of seventeen varieties. The best-known reds, Lago di Caldaro and Santa Maddalena, are soft and slightly almondy, while the best whites, based on Chardonnay, Müller-Thurgau, Silvaner, Gewürztraminer and Riesling, are light and delicate.

PIEDMONT: Big, full-bodied reds pre-eminently from the Nebbiolo grape. The classic wines are Barolo and the more amenable Barbaresco. The other important, but less distinguished, red grape is Barbera, grown best round Alba, Asti and Monferrato. Asti Spumante is a sweet and fruity sparkler, low in alcohol. The best white is Gavi, but it is unjustifiably expensive.

LOMBARDY: Some Nebbiolo-based red wines (Valtellina, Sassella, Grumello, Inferno) are comparable with the great Piedmontese reds.

VENETO: Light reds – notably Valpolicella and Bardolino – with slightly bitter tastes, best drunk young. Valpolicella's most memorable incarnations are as the strong, bitter-edged Amarone or as the sweet Recioto, both produced from semi-dried grapes. Raboso is powerful and needs age. Soave is famous but variable: often bland, but sometimes, well balanced and flowery.

FRIULI-VENEZIA GIULIA: The most successful varieties are Pinot Grigio, Sauvignon Blanc and Merlot; the most successful production area is Collio. In general, this region produces Italy's finest white wines.

TUSCANY: Most elegant of Italian reds – Chianti, the stronger and more fragrant Brunello di Montalcino, and Vino Nobile di Montepulciano. Tuscany is also the source of many of Italy's most innovative *Vini da Tavola,* sometimes based on the Chianti grape Sangiovese, sometimes on Cabernet Sauvignon, and sometimes on a blend between the two. These wines are often aged in small French casks to give a stylishly oaky finish.

UMBRIA: The classic white is Orvieto, traditionally semi-sweet, but now commonly dry. The best red is Rubesco di Torgiano, which is comparable with Chianti Classico.

MARCHES: Verdicchio dei Castelli di Jesi, a fresh, pale white, can be good, as can the Montepulciano-based red Rosso Conero, deeply flavoured and sturdy.

LAZIO: The only wine of note grown near Rome is Frascati which, at its best, is a softly nutty white. Most Frascati, however, is dull, industrial wine.

SICILY: This island has made great strides in recent years, and now offers a fine range of red and white table wines, often sold under brand names. Look out for Regaleali, Corvo, Donna Fugata and Terre di Ginestra among others.

SARDINIA: Cannonau, a full-flavoured red, and Vermentino, an aniseedy white, are Sardinia's most distinctive contributions.

SPAIN

Rioja and Penedés are the main regions producing quality wines. Other medium or full bodied reds include those of Navarra (Chivite, Ochoa), Valladolid (Vega Sicilia, Pesquera and Protos) and Jumilla. Rueda now produces fresh young whites. Mature Spanish table wines of high quality often have a characteristic vanilla flavour derived from storage in oak, though some fresh and fruity whites are now also being made for quicker consumption. Cava sparkling wines are made by the champagne method.

PORTUGAL

An under-rated producer. Solid reds and fruity dry whites come from the Dão and Bairrada regions. The Douro valley, home of port, produces some of Portugal's best table wines (Barca Velha, Quinta do Côtto), while in the south, the Alentejo is an exciting region to watch for both reds and whites. Top producers of class blends include José Maria da Fonseca Successores and JP Vinhos. Mateus rosé is a popular carbonated semi-sweet rosé. Vinho verde is made from barely-ripe grapes to give a 'green' taste.

CALIFORNIA

The wine industry has been much modernised in the past decade, and has taken the world by storm with good quality wines. Improvements continue to be made. The most successful varieties to date are Cabernet Sauvignon, the native Zinfandel, Chardonnay (outstanding) and Sauvignon (or Fumé) Blanc. Top names include Mondavi, Ridge, Chalone, Caymus, Bonny Doon, Heitz, Newton, Stag's Leap and Saintsbury.

AUSTRALIA

Wines to rival California's, and generally at more attractive prices. Labels are very informative and helpful. Prizes in shows for once mean a great deal. Reds tend to be powerful, broad and fat flavoured, particularly those made from Shiraz grapes. Cabernet Sauvignons are rich and blackcurrant. Watch out for wines from Penfolds, Wynns, Knappstein, Seaview, Cape Mentelle and Taltarni, though reliability is an Australian ace and many other names can be good, too. Among whites, Chardonnays and Semillon wines show great character, and are generally full-bodied in style, often with oaky flavours. Australia's Semillon ages better than its Chardonnay: look out for Lindemans, Rothbury and Tyrell. There are also gorgeous deep brown, sweet Muscat wines from Victoria.

NEW ZEALAND

The most rapidly advancing wine industry in the world, using classic varieties with modern and experimental methods to produce distinctive, characterful wines. White wines are more successful than reds, with Sauvignon Blanc (especially from the Marlborough area) and Chardonnay often being outstanding. Leading producers include Montana, Hunters, Corban's Stoneleigh Vineyard, Vidal, Babich and the celebrated Cloudy Bay.

CENTRAL EUROPE AND BALKANS

Wines from these countries offer great value for money, with quality tending generally to improve. Save in Greece, labelling follows the common pattern of matching place name with grape variety. Austrian wines are more full bodied, and lighter in alcohol, than German wines. Try examples of the peppery native white Grüner Veltliner. Austria also produces superb and inexpensive dessert wines, from villages such as Rust in the Neusiedlersee. Hungary provides lively whites and some sturdy, warming reds, and also the famous Tokay sweet wine, which resembles an oxidized Sauternes. Romanian and Yugoslavian wines are sound, good value, but undistinguished. Bulgaria has been the real success story of Eastern Europe, with reliable, well-aged and inexpensive reds based on Cabernet Sauvignon, Merlot, and the native varieties Mavrud and Gamza. White wines have lagged behind reds, but Chardonnay and Sauvignon Blanc are increasingly impressive.

Greece does not yet have the technology to produce top-quality wines in its hot climate, but the resin-flavoured Retsina is timeless and justifiably popular, while a few reds, like Boutari's Grande Reserve, achieve a rugged grandeur. Cyprus has improving standards and reliable brands of robust cheap red. Commandaria is a bargain dessert wine.

SOUTH AFRICA

South Africa has much to offer in terms of inexpensive whites and reds from the KWV, as well as an increasingly large and varied range of estate wines.

The country's best varieties are Cabernet Sauvignon, Merlot and Bordeaux-style blends for reds, and Sauvignon Blanc and Chardonnay for whites. Pinotage, a South African cross of Pinot Noir and Cinsaut, can also be very good. Look out for some of the excellent estate wines from Meerlust, Delheim, Kanonkop and Vriesenhof for reds, and Klein Constantia, Danie de Wet, Neil Ellis (a merchant/blender) and Backsberg for white wines.

OTHER WINE-PRODUCING COUNTRIES

English wines are produced on a small scale, but are highly priced for their quality. Swiss wines are sound, but expensive and little seen. North African reds are full-bodied and robust. Argentina and Chile both produce excellent Cabernet Sauvignon wines, and Argentina some

successful Chardonnay. Wines may also be found from Mexico, Israel, Turkey, Egypt, Lebanon (Château Musar is excellent), the Soviet Union and China.

SPARKLING WINES

Many sparkling wines are made by the champagne method, and state this on the label, though only a few of these approach the quality (and price) of Champagne itself. The other main method for producing sparkling wines is called the *cuve close* (or sealed tank). Asti Spumante is made by a process that combines the two methods. Most German Sekt (sparkling wine) is made by the *cuve close* method.

FORTIFIED WINES

The world's three greatest fortified wines are port (from Portugal's Douro valley), madeira (from the Atlantic island of Madeira) and sherry (from the Jerez region in Spain's Andalusia). Other fortified wines include Sicily's Marsala, Portugal's Moscatel de Setúbal, *Vins Doux Naturelles* from France, fine port-style wines from South Africa, Australia and California, and Liqueur Muscats from Australia.

PORT

Port is made from grapes grown in the upper valley of the Douro river and is shipped from Oporto. Port styles include the young and fruity *Ruby;* the lighter, nuttier *Tawny; Vintage Character,* a premium ruby; *Late Bottled Vintage,* a fruity port from a single year; *Crusted Port,* a blend of young ports from different years, bottled early and matured in bottle until a 'crust' (sediment) has formed; *10, 20, 30 and Over 40 Years Old* – all classic tawnies, matured for long years in wood; *Colheita Port,* a single-vintage tawny; and finally *Vintage Port,* fine port from a single year and perhaps a single *quinta* (farm), matured for long years in bottle.

Vintage port will always throw a crust, and therefore should always be decanted.

SHERRY

Sherry comes from the vineyards around the towns of Jerez de la Frontera, Puerto de Santa Maria and Sanlúcar de Barrameda. The third of these towns is the source of the special type of fino known as manzanilla (see overleaf).

Sherry is a blend of wines, matured by what is called the *solera* system, to ensure a continuing supply of wines of the same style and quality.

There are three main types of sherry.

FINO is a very dry, very pale and very tangy sherry, aged in cask under a special film of yeast called *flor*. It is best drunk chilled and fresh, and accompanies food well. Manzanilla is a soft style of fino from the seaside town of Sanlúcar.

AMONTILLADO should be a dry, aged fino that has lost its *flor* and its fresh yeasty quality and acquired a round, mellow yet slightly austere nuttiness instead. Most commercial Amontillados, however, are blended and sweetened with other, lesser sherries.

OLOROSO is a dry, dark sherry aged in cask without the cultivation of *flor*. Pure dry oloroso is fragrant and austere, but most are sweetened before export to produce 'cream' sherry. Pale cream, however, is a sweet blend partially based on fino.

MADEIRA

Madeira's distinguishing feature is the fact that it is 'cooked' in order to provide its characteristic burnt tang. For the finest, vintage madeiras, the 'cooking' takes place naturally, in casks placed in hot attics; for other madeiras, however, it takes place in sealed heated vats. Most madeira is still produced from the Tinta Negra Mole grape variety, and blended in order to correspond to the style established for the four classic grape varieties:

SERCIAL is the driest and lightest wine, a suitable aperitif, slightly chilled.

VERDELHO is medium dry, darker in colour.

BUAL is velvety, medium-sweet, deep golden-brown.

MALMSEY is the sweetest Madeira, rich and honeyed.

APERITIFS

Patent aperitifs are either wine or spirit based. French and Italian vermouths are among the most widely used wine-based aperitifs. Other aperitifs, generically called bitters, are made from distilled spirits distinctively flavoured with roots, herbs and barks.

VERMOUTHS

Dry, medium or sweet, they may be served chilled and straight or with ice cubes and/or soda water and a slice of lemon; or to make mixed drinks (dry white with gin for a dry Martini; sweet red with whisky for a Manhattan, for instance). Chambéry is the most subtle, delightful vermouth of France and has its own *appellation d'origine*. Made from light, dry wine of the southern Alps, its pink version, Chambéryzette, is flavoured with wild strawberries. Noilly Prat is the other bone-dry, pale, best-known French vermouth.

Cinzano, Martini and Gancia are famous Italian vermouth names. They can be red (sweet), white (dry) or *bianco* (meaning white, but on the sweet side of medium).

BITTERS

Campari, the best-known Italian bitters, is usually mixed with soda, as is the French Amer Picon. Campari mixed with red Italian vermouth, a splash of soda and a slice of lemon makes the popular drink called Americano. Suze is a very bitter, yellow, gentian-based aperitif, good as a restorative. Fernet-Branca and Underberg are ferocious looking-and-tasting medicinal bitters. Anis drinks – Pernod, Pastis, Ricard, Ouzo – are aniseed/liquorice-flavoured liquors that turn milky when water is added.

LIQUEURS

Liqueurs are *digestifs,* and so ideal as after-dinner drinks, though increasingly used in cooking sweet dishes, too. Alcohol, an essential ingredient in all liqueurs, may be in the form of grape spirit, grain spirit or fruit spirit. Sweetening is added and the variety of flavourings come from herbs, spices or fruit. Brandy is a spirit distilled from wine and is included here because of its popularity as an after-dinner drink. The list shows the more familiar liqueurs in this country, although many fascinating local ones can be discovered during travel to regions of their origin.

ADVOCAAT: A Dutch liqueur, thick and creamy, made from fresh egg yolks and brandy.

AMARETTO DI SARONNO: Italian fruit liqueur, flavoured with apricot kernels and almonds.

ANISETTE: A colourless aniseed-flavoured liqueur that comes from France, Spain and Italy. Marie Brizard, from Bordeaux, is the most famous.

AQUAVIT: Scandinavian national drink, made from grain, rye or potato and variously flavoured with caraway, aniseed or dill. Always served iced, but really best with open sandwiches or piquant snacks.

B AND B: Drier version of Bénédictine, in which the liqueur is ready-mixed half and half with brandy.

BAILEY'S IRISH CREAM: A low-strength liqueur of chocolate-flavoured whiskey and double cream.

BENEDICTINE: The most renowned and popular of herb-based liqueurs.

BOURBON WHISKEY: More full flavoured, robust and fruity than Scotch, but with less finesse.

BRANDY: A spirit distilled from wine, and the most famous brandy in the world is that produced at Cognac on the River Charente. Cognac's closest rival is the less subtle, earthier and more fiery Armagnac, produced in Gascony.

Fruit brandies are generally misnamed. The terms 'Cherry Brandy', 'Apricot Brandy', 'Peach Brandy' and so on are established names for sweet liqueurs made respectively from the fruits mentioned.

CALVADOS: Also called applejack, is an apple brandy that takes its name from Calvados, the centre of the Normandy apple orchards.

CASSIS: A blackcurrant-flavoured liqueur from Dijon, often added to dry white wine for a pretty, cooling summer drink called Kir.

CHARTREUSE: One of the most famous herb-flavour liqueurs originally compounded by the Carthusian monks at Chartreuse, near Grenoble, and still produced under their supervision. The yellow type is sweeter, the green higher in alcohol.

COINTREAU: A popular orange liqueur.

CRÈME DE CAÇAO: A very sweet dark cocoa-flavoured liqueur from the West Indies, sometimes drunk through a layer of cream.

CRÈME DE MENTHE: Green in colour with a pronounced peppermint flavour.

CURAÇAO: The original orange curaçao was made from citrus fruit from the island of Curaçao but the term is now generic and is used for various orange-flavoured liqueurs.

DRAMBUIE: A Scottish liqueur, golden coloured, with the flavour of whisky and heather honey.

EAUX-DE-VIE: These are dry, colourless fruit spirits. The best known are *kirsch* (cherry); *framboise* (raspberry); *fraise* (strawberry); *myrtille* (bilberry); *mirabelle* (golden plum); *quetsch* (Switzen plum); *prunelle* (sloe); *poire Williams* (pear); *houx* (holly berry); *coing* (quince); *sorbe alisier* (rowanberry); and in Germany and Switzerland *Enzian* (gentian).

GALLIANO: A golden spicy herbal Italian liqueur, made famous when combined with vodka and orange juice for Harvey Wallbanger cocktails.

GLAYVA: Scottish, whisky-based liqueur flavoured with honey and herbs.

GOLDWASSER: Aniseed-flavoured liqueur from Germany and Poland; colourless, with little gold particles in it.

GRAND MARNIER: The best known French brand of orange-flavoured liqueur.

IRISH MIST: Irish whiskey and heather honey.

IZARRA: Green and yellow herbal liqueurs based on armagnac and with a bouquet of mimosa honey, from the Basque country.

KAHLÚA: A Mexican coffee liqueur, quite different from Tia Maria.

KIRSCH: is an *eau de vie* based on cherries in which the crushed kernels are included with the fruit.

KUMMEL: A caraway-flavoured, colourless liqueur of Dutch origin.

MALIBU: A mixture of coconut and white rum.

MANDARINE NAPOLEON: Belgian proprietary liqueur, of tangerines macerated in aged Cognac.

MARASCHINO: A bitter-sweet liqueur made with maraschino cherries and their crushed kernels. It originated in Yugoslavia.

MARC: A spirit distilled from the leftover pips, skins and stalks produced by the pressing of grapes. Known as Grappa in Italy.

PARFAIT AMOUR: An exotic, sweet citrus-and-rosewater based liqueur made in several colours, mainly violet. It is scented and slightly spiced.

PISCO: A South American marc made from muscat grapes, aged in clay jars and traditionally said to have the taste and aroma of beeswax.

ROYAL MINT CHOCOLATE: A popular modern liqueur with a subtle flavour blend.

SAMBUCA: Italian liqueur tasting of elderberry and liquorice. It is traditional to float coffee beans on each glass and set fire to the liqueur for a few minutes to roast them, and release their flavour.

SLIVOVITZ: is a colourless, dry plum brandy, notably from the Balkans.

SLOE GIN: Rich, ruby red liqueur made by steeping sloe berries in gin. The traditional 'stirrup cup' of Old England.

SOUTHERN COMFORT: The most popular of America's indigenous liqueurs – a whiskey flavoured with peaches, oranges and herbs.

STREGA: An aromatic herb liqueur made from a centuries-old Italian recipe combining the flavours of some 70 herbs and barks.

TIA MARIA: A Jamaican rum liqueur, based on coffee extracts and local spices.

TRIPLE SEC: A strong white curaçao.

VAN DER HUM: South African liqueur, tasting of the *naartjie*, or tangerine.

(LA) VIEILLE CURE: A very potent liqueur made from some 40 aromatic plants and roots macerated in Armagnac and Cognac.

COCKTAILS, CUPS AND PUNCHES

This chapter contains a selection of the many party drink mixes which are based on spirits, sherry, port, wine, cider and ale. For non-alcoholic squashes and punches see pages 538-40.

COCKTAILS

Cocktails are alcoholic drinks based on mixtures of different wines, spirits and liqueurs, sometimes with the addition of fruit juice, coffee or cream. They are drunk on their own, never with meals. Although mixing cocktails is relatively simple in itself, there are a number of basic rules.

All cocktails are served cold and plenty of ice is needed to chill them. Crushed ice is more efficient at cooling than large blocks, so make your ice in a tray with fairly small sections and crush it, either with a special ice crusher or wrap in a tea towel and crush with a kitchen mallet or rolling pin. The ice should not melt in the drink, but remain in the base to cool it. To ensure it is really cold, use straight from the freezer.

Measuring is critical when making cocktails to get the right balance of ingredients. The classic cocktail measure – which you can buy – is 40 ml (1½ fl oz) but as long as you use a consistent measure for each ingredient you can use a small glass or something similar. Ideally, cocktails are mixed in a special shaker which incorporates a strainer, so that when it is poured out the ice which has chilled the drink remains behind.

They can also be mixed in a jug, in which case you will need a strainer, preferably the special bar type known as a hawthorne. In addition, you will need a long-handled spoon for stirring and measuring small quantities of flavourings, a corkscrew bottle opener, sharp fruit knife, citrus squeezer and chopping board.

Cocktails are made either by shaking, which produces a really cold but cloudy drink or by stirring which keeps it clear. Stir fizzy liquids lightly or they will quickly go flat. Some cocktails which include fresh fruit need to be puréed in a blender or food processor.

Classic cocktail glasses are stemmed with a straight-sided bowl that is considerably wider at the top than the base. They have a capacity of about 75-100 ml (4 fl oz) and are used for short drinks.

Long cocktails are served in tall, straight-sided glasses called highballs or Collins glasses. They have a capacity of about 200-300 ml (7-10 fl oz). Other glasses used for cocktails include whisky tumblers, wine glasses and champagne saucers and flutes. Glasses should be chilled in the refrigerator for at least an hour before cocktails are poured into them. If you want to frost the rims for a decorative effect, dip them first into egg white and then into caster sugar before chilling.

Part of the charm of cocktails is their range of colours and the garnishes used in them. Depending on the type of drink, you can garnish it with maraschino cherries, little cocktail onions, olives, fresh fruit – especially citrus fruit – mint or cucumber. Spices such as nutmeg are sometimes sprinkled on to cream cocktails.

Cocktails are often drunk through a straw and some cocktail glasses incorporate built-in glass straws. You can use wooden or coloured plastic cocktail sticks to spear some of the garnishes and give a decorative finishing touch with a small, coloured paper parasol.

Each of the cocktail recipes in this section will serve one person. Multiply the quantities according to the number of people you are intending to serving.

TOM COLLINS

2-3 ice cubes
juice of 1 lemon
15 ml (1 level tbsp) sugar
1 measure whisky
1 orange slice
soda water

1. In a shaker, mix the ice cubes, lemon juice, sugar and whisky until a frost forms.
2. Pour into a glass and add a slice of orange.
3. Top with soda water and stir before serving.

DRY MARTINI

2 parts French vermouth
1 part dry gin
crushed ice
1 stuffed olive or lemon rind curl

1. Shake the vermouth and gin together with some crushed ice in a shaker.
2. Pour into a glass and float a stuffed olive, or a curl of lemon rind on top. The proportions of a martini are a matter of personal taste; some people prefer 2 parts of gin to 1 of vermouth, others equal parts of gin and vermouth.

VARIATION:
Follow the recipe above, but use sweet vermouth and decorate with a cocktail cherry.

BRANDY ALEXANDER

1 part brandy
1 part crème de caçao
1 part double cream
a pinch of grated nutmeg

1. Mix together the brandy, crème de caçao and cream and shake well.
2. Dust with a little nutmeg and serve.

VARIATION
For a Gin Alexander, replace the brandy with gin.

BLACK RUSSIAN

2-3 ice cubes
2 parts vodka
1 part coffee-flavoured liqueur

1. Put the ice cubes in a tumbler and pour over the vodka and coffee-flavoured liqueur.

VARIATION
For a White Russian float cream on the top.

RUSTY NAIL

2-3 ice cubes
2 parts whisky
1 part Drambuie

1. Put the ice cubes in a tumbler and pour over the whisky and Drambuie.
2. Stir and serve on the rocks.

WHISKY SOUR

juice of ½ a lemon
5 ml (1 level tsp) sugar
1 measure rye whisky
crushed ice

1. Mix together the lemon juice, sugar and whisky and shake well with the ice.
2. Serve in a whisky tumbler.

PINK GIN

2-3 drops Angostura bitters
1 measure gin
2-3 measures iced water

1. Put the bitters into a glass and turn it until the sides are well coated.
2. Add gin and top up with iced water to taste.

BLOODY MARY

1 measure vodka
2 measures tomato juice
dash of Worcestershire sauce or Tabasco sauce
squeeze of lemon juice
crushed ice

1. Shake all the ingredients with the crushed ice in a shaker.
2. Strain into a cocktail glass.

SCREWDRIVER

2-3 ice cubes
1 measure vodka
juice of 1 orange
1 orange slice, to decorate

1. Put the ice cubes into a tall glass and pour in the vodka and orange juice.
2. Stir lightly and decorate with a slice of orange.

LEFT: Black Russians. RIGHT: Brandy Alexander

HARVEY WALLBANGER

2 parts vodka
6 parts orange juice
crushed ice
1 part Galliano

1. Pour the vodka and orange juice over the ice in a tall glass.
2. Float the Galliano on top.

DAIQUIRI

juice of ½ a lime or ¼ of a lemon
5 ml (1 level tsp) sugar
1 measure white rum
crushed ice
extra fruit juice and caster sugar for frosting

1. Mix the fruit juice, sugar and rum and shake well with the crushed ice in a shaker.
2. Dip the edges of the glass in a little more fruit juice and then into caster sugar to frost the rim before filling.

PINA COLADA

3 parts white rum
4 parts pineapple juice
2 parts coconut cream
crushed ice
1 pineapple slice and 1 cherry, to decorate

1. Blend together the rum, pineapple juice, coconut cream and crushed ice.
2. Pour into a large goblet or a hollowed-out pineapple half.
3. Decorate with a slice of pineapple and a cherry. Serve with straws.

MARGARITA

lemon juice
salt
4 parts tequila
1 part curaçao
1 part lemon or lime juice

1. Dip the edges of a chilled glass into lemon juice and then salt.
2. In a shaker, mix the tequila, curaçao and lemon juice.
3. Strain into the chilled glass and serve.

TEQUILA SUNRISE

5 ml (1 tsp) grenadine
1 part tequila
2 parts orange juice
ice cubes

1. Carefully pour the grenadine into the bottom of a chilled glass.
2. Stir the tequila and orange juice with ice in a mixing glass and strain into the glass so that it splashes on to the grenadine.
3. Add ice cubes and serve.

BUCKS FIZZ

1 part fresh orange juice
2 parts champagne

1. Chill the ingredients.
2. Fill a champagne glass about one-third full with orange juice and top up with champagne.

BLACK VELVET

1 part Guinness
1 part champagne

1. Chill the ingredients.
2. Pour equal quantities of Guinness and champagne into beer tankards and serve.

CUPS AND PUNCHES

Cups and punches are subtle mixtures of wines and/or spirits flavoured with fruit or spices. They
may be served hot or cold and are usually made in large quantities for parties.
When serving cups and punches, allow 200 ml (7 fl oz) per glass.

MIDSUMMER NIGHT'S DREAM

1 bottle Riesling
1 bottle Beaujolais
750 ml (25 fl oz) lemonade
50 ml (2 fl oz) orange-flavoured liqueur
1 dessert apple, cored and sliced
melon pieces
orange slices, quartered
a few strawberries
crushed ice
about 30 ml (2 tbsp) sugar

1. Pour the wines, lemonade and the orange-flavoured liqueur over the fruit and ice in a bowl. Chill and add sugar to taste.
2. Serve ice-cold.
MAKES ABOUT 2.3 LITRES (4 PINTS)

WHITE WINE CUP

crushed ice
3 bottles white wine
¾ bottle dry sherry
60 ml (4 tbsp) orange-flavoured liqueur
1 litre (1¾ pints) tonic water
cucumber slices, apple slices and borage sprigs

1. Mix all the ingredients together and chill before serving. Decorate with cucumber, apple slices and borage sprigs.
MAKES ABOUT 3.7 LITRES (6½ PINTS)

GLUHWEIN

600 ml (1 pint) red wine
75 g (3 oz) brown sugar
2 cinnamon sticks, each 5 cm (2 inches) long
1 lemon, stuck with cloves
150 ml (¼ pint) brandy

1. Put all the ingredients except the brandy in a saucepan, bring to simmering point, cover and simmer gently for 2-4 minutes.
2. Remove from the heat, add the brandy, strain and serve at once.
MAKES ABOUT 750 ML (1¼ PINTS)

BRANDY CIDER CUP

600 ml (1 pint) tea
50 g (2 oz) sugar
juice of 2 oranges
90-120 ml (6-8 tbsp) brandy
1 litre (1¾ pints) cider
1 lemon, thinly sliced

1. Infuse the tea for a few minutes and strain it on to the sugar in a bowl.
2. Cool and add the orange juice and brandy.
3. Just before serving, add the cider and decorate with the lemon slices.
MAKES ABOUT 2 LITRES (3½ PINTS)

KIR

4 parts dry white wine (Chablis or similar)
1 part crème de cassis

1. Thoroughly chill the wine before combining it with the cassis. Serve in a claret glass.

SLOE GIN

450 g (1 lb) sloes, stalks removed
75-100 g (3-4 oz) sugar
almond flavouring
1 bottle gin

1. Wash the sloes, prick all over with a darning needle and put into a screw-topped bottle.

2. Add the sugar and a few drops of almond flavouring. Fill up the bottle with gin, screw down tightly and leave in a dark place for 3 months, shaking occasionally.
3. At the end of this time, open the bottle and strain the liquor through muslin until clear.
4. Re-bottle and leave until required.

CLARET CUP

25 g (1 oz) sugar
thinly pared rind and juice of 1 lemon and 2 oranges
2 bottles claret
1 litre (1¾ pints) tonic water
few thin cucumber slices
borage sprigs (optional)

1. Put the sugar and the lemon and orange rinds in a saucepan and simmer for about 10 minutes.
2. Cool and add the strained juice of the lemon and oranges, together with the claret. Chill well.
3. Just before serving, add the tonic water, cucumber and borage, if using.
MAKES ABOUT 2.3 LITRES (4 PINTS)

DR JOHNSON'S CHOICE

1 bottle red wine
12 sugar cubes
6 cloves
150 ml (¼ pint) orange-flavoured liqueur
150 ml (¼ pint) brandy (optional)
freshly grated nutmeg

1. Heat the wine, sugar and cloves to near boiling point, then pour in 600 ml (1 pint) boiling water.
2. Pour in the orange-flavoured liqueur and the brandy, if using.
3. Pour into glasses and sprinkle with nutmeg.
MAKES ABOUT 1.7 LITRES (3 PINTS)

MULLED WINE

300 ml (½ pint) water
100 g (4 oz) sugar
4 cloves
1 cinnamon stick, 5 cm (2 inches) long
2 lemons, thinly sliced
1 bottle burgundy or claret
1 orange or lemon, thinly sliced, to decorate

1. Boil the water, sugar and spices together. Add the lemon slices, stir and leave to stand for 10 minutes.
2. Add the red wine, return to the heat and heat gently but do not boil.
3. Strain the wine into a bowl and serve hot, decorated with orange or lemon slices.
MAKES ABOUT 1.1 LITRES (2 PINTS)

JULGLOGG (CHRISTMAS WINE)

1 bottle aquavit or gin
2 bottles burgundy
75g (3 oz) seedless raisins
100 g (4 oz) sugar
15 ml (1 level tbsp) cardamom seeds (optional)
6 cloves
1 cinnamon stick, 5 cm (2 inches) long
small piece of lemon rind

1. Pour half the aquavit into a saucepan with the burgundy and add the raisins and sugar.
2. Tie the spices and lemon rind in muslin and add to the pan. Cover, bring very slowly to the boil and simmer for 30 minutes.
3. Add the remaining aquavit and remove from the heat. Take out the bag of spices just before serving and ignite the mixture with a match.
4. Serve in tumblers or punch glasses.
MAKES ABOUT 2.4 LITRES (4½ PINTS)

TEA, COFFEE AND SOFT DRINKS

There is now a wide range of teas and coffees to choose from. This section provides a guide to the different varieties and tells you how to prepare them for optimum flavour. Recipes for popular soft drinks are also included.

TEA

Tea was brought to Britain in the 17th Century although it had been drunk in China for many hundreds of years. It was a great luxury and very expensive. Ladies of grand houses would often keep the tea caddy under lock and key and the same tea leaves would be used for several brews. The custom of afternoon tea is thought to have started around 1840 by Anna, 7th Duchess of Bedford who wanted something to sustain her between lunch and dinner. The idea of afternoon tea was conceived around the same time as the Earl of Sandwich thought of putting a filling between two slices of bread!

The tea we enjoy today is made from the dried top leaf shoots of a type of camellia sinensis. Tea differs in taste and character depending on the soil, altitude and climatic conditions it is grown in. Although most of the tea we drink in Britain comes from India, Sri Lanka (Ceylon) and East Africa it is grown in approximately 25 countries. In recent years consumers have begun to take more interest in the tea they drink with many, many new varieties now on the market.

There are four main ways of producing tea:

BLACK TEA: The most popular type, sold in the UK. The leaves are fermented until they are dark brown and then dried.

GREEN TEA: The leaves are picked, withered on racks and steamed to stop oxidization and fermentation. This is the original tea and produces a weak brew, best drunk on its own or with lemon.

OOLONG TEA: After withering, the leaves are slightly crushed and half fermented before being dried. This produces a brown, delicately flavoured tea.

SMOKED TEA: These teas are dried over smoke giving them a distinctive flavour. They are produced in much smaller quantities than those described above.

Popular brand teas are a blend of between 15 to 40 different teas sold under a brand name. The best teas are those sold under their own name. The most common teas are:

ASSAM: Strong tea with a rich malty flavour.

CEYLON: Light, flavoursome tea with a slight lemony or astringent flavour.

DARJEELING: Indian tea with a delicate, 'grapey' taste, known as the champagne of teas.

EARL GREY: Usually a blend of China and Darjeeling tea, flavoured with citrus oil of bergamot.

ENGLISH BREAKFAST: Originally a fragrant blend of China teas, now usually a stronger blend of Ceylon and Assam tea, to be drunk with milk.

KEEMUM: Considered the best China tea available in the UK. It has an aromatic flavour strong enough to be drunk with milk.

LAPSANG SOUCHONG: China tea with a smoky aroma and taste.

OTHER TEAS:

FLAVOURED TEAS: These have flavours added from either fruit like passion fruit, herbs, such as sage or flowers like jasmine. These teas are a refreshing alternative to those drunk with milk. Jasmine tea, for example, is often enjoyed with

Chinese food. Make sure when buying these teas that the flavour added to them is not artificial, as these will often have an unpleasant taste and may contain added sugar.

HERBAL TEAS (OR TISANES): These don't contain any leaves from the tea plant but are made from the leaves of herbs or flowers. There are many of these on the market today as they are seen as more healthy than traditional tea. They are caffeine-free and drunk without milk.

Some herbal teas are said to have medicinal benefits. For example, camomile tea is believed to be good for soothing upset stomachs, coltsfoot for coughs and colds, whilst fennel tea is said to be good for relieving menstrual problems and helping stimulate the flow of milk in breast-feeding mothers. Tisanes can easily be made at home by drying the leaves, flowers or roots of a particular plant and then storing them in an airtight container until required.

DE-CAFFEINATED TEA: Although not a different blend this tea is treated to have the caffeine removed. These teas are becoming more popular and their flavour is improving.

MAKING TEA

- Tea should be bought in small quantities and stored in an airtight container to preserve the aroma and strength. Do not keep teas next to strong smelling foods as they will take on the flavour.
- When making tea in a pot, allow 5 ml (1 tsp) per person and 1 for the pot if there are more than three people.
- Leave Indian tea for 4-5 minutes to infuse in a pot; China tea needs only 2-3 minutes.
- Tea is calorie-free if drunk without milk or sugar and contains no artificial colouring or preservative.
- The average cup of tea contains about half the amount of caffeine that an average cup of coffee holds.

ICED TEA

1. Make tea in the usual way. Chill, then pour over the back of a spoon into a glass which has been half-filled with crushed ice.
2. Add sugar to taste and a slice of lemon to the glass.
3. Re-chill before serving.
SERVES 1

NOTE: Iced herbal teas (tisanes) are a refreshing summer drink. These can be made in the same way as Iced Tea using fresh or dried herbs. Camomile, hibiscus, lime, lemon verbena, peppermint and rosehip teas are all suitable for serving iced.

CINNAMON TEA

2 cloves
5 cm (2 inches) cinnamon stick
1.1 litres (2 pints) water
15 ml (3 tsp) tea
sugar to taste
50 ml (2 fl oz) orange juice
juice of 1 lemon

1. Place the cloves and cinnamon stick in a saucepan with the water. Bring to the boil.
2. Pour the boiling water over the tea and infuse for 4-5 minutes. Strain.
3. Add sugar to taste then stir in the orange and lemon juice. Serve hot.
SERVES 6

VARIATION: Serve with a cinnamon stick in each cup of tea.

SPECIAL CAMOMILE TEA

5 ml (1 tsp) dried camomile flowers
175 ml (6 fl oz) water
1 piece of orange rind
5 ml (1 tsp) honey

1. Boil the water then pour over the camomile flowers, orange rind and honey.
2. Stir well, then cover and leave to infuse for 8-10 minutes. Strain into a cup and serve hot, reheating if necessary.
SERVES 1

COFFEE

Coffee has been imported into the UK for three hundred years. It is made from the small, light green beans of the coffee tree. When ripe the fruit of the coffee tree is red and sweet and looks similar to a cherry. Inside each 'cherry' are two coffee beans. Once the ripe fruit has been picked, it is left to dry for 2-3 weeks. Once dried, the fruit is then crushed to extract the beans from the skins.

There are many different types of coffee but those with the finest flavour come from the tree known as *Coffea arabica*. These are the beans stocked by good coffee merchants. *Coffea robusta* has a coarser, poorer flavour and it is usually restricted to commercially prepared blends.

BUYING COFFEE

There are four main ways of buying coffee.

BEANS: It is possible to buy green coffee beans and roast them yourself, either in the oven, in a special electric roaster or in a heavy-based frying pan. The longer the coffee is roasted the darker and, usually, stronger it will become. If coffee is to be drunk with milk, a pale to medium roast is probably best. Dark roasted coffee is usually drunk black. Green beans keep indefinitely in a cool, dry place. Freshly roasted beans should be used within a few days or stored in the freezer.

READY GROUND: It is important to know how the coffee is going to be brewed when buying ground coffee (eg filter, espresso) as different grinds are needed for different machines (see opposite). After grinding, coffee should be used as soon as possible as it will loose flavour. The finer the grind, the quicker the flavour loss.

INSTANT COFFEE: This comes in powder and freeze-dried granules, the latter usually being more expensive but having more flavour. In Britain this is by far the most popular type of coffee drunk.

COFFEE ESSENCE: Usually mixed with chicory, coffee essence is best used in cooking or for making quick iced coffees.

TYPES OF COFFEE

There are many coffees to choose from and people often like to blend their own. The main types are:

BRAZILIAN: Smooth and mild in flavour with no bitterness or acidity.

COLUMBIAN: All varieties of Columbian coffee are rich in flavour.

COSTA RICAN: These high-grown coffees have a mild flavour with a fragrant aroma.

JAVA: A mature coffee from the East Indies with a subtle mellow flavour.

JAMAICAN: Mellow, sweet and aromatic. Jamaican beans should be medium-roasted to preserve their flavour.

KENYAN: Tart and aromatic coffee that blends well with other flavours.

MOCHA: The traditional Turkish coffee from Yemen with a slightly 'gamey' or 'cheesey' flavour.

MYSORE: A rich full flavoured coffee from Southern India.

MAKING COFFEE

Brewing coffee is merely a matter of infusion or boiling but there are many different machines and gadgets on the market. Infusion, particularly filtration is the most popular method of brewing coffee in the UK. Boiling water that has slightly cooled is poured over ground coffee, extracting the aromatic constituents and flavour and leaving behind the bitter parts.

MAKING COFFEE IN A JUG is one of the oldest ways of making coffee. Simply place ground coffee in a jug then add very hot (not boiling) water. Leave to infuse for a few minutes before serving. A strainer should be used when pouring.

CAFETIÈRE or the plunger method is similar to the jug method of coffee making but the plunger pushes the coffee grounds to the bottom of the pot so there is no need to strain the coffee when serving.

ELECTRIC PERCOLATORS use a different method. Water is brought to the boil in the percolator and forced over the coffee which is in a 'basket' in its top. Beware of the coffee becoming stewed when using this method.

VACUUM (CONA) MACHINES make coffee by forcing boiling water from a lower container to an upper one which contains coffee, the water then drips back into the lower jug from which it is served.

FILTER COFFEE is made by pouring water which is just off the boil over ground coffee which is in a filter. There are several versions of this method, some incorporating devices to keep the coffee hot once it has passed into the jug below.

ESPRESSO COFFEE is produced by steam being forced through coffee grounds. This produces strong, thick coffee, usually in small quantities. Expresso machines may be electric or for use on a hob. Hot milk can be added to espresso coffee to make cappuccino coffee.

COFFEE GRINDS

The best grinds for some of the most common brewing methods are:

METHOD	GRINDING GRADE
Filter/drips	Fine to medium
Jug	Coarse
Turkish	Very fine
Plunger (Cafetière)	Medium
Vacuum (Cona)	Medium fine or fine
Espresso	Very fine
Percolator	Medium or coarse

When choosing a coffee machine it is important to find the method which most suits your lifestyle and situation. For example, vacuum (Cona) machines are suitable for offices as a large amount of coffee can be made at one time, where as espresso machines which make only 1 or 2 cups are more suitable for home use.

When making ground coffee allow about 50 g (2 oz) coffee per 600 ml (1 pint) water. Coffee is best served hot but not boiling and should not be kept hot for too long after making or the flavour will deteriorate.

COFFEE AND HEALTH

In recent years there have been a number of reports which suggest that drinking excessive amounts of coffee can have adverse health effects, because of the high caffeine intake. It is recommended that one should not drink more than 6-10 cups of instant coffee per day (less of ground coffee). Any coffee that is stewed is thought to be more harmful than that which is freshly made. The more expensive arabica beans contain less caffeine than the cheaper robusta variety. De-caffeinated coffee is now widely available and has only a marginal loss of flavour.

IRISH OR GAELIC COFFEE

1 part Irish whiskey
5 ml (1 level tsp) brown sugar
3-4 parts double strength coffee
15-30 ml (1-2 tbsp) double cream, chilled

1. Gently warm a glass, pour in the whiskey and add the sugar.
2. Pour in black coffee to within 2.5 cm (1 inch) of the brim and stir to dissolve the sugar.
3. Fill to the brim with cream, poured over the back of a spoon and allow to stand for a few minutes before serving.
SERVES 1

VARIATIONS: Replace the whiskey with kirsch, rum, Cointreau, Tia Maria or Calvados.

ICED COFFEE

50 g (2 oz) ground coffee
900 ml (1½ pints) water
sugar to taste
ice cubes
double cream, whipped

1. Make some strong black coffee with the coffee and water.
2. While it is still hot, sweeten to taste with sugar. Cool and chill.
3. Pour into glasses, add an ice cube and top with whipped cream to serve.
SERVES 4

SOFT DRINKS

Homemade soft drinks are full of flavour and make refreshing thirst-quenchers on hot summer days. This section includes children's favourites such as lemonade, ginger beer, ice cream soda and fruit squashes, and punches.
Sterilise bottles, where necessary, as for jam jars (see page 464).

STRAWBERRY MILK SHAKE

300 ml (½ pint) milk
50 g (2 oz) strawberries, hulled and mashed
30 ml (2 tbsp) ice cream (optional)

1. Whisk all the ingredients together until frothy, or blend at maximum speed for 1 minute in a blender or food processor.
2. Pour into a large glass and serve immediately.
SERVES 1

VARIATIONS
Replace the strawberries with raspberries, or 1 banana, peeled and mashed.

COFFEE MILK SHAKE

150 ml (¼ pint) milk
150 ml (¼ pint) black coffee
30 ml (2 tbsp) ice cream

1. Whisk all the ingredients together until frothy, or blend at maximum speed for 1 minute in a blender or food processor.
2. Pour into a large glass and serve immediately.
SERVES 1

ICE CREAM SODA

1 glass soda water
15 ml (1 tbsp) ice cream

1. Whisk the soda water and ice cream together with a rotary whisk until frothy or blend at maximum speed for 1 minute in a blender or food processor.
2. Pour into a large glass and serve at once.
SERVES 1

VARIATIONS
GRAPEFRUIT OR LIME SODA
Follow the method (left) and whisk together ½ glass soda water, 30 ml (2 tbsp) grapefruit juice or 15 ml (1 tbsp) lime juice and 15 ml (1 tbsp) ice cream.

GINGER SODA
Follow the method (left) and whisk together ¾ glass ginger beer, ¼ glass lemonade and 15 ml (1 tbsp) ice cream.

STILL LEMONADE

3 lemons
175 g (6 oz) sugar
900 ml (1½ pints) boiling water

1. Remove the lemon rind thinly with a potato peeler.
2. Put the rind and sugar into a bowl or large jug and pour on the boiling water. Cover and leave to cool, stirring occasionally.
3. Add the juice of the lemons and strain the lemonade. Serve chilled.
MAKES ABOUT 1.1 LITRES (2 PINTS)

BITTER LEMON

2 lemons
600 ml (1 pint) water
100 g (4 oz) sugar

1. Cut the lemons into pieces, put in a saucepan with the water and bring to the boil.

2. Reduce the heat and simmer gently for 10-15 minutes, until the fruit is soft.
3. Add the sugar and stir until dissolved.
4. Remove from the heat, cover and cool. Strain before using. Serve with soda water, if liked.
MAKES ABOUT 900 ML (1½ PINTS)

QUICK LEMON SQUASH

juice of ½ a lemon
sugar to taste
soda water

1. Put the lemon juice and sugar into a glass and fill to the top with soda water.
SERVES 1

ORANGEADE

2 oranges
1 lemon
50 g (2 oz) sugar
600 ml (1 pint) boiling water

1. Thinly pare the orange rind, free of any pith.
2. Put the rinds and sugar into a bowl and pour over the boiling water.
3. Leave to cool, stirring occasionally, then add the strained juice of the oranges and lemon.
MAKES ABOUT 900 ML (1½ PINTS)

PINEAPPLE CRUSH

600 ml (1 pint) pineapple juice
juice of 1 orange
juice of 1 lemon
sugar
1.1 litres (2 pints) ginger ale (chilled in the bottle)

1. Combine the fruit juices, sweeten to taste with sugar and chill.
2. Just before serving, add the ginger ale.
MAKES ABOUT 1.7 LITRES (3 PINTS)

QUICK GINGER BEER

rind and juice of 1 large lemon
25 ml (5 level tsp) cream of tartar
450 g (1 lb) sugar
25 g (1 oz) fresh root ginger, peeled
2.3 litres (4 pints) boiling water
2.3 litres (4 pints) cold water
15 g (½ oz) fresh yeast
1 slice toast

1. Place the lemon rind, cream of tartar and sugar in a large bowl or plastic bucket. Bruise the ginger and add to the bowl.
2. Pour over the boiling water and stir until the sugar is dissolved. Add the cold water and lemon juice; cool until just warm to the hand.
3. Spread the yeast on the toast and float it on the mixture. Cover with a clean cloth and leave in a warm place for 24 hours until frothy.
4. Remove any scum from the top of the mixture, discard the toast and syphon the beer into sterilised bottles, avoiding any sediment.
5. Seal the bottles with screw tops or corks secured with wire. Leave for 3 days in a cool place before drinking. Drink within the following 3 days or the ginger beer will taste too yeasty.
MAKES ABOUT 5.1 LITRES (9 PINTS)

Use a rolling pin to bruise the root ginger.

Syphon from the bowl into sterilised bottles.

CITRUS PUNCH

juice of 2 grapefruit
juice of 2 lemons
juice of 5 oranges
150 ml (¼ pint) pineapple juice
sugar
1 litre (1¾ pints) tonic water (chilled in the bottle)
1 lemon, thinly sliced, to decorate

1. Strain fruit juices into a bowl. Chill.
2. Just before serving, add the sugar and tonic water. Decorate with lemon slices.
MAKES ABOUT 1.6 LITRES (2¾ PINTS)

Strain through a sieve.

SPICY FRUIT PUNCH

600 ml (1 pint) orange juice
300 ml (½ pint) pineapple juice
grated rind and juice of 1 lemon
2.5 ml (½ level tsp) freshly grated nutmeg
2.5 ml (½ level tsp) ground mixed spice
6 cloves
600 ml (1 pint) water
175 g (6 oz) sugar
1.1 litres (2 pints) ginger ale (chilled in the bottle)
crushed ice

1. Mix the fruit juices, lemon rind and spices in a large jug.
2. Put the water and sugar into a saucepan and heat gently to dissolve the sugar. Cool slightly and add to the other ingredients in the jug. Chill.
3. Strain the liquid and add the ginger ale and some crushed ice before serving.
MAKES ABOUT 2.8 LITRES (5 PINTS)

PINE-LIME SPARKLE

600 ml (1 pint) pineapple juice
45 ml (3 tbsp) freshly squeezed lemon juice
150 ml (¼ pint) lime juice cordial
50 g (2 oz) icing sugar
450 ml (¾ pint) bitter lemon (chilled in the bottle)
lime slices (optional)

1. Put the pineapple and lemon juices, and the lime cordial in a bowl and stir in the icing sugar. Chill.
2. Just before serving add the bitter lemon and some lime slices, if wished.
MAKES ABOUT 1 LITRE (1¾ PINTS)

Pine-Lime Sparkle

EQUIPPING YOUR KITCHEN

You can fill your kitchen with a vast array of allegedly labour-saving gadgets but may well find that not all of them get enough use to justify their initial purchase. Kitchen equipment suppliers might not agree but the fact is that the well equipped kitchen is one in which every item earns its keep on a regular – or infrequent but essential – basis and does not languish unused in a cupboard.

When equipping a kitchen from scratch there are some basic rules to consider before buying anything. They are:

- Do I need it?
- Will I use it?
- Is it easy to clean/will it go in a dishwasher?
- Is it easy to store?

If the answer to all of these is 'yes', you probably need the item in questions. And you can, of course, allow yourself some luxuries. Something like a lemon zester won't be in daily use but does do the job of creating thin strips of lemon rind better than a knife or potato peeler. And a fondue set also won't be utilized on a regular basis but might be something you enjoy using for informal entertaining from time to time.

It's only too easy to clutter up your kitchen with labour-saving gadgets that you don't use often enough to justify their purchase. And storage of these items may well make it more difficult to lay your hands on those kitchen tools you really do use on a regular basis.

STORING THINGS

Kitchens tend, on the whole, to be small, so storage space is precious. You want to be able to keep things near the place where they will be used – pans near the cooker, preparation tools near a work surface – and space given over to bulky items must really earn its keep.

Small electrical appliances can present a problem if you're short of work space. You're more likely to use them if they are out on a work top rather than buried in a cupboard but this can restrict your working area. Bear this in mind when thinking about which ones you really need.

CLEANING THINGS

Many items of kitchen equipment are so fiddly to clean that you spend more time cleaning them than they take to perform the task they are supposed to speed up. When buying any labour-saving gadget, think first whether you could perform its task equally well with, say, a sharp knife or a hand whisk. Obviously if you cook for large numbers, something which saves time when preparing food in quantity is helpful. But if you are preparing food for just one or two people, the time spent cleaning an item may eliminate any time saved on the task.

Items which can be cleaned in a dishwasher will save your time. Check on this when you buy.

COOKERS

Choosing a cooker today is like treading a minefield. The choice is enormous and unless you are familiar with the way different types of fuel perform and which special features add value, you are going to find selecting a model difficult. You can choose between free-standing, slot-in, built-in and split level models and between single and double ovens. Look for a simple model if it's your first purchase.

FUEL CHOICE

Your choice of fuel will depend on where you live. Electricity is the most widely available option, followed by gas which is available in most but not all areas of the UK. Oil is available as an option if you are buying a range cooker such as an Aga which can also be run on solid fuel, electricity and gas.

Range cookers such as Agas have the

advantage of also being able to heat domestic hot water and some central heating radiators but they do require some adjustments in cooking techniques. They may have two ovens; one hot for roasting and baking and one cooler for simmering and plate warming. Four-oven models provide a further range of temperatures and all have solid-top burners for hob cooking.

Ranges are, in general, more expensive to buy and install than conventional cookers and may, in some homes – particularly flats – require the kitchen floor to be reinforced because of their weight. Because a range keeps the kitchen warm all year round you may need some form of back up cooking appliance so that you can switch it off during hot weather.

HOBS

A hob may be an integral part of a free-standing cooker or a separate item. A particular advantage of a separate hob is that you can run it on a different fuel from your oven so that in the case of a power cut you still have the use of one appliance. A separate hob can be built into your worktop at a place which suits you and can also, if necessary, be fitted into a higher or lower housing unit to suit your personal height.

If you don't want a conventional four-ring/burner hob you could consider individual hob units consisting of single or double rings which might well be sufficient on their own if you are a small household and don't cook much.

GAS HOBS have instant heat and are easily controlled. Most have automatic ignition whereby the flame comes on when you operate the control; some have semi-automatic ignition where you have to activate both the fuel and the control. More sophisticated gas hobs have different-sized burners and rings – small for simmering and large for fast boiling.

ELECTRIC HOBS may have radiant rings, sealed hotplate rings, a ceramic surface, halogen lamps or magnetic induction. Radiant rings come in different kilowatt ratings for fast and slow cooking. Some have a dual element so you can switch on just the inner section when cooking in smaller pans.

Sealed hotplate rings take longer to heat up and cool down. They incorporate a pan sensor device for accurate heat control and turn down automatically to a preselected setting so there's no risk of boiling over.

Ceramic hobs provide a flush fit with worktops and are easy to clean. Some are rather slow to heat up and cool down and it's essential to keep an eye on the 'hob hot' light which will tell you when the surface is cool enough to touch.

Halogen cooking is done by very bright lamps so it's important to use a pan that fits over the cooking area or you will get glare.

Magnetic induction hobs require the use of ferrous metal pans to activate the force which produces heat. They operate only when a pan is place on the cooking area and go off the minute the pan is removed.

When choosing any hob look at ease of use and cleaning. Some have controls which are difficult to operate (try them in the shop) and some are sited where a small child could operate them. Check carefully for potential dirt traps and how difficult cleaning might be.

COOKER HOODS

Fitting a cooker hood or extractor fan will help to remove smells and moisture from the air in the kitchen and reduce the build-up of grease and dirt on surrounding areas.

A cooker hood may be the ducted or recirculating type. A ducted cooker hood has a duct running through an outside wall through which a fan evicts odours and moisture. A recirculating cooker hood works by a fan which passes air through replaceable grease and charcoal filters which remove moisture and smells before returning the cleaned air to the kitchen.

Most cooker hoods are fixed above the hob and may either remain permanently in position or be the retractable type which is pulled out when cooking is in progress but remains flush with wall units the rest of the time.

A further ducted type of extractor is fitted beside the hob at burner/ring level.

A cheaper alternative to a cooker hood is an extractor fan fitted into the glass of the kitchen window. It will not be as effective overall and will work efficiently only when the window is shut.

Under Building Regulations cooker hoods in new homes are required to make a specified number of air changes each hour. A ducted cooker hood must remove 30 litres of moisture laden air per second; an extractor fan 60 litres per second. If you are fitting new ventilation measures into an existing building it would be sensible to check with your local authority that the particular system you plan to install meets the requirements of the size of your kitchen.

OVENS

These may be part of a free-standing cooker with hob, built in or built under a worktop. Which you choose will depend on the layout of your kitchen. Some ovens have a separate grilling area; in others the grill is in the oven itself. When choosing an oven with a grill inside, check whether grilling is done with the door open or closed. If the door needs to be open you must be sure there is enough space for this and sufficient room to check the progress of food being grilled.

Ovens vary in the way they work. A conventional oven uses hot air convection currents from elements or burners to cook food. The temperature is usually hotter at the top than the bottom in British ovens with side elements, while in Continental ovens with top and bottom elements you get a different heat pattern.

FAN OVENS (sometimes called forced air convection ovens) offer a number of advantages over conventional ovens. They use less electricity and cook at a lower temperature. Temperature remains even so you can use all the shelves to full capacity. Browning is even and you don't have to reposition dishes to get even baking. Preheating is unnecessary for most foods since the oven heats up so fast.

Disadvantages include the noise from the fan and the fact that because there is no heat variation within the oven it is difficult to cook a complete meal where dishes require slightly different temperatures.

Multi-function ovens offer the choice of both conventional and fan cooking and are able to combine the heating elements and fan in different ways to create varied heat patterns for different combinations of dishes. The following are functions you may find in a multi-function oven although not all models have all of them:

Hot air grilling is fan cooking on the highest setting to produce the effect of a rotisserie. Instead of the food moving round a fixed heat source the hot air circulates round the food, browning and crisping on all sides.

Fan with grill (fan-assisted grilling) may consist of the fan and grill operating either alternately or simultaneously, producing an effect similar to hot air grilling.

Bottom element with fan enables heat to be circulated from below the food which is useful for crisping pastry and pizza bases.

Top and bottom heat with fan crisps and browns the underside of foods, which is useful for pizzas and pastry. This is also called the pastry function.

Top element with fan acts to create a hotter zone at the top of the oven. Useful where dishes require different temperatures.

Defrost enables the fan to operate without heat to defrost food more quickly than naturally, but not as fast as in a microwave.

Microwave combination is a feature of some models. These have an integral microwave which can be used alone or in combination with some of the other cooking functions.

OVEN LININGS

These are important in terms of keeping an oven clean since few of us are sufficiently well organised to follow the precept of wiping out the oven cavity while it is still warm.

Self-clean and stay-clean linings work by burning off deposited soil during cooking but only at medium to high temperatures. If you regularly cook at low temperatures you will need to have a burning off session from time to time.

When buying an oven with this type of lining do check that it goes all round the oven cavity if possible. Stay-clean sides will stay clean but if the base and top of the oven have ordinary linings you could spend some time employing elbow grease at the sink.

Pyrolitic cleaning is done at a very high temperature which will have its own special setting on the cooker. You do it when the oven becomes dirty and a safety lock ensures that the cooker can't be opened while the high heat programme is in progress.

OVEN FEATURES WORTH LOOKING FOR

Half grill facility for grilling small quantities economically.

Convenient controls which may be mechnical or digital. In a home with small children make sure they are in a safe position.

Warming area which may be a drawer in the base of the cooker or a rack below the grill. Some cookers with a double oven use the small one for plate warming.

Storage space for roasting tins and baking trays.

Automatic timer so you can set the oven to start and stop without you needing to be there. Bear in mind that it is not a good idea to put food in an oven in the morning and set it to be ready when you come home in the evening. Perishable foods (see page 556) should remain refrigerated until you are ready to cook them.

Minute minder tells you when cooking time is up.

Inner glass door to provide extra insulation and enable you to view the food inside without opening it and allowing the temperature to fall.
Lights so you can easily see the back of the hob and oven.

COOKER CHOICE

Read all sales literature carefully, all the time bearing in mind the kind of food you cook. Decide which – if any – of the myriad of special features would be useful to you and think whether you would use them often enough to justify their extra cost.

Consider whether you need a full sized cooker or combination or oven and hob. If you don't use an oven a great deal you might find a combination microwave (see page 551) or microwave with grill would cope with your conventional cooking needs. Or you could buy a table-top mini-oven which might also incorporate a grill. And if your kitchen is very small, consider a cooker that is narrower than the standard width. There is a good selection of these models available.

DISHWASHERS

A dishwasher is a valuable piece of kitchen equipment which will save you time and money. It washes better than you can, at a hotter, more hygienic temperature and is cheaper – year on year – than washing up by hand.

If you can't fit a standard-sized dishwasher into your kitchen, choose one of the narrow models available. Or consider a table-top model, although this will reduce worktop space and will not hold very many place settings.

You will need more crockery and cutlery than if washing up by hand after each meal or cooking session but that is the only drawback.

If you have a dishwasher, or plan to buy one in the future, make sure that any kitchen equipment you buy is dishwasher safe.

REFRIGERATORS AND FREEZERS

A refrigerator is an essential piece of kitchen equipment for storing perishable foods safely (see page 557 for approximate storage times). It may be built under a work surface, built into a housing unit at chest height or be free standing. Site it as near to the main food preparation area as possible so you are not constantly having to move between the two. Do not put a refrigerator next to a cooker or central heating boiler which will raise the temperature; the refrigerator motor will need to work harder to maintain the temperature and it will cost more to run. With most refrigerators there is the facility to hang the door on whichever side is more convenient.

Conventional refrigerators have a frozen food/ice-making compartment inside while 'larder' refrigerators do not. The latter therefore provides more refrigeration space within the same-sized cabinet and is also a better buy if you have a freezer in which you can store frozen food and make ice cubes.

Fridge/freezers combine a refrigerator and freezer in one appliance and thus save floor space. You can choose whether to have the freezer above the fridge or vice versa and also choose to have different size capacities within the one appliance. Freezers are described on page 558 but it's worth also noting that some (large) fridge/freezer models have a special compartment rated at 0°C which is designed for storing fresh meat, fish, fruit and vegetables at optimum temperature for long life in good condition.

Consider defrosting. Some models have a fan and are self-defrosting but will still need interior cleaning. Others may require manual defrosting (where you remove food and switch off) or have automatic defrosting which switches on when necessary and then resets the appliance.

Check the internal fittings of a refrigerator bearing in mind the kind of food you will be storing in it. Is there enough space for salad ingredients? Can you easily reach food at the back of the shelves? Is door storage high enough to take tall bottles and plastic containers of milk and fruit juice? Do you want a chilled drink dispenser? Is it easily wiped out and cleaned?

SMALL ELECTRICAL APPLIANCES

KETTLES

You can buy a non-electric kettle and heat it on your hob, or an electric model. Non-electric kettles are, on the whole less convenient, since they can boil dry and take longer to boil water than electric models.

A kettle should be well balanced, stable, easy to fill and pour from and have a comfortable handle. Useful features include a water gauge and indicator light. The choice lies between traditional shapes and the upright 'jug' shape. The advantage of a jug kettle is that you can boil just a small quantity of water at one time, eg enough for one cup of tea or coffee, whereas with the traditional shapes you require more water than may be needed in order to cover the element.

Electric kettles may be corded or cordless. The latter can be removed from the base for filling and pouring, obviating the need to unplug the flex.

COFFEE MAKERS

If you don't want to buy an electric coffee maker you can choose between an espresso machine that goes on the hob and the jug-and-filter or cafetière methods which require you to pour boiling water on to the coffee grounds in them. These do not keep coffee hot for a long period in the way that electric machines do. With electric machines the choice lies between filter, espresso and cappuccino.

FILTER COFFEE MAKERS heat water then pass it through a filter containing the ground coffee so that it drips through into a jug on a hotplate. Features to look for include an anti-drip device which prevents coffee spattering on the hotplate when the jug is removed; a swivelling filter holder so that you can remove grounds easily and a clear water level indicator so you can make the number of cups required. Some machines come with a thermal jug to keep coffee hot, instead of a hotplate.

ESPRESSO COFFEE MAKERS heat water which is then forced under pressure through a small metal container that holds closely packed, finely ground coffee. The resulting brew is strong and bitter. Electric espresso machines tend to be fiddly to clean. Cheaper models operate under steam pressure; more expensive ones use a pump to drive the water through the grounds under higher pressure and extract more of the authentic coffee flavour.

CAPPUCCINO COFFEE MAKERS are espresso machines with an extra facility for frothing milk.

WATER FILTERS

If you are not happy with the taste of the water from your tap or are concerned about the impurities it may contain you may choose to use a water filter. Fitting one into your domestic water system is expensive and most people opt for a jug with a filter cartridge.

When choosing a water filter, consider the capacity of the jug in relation to your needs and whether the model will fit into your refrigerator. Filtered water should be kept cool and used regularly. The filter itself (which should be changed as often as the manufacturer recommends) should always be kept wet.

JUICERS

If you choose a manual juicer you will only be able to obtain juice from citrus fruit. Electric juicers may be citrus-juice only, or the centrifugal type which can extract juice from a range of fruit and vegetables, eg apples and carrots. Electric juicers require more effort to operate and clean than manual models but produce clearer juice and they are faster in use. With citrus juicers you simply cut the fruit in half and place it on the rotating head; with centrifugal juicers you must first peel and prepare the fruit or vegetables.

COFFEE AND SPICE GRINDERS

Although most supermarkets now sell a variety of different grinds of coffee, suitable for different types of coffee-making machine, you may prefer to grind your own coffee beans freshly, as finely as you require.

Electric coffee grinders may be free-standing or they may operate as an attachment for a blender or mixer. You can also use them for grinding spices, but first clean them thoroughly by wiping out the container and then grinding one or two slices of bread to absorb any remaining odours. If you grind a lot of spices it is probably simpler to invest in two machines.

HERB MILLS

Small electric herb mills are useful for chopping large quantities of herbs and can usually also be used for puréeing baby food.

FOOD PREPARATION MACHINES

While tasks such as chopping, slicing, mixing, blending, grating and sieving small quantities can probably be done more quickly by hand and with less to clean afterwards, for large quantities a machine makes a big difference.

Your choice lies with blenders, stick blenders, food processors and hand and table food mixers. They don't all perform the same functions (although some overlap) and you may well need more than one machine to fulfil all your culinary needs.

BLENDERS

These are good for making batter, mayonnaise, pâté, purées, soup and baby food. Some can also be used to produce breadcrumbs and grated chocolate or cheese. They are generally better for smaller quantities.

Inspect the height of the blades before you buy; some are too high to cope with one-yolk mayonnaise and very small quantities of food. Variable speed is useful, as is a small hole in the lid through which to drip oil or add other liquids. Most goblets carry measurements down the side so you can check the quantity you are dealing with and add as necessary. A handle on the blender goblet is useful for lifting it off the base when it contains hot liquid.

For most blending tasks a good-size goblet – minimum 1 litre (2 pints) – is better, but if you deal with only small quantities a small one may be satisfactory. Some blender goblets can be put into a dishwasher; check if the manufacturer states 'top rack only'.

A blender may be an attachment to a food processor or table-top mixer. If free-standing it may be possible to fit a coffee or herb/spice grinder on to the motorised base.

FOOD PROCESSORS

Food processors have more functions than blenders but don't always blend smoothly because of the different shape of the bowl. They can slice, grate, chop, cream, knead and beat a wide selection of ingredients. They come with a variety of cutters, blades and whisks (all of which you have to store somewhere) and perform their tasks very quickly. You need to practise at first in order to avoid chopped onions turning into onion purée.

If you use your processor a lot it can be worth buying a second bowl to save having to wash up during a preparation session. Small food processors are available and handy for chopping herbs, baby food and small quantities. Some large food processors have a small bowl that can be fitted inside the large one to cope with small quantities of things like baby food.

HAND-HELD MIXERS

These may come with a bowl and stand and operate without being held. Or they may simply consist of a motorised head into which a selected of mixers, whisks and beaters can be fitted. They are compact, easy to clean and mix and beat well although they can't always cope with large quantities and dense mixtures.

There is little advantage in buying the type with a bowl and stand since these will have to be stored somewhere; beaters alone can be used in a suitable bowl that you own.

You can also buy cordless hand-held mixers which need to be stored on a recharging unit in between uses.

TABLE-TOP MIXERS

These are large and take up a lot of space. Because of their weight they can be left to operate without supervision and can deal with large quantities of mixture such as bread dough or fruit cake. They are only useful if you regularly cook large quantities of food which need to be pre-mixed. Some models can also be fitted with a variety of non-mixing attachments such as sausage-skin filler, pasta maker, bean slicer and so on.

STICK BLENDERS

Stick blenders are a cross between hand-held mixers and blenders. They consist of small rotating blades powered by a motor. They can be used in bowls or pans to liquidise ingredients or make a smooth sauce.

ELECTRIC CARVING KNIVES

These make light work of slicing through food such as meat or bread and can produce wafer-thin slices not always attainable manually.

ELECTRIC CAN OPENERS

These open cans smoothly and easily, retaining the lid on a magnet and are useful for anyone with weak wrists.

ICE CREAM MAKERS

These take the effort out of making ice cream by hand and having to beat it at regular intervals after removal from the freezer. They have revolving paddles which, because they rotate constantly during the freezing process, produce a smooth creamy result with no ice crystals.

Electric ice-cream makers may have their own built-in refrigerating equipment or may need to be used in your freezer. Those with their own refrigerating equipment tend to be heavy and fairly noisy in use. They make ice cream more quickly than the freezer type but are often fiddly to clean. Because they contain refrigerant they should not be moved around immediately before use. If stored in a cupboard, be sure to get your model into a working position and allow several hours for the refrigerant to settle.

Models which work in a freezer have a thin

power supply cord which does not prevent the seal on the freezer door from working correctly. When buying one of this type make sure that it will fit satisfactorily between the shelves of an upright freezer.

Most electric ice cream makers produce only small quantities of ice cream around 1 litre (2 pints) so are not suitable for bulk production to store in the freezer. In any case, for enjoyment of the texture at its best, ice cream made at home in this way is nicest eaten as soon as it is made. The relatively gentle action of these machines means that you can incorporate ingredients such as alpine strawberries or nuts without them being reduced to a purée.

SMALL ELECTRIC COOKING APPLIANCES

TOASTERS

When choosing a toaster consider a 'cool wall' model which won't burn anyone's fingers. Decide whether you want two or four slots and check whether they will take unusually-shaped bread and items such as crumpets, muffins and baps. Long wide slots which adjust to the size of the bread are more flexible than those which are of a fixed size.

Some models of toaster have a special setting for cooking bread from frozen.

DEEP-FAT FRYERS

Electric deep-fat fryers are safer and easier to use than a pan of oil on the hob. These have thermostatic control and more sophisticated models have a basket that can be raised and lowered from outside, a viewing window and 'cool' exterior wall so you don't burn your hands. Oil can be re-used several times (just as well, because you need lots), provided it is filtered between uses. If you don't possess a special filter jug use a strainer lined with piece of kitchen paper.

SANDWICH TOASTERS

Useful for making toasted sandwich snacks which seal in the filling. Buy one that will take decent-sized pieces of bread, preferably with removable toasting plates for easy cleaning.

SLOW COOKERS

These are free-standing electric casseroles which are useful for long slow cooking that won't boil over or burn and doesn't need watching. They are especially good for tenderising cheap, tougher cuts of meat and handy for having a complete one-pot meal ready to eat if you've been out of the house for several hours.

Some models have just one temperature; on others there may be automatic switch from an initial high temperature to a lower one. It's important not to lift the lid to stir or peer during cooking time unless it's essential for adding extra ingredients. If you do this you should add approximately half an hour to the recommended cooking time.

Bear in mind that because of the low temperature, liquid will not evaporate and meat and vegetables will not brown. Use less liquid than usual and fry off meat and vegetables before adding them.

POTS AND PANS

You can pay a few pounds for a basic saucepan or considerably more for one that's superior. Both will cook food so you have to decide between buying something with a short life that will need replacing and something which should last for years and years.

First consider your hob. If it's ceramic, sealed ring or halogen you will need pans with flat bases – some are specifically designed for these surfaces. If it's magnetic induction, in addition, you will need these flat bases to be made of ferrous metal.

Next, consider cleaning. If you own a dishwasher it's sensible to buy pans that can be cleaned in it. This may rule out some with wooden handles and knobs unless they have been specially treated. Check when you buy.

NON-STICK PANS

Non-stick is a marvellous surface for things like sauces, porridge and foods which tend to stick to uncoated pans. It's got much tougher in recent years but still needs to be treated with care. Even though some manufacturers claim you can use metal implements on non-stick surfaces, they won't stand up to cutting and scratching, nor can they stand very high heat. So although you'll probably want a non-stick frying pan, milk pan and general saucepan you may not need the coating on all your pans.

DURABILITY

Some saucepans are now fashion items and come in colours and designs that reflect current trends in kitchens decor and may match small electrical appliances, housewares and kitchen textiles. On the whole these tend to be cheaper pans which can't be expected to last for ever. Expensive pans could well last a lifetime if looked after carefully but if chosen with care both cheap and expensive saucepans should perform well during their lifetime.

POINTS TO CONSIDER

STABILITY: Check for a flat base either by putting a ruler across it or by rocking the pan on a flat surface. If necessary ask the shop assistant to remove the pan from its packaging so you can check it yourself.

LID FIT: Lids should fit well while moving just enough to allow steam to escape.

KNOBS: If these are not heat resistant you'll need to use an oven glove every time you lift the lid. The best knobs have a heat-resistant collar round them so that you don't burn your knuckles. If your knobs screw on, check that you can tighten the screws which will undoubtedly work loose with use.

HANDLES: These should be sufficiently long that they do not get too hot. In general, they should be comfortable to hold. Common faults are handles that are too narrow or too long. Large pans should have another handle opposite the main one to assist with lifting when full.

SHAPE: Look to see if there is a slight curve inside where the sides meet the base as this makes pans easier to clean. Pans with a bulge are good for recipes which need stirring or beating as spoons fit snugly into the bulge, but they are more difficult to clean than straight-sided pans.

POURING: A continuous pouring rim is best as it is not always easy to control thick liquids through a pouring lip – which may, in any case, be on the wrong side for left-handed people.

STORAGE: With unlimited cupboard space this obviously isn't a problem, but where storage space is limited look for pans that stack or can be hung up by their handles.

PAN SELECTION

Basic selection	Additional Pans
milk pan	omelette pan
two heavy-based 1.7 litre (3 pint) saucepans with lids	wok
	pressure cooker
two larger saucepans with lids	deep-fat fryer (electric)
heavy-based frying pan with lid	sauté pan with lid
steamer	crêpe pan
	double boiler
	preserving pan
	stock pot
	fish kettle

PAN MATERIALS

ALUMINIUM conducts heat evenly. Medium and heavy gauge aluminium are suitable for most fuels but lightweight aluminium is suitable only for gas and has a short life as it tends to distort. Note that aluminium will pit and discolour unless it has a non-stick or enamel lining.

In recent years, there has been concern about a possible link between aluminium and Alzheimer's disease. Research has shown that the transfer of aluminium from utensils into foodstuffs is negligible except with very acid foods. It is therefore prudent to cook very acid foods such as stoned fruit, chutney, etc in non-aluminium pans.

CAST ALUMINIUM AND CAST IRON are thick and heavy and are therefore good for long, slow cooking at low temperatures. They conduct heat well. Pans made of these materials which are coated with vitreous enamel are easier to clean.

Note that these materials are heavy so not suitable if you have difficulty lifting things. They are also liable to break if dropped on to a hard floor surface.

COPPER conducts heat brilliantly and is the choice of many professional chefs. It must be coated with tin, nickel or aluminium to prevent the copper reacting with very acid foods such as tomatoes and citrus fruit to produce an unpleasant taste. Copper is expensive and the pan exteriors will need regular polishing to keep them looking good.

HEATPROOF GLASS pans allow you to see what's cooking and conduct heat well. But they do tend to stick and may hot spot.

STAINLESS STEEL on its own does not conduct heat well and needs a layer of aluminium or copper bonded on to the base to improve this. Stainless steel pans are expensive but will, if looked after, last for ever.

VITREOUS ENAMEL (Vitramel (TM)) is a coating applied to various metals which on the exterior makes them more attractive and on the interior easier to clean. It is important to look for the trade mark and to avoid painted enamel finishes which chip easily. Vitramel (TM) is the trade mark of the Vitreous Enamel Development Council and denotes good quality enamel and its application. It should be cleaned only with products approved by the VEDC.

CASSEROLE CHOICE

Casseroles are made from virtually any material which is ovenproof. Some can be used on the hob; some in a microwave cooker. Some look good enough to serve from at the table; others are definitely destined only for the kitchen.

When choosing a casserole follow the guidelines outlined for selecting saucepans. And check particularly, since they don't have handles, that the grips and knobs can be held firmly when you're wearing oven gloves.

PRESSURE COOKERS
A pressure cooker cooks more quickly than an ordinary saucepan and is useful for making stock, cooking root vegetables and pulses and tenderising tough cuts of meat. Some people are wary of pressure cooking because they don't understand how it works. What happens is that it increases atmospheric pressure inside the sealed saucepan by allowing steam to escape only at a controlled rate. Water normally boils at 100°C (212°F) but at this high pressure the boiling point is increased to between 110°C-120°C (230°F-248°F) so food cooks more quickly.

When it comes to times and quantities it is important initially to follow the instructions supplied with your pan for accurate results. Some models come with automatic cut outs, timers and ringers. With other models you must keep an eye on pressure cooking.

TOOLS FOR THE KITCHEN
The range of non-electric kitchen tools available is enormous but in fact many of their various functions can be done with a sharp knife and hand grater. For those items that you believe you really need check the following points:
- quality and where appropriate sharpness
- comfort in use
- ease of cleaning
- ease of storage

KNIFE CHECKLIST

general kitchen knife
cook's knife
paring knife
filleting knife
carving knife and fork with guard
bread knife
palette knife
grapefruit knife
serrated knife for ham
knife sharpener (manual or electric)
knife storage (fabric sleeves, magnetic rack or
  a knife block)

YOU AND YOUR KITCHEN
On page 550 is a fairly comprehensive checklist of items that you might require in your kitchen, depending on how much you intend to cook. Many of them you may not need, especially if you are setting up home for the first time and working to a budget. You may, however, find the list a useful source of reference if you are composing a wedding list or restocking your kitchen.

Do not be deluded into thinking that you require unusual and expensive items for occasions when you are entertaining. For most people entertaining is a small part of life and what you really need is a selection of good quality everyday items of equipment that will really earn their keep. Items such as an asparagus steamer or raised pie mould are not worth having unless you use them a lot. Asparagus can be steamed in a large saucepan, propped up and tented with foil and a game pie can be made in a standard pie dish.

KITCHEN BASICS
The list below shows the essential basic kitchen equipment you'll need to follow recipes such as those in this book and produce food without having to improvise or wash up too much during a food preparation/cooking session.

Refer to the list on the following page for additional equipment you may want as your culinary skills or budget increase. Always remember the basic rules set out at the beginning of this chapter and consider need, likely use, cleaning and storage before you buy.

KITCHEN BASIC CHECKLIST

saucepans (see checklist)	casseroles
bakeware	roasting tin
carving dish	mixing bowls
processor/hand mixer	balloon whisk
potato peeler	hand grater
scissors	kitchen tongs
corkscrew	bottle opener
bread board	ladle
perforated draining spoon	potato masher
wooden spoons	spatulas
strainer	skewers
salt and pepper mills	rolling pin
knives (see checklist)	kitchen scales
measuring jug and spoons	ice cube trays
wire cooling rack	oven gloves
can opener (manual or electric)	storage containers

KITCHEN EQUIPMENT CHECKLIST

Cooking equipment

Selection of saucepans with lids

Large and small frying pans with lids

Selection of casseroles with lids

Roasting tin (with trivet)

Yorkshire pudding tin

Electric deep fat fryer (or chip pan)

Double boiler

Steamer or steaming baskets

Asparagus steamer

Omelette pan

Crêpe pan

Egg poacher

Wok

Sauté pan

Fish kettle

Pressure cooker

Griddle

Blanching basket

Stockpot

Flan tins

Flan rings

Flan dishes

Gratin dishes

Soufflé dishes

Pie dishes

Pudding basins

Griddle

Loaf tins

Bun tins

Cake tins

Baking sheets

Swiss roll tins

Dariole moulds

Springform cake tins

Madeleine sheet

Tartlet tins

Charlotte mould

Terrine mould

Raised pie mould

Jelly mould

Cream horn tins

Savarin mould

Bombe mould

Ramekins

Back-up cooking equipment

Wire cooling racks

Trivets (for keeping hot pans off worktops)

Carving dish, knife and fork

Colander/strainers

Weights, measures and temperatures

Kitchen scales

Measuring jug/spoons

Cook's timer

Thermometers (deep fryer, freezer, meat, microwave, oven, sugar)

Spaghetti measure

Kitchen utensils and other equipment

Knives (see page 549)

Knife sharpener

Chopping boards (ideally separate ones for meat, fish and vegetables)

Box grater (for cheese, carrots, etc)

Mincer (if no processor)

Salad shaker

Flour dredger

Pastry brush

Pastry wheel

Ceramic baking beans

Rolling pin

Pastry cutters

Pie funnel

Salt and pepper mills

Garlic press

Mixing bowls

Balloon whisk

Rotary whisk

Apple corer

Potato peeler

Bottle opener

Crown cap opener

Corkscrew

Ice cube trays

Kitchen scissors

Kitchen tongs

Palette knife

Ladle

Skimmer

Fish slice

Basting spoon

Slotted spoon

Potato masher

Flexible spatula

Wooden spoons

Wooden spatulas

Skewers

Kebab skewers

Trussing needles

Larding needles

Canelle knife

Bean slicer

Cheese slicer

Cheese wire

Splash guard (to prevent fat splashing)

Lemon squeezer

Gras-maigre (gravy separator)

Jar opener

Can opener

Poultry shears

Nutmeg grater

Potato/melon baller

Butter curler

Pestle and mortar

Mezzaluna (bowl with half-moon shaped curved blade for chopping herbs)

Cherry/olive stoner

Citrus zester

Ice cream scoop

Spiked potato baker

Chip cutter

Mandoline grater

Meat mallet

Nutcrackers

Pasta maker

Electrical appliances

Blender

Mixer/food processor

Kettle

Toaster

Coffee grinder

Coffee maker

Sandwich toaster

Ice cream maker

Juice extractor

Slow cooker (crockpot/electric casserole)

Deep-fat fryer

Yogurt maker

Carving knife

Can opener

Hot tray

Storage containers

Butter dish

Cheese dish/dome

Salt box/crock

Egg rack

Vegetable rack

Bread crock

Airtight containers for fridge/freezer

Airtight containers for dried goods

Holders/cutter boxes for kitchen foil, plastic film, etc.

Rumtopf

Specialist equipment

FOR CAKE DECORATION

Piping bag and nozzles

Icing turntable

Icing ruler

Icing nails

Serrated scraper

FOR PRESERVING

Preserving pan

Jam funnel

Jelly bag and stand

Sugar thermometer

MICROWAVE COOKING

Microwave cooking saves time and energy and is also cleaner than conventional cooking. Only you can decide whether you want to use your microwave as a back up to your main cooker or as a cooker in its own right. If the latter, you need to think carefully about the type of cooker you buy. If the former, go for a basic model with variable power and it will perform the tasks you require.

However sophisticated they are, all microwave cookers run off a 13 amp socket outlet and require no special installation. Models may be built in, built under a worktop or free-standing. They fall into two categories – microwave only and combination microwave – although some models in both categories include such refinements as temperature probes, weight or sensor cooking, special timers and hotplates on top.

If a microwave is to be your only form of cooker think carefully about what extra features would be useful. Study manufacturers' literature and ask people who own models with particular features if they really use them. If it's to be purely a back-up to your standard cooker, it probably makes sense to go for a simple model. Sizes vary and if your kitchen is small with no room for building in, you may want a compact model.

Outputs also vary. You will find that the most common is 650W and that most microwave instructions on food packaging and in recipe books are geared to this. If your output is lower or higher than this you will have to adjust cooking times accordingly.

COMBINED MICROWAVE COOKERS

These combine conventional microwave cooking with a fan oven cooking facility so you can either use microwaves alone or conventional cooking alone. You can also combine the two to reduce cooking time while taking advantage of the crisping and browning offered by conventional cooking. If you don't cook for large numbers or entertain a lot a combination microwave cooker is a good alternative to a standard oven and takes up considerably less space.

HOW MICROWAVE COOKERS WORK

Microwaves themselves are a form of electrical energy similar to that used for transmitting radio and television. They cannot pass through metal – and are indeed reflected back by it – so remain safely contained within the oven cavity.

Electricity is converted to microwaves by the magnetron – a key part of the appliance. Microwaves pass through non-metallic materials such as china, glass and rigid plastic but are absorbed by the moisture molecules in food, particularly those in fat and sugar. The microwaves cause the moisture molecules to vibrate at a rapid rate which produces an intense heat which cooks the food. Contrary to popular belief, microwaves do not cook from the inside outwards but penetrate food to around 5 cm (2 inches), after which the heat spreads through by conduction.

Microwave scare stories have made many people wary of their safety but this is unnecessary. All microwave ovens made to British Standards meet high safety standards and there is no need for concern. However it is sensible to have the door seals on your microwave checked at the intervals recommended by its manufacturer. Do not buy a cheap device for checking this yourself; most of them are inaccurate and easily damaged in use.

LOOKING AFTER YOUR MICROWAVE

CLEANING: Just wipe out the oven cavity with a damp cloth after use. Mop up any spills as they occur or the next use could burn them on to the surface. Excess spilled liquid can interfere with the oven's efficiency. If spills do get burned on, don't scrape them off as this could damage the oven's interior and distort the pattern of microwaves; elbow grease is the only answer.

For general cleaning, place a bowl of water in the oven cavity and turn the cooker on to full power until the water gives off steam. Remove the bowl and use a damp cloth wrung out in a solution of washing up liquid to clean the interior. Rinse with clear water and dry with a clean cloth. If smells build up in the oven cavity, heat a bowl of water with some lemon juice in it to clear them.

KEEP AIR VENTS CLEAR: Ensure that air can circulate round the oven and don't pile things on top of it.

NEVER SWITCH IT ON WHEN EMPTY: If there is no food to absorb the microwaves, they will bounce around the oven cavity and possibly damage the magnetron. If members of your household are careless about this or if small children can reach the controls it's a good idea always to leave a glass of water in the cooker to give the microwaves something to work on.

DON'T MOVE THE MICROWAVE COOKER AROUND unless it's really essential as this could result in damage to it.

MICROWAVE COOKWARE

Use only containers which are recommended as safe for microwave use. A simple test is to fill a container with water and microwave it on full power for 2 minutes. After that, check to see if the water is hot. If it is, fine. If not, but the container itself feels hot, it is not unsafe for use but is absorbing a lot of microwave energy which is therefore not getting through to the food. Ideally, choose containers which are made of materials through which microwaves pass easily, allowing them full contact with the food.

HEATPROOF GLASS is a good conductor of microwaves and has the advantage of allowing you to see what is being cooked. Glass dishes can also be used for serving food and will go in a dishwasher.

CHINA AND POTTERY vary in their ability to allow microwaves to pass through, so do the water test suggested earlier. Do not use china or pottery which has a metallic trim as this can cause 'arcing' – a distortion of microwave patterns which can damage the magnetron.

PLASTICS also vary in their ability to cope with microwaves. Most rigid plastics are satisfactory although flexible plastics tend not to be. Do the water test and, in general, avoid using plastics to cook foods with a high fat or sugar content as

these get very hot and may melt or distort the plastic. Some plastic containers are designed specifically for microwave use and state this on their packaging.

Plastic freezer bags can be used for short periods of thawing. Boiling bags can cope with microwave energy but must first be pricked to allow steam to escape and to avoid a build up of pressure which might cause bursting.

Cling film can be used for covering containers but it must be slit or pierced before cooking or it will initially dilate and then collapse and stick to the food being cooked. Check the packaging; not all types of cling film can be used in a microwave cooker. In any event, cling film should never come into direct contact with food.

STRAW, WICKER AND WOOD BASKETS can be used for quick heating of items like bread rolls, but because of their moisture content they will tend to dry out if used too often or given long exposure. Treat wooden containers with an occasional coating of vegetable oil from time to time to prevent them drying out.

PAPER is useful in a microwave cooker to prevent fatty foods spattering and things like bread and pastries from becoming soggy. Both greasepoof paper and absorbent kitchen paper work well.

If using paper napkins or plates as a basis for heating food, take care that they are white; coloured ones may bleed dye into the food. Avoid using waxed and plastic-coated cups and plates as the coating can melt into the food.

CONTAINER SHAPES AND SIZES

In general, round dishes are a better choice than square, oval or rectangular ones, as microwaves tend to cluster in the ends or corners and overcook the food. However, if you prefer square or rectangular containers in order to make better use of freezer space, use these for dishes which are stirred at regular intervals so that overcooking won't occur. Straight-sided containers are better for microwave cooking than those with sloping sides, which also lead to overcooking in parts. Shallow containers tend to cook more quickly and evenly than deep ones.

Never fill dishes more than two-thirds full; with liquids which are going to boil allow even more headspace.

MICROWAVE ACCESSORIES

These are best bought when you find you have a need for them. The following items might be helpful, depending how you use the appliance.

SPECIAL COOKWARE can usually also be used in a freezer. Buy shapes which suit the foods you cook.

ROASTING/BACON RACKS allow fat to drain away from the food being cooked.

THERMOMETERS tell you what temperature has been reached inside the food and are particularly useful for joints of meat and when reheating food.

BROWNING DISH has a special coating which when preheated sears and browns meat and poultry.

PLATE RINGS allow you to stack plated meals above each other for simultaneous cooking.

RING MOULDS allow microwaves access to both sides of things like cake mixtures. A good substitute is a glass tumbler placed in the centre of a round dish.

MICROWAVE COOKING TECHNIQUES

Microwave cooking really is quite different from cooking conventionally on a hob or in a 'conventional' oven and you will need to practice in order to get the best results. Because most people learn conventional cooking skills before they acquire a microwave cooker they tend to assume that they will instantly be able to master their new machine. But because of the speed of cooking, the importance of arranging food in the correct way and the allowance for standing time, cooking techniques are more precise.

Your microwave cooker's handbook will provide some guidance and it makes sense initially to follow recipes which have been designed specifically for microwave use. Once you are familiar with the way your cooker works you will be able to adapt your own standard recipes for microwave cooking.

As a rough guide, microwave cooking takes about a third to a quarter of the time required for conventional cooking but factors which also affect results include temperature, density and quantity. Foods from the refrigerator will take longer to cook than those at room temperature as will dense items such as joints and poultry.

The more food there is in the cooker, the harder the microwaves have to work but you don't need to add double the time for double the quantity. Allow roughly one third extra time when doubling a quantity and reduce the time to two thirds when halving it. With food cooked in a microwave it is always better to undercook since you can always return it for a few seconds/minutes longer if it proves underdone.

ARRANGING FOOD

How food is arranged in a microwave cooker affects how efficiently it is cooked. Because of the way the microwaves move around in the oven cavity it is easy to overcook some parts of food while others remain not ready. The following guidelines should help.

Try to leave a space in the centre of food – for example when cooking chops or small cakes – so that microwaves can reach as much surface area as possible. The ring mould (see above) is useful for this with wet mixtures.

Thicker parts of foods should be sited at the outside of the cooking container with thinner parts at the centre. Where there is a wide variation of thick and thin in one item – eg chops or fish – overlap the thinner parts or protect the thinner part with a covering of foil, shiny side in. This will slow cooking of the thinner part so that the whole item is ready at once. Remember to use only a small piece of foil so that the ratio of exposed food to foil remains high. Keep the foil smooth. If you notice any signs of 'arcing' remove the foil immediately.

Even with a turntable or stirrer fans, many foods benefit from being stirred during cooking. Obviously some dishes are unsuitable but where this is possible it should be done. It's useful to buy a plastic spoon/whisk suitable for microwaves so you can leave it in the dish during cooking time. Stir from the outside into the centre to get an even result. Where a dish genuinely can't be stirred without its texture or appearance being affected, turn it once or twice during cooking; more often if cooking time is longer than 10 minutes.

STANDING TIME

Standing time is an important factor in microwave cooking and thawing. Because food continues to cook by conduction after the microwaves have reached their maximum penetration of around 5 cm (2 inches), it will continue to cook after the power has been switched off. Recipes specifically for microwave cookers and food packs specify standing time, and it is important to adhere to this. Where no standing time is given – if you are adapting a conventional recipe – follow the advice given for a similar microwave recipe.

Standing time is particularly important with items like cakes and sponge-type puddings which come out of the oven looking very undercooked and need this period in which to firm up.

FOODS TO AVOID COOKING BY MICROWAVE

Not everything cooks well in a microwave although it scores over conventional cooking with items like fish and vegetables which retain all their nutrients, texture and colour. There are disadvantages with the following:

CASSEROLES AND SOUPS can be cooked but those which need long, slow cooking are better done in a conventional oven or slow cooker. They can, of course, be reheated in a microwave.

CAKES tend to look pale unless they contain ingredients such as chocolate or ginger. Icing will disguise this.

BREAD AND PASTRY are crisper and better cooked conventionally but can be warmed through in a microwave cooker.

RICE AND PASTA can be cooked satisfactorily but no more quickly than on a conventional hob. However they reheat very well in a microwave.

MEAT AND POULTRY cook well but do not have the crisp, brown appearance acquired in a conventional oven.

EGG AND CHEESE DISHES can be cooked but are easily ruined by just a few seconds too many. Whole eggs explode unless the yolk is pricked with a knife point or cocktail stick and need an exact temperature. Egg mixtures and cheese dishes can easily become rubbery if cooking is too long or the temperature too high.

SOUFFLÉS, YORKSHIRE PUDDING, BREADED AND BATTERED FISH don't cook well.

THAWING IN A MICROWAVE COOKER

One major advantage of a microwave cooker is the speed with which it thaws frozen food. This means you can leave deciding what to eat until you know how many people will want food and how hungry they are. Your microwave instructions will tell you how to thaw in your model.

MICROWAVING FROZEN FOOD

A freezer is an excellent complement to a microwave cooker and forward planning can make the freezer-to-microwave-to-table exercise one of the easier.

Freeze food in containers which can be used for thawing (if necessary) and reheating in the microwave and, if possible, serving at table.

Freeze food in small portions to give you greater flexibility. Single and double portions allow you to prepare exactly the quantity you need for any one meal. Dishes frozen in massive quantities take longer to thaw and reheat and may prove wasteful.

Cook double or greater quantities when preparing any recipe which can be frozen and then reheated in the microwave. Initial preparation and conventional cooking will take little longer and save time in the future.

COOK'S MICROWAVE TIPS

VEGETABLES

- Cut large vegetables into similar-sized pieces so they cook evenly.
- Don't add extra liquid to frozen vegetables.
- Pierce vegetables to be cooked in their skins to prevent bursting.

MEAT, POULTRY AND FISH

- Use a special microwave thermometer to check internal temperature.
- Improve browning by cooking in a covered glass dish.
- Don't salt meat, poultry or fish before cooking as this draws out moisture and toughens the texture.
- Slash the skin of whole fish to speed cooking time and prevent bursting, and brush with melted butter or oil to stop it drying out.
- Pierce the membrane on kidneys and liver to prevent bursting.

BAKING

- Underbake rather than overcook. You can always return the mixture to the microwave for a little extra time.
- Don't worry if a mixture looks wet after the recommended cooking time. Standing time will complete the baking process.
- Don't grease and flour containers or extra fat will leach into the mixture. Use greaseproof paper to line them.
- When converting recipes remember you'll need a wetter mixture. Add an extra 15 ml (1 tbsp) milk for each egg used.
- Always use a large container as baked mixtures tend to rise considerably. Never fill a container more than half full.
- Brush pastry cases with lightly beaten egg white to prevent the filling making the pastry soggy.
- Use a microwave roasting rack when baking so that microwaves can reach the underside.
- When thawing bread and cakes there is no need to cover them.
- When thawing raw pastry, start it off in the microwave and finish at room temperature to prevent it starting to cook.

READY MEALS

It is most important to cook ready meals until the whole dish is piping hot. Always stir if possible and follow the recommended cooking and standing times, adding extra cooking time if you are concerned. The dish should be too hot to eat immediately it comes out of the oven. The reason for this is that if any cold spots are present in the food (particularly likely if it is a dish that you can't stir), potentially harmful bacteria can survive. It is essential that all the food reaches a temperature of 70°C for a minimum of 2 minutes to prevent this. To ensure this you should:

- Allow a standing time of 2 minutes for small items and reheated foods.
- Stir soups, stews and any food which will not be spoiled by stirring, and then stand for 2 minutes.
- Stand containers of dense food which cannot be stirred for longer; eg 5 minutes for a shepherd's pie to serve 4 people.

BABY FOOD

Use your microwave to warm baby milk and to heat up baby food. Home-prepared dishes should be heated in suitable containers; commercially prepared foods can be heated either in their glass jars (with the lids removed) or decanted from cans and other containers into microwave-safe dishes. Always check all food and drink for babies to ensure it is not too hot before giving it to them. Remember to allow standing time as liquid and food will continue to heat up for a few minutes after removing from the oven.

MICROWAVE TIME-SAVERS

Even if you use your microwave simply for thawing and reheating and don't do much cooking from scratch in it, there are lots of ways in which it provides invaluable back-up to conventional cooking by cutting down on preparation time – and often extra dirty dishes. It is also useful for cooking small quantities of foods which could be more complicated or messy when cooked conventionally. An example is a small quantity of jam or chutney if you have only a small quantity of fruit to process.

- Warm bread rolls in a wicker basket.
- Soften or melt butter quickly.
- Reheat pancakes quickly.
- Soften sugar which has hardened in its packet.
- Liquefy hardened honey or golden syrup (glass jars only).
- Plump dried fruit in water.
- Toast nuts.
- Warm citrus fruit in order to produce more juice.
- Soften ice cream.
- Pierce chestnut skins and cook in minutes.
- Melt chocolate quickly.
- Warm milk for sauce making or serving with coffee.
- Make individual hot drinks.
- Bring cold red wine up to the correct temperature for drinking.
- Dissolve gelatine.
- Make porridge.
- Warm individual bowls of soup.
- Make scrambled egg in its serving dish.
- Cook jacket potatoes. They can be eaten immediately with a soft skin or transferred to a hot oven for a short time until crisp.
- Reheat rice and pasta.
- Dry herbs.
- Bake apples.
- Melt jelly cubes.
- Melt jam for coating a fruit cake before applying a layer of marzipan.
- Melt small quantities of hard or semi-hard fat for brushing on to foods which are to be grilled.
- Make small quantities of jam, lemon curd and chutney.
- Blanch small quantities of vegetables before freezing them.
- Partially cook chicken portions and chops before you put them on the barbecue to complete cooking.
- Toast flaked almonds.
- Eliminate the boiling stage for roast potatoes which can then be immediately transferred to a dish of hot fat in the conventional oven.
- Cook fillings for pastry cases while the pastry is baking blind in the conventional oven.
- Warm up individual snacks, eg baked beans put on a piece of ready-made toast.

ADJUSTING CONVENTIONAL RECIPES

Many recipes which give instructions for conventional cooking can be prepared equally satisfactorily in a microwave oven.

As you become more experienced at microwave cooking techniques you will be able to judge cooking and standing times ever more accurately. It is sensible to make (pencilled) notes on the conventional recipe once you are happy with its microwaved version.

FOOD STORAGE

Correct food storage is vitally important for ensuring that you avoid food poisoning, and for good nutrition. Today, most of us don't have a larder, but we do have freezers, refrigerators, and access to canned and dried foods – all of which extend the life of various foods and can cut down on the time spent shopping.

Good food storage requires planning and effort and doesn't just happen by chance. To start with your kitchen and food storage areas need to be hygienic.

RULES FOR KITCHEN HYGIENE

- Keep your kitchen as clean as possible.
- Pets should be kept out and certainly discouraged from walking or sitting on worktops.
- Wash down and dry surfaces, sinks, floor and the refrigerator regularly.
- Wash your hands before handling food and again between handling different types of food (eg raw and cooked meat where you could transfer bacteria from one to the other).
- Never put cooked or ready-to-eat foods on to a surface which has just had raw food on it.
- If you don't own a dishwasher, change drying up cloths and cleaning cloths every day.
- Scrub wooden chopping boards thoroughly, if necessary scraping them occasionally with a knife blade. Plastic chopping boards are more hygienic as they can be washed in very hot water or put in a dishwasher. Ideally keep separate boards for different foods, eg meat, fish and vegetables.
- Keep an eye open for weevils or pests, throw out any infested food and take the action necessary to eradicate them. This may require professional help.
- Even if your washing machine is in the kitchen, do not sort dirty laundry on the worktops. Wash your hands after handling dirty washing.
- If you cut yourself, cover the wound with a clean sterile dressing. Never handle food with an uncovered cut.

HANDLING PERISHABLE FOODS

- Do not shop for perishable foods unless you are taking them home immediately. Time spent in a shopping bag or car can cause growth of bacteria.
- Use a thermometer to check that your refrigerator is running at the correct temperature. This should be between 0°C and 5°C to prevent the development of micro-organisms. This temperature will not kill micro-organisms which are already present in food but keep them dormant, which is why it's vital to refrigerate perishables as soon as possible.
- Do not put warm or hot food in a refrigerator as it can raise the temperature of items already in there and cause bacterial growth.
- When cooking food which you intend to refrigerate, cool it as quickly as possible. Transfer it from the cooking container into a cool container and stand it on a rack to allow air to circulate all round. With large quantities, lower the container into a bowl of iced water which may need to be changed several times.
- If a refrigerator develops mould, wash and dry the interior thoroughly.
- Defrost the refrigerator regularly (unless it is self defrosting) and in any case wash it out from time to time with a solution of bicarbonate of soda in warm water. Detergent and washing up liquid should not be used because they tend to leave a smell which can transfer to food.
- Don't open the refrigerator door more often than necessary since this allows warm air to get in. Think what you need before opening.
- Don't overfill the refrigerator. Cool air needs to be able to circulate round the products.
- Keep all foods in covered containers.

REFRIGERATOR STORAGE

The following chart is an approximate guide to refrigerator storage times. You should adhere to the 'use by' dates on packaging. If you transfer something to another container use a chinagraph (freezer) pen to mark the date on which you opened it and by when you should use it. Your refrigerator should be set at an operating temperature between 1-5°C (34-41°F). You should regularly use a refrigerator thermometer to check this.

It is important to keep all food stored in the refrigerator covered so that cross-contamination of flavours does not occur. Strongly flavoured items like mature cheese and fish can easily affect less strongly flavoured foods such as milk and chicken.

Foods should be stored in particular parts of the refrigerator for two reasons:
- Because some areas are cooler than others.
- To prevent things like raw meat juices dripping on to other items.

APPROXIMATE REFRIGERATOR STORAGE TIMES

Raw meat		Cooked meat	
joints	3 days	joints	3 days
poultry	2 days	casseroles/stews	2 days
raw sliced meat	2 days	sliced meat	2 days
minced meat	1 day	ham	2 day
offal	1 day	meat pies	2 days
sausages	3 days		
bacon	7 days	**Dairy produce**	
bacon		milk (pasteurised,	
(in unopened vacuum pack)	2-3 weeks	homogenised)	4-5 days
fish	should be eaten	cheese, hard	7-14 days
	on day of	cheese, semi-hard	7-10 days
	purchase	cheese, soft	2-3 days
Vegetables		eggs (stored pointed end down)	2 weeks
salad leaves	2-3 days		
green vegetables	3-4 days		

WHERE TO STORE FOOD IN THE REFRIGERATOR

Top and centre shelves		Bottom shelf/shelves (above salad drawer)	
butter	lard	fresh meat	cooked meat
margarine	spreads	ham	sausages
cheese	preserves	fish	shellfish
salad dressings	mayonnaise	milk products	cream
sauces	eggs		
convenience foods	cooked items	NOTE: All meats should be packaged separately and raw meat and poultry stored below cooked meat and dairy products.	

Door			
milk	fruit juice		

Salad drawer	
fruit	vegetables

STORING FROZEN FOOD IN THE REFRIGERATOR

Some refrigerator models have a frozen food compartment for storing ready-frozen food. Only those which carry the four-star symbol **** can be used for freezing fresh food. An appliance with a lower star rating is only suitable for storing ready-frozen foods as follows:

*   up to 1 week
**   up to 1 month
***   up to 3 months

STORING CANNED FOOD

Canned food is commercially cooked in the can so that the food and its nutrients are sealed in, and the bacteria are sealed out. While canned food keeps longer than other preserved foods it is important to rotate your stock of cans and to check that they show no signs of rust, denting or 'blowing' at the seam which means the contents can be damaged.

Cans now carry a 'use by' date which means you can keep an eye on your stock and ensure that older cans are used up first.

Once opened canned food should be treated as fresh. Contents should be transferred to a clean, covered container, stored in the refrigerator and used within 2 days.

STORING DRIED FOOD

Dried food has a long life if stored correctly in clean, dry containers that are tightly sealed to prevent damp and infestation getting in. It is important never to add newly bought dried food, such as flour, to an existing half-used pack. It should be put into a separate container which has been washed and thoroughly dried.

Strongly flavoured dried foods such as coffee and spices should be bought in only small quantities as they quickly lose their aroma when exposed to air. Ideally they should be moved to ever-smaller containers as you use them up but since this is impractical it is best to buy in quantities which will be used up fairly quickly.

Check the 'use by' date on packaging to ascertain how long dried food can be stored.

Freezing

Freezing is an easy way of preserving food at home. Most foods, once frozen, keep for long periods of time. A well filled freezer will enable you to produce meals quickly – especially when combined with a microwave for thawing and reheating.

WHY FREEZE?

- Food can be stored for long periods without deteriorating.
- Home grown and 'free' hedgerow produce, such as blackberries, can be stored until required, rather than eaten immediately.
- Bargains in terms of special buys, Saturday afternoon offers and economy packs save money and can be frozen.
- Leftovers can be frozen so you don't have to eat the same food two days running.
- You can cook when it suits you and freeze the results – individual and double portions may be useful if your household is small or varies in numbers at mealtimes. These are also quicker to thaw than large quantities.
- You can keep a selection of out-of-season foods to make special dishes, eg raspberries, redcurrants and game.

CHOOSING A FREEZER

Freezers come in three types – chest, upright and combined fridge/freezers.

CHEST FREEZERS have a top-opening lid. They are cheaper to buy and run than other types but are most suitable if kept somewhere like a shed or garage rather than a kitchen where they take up a lot of space. It can also be difficult to find things in a chest freezer, partly because it has a tendency to become cluttered at the top. If you are below average height, you may have difficulty reaching items stored in the bottom. However the largest chest freezers are considerably bigger than the largest uprights so if you want to store a lot of food and have the space for one it could be your best choice.

UPRIGHT FREEZERS come in a variety of sizes and widths. You can buy models ranging from those which fit under a worktop to tall ones resembling wardrobes. Upright freezers are easier to load and unload than chest ones and will come with either shelves (usually fitted with a front baffle to keep cold air in when you open the door) or sliding drawers or baskets, both of which make it easier to see what is inside.

Some upright freezers are frost free which means there is no build up of frost in them. They are more expensive to buy and run but do eliminate the chore of defrosting and work at maximum efficiency all the time. A disadvantage is that because they use a fan to prevent frost build up they are noisier than standard models.

FRIDGE/FREEZERS combine two appliances in one and are useful in kitchens where space is tight. The size of the refrigerator and freezer compartments varies with different models so you can choose a small refrigerator and large freezer, large refrigerator and small freezer or one which has identical capacities.

All freezers run off a 13-amp socket outlet and need no special installation. However, it is important that the appliances should never be switched off (other than when defrosting), so if your plug is in a run of two or three it's sensible to tape the switch to the 'on' position or use a labelled or coloured plug to identify the freezer.

When choosing a freezer consider the controls on it. You need an external light to show that the appliance is working and preferably also an extra light which shows when you have the fast-freeze switch on – so you can remember to turn it off! It is also useful to have a temperature warning light which indicates if the internal temperature has fallen below the safe level. Some models provide a digital read-out enabling you to see exactly what the internal temperature is.

If you have small children buy a model which has controls which they cannot reach.

FREEZER EMERGENCIES

In the case of a power cut or if someone has accidentally switched off the power supply DO NOT PANIC. Frozen food takes a long time to thaw out and will be quite safe for a few hours. There are various things you can do:

- If you have advance warning from the electricity supplier that the power will go off, turn on the fast freeze switch, having first made sure that the freezer is completely full. Use old towels or rolled up newspaper to fill any gaps.
- Cover the freezer with a blanket or rug to

increase insulation but do not cover the condenser and pipes.
- Do not open the door until several hours after the appliance has begun working again.
- If it's just your freezer that's affected, ask neighbours if you can transfer food to their freezers.

In the case of a long period without power, note that food in a chest freezer should be safe for about 48 hours without power; food in an upright freezer for about 30 hours.

If all else fails, salvage what you can of the contents. Raw items can be cooked cooked, then frozen again afterwards; other items can be cooked and consumed. Throw away any item of food which you think may not be in edible condition. Don't risk food poisoning for the sake of saving a small amount of money.

Freezer insurance will cover you for the cost of spoiled food if, for example, your freezer breaks down while you are away. This can usually be done through your household contents policy and you should check how much you are covered for. When making a claim you may have either to save the food for someone from the insurance company to inspect or to itemise it with individual weights and values.

MOVING HOUSE

Ideally, you should run down your stock of frozen food before you move so that the freezer is empty, defrosted and clean. Some removal firms do have an electricity supply in their van but most do not.

FREEZING TECHNIQUES

Before freezing anything in a new model, check the manufacturer's handbook for information about control settings and quantities.

RULES FOR SUCCESSFUL FREEZING

- Freeze only good quality food. Freezing only preserves; it does not improve quality.
- Handle food as little as possible.
- Freeze in small quantities. You can always combine packs to make up the number of portions needed.
- Pack and seal food with care. If cold air or moisture get into the frozen food it will deteriorate and there is also the risk of cross flavouring.
- Don't put anything warm into the freezer as it will raise the temperature and cause frosting up and deterioration of other foods. If you

don't have time to cool something naturally, place the container in a bowl of iced water.

- Label and date food so you can easily identify what you need. Ideally, keep a freezer log book; add and delete items as you buy, cook and consume. That way you also don't have to keep opening the door and rummaging around to see what you've got.
- Never freeze more than one tenth of your freezer's capacity in any 24 hours or you will raise the internal temperature and risk damaging other foods.
- Except when freezing very small quantities, eg a loaf of bread or some leftovers, use the fast freeze switch. This overrides the thermostat and allows the temperature to drop below the normal storage temperature. The advantage of this is that food freezes faster, forming smaller ice crystals and retaining its original texture. Reducing the temperature also helps keep existing frozen food cold while the unfrozen items are freezing. The fast freeze switch should be turned on about six hours before you put new food in in.
- When freezing solid foods pack them tightly, removing as much air as possible. You can buy a vacuum pump which helps with this. Wrap them closely in foil or freezer film which fits where it touches. Use the correct sized container for the quantity and fill up any empty space with foil or freezer film.
- When freezing liquids leave room for expansion since frozen liquid expands by about one tenth of its volume and will push of lids if a container is filled too full.

FREEZER PACKAGING

For some frozen foods you will require special packaging; others can be stored in existing items from your kitchen such as plastic storage boxes and casseroles. Be sure that you do not freeze a meal in a casserole dish which you will want to use again before you consume its contents.

POLYTHENE BAGS: These should be heavy gauge (recommended for freezing) and will need to be sealed with twist ties or a special heat-sealant gadget. Extract as much air as possible before sealing. You can buy colour-coded bags – red for meat, blue for fish and green for fruit and vegetables – which make identification in the freezer easier.

FREEZER FILM: This is useful for covering items closely. It is also suitable to use as a lining for acidic foods to be over-wrapped in foil, and handy for packing small individual items which can be stored together in a polythene bag. Do not use ordinary cling film in the freezer.

FOIL: Ideally, buy special freezer foil which can be used in a single layer. Otherwise use standard kitchen foil in a double layer. Foil is good for wrapping round awkward-shaped items, such as a leg of lamb. Do not wrap acidic foods directly in foil or they may react with it.

INTERLEAVING: Pieces of greaseproof paper, polythene sheeting, foil or freezer film are good for keeping foods separate which might otherwise stick together, eg burgers, chicken pieces, sausages, chops and so on. You can buy ready-cut interleaves or make your own.

CONTAINERS: These may be foil, plastic or other materials suitable for the freezer, such as ceramics. In general square containers are more suitable than round ones since they stack better in the freezer and waste less space.

FREEZER TAPE: This sticks firm at low temperatures, unlike standard domestic sticky tape, and can be used for sealing most materials used in the freezer.

LABELS: However convinced you may be that you will recognise items you freeze when you put them in, after a few weeks they will look like everything else. Tales are legion of people mistaking borshch for blackcurrant ice cream and tomato sauce for strawberry purée. So buy special freezer labels (ordinary sticky labels won't stay on) and log details. If there's space put the contents, date and any further cooking instructions so that any anyone in the house can cook the dish from frozen.

OVERWRAP any item that looks as if its initial packaging is likely to come undone and let air in. With commercially packed foods make sure that you exclude air when you remove some of the contents. Things like fish fingers which come in a carton or packet should be repackaged in freezer film, foil or a polythene bag once some have been consumed, in order to keep them in good condition.

BUYING FOOD FOR THE FREEZER

When buying commercially frozen food for your freezer make sure you get it home as soon as possible to prevent it starting to thaw. Otherwise it will deteriorate and is also likely to affect the food already in the freezer.

When buying fresh food to be frozen, remember it is perishable and needs cold storage as soon as possible.

QUICK GUIDE TO FREEZER STORAGE TIMES

Item to be Frozen	Maximum Storage Time	Item to be Frozen	Maximum Storage Time
Dairy produce		**Meat and poultry**	
cream	6-8 months	beef and lamb	12 months
butter (unsalted)	6-8 months	pork and veal	4-6 months
butter (salted)	3-4 months	offal	2 months
cheese (hard)	4-6 months	sliced bacon and cured meat	2-3 months
cheese (soft)	3-4 months	bacon and ham joints	3-4 months
ice cream, mousses, etc	3-4 months	chicken and turkey	10-12 months
		duck and goose	4-6 months
Fish		venison	10-12 months
white fish	6-8 months	rabbit, hare and game	4-6 months
oily fish	3-4 months	sausages and sausagemeat	1 month
fish portions	3-4 months	minced red meat	3-4 months
shellfish	2-3 months		
		Prepared foods	
Fruit and vegetables		bread and bread rolls	2-3 months
fruit in syrup	9-12 months	other yeast products and pastries	3-4 months
fruit (without added sugar)	6-8 months	cakes	4-6 months
fruit purée	6-8 months	sandwiches	2-3 months
fruit juice	4-6 months	soups and sauces	3 months
vegetables (blanched – most varieties)	10-12 months	ready meals	4-6 months
		if highly seasoned	2-3 months
		boil-in-bag meals	4-6 months
		stock	6 months

THAWING FOOD

- Cover food loosely while it is thawing.
- Do not thaw food in a warm environment, as this provides ideal conditions for bacteria to multiply. Choose a cool place, such as a larder, or thaw in the refrigerator.
- If food is thawed in the refrigerator, make sure that it is completely defrosted before cooking. This is particularly important with large joints of meat and poultry, otherwise the internal temperature when cooking may not be hot enough to destroy any dangerous bacteria that may be present in the meat. The legs of poultry should be able to move freely and there should be no ice crystals in evidence.
- Cook food as soon as possible after thawing.
- Always throw away the liquid from thawing meat and poultry; it must never be allowed to contaminate other food.
- Do not refreeze food once it has thawed, unless it has been subsequently cooked. Raw meat can, therefore, be successfully refrozen.
- If the freezer breaks down, only refreeze food if it is still full of ice crystals and firm in the centre. Some foods, like ice cream and uncooked baked goods, will not retain their quality.
- Never refreeze any food that has been thawed accidentally over a period of days.

THAWING FOOD IN THE MICROWAVE

All microwave ovens vary. It is essential to follow the advice given in your instruction manual. Only thaw food in the microwave if it is going to be cooked or eaten immediately.

FREEZING VEGETABLES

Freeze only those vegetables which are really fresh – within 12 hours of their being picked. Most vegetables keep better for longer if blanched before freezing.

To blanch vegetables conventionally, immerse up to 450 g (1 lb) at a time in a large pan of boiling water (a preserving pan is good for this). Bring back to the boil (see chart for blanching times). Remove and put straight into a bowl of iced water to cool them. Blanching water can be used 6-7 times and the cooling water can be kept cool by the repeated addition of ice cubes or frozen ice blocks. A blanching basket makes this task easier; otherwise use a large square of muslin or a suitable strainer.

For small quantities blanching can be done in a microwave. Place the vegetables in a bowl containing 45 ml (3 tbsp) cold water and heat on full power for 3-5 minutes, stirring halfway through. Small diced or sliced vegetables need only a short time; large, dense root vegetables will need longer. Allow standing time of 1 minute before cooling as above and freezing.

Although blanching improves the texture of vegetables to be stored for some time, it is not essential to blanch those which will be eaten within a few weeks.

FREEZING VEGETABLES

Vegetable	Preparation	Blanching time
Artichokes, globe	Wash in cold water, add a little lemon juice to the blanching water, blanch, cool, and drain upside-down on absorbent kitchen paper. Pack in rigid containers.	4-5 minutes
Asparagus	Grade into thick and thin stems but don't tie into bunches. Wash in cold water, blanch, cool and drain. Tie into small bundles.	Thin – 1 minute Thick – 2 minutes
Aubergines	Peel and cut roughly into 2.5 cm (1 inch) slices. Blanch, cool and dry on absorbent kitchen paper. Pack in layers in rigid containers, separated by interleaving paper.	1-2 minutes
Beans, French, runner, broad	French: trim ends and blanch. Runner: slice thickly and blanch. Broad: shell and blanch. In each case, cool, drain and pack.	1 minute 1 minute 1½ minutes

Beetroot	Choose small beetroot up to 5 cm (2 inches) in diameter. Wash well and rub skin off after blanching. Beetroot under 2.5 cm (1 inch) in diameter may be frozen whole; others should be sliced or diced. Pack in rigid containers.
	NOTE: Long storage can make beetroot rubbery.
		Small whole –
		  5 minutes
		Large –
		  Cook until tender

Broccoli	Wash in salted water, and cut into small sprigs. Blanch, cool and drain. Pack in boxes in 1-2 layers, tips to stalks.	1 minute
Brussels sprouts	Make small cuts in stem. Blanch, cool and drain.	30 seconds – 1 minute
Carrots	If left whole scrape after blanching. Slice or cut into small dice. Blanch, cool, drain and pack.	2-3 minutes
Cauliflower	Break into small florets about 5 cm (2 inches) in diameter. Add the juice of a lemon to the blanching water to keep them white; blanch, cool, drain and pack.	1 minute
Celeriac	Cook until almost tender, peel and slice. Cool, then pack.	

Vegetable	Preparation	Blanching time
Celery	Cut into 2.5 cm (1 inch) lengths. Use for cooked dishes.	
Chillies	Remove stalks and scoop out the seeds and pithy part. Blanch, cool, drain and pack.	10 seconds
Corn on the cob	Select young yellow kernels, not starchy, over-ripe or shrunken. Remove husks and 'silks'. Blanch, cool and dry. Pack individually in freezer polythene or foil. NOTE: Freezing may cause loss of flavour and tenderness.	Small – 2 minutes Medium – 3 minutes Large – 4 minutes
Courgettes	Wash and cut into 1 cm (½ inch) slices. Blanch, cool, drain and pack.	10 seconds
Fennel	Trim and slice thinly. Blanch, cool, drain and pack.	30 seconds
Kohlrabi	Choose small roots, 5-7 cm (2-3 inches) in diameter. Cut off tops, peel and dice. Blanch, cool, drain and pack.	1 minute
Leeks	Cut into 1 cm (½ inch) slices and wash well. Blanch, cool, drain, pack and freeze. Only suitable for casseroles or soups.	30 seconds
Mangetout	Trim the ends. Blanch, cool, drain and pack.	10 seconds
Marrow	Choose young marrows. Peel, cut into 1-2.5 cm (½-1 inch) slices, blanch, cool, drain and pack.	10 seconds
Onions	Peel, finely chop, blanch and pack in small rigid containers for cooking later; packages should be overwrapped to prevent the smell filtering out. Button onions may be blanched whole and used in casseroles.	1 minute Button onions – 2 minutes
Parsnips	Choose young parsnips, trim, peel and cut into narrow strips. Blanch, cool, drain and pack.	1 minute
Peas, green	Shell and blanch. Shake the blanching basket from time to time to distribute the heat evenly. Cool, drain and pack in polythene bags or rigid containers.	1 minute
Peppers, sweet, green, red, yellow	Wash well, remove stems, seeds and membranes. Blanch as halves for stuffed peppers, or in thin slices for casseroles. For better colour, if storage is less than 6 months, do not blanch.	1 minute
Potatoes	Best frozen cooked as Croquettes or Duchesse Potatoes (see page 238).	1 minute
Spinach	Blanch in small quantities, cool quickly and press out excess moisture, or purée. Pack in rigid containers or polythene bags.	10 seconds
Tomatoes	Tomatoes are most useful frozen as purée. Small whole ones packed in bags and frozen can be used in cooked dishes. Purée: Skin the tomatoes, simmer in their own juice for 5 minutes, until soft. Rub through a nylon sieve or purée in a blender or food processor, cool and pack in small containers.	
Turnips	Trim and peel. Cut into small dice, about 1 cm (½ inch). Blanch, cool, drain and pack in rigid containers.	2½ minutes

FREEZING FRUIT

Fruit which is to be frozen should be perfectly ripe and free from any blemishes.

Overripe fruit can be frozen in the form of a purée. With fruits such as apples you will have to cook them first before puréeing, but fruits such as peaches can be peeled, stoned and puréed in their fresh form.

When freezing fruit first consider how you are likely to use it when you come to eat it and prepare accordingly. Small fruits which don't need peeling are best frozen as they are. Remove stalks where appropriate and spread them out either on special open-freezing trays or on baking sheets or trays lined with non-stick or greaseproof paper. Once frozen they can be stored in bags and will not stick to each other so you can easily remove just the quantity required.

Firm textured fruits and those which tend to discolour should be frozen in a syrup made up as indicated in the chart. Dissolve the sugar in the water, add lemon juice where indicated and leave to cool before putting in the fruit. Light fruits which tend to float to the surface should be kept below it by putting a damp, crumpled piece of non-absorbent paper on top. Leave 1-2 cm (about ½ inch) headspace for the liquid to expand. Most frozen fruit in syrup will keep for 9-12 months. Open frozen fruit and purées keep for 6-8 months; fruit juices 4-6 months.

FREEZING FRUIT

Fruit	Preparation
Apples, sliced	Peel, core and cut into 5 mm (¼ inch) slices. Drop into water and lemon juice. Blanch for 2-3 minutes and cool in ice-cold water before packing; useful for pies and flans.
Apples, puréed	Peel, core and stew in the minimum amount of water – sweetened or unsweetened. Purée or mash. Leave to cool before packing.
Apricots	Plunge them into boiling water for 30 seconds to loosen the skins, then peel. Then prepare in one of the following ways: • Cut in half or slice into syrup made with 450 g (1 lb) sugar to 1 litre (1¾ pints) water with the juice of a lemon added to prevent browning. Immerse the apricots by placing a piece of clean, crumpled, non-absorbent paper on the fruit, under the lid. • Leave whole and freeze in syrup. In time, an almond flavour may develop around the stone. • Purée cooked apricots.
Blackberries	Wash and dry fruit. Open freeze. Pack in rigid containers.
Blackcurrants	Use one of the following methods: • Use open freeze method for whole fruit. • Purée – cook to a purée with very little water and brown sugar, according to taste.
Blueberries or Bilberries	Use one of the following methods: • Open freeze. • Cold syrup – 900 g (2 lb) sugar dissolved in 1 litre (1¾ pints) water.
Cherries	Use one of the following methods: • Open freeze whole fruit; best used for pie fillings. • Cover with cold syrup – 450 g (1 lb) sugar to 1 litre (1¾ pints) water; leave headspace. Take care not to open until required, as fruit loses colour rapidly on exposure to the air.
Damsons	The skins are inclined to toughen during freezing. Best packing methods are: • Purée. • Halve, remove the stones and pack in cold syrup – 450 g (1 lb) sugar to 1 litre (1¾ pints) water; they will need cooking after freezing and can be used as stewed fruit. • Poached and sweetened.
Figs	Wash the figs gently to avoid bruising. Avoid freezing very ripe figs. Remove stems. Use one of the following methods: • Open freeze, either whole or peeled, then pack in polythene bags. • Peel and pack in cold syrup – 450 g (1 lb) sugar to 1 litre (1¾ pints) water. • Leave whole and wrap in foil; suitable for dessert figs.

Fruit	Preparation
Gooseberries	Use one of the following methods: • Open freeze; use for pie fillings. • Cold syrup – 900 g (2 lb) sugar to 1 litre (1¾ pints) water. • Purée – stew fruit in a very little water, rub through a nylon sieve and sweeten.
Grapefruit	Segment and pack in syrup (equal quantities of sugar and water – add any juice from fruit to syrup).
Greengages	Halve, remove stones and pack in syrup – 450 g (1 lb) sugar to 1 litre (1¾ pints) water, with the juice of 1 lemon added. Place in rigid containers. Do not open pack until required. Skins tend to toughen.
Lemons and Limes	Use one of the following methods: • Squeeze juice and freeze in ice-cube trays; transfer frozen cubes to polythene bags for storage. • Open freeze – whole lemons, slices or segments. • Remove all pith from the peel, cut into julienne strips, blanch for 1 minute, cool and pack; use for garnishing dishes.
Loganberries	Remove stalks and open freeze.
Mangoes, Papaya	Peel and slice ripe fruit into cold syrup – 450 g (1 lb) sugar to 1 litre (1¾ pints) water; add 30 ml (2 tbsp) lemon juice to each 1 litre (1¾ pints) syrup. Serve with additional lemon juice.
Oranges	Pack as for grapefruit, or use one of the following methods: • Squeeze out and freeze the juice; add sugar if desired and freeze in small quantities in containers or in ice-cube trays. • Remove all pith from the peel, cut into julienne strips, blanch for 1 minute, cool and pack; use for garnishing dishes. • Seville oranges may be scrubbed, packed in suitable quantities and frozen whole until required for making marmalade. (Do not thaw whole frozen fruit in order to cut it up before cooking as some discoloration often occurs – use whole fruit method for marmalade (see page 476). It is advisable to increase weight of Seville or bitter oranges or tangerines by one-eighth when freezing for subsequent marmalade making, in order to offset pectin loss.)
Peaches	Really ripe peaches are best skinned and stoned under running water, as scalding will soften and slightly discolour the flesh. Plunge firm peaches in boiling water for 30 seconds, then skin. Brush with lemon juice. • Pack halves or slices in cold syrup – 450 g (1 lb) sugar to 1 litre (1¾ pints) water, with the juice of 1 lemon added. Pack in rigid containers, leaving headspace. • Purée peeled and stoned peaches; mix in 15 ml (1 tbsp) lemon juice and 125 g (4 oz) sugar to each 450 g (1 lb) fruit – suitable for sorbets.
Pineapple	Peel and core, then slice, dice, crush or cut into wedges. • Pack unsweetened in layers, separated by non-stick paper, in rigid containers. • In cold syrup – 450 g (1 lb) sugar to 1 litre (1¾ pints) water, including any pineapple juice from the preparation – in rigid containers. • Pack crushed pineapple in rigid containers.
Plums	Halve and discard stones. Freeze in cold syrup – 450 g (1 lb) sugar to 1 litre (1¾ pints) water with the juice of 1 lemon. Pack in rigid containers. Do not open pack until required, as the fruit loses colour.
Redcurrants	Open freeze.
Rhubarb	Trim into 1-2.5 cm (½ -1 inch) lengths. Blanch in boiling water for 1 minute and cool quickly. • Pack in cold syrup, using equal quantities sugar and water. • Freeze chopped or pared. Use for pies and crumbles.
Strawberries and Raspberries	Remove stalks. Raspberries freeze well. Whole strawberries can be a disappointment; they are best frozen as a purée. Use one of the following methods: • Open freeze. • Purée; sweeten to taste – about 50 g (2 oz) sugar per 225 g (8 oz) purée; add a little lemon juice to strawberry purée.

GLOSSARY

A brief guide to the cooking methods, terms and ingredients which occur throughout the book. Where a fuller explanation to a particular technique is given elsewhere in the book, a cross reference is provided.

Agar-agar A tastless white powder, made from seaweed, which has useful gelling properties and can be used as a vegetarian substitute for gelatine.

Altitude Affects cooking times and temperatures. The higher the altitude the lower the temperature at which water boils.

Antipasto Italian phrase for a varied selection of hot or cold foods served as an appetiser. Literally means 'before the meal'.

Arrowroot Can be used as an alternative to cornflour as a thickening agent in liquids, such as sauces. It gives a clear gloss, unlike cornflour which produces a cloudy sauce.

Aspic jelly Savoury jelly used for setting and garnishing savoury dishes.

Au gratin Describes a dish which has been coated with sauce, sprinkled with breadcrumbs or cheese and finished by browning under the grill or in the oven. Low sided *gratin* dishes are used.

Bain-marie A low-sided container which is half filled with water kept just below boiling point. Containers of food are placed in it to keep warm or cook without overheating. A *bain-marie* is used for cooking custards and other egg dishes and keeping sauces warm. No special container is needed; a roasting tin will do. The term is also sometimes applied to a double boiler.

Baking Cooking in the oven by dry heat.

Baking blind The method used for cooking flans and tarts without their fillings (see page 380).

Baking powder A raising agent consisting of an acid, usually cream of tartar and an alkali (bicarbonate of soda) which react to produce carbon dioxide. This expands during baking and makes cakes and breads rise.

Barding Covering dry meat or the breast of poultry or game birds with pieces of bacon or fat to prevent the flesh drying out during roasting.

Basting Spooning the juices and melted fat over meat, poultry or game during roasting to keep it moist. The term is also used to describe spooning over a marinade. Use a large spoon.

Bean curd Also known as *tofu* and widely used in vegetarian and oriental cooking. It is made from a pressed purée of soya beans and sold fresh, dried and in cans.

Beating A method of incorporating air into an ingredient or mixture by agitating it vigorously with a spoon, fork, whisk or electric mixer. Also used to soften ingredients.

Béchamel Classic French white sauce, which is used as the basis for other sauces (see page 200) and a variety of savoury dishes.

Beurre manié Equal parts of flour and butter kneaded together to form a paste. Used for thickening soups, stews and casseroles. It is whisked into the hot liquid a little at a time at the end of cooking.

Bicarbonate of soda Sometimes used in baking to act as a raising agent.

Blanching Immersing food briefly in boiling water to whiten it, as in sweetbreads, or to remove the skin, such as peaches and tomatoes. Vegetables which are to be frozen and kept for a certain length of time are blanched to destroy enzymes and preserve the colour, flavour and texture.

Blanquette Stew usually made from white meat, such as veal or poultry, cooked in a white sauce enriched with cream and egg yolk.

Blender An electric machine usually consisting of a goblet with rotating blades in the base (see page 545). Used for puréeing wet mixtures and grinding dry ingredients. Ideal for making fresh breadcrumbs.

Boiling Cooking in liquid at 100°C (212°F). The main foods that are boiled are vegetables, rice and pasta. Syrups and glazes that need reducing and thickening are also boiled, as are some sauces.

Boning Removing the bones from meat or poultry, cutting the flesh as little as possible, so that it can be rolled or stuffed.

Bottling The term used for preserving food or preserves in glass jars under sterile conditions.

Bouchée Small round piece of cooked puff pastry served with a filling on top or inside. Should be no more than 4 cm (1½ inches) in diameter so that it can be eaten in one mouthful (its literal meaning).

Bouquet garni Small bunch of herbs – usually a mixture of parsley stems, thyme and a bay leaf – tied in muslin and used to flavour stocks, soups and stews.

Bourguignonne A French term applied to dishes in which burgundy and small braised button onions are used eg *boeuf bourguignonne*.

Braising A slow cooking method used for cuts of meat, poultry and game which are too tough to roast. It is also good for some vegetables. A pan or casserole with a tightly fitting lid should be used so that little liquid is lost through evaporation. The meat is first browned, then cooked on a bed of chopped vegetables (called a *mirepoix*), with just enough liquid to cover the vegetables. It may be cooked on the hob or in the oven.

Brining A method of preserving by immersing food in a salt and water solution.

Brioche An enriched yeast dough mixture baked in the shape of a cottage loaf. French in origin and usually eaten warm for breakfast.

Brochette Fish, meat or vegetables, cooked on a skewer or spit.

Broiling American term for grilling.

Broth The liquid produced by boiling meat or fish bones in water for a long time. Also sometimes called stock.

Brûlée A French term, literally meaning 'burnt' applied to a dish with a crisp coating of caramelised sugar.

Brut Means unsweetened and is a term used to describe dry wine and champagne.

Calorie A scientific term used in dietetics to measure the heat and energy producing quality of food.

Canapé Small appetisers, usually served with drinks and often consisting of a topping on a bread or pastry base.

Candying Method of impregnating pieces of fruit or peel with sugar to preserve them.

Caramel Substance obtained by heating sugar syrup very slowly until a rich brown colour.

Carbonade Rich stew or braise of meat which includes beer.

Casserole Strictly speaking, a dish with a tightly fitting lid used for cooking meat and vegetables. Now applied to the food cooked in this way.

Celsius Also known as Centigrade. A scale for measuring temperature in which the freezing point of water is 0° and the boiling point 100°. Now used for the oven settings on electric cookers, replacing the Fahrenheit scale which is gradually becoming obsolete in Europe.

Chantilly A classic French version of whipped cream which has been slightly sweetened and may be flavoured with vanilla.

Charcuterie The French term for cooked pork products, such as hams, sausages and terrines.

Charlotte A hot or cold moulded dessert. For a hot charlotte the mould is lined with bread and for a cold charlotte it is lined with sponge fingers.

Chasseur Literally translated means 'hunter-style'. Describes dishes cooked with mushrooms, shallots and white wine.

Chaudfroid A cold dish of jellied fish, poultry or game that is coated in a thick béchamel based or brown sauce, set under a layer of aspic.

Chilling Cooling food without freezing.

Chining Applied to joints of meat, this means severing the rib bones from the backbone by sawing through the ribs close to the spine. Joints such as loin or neck of lamb, veal or pork are best chined as this makes them easier to carve into chops or cutlets after cooking.

Chopping Cutting food into small neat pieces without damaging the tissues.

Chorizo Spanish sausage made of smoked pork and pimiento. Sold ready cooked.

Chowder An American dish somewhere between a soup and a stew, usually based on fish, eg clam chowder.

Citric acid A mild acid which occurs naturally in citrus fruit. Commercially produced citric acid is used mainly for preserving soft fruit drinks and in home wine making.

Clarifying Process of removing sediment or impurities from a food. Butter and dripping may be clarified so that they can be used for frying at higher temperatures.

To clarify butter, heat until melted and all bubbling stops. Remove from the heat and stand until the salt and sediment have sunk to the bottom, then gently pour off the fat, straining it through muslin. Chill and use as required. Clarified butter is also known as ghee.

To clarify dripping, melt the fat, then strain it to remove any particles. Pour over two to three times its volume of boiling water and allow to cool. The fat will rise to the top and become firm. Lift it off and wipe the underside with absorbent kitchen paper to remove any sediment.

Clarifying also means to clear a liquid or jelly, such as consommé, usually by adding egg white. The coagulation of the egg white throughout the liquid gathers up all the impurities and forms a scum on the surface which can be discarded.

Clotting A gentle heat applied to cream which produces the thick clotted cream of the south-west of England.

Cocotte Small earthenware, ovenproof container of single portion size. Also called a *ramekin*.

Coddling Method of soft boiling eggs.

Colander Perforated metal or plastic draining basket.

Compote Mixture of fruit stewed in sugar syrup. Served hot or cold.

Concasser A French term used to describe food that is finely or roughly chopped. It is most often applied to skinned, seeded and chopped tomatoes.

Conserve Whole fruit jam.

Consistency Term used to describe the texture of a mixture, eg firm, dropping or soft.

Consommé Concentrated stock which has been clarified.

Corned beef Pieces of beef cured in salt and sugar, pressed together into blocks and canned.

Cornstarch American name for cornflour.

Coulis A French term applied to a purée of vegetables, fish, poultry or fruit.

Court bouillon Seasoned liquid in which meat, poultry, fish or vegetables are boiled or poached.

Couscous Processed semolina in tiny pellets. Staple food in North African countries.

Crackling The crisp skin on roasted pork.

Cream of tartar (tartaric acid) A raising agent which is an ingredient of baking powder and self raising flour.

Creaming Beating together fat and sugar until the mixture resembles whipped cream in texture and colour (pale and fluffy). Used in cakes and puddings which contain a high proportion of fat and require the incorporation of a lot of air.

Crêpe French term for a pancake.

Crimping Decorating the edges of a pie, tart or shortbread by pinching it at regular intervals to give a fluted effect. The term may also refer to trimming cucumber, radishes, etc with a canelle knife or fork to produce a deckled cut finish.

Croquette Mixture of meat, fish, poultry, cooked potatoes or vegetables bound together and formed into roll or cork shapes, coated with egg and breadcrumbs and shallow or deep-fried.

Croûte A circle or rectangle of fried or toasted bread on which game and some main dishes and savouries are served. The term may also refer to a pastry crust, usually crescent shaped, served with savoury dishes.

Croûtons Small pieces of fried or toasted bread which are served with salads and soup.

Curd The parts of milk which coagulate when natural fermentation takes place, or when a curdling agent, such as rennet or an acid is added. The term also refers to a creamy preserve made from fruit (usually lemon or orange) and sugar, eggs and butter.

Curdle To separate fresh milk or a sauce either by adding acid (such as lemon juice) or by heating excessively. Also used to refer to creamed mixtures which have separated when the egg has been beaten in too quickly.

Cure To preserve fish, meat or poultry by salting, drying or smoking.

Dal The Indian collective term for pulses.

Daube Braising meat or vegetables in stock, often with wine or herbs.

Deep-fat Hot oil or fat in which food is totally immersed for deep-frying.

Deglaze To heat stock, wine or other liquid with the cooking juices left in the pan after roasting or sautéeing meat, stirring to dissolve the sediment.

Dégorge To draw out moisture from food, eg salting aubergines to remove bitter juices.

Dice To cut food into small cubes.

Dough A thick mixture of uncooked flour and liquid, usually combined with other ingredients. The term is used to refer to mixtures such as pastry, scones and biscuits as well as those made with yeast.

Drawing Removing the entrails from poultry and game.

Dredging Sprinkling food lightly with flour, sugar or other powdered coating. Fish and meat are often dredged with flour before frying, while cakes, biscuits and pancakes may be sprinkled with caster or icing sugar after cooking.

Dressing Plucking, drawing and trussing poultry and game. The term is also used to describe garnishing a dish, and coating a salad.

Dripping Fat obtained from roasting meat or pieces of fat which are rendered down deliberately (see also Rendering).

Dropping consistency Term used to describe the correct texture of a cake or pudding mixture just before cooking. Test for it by taking a spoonful of the mixture and holding the spoon on its side above the bowl. The mixture should fall off of its own accord within 5 seconds.

Drying Preserving food by dehydration. This is usually done commercially for foods such as rice, pasta and pulses, but it is possible to dry herbs and fruit at home.

Egg and crumbing Method of coating fish, rissoles, croquettes, etc before frying or baking.

Emulsion A mixture of two liquids which do not automatically dissolve into each other, eg oil and water. They can be made to emulsify by vigorous beating or shaking together, as when combining oil and vinegar in a French Dressing.

En croûte Term describing food which is wrapped in pastry before cooking.

En papillote A French term applied to food which is baked and/or served in baking parchment or greaseproof paper for a brief period and served in the parcel.

Enzyme Substances present in all foods which have not been subjected to processing. They work within foods continuously and are responsible for changes in food condition. Most enzymes are killed by cooking (see also Blanching).

Escalope A thin slice of meat, such as veal, turkey or pork, cut from the top of the leg and often egged and crumbed, then fried or grilled.

Espagnole Classic French rich brown sauce, used as the basis for other sauces (see page 202).

Extract Concentrated flavouring which is used in small quantities, eg meat extract, yeast extract.

Faggot A mixture of pork offal, onion and breadcrumbs which is baked and eaten with gravy. The term is also used to describe a small bunch of herbs tied like a miniature faggot of wood, such as a bouquet garni.

Fahrenheit System of measuring temperature which is being replaced with Celsius. Its freezing point is 32° and boiling point 212°.

Farce Alternative French term for stuffing.

Farina Fine flour made from wheat, nuts or potatoes.

Fermenting Term used to denote chemical changes deliberately or accidentally brought about by fermenting agents, such as yeast or bacteria. The process is utilised for making bread, yogurt and wine.

Fillet A term used for the undercut of a loin of beef, veal, pork or game; boned breasts of birds; and boned sides of fish.

Fines herbes Classic French mixture of chopped herbs, ie parsley, tarragon, chives and chervil.

Flambé Flavouring a dish with alcohol, usually brandy or rum, which is then ignited so that the actual alcohol content is burned off. Traditionally done to Christmas Pudding (see page 332) and Crêpes Suzette (see page 334).

Folding in (cutting and folding) Method of combining a whisked or creamed mixture with other ingredients so that it retains its lightness. Used mainly for meringues, soufflés and certain cake mixtures. Folding is best done with a metal spoon.

Fondue Dish cooked at the table over a fondue burner into which the diners dip food speared on long pronged fondue forks.

Fool Cold dessert consisting of puréed fruit with whipped cream or custard blended into it.

Forcemeat Stuffing for meat, fish or vegetables.

Fricassée White stew of chicken, rabbit, veal or vegetables, finished with cream and egg yolks (see also Blanquette).

Frosting American term for icing cakes. Also refers to the decorating of fruits, flowers and the rims of glasses, by coating with a fine layer of sugar.

Frothing Dredging the surface of roast meat, usually game, with flour and heating to a brown colour in a hot oven.

Frying Method of cooking food in hot fat or oil. There are various methods: shallow-frying in a little fat in a shallow pan; deep-frying where the food is totally immersed in oil; dry-frying in which fatty foods, such as bacon and sausages, are cooked in a non-stick pan without extra fat; see also Stir-frying.

Galantine A dish of white meat which has been boned, sometimes stuffed, rolled, cooked, pressed and glazed with aspic to be served cold.

Garnish A decoration, usually edible, such as parsley, watercress, or lemon which is added to a savoury dish to enhance its appearance.

Gelatine An animal-derived gelling agent sold in powdered form in sachets, and as leaf gelatine.

Genoese Sponge cake made with a whisked egg mixture enriched with melted butter.

Ghee Clarified butter widely used in Indian cookery (see also Clarifying).

Glacé French word meaning iced or glossy.

Glaze Food used to give a glossy coating to sweet and savoury dishes to improve their appearance and sometimes flavour. Ingredients for glazes include beaten egg, egg white, milk and syrup.

Gluten A protein constituent of wheat and other cereals. The amount present in flours varies and accounts for the different textures of cakes and breads.

Granita An Italian half-frozen water ice.

Grating Shredding cheese, carrots and other hard foods with a grater or food processor attachment.

Grecque, à la Strictly, this term should only be applied to dishes of Greek origin but this is seldom the case. It is now more often used to describe dishes of general Mediterranean origin, usually flavoured with olive oil, lemon and various spices.

Griddle A flat, heavy, metal plate used on top of the cooker for cooking scones, crumpets etc.

Grinding Reducing foods to small particles in a food mill, pestle and mortar, electric grinder or food processor. Foods ground include coffee beans, nuts and spices.

Grissini Long, slim, brittle Italian bread sticks.

Gut To clean out the inside of a fish, removing all the entrails.

Hanging Leaving meat or game suspended in a cool, dry place to allow air to circulate around it to tenderise the flesh and develop the flavour.

Hard sauce Creamed butter and sugar flavoured with brandy, rum or whisky and chilled until firm; also called brandy or rum butter. Served with hot puddings.

Hors d'oeuvre Often used as a term for a starter but, strictly speaking, means a selection of cold foods served together as an appetiser.

Hulling Removing the calyx from soft fruits, eg strawberries.

Infusing Method of imparting flavour to a liquid. Flavourings, such as aromatic vegetables, herbs, spices, vanilla pod or coffee beans, are added to milk or water, sometimes brought to the boil, then left to soak.

Jardinière Refers to dishes garnished with mixed fresh spring vegetables or green peas and sprigs of cauliflower.

Jugged Traditional method of cooking hare in a tall covered pot until very tender and rich dark brown in colour. The blood is added at the end of the cooking time.

Julienne Vegetables or fruit rind cut into very fine strips to use as a garnish or ingredient.

Kebab General name for a dish comprising cubes of meat, fish, shellfish, fruit and vegetables which are cooked on skewers under a grill or on a barbecue.

Knead To work dough by pummelling with the heel of the hand.

Knock back To knead a yeast dough for a second time after rising, to ensure an even texture.

Kosher Food prepared according to orthodox Jewish laws.

Kugelhopf A sweetened yeast cake which contains dried fruit and is baked in a special deep fluted tin.

Langues de chats Literally means cats' tongues. Small thin flat crisp biscuits served with ice creams and mousses.

Larding Inserting small strips of fat bacon into the flesh of game birds, poultry and dry meat before cooking. It is done with a special larding needle.

Leaven The raising agent in dough, usually yeast or baking powder.

Liaison Term used to describe any combination of ingredients which is used for thickening or binding. The ingredients of a liason are usually flour, cornflour, arrowroot, rice or potato flour, or egg yolk.

Lukewarm In cookery, this term is used to describe the temperature of a substance, usually a liquid, when it is about blood temperature, ie approximately 37°C (98.4°F).

Macédoine The French term for a mixture of fruit or vegetables cut into even-sized dice. Usually used as a garnish.

Macerate To soften and flavour raw or dried foods by soaking in a liquid.

Marinate To soak meat, poultry or game in a mixture of oil, wine, vinegar and flavourings to tenderise it and add flavour. The mixture, which is known as a *marinade,* may also be used to baste the food during cooking.

Marmite A French metal or earthenware pot used for long slow cooking of casseroles on top of the stove or in the oven.

Medallions French term for small rounds of meat, usually beef or veal.

Meringue Egg white whisked until stiff, mixed with caster sugar and dried slowly in a low oven until crisp.

Meunière A French term which refers to food cooked in butter, seasoned with salt, pepper and lemon juice and finished with parsley. Usually applied to fish dishes.

Milling Reducing to a powder or paste (see also Grinding).

Mincing Chopping or cutting food into very small pieces. It may be done with a knife, a manual mincing machine or in a food processor.

Mirepoix A mixture of cut vegetables, usually carrot, celery and onion, with a little added ham or bacon, used as a bed on which to braise meat.

Mocca A term which has come to mean a blend of chocolate and coffee.

Monosodium glutamate (MSG) A powder with little flavour of its own, but which enhances the flavour of ingredients it is added to. A principal ingredient in processed foods and Chinese cookery.

Navarin Lamb stew with onions and potatoes.

Noisettes Neatly trimmed and tied boneless pieces of lamb, not less than 1 cm (½ inch) thick, cut from the loin or best end of neck.

Panada A thick roux-based sauce used for binding croquettes and similar mixtures.

Par-boiling A term used to describe boiling food for part of its cooking time before finishing it by another method.

Paring Thinly peeling and trimming vegetables or fruit.

Pasteurising Sterilising milk by heating to 60-92°C (140-180°F) to destroy bacteria.

Pasty An individual savoury pastry pie made without a dish on a baking sheet.

Pâte The French word for pastry, familiar in *pâte sucrée,* a sweet flan pastry.

Pâté A savoury mixture made from minced meat, flaked fish and/or vegetables cooked to form a solid mass. Smoked fish pâtés are rarely cooked.

Patty Small pie or *vol au vent,* often of puff pastry.

Paunching Removing the stomach and intestines of a rabbit or hare.

Paupiettes Slices of meat or fish rolled around a stuffing, usually braised or fried.

Pectin A naturally occuring substance found in most fruit and some vegetables which is necessary for setting jams and jellies.

Pickling Preserving fresh raw, or lightly cooked food in vinegar (see page 488).

Piping Forcing cream, icing, mashed potato, cake mixtures and meringue through a nozzle fitted into the end of a nylon or greaseproof paper piping bag to create fancy patterns.

Pith White lining under the rind of citrus fruit.

Plucking Removing feathers from poultry and game.

Poaching Cooking food gently in liquid at simmering point, so that the surface of the liquid is just trembling.

Pope's eye The small circle of fat in the centre of a leg of lamb or pork. In Scotland, it is the name for prime rump steak.

Pot roasting A method of cooking meat slowly in a covered pan with fat and a little liquid.

Potage The French term for a thick soup.

Praline Almonds caramelised in sugar, then crushed and used to flavour sweet dishes.

Preserving Keeping food in edible condition by freezing, canning, pickling, crystallising, irradiation, drying, smoking etc.

Pressure cooking Cooking food quickly in steam under pressure.

Prosciutto Italian raw smoked ham.

Proving The term used for leaving bread dough to rise after shaping.

Pulses The generic name given to all dried peas, beans and lentils. These are valued for their high protein and fibre content.

Purée Fruit, vegetable, meat or fish which has been pounded, sieved or liquidised to a smooth pulp. Purées often form the basis for soups, sweet and savoury sauces.

Quenelles Fish, meat or poultry which has been blended to a fine forcemeat, shaped into rounds or ovals, then cooked in liquid and served either as a garnish for soup or as a main course.

Ramekin Individual round ovenproof dish.

Réchauffé French term for reheated leftovers.

Reducing Fast-boiling a liquid in an uncovered pan to evaporate water and produce a more concentrated flavour.

Refresh To pour cold water over blanched and drained vegetables to set the colour and stop the cooking process.

Rendering Extracting fat from meat trimmings by cutting them into small pieces and heating in a cool oven at 150°C (300°F) mark 2 until the fat runs out and can be strained.

Rennet A substance extracted from a calf's stomach which will curdle or coagulate milk. The process is used for junket and cheese-making. Vegetarian rennet is also available.

Rice paper Edible paper made from the pith of a Chinese tree. Used as an edible base for sticky baked goods such as macaroons.

Roasting Cooking meat by dry heat in an oven or over an open flame.

Roulade Meat, cake or soufflé mixture served in a roll.

Roux A mixture of equal amounts of fat and flour cooked together to form the basis of many sauces.

Rubbing in Method of incorporating fat into flour when a short texture is required. It is used for pastry, cakes, scones and biscuits.

Salmis A stew made from game birds; the bird is partly roasted and then cooked with wine or port.

Salting A method of preserving food in dry salt or a brine solution.

Sautéeing Cooking food in a small quantity of fat in a sauté pan (a frying pan with straight sides and a wide base), which browns the food quickly.

Scalding Pouring boiling water over food to clean it, loosen hairs or remove the skin. Food should not be left in boiling water or it will begin to cook. It is also the term used for heating milk to just below boiling point, to retard souring or infuse it with another flavour.

Scalloping Decorating the double edge of a pastry pie with small horizontal cuts which are pulled up with the back of a knife to produce a scalloped effect (see page 379).

Scoring To cut narrow parallel lines in the surface of food to improve its appearance or help it cook more quickly (see also Crackling).

Searing Browning meat quickly in a little hot fat before grilling or roasting.

Seasoned flour Flour mixed with a little salt and pepper, for dusting meat and fish before frying.

Seasoning Adding salt, pepper, herbs and spices to a dish for added flavour.

Shredding Grating cheese or slicing raw vegetables into very fine pieces or strips.

Sieving Pushing food through a perforated sieve to get a soft, even texture.

Sifting Shaking dry ingredients through a sieve to remove lumps.

Simmering Keeping a liquid just below boiling point.

Singeing Using a flame to burn off any residual traces of feather on plucked game or poultry.

Skimming Removing froth, scum or fat from the surface of stock, gravy, stews and jam. Use either a skimmer, a spoon or absorbent kitchen paper.

Skinning Removing the skin from meat, fish, poultry, fruit or vegetables.

Smoking The process of curing food by exposure to wood smoke.

Souring Adding acid, often in the form of lemon juice to cream to give it a sour taste.

Sousing Pickling in brine or vinegar.

Spit Rotating rod on which meat, poultry or game is cooked either in the oven or over a fire.

Steaming Cooking food in the steam of rapidly boiling water.

Steeping Covering food with hot or cold water and leaving it to stand, either to soften it or extract its flavour and/or colour.

Sterilising Destroying bacteria in foods by heating.

Stewing Long, slow cooking method where food is placed in liquid which is kept at simmering point. Good for tenderising coarse meat.

Stir-frying Quick method of frying in shallow fat. The food must be cut into small, even-sized pieces and moved around constantly until coated. Stir-fried food is usually cooked in a *wok*.

Stock The liquid produced when meat, bones, poultry, fish or vegetables are simmered in water with herbs and flavourings for several hours to extract their flavour (see page 19).

Suet Hard fat found around the kidneys in beef or mutton. Usually bought in packets rather than fresh. Use in pastry and steamed puddings.

Sweating Gently cooking food (usually vegetables) in melted fat in a covered pan, until the juices run.

Syrup A concentrated solution of sugar in water, used in making water ices, drinks and fruit juices.

Tenderising Beating raw meat with a spiked mallet or rolling pin to break down the fibres and make it more tender for grilling or frying.

Tepid The term used to describe temperature at approximately blood heat.

Terrine China or earthenware dish used for pâtés. Also used to refer to the food cooked in it.

Texturised vegetable protein (TVP) Meat substitute made from vegetables, usually soya beans. It generally takes on the flavour of anything it is cooked with.

Truffle Rare black or white fungus of the same family as the mushroom. Due to the cost, truffles are used mainly for garnishing.

Trussing Tying or skewering into shape before cooking. Applied mainly to poultry and game.

Unleavened Bread without a raising agent.

Vanilla sugar Sugar in which a vanilla pod has been stored to release its flavour.

Vol au vent A round or oval puff pastry case which is filled with diced meat, poultry, fish or vegetables in sauce.

Whipping (whisking) Beating air rapidly into a mixture either with a manual or electric whisk.

Wok Chinese pan used for stir-frying. The food cooks on the sloping sides of the pan as well as in the rounded base.

Zest The coloured outer layer of citrus fruit which contains essential oil.

INDEX

A

Accompaniments, for soups 17
Acid curd cheese 281
Aduki beans 242
Adzuki beans *see* Aduki beans
Agar-agar 359, 566
Agas 541-2
Aïoli 256
Alcohol, fruit in 482-3
Alfalfa: radicchio and alfalfa salad 260
Allspice 190
Almond essence 194
Almond oil 253
Almond paste (marzipan) 426
  celebration cakes 423
  marzipan 'oranges' 507
  Danish pastries 457
  Neapolitan slices 497
  Simnel cake 428
Almonds 324
  almond and cherry flan 336
  almond butter cream 433
  almond chocolate biscuits 445
  almond crisps 439
  almond fingers 398
  almond stars 447
  almond truffles 502
  Bakewell pudding 335
  broccoli amandine 228
  cauliflower and almond cream soup 23
  creamy courgettes and almonds 232
  praline ice cream 367
  trout and almonds 78
Alsace wines 523
Altitude 566
Alto Adige wines 523
Aluminium pans 548
American frosting 420, 434
Anchovies 58
  hors d'oeuvres 34
  anchovy butter 207
  anchovy sauce 199
  Scotch woodcock 52
Anchovy essence 194
Angelica 187, 424
Angels on horseback 52
Angler fish *see* Monkfish
Angostura bitters 194
Anise pepper 190
Aniseed 190
Antipasto 566
Aperitifs 526
Apples 314
  dried 323
  freezing 564
  apple and blackberry charlotte 328

apple and celery stuffing 185
apple and hazelnut layer 338
apple cheese 479
apple chutney 486
apple pie 337
apple sauce 205
apple strudel 343
apricot, apple and prune stuffing 186
baked apples 328
blackberry and apple jam 468
braised red cabbage with apple 228
casseroled pigeons with cider and apple 173
Eve's pudding 327
French apple flan 337
layered sausage pie 145
marrow and apple chutney 486
mint and apple jelly 472
Normandy pork 128
pasta, prawn and apple salad 264
poached in sugar syrup 344
red cabbage and apple salad 259
sautéed liver with sage and apple 139
Somerset apple cake 414
toffee apples 499
Waldorf salad 258
Apricots 314
  dried 323
  freezing 564
  apricot and pistachio rolls 389
  apricot, apple and prune stuffing 186
  apricot glaze 425
  apricot jam 467
  apricot nut teabread 405
  apricot oat crunchies 444
  apricot savarin 346
  apricot stuffing 186
  dried apricot jam 468
  fresh apricot flan 338
  hot apricot soufflé 358
  rolled stuffed breasts of lamb 115
  spiced apricot upside-down pudding 329
  wholewheat and apricot salad 266
Arborio rice 307
Arrowroot 566
  sauces 197
Artichokes *see* Globe artichokes; Jerusalem artichokes
Asafoetida 190-1

Ascorbic acid 13
Asparagus 211-12
  freezing 562
  asparagus Maltaise 224
  asparagus rolls 48
  asparagus scramble 274
  cheese and asparagus tart 294
  chilled asparagus soup 32
  prawn and asparagus mousse 44
  turkey escalopes with asparagus 167
Aspic 566
  chaudfroid sauce 200
  chicken chaudfroid 161
  salmon in aspic 78
  salmon mousse 43
Au gratin 566
Aubergines 212
  freezing 562
  aubergines with ham 226
  Middle Eastern meatballs 122
  moussaka 121
  ratatouille 236
  tortellini al forno 306
Aurore sauce 201
Australian wines 524
Austrian wines 525
Automatic timing, ovens 543
Autumn pudding 347
Avocado 314
  salads 250
  avocado mousse 42
  chilled avocado soup 32
  dressed avocados 37
  guacamole 47
  lemon-dressed avocado salad 262
  smoked salmon and avocado pizza 290
  tomato and mozzarella salad 36

B

Babaco 314
Baby corn, salads 250
Baby food, microwave cooking 555
Bacon: cures 132
  cuts 132-3
  rashers 133
  storage 133
  bacon and egg croquettes 275
  bacon or ham stuffing 185
  bacon rolls 154
  baked and glazed bacon 135
  boiled bacon joint 134
  braised bacon 134

devils on horseback 52
fresh spinach salad with hot bacon dressing 262
omelette 277
quiche Lorraine 294
snippets 141
spaghetti alla carbonara 300
swede and bacon bake 239
Bacteria 556
Baden, wines 523
Bain-marie 566
Baked Alaska 369
Baked puddings 326-9
Bakewell pudding 335
Baking 566
  eggs 269
  fish 57
  microwave cooking 554
  salmon 76
  sausages 144
Baking blind 380, 566
Baking powder 376, 393, 448, 566
Baklava 342
Balkan wines 525
Ballontine of turkey 163
Balm 187
Balsamic vinegar 253
Bamboo shoots 212
Bananas 315
  dried 323
  banana and honey teabread 404
  flambé bananas 346
  fried bananas 154
  yogurt and banana dessert 357
Baps, floury 454
Barbados sugar 392-3
Barbecue sauce 206
Barbecued fish 56
Barbecued spare ribs 129
Barbecuing: lamb 113
  meat 93
  pork 124
  steaks 96
Barding 566
Barley 240
Basil 187-8
  fresh tomato soup with basil 21
  pesto 256
  sweet pepper and basil flan 293
  tomato salad with basil 257
Baskets, meringue 372
Basmati pilaff 309
Bass 58
Basting 566
Batavia lettuce 252
Bath chaps 137
Battenberg cake, chocolate 410

Batter puddings 333-4
Bavarois: chocolate 354
  coffee 354
Bay 188
Bean curd 566
Bean sprouts 212
  bean sprout and brown rice salad 260
  bean sprouts with Chinese egg strips 227
Beans *see also* Broad beans; Haricot beans etc.
  canned 241
  cooking time 242
  dried 241-2
  mixed bean salad 261
Béarnaise sauce 204
Beating 566
Beaujolais wines 522-3
Béchamel sauce 200, 566
Beef: carving 94
  cuts 95-6
  roasting 94
  steaks 96
  brisket:
    braised brisket with red wine 97
  cooked meat:
    cottage pie 106
    rissoles 105
  fillet steak:
    fillet of beef Wellington 98
    fondue bourguignonne 100
    steak Diane 101
  minced beef:
    beefburgers 106
    chilli con carne 106
    lasagne 303
    meat balls in tomato sauce 107
    spaghetti Bolognese 299
  quick-fry steaks:
    steak and Stilton parcels 102
  rump steak:
    beef stewed in red wine 100
    boeuf Stroganoff 104
    chilli beef with noodles 107
    steak and kidney kebabs 102
  shin:
    beef stock 19
    Scotch broth 28
  silverside:
    spiced silverside 99
  sirloin:
    peppered beef sauté 103
    roast beef with Yorkshire pudding 97
    steak au poivre 101
  stewing steak:
    carbonade of beef 99
    classic beef stew 99
    Cornish pasties 105
    steak and kidney pudding 104
    steak and mushroom pie 105
  topside:
    beef olives 101
    boeuf bourguignonne 100

Beer: carbonade of beef 99
Beetroot 212-14
  freezing 562
  salads 250
  baked beetroot 228
  beet relish 487
  beetroot in caraway dressing 261
  beetroot with orange 227
  borshch 31
  pickled beetroot 490
Beignets de fruits 334
Belfast ham 133
Beta-carotene 11-12
Beurre manié 566
Bicarbonate of soda 393, 448, 566
Bilberries 315
  freezing 564
  bilberry jelly 474
Binding sauce 198
Biotin 12
Biscuits and cookies *see also* Petits fours
  baking 435
  storing 435
  almond chocolate biscuits 445
  almond crisps 439
  apricot oat crunchies 444
  brandy snaps 441
  cheese straws 49
  cherry and walnut biscuits 439
  cherry garlands 443
  chocolate chip cookies 443
  chocolate nut snaps 437
  chocolate Viennese fingers 442
  cigarettes russes 440
  coconut macaroons 440
  date crunchies 444
  Easter biscuits 437
  flapjacks 444
  Florentines 440
  ginger biscuits 442
  gingerbread men 438
  Grantham gingerbreads 438
  langues de chats 443
  madeleines 439
  peanut butter cookies 438
  pinwheel biscuits 436
  refrigerator biscuits 445
  Shewsbury biscuits 436
  shortbread rounds 437
Bismarcks 59
Bisque, mussel 31
Bitter lemon 539
Bitters 526
Black beans 242
Black-eyed beans 242
Black Forest gâteau 416
Black Russian (cocktail) 529
Black velvet (cocktail) 531
Blackberries 315
  freezing 564
  apple and blackberry charlotte 328

blackberry and apple jam 468
  bramble jelly 473
  damson and blackberry cheese 480
Blackcurrants 316
  freezing 564
  blackcurrant jam 468
  blackcurrant mousse 362
  double-crust blackcurrant pie 339
Blackgame 172
Blanching 566
Blancmange 352
Blanquette de veau 112
Blanquettes 566
Blenders 545-6, 567
Bloaters 79
Bloody Mary (cocktail) 530
Blue cheese: blue cheese butter 207
  blue cheese dip 47
  blue cheese dressing 254
  celery and Stilton soup 24
  cheese and olive pick-ups 48
  pasta baked with mushrooms and cheese 303
  Roquefort quiche 294
  steak and Stilton parcels 102
  Stilton bites 49
  Stilton soufflé 270
Blueberries 315
  freezing 564
  blueberry curd 480
Boeuf bourguignonne 100
Boeuf en croûte 98
Boeuf Stroganoff 104
Boiling 567
  eggs 268
  meat 93
  potatoes 220
  sugar 494
Boning 567
  poultry 147
Boodle's orange fool 356
Borage 188
Bordeaux wines 522
Borlotti beans 242
  smoked haddock and bean salad 263
Borshch 31
Boston beans 248
Boston brownies 400
Bottling 567
Bouchées 386, 567
Bouillabaisse 30
Bouquet garni 195, 567
Bourgeois (snapper) 60
Bourguignonne 567
Bradenham ham 133
Brains 136-7
  brains in black butter sauce 143
Braising 567
  meat 93
Bramble jelly 473
Brandy 527
  brandied cherries 482

brandied peaches 483
brandy Alexander 529
brandy butter 210
brandy cider cup 532
brandy snaps 441
Brawn 144
Brazil nuts 324
  peach and nut stuffing 186
Bread *see also* Buns; Rolls; Toast
  ingredients 448-51
  making 451-2
  microwave cooking 554
  quick breads 462-3
  traditional shapes 451
  apple and blackberry charlotte 328
  bread and butter pudding 353
  bread sauce 206
  brown bread ice cream 369
  caraway rye bread 462
  chappatis 462
  cheese loaf 456
  croûtons 17
  dark rye bread 455
  granary bread 453
  herbed cheese bread 463
  hot garlic bread 514
  malt bread 459
  parathas 463
  quick wholemeal bread 454
  sage and onion bread 455
  soda bread 462
  Stollen 460
  tortillas 463
  white bread 453
  wholemeal bread 454
Bread and butter pickle 492
Breadcrumbs: stuffings 181
  fried crumbs 171
Bream, Emperor 58
Bream, sea 58
Brill 58
Brining 567
  pickles 488
Brioche 459, 567
Broad beans 212
  freezing 562
  broad bean bake 247
  broad beans in lemon parsley sauce 226
  pasta with courgettes and broad beans 300
  three bean salad 516
Broccoli 214
  freezing 562
  broccoli amandine 228
Brochettes 567 *see also* Kebabs
Broiling 567
Broth 567
Brown flour, for bread 450
Brown sauces 202-3
Brown sugar 392
Brown trout 75
Browning dishes, microwave cookers 553
Brûlées 567

Brussels sprouts 214
  freezing 562
  Brussels sprouts and
    chestnuts 228
Brut 567
Buck rarebit 286
Buckling 79
Bucks fizz (cocktail) 531
Buckwheat 240
Buckwheat flour 450
Buffet parties 512
  menus 514-19
  quantities 513
Bulgar wheat *see* Bulghur
Bulgarian wines 525
Bulghur 240
Buns: Chelsea buns 460
  hot cross buns 460
Burgers: beefburgers 106
  pork and oat burgers 131
  savoury nut burgers 248
Burgul *see* Bulghur
Burgundy wines 522
Burnet 188
Butter 9
  for cakes 393
  clarifying 568
  for pastry 376-7
  savoury 207
  anchovy 207
  black butter sauce 143
  blue cheese 207
  brandy 210
  cinnamon 457
  curry 207
  garlic 207
  golden 207
  green 207
  ham 207
  horseradish 207
  lobster 207
  maître d'hôtel 207
  onion 207
  tarragon 207
Butter beans 242
  carrot and bean soufflés 244
Butter cream 433
Buttermilk 393
Butternut squashes 222
Butters, fruit *see* Fruit butters
Butterscotch 499
Butterscotch sauce 208

C

Cabbage 214
  salads 250
  cabbage with juniper berries
    229
  coleslaw 258
  party coleslaw 518
  savoury white cabbage 229
Caerphilly cheese 279, 281
Caesar salad 260
Caffeine 537
Cake boards 423, 424
Cakes 392-434
  see also Meringues; Pastries

cake making methods 394-6
cake tins 396-7
celebration cakes 421-31
  cooling 397
  decorating 423-5
  heating the oven 397
  ingredients 392-4
  microwave cooking 554
  problems 397
  small cakes 398-400
  testing 397
  unusual shapes 430
  wedding cakes 421-3
  almond fingers 398
  Boston brownies 400
  carrot cake 408
  celebration cake 429, 510
  chocolate Battenberg cake
    410
  chocolate biscuit cake 411
  chocolate crackles 399
  chocolate slab cake 410
  devil's food cake 420
  English madeleines 400
  fairy cakes 400
  farmhouse sultana cake 411
  frosted coconut cake 414
  Genoese sponge 406
  honey cake 409
  Madeira cake 412
  maids of honour 399
  marbled chocolate cake 415
  novelty clown cake 430-1
  rich cherry cake 411
  rock buns 399
  rosebud wedding cake 427
  Simnel cake 428
  Somerset apple cake 414
  sponge fingers 399
  Swiss roll 407
  Victoria sandwich cake 406
  walnut layer cake 409
  whisked sponge cake 407
  Yule log 429
Calcium 13
Californian wines 521, 524
Calories 16, 567
Calvados 527
Calves' liver *see* Liver
Camomile tea 535
Can openers, electric 546
Canapés 33-4, 567
Candying 567
Canned beans 241
Canned food 558
Canned herrings 59
Cannellini beans 242
  bean and coriander potage
    27
Cannelloni 295-7
  fish-stuffed cannelloni with
    cheese 304
Cape gooseberries 315
Capercaillie 172
Capers: caper mayonnaise 254
  caper sauce 199
  Oxford John steaks with
    caper sauce 123

skate with black butter 66
Carambola 322
Caramel 494, 567
  crushed 508
  crème brûlée 356
  crème caramel 353
  oranges in caramel 345
Caraque, chocolate 508
Caraway 191
  beetroot in caraway dressing
    261
Caraway seeds 451
  caraway rye bread 462
Carbohydrates 10
Carbonades 567
  beef 99
Cardamom 191
Cardoon 214
Carp 75
Carrots 215
  freezing 562
  garnishes 506
  salads 250
  carrot and bean soufflés 244
  carrot and orange soup 22
  carrot cake 408
  carrots with mint and lemon
    230
Carving: game 172
  meat 94-5
  turkey 148
Cashew nuts 324
  spiced chicken with cashew
    nuts 153
  turkey with cashew nuts and
    mushrooms 166
Cassava 215
Casseroles 567
  casserole dishes 548-9
  meat 93
  microwave cooking 554
  beef stewed in red wine 100
  casseroled pigeons with cider
    and apple 173
  chunky fish casserole 71
  classic beef stew 99
  coq au vin 160
  creamed quail casserole 173
  Eastern casserole of lamb
    515
  Irish stew 121
  jugged hare 177
  lamb and kidney bean
    casserole 123
  lamb's heart casserole 140
  Lancashire hot pot 120
  navarin of lamb 117
  pheasant with port 174
  poulet en cocotte 158
  quick pork cassoulet 126
  red kidney bean hot-pot 246
  rich venison casserole 179
  salmis of pheasant 175
  sausage and bean stew 145
  Somerset pork stew 128
  sweet-sour rabbit with prunes
    177
  veal goulash 110

Cast iron pans 548
Caster sugar 392
Castle puddings 326
  steamed 330
Catfish 58
Cauliflower 215
  freezing 562
  cauliflower and almond
    cream soup 23
  cauliflower cheese 230
  cauliflower Polonaise 230
  crispy cauliflower salad 257
Caviar, hors d'oeuvres 34-5
Cayenne 191
Celebration cakes 421-31, 429
Celeriac 215
  freezing 562
  salads 250
  celeriac and onion bake 231
Celery 215
  freezing 563
  garnishes 505
  salads 250
  apple and celery stuffing 185
  braised celery with walnuts
    231
  celery and Stilton soup 24
  Waldorf salad 258
Celery seeds 191, 451
Cellophane noodles 297
Celsius 567
Central European wines 525
Cèpes 218
Ceramic hobs 542
Ceramics, for microwave 552
Ceviche 69
Chablis wines 522
Champagne 523, 525
  black velvet 531
  buck's fizz 531
Chanterelles 218
Chantilly 567
Chappatis 120, 462
Char 75
Charcuterie 567
Chard, Swiss *see* Swiss chard
Charlottes 567
  apple and blackberry 328
  charlotte russe 355
Chasseur 567
Château potatoes 238
Chaudfroid 567
Chaudfroid sauce 200
Chayote 215
Cheddar cheese 279, 280, 283
Cheese 279-85
  see also Blue cheese; Cheese,
    soft; Gratins
  buying 279
  microwave cooking 554
  storing 279
  buck rarebit 286
  cauliflower cheese 230
  cheese and asparagus tart
    294
  cheese and potato cakes 287
  cheese fondue 287
  cheese loaf 456

cheese omelette 277
cheese palmiers 50
cheese pastry 381, 383
cheese sauce 199
cheese scones 402
cheese soufflé 270
cheese straws 49
croque monsieur 286
eggs Florentine 272
Feta cheese puffs 286
fish-stuffed cannelloni with
    cheese 304
herbed cheese bread 463
hot fish terrine with Gruyère
    sauce 71
individual quiches 49
macaroni cheese 302
Mornay sauce 200
pesto 256
potted cheese with mint 287
prawn and feta purses 50
quiche Lorraine 294
spaghetti with butter and
    Parmesan 299
spicy cheese and tomato dip
    47
tomato and mozzarella pizza
    289
tomato and mozzarella salad
    36
vegetarian roast 244
Welsh rarebit 286
Cheese, soft 280-1
cheese gnocchi 313
coeurs à la crème 356
crab and Ricotta quiche 294
lemon cheese jelly 365
savoury choux puffs 51
spinach gnocchi 313
stuffed egg mayonnaise 273
tiramisu 363
tortellini al forno 306
Cheesecakes: hot chocolate 349
lemon 348
redcurrant 350
traditional baked 348
Cheeses, fruit see Fruit cheeses
Chelsea buns 460
Cherries 315
freezing 564
almond and cherry flan 336
Black Forest gâteau 416
brandied cherries 482
cherry and walnut biscuits
    439
cherry fudge 500, 501
cherry garlands 443
cherry jam 470
rich cherry cake 411
Chervil 188
Chestnuts 324-5
Brussels sprouts and
    chestnuts 228
chestnut and orange soup 29
chestnut stuffing 185
chocolate and chestnut
    cream Vacherin 374
pheasant with chestnuts 175

sausagemeat and chestnut
    stuffing 185
Chick peas 242
hot spiced chick peas 245
hummus 48
Chicken see also Liver; Smoked
    chicken
types of chicken, 146
chicken stock 19
breasts:
chicken and prawn risotto
    311
chicken chaudfroid 161
chicken Kiev 153
chicken with tarragon sauce
    152
poached chicken breasts 151
shredded chicken with
    mushrooms and walnuts
    157
spiced chicken with cashew
    nuts 153
stir-fried chicken with
    courgettes 156
cooked meat:
chicken bouchées 51
pancake rolls 162
drumsticks:
paella 312
sesame lemon chicken 154
oven-ready:
chicken galantine 150
chicken Maryland 154
chicken puff pie 161
chicken soup with dumplings
    27
Coronation chicken 266
French-style roast chicken
    149
fricassée of chicken 155
Italian stuffed chicken 149
poached chicken 151
poulet en cocotte 158
roast chicken 149
spiced rice with chicken 311
portions:
baked chicken quarters 151
chicken au gratin 155
chicken cacciatora 159
chicken Marengo 159
chicken with cumin and
    cider 152
chicken with vermouth and
    olives 158
coq au vin 160
fried chicken 151
grilled chicken or poussin
    151
stoved chicken 159
Tandoori chicken 155
poussins:
devilled poussins 150
grilled chicken or poussin
    151
herby orange poussins 150
Italian-style poussin 160
Oriental-style poussins 150
Chicory 215-16

salads 250
braised chicory 231
Florida chicory salad 262
Chiffon pie, rhubarb and
    orange 340
Chilli peppers 219
freezing 563
harissa 196
Chilli powder 191
chilli beef with noodles 170
chilli con carne 106
turkey kebabs with chilli
    peanut sauce 165
Chilling 567
China, microwave cookware 552
Chinese gooseberries see Kiwi
    fruit
Chinese lanterns 315
Chinese leaves 216
salads 250
stir-fried Chinese leaves 231
Chinese-style fried liver 137
Chining 567-8
Chipped potatoes 220
Chips, game 171, 220
Chives 188
Chocolate: chocolate dipped
    fruit 504
decorations 424, 508
dipped chocolates 504
Easter eggs 504
melting 504
almond chocolate biscuits
    445
Black Forest gâteau 416
Boston brownies 400
chocolate and chestnut
    cream Vacherin 374
chocolate and vanilla
    roulade 416
chocolate Battenberg cake
    410
chocolate bavarois 354
chocolate biscuit cake 411
chocolate butter cream 433
chocolate chip cookies 443
chocolate crackles 399
chocolate cream sandwiches
    436
chocolate crème au beurre
    433
chocolate flake ice cream
    367
chocolate frosting 434
chocolate fudge 501
chocolate fudge frosting 434
chocolate ginger flan 339
chocolate glacé icing 432
chocolate hazelnut clusters
    503
chocolate ice cream 367
chocolate ice cream log 407
chocolate mousse 364
chocolate nut snaps 437
chocolate nut truffles 502
chocolate orange soufflé 361
chocolate pear upside-down
    pudding 329

chocolate sandwich cake 406
chocolate slab cake 410
chocolate sponge pudding
    326, 330
chocolate Swiss roll 407
chocolate Viennese fingers
    442
collettes 503
devil's food cake 420
Florentines 440
hot chocolate cheesecake
    349
hot chocolate soufflé 358
marbled chocolate cake 415
profiteroles 343
rich chocolate rum truffles
    502
rich chocolate sauce 209
Sachertorte 419
Yule log 429
Cholecalciferol 13
Cholesterol 9-10
Chopping 568
Chorizo 568
Choux pastry 376, 388
gâteau St. Honoré 342
gougère 388
profiteroles 343
savoury choux puffs 51
smoked haddock gougère 80
Chow-chow 215
Chowders 568
mixed fish 30
Christmas cake 421-2
white Christmas cake 428
Christmas pudding 332
iced 369
Christmas wine 533
Chutneys 484
apple 486
green tomato 485
hot Indian 486
marrow and apple 486
peach 485
sweet mango 485
Cider: brandy cider cup 532
casseroled pigeons with cider
    and apple 173
chicken with cumin and
    cider 152
Cider vinegar 253
Cigarettes russes 440
Cinnamon 191
cinnamon butter 457
cinnamon ice cream 367
cinnamon tea 535
Citric acid 568
Citrus fruit see also Lemons;
    Oranges
juicers 545
julienne 507
marmalade 475
Citrus punch 540
Clams 81
preparation 81
mussels and clams with
    tomatoes 89
Claret cup 533

Claret jelly 365
Clarifying 568
Classic green salad 257
Cleaning: equipment 541
    kitchen hygiene 556
    microwave cookers 551-2
    ovens 543
    pots and pans 547
Clementines 320
Cling film: for freezers 560
    in microwave cookers 552
Clotting 568
Cloves 191
Clown cake 430-1
Coating sauce 198
Cobalamin 12
Cockles 84
    hors d'oeuvres 35
    preparation 84
Cocktails 528-31
Coconut 325
    coconut ice bars 500
    coconut ice cream 367
    coconut macaroons 440
    frosted coconut cake 414
    Malaysian-style prawns 88
Cocottes 568
    see also Smoked cod's roe
    cod in white wine 63
    marinated cod steaks 69
    spiced fish steaks 72
    spinach and seafood pasties
        63
Coddled eggs 268, 568
Coeurs à la crème 356
Coffee 536-7
    grinders 545
    coffee bavarois 354
    coffee butter cream 433
    coffee crème au beurre 433
    coffee fudge 501
    coffee fudge frosting 434
    coffee gâteau 417
    coffee glacé icing 432
    coffee ice cream 367
    coffee milk shake 538
    coffee sandwich cake 406
    iced coffee 537
    individual coffee bombes 370
        Irish coffee 537
    tiramisu 363
    walnut and coffee fudge 501
Coffee essence 194
Coffee makers 545
Colanders 568
Coleslaw 258
    party coleslaw 518
Coley 58
Collettes 503
Combined microwave cookers
    551
Combs, icing 423
Compotes 568
Concasser 568
Conchiglie 297
Conger eel 58
Conserves 568
    see also Jam

Consistency 568
Clarifying 568
Consommé 20, 568
    consommé à la jardinière 20
    consommé à la royale 20
    consommé julienne 20
    jellied consommé 20
Containers: for freezers 560
    microwave cookers 552
Cooker hoods 542
Cookers 541-4
    microwave 551-2
Cookies see Biscuits
Copper pans 548
Coq au vin 160
Coquilles St. Jacques 90
Coriander 188
    bean and coriander potage
        26
    spiced honey and coriander
        dressing 255
Coriander seeds 191
Corn (maize) 240
    see also Sweetcorn
    baby corn 222
    freezing 563
Corn fritters 154
Corn salad see Lamb's lettuce
Corned beef 568
Cornflour 240
    sauces 197
Cornish pasties 105
Cornmeal 240
Cornstarch 568
Coronation chicken 266
Cos lettuce 252
Cottage cheese 281
Cottage pie 106
Coulis 197, 568
Courgettes 216
    freezing 563
    salads 250
    creamy courgettes and
        almonds 232
    pasta with courgettes and
        broad beans 300
    ratatouille 236
    stir-fried chicken with
        courgettes 156
Court bouillon 56, 568
Couscous 241, 568
    vegetable couscous 243
Crab 81
    baked crab ramekins 40
    crab and Ricotta quiche 294
    crab salad 264
    dressed crab 85-6
Crab apples 315
    spiced crab apples 489
Cracked wheat 241
Crackling 568
Cranberries 315
    cranberry sauce 206
Crawfish 81
Crayfish 82
Cream 351
    piped 507
    ginger cream 341
    syllabub 354

Cream cheese 280
Cream horns 390
Cream of tartar 393, 448, 568
Cream sauce: curry 254
    mustard 200
Creaming 568
Creaming method, cakes 394
Crème au beurre 433
Crème brûlée 356
Crème caramel 353
Crème de cassis, kir 532
Crème fraîche 351
Crème pâtissière 210
    gâteau St. Honorè 342
Crêpes 568
    see also Pancakes
Crêpes Suzette 334
Crimping 379, 568
Croissants 458
Croque monsieur 286
Croquembouche 388
Croquettes 568
    bacon and egg 275
    walnut 243
Croûtes 568
Croûtons 17, 568
Crown roast of lamb 114
Crown roast of pork 125
Crumbles, fruit 328
Crumbs see Breadcrumbs
Crumpets 456
Crystallized flowers 424
Cucumber 216
    garnishes 506
    salads 250
    cucumber mayonnaise 254
    cucumber sauce 205
    sautéed cucumber with herbs
        232
    tzatziki 46
Cumberland ham 133
Cumberland sauce 206
Cumin 191
Cups and punches 532-3
Curdle 569
Curds 569
Curds, fruit see Fruit curds
Cure 569
Currants see Blackcurrants;
    Redcurrants; White currants
Currants (dried) 323
Curries: curry powder 195
    Coronation chicken 266
    curried okra 234
    curried parsnip soup 24
    curry butter 207
    curry cream sauce 254
    Indonesian fish curry 68
    lamb korma 116
    mild curry sauce 199
    vegetable curry 249
Curry plant 188
Custard: baked custard 352
    crème caramel 353
    custard cream 357
    egg custard sauce 208
    floating islands 357
Custard apples 316

Custard marrow 222
Cuttlefish 58
Cyprus wines 525

D

Dab 58
Daikon radish 221
Daiquiri (cocktail) 531
Dairy produce: freezing 561
    storage 557
Dal 569
Damsons 322
    freezing 564
    damson and blackberry
        cheese 480
    damson cheese 480
    damson jam 470
Dandelion, salads 250
Danish pastries 457
Dasheen 216
Dates 316
    dried 323
    date and raisin teabread 404
    date crunchies 444
    pickled dates 492
Daubes 569
Decorations 507-8
    cake 423-5
Deep-fat fryers 547, 569
Defrosting, refrigerators and
    freezers 544
Deglaze 569
Dégorge 569
Demerara sugar 392
Demi-glace sauce 202
Desserts: baked puddings 326-9
    batter puddings 333-4
    cheesecakes 348-50
    cold soufflés, jellies and
        mousses 359-65
    fruit 344-7
    ices and iced desserts 366-70
    meringues 372-5
    milk, custard and cream
        puddings 351-7
    pies, flans and pastries
        335-43
    steamed puddings 330-2
Devilled mushroom 'pizzas' 291
Devilled poussins 150
Devilled turkey drumsticks 164
Devil's food cake 420
Devils on horseback 52
Diabetic marmalade 476
Dice 569
Dietary fibre 10, 15
Dieting 15-16
Dill 188
    stuffed mushrooms with dill
        37
Dips: blue cheese 47
    guacamole 47
    hummus 48
    mustard 47
    spicy cheese and tomato 47
    taramasalata 47
    tzatziki 46

Dishwashers 544
Dolmas 121
Dough 569
Dover sole 60-1
Dragees, silver 424
Drawing 569
Dredging 569
Dressing 569
Dressings *see* Salad dressings
Dried food, storage 558
Dried fruit 323
   see also Fruit cakes;
     Mincemeat; Teabreads
   fruit biscuits 436
   fruit squares 436
   iced Christmas pudding 369
   rich Christmas pudding 332
   stewed dried fruit 344
Drinks: cocktails 528-31
   coffee 536-7
   cups and punches 532-3
   liqueurs 526-7
   soft drinks 538-40
   tea 534-5
   wines 520-6
Dripping 569
Drop scones 403
Dropping consistency 569
Dry brining, pickles 488
Dry-frying 570
   spices 196
Dry martini 529
Drying 569
   herbs 187
Dublin Bay prawns *see* Scampi
Duchesse potatoes 238
Duck eggs 268
Duckling 168
   see also Wild duck
   apricot stuffing 186
   crispy duck breast with
     mangetout 169
   duck and orange terrine 42
   duckling with orange sauce
     168
   roast duckling 168
   spiced duckling and orange
     salad 266
Dudi 216
Dumplings 18
   see also Gnocchi
   chicken soup with dumplings
     27
Dundee cake 412
Durian 316
Dutch cabbage 214

E

Easter biscuits 437
Easter eggs 504
Eastern casserole of lamb 515
Eccles cakes 384, 390
Eclairs 391
Eddoe 216
Eels 75
   see also Conger eel; Smoked
     eel

Egg and crumbing 569
Egg noodles 297
Egg plant *see* Aubergines
Eggs 267-9
   see also Meringues;
     Omelettes; Soufflés
   baking 269
   boiled 268
   buying 267
   for cakes 393
   coddled 268, 568
   egg-based sauces 203-4
   egg mollet 268
   frying 268
   microwave cooking 554
   poached 268
   safety 267
   scrambled 269
   separating 268
   sizes 267
   storing 267
   asparagus scramble 274
   bacon and egg croquettes
     275
   baked egg and vegetable pots
     274
   baked eggs with mushrooms
     272
   bean sprouts with Chinese
     egg strips 227
   buck rarebit 286
   egg custard sauce 208
   egg custard tart 335
   egg mayonnaise 273
   egg sauce 199
   eggs Bénédict 274
   eggs Florentine 272
   pickled eggs 490
   pipérade 272
   Scotch eggs 273
   spaghetti alla carbonara 300
   stuffed egg mayonnaise 273
   stuffed eggs with pâté 273
Elderberries 316
   elderberry jelly 474
Electric cookers 541, 542
Electrical appliances 541, 544-7
Emperor bream 58
Emulsion 267, 569
En croûte 569
En papillote 569
Endive 252
English madeleines 400
English wines 525
Enzymes 569
Equipment 541-50
   cookers 541-4
   dishwashers 544
   electrical appliances 544-7
   pots and pans 547-9
   refrigerators and freezers
     544
Escalopes 569
Escarole 252
Espagnole sauce 202, 569
Espresso coffee makers 545
Essences 194
Eve's pudding 327

Exotic fruit salad 519
Extract 569
Extractor fans 542

F

Faggots 569
Fahrenheit 569
Fairy cakes 400
Fan ovens 543
Farce 569
Farfalle 297
Farina 569
Farmhouse sultana cake 411
Fats *see also* Butter; Oils
   for bread 450
   for cakes 393
   for pastry 376-7
   and health 9-10, 15
Feather Icing 432
Feijoas 316
Fennel 188, 216
   freezing 563
   salads 252
   braised fennel 232
   fennel and radicchio salad
     519
   fennel and tomato salad 261
   salmon with fennel sauce 77
Fennel seeds 193, 451
Fenugreek 191
Fermenting 569
Feta cheese 280, 283
   feta cheese puffs 286
   prawn and feta purses 50
Fettucine 298
Fibre 10, 15
Figs 316
   dried 323
   freezing 564
Fillet 569
Filleting, fish 54-6
Filo pastry 376, 389
Filters: coffee makers 545
   water 545
Fines herbes 188, 195, 569
Fines herbes omelette 277
Finger food 33, 48-51
Finnan haddock 79
Fish 53-80
   see also Cod; Salmon etc.
   baked 57
   barbecued 56
   buying 53
   cleaning 53-4
   deep-frying 57
   filleting 54-6
   freezing 561
   freshwater fish 75-8
   grilling 56
   hors d'oeuvres 34-5
   microwave cooking 57, 554
   poaching 56
   sea fish 58-74
   shallow-frying 57
   skinning 54
   smoked fish 79-80
   steaming 57

   bouillabaisse 30
   fish cakes 64
   fish soufflé 270
   fish stock 19
   fritto misto di mare 73
   glazed seafood platter 91
   mixed fish chowder 30
   mixed seafood brochettes 91
   omelette 277
   parchment baked fish 67
Five-spice powder 195
Flageolet beans 242
Flaked pastries 384-6
Flaky pastry 384
Flambé 570
Flambé bananas 346
Flan rings 396, 397
Flans: pastry for 377, 380
   savoury *see* Quiches and flans
   sweet *see* Tarts
Flapjacks 444
Flavourings 194
   for cakes 393
Fleurons 158
Floating islands 357
Florence fennel *see* Fennel
Florentines 440
Florida chicory salad 262
Florida cocktails 36
Flounder 59
Flour: for bread 450
   for cakes 392
   for pastry 376
   seasoned 573
Floury baps 454
Flowers: crystallized 424
   frosted 507
   jelly 507
   in salads 253
Fluoride 14
Fluting pastry 379
Foil, for freezers 560
Folding in 570
Folic acid 12
Fondant: boiled fondant 495
   peppermint creams 495
   uncooked fondant 495
   uncooked peppermint
     creams 496
Fondues 570
   cheese fondue 287
   fondue bourguignonne 100
Food preparation machines
   545-6
Food processors 546
Fools 570
   Boodle's orange fool 356
   gooseberry fool 344
Forcemeat 570
Forcemeat balls 183
Fork-mix pastry 383
Fortified wines 525-6
Freezer film 560
Freezer tape 560
Freezers 544, 558-9
French apple flan 337
French beans 212
   freezing 562

French bean soup 29
French beans with thyme 226
French beans with tomatoes 227
three bean salad 516
French dressing 255
French onion soup 23
French-style roast chicken 149
French wines 520, 522-3
Freshwater fish 75-8
Fricassées 570
chicken 155
lamb's tongues 141
rabbit 178
Fried crumbs 171
Frikadeller 131
Frisée see Endive
Fritters: batter 334
beignets de fruits 334
corn 154
Fritto misto di mare 73
Fromage frais 283-4
Frosted coconut cake 414
Frosted fruits and flowers 447, 507
Frostings 570
American 420, 434
chocolate 434
coffee fudge 434
seven-minute 434
vanilla 434
Frothing 570
Frozen food 558-65
fish 53
fruit 564-5
microwave cooking 554
storing 558
thawing 561
vegetables 562-3
Fruit 314-23
see also Apples, Pears etc. and Dried fruit
in alcohol 482-3
for cakes 394
chocolate-dipped 504
coulis 197
desserts 344-7
freezing 561, 564-5
frosted 447, 507
fruit butters 479
jams 466
jellies 359, 472
marzipan 497
starters 35-9
vinegars 253
vitamin content 14
autumn pudding 347
beignets de fruits 334
créme au beurre 433
everyday fruit scones 402
fresh fruit tartlets 391
frozen fruit yogurt 366
fruit crumble 328
fruit ice cream 367
fruit sponge pudding 330
meringues with summer fruits 516
poached fruits in syrup 344

Rumpot 483
summer pudding 347
Fruit cakes 421
covering with almond paste 426
Dundee cake 412
half-pound cake 413
one-stage fruit cake 412
rich fruit cake 421, 422
white Christmas cake 428
Fruit cheeses 479
apple 479
damson 480
Fruit curds 479
blueberry 480
lemon 480
orange 480
Fruit salads: exotic fruit salad 519
fresh fruit salad 345
Frying 570
eggs 268
fish 57
lamb 113
meat 93
pork 124
sausages 144
steaks 96
Fudge 500
cherry 500, 501
chocolate 501
coffee 501
vanilla 500
walnut and coffee 501
Fuel, cookers 541-2

G

Gaelic coffee 537
Galangal 192
Galantine 570
chicken 150
Game 171
see also Quail; Venison etc.
accompaniments 171-2
carving 172
cooking and serving 171
open seasons 172
storing 171
raised game pie 178
Game chips 171, 220
Gammon 132
see also Bacon
Garam masala 196
Garbanzos see Chick peas
Garlic 188
aïoli 256
coarse garlic pâté 46
croûtons 17
garlic butter 207
hot garlic bread 514
prawns fried in garlic 88
rich garlic dressing 255
roast lamb fillets with garlic 118
Garnishes 505-6, 570
pastry 158, 379
for soups 17

Gas cookers 541, 542
Gâteaux: Black Forest 416
coffee 417
gâteau St. Honoré 342
hazelnut meringue 375
raspberry torte 418
Sachertorte 419
Gazpacho 31
Gelatine 359, 570
Genoese sponge 406, 570
German wines 520, 523
Ghee 570
Gherkins: garnishes 506
pickled gherkins 490
Gin: pink gin 530
sloe gin 533
Ginger 191
chocolate ginger flan 339
ginger biscuits 442
ginger cream 341
ginger custard cream 357
ginger sauce 209
ginger sponge pudding 326
ginger Swiss roll 407
gingerbread 405
gingerbread men 438
Grantham gingerbreads 438
marrow and ginger jam 470
melon and ginger sorbet 368
oatmeal parkin 405
quick ginger beer 539
rhubarb and ginger jam 471
Glacé 570
Glacé icing 432
Glass: cocktail glasses 528
microwave cookware 552
Glazed fruit sponge flan 340
Glazed onions 235
Glazed seafood platter 91,
Glazes 570
for bread 450-1
apricot 425
spiced marmalade and honey glaze 135
Globe artichokes 211
freezing 562
stuffed globe artichokes 225
Globe onions 218
Gluhwein 532
Gluten 392, 450, 570
Glutinous rice 307
Gnocchi 313
cheese gnocchi 313
gnocchi alla Romana 313
spinach gnocchi 313
Goat's milk cheeses 280
Golden butter 207
Golden cutlets 79
Golden syrup 393
Good King Henry 222
Goose 169
wild goose 172
roast goose 169
Goose eggs 268
Gooseberries 318
freezing 565
gooseberry cheese 480
gooseberry fool 344

gooseberry jam 469
gooseberry sauce 204
poached in sugar syrup 344
Gougére 388
smoked haddock 80
Goujons, hake 64
Goulash, veal 110
Grains 240-1
Granadilla 318
Granary bread 453
Granary flour 450
Granita 570
Grantham gingerbreads 438
Granulated sugar 392, 466
Grapefruit 318
freezing 565
citrus punch 540
Florida cocktails 36
grapefruit starter 35
spiced hot grapefruit 35
three-fruit marmalade 475
Grapes 318
sole Véronique 70
Grapeseed oil 253
Grating 570
Gratins 566
chicken au gratin 155
gratin Dauphinois 236
ham and leeks au gratin 135
leeks au gratin 233
pasta, veal and rosemary gratin 304
Gravad lax 35
Gravy 202
thin gravy 171
Grayling 75
Greasing cake tins 396
Grecque, à la 570
Greek salad 259
Greek-style new potatoes 237
Greek wines 525
Green beans see French beans
Green butter 207
Greengages 322
freezing 565
greengage jam 470
Grey mullet see Mullet, grey
Griddle scones 401, 403
Griddles 570
Grilling: fish 56
lamb 113
meat 93
pork 124
salmon 76
sausages 144
steaks 96
Grills 543
Grinding 545, 570
Grissini 570
Grits 240
Ground nuts see Peanuts
Groundnut oil 253
Grouse 172
Gruyère cheese 280, 284
hot fish terrine with Gruyère sauce 71
Guacamole 47
Guard of honour 114

Guavas 317, 318
Guinea fowl 169
  roast guinea fowl 169
Guinness: black velvet 531
Gurnard 59
Gurnet 59
Gut 570

H

Haddock 53, 59
  see also Smoked haddock
  ceviche 69
  Indonesian fish curry 68
  old fashioned fish pie 67
Hake 59
  hake goujons 64
  hot fish terrine with Gruyère
    sauce 71
Half cream 351
Half-pound cake 413
Halibut 53, 59
  see also Smoked halibut
Halogen hobs 54
Ham 153
  aubergines with ham 226
  bacon or ham stuffing 185
  croque monsieur 286
  eggs Bénédict 274
  ham and leeks au gratin 135
  ham butter 207
  ham soufflé 270
  melon and Parma ham 39
  omelette 277
  tagliatelle with Parma ham in
    cream sauce 302
  veal and ham pie 110
  veal escalopes with ham and
    Marsala 109
Hanging 570
Hard sauce 210, 570
Hare 176
  preparation 176
  jugged hare 177
  roast hare 176
Haricot beans 242
  Boston beans 248
Harissa 196
Harvey Wallbanger (cocktail)
  531
Hasselback potatoes 238
Hazelnut oil 253
Hazelnuts 325
  apple and hazelnut layer 338
  apricot nut teabread 405
  brown sugar and hazelnut
    meringues 373
  chocolate hazelnut clusters
  hazelnut meringue gâteau
    375
Heart 136
  lamb's heart casserole 140
Herbs 187-90
  drying 187
  garnishes 505
  herb mills 545
  in salads 253
  vinegars 253

bouquet garni 195
fines herbes 195
herb jellies 472
herb pasta 298
herb pastry 381
herbal teas 535
herbed cheese bread 463
hot herb bread 514
Herrings 53, 59
  see also Kippers
  hors d'oeuvres 35
  preparation 56
  herrings in oatmeal 64
  soused herrings 64
Hiring equipment 511-12
Hobs 542, 547
Hollandaise sauce 203
Hominy 240
Honey 393
  baklava 342
  banana and honey teabread
    404
  honey-baked ham 133
  honey cake 409
  honey jumbles 445
  spiced honey and coriander
    dressing 255
  spiced marmalade and honey
    glaze 135
Hoods, cooker 542
Hors d'oeuvres 34, 570
Horse mackerel 59
Horseradish 191
  horseradish butter 207
  horseradish cream 205
Hot cross buns 460
Hot water crust pastry 386
Hulling 570
Humbugs, peppermint 499
Hummus 48
Hungarian wines 525
Huss 59
Hygiene 556

I

Ice, for cocktails 528
Ices and ice creams; *see also*
  Sorbets and water ices
  freezing 366
  ice cream makers 546-7
  machines 366
  baked Alaska 369
  brown bread ice cream 369
  chocolate 367
  chocolate flake 367
  cinnamon 367
  coconut 367
  coffee 367
  frozen yogurt 366
  fruit 367
  ice cream soda 538
  iced Christmas pudding 369
  iced raspberry meringue 370
  individual coffee bombes 370
  Pernod parfait 370
  praline 367
  vanilla ice cream 367

Iced coffee 537
Iced petits fours 447
Iced tea 535
Icing sugar 392
Icing sugar patterns 508
Icings: celebration cakes 423
  decorating cakes 423-5
  piping 424-5
  American frosting 420, 434
  butter cream 433
  chocolate frosting 434
  coffee fudge frosting 434
  crème au beurre 433
  glacé 432
  royal 423, 426-7
  seven-minute frosting 434
  vanilla frosting 434
Indian chutney 486
Indonesian fish curry 68
Infusing 570
Insurance, freezers 559
Interleaving, for freezers 560
Iodine 14
Irish coffee 537
Irish stew 121
Iron, cast iron pans 548
Iron (mineral) 14
Italian pasta soup 26
Italian red onions 218
Italian stuffed chicken 149
Italian-style poussin 160
Italian wines 521, 523-4

J

Jacket baked onions 235
Jacket potatoes 220
Jackfruit 318
Jam *see also* Marmalade
  equipment 464
  fruit 466
  potting and storing 467
  pressure cooking 478
  testing 466-7
  apricot 467
  blackberry and apple 468
  blackcurrant 468
  cherry 470
  dried apricot 468
  gooseberry 469
  light set raspberry 471
  marrow and ginger 470
  plum 470
  raspberry 471
  rhubarb and ginger 471
  rose petal 468
  strawberry 469
  strawberry conserve 469
  uncooked freezer jam 471
Jam jars 464
Jam roly-poly 331
Jam sponge pudding 326, 330
Jam suet pudding 331
Jamaica pepper 190
Japanese medlars 319
Japonicas 318
Jardinière 570
Jellied consommé 20

Jellies (fruit) 472
  pressure cooking 478
  bramble 473
  elderberry 474
  herb 472
  mint and apple 472
  quince 474
  redcurrant 474
  rosehip 473
Jelly 359-60
  flower decorations 507
  aspic 43
  claret jelly 365
  lemon cheese jelly 365
  milk jelly 365
Jerusalem artichokes 211
  cream of artichoke soup 21
  in nutmeg cream 225
Job Gris 60
John Dory 59
Jointing poultry 147
Jugged hare 176, 571
Juicers 545
Julglogg 533
Julienne 571
  citrus 507
Juniper berries 191
  cabbage with juniper berries
    229
Junket 351

K

Kale 217
Karella 217
Kashmiri-style lamb 116
Kebabs 571
  lamb kebabs 122
  mixed seafood brochettes 91
  monkfish and mussel
    brochettes 65
  pork kebabs 131
  quorn satay 248
  steak and kidney kebabs 102
  turkey kebabs with chilli
    peanut sauce 165
Kedgeree, smoked haddock 80
Kentucky ham 133
Kettles 544-5
Kidney beans *see* Red kidney
  beans
Kidneys 136
  braised kidneys in port 139
  creamed kidneys in wine 140
  grilled kidneys 138
  steak and kidney kebabs 102
  steak and kidney pudding 104
Kippers 79
Kir 532
Kiwi fruit 318
Kneading 451, 571
Knives 549
  electric carving knives 546
Knock back 571
Knocking up pastry 379
Kohlrabi 217
  freezing 563
  scalloped kohlrabi 232

Korma, lamb 116
Kosher 571
Koulibiac, fish 73
Kugelhopf 571
Kumquats 319

L

Labels, for freezers 560
Lacto-vegetarians 15
Lamb: see also Heart; Kidneys;
  Liver; Tongue
  barbecuing 113
  carving 94-5
  cuts 113
  frying113
  grilling 113
  roasting 94, 113
  best end:
  crown roast of lamb 114
  guard of honour 114
  lamb paprika 117
  navarin of lamb 117
  breast:
  lamb and kidney bean
    casserole 123
  rolled stuffed breast of lamb
    115
  chops:
  lamb chops with leeks and
    lentils 119
  cooked meat:
  shepherd's pie 106
  cutlets:
  lamb cutlets en croûte 115
  fillet:
  lamb korma 116
  spiced lamb with wholewheat
    120
  leg:
  Kashmiri-style lamb 116
  lamb escalopes with oatmeal
    118
  lamb in redcurrant sauce 123
  lamb kebabs 122
  Oxford John steaks with
    caper sauce 123
  middle neck chops:
  Irish stew 121
  Lancashire hot pot 120
  minced and cubed:
  Eastern casserole of lamb
    515
  Middle Eastern meatballs
    122
  moussaka 121
  stuffed vine leaves 121
  neck fillets:
  roast lamb fillets with garlic
    118
  shoulder:
  spinach stuffed shoulder of
    lamb 117
Lamb's lettuce 252
Lancashire hot pot 120
Lancashire tripe and onions 140
Languedoc wines 523
Langues de chats 443, 571

Laos powder 192
Lard, for pastry 376-7
Larding 571
Lasagne 295,298
  recipe 303
Lattice work, pastry 379
Layered sausage pie 145
Lazio, wines 524
Leaven 571
Leaves: chocolate 508
  pastry 379
Leeks 217
  freezing 563
  ham and leeks au gratin 135
  lamb chops with leeks and
    lentils 119
  leek and onion flan 292
  leek and split pea soup 28
  leeks au gratin 233
  pasta with mushroom and
    leek sauce 300
  vichyssoise 32
Lemon balm 187
Lemon grass 188
Lemon sole 61
Lemons 319
  freezing 565
  garnishes 505
  baked trout with lemon 78
  bitter lemon 539
  broad beans in lemon parsley
    sauce 226
  carrots with mint and lemon
    230
  citrus punch 540
  lemon and mustard mackerel
    70
  lemon and yogurt mousse
    365
  lemon butter cream 433
  lemon cheese jelly 365
  lemon crème au beurre 433
  lemon curd 480
  lemon-dressed avocado salad
    262
  lemon glacé icing 432
  lemon layer pudding 327
  lemon meringue pie 373
  lemon sandwich cake 406
  lemon sauce 209
  lemon shred marmalade 477
  lemon sorbet 368
  lemon soufflé 360
  lemon sponge pudding 330
  orange and lemon sponge
    pudding 326
  quick lemon squash 539
  sesame lemon chicken 154
  still lemonade 538
  three-fruit marmalade 475
  turkey sauté with lemon and
    walnuts 166
Lentils 241, 242
  lamb chops with leeks and
    lentils 119
  roasted peppers with lentils
    244
  winter lentil soup 26

Lettuce 217
  salads 252
  lettuce soup 21
  petits pois à la Française 235
Liaisons 571
'Lights' 137
Lima beans see Butter beans
Limes 319
  freezing 565
  ceviche 69
  monkfish with lime and
    prawns 65
Lining cake tins 396-7
Liqueur glacé icing 432
Liqueurs 526-7
Liver 136
  chicken liver pâté 45
  chicken livers on toast 52
  Chinese-style fried liver 137
  coarse garlic pâté 46
  lamb's liver and mushrooms
    138
  liver and onions 137
  liver Marsala 137
  pâté en croûte 518
  pork and liver pâté with
    black olives 45
  sautéed liver with sage and
    apple 139
Loaf tins 396, 397
Lobster 82
  preparation 82
  grilled lobster 87
  lobster butter 207
  lobster mayonnaise 86
  lobster Newburg 87
  lobster salad 86
  lobster thermidor 87
Loganberries 319
  freezing 565
Loire wines 523
Lollo rosso 252
Lombardy wines 523
Loquats 319
Lovage 188
Lukewarm 571
Lungs 137
Lychees 319

M

Macaroni 295
  macaroni cheese 302
Macaroons, coconut 440
Mace 192
Macédoine 571
Macerating 571
Mâché see Lamb's lettuce
Mackerel 53, 59
  see also Smoked mackerel
  hors d'oeuvres 35
  preparation 56
  lemon and mustard mackerel
    70
Madeira cake 412
Madeira wine 526
Madeleines 439
  English 400

Magnesium 13-14
Magnetic induction hobs 542
Maids of honour 399
Maître d'hôtel butter 207
Maize 240
Malaysian-style prawns 88
Mallard 172
Malt bread 459
Malt extract 393
Malted fruit loaf 404
Mandarins 320
Mangetout 219
  freezing 563
  crispy duck breast with
    mangetout 169
  mangetout and mushroom
    salad 259
  stir-fried mangetout 234
Mangoes 319
  freezing 565
  mango mousse 362
  sweet mango chutney 485
Mangosteens 319
Manioc 215
Marbled chocolate cake 415
Marches, wines 524
Margarine 376-7, 393
Margarita (cocktail) 531
Marinades 571
Marjoram 188
Marmalade 475
  pressure cooking 478
  diabetic 476
  orange shred 477
  Seville orange 476
  spiced marmalade and honey
    glaze 135
  three-fruit 475
Marmites 571
Marrow 217
  freezing 563
  marrow and apple chutney
    486
  marrow and ginger jam 470
  spiced marrow 234
Marsala: liver Marsala 137
  veal escalopes with ham and
    Marsala 109
  zabaglione 362
Marzipan see Almond paste
Masa harina 240
  tortillas 463
Mascarpone cheese 284
  tiramisu 363
Matjes herrings 59
Mayonnaise 254
  aïoli 256
  blue cheese dressing 254
  caper mayonnaise 254
  cucumber mayonnaise 254
  curry cream sauce 254
  egg mayonnaise 273
  lobster mayonnaise 86
  rémoulade sauce 254
  shellfish cocktails 41
  stuffed egg mayonnaise 273
  tartare sauce 254
  Thousand Island 254

Meat 92-5
see also Beef; Lamb etc.
barbecuing 93
boiling 93
braising 93
buying 92
carving 94-5
freezing 561
frying 93
grilling 93
hors d'oeuvres 34
roasting 93-4
spit-roasting 94
stewing and casseroling 93
storage 92-3, 557
Meatballs: frikadeller 131
meat balls in tomato sauce
107
Middle Eastern meatballs
122
sweet-sour pork balls 129
Medallions 571
Medlars 320
Melba sauce 209
Melba toast 18
Melon 320
melon and ginger sorbet 368
melon and Parma ham 39
melon balls 38
melon slices 38
Melting chocolate 504
Melting method, cakes 394-5
Menus, for parties 509-10
Meringues 372, 571
baskets 372
nests 372
brown sugar and hazelnut
meringues 373
chocolate and chestnut
cream Vacherin 374
baked Alaska 369
floating islands 357
hazelnut meringue gâteau
375
iced raspberry meringue 370
Italian meringue 372
lemon meringue pie 373
meringue cuite 372
meringue petits fours 446
meringue Suisse 372
meringues with summer
fruits 516
queen of puddings 354
raspberry Pavlova 373
Meunière 571
Microwave cooking 551-5
baby food 555
baking 554
combination ovens 543
cooking techniques 553-4
cookware 552-3
fish 57, 76, 554
meat and poultry 554
ready meals 555
thawing food in 554, 561
vegetables 554
Middle Eastern meatballs 122
Midi wines 523

Midsummer night's dream
(punch) 532
Milk 351
for cakes 393
coffee milk shake 538
milk bread 453
strawberry milk shake 538
Milk puddings: blancmange
352
junket 351
milk jelly 365
rice pudding 352
semolina pudding 352
yogurt 351
Mille feuilles 343
Millet 241
Milling 571
Mincemeat 481
mince pies 339
mincemeat surprise pudding
330
Mincing 571
Mineolas 320
Minerals 11, 13-14
Minestrone 28
Mint 188
carrots with mint and lemon
230
mint and apple jelly 472
mint and rosemary stuffing
183
mint sauce 205
minted pear vinaigrette 36
potted cheese with mint 287
Mirepoix 571
Mixed herbs 190
Mixed spice 196
Mixers 546
Mocha 571
mocha butter cream 433
mocha glacé icing 432
mocha truffles 502
Monkey nuts *see* Peanuts
Monkfish 59
mixed fish stir-fry 72
monkfish and mussel
brochettes 65
monkfish with lime and
prawns 65
Monosodium glutamate (MSG)
194, 571
Monounsaturated fats 9-10
Mooli 221
Morels 218
Mornay sauce 200
Mosel-Saar-Ruwer wines 523
Moulds: lining with jelly 355
pastry 377
raised pies 378
unmoulding 360
Moules marinières 89
Moussaka 121
Mousseline sauce 203
sweet 210
Mousses: avocado 42
blackcurrant 362
chocolate 364
lemon and yogurt 365

mango 362
prawn and asparagus 44
salmon 43
smoked trout 44
strawberry and orange 364
Mozzarella cheese 280, 284
tomato and mozzarella pizza
289
tomato and mozzarella salad
36
Muesli yogurt, frozen 366
Muffins 403
quick muffin 'pizzas' 291
Mulberries 320
Mulled wine 533
Mullet, grey 59
Mullet, red 59
red mullet in tomato sauce
66
Mulligatawny soup 25
Mung beans 242
Mushrooms 218
garnishes 506
salads 252
baked eggs with mushrooms
272
creamed mushrooms 234
devilled mushroom 'pizzas'
291
lamb's liver and mushrooms
138
mangetout and mushroom
salad 259
marinated mushrooms 260
mushroom bouchées 51
mushroom sauce 199
mushroom soufflé 270
mushroom soup 25
mushroom stuffing 186
mushrooms à la Grecque 37
omelette 277
pasta baked with mushrooms
and cheese 303
pasta with mushroom and
leek sauce 300
pickled mushrooms 491
shredded chicken with
mushrooms and walnuts
157
sole bonne femme 70
steak and mushroom pie 105
stuffed mushrooms with dill
37
turkey with cashew nuts and
mushrooms 166
veal escalopes in mushroom
sauce 111
vegetarian roast 244
Mussels 82
hors d'oeuvres 35
preparation 82
monkfish and mussel
brochettes 65
moules marinières 89
mussel bisque 31
mussels and clams with
tomatoes 89
paella 312

Mustard 192
lemon and mustard mackerel
70
mustard cream sauce 200
mustard dip 47
mustard relish 487
turnips in mustard sauce 239
Mustard and cress 252

N

Nails, icing 423
Nasturtium leaves 252
Navarin of lamb 117, 571
Neapolitan slices 497
Nectarines 320
Nests, meringue 372
New Zealand wines 524
Niacin 12
Nicotinamide 12
Nicotinic acid 12
Noisettes 571
Non starch polysaccharides
(NSP) 10
Non-stick pans 547
Noodles 295, 297
chilli beef with noodles 107
Normandy pork 128
Normandy sauce 201
Norway haddock *see* Red Fish
Novelty clown cake 430-1
Nozzles, icing 423-4
Nutmeg 192
Jerusalem artichokes in
nutmeg cream 225
Nutrition 9-16
Nuts 324-5
see also Chestnuts; Walnuts
etc.
buying 324
for cakes 394, 424
storing 324
toasting 324
butterscotch sauce 208
chocolate nut truffles 502
nut pastry 381
nut stuffing 184
savoury nut burgers 248

O

Oatmeal 241
apricot oat crunchies 444
flapjacks 444
herrings in oatmeal 64
lamb escalopes with oatmeal
118
oatmeal and prune stuffing
184
oatmeal parkin 405
pork and oat burgers 131
Obesity 15-16
Ocean perch *see* Red fish
Octopus 60
preparation 60
Offal 136-7
see also Kidneys; Liver etc.
Oil pastry 383

Oils: for cakes 393, 396
 for pastry 376
 salad dressings 253
Oily fish 53
Okra 218
 curried okra 234
Old English trifle 355
Old-fashioned fish pie 67
Old-fashioned treacle tart 336
Olive oil 253
Olives: cheese and olive pick-
 ups 48
 chicken with vermouth and
 olives 158
 pizza Niçoise 289
 pork and liver pâté with
 black olives 45
Omelettes 276
 fillings 277
 omelette Arnold Bennett 278
 plain omelette 276
 prawn and tarragon omelette
 278
 soufflé omelette 277
 Spanish omelette 277
One-stage method, cakes 394
Onions 218
 freezing 563
 celeriac and onion bake 231
 French onion soup 23
 glazed onions 235
 jacket baked onions 235
 Lancashire tripe and onions
 140
 leek and onion flan 292
 liver and onions 137
 onion butter 207
 onion sauce 199
 pickled onions 490
 sage and onion bread 455
 sage and onion stuffing 182
 soubise sauce 201
Orange flower water 194
Oranges 320
 see also Marmalade
 freezing 565
 garnishes 506
 asparagus Maltaise 224
 beetroot with orange 227
 Boodle's orange fool 356
 buck's fizz 531
 carrot and orange soup 22
 chestnut and orange soup 29
 chocolate orange soufflé 361
 citrus punch 540
 duck and orange terrine 42
 duckling with orange sauce
 168
 Florida cocktails 36
 orange and lemon sponge
 pudding 326
 orange butter cream 433
 orange crème au beurre 433
 orange curd 480
 orange glacé icing 432
 orange Madeira cake 412
 orange sandwich cake 406
 orange sauce 209

 orange sponge pudding 330
 orange water ice 368
 oranges in caramel 345
 orangeade 539
 rhubarb and orange chiffon
 pie 340
 smoked chicken and orange
 appetiser 38
 spiced duckling and orange
 salad 266
 spicy fruit punch 540
 strawberry and orange
 mousse 364
 sweet potatoes with orange
 239
 walnut and orange pudding
 329
'Oranges', marzipan 507
Oregano 190
Oriental salad 518
Oriental-style poussins 150
Ortaniques 320
Osso buco 112
Oven scones 402
Ovens 543-4
**Oxford John steaks with caper
 sauce** 123
Oxtail 136
 braised oxtail 141
 oxtail paprika 142
Oyster mushrooms 218
Oysters 82
 hors d'oeuvres 35
 angels on horseback 52
 oysters au naturel 87

P

Packaging for freezers 560
Paella 312
Palm hearts 219
Palmiers 390
 cheese 50
Panada 571
Pancakes 333
 crêpes Suzette 334
 pancake rolls 162
 Scotch 403
 seafood pancakes 40
Pantothenic acid 12
Papayas 317
 freezing 565
Paprika 192
 lamb paprika 117
 oxtail paprika 142
Par-boiling 571
Parathas 463
Parchment baked fish 67
Parfait, Pernod 370
Paring 571
Parkin, oatmeal 405
Parma ham 133
 melon and Parma ham 39
 tagliatelle with Parma ham in
 cream sauce 302
Parmesan cheese 280, 284
 spaghetti with butter and
 Parmesan 299

Parrotfish 55, 60
Parsley 190
 broad beans in lemon parsley
 sauce 226
 maitre d'hôtel butter 207
 parsley sauce 199
Parsnips 219
 freezing 563
 curried parsnip soup 24
 parsnip bake 235
Parties 509-19
 drinks 512
 menus 514-19
 planning menus 509-10
 quantities 512, 513
Partridge 172
Passion fruit 321
Pasta 295-7
 see also Macaroni; Spaghetti
 etc.
 cooking 297
 microwave cooking 554
 storing 297
 herb pasta 298
 homemade pasta dough 298
 pasta, prawn and apple salad
 264
 pasta, veal and rosemary
 gratin 304
 pasta verde 298
 pasta with mushroom and
 leek sauce 300
 pasta with spicy sausage and
 tomato sauce 302
 pork and pasta stir-fry 127
 red pasta 298
 traditional Italian pasta soup
 (pasta in brodo) 26
Pasteurising 571
Pasties 571
 Cornish 105
 spinach and seafood 63
Pastries *see also* Choux pastry
 apple strudel 343
 apricot and pistachio rolls
 389
 baklava 342
 cheese palmiers 50
 cream horns 390
 Danish pastries 457
 Eccles cakes 390
 éclairs 391
 feta cheese puffs 286
 mille feuilles 343
 mushroom bouchées 51
 palmiers 390
 prawn and feta purses 50
 smoked salmon samosas 50
Pastry: baking blind 380
 garnishes 379
 ingredients 376-7
 microwave cooking 554
 quantity guide 380
 rolling out 377
 shaping 377-8
 cheese 381, 383
 choux 376, 388
 crescents 158

 filo 376, 389
 flaky 384
 herb 381
 hot water crust 386
 nut 381
 oil or fork-mix 383
 one stage short pastry 383
 pâte sucrée 382
 puff 376, 385-6
 rich shortcrust 382
 rough puff 385
 shortcrust 381-2
 suetcrust 376, 387
 wholemeal 381
Pastry cream 210
Pâté 571
Pâte sucrée 382
Pâtés 571-2
 chicken liver 45
 coarse garlic 46
 pâté en croûte 518
 pork and liver pâté with
 black olives 45
 potted prawn 46
 smoked mackerel 45
 smoked salmon 39
 stuffed eggs with pâté 273
Patties 572
Patty pan squashes 222
Paunching 572
Paupiettes 572
Pavlova, raspberry 373
Paw paws *see* Papayas
Peaches 321
 dried 323
 freezing 565
 brandied peaches 483
 peach and nut stuffing 186
 peach chutney 485
 poached in sugar syrup 344
Peanut butter cookies 438
Peanuts 325
 peanut brittle 498
 turkey kebabs with chilli
 peanut sauce 165
Pears 321
 dried 323
 chocolate pear upside-down
 pudding 329
 fresh pear shortcake 346
 minted pear vinaigrette 36
 pears in port 345
 poached in sugar syrup 344
 spiced pears 489
Peas 219
 freezing 563
 petits pois à la Française 235
 Shropshire pea soup 25
Peas, dried 241-2
 leek and split pea soup 28
Pecan nuts 325
 pecan pie 335
Pectin 466, 572
Peel, candied 394
Penne 297
 spring vegetable pasta 305
Peppercorns 192
 peppered beef sauté 103

skate in pepper butter 66
steak au poivre 101
Peppermint: peppermint
  creams 495
  peppermint humbugs 499
  uncooked peppermint
    creams 496
Peppers 219
  freezing 563
  salads 252
  pipérade 272
  pork steaks with peppers 130
  red pasta 298
  roasted peppers with lentils
    244
  sweet pepper and basil flan
    293
Perch 75
Pernod parfait 370
Persimmons 321
Pesto 256
  rolled plaice with pesto 62
Petits fours 446
  almond stars 447
  iced petits fours 447
  meringue petits fours 446
Petits pois à la Française 235
Pheasant 172
  pheasant with chestnuts 175
  pheasant with port 174
  roast pheasant 174
  salmis of pheasant 175
Phosphorus 14
Phyllo pastry see Filo pastry
Piccalilli 492
Pickle jars 484
Pickles 488, 572
  beetroot 490
  bread and butter 492
  dates 492
  eggs 490
  gherkins 490
  mixed pickle 492
  mushrooms 491
  onions 490
  piccalilli 492
  plums 491
  red cabbage 491
  spiced crab-apples 489
  spiced pears 489
  spiced vinegar 489
  sweet spiced vinegar 489
Pickling onions 218
Pickling spice 196
Pie dishes, pastry 377-8, 380
Piedmont wines 523
Pies: raised pies 378
  apple pie 337
  chicken puff pie 161
  cottage pie 106
  double-crust blackcurrant
    pie 339
  layered sausage pie 145
  mince pies 339
  old fashioned fish pie 67
  poacher's pie 177
  raised game pie 178
  shepherd's pie 106

steak and mushroom pie 105
  veal and ham pie 110
  wholemeal vegetable and
    herb pie 247
Pigeons 172
  casseroled pigeons with cider
    and apple 173
Pignoli see Pine nuts
Pike 75
Pilaff (pilau): basic pilau rice
  308
  basmati pilaff 309
  brown rice pilaff 515
Pilchards 60
Pina colada (cocktail) 531
Pine nuts 325
  pesto 256
Pineapple 321
  freezing 565
  pine-lime sparkle 540
  pineapple crush 539
  pineapple tarte tatin 341
  pineapple upside-down
    pudding 329
Pink gin (cocktail) 530
Pinto beans 242
Pinwheel biscuits 436
Pinwheels, smoked salmon 48
Pipérade 272
Piping 572
  choux pastry 388
  cream 507
  icing 424-5
Piping bags 424-5
Pistachio nuts 325
  apricot and pistachio rolls
    389
Pith 572
Pizzas: basic pizza dough 288
  devilled mushroom 'pizzas'
    291
  hot sausage and salami pizza
    289
  pizza Niçoise 289
  quick muffin 'pizzas' 291
  quick pizza dough 288
  smoked salmon and avocado
    pizza 290
  tomato and mozzarella pizza
    289
Plaice 53, 60
  plaice and spinach flan 292
  rolled plaice with pesto 62
Plain flour 376, 392, 450
Plantains 219
Plastics, microwave cookware
  552
Plucking 572
Plums 322
  freezing 565
  pickled plums 491
  plum jam 470
  poached in sugar syrup 344
Poacher's pie 177
Poaching 572
  eggs 268
  fish 56
  salmon 76

Polenta 240
Polythene bags, for freezers 560
Polyunsaturated fats 9
Pomegranates 322
Pope's eye 572
Poppadoms 120
Poppy seeds 192, 451
Pork: see also Sausagemeat;
  Sausages
  barbecuing 124
  carving 95
  cuts 124
  frying 124
  grilling 124
  roasting 94, 124
  belly:
  brawn 144
  coarse garlic pâté 46
  pork and liver pâté with
    black olives 45
  Somerset pork stew 128
  chops:
  baked stuffed pork chops
    128
  fillet:
  Normandy pork 128
  pork escalopes with sage 129
  loin:
  crown roast of pork 125
  golden grilled pork steaks
    126
  pork steaks with peppers 130
  minced and cubed:
  frikadeller 131
  pork and oat burgers 131
  pork kebabs 131
  sweet-sour pork balls 129
  spare ribs:
  barbecued spare ribs 129
  streaky rashers:
  quick pork cassoulet 126
  tenderloin:
  pork and pasta stir-fry 127
  roast pork tenderloin 125
Port 525
  braised kidneys in port 139
  pears in port 345
  pheasant with port 174
Portuguese wines 521, 524
Pot roasting 572
Potage 572
Potassium 14
Potatoes 220-1
  chipped 220
  cooking methods 220-1
  freezing 563
  jacket 220
  roast 221
  château potatoes 238
  cheese and potato cakes 287
  cottage pie 106
  duchesse potatoes 238
  fish cakes 64
  game chips 171, 220
  gratin Dauphinois 236
  Greek-style new potatoes 237
  Hasselback potatoes 238
  Irish stew 121

Lancashire hot pot 120
  layered sausage pie 145
  new potatoes with tarragon
    cream 237
  old fashioned fish pie 67
  potato salad 257
  rissoles 105
  scalloped potatoes 236
  shepherd's pie 106
  smoked mackerel salad 264
  Spanish omelette 277
  stoved chicken 159
  Swiss rosti 238
  vichyssoise 32
Potatoes, sweet see Sweet
  potatoes
Pots and pans 547-9
Potted cheese with mint 287
Potted prawn pâté 46
Pottery, microwave cookware
  552
Poulet en cocotte 158
Poultry 146-8
  see also Chicken; Duck etc.
  boning 147
  freezing 561
  hygiene 147
  jointing 147
  microwave cooking 554
  stuffing 148
  thawing 148
  trussing 148
Pouring sauce 198
Poussins see Chicken
Praline 572
  praline ice cream 367
Prawns 83
  see also Shrimps
  hors d'oeuvres 35
  to peel 83
  chicken and prawn risotto
    311
  Malaysian-style prawns 88
  monkfish with lime and
    prawns 65
  omelette 277
  pasta, prawn and apple salad
    264
  potted prawn pâté 46
  prawn and asparagus mousse
    44
  prawn and feta purses 50
  prawn and tarragon omelette
    278
  prawn bouchées 51
  prawns fried in garlic 88
  shellfish cocktails 41
  spinach and seafood pasties
    63
  stir-fried prawns 88
  warm seafood salad 265
Presenting food 505-8
Preserving 572
Preserving pans 464, 484
Pressed ox tongue 142
Pressure cookers 549, 572
  marmalades, jams and jellies
    478

Prickly pears 322
Profiteroles 343
Prosciutto 133, 572
Protein 11
Provence, wines 523
Proving 572
Prunes 323
 apricot, apple and prune
 stuffing 186
 devils on horseback 52
 oatmeal and prune stuffing
 184
 sweet-sour rabbit with prunes
 177
Ptarmigan 172
Puddings see Desserts
Puff pastry 376, 385-6
Pulses 241-2, 572
 cooking times 242
Pumpkin 221
Punches and cups 532-3
Purées 572
Pyridoxine 12
Pyrolitic cleaning 543

Q

Quail 172
 roast quail 173
 creamed quail casserole 173
Quail eggs 268
Quark 284-5
Queen of puddings 354
Quenelles 74, 572
Quiches and savoury flans:
 cheese and asparagus tart
 294
 crab and Ricotta quiche 294
 individual quiches 49
 leek and onion flan 292
 plaice and spinach flan 292
 quiche Lorraine 294
 Roquefort quiche 294
 sweet pepper and basil flan
 293
Quinces 322
 quince jelly 474
Quorn 240
 quorn satay 248

R

Rabbit 176
 preparation 176
 fricassée of rabbit 178
 poacher's pie 177
 sweet-sour rabbit with prunes
 177
Radicchio 252
 fennel and radicchio salad
 519
 radicchio and alfalfa salad
 260
Radishes 221
 garnishes 506
 salads 252
Rainbow trout 75

Raised pies 378
 game pie 178
Raising agents: for bread 448
 for cakes 393
 eggs 268
 for pastry 376
 for scones 401
Raisins 323
 date and raisin teabread 404
Rambutans 322
Ramekins 572
Range cookers 541-2
Raspberries 322
 freezing 565
 iced raspberry meringue 370
 light set raspberry jam 471
 Melba sauce 209
 raspberry jam 471
 raspberry Pavlova 373
 raspberry rings 436
 raspberry roulade 420
 raspberry soufflé 360
 raspberry torte 418
 strawberries with raspberry
 sauce 516
 uncooked freezer jam 471
Ratatouille 236
Ravioli 297
 ravioli stuffed with spinach
 306
Réchauffé 572
Red cabbage 214
 braised red cabbage with
 apple 228
 pickled red cabbage 491
 red cabbage and apple salad
 259
Red fish 60
Red herrings 79
Red kidney beans 242
 chilli con carne 106
 lamb and kidney bean
 casserole 123
 quick pork cassoulet 126
 red kidney bean hot-pot 246
 sausage and bean stew 145
 three bean salad 516
Red mullet see Mullet, red
Red snapper 60
Red wines 521-2
Redcurrant sauce, lamb in 123
Redcurrants 316
 freezing 565
 redcurrant cheesecake 350
 redcurrant jelly 474
Reducing 572
Reform sauce 203
Refreshing 572
Refrigerator biscuits 445
Refrigerators 544, 556-8
Relishes 484
 beet 487
 mustard 487
 tomato 487
Rémoulade sauce 254
Rendering 572
Rennet 572
Retinol 11

Rheingau wines 523
Rheinhessen wines 523
Rheinpfalz wines 523
Rhône wines 523
Rhubarb 322
 freezing 565
 poached in sugar syrup 344
 rhubarb and ginger jam 471
 rhubarb and orange chiffon
 pie 340
Riboflavin 12, 14
Rice 307
 cooking 307
 microwave cooking 554
 stuffings 181
 basic pilau rice 308
 basmati pilaff 309
 bean sprout and brown rice
 salad 260
 boiled rice 308
 brown rice pilaff 515
 brown rice risotto 312
 chicken and prawn risotto
 311
 herby rice 308
 oven-cooked rice 308
 paella 312
 rice pudding 352
 rice salad ring 258
 rice stuffing 183
 risotto alla Milanese 311
 saffron rice 308
 savoury rice 310
 smoked haddock kedgeree
 80
 special fried rice 309
 spiced rice with chicken Thai
 fried rice 310
 turmeric rice 308
 vegetarian roast 244
Rice noodles 297
Rice paper 572
Rich shortcrust or flan pastry
 382
Ricotta cheese 279, 285
 crab and Ricotta quiche 294
Rigatoni 297
Risotto: brown rice 312
 chicken and prawn 311
 risotto alla Milanese 311
Rissoles 105
River trout 75
Roasting 572
 lamb 113
 meat 93-4
 pork 124
 potatoes 221
 turkey 148, 162
Robert sauce 203
Rock buns 399
Rocket 252
Roe, cod's 58
 see also Smoked cod's roe
Rollmops 59
Rolls: floury baps 454
 white rolls 453
Romanian wines 525
Roquefort cheese 280, 285

Roquefort quiche 294
Rose petal jam 468
Rose water 194
 glacé icing 432
Rosé wines 521
Rosebud wedding cake 427
Rosehip jelly 473
Rosemary 190
 mint and rosemary stuffing
 183
 pasta, veal and rosemary
 gratin 304
Rough puff pastry 385
Roulades 572
 chocolate and vanilla 416
 raspberry 420
 spicy spinach 271
Roussillon wines 523
Roux 197, 572
Royal icing 423, 426-7
Rubbing in 394, 572
Rulers, icing 423
Rum: daiquiri 531
 pina colada 531
 rich chocolate rum truffles
 502
 rumpot 483
Runner beans 212
 freezing 562
 spiced runner beans 227
Ruotini 297
Rusty nail (cocktail) 529
Rye 241
Rye flour 450
 caraway rye bread 462
 dark rye bread 455

S

Sabayon sauce 210
Sachertorte 419
Saffron 192
 saffron rice 308
Sage 190
 pork escalopes with sage 129
 sage and onion bread 455
 sage and onion stuffing 182
 sautéed liver with sage and
 apple 139
St. Peter's fish 75
Saithe see Coley
Salad burnet 188
Salad dressings 253
 aïoli 256
 French dressing 255
 mayonnaise 254
 pesto 256
 rich garlic dressing 255
 spiced honey and coriander
 dressing 255
 tomato and yogurt dressing
 256
 yogurt dressing 256
Salad oils 253
Salads 250-3
 herbs and flowers 253
 bean sprout and brown rice
 260

beetroot in caraway dressing 261
Caesar 260
classic green salad 257
coleslaw 258
Coronation chicken 266
crab 264
crispy cauliflower 257
fennel and radicchio 519
fennel and tomato 261
Florida chicory 262
fresh spinach salad with hot bacon dressing 262
Greek 259
green salad with croûtons 519
lemon-dressed avocado 262
lobster 86
mangetout and mushroom 259
mixed bean 261
oriental 518
party coleslaw 518
pasta, prawn and apple 264
potato 257
radicchio and alfalfa 260
red cabbage and apple 259
rice salad ring 258
salade Niçoise 263
salade tiède 39
shredded red salad 515
smoked haddock and bean 263
smoked mackerel 264
spiced duckling and orange 266
three bean 516
tomato and mozzarella 36
tomato salad with basil 257
Waldorf 258
warm seafood 265
wholewheat and apricot 266
Salami: hot sausage and salami pizza 289
Salmis 572
pheasant 175
Salmon 75
see also Smoked salmon
hors d'oeuvres 35
baked salmon 76
fish koulibiac 73
fish-stuffed cannelloni with cheese 304
grilled salmon 76
microwave cooking salmon 76
poached salmon 76
salmon in aspic 78
salmon mousse 43
salmon with fennel sauce 77
Salmon trout *see* Sea trout
Salmonella 267
Salsify 221
Salt 11, 15, 194
for bread 450
in pastry 376
Salt cod 58
Salt herrings 59

Saltimbocca alla Romana 109
Salting 572
Samosas, smoked salmon 50
Sandpaper 424
Sandwich tins 396, 397
Sandwich toasters 547
Sandwiches: asparagus rolls 48
croque monsieur 286
smoked salmon pinwheels 48
Sardines 60
hors d'oeuvres 35
fresh sardines with herbs 66
Sardinian wines 524
Satsumas 320
Saturated fats 9, 15
Saucepans 547-8
Sauces 197-8
see also Salad dressings
arrowroot 197
brown 202-3
cornflour 197
coulis 197
egg-based 203-4
liquid for 197
roux-based 197
sweet 208-10
traditional 204-7
vegetable purées 197
white 198-201
anchovy 199
apple 205
aurore 201
barbecue 206
Béarnaise 204
Béchamel 200
brandy butter 210
bread 206
butterscotch 208
caper 199
chaudfroid 200
cheese 199
chocolate 209
cranberry 206
crème pâtissière 210
cucumber 205
Cumberland 206
curry, mild 199
curry cream 254
demi-glace 202
egg 199
egg custard 208
espagnole 202
ginger 209
gooseberry 204
gravy 202
Hollandaise 203
horseradish cream 205
lemon 209
Melba 209
mint 205
Mornay 200
mousseline 203
mushroom 199
mustard cream 200
Normandy 201
onion 199
orange 209
parsley 199

Reform 203
rémoulade 254
Robert 203
sabayon 210
soubise 201
suprême 201
sweet mousseline 210
sweet white 208
tartare 254
tomato 207
velouté 201
white 198-9
Sausagemeat: cooking methods 144
stuffings 181
forcemeat balls 183
sausagemeat and chestnut stuffing 185
Scotch eggs 273
Sausages: cooking methods 144
hot sausage and salami pizza 289
layered sausage pie 145
pasta with spicy sausage and tomato sauce 302
sausage and bean stew 145
sausage rolls 144
toad in the hole 145
Sautéeing 572
potatoes 220
Savarin, apricot 346
Savory 190
Savouries, after-dinner 35, 52
Savoury butters 207
Savoy cabbage 214
Scad 59
Scalding 572
Scalloped kohlrabi 232
Scalloped potatoes 236
Scalloping 379, 573
Scallops 83
preparation 83
coquilles St. Jacques 90
mixed fish stir-fry 72
warm seafood salad 265
Scampi 83
deep-fried scampi 90
scampi Provençal 90
Scones 401
cheese scones 402
drop scones 403
everyday fruit scones 402
griddle scones 401, 403
oven scones 402
rich tea scones 402
wholemeal scones 402
Scoring 573
Scorzonera 221
Scotch broth 28
Scotch eggs 273
Scotch pancakes 403
Scotch woodcock 52
Scrambled eggs 269
Screwdriver (cocktail) 530
Sea bass *see* Bass
Sea bream 58
Sea fish 58-74
Sea trout 75

Seafood *see* Fish; Shellfish
Seafood pancakes 40
Seafood starters 39-41
Seakale 221
Seakale beet 222
Searing 573
Seasoned flour 573
Seasoning 573
Seed cake 412
Self raising flour 376, 392, 401, 450
Semolina pudding 352
Sesame lemon chicken 154
Sesame seeds 192, 451
Seven-minute frosting 434
Seville orange marmalade 476
Shallots 218
Shallow-frying 570
fish 57
Shark 60
Sharon fruit 321
Shellfish 81-91 *see also* Crab; Prawns etc.
buying 53
hors d'oeuvres 34-5
bouillabaisse 30
glazed seafood platter 91
mixed seafood brochettes 91
shellfish cocktails 41
Shepherd's pie 106
Sherry 525-6
Sherry vinegar 253
Shiitake mushrooms 218
Short pastries 381-3
Shortbread rounds 437
Shortcake, fresh pear 346
Shortcrust pastry 381-2
Shredding 573
Shrewsbury biscuits 436
Shrimps 83
omelette 277
see also Prawns
Shropshire pea soup 25
Sicily, wines 524
Sieving 573
Sifting 573
Silver dragees 424
Silverskin onions 218
Simmering 573
Simnel cake 428
Singeing 573
Skate 60
skate in pepper butter 66
skate with black butter 66
Skimming 573
Skinning fish 54
Slimming 15-16
Sloes 322
sloe gin 533
Slow cookers 547
Smelt 60
Smoked chicken and orange appetiser 38
Smoked cod 79
Smoked cod's roe 79
taramasalata 47
Smoked eel 79
hors d'oeuvres 35

Smoked fish 79-80
Smoked haddock 79
  fish soufflé 270
  mixed fish chowder 30
  omelette Arnold Bennett 278
  seafood pancakes 40
  smoked haddock and bean
    salad 263
  smoked haddock gougère 80
  smoked haddock kedgeree
    80
Smoked halibut 79
Smoked herring 79
Smoked mackerel 79
  smoked mackerel pâté 45
  smoked mackerel salad 264
Smoked salmon 79
  hors d'oeuvres 35
  savoury choux puffs 51
  smoked salmon and avocado
    pizza 290
  smoked salmon pâté 39
  smoked salmon pinwheels 48
  smoked salmon samosas 50
Smoked sprats 79
Smoked sturgeon 79
Smoked trout 79
  smoked trout mousse 44
Smoked tuna 79
Smokies 79
Smoking 573
Snapper 60
Snipe 172
Soda bread 462
Soft drinks 538-40
Sole 53, 60-1
  chunky fish casserole 71
  sole bonne femme 70
  sole meunière 70
  sole Véronique 70
  stuffed sole paupiettes 68
Somerset apple cake 414
Somerset pork stew 128
Sorbets and water ices:
  lemon sorbet 368
  melon and ginger sorbet 368
  orange water ice 368
  strawberry sorbet 368
Sorrel 221
Soubise sauce 201
Soufflé omelette 277
Soufflés: hot savoury 269-71;
  cold sweet 360; hot sweet
    358
  apricot 358
  carrot and bean 244
  cheese 270
  chocolate 358
  chocolate orange 361
  fish 270
  ham 270
  lemon 360
  mushroom 270
  raspberry 360
  spinach 269
  Stilton 270
  strawberry 360
  vanilla 358

Soups 17
  garnishes and
    accompaniments 17
  microwave cooking 554
  bean and coriander potage
    27
  borshch 31
  bouillabaisse 30
  carrot and orange 22
  cauliflower and almond
    cream 23
  celery and Stilton 24
  chestnut and orange 29
  chicken with dumplings 27
  chilled asparagus 32
  chilled avocado 32
  consommé 20
  cream of artichoke 21
  cream of spinach 24
  curried parsnip 24
  French bean 29
  French onion 23
  fresh tomato with basil 21
  gazpacho 31
  leek and split pea 28
  lettuce 21
  Minestrone 28
  mixed fish chowder 30
  Mulligatawny 25
  mushroom 25
  mussel bisque 31
  Scotch broth 28
  Shropshire pea 25
  traditional Italian pasta 26
  vichyssoise 32
  watercress 22
  winter lentil 26
Souring 573
Soused herrings 64
Sousing 573
South African wines 525
Soy sauce 194
Soya bean curd see Tofu
Soya beans 242
Soya oil 9
Spaghetti 295
  spaghetti alla carbonara 300
  spaghetti Bolognese 299
  spaghetti Napoletana 299
  spaghetti with butter and
    Parmesan 299
Spaghetti marrow 222
Spanish black radish 221
Spanish omelette 277
Spanish onions 218
Spanish wines 521, 524
Spare ribs, barbecued 129
Sparkling wines 525
Spices 190-4
  for cakes 393
  dry-freezing 196
  grinders 545
  curry powder 195
  five-spice powder 195
  garam masala 196
  harissa 196
  mixed spice 196
  pickling spice 196

Spice biscuits 436
Spider's web, icing 432
Spinach 222
  freezing 563
  cream of spinach soup 24
  creamed spinach 238
  eggs Florentine 272
  fresh spinach salad with hot
    bacon dressing 262
  hot spinach soufflé 269
  pasta verde 298
  plaice and spinach flan 292
  ravioli stuffed with spinach
    306
  spicy spinach roulade 271
  spinach and seafood pasties
    63
  spinach gnocchi 313
  spinach stuffed shoulder of
    lamb 117
  veal chops with spinach
    purée 108
Spinach beet 222
Spiny lobster see Crawfish
Spit-roasting 94, 573
Sponge cakes 395-6
  Genoese sponge 406
  whisked sponge cake 407
Sponge fingers 399
Sponge puddings 326-7, 329
  see also Steamed puddings
Spotted Dick 331
Sprats 61
  see also Smoked sprats
Spring onions 218
  garnishes 505
  salads 252
Spring-release tins 396
Spring vegetable pasta 305
Squashes 222
Squid 61
  cleaning 61
  fritto misto di mare 73
Stainless steel pans 548
Standing time, microwave 553
Star anise 192-4
Star fruit 322
Starters 33-52
Steak and kidney kebabs 102
Steak and kidney pudding 104
Steak and mushroom pie 105
Steaks 96
  for recipes see Beef
Steamed puddings 330-2
Steaming 573
  fish 57
  potatoes 220
Steeping 573
Sterilising 573
Stewing 573
  see also Casseroles and stews
Stilton cheese 280, 285
  celery and Stilton soup 24
  pasta baked with mushrooms
    and cheese 303
  steak and Stilton parcels 102
  Stilton bites 49
  Stilton soufflé 270

Stir-frying 573
Stocks 18, 573
  beef 19
  chicken 19
  court bouillon 56
  fish 19
  vegetable 19
Stollen 460
Stoneground flour 450
Storage: equipment 541
  freezers 558-65
  hygiene 556
  pots and pans 548
  refrigerators 557-8
Stoved chicken 159
Strawberries 322-3
  freezing 565
  glazed fruit sponge flan 340
  strawberries with raspberry
    sauce 516
  strawberry and orange
    mousse 364
  strawberry conserve 469
  strawberry jam 469
  strawberry milk shake 538
  strawberry sorbet 368
  strawberry soufflé 360
Strudel, apple 343
Strudel pastry see Filo pastry
Stuffings 181
  stuffing poultry 148
  apple and celery 185
  apricot 186
  apricot, apple and prune 186
  bacon or ham 185
  chestnut 185
  festive turkey 182
  mint and rosemary 183
  mushroom 186
  nut 184
  oatmeal and prune 184
  peach and nut 186
  rice 183
  sage and onion 182
  sausagemeat and chestnut
    185
  veal 184
Sturgeon 61
  smoked 79
Suet 573
  see also Steamed puddings
  suet puddings 387
  dumplings 18
  jam suet pudding 331
  steak and kidney pudding
    104
  suetcrust pastry 376, 377, 387
Suffolk ham 133
Sugar 10-11, 15
  boiling 494
  for cakes 392-3
  icing sugar patterns 508
  for jam 466
  for pastry 377
  thermometers 493
  brown sugar and hazelnut
    meringues 373
  vanilla 573

Sugar coffee beans 424
Sugar snap peas 219
Sultanas 323
  see also Dried fruit
  farmhouse sultana cake 411
Summer pudding 347
Sunflower oil 253
Suprême sauce 201
Sweating 573
Swedes 222
  swede and bacon bake 239
Sweet potatoes 223
  sweet potatoes with orange 239
Sweet-sour pork balls 129
Sweet-sour rabbit with prunes 177
Sweet white wines 522
Sweetbreads 136
  creamed sweetbreads 143
Sweetcorn 222
  baby corn 222, 250
  freezing 563
  corn fritters 154
Sweets: *see also* Petits fours
  boiling sugar 494
  cake decorations 424
  chocolate dipped fruit 504
  chocolate Easter eggs 504
  dipped chocolates 504
  equipment 493-4
  storing 494
  almond truffles 502
  butterscotch 499
  chocolate fudge 501
  chocolate hazelnut clusters 503
  chocolate nut truffles 502
  coconut ice bars 500
  coffee fudge 501
  collettes 503
  fondants 495-6
  marzipan 497
  mocha truffles 502
  peanut brittle 498
  peppermint creams 495-6
  peppermint humbugs 499
  rich chocolate rum truffles 502
  toffee apples 499
  treacle toffee 498
  vanilla fudge 500
Swiss chard 223
Swiss roll 407
Swiss roll tins 397
Swiss rosti 238
Syllabub 354
Syrup 573
  golden syrup 393
  old-fashioned treacle tart 336
  syrup sponge pudding 330

T

Tabasco sauce 194
Tagliatelle 298
  pasta baked with mushrooms and cheese 303

pasta with courgettes and broad beans 300
tagliatelle with Parma ham in cream sauce 302
tagliatelle with sun-dried tomato sauce 301
Tahini 194
  hummus 48
Tamarillos 323
Tamarind 194
Tamarind juice 196
Tandoori chicken 155
Tangelos 320
Tangerines 320
Taramasalata 47
Tarragon 190
  chicken with tarragon sauce 152
  new potatoes with tarragon cream 237
  prawn and tarragon omelette 278
  tarragon butter 207
Tartare sauce 254
Tartaric acid 568
Tarts and sweet flans:
  pastry 377, 380
  almond and cherry flan 336
  apple and hazelnut layer 338
  Bakewell pudding 335
  chocolate ginger flan 339
  egg custard tart 335
  French apple flan 337
  fresh apricot flan 338
  fresh fruit tartlets 391
  glazed fruit sponge flan 340
  lemon meringue pie 373
  old-fashioned treacle tart 336
  pecan pie 335
  pineapple tarte tatin 341
  rhubarb and orange chiffon pie 340
Tassels, pastry 379
Tayberries 319
Tea 534-5
  cinnamon tea 535
  iced tea 535
  special camomile tea 535
Teabreads 401
  apricot nut teabread 405
  banana and honey teabread 404
  date and raisin teabread 404
  malted fruit loaf 404
Teal 172
Tenderising 573
Tepid 573
Tequila: margarita 531
  tequila sunrise 531
Terrines 573
  duck and orange 42
  hot fish terrine with Gruyère sauce 71
  vegetable 41
Texturised vegetable protein (TVP) 573
Thai fried rice 310

Thawing 561
  in microwave cookers 554, 561
  poultry 148
Therese (snapper) 60
Thermometers: microwave cookers 553
  sugar 493
Thiamin 12
Thickening agents, eggs 268
Thousand Island mayonnaise 254
Three bean salad 516
Thyme 190
  French beans with thyme 226
Timers, oven 543
Tiramisu 363
Tisanes 535
Toad in the hole 145
Toast: chicken livers on 52
  game birds on 171-2
  Melba toast 18
  Welsh rarebit 286
Toasters 547
Toasting nuts 324
Tocopherols 13
Toffee 498
  butterscotch 499
  peanut brittle 498
  toffee apples 499
  treacle toffee 498
Tofu 240
Tom Collins 529
Tomatoes 223
  freezing 563
  garnishes 506
  salads 252
  aurore sauce 201
  basic tomato sauce 207
  fennel and tomato salad 261
  French beans with tomatoes 227
  fresh tomato soup with basil 21
  gazpacho 31
  green tomato chutney 485
  meat balls in tomato sauce 107
  mussels and clams with tomatoes 89
  omelette 277
  oxtail paprika 142
  pasta with spicy sausage and tomato sauce 302
  quick tomato sauce 207
  ratatouille 236
  red mullet in tomato sauce 66
  spaghetti Napoletana 299
  spicy cheese and tomato dip 47
  stuffed tomatoes 36
  tagliatelle with sun-dried tomato sauce 301
  tomato and mozzarella pizza 289
  tomato and mozzarella salad 36

tomato and yogurt dressing 256
tomato relish 487
tomato salad with basil 257
tortellini al forno 306
Tongue 136
  fricassée of lamb's tongues 141
  pressed ox tongue 142
Tools 549
Torbay sole 61
Tortellini 297
Tortellini al forno 306
Torte, raspberry 418
Tortillas 463
Traditional Italian pasta soup 26
Transparent noodles 297
Treacle 393
  treacle tart 336
  treacle toffee 498
Trifle, old English 355
Tripe 136
  Lancashire tripe and onions 140
Trotters 137
  brawn 144
Trout 53, 75
  see also Smoked trout
  hors d'oeuvres 35
  baked trout with lemon 78
  trout and almonds 78
Truffles 218, 573
Truffles (sweets): almond 502
  chocolate hazelnut 503
  chocolate nut 502
  collettes 503
  mocha 502
  rich chocolate rum 502
Trussing 148, 573
Tuna 61
  smoked 79
  pizza Niçoise 289
  quick muffin 'pizzas' 291
  salade Niçoise 263
  vitello tonnato 112
Tunny *see* Tuna
Turbot 61
Turkey 147
  carving 148
  roasting 148, 162
  ballotine of turkey 163
  devilled drumsticks 164
  festive turkey stuffing 182
  forcemeat balls 183
  roast turkey 162
  stuffed turkey drumsticks 164
  turkey à la King 167
  turkey escalopes with asparagus 167
  turkey in spiced yogurt 165
  turkey kebabs with chilli peanut sauce 165
  turkey sauté with lemon and walnuts 166
  turkey Stroganoff 164
  turkey with cashew nuts and mushrooms 166

Turkey eggs 268
Turmeric 194
turmeric rice 308
Turnips 223
freezing 563
turnips in mustard sauce 239
Turntables, icing 423
Tuscan wines 524
T.V.P. (textured vegetable
protein) 240
Tzaziki 46

U

Ugli fruit 320
Umbrian wines 524
Unleavened bread 573

V

Vacherin, chocolate and
chestnut cream 374
Vandyking oranges 506
Vanilla 194
essence 194
sugar 573
chocolate and vanilla
roulade 416
hot vanilla soufflé 358
vanilla frosting 434
vanilla fudge 500
vanilla ice cream 367
Veal: cuts 108
roasting 94
blanquette de veau 112
escalopes fines herbes 109
osso buco 112
pasta, veal and rosemary
gratin 304
veal and ham pie 110
veal chops with spinach
purée 108
veal escalopes in mushroom
sauce 111
veal escalopes with ham and
Marsala 109
veal goulash 110
veal stuffing 184
vitello tonnato 112
Wiener schnitzel 109
Vegans 15
Vegetable pear 215
Vegetables 211
see also Cabbage; Tomatoes
etc. and Salads
coulis 197
freezing 561,562-3
microwave cooking 554
pickles 488
starters 35-9
storage 557
vegetable purée sauces 197
vitamin content 14
baked egg and vegetable pots
274
spring vegetable pasta 305
stir-fried mixed vegetables
246

vegetable couscous 243
vegetable curry 249
vegetable stock 19
vegetable terrine 41
vegetarian medley 246
wholemeal vegetable and
herb pie 247
Vegetarian medley 246
Vegetarian roast 244
Vegetarianism 15, 240-9
Velouté sauce 201
Veneto, wines 524
Venison 179
marinated venison 179
rich venison casserole 179
roast venison 179
venison escalopes with red
wine 180
Vermicelli (coloured), cake
decorations 424
Vermicelli (noodles) 295
Vermouth 526
chicken with vermouth and
olives 158
dry martini 529
Vichyssoise 32
Victoria sandwich cake 406
Viennese fingers, chocolate
442
Vinaigrette, minted pear 36
Vine fruits 323
Vine leaves 223-4
stuffed vine leaves 121
Vinegars: fruit 253
herb 253
for pickles 488
salad dressings 253
spiced vinegar 489
sweet spiced vinegar 489
Virginia ham 133
Vitamins 11-13, 14
Vitamin A 11-12
Vitamin B complex 12, 14
Vitamin C 13, 14
Vitamin D 13
Vitamin E 13
Vitamin K 13
Vitello tonnato 112
Vitreous enamel pans 548
Vodka: Black Russian 529
bloody Mary 530
Harvey wallbanger 531
screwdriver 530
Vol-au-vents 386, 573

W

Waffles 333
Waldorf salad 258
Walnut oil 253
Walnuts 325
baklava 342
braised celery with walnuts
231
cherry and walnut biscuits
439
chicken with mushrooms
and walnuts 157

turkey sauté with lemon and
walnuts 166
walnut and coffee fudge 501
walnut and orange pudding
329
walnut creams 496
walnut croquettes 243
walnut layer cake 409
Water filters 545
Water ices *see* Sorbets and water
ices
Watercress 224
salads 525
green butter 207
watercress soup 22
Watermelon 320
see also Melon
Wedding cakes 421-3
rosebud wedding cake 427
Weight reducing diets 15-16
Welsh rarebit 286
Wet brining, pickles 488
Wheat 241
see also Wholewheat
cracked wheat 241
Wheatgerm 241
Wheatmeal flour 450
Whelks 84
hors d'oeuvres 35
preparation 84
Whipping 573
Whisked sponge cake 407
Whisking 573
cakes 395-6
Whisky/whiskey: Irish coffee
537
rusty nail (cocktail) 529
Tom Collins 529
whisky marmalade 476
whisky sour 529
White bread 453
White cabbage 214
White Christmas cake 428
White currants 316
White flour 450
White sauce 198-9
White wines 521, 522
Whitebait 61
hors d'oeuvres 35
fried whitebait 74
Whiting 53, 61
fish koulibiac 73
quenelles 74
Wholemeal bread 454
Wholemeal flour 376
for bread 450
for cakes 392
Wholemeal pastry 381
Wholemeal scones 402
**Wholemeal vegetable and herb
pie** 247
Wholewheat 241
spiced lamb with wholewheat
120
wholewheat and apricot salad
266
Wiener schnitzel 109
Wigeon 172

Wild duck 172
Wild goose 172
Wild rice 307
Wine 520-6
to accompany food 521-2
ageing 521
aperitifs 526
to chill 512
countries 522-5
cups and punches 532-3
fortified 525-6
labels 520-1
for parties 512
serving 521
storing 521
beef stewed in red wine 100
braised brisket with red wine
97
claret jelly 365
cod in white wine 63
coq au vin 160
creamed kidneys in wine
140
mulled wine 533
syllabub 354
venison escalopes with red
wine 180
Wine vinegar 253
Winkles 84
hors d'oeuvres 35
Winter lentil soup 26
Witch 61
Woks 573
Woodcock 172
Woodpigeon 172
see also Pigeon
Worcestershire sauce 194

Y

Yams 224
Yeast 448
Yogurt 351
to make 351
frozen fruit yogurt 366
frozen muesli yogurt 366
frozen yogurt 366
lemon and yogurt mousse
365
tomato and yogurt dressing
256
turkey in spiced yogurt 165
tzaziki 46
yogurt and banana dessert
357
yogurt dressing 256
York ham 133
Yorkshire pudding 97
Yucla 215
Yugoslavian wines 525
Yule log 429

Z

Zabaglione 362
Zest 573
Zinc 14
Zite 295

ALICE and the FLY

ALICE
and the
FLY

JAMES RICE

HODDER &
STOUGHTON

First published in Great Britain in 2015
by Hodder & Stoughton
An Hachette UK company

A CIP catalogue record for this title is available from the British Library

Hardback ISBN 978 1 444 79010 8
Trade Paperback ISBN 978 1 444 79951 4
eBook ISBN 978 1 444 79011 5

Typeset in Warnock Pro by Palimpsest Book Production Ltd,
Falkirk, Stirlingshire

Printed and bound by Clays Ltd, St Ives plc

Hodder & Stoughton policy is to use papers that are natural, renewable and
recyclable products and made from wood grown in sustainable forests. The logging
and manufacturing processes are expected to conform to the environmental
regulations of the country of origin.

Hodder & Stoughton Ltd
338 Euston Road
London NW1 3BH

www.hodder.co.uk

For my parents, who are not the parents in this book – you are amazing and you raised me well.

Also for Nat, who is my favourite human being.

I

The bus was late tonight. It was raining, that icy winter rain, the kind that stings. Even under the shelter on Green Avenue I got soaked because the wind kept lifting the rain onto me. By the time the bus arrived I was dripping, so numb I couldn't feel myself climbing on board.

It was the older driver again, the one with the moustache. He gave me that smile of his. A hint of a frown. An I-know-all-about-you nod. I dropped the fare into the bowl and he told me I'd be better off buying a weekly pass, cheaper that way. I just tore off my ticket, kept my head down.

The bus was full of the usual uniforms. Yellow visibility jackets, Waitrose name badges. A cleaner slept with her Marigolds on. No one who works in Skipdale actually lives here, they all get the bus back to the Pitt. I hurried up the aisle to my usual seat, a couple of rows from the back. For a few minutes we waited, listening to the click-clack of the indicator. I watched the wet blur of rain on the window – the reflection of the lights, flashing in the puddles on the

3

pavement. Then the engine trembled back to life and the bus pulled off through Skipdale.

I got a little shivery today, between those first couple of stops. Thinking now about all those passengers on the bus, it makes me wonder how I do it every night. It's not people so much that bother me. It's **Them**. I heard once that a person is never more than three metres away from one of **Them** at any time, and since then I can't help feeling that the more people there are around, the more there's a chance that one of **Them**'ll be around too. I know that's stupid.

We soon reached the Prancing Horse. Even through the rain I could make out the small crowd huddled under the shelter. The doors hissed open and Man With Ear Hair stumbled through, shaking his umbrella, handing over his change. He took the disabled seat at the front and made full use of its legroom. Woman Who Sneezes was next, squeezing beside a Waitrose employee, her bulk spilling over into the aisle. A couple of old ladies showed their passes, riding back from their day out in the crime-free capital of England. 'It's such a nice town,' they told the driver. 'It's such a nice pub, it was such nice fish.' Their sagging faces were so expressionless I could have reached out and given them a wobble.

And then there was you, all red curls and smiles, stepping up to buy your ticket, and the warmth rose through me like helium to my brain.

You were wet today. Shivering. You smelt of disinfectant, stronger than any other work-smell on the bus. Is it legal for you to work there? The landlord probably doesn't realise how young you are. You look older. You're not the prettiest girl in school, conventionally speaking. There's a gap in your teeth and your hair's kind of a mess with your roots coming through, and you always wear those thick black sunglasses, which is kind of weird. You have an amazing smile, though. Once I walked right past you and you smiled, right at me, as if we knew each other. It was only a slight smile, your cheeks bunching at the corners just the right amount, but it made me want to reach out and stroke them, brush them with the backs of my knuckles, like Nan used to with mine. I know that's sad but it's true.

You took your seat, on the front row. Working after school must tire you out because you always drift off as soon as you sit, sunglasses clinking the window with each back-and-forth roll of your head. We pulled off through the square, past Hampton's Butcher's. I couldn't help thinking of your dad and the others, shivering with all that slippery meat while I was on the bus with you.

Then we turned onto the dual carriageway and sped out to the Pitt.

I wonder what it's like, living in the Pitt. Do you tell anyone? I can't think of a single kid who'd admit to living in the Pitt.

It's odd you have Skipdale friends, very few Pitt kids get into Skipdale High and even then they tend to stick to their own. Their families are always trying to set up in Skipdale but it does its best to keep them out. We have a Pitt neighbour: Artie Sampson. I've lost count of the number of times Mum's peered out of the dining-room window and complained about him. She tells Sarah and me to keep away. 'He's trying to climb too high in the property market. He'll fall and he'll break his neck.'

There's a physical descent into the Pitt, ear-popping and stomach-churning at the speeds the bus reaches, which might be why you choose to sleep through it. My father calls it the 'Social De-cline'. I remember when I was little I'd play a game along the Social De-cline where I'd try and count how many houses were boarded up, how many were burnt out. Sometimes I'd find a house that was boarded up and burnt out. It was hard because Mum always drove the Social De-cline so fast, even faster than the bus does. It was as if the very air could rust the BMW.

Of course, you slept right through. Every pothole, every bend, every sudden break at traffic lights that threw us from our seats. The bus jerked and rattled so much it felt as if it might come apart, but you just slumped there, face pressed to the window. We stopped by the retail park and Old Man BO got on and sat right beside you but even then you didn't wake up, didn't even squirm from the stink of him. You stayed slumped, lolling like a rag doll, completely at the mercy of the rhythm of the bus. I watched you in the mirror for as long as I could, only looking away when the driver caught my eye.

We turned at the lights, past Ahmed's Boutique. As always you woke the moment we passed the church, Nan's church, just in time to miss the large black letters spanned over its sign:

LIFE: THE TIME GOD GIVES YOU TO DECIDE HOW TO SPEND ETERNITY

You rang the bell. The bus pulled up at the council houses behind the Rat and Dog. You stood and thanked the driver, hurried down the steps with your coat over your head. I wiped the mist from the window and watched you blur into the rain. I felt that pull in my stomach, like someone clutching my guts. I wished you had an umbrella.

The trip back was even harder. I got shivery again, goose-pimpled. There were a lot of gangs out tonight, mounting bikes on street corners, cigarettes curling smoke from under their hoods. I nearly fell out of my seat when one of them threw a bottle up at the window. I wasn't too bothered about people any more, though – all I could think about was **Them**. I lifted my feet up onto the seat. I knew they were everywhere I wasn't looking. I had to keep turning my head, brushing any tickles of web on my neck, checking the ceiling and floor. They're sneaky.

We ascended the Social In-cline. The houses grew and separated. Potted plants congregated in front gardens. The rain eased. Eventually we came back through the square and the bus hissed to a stop at Green Avenue. As I stepped down the driver gave me that smile again. The smile he always gives me when I get off at Green Avenue. The smile that knows it's the same stop I got on at just half an hour ago.

Miss Hayes has a new theory. She thinks my condition's caused by some traumatic incident from my past I keep deep-rooted in my mind. As soon as I come clean I'll flood out all these tears and it'll all be OK and I won't be scared of **Them** any more. I'll be able to do P.E. and won't have any more episodes. Maybe I'll even talk – and talk properly, with proper 'S's. The truth is I can't think of any single traumatic childhood incident to tell her about. I mean, there are plenty of bad memories – Herb's death, or the time I bit the hole in my tongue, or Finners Island, out on the boat with Sarah – but none of these caused the phobia. I've always had it. It's **Them**. I'm just scared of **Them**. It's that simple.

I thought I was in trouble the first time Miss Hayes told me to stay after class. She'd asked a question about *An Inspector Calls* and the representation of the lower classes and nobody had answered and so she'd asked me because she'd known I knew the answer because I'd just written an essay all about *An Inspector Calls* and the representation of the lower classes and I'd wanted to tell her the answer but the rest of the class had hung their heads over their shoulders and set their frowning eyes upon me so I'd had to just sit there with my head down, not saying anything.

Some of them started to giggle, which is a thing they like to do when I'm expected to speak and don't. Some of them whispered. Carly Meadows said the word 'psycho', which is a word they like to use. Then the bell rang and everyone grabbed their things and ran for the door and Miss Hayes asked me to stay behind and I just sat there, waiting for a telling-off.

Miss Hayes perched on the edge of my desk (which worried me at the time, it still being wobbly after Ian and Goose's wrestling). She crossed one leg over the other and then crossed one arm over the other and said she'd given me an A- for that *An Inspector Calls* essay. She said I was a natural at English. I wish I'd said something clever like, 'Well, I've lived in England all my life', but I can never think of these things at the time so I just nodded. She said she'd spoken to the school nurse about me and about **Them** and about my condition and she wanted to know if I'd come with her to her office for a little chat. I didn't know what to say to that either. I just nodded again.

Since then I've been waiting behind every Tuesday for a little chat in Miss Hayes' office. We never chat, though. We tend to just sit in silence. I pick the dry skin from my hands while she twists that ring on her finger, like I'm an old-fashioned TV set and she's trying to turn up the volume knob. It doesn't bother me, silence. People talk too much. They make awkward talk every five minutes about school or my parents or how my sister's dancing's going. It's nice to sit in silence for an hour in the same room as Miss Hayes, just knowing we're both there experiencing that silence together. It gives me a bit of a warmth.

Miss Hayes doesn't think silence is very progressive. A couple of weeks ago she gave me this little leather book and said writing stuff down might help me express myself. I asked her what I should write. She said, 'This isn't an assignment, just write down your thoughts. Your feelings.'

Tonight she asked if I'd written down any of my thoughts or feelings and I said I'd written one thing, last week, but it wasn't much, only a few pages. I didn't know what to write so I ended up writing about a bus ride I took.

'It's OK to write about a bus ride,' she said. 'You can write about anything.'

I told her it's hard writing to myself because I already know everything I have to say. I said that last time I pretended to be writing to someone else and that helped. She said that's OK too. I don't have to write to myself. Her diary's called Deirdre and she finds Deirdre very easy to write to. I asked her who Deirdre was and she just swallowed and said, 'Nobody.'

Well, Miss Hayes may write to nobody, but I think writing to nobody's pretty stupid. That's why I've decided to keep writing to you. I hope you don't mind, you just seem like a good way of getting the words on the page. I know you don't know me, but nobody knows me, and by knowing that you now kind of know me better than anyone.

My name's Greg, by the way.

We live in one of the avenue's corner houses with a total of ten rooms and every couple of months my father gives Mum his credit card and she goes to work on one. New style, new theme, new colour scheme. Sometimes she gets walls knocked down or fireplaces installed. Last summer she had little lights set into the dining-room wall like stars, but they looked too tacky so she had them ripped out and the foundations gave and I spent weeks with my head under my pillow while hairy Pitt people hammered and plastered and swore in loud voices.

At the minute Mum's re-envisioning the lounge. Everything's hospital-white, from the carpet to the curtains to the candlesticks. There are piles of catalogues under the coffee table and Mum spends most of the day flipping through them, making phone calls. She's still waiting for the Italian leather couch. She's designed the room around it. It's the most expensive item of furniture she's ever encountered. My father said it costs more than the rest of the room combined, including the decorators' wages. He's had to take on three new clients to afford the initial deposit. The last time we saw my father was Sunday. Mum told me not to tell anyone this. I don't know who she thinks I'm going to tell.

Today's decorators were a father-and-son plastering firm, smoothing over the cracks in the lounge ceiling. (My sister's room is above the lounge. My sister dances.) By the time I was dressed and packed up for school they'd stopped for a coffee break. They were sitting on the dining-room window seat, the cafetière steaming between them. Both plasterers wore grey vests and khaki camouflage trousers. The father's belly was slipping out of the bottom of his vest. He had a lot of moles.

I sat at the top of the stairs and waited for them to get back to work. I wanted to slip down for breakfast unnoticed. Decorators make me nervous. They scratch their armpits and sniff their fingers. They speak loudly as if they don't care who hears them. Sometimes they say stuff to me or try and joke with me and I don't know how to reply. I always feel bad for not giving them a hand.

They make Mum nervous too. If she saw one shopping in Waitrose she'd tut and give them her sour-face but when they're in her home she's all smiles and 'Can I get you some more coffee?' This morning she came to collect their empty coffee mugs and noticed the dustsheets they'd laid down were old bed sheets and joked, 'Are you going to have to wash these

14

before bedtime tonight?' grinning like she was advertising toothpaste. They were pretty good-natured about it. They laughed along. Then they watched Mum's legs as she stepped back out into the hall. The son spotted me at the top of the stairs and winked. I left without eating breakfast.

The rest of the morning was pretty normal. I guess I don't lead a very crazy life. If Ian Connor was writing this then he'd have all kinds of stories to tell you but all I did this morning was go to my lessons. First lesson was P.E. This month they're doing football. I sat in the sports hall and watched them out on the field, breathing white and shivering. They still laughed, though. To be honest I'd be fine out on the field, but I don't think Mr McKenzie wants me to join in with P.E. any more. Not after last time. He doesn't even ask me for a note now, he just says, 'You sitting out again, Greg, yeah?' at the start of each class and I just nod and head for the sports hall.

Second lesson was Chemistry. We sterilised the desks. We covered them in alcohol and set them alight, watched a blue tide of flames spread over the wood. I guess that's exciting enough to write down.

Third lesson was History with Mr Finch. We did nothing in History exciting enough to write down.

Right now I'm sitting in the library. I come here every lunchtime. It's quiet. I can hear my pen scratching the paper. There's just the murmur of the crowds out on the playground, the tick of the clock, the steady waves of Miss Eleanor's ultra-loud breathing: in and out, in and out. Sometimes she stops on an in and I hold my own breath waiting for the out. It always comes, eventually.

I saw you a few minutes ago. You were sneaking across the field with Angela Hargrove. I stepped over to the window, as quietly as possible to avoid waking Miss Eleanor. You were wearing that coat again, the one with the red fur trim. You were wearing your sunglasses. You were laughing at some sort of impression Angela was doing, waving her hands about her head. When you laugh you always cover your teeth, try and hide the gap, which is stupid because the gap is the most unique and amazing part of your smile. That's the third day in a row you two have snuck out through the gap in the hedge. Only sixth-formers are allowed to leave the grounds during school-time. I guess you know that.

I haven't always hidden away in the library. I used to sit out at lunch, on the wall over by the Lipton Building. I didn't care that I was on my own because there was this family of magpies that nested just the other side of the fence and I liked to watch them, leaping out over the crowds, snatching things for their nest in the trees. Then one day a gang of Pitt kids noticed me there. One of them was your brother. (This was a couple of years back, when he was still in school.) They crowded round me and began to say things, the usual things, about my condition and my lisp and how weird I was and how pathetic it was that I was sitting out there on my own, etc. etc., but the magpies were out that day so I wasn't really paying attention, I was too busy watching them, too busy listening to that little cackle they have, that miniature machine-gun squawk. Then your brother hunched down to eye level and demanded I 'say something'. I didn't know what to say. I was straining over his shoulder to see the magpies, picking through the bin. It made me smile because it was as if they knew exactly what they were looking for. Then one of the other Pitt kids bent down alongside your brother and reminded me that your brother had asked me to say something and told me I'd better 'say something quick, or else', only one of the magpies had caught something small and wriggling in its beak and I was too busy trying to make out what it was. Next thing I knew the whole gang was screaming 'Say something!' right in my face and they were over-pronouncing their 'S's and a crowd had gathered including Carly Meadows and a couple of other Vultures from my year and some people in the crowd were calling me a psycho and chanting, 'Say "psycho", say "psycho",' because they knew 'psycho' was a word I couldn't say properly. It was at this point I realised I was scratching at my arm, which is something I do when I'm nervous. I lost sight of the magpies when one of the Pitt kids reached forward and poured a can of Tango over my head. Everyone stopped shouting then, started laughing instead, staring at me and laughing as Tango trickled down my neck, soaking into my collar. A few of them pointed, which was kind of stupid because everyone knew what they were laughing at. I breathed as slowly as I could, counting each drip from my fringe as it hit the pavement. After a minute they stopped laughing and just stared. It was then that I realised there were other drips hitting the pavement, red droplets of something thicker, something that splattered as it landed. The arm of my shirt was spotted red. Some of the Vultures said I was disgusting and a few made that wrinkle-face but most just stared. Then they left. I think that was the only time I ever saw your brother in uniform.

That afternoon I kept my blazer on. I had Maths and my hair went all hard and sticky from the Tango but nobody noticed.

TRANSCRIPT

Extract of interview between Detective
Sergeant Terrence Mansell (TM) and Gregory
Hall's classmate, Ian Connor (IC).

TM: Thank you for agreeing to talk with me.
IC: S'all right.
TM: As you probably know, we're here to
    discuss Greg.
IC: Um . . . well, yeah.
TM: How well do you know Greg?
IC: Well, he's in my class.
TM: You sit next to him.
IC: In a few lessons, yeah. English. A few
    others.
TM: Would you consider him a friend?
[IC laughs.]
IC: God, no.
TM: So, what do you think of him?

IC: Same as everyone else.

TM: Which is?

IC: He's nuts.

TM: Can you elaborate?

IC: He's psycho nuts.

TM: What makes you say that?

[IC laughs nervously.]

IC: Erm . . . ?

TM: I mean aside from the events of the past few days. I mean, what gave Greg this reputation?

IC: It's just how he is.

TM: 'Is'?

IC: The way he walks. The way he . . . watches. And there's the scratching. The mumbling. He's on meds, too. Did you know that? We found them, me and Goose. 'Antipsychotic'.

TM: Right.

IC: And then there's the way he is with girls. He's always, like, looking at the girls in class. You know? Like, staring at them.

TM: You never look at girls?

IC: Not in that way. Not, like, creepy, like he does.

TM: Are you aware you feature in his journal?

IC: Me?

TM: You.

IC: What's he say about me?

TM: He alludes to your . . . involvement
. . . with certain girls from your year.

IC: Really?

TM: And girls from younger years.

IC: Younger?

TM: Angela Hargrove?

IC: I had nothing to do with that.

TM: With what?

IC: New Year's. I know she was saying stuff
when the police showed up. Stuff about Goose
and Darren. That had nothing to do with me.
I was passed out.

TM: This is the party at Wallaby Drive? The
Lamberts'?

IC: Goose's, yeah.

TM: Did you see Greg that night?

IC: Not that I remember.

TM: But he was at the party?

IC: He might have been. I didn't notice.

TM: You didn't notice?

IC: He's very unnoticeable. That's part of his

creepiness too. His psycho-nuttiness. And, as I said, I was out of it that night.

TM: We're getting off topic here. I'm just trying to get a feel for Greg. What he's like as a person. You've sat next to him for, what, three years? Isn't there anything you can tell me?

IC: Only what I've told you already. He's a creep.

TM: Nothing else?

IC: It's the way he looks at you. That's it, it's the eyes. It's all in the eyes.

TM: The eyes?

IC: Exactly. Just look into those eyes. Everything you need to know's right there. In the eyes.

TM: That's all you've got to say?

IC: Sorry. I'm not trying to waste your time or anything. It's just, I don't really know the guy. I don't remember ever even having a conversation with him.

TM: Well, who does know him?

[Pause.]

IC: I don't know. He didn't have any friends, as far as I know. I guess nobody knows him.

That's the thing. You could interview the whole class and you wouldn't find a single person that knows him. Not really. I guess that's what makes him creepy. I guess that's what makes him psycho, really. How alone he is.

TM: Right.

IC: That and the eyes.

TM: Thanks.

21/11

Saturdays I work at Hampton's in the square. Your dad might have mentioned the back-lad? Probably not. I work alone in the kitchen, tucked away between the industrial freezers. There's a metal basin, a worktop for dishes to dry on and a single shelf with a kettle and tea bags and soft crumbly biscuits. The air in the kitchen is even colder than inside the freezers. I try not to breathe through my mouth because the cold hurts the hole in my tongue.

Your dad works with Phil on the fresh-meat block. They're obscured from the front of the shop by the chicken oven. I guess the customers don't like to see all that hacking and tearing. Their block is only metres from the kitchen so I always hear them joking around. Phil gives your dad a bit of stick for his ponytail but Phil's only twenty-two and he's going bald, so he's not really qualified to be making hair jokes. Sometimes your dad snatches Phil's hat and holds it in the air and Phil jumps up trying to reach it, one hand over his bald spot. Your dad just laughs. He's got one of the biggest laughs I've ever heard.

He laughs 'Heh' instead of 'Ha'. 'Heh heh heh'. All day long.

Sometimes your dad talks about you in work. He tells Phil about how you're into art, how one day you're going to university. He never talks about your brother. This morning Phil was discussing baby names and your dad said he named you the morning you were born. He'd overdosed on Dutch courage and spent the night watching a VHS of *Alice in Wonderland*, over and over, rewinding and playing it till the birds starting singing and the telephone started ringing and he found out you existed. I wonder if you know that story? Whenever they're talking about you I tend to turn off the kitchen tap and just stare at the bubbles in the water.

There's an older butcher called Charlie who works on the fresh-meat side, slicing ham and cooked chicken. His face is shrivelled to a point and he looks a lot like a chicken himself, especially with those little round glasses. (I know chickens don't wear glasses, but if you saw him you'd know what I mean.) He's always telling Phil and your dad to grow up and calling your dad a hippy. They call him the Miserable Old Cunt. Sometimes they shout back to me, 'The Miserable Old Cunt needs a fresh bucket,' and I have to fill a bucket with soap and steaming water and bring it out to him. I feel guilty responding when they call him the Miserable Old Cunt, it's like I'm agreeing with them. He never even looks at me when I deliver his bucket. I guess he is a bit miserable.

25

There's also this pack of four Vultures that serve out front in the shop. They're in your year, which means it's technically illegal for them to work, but it's money in an envelope so I guess it doesn't matter. Most of them take dance class with my sister and have the same bleached hair, long nails and powdery orange skin. They smell like cherries.

And then there's me. The back-lad. I just keep my head down, concentrate on my work. In the morning I have to wash the walls and the floor and the insides of the fridges. It's blood, mainly. Fresh blood wipes off easily but as soon as the cold gets to it it gets all hard and sticky and needs bleach and boiled water. They have all kinds of meat hanging in the fridge and I have to shift it around to clean. Sometimes there are cow legs or whole ribcages hanging there. Sometimes there are pig heads, with hardened snouts and icicles for eyelashes.

Twice a day I have to empty the fat from the chicken oven. It gathers in this large metal tray underneath. It's very heavy and hard to manoeuvre. I have to slide it all the way out, till I can feel the heat of the fat on my face. I have to unscrew the stopper and let the molten fat dribble into a bucket, then empty the bucket into a bin out the back. Molten fat looks and smells like thick pee. The Vultures hate it. Their noses wrinkle in disgust. They don't have a problem with meat and blood, just fat.

I make tea and coffee too, when they ask me. I have to make

drinks for everyone and it's awkward because the Vultures have never told me their names so I have to just wait for them to stop serving and notice me before I can ask what they want to drink. Sometimes they just ignore me, or do that wrinkle-face and giggle to each other.

I spend the rest of the day in my kitchen, watching the tap. I can watch that tap for hours, the water gurgling, steam in my face, warmer and warmer as the surface rises. I used to love baths when I was little. My sister and I had to share. We had this toy boat she was obsessed with. We've got some film of it somewhere, us both in the bath, playing with that boat. My sister never wanted the bath to end, she'd just refuse to get out. Maybe that's what dried out her skin so much. That was before Finners Island, before I moved to Nan's. I think about the old days when I'm watching the tap. I think about all kinds of stuff. The kitchen gets all foggy with steam.

It's not too bad, really, being the back-lad. I keep to myself. I have my own kitchen and nobody bothers me. I've heard them talk about me a couple of times but nowhere near as much as they do in school. The only thing that bothers me is when the Vultures come out the back for their buckets. They need buckets to clean the counters and the only tap's in my kitchen and the kitchen's only really big enough for me, which means they have to stand right next to me, so close I can feel their warmth. It takes a long time for those buckets to fill so usually I close my eyes. I try and think about all the pigs and chickens in the freezer, how cold they are. I try and just listen to the rushing water.

Sometimes I don't even realise they've gone until I can't smell cherries any more.

My bedroom window's the fire-escape window. It's the window that, in the event of a fire, my family would supposedly crawl out of onto the safety of the roof. A couple of years ago one of my favourite things in the world was to open this window as wide as I could on rainy winter nights and feel the chill of the rain battering the roof tiles just an arm's length from my face. Sometimes I used to reach my arm out into the night and let the rain patter and pool into the palm of my hand, numbing it out of all existence and, when it was so numb I could no longer even feel the rain, when with a reach and poke of my warm and living hand that white-dead hand felt like a hunk of frozen pork thawing in the fridge, and when the white-dead hand couldn't even feel the poking of the warm and living hand, I would pull both hands down under my bed sheets and curl my whole body around them and the white-dead hand would burn back to life. On those nights I'd always have the best dreams. I'd dream I hadn't even been born yet.

Then this one night I woke and saw it was raining and

decided to have a go at my arm-reaching-out thing but I must have been very tired because after what must have been only a minute of hand-numbing I fell asleep, my arm still stretched out on the window ledge. By the time I woke the rain had stopped. The sun hadn't quite risen and the garden was filtered with that golden light they film Corn Flakes adverts in. My hand was numb, resting there on the window ledge, and my first thought was to drag it into the warmth beneath the duvet. But, before I'd even had the chance to drag it into the warmth beneath the duvet, one of **Them** had dropped from the sky, right through the window, dropped right into the palm of my hand and just sat there, perfectly still, its legs spread wide in its landing.

Later, after my fitting and my vomiting and the seemingly impossible task of regaining my breathing, my father had said that they can sometimes ride their webs like paragliders, floating for miles on the wind. He saw it once in a documentary. He said they were fascinating creatures. Then he saw Mum and I staring up at him and he stopped saying things and went back to bed.

My window's been locked ever since. Mum's always searching for the key. She says it's dangerous. We could all burn to death. And anyway, my room smells like teenage boy. I'm used to it. I keep the key in with my secret things, in my *Casablanca* video-case. I used to keep my secret things in my *Brief Encounter* video-case but last week I finally watched *Casablanca* again and immediately swapped them because *Casablanca* became my new all-time favourite and therefore has to be my Secret Case. I designed the cases myself, during Retro Hollywood Season on Channel 4, when my video recorder pretty much constantly had its REC light showing. I wrote the name of each film on the sleeve of each case in my best cursive handwriting – drawing two thin lines in pencil, making sure the top of each letter touched the top line and the bottom touched the bottom line and waiting for the ink to dry and rubbing out the pencil and being left with titles both neat and straight. They look great on my shelf, lined up in their cases. At first I enjoyed the prospect of browsing the neat and straight titles and deciding which film to choose, but then the first film I chose was *Brief Encounter* and it instantly became my favourite film of all time. I couldn't stop watching it, over and over. Every time I came to choose a film I would start out wanting something new to watch and then think of Alec and Laura standing on that platform and Alec giving Laura's shoulder a squeeze and that shoulder-squeeze being the only way he could ever tell her that she's his one true love, his run-away-together kind of love, and that he's sorry that they'll never be together and how getting on that train is the saddest thing he'll ever have to do but he has to do it anyway, and it gave me a kind of inflation in my chest, a kind of beautiful indigestion, and I ended up choosing *Brief Encounter* every time.

I've since devised a brutal-but-fair rule for film-watching. I am absolutely (under no circumstances) allowed to watch the same film twice in a row. It's a hard rule to stick to but it's the only way I can stop myself watching the same ones over and over. I've also decided to store my videos in the wrong cases, so whatever film I choose is not the film I watch. This means every film is watched a relatively equal number of times. It also means (as the videos are no longer assigned to specific cases and as there is always a video in the VCR) that there is always an empty video-case. This video-case is my Secret Case. At the moment my Secret Case is *Casablanca*.

The other things I store in *Casablanca* are as follows:

- Nan and Herb's wedding photo.
- The ticket stub from a bird-watching walk on Finners Island. (It's years since we've been to Finners Island. I don't even know if they have bird-watching walks there any more.)
- The black button-eye of Mr Snow, my old white bear (which luckily came off before I buried him in the sand on Finners Island, losing him forever).
- The spare key to my father's study.
- Money.
1. The slick black feather of an American bald eagle.

Apart from my video shelf, my bed, my wardrobe, my TV stand and my brown and green striped draught-excluder snake 'Sammy' that lies over the crack at the bottom of my door, my room is virtually empty. Mum calls it minimalist. I just don't like clutter. I like to be able to see every possible inch of my bedroom at all times. I also like parcel tape and have used it extensively, taping the edge of my carpet to my skirting board and the foot of my bed to my carpet and taping all the cracks in all the walls and even taping over the air vent, leaving my room pretty much impenetrable.

Nan and I always used to tape the cracks back at Kirk Lane. We'd do it every winter because winter's when they come inside, trying to escape the cold. Nan called it the Great Influx. She'd say, 'We need to prepare for the Great Influx.' To be honest the term 'Great Influx' probably didn't help reassure me, but the parcel-taping did – it let me relax a little. She used to collect conkers, too, down at Crossgrove Park, scatter them all over the house. Apparently it was meant to scare **Them** away. I don't know, it's not something I've carried on since moving back because rummaging through leaves on the ground is the last thing I want to be doing if I'm hoping to avoid **Them**.

Mum won't let me parcel tape downstairs so I seal myself into my bedroom. It's the one place I don't have to worry about **Them** so much. I don't have to shake out my bed sheets or shine a torch down the back of my desk or check the insides of my slippers before use. I still do these things, but more out of routine than anything. It's just nice to lean my head against the wall without worrying about anything dropping down the back of my neck.

Sundays are hard. Saturdays are OK because I'm with your dad and occasionally he'll talk about you, but Sundays I have to just sit here with nothing to do all day but think. I think of our bus rides. I think of the times I've seen you in school, laughing out on the field with Angela Hargrove. I think back to under the bridge, back to the first time we met. Sometimes my thoughts stray to bad times, unwanted memories, and I try and think about nothing instead, try and just clear my head.

Today I watched *Gone with the Wind* (one of Nan's old favourites – a lucky selection from my random video system). Trust me, there's nothing like a four-hour-long epic romance to clear your head. Especially when there's Vivien Leigh and Clark Gable up on the screen with all their quick one-liners and chemistry, Clark clutching Viv in that kissing-embrace of his, all slicked-back hair and moustache. That's the thing I love about old movies – they had taste back then. They knew that all they needed was a kiss, an occasional shoulder-squeeze. That's the difference. In old movies, whenever the characters are kissing, it always cuts to black. A kiss is enough.

The rest is left to the imagination. In modern movies a kiss is never enough. They never cut to black. Nothing is left to the imagination. It's like that's the whole point of the film: the non-cut-to-black parts. It's disgusting.

I'd just fast-forwarded through the intermission when Sarah woke up. Sarah's time is spent sleeping or dancing. I can tell when she's awake by the dull thud of bass through the wall. She only leaves her bedroom for school and dance-rehearsals. (Sometimes she comes out at night, too, to do whatever it is that keeps her out past 04:00 and makes her fall asleep on the stairs with lipstick smeared down her chin.) Her room is like a house of mirrors in a fairground – if you peer through the crack in the door, fifteen other yous peer in from fifteen different crack-in-the-doors all over the walls and ceiling. A dancer needs to make sure they look good from every angle.

Sarah's been dancing to a new song this week. It goes:

> *Ooo you got me screamin' boy,*
> *Eat me like a cannibal.*
> *Butt in the air boy,*
> *Take me like an animal.*

It's the song she'll dance to at the Christmas Dance Fantastical. She's working on her routine. She's decided that, until that night, she's going to use all her available time to practise.

By 16:14 the dull thud of bass was giving me a headache. It was impossible to concentrate on *Gone with the Wind*. I went down to the dining room, huddled on the window seat. Mum was preparing dinner. A few years ago Mum knocked down most of the ground-floor walls. ('Open-plan.') It's pretty draughty but it means I can see right through to the kitchen from my place in the dining room.

Mum doesn't suit the kitchen. Her hair kept slipping from its bouffant and she spent several minutes tutting and fiddling in the crème brûlée mixture with a bread knife, trying to pick out what I assume was a chipped nail. Mum doesn't suit doing many things any more. Except drinking cocktails. She can stand and drink cocktails better than anyone I've ever met.

Mum's worried because the Hamptons are coming over in a couple of weeks. Ken and Ursula Hampton are Mum's best friends. Ursula Hampton uses words like 'Golly' and 'Jolly', which makes her hard to trust. Ken Hampton has a stake in several of Skipdale's most successful local businesses, including my father's clinic. He owns several sports cars and sometimes goes to parties with the mayor. It was Ken who gave me the back-lad job. He told Mum I needed to socialise more, that the work environment of the butcher's would be good for my confidence. It'd turn me into 'one of the lads'. Ken Hampton's about five foot tall. He used to be ginger, properly carrot-coloured, till one day his hair just turned black, overnight, which we're not allowed to mention.

The Hamptons come over from time to time for meals. My sister and I make ourselves scarce. Mum has to cook. My father has to socialise. I don't think they enjoy it, no matter how much they pretend to. Every meal tends to serve a purpose. This time it's to show the Hamptons the new white Italian leather couch. It also pretty much guarantees Mum a place at the Hamptons' New Year's bash, which is a hotbed of social activity. Today Mum tried out her latest menu: blackened fillet of salmon with chipotle squash purée and mango rice. For dessert Mum baked individual crèmes brûlées with cranberries and orange cream. Crème brûlée is Mum's signature dish. She has her own blowtorch.

My father spent most of the day in his study – a room he refused to let Mum de-wall in her open-planning. He has a heavy oak-effect door he keeps locked at all times. He doesn't know I have his spare key. My father is a surgeon and a part-owner of Burke's Clinic. (Who 'Burke' is, I've never found out. I think they just made the name up.) He helps lift people's confidence through surgical improvement. Burke's Clinic has pictures of all their employees on their website. (It is important for a business to have a public face.) In my father's photo he is standing in a white surgical room in blue cap and gown, a facemask hung round his neck. He is smiling, one hand holding a raised scalpel, the other giving a thumbs up. Beneath it says: 'Howard Hall: Breast Man'.

My father's latest secretary is called Joanna Hewitt. He calls her 'Jo'. Joanna's Burke's Clinic picture is cut from a group holiday photo. She has long blond hair and a low-cut top. She is both pouting and winking at the camera. There is a definite resemblance to a young Pamela Anderson, especially the breasts (which I'd guess to be at least a size DD), and also the nose, which is narrow with that distinctive bump at the end. I'd love one day for my father to employ a male secretary, flat-chested with natural black hair and a fat nose. I think it'd stop Mum getting so tense.

At 17:02 Mum shouted that dinner was served. I switched from the window seat to my seat at the table. Mum laid out four plates of blackened salmon. She was wearing a blue strapless dress with earrings: diamonds. Her nails were also blue, as were the heels she was trotting around the table in. She laid out napkins beside each plate before taking her seat, to the left of me. She smiled, not at me but occasionally glancing over to me. Sundays are becoming kind of a big deal because it's the only night my father eats with us.

After a few minutes my father emerged from his study. He took his seat beside me, opposite Mum. My father is an extremely handsome man, especially for someone in his fifties. He's well groomed. He still has all of his hair, which he gels daily. When I was little I remember it being longer and blacker and always slicked back, and over the past couple of years his hair has not so much greyed, as silvered. At one of their dinner parties, whilst complimenting his work on Ursula's implants, Ken Hampton described my father as 'the George Clooney of breast augmentation'.

Tonight he was holding a collection of photographs of inframammary infections, which he set out on the table to browse through whilst he ate. He was also nursing a glass of either whiskey or Scotch (I've never worked out the difference). He smelt of cigarettes, which is what he usually smells of nowadays, since he promised Mum he'd quit and so has to kneel on his office chair, smoking out of the study window. As soon as he'd sat down my father started on his salmon, separating the blackened and non-blackened parts with his fork, scooping the least burnt bits to his mouth. Mum frowned. She asked if maybe we could have some manners for once and wait until everyone's seated before stuffing our faces? My father sighed and let his fork fall to the table. It landed with a sort of semi-silenced clatter, speckling the tablecloth with salmon crumbs. My father didn't seem to notice, he was still looking at his photos. Mum's eyes stayed fixed on the fork for a good thirty seconds before she turned to shout for Sarah again.

Then Mum turned to me, as if she'd just remembered something of great importance. She asked if I'd taken my pill today.

I nodded. She always asks at dinner whether I've taken my pill and I always nod because I take it first thing in the morning. I used to take it at school on my lunch break but then Goose found them in my bag and showed them to Ian and he stood up and read the label out in front of everyone and so now I keep them at home. They're powdery, horrible-tasting pills and I have to let them dissolve on my tongue, so I take one just before I brush my teeth. I don't know why Mum feels the need to keep asking me about them at dinner. I think maybe she's just making conversation.

After a few minutes my sister came galloping down the stairs. She was wearing her dance leotard, earphones tap-tapping away. She took her seat opposite me, between Mum and my father. She smelt like dancing.

Mum gave a single nod and we began. The salmon tasted charred. I tried my best to eat it but the blackened parts were hard and reminded me of burnt toast. Sarah picked at her rice. She nodded a beat as she ate. Sarah is a slave to the rhythm.

My father continued one-handed. Mum always sets him a knife out just in case but I've only ever seen him use it once, on a particularly well-done piece of steak, and he sighed and muttered the whole time as if he wasn't sure how to use the thing. This uncertainty with knives is odd, considering his profession. It's possible my father's not-using-a-knife is to distance the concept of food from that of surgery. Or, more likely, my father's such a busy person he can only dedicate one of his hands to the task of eating. Mum kept smiling, watching him sip from his tumbler, watching him turn a page, watching him scoop and swallow his salmon.

Mum was the first to speak. She asked my father what he thought. He said, 'About what?' and she said this was her Hamptons meal and my father nodded and said, 'Very good.' He lifted a photograph from the bottom of the pile. It showed a woman with two different-sized breasts, one red and bulbous, far beyond the level of regular post-op swelling. He put his fork down and reached into his top pocket to retrieve his glasses.

Mum turned to Sarah. 'What do you think?'

'What?' she shouted.

'Do – you – like – it?'

She pulled out one of the buds of her earphones.

'What?'

'Never mind.'

I waited for Mum to ask me. I had all these answers prepared in my head about how delicious it was. About how flavoursome the blackened parts were. About how it was definitely not weird to mix mango with rice. But Mum didn't ask me. She just smiled at her salmon.

She said, 'I bet Ursula Hampton doesn't even know what a chipotle is.'

And I knew then, that this was not the end. That this was one of her long-term projects. That every night until the Hamptons' meal Mum will cook blackened fillet of salmon with chipotle squash purée and mango rice and will want to know if the salmon tastes any more perfect and, even if she asks me, I won't know what to say, because to me it will taste exactly the same. My favourite meal is Waitrose Maple Triple Nut Muesli (with the clusters). My favourite drink is the sweet milk that's left at the end, the odd raisin floating in it. I eat breakfast alone so I can drink it straight from the bowl.

My sister swallowed a couple of forkfuls of salmon before excusing herself and bounding back upstairs. I ate as much as I could but I never have much of an appetite and it put me off altogether when she starting heaving in the bathroom. Sarah always forgets she shouldn't dance straight after eating.

My father frowned at one of his photographs. He turned it upside down. Then his BlackBerry began to hum-hum and he stood and said, 'Hey, Jo,' and Mum looked down at her plate again. Mum rarely challenges my father's work. Once or twice I've heard her comment on his long hours but he just sighs and gives her that glare over the top of his glasses and says, 'Credit cards have interest, Deb,' and Mum looks around at her house and furnishings and the vases of black glittering twigs and nods and carries on smiling.

I tried my best to show Mum I was enjoying the salmon. I

smiled and hummed a few yummy noises. I even waited around after I'd finished, waited for the crème brûlée. I'm not sure she noticed. She was too busy nibbling and staring at her plate. She said the rice needed more mango. I don't know if she was talking to me.

Not a single person in my set has a surname beginning D, E, F or G, so for a lot of lessons I sit next to Ian Connor. I was there the time he snorted four lines of pepper in Media Studies. I was there the time he chewed that massive golf ball of sugar-free gum, telling everyone that the sugar equivalent was a laxative and having to run home with his hand down the back of his trousers. I was even standing at the window the time he rode the cafeteria trolley down that slope by the Lipton Building and crashed into Mr Cullman's Ford Capri, littering the bonnet with chocolate éclairs. Although we've never actually spoken I still know Ian better than Goose or Sam Johnson or any of those skater kids that follow him around at lunch. I know that he draws bar codes on the back of all his exercise books and writes swear words as their ISBNs. I know that at the start of every lesson he biros over the lines of the smiley face on the palm of his hand, so hard that by now it's tattooed into the creases of his skin. I know that at least twice a day his mum texts to see if he's OK and that, although he takes his time reading the texts, he never responds.

Ian and I sit on the back row in English Lit. Goose sits on the table opposite. I don't really get why they call George Lambert 'Goose'. I used to think it was his laugh (quite nasal and quack-like) but once I heard Ian say it's because he looks like someone in the year above whose nickname is also Goose. Nicknames are funny things. There's this one kid in class, one of the Oxbridge kids that sit at the front: 'Eggy'. Apparently he farted once in assembly in year seven. That's it. Now he's 'Eggy' for the rest of his life. I'd like it if someone just called me 'Greg'. 'Psycho' is a hard nickname to live down.

Today Ian and Goose spent English Lit passing notes. Ian scribbles notes to Goose on scraps of paper, usually ripped from the book we're studying and chucks them across to his desk. Goose scribbles a few lines and throws them back. It's like very slow tennis. When most people read or write notes they tend to cover what they're reading or writing with their arm, but Ian doesn't bother. He writes about girls a lot. Today the notes were about Ian and Lucy Marlowe getting together at the Halloween party a few weeks back and Ian not remembering and Goose saying Lucy must have slipped something into his drink and taken advantage of him. They didn't use terms like 'getting together' or 'taken advantage of' though. I still remember Lucy Marlowe from year seven, sitting out on the steps of the Lipton Building with her glasses and her *Star Trek* lunchbox while the boys kicked their football at her. I wouldn't have believed it was the same girl if I hadn't stayed in her set through school. If I hadn't witnessed the slow transformation: the fake tan, the contact lenses, the pink fur-collared coat. If I hadn't been there the day she came to class with an explosion of dyed-blond extensions and heard Mr Cullman say, 'Well, Lucy, it's nice to see you've finally found yourself.'

Lucy's been absent since Thursday. Goose wrote that last week he and Sam Johnson snuck into the girls' changing rooms during hockey and painted 'Flat-Chested Slut' in Tipp-Ex on the back of her blazer. Apparently Lucy spent all last lesson without even realising the sniggers were about her (and it was History with Mr Finch so he wasn't likely to notice). She probably walked all the way home without realising. She probably sat down and relaxed and watched TV (maybe even the odd episode of *Star Trek* for old times' sake), completely oblivious, until her mum arrived home from the health spa and screamed at the flaky white letters dried into her daughter's back . . . hand to her mouth . . . face Tipp-Ex white . . .

The notes became a discussion of the possible reasons for Lucy's absence. Goose's theory was that when Ian had had intercourse with her he was so big he'd ruptured her ovaries and over the last nine days bits of her insides had been slipping out when she peed and this morning she woke up screaming in a bed of blood with the remainder of her womb smeared across the mattress. Ian giggled at this. I had to look away, had to scratch at my leg under the table. It makes me sick, that kind of talk.

Neither of them has yet considered the possibility that Lucy is pregnant. Teenage pregnancy statistics are high in the Pitt but I've never known a pregnant teenager in Skipdale. I wonder if it's because in Skipdale we don't have as much of that stuff going on, or because our parents have enough shame to march the kid straight down to the appropriate clinic and get it dealt with.

I didn't get a chance to read the last note Goose threw over but it must have been hilarious because Ian spent the rest of the lesson giggling with his head in his hands. Miss Hayes carried on reading. Miss Hayes once intercepted one of Ian and Goose's notes. It was one of Ian's girl stories and was full of swearing and graphic sexual imagery but Miss Hayes read it out to the whole class the same enthusiastic way she reads *An Inspector Calls*. I think she wanted to embarrass Ian but he laughed louder than anyone. He said, 'Don't worry, Miss, I'll give you a go too, if you want.' He got two weeks' detention for that. He still passes notes but Miss Hayes tends to ignore them.

After English was lunch. I went to the library again. I was going to spend the hour writing but then I saw you and

Angela sneaking out across the field. I'd spent all weekend without you and this time I just had to follow. I waited till you'd disappeared through the gap in the hedge before hurrying out through the fire door after you.

You crossed the carriageway to the estate behind the square. By the time I caught sight of you again you were stepping through the gate of what must have been Angela's back garden. It was hard to make out, through the trees, but I could just about see you, the two of you, laid out on the wooden skeletons of her parents' sun-loungers. You were giggling and passing a rolled-up cigarette, letting smoke crawl out amongst your white and steaming breath. I sat in the bus stop across the street, hood up, hugging my parka shut. I ate my tuna sandwich. I found that, if I tapped my feet together, I could keep them from going numb.

It's strange to think that a few months ago you weren't a part of my life. That I only knew you vaguely, as The Girl In The Shades or Miss Cool or (through Ian and Goose's notes) as a little coloured-in symbol the shape of a pair of sunglasses. I knew you in the same way I know the names of the TV shows or songs people talk about, without having seen/heard them. I must have seen you around school once or twice but I'd never really registered you. Not until under the bridge. Not until your smile.

It's hard to remember now what Goose and Ian used to

write about you in their note-tennis. They haven't written about you recently so I've not been able to properly pin down your social status. You're just one of those unpindownable people. If you were popular I'd know who you were, I would at some point have been pushed to the ground or had Tango poured over me or have been asked to 'say something' in front of you in some kind of attempt to impress. But if you were unpopular then I would have more than likely witnessed you as a victim of similar pushings-over/Tango-pourings. So I'm guessing you lie somewhere in Skipdale High's social middle class. Therefore it's pretty impressive you've landed a friendship with Angela Hargrove.

When Sarah first started at Skipdale her form teacher had asked the class what they wanted to be when they grew up and Angela Hargrove said she wanted to be 'Every man's wet dream'. My sister retold this story that night at the dinner table. Mum was so shocked she let a half-chewed forkful of cannelloni fall from her mouth onto the tablecloth. I think that's what my sister loves the most about Angela – her ability to hang-mouth adults. Sarah's never actually managed to make friends with her, instead becoming one of her crowd of backing dancers at school dance shows. (Angela Hargrove is the Dancing Queen. She moves like silk. My sister says Angela has her own fifteen-minute dance solo in the Christmas Dance Fantastical and my sister, whose own part is five minutes, at the back, along with three Vultures, says this with genuine, head-shaking admiration. Awe even.)

How have you managed to get in with Angela? I bet she doesn't know you live in the Pitt, does she? No way would she hang around with anyone from the Pitt. She pulls her disgusted wrinkle-face if she sees a Pitt kid the other side of the playground, never mind sharing a cigarette on adjacent sun-loungers. The two of you seemed pretty merry with each other at lunch. You couldn't stop laughing. In the end Angela laughed so much she slid off the front of her lounger, disappearing from view behind the tree stumps. Then you started your own giggle-fit, rocking too far on your lounger and tumbling right off the back. I had to climb up on the bench to see you. You didn't seem to be hurt, though. You were still laughing.

You remained on the ground, then, the two of you. You left your sun-loungers with their legs in the air and just lay there, mumbling and smoking and giggling. I decided to head back to school. I wanted to get back to the warmth of the library, but it was starting to rain by the time I reached the dual carriageway and I knew better than to linger in the rain – it was lingering in the rain that made me sick a few months back. So I climbed down to the canal path, took shelter under the bridge instead. Usually I do my best to avoid bridges, or archways, or anywhere else one of **Them** could suddenly drop down upon me, but the canal bridge is different, I like it under there. I feel safe. Sometimes, if I don't want to go home between school and our bus, I go there and wait for you to finish work.

Today was particularly cold and parts of the canal had frozen into these little white islands. There were half a dozen ducks perched on the bank, inspecting the water like it was some lifestyle choice they'd yet to decide on. I balled into my warm-position: legs tucked into chest, coat over knees, hood pulled tight. I wondered if the ducks were cold. They seemed perfectly happy standing there, aiming their beaks at the surface of the water.

I closed my eyes and thought of you. I imagined you and Angela, lying there on your sun-loungers. Pictured you, staring up into the sky, raindrops speckling the lenses of your sunglasses.

By the time I opened my eyes again I was late for form. All the ducks had snuck off and left me.

DATE UNKNOWN

A couple of months ago I got sick. Like, really sick. Like, spend-three-days-rolled-up-in-my-duvet-like-a-frozen-sausage-roll sort of sick.

I got sick because back then I always waited in the library after school for the crowds to disappear before walking home and so by the time I was ready to leave the sky had gone black and the wind had picked up and I had trekked across the field and out through the gap in the hedge onto the dual carriageway to avoid your brother and the rest of that gang of Pitt kids who had nothing better to do than hang around the gate after school and throw stones at the orchestra who had stayed late to practise and I had walked down towards the square and I had put my bag on both shoulders because it was really heavy because at lunchtime I had gone down to Waitrose and bought three 4-packs of videotapes to record old movies that were showing that week as part of Channel 4's Retro Hollywood Season and I had had to carry them around all day and my shoulders were really aching and the skin where my neck joins my shoulders was really stinging from the pulling and scraping of my shoulder straps and I was cold because I couldn't hug my coat together to keep warm that day because I had to keep my thumbs under my shoulder straps to keep my bag hoisted on my back to stop one of the corners of one of the 4-packs of videotapes from nuzzling my spine and the wind had been hissing at me that day like Nan's cat Mr Saunders used to hiss when I would try and move him off my bed so Herb wouldn't catch him and literally kick him off the bed instead and the wind had been getting right under my shirt that had untucked and was flapping against my skin that was all tight and goose-pimpled and there had been a mist of ice-water in the wind and it had stuck my shirt to my skin and my hood had blown down so the mist of ice-water in the wind had got into my eyes too and made them water which I had been glad of in a way because at least the tears on my face were warm and I hadn't been able to cross the dual carriageway because I couldn't see properly and it's dangerous to cross a dual carriageway when you can't see properly so I had half stepped half slid down the embankment to the canal to take cover under the bridge so that I could reposition the videotapes in my bag so that I could release my thumbs and put my hood up and walk with my hands in my coat pockets and wrap my coat around myself and hopefully stop the icy mist of rain getting in and also cover my nipples which were sharp and straight like drawing pins but in the end I hadn't been able to fix my bag or my coat or my nipples because instead of finding peace in the-safety-and-solitude-of-under-the-bridge I had stumbled down to find you waiting in the-safety-and-solitude-of-under-the-bridge and I had had to just keep on walking with my head down and pretend that I was just passing through the-safety-and-solitude-of-under-the-bridge because your big eyes were there and they were unsunglassed and blue and aimed right at me and I'd had to try my best to not look at them whilst trying to work out who you were and what year you were in because you were wearing Skipdale uniform but I hadn't recognised you at the time without those thick dark glasses and I had kept walking and the wind hadn't hissed under the bridge like Mr Saunders because it had been sheltered and silent under the bridge and for some reason as I passed you I had lifted my head which had been a very strange thing for me to have done because when I'm walking past people I always just watch my shoes and count to ten and I'm still not entirely sure whether I did in fact lift my head or whether I might have just imagined lifting my head and imagined seeing that your hair was wet and imagined that the dye had streaked red lines down your face like blood and imagined that your big eyes had fixed on mine and imagined that smile that smile and I can't remember if I had smiled back or if I had even imagined smiling back if in fact your smile had just been imagined by my imagination because all I can remember is how much I had concentrated on walking because walking had seemed only possible if I concentrated very carefully on it and I had managed one step at a time to keep walking through the rest of the-safety-and-solitude-of-under-the-bridge until I had come out the other side onto the canal path again and that's where I had stopped and I hadn't been able to walk any more and I'd sat down in the icy mist of the rain and watched the ducks for a while and then watched the ducks for a while longer until I was very cold and very wet and sick.

And even if I didn't smile back at you at the time, imaginarily or realitarily, it didn't really matter, because even through my sickness and my shaking and my headaches and my chattering teeth I kept smiling for the next three days.

Miss Hayes has a new theory. She thinks I'm not reading enough. Today she brought in two handle-stretched Waitrose bags bulging with books. It was hard work heaving them to the bus stop and the bus was so packed with rush-hour commuters I ended up having no place to store them but on my seat, which meant I had nowhere to sit but on top of them, which is why I may have seemed taller today.

Miss Hayes thinks reading will help me interact with my peers. If I made more of an effort to fit in then maybe I could make some friends. If I had some friends maybe I could stop thinking about **Them** so much. I did have a friend once, back in St Peter's. His name was Andrew Wilt. I used to stay in the classroom at lunch and play chess with him. Everyone else was out playing football but he had to stay inside because he had leukaemia and his body was weak. He was a bastard. He used to jab me with a pencil and call me Freak Boy. I guess he had the right to be a bastard, what with the leukaemia, but he'd always sharpen the pencil before he jabbed me and once the tip broke off and stayed in my hand, a little grey freckle I have to this day. The teachers thought I was very noble to stay with Andrew at lunch but he said I was just a freak with no choice. He always went on about how bad I was at chess. Then, when no one was looking, he'd jab me. In year six Andrew Wilt finally died of leukaemia and from then on I sat alone at lunch and played chess on my own. I actually preferred it that way.

I didn't tell Miss Hayes any of this. She was sitting there smiling, just waiting for me to talk, but I didn't know where to begin. She asked if I'd written anything in my journal this week and I nodded. She grinned and leant forwards, so far I could see the white of her bra. She asked if it had worked, if I felt any different. I wanted to say yes, especially with Miss Hayes literally perched on the edge of her seat like that, but I couldn't think of any effect it had had on me (except for cramping my hand a little) and I didn't want to lie, so I just shook my head and watched Miss Hayes' smile disappear, watched that frown crawl back as she slouched into her seat again. She tapped her pencil against her lips.

She said these things take time. She said I need to be more honest in my writing. She said: 'Remember, nobody will read it.' I promise that I'm being as honest as possible. I'm writing as much as I can but it's hard when you don't know what to write. I never know if I'm writing the right thing.

That's when Miss Hayes went out for the books. She had to go to her car to get them and when she got back her hair had frizzed in the rain. Her blouse was stuck to her chest and I could see her bra without her even having to bend over. I tried not to stare. I could feel this pressure, building inside me. My head ached. I was scratching my arm. She put the pencil to her lips again. I tried to concentrate on the books, tried to read the titles, but I couldn't seem to focus.

Miss Hayes said I was very lucky to have someone lend me all these books. She said that when she was my age she was good at English too and if her English teacher had given her time and encouragement and a big pile of books like this she would have found her calling earlier on in life. She said books can save people. She said books can change the world. I can't really see how a book could change the world – nobody even reads them any more. Everyone in class talks about music and TV, not books.

Miss Hayes said it was Mr Cullman who introduced her to books. She said that Cullman may teach Geography but his real passion is literature. He has a library in his house. She said she's only marrying him for his library and winked. By the time I realised I was meant to laugh it was too late.

Then she asked if I had 'someone'. I wasn't sure how to answer, so I didn't.

'You know, like a girl,' she said. 'A girl you like? Or likes you?

It's important, you know, to have someone. Even a boy . . .'

I stared at the carpet.

'You need someone you can confide in. Someone you can love. It's important to find a home for your love. Do you understand? These books are a start, but you'll need people, too. We all need people.'

Now I'm back home. Miss Hayes' books are stacked in the corner of my bedroom. They're adding an uncomfortable level of clutter to my room. I might stash them away, at the bottom of my wardrobe. I can always pretend I've read them.

TRANSCRIPT

Extract of interview between Detective
Sergeant Terrence Mansell (TM) and Gregory
Hall's teacher, Miss Rachel Hayes (RH).

TM: Thanks for coming in.

RH: That's OK.

TM: I presume you know why you're here.

RH: I've read the newspapers. I don't exactly
know the details.

TM: I can't discuss details anyway.

RH: Right.

TM: All I'm after here is some basic information.

RH: Mm-hm.

TM: Stuff on your relationship with Greg.

RH: OK.

TM: So, tell me about your relationship with
Greg.

RH: Well, I'm his teacher.

TM: What subject?

RH: English.

TM: And you also spent time together outside of school?

RH: You know, it'd be easier all round if you didn't make me answer questions you already know the answers to.

TM: I'm just trying to establish the facts here.

RH: You know the facts. You know I saw Greg outside of school. That's why I'm here. That's why you've brought me in.

TM: To be honest, Miss Hayes, it'd actually be easier if you just answered the questions. Then I can tick them off my list. Then you can go home.

RH: Fine, yes, I saw Greg. After school. Every Tuesday.

TM: Why?

RH: The idea was that he could discuss any problems he was having. In school, at home. Whatever. But he stopped coming. A few weeks ago.

TM: Why was that?

RH: I don't know exactly. There was the stuff

with my fiancé, I don't know if that might have scared him off.

TM: Right.

RH: A lot of people were . . . different after that. It's stupid, though, really. I mean, with Greg. It had no bearing on our meetings.

TM: When did these 'meetings' first start?

RH: A few months ago. October, I think.

TM: And you knew about his condition?

RH: Yes.

TM: And that he was on medication?

RH: Yes. Well, I learnt about everything, you know, the phobia and everything, from the school nurse beforehand. I found out about the pills in class, actually, when one of the other pupils stole them from his school bag. Showed them to everyone.

TM: That must have made things difficult for him.

RH: To be honest we never really talked about any of that, the bullying. There was a fair bit of bullying, it's true, but I didn't want to fixate on that.

TM: What did you talk about?

RH: Not much, really. He wasn't one for baring his soul.

TM: Right.

RH: I tried all kinds of approaches but it made no difference.

TM: What did you try?

RH: Well, I'd ask him questions. Tell him things, about me, about my life. I wanted to just make some sort of connection, you know? I gave him some books once, some of my fiancé's. Of course that's probably the last we'll see of them.

TM: But you never made this 'connection'?

RH: He was unreachable.

TM: Disconnected.

RH: Right.

TM: What was it exactly that made you want to set up these meetings?

RH: What do you mean?

TM: Well, why did you want a connection? What did you hope to get out of it?

RH: I just wanted to help him. I thought he was intelligent. Misunderstood. I thought eventually he'd open up. Obviously at this point I didn't know, you know, what he was capable of.

TM: It had nothing to do with your own
   personal history?

RH: No. I mean . . . what's that got to do
   with anything?

TM: Just a question. It's not important really.

RH: Well, I mean, I did have a tough time
   growing up. And he seemed to also be having
   a tough time. So there was that, yes. I
   wanted to help. I felt compelled to help.

TM: Right.

RH: But the emphasis was always on Greg.

TM: Of course.

RH: What do you mean, anyway — my 'own
   personal history'?

TM: Just referring to what I've read. The
   parts Greg's mentioned.

RH: Mentioned?

TM: In the journal.

RH: Journal?

TM: His journal. That was your idea, right?
   You gave him the journal?

RH: Yes, I gave him a journal. In one of our
   sessions. I didn't think he used it much.

TM: Oh, he used it all right. There're
   hundreds of pages' worth back at my office.

RH: Really?

TM: It took me all night to read through them. Not to mention the stuff transcribed from the walls.

RH: The walls? It was that bad, huh? I mean, I read the stuff in the papers. About the house. I didn't know how much to believe . . .

TM: Let's just stick to the journal. You didn't know he was using it?

RH: No. But, well, I'm glad he did. That he found some use for it. I was seeing him regularly by the time I gave him that. He came voluntarily, so he obviously wasn't opposed to the idea of sitting with me. The idea of help. It was speaking he had a problem with. I think he was embarrassed, you know, about the lisp? I thought that if he wouldn't talk to me, maybe he'd talk to himself, you know? Write to himself. You know what I mean? It's a fairly common technique.

TM: Common?

RH: Yes.

TM: To whom?

RH: Well, psychiatrists.

TM: Right.

RH: Writing as a sort of therapy.

TM: Yes, I get the concept.

RH: Obviously it worked on some level. I mean, it clearly sparked something inside him.

TM: Do you have any prior training in this field?

RH: Psychiatry?

TM: Are you qualified in any way?

RH: I studied psychology.

TM: Where?

RH: Sixth-form.

TM: So, like, A-level?

RH: Look, to be honest I've had just about enough of these interviews recently, OK?

TM: I believe this to be your first with me.

RH: I'm talking about my fiancé.

TM: That's a separate case.

RH: Still.

TM: I'd like to stick with Greg if possible.

RH: I'm getting a little tired of the accusatory tone.

TM: I'm not accusing you of anything. I'd like to be clear on that. It's just that you're mentioned frequently in the journal and I need to work out whether what's written there is accurate or not.

RH: Accurate?

TM: I need you to shed some light on a few things.

RH: Well . . .

TM: Several of these extracts have been disputed.

RH: Really?

TM: I just want to clear a few things up.

RH: Fine. Let's clear this up first, then: the whole time I was meeting with Greg there was never any indication he was violent. If there had been, I would have told someone. I would have asked to speak to his parents, his doctor, whoever. As far as I was concerned he was just a mixed-up teenager who needed a friend. Someone to talk to. And that's what I was trying to be. A friend.

TM: And Greg saw you as a friend?

RH: I hope so.

TM: Do you think he ever thought of you as more than a friend?

RH: More?

TM: Do you think Greg may have found you sexually attractive?

RH: What's that got to do with anything?

TM: It's a straightforward question.

RH: I couldn't really say. He was never one to announce his sexuality. Not like others in his class. I thought he might be gay, actually, at one point . . .

TM: You never picked up on anything? Any . . . feelings?

RH: Well, I noticed him looking at my chest a couple of times. But all teenage boys do that. They're fascinated by that stuff. You know, stuff they don't have. I'm aware that I'm young and therefore attractive, by teacher standards.

TM: He alludes to your breasts at one point, in the journal.

RH: Oh?

TM: He describes how he can see your bra. Due to the wet nature of your blouse.

RH: Well, OK, but I'm not sure that's important. I mean, I fancied my teacher once. I remember what it's like. It doesn't mean anything.

TM: So you did nothing to encourage this
behaviour?

RH: Excuse me? You're telling me that's not
accusatory? 'Encourage'? No, I encouraged
nothing of the sort.

TM: But you admit to the possibility that Greg
could have been attracted to you? Could have
been repressing some sort of sexual urge?

RH: I don't know. It could have been a part
of it. I didn't get that . . . erm . . .
vibe, myself. But as I've said, I didn't get
much of anything, other than silence. It
could have been a part of it, yes, I
suppose.

TM: Did he ever mention Alice to you?

RH: Not to me, no.

TM: How about her father?

[RH shakes head.]

TM: Could you answer? For the tape, please.

RH: No.

TM: How about his sister? Did he ever talk
about a place called Finners Island? About
the troubles with his family?

RH: I know it's not very helpful, but he
didn't really speak, like, at all. We'd just

sit together. That was the relationship we had. I'd try and help him and he'd just sit there.

TM: Right.

RH: Sometimes he'd nod. Or he'd answer 'yes' or 'no', but apart from that . . .

TM: OK.

RH: I mean, can you understand how infuriating it was? I tried to help him, I really did. And when he stopped coming, you know, near the end, when he started avoiding me, it was a real slap in the face. Like, we were just on the brink of making real progress and he decided to pull the plug. It was ungrateful, is what it was.

TM: I can imagine.

RH: And it's hard not to blame yourself. I mean, you read about stuff like this all the time, but to be a part of it . . . To know him. To have played some part in his life. I just wish I could have helped, you know?

TM: It's not your fault.

RH: I know, but still. I just wish he would have listened.

TM: Right.

RH: I just wish all of this could have been avoided.

Mum cut my hair last night. She used to be a full-time hair-dresser, back in the Pitt. She worked at a salon called Ahmed's Boutique, just round the corner from Kirk Lane. It's shut now, boarded up, like most Pitt places. We pass it every night on the bus but by then you're always asleep.

Now Mum does part-time, mobile hairdressing instead. It started with Mrs Jenkins next door. Mum doesn't really like Mrs Jenkins because she's old and smells like pee and some-times spends days at a time in the loft. She does like Mrs Jenkins' old-lady-conversational-streak though because a few years ago Mrs Jenkins recommended Mum's hairdressing skills to Karen Mosley in church and then Karen Mosley recom-mended Mum's hairdressing skills to Sandra Peterson and Sandra Peterson recommended Mum's hairdressing skills to Sally Anderson and Sally Anderson's gym buddies with Ursula Hampton and so now Mum's going round to Ursula Hampton's every week, styling Ursula Hampton's hair in all kinds of fabu-lous curls and inviting Ursula and Ken around for meals and over the last couple of years Ken has invested heavily in my father's clinic and this year they may even get an invite to the Hamptons' famous New Year's bash, which makes Mum truly, truly happy. Mum has friends, not customers. Hairdressing's a hobby and she enjoys it. It's not like we need the money. (These are the first things she tells Karen or Sandra or Sally or Ursula or any other friends whose hair she cuts.)

She cuts her friends' hair in the kitchen. Sometimes I sit on the stairs so I can listen to them. It's amazing how much they can talk, how they can keep thinking up things to say. As soon as they perch on that stool in the kitchen their words fill the house, echoing through the open-plan downstairs. Sally Anderson likes to talk about Karen Mosley and Karen Mosley likes to talk about Ursula Hampton and Ursula Hampton likes to talk about Sally Anderson. They talk about how such-and-such's new carpet is awful and how such-and-such has the worst dress sense and how such-and-such's nephew is getting a sex change in the summer and wants to be called Rennet and they never should have let him have that Barbie when he was a child. Her friends must know Mum talks about them with her other friends but that doesn't stop them talking about each other. It's like Mum has some kind of hold over them. Maybe it's the scissors. If Mum does get an invite to the Hamptons' New Year's bash then the Mosleys and the Petersons and the Andersons are all going to be there. I don't know what they'll all talk about.

I never know what to say when Mum cuts my hair. Last night she asked how school was. I told her it was OK. She asked how my after-school lessons were going. I've never told Mum I have after-school lessons. A few weeks ago I mentioned the meetings with Miss Hayes and since then she's assumed that's where I've been going every night. I didn't want to lie so instead I changed the subject. I told her I've been doing well with my *An Inspector Calls* essays, that I got an A- for one of them. She said, 'Very good,' and nodded. Then she asked what subject my *An Inspector Calls* essays are for and I told her English and she said, 'English?' and I said, 'Yes,' and she nodded again, smiling at me in the mirror. She asked if I want to do something English-related when I leave school, like become an English teacher or something. I said I didn't know.

Then Mum stopped talking so she could concentrate on my hair. My hair is Mum's greatest challenge. Its default setting is Scruffy Bowl. Mum says she tries her best to make me look good, with the haircuts and the clothes she buys me, but somehow I always manage to look a disgrace. She says I have a 'Natural Trampness'. I closed my eyes, felt Mum's nails navigate my scalp. Listened to the hum of the fridge, the rain on the window. The whispering snips of the scissors.

Right now I'm sitting on the bus. Even with last night's haircut my hair's still quite long, and long hair's kind of nerve-racking out in the Pitt. I know your dad's got a ponytail but he's a big bloke, he can get away with it. I'm just a kid and Pitt kids don't have long hair. There's two slouched at the back of the bus right now, heads shaved to the bone. Just enough hair to scratch your fist on. Every time I look up they're staring at me.

Now, this is a bit embarrassing, but I did some looking in the mirror this morning. Just a quick look, while I was getting washed. My new hair's about the same length as Ian's – just long enough to nibble my fringe. I stroked it down over my face the way he does, a kind of moody artistic way, like a rock star. It could never look exactly like Ian's but it was a start. (Ian scrubs his hair with shampoo, then doesn't wash it out, so it's always a bit crunchy and straggly looking. He likes it when he's walking down the street and it starts to rain and his head starts foaming.)

I had to fix my hair back to its scruffy bowl before school, so nobody would notice it'd been cut. I tried to rearrange it as I waited with the ducks but the canal isn't very reflective so I couldn't be sure whether I looked like a rock star or not. I always keep my hood up and head down on the bus, so nobody usually sees my hair, but tonight I'd planned a lean-back-with-my-fringe-over-my-face pose. I'd planned to give you a bit of a smoky-eyed glance, too, but it's hard to do anything when you step on board, my head fills with static. Did you notice? You looked over but only in that glance-around way that people assess their situation. Those vinyl-black glasses don't give much away. I think you gave the Pitt kids at the back quite a stare. Does the fact that your dad has long hair make it more or less likely for you to like it? I wish I knew psychology.

You kept your head down the rest of the journey. The Pitt kids kept playing that thud-thud music (although it was more like a tap-tap through their phone speakers). They kept staring at me, I could feel it. I wanted to turn around and tell them to shut up. You were trying to sleep.

Today the church sign said:

JESUS
LUVS
U
(EVEN WEN NO 1 ELSE WILL)

You pressed the STOP bell and we pulled up round the back of the Rat and Dog. You rubbed your eyes and stepped off without even a glance back at me and my hair. You just left me here with these Pitt kids and nothing to do but write and writing on the bus is making me sick.

I wish I could have gone with you.

Today was one of my bad days. One of my neck-rubbing collar-brushing goose-pimpling web-tickling shaking kind of days. One of those days when every time I close my eyes – every time I even blink – I see **Them**, hundreds of **Them**, massing in my head. At lunch I couldn't sit still. I kept jumping up every time my hair brushed my neck and the scraping of my chair kept waking Miss Eleanor and she kept shushing me with that big librarian finger of hers. In the end I had to go down to the toilets and sit in a cubicle in my balled-up position and stare at the wall. I had to picture your face. I knew that, if I saw you, everything would be OK.

And it was. For the whole bus ride I sat and stared at your red curls and didn't think about **Them**. I didn't even think about the fact that I wasn't thinking about **Them**. But then you got up to leave and it ached me to see you, clutching the rail, rocking from side to side as we slowed outside the Rat and Dog, knowing that any second you would step off the bus and disappear into the darkness and I would have to wait all weekend to see you again. I found myself sliding to the edge of my seat, I found myself clutching my bag to my chest, and as Man With Ear Hair and Woman Who Sneezes both stood and blocked you and I could only see a tiny patch of your hair in the driver's mirror, I found myself standing and joining the queue. It felt like the first time I'd ever used my legs.

We shuffled along the aisle of the bus, past the fat and frowning face of the driver (a face that said, 'This is not Green Avenue, this is not your usual stop') and down the steps to the pavement. For a second we stood, watching the bus pull away. You lit a cigarette, cupping your lighter to protect the flame, a yellow flash that soon flickered and faded in the darkness. I wondered how you could see with your sunglasses on.

The crowd dispersed. Man With Ear Hair and Woman Who Sneezes disappeared up the side of the Rat and Dog. My breath was steaming and my feet were numb but I still felt that warmth inside to know you were there, to hear the click of your heels as you hurried up the street. I waited till you were a black and red figure, too far away to hear my footsteps, before I began to follow.

Once my father had a bump in his company Audi and he had to drive Mum's BMW over to the garage to collect it and I remember Mum muttering the whole journey about a 'two-second stopping distance' between vehicles. The two of them sharing polite gritted-toothed words about what a 'two-second stopping distance' actually was – the disagreement, we found out eventually, caused by my father's use of 'and' to separate seconds differing from Mum's 'Mississippi'. I tried to use a similar distance-method for our walk, maintaining a twenty-second stopping distance (using Mississippis), which I think is an appropriate translation from car to foot.

It was hard maintaining the twenty-second stopping distance, though, because you kept turning corners and disappearing from view and I kept having to hurry to the corner and wait, lingering in the scent of your cigarette, watching you gain enough distance before I could start walking again. A couple of times you stopped and I stopped too, begging you not to turn around, because if you turned you would see me and I might scare you. I pleaded with you to keep on walking, to just let me follow, let me watch the swaying curls of your hair. Both times you did.

It was strange, walking through the Pitt again. It seems different now. Most of it's unchanged, really – St Peter's still looks the same (except for those tall green fences around it) and Crossgrove Park still has the swings and that rusted old climbing frame. Maybe it seems different because it's winter and it's dark or because it's even scruffier and even more overgrown with even more misspelt graffiti, or maybe it's because I know that Nan's not there any more, not really, not the Nan I knew. We walked all the way down Brook Road and through the park to the estates. I didn't see or hear a single other person, just you and your heels, echoing up each empty street. It was as if we were the only two people in the whole Pitt.

And then you disappeared. This time where I couldn't follow: up your driveway. I crossed the road and quickened my pace but by the time I reached your house your peeling red door had slammed shut. I remembered where I was, out in the furthest reaches of the bus route. I remembered the gangs of Pitt kids I'd seen from the window, pitching stones at the cars on the carriageway. I could hear laughter, somewhere, a couple of streets away. I didn't even know if I'd remember the way back.

But then I noticed something: a thin thread of smoke, rising from the end of your path. Your cigarette butt, lying there, smouldering. It gave me the same feeling of dread I get when I see a snail in the middle of the road. A cigarette that had been sitting in a packet in your pocket all day, that had travelled the bus with us, that had been to your lips and felt your suck and burnt down for you – it was just lying there, dying on the cold pavement. I glanced around but the street was deserted. I picked it up, held it in my pocket.

I ran back to the bus stop. I didn't try to remember the way, I just remembered, instinctively. It was only seven minutes till the next bus so I sat and listened to my breathing, the butt burning into the palm of my hand. I didn't dare remove it from my pocket, didn't dare examine it in case, in the yellow light of the bus stop, I realised it was just a cigarette butt, and threw it away.

Later, when my sister was thudding away in her room and Mum had taken up her nap-position in the lounge, I crept out into the garden and sat on the edge of one of Mum's plant pots and took the butt from my pocket. It was smaller than I remembered, smaller than it felt. The tip of the filter was crumpled pink from your lipstick. I smelt it, thinking it would smell of something other than cigarettes.

I held it in my lips. I clicked the trigger of Mum's crème brûlée blowtorch (the only light I'd been able to find). Its flame was blue and extremely hot and it was hard to light the butt without singeing my nostrils. I breathed deep, sucking the heat into my chest. I don't know what I was expecting – something smooth, maybe. Cigarette smoke always looks so silky but it felt more like gravel clawing down my throat. I coughed and dropped the butt into the flower bed.

It was hard to find in the darkness. Mum's blowtorch doesn't give much light. It was only as I crouched there, searching, that I noticed the burn on the palm of my hand, the weeping pink hole the cigarette had left when I grasped it.

I found the butt, eventually. It was lodged under one of the plant tubs, speckled with soil. I slipped it back into my pocket and came inside.

By the way, I wouldn't let your dad find out you smoke.
Whenever Phil smokes, your dad gets very upset. He says,
'You're sucking the dick of death, man.' Phil sometimes offers
him a cigarette as a little joke but your dad never laughs. He
just gives Phil that stony-faced look.

This morning Phil was helping your dad carry some dead
pigs to the freezer. Your dad lifted them no problem, hoisting
them over his shoulder like a fireman, but Phil's small and
skinny and by the end he was panting his way past the kitchen
like a wounded solider carrying a comrade.

Afterwards Phil was exhausted. He wanted a smoke. He
looked everywhere for his tobacco pouch but it was gone. He
got pretty angry, in a breathless sort of way, and kept asking
your dad where it was, but your dad just gave one of his heh-
heh-heh laughs and said he didn't know and that smoking was
the reason Phil was out of breath in the first place. He said,
'You're sucking the dick of death, man. Do you want your kid
to grow up without a daddy?'

They didn't speak for a while after that. Phil just hacked away at the meat. The Top 40 Chart Show was playing on the radio, that song my sister's always dancing to. 'Ooo you got me screamin' boy . . .' Eventually your dad took the tobacco pouch from his pocket and slapped it on the block and Phil snatched it and hurried out the back of the shop. I just kept my head down, mopped out the fridge. This week the Top 40 Chart Show was sponsored by Burke's Clinic: 'THE place for your boob job.'

After lunch Phil came into my kitchen, smelling like a whole lot of smoke. He gave me a handful of coins and a slip of paper and told me to go to the bookies for him. I said I was too young to go the bookies and he said not to worry, I looked old enough, and if there was any trouble to just say his name. He said not to tell anyone (meaning your dad) where I was going. I went out the back door. It was busy in the bookies so I had to queue. I handed the slip of paper and the coins to the guy with the beard behind the counter and he gave me a different slip of paper without even looking up and I went back and gave Phil the new slip of paper and he tucked it into his pocket. Nobody asked where I'd been.

In the afternoon the Top 40 Chart Show finished and there was football instead. Phil stood by the radio, scratching at his neck with mince-covered fingers. The commentators were angry with the players, shouting and calling them a disgrace. It got me thinking about Lucy Marlowe again. I remembered those times she'd sit on the steps to the Lipton Building, trying to eat her lunch in peace, whilst the boys took it in turns to kick their football at her. How they'd snigger and ask her to throw it back. How she'd still always throw it back. I remember once they hit her *Star Trek* lunchbox and it clattered down the stairs and smashed open and her ham and ketchup sandwich landed in the gutter and she ran inside crying and nobody even picked up her sandwich and it lay there all day soaking up rainwater until the bread had melted, ketchup veining out across the playground. The boys used to say Lucy Marlowe was a nerd because she was passionate about *Star Trek* and wore this baggy Mr Spock T-shirt on own-clothes day that would probably still fit her now. I didn't understand because they all wore matching football shirts on own-clothes day and I think football's much nerdier than *Star Trek*. It's not like *Star Trek* host radio shows every weekend with phone-ins and episode-by-episode analysis. It's not like *Star Trek* fans stand by the radio scratching their necks and chewing their lips, looking like the entire world depends on what the commentator says next.

Someone scored and Phil jumped and punched the air. He kept grinning till the match was over. Then he winked at me and went back out to his block. I didn't wink back but I couldn't help smiling when he started singing. He danced around your dad. He gave him a big kiss on the side of his stony face.

Your dad just laughed.

'Heh-heh-heh.'

Miss Hayes has a new theory. She thinks I'm not really scared of **Them**. She thinks they're just something to blame my anxiety on. She thinks I hide my real fears behind Metaphorical Phantoms. Miss Hayes said when she was little her dad gave her a ventriloquist's doll, a clown, called Mr Fungal. Mr Fungal was her favourite toy in the world. Her and Mr Fungal used to joint-host shows for her mum and she'd swear she couldn't see her lips move. She said that when she was a little older her and her dad had a falling-out. Well, she said it was like a falling-out, only secret. She couldn't tell anyone. She said she fell out with Mr Fungal, too. She'd wake up in the night crying and Mr Fungal would be there, grinning away from her bedside table. She hated him. She couldn't even stand to be in the same room as him. She wanted to throw Mr Fungal out but then her mum would want to know why she didn't like him any more. Mr Fungal belonged to her dad and by this point her dad had gone and her mum liked to keep the few things he'd left behind.

Miss Hayes said that she stuffed Mr Fungal right down at the bottom of her wardrobe, under her boxes of books and cuddly toys and shoes. She ignored him for a while but in the back of her mind she always knew he was still there, grinning. By then she was becoming a teenager and going through a rebellious time, so she took Mr Fungal out to the woods. She walked for hours without even thinking. She came to a clearing and sat Mr Fungal right in the middle, on the dry grass, and poured a bottle of methylated spirit over his head and set fire to him. She said he gave off a lot of smoke, a big column of it pointing into the sky. She said he crackled. She couldn't leave till she was sure he was all burnt away, till she was sure he wouldn't end up back on her shelf the next day, grinning with his lips all blistered and popped.

By this point in the story Miss Hayes' voice was breaking. She clutched her skirt. Her hands were red but for a thin border of white round her engagement ring. There was silence – and not a nice silence. Miss Hayes wiped the side of her face. She said that sometimes our Metaphorical Phantoms can seem like the root of all evil but they're not, they're just a barrier between us and our real problems. She said that even if there was some natural phenomenon and all of **Them** were wiped out forever, I still wouldn't be happy. She said they're just a symbol.

I've heard similar theories. A couple of years ago when my phobia was getting out of hand again Mum took me to see her doctor, Dr Filburn. Dr Filburn was different to the other doctors I saw because he was a doctor of the mind. He wasn't like the others who just palmed me off with pills. Dr Filburn was going to cure me.

Dr Filburn said it was the concept of **Them** that scared me. He said I could happily coexist with **Them** if I could just overcome my irrational brain. Dr Filburn also used the term 'Metaphorical Phantoms', only he said I needed to face my Metaphorical Phantoms head-on. Dr Filburn was old. Not age-wise – he just looked like he belonged in the past. He had a moustache. Mum seemed to like him, though. He really helped her when she went through her sick stage. The whole time I lay in that comfy white chair Mum stood there, smiling back and forth between us. It was that same smile she dons while showing off a new item of furniture – the smile that forces you to smile right back.

Dr Filburn told me to close my eyes. With the click of a remote his office was engulfed in low, moaning whale music. After a few minutes he began to speak, softly. He told me to imagine a mountainside, shrouded in mist. He told me to pretend I was walking through the mist, searching for something, an animal. He told me to find the animal. I found an American bald eagle. It was perched on a rock overlooking a misty beach. Apparently this was my 'Safety Animal', and Dr Filburn told me to approach it, which I did. Then he told me to stroke it, which I also did and which, I have to admit, felt relaxing. Its wings were spread and I could feel the ribbed bones beneath. It made me feel light-headed.

Dr Filburn told me to open my eyes. He placed my right hand on his desk, which was empty apart from a pen, a pad and a picture of a blonde lady that could have been his wife or his daughter. Then he left the room, returning with a little plastic one of **Them**. He told me to maintain the peaceful state of mind I'd created stroking my Safety Animal. Mum was still smiling.

Dr Filburn placed the plastic one of **Them** on his desk. He asked if I was OK with the plastic one of **Them** on his desk and I nodded. He told me to close my eyes and imagine my animal. When he asked me to open them again the plastic one of **Them** had moved across the desk, a little closer to me. He asked if I was still OK. I nodded again. He told me to close my eyes again.

This continued until the little plastic one of **Them** was perched right in front of me. Then Dr Filburn lifted the plastic one of **Them** and placed it in the palm of my hand. He asked if I still felt scared. I wanted to explain that I'd never been scared of the little plastic one of **Them** because it was plastic and right at the start I could have just walked over and picked it up, Safety Animal or no Safety Animal. Instead I just shook my head. Dr Filburn nodded and left the room again.

He returned with a jar. Before the lid was even off I was clutching the leather and starting to fit. Everything went cold and dark. Mum was screaming. That was the day I bit the hole through my tongue. I never saw Dr Filburn again. I remember how angry he was when I bled all over his comfy white chair.

But anyway, they're not real. I guess that's the point. That's what I have to remember.

They're just Metaphorical Phantoms.

They're not real.

It hurts because you are still there and I know you are there and I don't know how to take you away. And it's not your fault but you could have come to school. You could have to come to school anyway and just worn your glasses and nobody would have known and I would have walked you home and everything would be the same.

But nothing is the same.

And it was hard for me. I waited for you. At 08:18 I was pressed against the gate, holding my breath, watching your bus arrive. I was examining each Pitt kid as they stumbled from the steps. By the time the last kid had departed and the bus had pulled away I'd nearly forgotten how to breathe.

And I waited again, at lunch, in the library, staking out the hole in the hedge. But Angela Hargrove crawled out through it alone and returned, an hour later, still alone.

And all I could think about was you. The lack of you.

So at 15:30 when the final bell rang I waited one more time, in my usual waiting-place, with the ducks. I waited for the

17:32. I guess some part of me still expected to see you, shivering at the bus stop outside the Prancing Horse, but you hadn't gone to work either.

But I stayed on our bus. I rode it all the way out to the Pitt. I closed my eyes and pictured your sleeping face in the driver's mirror. I told myself you were OK. You were fine. You were at home. You had not been hit by a bus. You had not been attacked by a gang in the Pitt. You were not at the hospital having contracted cancer from all that smoking and you were not going to die like Andrew Wilt, shaky and milky and bald. I got off at our usual stop, walked our usual route. I watched my feet. That way I could pretend you were up ahead of me. I could imagine the click of your heels on the pavement. I could even sniff for your cigarette – I swear at one point I could even smell it. But you seemed further ahead than usual. I couldn't keep up with you. Every time I lifted my head you'd disappear again and I'd be alone again and in the end I started to run, up all the dark and empty streets, run with the cold air biting my face.

By the time I reached your house I was panting. I sat on the wall opposite. The air was cold and stung the hole in my tongue. I focused on your red and peeling door. Your curtains were drawn. Your father's car sat outside, rusted browny-green, its backseats packed with Hampton's cardboard boxes. I could hear a sound, a voice. Canned laughter.

Your house backs onto Crossgrove Park. I hurried across the field, counting the houses till I reached your back hedge. Your garden was overrun with weeds, foot-long grass, white plastic patio furniture. Any intentional plant life was dead – the hedge patchy, the few scattered plant tubs at the back housing only shrivelled brown remains. Your father was spread across the couch in the lounge, lit by the TV. Laughter murmured behind the glass. Your father wasn't laughing, he was swigging from a bottle. His eyes were shut and he was swigging from a bottle.

There was a shed in the corner: shelter from the light of the house. I found a gap in the hedge just behind it. The shed itself was rotten. There were several crooked or missing planks. The roof was held up by four wooden beams, one in each corner, planted into the surrounding mud.

A strip of light shone from the first floor of the house. A bedroom. The curtains were thick and purple, giving nothing away but a thin square of light round the edges. Every few seconds a shadow passed over it, flickering, back and forth. Back and forth.

That's when I heard a growl – deep, nearby. I was leaning on the shed and I assumed it was the boards creaking but as I turned the growling increased, snarling and guttural. I turned too sharply, slipped in the mud. The wet grass broke my fall. A sharp pain spread from my palm – the burn, the scab from your cigarette butt, I'd grazed it on the side of the shed and now it was bleeding. There was mud and blood on the arm of my coat. I tried to wipe it but my hands were muddy too, even muddier than my arm and all I could do was make things muddier and bloodier and worse.

That's when the barking started. I could see it now, the dog, through a gap in the shed. Its head was long and snouted, just a foot or two from mine. Its breath was hot and smelt like boiled ham. The only thing holding it back was a length of chain, knotted round its neck. I don't know one breed of dog from another but it was a pretty mean-looking dog. It had lots of teeth, most of them yellow with black bits in between. Its gums were the colour of chopped liver.

I was halfway to standing when the back door opened. Your father's voice echoed out across the garden. I dropped to the ground, once again facing the roaring stinking dog. Your father shouted for a minute, stuff like 'Shut up, Scraps' and 'I'll give you something to bark about' but the dog didn't shut up, if anything it got louder. I closed my eyes. The barking stabbed into my ears. Everything was wet and tasted like soil.

And then there was you. All it took was your mumble across the garden and the dog stopped its barking and turned to face the house. It whined from deep inside itself. You told your father to go back indoors. Liquid clunked from his bottle. He coughed and swallowed and breathed.

He said, 'If you don't shut it up, I will.' And the back door slammed shut.

I tried to catch a glimpse of you then, strained to see over the long grass. Your feet rustled past. They slowed to step over the patio furniture, slapped the concrete steps up to the shed. The dog scrambled over to greet you. I glanced at the house. Your father was across the couch again, head back, swigging at his bottle.

Your footsteps creaked into the shed. I saw you then, kneeling beside the dog, scratching its ears as it whined. You had your back to me, your hair tied in pigtails. You wore a pink dressing gown, a pair of black Wellington boots. You rubbed the dog's head, pulling the skin back to show the red of its eyes.

You told it, 'There-there.'

Then you stood and reached, high up into the shed, returning with a clear plastic bag of bone-shaped biscuits. You rattled a few into your palm. The dog chewed noisily. It drooled onto your dressing gown. When it'd finished it rested its head on your lap. You stroked its belly. Rubbed its ribs.

You said, 'Good boy, Scraps. Good boy.'

You lay its head beside me. Facing me. It breathed, soft and warm. The boiled ham smell was stronger than ever, probably because of the biscuits.

It closed its eyes, let its tongue loll onto the shed floor. Its ribs rose and fell in time with my own.

I closed my eyes.

You locked the shed. You crunched across the lawn, back to the house. I waited till I heard the kitchen door, then climbed to my feet.

You had stopped in the doorway. You were staring over at the shed, right at me. I hunched down. You mustn't have seen me because a second later you turned and disappeared inside, locking the door behind you.

I can still see you now, that image of you I glimpsed for just a second. Your red hair parted, your eye all swollen and black.

This morning I watched your father through the blinds of the back fridge. He hacked at the hunks of meat on his block. He sipped tea and read the paper. He joked with Phil, holding his hat in the air with that big hand of his, too high for Phil to reach. Always with that laugh: 'Heh-heh-heh.'

I only realised how long I'd been standing there when Phil stepped in and asked me to go the bookies. I was shivering but he thought I was nodding so he just placed the money in my hand and gave me a thumbs up.

It was 09:55. I had to sit on the step and wait till 10:00 for the bookies to open. The square was empty. There were two pigeons hopping around the car park. One of them was missing a leg. The other was missing an eye. They picked at a carton of chips. When the man from the bookies opened the door they scrambled into flight, landing the other side of the square. Pigeons never fly very far.

When I got back to Hampton's your father was in the kitchen. He was enormous in my tiny kitchen, his head right up near the ceiling, where the steam gathers. He smiled down at me. I smiled back. I was numb and empty and smiling back seemed almost natural. He asked me to make him and Phil a tea. Phil shouted back that he wanted a coffee. Your father said cheers and called me 'mate'.

In Hampton's we use T-Rex Bleach. It's 'The wild way to clean'. The bottle has T - R E X written across it in jungle-style font, a teeth-marked chunk missing from the T as if an actual T-rex has taken a bite. Bleach is something I've got used to, working as a cleaner. It stings my nostrils and makes my fingers peel and sometimes at night I can still taste it, burning the back of my throat, but it's the only way to shift real grime – the kind of grime that's hard and black and no longer resembles what it used to be.

I put half a teaspoon of T-Rex Bleach in your father's tea. Mum uses bleach to keep her mugs white and I know from experience that it's only after a few sips the burning taste is noticeable and you realise you should have washed the cup more. I'm guessing T-Rex Bleach is stronger than the spray Mum uses. It says I N D U S T R I A L across it. The lid is childproof, with a black and yellow X on it. I can't help but wonder why, if they didn't want children to play with it, they put a T-rex on the front of the bottle.

Your father was over at the mincer, one hand shovelling hunks of steak down the funnel, the other covering the plate where the mince worms out. It's important to cover the mince as it worms out or else it can pop and splatter the walls. I placed his tea on the block. I waited for him to notice me, so I could point to the mug. Eventually he did and I pointed and he nodded and pushed the big red STOP button and lifted the mug with his enormous mince-covered hand and slurped in the newfound silence. He coughed. He slurped again. Then he sat the mug back on the block and the whirr of the mincer started up again. He didn't look up so I went back to my kitchen.

In *An Inspector Calls* there's a character called Eva Smith who kills herself by drinking bleach. I think you'd have to drink a lot of bleach to kill yourself. If you brewed a tea bag in bleach and added milk and sugar and heated it in the microwave till it was steaming and gulped it down, that might kill you. I doubt half a teaspoon of T-Rex Bleach could kill anyone. Especially not someone as big as your father.

It was only after I'd delivered the tea that I remembered my first day at Hampton's – your father showing me the racks at the back where the cleaning stuff's kept, pointing to a white plastic dish containing green, plastic-looking pellets on the floor right at the back and telling me never to touch it, telling me it was rat poison. How many teaspoons of rat poison would it take to kill someone? How many to just make them really sick?

Your father didn't ask for another cup of tea.

Today I walked down to the canal. I needed to be somewhere I could think. I took some bread because all last week as I waited for our bus the ducks came venturing over the ice to peck at my feet. I guess when the canal's frozen they don't eat. They went crazy at the sight of bread. I only had four slices (all that was left in the bread bin) and they gobbled it up in no time. Then they stood there, glaring at me. It was kind of awkward, like they were weighing up my edibility.

At 15:15 I heard mumblings from above. I recognised the voices: Ian and Goose. Their feet were hanging over the mouth of the bridge. Ian wears these black trainers with luminous shoelaces and they glowed like green dangling worms. The ducks waddled out, staring up at them. I guess they thought they were food.

Ian was talking but I couldn't hear what about. The usual stuff, probably. Girls. Parties. At one point he flicked a cigarette butt down onto the ice and the ducks went crazy again, swarming and pecking to the squeals of Goose's high-pitched laughter.

I huddled into my warm-position and waited. I figured they'd leave soon and I could be alone with the ducks. Be alone to think. Only the longer I sat there the less I could think about anything other than **Them**. It was different, with Ian and Goose there – I couldn't seem to summon the usual safety-and-solitude feeling of under the bridge. Instead I was very aware that I was under a bridge – that normally that'd be the kind of place that would terrify me. That there was a very real chance one or more of **Them** were above me, in the darkness, waiting to descend. I began to panic. I thought I might even have one of my attacks. I tried to picture you, but each time I'd see that eye of yours, all black and swollen.

After ten minutes or so Ian and Goose left and I was able to climb up to the carriageway and head home. I don't think either of them saw me.

I got home just as Mum was serving dinner. My father wasn't there. I didn't ask where he was but I assume the answer would have been that he was working. Who has breast augmentation on a Sunday afternoon? We ate our salmon in silence. Then Sarah and I went up to our rooms. Sarah was dancing to that song again. 'Ooo you got me screamin' boy . . .'

I waited till 21:30, then crept down to my father's study. Sometimes at night I sneak down there for internet research. Mum's always had an issue with closed spaces and locked doors (she pretty much knocked down half the house under

Dr Filburn's guidance to make it 'an open and honest place to live'), so she definitely has a problem with my father's locked study. I don't know what upsets her more, the thousands of photos of women's breasts he has stashed away in there or the fact that she can't get in to polish the woodwork, but each time my father clicks that lock Mum's lip does some serious twitching. It's as if, for a split-second, the left half of her mouth is trying to out-smile the right.

I happen to know that my father has little of interest inside his study. There's a desk, a filing cabinet, a black leather chair and a bookcase. The bookcase contains six shelves of breast augmentation journals and one shelf of *Baywatch* videos. The filing cabinet's scattered with plastic models of different-sized and -shaped breasts. There is a large poster of Pamela Anderson pinned over the desk. My father says Pamela Anderson is an icon of his generation. He says it's a shame that all our generation has in the way of a strong female role model is Katie Price.

It's the click of the study door unlocking that I always think will wake Mum. Occasionally her sleeping face twitches but that's it. Mum's an expert napper. She can nap through anything. Her usual nap-place was the couch but, as we're still waiting on the white Italian leather couch, we're now in a transitional period couch-wise, and so Mum has taken to napping on the lounge carpet instead, her body horizontal across the floor, her head vertical against the white-painted wall. Tonight I stood outside my father's study for a few minutes, just watching the light of the television flicker across her, sometimes lighting her legs, sometimes the rise and fall of her chest beneath her dressing gown, sometimes the sag of her cocked, unsmiling head. Mum never smiles when she sleeps.

Tonight's internet research was a regular of mine: Finners Island. Finners Island's a dot on the map just off the southern coast of England. We used to go there when I was little. Half the island's wetland and my father was a big fan of its constant photo opportunities. There were all sorts of beautiful birds there. There were a lot of ducks, too, but my father rarely took photos of them. There was a bald eagle there, somewhere, according to legend. My father never managed to get a photo of the bald eagle, which to him was proof enough of its non-existence. But Nan and I knew better. We saw it.

I've tried to find the Finners Island photos many times over the years, but I think Mum must have thrown them out. She doesn't want to be reminded of it – of what happened to Sarah. Now I use the internet for photos. Of course none of the internet photos of Finners Island include Mum or Nan or Sarah and I (or the bald eagle – even Finners Island's official website seems to doubt its existence) but there are some of the ducks and the woods and the beach. It's nice, clicking through the photos. Finners Island has always been a place I can go to when Skipdale gets too much, and it's nice seeing that there's this one little part of the world that never changes.

Mum was still in her nap-position when I relocked the study, the light of BBC News 24 washing over her. It was 22:10. The earliest my father's arrived home from work in the past six months is 23:07. By then I'm always well out of his study and up in my room and Sarah's thudding has usually stopped and all he has to do is unplug the TV and fireman's-lift Mum upstairs to bed. Some nights my father doesn't arrive home from work at all. He's a very important man. Mum says that Burke's Clinic wouldn't be half as successful if it weren't for my father's mix of long hours and surgical expertise. My father's patients are more like friends than clients.

I crouched there with Mum for a while. The lounge seems so empty, couchless. So cold. The whole house seems cold since she had it open-planned. I sipped her glass of wine. I'm not meant to drink, really, because of my medication, but I thought I'd try a sip. I wish I hadn't – I can still taste it now. Wine tastes like blackcurrant and perfume.

BBC News 24 was all about this winter and how it's going to be the coldest in thirty years. It showed footage of Scotland covered in snow, kids sliding down hills on bin bags, a woman falling over in the street while people carefully hurried by. Mum likes to keep up to date with the news for when the Hamptons discuss current affairs. Ken Hampton reads the

Guardian. I don't think Mum's ever watched a full report before drifting off.

I put down the wine and unplugged the TV. I left Mum laid out on the lounge carpet, ready for when my father gets home.

Today you still weren't in school so I had to catch the bus alone and walk to your house alone and climb in through the back hedge. Your father was drinking in the TV light again. Scraps was snoring in the shed. I knelt till I could make out his sleeping head through the missing-plank gap. I whistled. He raised an ear but the rest of him stayed asleep. I whistled again and tapped the side of the shed and he yawned and turned to me. He scrambled to his feet to bark but before he had the chance I reached in with a bag of leftovers: yesterday's blackened salmon. He stopped and sniffed and trotted towards me, as far as his chain would allow. He picked the salmon from my hand and carried it to his corner.

It was a tight squeeze through the missing-plank gap. The shed shuddered so much I thought it might collapse. Scraps tilted his head to watch me. I told him 'there-there'. I tickled his ear. He whined and carried on eating. The shed smelt of metal. The only light came from a shaft of moonlight, spilling through a gap in the ceiling. Various rusted garden tools hung from various nails, their shadows dancing up the walls.

We used to have a shed. Nan called it 'Herb's pigeon coop' but I never saw any pigeons (and besides the Herb I knew didn't go near the shed – he spent the whole time in his chair). I used to have nightmares about that shed – the webs in the corner, scattered with dead flies and egg sacs and **Them**. My father called it 'The Lair'.

Of course your shed was a lair too. I could feel **Them** – their many eyes watching from the top shelves, where the moonlight doesn't shine. But I concentrated on you. I sat on the tool chest by the window. I could hear **Them**, their usual whispers. I just ignored **Them**. The window was stained and murky but I could still make out the glow of your bedroom.

Scraps finished eating and lay beside me, head on my lap. He sniffed at my pocket. I apologised, I didn't have any more salmon. I imagined Scraps sitting there, every night, staring up at your room. I rubbed his head the way you did, dragging his eyelids back. I didn't rub his belly because it was all black and bruised.

There was a tool hanging by the window, the size and shape of a gun only with a cartridge at the bottom, packed with nails. I remember Miss Hayes once saying that a gun is an omen. If there's ever a gun somewhere in a story then by the end one of the characters will be dead. I don't know if this applies to nail guns. I unhooked the gun and held it on my lap. Your father lay, flat out, on his couch. His bottle slipped to the carpet, rocking in the cradle of his hand.

I wrapped my arm round Scraps, hugging his head to my chest. It's usually hard to see stars in the Pitt because of the light pollution but tonight it was so clear we could make out each and every one. I pointed them out to Scraps. His mouth opened and for a moment I thought he was awestruck but then he closed his eyes and sneezed on my hand.

We watched and waited. Your curtains remained shut. At one point I thought I saw a shadow pass over them but it didn't pass again. I thought Scraps might have kept me warm but he turned out to be even colder than I was. I'd have been better off hugging the tool chest. I began to tremble and eventually he stood and stumbled away, curling in the corner, just to get some rest.

When it reached 21:00 I hung the nail gun back in its place and crawled over to the plank gap. I promised Scraps I'd be back, I'd bring him more blackened salmon. When I reached the hedge I looked back one last time. Your father was spread across the floor in the lounge. His bottle had rolled to the other side of the room.

On the bus back I thought about your father. I thought about you, up in your room, waiting to make your escape. I thought about Finners Island. I'd always planned to live on Finners Island. I never thought what I'd actually do there — there are only six or seven people who live on the island and they all work for the National Trust. I don't think I'd be very good at working for the National Trust. You would — you like animals (well, you like Scraps). You could paint, too — there are plenty of picturesque landscapes. Perhaps I could work on the mainland. Become an English teacher. We could walk Scraps in the woods.

When I got home Mum was asleep on the lounge floor. I heard voices coming from Sarah's room. A girl said, 'You just need to curve your back more, pretend you're liquid.' Sarah said, 'OK.'

Sarah's door was ajar. I could see her reflection in the large ceiling-mirror, her and one of her Vulture friends. It could have been one of the Vultures from work, there's no way of knowing. They were both in their Dance Fantastical leotards, a violent glittering red against the orange of their skin. My sister reached for the remote. Music burst from the TV.

I stepped closer till I could make out the reflection of the screen. There was a music video playing. The singer was scrawny. Blond hair swayed around her body as she moved. It was that song again: 'Ooo you got me screamin' boy . . .' The singer's legs were sliding about in black latex trousers, skintight, glistening like oil. On the line, 'Butt in the air boy', she crawled onto her knees, sliding her rear up towards the camera. The air was warm and sweet like cherries.

The song finished. My sister and the Vulture were staring at me. My sister told me to get the fuck out of her room.

Miss Hayes has a new theory. She hasn't told me it yet, but she has a brand new set of questions, mostly about my relationship with my parents. She asked if I think I'm a good son. I didn't really know what to tell her. I don't smoke. On the other hand I don't do the washing-up (I'm too scared of breaking the china). I can't be a bad son because I don't really do anything. I'm a nothing son. It's like in Chemistry when we studied acids and alkalis, dipping those purple strips of litmus paper into beakers of vinegar and lemon juice to determine their pH level. I am the tap water. I am pH7. Neutral. I remain purple.

In the end I couldn't decide what to say and too much silence had passed to say anything, so I said nothing.

I didn't go to the bus stop afterwards. I couldn't face the ride without you so I just walked home. Mum was on the floor in the living room, reciting a shopping list she was writing in permanent marker on the back of an old *House Proud Magazine*. The list consisted of more salmon and more mango and more rice and more chipotle and more butternut squash and more of pretty much everything else needed for the Hamptons' meal. The big night's getting closer and not only is Mum's starter not quite perfect but the new couch still hasn't arrived. I'm not sure if Mum invites the Hamptons over because she's decorated or if she decorates because they're coming over. I don't think even she knows.

I didn't like the thought of Mum having to cart all that rice and mango and fish around Waitrose alone so I collected the reusable bags and waited in the car. I used to go shopping with Mum when I was little. We'd go to the outlet store. They had jars of mayonnaise the size of my head. I haven't gone with her the past few years because she always goes to Waitrose and it's so cold in Waitrose. It's like every aisle's the frozen aisle.

It was another ten minutes or so before Mum tottered across the driveway. Her heels caught in the cobbles and she had to keep reaching out to maintain her balance. Mum says a girl should always wear heels because she never knows who she might run into. (Mum can't run anywhere in heels.) I think Mum got a bit of a fright when she noticed me, sitting there in the passenger seat. She gave me a glance of The Eyebrow. 'No after-school classes tonight?' I shook my head. She sighed and pressed the start-engine button and Elvis swooned into life with 'Are You Lonesome Tonight?' Mum skipped to 'Suspicious Minds'. 'Suspicious Minds' is Mum's favourite. It's the only time I know for a fact that her smile's genuine – when

Elvis announces he's 'caught in a trap'. Halfway down the avenue Mum got all bouncy and turned the volume knob, round and round, again and again, even when it said VOLUME MAX. By the time we reached Derby Lane Elvis was roaring and Mum was singing along, aiming too high and holding the notes for as long as she could, which didn't really suit 'Suspicious Minds'. I'm not too big a fan of Elvis myself but I like his effect on Mum. Ken and Ursula listen to slow jazz covers of 'Singin' In The Rain' and 'Feeling Good'. They'd never listen to Elvis.

Waitrose is always the same level of busy: not very busy at all. Mum says that's why she likes it. She says high food prices are worth the exclusive shopping experience. This is why Mum hates the Waitrose Essentials range. She says Waitrose shouldn't down-market their produce to people who can't afford to shop there. My problem with the Waitrose Essentials range is that it includes stuff like couscous. I don't think couscous is very essential.

Mum set about replacing the food for her dinner party. Mum shops in the order in which her food will be served and a good dinner party always starts with nibbly bits, which are the far side of the shop. Salted chilli almonds, marinated onions, bean dip with crudités. Waitrose is nibbly-bit heaven. It has its own olive bar – tray after tray of rubbery black grapes that taste like the sea. Mum says appetisers are imperative. A guest should be greeted with something to eat so that they're not just standing there, having to talk to each other. Nibbles are foreplay.

Mum's starter is baked aubergine, stuffed with rice and blue cheese. Aubergines, rice and blue cheese are situated in different corners of the shop so Mum had to hurry back and forth between aisles, leaving little black heel-scrapes wherever she went. She was constantly mumbling but I was trailing behind with the trolley and couldn't hear what she was saying. By the time we reached the seafood counter Mum was out of breath. The fishmonger was nice enough to wait. Mum leant on the glass, gulping down that icy air, the fish glaring up at her, their mouths gaping. Eventually Mum coughed and sighed and smiled and said she would like the finest Scottish salmon the fishmonger had to offer, please. She said that the salmon needs to be the climax of her meal. It has to be perfection. Mum's favourite phrases are: 'Immaculate', 'Perfection' and 'Wow Factor'. The fishmonger was only a teenager and didn't really know how to reply. He just kept saying, 'It's good fish, this. It's fresh.'

Once the trolley was stacked with salmon we hurried over to the drinks corner. The floor of Waitrose's drinks corner is wooden to give it the look of an authentic wine cellar. Ursula Hampton only drinks champagne (other drinks give her heartburn) so Mum collected a few bottles and slotted them into the front of the trolley. Finally, the Hamptons are to be served coffee. Mum says a person's coffee tells you a lot about them. Mum has a large machine that grinds beans and froths cream. She polishes her cafetière daily. Waitrose has an unprecedented range of coffee: Brazilian Daterra, Colombian Supremo, Kenya AA, Kwonggi Mountain, Monsoon Malabar, Colombian Reserve, Sumatra Mandheling, Mocha Sidamo. Mum had to try and figure out which flavour of coffee was most appropriate. She kept muttering, 'I just don't know, I just don't know.' She lifted a packet of Colombian Supremo and sniffed it. She examined the description on the back.

I wished she would relax about the whole thing. I kept thinking about the Prancing Horse around the corner and wondering if they served cocktails and if they'd serve me. I wanted to ask Mum if she fancied a cocktail, to relax her. I know she prefers places in the city with leather seats and atmosphere but I thought I might as well ask. I didn't know what we'd talk about. I wasn't giving much thought to it at all, actually – my mind was full of Elvis. I just wanted to buy her a drink so she wouldn't go home and cook another blackened salmon, tottering around the kitchen in her heels, whilst all the time smiling and smiling. It must be exhausting. In my head I kept saying, 'Do you fancy a cocktail?' I thought, 'I'll say it on three,' and counted 'One' and counted 'Two'.

But then Mum dropped the Colombian Supremo and pushed the trolley into my stomach, forcing me back behind the bread stand. She shushed me, even though I wasn't saying anything. She peered around the corner. After a minute I peered too. Ursula Hampton was at the olive bar, a basket hung over her arm, spooning olives into a little plastic tub.

'I can't bump into her,' Mum said. 'Not like this.'

I couldn't work out why. Mum was wearing her heels and her hair and makeup were perfect. She looked beautiful. She kept repeating the word 'No,' over and over, under her breath. 'No, no, no, no, no.' Then she turned to me and said, 'Just promise me, if she sees us, just promise me you'll try and be normal.'

I didn't reply to that because I didn't know how to reply. I didn't know how I could promise something I had failed to do my whole life. Ursula flipped through a couple of magazines, then headed to the checkout. A man came up behind us wanting a baguette and Mum apologised and passed him the largest one she could find. We waited until Ursula was out into the car park before making our way to the tills.

At the checkout Mum's cards kept beeping. She kept rummaging in her bag for card after card, her protests quietening as the queue grew. In the end she split the bill over four cards and we left without looking back.

She didn't play any Elvis on the way home.

It's been a long day. I've spent the past ten minutes or so sitting here in the snow, trying to remember how exactly it all began, and it's just come to me. Of course: the Italian leather couch came. This morning was the last possible morning it could arrive in time for the Hamptons' meal. And this morning it arrived.

I waited until the van had rolled off down the avenue before I left my room. Mum was so excited she'd forgotten to pour the Colombian Supremo for the delivery guys and the cafetière was still steaming on the dining-room table. I headed straight to the front door but she rushed out of the living room, grinning and whispering to 'Come and see, come and see.'

The living room looks much smaller with the couch. It's a leather corner-suite. White. Mum kept stroking it with the tip of her finger. I know she wanted me to comment on its beauty, on how the white leather matched the white walls or something, but I don't know about that stuff and I can never think of what to say at the time. In the end I just nodded encouragingly. Then she got all serious and told me under no circumstances was I to sit on it. I nodded again and stepped out to the hallway. She didn't follow so I left for school.

First lesson was Geography. Ian and Goose were passing notes again, which is more geographically difficult than in English Lit., since Ian and I sit front left and Goose sits back right. It means that sometimes Goose's notes (which he scrunches into tight little balls) land in my collar or bounce off the back of my head. They were discussing Lucy Marlowe again. Goose's latest theory was that, after Ian had shown her the 'magic of sex', Lucy had realised how much she loved it. How much she needed it. He wrote that since Halloween she's been out every night picking up guys just to try and relive the experience. He wrote that she's now quit school to pursue a career as a prostitute.

Before Ian could respond the door opened at the back of the class and Lucy entered and Mr Cullman stopped explaining the possible outcomes of the collision of tectonic plates and just stared at her, every member of the class straining over their shoulders to join in with the staring. Lucy lingered in the doorway, one hand on her hip. Goose whistled. Lucy stepped past him to the front of the class and sat at the table alongside Ian. I didn't want to stare like everyone else because I know it's not nice being stared at, so I kept my head down. I just glanced up occasionally.

At first it seemed as if Lucy had stuffed two footballs down her blouse, but on closer inspection the tops of the footballs were bursting from the top of the blouse and they were clearly not footballs as they were covered with skin and frilled with the pink lace of a bra. Lucy kept her head up. She looked serious and sophisticated. After a minute Mr Cullman managed to look her in the eye. He muttered a welcome back and turned to the whiteboard.

Ian continued to stare. Eventually Lucy turned to him and said, 'Do you mind?' and Ian grinned in response, not looking up from her chest. She tried to carry on looking all pissed off and sophisticated but she couldn't help smirking. She took a deep breath and her chest swelled, almost bursting from her blouse. Ian let out a squeal of excitement. I felt sick, light-headed. I don't think Lucy's Mr Spock T-shirt would fit her any more.

After lunch was English. We were studying act three of *An Inspector Calls*, which is Miss Hayes' favourite part. Miss Hayes got excited reading it to us. She folded the book over, holding it with one hand so she could convey the words with the other. She circuited the room, stopping at her favourite passages to gauge our reaction. She adopted different voices for each of the characters. Ian and Goose were passing notes again but Miss Hayes just ignored them and concentrated on her reading.

I tried to concentrate on her reading too but it became hard not to glance at Ian and Goose's notes. They were still discussing Lucy. Goose asked if Ian'd had a go on her implants at lunch but Ian wrote back that she wouldn't let him because they were in school and if he got caught fondling they might get suspended. He could look at them as much as he wanted, though. He drew a picture of them. He wrote that after school he was going to Lucy's house and he was sure they'd get up to you-know-what and he'd have a proper go on them then.

Then Goose started drawing pictures. The pictures were of the possible scenarios you-know-what might entail. In most of them Lucy was bent over, screaming with her eyes closed while Ian stood behind her, a big smile on his face. I felt that pressure building inside me again. I tried to concentrate on picking my fingers. It takes a few days for the effects of T-Rex Bleach to show on my hands but when it does they're plagued. It's like picking glue except it stings, the skin underneath's so soft and pink and raw.

Then Goose's notes were about you. About how you've also been off the past couple of weeks. He thought maybe you'd gone in for surgery, too. He drew more pictures, this time with your screaming face. He even drew your sunglasses. Ian just replied 'Haha' but Goose carried on, note after note after note. My head ached. I picked and picked till my fingers bled, till my copy of *An Inspector Calls* was patterned with bloody prints.

The bell rang. Everyone hurried from class. Miss Hayes smiled over at me, as if she wanted one of our little chats, but I kept my head down and left. Goose and Ian set off over the field. Last period was P.S.H.E. but Ian and Goose never go to P.S.H.E., they always sneak off somewhere, usually with a couple of girls.

Lucy was waiting for them, over by the sandpit. When Ian saw her he ran and hoisted her into the air. She screamed and laughed and slapped his shoulders, shouting for him to be careful: 'They're still sensitive!' They sat together in the sand. Goose sat with them. They started kissing and Goose just sat there, watching.

I waited over by the bins. Eventually Ian leant over and whispered something to Goose and Goose nodded and stood and retreated to the hole in the hedge. By the time I crossed the field he'd disappeared onto the dual carriageway. Ian and Lucy were laid out, kissing in the sand.

It was 14:36. The dual carriageway was dull and empty. The sky was thick like cream. Goose was sitting on the wall of the canal bridge, his legs dangling over the edge. He was smoking a cigarette.

I put my hood up. I placed my hands in my coat pockets and crossed the carriageway. There was no wind but the air was very cold and each breath stung the hole in my tongue. I wrapped my coat as tightly as I could but the cold was somehow still seeping inside, clutching my bones and making me shiver. I tried to think of you, but all I could see was the version of you in Goose's drawings, bent over, screaming.

I reached the canal bridge. I could just make out the tapping of Goose's earphones. I gripped the insides of my pockets. My entire body was trembling. I thought any second he'd hear me, the slight swishing of my parka as I edged towards him, but he was too busy nodding his head to the music. There were strips of web hanging from his hair, clinging to his left shoulder, dancing in the air.

Whatever Goose was listening to was tap-tapping into some sort of climax. I took my hands from my pockets. My finger-tips ached in the cold. I leant forward, till I could feel the warmth of his fleece on my face, till I could smell the sour mix of sweat and cigarettes.

That's when I saw it: one of **Them**, emerging one leg at a time from the collar of his fleece. It wasn't a particularly large one – about the size of a two-pence piece, including leg-span – but I froze all the same as it scurried down his back. It drew to a stop between his shoulder blades, level with my face. The earphones ceased their tapping. There was a silence in the air.

It perched there, still for a second, before extending a leg out towards me.

I pressed my hands into Goose's back. The soft fleece burnt my stinging fingers. I half expected the fall to be in slow motion,

like a fall in a film, but Goose barely had time to lift his arms
before he hit the ice. The ducks scattered, squawking in alarm.
Goose's body lay there, arms spread, like he was making snow
angels. Blood veined from his mouth across the frozen canal.
The ducks watched him. I watched him. They moved in slowly,
pecking at his sides and his back. I breathed.

Then I ran. My feet were numb and ached in the cold but
I just kept on running. I must have kept running for nearly
an hour. There weren't many cars about and for a while I ran
right along the middle of the carriageway, but then the school
traffic started and I carried on along the pavement. I ignored
the pain of my breathing, the stitch in my side. I ran the bus
route, all the way down the Social De-cline. All the way out
to the Pitt. I needed to see you. I knew that once I did, everything would be OK.

By the time I reached the church it was starting to snow. I
leant against the wall, breathing deeply.

The sign said:

FORGIVE AS THE LORD FORGAVE YOU

I passed the Rat and Dog and turned, heading down towards
the park. I crossed over to your estate.

And then I stopped. Scraps was there. He was standing in
the middle of the road, sniffing at a pigeon that was spread

across the tarmac. He stared at me for a second, recognition in his eyes. He bounded over.

I knelt to him. We were both panting. He sniffed at my pocket, licked my hands. I told him I didn't have any salmon, sorry. I asked what he was doing out in the street.

Then I looked up and saw you, standing at the corner. I stepped back from Scraps. He woofed at me.

'There you are,' you said. You were talking to Scraps. He trotted over and you took hold of his collar and rubbed his head and told me you were sorry, glancing sideways through your red curling hair. You weren't wearing your sunglasses.

In my head I said, 'Say something, say something, say something,' but I didn't say anything.

Then you walked away. I thought maybe that was it. I was too scared to speak but inside I was aching for you to say something else, anything else.

You'd nearly reached the corner again when you stopped and turned to me.

You said, 'You're in my school, aren't you?' and I nodded and you smiled and said, 'I've seen you on the bus. You live round here?'

I nodded again. It's not lying, really, it was just nodding.

You asked my name and I told you.

You said, 'I'm Alice.'

I tried my best to think of what to say next but my mind

wasn't processing anything. The snow was getting thick. It gathered in your hair.

'Well, see you around.' You walked to the corner, holding Scraps by his collar. Scraps looked back over his shoulder a few seconds before turning back to you. I just stood there, watching through the snow.

At the corner you turned back one last time. You said, 'By the way, you shouldn't stand there.'

I swallowed.

'On three grids,' you said.

I looked down. You were right – I was standing on a set of three grids. I stepped off onto regular plain pavement.

'It's unlucky.'

DATE UNKNOWN

So Mum and my father and Ken Hampton and Ursula Hampton are sitting at the dining-room table with knives and forks and big white plates of blackened salmon and mango rice and chipotle-whatever-it's-called and they're smiling and there are trumpets sounding softly from over in the lounge and nobody's talking because everybody's politely waiting to see who'll be the first to take that first bite of delicious-looking salmon and Mum thinks but isn't sure that one of the Hamptons should be the first to take a bite because after all they're the guests but Ursula Hampton is sure that Mum should be the first to take a bite and 'lead the meal' because after all she's the host and the only sounds are the long swooping trumpet-notes as they glide from Mum's subwoofer in the lounge, past the vases of glittering black twigs and tall glass candlesticks supporting thick purple red-grape-scented candles to harmonise over the heads of the four diners, who still sit and still smile and still wait for someone to start eating and in the end it's Ken Hampton who takes the initiative and under the polite-smiling gaze of

126

the other three diners cuts a small slice of salmon and spreads it with mango rice and chipotle-whatever-it's-called until his fork is loaded with an even mixture of the textures and flavours compiled on his steaming plate, nodding in turn to each of the diners before raising his fork to his lips, however as he does so there's this small but audible clink, Ken's fork stopping dead before his face, Ken's red and bushy eyebrows crawling into a frown upon his forehead and as a third trumpet joins the two soft trumpets playing a slightly louder, slightly sadder note it becomes clear that although Ken's smiling lips have parted, his white wall of smiling teeth beneath have not and no matter how much Ken strains against the locked hinges of his jaw he cannot seem to part his teeth, cannot allow the blackened salmon and mango rice access to his mouth, cannot experience that smoky Mexican chipotle flavour, cannot do anything in fact but let the forkful of food slip back to his plate, splattering amongst his rice and splashing mango sauce up onto his salmon-pink shirt and by now several more trumpets have joined the increasingly sad trumpet music, this time playing even lower and more sustained notes, thick and deep like subtle but relentless foghorns and the focus of the diners has shifted to Ursula who's attempting to take some of the limelight off Ken by slicing into her own plate of blackened salmon and mango rice and chipotle-whatever-it's-called, delicately arranging a mixture of fish and rice on her fork before lifting it to her still-smiling lips, but as Ursula attempts to take a bite she too is met by a small but audible clink and she too finds her teeth unopenable and she too strains against her jaw-locked mouth but cannot get a single ounce of Mum's delicious-looking blackened salmon past her gleaming white teeth and so she too finds her forkful of salmon splashing back into the mango sauce, speckling the tablecloth with a scattering of sauce spots and so as the trumpet music squeals ever louder from the subwoofer speakers in the lounge the focus of the four smiling diners turns to Mum who, even through her beaming smile, is clearly so appalled and embarrassed at her disaster-of-a-dinner-party that she has no choice but to take control, to 'lead the meal', to politely smilingly dig into her own plate of blackened salmon, mango rice, chipotle-whatever-it's-called and show them how it's done but as Mum obligingly slices into the food on her plate it becomes pretty obvious before she even raises her fork that her chances of success are likely to be similar to Ken and Ursula's, that Mum is more than likely also going to suffer the inevitable clink, the inevitable jaw-lock, the inevitable slip-of-food-from-fork, yet still Mum persists, still raising her fork, still parting her lips, still trying her best to jab that fork through her still-sealed teeth and by now several more trumpets have joined the increasingly loud trumpet music, squealing chaotically and distorting harshly and far surpassing the appropriate volume for background music and my father is also trying to join in and eat some salmon and so now all four diners are attempting to open their jaws, to break past their smiles, to eat the food that Mum has spent so long preparing but no matter how much they fork, how desperate their eyes look, how many drips of sweat fleck the plates before them, they can't seem to manage to stop smiling long enough to get a single forkful of salmon into the warm wetness of their mouths and the trumpets are wailing now, sustaining unmatching notes for far longer than any trumpeter could possibly blow and the diners are practically stabbing the cutlery into their faces, my father resorting to holding his fork towards him like a samurai when they stab themselves in old movies and he's thrusting with all his might at his mouth and Ursula Hampton's hair has slipped down over her eyes and she is hack-hack-hacking away at her face until eventually she misses her teeth and hacks off a hunk of the side of her cheek and Mum is now trying to pry open her jaw with her stainless steel knife and Ursula's blood is staining the tablecloth and the jazz is building into a sort of swarming buzzing free-style-jazz frenzy and as Ken Hampton finally breaks through his two front teeth two long curling black legs begin to wriggle out through the gap and

II

It's official: Christmas is coming. Mum's decorations arrived this morning. We have two new artificial Christmas trees. Mum buys new trees every year. She says she can tell when a tree's spent eleven months in the loft.

Mum's down in the dining room, singing 'Suspicious Minds'. She got the call from the Hamptons yesterday: she and my father are invited to the New Year's bash. Mum's been singing Elvis non-stop all morning. Every so often she comes up to show me a new bauble or strip of tinsel or the various twinkle-settings of her White-Gold Icicle fairy lights. My father hasn't been home since Tuesday.

I feel better today but Mum won't let me out of bed. She says she wants me strong for work. She doesn't want to let Ken Hampton down. I doubt Ken Hampton would care if I wasn't strong for work (I've never even seen him set foot in the butcher's) but it's not bad spending a few days in bed. I haven't had to get dressed or eat at the dinner table. I haven't had to wade out through the snow to school. All I do is lie here, watching film after film from my Retro Hollywood video collection. This morning I watched *Breakfast at Tiffany's*. I snuck a box of Waitrose Maple Triple Nut Muesli up to my room and crunched my way through two hours of 1940s-New-York-related bliss. That final scene gets me every time: Holly and Fred and the little wet cat in the rain. Audrey Hepburn clutching the collar of George Peppard's coat. I think you're prettier than Audrey Hepburn.

Mum's spent the last few days looking for my window-key. She wants to air my room before the sick-smell contaminates the rest of the house. She says a house should smell like nothing but fresh air. It was fresh air made me sick in the first place. On Monday, after you spoke to me, I spent hours out in the cold. I was out in the Pitt all alone and I needed some time to think.

I thought about going to Nan's old house, on Kirk Lane, but sometimes my father goes there with his secretaries and in the end I decided against it. I walked to the church instead. I sat on the wall outside. I wrote in my journal. I watched the snow transform the Pitt around me, cars and walls and bins and cans and bottles becoming shapes, carpeted in white.

At one point a gang of kids emerged from the houses up the road, their upturned faces amber in the street lights. They set about building a snowman – some rolling the snow while others ran home to collect the facial fruits. They constructed it out on the corner, a mountain of a thing with two cooking apples for eyes. It was only when they'd finished that I realised the snow was covering me, gathering in my hair and the fur of my parka. I was becoming a snowman myself. I stood and shook off and one of the kids pointed and screamed and turned and ran and the others followed, disappearing into the ever-whitening Pitt.

I waded back to Skipdale. The snow was up to my knees. It twirled around me like leaves in a breeze. The cars on the dual carriageway were rolling along the same speed I was wading. I don't know what time it was when I arrived home. As I stepped into the hallway I heard mumbling voices, clinking cutlery, slow jazz. I heard the correctly pronounced 'ha-ha's in Ursula Hampton's laughter. I heard the door slip shut behind me. I heard the slow jazz end and the talking cease and then silence, real silence.

I swallowed and stepped into view. There they were: Ursula, Ken, my father, all perched in the candlelight with wide eyes and smiles and plates of blackened salmon. Mum had her back to me. She kept her head down. I was glad in a way because even if she'd turned I don't think I'd have been able to look her in the eye. The slow jazz started up again – a trumpet wailing.

Ken Hampton said my name. He said it as if it were a question, raising his eyebrows, closing the gap between them and his thick black hair. He was wearing a pink shirt, the three undone buttons causing it to clash with the fuzzy layer of orange on his chest. He said he didn't know I was joining them this evening and my father immediately said that I wasn't, that he thought I was at a friend's, why wasn't I at a friend's? My father's voice was loudening. This was a bad sign. He kept glancing at Mum, chewing the inside of his cheek.

'Beautiful night,' Ursula said. I nodded. I was still shivering from the wade back. The bottoms of my trousers were caked in snow. The smell of salmon churned my stomach. It dawned on me that my current symptoms – nausea, shivering, tight-locked jaw – were the same ones I get as a result of seeing one of **Them**. It further dawned on me that I had in fact seen one of **Them**, only a few hours earlier, creeping down the back of Goose's fleece and that I hadn't yet experienced any of the usual effects. I waited a few seconds, breathing deeply, staring at the floor, unsure whether to continue upstairs to my room.

Somebody spoke. At first the words didn't register and I glanced from face to face, waiting for whoever it was to repeat what they'd said. We'd entered into a conversation now and I knew I'd have to wait there, under the Hamptons' gaze. Wait until they deemed it fit to let me go, until they gave me the opportunity to run up to my pretty-much-impenetrable bedroom, to close my door and position my brown and green striped draught-excluder snake and crawl into my bed, safe and warm and alone.

It must have been Ken who'd spoken because he repeated his question. He asked how I was finding things at the butcher's. In my head I told him I hated it. I told him I didn't even need his money, that it was just building up in a video-case in my room. I told him, 'Shove your job up your ass.' The whole time I was in my head telling him these things there was slow jazz and smiling faces. Ursula sipped her champagne. My legs were trembling. I wasn't saying anything. I was just standing there not saying anything. Mum raised her hand to her forehead.

Then Ursula asked me how school was. I nodded an 'OK' and tried to smile but I couldn't tell if they even noticed my smile because they were all already smiling, even my father, who never smiles.

'He's doing very well at English, aren't you, Greg?' my father said.

Ursula Hampton repeated the word 'English' and asked if I wanted to be an English teacher when I grew up and I nodded again, like it was appropriate to just stand there and nod at everything they said, which, by the look on Ursula's face, it wasn't. Ken also nodded for a few seconds, his brow creasing into three distinct lines like the claw of some wild animal, whilst he thought of something else to say. He asked what I thought of the new couch. Ursula shot him a frown. She turned back to me and smiled.

'Lovely, isn't it?'

I wanted to say that I loved the couch. I wanted to say it was the most beautiful piece of furniture I'd ever seen, that it was even more white and pure and beautiful than the snow outside. I wanted to tell them about its Italian origins and how it complements the curtains and prove to Mum that all this time I have been listening, I've just never known how to reply. But I didn't. I just stood there wondering how long it would take them to notice my trembling legs. Wondering how I could leave without making things worse.

That's when I vomited. It started as a cough – it was only after three or four coughs that I could taste the thin, hot bile, a similar taste to mum's chipotle squash purée. From then on memories are vague. I remember sinking to the floor but that's when I must have blacked out because next thing Mum was kneeling over me, her nails scratching my neck in search of a pulse, probing my mouth to scoop out sick, pinching my skin as she struggled to lift me. I heard my father telling the Hamptons to sit, finish their meal. I heard him remark on the blackened salmon.

The voices faded. Mum carried me up to the bathroom. At the time I was certain it was you carrying me. Each time I opened my eyes I saw that image of you, out in the snowy street with Scraps by your side. I don't remember much of Mum undressing me, just the cold sting of bathroom tiles, the rumble of the bathtub filling with water, my head rocking as she peeled off my sick-covered trousers. I didn't regain full consciousness till I was in the bath and even then it came more as a slow realisation that I wasn't dreaming.

Mum was kneeling beside me, holding my head above the surface of the water. Her dress was wet, clinging to her arms and stomach. She wasn't smiling. I didn't know what to say so I just lay there, staring back at her. The water felt like a blanket. Sweat or steam gathered into a droplet at the end of my nose. I was very aware of being naked.

'I'm sorry,' I said.

Mum shushed me. She slicked my fringe out of my eyes.

She told me it'd all be OK.

I didn't let Ken Hampton down. I got up extra early and waded to work. It was easier wading in the road because the snow wasn't as deep but every so often a car would approach and I'd have to clamber back up onto the pavement. I don't think I stepped on any sets of three grids but it was impossible to be sure. I was eighteen minutes late. As I arrived your father cheered and called me a 'Snow Hero'.

I spent most of the morning making coffee. Phil's got a night job driving up to the woods in his brother's van to collect Christmas trees. He said that, what with the new baby, he's saving for the best Christmas ever. I made fresh coffee every half-hour, using twice the normal amount of granules, like my sister does when she wants to maintain her dancer's energy. I didn't want Phil to lose concentration and cut off one of his fingers.

The coffee-drinking played havoc with Phil's waterworks. He was rushing back every ten minutes to empty his bladder. The pipes had frozen and the toilet wouldn't flush, so all day the aroma of coffee and urine lingered in the back of the shop. Every time the Vultures came out for a bucket they'd frown their wrinkle-faces and Phil'd just laugh and say, 'Merry fucking Christmas.'

Eventually home time came. I'm meant to finish at 17:00 but I never get out till at least 17:15 because I have to wait in the safety and solitude of my kitchen until the Vultures (who also finish at 17:00) have vacated the premises. The Vultures take their time vacating the premises. Since Ken Hampton insisted every employee wear a black Hampton's Butcher's cap the Vultures have ended their Saturdays gathered in the cloak-room, trying to fix their hat-hair. They do this with a mixture of combing and spraying and applying metal clips. They like to talk about their night ahead: which bars they will go to, which songs they will dance to, which boys they will kiss. I stand in the kitchen and pretend to be mopping the long-since-clean 5ft^2 tile floor. Once I tried running the tap to drown out the Vultures' giggling but one of them appeared at the kitchen doorway and reached in and turned the tap off and said, 'Do you mind? We're trying to talk here,' so now I just stand there and wait for them to leave.

Once they'd gone I stepped out front for my wages. Your father and Phil were sitting on the counter. Your father asked if the cleaning was all done and I nodded. He said he had one more job for me.

He took me out the back to the car park. There was only one car – ploughed bonnet-deep in the snow. Your father said he'd had a little trouble getting into his usual parking space this morning. He grinned and handed me a shovel.

The snow had hardened to ice in the darkness. I hacked away, piling shovelful after shovelful by the bins in the alley. It was getting on for 17:30 and I knew I was no longer being paid but still I shovelled, all around the car and behind the four wheels. I even cleared a path to the street so your father could reverse out easily. My feet numbed and my hands stung and the ice lost all texture. I could hear your father and Phil, laughing inside.

It was just as I was finishing, hacking the snow out from under the exhaust, that I smashed a tail light. I don't know what happened, my arm just suddenly jerked. The force of it ached my hand (the palm's still sensitive from that cigarette burn). The bulb was bare and broken and there was red glass scattered over the ice. I considered running home, abandoning the snow and the shovel and the envelope with my wages that lay on the counter inside. I even dropped the shovel. Then I picked it up again. I buried the shards and went back inside.

The lights were off. Phil had gone. Your father was waiting in the darkness.

'All done?' he said.

I nodded.

He took the shovel and rested it in the corner with the brushes. He padlocked the back door and led me out into the shop. I stepped into the square and hugged my coat around myself.

He handed me my wages.

'See you next week.'

It's hard returning to school after an absence. It's only when I reappear that people realise I've been gone. People notice me. People talk.

There was more pressing news this morning, though. Cullman was off. According to the whispers of the Vultures in form, he's been suspended. Ian and Goose were also absent so I wasn't able to obtain any further details via their note-tennis.

At break I went to the library. As soon as I entered I knew something was different. It was the smell. There's normally that book smell of ink and dusty paper (which is what Miss Eleanor smells like too, I've noticed, when passing her in the corridor) but today the air was sweet and thick, like Mum's chipotle squash purée. Miss Eleanor was nowhere to be seen.

There was mumbling from the bookshelves at the back. I knew it'd more than likely be other pupils up to no good.

I'd half retreated to the door when I heard your laugh.

You were in the Fiction aisle. When I knelt I could see you, through a gap in the shelves, cross-legged in the corner by

Poetry. It's days since I've caught your bus, days without even a sight of you and now this – you – here in my library. I couldn't imagine what would happen if you saw me. Would you recognise me again? Would you speak to me? Your head was back as if in mid-yawn. Smoke rose from your mouth, a great curling mist of it, growing and gathering at the duct-taped fire alarm. Angela's head rested on your shoulder, glaring at the cigarette between your fingers.

'Holy shit,' she said.

You took another drag. The two of you began to giggle but I couldn't work out why.

Then came Ian's voice.

'My turn, ladies.'

I crawled along the aisle. Ian was over by the audiobooks, leaning back on his elbows, tie round his head, Rambo-style. Goose was beside him, grinning, waiting for his turn with the cigarette.

'Just a second, babe.'

Angela slid down into your lap for another drag. The tip flared in your sunglasses.

I huddled against the bookcase. I shut my eyes. I pictured Goose as I'd seen him last, laid out on the canal, ducks surrounding him on the ice. I felt the static of his fleece on my fingers. Now here he was, here in my library. Not a scratch on him. Grinning away without even a chipped tooth.

Here you all were, you and Goose and Ian and Angela, here in my library.

This is what happens when I don't see you. This is what always happens to pure perfect things, given time. Circumstances change. People change. The world moves on and I am left behind. I wanted to rewind to when it was just me and you, standing in the street. Me, you and Scraps, in the snow.

I tuned in and out of the conversation. You remained silent but Angela spoke of several things: the quality of the cigarette you were smoking, an upcoming party at Goose's, the Christmas Dance Fantastical. Angela ranted about Cullman. Apparently he's been suspended for having indecent images on his computer. Angela says the images were of Lucy Marlowe. She says Lucy sent pictures of her post-op breasts to Cullman in an effort to secure herself a place in the Fantastical. She said Lucy was a little bitch for trying to muscle in on her dance show. Now there are rumours the Fantastical's been suspended, that they may be reorganising it after Christmas. Whoever heard of a Christmas Dance Fantastical after Christmas?

Angela snorted. I turned back to the missing-book gap. She was kneeling on all fours in the aisle, her face twisted in a state of extreme silent laughter. She looked like Nan's cat Mr Saunders used to, coughing up a fur-ball.

Ian said, 'What?' He started laughing too. 'What?'

'It's just Cullman,' she panted between giggles, 'the old paedo. I can't believe he finally got caught!'

Angela dropped head first into Ian's lap. Ian took the opportunity to lift the cigarette from her fingers. He inhaled. You were slumped back against the bookcase, that smile still over your face. Goose shuffled over and sat beside you. He kept staring at you. You were wearing your sunglasses but I could tell from the tilt of your head you were sleeping.

'Fuck Lucy,' Ian said, letting the smoke crawl out with his speech. 'I don't even care about her and her tits. She never even let me touch them.' He held the cigarette out. Goose took it without shifting his gaze from you.

'Younger girls are more fun.' Ian lifted Angela's hand and kissed it like a gentleman.

'Is that right?' she said.

That's when Ian and Angela started kissing. I turned away again. All I could make out was the wet popping and peeling of lips. Angela moaned. The bookcase wobbled. A hardback of *Pride and Prejudice* tipped onto its side. The smoke was giving me a headache. I shut my eyes.

Then Angela said, 'I'm bored, let's go get some food,' and climbed to her feet. She must have used the bookshelf to balance because it wobbled again and this time *Pride and Prejudice* slipped from the shelf, landing corner first on my knee. I huddled up against the wall, over by History, trying to rub the pain away.

You appeared one by one, stumbling down the aisle to the fire escape. Ian was holding Angela's hand. Goose was holding yours. You spilt out through the doorway into the playground.

Your laughter grew quieter and quieter and quieter. Then it disappeared.

I waited in the library till the bell sounded. Then I went to English. Ian and Goose didn't show up. They must have stayed with you and Angela. Miss Hayes didn't show up either. The rest of us waited fifteen minutes, then left. The rule (for our year at least) is that if a teacher hasn't shown up for class within fifteen minutes, the class is allowed to leave. I'm pretty sure this is not an actual Skipdale High rule.

I went to Miss Hayes' office. The door was closed. I knocked but there was no answer. I checked the car park – her car was still there.

I went and knocked again.

'What?'

I told her it was me. I asked if I could come in. She didn't say no so after a few seconds I entered.

Miss Hayes was at her desk. Her mascara had run, gathering in the wrinkles under her eyes. I asked if she was OK but she didn't respond. I took my usual seat.

'What are you doing?' she said.

I told her I'd come for our meeting. I'd missed the last one because I was absent, I was sick, and for that I apologised.

Miss Hayes laughed. Not a proper laugh, just a single 'Ha'. She stared at her hands, one holding the other on her lap. She'd placed her engagement ring in the middle of the desk.

'I guess you've heard the rumours,' she said. 'You're here to see if they're true.'

I shook my head. I told Miss Hayes I had come for me. I needed her help. I asked if she had any new theories.

'What's the point?' she said. 'I'll sit here and try to help you and you'll sit there and won't say a word.'

I didn't know what to say to that so I just sat there and didn't say a word.

'Have you even read any of those books I lent you?'

I stared at her engagement ring.

'Thought not.'

I wanted to show Miss Hayes my journal. Show her how I've used it. Show her how it's so filled with words that the pages can't take it any more. Show her how the spine is so cracked and worn I have to hold it together with an elastic band. I wanted to explain that it didn't matter if I answered or not when she spoke to me, that it was OK for us to just sit in silence.

But I didn't say anything. I just stared at the desk.

'Just go away,' Miss Hayes said.

So I did.

This morning as I came down for breakfast Mum was kneeling on the dining-room window seat, splitting the blinds with her thumb and finger. She was shaking her head.

'Have you seen this?' she said. 'Have you seen it?'

I didn't need to split the blinds. Even through the frosted glass of the porch I could make out the outline of the seven-foot inflatable Father Christmas Artie Sampson had erected on his front path. It grinned proudly. It nodded in the breeze. I wondered how he'd get his car in and out of the garage.

'We all agreed,' Mum said, 'but he just couldn't stick to it, could he?'

Mum's Christmas light petition started in August. Everyone in the avenue agreed on the same White-Gold Icicle fairy lights with the same product number from the same catalogue, agreeing to hang them from the same points on the arch of their roof. Even Mrs Jenkins next door agreed. But Mum knew Artie Sampson was up to something. She knew it from his vacant smile when she showed him the pictures in the catalogue, from his assurance he'd remember the product number and didn't need to write it down. Mum had told him how she just wanted the avenue to look nice for the festive period and Artie Sampson had nodded and winked and said, 'Oh, don't worry, it will,' and Mum had just known he'd pull a stunt like this.

Mum finished her Christmas decorations last night. Our house is near enough a replica of the *House Proud Magazine* Christmas special. The magazine calls it 'modern-traditional' – traditional lights, garlands and presents juxtaposed with an enormous porcelain snowman and wire-figure nativity. In the centre of the lounge ceiling hangs an upside-down Christmas tree. Mum spent over an hour on the stepladder, gluing each decoration onto its PVC branches. She says it has Wow Factor.

Mrs Jenkins next door hasn't put her White-Gold Icicle lights up yet either. I was the only one dressed, so Mum sent me round this morning to see if she needed any help nailing them to her porch. There was no answer. She was probably in the loft. Mrs Jenkins spends days at a time up in the loft, playing the piano. Every so often, late at night, I can hear her, the tinkling of her piano keys. I knocked four or five times, then retreated down the path. Artie was standing on his doorstep with his wife, admiring the Father Christmas. He shouted over, 'Good morning!' then noticed Mum, kneeling there at the dining-room window and waved, gesturing at the inflatable figure on his path with a grinning thumbs up. Mum smiled and waved back. As I entered she turned from the window, rubbing the image from her eyes.

She frowned at the floor for a few seconds. Then she shook her head and said, 'It'll take more than Artie Sampson to ruin this Christmas,' and disappeared into the lounge.

I carried on through to the kitchen. Sarah was there. She was over by the cafetière. Normally Sarah won't leave her room till she's all made up and lacquered and squeezed into her uniform but this morning she was still in her dressing gown, hair tied back, face pale and clean. She looked like a child again.

I went to the cupboard for a bowl and began to fill it with Waitrose Maple Triple Nut Muesli. Sarah was getting her usual morning coffee-shot. She spooned some Colombian Supremo beans into a mug, waiting for the kettle to boil. Her eyes were narrow. There were a couple of angry spots on her forehead. The kettle clicked and she quarter-filled the mug, swilling the beans, softening them in the water. I offered the milk but she ignored me, draining the beans over the sink, knocking them back, chewing them noisily as she hurried upstairs.

I left my muesli and followed. Mum was in the living room, scrubbing at the couch. Her latest enemy is gravity, which was littering the white Italian leather with glitter and PVC pine needles, courtesy of the upside-down tree. She was too busy scrubbing to hear me tiptoe upstairs, to hear the creak of the floorboards as I knelt at Sarah's door.

Sarah was at her dressing table, frowning at her pale clean face. She reached for her vanity case and began dabbing foundation, powdering herself a blank canvas. I never thought Sarah'd be able to wear makeup. She got into Mum's blusher once, when we were little, and had to be rushed to A&E. It was her skin, she had a reaction. She was always having trouble with her skin. It was too dry. It was always peeling. The kids at school called her 'Flake'.

Dust was the problem, that's what the doctors said. Dust was the enemy. Dust made her scratch and when she scratched her skin it turned to dust. It was a vicious circle. Mum used to tell her off for scratching, used to make her wear oven mitts to bed, but there was no stopping her. I'd often hear her in the night, that sht-sht-sht of her little claws as she shed into her bedspread. I still remember the two of us, jumping up and down on her mattress, watching the particles of dust, Sarah's skin, dance in the sunlight around us.

That was before the time on Finners Island, before I moved to Nan's. When I came back there was a different Sarah, a popular Sarah, who wore makeup and danced on stage and was never called 'Flake' by anyone. I sat in the hall and watched her this morning. I had to see the transformation for myself, had to witness her paint herself into a woman again. Otherwise I'd never have believed it was the same girl.

TRANSCRIPT

Extract of interview between Detective
Sergeant Terrence Mansell (TM) and Gregory
Hall's sister, Miss Sarah Hall (SH).

TM: I promise this won't take long.

SH: That's OK.

TM: I just need to talk. About what's gone on
   with your brother.

SH: I figured.

TM: How are you dealing with everything?

[SH shrugs shoulders.]

SH: OK, I guess.

TM: OK?

SH: I mean, I don't know. I suppose. What do
   you want me to say?

TM: Just the truth.

SH: Well, Mum's having another breakdown.

Everyone at school now hates me, so there's that.

TM: Because of Greg?

SH: They call me 'Psycho Sister'.

TM: Nice.

SH: This girl in my year, Angela, she came over and spat on me the other day. Actually spat on me. On my neck.

TM: Kids can be . . . you know.

SH: Yeah.

TM: I guess you're right then. 'OK' probably is the best word. 'OK' under some very difficult circumstances.

SH: Right.

TM: Have you seen Greg at all?

[SH shakes head.]

TM: You don't want to?

[SH shrugs shoulders.]

TM: What's your relationship like?

SH: With Greg?

TM: Yeah.

SH: Well, he's my brother.

TM: And?

SH: That's about it, I guess.

TM: You aren't close?

SH: He's a bit strange. Like, creepy. I mean,
he can't help it, it's not his fault. It's
just the way he is. He never says much.
He's always just there, lingering.

TM: I believe you lived apart when you were
younger?

SH: He lived at Nan's.

TM: So you didn't see each other much?

SH: Mum wouldn't let us. She went over to see
him at weekends but she never let me go
with her. She said it was because of the
cat. I had eczema. She said the cat was bad
for my skin.

TM: You didn't believe her?

SH: Well, that never explained why Greg
couldn't come here, did it?

TM: I guess not.

SH: It never explained why we'd have to go on
separate days out. Why we never went on
holiday any more. Why, during the odd time we
were together, like Christmas or my birthday,
she'd sit us at opposite ends of the table.
Like, what, he had too many cat hairs on
him? Like, they couldn't just brush him off

or something? I mean, I was allowed to go to Nan's for New Year's, to watch the fireworks. But even then I'd sit one end of the kitchen and he'd sit the other. Everyone just acted as though it was, you know, normal.

TM: Why do you think she wanted to keep you apart?

SH: Because of how he was. Because of the whole Finners Island thing. Although if you mention that to Mum, it's like there's no such place. She's so fucking repressed.

TM: Enlighten me, what's 'the whole Finners Island thing'?

SH: Some place we used to go when we were little. I can't really remember.

TM: But something happened there? There was an . . . incident?

SH: I think I was like eight or something. I remember I wanted to go in a boat, but they wouldn't let me in the boat. And then Greg took me out in the boat. I don't remember much after that, just being in hospital.

TM: And that's when Greg moved away?

SH: Yeah. Suddenly it was like, 'Oh, he's just going to Nan's for a bit'. And then, 'Oh, they're having so much fun he's going to stay'. And then, five years later, when Nan went cuckoo, when she had to go in a home, it was like, 'OK, well look who's back'.

TM: Was that strange, having him back?

SH: Well, yeah. It was weird. Because I'd still seen him, every so often, but then suddenly he was there, like, all the time. Like I said, lingering.

TM: You'd prefer he hadn't come back?

SH: No. I wouldn't say that. I mean, he's my brother. I just don't know him. And he never, you know, tried to get to know me either. We just steered clear of each other, when he came back. We were used to steering clear of each other.

TM: What about when he went missing?

SH: What about it?

TM: How did you feel?

SH: Well, I saw him. You know, that night? At the party? I was the last one to see him.

TM: This is the Wallaby Drive party? The Lambert house?

SH: Right. So I told Mum and Dad and they were all like, 'What? A party?' And I was like, 'Yeah'. I actually thought it was pretty cool he came to the party. I mean, I never thought he would. It took some balls, with his reputation.

TM: What time did he get there?

SH: It was about eleven when I saw him, I think.

TM: And how was he?

SH: Alone, as usual. He said he was looking for someone. I think we can all guess who that was. And he was drunk, I think. They made a big deal about that. The drinking. Because he's not meant to drink, you know, on his meds. But I didn't think it could hurt. I mean, he's got to get drunk sometime, right? He's a teenager, for god's sake. That's what he's supposed to do.

TM: Did you speak to him at the party?

SH: I told him to go home. I felt bad about that afterwards, but what was I supposed to do? I thought he was going to get himself beaten up.

TM: And that was the last you saw of him?

SH: Yeah.

TM: You didn't see him take the knife?

SH: I didn't see him take anything.

TM: And what about the accusations?

SH: What about them?

TM: Do you think he's guilty?

SH: No.

TM: How come?

SH: Well, I mean, I guess he is. But not like properly guilty. It's a disease, right? How can he be guilty of a disease? If you're looking for someone to blame, you should blame us.

TM: 'Us'?

SH: All of us. We should have been keeping an eye on him. We should have been dealing with it. Instead we were ignoring him. Hoping it'd all just go away. That's what I was doing, at the party.

TM: It's wrong to blame yourself.

SH: Yeah, right.

TM: I'm serious.

SH: Well I blame the disease, then. I blame the pills. Whatever.

TM: Just don't blame yourself. You're too young for that kind of guilt. It eats you up, that kind of guilt.

SH: Right.

TM: You've done nothing wrong.

SH: Whatever.

TM: I promise.

SH: Can I go now?

I haven't been to the library since Monday. At breaks I sit on the steps behind the technology block. I ball into my warm-position. Nobody ever goes back there.

Today I watched the rain out over the field, dissolving the last of the snow. My mind must have wandered because I didn't hear the bell and ended up late to third lesson.

Third lesson was also last lesson, with it being the last day of term. We had English Lit. As I arrived Miss Hayes was waiting in the corridor. She was soaked from the rain, her bra showing through her blouse again. She told me she was sorry for being so rude the other day. She said I could stay behind after English, we could talk. I nodded. She clutched my arm. Her hand was cold and wet and she was wearing her engagement ring and it had turned on her finger so its diamond stabbed into my wrist. She told me she really was sorry. I nodded again, then pulled away and hurried inside.

The class silenced as I entered. They watched me cross the room to my desk at the back. Only half of them were present

– a typical turnout for the last day of term. Most had abandoned the seating plan and were sitting with friends. A gang of Vultures were gathered in the corner: Lucy Marlowe, Carly Meadows, a few others. They'd formed a circle with their chairs and were whispering amongst themselves.

Miss Hayes kept her head down as she entered. She avoided eye contact with Lucy and the Vultures. She also avoided my corner – she was probably scared of seeing Ian and Goose there, grinning from the back of the room, but they never come in for half-days. I took my copy of *An Inspector Calls* from my bag. Nobody else had taken their copy of *An Inspector Calls* from their bags except for Eggy and Dan Bradey. Eggy and Dan Bradey always have their copies of *An Inspector Calls* out well in advance so they can get a head start with the reading. They like to make notes and ask Miss Hayes questions about Priestley's socialist principles. They're going to Oxbridge.

Miss Hayes sat at her desk. She glanced over at the door, or perhaps the clock above it, awaiting any latecomers. By 11:30 no one else had arrived so she began to read.

Miss Hayes was quiet today. She stumbled on words and had to repeat them. She kept her eyes on the page, not once adopting any character voices. There were twenty pages remaining of *An Inspector Calls*. We'd reached the climax, where Inspector Goole shouts at all the other characters for being so nasty to Eva Smith. On paper the speech is strong and passionate and Miss Hayes' mumbling didn't really do it justice. Most of the class were sleeping or watching raindrops snake the windows. Sam Johnson was picking shards of soil from his trousers. The Vultures were whispering in their corner. The only people paying attention were Eggy and Dan Bradey.

I tried to concentrate on *An Inspector Calls* but my mind kept drifting. I kept thinking of you, that image of you, cross-legged in the library with Goose and Ian and Angela. I tried to remember happier times – our bus rides, under the bridge, the time you spoke to me in the street – but all I saw was Goose, leering at you in the Poetry aisle. The flare of your cigarette in vinyl-black lenses. Ian and Angela's wet-sucking kisses. Miss Hayes' voice was breaking. I glanced up at first but soon learnt to keep my head down. I couldn't stand it, watching her. Her hair was still wet and it might have just been the rainwater lining her face, but it looked like she was crying. Carly Meadows soon noticed and muttered to the other Vultures. Lucy snorted, stifling a laugh. Miss Hayes just ignored them, carried on reading.

I followed her reading in my book. I underlined each word with my finger as she read it. I thought that maybe if I showed Miss Hayes how much I was concentrating, she'd realise that she was doing a good job and become a more confident reader. It was just as Goole's speech was ending, just as she stopped to turn the page, that I glanced up at Miss Hayes again and noticed one of **Them**, at the front of the class, descending from the ceiling above her.

I haven't had many attacks at school. There was the time in P.E. with the one of **Them** in my trainer and the time I felt a web brush my face in the stationery cupboard but apart from that school's been relatively fit-free. In the winter they tend to inhabit warm places (i.e. the Great Influx) and – with its high ceilings and un-double-glazed windows and constantly left-open double doors – Skipdale High isn't exactly warm.

Today was different. Today one had crept into English Lit and was hanging there, right at the front of the class. At first I didn't know how to react. It was so out of place, so alien, dangling there over Miss Hayes. It was its blackness that struck me – maybe it was just the contrast between it and the white-board behind it, but its blackness was almost a void, like a hole in the fabric of reality. The Vultures were still giggling in their corner. Sam Johnson was still de-soiling his trousers. Even Eggy and Dan Brady – who were both staring right at Miss Hayes, so it was clearly in their sightline – just carried on jotting notes in their copies of *An Inspector Calls*.

Miss Hayes kept on reading. Her words were just noise now, a slow hum to accompany the descent. Little by little it closed the gap between itself and her head. It drew to a stop, inches above her. It hung there for a second, rocking in the breeze, front legs twitching in anticipation. Then it dropped into her hair.

My fits tend to come in stages. First my body seizes up. The term 'frozen to the spot' is pretty accurate because the seizing has a coldness to it, as well as a prickliness that gathers at the base of my spine. Sound fades. Blood pulses. My head aches. It's often worse when I can't actually see the one of **Them**, when the one of **Them** is there one minute, then suddenly hidden from view. Like the one in Miss Hayes' hair.

I tried to fix my mind on the play but by then my copy of *An Inspector Calls* was shaking violently. I shut my eyes. I breathed. I followed Miss Hayes' words in my head. Word after word after word. The only other sounds were the hiss of the rain, the Vultures' occasional giggling. Then Miss Hayes stopped to clear her throat and I couldn't help but glance up at her again, couldn't help but notice it, creeping out across her forehead.

That's when Lucy and Carly Meadows turned to glare at me. Carly muttered something to Lucy and Lucy snorted and I realised I'd clenched my fists, ripping a handful of pages from my copy of *An Inspector Calls*. My breathing was fast and probably loud. I dropped the book and clutched the sides of my desk. Each time I closed my eyes I kept seeing you, sitting in the poetry aisle with Goose, only now it was Goose kissing you. Now it was yours and Goose's lips, popping and peeling. The one of **Them** crawled further down Miss Hayes' forehead. It slowed, struggling to clamber over her eyelashes before scurrying down the left side of her nose. The desk rattled from my trembling. Others were turning. Sam Johnson abandoned his mission to de-mud his trousers and just glared at me. Even Eggy and Dan Brady glanced over, muttering to each other, tutting. Miss Hayes just kept reading, reading and reading and reading, all those words that had long since lost all meaning, as it sat there, balanced upon her lip, bouncing to the rhythm of her speech. She stopped to turn the page and it finally disappeared, slipping out of sight into her open mouth.

I must have toppled my desk when I bolted because there was a sudden scraping and a clattering and my copy of *An Inspector Calls* skated out across the classroom floor. Somebody laughed. One of the Vultures screeched the word 'Psycho'. I ran down the echoing corridor of the Lipton Building. I ran out across the field. I kept running, through the gap in the hedge and up the dual carriageway. The rain fell in sheets, drowning the world around me. A river cascaded the pavement. When I reached the relative dryness of the bus stop I just sat, hugging myself into my warm-position.

I threw up. It was phlegm, mostly, plus a couple of raisins from breakfast. I felt better after that. I sat, shivered, watched the rain wash the phlegm away. The whole time I sat there I half expected to see Miss Hayes, skittering up the carriageway after me. But she never came.

At 12:02 the bus pulled up and I climbed on board. I took my seat at the back. I concentrated on the view, the rainy blur of the Social De-cline, the ever-rusting bridges that pre-empt the Pitt.

The church sign said:

WHAT IS MISSING FROM 'CH CH'?
U R

I got off at our usual stop. By then the rain had slowed to a spit. There was a mound of snow still out on the corner by the church, an apple rotting on the pavement. The remains of the Pitt kids' mountain of a snowman.

I hurried round to the park. I crossed the field to the houses at the back. I just needed to see you. Alone. Without Goose and Ian and Angela. I needed it to be just the two of us. Like before.

I counted the gardens till I reached yours. I was halfway through the hedge when a shout came from the play area. It didn't sound like any human shout – more like the angered cry of some prehistoric animal. I turned back to the field.

There was a gang of four Pitt kids perched on the bars of the climbing frame, glaring over at me from under their hoods. It reminded me of that scene from *The Birds*, where Melanie Daniels turns and sees all those crows gaping down at her.

Then, one by one, they slid from the bars, crossing the park towards me.

The leader was your brother. I could tell from that walk of his – the way he bows his head, fixes his glare, lets his arms just hang there by his sides. I should have run as soon as I saw him, I realised that, but in no time he and his friends had surrounded me and it was clear I was going nowhere.

I'd interrupted your brother mid-smoke and for a minute he just stood there, savouring the last few drags of his cigarette. The other Pitt kids waited either side, grinning to each other. One of them tossed a football from one hand to the other. Your brother flicked his cigarette into the hedge and bent down to exhale in my face. His deodorant was strong, sour in my throat.

'What do you think you're doing?'

It seemed a strange question at the time. My mind had blanked and I didn't really know what I was doing. I was in class listening to Miss Hayes reading and then suddenly I was out in the Pitt. There was no logical explanation. All I could do was stand there, trying to mouth words, but what those words were I've no idea. The other Pitt kids were still grinning but your brother's face seemed locked into a frown.

'I'll ask again,' he said, slowly. 'What the fuck are you doing sniffing round my garden?'

His eyes bore into me, the same glittering blue as yours. I

tried to concentrate on my breathing, the trembling in my ever-weakening legs. All I could think about was the time with the Tango. I'd have loved for one of them to pour Tango over me. I kept thinking 'Just pour Tango over me and leave. Just pour Tango on me and leave.'

Your brother turned to one of the Pitt kids, the one with the football. He muttered something into his ear. The Pitt kid laughed and nodded. Your brother turned back to me.

He smiled.

He lifted his hand from the pocket of his hoodie. I expected a knife or a broken bottle but there were only his fingers. His hand was bunched into a fist with his index and his middle finger pointing towards me like a gun. He turned his hand and spread the fingers into a V, so he was swearing at me. His mates giggled. My stomach quaked. Maybe that was it – he was just going to swear at me. All things considered it wasn't that bad.

Then he pressed his fingers into my eyes. I backed as far as I could into the hedge, so far that the branches were stabbing into my neck, but your brother just kept on pushing. Deeper and deeper and deeper and deeper. He hooked his thumb under my chin, grasping my head like a bowling ball.

At first the pain was sharp and stinging but the longer and harder he forced his fingers the more it swelled into a deep, brain-splitting ache. I clutched the branches of the hedge, thorny against my palms. The soft skin of my burn-wound throbbed. The warm wetness of what I hoped were tears ran down my cheeks.

The Pitt kids laughed.

Somewhere a dog barked.

Your brother hissed into my ear. I can't remember the exact words but it was the usual kind of stuff. He called me a psycho and told me I shouldn't be snooping round people's gardens and said that if I ever came back he'd more than blind me. He pressed harder and harder, in keeping with the rage in his voice. A pressure built in my forehead. Any moment my eyes would burst like ripe tomatoes. His fingers would split through into my skull.

Such is the danger of being noticed. I should have checked the field first. It was stupid not to. I would pay for my stupidity. Your brother would blind me, out in Crossgrove Park, the park I used to play in as a child. The park Nan used to take me to, to look for conkers. He would blind me and I would never see your face again. This is what I thought as I sank down into your hedge.

Only then, a voice came. It said, 'What do you think you're doing?' just like your brother's had, only softer. And I knew instantly it was you.

The pressure eased then, the fingers withdrew. I slipped down to the ground. I pressed the heels of my hands into my eyes, trying to rub out the pain. All I could see were purple and yellow shapes, swooping and popping like fireworks. I really wanted to get up and look like I was OK. But I wasn't OK.

You told your brother to leave me alone.

Laughter.

You said, 'I mean it, Sean.' You talked about whiskey, about how your brother had taken some from the shed, how you'd tell your father. You said you'd tell him about the smoking, too.

'You know what he'll do if he finds you've been smoking.'

Seconds passed. Raindrops rattled in the hedge around me.

The warmth of your brother at my cheek:

'Next time, mate . . .'

And then he was gone. The patting of feet grew distant over the field. All that remained was clean cold air.

'You OK?' you said.

I nodded. It was hard to tell how powerful a nod without being able to see. I added a 'Yes.'

'I don't think you are.'

I tried to stand up but it was hard to know which way up was, I had no idea which direction I was facing. I clutched the hedge for support but its leaves were wet and I slipped and scratched my face on a branch.

'You're definitely not OK,' you said. 'Come here.'

Your hands were small and cold in mine. You were stronger

than I expected – in seconds I was hoisted from the hedge, dragged forward till my feet found the ground. I brushed the leaves from my hair.

'It's me, Alice,' you said. 'We've met before. Remember?'

I nodded, this time it was a big nod, to be sure you saw it. My legs were still shaking. Traffic hummed from the dual carriageway in the distance. It couldn't be real. You couldn't be there, before me. I decided I wouldn't believe it till I'd seen it, till I'd seen you. I tried to open my eyes but everything was a bright blinding white.

'Come on.' You took hold of the sleeve of my coat. You dragged me out across the field. You must have been running because I stumbled to keep up. The grass was boggy and soon my socks were soaked. Somewhere along the way I'd lost my school bag, but it didn't seem to matter.

We stopped. Your hands pressed into my shoulders. You told me to sit. You guided me onto a hard, swaying seat. When I lifted my hands and found the chains I realised it was a swing. We'd reached the play area.

'Just sit here a minute,' you said.

'I'm blind,' I said.

'You're not blind,' you said, 'trust me. Just give it a minute.'

I gave it a minute. The rain had stopped. Somewhere to my right there was a panting sound.

'How many fingers am I holding up?'

I opened my eyes. The world was still a flash of stinging white.

'Three?'

'No. You're right. You must be blind.'

I couldn't see if you were smiling. I lowered my hands to my lap. Something warm slid over my fingers. I jerked.

'That's just Scraps,' you said. 'He's harmless.'

I reached and found Scraps' head. I could feel every notch and socket of his skull. You told me that he doesn't usually like strangers. I must be special. I waited another couple of minutes before opening my eyes again. This time the grass and the sky and the rows of houses were there, only caught in a bright swirling mass of colour.

I shut my eyes again.

'Better?'

I nodded.

I waited another few minutes. I could smell smoke, that sweet chipotle smoke I'd smelt in the library. You must have seen me sniffing because all of a sudden you said, 'Do you want some?' Before I'd even had a chance to say, 'No thank you,' the paper tip of a cigarette was stuck to my lips and you were saying, 'Go on, just try it – breathe it in – it'll relax you.' So I did. I took a short sharp mouthful. It caught in my throat and I coughed, so much I nearly lost my balance. I had to clutch the chains of the swing.

You snorted, trying to hide your laughter.

'Try again.'

This time I inhaled slowly. You said to hold the smoke in my chest. As I breathed out I felt a lightness crawl up through me. I opened my eyes. I could see the outline of the world around us – the park, the houses, the slide. You. The sky was bright and at first I had to squint. You said, 'Here,' and slid your sunglasses over my eyes. The world was tinted pink but it was there and in its right place and so were you, smiling from the swing beside me. You were wearing that coat you sometimes wear for school, the one with the red fur trim. You were squinting now. I realised what it was then, from that close up, what was so strange about your un-sunglassed eyes. I noticed for the first time that you don't have any eyelashes.

You lifted the cigarette to your mouth.

'Look,' you murmured. 'You're meant to hold it in your lungs. Right? I'll show you the proper way. You ready?'

You placed the cigarette to your lips and closed your eyes. The end flared, your neck flexed. You opened your mouth into an O. The faintest wisp of smoke spilt out into the air, just for a second, before you sucked it back down inside. And then time stopped. You froze. You didn't breathe. Your mouth remained O. Your eyes were shut, so pale and naked without their lashes. Slowly smoke reappeared, crawling from inside you, out into the air around us.

175

You smiled.

'See?'

I scanned the park. You told me to relax. You said your brother's an asshole, he'd be off playing on the railway line by now. My coat-sleeve was muddy and my hands were scratched from the hedge. My palm was bleeding again, that burn from your cigarette that just won't heal. I was shivering. Scraps bounded off across the field, chasing a flock of pigeons. They scattered into the air.

You passed me the cigarette and I took a drag. It was easier the second time but there was no way I could hold it inside for as long as you had. After less than a second it all came spluttering out.

I remembered I was still wearing your sunglasses and apologised and passed them to you. You slipped them on.

You said, 'You probably think it's pretty weird, me always wearing these . . .'

I shook my head.

'Everyone does. They call me "Miss Cool".'

'You look like Audrey Hepburn,' I said, 'in *Breakfast at Tiffany's*.'

You said you hadn't seen it.

'You have to.'

But by then you'd stopped listening. You were frowning. I couldn't tell what you were frowning at because you were wearing your sunglasses. You leant forward, towards me. You reached for my eyes, just as your brother had, only this time I didn't flinch or back away. I pressed my feet into the grass to stop the rocking of the swing. You stroked the underside of my eyelid and gently withdrew your hand. There was a single eyelash curled over your fingertip.

You held it out to me.

'Make a wish,' you said.

I didn't know what you were saying. I was too busy staring, my reflection staring back from the lenses of your sunglasses. You were still frowning.

'You have to blow and make a wish,' you said. 'Each of your eyelashes is a wish. Don't you know that?'

So I did as you said. I closed my eyes and blew and when I opened them again your finger was bare. You put your hand back into your pocket. You turned from my gaze to scan the park, the backs of the houses.

You turned back to me, frowning again.

'I have to go.'

You picked up your bag and stood from the swing.

'Oh,' I said.

'I'll see you around.'

You hurried across the field to your house, your feet patting the wet grass. You reached the hedge and called out to Scraps before disappearing down the side of the shed. Scraps glanced back once and followed. I kept waiting for you to look back but you didn't.

I stubbed the cigarette out and stood to leave. It was only then that I noticed your father, staring down from your bedroom window.

DATE UNKNOWN

So its the middle of the night and Im huddled in bed and from the weight of my head Im certain Im sleeping when suddenly a sound like taptaptap comes from the glass of my fireescape window and at first I try to ignore the sound try to keep my eyes shut try to pretend Im asleep but as the sound persists I cant help but wake cant help but sit up cant help but notice you out in the darkness your palm against the glass your breath white and shivering in the silver glaze of moonlight and at first Im confused and a little scared because it can be a little scary and confusing to wake in the night with someones face at the window but as you raise your hand and tap once more and fix those wideblue eyes upon me all my fear and confusion subsides and turns within my stomach and I see that smile that smile and all I want is to let you in to peel back that wall of doubleglazed glass between us and admit you into the safety of my room into the softwarmness of my bed however as I reach for my fireescape windowhandle I find the windowhandle hard and immovable and my fireescape window fixed and unopenable and lockeduptight and of course my fireescape window is lockeduptight my fireescape window has been lockeduptight for years my fireescape window has been locked-uptight ever since that incident with the paragliding oneof**THEM** and so as I scramble out of bed to my videoshelf to retrieve the windowkey from my *Brief Encounter* videocase to peel back the wall of doubleglazed glass between us and admit you into the softwarmness of my bed you can imagine my shock and horror to find the videocase completely sealed in a prettymuchimpenetrable layer of crinkled brown parceltape my frustration when I cant seem to be able find any kind of seam from which I can peel back the parceltape my despera-tion as the taptaptapping resumes and I glance up and see you there still with those eyes fixed upon mine still with that smile that smile and all I can do is tell you that Im sorry Im sorry but not to worry not to worry Ill soon have the videocase open Ill soon have the windowkey Ill soon peel back that wall of doubleglazed glass between us and admit you into the soft-warmness of my bed and everything will be OK everything will be OK everythingwillbeOK but to be honest Im not entirely sure everything will be OK in fact Im not entirely sure you can even hear me because afterall the windows doubleglazed and Im speaking fairly quietly so as not to wake any of my family and your face isnt showing any sign of having heard me and is still fixed in that same vacant smile and small white flakes of snow are now drifting through the darkness settling on your hair your dressing gown the black rubber toes of your Wellington boots and youre shivering and still tapping at the window still waving and so when I do finally discover a seam in the parceltape seal of the *Brief Encounter* videocase you can imagine my relief as well as my urgency and frustration when I set about peeling and peeling and peelingpeelingpeeling only to find that there seems to be no end to the parceltape that no matter how much I peel the parceltape just keeps on going on and on layer after layer like some kind of passtheparcel parceltape nightmare gathering in reams like an enormous parceltape snake coiled on my prettymuchimpenetrable bedroom floor and so as another taptaptap comes from the glass of my fireescape window I glance up and see that the snows coming down heavy now your shivering growing into a shaking and all I want with every ounce of my soul is to unlock that window to peel back the glass to let the ovenwarmth of my bedroom settle upon you to hold and hold and hold you in the softwarmness of my bed but no matter how much parceltape I tear from my *Brief Encounter* videocase I just cant seem to get inside to that key that tiny bit of metal Ive kept hidden away for so long without ever thinking it would be so important and unobtainable and Im clawing at the parceltape now and biting at it and Im sweating and my hands are sticking to the hot wet plastic and your shaking is growing into more of a rattling and your taptaptapping more of a knockknock-knocking on account of the layer of ice thats hardened over your knuckles and each time I look up at your everwhitening face youre still smiling with those everwhitening lips that smile that smile that smile and Im screaming now screaming for help from anyone who can help but theres not a sight nor sound from the rest of my family and Im trying to get the box open really I am but I cant get the box open I cant get it open and your face is frosting over like one of the pig heads in Hamptons freezer and Im smashing the *Brief Encounter* videocase against my videoshelf and Im hurling the case to the ground and stamping on it and Im on my knees clawing at it and finally as I claw through the plastic your banging halts your skin white as snow your hair frozen into solid curls of ice and as I tear back the broken box with my hot and bleeding fingers all I find is **THEM** hundreds of **THEM** thousands of **THEM** spilling from the shattered shards of plastic wriggling through my fingers spreading across my bedroom floor and

The shop was empty when I arrived. Charlie and the Vultures don't get there till 08:30 but your father and Phil are usually at their block first thing, slicing steaks for the counter. I checked the kitchen, the toilet, even the freezer at the back but there was no sign of anybody.

My first job was to empty last night's fat from the chicken oven. I dragged out the fat-tray, scraped the contents into the green plastic bucket and hauled it out the back to the bins. There was Phil, sitting on the steps in the alley, smoking, counting a wad of £20 notes. He scrambled to his feet, forcing the wad down the front of his jeans. He laughed when he realised it was me.

'Gave me a heart attack.'

I lifted the lid off the fat-bin. Phil said your father had gone to the abattoir to pick up the Christmas turkeys. I tipped the bucket. I had to turn from the smell as the fat glugged out, slapping and spreading a new surface. Phil scratched his neck. He glanced over at the empty car park. He kept one hand on the buckle at the front of his jeans.

'Do you know what happens to that?' He nodded at the fat.

I glanced into the bin, then back to Phil. I shook my head.

'It's taken to the rendering plant,' he said, 'recycled. Used in glue and chemicals and stuff. Makeup, too. That's why when your bird wakes up in the morning she's always covered in spots – all the grease in the makeup.'

I shook the bucket, watching the last few lumps slip into the bin.

'Did you know that?'

I shook my head. I slid the lid back and turned to the shop. Phil was blocking the doorway.

He rubbed his chin.

'You won't tell anyone,' he said. 'About me being out here?'

I shook my head again.

He looked up to the sky. He clawed his neck with his nails. The fat-bucket was sticky. It smelt like rotten chicken. I wanted to go inside and wash my hands. Phil nodded, slowly. He smiled.

'Come on then,' he said, and turned and disappeared inside.

Phil kept his head down the rest of the morning. He didn't turn on the radio or send me to the bookies or even try to wind up Charlie. I hoped that's how the day would play out: Phil at his block, me in my kitchen, your father off at the abattoir. Next Saturday's Boxing Day and Hampton's is closed and I liked the prospect of going two whole weeks without seeing your father. Then, just as I dragged off my rubber gloves and turned to go to lunch, he appeared in the kitchen doorway. He wasn't smiling.

He told me to follow him.

There was a van out in the car park, backed up to the alleyway. Your father opened the doors to reveal stacks and stacks of turkey-crates. The turkeys were enormous, especially when you consider that lumpy white carcass is just the torso. Some of those turkey torsos were as big as yours.

'Grab a crate,' he said.

They were even heavier than I thought. As I lifted a pain ached, not just in my scarred palm this time, but all the way up my arms and neck to my forehead. Your father pointed out where to stack them, up on the shelves of the big empty freezer. The freezer was misty and layered with ice. I nearly slipped as I hoisted the first turkey-crate. Your father disappeared into the shop. He returned a few minutes later with Phil, leading him past me to the van outside.

I stepped out for another crate. Your father was rummaging through the glove box. He retrieved a bottle of mulled wine – a present from the guys at the abattoir. He poured two mugs and handed one to Phil and they leant against the van, drinking, watching as I shifted the turkey-crates. A couple of times a crate slipped and I had to catch it with my knee and your father told me to be careful not to dirty any turkeys. Hampton's customers had pre-ordered months in advance and each and every turkey was spoken for.

Phil chewed his lip. He tapped the side of his mug.

'Let's give him a hand, eh?' he said. He was shaking. Sweating. He must have been up all night delivering Christmas trees.

Your father said nothing.

'Ah, come on,' Phil said. 'It'll be quicker.' He placed his mug on the roof of the van and stooped to reach inside for a crate.

Your father didn't help. He probably could have lifted a crate on each shoulder, but instead he just leant against the wall, watching Phil and I struggle up the steps to the freezer. We had to stack the turkey-crates quite tightly to fit them inside, piling them as high as possible. Phil piled his to the left, I piled mine to the right. Slowly the two piles began to join.

We got a system going, taking it in turns to grab a crate from the van. It got to the point where Phil and I only passed each other in the doorway. Where, when I was stacking a crate in the freezer, he was fetching one from the van, and vice versa.

I was out in the van when I heard the screaming. It was a squealing sort of scream. Ear-stabbing. By the time I scrambled out into the alley your father had dropped his mug and disappeared inside.

For a few seconds it was hard to tell what was happening. The freezer was narrow and misty and Phil was thrashing about, fist in the air, blood lining the front of his apron. It was only when he fainted, his body hanging there like a passenger clutching the rail of the bus, that it became clear his arm was caught on a meat hook. Your father took his legs, lifted them over his shoulder. He hoisted Phil hook and all from the freezer and carried him out to the butcher's block. The hook had pierced the back of Phil's hand, its tip jutting from his wrist. Your father wrapped Phil's arm in an apron. Blood steamed from a pool in the freezer. It had trickled down the steps, curling round the grouting of the tiles. One of the Vultures stepped out the back to check what all the commotion was. She squealed, 'Eeeee!' and ran back to tell the others.

Your father told me to clean up. Wipe the turkeys and get them back in their crates. He carried Phil to his car and sped off down the carriageway. By the time I got to the blood it had frozen and I had to scrape it away with a knife. I transported the rest of the crates on my own. It took all afternoon. I kept having to stop, leaning against the van to catch my breath. At one point I leant too hard and Phil's mug of mulled wine toppled from the roof, bouncing from my shoulder and shattering in the alley. I shovelled the shards away and carried on shifting the turkeys.

When your father returned he went straight to his counter. I didn't ask about Phil and he didn't tell me. Without the radio all I could hear was the banging of his cleaver, the laughter of the Vultures out the front in the shop.

I tried my best to finish my cleaning early so I could leave before the Vultures' congregation in the coat cupboard, but transporting those turkeys put me behind all day. At 16:55 I still had a stack of chicken trays to clean. And chicken trays are the worst — all that baked-on fat. I have to boil the kettle and leave it to soak with detergent and T-Rex Bleach and even then (even through my rubber gloves) I still grate the skin from my fingertips. 17:00 came and went and the Vultures fixed their hair and set off into the cold and I was still scrubbing at chicken trays.

By the time I went out the front for my money it was 17:27. Your father was alone at the counter, sorting through piles of £20 notes. I picked up my envelope and headed for the door.

'You going to leave without saying merry Christmas?' your father asked.

He kept his head down, counting.

'Merry Christmas.' I tried the door. It was locked.

'You'll never guess what happened to my car last week.'

He slid a rubber band round a wad of twenties. I tried to say, 'What?' but all that came out was an unrecognisable grunt.

'Some son of a bitch smashed my tail light. Can you believe it?'

Your father looked up. He smiled. He stepped round the

counter and crossed the shop towards me. His trousers were still speckled with Phil's blood.

He stopped beside me, at the door. He stared down at me for a few seconds. The keys hung there on their chain on his belt but he didn't reach for them. Instead he leant forwards, took his large hand from his pocket and placed it on my head.

'I see things,' he said. 'You know?'

The tail of a dragon tattoo was curling out from the sleeve of his T-shirt. I tried to nod but he kept tight hold of my skull.

'I know you know what I'm talking about. I saw you. You know I saw you. From now on you keep away from her. OK?'

I swallowed. I was about to say, 'OK,' when he nodded my head with his hand.

'She's very special. Too special for you. OK?'

Nod.

'I know you have your problems, but Ken gave you the job here to try to help you. To normalise you. Not so you could go sniffing round your boss's daughter. She is out of bounds. Otherwise you become my problem. OK?'

Nod.

'I find out you've been near her again, that's it. There is no second warning.'

He kept hold of my head a few seconds longer. I thought maybe he was going to pop it, like a watermelon, but the pressure eased and he let me go. I glanced over at the selection of turkeys, hanging in the window. The clock behind the counter said 17:30. Your father turned to it and grinned.

'Your mam'll be worried about you,' he said. 'Best run on home, eh?'

He patted me on the shoulder.

'You're all right really, aren't you?' he said. 'We're all right?'

I nodded on my own this time. My neck ached from his grip. He told me I was all right a few more times as he unhooked the keys from his belt. He unlocked the door and held it open. I stepped out into the darkness.

'Oh, and kid . . . ?' he said.

I turned back. He took out his wallet and removed a £20 note. He held it out to me.

'Merry Christmas.'

I swallowed.

'Go on,' he said. 'Merry Christmas.'

I took the £20 note and scrunched it in my pocket. I hurried away. I kept expecting him to call out again but he didn't. As I turned from the square I heard the bolt of the door.

When I reached Green Avenue I turned back one last time. I could still see his shape in the window, his head amongst the raw hanging turkeys.

Today started like today starts every year, with the creak of the door and the click of the light switch and Mum's grinning face: 'It's Christmas!' She sat a glass of orange juice on my bedside table and told me I'd best come downstairs: 'Santa's been!' With that she was gone, off to wake the others.

I went down to the lounge. My father was there, perched on the edge of the couch. He too was clutching a glass of orange juice. He was wearing the Ted Baker ensemble Mum bought him last year: light brown trousers, green V-neck sweater. He smelt of aftershave. Mum buys us new clothes and aftershave every Christmas but my father always makes the mistake of getting dressed and applying his aftershave before we open our presents, then has to get rewashed and redressed afterwards. In the centre of the carpet was an enormous pile of presents, neatly wrapped in white paper. Usually we store presents at the foot of the Christmas tree but this year the foot of the Christmas tree is nailed to the lounge ceiling. I took a moment deciding whether to sit beside my father on the couch, before Mum appeared behind me.

'Don't you want to sit on the floor?' she said. 'With the presents?'

I told her I couldn't sit on the floor. I had to always sit on a couch, with my feet up. Because of **Them**. Remember?

'Fine. That's fine. Sit, sit. Make yourself comfortable.'

My father slid up to make room for me. Mum lingered for a few seconds, watching as I lifted my feet to sit cross-legged.

'Just please be careful.'

Mum disappeared upstairs then, to try to wake Sarah again. I took a sip of orange. My father chewed the inside of his cheek. Mum mumbled from Sarah's room. The mumbling faded for a few seconds then started up again. Then Sarah screamed, 'Just fuck off and leave me alone,' and Mum retreated back downstairs. She stopped and smiled in the doorway before taking a seat between me and my father. The upside-down Christmas tree hung between us like a giant twinkling drill about to bore into the centre of the carpet. My father took a sip of his orange juice and from the bubbles I realised that his wasn't actually orange juice at all, but Buck's fizz, which is like orange juice only fizzed with champagne. I'm not allowed Buck's fizz because of my medication. I don't mind so much because I tried a sip once and Buck's fizz is disgusting.

Eventually Sarah limped down to the lounge and we were

able to start unwrapping presents. Mum goes a little overboard at Christmas so everyone had several presents to unwrap. My main present was a DVD player. Mum said she knew I liked watching films and it was about time I caught up with the twenty-first century. I don't actually own any DVDs, but I didn't mention this to Mum because it was still a very thoughtful gift. My other presents were the usual: aftershave, trousers, a grey Armani jumper. I folded the jumper and trousers and placed them on the floor beside me and Mum knelt and refolded them, smiling and muttering something indistinguishable. Mum had bought my father a new aftershave/trousers/jumper set too and he moaned, 'I'll have to go and get changed now,' in a fake-angry sort of way. He'd bought Mum chocolates and some new cleaning fluids for the couch. Apparently they were very expensive.

I handed out my presents. I'd tried my best to find lounge-colour-scheme-matching wrapping paper but the best I could manage was white with a scattered array of *Winnie-the-Pooh* characters. It didn't seem to matter: Mum tore the paper to shreds before it even had a chance to register. I'd bought her a box set of Elvis Presley CDs and as soon as she saw his black and white grin she gasped and told everyone to stop unwrapping while she put some music on. My father was next to open his present – a bottle of Scotch and a poster of Marilyn Monroe. I told him Marilyn Monroe was the Pamela Anderson of her day. He nodded and chewed the inside of his cheek. One

Christmas my father chewed his cheek so much he bled, spotting his new Ralph Lauren shirt with red stains. Mum used to say he'd one day chew a hole right through and end up with two mouths, but Mum never says that any more.

Sarah was the last to open presents. She had to be coaxed a little by Mum, who was rubbing her arm and whispering, 'Come on, your turn, love.' Sarah's been practising extra hard these past few weeks. Since the allegations against Cullman the Christmas Dance Fantastical's been delayed and so now Sarah has to keep practising right through till the twenty-eighth. Sarah placed her Buck's fizz on the floor and slowly peeled back the paper of her main gift: a crate of Hi-Wizz Vitamin Energy Shake. She nodded (a crate of Hi-Wizz Vitamin Energy Shake was what she'd asked for). She also received the usual makeup and pyjamas and perfume. What Sarah really wants is breast enhancement surgery but Mum says she's not allowed to until she's at least in her twenties. Apparently Mum was in her twenties when she first got her breasts enhanced. Sarah says that's not fair because there are girls in school (e.g. Lucy Marlowe) who've had the op., but Mum's word is final. I bought Sarah *Singin' in the Rain* because there's lots of great dancing in it. Sarah muttered that she didn't know we were buying each other presents this year.

By the time we'd finished it was getting light. Sarah disappeared upstairs to bed, my father to his study, Mum to the kitchen to prepare Christmas dinner. I sat on the dining-room window seat and watched her rubbing oil onto the turkey carcass. Occasionally my father ventured out of his study for some nuts or a mince pie. He opened the bottle of Scotch I'd bought him. Mum gave him a glance of The Eyebrow but my father just smiled and said, 'It's Christmas, you can start early at Christmas,' rummaging through the cupboard for a glass. He poured. He asked Mum if she wanted him to drive. She didn't reply.

'If you want me to drive I won't drink,' he said.

Mum washed her hands. She lifted a bowl of stuffing from the fridge and tipped it onto the chopping board. She shook her head.

'OK.' My father knocked back the drink, poured another and disappeared back into his study.

Once dinner was in the oven we left for Golden Pines. Mum drove. It was starting to rain. I thought Mum might have brought her Elvis CD to listen to on the way but she didn't and we listened to the rain instead.

Halfway down the Social De-cline my father got bored of listening to the rain and switched on the radio. Sarah's dance song was playing. Apparently it's called 'Screemin Boi' by someone called Miss X. According to the radio it's the Christmas number one. It thudded from the speakers the whole way out to the Pitt but Sarah didn't once try and dance. She just watched the passing cars, the rain on the windows.

Mum exited the carriageway by the industrial estate, taking the back roads through the Pitt. Mum always takes the back roads through the Pitt because it means she doesn't have to pass Kirk Lane or Ahmed's Boutique or the church or any of those old places. By the time we pulled into Golden Pines the rain was heavy. My father asked if Mum had her umbrella.

She shook her head.

'Guess we'll just have to run for it, then.'

The reception was empty. Mum stood for a while by the desk, staring at the 'Ring For Attention' bell. My father and Sarah sat on the couch. I stood beside Mum, counting the drips from my coat soaking into the carpet. The phone behind reception started to ring. It rang six times and stopped. Then it rang again. The receptionist stepped out. It was a different receptionist to the one at Nan's birthday. This one's badge said 'Evon'.

Evon led us past the TV room. The other old ladies were all together, slumped in various mismatched armchairs. A few were alone but most had family members gathered around them. Mum asked why Nan wasn't in the TV room. Evon said it hadn't been one of Nan's good days.

Nan was in bed. There was a nurse kneeling at her side, guiding her arm into a beige dressing gown. Nan's whole room was beige. There were beige curtains and beige walls. They'd tried to decorate it for Christmas, an assortment of tinsel-scraps and paper snowflake streamers hung round her window frame, but these only emphasised the beigeness. There was a small fibre-optic tree on the bedside table. Mum watched the pulse of its glow. She didn't look at Nan.

The nurse turned to us and said she was just getting Nan 'all cosy'. I recognised the nurse from last time. She was wearing a badge that said 'Jade' but I didn't recognise the name Jade so maybe it was a different nurse or maybe I just didn't read her name badge last time or maybe I've just forgotten the name Jade since then. It was a while back. Jade tied Nan's dressing gown in a double knot. She pressed her jaw closed. 'Don't want to go catching any flies,' she said.

There was a tray on Nan's knee and on the tray was a plate and on the plate was a Christmas dinner and on the Christmas dinner was a layer of gravy, long since congealed. Jade said it seemed Nan wasn't hungry. I'm not sure if Jade doesn't know about Nan's not eating, or was just being polite in not mentioning it. She lifted the tray from Nan's lap. The gravy wobbled like jelly. She wished us a merry Christmas and stepped out into the hall.

Mum sat on the chair beside Nan. She reached out and held her hand for a second, then held her own hands together on her lap. There were several tubes draped over the headboard, connecting Nan's arm to a hooked-up bag of clear liquid in the corner. Sarah sat at the end of the bed, next to the bump of Nan's toes. My father stepped over to stare out of the window. The rain hissed out in the car park, drumming the roofs of the cars.

'Hi, Mum,' Mum said.

Nan stared straight ahead. Her face was more skeleton-like than ever. It still had that thin layer of ultra-fine, white hair I could never stop staring at as a child. The tray had left a rectangle of flattened duvet on her lap. A metallic tap-tap-tap came from the corner as Sarah began to nod along to her earphones.

'We brought you some cake.' Mum took a wad of silver foil out of her bag and placed it on Nan's dressing table. She peeled it open to reveal a slice of Christmas cake.

Nan didn't acknowledge the cake. She was staring at the cross above the door. That's what she does when we visit – stares at the cross above the door. My father used to say it's because she's cross. He used to say, 'She's cross, that's what she's trying to tell us. She's cross.' He doesn't say that any more. He just stares out of the window. He stares out of the window and Nan stares at the cross and Mum stares at her hands and Sarah stares at her iPod and I don't know where to stare. Usually I stare at Nan's feet, the bump they make in the bed sheets. Today her big toe was sticking out from under the blanket. Her toenail was longer than I've ever seen it. Whose job is it to cut her toenails? Jade's? Evon's?

Ours?

'Merry Christmas, Mum,' Mum said.

Nan stared at the cross.

'Have you had a nice day?'

Nan stared at the cross.

'We went to church this morning, the whole family. We really enjoyed it.'

Nan stared at the cross.

Last Christmas, as Nan was staring at her cross, she started mouthing a couple of words, over and over. It took us the whole visit to work out what she was mouthing. At first Mum though it was 'pyjamas' and told Nan she was already wearing pyjamas, but then my father realised it was 'praise Jesus'. He was made up when he realised – we all were. We couldn't stop smiling at how clever he was.

We all sat there, smiling, as Nan praised Jesus.

Nan didn't start with religion till Herb died. That was when she began to change. Mum said she'd have been better off dying beside him that night, but I don't know if that's true. Nan and I had some of our happiest times in those final couple of years. It was me who found her that afternoon. It was back when I was living with her. Nan was meant to be picking me up from school and I thought it odd, her not being there at the gate when we finished, but she always baked on Fridays and baking made her absentminded. It was only when I got back to the house and found the milk still on the step, the paper still in the letterbox, Mr Saunders pacing the porch, crying to be fed, that I knew there was something seriously wrong.

I went round to the alley and climbed over the wall into the yard. I got in through the kitchen window. There's a way to jiggle the lock so it falls right out. I called to Nan and she called right back to me and she sounded frightened, more frightened than I'd ever heard her.

I tried my best to lift Herb off the bed but he was so stiff and cold and unmovable. I phoned an ambulance. After that we waited. At first I sat on the floor. I told Nan about my day at school. This was during the Andrew Wilt period and I knew that the best way to take Nan's mind off things was to talk about our chess games. It was only when Nan started crying that I climbed into bed with her, forcing myself between her and Herb. She couldn't get over him, that was the problem. Her side of the bed was against the wall and Herb always slept on top of the duvet. Nan held me to her chest so I couldn't see her tears but I still felt them, running down the back of my neck.

Like that we waited for the ambulance.

By the time we arrived home the rain had stopped. Mum served the turkey. Nobody ate much. Mum picked but I didn't see her actually eat any. Each time she caught me looking she smiled and I smiled back and carried on eating, trying my best to finish as much as possible. She didn't ask if I'd taken my medication. At one point a piece of turkey slipped from my fork, splashing gravy onto my new Christmas jumper, but Mum didn't even look, she just kept smiling down at her plate. Elvis crooned from the living room. The Sampsons' inflatable Santa grinned from across the street. My father ate using only his right hand, his left hand cradling the rim of his Scotch glass. He stared at the tablecloth, at the spot where he'd usually place his inframammary infection photos. The only sound was the clinking of cutlery.

After dinner Sarah went to her bedroom. My father went to his study. It was just Mum and I sitting in the lounge, at opposite ends of the couch. We watched BBC News 24. The only news was that it was Christmas. They cut to a shot of a reporter, supposedly in the North Pole, supposedly interviewing the real Father Christmas.

I waited till Mum began to snore, then retrieved my coat and your present. I took some turkey, too, and a little leftover Christmas pudding, for Scraps, and headed off down the carriageway to the Pitt.

I stopped off at the canal on the way, to see the ducks. I figured people probably don't bother taking bread on Christmas Day and it's only fair that they eat too. I could give them Scraps' Christmas pudding. He wouldn't mind – he'd still have the turkey.

The canal had melted in the rain. It had formed those little white islands again. Only today the ducks were nowhere to be seen. I walked up and down for a full fifteen minutes but I couldn't find a single one of them. Then it struck me: the ducks have left. They've given up on Skipdale. They've flown south, where it's warmer. They've finally seen sense and got the hell out of here.

I followed the carriageway down the Social De-cline. I couldn't stop smiling about the ducks, the thought of them, off some-where warm. Pitt families go all out with Christmas decorations. The boarded-up houses were still in darkness but those inhab-ited were bright enough to compensate. There were flashing lights, nativity scenes, 'Santa Stop Here' signs. Five different houses had one of Artie Sampson's inflatable Father Christmases. Even your father had made the effort. The front of your house was lit by a string of electric-blue lights, pinned along the gutter. A nodding Rudolph grinned from his dashboard.

I crossed Crossgrove to your back hedge. I scanned the field for your brother but he was nowhere to be seen. I slipped in through the hedge gap. I took the turkey from my pocket. It was only as I knelt to the missing-plank gap that I realised Scraps was missing, his chain lying limp on the shed floor. Your living room was brighter than usual due to the Christmas tree, twinkling its various light-sequences. Scraps was laid out in front of the fire. You were kneeling beside him, rubbing his belly. Your father was on the couch in his usual position, sipping from what looked like (though from a distance it was hard to verify) a snowman-shaped mug.

I crawled up into the shed anyway. Where else would I go? It was especially cold tonight – Scraps must give off more heat than I gave him credit for. I dragged the toolkit over to the window and sat, forehead against the glass. You were wearing your dressing gown. Sunglasses. Your hair was tied up, covered in small squares of tinfoil. You were stroking the side of Scraps' head, eyes fixed on the TV. Your father had freed his hair from its ponytail. It flowed down the back of the couch, right to the floor. Occasionally you'd turn to your father and say something. Occasionally he'd turn back. Occasionally you'd both burst out laughing.

I hadn't expected this. You and your father and Scraps, together in the living room. Me, out here, alone. This was new.

After a while I began to sense **Them**. I could feel **Them**, glaring down from the tops of the shelves, the dark corners. I unhooked the nail gun and held it on my lap. It helped. I realised it wasn't fear I was feeling, it was anger. There was an anger in me. I don't know if I was angry at you or your father or Scraps or **Them**, but the anger was there. This was also new.

I took the turkey and the Christmas pudding from my

pocket. I placed them over in Scraps' corner. I figured he'd find them, eventually. Then I took out your present: *Breakfast at Tiffany's.* I fixed the ribbon, brushed off a few scattered pudding crumbs. I tried to think of somewhere I could leave it for you, somewhere only you would go. I couldn't think of anywhere, so I just held it on my lap, next to the nail gun.

Soon I could hear **Them**. They hissed from the shelves at the back. I shut my eyes but I could still sense **Them**, crawling through the darkness. I held the nail gun out in front of me and squeezed the trigger. The gun jerked, cracking like a whip, spitting a glittering nail into the far wall of the shed. A warning shot. I fired again. The hissing ceased, the crack of the wood emphasising the silence.

I shot out a few more nails, just to be sure.

Then I placed my cheek against the glass. I concentrated on you. Nobody moved, neither you, nor your father, nor Scraps, nor I. I found that if I closed my left eye I couldn't even see your father. He'd disappear into the darkness. Gone in the blink of an eye. I kept my left eye shut for a while.

Then I must have shut my right eye.

I don't know how long I slept but next thing the door was creaking open, cracking as it struck the corner of the toolkit. Next thing someone was stoop-stumbling into the shed. From the snorting and grunting and the gagging whiskey smell, I knew it wasn't you.

My cheek was frozen to the glass, frosted by my breath. I knew the door must be partly obscuring me but to what extent I'd no idea. I was sure any second he would notice me, perched there in the corner. He creaked over to the back, where Scraps usually lies. As my eyes adjusted I noticed Scraps still inside the house, laid out in front of the fire. You were beside him, sleeping.

I peeled my cheek from the window, as quietly as possible. Your father was hunched, rummaging through the jars and rusted tins that layer the shed's shelves. He was grunting, shaking his head, hair dancing down his back. He dislodged a paint tin, which rolled across the floor, clinking against the toolkit between my knees.

There was a square patch of ceiling, silver-lit by moonlight. As your father rummaged one of **Them** scurried out, its shadow stretched limb-long. Your father gasped. He'd caught his arm on a nail in the wall. He examined the small patch of nails, plucked one from the wall and held it to the moonlight. I realised I was still clutching the nail gun. He dropped the nail and turned back to the shelves, reached to the back, dislodging something, a bottle, holding it up to the light to examine its quarter of amber liquid. He unscrewed the lid and sniffed its open neck.

Another one of **Them** crept out, joining the one of **Them** in the centre of the ceiling, their merging shadows creating a new, indefinable, stretched-out silhouette. Your father took a swig from his bottle. He swilled and he swallowed. He sighed. He took another swig. Another one of **Them** crawled out. Another. Another.

Then your father noticed something on the floor. He knelt, the old boards creaking with his weight. He lifted something and examined it in the moonlight. The piece of turkey I'd left for Scraps. He sniffed it, took another swig, never taking his eyes from the turkey. My shaking began to rattle the metal-flapped lid of the toolkit. I lifted the nail gun from my lap. I didn't know whether to aim at your father or at **Them**. All I could hear was their mass hissing.

More of **Them** were creeping from the shadows.

Your father took another swig.

I dropped the nail gun and scrambled to the door. The toolkit tipped, its contents spilling over the floorboards. Your father cried out, his bottle shattering as I leapt the stairs. I slipped on the grass, twisted my ankle. I stumbled down the side to the hedge and tore out across the field. It was raining. Your father shouted – slurred shouts, contradictory:

'Come back here, you little shit . . . You'd better run . . .'

I did run. I ran through the estate, up past the Rat and Dog. I ran till I reached the church, till my legs and my lungs couldn't take any more. I leant on the church wall. The rain was heavy. My ankle ached. I was shaking all over. Beads of rain dripped from the hood of my parka.

I breathed, slow deep breaths to keep the vomit down. After a few minutes my stomach had settled and the pounding in my head had stopped and I began to make out singing. It was hard to hear through the hiss of the rain, but it was there. Delicate. Choir-like. 'Silent Night'.

The church sign said:

CHRISTMAS CHOIR SERVICE
ALL WELCOME

Rain rippled the puddles around me. I hugged myself through my coat. Your father's words rang out over the choir music:

'You'd better run . . .'

And I knew he was right. We have to run. We have to leave, like the ducks. It's simple, really.

I waited for the song to finish, then limped back up to the carriageway. As I reached the canal bridge I checked my pocket and realised I'd left your present in the shed.

Sarah didn't go to bed last night. She danced right through till morning.

Thud – thud – thud – thud – thud – thud – thud – thud – thud – thud – thud.

At 05:32 I gave up trying to sleep and hobbled down to the kitchen. I ate a bowl of Waitrose Maple Triple Nut Muesli. I checked Mum's Colombian Supremo but there were only a few beans left so I microwaved a half-drunk mug from last night instead, being sure to wipe Mum's lipstick from the rim. I wanted to be alert for the Christmas Dance Fantastical. Sarah said everyone would be at the Christmas Dance Fantastical. This meant you would be at the Christmas Dance Fantastical. The coffee was very bitter. I added milk and sugar but it made little difference. Coffee's a taste that lingers.

Mum was at the foot of the couch, sprawled across the carpet. BBC News 24 looped the same old snow footage. The rolling news bar said: SNOW WARNING! . . . SNOW

TO RETURN WITHIN ONE WEEK! . . . The television was muted, the only sound the dull thud of Sarah's dancing. Occasionally she'd leap across her room and the upside-down Christmas tree would shudder, its baubles clinking above me.

I sat cross-legged on the couch, next to Mum's sleeping head. Sarah's music didn't cut out till 08:02. It ended mid-song, leaving a buzz of silence. Mum sat up and wiped her chin. She climbed to her feet, shuffled out to the kitchen and popped the lid from her coffee tin. She sighed. It was most likely Sarah who'd used all the beans, in her morning coffee-shots. The kettle hissed. There was the familiar rattle of the grinder and Mum returned with a steaming mug and perched on the couch beside me. She sipped.

The snow footage looped again and again. Kids still sliding down the hill on their bin bags. That green-hatted woman ever-slipping on the ice, never catching the wall as she fell, people passing by without ever stopping to help.

The rolling news bar said: . . . TEMPERATURES REACH RECORD LOW ACROSS EUROPE . . .

At 8:33 Sarah thundered down the stairs. She was wearing her Christmas Dance Fantastical leotard. She said she was late for dress rehearsal. Mum asked what time the Fantastical started and Sarah told her it was 19:30, like it said on the tickets. Mum told her to take a coat but Sarah said it was good to be cold, the colder she was the more she'd dance and the more she'd dance the more practice she'd get and after all practice makes perfect. She took a few bottles of Hi-Wizz Vitamin Energy Shake from the fridge and hurried out the door.

Soon after that the doorbell rang. It was Old Mrs Jenkins' niece, Gretna. Old Mrs Jenkins is dead. Another victim of the winter, Gretna said. Too much time in that draughty attic. Apparently Gretna comes over every year for Boxing Day supper and usually Mrs Jenkins hears her bike roaring from the dual carriageway and is waiting on the doorstep for her to arrive, but this year she was nowhere to be seen. She wouldn't even answer the doorbell. Apparently when Gretna peered in through the letterbox she fainted, right there on the doorstep. The smell just knocked her out. And Gretna's a big woman.

Mum went for a lie-down once Gretna had gone. Mrs Jenkins had been her first ever Skipdale customer, the one who'd first recommended her hairdressing skills. The two hadn't spoken for a couple of years now but Mum still had a soft spot for her. She didn't come down till dinnertime. We had turkey sandwiches. Mum laid out stuffing and cranberry and horse-radish in little bowls across the table but we both ate our sandwiches dry, with just a little salt and butter. I could tell she'd been crying but I didn't mention it.

19:30 came and went but my father never arrived home from work. Mum said we could always leave my father's ticket on the mantelpiece. He could catch us up if he wanted. If he had time.

We arrived at Skipdale High at 19:45. A group of sixth-formers manned the gates – high-visibility jackets, P.E. whistles bit between their teeth. They waved us over to a space in the corner of the field. It was a muddy patch and Mum had concerns about the BMW's paintwork but she parked up there anyway. We hurried across the field to the sports hall, as fast as Mum's heels would allow.

The hall was dark when we entered. Silent. Rows of parents stared up at the stage from a sea of plastic chairs. Mum scanned for empty seats but the room was packed. I searched amongst the crowd but it was impossible to find you in the darkness. There was a silence in the room that can only be described as The Calm Before the Storm.

The stage was T-shaped, a catwalk running out through the crowd. A spotlight flickered and there was Angela Hargrove, halfway up the catwalk, dressed as a scantily clad Christmas Fairy, perched upon a Christmas tree. (The tree was actually a stepladder with two green cardboard tree-shapes glued either side but in theatre you have to suspend your disbelief.) Angela welcomed everybody to this year's Christmas Dance Fantastical.

She said that this year Santa was going to bring a very special present for all the boys and girls of Skipdale High. (It's actually December the twenty-eighth but again: suspension of disbelief.) There was a group of sixth-formers in the corner of the hall, leaning against the monkey bars. Mum stared at each of them in turn but they were too busy glaring up at Angela to notice us. Then a dance remix of 'Santa Baby' kicked in and Angela skittered down the stepladder to the front of the catwalk-stage. Lights flashed. Six girls in C.D.F. leotards poured on from either side, strutting up the catwalk, circling Angela. It was hard to tell if any of the dancers was Sarah, they were all moving so quickly and the lights were flashing so dramatically. All I could make out was red Lycra and flesh.

'Santa Baby' ended. The audience applauded. Angela descended the catwalk, disappearing stage right. One of the sixth-formers noticed us and directed us to seats in separate corners of the back row. Mum mouthed that she'd meet me by the car after the show. Another song began, the six Vultures continuing their backing dance. I realised that none of them could be my sister because my sister's only part was during 'Screemin Boi', which was the grand finale.

I scanned the crowd again. In one particularly bright flash of light I noticed Ian, crouching stage left, glaring up at the dancers. In the next flash I saw you, sitting in the row behind. From then on I kept my eyes fixed on that point. Each time the spotlights crossed the catwalk I could just make you out, Goose beside you, whispering into your ear. You were smiling. Occasionally you were laughing.

There were themes to the Fantastical's various dances. Some were Christmas-related, others I think were popular songs, most of which I didn't recognise. The backing dancers all wore C.D.F. leotards but Angela Hargrove had a range of different costumes. 'Rudolph The Red-Nosed Reindeer' began and Angela took to the stage once again – fairy-lit antlers, diamanté-encrusted nose. Another monologue: this time about her red nose, her responsibilities to Santa, how the other reindeers never let her join in with their reindeer games. Ian was watching from the very edge of his seat. He was practically foaming at the mouth. You still had Goose at your ear, only now he'd put his arm round you. You weren't smiling any more.

Then the Rudolph remix kicked in and a swarm of dancers flooded the stage, the lights strobing on/off/on/off/on/off, transforming everything into a series of images, segmented by blackness: Angela dropping to the floor. BLACK. Angela, jerking her head back. BLACK. The swarm of backing dancers, pouring in behind her. BLACK. The backing dancers forming a line. BLACK. The backing dancers kicking their legs out. BLACK. Angela writhing across the floor, nose held high. BLACK. A sea of parents' faces, staring hang-mouthed at the stage. BLACK. Ian, grinning, straining to see up Angela's skirt from the side of the stage. BLACK. Goose, huddling close to you. BLACK. Goose, nuzzling your neck. BLACK. You, pushing Goose away. BLACK. Goose's tongue against your neck. BLACK.

You, standing.

BLACK.

You, pushing Goose down into his seat.

BLACK.

You, clutching your sunglassed eyes.

BLACK.

You, dragging your hood up over your head as you step through the crowd to a doorway, stage left.

BLACK.

And that's when I found myself standing, following. It was hard, crossing the hall in the strobing lights but at least with the dancing nobody seemed to notice me. I headed to the doorway, stage left.

The doorway led to the Lipton Building. The light was dim but constant, the Rudolph remix a dull hum.

The corridor was empty. I checked every classroom till I reached Miss Hayes' office at the end but you were nowhere to be seen.

I retraced my steps.

It was only when I'd lapped the corridor a third time that I noticed the caretaker's closet, the door slightly ajar.

I pressed my cheek to the wood. I shut my eyes. I could hear you breathing inside.

I considered going back to the hall, sitting across from Mum and waiting for the show to end. I considered going out to the car park, waiting it out with the BMW.

Then I opened the door.

There you were, huddled in the corner by the brooms, head in your hands.

'Fuck off,' you said.

I told you it was me, Greg. You shuffled a little, trying to block out the light with your folded arms.

'Oh,' you said. 'OK.'

You shuffled back a little further.

'Well, if you're going to come in, come in.'

I asked if you were OK.

'Just come in.'

I stepped inside. It was only a small closet and stepping inside meant my knees were right beside your face.

'Shut the door.'

I asked why.

'I can't deal with the light right now,' you said. 'Just shut the door.'

I shut the door. BLACK. I stood for a while. Then I crouched. I thought about sitting but there wasn't room, what with the piles of mop heads and bleach bottles behind me.

'It's just my eyes,' you said. 'The lights.'

I said it was OK.

I could feel your breath, warm against my arm. Here we were in the caretaker's closet, in darkness once again. I always seem to lose my sight when I'm with you. I wanted to ask about Goose. I wanted to ask about your father. I wanted to ask if you found your present. I wanted to tell you about Finners Island, about my plan for us to run away. But I didn't.

I don't know how long we stayed like that, you huddled there with me crouched over you. By the end my legs ached. Music hummed from the hall. I could make out the odd lyric of 'Screemin Boi'. Then it stopped. You didn't say anything, you just breathed. You sniffed a few times. Everything smelt of disinfectant.

Then suddenly you stood.

'I'd best get going,' you said.

I asked if you were OK again. I was aware of repeating myself.

'Just a migraine,' you said. 'Happens sometimes.'

Light flooded back into the room. You were standing in the doorway. You might have been staring at me. I don't know. You were wearing your sunglasses.

'Thanks for checking on me,' you said. 'I am OK. Honest.'

I nodded.

'I guess I'll see you at the party.'

I asked what party.

'Goose's party. New Year's.'

I said I hadn't been invited.

'Everyone's invited.'

I didn't know what to say to that so I just crouched there, staring up at you, not saying anything.

'Whatever,' you said. 'Might see you there.'

You turned, let the door shut.

BLACK.

It came again this morning, the rain. The steady hiss. The house has seemed so quiet since Sarah's rehearsals have finished and it was nice just to listen to it, battering the windows, gurgling over the brim of the gutter, spilling and slapping on the pavement out back.

Mum said it's supposed to rain at funerals. 'Washes all sins away.' She was fixing her fascinator in the dining-room mirror. She bought it especially – black lace, embroidered with tiny black roses. Across the road lay Artie Sampson's inflatable Santa, a crumpled red puddle on his path. At first Artie had tried to fix the gash with parcel tape, but each time he got it standing the tape'd peel and it'd bow again and Artie'd sink to his knees, clutching what's left of his hair. I considered telling him that duct tape would be a better idea (Nan and I would sometimes use duct tape on outdoor cracks, where parcel tape wasn't quite enough) but I knew Mum would kill me so I kept quiet. Since the rain came he's given up. Occasionally his face appears at the window, but that's it.

Mum asked if I was going to get ready. I told her I was ready. I was wearing my school blazer. It's the only black jacket I own. I unstitched the Skipdale badge so there's no way to tell it's a school blazer.

Mum gave me a glance of The Eyebrow.

'Wouldn't you rather wear your new Christmas clothes?' she said.

I told Mum my Christmas clothes are grey. Are you allowed to wear grey at a funeral?

Mum said grey was fine. She'd cut my hair last night, blow-dried it into a bowl, managing to keep all the curls down. She wanted me to look smart for once. Was that too much to ask?

Mum was in a good mood today. The past couple of days have been hard for her. I went over to Goose's on Monday, to stake out the place before the party, and when I got back Mum was in the car, crying, 'Suspicious Minds' roaring from the speakers. Artie Sampson's Father Christmas was half deflated over the road, still with Mum's hairdressing scissors jutting from its belly. It was only when the car battery died and Elvis cut out that she finally stumbled over to the house.

My father and I waited in the hall. For a full minute she just stood there, smiling from the doorway. My father asked if she was OK. She nodded. He asked if she'd like a cup of coffee. Again, she nodded.

219

'I'll make it,' she said.

She turned to lock the car. I don't know if it was the flat battery or that Mum was just pressing the wrong button on her key fob but it wouldn't lock. After four or five tries she dropped the keys on the porch floor. Two steps into the hallway she collapsed.

It turned out Mum had been to the Hamptons' that morning. Ursula bought the couch. The exact same white Italian leather couch. The exact same product number from the exact same catalogue. Apparently it looks fabulous in Ursula's living room, which is twice the size of our living room. It has more Wow Factor than Mum could ever dream of. It'll be the talk of the Hamptons' New Year's party.

My father chewed his cheek. He left Mum on the floor whilst he went to the kitchen for the coffee. There was no Colombian Supremo left so he had to use instant. He filled two mugs and brought them through to the hall. Then he knelt beside Mum, lifting her head, forcing her to sip from one of the mugs. Coffee ran down her chin, joining the trail of snot and mascara.

He told her it was OK. He told her he'd had a couple of new clients recently. He told Mum we could afford a little redecorating. She could start the room over again. She could decorate a brand new room if she wanted to. Whatever she thought best. Mum clutched the sleeves of his shirt. She sobbed into his lap. My father assured her that everything would be OK.

We left for the funeral at 15:40. The service was at St Mary's. Mum and I sat in the second row. There was only Gretna and her sister Molly in the first row but Mum said that's how it was meant to be, family only. There were others dotted around, old ladies mostly. Artie Sampson and his wife appeared, taking a pew at the back. They ignored us and we ignored them.

For the first five minutes the vicar spoke about Mrs Jenkins, about how she was a well-loved member of the community and a regular at the church and how concerned they all were when she stopped showing up for service. He said Mrs Jenkins had had a lot of tragedy in her life but she fought through it all. She was a fighter. Then he spoke about Jesus, about the tragedy Jesus had had in his life. He spoke about Jesus for about half an hour. Then the funeral ended.

It was still raining as we left. We ran to the car. I wasn't bothered about getting wet but Mum was worried about my hair and my Christmas clothes so I stooped under the umbrella with her. The spokes kept catching my scalp.

Mum said she didn't want to be the first to arrive at the wake so we waited in the car for a while, watching the rain. She switched on the CD player. I thought she was going to play 'Suspicious Minds' but instead she skipped to 'Are You

Lonesome Tonight?' She stared up at the church. I could tell she was thinking about Nan. Church always makes her think of Nan, that's why she never goes. We listened to the entire song, start to finish, twice, before she switched off the CD player and started the engine.

The wake was at the Prancing Horse. There was a table in the corner with a 'Reserved' sign and a buffet of finger sandwiches – ham, egg, cheese and pickle. Gretna was sitting at the table, chatting to two old ladies. Gretna's sister was standing at the buffet, peeling back the sandwiches to study their fillings.

Gretna waved us over. She said, 'Wasn't it a lovely service?' and Mum said, 'It was.' The old ladies smiled up at us. Gretna's sister returned from the buffet and Gretna introduced her as Molly. Molly invited us to help ourselves to a drink at the bar, there was a tab. The old ladies and Gretna and Molly were all drinking pineapple juice but Mum said we'd need something stronger. She ordered us both a cosmopolitan, which is a type of cocktail. I said maybe I shouldn't, what about my medication?

'Just one won't hurt,' she said.

We took two stools at the reserved table. At first Gretna asked about my age, my school, what I wanted to be when I grew up. Mum said I was very good at English and Gretna asked if I was going to be an English teacher and I nodded and smiled and sipped my cocktail. It tasted like cranberry juice.

For a while Gretna talked about her life on the road. She's a Heaven's Angel. The Heaven's Angels are a Christian biker gang. They travel the country, trying to recruit other Christian bikers. Gretna never said what would happen when they'd recruited enough Christian bikers. Molly was also a Heaven's Angel. They both had leather jackets hung over their chairs, a picture of a smiling Jesus stitched to the back. They held hands under the table. I couldn't help but doubt what Mum had said about them being sisters.

Mum ordered us two more cocktails, margaritas this time, which tasted like lime juice. Then Mum began to tell Gretna and Molly and the old ladies about the kitchen she's planning, how she's going to knock through the lounge and extend the back of the house to make room for it, how we're saving for an Aga cooker. She'll probably need planning permission and so Gretna might have to sign something at some point, 'But it's not going to be unsightly or anything, don't worry.' Gretna nodded and smiled and sipped her pineapple juice. I ate an egg sandwich. It was gritted with shell. I washed it down with more margarita.

I kept an eye out for you. I thought I might catch a glimpse of you in your Marigolds but I didn't. I'm not sure if you even work at the Prancing Horse any more. It didn't matter too much, tomorrow is Goose's party. Tomorrow we're going to run away together and I'll see you every day then. It's strange to think I'll probably never see Mum again. That's why I kept drinking those cocktails with her. Some of them were disgusting but I didn't want Mum to know that. I figured it was a good memory she could have of us. A good way to say goodbye.

The rain was heavy when we left, even heavier than it'd been all day. We planned to make a run for the car but as soon as we set off Mum tripped in her heels. She kicked them off and tucked them under her arm and the two of us sprinted across the car park. Mum squealed at the icy rain on her toes. I tried to protect her with the umbrella.

By the time we reached the car we were shivering. Mum set the air-con to HEAT, lifting her feet to the dashboard. There are floor heaters in the BMW but Mum doesn't know how to turn them on.

'That was pretty fun,' she said. 'For a funeral.'

We listened to 'Are You Lonesome Tonight?' again. Mum sang along. She started the engine and pulled out of the car park. It was dark by now. Even with the wipers on full it was hard to see through the blur of the rain. I put my seat belt on. Mum said she was going to make Singapore slings when we got home.

'Have you ever had a Singapore sling?'

I shook my head.

'They're fabulous.'

We pulled out of the square onto the dual carriageway. Mum

started to tell me about Singapore slings, how you shake everything up with the ice before serving, how you have to be careful not to add club soda until after it's been shaken or else it explodes all over the kitchen. We'd just passed the canal bridge when we heard the squeal. The car bounced a little.

'What was that?'

I shrugged.

'The tyre?'

Mum frowned in the rear-view mirror. She pulled into the bus stop and stared over her shoulder.

'What is that? Can you see that? In the road?'

I told Mum I couldn't see anything.

'Wait here.'

She opened the umbrella and stepped out into the rain. The hazard lights clicked and flashed and clicked and flashed. Rain hammered the windscreen. I closed my eyes.

Next thing Mum was back, knocking on my window.

'Greg,' she cried. 'Get out, Greg.'

I climbed out of the car. The rain washed over me. It flattened my hair. It soaked my sweater. It ran down the collar of my shirt. I hunched, as if hunching would keep me dry. A river of rain cascaded over the street, flashing red in the hazard lights. A white feather floated by, disappearing under the car.

Mum was standing in the middle of the carriageway. The

umbrella lay beside her, filling with rain. She was staring at a white fluffy ball in the road.

It was a mallard. Its neck was flattened, worms of what looked like mince smeared in all directions. One of its legs was pressed into the tarmac, the other flapping wildly in the rain.

'What is it?' Mum said.

I told her it was a duck.

'What the hell's it doing here?' she screamed. 'Out on its own? Don't they emigrate?'

I told her I thought they did. I thought they had.

'Should we kill it?'

I didn't know.

'We can't just drive off,' she said. 'We can't just leave it.'

The rain soaked through my jumper. It snaked my back, gathering at the lip of my boxers. My fringe was starting to curl. I was surprised how little blood there was, just feathers and meat.

Every few seconds the duck let out a squawk. It sounded like it was coughing.

'We've got to do something,' Mum said. 'What if I reversed over it?'

The rain lightened. Spitting. Its hiss died.

Everything went quiet.

'What do we do?'

TRANSCRIPT

Extract of interview between Detective
Sergeant Terrence Mansell (TM) and Gregory
Hall's mother, Mrs Deborah Hall (DH).

TM: Let's talk about Greg's condition.

DH: OK.

TM: He's schizophrenic.

DH: Apparently.

TM: You don't believe he is?

DH: Sometimes. Sometimes I'm not so sure.

TM: Why?

DH: That doctor, he . . . he just assumed
   that's what it is, straight off. That first
   time we saw him. And there's no proper test.
   It's not like they can ever know for sure. I
   . . . I don't know. It just seems too easy.

TM: Easy?

DH: It's like a cop-out. Like, an excuse for

the way he is, rather than an explanation.

TM: But his hallucinations? His episodes? This would suggest schizophrenia?

DH: He sees things, yes. Things we can't see. Sometimes I think he's making it up, but then sometimes I think maybe he's just overreacting because he's actually seen something, a cobweb or something, and it's sent him into over-drive. I don't know. I think maybe it's a bit of both. He doesn't know, when he sees some-thing, whether it's real or not. I mean, to him it is real. I guess it doesn't matter.

TM: But that's what schizophrenia is, right? Paranoia? False beliefs?

DH: I suppose.

TM: You're still unconvinced?

DH: There's no proper test. That's all I'm saying.

TM: How old was he when he was diagnosed?

DH: Sarah was four at the time, so he must have been, what, six or seven.

TM: That seems young.

DH: It is young. Very young. Dr Hughes said it was the youngest he'd ever seen.

TM: But he was certain it was schizophrenia?

DH: He was determined. Mind you, almost everyone since has agreed. We have check-ups less regularly now, but at first we were going back every couple of months, not always to the same doctor. The only person who ever even considered another possibility, who ever considered Greg could be cured, was my psychiatrist, Dr Filburn.

TM: What about your husband? What does he think?

DH: I don't know. At first he thought Greg was just doing it for attention. Now, I don't know. You'd have to ask him.

TM: But he is a doctor?

DH: Not any more, he's a surgeon.

TM: But presumably he was? Presumably he went to medical school?

DH: Well, yes.

TM: And he didn't notice anything? Any signs? Before the diagnosis?

DH: I think he was hoping it was just a stage. I don't know. He was thinking that it was, you know, attention.

TM: It must have been hard.

DH: It is.

TM: Not just for Greg, but for you all. There's quite a stigma.

DH: We kept it private. We keep ourselves to ourselves. We're that sort of family.

TM: What was it that made you get him checked out in the first place?

DH: It was Sarah. How he was with Sarah.

TM: They didn't get on?

DH: They got on fine, at first. He was fascinated by her.

TM: In what way?

DH: Well, when we first brought her home he'd stand at the end of the cot for ages, staring at her. It was like he didn't believe she was real. It was only when she got older he started acting up.

TM: How?

DH: There were incidents.

TM: Like what?

DH: We found him in her room a couple of times, at night.

TM: Doing what?

DH: Watching her. Crying.

TM: Crying?

DH: He said it was, you know, 'them'. He said

she had them all over her. This was the first we heard about 'them'. To start with I didn't know what the hell he was talking about. By then she'd be crying too. This was when she was about eighteen months and he used to scare her, doing that. So I'd lift her out of bed and I'd lift her pyjamas up to show him how clean she was, show him there was nothing there, nothing on her, but it made no difference. He'd just keep crying, telling me I had to help her. Telling me I had to get them off her.

TM: So what did you do?

DH: I didn't know what to do. I wasn't sleeping much. I was working at the salon then. Howard was still planning the surgery, so it was a stressful time. I was the one who always had to get up in the night. But I figured it was a stage, it'd pass.

TM: But it didn't pass.

DH: It got worse when she was about four. That's when he started scratching at her.

TM: Scratching?

DH: Well, she had eczema. Really bad eczema. She was always scratching, always covered in scratches anyway, so we didn't know, at first, that he was doing it too. Then we were at the supermarket one day and I heard her screaming and turned round and she was cowering from him, and he was over her, standing over her, clawing at her. He was six so he was bigger, a lot stronger. He started saying it again, the same old stuff, that she had 'them' all over her. That he had to get them off.

TM: He thought they were something to do with her eczema?

DH: He'd muddled the two things in his mind somehow. He'd sit there watching her scratch, saying stuff like, 'Help her. Get them off her. They're all over her.' And I'd try and explain there was nothing there, but he wouldn't listen. They were real. To him they were real and that was that.

TM: So you took him to the doctor.

DH: Howard didn't want to. I don't know why. We never talked about it all that much, he just told me not to be dramatic. Told me it was just attention-seeking. He didn't witness it first hand, though, and it was hard to explain how . . . how horrific it was. How obvious it was that Greg really believed in them. Believed that they were real. Until Finners Island.

TM: Finners Island?

DH: That was when he crossed a line. When I decided to split them up.

TM: What happened?

DH: We don't know, exactly. [Sighs.] Look, I feel I'm giving the wrong impression. He's not . . . violent. He's a very peaceful person, very calm. It's just his condition. He can't seem to help it.

TM: What happened on Finners Island?

DH: He had some kind of episode. It was out on the water. Sarah always loved the boats . . .

TM: The boats?

DH: There were these boats you could go out to sea in. These little inflatable things. What are they called?

TM: Dinghies?

DH: Yeah, like rubber dinghies. Anyway, we wouldn't let her out in them because she was only four. But she really wanted to, she

kept going on about it. Then one morning
Howard and I went into the woods for a
walk. My parents were with us and they were
supposed to be watching the children.

TM: Are these the grandparents Greg went to
live with?

DH: Yeah. Don't get me wrong, they were
reliable, usually, and responsible. But
they were old, even then, especially Herb.
I think those holidays took a lot out of
them. Anyway, they must have both fallen
asleep or something because when we got
back the kids were gone. Mum and Herb were
frantic, obviously — we all were. We had
no idea where they'd gone.

TM: They'd gone out in a dinghy.

DH: Yeah. Though they weren't in the dinghy
any more by this point. I just saw this
splashing, something splashing out in the
water, and then Howard was gone, running out
across the beach like something from one of
his *Baywatch* videos.

TM: He saved them.

DH: He was the hero, yes. Sarah was unconscious

but Howard brought her round. He had to
resuscitate her. That was the worst moment
of my life, watching him do that. You know,
that thing with the hands? The kiss of
life? She was too young for all that. Her
body was so small. It seemed absurd. It was
only when we got back to the hotel we
realised she was all scratched up. Greg was
throwing up in the reception, into a bucket
from this bucket-and-spade set we had.
Sarah was bleeding quite a bit and it was
obvious he'd been scratching at her. That
he'd had some kind of episode, out in the
boat.

TM: That's why you sent him off, to live with
your parents.

DH: I had to be sure he wouldn't hurt Sarah.
I had to protect her.

TM: That's understandable.

DH: I didn't want him to be away from us. I
didn't want to only see him once a week. I
just . . . I had no choice. I took him to
the doctors. Got him diagnosed. Got him on
medication.

TM: And did things improve?

DH: They seemed to. I don't know if it was the pills or the fact he was apart from Sarah, but he had fewer and fewer episodes. He'd talk about 'them' less. For years he was fine. Until he was about eleven.

TM: Then what happened?

DH: That was when my mother . . . she had a breakdown. It was after Herb died, she never really recovered from that. She got even more religious. We sometimes thought maybe she was . . . well, you know. If Greg is then there's no reason she couldn't be as well. They say it runs in families. And she was always big into church. That's a part of it, I think, the religion. Believing all that stuff, believing in imaginary people, right? Anyway, she got Greg's condition and her own all jumbled. She was trying to help him but she was making it worse, going on about 'them' all the time, taping up all the cracks in the house.

TM: The parcel tape?

DH: That was her, got him doing that. We had

to step in eventually. She was . . . we had
to have her put in a home. Greg had to come
back to the family.

TM: And how was he?

DH: Good. Well, as good as he ever was. He
was still very quiet, but he was fine with
Sarah. He rarely had any fits or anything,
just the occasional episode. Maybe like once
a year or something.

TM: You didn't know it had come back then,
recently? That he was having problems again?

DH: No. I mean, there was an incident, a few
weeks ago. He was sick in the house, at a
dinner party. But I thought that was just
one of these stand-alone episodes. I didn't
know it meant anything. I didn't know he
was going to do anything . . . like this.

[Pause.]

[DH starts crying.]

TM: We can have a break if you want.

DH: If I'd known, I would have done something.
I would have.

TM: Do you need a minute?

DH: I'll be OK. I just . . . I'll be OK.

[Pause.]

TM: It's not your fault.

DH: Yes, I think I'd like a minute, actually.

TM: OK.

DH: Just a minute. I'll be fine in a minute.

III

OK, so I'm just going to try to be honest here. A lot has happened and I want to get it all down and the only way I can think of is just to write it, as best as I can remember. I have to ignore the cold and the tiredness and the pain in my palm and just write.

So here goes.

I opened my window. That's how it started, for me, New Year's Eve. The end-of-year celebrations. I retrieved the key from my *Breakfast at Tiffany's* video-case and opened my fire-escape window. It was hard, after all that time locked up. Stiff. It made this sort of sucking sound, the rubber inlay peeling from the plastic.

I sat out on the roof. The air was icy so I balled into my warm-position. I smoked. I thought I'd better practise for the party. I didn't want to cough all over you like last time. I'd managed to buy some beers, too, from Waitrose, so I practised drinking a few of them. Sarah and Mum were getting ready in their rooms. My father was locked away in his study. And there I was, sitting on the rooftop, sipping a Bud and watching the stars.

After a while I felt tired. I was worried I'd fall asleep, slip and fall down into the garden, so I climbed back inside and lay on my bed.

By the time I woke everyone had left: my parents had gone to the Hamptons', my sister gone off with the Vultures from her year. The room was icy from having left the window open. I had a headache. I huddled under the sheets for an hour, forced down another beer. I tried not to think of the night ahead – the party. I tried to concentrate on what really mattered: you. You had invited me. You'd said you'd see me there. No matter what happened I had to ensure you did.

I packed a few things. Some clothes, deodorant, a toothbrush, stashed in the rucksack with my beers. I took my *Breakfast at Tiffany's* video-case. I figured we'd need money and I now have over £454, built up in Hampton's wage packets – more than enough to get the train down to the coast. More than enough to get the ferry to Finners Island.

I waited till 22:07, then walked to Goose's. I figured this was a good time to arrive. The party would be well underway by then. You'd be there by then. As I reached the corner of Wallaby

Drive I began to make out the chorus of Miss X's 'Screemin Boi'. As I approached number 7 the song had reached the breakdown, where Miss X pants erotically over the steady thud-thud of the bass drum. There were a couple of partygoers, year tens by the looks of it, asleep on the front path – one curled by the flower tubs, the other face down beneath the vomit-splattered bonnet of Goose's parents' Mercedes. The front door was wide open, the hallway beyond it heaving with bodies.

It was even more packed than I'd expected. People were squeezed into every corner, slouched in every doorway, perched on every step of the staircase. They laughed, smoked, swigged various coloured liquids from various cans and bottles. They smelt of beer, cigarettes, cherries and sweat. You were nowhere to be seen. It dawned on me that I was overdressed: the girls were dolled up – tight-fitting dresses, the usual Vulture hair and makeup – but the boys were all wearing T-shirt-and-jean combos. A few had styled their hair with gel but that was the only evidence of any pride in their appearance.

I stepped back out into the front garden. I inhaled a couple of lungfuls of icy night air. The beer-buzz seemed to be wearing off and my hands were trembling, rattling my backpack, clinking the bottles inside. I rested the backpack on the doorstep and dragged off my Christmas jumper. I untucked my shirt and ruffled my hair. One of the year tens raised his head and asked if I had a glass of water. I told him I didn't. I had beer, though.

'That'll do.'

I handed him a bottle. He gave me a thumbs up and hugged it to his chest. He lay his face on the gravel. I didn't want to disturb him with the offer of a bottle-opener so I turned and stepped inside the house again.

I squeezed my way in through the hall crowd. At first the mass body heat was a relief from the cold but it took mere seconds to increase to that uncomfortable neck-sweat stage. I apologised pretty much constantly for the amount of bodily contact I was making but I don't think anyone could hear me. Miss X was still playing, a new song now, the phrase 'Pleaser teaser' or possibly 'Teaser pleaser' repeating over and over and over and over and over leaving the partygoers with no communicatory option but to lean in and scream into one another's ears. All around me were voices but I couldn't make out a single word they were saying. I searched for your face, the red curls of your hair, but the hall was so dark and the crowd was so vast and I couldn't find you.

I pressed on to the kitchen. I figured it might be quieter there, I could cool off, catch my bearings, put my beers in the fridge. Only the kitchen was even livelier than the hallway. The fridge was open, its contents spread across the table and floor. Several foodstuffs were smeared up the walls – ketchup, dog food, something white and gloopy, possibly mayonnaise or fresh yoghurt. Most of the crowd congregated at the entrance to the conservatory, surrounding some fat kid who was standing on the pool table. Ian was over by the sink with Angela, pouring green liquid into two eggcups. They linked arms and downed the contents – Angela coughing, Ian laughing and slapping her back. Miss X was still playing, yet another song now, the chorus: 'Foot fetish / Fetish feet / Give me something good to eat'.

The fat kid on the pool table was Eggy, one of the Oxbridge kids from my class. He was shouting something but it was impossible to distinguish over the music. He lifted an egg high above him, attempting that trick where you squeeze it between your thumb and finger to demonstrate the strength of the shell – only each time Eggy squeezed the egg burst in his hand, spilling yolk down his arm, splattering his shoes and the felt of the pool table. There were stacks of egg boxes piled beside him. People were laughing, shouting things over the music like 'Go on, Eggy!' and 'You can do it, you smelly bastard!' and a variety of other encouragements. Eggy kept trying, egg after egg after egg, angrier and angrier at each pop and splatter.

I pressed on to a section of unsplattered work-surface in the corner, over by the recycling box. I took a beer from my bag and cracked it open. I sipped, thumb-plugging the bottle to keep it from foaming. The beer was warm. It tasted like fizz. It made me thirsty, which is the opposite of what a beverage should do.

There were two partygoers sitting on the work-surface beside me. Hawaiian shirts, three-quarter-length trousers, sandals. One of them was bald but for a single strip of black hair, running from his forehead to the back of his neck. The other was blond, hair down to his shoulders.

Halfway through my beer I began to make out the odd stray shout of their conversation. They were discussing Lucy Marlowe. The near-bald kid was questioning her attractiveness. He thought her new boobs were too big, they looked out of place. He said Lucy was too short to pull them off. The blond kid disagreed, in his opinion there was no such thing as 'too big'. I couldn't help but glance over, following their conversation. The blond kid noticed my glances. Each time he'd catch my eye I'd look away, back over at Eggy and his egg-popping.

Then the blond kid slid from the work-surface, leaning over to scream in my ear.

'Do I know you, man?'

I shook my head. He squinted at me. He leant over again.

'What's your name?'

I leant to his ear and told him.

'What year are you in?'

I told him.

'Hey, you in Lucy Marlowe's class?'

I nodded. He grinned. The near-bald kid screamed 'What?' and the blond kid shouted something into his ear. Then the blond kid told me how lucky I am. He explained how attractive Lucy Marlowe is since her breast enhancement surgery. He asked if I'd got a good look at her post-op breasts. I told him I hadn't. The blond kid advised me to keep an eye out for any breast-glimpse opportunity. He had a friend in the same class as Angela Hargrove and once she'd been running late and got changed for dance practice right in the middle of her Geography class and his friend had seen one of her nipples. I didn't know how to respond to this. More and more party-goers were forcing their way into the kitchen to watch Eggy. He'd given up popping and was now trying to juggle the eggs. Ian was filling a dog bowl with green liquid. The dog was on the conservatory patio, roaring at the army of intruders in its house, barking a diamond of condensation onto the glass. Miss X was still playing, lyrics indecipherable.

You were still nowhere to be seen.

The blond kid asked who I fancied more, Lucy Marlowe or Angela Hargrove. I said I didn't know.

'You've got to know! If you don't know, who does?'

I didn't want to talk about girls any more so I told him I had a girlfriend. I thought that would stop him asking but he just whit-wooed and winked at the near-bald kid and asked even worse questions, which I won't repeat here. I told him that what he was referring to was private, between me and my girl. I don't know what his reaction to this was because by now I was concentrating solely on Eggy. The crowd had bored of his juggling and were hurling stuff at him, other foodstuffs – avocados, rashers of bacon, spoonfuls of the white gloopy substance.

They began to chant: 'E-ggy! E-ggy! E-ggy!'

'Wait, I know you!' the blond kid shouted. 'You're that kid in Ian's class! The psycho!'

The bald kid frowned. The blond kid leant to his ear and shouted something and they both laughed. I sipped my beer. The blond kid leant to my ear.

'I know who you're shaggin'! It's Miss Hayes!'

Ian dropped the dog bowl and began to nibble at Angela's neck. She laughed and tried to push him away. Eggy was retaliating, launching eggs out into the crowd. One splattered across the window, above the dog, and it leapt to bite at it from the other side of the glass. Miss X seemed to be getting louder and louder. The blond kid was saying something about Miss Hayes, about our weekly meetings. The crowd was still chanting.

You were still nowhere to be seen.

I placed my empty beer bottle in the recycling box, smiled once more at the Hawaiian-shirt kids and stepped out into the hallway. I was shaking so much I could feel the bottles in my backpack, clinking together. One of the bottles had dislodged from its cardboard sleeve and was nuzzling my spine. The Hawaiian-shirt kids were grinning. They may have been laughing, I don't know – there was laughter everywhere and it was impossible to single out theirs.

I knew I needed to find you. I needed to say what I had to say and get away from Goose's, before more people noticed me. There were three other doorways across the hall and I squeezed through to each of them in turn. The first was locked. The second led to the dining room, which was in darkness, empty but for a couple perched on the window seat, kissing aggressively.

The third led to the living room. A gang of year tens were cross-legged in the centre of the room, sitting around a Monopoly board. They'd built a small town out of the game's green and red plastic buildings and one of them was flooding the town with beer. The rest were rolling cigarettes using £500 notes. The TV was on, a channel with a topless woman who rolls on the floor while speaking into a telephone, but nobody was watching, everyone was drinking and shouting into one another's ears. Lucy Marlowe and Carly Meadows were over in the corner, stabbing the keys of the Lamberts' piano, roaring with laughter. It was impossible to hear anything over Miss X, still screeching from the stereo:

L–O–V–E,
It is an accessory

I returned to the dining room. I sat. I figured I'd wait it out. I had to see you eventually. It was impossible to spend the whole night in the house with you and not see you. Fate had thrown us together in the past and it would again. I just had to be patient.

I took my four remaining beers from the plastic Waitrose bag and lined them up on the dining table, along with the cigarettes and box of cooking matches. The kissing couple didn't notice, or if they did then it didn't affect the aggressiveness of their kissing. The party hummed around us, the odd Vulture-screech penetrating the music. At one point there was an almighty crash, followed by mass laughter and applause, which I assume was Eggy slipping from the pool table. Eventually the kissers departed, giggling and handholding. Finally the music died. By the time I'd opened my third beer it was 23:07.

The hallway had cleared when I left the dining room. Its carpet was littered with cans and bottles, reams of toilet roll. The partygoers had raided a box of fireworks and were setting them off in the garden – cheering along with their screeches and pops. I wondered how they'd celebrate the stroke of midnight. They'd already trashed the house, already set off the fireworks. The only possible climax was some sort of explosion, destroy the house completely. Some sort of human sacrifice, perhaps.

I needed the toilet. I stepped over to the stairs. As I passed the living room something gasped.

'Oh my god!'

It was Carly Meadows. She was laid out on the couch, glaring up at me.

'You're that guy from class,' she said.

I nodded. The living room had also pretty much emptied. There was Monopoly money everywhere. A different woman was topless on the TV, sucking a telephone like it was an ice-lolly.

'Lucy, look,' Carly said. 'That guy from English is here.'

Lucy Marlowe sat up from behind the couch. She was chewing gum, clutching a half-drunk bottle of Navy Rum. Her top had slipped down so much that one of her nipples was sticking out. She looked me up and down.

'Fuckin' hell,' she said.

I nodded. I sipped my beer, coughing as I swallowed. I tried not to look at the nipple.

'That was amazin' when you ran out of class the other day,' Carly Meadows said. 'Wasn't that amazin' when he ran out of class the other day, Lucy?'

'It was amazin'.'

'Amazin'.'

I thanked them, still nodding, still sipping my beer. Carly and Lucy glared up at me and I sipped until my bottle was empty. Then I picked at the label. The woman on the TV turned and raised her backside to the camera. She reached back and wobbled her bum cheeks.

I asked the girls if they'd seen Ian anywhere. Or Angela. Or even Goose.

They laughed.

'What the fuck do you want with Angela?' Carly Meadows said.

I asked if they'd seen you at all. They laughed again.

'Alith? Have we theen Alith?'

'Who the fuck'th Alith?'

I rubbed my tongue against the roof of my mouth. Sometimes this helps my lisp. A rocket struck the window, ricocheting into the crowd. The partygoers swarmed in circles, laughing, screaming. The dog bounded between them, howling.

I asked the girls to excuse me. They laughed again.

'Excuthe me!'

'Excuthe!'

I stepped back through the hall. Lucy and Carly carried on talking. One of them used the world 'psycho' but I ignored it and carried on up the stairs. They were slick with sick and spilt beer and various partygoers were curled in various positions, sleeping in one another's arms. At the top of the stairs were a guy and girl, huddled, aggressive-kissing. The guy was sucking the girl's neck, pressing her face into the wall with one hand, thumb-rubbing her nipple with the other. The girl murmured. She clutched a bottle of Lambrini, tipping it too far, hissing a waterfall down the top three stairs.

The girl's eyes opened.

It was Sarah.

She squealed and pushed the guy from her neck. It was the blond Hawaiian-shirt kid from the kitchen. He smirked. He wiped his mouth. Sarah frowned at me. It was that same frown she used to give the St Peter's kids when they called her 'Flake' in the playground, like she was angry at my very soul.

Sarah excused herself, standing, fixing her top. She dragged me across the landing to the bathroom. The blond kid shouted, 'Hey, she's mine!' but Sarah shushed him and slammed and locked the door.

The bathroom was vast and granite-tiled, adorned with candles, seashells, scented hand soaps. It made me think of Mum. The sink was brimming with water, wadded with toilet paper and some sort of green leafy foodstuff – spinach, maybe, or rocket salad. Sarah dragged me over to the shower. The curtain was pulled right across. It was patterned with little grey ducks.

'Why are you here?'

I told Sarah that Goose was in my year. I came because of the party. It was New Year's.

She continued to frown. 'Who invited you?'

I couldn't think of any names off the top of my head so I just said, 'Ian Connor.'

She snorted. 'As if.'

The shower curtain danced slightly in the breeze. The ducks swayed back and forth. Behind it lay a blurred pink figure. Sarah started to speak again but I had no idea what she was saying – I was too busy trying to work out if the pink figure was in fact a living, breathing, possibly naked person, listening in on our conversation. Sarah stopped talking. She turned her frown to the shower curtain. She turned to me. She tore the curtain back.

There was a woman, slumped in the foot of the shower, skin pink and glistening, mouth lipstick-red and open in an O. She was wearing a shower cap, which was pointless as she was made entirely of plastic and therefore already waterproof. The words 'Flat-Chested Slut' were painted across her inflated breasts in Tipp-Ex.

Sarah sighed and grabbed the woman and slung her across the room. She bounced off the door before settling, head wedged beneath the sink. Sarah dragged me into the shower and pulled the curtain across.

'Look,' she whispered, 'you're not going to fit in here. It's just not going to happen. Plus Tony said a gang of Pitt kids are coming to trash the place any minute and let's face it, if anyone's getting a beating, it's you.'

I told Sarah that I had to find somebody.

'Who?'

I couldn't say.

'Whatever. Just hurry up and get out of here. If anyone asks, we're not related, OK?'

I nodded. I thanked Sarah for the warning. She said, 'Whatever,' again and stepped out from the shower. After a quick mirror-check she left, slamming the door behind her.

I stepped over to the toilet. I placed my beer on the basin and took a pee. It was the longest pee of my life. Halfway through I noticed the plastic woman, still slumped on the floor, watching me, her mouth still shocked into an O.

By the time I stepped out onto the landing again, Sarah and the blond kid had gone. Out in the garden someone was screaming, possibly a victim of a ricocheted firework. The dog was barking. There were three doors along the landing, all of which were shut. At the far end was another stairway, leading up to some sort of attic room. I could make out giggling. A lingering chipotle-smoke smell.

I climbed the stairs. The giggling was accompanied by a squeaking. At the top of the stairs was another door, slightly ajar. I could make out Ian, or half of him at least, cross-legged at the foot of a wardrobe, holding his face. His shirt was torn, chin resting on his bare white chest, fringe curled over his knuckles. He was rocking back and forth and at first I thought the squeaking was coming from him, perhaps from his back pressing against the wardrobe behind him. But as I crept closer to the door-crack it was clear the squeaking was coming from the other side of the room, along with Goose's laughter and a faint repetitive slapping.

I pressed the door open. A TV glared from the wall, broadcasting a blizzard of static. Goose's bed was over by the window. There was a girl on it. At first I thought it might be you but I quickly recognised Angela. Her head bobbed, hang-mouthed, off the side, chin in the air, hair swaying into a puddle of vomit on the carpet. Goose stood beside her, giggling, tipping a bottle of beer onto her chest. It fizzed over her face, trickling through her hair into the ever-expanding vomit-puddle. Beer bubbles glistened on her forehead and eyelashes. The near-bald Hawaiian-shirt kid was there, hunched halfway down the bed, teeth gritted, gripping the mattress. He was jerking back and forth. His Hawaiian shirt was open, flapping about him. His eyes were closed, tight – his forehead locked into a frown.

Every few seconds Angela's head turned from side to side, as if by turning her head she could avoid the sticky torrent of beer, but Goose was relentless in his pouring. When the bottle was empty he reached for another from a box beside the bed, cracking the lid with his teeth. I wasn't sure if he'd noticed me – if any of them had. It didn't seem to matter. Occasionally Angela would let out a sound – a grunt, or a short sharp intake of breath – and the Hawaiian-shirt kid would repeat the sound, imitate it. I'm not sure if he was aware he was doing this. The static light washed over them all. It danced chaotically, especially on Angela. Shadows flickered over her, like **Them**, hundreds of **Them**, swarming on her cold white skin.

As I retreated to the attic stairs Ian looked up from his lap. He took a second to focus on me but when he did he gave me a thumbs up. Then he shook his head, let it slide back into his hands.

I sat in the bathroom for a while. I don't know how long. First I was sick in the sink and then I just sat on the side of the bath, watching my vomit chunks float amongst the leafy green stuff. I thought over the situation. If you weren't up there with Goose, then you weren't at the party. If you weren't at the party then you must be at home. You must have a reason for staying at home and that reason was more than likely your father.

I knew then, what I had to do. Things were going to be more complicated than I'd thought. I wasn't able to just meet you at the party, that was too easy. I was going to have to go out to the Pitt and get you.

A banging came from downstairs. I thought it was the party-goers. I assumed they'd decided to set off their fireworks indoors. The big New Year's climax.

When I reached the foot of the stairs I realised it was the Pitt kids – a gang of them had arrived with baseball bats and were in the process of destroying the kitchen. The partygoers were still out in the garden. They'd built a bonfire from the last of the fireworks (the least entertaining ones – fountains, roman candles, Catherine wheels) and were sitting in a circle watching the screaming flames, crackling and flashing in various colours.

There were four Pitt kids in total. One of them was wearing a blue hoodie, not unlike your brother's. I couldn't be sure it was him because of the scarf covering his mouth, and he wouldn't stay still long enough for me to assess the blueness of his eyes. He brought his bat down on the kitchen sink, the porcelain splitting clean down the middle. Two others were smashing the crockery. Another was dragging out the drawers, emptying them out onto the floor.

I knew that if I was going to face your father I couldn't go empty-handed. I considered the Pitt kids' bats. They were threatening enough but there was no way I could do any real damage, if it came to it. Not against your father. I doubt I could even reach his head.

Then one of the Pitt kids emptied the knife drawer and a selection of knives clattered across the tiles.

I crossed the kitchen to the knives. The Pitt kids stopped their smashing and stared at me, bats loose in their hands.

They glared from under their hoods. I chose a knife, a large carving knife, like the ones at the butcher's. I could feel the Pitt kids' eyes on me as I examined it. Then I crossed the room again, to the door, and left.

The Pitt's always been firework crazy. I remember those New Years with Nan and Herb, how they'd always make a big deal about getting fireworks. They wanted to make it special because at Christmas and birthdays we went to Skipdale – this was the only night my parents brought Sarah down to the Pitt. It was the only night I remember Herb leaving his chair. I used to believe Herb spent all year plugged into the wall, charging, waiting to launch into New Year's Eve – into the drinking of Guinness and roasting of chestnuts and piling of rockets on the kitchen table, which I would inspect thoroughly. I'd pick the order in which the fireworks were to be launched, which would depend on the size of the rockets and the tradition of saving the biggest, most orbit-likely till last. Every year Herb would tell me we'd get at least one of the bastards into space.

Herb did the dangerous stuff. The garden was concrete so he couldn't stab the tubes into soil the way the instructions said. Instead he'd arrange the rockets in their own individual plant pots. The garden was only twenty foot long, so the hundred-foot safety distance was out of the question, but for this one night of the year Herb would take a 'Whatever happens, happens' attitude (perhaps due to the Guinness) and would light as many rockets as he could, only hobbling to the relative safety of the kitchen doorway when the first few were screaming into the air. It seems odd but when I think back to New Years, to Herb skipping about with his safety lighter and Sarah balanced on Mum's knee scratching at her toes and all the fireworks in their plant pots with all their screaming light and banging, my favourite part is still thinking about Nan, sitting in silence at the back of the kitchen, Mr Saunders curled on her knee. Thinking about Nan's furry face as it followed each rocket up into the sky. It was as if after all those years she still wasn't sure how it was done.

Tonight was no different. Rockets screeched from every garden, thundering and flowering through the murk of the sky, bathing the streets in light: red, green, golden yellow. The streets were misted in smoke. It was like a war zone. I crossed at the Rat and Dog. A crowd of drinkers had spilt from its doorway and were standing in a circle, linking arms and singing. Music hummed from the pub – chatter, laughter, shattering glass. I pulled my hood up and kept my head down. I hurried to the estates.

The knife was still tucked into my belt, cold against my hip. I couldn't help but imagine it, pressing it into your father's stomach, the resistance at first, before his belly gave way to it. It was a large belly and I'd need to give it some force. I'd need to be quick, if it came to it.

I stopped at the end of your road. I leant against the wall and heaved. Nothing came up. I couldn't help but feel it, again and again, the knife popping your father's stomach. I remembered Artie Sampson's Father Christmas, doubled over on the pavement. That's how your father would fall, sinking slowly till his face pressed into the ground. I clutched the handle of the knife and thought of you, your eye all swollen and black.

Your house was in darkness. Your father's car was missing. I rang the bell. I couldn't hear the ring so I tried knocking instead. I knocked again. Nothing. I knelt to the letterbox and pressed it open but it was too dark to see anything. It was only then I realised how much I was trembling. How much I was gritting my teeth.

I stood and knocked again, repeatedly.

A voice called out, 'Are you the police?'

I stepped back, hiding the knife under the hem of my jumper. I scanned the front of the house but I couldn't see where the voice was coming from.

'You're not the police.'

There was an old woman, squinting down at me from next-door's bedroom window. She was wearing a fluffy red dressing gown, a large pair of glasses dangling from a cord round her neck.

'He's not in,' she said. 'Did all his roaring then left. As always.'

I asked if she knew where you were.

'There'll be hell to pay when the police get here.'

I knocked again. I waited a couple more minutes, the old lady still squinting down at me. Then I walked round to the park.

The back of the house was as quiet as the front. Your TV lay on the floor in the middle of the lounge, projecting its light up the far wall. The rest of the house was in darkness.

I crawled in through the hedge. A whining came from the shed, high-pitched like Scraps, only interspersed with short sharp sobs. I knelt to the missing-plank gap. There you were, a moonlit silhouette in the corner, Scraps across your lap. You hugged his head over your shoulder, nuzzling his chest. You rubbed the side of his face, dragging the skin back to reveal the white of his eye.

I stood, brushing the mud from my palms and my knees. I dragged my hood down and fixed my hair the best I could, though there was no reflective surface to check my appearance. I took the knife from my belt and stashed it in my backpack. I stepped round to the front of the shed. The grass was frozen and crunched beneath my feet. As I stepped up to the door the whining stopped.

I knocked.

'What?' you said.

I couldn't think of anything to say so I just knocked again.

'What the fuck do you want?'

'I . . .'

The floorboards creaked. You sniffed.

'Well if you're going to come in, then come in.'

I opened the door.

And then came the shot. I must have registered you somehow, in that split-second, standing there in the shed doorway, because I can still picture your face as it was at that moment – stern, frowning, unsunglassed. I can still see the hate in your eyes. I must have seen the gun, too, because I raised my arm the instant the trigger cracked, hand spread as if commanding you to stop. When the pain hit I found myself outside again, stumbling from the steps to the lawn.

I landed on my back. My jaw locked. Each breath hissed through my teeth. I was holding the hand above me by its wrist, limp and clawed and burning, a hot-sharp sting that spread from my palm to the tips of my fingers. Next thing you were kneeling beside me. You were telling me how sorry you were. You were still holding the nail gun but as soon as you realised you tossed it into the hedge. You reached for the hand but I clutched it to my chest.

'It's fine,' I hissed. 'It's nothing.' My lisp sounded even worse through clenched teeth.

Then you saw the blood.

'Shit.'

You clutched your hair. You rubbed your palms into your eyes. You shook your head. You were wearing that pink dressing gown, beneath it a white dress, patterned with blue flowers.

I wanted to reassure you but the pain was clouding my thoughts. All I seemed to be able to do was lie there, gritting my teeth, so hard my gums ached.

'Wait there,' you said.

You disappeared into the shed again. The toolbox rattled. My hand was shaking and I struggled to hold it still. My stomach was churning. I breathed slowly. Within seconds you were back at my side, clutching a pair of pliers.

'Come on.'

You reached under my armpits and hoisted me to my feet, took hold of my un-pierced hand and led me over to the house. You were shaking as much as I was but your crying seemed to have stopped, replaced by a frown of deep concentration.

The kitchen was in darkness. I waited at the doorway while you switched on the light – a bare bulb hanging from the ceiling. It was small for a kitchen, like Nan's used to be – more of a utility room, only with a cooker and a stack of dirty plates on the side.

There was a single stool over in the corner and you told me to sit. You scrambled about, emptying every drawer and cabinet

– utensils, shopping bags, half-empty cereal boxes. I nursed my hand on my lap like a bird with an injured wing. It was only in the light of the single bare bulb that I noticed the bloodstain, spread across the hem of your dress. I looked down at my hand again. It made me light-headed. I should have known, really, that it wasn't my blood on your dress, because it had already blackened to that sticky stage.

You ran out through the hall, up the stairs, shouting for me to wait where I was. I don't know where you thought I was going to go. My hand was still trembling, coat-sleeve sticky with blood, all the way down to my elbow. I cupped my right hand beneath my left, to catch the drips.

You arrived at the doorway again. You placed a pair of tights and a bottle of whiskey on the sideboard. Then you knelt and reached for my hand.

I pulled away.

'Show me.'

I shook my head. 'It's fine.'

'It's not fine.'

'It is.'

You sighed. 'We need to get it out before the tetanus kicks in.'

'I don't think that's how it works.'

You looked me in the eye.

'Show me.'

I uncurled my hand as much as I could. You took my wrist and held it to the light. My palm was cupping a pool of blood. You turned it, examining it, not seeming to mind when the blood spilled onto the floor tiles. I retched. Not because of the pain (although that in itself was pretty intense) but because of the sight of it – the nail – jutting from the back of my hand like some sort of small metallic fang. I couldn't believe what a good shot it had been, right through that cigarette burn on my palm, the scab that was finally healing.

'Here.' You handed me the whiskey bottle. I thought you just wanted me to hold it but then you said, 'Drink, it'll help.' I tried to open the bottle with my teeth but it was tightly screwed. You apologised, resting my hand on the side while you twisted the top off for me.

I took a swig. I retched again.

You told me to look away. I tried to concentrate on the light bulb. It was rocking slightly in the breeze. I could already feel the whiskey, warming its way up through me.

I couldn't help but glance up as you placed the teeth of the pliers on the nail head.

'On three, OK?'

I nodded.

'One . . .'

I gritted my teeth.

'Two . . .'

You yanked. My arm jerked. The pain burnt right up to my elbow. I screamed out and stumbled from the stool to the far side of the room. I crouched in the doorway, biting into the collar of my coat.

I held my hand to the light. The nail was still there.

'You said on three,' I said. I was sweating and shaking and my lisp sounded worse than ever.

'It's wedged right in there,' you said. 'We'll have to go again.'

I told you I thought we were maybe better off calling an ambulance. You shook your head. You said it was never a good idea to get the authorities involved in situations like this. Besides, by the time they got here my arm would be riddled with the tetanus.

I perched on the stool again.

'On two or on three this time?' I asked.

'On three.'

But that was another lie. This time you didn't count at all. As soon you'd gripped the nail you tugged, so hard that, when the nail did break free, you stumbled right across the kitchen into the sideboard, tipping the pile of plates onto the floor. The pain was like nothing I'd ever felt. It was like you'd ripped out one of my bones. I managed not to cry out this time but I still stumbled forwards and dropped my rucksack. My *Breakfast at Tiffany's* video-case clattered across the kitchen floor the same moment the plates did, my journal and wage packets and various keys and trinkets scattering amongst the shattered ceramic.

You examined the nail in the light.

'We got it!'

I bent to gather the contents of my video-case. I tried to piece together the pages of my journal but I was getting blood all over everything. You knelt, trying to help.

'What is this stuff?'

'Don't read it,' I said. 'It's private.'

It was only after I'd spoken that I realised how hostile I'd sounded. You lifted the video-case and starting stuffing the pages inside. You glanced at the title on the spine.

'It's just a box,' I said. 'It's where I keep things.'

'What things?'

'Just things.'

You picked up the cigarette butt. The one I saved from outside your house.

'Is this one of your things?'

I nodded. You weren't paying attention, you were too busy studying it. I added a 'Yes' and you looked up and placed it in the box. Then you reached for the pliers from the sideboard. You held out the nail.

'You want this? For your box?'

You didn't wait for an answer. You dislodged the nail and wrapped it in kitchen roll, placing it in the video-case with everything else.

'Here, keep it,' you said. 'From now on you can always look at it and remember the time that crazy bitch fucked up your hand.'

The box clicked shut. You smiled.

'How does it feel?'

'The hand?'

'The hand.'

'Like the mother of all bee stings.'

You stood and passed me the video-case. I slipped it back into my bag.

'Now we just need to sterilise it.'

I sat on the stool again. You reached into the cupboard for a couple of mugs and poured us both a shot of whiskey. You poured the rest of the bottle over my hand, washing all the blood away. It stung like crazy but by now my hand had been stinging so consistently it was almost expected. I could pretty much remove my mind from the pain. What really bothered me was the smell.

You stretched out the tights and bound my palm. You apologised for your lack of bandages, assuring me the tights were clean. I said it didn't matter. After a few minutes you looked up, eyes fixed on mine.

'Sorry I shot you,' you said. 'I didn't know you were you.'

I nodded. 'It was a mistake. People make mistakes.'

You took a pin from your pocket, fixing the tights in place.

'You weren't at the party,' I said. 'I just came to check you were OK.'

You stared down at your lap, the black stain on your dress. You glanced out at the shed.

'I'm not.'

We crossed the garden to the shed. You stopped at the steps and sat, rubbing your eyes. I stood beside you, waiting. You told me it wasn't pretty and I said it was OK. I raised my hand and told you that, after what we'd just been through, I was ready for anything.

You smiled. You stood again. You stepped up to the shed door.

Under the spotlight of your torch we examined the mess. Various tools had fallen from their nails on the wall. The toolkit lay side-on, its contents spread across the floorboards. Scraps was laid out in his corner, mouth hanging open, tongue limp on the shed floor. There was a black patch across his face I tried not to fixate on. Several black boot marks patterned his ribs.

You switched off the torch then and all we could make out was our breath, curling before us in the moonlight.

'We should bury him,' I said.

You nodded. 'The park. He liked the park.'

I slid off my coat and wrapped it over Scraps. The blood had hardened. It was sticky in the cold air and peeling him from the boards was more difficult than I expected. His legs had stiffened, bobbing as I lifted. He ached my hand a little but the pain eased when I shifted his weight into the crook of my arm. I caught a glimpse of the right side of his skull, buried in the hood of my coat: face caved, fur black and bloody. His right eye was missing, or maybe just so far buried into its socket it was no longer visible. You unhooked a shovel from the wall and led us, out through the hedge gap and across the field.

By then the fireworks had finished and the Pitt was quiet again. I couldn't hear any traffic out on the carriageway. The only sound was our feet, crunching the grass.

You stopped over by the climbing frame.

'Here.'

I laid Scraps down. You sat on one of the swings, beside him, rocking back and forth slightly, reaching down to stroke the un-caved side of his face. I lifted the shovel. It was cold, the metal sticking to my fingers. I hacked it into the ground, gasping at the sting in my palm.

'Sorry,' you said. 'Of course. Here. Let me.'

You took the shovel and told me to sit. I took the other swing. I wanted to reach down and stroke Scraps like you had but I just played with the fur on the hood of the parka instead.

You placed the blade of the shovel onto the grass and stamped. Nothing. The ground wouldn't give. You stamped again. Nothing.

'It's frozen.'

You stamped one more time and the shovel cracked, the blade dislodging from its handle.

'Fuck.'

You laughed and looked up to the sky. The fog of the fireworks was clearing. The stars glittered above us.

'I have a better idea.'

You tossed the shovel and lifted Scraps, nursing him over your shoulder like a baby. You led us back across the field, back through the hedge and over to the shed. You laid Scraps in his corner. I waited at the doorway with the torch as you knelt beside him, whispering to him. Then you started rummaging through the shelves at the back. You lifted out a half-empty bottle of whiskey and placed it on the floor beside you. You lifted out another, two more, not stopping till there were half a dozen, lined up across the shed floor, each with varying amounts of alcohol inside. You placed one bottle – about a third full – in your dressing-gown pocket. The others you opened, one by one, emptying them over Scraps, my coat, the floor of the shed, washing the blood through the cracks between the boards.

You stepped down. You took the last bottle of whiskey from your pocket and splattered half across the steps. You asked me for a match. I offered you the box and you snatched them from me, lighting them and dropping them one by one onto the steps. I waited over by the patio furniture. Eventually the whiskey caught, a blue tide of flames spreading, then engulfing the shed.

I tore two plastic patio chairs from the overgrown grass. We sat. We watched the fire. We listened to it crackle. You put on your sunglasses, the flames dancing in their lenses. The heat baked our faces. After a while there was a crash and a billowing of sparks as the roof fell in. We moved our chairs back a little. A column of smoke towered up into the sky.

'Do you have any cigarettes?'

I offered you the packet. You took one and stepped over to the fire, holding the tip to the flames. Then you sat again and we smoked, passing the cigarette back and forth. I could smell Scraps. He smelt like any other burning meat. I was sure you could smell him too, but neither of us mentioned it. You took out the half-bottle of whiskey and we drank, a taste hotter than the fire. By the end I'd learnt not to grimace as I sipped.

Then the sirens started. I asked what you wanted to do.

'Can we go somewhere?' you said. 'I don't think I want to be here any more.'

I nodded. 'I know somewhere we can go.'

By the time we left the house a crowd had gathered. They let out a collective gasp when they saw us, as if they were shocked anything could have survived the fire. Somewhere the sirens still whirred. The old lady from next door shuffled over, still in her dressing gown.

'Are you OK, dear?' she said. 'Are you OK?'

'Fine,' you said.

You tried to hurry past but the old lady grabbed you, hugging you to her chest.

'Don't you worry, love, they're on their way.'

You wriggled free and pushed on through the crowd. The old lady cried out your name but you just wiped your eyes and screamed that she should fuck off and mind her own business. The crowd glared.

I kept my head down and followed. You didn't stop till you reached the corner. You glanced in both directions, then leant against the wall, hood up, head slumped.

'I don't even know where we're going.'

I led us the rest of the way. You were wrapped in your coat, the one with the red fur trim. My parka had burnt up with Scraps so you'd lent me your father's leather jacket, which was enormous on me, the sleeves hanging to knee-level. It was the smallest you'd been able to find. You held on to the cuff, head down, occasionally sniffing.

Then the snow started. You were shaking and I wanted to hug you to me, to keep us both warm, but I didn't. The sirens were getting louder. At one point you shoved me, stumbling from the pavement, into the street. There was a set of three grids, veiled by the thin layer of snow.

'Sorry,' I said. 'Didn't see it.'

You nodded and took my sleeve again.

We didn't stop again till we reached the Rat and Dog. You wanted to scavenge for booze. The pub was shut, the crowds having returned home, but you found a half-drunk bottle of wine under one of the tables out front and we carried on walking, you taking the occasional swig.

As we crossed the dual carriageway the fire engine came roaring past us, lights flashing, sirens screaming. By the time we reached the church its sirens had ceased and the only sound was our feet, creaking on the snow.

I asked if you'd ever been inside the church.

'Once, maybe.'

'I used to go there when I was little,' I said. 'My nan used to take me.'

'What does that mean?'

You nodded to the church sign.

It said:

GOD WELCOMES ALL
INTO THE KINGDOM OF HEAVEN

'I guess it's to try get people inside. All different sorts of people. Rather than just old ladies.'

'You reckon it's ever worked?'

I shrugged.

You downed what was left of the wine and tossed the empty bottle at the sign. It shattered, dislodging some of the letters.

Now it said:

GOD WE OMES ALL
INTO THE KI G OM OF HEAVEN

'Why'd you do that?' I said.

You shrugged.

I crossed the lawn and picked up the letters and slotted them back into place. I kicked the broken glass into the flower bed. You sat on the wall and watched. Then you took my sleeve and we carried on, across the street to Kirk Lane.

It's always a shock to see Nan's house again. It's amazing how much damage we did just by leaving, just by not being there. The front windows are long since smashed (presumably by Pitt kids) and boarded (presumably by my father), the front garden a mass of overgrown brambles and grass. I doubt it's still on the market. The 'For Sale' sign's still there but it's slipped down the side of the hedge now, just the F and the O visible through the leaves.

I remember when we first moved out Mum wanted to lower the price and get rid, but my father said she couldn't just give away her childhood home like that. My father had this theory that one day the government were going to bulldoze the Pitt and they'd give us a good price for the place. A year or so later (when the government still hadn't bulldozed the Pitt) my father organised a few viewings, though nothing ever came of them. Since then they've stopped discussing it. My father still comes down here sometimes, though, with his secretaries.

'This it?' you said.

I nodded. You looked it up and down, frowning, as if you didn't believe someone could live there. I explained that I didn't have keys, that the only way in was round the back. Were you OK to wait?

You glanced up the street. Everything was still and silent now that we'd stopped walking. I thought I could make out the sigh of each snowflake, landing on the shoulders of your father's jacket.

You nodded.

I hurried through the alley to the back wall. Climbing over was tricky, due to the usual broken-glass-scattered-across-the-top-of-the-wall-like-rows-of-glittering-shark-teeth Pitt trespassing deterrent. The bricks were slick with ice and the hole in my hand was screaming with pain and at one point I slipped and caught my elbow on the glass and tore your father's jacket.

The garden is still a graveyard of Nan's old plant tubs and there was a fairly large one (more like a trough, really) running along the back wall, packed with soil, which helped break my fall. I stumbled over to the kitchen window and climbed up, only then realising I'd left a shoe behind in the plant tub. There were more important things to think of, though. You were still out there, out front, alone. I had to get inside and let you in.

There's a trick to the window. Jiggle the handle and the lock falls right out. It was stiff and stuck to the frame with grime but I forced it open as wide as I could and wriggled through, tumbling head first into the kitchen. The tiles were furred with a layer of dust. I tried not to think of how many potential webs were about. I reached for the light switch and was relieved to find the lights still worked, the electricity was still on. It was a shock to see it again, the kitchen. It didn't look the same somehow. It was all there – the table and chairs, the old gas cooker, the fridge complete with photographs of Sarah and me, held in place by various colourful magnetic letters – but something wasn't right about it, something wasn't the same. It was like a replica, like a display in some museum. I didn't linger for long. I hurried out through the hallway to the front door. I knew I had to find you. I knew I had to get you inside.

The street was empty. All was still but for the snow – thick now, falling fast. I figured you had run home. To a friend's, maybe. Angela's. Ian's. Goose's. I figured you'd sobered in the cold and thought better of me.

Then I noticed your hair, spilt across the pavement at the end of the path.

I waded through the grass to the front gate. You were laid out, shivering, flecked with snow. I dragged the gate open. I knelt to you.

'Alice.' I shook your shoulder. 'Alice.'

You turned away from me.

'Let's go inside,' I said.

'I'm tired.'

'Me too. Let's go inside.'

I helped you to your feet, brushing the snow from the fur of your coat. By now you must've forgotten about the hole in my hand because you held it tight, clutching for balance. You didn't let go till we'd crossed the lawn, till we were safely inside the house.

You sat on the stairs while I bolted the door.

'This is where you live?'

I thought about explaining but I couldn't think of how to explain, so I just nodded.

'It's even colder than out there.'

I bent down to the cupboard under the stairs. 'I'll switch on the boiler. It'll warm up soon.'

You picked at the sleeve of your coat. 'I want to sleep. Where can I sleep?'

'I'll show you.'

I led you upstairs. I weighed up the options. Nan's room was safest, but I thought all the parcel tape might freak you out, so I took you over to my old room instead. The window was adequately boarded so I figured it'd be warm enough, plus there'd be less light to disturb you in the morning. You bobbed down onto the mattress. There was still that old bedding on it, the *Peanuts* bedding, with Snoopy and Charlie Brown and all the rest. 'Happiness is being part of the gang' it says. You stared down at your lap.

After a minute or two you appeared to be asleep. I turned to leave.

'Wait,' you said.

I stopped in the doorway.

'Stay.'

I shut the door. I sat beside you on the bed. I don't know how long we sat there. You continued to stare at your lap. You stroked your coat cuff. You kept opening your mouth as if to speak, then closing it again and shaking your head. The pipes clunked around us. They made sounds like bowling balls, rolling through the walls.

'It's the heating,' I said. 'It's temperamental.'

You nodded. You motioned to my hand. Blood had soaked through the tights, leaking onto the quilt between us. My fingers were sticky with it. I wiped them on my trousers.

My new Christmas trousers, stained with blood. I felt sick.

'You need a new bandage.'

'It's OK,' I said. Then, after a few seconds, 'I cut my elbow, too.' I showed you the tear in your father's jacket. 'Sorry.'

You didn't look up. You were staring at something.

'You lost a shoe,' you said.

I glanced at my sock, caked in mud. I told you I'd lost it in a flower tub. You snorted a laugh. Then you squealed. I glanced around – at first I thought it was the pipes. Then you did it again, a short sharp squeal. You giggled, looking up at me, hand over your mouth. You pointed to your throat. You did it again, shoulders jerking.

Hiccups.

I laughed too. With each squeal our laughter grew, which only made the hiccupping worse. Tears spilt from under your glasses, lining your cheeks. I asked if you wanted a glass of water. You shook your head and coughed the word 'Cigarette' and I took the packet from my pocket and gave it to you. You lit up. You hiccupped the first drag, spilling its smoke into the air around us.

The second you breathed down, held in your chest.

You sighed.

'Sorry,' you said, the smoke escaping with your words. 'I'm not a regular drinker.'

'Me neither.'

You offered me the cigarette. I took a drag and passed it back and you placed it between your lips. You coughed a couple of times but you didn't hiccup again.

After a while, you sighed. 'It was my dad.'

'I know.'

'He's not a bad man. Not really.'

I didn't reply.

'He just loses it sometimes. Takes it out on others. Scraps . . .'

'That's why you wanted to shoot him?'

'Yes. I still am going to shoot him. Next time I see him. And not in the hand.' You shook your head. 'That's if I ever see him again. Which I won't. I'm not going back there. Not now Scraps is gone.'

'I know somewhere we can go.'

'We?'

I looked down at my feet. My one shoe. You took another drag.

'We,' you said, as if answering your own question.

You rested your head on my shoulder. Your hands lay palm-up on your lap. Your hair smelt of smoke.

'You went to the party, right?'

'Right.'

'How was it?'

'Busy.'

'You see Goose? Was he sad? Was he missing me?'

Before I could answer you snorted, a sort of laugh I couldn't equate to anything.

'No,' I said. 'I didn't see him.'

We didn't speak for a while. I don't know how long. I could feel the warmth of your body next to mine. The weight of your head on my shoulder.

'I forgot to say,' you said. 'Happy New Year.'

'Happy New Year.'

Soon after that you began to snore. I shifted so I could see you – mouth hanging open, cigarette smouldering. I peeled the butt from your bottom lip and stubbed it out on the head-board.

I stood, laying you out on the mattress.

'Goodnight,' I said.

I slid the quilt out from under you. You shuddered in your sleep. I was in the process of tucking you in when you sat up, your face inches from mine.

You glanced round the room.

'It's OK,' I said. 'You're here.'

You lifted your glasses, propping them in your hair like a headband. Your eyes were wide, pupils dilated into two black coins. Your eyelashes had begun to grow back, just bristles at the moment. Half-formed wishes in the making.

You examined my face, from my scruffy bowl of hair to the

tip of my chin. Then you shut your eyes and leant forward, all the way forward, until your cold lips were pressed against mine. You smiled, sighing through your nose, your breath hot against my chin. I didn't dare move. I didn't dare breathe. I just crouched there, watching.

Your eyes opened again.

'Happy New Year.'

Your head tipped forward, your eyes focusing on my shirt collar. A frown dipped your brow. I glanced down, thinking there was maybe a stain or something.

Then you heaved. Your sick splattered my chest, warm and whiskey-stinking. It ran down the front of my Christmas jumper. You heaved again, all down the front of your dress this time. Your sunglasses slipped back over your eyes. You retched twice more but nothing came.

Then you slumped back, asleep.

For a minute I just crouched there, counting each vomit-drip as it dotted the duvet. You lay still, mouth open, chin glistening. Your lap was puddled, a pale red-wine liquid the consistency of spit. The odd fleck of unidentifiable foodstuff.

'Alice,' I said.

I shook your shoulder. Everything smelt of whiskey.

'Alice? You OK?'

Nothing.

'Alice.'

I stepped through to the bathroom. The door was stiff and at first I thought it was locked but then I remembered the bathroom door was always stiff, that you have to sort of barge it with your hip to get it open. The bathroom's still the same – same towels, same toilet-roll holder, even Nan's facecloth, still curled at the side of the sink. I wasn't really paying attention to all this at the time, though – I was thinking about the vomit, dripping from the hem of my jumper, dotting the dusty tiles. I examined myself in the mirror. My hair was sticking up in ways I'd never thought possible, far surpassing my usual scruffy bowl. Two large curls corkscrewed from my fringe like horns. I was still feeling the buzz of the whiskey and I ended up standing there for I don't know how long, staring at my own reflection.

I dragged off your father's jacket, draped it over the toilet seat. I peeled off my jumper, my shirt, slid off my one remaining shoe, my socks, trousers, boxers. I stepped into the bathtub. It was layered with dust, gritty and dry between my toes. I held the showerhead to my chest, the pipes clunking and shuddering as water glugged out, cold and brown at first, then steaming, hot and clear. It scalded my chest, my stomach, my legs. It burnt like crazy but I didn't add any cold. I just stood and watched it, pooling at my feet, blackened with grit and dust, gurgling down the plughole.

Once I was clean I stepped through to the bedroom again and fetched some fresh clothes from my bag. I hadn't thought I'd need them so soon. You were still on the bed, head tipped to the side. A string of spit hung from your mouth.

I leant over you, shook your shoulder.

'Alice?'

Nothing.

I told you you could sleep soon, but wouldn't you rather get out of those sick-splattered clothes?

Nothing.

I slid my arms beneath you, one under your neck, the other under your legs. I hoisted. A pain shot through my hand. You were much heavier than Scraps had been. You struggled in your sleep and I told you there-there, told you it was OK. Halfway to the bedroom door I had to stop and crouch, your weight on my knee while I re-gathered my strength. I stood again, heaving you over my shoulder into a fireman's lift, before stoop-stumbling out across the landing.

I lay you on the bathroom floor. You shivered in your sleep. I rinsed and plugged the bathtub and turned on the hot tap. The water rose. Steam fogged us, misting the mirror, gathering at the ceiling.

I took off your coat. I had to guide your arms out then drag it from under you. There didn't appear to be any vomit on it except for a few strands of drool, dried across the collar. I cupped some water from the bathtub and scrubbed them away. Next I peeled off your dress and tights, which were saturated, clinging to your legs with webs of spit. Finally I removed your sunglasses. I carried your clothes through to my old room, everything whiskey-stinking together in the corner, and shut the door behind me.

You looked so cold, lying there in your underwear on the bathroom floor, so I sat beside you, back against the tub and held you, icy in my arms. I pressed my face into your hair, breathed in the smell of whiskey and smoke, trying my best to ignore the tang of bile. The bath rumbled behind us. The pipes clunked in the walls. Once the water had reached the three-quarter mark I stood and lifted you. It was hard because I didn't have your clothes to cling to, just your skin, so cold and goose-pimpled. You struggled at first, flinging your arms in your sleep. I nearly dropped you. You soon settled once I'd lowered you into the water. I cradled your head above the surface. I was shocked at first to see blood, spreading from the back of your neck, clouding the water, but then I remembered the hole in my palm and passed your head to my right hand, holding my left in the air to try decrease the blood flow. Once the bath had filled I reached over and turned off the taps and just knelt there, holding you.

I tried not to look at you – your body, I mean. I kept my eyes fixed on your face. For a few minutes the tap dripped, rippling the water. Then the dripping stopped and the water was still and what was left was a near-perfect silence. I thought maybe I should break the silence, talk to you, only I didn't know what to say. My knees ached against the floor tiles. How long are you supposed to bathe someone? I checked my watch but the screen was blank. I rubbed it with my thumb, the ink of the digits blurring beneath. I must have submerged it. I guess it wasn't waterproof.

I decided to wash your hair. I know girls can be particular about exactly when and where they wet their hair but the ends were crunched with dried vomit and I thought it best I rinse them. I dipped your head back – your red curls danced below the surface. Their redness mixed with the tinge of my blood, tinting the water pink. I spread my fingers across your scalp, massaging every notch and socket of your skull. I thought of the times Mum'd wash my hair, the feel of foreign hands on my head. There wasn't any shampoo but I figured that didn't matter too much, so long as I got the sick out.

Somewhere outside a firework screeched. I lifted you from the water, picking the loose strands of hair that clung to your forehead. You looked so beautiful, your face pale and clean, glittering with beads of bathwater. I wanted to kiss you but we'd already had one failed kiss and our next had to be romantic, an embrace on a station platform, hand-holding at sunset on Finners Island beach. I thought of Finners Island again and couldn't help but smile. I hadn't had a chance to tell you where we were going yet, but there'd be time for that later. Plenty of time for that later.

You murmured in your sleep. Another firework crackled outside. It flowered at the window, giving the room a green glow. I turned to watch it descend. It was then I caught a glimpse of you, the rest of you, your body, blurred beneath the water. I'd shifted slightly when I turned and the movement was still passing through you, your legs bobbing, your breasts rising then sinking. Your feet were crossed. Your hands lay motionless on your belly. Your bra was plain black but your knickers were grey with a sort of pink frill. Something was swelling inside me, some pressure, rising from my stomach to my forehead and I turned away, glanced up at the ceiling, and that's when I noticed one of **Them**, wriggling out through the slats in the air vent.

I kept my head down. I concentrated on you. Your sleeping face. I figured that, if I ignored it, then maybe it could be like I hadn't seen it. We could carry on our bath in peace. Only it doesn't work like that. Once I knew one of **Them** was there I couldn't help but glance above me. Couldn't help but notice it, edging along the wall towards us. Just as it reached the window another firework burst outside, red this time, spreading its gangly shadow across the white-tiled wall. The water rippled out around you. You were shivering. No, not you, *I* was shivering. I was shivering and you were just lying there, sleeping, shaking in my arms.

I should have lifted you out then, should have carried you through to the safety and solitude of Nan's parcel-taped bedroom, only I was determined we weren't going to be disturbed by **Them**. I wasn't going to let **Them** do it again. They're Metaphorical Phantoms, all I had to do was block **Them** out of my mind and there was nothing they could do to harm us. I kept telling myself this. I may have said it aloud as well, I don't know – everything from then on seems blurred – my head was still throbbing from the whiskey.

Then a scratching started over at the sink and I turned in time to see another, crawling out from behind the mirror. This one was enormous, about the size of your hand – which I was holding now, clutching in my bloodied fist – and it too approached the bathtub, only quicker than the first, not so slow and steady but in these short scurrying bursts. Two more followed from behind the toilet cistern. I noticed another, over by the extractor fan. Another, up on the rings of the shower curtain. I breathed steadily. I closed my eyes. I told myself I had nothing to fear, they were Metaphorical Phantoms. They were Metaphorical Phantoms. They were Metaphorical Phantoms. Then one of the tiles slipped, bouncing from the bathtub and shattering across the floor and a swarm of **Them** scrambled through the hole, spreading up the bathroom wall.

By this point the fitting had started. I was shaking violently, my arms slapping the surface of the water. You were shaking with me, your head rocking over the crook of my arm. I clutched you tight to my chest, trying to hold you still, your eyelids flickering, beads of bathwater quivering on your forehead, but I couldn't seem to hold you, couldn't seem to stop you from shaking with me. Blood ran down my chin, dripped onto your cheek and I realised I'd bitten into my tongue. The water was splashing right over the side of the bath, splattering on the dusty floor.

They started to hiss. The usual stuff, calling me a psycho and a pervert, etc. I tried to concentrate on something else, some pure, happy thought – Finners Island, that day with Nan, that time with the eagle. I started to tell you about it, about Finners Island, about how we could live so happily there, the two of us – whispering to you, my face pressed against your hot wet scalp, but with my tongue bitten up I was lisping more than ever and I found it hard even to understand myself. Your hair was getting in my mouth, matted with blood from my tongue. I retched. I glanced up one last time. By now there must have been hundreds of **Them**, a great black tide of **Them**, spreading out across the ceiling. Steam collected around **Them**, their bodies glistening like a sea of fat black olives. I remember laughing. I remember wondering how they could keep a grip on the bathroom ceiling when everything was so damp and then, right on cue, one slipped and thudded to the floor, wriggling on its back. A couple plopped down into the water. Others began to descend on webs.

I shut my eyes. Pressed my forehead to yours. I told myself they weren't there, they weren't real, but the truth is they were. I could feel **Them**. On my neck, my arms, crawling down the back of my shirt. I could hear **Them**, their mass hiss growing, surrounding us. I could see **Them**. Even with my eyes shut I could see **Them**. Wriggling from their cracks in the ceiling, from the collar of Goose's fleece, from the dark corners of your shed, the Lair. More and more of **Them**, every second. I saw **Them** on your father as he sucked at his whiskey bottle, on the Vultures as they danced around the stage in their leotards, on Mum and my father and Ursula and Ken as they sat scooping forkful after forkful of burnt salmon into their fat grinning mouths. I saw **Them** on Miss Hayes, creeping out over her face as she read at the front of class, all those pointless words that don't mean a thing. I saw **Them** in the meat at Hampton's counter, wriggling between the folds of flesh. Infested. I saw **Them** pouring from Mum's Italian leather couch, its stitches splitting, its white folds parting like some great sagging mouth, vomiting a sea of **Them** out across the living-room carpet. I saw **Them** on Angela Hargrove as she lay unconscious on Goose's bed, head bobbing to the thrusts of the near-bald Hawaiian-shirt kid. I saw **Them** spilling from the

belly of your fat fuck of a father as I forced the knife into him
again and again and again and the tide of **Them** just kept on
coming, on and on. Metaphorical Phantoms. I saw Sarah, not
as she is now, but when she was little, when she'd scratch and
scratch at **Them**, just like I was scratching at you now, trying
my best to claw **Them** from your skin, but there were just so
many, too many. It was like the time in the boat all over again,
the other time on Finners Island, the time I try not to think
about, with all that splashing and shaking, your head dipping
back below the surface just like Sarah's, mouth open as if
screaming, only silent, bubbles rising through the water.
Metaphorical Phantoms. My jaw locked, my shaking churning
the bathwater.

Metaphorical Phantoms.

Clutching you to my chest, as tight as possible, everything
getting dark until there's only the warm metal taste of blood.

Metaphorical Phantoms.

Metaphorical Phantoms.

Metaphorical Phantoms.

The robin's back. I haven't told you about him yet, have I? The robin? He appeared first thing this morning, woke me up. I was on the lounge carpet. I don't know what time this was because my watch is still blurred from the water, but I sat up as soon I heard him cheeping. He was perched on those boards across the lounge window, head poking through the gap. By the time I stood he'd gone again but he's been back about five or six times since. Each time he does the same thing – pokes his head through, cheeps at me, then disappears. It's been going on for about two hours now. I don't know what he wants. I just can't work it out.

It's strange, being back at 1 Kirk Lane. I know I said so last night, but here in the daylight it's even worse. Right now I'm sitting in the lounge and the longer I sit here the more unfamiliar everything gets. There's something missing, that's the only way I can describe it. And I know Nan's missing, I know that's the obvious answer, but it's more than that. The colours are wrong – everything's too dark, the boarded windows murking everything in this veil of gloom. There's a strange smell. The damp's got to the wallpaper, giving the various floral designs this warped, wrinkled effect. Everything's so much smaller. I found a bag of half-knitted jumpers, Nan's final batch, tucked down the side of the armchair – how did I ever fit into those jumpers? And those plates, those cat plates that line the stairway wall, the ones Nan sent off for each week from *Love Cat Magazine*, each decorated with a different-coloured cat, they used to seem enormous, the cats' heads as big as mine, but now they're no more than saucers.

What really gets me, though, is the silence. All I can hear is my pen, scratching the paper. The steady rasp of my breathing. In and out. In and out. It's far quieter than I ever remember. I've been trying to put my finger on why all morning and it wasn't until just before, when I went up to check on you, that I finally realised. It's the grandfather clock in the hall. It's stopped, forever reading five to twelve. Forever losing its steady tick.

I'm sitting in Herb's armchair. It's the first time I've ever sat here. We'd never use the armchair, Nan and I – we'd share the couch, hunched together with our necks straining so we could see the TV. That's how we sat every night, watching those old movies. It seemed wrong, once Herb was gone, for one of us to switch to the armchair, just for the sake of comfort. The house is freezing again. The heating must have given out. I hope you're OK up there. I wrapped you as snug as I could, using Nan's old sheets, as well as my Snoopy duvet. 'Happiness is being part of the gang'. I put you in Nan's room. I thought it'd be safer, what with all the parcel tape.

Nan and I spent vast amounts of time and resources securing this house, barricading **Them** out. We went to such extremes that Mum feared we'd seal the place completely, that it'd become some sort of airtight tomb and the two of us would suffocate in the night. Mum banned us from parcel-taping downstairs so Nan and I concentrated our efforts on her bedroom, taping the walls and windows and Herb's old wardrobe, transforming it into a pretty-much-impenetrable parcel-taped nest. For the last few months she was taping pretty much constantly, buying the entire stock down at the post office each time she went to pick up her pension, stockpiling. All she ever talked about was the Great Influx. That and the Devil. I think Nan knew what my parents were planning. Somewhere deep in the jumbled logic of her brain she knew I was moving back to Skipdale. She knew about Golden Pines. She was sealing off her bedroom from her own versions of **Them**.

The snow's started up again. I went out before, to the shed, to get more boards. The shed, the plant tubs, the back wall, they're all iced in whiteness. I doubt we could leave today even if you were up to it. The buses are probably all cancelled. I doubt we could even get through the front door, with the snow.

My tongue-hole feels wider than usual. I must have chewed it pretty badly up in the bathroom. My hand keeps bleeding too. I've still got your tights wrapped around it. I should find a new bandage. I keep meaning to. I keep finding bloodied prints everywhere and wondering whose they are and realising they're mine. I just can't seem to focus on anything.

I've boarded the back windows. I figured if we're going to stay a while I'd better secure the place. We need to at least try and keep **Them** out. It's hard, hammering the boards with my hand messed up. I have to hold each board in place with my shoulder or my elbow and the boards keep slipping and to be honest I could really do with your nail gun. I boarded the gap in the lounge window too. Sorry, Mr Robin. Whatever it was you wanted, I hope you find it somewhere else.

I checked Nan's wardrobe and there're still rolls and rolls of parcel tape up there. The stockpile. I've counted it out: twenty-seven rolls. It should hopefully be enough. It'll have to be enough.

I've just been up to check on you. You look better now, in Nan's room, all wrapped up. I hated seeing you like that, in the bathtub. You were so silent, so still. The water had settled over you and your hair had settled in the water and you looked frozen. You looked as if you were frozen in glass. There was no sign of **Them**, of course, by then. No chipped plaster or tiles missing from the walls. They crawl back to their holes once the fitting's over and then everything's back to normal. I can still feel that chill as I reached into the water. The cold sting. The splashing and trickling as I lifted you. You were stiff and your stiffness made you hard to carry but I carried you anyway, across the hallway to Nan's room, the only safe room left in the house. I lay you on Nan's bed. I wrapped you up. I wanted to keep you warm but also to cover you, to cover those scratches, the marks I must have made when I was fitting. I kissed you once on the forehead and sat there for a while, beside you, on the bed. I felt as if I wanted to say something but I didn't know what, so that's when I came downstairs.

I just retrieved my *Breakfast at Tiffany's* video-case. I emptied it, laid out our money, the feather, the button-eye of Mr Snow. I laid out all the entries of my diary. There's so much writing, all those words, even more than I thought. Poor Miss Hayes, she never even got to see it.

I took the journal upstairs, read you a few extracts. Only short ones. I just wanted to break the silence – I can't stand it. I read the parts about you and the parts about Nan and the parts about Finners Island. Then I got distracted – I told you all about Finners Island, about the birds and the church and the beach. I told you about the opportunities for an artist there, the beauty of the landscape. I told you that maybe we could get another dog, call it Scraps II or something. Then I realised how insensitive that was and apologised and assured you we could never replace Scraps, we'd have to think of a new name, or get a different animal altogether. Maybe the animals that already live on Finners Island could be our pets instead – all the different birds, the exotic ones and the regular ones. The ducks. They could all belong to us.

Then I told you about the eagle. I've never told anyone about that. I promised Nan I wouldn't.

After that I tried to sleep. The throb in my hand wouldn't let me. Maybe you were right, maybe I left it too long and the tetanus set in. Maybe it's working its way up my arm to my brain. Sorry to bring that up again. I don't blame you. It just hurts, you know? Maybe I need a doctor or something.

I haven't taken my medication today. I forgot my pills, can you believe that? I brought my clothes and my toothbrush and my money and deodorant, but somehow forgot my pills. I hate to think what Mum'd have to say about that.

It's kind of gloomy here, in Nan's nest. It got bad near the end, with Nan. It got to the point where I was the only person she'd let enter her parcel-taped bedroom. I'd bring her meals and medicine and more and more rolls of tape, picking up what I could on the way home from school. The two of us would watch our movies. She'd even let me sleep in here, sometimes. She always called me 'Fly'. Even when she'd forgotten everyone else, when she was calling Mum 'Ellie' and my father 'Herb' and Sarah 'Mr Saunders', she'd still smile when she saw me, she'd still say, 'Hi, Fly – fancy a movie?'

The sun's just about risen over Crossgrove Park, the snow glittering in its glow. I peeled some of the parcel tape from the window so we could see. Not a single person's passed in the last two hours, by car or foot, the snow remaining clean, untouched. It's impossible to make out your house from this side of the park, or your garden, or even what's left of the shed, but each time I press my face up to the window I can detect that singed scent in the air. A hint of barbecue-char from the fire we made.

Your hair's dry now. It seems to have faded since last night. Perhaps I shouldn't have washed it. You probably have some special kind of shampoo, to keep the colour in. It's strange, I'm so used to watching you on the bus, your head rocking against the window and it's amazing how peaceful you look, laid out on Nan's bed. How calm. It makes me feel calm just looking at you.

I'm going to try and sleep again. That's all I really want, to lie beside you and sleep. That's all that's really left to do.

TRANSCRIPT

Extract of interview between Detective
Sergeant Terrence Mansell (TM) and Gregory
Hall's father, Dr Howard Hall (HH).

TM: Thanks for coming in.

HH: That's OK.

TM: I realise this is a difficult time.

HH: I just want to get it over with.

TM: Understandable.

HH: Whatever this is. What is this, a follow-
up?

TM: I just want to clarify a few things.
That's all we're doing today.

HH: Right.

TM: About that night. January third.

HH: OK.

TM: About Greg.

HH: Right.

TM: How is Greg?

HH: They're looking after him.

TM: He hasn't said anything?

HH: Not yet.

TM: And Deborah?

HH: She's . . . it's hit her hard. I don't
think it helps, seeing him like this. She's
been through rough patches before, but she's
struggling to get through this time.

TM: Right.

HH: The whole thing's just . . . it's a mess.
You know?

TM: It's a terrible situation.

HH: It's a mess.

TM: For all of you.

HH: Yes, but especially for her. I mean,
I haven't always been the best father. I
haven't always been there. But her . . .

TM: Shall we get this over with, then?

HH: I guess.

TM: Then you can get back to her. To them.

HH: What is it you want to know?

TM: Well, as I've said, I'd like to start
with that night, January third.

HH: OK.

TM: Why don't you talk me through what
  happened.

HH: I did make a statement at the time.

TM: I've read the statement. I know what's in
  the statement. I'd just like to hear it
  first-hand, if that's OK.

HH: I guess.

TM: I just want to go through, step by step.
  See if there's any stone . . . you know
  . . . unturned.

HH: Right.

TM: So, January third. What happened?

HH: Well, we went to the house.

TM: We?

HH: Yeah, the two of us. Miss Hewitt and I.

TM: And Miss Hewitt is?

HH: My secretary.

TM: And the reason for your visit to the
  house?

HH: Is that important?

TM: I don't know, is it?

HH: Not really, it was just I was showing her
  around. She was thinking of buying the
  place.

TM: Buying it?

HH: Yeah.

TM: OK . . .

HH: Why?

TM: It's not exactly a show home.

HH: She wanted somewhere with potential, she
    said. Somewhere to renovate.

TM: So you took her for a viewing?

HH: That's right.

TM: At a time when your son, Greg, was
    missing. Had been missing for three days.

HH: No. I mean, we didn't know he'd gone
    missing. Not for sure. Deborah was freaking
    out, obviously, but I thought he was probably
    staying at a friend's or something.

TM: A friend's?

HH: Yeah. I mean, I know it was unusual, for
    him to stay away like that, for a couple of
    nights. But it was the school holidays. He'd
    been to a party. He'd been drinking,
    according to Sarah. And then there was the
    snow. Snow brings everything to a halt. I
    was sure he was staying with someone. I was
    sure he'd show up.

TM: You weren't worried?

HH: Not like Debbie, no. And may I remind you

that's exactly what your people said too, when
she called them. 'He'll be at a friend's.'

TM: Right.

HH: Plus we didn't know about her then. About
the girl, I mean. Her father hadn't reported
it.

TM: No.

HH: Anyway, look, this isn't important, OK? Jo
wanted to see the house and so I took her.
So we were there. I mean, that's what's
important right? That we were there? That we
found him?

TM: What time was this?

HH: Half-nine, maybe?

TM: And I'm guessing you expected the house to
be empty?

HH: Well, obviously. It has been for years.

TM: You hadn't considered the possibility Greg
might go there?

HH: It makes sense now. Why he'd go there. It
was his home, once. I hadn't considered it at
the time, otherwise I'd have gone and got
him. I obviously wasn't expecting . . . that.

TM: And so when did you realise the house
wasn't empty?

HH: Well, I knew something was wrong when the door wouldn't open. I mean, my keys worked, the door unlocked, I just couldn't get it open. I tried kicking it. Barging it.

TM: He'd sealed it.

HH: Right. So then I went round the back. I still didn't know it was Gregory at that point. I didn't know what it was. I thought maybe the cold had warped the frame or something. So I got this shovel from the shed. I figured I could pry it open. The door, that is. That's when I noticed the extra boards, at the back of the house.

TM: Extra boards?

HH: I'd put some up over the windows years back, the ones that were broken. But there were more now, even on the unbroken ones. That's when I started to panic. I cut my hand climbing back over, see? Just there? There's all this glass on the back wall Deb's mum put there, probably to stop trespassers, but I'd forgotten all about it, hadn't realised until it was too late. Anyway, I managed to climb back over and went back round the front and wedged the shovel under the door and pried it. That's when I knew something was really wrong. Because that's when I could . . . well . . . smell it.

TM: What was Miss Hewitt doing at this point?

HH: Freaking out.

TM: She was suspicious?

HH: She wanted to wait for the police.

TM: So this was after the 999 call?

HH: Yeah. She rang straight away. While I was still in the shed.

TM: She no longer wanted to buy the house I take it?

HH: She wanted to get back in the car. She wanted to lock the doors and wait for the police.

TM: But you didn't?

HH: No. I probably should have. I mean, I still wasn't sure it was Gregory in there. But I knew I had to find out what was going on. I ended up hacking the door to pieces with that shovel. The smell was terrible, he'd sealed that place up pretty good it was all . . . festering . . . you know? And I could see him, over in the corner, head down. I could see him and I thought . . . well, I don't know what I was thinking really. I mean, he wasn't moving. I saw he wasn't moving. And then the adrenaline took over.

TM: And you got inside?

HH: Eventually. It seemed to take forever, but I tore my way inside. There was all that tape . . .

TM: The parcel tape.

HH: Right. He'd sealed the place up pretty tight.

TM: And what kind of state was Greg in?

HH: I don't think he knew I was there.

TM: He was unresponsive?

HH: I don't think he knew what was going on. He seemed to just be staring into space. His face was just blank. There was, like, zero expression. The least expression I've ever seen on the face of a living human. Bear in mind that I'm a plastic surgeon.

TM: I've seen the website.

HH: Yes, well . . .

TM: 'Breast Man.'

HH: Right. But as I said, he was just sat there, glaring at the ceiling. And he was wearing this massive leather jacket. And his

hand was all bloody. And he was holding
something, a video-case with all this stuff
in, leaflets and papers and stuff, spread out
over his lap. Oh, and money, there was a wad
of money. And a cigarette butt. There was
this cigarette butt in his other hand, the
non-bloody one. I know it's a strange thing
to notice, but it struck me as odd at the
time because Gregory's never been the kind to
smoke. Not like me, I love a smoke. I could
do with a smoke right now, actually . . .

TM: So then what?

HH: Well that's when Jo arrived at the
doorway. She took one look and ran out,
screaming. I was annoyed at the time because
I thought that was the last thing he
needed, some screaming bimbo. Though to be
honest I don't think he even noticed.

TM: So you took Greg outside?

HH: Well, first I tried to talk to him. I
slapped his face a little and got nothing.
But yeah, I knew I had to get him out of
there. Get him warmed up. Get him away from
that smell. So I carried him out to the
car. He felt like ice. I sat him in the

passenger seat and put the heaters on. I
had this bottle of water. I remember trying
to get him to drink and it just running
down his chin, all down the front of him.

TM: And where was Miss Hewitt at this point?

HH: Sat on the kerb. She wouldn't come
anywhere near us.

TM: Did she know Greg was your son?

HH: Probably not, actually. I presumed she
would have at the time, but thinking back
. . . She's pretty dense, to be honest.

TM: Right.

HH: I'd love a cigarette right now.

TM: We can take a break soon.

HH: I'm guessing it's against the rules,
smoking? In here, I mean?

TM: Yes.

HH: So I'm not allowed to smoke in here?

TM: Unfortunately not, no.

HH: Right. It's fine.

TM: So you waited in the car until the
officers arrived?

HH: Yes. Except for Jo. She stayed out on the
kerb.

TM: You didn't venture upstairs?

HH: No.

TM: Neither you nor Miss Hewitt?

HH: No. Neither of us saw upstairs.

TM: Right.

HH: And if you're about to show me pictures I don't want to see it.

TM: I wasn't.

HH: I know all about her. The girl. I know all about it.

TM: OK.

HH: I mean, anything you want to show me, it can't be worse than what's in my head, believe me. I mean, really we should be made to see, Debs and I. We're to blame, really.

TM: No one's to blame here.

HH: Of course someone's to blame. Someone's always to blame. That's the whole point, right? That's why I'm here, that's why you're involved. And the truth is it has to be us. We're the parents.

TM: I'm not blaming anyone. I'd like to be clear on that. I'm just trying to get the facts straight.

HH: The facts?

TM: That's all I want.

HH: This isn't the first time this has happened. Did you know that? Were you aware of that fact?

TM: I've spoken with your wife. I know about Sarah, if that's what you mean.

HH: His sister. His own sister. Our own daughter. I mean, we should have known it'd happen again. It was obviously going to happen again. And what did we do? We just sent him away. We just ignored it.

TM: Dr Hall?

HH: And I know we got him on diagnosed. And I know we got him medicated. But we weren't there for him. He needed us and where were we?

TM: Dr Hall.

HH: At the fucking Hamptons' that's where. I don't know. I don't even know. I . . .

[HH takes a cigarette from his pocket and lights it.]

TM: Take a minute if you want.

HH: No, you're right. I'm sorry. I . . .

TM: It's OK.

HH: Sorry, I'm just venting here. It's just

. . . I have no one . . . I mean, Debs is
ill, I can't talk about this stuff with
her, and Sarah . . . she's too young to lay
this on. I have no one. I'm a fifty-three
year old man with no one in his life to
have an adult conversation with. Not about
this, anyway.

TM: Are you OK?

HH: There's nothing we can do. We just need
to be there for him now. I know that now. I
know that.

TM: I'm sure he'd appreciate your support.

HH: And when I think back to that day,
holding him my arms, trying to get him to
drink from that bottle of water. Telling him
it was all going to be OK. And there was
nothing, you know? Nothing there. Just that
blank expression. That was the scariest day
of my life.

TM: I can imagine.

HH: Do you have kids, Detective?

TM: I do.

HH: Then you know.

TM: We can take a break if you want.

HH: You know.

IV

07/03

I know I haven't written in a while. I'm sorry for that. And I'm sorry about my handwriting – I can't seem to stop shaking, I think it's this new medication. I hope you don't mind but I've decided this is the last time I'll write to you. It was Dr Howard's idea. She said that, since I didn't get to go to the funeral, this would be a good way of saying goodbye.

It was my father who found us, back at the house. I don't remember any of that. Or them bringing me here. Those first few days are a complete blank, the weeks that followed sketchy at best. Being here dawned on me gradually, more like a slow realisation that I wasn't dreaming. When I did dream it was about you, Finners Island, Scraps. At the time I wasn't sure which parts were real, which parts were dreams or nightmares. And then there was **Them**. It was a hard time.

Things are getting better. I'm into more of a routine now, especially with my sleeping. My hand's finally healed. Apparently it was badly infected when they found us but now all that's left is a scar, a numb white spot in the centre of my palm. It's not too far from that little grey fleck Andrew Wilt's pencil left. Sometimes at night I press the scar, hard, until it starts to ache. I don't know why. I just like to feel it.

Mum hasn't visited much. She's seeing Dr Filburn again and he's advised against regular visits. Even when she does come, she never says much. She always starts crying halfway through and has to leave the room. She's sure to return, right at the end, to tell me not to worry. I'm not the cause of the tears, she says. They've been building up for years. This whole thing's just opened the floodgates.

Dad and Sarah visit more regularly, usually every other day. It's getting warmer now and yesterday we sat out and ate together on the grass. Dad brought tuna sandwiches (he knows I don't like the food here) and Sarah lent me one of her earphones so I could tap my head along to her thud-thud music. It was actually quite relaxing, in a weird way, even though the music is horrific. Sarah's eczema's back. I've noticed the odd patch of flaked skin, on her neck and the backs of her hands. She only scratches when she thinks nobody's looking. It's probably stress – the doctor said it could come back in times of stress. This has been a time of much stress.

Dr Howard is nice. She reminds me of how Miss Hayes used to be. She lets us just sit in silence. She's just there to talk to, she says, if I ever need somebody to talk to, though the truth is I haven't spoken since New Year's. I can't seem to get any words out. The more I try, the harder it is. Dr Howard told me to stop trying so hard and just relax. The words will come when they're ready, she says.

A lot of people went to your funeral. That's what Sarah said. She didn't go, of course, but her classes were nearly empty that day and Miss Hayes let the rest of them go early as a mark of respect. I haven't seen or heard from your father. I know he's no longer at the butcher's. The rumours are that he hacked off three of his fingers, drunk on the job, but I don't know how true that is. Sarah said she heard it from one of the girls in her year, but it was hard to verify because not many of the girls in her year are talking to her. My father couldn't verify it either because he hasn't spoken to Ken Hampton in over a month. Sarah said they've had to close the clinic for the time being. Dad's never mentioned this. He only talks about the weather or lunch. He doesn't like to talk about serious stuff.

I know you won't read this, by the way. I know now that I'm not really writing to you, that I was never really writing to you. That you never got to read any of what I wrote. I know now that there were in fact two yous – the real you, who I shared a few chance encounters with, and the you I wrote to, the you I found myself talking to, in my head. Right now I don't know which you I'm writing to. Both, I guess. And myself. Ultimately I know I'm writing to myself.

Spring's just about here. Every morning I wake to the sound of the birds. They're so loud, I forgot just how loud they are. They're the perfect alarm clock. Without them I'm not sure I'd ever wake up. I've been pulling out my eyelashes. It's a new habit. Dr Howard advises against it. She says it's a problem, but not such a problem, considering my other problems. This morning I discovered a couple of fresh ones, just starting to show. I managed to pluck them. I went out to the gardens at lunch with them cradled in my palm. I shut my eyes and blew them away. I can't tell you what I wished because then it might not come true. But there was a good breeze today. I'm sure they'll go far.

DATE UNKNOWN

I remember it was sunny when we left the hotel but by the time we reached the forest the rain had come. It fell in waves, like the sea had taken to the sky. It hissed through the leaves above us, rattling the hoods of our raincoats.

Nan said she knew a short cut, a secret path down to the lily pond. We loved feeding the ducks. It was our favourite part of the day. Sarah, my parents, they weren't bothered, they'd given their sandwich crusts to us and we'd headed off straight after lunch. Nan kept saying we had to go west, pointing: *this way's west* and *that way's west,* but I doubt if she knew which way west actually was. It seemed to me we were going in circles.

After a while Nan began to panic. 'How can you get lost on an island this small?' she said. 'This is the sixth time I've been here.'

Eventually we found a cliff edge but there was no secret path. Nan was exhausted and needed to sit for a while so we took shelter under an overgrown blackberry bush. We watched the rain, fizzing like static on the surface of the

321

sea. Nan said not to eat the blackberries, just in case they were poisonous.

After a few minutes the rain died. After another few minutes the sun came out, so hot we began to steam. Nan said it was a true British holiday, all weathers at once. That's when I first noticed it, perched there in the branches above us. I nudged Nan and pointed. I couldn't stop staring at it.

'Look away,' Nan whispered. 'Else it'll claw your eyes out.'

Nan and I huddled there, staring at our shoes while it perched above us, scanning the horizon. I asked Nan what it was doing here and she said there were several theories. One was that it escaped from a zoo. I asked if there was any chance it had flown here by choice but Nan said she doubted it could have made it all the way from America.

As its shadow passed over us we couldn't help but look, couldn't help but watch it cross the sky. It soared low over the sea, disappearing behind the trees that lined the far side of the cove.

'We don't tell anyone about this,' Nan said. 'It's our secret. It's just for me and you.'

We waited, just in case it circled back. It didn't. Then we waited a while longer, just sitting there in silence.

Nan stood. She sighed and smiled. She said, 'We'd best get back, Fly, else your parents'll think we've drowned in the rain.'

I nodded and stood too and we both headed off through the forest. We still didn't know which direction we were supposed to be heading in, but for some reason it didn't seem to matter any more.

Acknowledgements

Thanks to everyone on my MA, especially Robyn Donaldson, Mike Holloway, Paul Abbot, Denise Bundred and Christof Häberle. To my inspiring teachers Alicia Stubbersfield and Jim Friel. To 'The Dicks', Josh Mansell, Matty Herring and Liam Sillett. To Mike Morris and everyone at Writing on the Wall. To Niall Griffiths and Julia Bell for making me feel like a writer. To Luke Brown for the encouragement and Karolina Sutton, Norah Perkins and Kate Howard for making all my childhood dreams come true.

To my friends, my family, Nat and my cats.

And to anyone that reads it, cheers.

READING GROUP QUESTIONS

1. The social disparity between Skipdale and The Pitt sets the scene for the novel. Why do you think this is important?

2. What motivates Greg to tell his story?

3. How does the inclusion of the police transcript add to the narrative? Does it alter your opinion of Greg's reliability as a narrator?

4. Did this novel contribute to your understanding of phobias?

5. What role does the notion of obsession play in the novel?

6. Greg's parents are fixated on projecting a perfect image. How does this contrast to the reality of their situation?

7. Can we see Greg's obsession with classic Hollywood films influencing his own outlook on life and on romance in particular?

8. 'Miss Hayes has a new theory. She thinks I'm not really scared of **Them**. She thinks they're just something to blame my anxiety on. She thinks I hide my real fears behind Metaphorical Phantoms'. What do you think of Miss Hayes' theory? Are there other characters in the novel besides Greg and Miss Hayes with their own 'Metaphorical Phantoms'?

9. Do you feel sympathy for Greg's mother?

10. What is the significance of Finners Island?

11. This novel deals with some difficult social issues and the world that Greg inhabits is almost dystopian. Is there room for happiness in a world like this?

12. How far do you think the author has used Greg's social alienation to expose intricate truths about our modern lives?

13. Sarah accuses her mother of being repressed. What part does repression play in the novel as a whole and how does it manifest?

14. Greg's father claims that 'someone is always to blame'. Do you think this is the case in this situation?